Matrix Algorithms in MATLAB®

Matrix Algorithms in MATLAB®

Ong U. Routh

AMSTERDAM • BOSTON • HEIDELBERG • LONDON
NEW YORK • OXFORD • PARIS • SAN DIEGO
SAN FRANCISCO • SINGAPORE • SYDNEY • TOKYO

Academic Press is an Imprint of Elsevier

Publisher: Joe Hayton
Senior Editorial Project Manager: Kattie Washington
Project Manager: Anusha Sambamoorthy
Designer: Maria Ines Cruz

Academic Press is an imprint of Elsevier
125, London Wall, EC2Y, 5AS
525 B Street, Suite 1800, San Diego, CA 92101-4495, USA
50 Hampshire Street, 5th Floor, Cambridge MA 02139, USA
The Boulevard, Langford Lane, Kidlington, Oxford OX5 1GB, UK

Library of Congress Cataloging-in-Publication Data
A catalog record for this book is available from the Library of Congress

British Library Cataloguing-in-Publication Data
A catalogue record for this book is available from the British Library.

ISBN: 978-0-12-803804-8

For information on all Academic Press publications
visit our website at www.elsevier.com

Working together
to grow libraries in
developing countries

www.elsevier.com • www.bookaid.org

This book is dedicated to my wife Kathy, and two children Jeffrey and Jennifer

Contents

List of Figures

Preface

About Matrix Algorithms

Matrix computations are very important to many scientific and engineering disciplines. Many successful public and commercial software packages for the matrix computations, such as LAPACK and MATLAB,[1] have been widely used for decades. LAPACK stands for *Linear Algebra PACKage*. It is a Fortran library of routines for solving linear equations, least square of linear equations, eigenvalue problems and singular value problems for dense and band of real and complex matrices. MATLAB stands for *MATrix LABoratory*. It is an interpretive computer language and numerical computation environment. It includes a lot of built-in matrix computation algorithms, most of which are built upon LAPACK. Its powerful sub-matrix indexing capability makes it a good tool for the rapid prototype of numerical algorithms. Vast amount of various computer programs for the matrix computations in different computer languages can also be easily found through the search facilities of the internet. Notably two internet resources, GAMS[2] and NETLIB,[3] provide free access to documentation and source codes of many reusable computer software components, most of which are about matrix computations.

In spite of the wide availability of different kinds of computer programs for the matrix computations, the matrix computations remain an active research and development area for many years. New applications, new algorithms and improvements to old algorithms are constantly emerging. Due to their sheer importance, the matrix computations are taught from the middle school to many doctorate majors of science and engineering. There are many good books available for different readers. *Matrix Computations* by Gene H. Golub and Charles F. Van Loan [29] builds a systematic framework for the broad discipline of the matrix computations and gives an excellent description of algorithms and in-depth analysis of the properties of algorithms. Furthermore the book contains a vast amount of references to the interested readers. [5, 7] can be consulted for algorithmic matters in equation solutions and eigenvalue solutions. [3, 42, 51] cover the coding matters. For the complete coverage of the field, the two volume treatise by G.W. Stewart [68, 69] can be consulted.

Some of these books present matrix algorithms as MATLAB-like pseudo codes. The first time readers of these books will find the MATLAB pseudo codes useful to gain a preliminary understanding of the algorithms. However, algorithms are best studied through the use of the real computer codes. Through the running and debugging of the real codes, readers can expect to understand the mathematical properties of algorithms and all the subtlety of numerical computations. Readers cannot gain any insight of how an algorithm works by simply studying pseudo codes. On the other hand, many public domain codes, such as LAPACK, are too large to learn. Often the data structure obscures the essence of algorithms.

What is *Matrix Algorithms in MATLAB*

This book tries to shorten the wide gap between the rigorous mathematics of matrix algorithm and complicated computer code implementations. It presents many matrix algorithms using real MATLAB codes. For each algorithm, the presentation starts with a brief but simple mathematical exposure. The algorithm is usually explained with a small matrix, step by step, in the same order that the algorithm is

---

[1] MATLAB is a registered trademark of The MathWorks, Inc.

[2] http://gams.nist.gov.

[3] http://www.netlib.org.

executed on a computer. Then the MATLAB codes for the algorithm are listed. Mostly due to its natural notation of the sub-matrices, the MATLAB codes do not look very different from pseudo codes. For the sake of clarity of the representation, most of the MATLAB codes presented in the book are kept within 100 lines. At the beginning of each MATLAB code is some comments about the functions, input and output of the code, which can be accessed by MATLAB's *help* system. Therefore the core codes for each algorithm is even shorter and easier to understand. After the list of codes, a few numerical examples are given. The purpose of the examples has three folds. Firstly, examples verify the code implementation. Secondly, the examples demonstrate the usage of the MATLAB codes. Thirdly, the examples show the mathematical properties of the algorithm.

The algorithms covered in the book include some common algorithms found in MATLAB, such as algorithms in *lu*, *qr*, *eig* and *svd* etc. The MATLAB codes represented in the book for these common algorithms offer more options. For example, restart, different permutations, accuracy and output controls are offered in *lu*, *qr* and the other algorithms. The book contains over 15 different equation solution algorithms, over 10 different eigenvalue algorithms and singular value algorithms. The algorithms covered in the book include many other algorithms not found in MATLAB nor even in LAPACK. For example, the decomposition of symmetric indefinite matrix of [12] and [1], the solution of Vandermonde matrix, various iterative equation solution algorithms with assumed pre-conditioners, iterative eigen solution algorithms of symmetric and non-symmetric matrices. All the MATLAB codes presented in the book are tested with thousands of runs of MATLAB randomly generated matrices. The validity of the computation is verified by the mathematical identity for each computation. No errors are found! The clarity of the presentation of the algorithms is the goal of the MATLAB codes of the book. The efficiency of the codes is the secondary consideration. However, the CPU time of most common algorithms is usually within 5 times of the MATLAB built-in algorithms for same matrices. When running the MATLAB codes, a big part of the CPU time is spent on the interpretation of the codes. Only real matrices are covered in the book. The extension to the complex matrices is usually straight forward for most algorithms. Band and sparse matrices are not treated in most algorithms. But in the iterative equation solution algorithms and eigen solution algorithms, the special considerations of band and sparse matrices can be supplied by user routines as input arguments to the algorithms.

In Chapter 1, *Introduction*, a brief introduction of MATLAB will be made together with most notations used in the book. A summary of the basic theory of matrix computations, a systematic view of different algorithms, the classifications of matrices, the storage of special matrices, reordering of sparse matrices and some utility MATLAB codes will be covered in Chapter 1.

Chapters 2 and 3, *Direct Algorithms of Decompositions of Matrices by Non-orthogonal/Orthogonal Transformations*, address the decompositions of a general matrix and some special matrices. The decomposition of a matrix is itself an important matrix computation problem, but also the foundation of other matrix algorithms. Chapter 2 starts with Gauss zeroing matrix. Then it presents LU and LDU decompositions for general matrices, congruent transformation algorithms (LDLt, LTLt, LBLt decompositions) for symmetric matrices, LLt (Cholesky) for symmetric positive definite matrices and xLLt (a modified Cholesky) for symmetric matrices. It continues with 3 similarity transformation algorithms (LHLi and GTGi) and lastly GTGJGt algorithm that simultaneously transforms one symmetric matrix to a symmetric tri-diagonal and another symmetric matrix to a diagonal of only ±1s and possibly 0s. Chapter 3 is parallel to Chapter 2, but only orthogonal transformations are used in algorithms. Corresponding to Gauss matrix is Householder matrix and Givens matrix. Corresponding to LU, LDU are QR, QLZ and QBZ decompositions. Corresponding to LHLi and GTGi are QHQt and QTQt decompositions. Corresponding to GTGJGt is QHRZ algorithm that simultaneously transforms one matrix to Hessenberg and another matrix to upper triangle. Most algorithms in Chapters 2 and 3 are presented in more than one flavors, transforming, decomposing and multiplying, according to the classifications of matrix algorithms made in Chapter 1.

Chapter 4 presents *Direct Algorithms of Solution of Linear Equations*. The first 3 sections introduce several theoretical tools for the solution of linear equations, pseudo inverse, minimum norm/residual solutions, solutions with linear constraints. It begins the algorithms of 5 special structured matrices: zero matrix, diagonal matrix, orthogonal matrix and lower/upper triangular matrix. Then it presents 4 elimination algorithms: Gauss and Gauss-Jordan eliminations by non-orthogonal transformations, Householder and Givens eliminations by orthogonal transformations. It follows by decomposing algorithms that utilize all the matrix decomposition algorithms of Chapters 2 and 3. Lastly it presents two special algorithms arising from the interpolation problems: Vandermonde matrix and Fast Fourier Transform.

Chapter 5 presents *Iterative Algorithms of Solution of Linear Equations*, which are better suited for large and sparse matrices. Presented algorithms include Jacobi ierations, Gauss-Seidel iterations, 3 algorithms based on Lanczos (Conjugate Gradient, Minimum Residual and Minimum Error) for symmetric matrices, 11 algorithms based on Arnoldi (Full Orthogonalization, Generalized Minimum Residual, Generalized Minimum Error, and 8 other variants) for unsymmetric matrices, 4 special algorithms for normal equations. The algorithms are complemented by an overview of iterative algorithms and plots of convergence patterns. The last section briefly touches 4 important topics: pre-conditioning, parallel computation, algebraic multigrid method and domain decomposition method.

Chapter 6 presents *Direct Algorithms of Solution of Eigenvalue Problem*. Section 6.1 provides the simple algorithm for 2×2 matrix, which is used in Jacobi iteration algorithms of Section 6.8 and other algorithms as a building block. The third section builds 4 auxiliary tools for the symmetric eigenvalues, to count how many eigenvalues in a given interval and to approximate the lower and upper bounds of a given eigenvalue. Section 6.4 is on the key QR iteration algorithms for both unsymmetric and symmetric matrices. Sections 6.5 and 6.6 are on the calculation of invariant subspace: inverse iteration to calculate an eigenvector by a given eigenvalue and eigenvalue reordering. Section 6.7 presents two more special algorithms for symmetric tri-diagonal matrices: bisection and divide-and-conquer. Sections 6.9–6.11 present 3 algorithms for generalized eigenvalue problems, symmetric positive definite pencils, unsymmetric pencils and symmetric positive indefinite pencils.

Chapter 7 presents *Iterative Algorithms of Solution of Eigenvalue Problem*, which are better suited for large and sparse matrices. The first algorithm is the power/subspace iteration. Sections 7.3 and 7.4 have full presentations of two celebrated algorithms, Lanczos for symmetric matrices and Arnoldi for unsymmetric matrices. All the algorithms are complemented by an overview of iterative algorithms and plots of convergence patterns. The last section discusses briefly 3 important topics: generalized eigenvalue problem, nonlinear eigenvalue problem and Jacobi-Davidson iterations.

Chapter 8 presents *Algorithms of Solution of Singular Value Decomposition*. Section 8.1 discusses the connection between the singular value decomposition and eigenvalue decomposition of a symmetric matrix. The connection shows how to construct the algorithms for singular value decompositions from the eigenvalue algorithms of Chapters 7 and 8. Section 8.2 presents the simple algorithms for row/column vectors and 2×2 matrices. Built upon the simple algorithm of Section 8.2, Section 8.3 presents the relatively simple Jacobi algorithm. Section 8.4 is the counter part of Section 6.4 in singular value decomposition, QR iteration. Section 8.5 presents two special algorithms for a bi-diagonal matrix: bisection and divide-and-conquer. For large and sparse matrices, Section 8.6 discusses the Lanczos singular value algorithm.

Who Reads *Matrix Algorithms in MATLAB*

This book is intended for people working in the field of matrix computations, who need to master, implement and improve the matrix algorithms. Students in computer science, applied mathematics, computer engineering and other engineering disciplines can benefit from studying the book. The book is also useful to researchers and professionals in numerical analysis of engineering and scientific research.

How to Read *Matrix Algorithms in MATLAB*

The book can be used in the traditional way, reading. At first, readers can read the brief discussions of mathematical exposures. Then follow the step-by-step explanation of an algorithm by simple examples. The most efficient way of reading it is to run and debug the examples on computers on which a MATLAB program is installed. With 3–5 rounds of debugging and more numerical experiments by readers, readers can expect to have a solid understanding of the algorithm. Because MATLAB codes are very close to any pseudo codes, no computer programming knowledge is required. For readers with experience in MATLAB, Section 1.2 can certainly be by-passed; otherwise readers can read Section 1.2 to jump start.

Acknowledgments

Writing this book was my personal endeavor to sharpen my skills in numerical computations. Nevertheless, the many supports I received over many years are necessary to make it happen.

First and foremost, I acknowledge the great contribution and sacrifice of my wife, Kathy, and two children, Jeffrey and Jennifer. For many days and nights, Kathy shoulders the responsibility of taking care of the family, raising and educating the two children. She fully supports my endeavor of studying mechanics and numerical computations, in either shining or raining days. Her love gives me the strength to persist. Jeffrey and Jennifer missed my fatherhood when they needed it the most. I apologize to them my absence and impatience, while I was focusing on my study. Without their contribution and sacrifice, writing this book is impossible. Therefore I dedicate *Matrix Algorithms in MATLAB* to them, my dear wife, Kathy, and two wonderful children, Jeffrey and Jennifer.

I am very proud of my humble origin, the son of my uneducated parents, Shang Z. and Allyn. Their unconditional love and belief in me being excellent were my only source of strength for many years. They will live in my heart forever.

I express my great appreciation to my Publisher, Joe Hayton, and my Editorial Project Manager, Kattie Washington, at Elsevier, and to my Production Project Manager, Anusha Sambamoorthy. It was my great honor to have the opportunity to work with Joe, Kattie, and Anusha in publishing this book. I am thankful to Maria Ines Cruz at Elsevier for the cover design. I am also thankful to the anonymous manuscript reviewers for their time reviewing the book and making suggestions to improve the book.

Finally I wish to acknowledge two people I have never met: Cleve Moler, the creator of MATLAB and co-founder of Mathworks, for lending me the excellent tool to implement and present matrix algorithms; and Donald Knuth, for lending me LaTeX to write the book.

Ong U. Routh
December 9, 2015

License Terms

You need to read this section if you want to use any MATLAB codes in this book on a computer.

The author makes no warranties, explicit or implied, that the programs contained in this book are free of errors. They should not be relied on solving a problem whose incorrect solution could result in injury to a person and/or to loss of a property. If you use the programs in such a manner, it is at your own risk. The author and publisher disclaim all liability for direct or consequential damages resulting from your use of the programs.

This book and all the programs contained are protected by copyright laws. Under the copyright laws, all derivative works (modified versions or a translation into another computer language) also come under the same copyright laws as the original work. Copyright does not protect ideas, but only the expression of those ideas in a particular form. If you analyze the ideas contained in any programs contained in the book, and then express those ideas in your own completely different implementation; that new implementation belongs to you. That is what I have done for all the programs in this book that are entirely of my own devising. I do attempt to give proper attributions to the originators of those ideas. Unfortunately, the study of matrix algorithms has a long history and many ideas are attributed to more than one person. The author cannot claim the accuracy of each attribution.

The programs contained in this book are allowed to use under the following license terms.

1. You purchase this book. You can use MATLAB M-file editor or any text file editors to type a program and save it onto your computer. You are not authorized to transfer or distribute a machine-readable copy to any other person or any other computer. I authorize you to use the program that you type onto you computer on that computer for your own personal and noncommercial purposes. This license is termed as *License by Book Purchasing*.

2. You pay a nominal fee to download all the MATLAB programs contained in the book electronically from the author-hosted companion website, www.matrixalgorithmsinmatlab.com. You are not authorized to transfer or distribute all or any part of the downloaded codes to any other person or more than one computer. I authorize you to use all the programs on that computer for your own personal and noncommercial purposes. This license is termed as *License by Program Purchasing*.

3. Instructors at accredited educational institutions who have adopted this book for a course, and who have already obtained a license by either *License by Book Purchasing* or *License by Program Purchasing*, may license the programs for use in that course as follows: e-mail your name, title, and address; the course name, number, dates and estimated enrollment; and advance nominal payment per (estimated) student to matrixalgorithmsinmatlab@gmail.com. You may receive by return e-mail a license authorizing you to make copies of the programs for use by your students, and/or to transfer the programs to a machine accessible to your students, for the duration of the course.

Introduction

INTRODUCTION

In this chapter, we will first have a brief review of the theory of linear algebra that are important to the presentation of the book [29, 55, 68, 69] and the vast references of those books have much more in-depth presentations with regard to the theoretical matters. In the second section, we will give a brief introduction to the syntax of the MATLAB®. The introduction focuses only on those related to the matrix computations. For a more detailed coverage, the MATLAB User's Guide [35] and the MATLAB tutorial [43, 50] can be consulted. [42] offers a brief introduction of MATLAB in its first chapter. When designing a matrix algorithm, it is necessary to take into account the special structures and properties of the matrix. Section 1.3 will introduce some of the important types of the matrices encountered in practice. Matrix algorithms are broad and complex. An effective overview of matrix algorithms is certainly beneficiary. We hope Section 1.4 can serve that purpose. In Section 1.5, three reordering algorithms of sparse matrices are presented. In the last section, Section 1.6, some simple utility MATLAB codes that are used in the algorithms to be presented in later chapters are listed, so that the reader can find what these utility functions do. Several utility algorithms for band and sparse matrices, such as the matrix–vector product, which are useful in the iterative equation and eigenvalue solutions of the band and sparse matrices, are also presented in this section.

A word about the notations: we use a capital letter to represent a matrix, a lower case letter to represent a vector. In both the equations and the MATLAB codes discussed in the book, we stick to this convention. We usually use i, j, k, l, m, n for the integers, such as a matrix index and a loop counter. In equations, we use a lower case Greek letter to present a scalar. In MATLAB codes, the Greek letter representing the scalar is its Latin name, for example, alpha for α, beta for β, etc. To keep a smooth transition from the algorithm to the MATLAB code implementation, the notations will follow closely the MATLAB style. Most of the notations used in the book will be introduced on the fly in Sections 1.1 and 1.2.

1.1 ELEMENTS OF LINEAR ALGEBRA

This book focuses on the algorithmic aspect of the matrix computations. The theoretical discussion and error analysis of each algorithm can be found elsewhere, for example, [29, 56, 68, 69] and the vast amounts of the references cited in these books. However, some background of theoretical information is necessary to start the presentation of any algorithms of matrix computations. This section serves as a brief introduction and an overview of the broad field of matrix computations.

Matrix Algorithms in MATLAB. DOI: 10.1016/B978-0-12-803804-8.00007-6

1.1.1 DEFINITIONS

Let $\mathbb{R}$ be a real field. $\alpha \in \mathbb{R}$ is a scalar. $\mathbf{a} \in \mathbb{R}^n$ is a column vector of size n. Its transpose $\mathbf{a}'$ is a row vector of size n. In Eq. (1.1), a_i or $a(i)$ is the ith component of $\mathbf{a}$; $\mathbf{a}(1:m)$ is the components from the first position to the mth position,

$$\mathbf{a} = \begin{bmatrix} a_1 \\ a_2 \\ \vdots \\ a_n \end{bmatrix} = [a_i] = [a(i)] = \begin{bmatrix} a_1 \\ \vdots \\ a_m \\ a_{m+1} \\ \vdots \\ a_n \end{bmatrix} = \begin{bmatrix} \mathbf{a}(1:m) \\ \mathbf{a}(m+1:n) \end{bmatrix}, \tag{1.1a}$$

$$\mathbf{a}' = (a_1, a_2, \ldots, a_n) = (a_i). \tag{1.1b}$$

In this book, a scalar is denoted as a lower case Latin or Greek letter; a vector is denoted as a **bold** lower case Latin letter. The component of a vector is denoted by the same Latin letter with a subscript denoting its location. In Eq. (1.1), we introduced five notations for a vector. Depending on the context, all the five notations will be used interchangeably within the same equation.

In $\mathbb{R}^n$, we define two operations, the addition and scalar product.

$$\mathbf{c} = \mathbf{a} + \mathbf{b}, \qquad c_i = a_i + b_i, \tag{1.2a}$$

$$\mathbf{b} = \alpha \mathbf{a}, \qquad b_i = \alpha a_i. \tag{1.2b}$$

With the addition and scalar product defined as Eq. (1.2), $\mathbb{R}^n$ becomes a linear space. Further we define the metric, norm, and inner dot product in $\mathbb{R}^n$. With these definitions, $\mathbb{R}^n$ becomes a metric space, a normed space, and an inner product space,

$$\|\mathbf{a}\|_p = \left(\sum_{i=1}^{n} a_i^p \right)^{\frac{1}{p}}, \tag{1.3a}$$

$$p = 1: \quad \|\mathbf{a}\|_1 = \sum_{i=1}^{n} |a_i|, \tag{1.3b}$$

$$p = 2: \quad \|\mathbf{a}\|_2 = \sqrt{\sum_{i=1}^{n} a_i^2} = \sqrt{a_i a_i}, \tag{1.3c}$$

$$p = \infty: \quad \|\mathbf{a}\|_\infty = \max_{i=1}^{n} |a_i|, \tag{1.3d}$$

$$(\mathbf{a}, \mathbf{b}) = \mathbf{a}'\mathbf{b} = \sum_{i=1}^{n} a_i b_i = a_i b_i, \tag{1.3e}$$

$$\|\mathbf{a} - \mathbf{b}\| = \sqrt{\sum_{i=1}^{n} (a_i - b_i)(a_i - b_i)} = \sqrt{(a_i - b_i)(a_i - b_i)}. \tag{1.3f}$$

In Eq. (1.3), we adopted Einstein's summation convention, which rules that the indices repeated twice in a term are summed over the range of the index.

If the norm of a vector is one, the vector is a unit vector. If the dot product of two vectors is zero, the two vectors are orthogonal.

A matrix is defined as an ordered data table in rows and columns. Let $\mathbf{A} \in \mathbb{R}^{m \times n}$ be a matrix. It has m rows and n columns shown in Eq. (1.4), where A_{ij} or $A(i,j)$ are the data at ith row and jth column; $\mathbf{A}(i,:)$ is the ith row vector; and $\mathbf{A}(:,j)$ is the jth column vector. It should be noted the different notations for the same matrix in Eq. (1.4). In this book, the **bold** UPPER CASE Latin letter is used to represent a matrix,

$$
\begin{aligned}
\mathbf{A} &= \begin{bmatrix} A_{11} & A_{12} & \cdots & A_{1n} \\ A_{21} & A_{22} & \cdots & A_{2n} \\ \vdots & \vdots & \ddots & \vdots \\ A_{m1} & A_{m2} & \cdots & A_{mn} \end{bmatrix} \\
&= \left[A_{ij} \right] = \left[A(i,j) \right] \\
&= \begin{bmatrix} \mathbf{A}(1,:) \\ \mathbf{A}(2,:) \\ \vdots \\ \mathbf{A}(m,:) \end{bmatrix} = \left[\mathbf{A}(i,:) \right] \\
&= \left(\mathbf{A}(:,1), \mathbf{A}(:,2), \ldots, \mathbf{A}(:,n) \right) = \left(\mathbf{A}(:,j) \right) \\
&= \begin{bmatrix} \mathbf{A}(1:k,1:l) & \mathbf{A}(1:k,l+1:n) \\ \mathbf{A}(k+1:m,1:l) & \mathbf{A}(k+1:m,l+1:n) \end{bmatrix}.
\end{aligned} \tag{1.4}
$$

The addition, scalar product, metric, norm, and inner product of $\mathbb{R}^{m \times n}$ are defined similarly to those corresponding to $\mathbb{R}^n$,

$$\mathbf{C} = \mathbf{A} + \mathbf{B}, \qquad C_{ij} = A_{ij} + B_{ij}, \tag{1.5a}$$

$$\mathbf{B} = \alpha \mathbf{A}, \qquad B_{ij} = \alpha A_{ij}, \tag{1.5b}$$

$$\|\mathbf{A} - \mathbf{B}\| = \sqrt{\sum_{i=1}^{m} \sum_{j=1}^{n} (A_{ij} - B_{ij})(A_{ij} - B_{ij})}, \tag{1.6a}$$

$$\|\mathbf{A}\| = \|\mathbf{A}\|_F = \sqrt{\sum_{i=1}^{m} \sum_{j=1}^{n} A_{ij} A_{ij}} = \sqrt{A_{ij} A_{ij}}, \tag{1.6b}$$

$$\mathbf{A}:\mathbf{B} = \sum_{i=1}^{m} \sum_{j=1}^{n} A_{ij} B_{ij} = A_{ij} B_{ij}. \tag{1.6c}$$

Again within Eq. (1.6), the Einstein's summation convention is adopted. In the sequel, we will omit the summation symbol; if not stated otherwise, the summation is always assumed for the repeated indices within one term. With the definitions Eq. (1.5) and Eq. (1.6), $\mathbb{R}^{m \times n}$ becomes a linear space, a metric space, a normed space, and an inner product space.

The matrix norm defined in Eq. (1.6) is also called Frobenius norm. Another more often used matrix norm is defined based on the norm of the vector, Eq. (1.3),

$$\|\mathbf{A}\|_p = \max_{\mathbf{x} \in \mathbb{R}^n, \mathbf{x} \neq 0} \frac{\|\mathbf{A}\mathbf{x}\|_p}{\|\mathbf{x}\|_p} = \max_{\mathbf{x} \in \mathbb{R}^n, \|\mathbf{x}\|_p = 1} \|\mathbf{A}\mathbf{x}\|_p. \tag{1.7}$$

Based on this definition of the matrix norm, we have the following important inequality relation:

$$\|\mathbf{A}\mathbf{x}\|_p \leq \|\mathbf{A}\|_p \|\mathbf{x}\|_p. \tag{1.8}$$

The important instances of 1-norm and ∞-norm of $\mathbf{A}$ can be easily calculated as

$$\|\mathbf{A}\|_1 = \max_{1 \leq j \leq n} \sum_{i=1}^{m} \|A_{ij}\|, \quad \|\mathbf{A}\|_\infty = \max_{1 \leq i \leq m} \sum_{j=1}^{n} \|A_{ij}\|. \tag{1.9}$$

However, the calculation of $\|\mathbf{A}\|_2$ is more complicated, as can be see by the necessary condition $\mathbf{A}'\mathbf{A}\mathbf{z} = (\mathbf{z}'\mathbf{A}'\mathbf{A}\mathbf{z})\mathbf{z}$ to maximize the function $\mathbf{x}'\mathbf{A}'\mathbf{A}\mathbf{x}/\mathbf{x}'\mathbf{x}$. Fortunately if the objective is to get an estimate of $\|\mathbf{A}\|_2$, the following inequalities are helpful,

$$\|\mathbf{A}\|_2 \leq \|\mathbf{A}\|_F \leq \sqrt{n}\|\mathbf{A}\|_2, \tag{1.10a}$$

$$\max_{i,j}|A_{ij}| \leq \|\mathbf{A}\|_2 \leq \sqrt{mn} \max_{i,j}|A_{ij}|, \tag{1.10b}$$

$$\frac{1}{\sqrt{n}}\|\mathbf{A}\|_\infty \leq \|\mathbf{A}\|_2 \leq \sqrt{m}\|\mathbf{A}\|_\infty, \tag{1.10c}$$

$$\frac{1}{\sqrt{m}}\|\mathbf{A}\|_1 \leq \|\mathbf{A}\|_2 \leq \sqrt{n}\|\mathbf{A}\|_1, \tag{1.10d}$$

$$\|\mathbf{A}\|_2 \leq \sqrt{\|\mathbf{A}\|_1\|\mathbf{A}\|_\infty}. \tag{1.10e}$$

For square matrices, we have two more important definitions, trace and determinant,

$$\text{tr}(\mathbf{A}) = \sum_{i=1}^{n} A_{ii} = A_{ii}, \tag{1.11}$$

$$\det(\mathbf{A}) = \sum_{\mathbf{p},\mathbf{q} \in \mathbf{P}} \text{sign}(\mathbf{p})\,\text{sign}(\mathbf{q}) \prod_{i=1}^{n} A(p_i, q_i),$$

$$= \sum_{\mathbf{p} \in \mathbf{P}} \text{sign}(\mathbf{p})A(p_1, 1)A(p_2, 2) \cdots A(p_n, n), \tag{1.12}$$

$$= \sum_{\mathbf{q} \in \mathbf{P}} \text{sign}(\mathbf{q})A(1, q_1)A(2, q_2) \cdots A(n, q_n),$$

where $\mathbf{P}$ stands for all permutations of $(1, 2, \ldots, n)$, $\text{sign}(\mathbf{p}) = 1$ for even permutations and $\text{sign}(\mathbf{p}) = -1$ for odd permutations. We can take $\mathbf{p} = \mathbf{q}$ in the definition.

With the definition of the matrix, we can give the outer product of two vectors. The outer product of two vectors $\mathbf{a} \in \mathbb{R}^m, \mathbf{b} \in \mathbb{R}^n$ is a matrix $\mathbf{C} \in \mathbb{R}^{m \times n}$ defined as follows:

$$\mathbf{C} = \mathbf{a} \otimes \mathbf{b} = \mathbf{a}\mathbf{b}', \qquad C_{ij} = a_i b_j. \tag{1.13}$$

The dot products between a matrix and a vector and between two matrices as defined below are fundamental to the matrix algorithms,

$$\mathbf{Ab} = \left[A_{ij}b_j\right] = \left[\mathbf{A}(i,:)\mathbf{b}\right] = \mathbf{A}(:,j)b(j), \tag{1.14a}$$

$$\mathbf{AB} = \left[A(i,k)B(k,j)\right] = \left[\mathbf{A}(i,:)\mathbf{B}(:,j)\right] = (\mathbf{A}(:,j)B(j,k)) = \mathbf{A}(:,j)\mathbf{B}(j,:). \tag{1.14b}$$

In Eq. (1.14), the dot product of $\mathbf{Ab}$ can be viewed as the dot product of row vectors $\mathbf{A}(i,:)$ and $\mathbf{b}$ or as a linear combination of the column vectors $\mathbf{A}(:,j)b_j$. Similarly each component of $\mathbf{AB}$ is the dot product of vectors $\mathbf{A}(i,:)\mathbf{B}(:,j)$. Each column of $\mathbf{AB}$ can be interpreted as a linear combination of column vectors $\mathbf{A}(:,j)B(j,k)$. Further $\mathbf{AB}$ can be represented as the summation of n vector outer products of $\mathbf{A}(:,j)\mathbf{B}(j,:)$.

The outer product between two matrices $\mathbf{A} \in \mathbb{R}^{m\times n}$ and $\mathbf{B} \in \mathbb{R}^{p\times q}$ is a matrix of size $mp \times nq$ defined below,

$$\mathbf{C} = \mathbf{A} \otimes \mathbf{B} = \left[A_{ij}B_{kl}\right]$$

$$= \begin{bmatrix} A_{11}\mathbf{B} & A_{12}\mathbf{B} & \cdots & A_{1n}\mathbf{B} \\ A_{21}\mathbf{B} & A_{22}\mathbf{B} & \cdots & A_{2n}\mathbf{B} \\ \vdots & \vdots & \vdots & \vdots \\ A_{m1}\mathbf{B} & A_{m2}\mathbf{B} & \cdots & A_{mn}\mathbf{B} \end{bmatrix}. \tag{1.15}$$

1.1.2 LINEAR INDEPENDENCE AND RELATED CONCEPTS

Given n nonzero vectors $\mathbf{a}_1, \mathbf{a}_2, \ldots, \mathbf{a}_n \in \mathbb{R}^m$, if there exists n scalars $b_1, b_2, \ldots, b_n$, such that

$$b_1\mathbf{a}_1 + b_2\mathbf{a}_2 + \cdots + b_n\mathbf{a}_n = \mathbf{0} \quad \text{and} \quad b_1 b_2 \cdots b_n \neq 0, \tag{1.16}$$

we say $\mathbf{a}_1, \mathbf{a}_2, \ldots, \mathbf{a}_n$ are linearly dependent. Otherwise,

$$b_1\mathbf{a}_1 + b_2\mathbf{a}_2 + \cdots + b_n\mathbf{a}_n = \mathbf{0} \iff b_1 b_2 \cdots b_n = 0 \tag{1.17}$$

we say $\mathbf{a}_1, \mathbf{a}_2, \ldots, \mathbf{a}_n$ are linearly independent.

Let $\mathbf{A} = (\mathbf{a}_1, \mathbf{a}_2, \ldots, \mathbf{a}_n)$ and $\mathbf{b}' = (b_1, b_2, \ldots, b_n)$. Eq. (1.16) is equivalent to say the columns of the matrix $\mathbf{A}$ are linearly dependent if

$$\mathbf{Ab} = \mathbf{0} \quad \text{and} \quad \mathbf{b} \neq \mathbf{0}. \tag{1.18}$$

Eq. (1.17) is equivalent to say the columns of the matrix $\mathbf{A}$ are linearly independent if

$$\mathbf{Ab} = \mathbf{0} \iff \mathbf{b} = \mathbf{0}. \tag{1.19}$$

The number of linearly independent columns of a matrix is the column rank of a matrix. Similarly, the number of linearly independent rows of a matrix is the row rank of the matrix. One of the fundamental theorem of linear algebra states that the row rank and column rank of any matrices, namely, the rank of the matrix, are equal. If the rank of the matrix is less than $\min(m,n)$, the matrix is rank deficient; otherwise it is full rank.

If a matrix is square and has full rank, it is non-singular or invertible, otherwise singular or non-invertible. If a matrix $\mathbf{A}$ is non-singular, there exists a matrix $\mathbf{B}$ such that

$$\mathbf{AB} = \mathbf{BA} = \mathbf{I}, \tag{1.20}$$

where **I** is the identity matrix. **B** is the inverse of **A**, denoted as $\mathbf{B} = \mathbf{A}^{-1}$. **A** is also the inverse of **B**.[1] The necessary and sufficient condition for the non-singularity of **A** is $\det(\mathbf{A}) \neq 0$. With the introduction of the identity matrix and the definition of the inverse, the non-singular matrices of $\mathbf{A} \in \mathbf{R}^{n \times n}$ form a group.

The kernel or the null space of **A** is a linear space defined by

$$\text{null}(\mathbf{A}) = \{\mathbf{b} \in \mathbb{R}^n \mid \mathbf{Ab} = \mathbf{0}\}. \tag{1.21}$$

The range of **A** is another linear space defined by

$$\text{range}(\mathbf{A}) = \{\mathbf{Ab} \mid \mathbf{b} \in \mathbb{R}^n\}. \tag{1.22}$$

Another fundamental theorem of linear algebra is stated by the following equations, where $\mathbf{A} \in \mathbb{R}^{m \times n}$:

$$\dim(\text{range}(\mathbf{A})) + \dim(\text{null}(\mathbf{A}')) = n, \tag{1.23a}$$
$$\dim(\text{range}(\mathbf{A}')) + \dim(\text{null}(\mathbf{A})) = m. \tag{1.23b}$$

As can be seen by Eq. (1.23), the whole space $\mathbb{R}^n$ is a sum of two complementary subspaces, range(**A**) and null(**A**′). A set of orthogonal basis can be constructed from range(**A**), for example, by Gram–Schimdt algorithm. Another set of orthogonal basis can also be constructed from null(**A**′). Then the whole space $\mathbb{R}^n$ is a direct sum of the two sets of orthogonal basis. Now let us take range(**A**) as an example to show the construction of orthogonal bases. Each column of **A** is a base vector of range(**A**). An orthogonal basis can be constructed by following Algorithm 1.1. In Algorithm 1.1, line 5 is the essence of the Gram–Schimdt algorithm. Numerically, line 5 is not stable. We will present a numerically stable Gram–Schimdt algorithm in Chapter 3.

Algorithm 1.1 Gram–Schimdt Algorithm

1: Empty Orthogonal Vectors **Q**.
2: **for** $j = 1, 2, \ldots, n$ **do**
3:    $\mathbf{q} = \mathbf{A}(:, j)$.
4:    **if Q** is not empty **then**
5:       $\mathbf{q} = \mathbf{q} - \mathbf{Q}(\mathbf{Q}'\mathbf{q})$.
6:    **end if**
7:    $\alpha = \sqrt{\mathbf{q}'\mathbf{q}}$.
8:    **if** $\alpha > 0$ **then**
9:       $\mathbf{Q} = [\mathbf{Q}, \frac{\mathbf{q}}{\alpha}]$.
10:    **end if**
11: **end for**

In the group of non-singular matrices, there is one special subgroup called orthogonal that the inverse of its member is the member's transpose,

$$\mathbf{Q}'\mathbf{Q} = \mathbf{QQ}' = \mathbf{I}. \tag{1.24}$$

---
[1] If **A** is non-square or rank deficient, there exists various kinds of generalized inverse. We will not discuss the generalized inverse in this book. Refer to [34] for some information.

If a matrix is orthogonal, each of its column and row are unit vectors, and the dot product between columns and rows are zeros. This means the columns and rows of an orthogonal matrix are maximally linearly independent. One of the important properties of an orthogonal matrix is that it preserves the dot product of any two vectors,

$$(\mathbf{Qx})'(\mathbf{Qx}) = \mathbf{x}'\mathbf{Q}'\mathbf{Qx} = \mathbf{x}'\mathbf{x}, \tag{1.25a}$$

$$(\mathbf{Qx})'(\mathbf{Qy}) = \mathbf{x}'\mathbf{Q}'\mathbf{Qy} = \mathbf{x}'\mathbf{y}. \tag{1.25b}$$

1.1.3 SOLUTION OF LINEAR EQUATIONS

Properties of Solutions Given $\mathbf{A} \in \mathbb{R}^{m \times n}$, the homogeneous problem is to find $\mathbf{x}_0 \in \mathbb{R}^n$ to satisfy $\mathbf{Ax}_0 = \mathbf{0}$. According to the definition of null($\mathbf{A}$) of Eq. (1.21), the solution $\mathbf{x}_0$ is in the null space of $\mathbf{A}$. There are nonzero homogeneous solutions if and only if $r = \text{rank}(\mathbf{A}) < n$. The inhomogeneous problem is to find $\mathbf{x}_1 \in \mathbb{R}^n$ to satisfy $\mathbf{Ax}_1 = \mathbf{b}$, here $\mathbf{b} \in \mathbb{R}^m$. There are solutions if and only if $\text{rank}(\mathbf{A}) = \text{rank}([\mathbf{A},\mathbf{b}])$, that is, $\mathbf{b}$ is in the range space of $\mathbf{A}$, in another word, the equations $\mathbf{Ax} = \mathbf{b}$ are consistent. If $\text{rank}(\mathbf{A}) < \text{rank}([\mathbf{A},\mathbf{b}])$, the equations $\mathbf{Ax} = \mathbf{b}$ are not consistent. If the solution exists, the solution can be written as $\mathbf{x} = \mathbf{x}_0 + \mathbf{x}_1$, where $\mathbf{Ax}_0 = \mathbf{0}$ and $\mathbf{Ax}_1 = \mathbf{b}$.

When the solution exists but is not unique, the purpose is often to find a representative solution called the minimum norm solution, $\mathbf{x}$: $\mathbf{Ax} = \mathbf{b}$ and $\|\mathbf{x}\|_2$ is minimum. When the solution does not exist, for any $\mathbf{x} \in \mathbb{R}^n$, $\mathbf{Ax} - \mathbf{b} \neq \mathbf{0}$. The purpose is often to find one $\mathbf{x}$ so that $\mathbf{b} - \|\mathbf{Ax}\|_2$ is minimum; such $\mathbf{x}$ is called a minimum residual solution. If $\text{rank}(\mathbf{A}) < n$, the minimum residual solution is not unique. In such a case, we want to find one minimum residual solution with the minimum norm: $\mathbf{b} - \|\mathbf{Ax}\|_2$ is minimum and $\|\mathbf{x}\|_2$ is minimum.

If $m = n$, $\mathbf{A}$ is a square matrix. The condition of the existence of any solutions of $\mathbf{Ax} = \mathbf{b}$ is same as the case $m \neq n$ discussed in the last paragraphs. Further in case of the square matrix, we have the unique solution if and only if $r = \text{rank}(\mathbf{A}) = m$. The unique solution can be written as $\mathbf{x} = \mathbf{A}^{-1}\mathbf{b}$.

Depending on the conditions imposed by the given linear equations, $\mathbf{Ax} = \mathbf{b}$, the problem of the solution of linear equations is to find the unique solution, the unique minimum norm solution or the unique minimum residual solution. Many algorithms to solve such a problem will be presented in Chapters 4 and 5.

Permutations When solving linear equations, permutations are an important operation. Now let us look at a simple example,

$$\begin{aligned} x_1 + 33x_2 + 2x_3 &= 10, \\ 11x_1 + 2x_2 + x_3 &= 20, \\ x_1 + 2x_2 + 22x_3 &= 30. \end{aligned} \tag{1.26}$$

We can rewrite Eq. (1.26) in a different order as follows:

$$\begin{aligned} 11x_1 + 2x_2 + x_3 &= 20, \\ x_1 + 2x_2 + 22x_3 &= 30, \\ x_1 + 33x_2 + 2x_3 &= 10. \end{aligned} \tag{1.27}$$

Then, we relabel the unknowns as $x_1 \mapsto y_1, x_2 \mapsto y_3, x_3 \mapsto y_2$ and write Eq. (1.27) in terms of y_1, y_2, and y_3,

$$
\begin{aligned}
11y_1 + y_2 + 2y_3 &= 20, \\
y_1 + 22y_2 + 2y_3 &= 30, \\
y_1 + 2y_2 + 33y_3 &= 10.
\end{aligned}
\tag{1.28}
$$

New equations (1.28) are obviously equivalent to original equations (1.26). After solving Eq. (1.28) and reversing the unknowns $y_1 \mapsto x_1, y_3 \mapsto x_2, y_2 \mapsto x_3$, we obtain the solution to original equations (1.26). Compared with original equations (1.26), new equations Eq. (1.28) have better numerical properties—it has less numerical error when solved using Gaussian eliminations and is convergent when solved using Jacobi iterations. Therefore, when we solve equations such as Eq. (1.26), we need to first transform them to a form similar to Eq. (1.28). The basic transformations are changing equations order, relabeling unknowns and reversing the relabeling of unknowns. The basic transformations are represented as permutations. For example, the reordering of equations, $p_1 = [2,3,1]$; the relabeling of unknowns, $p_2 = [1,3,2]$ and reversing the relabeling of unknowns, $p_3 = [1,3,2] = p_2^{-1}$.

Woodbury–Sherman–Morrison Formula We will use the following linear equations with special block matrices to prove the Woodbury–Sherman–Morrison formula [51]

$$
\begin{bmatrix} \mathbf{A} & \mathbf{B} \\ \mathbf{C'} & -\mathbf{I} \end{bmatrix}
\begin{bmatrix} \mathbf{X} \\ \mathbf{Y} \end{bmatrix} =
\begin{bmatrix} \mathbf{I} \\ \mathbf{0} \end{bmatrix}.
$$

The second equation gives $\mathbf{Y} = \mathbf{C'X}$. Introducing $\mathbf{Y} = \mathbf{C'X}$ to the first equation gives $(\mathbf{A} + \mathbf{BC'})\mathbf{X} = \mathbf{I}$. Therefore, the solution $\mathbf{X}$ is the inverse of $\mathbf{A} + \mathbf{BC'}$. Now by the first equation, $\mathbf{X} = \mathbf{A}^{-1}(\mathbf{I} - \mathbf{BY})$. Introducing this expression into the second equation and solve for $\mathbf{Y}$, we obtain $\mathbf{Y} = (\mathbf{I} + \mathbf{C'A}^{-1}\mathbf{B})^{-1})\mathbf{C'A}^{-1}$. Now substituting the solution of $\mathbf{Y}$ into the expression for $\mathbf{X}$, we obtain the Woodbury–Sherman–Morrison formula

$$
(\mathbf{A} + \mathbf{BC'})^{-1} = \mathbf{A}^{-1} - \mathbf{A}^{-1}\left(\mathbf{I} + \mathbf{C'A}^{-1}\mathbf{B}\right)^{-1}\mathbf{C'A}^{-1}.
\tag{1.29}
$$

The Woodbury–Sherman–Morrison formula is useful to extend the applicability of some algorithms of linear equation solutions. For example, the solution of symmetric positive definite system by Cholesky algorithm is efficient. The matrix of another system of linear equations is only slightly different from the symmetric positive definite, with differences in a few locations or with a low rank update of $\mathbf{BC'}$. By applying the Woodbury–Sherman–Morrison formula, the new system of linear equations may be solved more efficiently with Cholesky algorithm than a general linear equation solution algorithm.

Block Matrix Algorithms Many algorithms of linear equation solutions have a block matrix form. No block matrix form of algorithms will be discussed in this book. However, all the algorithms to be presented can be extended to the block matrix form. The way to extend these algorithms to block matrix forms is illustrated with the following examples.

First, we study linear equations in block matrix form,

$$
\mathbf{Ax} = \begin{bmatrix} \mathbf{A}_{11} & \mathbf{A}_{12} \\ \mathbf{A}_{21} & \mathbf{A}_{22} \end{bmatrix}
\begin{bmatrix} \mathbf{x}_1 \\ \mathbf{x}_2 \end{bmatrix} =
\begin{bmatrix} \mathbf{b}_1 \\ \mathbf{b}_2 \end{bmatrix} = \mathbf{b}.
\tag{1.30}
$$

We obtain the solution by eliminating $\mathbf{x}_1$ from the second equation or by eliminating $\mathbf{x}_2$ from the first equation. The equation is written as $\mathbf{x} = \mathbf{A}^{-1}\mathbf{b}$, where $\mathbf{A}^{-1}$ is as follows:

$$
\mathbf{A}^{-1} = \begin{bmatrix} \mathbf{A}_{11}^{-1} + \mathbf{A}_{11}^{-1}\mathbf{A}_{12}\mathbf{B}_{22}^{-1}\mathbf{A}_{21}\mathbf{A}_{11}^{-1} & -\mathbf{A}_{11}^{-1}\mathbf{A}_{12}\mathbf{B}_{22}^{-1} \\ -\mathbf{B}_{22}^{-1}\mathbf{A}_{21}\mathbf{A}_{11}^{-1} & \mathbf{B}_{22}^{-1} \end{bmatrix}
$$
$$
= \begin{bmatrix} \mathbf{B}_{11}^{-1} & -\mathbf{B}_{11}^{-1}\mathbf{A}_{12}\mathbf{A}_{22}^{-1} \\ -\mathbf{A}_{22}^{-1}\mathbf{A}_{12}\mathbf{B}_{11}^{-1} & \mathbf{A}_{22}^{-1} + \mathbf{A}_{22}^{-1}\mathbf{A}_{21}\mathbf{B}_{11}^{-1}\mathbf{A}_{12}\mathbf{A}_{22}^{-1} \end{bmatrix}, \tag{1.31}
$$

where $\mathbf{B}_{22} = \mathbf{A}_{22} - \mathbf{A}_{21}\mathbf{A}_{11}^{-1}\mathbf{A}_{12}$ and $\mathbf{B}_{11} = \mathbf{A}_{11} - \mathbf{A}_{12}\mathbf{A}_{22}^{-1}\mathbf{A}_{21}$ are both called Schur complement. Here, we assume $\mathbf{A}_{11}$ and $\mathbf{B}_{22}$ are invertible in the first equation of (1.31), and $\mathbf{A}_{22}$ and $\mathbf{B}_{11}$ are invertible in the second equation of (1.31).

The block form of LU decomposition of $\mathbf{A}$ is shown below,

$$
\mathbf{A} = \begin{bmatrix} \mathbf{A}_{11} & \mathbf{A}_{12} \\ \mathbf{A}_{21} & \mathbf{A}_{22} \end{bmatrix} = \begin{bmatrix} \mathbf{L}_{11} & \mathbf{0} \\ \mathbf{L}_{21} & \mathbf{L}_{22} \end{bmatrix} \begin{bmatrix} \mathbf{U}_{11} & \mathbf{U}_{12} \\ \mathbf{0} & \mathbf{U}_{22} \end{bmatrix}
$$
$$
= \begin{bmatrix} \mathbf{L}_{11}\mathbf{U}_{11} & \mathbf{L}_{11}\mathbf{U}_{12} \\ \mathbf{L}_{21}\mathbf{U}_{11} & \mathbf{L}_{21}\mathbf{U}_{12} + \mathbf{L}_{22}\mathbf{L}_{22} \end{bmatrix}. \tag{1.32}
$$

By equating each block of the second matrix and fourth matrix of (1.32), we obtain each of the block matrices,

$$
\mathbf{L}_{11}\mathbf{U}_{11} = \mathbf{A}_{11} \quad \text{by LU}, \tag{1.33a}
$$
$$
\mathbf{U}_{12} = \mathbf{L}_{11}^{-1}\mathbf{A}_{12}, \tag{1.33b}
$$
$$
\mathbf{L}_{21} = \mathbf{A}_{21}\mathbf{U}_{11}^{-1}, \tag{1.33c}
$$
$$
\mathbf{L}_{22}\mathbf{U}_{22} = \mathbf{A}_{22} - \mathbf{L}_{21}\mathbf{U}_{12} \quad \text{by LU}. \tag{1.33d}
$$

If the block matrices have special structures, they should be exploited. The following special form of equations are found very often in practice and can be solved in the block matrix form with the ideas presented above,

$$
\begin{bmatrix} \mathbf{A} & \mathbf{B}' \\ \mathbf{B} & \mathbf{0} \end{bmatrix} \begin{bmatrix} \mathbf{x} \\ \mathbf{y} \end{bmatrix} = \begin{bmatrix} \mathbf{b} \\ \mathbf{c} \end{bmatrix}. \tag{1.34}
$$

1.1.4 SOLUTION OF EIGENVALUE PROBLEM

General Matrix For a square $\mathbf{A} \in \mathbb{R}^{n \times n}$, the eigenvalue problem is to find a $\mathbf{x} \in \mathbb{R}^n \neq \mathbf{0}$ and a scalar λ such that $\mathbf{A}\mathbf{x} = \lambda\mathbf{x}$. λ is called an eigenvalue of $\mathbf{A}$, denoted as $\lambda(\mathbf{A})$, and $\mathbf{x}$ is the eigenvector corresponding to λ. We can rewrite $\mathbf{A}\mathbf{x} = \lambda\mathbf{x}$ as $(\mathbf{A} - \lambda\mathbf{I})\mathbf{x} = \mathbf{0}$. For the nonzero $\mathbf{x}$ to exist, it is necessary and sufficient that $\det(\mathbf{A} - \lambda\mathbf{I}) = 0$. And this forms the essence of the solution of the eigenvalue problem: find the eigenvalue λ by the characteristic equation $\det(\mathbf{A} - \lambda\mathbf{I}) = 0$, then find the eigenvector $\mathbf{x}$ by solving the linear equations $(\mathbf{A} - \lambda\mathbf{I})\mathbf{x} = \mathbf{0}$,

$$
\det(\mathbf{A} - \lambda\mathbf{I}) = \det(\mathbf{A}' - \lambda\mathbf{I})
$$
$$
= \det(\mathbf{A}) - c_1\lambda + \cdots + (-1)^{n-1}\operatorname{tr}(\mathbf{A})\lambda^{n-1} + (-1)^n\lambda^n \tag{1.35}
$$
$$
= (\lambda - \lambda_1)^{\alpha_1}(\lambda - \lambda_2)^{\alpha_2} \cdots (\lambda - \lambda_s)^{\alpha_s} = 0.
$$

Eq. (1.35) is an algebraic equation of polynomial of order n, and α_i is the algebraic multiplicity of a distinct root $\lambda_i, i = 1, 2, \ldots, s$. By the fundamental theorem of algebra, $\alpha_1 + \alpha_2 + \cdots + \alpha_s = n$. For a real matrix, the coefficients of the characteristic equation are all real. The roots of the characteristic equation can be complex; however, they always appear as complex conjugate pairs. Their corresponding eigenvectors are also complex conjugate pairs. If n is odd, at least one eigenvalue is real. For each distinct λ_i, $\beta_i = \dim(\text{null}(\mathbf{A} - \lambda_i \mathbf{I}))$ is called the geometrical multiplicity of λ_i. In other words, the geometrical multiplicity of an eigenvalue is the number of linearly independent eigenvectors corresponding to that eigenvalue. In linear algebra [14, 49, 59], it proves that $1 \leq \beta_i \leq \alpha_i, i = 1, 2, \ldots, s$. As a result of this inequality, the number of all the linearly independent eigenvectors of a matrix can be less than and at most equal to the matrix order.

If $\beta_i = \alpha_i, i = 1, 2, \ldots, s$, then $\mathbf{A}$ has n linearly independent eigenvectors. If $\alpha_i = 1$, then $\beta_i = \alpha_i = 1$. When $\mathbf{A}$ has n linearly independent eigenvectors, we can write all $\mathbf{A}\mathbf{x}_i = \lambda_i \mathbf{x}_i, i = 1, 2, \ldots, n$ as a matrix equation,

$$\mathbf{A}[\mathbf{x}_1, \mathbf{x}_2, \ldots, \mathbf{x}_n] = [\mathbf{x}_1, \mathbf{x}_2, \ldots, \mathbf{x}_n] \text{diag}(\lambda_1, \lambda_2, \ldots, \lambda_n), \tag{1.36}$$

where $\lambda_1, \lambda_2, \ldots, \lambda_n$ are possibly not distinctive. Naming $\mathbf{X} = [\mathbf{x}_1, \mathbf{x}_2, \ldots, \mathbf{x}_n]$ and $\Lambda = \text{diag}(\lambda_1, \lambda_2, \ldots, \lambda_n)$, then we can write Eq. (1.36) equivalently as

$$\mathbf{A}\mathbf{X} = \mathbf{X}\Lambda, \tag{1.37a}$$

$$\mathbf{X}^{-1}\mathbf{A} = \Lambda\mathbf{X}^{-1}, \tag{1.37b}$$

$$\mathbf{A} = \mathbf{X}\Lambda\mathbf{X}^{-1}, \tag{1.37c}$$

$$\mathbf{X}^{-1}\mathbf{A}\mathbf{X} = \Lambda. \tag{1.37d}$$

In this case, $\mathbf{A}$ is similar to a diagonal matrix, or is diagonalizable, or non-defective.

On the other hand, for λ_i, when $\alpha_i > 1, 1 \leq \beta_i < \alpha_i$, for any $i \in (1, 2, \ldots, s)$, $(\mathbf{A} - \lambda_i \mathbf{I})\mathbf{x}_i = \mathbf{0}$ cannot provide enough linearly independent eigenvectors to satisfy Eq. (1.36). In this case, $\mathbf{A}$ cannot be diagonalized or defective. The closest form to a diagonal matrix $\mathbf{A}$ is similar to is the Jordan canonical form

$$\mathbf{X}^{-1}\mathbf{A}\mathbf{X} = \text{diag}(\mathbf{J}_1, \mathbf{J}_2, \ldots, \mathbf{J}_s), \tag{1.38}$$

where $\mathbf{J}_i$ is the Jordan block corresponding to $\lambda_i, i = 1, 2, \ldots, s$. The Jordan block $\mathbf{J}_i$ is bi-diagonal, whose diagonal has values of λ_i and super-diagonal has values of 1s or 0s, as illustrated in the following example:

$$\mathbf{J}_i = \begin{bmatrix} \lambda_i & 1 & & & & \\ & \lambda_i & 0 & & & \\ & & \lambda_i & 1 & & \\ & & & \lambda_i & 1 & \\ & & & & \lambda_i & 0 \\ & & & & & \lambda_i \end{bmatrix} = \lambda_i \mathbf{I}_i + \mathbf{N}_i. \tag{1.39}$$

The size of $\mathbf{J}_i$ is α_i, the algebraic multiplicity of λ_i. The 0s on the super-diagonal divide $\mathbf{J}_i$ into a number of Jordan sub-blocks. A Jordan sub-block has only 1s on the super-diagonal or is 1×1. The number of Jordan sub-blocks in $\mathbf{J}_i$ is β_i, the geometrical multiplicity of λ_i. The size of each Jordan sub-block in $\mathbf{J}_i$ and the corresponding columns $\mathbf{X}_i$ of $\mathbf{X}$ in Eq. (1.38) are obtained through the solution of null space of $(\mathbf{A} - \lambda_i \mathbf{I})^k$, for $k = 1, 2, \ldots, l$. Here, l is the minimum l such that $\dim\left(\text{null}(\mathbf{A} - \lambda_i \mathbf{I})^{l+1}\right) = \dim\left(\text{null}(\mathbf{A} - \lambda_i \mathbf{I})^l\right) = \alpha_i$.

By Eqs. (1.38) and (1.39), we have

$$\dim\left(\text{null}\,(\mathbf{A} - \lambda_i\mathbf{I})^k\right) = \dim\left(\text{null}\left(\mathbf{N}_i^k\right)\right). \tag{1.40}$$

By the special structure of $\mathbf{N}_i$ of Eq. (1.39), we can see that $\dim\left(\text{null}\left(\mathbf{N}_i^k\right)\right) - \dim\left(\text{null}\left(\mathbf{N}_i^{k-1}\right)\right)$ determines the number of Jordan sub-blocks with a size of at least k. Therefore, the number of Jordan sub-blocks with the size k is determined by

$$2\dim\left(\text{null}\left(\mathbf{N}_i^k\right)\right) - \dim\left(\text{null}\left(\mathbf{N}_i^{k+1}\right)\right) - \dim\left(\text{null}\left(\mathbf{N}_i^{k-1}\right)\right). \tag{1.41}$$

By Eq. (1.40), this number can be calculated as follows:

$$2\dim\left(\text{null}\,(\mathbf{A} - \lambda_i\mathbf{I})^k\right) - \dim\left(\text{null}\,(\mathbf{A} - \lambda_i\mathbf{I})^{k+1}\right) - \dim\left(\text{null}\,(\mathbf{A} - \lambda_i\mathbf{I})^{k-1}\right). \tag{1.42}$$

Further we have $\text{null}\,(\mathbf{A} - \lambda_i\mathbf{I})^{k+1} \supseteq \text{null}\,(\mathbf{A} - \lambda_i\mathbf{I})^k$. Therefore, by comparing $\text{null}\,(\mathbf{A} - \lambda_i\mathbf{I})^{k+1}$ and $\text{null}\,(\mathbf{A} - \lambda_i\mathbf{I})^k$, we can ascertain the location of each solution of $\text{null}\,(\mathbf{A} - \lambda_i\mathbf{I})^k$ in $\mathbf{X}$ of Eq. (1.38).

From the above discussion, we can see that the Jordan canonical form always exists and is unique up to the permutations of $\mathbf{J}_i$s and the permutations of Jordan sub-block in each $\mathbf{J}_i$. If the size of all Jordan blocks is 1, Eq. (1.38) is reduced to Eq. (1.36), the case that $\mathbf{A}$ is diagonalizable.

However, the determination of Λ and $\mathbf{J}$ according to Eq. (1.36) and Eq. (1.38) is a difficult task, because of the conditioning of $\mathbf{X}$ in Eqs. (1.36) and (1.38) and inevitable errors in any numerical calculations. A numerical stable algorithm can be obtained if we use orthogonal matrix $\mathbf{Q}$ in the similarity transformation. Suppose we obtained an arbitrary eigenvalue λ_1 and a unit length eigenvector $\mathbf{q}_1$, $\mathbf{A}\mathbf{q}_1 = \lambda_1\mathbf{q}_1$. From $\mathbf{q}_1$, we can construct an orthogonal complementary matrix $\mathbf{Q}_{1\perp} \in \mathbb{R}^{n\times(n-1)}$ by Algorithm 1.1, so that

$$\left(\mathbf{q}_1, \mathbf{Q}_{1\perp}\right)' \mathbf{A}\left(\mathbf{q}_1, \mathbf{Q}_{1\perp}\right) = \begin{bmatrix} \mathbf{q}_1'\lambda_1\mathbf{q}_1 & \mathbf{q}_1'\mathbf{A}\mathbf{Q}_{1\perp} \\ \mathbf{Q}_{1\perp}'\lambda_1\mathbf{q}_1 & \mathbf{Q}_{1\perp}'\mathbf{A}\mathbf{Q}_{1\perp} \end{bmatrix} = \begin{bmatrix} \lambda_1 & \mathbf{A}_{12} \\ \mathbf{0} & \mathbf{A}_{22} \end{bmatrix}. \tag{1.43}$$

Now suppose we obtained another arbitrary λ_2 and $\mathbf{q}_2$: $\mathbf{A}_{22}\mathbf{q}_2 = \lambda_2\mathbf{q}_2$. And we construct an orthogonal complementary matrix $\mathbf{Q}_{2\perp} \in \mathbb{R}^{n\times(n-2)}$, so that

$$\begin{aligned} &\begin{bmatrix} 1 & \mathbf{0} & \mathbf{0}' \\ \mathbf{0} & \mathbf{q}_2 & \mathbf{Q}_{2\perp} \end{bmatrix}' \begin{bmatrix} \lambda_1 & \mathbf{A}_{12} \\ \mathbf{0} & \mathbf{A}_{22} \end{bmatrix} \begin{bmatrix} 1 & \mathbf{0} & \mathbf{0}' \\ \mathbf{0} & \mathbf{q}_2 & \mathbf{Q}_{2\perp} \end{bmatrix} \\ &= \begin{bmatrix} \lambda_1 & \mathbf{A}_{12}\mathbf{q}_2 & \mathbf{A}_{12}\mathbf{Q}_{2\perp} \\ 0 & \mathbf{q}_2'\lambda_2\mathbf{q}_2 & \mathbf{q}_2'\mathbf{A}_{22}\mathbf{Q}_{2\perp} \\ \mathbf{0} & \mathbf{Q}_{2\perp}'\lambda_2\mathbf{q}_2 & \mathbf{Q}_{2\perp}'\mathbf{A}_{22}\mathbf{Q}_{2\perp} \end{bmatrix} = \begin{bmatrix} \lambda_1 & A_{12} & \mathbf{A}_{13} \\ 0 & \lambda_2 & \mathbf{A}_{23} \\ 0 & 0 & \mathbf{A}_{33} \end{bmatrix}. \end{aligned} \tag{1.44}$$

The above process can be repeated for n steps. We then proved the Schur decomposition of $\mathbf{A}$,

$$\mathbf{Q}'\mathbf{A}\mathbf{Q} = \mathbf{T}, \tag{1.45}$$

where $\mathbf{T}$ is an upper triangular matrix with the eigenvalues of $\mathbf{A}$ on the diagonal and $\mathbf{Q}$ is an orthogonal matrix obtained from

$$\mathbf{Q} = \left[\mathbf{q}_1, \mathbf{Q}_{1\perp}\right]\begin{bmatrix} 1 & \mathbf{0} & \mathbf{0} \\ \mathbf{0} & \mathbf{q}_2 & \mathbf{Q}_{2\perp} \end{bmatrix}\cdots \tag{1.46}$$

Avoid Complex Arithmetic For a real matrix, the complex eigenvalues and eigenvectors appear as complex conjugate pairs. Suppose λ and $\mathbf{x}$ are a pair of complex eigenvalue and eigenvector: $\lambda = \xi + i\eta$ and $\mathbf{x} = \mathbf{x}_1 + i\mathbf{x}_2$. We can avoid the complex arithmetic following the procedures discussed below.

For the diagonal decomposition Eq. (1.36), $\mathbf{A}\mathbf{x} = \lambda\mathbf{x}$ can be written as follows:

$$\mathbf{A}\left[\mathbf{x}_1, \mathbf{x}_2\right] = \left[\mathbf{x}_1, \mathbf{x}_2\right]\begin{bmatrix} \xi & \eta \\ -\eta & \xi \end{bmatrix}. \tag{1.47}$$

For the Jordan decomposition Eq. (1.38), $\mathbf{A}\mathbf{y} = \mathbf{x} + \lambda\mathbf{y}$, where λ and $\mathbf{x}$ are shown above and $\mathbf{y} = \mathbf{y}_1 + i\mathbf{y}_2$, can be written as follows:

$$\mathbf{A}\left[\mathbf{x}_1, \mathbf{x}_2\,\mathbf{y}_1, \mathbf{y}_2\right] = \left[\mathbf{x}_1, \mathbf{x}_2, \mathbf{y}_1, \mathbf{y}_2\right]\begin{bmatrix} \xi & \eta & 1 & 0 \\ -\eta & \xi & 0 & 1 \\ 0 & 0 & \xi & \eta \\ 0 & 0 & -\eta & \xi \end{bmatrix}. \tag{1.48}$$

For the Schur decomposition, Eq. (1.45), the orthogonal transformation matrix $\mathbf{Q}$ is built in the following way. From Eq. (1.47), we can expect $\left[\mathbf{x}_1, \mathbf{x}_2\right]$ are linearly independent, otherwise $\eta = 0$ and this contradicts the assumption of the complex eigenvalue. We can construct two orthogonal vectors $\mathbf{q}_1, \mathbf{q}_2$ by Algorithm 1.1, such that

$$\left[\mathbf{x}_1, \mathbf{x}_2\right] = \left[\mathbf{q}_1, \mathbf{q}_2\right]\begin{bmatrix} r_{11} & r_{12} \\ 0 & r_{22} \end{bmatrix}.$$

Then, we can write Eq. (1.47) as follows:

$$\mathbf{A}\left[\mathbf{q}_1, \mathbf{q}_2\right] = \left[\mathbf{q}_1, \mathbf{q}_2\right]\begin{bmatrix} r_{11} & r_{12} \\ 0 & r_{22} \end{bmatrix}\begin{bmatrix} \xi & \eta \\ -\eta & \xi \end{bmatrix}\begin{bmatrix} r_{11} & r_{12} \\ 0 & r_{22} \end{bmatrix}^{-1}$$

$$= \left[\mathbf{q}_1, \mathbf{q}_2\right]\begin{bmatrix} \xi - \frac{r_{12}}{r_{11}}\eta & \left(\frac{r_{11}}{r_{22}} + \frac{r_{12}^2}{r_{11}r_{22}}\right)\eta \\ -\frac{r_{22}}{r_{11}}\eta & \xi + \frac{r_{12}}{r_{11}}\eta \end{bmatrix} = \left[\mathbf{q}_1, \mathbf{q}_2\right]\mathbf{D}.$$

An orthogonal complementary matrix $\mathbf{Q}_{12\perp}$ of $\left[\mathbf{q}_1, \mathbf{q}_2\right]$ can be constructed. Then,

$$\left[\mathbf{q}_1, \mathbf{q}_2, \mathbf{Q}_{12\perp}\right]'\mathbf{A}\left[\mathbf{q}_1, \mathbf{q}_2, \mathbf{Q}_{12\perp}\right]$$
$$= \begin{bmatrix} \left[\mathbf{q}_1, \mathbf{q}_2\right]' \\ \mathbf{Q}_{12\perp}' \end{bmatrix}\left[\left[\mathbf{q}_1, \mathbf{q}_2\right]\mathbf{D}, \mathbf{A}\mathbf{Q}_{12\perp}\right] = \begin{bmatrix} \mathbf{D} & \left[\mathbf{q}_1, \mathbf{q}_2\right]'\mathbf{A}\mathbf{Q}_{12\perp} \\ 0 & \mathbf{Q}_{12\perp}'\mathbf{A}\mathbf{Q}_{12\perp} \end{bmatrix}. \tag{1.49}$$

The same process can be applied to $\mathbf{Q}_{12\perp}'\mathbf{A}\mathbf{Q}_{12\perp}$. Then, $\mathbf{A}$ is transformed to a quasi upper triangular matrix with orthogonal similarity transformations. The diagonal of the quasi upper triangular matrix is made of 1×1 and 2×2 blocks of eigenvalues of $\mathbf{A}$.

Transposed Matrix In Eq. (1.37b), we rename $\mathbf{Y}' = \mathbf{X}^{-1}$ and rewrite Eq. (1.37b) as follows:

$$\mathbf{Y}'\mathbf{A} = \Lambda\mathbf{Y}'. \tag{1.50}$$

We call $\mathbf{Y}$ the left eigenvectors of $\mathbf{A}$. In this perspective, we call $\mathbf{X}$ in Eq. (1.37a) the right eigenvectors of $\mathbf{A}$. Taking the transpose of Eq. (1.50), we rewrite it as follows:

$$\mathbf{A}'\mathbf{Y} = \mathbf{Y}\Lambda' \tag{1.51}$$

and we see that $\mathbf{Y}$ is the eigenvector of $\mathbf{A}'$. If $\mathbf{A}$ is diagonalizable, we can always choose $\mathbf{X}$ and $\mathbf{Y}$ to be of the form $\mathbf{Y}' = \mathbf{X}^{-1}$. If $\mathbf{A}$ is real, from Eq. (1.35), we see that the coefficients of the characteristic polynomial of $\mathbf{A}$ and $\mathbf{A}'$ are same, so the eigenvalues of $\mathbf{A}$ and $\mathbf{A}'$ are same.

If $\mathbf{A}$ is not diagonalizable, we can have similar conclusions from Eq. (1.38). In Eq. (1.38), we rename $\mathbf{Y}' = \mathbf{X}^{-1}$, take the transpose of Eq. (1.38) and we get $\mathbf{A}'\mathbf{Y} = \mathbf{Y}\mathbf{J}'$.

Symmetric Matrix If $\mathbf{A}$ is symmetric, most conclusions of this section can be simplified. First of all, a symmetric matrix can always be diagonalized with orthogonal transformations. From Eq. (1.45), $\mathbf{Q}'\mathbf{A}\mathbf{Q} = \mathbf{T}$, take the transpose and note that $\mathbf{A}' = \mathbf{A}$, we see that $\mathbf{T}' = \mathbf{T}$. But $\mathbf{T}$ is upper triangular; therefore, the Schur decomposition of a symmetric matrix must be diagonal. Second, the eigenvalues of a symmetric matrix must be real. Take the conjugate transpose of $\lambda = \mathbf{q}'\mathbf{A}\mathbf{q}$, we have $\lambda' = \mathbf{q}'\mathbf{A}'\mathbf{q} = \mathbf{q}'\mathbf{A}\mathbf{q} = \lambda$. Therefore, λ is real. Because all the eigenvalues are real, we can order them from small to large and order the columns of $\mathbf{Q}$ accordingly,

$$\lambda_1 \le \lambda_2 \le \lambda_3 \le \cdots \le \lambda_n$$
$$[\mathbf{q}_1, \mathbf{q}_2, \ldots, \mathbf{q}_n]' \mathbf{A} [\mathbf{q}_1, \mathbf{q}_2, \ldots, \mathbf{q}_n] = \mathrm{diag}(\lambda_1, \lambda_2, \ldots, \lambda_n). \tag{1.52}$$

For any vector $\mathbf{v} \in \mathbb{R}^n$, we define the Rayleigh quotient as follows:

$$r(\mathbf{v}) = \frac{\mathbf{v}'\mathbf{A}\mathbf{v}}{\mathbf{v}'\mathbf{v}}. \tag{1.53}$$

If we take the stationary condition of $r(\mathbf{v})$,

$$\frac{\partial r(\mathbf{v})}{\partial \mathbf{v}} = \frac{1}{\mathbf{v}'\mathbf{v}}(\mathbf{A}\mathbf{v} - r\mathbf{v}) = \mathbf{0} \tag{1.54}$$

we see that the gradient of $r(\mathbf{v})$ is zero at any eigenvectors and the stationary value of $r(\mathbf{v})$ is an eigenvalue.

The columns of $\mathbf{Q}$ form orthonormal bases of $\mathbb{R}^n$. Any vector $\mathbf{v} \in \mathbb{R}^n$ can be decomposed in $\mathbf{Q}$ as

$$\mathbf{v} = \mathbf{Q}(\mathbf{Q}'\mathbf{v}) = \mathbf{Q}\mathbf{v}_+. \tag{1.55}$$

Then, the Rayleigh quotient can be calculated in terms of $\mathbf{v}_+$ as follows:

$$r(\mathbf{v}) = \frac{\mathbf{v}_+'\mathbf{Q}'\mathbf{A}\mathbf{Q}\mathbf{v}_+}{\mathbf{v}_+'\mathbf{Q}'\mathbf{Q}\mathbf{v}_+} = \frac{\mathbf{v}_+'\Lambda\mathbf{v}_+}{\mathbf{v}_+'\mathbf{v}_+} = \frac{\sum_{i=1}^n \lambda_i v_{+i}^2}{\sum_{i=1}^n v_{+i}^2} = \sum_{i=1}^n \beta_i \lambda_i, \tag{1.56}$$

where $0 \le \beta_i \le 1$ and $\sum_{i=1}^n \beta_i = 1$. From this we obtained the following important property:

$$\lambda_1 \le r(\mathbf{v}) \le \lambda_n, \quad \forall \mathbf{v} \in \mathbb{R}^n,$$
$$\lambda_1 = \min_{\mathbf{v}\in\mathbb{R}^n} r(\mathbf{v}), \quad \lambda_n = \max_{\mathbf{v}\in\mathbb{R}^n} r(\mathbf{v}). \tag{1.57}$$

If $\mathbf{v}$ has constraints, the minimum of $r(\mathbf{v})$ will increase and the maximum of $r(\mathbf{v})$ will decrease. For example, $\forall \mathbf{v} \in \mathbf{Q}_k = \mathrm{span}(\mathbf{q}_1, \mathbf{q}_2, \ldots, \mathbf{q}_k)$, $\lambda_k \ge r(\mathbf{v})$, and $\forall \mathbf{v} \in \mathbf{Q}_{n-k+1} = \mathrm{span}(\mathbf{q}_k, \mathbf{q}_{k+1}, \ldots, \mathbf{q}_n)$, $\lambda_k \le r(\mathbf{v})$.

Let $\mathbf{V}_k$ and $\mathbf{V}_{n-k+1}$ are two arbitrary subspaces of $\mathbb{R}^n$,

$$\mathbf{V}_k = \{\mathbf{V} \subset \mathbb{R}^n \mid \dim(\mathbf{V}) = k\}$$
$$= \left\{\mathbf{v} \in \mathbb{R}^n \mid \mathbf{w}_j'\mathbf{v} = 0, \forall \mathbf{w}_j \in \mathbb{R}^n, j = 1, \ldots, n - k\right\},$$
$$\mathbf{V}_{n-k+1} = \{\mathbf{V} \subset \mathbb{R}^n \mid \dim(\mathbf{V}) = n - k + 1\}$$
$$= \left\{\mathbf{v} \in \mathbb{R}^n \mid \mathbf{w}_j'\mathbf{v} = 0, \forall \mathbf{w}_j \in \mathbb{R}^n, j = 1, \ldots, k - 1\right\}.$$

Because $\mathbf{V}_k \supset \mathbf{Q}_k$ and the minimum of a function cannot increase in a larger domain, we must have $\min \max_{\mathbf{v} \in \mathbf{V}_k} r(\mathbf{v}) \leq \max_{\mathbf{q} \in \mathbf{Q}_k} r(\mathbf{q}) = \lambda_k$. Further $r(\mathbf{q}) \leq \lambda_k$ for any $\mathbf{q} \in \mathbf{V}_k \cap \mathbf{Q}_{n-k+1}$ and the maximum of a function cannot decrease in a larger domain, we must have $\min \max_{\mathbf{v} \in \mathbf{V}_k} r(\mathbf{v}) \geq r(\mathbf{q}) \geq \lambda_k$. Considering the two inequalities, we obtained the Courant–Fischer min–max theorem

$$\lambda_k = \min_{\mathbf{v} \in \mathbf{V}_k} \max r(\mathbf{v}). \tag{1.58}$$

Based on the same reasoning for $\mathbf{v} \in \mathbf{V}_{n-k+1}$, we can have another form of the min–max theorem

$$\lambda_k = \max_{\mathbf{v} \in \mathbf{V}_{n-k+1}} \min r(\mathbf{v}). \tag{1.59}$$

The min–max theorem tells us that any eigenvalues of a symmetric matrix $\mathbf{A} \in \mathbb{R}^{n \times n}$ can be understood to be the minimum or maximum of the Rayleigh quotient in a properly constrained subspaces of $\mathbb{R}^n$. Eq. (1.58) and Eq. (1.59) are extensions of Eq. (1.57).

Generalized eigenvalue Problems For two square matrices, $\mathbf{A}, \mathbf{B} \in \mathbb{R}^{n \times n}$, the generalized eigenvalue problem is to find a $\mathbf{x} \in \mathbb{R}^n \neq \mathbf{0}$ and a scalar λ such that $\mathbf{Ax} = \lambda \mathbf{Bx}$. λ is called an eigenvalue of the pair $(\mathbf{A}, \mathbf{B})$, denoted as $\lambda(\mathbf{A}, \mathbf{B})$, and $\mathbf{x}$ is the eigenvector of the pair $(\mathbf{A}, \mathbf{B})$ corresponding to λ. For the nonzero $\mathbf{x}$ to exist, it is necessary and sufficient that $\det(\mathbf{A} - \lambda \mathbf{B}) = 0$. And this forms the essence of the solution of the generalized eigenvalue problem: find the eigenvalue λ by the characteristic equation $\det(\mathbf{A} - \lambda \mathbf{B}) = 0$, then find the eigenvector $\mathbf{x}$ by solving the linear equations $(\mathbf{A} - \lambda \mathbf{B})\mathbf{x} = \mathbf{0}$,

$$
\begin{aligned}
\det(\mathbf{A} - \lambda \mathbf{B}) &= \det(\mathbf{A}' - \lambda \mathbf{B}') \\
&= \sum_{j_1, \ldots, j_n} \pm A_{1j_1} A_{2j_2} \cdots A_{nj_n} P_n(\lambda) \\
&= \det(\mathbf{A}) - c_1 \lambda^1 + c_2 \lambda^2 + \cdots + (-1)^n \lambda^n \det(\mathbf{B}).
\end{aligned} \tag{1.60}
$$

The summation is done over all the permutations of $(1, 2, \ldots, n)$. The term is positive if the permutation is even, negative otherwise. $P_n(\lambda)$ is a polynomial of λ defined below,

$$
\begin{aligned}
P_n(\lambda) = 1 &- \lambda \sum_{a=1}^{n} \frac{B_{aj_a}}{A_{aj_a}} + \lambda^2 \sum_{a=1}^{n-1} \frac{B_{aj_a}}{A_{aj_a}} \sum_{b=a+1}^{n} \frac{B_{bj_b}}{A_{bj_b}} \\
&- \lambda^3 \sum_{a=1}^{n-2} \frac{B_{aj_a}}{A_{aj_a}} \sum_{b=a+1}^{n-1} \frac{B_{bj_b}}{A_{bj_b}} \sum_{c=b+1}^{n} \frac{B_{cj_c}}{A_{cj_c}} + \cdots \\
&+ (-1)^n \lambda^n \sum_{a=1}^{1} \frac{B_{aj_a}}{A_{aj_a}} \sum_{b=a+1}^{2} \frac{B_{bj_b}}{A_{bj_b}} \cdots \sum_{z=y+1}^{n} \frac{B_{zj_z}}{A_{zj_z}}.
\end{aligned} \tag{1.61}
$$

From Eq. (1.60), we can see that the number of $\lambda(\mathbf{A},\mathbf{B})$ is equal to the order of the characteristic polynomial. The number of $\lambda(\mathbf{A},\mathbf{B})$ is n if and only if $\det(\mathbf{B}) \neq 0$. If $\det(\mathbf{B}) = 0$, the number of $\lambda(\mathbf{A},\mathbf{B})$ can be less than n. If all the coefficients of the characteristic polynomial are zeros, all the complex numbers are eigenvalues. If $\det(\mathbf{A}) \neq 0$ and all other coefficients are zeros, there are no eigenvalues. If $0 \neq \lambda \in \lambda(\mathbf{A},\mathbf{B})$, then $1/\lambda \in \lambda(\mathbf{B},\mathbf{A})$. If $\mathbf{A}$ and $\mathbf{B}$ are real matrices, the existing complex $\lambda(\mathbf{A},\mathbf{B})$ and its corresponding eigenvectors are in complex conjugate pairs.

If $\det(\mathbf{B}) \neq 0$, $\lambda(\mathbf{A},\mathbf{B})$ can be calculated as $\lambda(\mathbf{A},\mathbf{B}) = \lambda(\mathbf{B}^{-1}\mathbf{A}) = \lambda(\mathbf{A}\mathbf{B}^{-1})$. However, if $\mathbf{B}$ is not well-conditioned. the calculation of the inverse of $\mathbf{B}$ will have a negative impact on the accuracy of $\lambda(\mathbf{B}^{-1}\mathbf{A})$ or $\lambda(\mathbf{A}\mathbf{B}^{-1})$. A better approach is to transform $[\mathbf{A},\mathbf{B}]$ simultaneously by well-conditioned $\mathbf{U}$ and $\mathbf{V}$ to some simpler forms, such as diagonal, triangular, or Hessenberg, by observing that $\lambda(\mathbf{A},\mathbf{B}) = \lambda(\mathbf{UAV},\mathbf{UBV})$. In Chapters 5 and 6, we will present various algorithms to solve $\lambda(\mathbf{A},\mathbf{B})$.

If $\mathbf{A}$ and $\mathbf{B}$ are symmetric matrices, we need to use the congruent transformation of the form $\lambda(\mathbf{A},\mathbf{B}) = \lambda(\mathbf{X}'\mathbf{A}\mathbf{X},\mathbf{X}'\mathbf{B}\mathbf{X})$ to preserve the symmetry. If $\mathbf{B}$ is not positive definite, the symmetry of $\mathbf{A}$ and $\mathbf{B}$ cannot guarantee $\lambda(\mathbf{A},\mathbf{B})$ is real. If $\mathbf{B}$ is positive definite, the $\lambda(\mathbf{A},\mathbf{B})$ of the symmetric pair $[\mathbf{A},\mathbf{B}]$ is real. In this case, the eigenvectors $\mathbf{X}$ have the following orthogonal properties:

$$\mathbf{X}'\mathbf{A}\mathbf{X} = \Lambda, \qquad \mathbf{X}'\mathbf{B}\mathbf{X} = \mathbf{I}, \qquad \mathbf{A}\mathbf{X} = \mathbf{B}\mathbf{X}\Lambda. \tag{1.62}$$

1.2 A BRIEF INTRODUCTION OF MATLAB

In MATLAB, all the variables do not have an explicit type. They are created, assigned, and changed on the fly. A matrix variable can be assigned to a scalar variable or a vector variable can be assigned to a matrix variable. For the notation purpose, we do not show these kinds of assignments in this introduction and will not use them in the MATLAB codes.

In the MATLAB command window at the symbol $\gg$, enter the following input, where $\gg$ is the MATLAB command prompt.

```
>> u=[1,2,3,4,5]
u =
      1     2     3     4     5
```

The above input creates a row vector u of five columns. [1,2,3,4,5] is a row vector. For the row vector, each column is delimited by a comma. Then MATLAB outputs the execution of the input, in this case, the contents of the created u. The next example shows how the component of u is accessed.

```
>> u(3)=33
u =
      1     2    33     4     5
```

Here u(3)=33 assigns 33 to the third component of u. In MATLAB, the index of a vector or matrix starts with 1.

```
>> u(2:4)
=     2    33     4
```

u(2:4) shows the components of 2 to 4 of u, where 2:4 is actually another way of creating a row vector.

```
>> 2:4
=     2     3     4
```

2:4 means creating a row vector with the first component 2 and end component 4 in the increment of 1. More generally begin:stride:end creates a row vector with the first component begin in the increment of stride until reaching end. If stride=1, begin:1:end can be shortened as begin:end.

We can change u(2:4) as follows.

```
>> u(2:4)=[2.2,3.3,4.4]
u =
    1.0000    2.2000    3.3000    4.4000    5.0000
```

Here u(2:4)=[2.2,3.3,4.4] assigns [2.2,3.3,4.4] to the 2–4 components of u.

MATLAB is an interpretive computation environment. MATLAB will output the result of the execution of each input as shown in all the above examples. If we do not want to see the output, especially the outputs of many intermediate results of a long computation, we can add a semicolon to the end of the input. The semicolon at the end of the input will suppress the output.

```
>> u(2:4)=[22,33,44];
```

Now u(2:4) is changed to [22,33,44]. To confirm this, simply enter the name of the vector u at the command prompt >>.

```
>> u
u =
    1    22    33    44    5
```

The transpose of a row vector is a column vector. The following input u=u' assigns the transpose of u to itself. Apostrophe "'" is the symbol for the transpose.

```
>> u=u'
u =
    1
    22
    33
    44
    5
```

For the column vector, its components are accessed in the same way as the row vector, such as u(3) and u(2:4).

```
>> u(2:4)=[2.2;3.3;4.4];
```

Here u(2:4)=[2.2;3.3;4.4] assigns [2.2;3.3;4.4] to u(2:4). [2.2;3.3;4.4] itself is a column vector. For the column vector, each row is delimited by a semicolon.

Vector computations, scalar product, addition, dot(inner) product, and outer product are demonstrated in the following four examples.

```
>> v=1.1*u
v =
    1.1000
    2.4200
    3.6300
    4.8400
    5.5000

>> v=v+0.1*u
v =
    1.2000
    2.6400
```

```
     3.9600
     5.2800
     6.0000

>> alpha=u'*v
alpha =
    73.3080

>> A=u*v'
A =
     1.2000      2.6400      3.9600      5.2800      6.0000
     2.6400      5.8080      8.7120     11.6160     13.2000
     3.9600      8.7120     13.0680     17.4240     19.8000
     5.2800     11.6160     17.4240     23.2320     26.4000
     6.0000     13.2000     19.8000     26.4000     30.0000
```

The following input redefines the matrix A, which has three rows and five columns. Each row is delimited by a semicolon. Each column is delimited by a comma or space.

```
>> A = [11,12,13,14,15;
        21,22,23,24,25;
        31,32,33,34,35]
A =
    11    12    13    14    15
    21    22    23    24    25
    31    32    33    34    35
```

The access of components of A is demonstrated by the following example:

```
>> A(1,2)=1.2
A =
    11.0000     1.2000    13.0000    14.0000    15.0000
    21.0000    22.0000    23.0000    24.0000    25.0000
    31.0000    32.0000    33.0000    34.0000    35.0000
```

Here A(1,2)=1.2 assigns 1.2 to row 1 and column 2 of A.

```
>> A(2,:)
=    21    22    23    24    25
```

Here A(2,:) shows the contents of row 2 of A.

```
>> A(2,:) = [2.1,2.2,2.3,2.4,2.5]
A =
    11.0000     1.2000    13.0000    14.0000    15.0000
     2.1000     2.2000     2.3000     2.4000     2.5000
    31.0000    32.0000    33.0000    34.0000    35.0000
```

Here A(2,:)=[2.1,2.2,2.3,2.4,2.5] assigns [2.1,2.2,2.3,2.4,2.5] to the second row of A.

```
>> A(:,2)=[12;22;32];
```

Here A(:,2)=[12;22;32] assigns [12;22;32] to the second column of A.

```
>> A(2:3,2:4)=[22,23,24;3.2,3.3,3.4]
A =
    11.0000    12.0000    13.0000    14.0000    15.0000
     2.1000    22.0000    23.0000    24.0000     2.5000
    31.0000     3.2000     3.3000     3.4000    35.0000
```

Here A(2:3,2:4)=[22,23,24;3.2,3.3,3.4] assigns [22,23,24;3.2,3.3,3.4] to the rows 2 and 3 and columns 2 and 4 of A.

```
>> B=A(1:3,1:3);
>> B=0.5*(B+B')
B =
    11.0000     7.0500    22.0000
     7.0500    22.0000    13.1000
    22.0000    13.1000     3.3000
```

Here B=A(1:3,1:3) assigns the first three rows and columns of A to a new matrix B. Then B=0.5*(B+B') sets B's symmetric part to itself.

We, as MATLAB users, do not need to worry about the memory allocation and deallocation of any variables. However, to improve the efficiency of the MATLAB memory management, it is recommended to set up the size correctly with the MATLAB's zeros function for a matrix or vector.

```
>> v1 = zeros(8,1);
>> v2 = zeros(1,8);
>> V = zeros(8);
for j=1:8
    v1(j) = j;   v2(j) = 2*j;
    for k=1:8
        V(j,k) = j+2*k;
    end
end

>> v1
v1 =
    1
    2
    3
    4
    5
    6
    7
    8

>> v2
v2 =
    2    4    6    8   10   12   14   16

>> V
V =
    3    5    7    9   11   13   15   17
    4    6    8   10   12   14   16   18
    5    7    9   11   13   15   17   19
    6    8   10   12   14   16   18   20
    7    9   11   13   15   17   19   21
    8   10   12   14   16   18   20   22
    9   11   13   15   17   19   21   23
   10   12   14   16   18   20   22   24
```

As can be seen from the MATLAB output, v1 = zeros(8,1) defines v1 to be a column vector of 8, v2 = zeros(1,8) defines v2 to be a row vector of 8, and V = zeros(8) defines a square matrix of 8×8. It is noted that V = zeros(8) is equivalent to the input V = zeros(8,8). More generally, to set up a matrix of

$m \times n$, we can use zeros(m,n). Besides zeros, eye and ones are other two MATLAB functions of creating matrices. They are demonstrated by the examples below.

```
>> I=eye(3)
I =
     1     0     0
     0     1     0
     0     0     1

>> Y=ones(3,8)
Y =
     1     1     1     1     1     1     1     1
     1     1     1     1     1     1     1     1
     1     1     1     1     1     1     1     1
```

The zeros, eye, ones functions bring up the MATLAB's help system. To find how to use zeros, issue help zeros. MATLAB outputs the following:

```
>> help zeros
 ZEROS  Zeros array.
    ZEROS(N) is an N-by-N matrix of zeros.

    ZEROS(M,N) or ZEROS([M,N]) is an M-by-N matrix of zeros.
...

 Example:
      x = zeros(2,3,'int8');
```

The MATLAB help system can be explored by using help help.

```
>> help help
 HELP Display help text in Command Window.
    HELP, by itself, lists all primary help topics. Each primary topic
    corresponds to a directory name on the MATLABPATH.

    HELP / lists a description of all operators and special characters.

    HELP FUN displays a description of and syntax for the function FUN.
    When FUN is in multiple directories on the MATLAB path, HELP displays
    information about the first FUN found on the path and lists
    PATHNAME/FUN for other (overloaded) FUNs.
...
```

MATLAB provides a series of functions to inquire a defined vector or matrix. We will use the above defined v1,v2,v to show the usage of a few of the functions which are used often in the MATLAB codes presented in the book. To be brief, exist('v1','var') checks if a variable with the name 'v1' exists in the current scope. size(v1) returns the size of v1. Both norm(v1) and norm(v1,2) calculate the 2-norm of v1. Both norm(V) and norm(V,2) calculate the largest singular value of V. The full detail of each function can be found using the MATLAB help system. For example, help exist, help size, help length, help norm, etc.

```
>> [exist('v1','var'),exist('V','var'),exist('v3','var')]
=    1    1    0

>> [size(v1);size(v2);size(V)]
=    8    1
     1    8
     8    8

>> [size(v1,1),size(v1,2),size(v2,1),size(v2,2),size(V,1),size(V,2)]
=    8    1    1    8    8    8

>> length(v1)==length(v2) && length(v2)==length(V)
=    1

>> [norm(v1),norm(v1,2),norm(v1,1),norm(v1,inf),norm(v1,-inf)]
=  14.2829    14.2829    36.0000    8.0000    1.0000

>> [norm(v2),norm(v2,2),norm(v2,1),norm(v2,inf),norm(v2,-inf)]
=  28.5657    28.5657    72.0000    16.0000    2.0000

>> [norm(V),norm(V,2),norm(V,1),norm(V,inf),norm(v2,'fro')]
=  115.3693   115.3693   164.0000   136.0000    28.5657
```

A few more MATLAB functions will be introduced in the subsequent sections when they arise.

We, the MATLAB users, can also write MATLAB functions to perform any computations. The syntax of the function and way to call it are demonstrated by the following simple example:

```
function [v1,v2,V] = foo(n)

v1 = zeros(n,1);   v2 = zeros(1,n);   V = zeros(n);
for j=1:n
    v1(j) = j;   v2(j) = 2*j;
    for k=1:8
        V(j,k) = j+2*k;
    end
end
end
```

Save the above MATLAB code to foo.m and keep it in a directory in the MATLAB search path. Then in the MATLAB command window or in another MATLAB function, we can call the defined function as follows:

```
[u1,u2,U]=foo(8);
```

This will create two vectors u1,u2 and a matrix U which are identical in contents to the already defined v1,v2,V. To create these vectors and matrix of a different size, we can do it similarly.

```
>> [w1,w2,W]=foo(3)
w1 =
     1
     2
     3
w2 =
     2    4    6
W =
     3    5    7    9    11    13    15    17
     4    6    8    10   12    14    16    18
     5    7    9    11   13    15    17    19
```

MATLAB is an interpretive computation environment as well as an interpretive computer language. It provides the constructs found in most computer languages, such as conditional blocks and loops. The keywords for these constructs, e.g. if,else,for,while, are very similar to C or FORTRAN. MATLAB also provides very similar operators to those in C, such as &&, ||, ~ for logic *and, or, not* and +,-,*,/ for additions and multiplications of matrices and vectors. The meaning and usage of all the keywords and operators are obvious. They can also be explored using the MATLAB help system. For example, help if, help &&, and help *.

Vectors and matrices store numerical data. Cells can store a mixed type of data, such as strings and numbers, vectors and matrices of different sizes. Cells are useful to organize related data as a single object and used as input arguments to MATLAB functions. The way to create cells and access them is demonstrated by the following examples.

```
>> C=cell(3)   %create 3x3 cells
C =
      []      []      []
      []      []      []
      []      []      []
>> C(:,1)={'One1','Two1','Three1'};
>> C{2,2}=[1,2;3,4];
>> C{1,2}=[1,2];
>> C{3,2}=[1;2];
>> C
C =
    'One1'        [1x2 double]      []
    'Two1'        [2x2 double]      []
    'Three1'      [2x1 double]      []

>> C{1,3}=[1,3];
>> C{2,3}=C{1,3};
>> C{2,3}   %{} access content
=    1    3
>> C(2,3)   %() access cell
=   [1x2 double]
>> C{2,3}=[2;3];
>> C{2,3}
=    2
     3
```

```
>> C{3,3}={C(:,1);C{2,2};C(1:2,3)}
C =
    'One1'      [1x2 double]    [1x2 double]
    'Two1'      [2x2 double]    [2x1 double]
    'Three1'    [2x1 double]    {3x1 cell }
>> C{3,3}      %a cell contains multiple cells
=   {3x1 cell  }
    [2x2 double]
    {2x1 cell  }
>> C{3,3}{1}
=   'One1'
    'Two1'
    'Three1'
>> C{3,3}{2}
=    1    2
     3    4
>> C{3,3}{3}
=   [1x2 double]
    [2x1 double]
>> C{3,3}{3}{1}
=    1    3
>> C{3,3}{3}{1:2}
=    1    3
=    2
     3
```

Before closing this brief introduction of MATLAB, two more points, the MATLAB code comment and continuation, need to be clarified. In computer languages, comments are ignored by computer compilers or interpreters and are just useful for people studying the codes. In MATLAB codes, in a line anything after the symbol % are comments. Unlike C, one MATLAB instruction cannot spread to multiple lines. If a MATLAB instruction is too long for one line, use the ellipsis symbol ... at the end of the line then continue the code in the next line.

1.3 TYPES OF MATRICES

It is well-known that the computational efficiency of a matrix algorithm can be greatly improved and the required computer memory for such an algorithm can be greatly reduced if we can take advantage of any structures and properties a matrix has. The matrices arising in a specific application area often have special structures and properties. This makes the special matrix algorithms for different matrix types necessary. This also tells us that types of matrices can be made according to different criteria, that is, according to the algorithms we are interested in. Matrix computation algorithms are many, so are the types of matrices. In this section, we will discuss a few types of matrices that are important to the topics of the book.

1.3.1 SQUARE VS. NON-SQUARE MATRICES

If the number of rows and the number of columns of a matrix are equal, the matrix is a square matrix; otherwise the matrix is a rectangular matrix. Some algorithms, such as inverse and eigenvalue analysis, are applicable to square matrices only, while some other algorithms, such as LU, QR, and singular value analysis, are applicable to both square and non-square matrices.

1.3.2 SYMMETRIC VS. NON-SYMMETRIC MATRICES

In the linear space of square matrices, there is a special sub-space of symmetric and anti-symmetric matrices. If a matrix A of $R^{n \times n}$ is symmetric, it satisfies $A = A'$, that is, $A(i,j) = A(j,i), 1 \leq i,j \leq n$. If a matrix A of $R^{n \times n}$ is anti-symmetric, it satisfies $A = -A'$, that is, $A(i,j) = -A(j,i), A(i,i) = 0, 1 \leq i,j \leq n$. For a general square matrix A, we can split it to a symmetric part $\frac{1}{2}(A + A')$ and anti-symmetric part $\frac{1}{2}(A - A')$. More efficient LU algorithm, e.g. LDLt algorithm exists for symmetric matrices. We have already seen the importance of symmetric matrices in eigenvalue analysis in Section 1.1.

1.3.3 FULL RANK VS. DEFICIENT RANK MATRICES

```
>> A=randn(3,6)
A =
    1.4789   -1.2919   -0.8436   -0.5465    0.6630   -0.1199
    1.1380   -0.0729    0.4978   -0.8468   -0.8542   -0.0653
   -0.6841   -0.3306    1.4885   -0.2463   -1.2013    0.4853
```

All three rows are linearly independent. The rank of the matrix A is *3*, which is equal to min(3,6), i.e. the minimum of number of rows and number of columns—it is full rank.

```
>> rank(A)
=    3
```

If the last two rows are proportional to the first row, the rank of A is only *1*, which is less than min(3,6), i.e. the minimum of the number of rows and the number of columns—it is rank deficient.

```
>> A(2,:) = A(1,:)*rand;
>> A(3,:) = A(1,:)*rand + A(2,:)*rand;
>> rank(A)
=    1
```

It is obvious that the following A is very close to the previous rank deficient matrix. But its rank abruptly changed to 3 from 1.

```
>> A = A+1.0e-10*rand(3,6);
>> rank(A)
=    3
```

Full rank matrices are dense around the neighborhood of any rank deficient matrices. Therefore, the rank deficiency is usually detected within a range of numerical tolerance. The most reliable numerical method to calculate the rank of a matrix is the singular value decomposition (SVD).

1.3.4 SINGULAR VS. NON-SINGULAR MATRICES

Let us look at a simple example.

```
>> A=[11,12,310;21,22,320;310,320,330]
A =
    11    12   310
    21    22   320
   310   320   330
>> X=mdivideByGauss_(A,eye(3))
X =
   -3.2034    3.2067   -0.1003
    3.1067   -3.1135    0.1007
   -0.0034    0.0067   -0.0003
```

Here `mdivideByGauss_(A,eye(3))` is the function to find X such that $AX = I$. Therefore, X is the inverse of A. See Section 4.4 for the discussion of the MATLAB function `mdivideByGauss_.m`. Now if we make the columns of A linearly dependent, calculating the inverse of A in MATLAB will prompt a warning.

```
>> A(:,2)=2.0*A(:,1)
A =
    11    22   310
    21    42   320
   310   620   330

>> X=mdivideByGauss_(A,eye(3))
Warning: mdivideByGauss_: A*x=b(:,1) inconsistent.
> In mdivideByGauss_ at 50
Warning: mdivideByGauss_: A*x=b(:,2) inconsistent.
> In mdivideByGauss_ at 50
Warning: mdivideByGauss_: A*x=b(:,3) inconsistent.
> In mdivideByGauss_ at 50
X =
  -0.000713744998378        0    0.000670487725749
  -0.001427489996756        0    0.001340975451498
   0.003352438628744        0   -0.000118957499730
```

Because now A is rank deficient or singular, it does not have an inverse. If we add a small perturbation to the singular A, it will become non-singular again. But its inverse of the perturbed singular A will have very large numbers. The calculation of its inverse by most numerical algorithms other than the SVD will be prone to the numerical inaccuracy.

```
>> A(2,2)=(1+100*eps)*A(2,2)
A =
    11.0000    22.0000   310.0000
    21.0000    42.0000   320.0000
   310.0000   620.0000   330.0000

>> X=mdivideByGauss_(A,eye(3),1,10*eps)
X =
  1.0e+012 *
   2.160509113233579   -2.165192128543508   0.070011078883372
```

```
  -1.080254556616792    1.082596064271754   -0.035005539441684
   0.000000000000003                    0   -0.000000000000000
```

Just as any full rank matrix is dense around the neighborhood of a rank deficient matrix, a non-singular matrix can be arbitrarily close to a singular matrix. The best measurement of the nearness of a matrix to a singular matrix is its condition number, i.e. the ratio of its largest singular value to its smallest singular value.

```
>> cond(A)
= 2.8932e+015
```

It is noted that the smallest singular value alone cannot measure the nearness to the singularity. For example, A=realmin*eye(3), A's smallest singular value is realmin, that is, 2.2251e-308, on a Windows PC. However, the condition number of A equals 1, it is perfectly conditioned.

1.3.5 ORTHOGONAL VS. NON-ORTHOGONAL MATRICES

To show some properties of orthogonal matrices, we use QR_ to generate an orthogonal matrix.

```
>> A=randn(3)
A =
     1.1908   -0.1567   -1.0565
    -1.2025   -1.6041    1.4151
    -0.0198    0.2573   -0.8051
>> [Q,R]=QR_(A)
Q =
    -0.7036   -0.6926    0.1588
     0.7105   -0.6894    0.1412
     0.0117    0.2122    0.9772
R =
    -1.6925   -1.0264    1.7394
          0    1.2690   -0.4147
          0         0   -0.7547
```

Q is orthogonal, A is non-orthogonal. We can verify $\mathbf{Q'Q}$ and $\mathbf{QQ'}$ are a 3×3 identity matrix. $\mathbf{A'A}$ and $\mathbf{AA'}$ are calculated below.

```
>> A'*A
=    2.8644    1.7371   -2.9438
     1.7371    2.6639   -2.3116
    -2.9438   -2.3116    3.7669
>> A*A'
=    2.5588   -2.6756    0.7867
    -2.6756    6.0216   -1.5283
     0.7867   -1.5283    0.7148
```

$\mathbf{A}(:,2)$ has a component of 1.0264 in the direction of $\mathbf{A}(:,1)$. $\mathbf{A}(:,3)$ has a component of 1.7394 in the direction of $\mathbf{A}(:,1)$ and a component of 0.4147 in the direction of $\mathbf{A}(:,2)$.

In the following example, Q1 is the first and second row of Q. The two rows of Q1 are still orthogonal. But the columns of Q1 are not orthogonal anymore, because the last components of the three orthogonal columns are removed.

```
>> Q1=Q(1:2,:)
Q1 =
    -0.7036   -0.6926    0.1588
     0.7105   -0.6894    0.1412
```

```
>> Q1'*Q1
=    0.9999   -0.0025   -0.0114
    -0.0025    0.9550   -0.2074
    -0.0114   -0.2074    0.0452
>> Q1*Q1'
=    1.0000   -0.0000
    -0.0000    1.0000
```

In the following, Q2 is the second and third column of Q. The two columns of Q2 are still orthogonal. But the rows of Q2 are not orthogonal anymore, because of the first components of the three orthogonal rows are removed.

```
>> Q2=Q(:,2:3)
Q2 =
   -0.6926    0.1588
   -0.6894    0.1412
    0.2122    0.9772
>> Q2'*Q2
=    1.0000         0
          0    1.0000
>> Q2*Q2'
=    0.5049    0.4999    0.0082
     0.4999    0.4952   -0.0083
     0.0082   -0.0083    0.9999
```

1.3.6 DEFECTIVE VS. NON-DEFECTIVE MATRICES

Now let us look at an example

```
>> A = [-5.870948603197477   -4.322390657029254   -5.882971695637162;
         4.890937204469293    4.695954968340351    3.908969795706609;
         6.921235483660148    3.800922593234762    7.174993634857128];

>> [s,V]=eigUnsymByQR_(A,100*eps,'long')
s =
   3.000000000000018
   0.999999999999994
   1.999999999999996
V =
  -0.631930043712464    0.720490583577060   -0.460702104940496
   0.539150948776833   -0.284639640544552    0.886855906827696
   0.556759081009555   -0.632355591425786   -0.035216062077156
```

Here eigUnsymByQR_ is the MATLAB function for the eigenvalue calculation of a unsymmetrical matrix. See Section 6.4. For the given matrix A, the calculated s and V approximately verify $\mathbf{V}^{-1}\mathbf{AV} - \mathbf{S} = \mathbf{0}$. s are the eigenvalues and V are the eigenvectors. The given A is non-defective or diagonalizable.

```
>> inv(V)*A*V-diag(s)
= 1.0e-013 *
  -0.088817841970013   -0.017763568394003   -0.135447209004269
  -0.095479180117763    0.011102230246252   -0.058009153036664
   0.053290705182008   -0.017763568394003    0.053290705182008
```

For a real matrix **A**, even if it is non-defective, **V** and **S** may not be real. Now let us look at another example.

```
>> A=[-0.203690479567358    1.592940703766015   -0.078661919359452;
       -2.054324680556606    1.018411788624710   -0.681656860002363;
        0.132560731417280   -1.580402499303162   -1.024553057429032];
>> [S,V]=eigUnsymByQR_(A,100*eps,'long')
S =
     0.541082840390260    1.506244111129035
    -1.506244111129035    0.541082840390260
    -1.291997429152201                    0
V =
    -0.622797781701984   -0.002655205689615   -0.152556352123276
    -0.268622408060853   -0.580510238128184    0.152446888846097
     0.406095047298063    0.195070630454114    0.976466336085369
```

For this matrix A, its eigenvectors and eigenvalues include complex values. Because A is real, the complex S and V are in complex conjugate pairs. To avoid the complex arithmetic, we slightly lose the requirement that S is diagonal by allowing that S is a block diagonal of 1×1 and 2×2 blocks. Such a block diagonal of 1×1 and 2×2 blocks is called block diagonal. The calculated eigenvalues are $S(1,1) \pm S(2,1)i$ and $S(3,1)$. The corresponding eigenvectors are $V(:,1) \pm V(:,2)i$ and $V(:,3)$. S and V approximately verify $AV - VS = 0$.

```
>> A*V(:,1:2)-V(:,1:2)*S(1:2,1:2)          >> A*V(:,3)-V(:,3)*S(3,1)
= 1.0e-014 *                               = 1.0e-015 *
   -0.144328993201270   -0.077715611723761     -0.138777878078145
   -0.066613381477509    0.122124532708767                     0
   -0.077715611723761                    0                     0
```

A given real square matrix **A** can be defective, that is, a non-singular **V** cannot be found such that a diagonal or block diagonal **S** verifies $AV = VS$. Look at the following example. Refer to Chapter 6 for the discussion of the input arguments of eig_.

```
>> A=[3.203243570535541  -1.912986509597475  -0.493828668312728;
       0.765810280107482   0.780756356738926  -0.335947757509164;
      -0.425393609032944   0.584584431903387   1.016000072725533];

>> [S,V]=eigUnsymByQR_(A,100*eps,'long')
S =
     2.000000033466015
     1.999999966533981
     1.000000000000000
V =
    -0.840695113136516   -0.840695101721086   -0.454771909218991
    -0.539819420672857   -0.539819439496804   -0.308059661494443
     0.042740142872968    0.042740129662041   -0.835632548160519
```

V(:,1) and V(:,2) are almost linearly dependent. We can show that cond(**V**) = 1.001150721099201$e +$ 008. An exact singular **V** is rarely obtained numerically. When a matrix **A** is defective or close to defective, any numerical algorithms to calculate the eigen decomposition in the form of Eq. (1.36) are very prone to numerical errors. A numerical stable algorithm is the Schur decomposition in the form of Eq. (1.45).

```
>> [S,V]=eigUnsymByQR_(A,1000*eps,'short')
S =
     2.043493777304260    2.606216786031949    0.929180859519115
    -0.000725844708825    1.956506222696014    0.607032256100132
                     0                    0    0.999999999999722
```

```
V =
    0.847997070503732     0.430530850394007     0.309102176110266
    0.527510393262169    -0.742081265121680    -0.413579715358233
   -0.051320107340879    -0.513768997521668     0.856392237101727
```

Now V is orthogonal. The block diagonal of S gives the eigenvalues. A direct calculation of $S(1:2,1:2)$ shows that its eigenvalues are $2.000000000000137 \pm 0.000000103508947i$. The theoretical solution of the eigenvalues of the given A is $(1,2,2)$. The difference is due to the numerical error. We can reduce the numerical error by a tighter tolerance.

```
>> [S,V]=eigUnsymByQR_(A,100*eps,'short')
S =
    2.000000033466014     2.606942630740349    -0.918922472969734
                    0     1.999999966533981    -0.622452181550222
    0.000000000000000                     0     1.000000000000000
V =
   -0.840695113136516    -0.444620705177072     0.309102176110463
   -0.539819420672856     0.733175839828580    -0.413579715358572
    0.042740142872969     0.514553803231012     0.856392237101492
```

Now let us look at another example.

```
A = [1      0      0;
     0      2      1;
     0      0      2];
```

Simple calculation shows only two linearly independent eigenvectors can be found for such A. Such A is a defective matrix. Similarly to the difficulty to detect the singularity of a matrix, it is equally difficult to detect the defectiveness of a matrix.

However, if a matrix **A** is real and symmetric, it is always diagonalizable. It can be proved that all the eigenvalues are real and eigenvectors are orthogonal [29]. For a brief account, refer to 1.1. The eigen decomposition of symmetric matrices does not suffer from the numerical difficulty associated with the eigen decomposition of non-symmetric matrices. The eigenvalues of the symmetric part of the last given A can be accurately calculated by many algorithms. Refer to Chapter 5 for the presentation of the algorithms of the eigenvalue analysis of symmetric matrices.

```
>> A=0.5*(A+A')
A =
    1.000000000000000                     0                     0
                    0     2.000000000000000     0.500000000000000
                    0     0.500000000000000     2.000000000000000

>> [S,V]=eigSymByQR_(A,100*eps,'long')
S =
    1.000000000000000
    2.500000000000000
    1.500000000000000
V =
    1.000000000000000                     0                     0
                    0     0.707106781186547    -0.707106781186547
                    0     0.707106781186547     0.707106781186547
```

Here eigSymByQR_ is the MATLAB function for the eigenvalue calculation of a symmetrical matrix. See Section 6.4.

1.3.7 POSITIVE (SEMI-)DEFINITE VS. POSITIVE INDEFINITE MATRICES

A positive (semi-)definite matrix is a square matrix with the following property:

$$\mathbf{x}'\mathbf{A}\mathbf{x} = \mathbf{x}'\frac{1}{2}(\mathbf{A} + \mathbf{A}')\mathbf{x} \geq 0, \quad \forall x. \tag{1.63}$$

If the inequality is strictly greater, it is positive definite, otherwise positive semi-definite. From the definition, we can see that **A** is positive (semi-)definite iff its symmetric part is positive (semi-)definite. Therefore, we can limit the discussion of positive (semi-)definite to symmetric matrices. By the eigen decomposition, $\mathbf{A} = \mathbf{VSV}'$, we can see that

$$\mathbf{x}'\mathbf{A}\mathbf{x} = (\mathbf{Vx})'\,\mathbf{S}\,(\mathbf{Vx}) = \mathbf{y}'\mathbf{Sy} = s_1 y_1^2 + s_2 y_2^2 + \cdots + s_n y_n^2 \geq 0, \quad \forall x, y. \tag{1.64}$$

A is positive (semi-)definite iff its eigenvalues are positive (non-negative). On the other hand, **A** is positive indefinite iff its eigenvalues include positive and negative. If **A**'s eigenvalues include zeros, **A** must be singular.

```
>> A=randn(3);
>> A=0.5*(A+A')
A =
      1.7701      0.4729     -0.4919
      0.4729      1.2698     -0.5175
     -0.4919     -0.5175     -1.1634
>> eigSymByQR_(A)
=     2.1973
      0.9987
     -1.3194
```

A in the above example is positive indefinite.

```
>> A=A+2*eye(3);
>> eigSymByQR_(A)
=     4.1973
      2.9987
      0.6806
```

Now the modified A is positive definite.

If **A** is positive (semi-)definite, it can have a special LU decomposition, that is, more efficient Cholesky decomposition. Other than the Cholesky decomposition, another important decomposition is square root. See [32]. The importance of positive definite matrix appears again in the generalized eigen problem $\mathbf{AV} = \mathbf{BVS}$. See Sections 1.1.4 and 6.9. If neither **A** nor **B** is positive definite, the generalized eigen problem is more difficult to solve.

1.3.8 ZERO STRUCTURED VS. FULL MATRICES

We will use MATLAB functions to generate various zero structured matrices from a full matrix to introduce more MATLAB functions. But remember that most zero structured matrices occur naturally in real applications. Zeros are important factors to exploit to improve the algorithm efficiency and reduce the memory.

```
A = [11     12     13     14     15     16     17     18;
     21     22     23     24     25     26     27     28;
```

```
31    32    33    34    35    36    37    38;
41    42    43    44    45    46    47    48;
51    52    53    54    55    56    57    58];
```

Diagonal Matrix A diagonal matrix appears most often as a factor in the factorization of a general matrix. For now we create a diagonal matrix from A. The MATLAB function diag on a matrix creates a vector from the diagonal of the matrix.

```
>> d=diag(A)'
d =
    11    22    33    44    55
```

The MATLAB diag function on a vector creates a diagonal matrix.

```
>> D=diag(d)
D =
    11     0     0     0     0
     0    22     0     0     0
     0     0    33     0     0
     0     0     0    44     0
     0     0     0     0    55
```

A diagonal matrix can be non-square. We can increase D to the same size of A as follows.

```
>> D=[D,zeros(5,3)]
D =
    11     0     0     0     0     0     0     0
     0    22     0     0     0     0     0     0
     0     0    33     0     0     0     0     0
     0     0     0    44     0     0     0     0
     0     0     0     0    55     0     0     0
```

Bi-diagonal Matrix A bi-diagonal matrix has nonzero components on the diagonal and super (or sub) diagonal. It can be a factor in a factorization of a general matrix. It plays an important role in an algorithm of singular value calculation, referring to Sections 8.4, 8.5 and 8.6. Two examples of bi-diagonal matrices are shown below.

```
>> d1=diag(A,1)'
d1 =
    12    23    34    45    56

>> Bd1=diag(d)+diag(d1(1:4),1)
Bd1 =
    11    12     0     0     0
     0    22    23     0     0
     0     0    33    34     0
     0     0     0    44    45
     0     0     0     0    55

Bd2 = D;
for j=1:5
       Bd2(j,j+1) = d1(j);
end
>> Bd2
Bd2 =
    11    12     0     0     0     0     0     0
     0    22    23     0     0     0     0     0
     0     0    33    34     0     0     0     0
```

| 0 | 0 | 0 | 44 | 45 | 0 | 0 | 0 |
| 0 | 0 | 0 | 0 | 55 | 56 | 0 | 0 |

Tri-diagonal Matrix A tri-diagonal matrix has nonzero components on the diagonal, super-, and sub-diagonal. Tri-diagonal matrices appear in matrix factorizations and Lanczos reduction of matrices, referring to Sections 2.4.3, 2.5.2, 2.5.3, and 3.6. We show two examples of tri-diagonal matrices by creating them with the MATLAB functions.

```
>> d2=diag(A,-1)'
d2 =
    21   32   43   54
```

```
Td1 = Bd1;
>> Td1 = Td1 + diag(d2,-1)
Td1 =
    11   12    0    0    0
    21   22   23    0    0
     0   32   33   34    0
     0    0   43   44   45
     0    0    0   54   55
```

```
Td2 = Bd2;
for j=1:4
        Td2(j+1,j) = d2(j);
end
>> Td2
Td2 =
    11   12    0    0    0    0    0    0
    21   22   23    0    0    0    0    0
     0   32   33   34    0    0    0    0
     0    0   43   44   45    0    0    0
     0    0    0   54   55   56    0    0
```

Band Matrix A band matrix has nonzero components along a narrow band of the diagonal.

$$|B(i,j)| \geq 0 \quad j = \max(1, i - b_l) : \min(n, i + b_u), \tag{1.65}$$

where n is the number of columns, b_l is the lower bandwidth, and b_u the upper bandwidth. If $b_l + b_u + 1 \ll n$, the matrix is considered banded. Diagonal, bi-diagonal, and tri-diagonal matrices are all special band matrices. For diagonal, $b_l = b_u = 0$; bi-diagonal, $b_l = 0, b_u = 1$ or $b_l = 1, b_u = 0$; tri-diagonal, $b_l = b_u = 1$. In the following, we create one band matrix from A with the MATLAB commands.

```
>> d3=diag(A,2);
>> B=Td1;
>> B=B+diag(d3(1:3),2)
B =
    11   12   13    0    0
    21   22   23   24    0
     0   32   33   34   35
     0    0   43   44   45
     0    0    0   54   55
```

Band matrices can be stored as a full matrix of size of $m \times (b_l + b_u + 1)$. Given the band matrix B in the full storage, we can use the following function to convert it to the band storage.

Algorithm 1.1

Convert a band A in full format to band format.

```
function [B,lbw,ubw,m,n] = full2band_(A,lbw,ubw)

[m,n] = size(A); lbw1 = lbw + 1;
B = zeros(min(m,n+lbw),lbw1+ubw);

for i=1:m
    for j=max(1,i-lbw):min(i+ubw,n)
        B(i,j-i+lbw1) = A(i,j);
    end
end
```

The following is the same band matrix B in the band storage. Here, the saved memory is tiny. If $b_l + b_u + 1 \ll n$, the saved memory will be considerably large.

```
>> Bb=full2band_(B,1,2)
Bb =
      0    11    12    13
     21    22    23    24
     32    33    34    35
     43    44    45     0
     54    55     0     0
```

Given the band matrix Bb in band storage, we can use the following function to convert it to the full memory storage.

Algorithm 1.2

Convert band B in band format to full format.

```
function A = band2full_(B,lbw,ubw,m,n,sym)

if (~exist('m','var') || isempty(m)) m = size(B,1); end
if (~exist('n','var') || isempty(n)) n = m; end
if (~exist('sym','var') || isempty(sym)) sym = 0; end
A = zeros(m,n); lbw1 = lbw + 1;

for i=1:m
    for j=max(1,i-lbw):min(i+ubw,n)
        A(i,j) = B(i,j-i+lbw1);
        if (sym == 1) A(j,i) = A(i,j); end
    end
end
```

B=band2full_(Bb,1,2,5,5) creates the original band matrix B in full storage.

Lower(Upper) Triangular Matrix A matrix with nonzeros below (or above) the diagonal is a lower (or upper) triangular matrix. It plays an important role in matrix factorizations and equation solution as well as eigen solution problems. It is shown in the example below.

```
>> T1=tril(A)
T1 =
     11     0     0     0     0     0     0     0
     21    22     0     0     0     0     0     0
     31    32    33     0     0     0     0     0
     41    42    43    44     0     0     0     0
     51    52    53    54    55     0     0     0
```

```
>> T2=triu(A)
T2 =
    11    12    13    14    15    16    17    18
     0    22    23    24    25    26    27    28
     0     0    33    34    35    36    37    38
     0     0     0    44    45    46    47    48
     0     0     0     0    55    56    57    58
```

It can be shown by a direct calculation that the product of two square lower (upper) triangular matrices remains square lower (upper) triangular matrix.

Lower(Upper) Hessenberg Matrix A lower (upper) Hessenberg matrix has one extra nonzero above (below) the diagonal in the lower (upper) triangular matrix. A Hessenberg matrix appears in matrix factorizations and Arnoldi reduction of matrices, referring to Sections 2.5.1 and 3.5.

```
>> H1=T1(:,1:5);
>> H1=H1+diag(d1(1:4),1)
H1  =
    11    12     0     0     0
    21    22    23     0     0
    31    32    33    34     0
    41    42    43    44    45
    51    52    53    54    55
>> H2=H1'
H2  =
    11    21    31    41    51
    12    22    32    42    52
     0    23    33    43    53
     0     0    34    44    54
     0     0     0    45    55
```

It can be shown by a direct calculation that the product of a lower (upper) Hessenberg matrix and a lower (upper) triangular matrix remains a lower (upper) Hessenberg matrix, and the product of two lower (upper) Hessenberg matrices has two nonzero sub-diagonals (sup-diagonals).

Sparse Matrix If a matrix has a lot of zeros but the location of zeros does not have a clear pattern, the matrix is categorized as a sparse matrix. For example,

```
A  = [11    12     0     0     0     0     0    18;
       0    22     0    24    25     0    27     0;
       0     0    33     0     0     0     0    38;
       0     0     0    44     0     0     0     0;
       0     0     0     0    55    56     0    58];
```

We only need to keep nonzeros and their locations in the memory. There are many options to store a sparse matrix. All the matrix algorithms applied to a sparse matrix will be shaped strongly in the implementation level by the data structure chosen to store the sparse matrix. One data structure may be slightly or considerably more efficient than another data structure for a particular problem. The difference is strongly problem dependent and computer architecture dependent. Fortunately all the data structures are very similar and easy to convert between each other. We will discuss only two data structures, coordinate format (IJD) and compressed sparse row (CSR) format. Refer to [56] for more information about the storage schemes.

In IJD format, we have one vector dA to store all the nonzeros, one integer vector iA to keep the row index and another integer vector jA to keep the column index of each nonzero. The three vectors have the same length. For the above listed sparse matrix A in the full format, the three vectors are as follows. The meaning of each data should be obvious.

```
iA = [1,1,1,2,2,2,2,3,3,4,5,5,5];
jA = [1,2,8,2,4,5,7,3,8,4,5,6,8];
dA = [11,12,18,22,24,25,27,33,38,44,55,56,58];
```

IJD format is useful for the matrix input. The data in iA,jA,dA do not need to follow any order. Applying a reversing or any permutation to iA,jA,dA does not change the data of the sparse matrix A. Duplicate (i, j) entries in IJD format imply the summation of all the duplicates. This makes the IJD format ideal for the construction of the finite element matrices.

In IJD format, if the data are listed by row and then the column as shown in the above example, the vector iA contains redundant information (it has duplicated 1's, 2's, 3's and 5's). To eliminate the redundant information, we replace it with a vector rA which holds the location of the first nonzero component of each row in dA and jA. The length of rA is always the number of rows plus 1. The last component of rA is the number of nonzeros plus 1. The new format is CSR. For the above listed sparse matrix A in the full format, the three vectors are as follows. The contents of dA and jA are same as in IJD format. The length of rA is reduced to 6, which is size(A,1)+1. For $1 \leq i \leq 5$, rA(i) is the location of the first nonzero component of row i in dA and jA. rA(6)=13 tells that the number of nonzeros in A is $13 - 1 = 12$.

```
rA = [1,4,8,10,11,13];
jA = [1,2,8,2,4,5,7,3,8,4,5,6,8];
dA = [11,12,18,22,24,25,27,33,38,44,55,56,58];
```

In real applications involving sparse matrices, a data conversion between the sparse format and full format is rarely needed, because sparse matrices are usually created and operated in a sparse format. However, the following MATLAB functions for the data format conversions between the sparse format and full format are helpful for the further explanation for the sparse storage schemes.

Algorithm 1.3

Convert a sparse matrix in IJD to full format. Duplicate (i, j)s are summed.

```
function A = ijd2full_(iA,jA,dA,m,n)

if (~exist('m','var') || isempty(m)) m = max(iA); end
if (~exist('n','var') || isempty(n)) n = max(jA); end
nnz = length(dA);

A = zeros(m,n);
for k = 1:nnz
    i = iA(k);   j = jA(k);
    A(i,j) = A(i,j) + dA(k);
end
```

Algorithm 1.4

Convert a sparse matrix in full format to IJD format.

```
function [iA,jA,dA,m,n] = full2ijd_(A)

[m,n] = size(A);   nnz = 0;   iA = [];   jA = [];   dA = [];

for i=1:m
```

```
    if (length(dA)-nnz < n)
        iA = [iA,zeros(1,n)];  jA = [jA,zeros(1,n)];  dA = [dA,zeros(1,n)];
    end
    for j=1:n
        if (A(i,j) ~= 0.0)
            nnz = nnz + 1;
            iA(nnz) = i;  jA(nnz) = j;  dA(nnz) = A(i,j);
        end
    end
end
iA = iA(1:nnz);   jA = jA(1:nnz);   dA = dA(1:nnz);
```

Algorithm 1.5

Convert a sparse matrix in CSR format to full format.

```
function A = csr2full_(dA,rA,jA,m,n)

if (~exist('m','var') || isempty(m)) m = length(rA)-1; end
if (~exist('n','var') || isempty(n)) n = max(jA); end

A = zeros(m,n);
for i=1:m
    for k=rA(i):rA(i+1)-1
        j = jA(k);  A(i,j) = dA(k);
    end
end
```

Algorithm 1.6

Convert a sparse matrix in full format to CSR format.

```
function [dA,rA,jA,m,n] = full2csr_(A)

[m,n] = size(A);   nnz = 1;   dA = [];   rA = zeros(1,m+1);   jA = [];

for i=1:m
    rA(i) = nnz;
    if (length(dA)-nnz < n)
        dA = [dA,zeros(1,n)];   jA = [jA,zeros(1,n)];
    end
    for j=1:n
        if(A(i,j) ~= 0.0)
            dA(nnz) = A(i,j);  jA(nnz) = j;  nnz = nnz + 1;
        end
    end
end
dA = dA(1:nnz-1);   rA(m+1) = nnz;   jA = jA(1:nnz-1);
```

IJD format and CSR format can be converted to each other with the following MATLAB functions.

Algorithm 1.7

Convert a sparse matrix in IJD to CSR format. Duplicate (i, j)s are summed.

```
function [Arc,rA,cA,m,n] = ijd2csr_(Aij,iA,jA,m,n)

if (size(Aij,2) == 1) Aij = Aij'; end
if (size(iA,2) == 1) iA = iA'; end
```

```
if (size(jA,2) == 1) jA = jA'; end
[iA,p] = sort(iA,'ascend');
Aij = Aij(p);   iA = [iA,m+1];   jA = [jA(p),n+1];

i1 = 1;   r = 0;   inz = 1;   nnz = length(Aij);
Arc = [];   rA = zeros(1,m+1);   cA = [];

while(i1 <= nnz)
    if (length(cA)-inz < n)
        Arc = [Arc,zeros(1,n)];   cA = [cA,zeros(1,n)];
    end

    i2 = i1 + 1;
    while(iA(i2) == iA(i1))
        i2 = i2 + 1;
    end
    r = r + 1;   rA(r:iA(i1)) = inz;   r = iA(i1);

    [jA(i1:i2-1),p] = sort(jA(i1:i2-1),'ascend');
    Aij(i1:i2-1) = permute_(p,Aij(i1:i2-1),'row');

    j1 = i1;   j2 = j1 + 1;
    while(j1 < i2)
        while (j2<i2 && jA(j2)==jA(j1))
            j2 = j2 + 1;
        end
        Arc(inz) = Aij(j1);
        cA(inz) = jA(j1);
        for j=j1+1:j2-1
            Arc(inz) = Arc(inz) + Aij(j);
        end

        j1 = j2;   j2 = j1 + 1;   inz = inz + 1;
    end

    i1 = i2;
end
Arc = Arc(1:inz-1);   rA(r+1:m+1) = inz;   cA = cA(1:inz-1);
```

Algorithm 1.8

Convert a sparse matrix in CSR format to IJD format.

```
function [Aij,iA,jA,m,n] = csr2ijd_(Arc,rA,cA,m,n)

if (~exist('m','var') || isempty(m)) m = length(rA)-1; end
if (~exist('n','var') || isempty(n)) n = max(cA); end
if (m ~= length(rA)-1) error('csr2ijd_:_matrix_size_differs.'); end

Aij = Arc;   jA = cA;   iA = zeros(1,length(jA));
for i=1:m
    iA(rA(i):rA(i+1)-1) = i;
end
```

1.4 OVERVIEW OF MATRIX COMPUTATIONS

Four Forms of Matrix Algorithms   Given a matrix $A \in \mathbb{R}^{m \times n}$, we find two non-singular matrices $U \in \mathbb{R}^{m \times m}$ and $V \in \mathbb{R}^{n \times n}$ and perform $U^{-1}AV^{-1} = B$ or equivalently $A = UBV$, $AV^{-1} = UB$, $U^{-1}A = BV$. Many matrix computations can be presented as one of the four forms.

We call $U^{-1}AV^{-1} = B$ a transforming algorithm. In this kind of algorithm, according to the required form of B, choosing the appropriate U_1^{-1} and V_1^{-1}, calculate $A_1 = U_1^{-1}AV_1^{-1}$. Repeat $A_i = U_i^{-1}A_{i-1}V_i^{-1}$ for a fixed or variable number of steps until the final A_i assume the required form of B. In the implementation, A_1 will overwrite A and A_i will overwrite A_{i-1}. U_i^{-1} and V_i^{-1} are not needed to be saved. The final U^{-1} and V^{-1} are continuously updated from U_i^{-1} and V_i^{-1} of each step. It should be emphasized that it is U_i^{-1} and V_i^{-1} that are determined and no inverse calculation is needed. The Gauss elimination algorithm and QR algorithm using Householder reflection or Givens rotation all belong to this category of algorithms.

The second form $A = UBV$ is called a decomposing algorithm. If an assumed form of $A = UBV$ can be proved valid mathematically, we can write the equality condition of each row or column of the left and right hand sides. We will then be able to construct U, V and B row by row or column by column, from the top row to the bottom row, or from the left column to the right column, or vice versa. The Crout algorithm, Cholesky algorithm and Gram–Schimdt algorithm are examples of the second category.

The third form $AV^{-1} = UB$ and the fourth form $U^{-1}A = BV$ are called a multiplying algorithm.[2] They are mostly used in iterative matrix algorithms. If an assumed form of $A = UBV$ exists and it is proved mathematically that U, V^{-1}, and B can be non-unique. Of course U, V^{-1}, and B cannot be arbitrary; they must have the required forms and satisfy $AV^{-1} = UB$ and $U^{-1}A = BV$. The non-uniqueness and the imposed conditions make the multiplying algorithm possible: The first row (or column) of U and V^{-1} can be arbitrary. Once the first row (or column) of U and V^{-1} is determined, all U, V^{-1} and B are becoming unique. The extra flexibility of choosing the first row (or column) of U or V^{-1} and the special form of B (bi-diagonal, tri-diagonal, or Hessenberg) allows us to determine U, V^{-1}, and B column by column, or row by row by using $AV^{-1} = UB$ and $U^{-1}A = BV$. Lanczos algorithm and Arnoldi algorithm are examples of the third category. In these types of algorithms, A is not altered and used only in the matrix–vector product, such as Av or uA. Because of this property, A can be not only an ordinary matrix but also any general linear transformation in factored form of matrices and inverse matrices.

In most cases, the purpose is to find the numerically good U and V and suitably structured form of B. With the given matrix A, the different choices of the numerical properties of U and V, the pursued structure of B and the required algorithmic efficiency, we will have different algorithms.

First of all, the available structure and numerical property of A will determine the applicable algorithms. In the previous section, we had a classification of matrices. Second, the choices of U, V, and B and the algorithmic efficiency are intricately dependent on each other. Roughly speaking, striving to offer the numerically best possible U, V, and B under the constraint of the required efficiency and the limited computer memory forms the bulk of the research of the matrix computations.

About the numerically good U and V, we require U and V to be non-singular, because we want B keeps all the information carried by A. A higher requirement is that U and V are not only non-singular but also well-conditioned. A non-singular but bad conditioned U and V will magnify the

---

[2]Transforming algorithm, decomposing algorithm, and multiplying algorithm are not the commonly accepted terminology, but just a terminology adopted for the discussion of this section.

errors inevitably present in both the original matrix $\mathbf{A}$ and the numerical computations. The best conditioned matrices are orthogonal matrices. Permutations, rotations and reflections are examples of orthogonal matrices. The orthogonal matrices lead to orthogonal transformations. The orthogonal transformations keep the norm and dot product and therefore will not magnify nor reduce the errors—they are numerically the utmost stable. QR and SVD are examples of orthogonal transformations. Sometimes we lower the requirement to have orthogonal $\mathbf{U}$ and $\mathbf{V}$ to make gains in other areas, such as computational efficiency or the preferred form of $\mathbf{B}$ achievable by non-orthogonal transformations. LU is an example of the non-orthogonal transformations. In most non-orthogonal transformation algorithms, we usually have to mix the orthogonal transformations to minimize the errors. In LU-type of algorithms, pivoting is the permutation (orthogonal) introduced between the successive Gaussian zeroing steps.

Other than the conditioning of $\mathbf{U}$ and $\mathbf{V}$, we may also have the requirement to the forms of $\mathbf{U}$ and $\mathbf{V}$. The most common forms of $\mathbf{U}$ and $\mathbf{V}$ are the following: (a) $\mathbf{U}$ or $\mathbf{V}$ is an identity matrix; (b) $\mathbf{U}$ or $\mathbf{V}$ is a lower (upper) triangular matrix; (c) $\mathbf{V} = \mathbf{U}^{-1}$; or (d) $\mathbf{V} = \mathbf{U}'$. If $\mathbf{U}$ or $\mathbf{V}$ is an identity matrix, the transformation is one-sided: $\mathbf{U}$ performs the row transformation; $\mathbf{V}$ performs the column transformation. LU and QR are examples of this kind of transformation. If $\mathbf{V} = \mathbf{U}^{-1}$, the transformation is called a similarity transformation. A similarity transformation preserves the eigenvalues. If $\mathbf{A}$ is symmetric, transformations with $\mathbf{V} = \mathbf{U}'$ will keep the symmetry of the matrix. If $\mathbf{V} = \mathbf{U}'$, the transformation is called a congruent transformation. A congruent transformation preserves the inertia of a matrix, i.e. the signs of the eigenvalues of the matrix. If $\mathbf{U}$ is orthogonal, $\mathbf{V} = \mathbf{U}'$ is also $\mathbf{V} = \mathbf{U}^{-1}$, a congruent transformation is also a similarity transformation. If $\mathbf{V} = \mathbf{U}^{-1}$ or $\mathbf{V} = \mathbf{U}'$, it is necessary that $\mathbf{A}$ and $\mathbf{B}$ are square matrices.

Under the given requirement of the conditioning and forms of $\mathbf{U}$ and $\mathbf{V}$, the goal of many algorithms of matrix computations is to find the simplest structured form of $\mathbf{B}$. A diagonal $\mathbf{B}$ is often the goal. However, a diagonal $\mathbf{B}$ may not exist with the given forms of $\mathbf{U}$ and $\mathbf{V}$ or impossible to achieve with a direct algorithm.[3] In such a case, we have to use an iterative algorithm or we may lower the expectation for a diagonal $\mathbf{B}$ to a bi-diagonal, tri-diagonal, lower (upper) triangular, or Hessenberg matrix. On the other hand, if we keep the expectation for a form of $\mathbf{B}$, we may lower the restriction to $\mathbf{U}$ and $\mathbf{V}$, for example, from orthogonal to non-orthogonal, from one-sided to two-sided, or from requiring $\mathbf{V} = \mathbf{U}^{-1}$ or $\mathbf{V} = \mathbf{U}'$ to independent $\mathbf{U}$ and $\mathbf{V}$.

Under the given conditions, if the required form of $\mathbf{B}$ exists, we may still have to rely on the iterative algorithms to find $\mathbf{B}$. For example, the eigenvalue problems and singular value problems are to find the roots of polynomials. The fundamental theorem of algebra states that no explicit formula exists for the root of polynomials of the order higher than four. Thus, it rules out any possibility of direct algorithms for the eigenvalue problems and singular value problems. When we have to use the iterative algorithms, for the efficiency, we usually split the problem into two smaller problems. First, we use a direct algorithm to transform $\mathbf{A}$ to a form different from the required $\mathbf{B}$ but significantly simpler than $\mathbf{A}$. In the second stage, we apply an iterative algorithm to the simplified $\mathbf{A}$.

Under a different condition, we may also have to rely on iterative algorithms even if the problem can be solved mathematically by means of direct algorithms. One such example is to solve a large scale sparse linear equation. Given a sparse $\mathbf{A}$, any direct algorithms of the linear equations solutions will produce a full $\mathbf{U}$, $\mathbf{B}$ or $\mathbf{V}$. Thus, the efficiency and computer memory limitation will rule out the application of direct algorithms. When solving linear equation solution or eigenvalue solution of large matrices, computer memory limitation requires the problem to be solved in a smaller linear space than

---

[3]An algorithm is direct if it is applied to a computation, the computation can finish with a pre-determined set of operations. Otherwise, the algorithm is iterative.

the original linear space empowered by **A**. The smaller linear space has to be generated with the third kind or fourth kind of the algorithms, namely, the multiplying algorithm discussed above. The original problem in the bigger linear space is projected onto the smaller linear space and emulated in the updated smaller linear spaces iteratively.

Given a matrix **A**, the four forms of matrix algorithms will produce the desired form of the matrix **B** with suitably chosen **U** and **V**. All the matrix algorithms requires certain steps to finish. The steps of a direct algorithm depend only on the size of **A**. The steps of an iterative algorithm depend not only on the size of **A** but also on certain properties (or in other words, certain conditioning) of **A**. The matrices **B**, **U** and **V** change continuously in each step of an algorithm. What remains invariant in all the steps of all the matrix algorithms are the four mathematically equivalent relations $\mathbf{U}^{-1}\mathbf{A}\mathbf{V}^{-1} = \mathbf{B}$, $\mathbf{A} = \mathbf{UBV}$, $\mathbf{A}\mathbf{V}^{-1} = \mathbf{UB}$ or $\mathbf{U}^{-1}\mathbf{A} = \mathbf{BV}$. In theory and practice, all the matrix algorithms can stop in any intermediate steps and restart the calculation from the stopped step. Most matrix algorithms to be presented in the book are provided with a restart capability. Therefore, the user can check the form of **B**, **U** and **V** in any intermediate steps of an algorithm. The user can even run an algorithm step by step to understand the progress of the algorithm.

Numerical Errors As we can see, the four kinds of algorithms are mathematically equivalent. However, they offer different numerical properties and places different requirement on the original matrix and computer resources. Much of the complexity of many matrix algorithms is due to the inevitable errors in any floating point calculations. This book does not go to the details of error analysis of different matrix algorithms. There are a lot of research done in that area. Refer to [33] and [70] for the complete coverage. Some sections of [29] also offer some in-depth discussions. Briefly, in direct matrix algorithms, the errors are due to the floating point calculations. In iterative matrix algorithms, the errors are two folds. One is the floating point calculation. The other is the approximation introduced in finding solutions in a smaller space.

The floating point error is due to the modeling of infinite and continuous real numbers by a finite and discrete set of numbers with only fixed number of digits. There is error in the representation of real numbers in the computer and also error in the results of any floating point calculations. The matrix algorithms are designed to avoid the increase of floating point errors in all the calculation steps. Roughly speaking, they are designed in such a way that very large numbers and very small numbers will not occur in the calculations. Ideally, the numbers are kept close to one, where the floating point representation of real numbers is the best. There are two ways of measuring errors of a matrix algorithm. One is the forward error, the error in the result between the exact solution and the numerical solution. Because the exact solution is unknown, the forward error analysis is difficult to apply. The other kind of error measurement is the backward error. The error-prone result of a numerical algorithm is interpreted as the exact result of slightly different input data. The difference between the actual input data to the numerical algorithm and that slightly different input data is the backward error.

The approximating errors in the iterative matrix algorithms can be reduced by improving the approximating power of the smaller space and are controlled by the set tolerance.

In most matrix algorithms to be presented in the book, there is an input argument named `tol`. It is used to check the closeness of a quantity to zero. For example, in LU decomposition, we need to check if the pivot is close to zero. In the iterative algorithms, we need to check if the error is close to zero. Depending on the quantity under checking, some reference value is adopted. When we say a scalar, a vector or a matrix is zero, we mean it is close to zero measured by `tol` and some reference value in the sense illustrated by the following code snippet.

```
A = randn(8);
A(2,:) = 1.0e-12*A(2,:);
tol = 100*eps;
epsilon = tol*max(1.0, norm(diag(A)));    %example: use norm(diag(A)) as reference
if (abs(A(2,2)) < epsilon)
    %treat A(2,2) as zero
end
if (norm(A(2,:)) < epsilon)
    %treat A(2,:) as zero
end
```

Direct Algorithms of Linear Equations Solution [29] For the generality, we consider $\mathbf{Ax} = \mathbf{b}$, where $\mathbf{A} \in \mathbb{R}^{m \times n}$. All the direct algorithms of solving linear equations can be presented in one of the two forms as shown below,

$$(\mathbf{UAV})\left(\mathbf{V}^{-1}\mathbf{x}\right) = \mathbf{By} = \mathbf{Ub} = \mathbf{c}, \tag{1.66a}$$

$$\left(\mathbf{U}^{-1}\mathbf{BV}^{-1}\right)\mathbf{x} = \mathbf{b}. \tag{1.66b}$$

In the form of Eq. (1.66a), we choose $\mathbf{U}$ and a simple enough $\mathbf{V}$ to introduce zeros to $\mathbf{A}$, so that $\mathbf{B} = \mathbf{UAV}$ is a simple structured matrix, such as a diagonal (or even better an identity) or triangular matrix. The final solution is obtained in two steps,

$$\mathbf{y} = \mathbf{B}^{-1}\mathbf{c}, \qquad \mathbf{x} = \mathbf{Vy}. \tag{1.67}$$

Because of the simple form of $\mathbf{B}$ achieved by the well-chosen $\mathbf{U}$ and $\mathbf{V}$, the solution of $\mathbf{y} = \mathbf{B}^{-1}\mathbf{c}$ is easy.

In Eq. (1.66a), $\mathbf{U}$ applies transformation to $\mathbf{A}$ and $\mathbf{b}$ at the same time, and we do not need to keep $\mathbf{U}$. In most popular algorithms, $\mathbf{U}$ or $\mathbf{V}$ is chosen as an identity matrix. For example, in a typical Gaussian elimination algorithm, $\mathbf{V} = \mathbf{I}$ and $\mathbf{U}$ is chosen so that $\mathbf{B}$ is an upper triangular matrix, and in a Gauss–Jordan elimination algorithm, $\mathbf{V} = \mathbf{I}$ and $\mathbf{U}$ is chosen so that $\mathbf{B}$ is an identity matrix.

In the form of Eq. (1.66b), we choose a simple structured $\mathbf{U}^{-1}$ and a simple structured $\mathbf{V}^{-1}$, so that $\mathbf{B}$ is also a simple structured. The final solution is obtained in three steps,

$$\mathbf{z} = \left(\mathbf{U}^{-1}\right)^{-1}\mathbf{b}, \qquad \mathbf{y} = \mathbf{B}^{-1}\mathbf{z}, \qquad \mathbf{x} = \left(\mathbf{V}^{-1}\right)^{-1}\mathbf{y}. \tag{1.68}$$

In most popular algorithms, $\mathbf{U}^{-1}$ or $\mathbf{V}^{-1}$ is chosen as an identity matrix. For example, in LU or QR algorithms, $\mathbf{V}^{-1}$ is an identity matrix. Because of simple structured $\mathbf{U}^{-1}$, $\mathbf{B}$ and $\mathbf{V}^{-1}$, the equation solutions of Eq. (1.68) are easy.

Iterative Algorithms of Linear Equations Solution [29, 56] In the iterative algorithms, we make an assumption for the solution $\mathbf{x} = \mathbf{x}_0 + \mathbf{Ky}$, where $\mathbf{K} \in \mathbb{R}^{n \times s}, s \ll n$. Introducing $\mathbf{x} = \mathbf{x}_0 + \mathbf{Ky}$ to $\mathbf{Ax} = \mathbf{b}$, we usually have an error in the equations (residual),

$$\mathbf{r} = \mathbf{A}\left(\mathbf{x}_0 + \mathbf{Ky}\right) - \mathbf{b} = \mathbf{Ax}_0 - \mathbf{b} + \mathbf{AKy} = \mathbf{r}_0 + \mathbf{AKy} \neq \mathbf{0}. \tag{1.69}$$

To determine $\mathbf{y}$, we introduce s equations

$$\mathbf{L}'\mathbf{r} = \mathbf{L}'\left(\mathbf{r}_0 + \mathbf{AKy}\right) = \mathbf{0}, \tag{1.70}$$

where $\mathbf{L} \in \mathbb{R}^{m \times s}$. To determine $\mathbf{y}$ uniquely, we require $\mathbf{L}'\mathbf{AK}$ to be non-singular, so that an improved solution can be obtained in two steps,

$$\mathbf{y} = -(\mathbf{L}'\mathbf{AK})^{-1}\mathbf{L}'\mathbf{r}_0, \quad \mathbf{x}_1 = \mathbf{x}_0 + \mathbf{Ky} = \mathbf{x}_0 - \mathbf{K}(\mathbf{L}'\mathbf{AK})^{-1}\mathbf{L}'\mathbf{r}_0. \tag{1.71}$$

From the improved approximate solution $\mathbf{x}_1$, we calculate a new residual $\mathbf{r}_1 = \mathbf{Ax}_1 - \mathbf{b}$. From the norm of $\mathbf{r}_1$, we can accept $\mathbf{x}_1$ as the solution or start a new iteration. In the new iteration, we will take $\mathbf{x}_1$ as $\mathbf{x}_0$ and can generate a better set of $\mathbf{K}$ and $\mathbf{L}$ from the information of $\mathbf{r}_1$.

The choice of $\mathbf{K}$ and $\mathbf{L}$ and the way to construct them determine various kinds of iterative algorithms. To improve the convergence of an iterative algorithm, we can apply the iterative algorithm to $\mathbf{B} = \mathbf{UAV}$. $\mathbf{U}$ and $\mathbf{V}$ are chosen to make $\mathbf{B}$ at least better conditioned and even better close to an identity matrix. $\mathbf{U}$ and $\mathbf{V}$ are called pre-conditioners in this perspective.

Because iterative algorithms are mostly applied to the sparse matrices, the sparsity of the matrices has to be taken into account when constructing $\mathbf{K}$ and $\mathbf{L}$, as well as the pre-conditioners, $\mathbf{U}$ and $\mathbf{V}$.

Direct Algorithms of Eigenvalues Solution [29][4] Among the direct algorithms, QR iteration algorithm is the most widely applicable. It is rooted in the simple power method. Suppose $\mathbf{A}$ is diagonalizable: $\mathbf{A} = \mathbf{X}\mathbf{\Lambda}\mathbf{X}^{-1}$. The eigenvectors are ordered according to the magnitude of eigenvalues: $|\lambda_1| \geq |\lambda_2| \geq \cdots \geq |\lambda_n|$. An arbitrary vector $\mathbf{q}_0$ is decomposed in the eigenvectors,

$$\mathbf{q}_0 = a_1 \mathbf{X}(:,1) + a_2 \mathbf{X}(:,2) + \cdots + a_n \mathbf{X}(:,n). \tag{1.72}$$

If $a_1 \neq 0$ and $|\frac{\lambda_2}{\lambda_1}| < 1$,

$$\mathbf{A}^k \mathbf{q}_0 = a_1 \lambda_1^k \left(\mathbf{X}(:,1) + \frac{a_2}{a_1}\frac{\lambda_2^k}{\lambda_1^k}\mathbf{X}(:,2) + \cdots + \frac{a_n}{a_1}\frac{\lambda_n^k}{\lambda_1^k}\mathbf{X}(:,n) \right) \longrightarrow a_1 \lambda_1^k \mathbf{X}(:,1). \tag{1.73}$$

To avoid overflow or underflow, after each multiplication by $\mathbf{A}$, we perform a normalization. Then, we obtain the power iteration algorithm. Under the assumptions, λ approaches λ_1 and $\mathbf{y}$ approaches $\mathbf{X}(:,1)$. The convergence depends on $\frac{\lambda_2}{\lambda_1}$. If the ratio is close to 0, the convergence is fast. If the ratio is close to 1, the convergence is slow. Algorithm 1.2 presents the simple power iteration.

Algorithm 1.2 Power Iteration Algorithm

1: Input an arbitrary vector $\mathbf{y}$.
2: **for** $k = 1, 2, \ldots$ **do**
3:     $\mathbf{q} = \mathbf{y}/\|\mathbf{y}\|_2$
4:     $\mathbf{y} = \mathbf{Aq}$.
5:     $\lambda = \mathbf{q}'\mathbf{y}$.
6: **end for**

Given an arbitrary matrix $\mathbf{Y} \in \mathbb{R}^{n \times s}, 1 \leq s \leq n$, we generalize the power iteration to calculate more than one eigenvalue and eigenvector, which gives us the sub-space iteration of Algorithm 1.3. We can see that the QR decomposition in the sub-space iteration algorithm replaces the vector normalization in

---

[4] Quote [5]: Note that 'direct' methods must still iterate, since finding eigenvalues is mathematically equivalent to finding zeros of polynomials, for which no noniterative methods can exist. We can call a method *direct* if experience shows that it (nearly) never fails to converge in a fixed number of iterations.

the power iteration algorithm and the other steps are similar. If the initial input matrix is not orthogonal to the eigenvector subspace span $(\mathbf{X}(:,1),\mathbf{X}(:,2),\dots,\mathbf{X}(:,s))$ and $\lambda_s > \lambda_{s+1}$, by the similar argument, we can imagine $\mathbf{Q}$ approaches span $(\mathbf{X}(:,1),\mathbf{X}(:,2),\dots,\mathbf{X}(:,s))$ and $\mathbf{T}$ approaches an upper triangular matrix (the Schur form).[5] From the theoretical point of view, the QR decomposition, just as the normalization in the power iteration, is not needed for the convergence and can be replaced by LU decomposition. QR decomposition is used for the sake of numerical stability. Because $\mathbf{R}$ in the algorithm is an upper triangular matrix, the spanned spaces of $\mathbf{Y}$ and $\mathbf{Q}$ are same.

Algorithm 1.3 Sub-space Iteration Algorithm

1: Input an arbitrary matrix $\mathbf{Y} \in \mathbb{R}^{n\times s}$.
2: **for** $k = 1,2,\dots$ **do**
3:   QR decomposition: $\mathbf{Y} = \mathbf{QR}$, $\mathbf{Q} \in \mathbb{R}^{n\times s}$ orthogonal, $\mathbf{R}$ upper triangle.
4:   $\mathbf{Y} = \mathbf{AQ}$.
5:   $\mathbf{T} = \mathbf{Q}'\mathbf{Y}$.
6: **end for**

If the initial input matrix $\mathbf{Y} = \mathbf{I} \in \mathbb{R}^{n\times n}$, the sub-space iteration becomes the whole space iteration. In this case, we can present it in a mathematically equivalent but more convenient form, that is, the QR iteration algorithm. Let us analyze the matrix $\mathbf{T}$ calculated by Algorithm 1.3 in two consecutive steps,

$$\mathbf{T}_{k-1} = \mathbf{Q}'_{k-1}\mathbf{Y}_{k-1} = \mathbf{Q}'_{k-1}(\mathbf{Q}_k\mathbf{R}_k) = (\mathbf{Q}'_{k-1}\mathbf{Q}_k)\mathbf{R}_k = \mathbf{P}_k\mathbf{R}_k,$$
$$\mathbf{T}_k = \mathbf{Q}'_k\mathbf{Y}_k = (\mathbf{Q}'_k\mathbf{AQ}_{k-1})(\mathbf{Q}'_{k-1}\mathbf{Q}_k) = (\mathbf{Q}'_k\mathbf{Y}_{k-1})(\mathbf{Q}'_{k-1}\mathbf{Q}_k) = \mathbf{R}_k(\mathbf{Q}'_{k-1}\mathbf{Q}_k) = \mathbf{R}_k\mathbf{P}_k.$$

By the comparison of $\mathbf{T}$ calculated in steps $k-1$ and k, we can simplify the whole space iteration to QR iteration. The core of QR iteration algorithm is presented in Algorithm 1.4. If we do not need to keep $\mathbf{A}$, it can replace $\mathbf{T}$ in Algorithm 1.4. Here, $\mathbf{T}$ is used to emphasize it is the same $\mathbf{T}$ calculated in the whole space iteration, which approaches the Schur form of $\mathbf{A}$.

Algorithm 1.4 QR Iteration Algorithm

1: $\mathbf{T} = \mathbf{A}$.
2: **for** $k = 1,2,\dots$ **do**
3:   QR decomposition: $\mathbf{T} = \mathbf{QR}$, $\mathbf{Q}$ orthogonal, $\mathbf{R}$ upper triangle.
4:   $\mathbf{T} = \mathbf{RQ}$.
5: **end for**

QR iteration algorithm as shown in Algorithm 1.4 is too costly. Three important improvements are available. First reduce $\mathbf{A}$ to an upper Hessenberg matrix $\mathbf{H}$, then apply QR iteration to $\mathbf{H}$. Second use implicit shift. If we have an estimate μ for the eigenvalue λ_i. Then, the QR iteration applied to $\mathbf{H} - \mu\mathbf{I}$ will converge in $[(\lambda_i - \mu)/(\lambda_{i-1} - \mu)]^k$. If $\lambda_i - \mu \ll \lambda_{i-1} - \mu$, the convergence is fast. Third deflate when an eigenvalue converges. Then, the subsequent QR iteration is applied to a smaller $\mathbf{H}$. The complete QR iteration algorithm with the MATLAB code will be presented in Chapter 5.

If $\mathbf{A}$ is symmetric, the reduced Hessenberg $\mathbf{H}$ becomes symmetric tri-diagonal. The QR iteration algorithm applied to a symmetric tri-diagonal is even more efficient. There are two other special

---
[5]Refer to [29] for the rigorous proof.

algorithms for the symmetric tri-diagonal matrix. One is the bisection method based on the calculation of $\det(\mathbf{H} - \lambda\mathbf{I})$. Because $\mathbf{H}$ is tri-diagonal, $\det(\mathbf{H} - \lambda\mathbf{I})$ can be efficiently calculated. The other is the divide-and-conquer method. The tri-diagonal matrix can be deflated into two smaller tri-diagonal matrices with the addition of an rank-1 matrix. The two smaller tri-diagonal matrices can be deflated recursively until a series of very small tri-diagonal matrices are obtained. The eigenvalues of each small tri-diagonal matrix can be calculated by any suitable means. Then, the small decoupled tri-diagonal matrices are stitched to form a bigger tri-diagonal matrix. The eigenvalues of the bigger tri-diagonal matrix are obtained based on the eigenvalues of a diagonal matrix plus a rank-1 update. The whole process is recursive and can be parallelized. These algorithms with MATLAB codes will be presented in Chapter 5 together with other algorithms not mentioned here.

Iterative Algorithms of Eigenvalues Solution [29, 55]   Similarly to the iterative algorithms for the linear equation solutions, we make an assumption for the eigenvector $\mathbf{x} = \mathbf{Ky}$, where $\mathbf{K} \in \mathbb{R}^{n\times s}, s \ll n$. Corresponding to $\mathbf{K}$, we construct $\mathbf{L'K} = \mathbf{I}$.[6] Now we solve a reduced eigenvalue problem to obtain μ and $\mathbf{y}$,

$$(\mathbf{L'AK})\,\mathbf{y} = \mathbf{By} = \mu\mathbf{y}. \tag{1.74}$$

Introducing $\mathbf{x} = \mathbf{Ky}$ to $\mathbf{Ax} = \mu\mathbf{x}$, we usually have an error in the equations (residual),

$$\mathbf{r} = \mathbf{Ax} - \mu\mathbf{x} = \mathbf{AKy} - \lambda\mathbf{Ky} \neq \mathbf{0}. \tag{1.75}$$

From the obtained residual $\mathbf{r}$, we can make an improved $\mathbf{K}$ and $\mathbf{L}$ to start a new iteration until the residual is smaller than a set tolerance.

The choice of $\mathbf{K}$ and $\mathbf{L}$ and the way to construct them determine various kinds of iterative algorithms. Because iterative algorithms are mostly applied to the sparse matrices, the sparsity of the matrices has to be taken into account when constructing $\mathbf{K}$ and $\mathbf{L}$.

In the subsequent chapters, all the algorithms to be presented are merely the applications of the ideas discussed in this section.

Signature of Matrix Algorithm Function   The naming of the presented MATLAB functions follows `fun_`, that is, an alphabetic name following an underscore `_`. For example, `LU_` for LU decomposition, `QR_` for QR decomposition, `eig_` for eigenvalue solution, `svd_` for singular value solution. Generally, the functions of the direct factorization algorithms, such as LU and QR, are in upper case. Others, such as equation solutions and eigenvalue solutions, are in lower case. If MATLAB has a built-in function for the same algorithm, the alphabetic name of the presented algorithm is same as the MATLAB built-in function, such as `LU_` and the examples cited above. The following lists all the functions with names starting with *mdivide*. These functions are algorithms for equation solutions, see Chapter 4.

```
>> ls mdivide*.m
```

```
mdivideBandByGauss_.m        mdivideBandUpperTriangle_.m    mdivideByHouseholder_.m
mdivideOrthogonal_.m         mdivideBandByGivens_.m         mdivideByDecomposing_.m
mdivideDiagonal_.m           mdivideUpperTriangle_.m        mdivideBandLowerTriangle_.m
mdivideByGauss_.m            mdivideLowerTriangle_.m
```

In the beginning of each function, there are short comments briefing the purpose of the function, the meaning of the input and output arguments. The comments can be accessed by MATLAB help system. For example in MATLAB, issue `help LU_`, we will get the following output.

---

[6]$\mathbf{L'}$ is the left inverse of $\mathbf{K}$.

```
>> help LU_
 function [L,U,p,q] = LU_(A,algo,pivot,tol,format,f1st,last,p,q)
 LU: P*A*Q'=L*U.L lower,U upper triangle, P row, Q column permutation.
 algo='Gauss' or 'Crout'
 pivot=0, no pivot; =1 min row pivot to allow LU to finish;
        =2 row pivot |lij|<=1; pivot=3, =2+column pivot;
        =4, complete pivoting
 tol=tolerance to check 0s.
 format='long':  L(m,m),U(m,n), P,Q permutation matrices.
        ='short': rows of U w/ zeros are removed. p,q in vector form.
 f1st,last,p,q: restart parameters.
```

In many matrix algorithms to be presented in the book, there is an input argument named format. It is used to control the format of the output of the algorithms. It has at least two possible input values, 'short' and 'long'. When format='short', the output arguments are in short formats—all permutations are in permutation vector forms and all zero rows or columns in the output matrices are removed. When format='long', the output arguments are in long formats—all permutations are in permutation matrix forms and all zero rows or columns in the output matrices are retained to their full sizes. Besides the long and short formats, the algorithms of the matrix decompositions to be presented in Chapters 2 and 3 have a compact format and a brief format. The compact format contains all the information of the decompositions, but is hard to read. Some algorithms of the matrix decompositions have a driver which changes the compact format to a long format or short format for better readability. The brief format does not calculate and keep the transformation matrices, that is, **U** and **V** are not calculated and saved in the calculation of **A** = **UBV**. The different output formats will be explained with examples in Section 2.2 of Chapter 2 and Section 3.2 of Chapter 3.

The input and outputs arguments to all the MATLAB functions to be presented in the book are organized in such a way to facilitate the usage. The necessary input arguments are placed at the beginning of the input argument lists. Many input arguments to the end of the argument lists have default values set in the MATLAB codes. The input arguments are checked for their validity. Let us take a look at the input arguments and output arguments of LU_. The following MATLAB code is the first 24 lines of codes from LU_.m.

```
%function [L,U,p,q] = LU_(A,algo,pivot,tol,format,f1st,last,p,q)
%LU: P*A*Q'=L*U.L lower,U upper triangle, P row, Q column permutation.
%algo='Gauss' or 'Crout'
%pivot=0, no pivot; =1 min row pivot to allow lu to finish;
%       =2 row pivot |lij|<=1; pivot=3, =2+column pivot;
%       =4, complete pivoting
%tol=tolerance to check 0s.
%format='long':  L(m,m),U(m,n), P,Q permutation matrices.
%       ='short': rows of U w/ zeros are removed. p,q in vector form.
%f1st,last,p,q: restart parameters.
function [L,U,p,q] = LU_(A,algo,pivot,tol,format,f1st,last,p,q)

[m,n] = size(A);
if (~exist('algo','var') || isempty(algo)) algo = 'Gauss'; end
if (~exist('pivot','var') || isempty(pivot)) pivot = 2; end
if (~exist('tol','var') || isempty(tol)) tol = sqrt(eps); end
if (~exist('format','var') || isempty(format)) format = 'short';  end
if (~exist('f1st','var') || isempty(f1st)) f1st = 1;  end
```

```
if (flst < 1) flst = 1; end
if (~exist('last','var') || isempty(last)) last = min(m,n); end
if (last > min(m,n)) last = min(m,n); end
if (~exist('p','var') || isempty(p)) p = 1:m; end
if (~exist('q','var')  || isempty(q)) q = 1:n; end
```

The first 10 lines are comments, which was displayed by help LU_. LU_ has 9 input arguments. The first input argument A is the matrix to be decomposed by LU. The second to the last input arguments controls the details of the LU decomposition. In many cases, the default values for the last eight input arguments are valid. Therefore, the call to LU_.m can be simply [L,U,p]=LU_(A). However, if the Crout algorithm is preferred to the default Gauss algorithm, the syntax can be simply [L,U,p]=LU_(A,'crout'). If the complete pivoting of Gauss algorithm and the long output format are preferred to the default settings, the syntax is [L,U,P,Q]=LU_(A,'gauss',4,[],'long'). The third input argument pivot=4 sets the complete pivoting. The fourth output argument Q recording the column permutations, which were omitted in the two previous calls with only row permutations, becomes necessary in the output argument list. It does not harm to include q in the output argument list in [L,U,p,q]=LU_(A) or [L,U,p,q]=LU_(A,'crout'). In both cases, the output q is just [], an empty array of MATLAB. In [L,U,P,Q]=LU_(A,'gauss',4,[],'long'), the fourth input [] acts as a place holder, because the fifth input format='long' is not the default value of format='short'. The second input algo='gauss' is indeed the default value, which therefore can be replaced by a place holder []. The last four input arguments to LU_.m are only needed for partial LU decomposition and restart LU decomposition. See Section 2.2 for the demonstration examples of LU_.m.

Another MATLAB facility, a cell array, is adopted to organize a long input argument list into groups. A cell array provides a storage mechanism for dissimilar types of data as the following example shows. In multiplying algorithms, such as the Lanczos algorithm to transform a symmetrical matrix **A** into a symmetrical tri-diagonal matrix **T**, see QTQtByLanczos_.m in Section 3.6.3.

```
>> B=randn(8);   B=0.5*(B+B');      %B=B'
>> [L,D,p]=LDLt_(B);                %P*B*P'=L*D*L', LDLt decomposition
```

In QTQtByLanczos_.m, the basic calculation is the matrix–vector product, **Aq**. In this example, **A** is not directly given, but $\mathbf{A} = \mathbf{B}^{-1} = \mathbf{P}'\mathbf{L}'^{-1}\mathbf{D}^{-1}\mathbf{L}^{-1}\mathbf{P}$. However, **A** can be completely determined by cell data as follows. Then **A** and **B** are input to QTQtByLanczos_.m in the same way.

```
>> A=cell(1,6);
>> A{1}={'size',[8,8]};
>> A{2}={'mdividePermute_',p};
>> A{3}={'mdivideUpperTriangle_',L'};
>> A{4}={'mdivideDiagonal_',D};
>> A{5}={'mdivideLowerTriangle',L};
>> A{6}={'mtimesPermute_',p}
A =
    {1x2 cell}    {1x2 cell}    {1x2 cell}    {1x2 cell}    {1x2 cell}    {1x2 cell}
```

where mdividePermute_, mdivideUpperTriangle_, mdivideDiagonal_, mdivideLowerTriangle_ and mtimesPermute_ are all MATLAB function names.

Verification of Matrix Algorithm Function We mention briefly how the MATLAB algorithm functions presented in the book are verified. We take LU decomposition as an example. LU decomposition factorizes the permuted form of a given matrix A into a product of a lower triangular matrix L and an upper triangular matrix U. **PA = LU**, **P** is a permutation matrix. MATLAB built-in function lu does this calculation. Issue help lu in MATLAB for more information of LU. See the following example.

```
>> A=10+(20-10)*rand(3)
A =
   18.1730   13.9978   14.3141
   18.6869   12.5987   19.1065
   10.8444   18.0007   11.8185
>> [L1,U1,P1]=lu(A)
L1 =
    1.0000        0         0
    0.5803    1.0000        0
    0.9725    0.1633    1.0000
U1 =
   18.6869   12.5987   19.1065
        0   10.6894    0.7307
        0        0   -4.3862
P1 =
    0    1    0
    0    0    1
    1    0    0
```

where `A=10+(20-10)*rand(3)` creates a matrix `A` of 3×3 whose components are the pseudo-random numbers of uniform distribution in the interval $[10, 20]$. The LU decomposition of `A` verifies the following identity:

$$P_1 A - L_1 U_1 = 0.$$

This identity can be verified.

```
>> norm(P1*A-L1*U1) < 10.0*eps*max(abs(diag(U1)))
=    1
```

where `max(abs(diag(U1)))` calculates the maximum of the absolute of the diagonals of `U1`, and `eps` is a MATLAB constant of the machine precision.[7] The above calculation shows the identity $P_1 A - L_1 U_1 = 0$ is verified to the machine precision.

The demonstrating MATLAB code for LU decomposition is `LU_.m`. Refer to Section 2.2 for the discussion of `LU_.m`.

Using the demonstrating `LU_.m`, we can do the same calculation of `A`.

```
>> [L2,U2,P2]=LU_(A)
L2 =
    1.0000        0         0
    0.5803    1.0000        0
    0.9725    0.1633    1.0000
U2 =
   18.6869   12.5987   19.1065
        0   10.6894    0.7307
        0        0   -4.3862
P2 =
    0    1    0
    0    0    1
    1    0    0
```

The output `[L2,U2,P2]` of `LU_` is compared with `[L1,U1,P1]` of the built-in `lu` of MATLAB. For each algorithm presented in the book, if MATLAB has a built-in function, the calculation of the algorithm will be first compared with the output of the built-in MATLAB function. But the extensive verifications are performed using a MATLAB script similar to the following code:

---

[7]On Dell Inspiron 1545, the value of eps equals `2.2204e-016`. It can be checked by issuing >> eps in MATLAB.

```
m = 6; n = 8;
for j = 1:100
    A = 10.0 + (20.0-10.0)*rand(n);
    [L,U,P] = LU_(A);
    if (norm(P*A-L*U) > 10.0*eps*max(abs(diag(U))))
        error ('possible error in LU_');
    end

    A = 10.0 + 2.0*randn(m,n);
    [L,U,P] = LU_(A);
    if (norm(P*A-L*U) > 10.0*eps*max(abs(diag(U))))
        error ('possible error in LU_');
    end
end
```

where randn(m,n) is another way of creating random testing matrices. A = 10.0 + 2.0*randn(m,n) creates a matrix of $m \times n$ with components of pseudo-random numbers of normal distribution with mean equal to 10.0 and the standard deviation equal to 2.0. In this way, hundreds and thousands of tests of LU decomposition of matrices of different sizes and values can be performed easily and quickly. All the algorithms presented in the book are verified by similar means.

1.5 REORDERING OF SPARSE MATRICES

A sparse matrix has a lot of zeros but the location of zeros does not have a clear pattern. By reordering a sparse matrix, we can obtain some wanted pattern of zeros to suit different needs of different algorithms. One example is to reorder a sparse matrix to a band matrix with a small bandwidth. A band matrix is more suitable for LU-type-based equation solutions. Another example is to group together the columns which are not coupled, so that the permuted sparse matrix has a block structure in which the diagonal blocks include one or more diagonal sub-matrices. The diagonal block structure is more suitable for Jacobi or Gauss–Seidel iterative equation solutions. The optimum solutions to these reordering problems are NP-complete or NP-hard [52]. However, efficient algorithms to solve these problems based on some heuristics are available [56]. They are usually presented in the context of the adjacency graph of a sparse matrix. The vertices of the adjacency graph of a sparse matrix are the column numbers. There is an edge between any two vertices i and j if $A(i,j) \neq 0$. The adjacency graph is undirected if $A(j,i) \neq 0$ whenever $A(i,j) \neq 0$ and directed otherwise.

For simplicity, we consider only undirected graph and symmetric reordering in this section. Symmetric reordering means that the same permutations are applied to the rows and columns of the matrix. To the adjacency graph, symmetric reordering means relabeling the vertices without changing the edges.

The two integer vectors rA and jA of the CSR format of a sparse matrix include all the information of the adjacency graph. For a column (or vertex) j, the number of columns (or vertices) which are coupled with (or adjacent to) the column (or vertex) j, i.e. the degree of the vertex j, is

$$\deg(j) = rA(j + 1) - rA(j). \tag{1.76}$$

All the columns (or vertices) coupled with (or adjacent to) the column (or vertex) j, i.e. the adjacent vertices of the vertex j, are

$$\text{adj}(j) = jA(rA(1) : rA(j + 1) - 1). \tag{1.77}$$

symrcmCSR_ in the following is known as reverse Cuthill–McKee (RCM) algorithm in the literature [16, 27, 28, 77]. It picks one of the vertex which has the minimum degree among all the vertices, then relabels each adjacent vertex and the adjacent vertices of the next level in the order of increasing degree. The algorithm is to make the bandwidth as small as possible. It has a MATLAB built-in counterpart, symrcm.

Algorithm 1.9

RCM Algorithm: Reorder a sparse matrix in CSR format to minimize bandwidth.

```
function p = symrcmCSR_(rA,jA)

m = length(rA)-1;   o = zeros(1,m);   p = [];

while(length(p) < m)
    dmin = m;
    for j=1:m
        if (o(j) == 0) dmin = min(dmin, rA(j+1)-rA(j)); end
    end
    j1 = [];
    for j=1:m
        if (o(j)==0 && dmin==rA(j+1)-rA(j)) j1 = [j1,j]; end
    end
    q = j1(1);   %or q(j),1<=j<=lenth(q)
    while (~isempty(q))
        q1 = q(1);   q = q(2:end);
        if (o(q1) == 0)
            o(q1) = 1; p = [p,q1]; q = [q,jA(rA(q1):rA(q1+1)-1)];
        end
    end
end

for j=1:floor(m/2) pj = p(j); p(j) = p(m-j+1); p(m-j+1) = pj; end %reverse
```

The application of symrcmCSR_ to a sparse matrix is demonstrated by the following MATLAB script.

```
load('west0479.mat');
S = west0479;            %S from a portion of Harwell-Boeing matrix, west0479.
A = S*S';                %A in MATLAB internal sparse format
[iA,jA,dA] = find(A);    %convert A to IJD format
[rA,jA,dA,m,n] = ijd2csr_(iA',jA',dA',size(A,1),size(A,2));
p = symrcmCSR_(rA,jA);   %p a permutation vector, (rA,jA) CSR's integer's vectors.
subplot(1,2,1),spy(A), title('A:_sparse_matrix_before_RCM');
subplot(1,2,2),spy(A(p,p)),title('A:_sparse_matrix_after_RCM');
```

The MATLAB function spy visualizes the sparsity pattern of a matrix. The two spy commands plot Fig. 1.1.

The reordering algorithm maxCut_ finds a set of vertices that any two vertices in the set are not adjacent. The algorithm is to make this set as large as possible according to the criterion. A permuted sparse matrix based on the maximal independent set has a diagonal submatrix in the diagonal.

Algorithm 1.10

Find a maximal independent set of columns from a sparse matrix in CSR format.

```
%Find a maximal independent set of columns from a sparse matrix in CSR format.
```

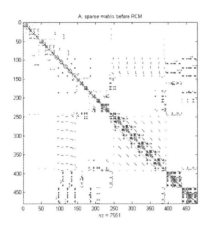
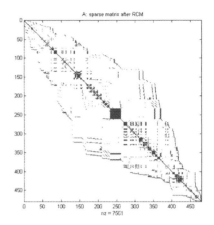

FIGURE 1.1

Sparsity pattern before and after RCM reordering.

```
function p = maxCut_(rA,jA)

m = length(rA)-1;  o = zeros(1,m);  d = zeros(1,m);  p1 = [];  p2 = [];
for j=1:m  d(j) = rA(j+1) - rA(j);  end
[d,q] = sort(d,'ascend');

for j=1:m
    qj = q(j);
    if (o(qj) == 0)
        adj = jA(rA(qj):rA(qj+1)-1);
        for k=1:length(adj)
            if (adj(k) == qj)  p1 = [p1,qj];
            elseif (o(adj(k)) == 0) p2 = [p2,adj(k)]; end
        end
        o(jA(rA(qj):rA(qj+1)-1)) = 1;
    end
end

p = [p1,p2];
```

The reordering algorithm `minColor_` is known as vertex coloring in graph theory [56]. It groups together each independent set of columns which are not adjacent to each other. It is equivalent to coloring each vertex with a different color from its adjacent vertices. The algorithm is to use as few colors as possible to color all the vertices according to the criterion. A permuted sparse matrix based on the vertex coloring has several diagonal submatrices in the diagonal. The number of diagonal submatrices equals to the number of colors coloring all the vertices.

Algorithm 1.11

Color all columns of a sparse matrix in CSR format.

```
%Color all columns of a sparse matrix in CSR format.
%Criteria: no adjacent columns in same color, as few colors as possible.
function p = minColor_(rA,jA)
```

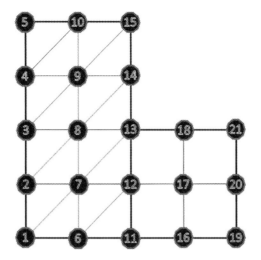

FIGURE 1.2

Finite element mesh.

```
m = length(rA)-1;  n = max(jA);  o = zeros(1,m);  c = zeros(1,m);

for j=1:m
    adj = jA(rA(j):rA(j+1)-1);  d = length(adj);
    cadj = sort(c(adj),'ascend');
    cmin = cadj(1);  cmax = cadj(end);

    for cj=1:cmax+1
        oldc = 0;
        if (cmin<=cj && cj<=cmax)
            for k=1:d
                if (cj == cadj(k)) oldc = 1; end
            end
        end
        if (oldc == 0) c(j) = cj; break; end
    end
end

[c,p] = sort(c,'ascend');
```

We apply the two reordering algorithms maxCut_ and minColor_ to the sparse matrix of the finite element mesh shown in Fig. 1.2. For simplicity, we assume each finite element node has only one unknown. The adjacency graph of the sparse matrix is determined by the mesh topology.

In the first step, we create the element node vectors which relate local node numbers to global node numbers. This is known as meshing the model in a finite element analysis.

```
elem=cell(1,20);   %We use cell array, because of different length of members of elem
elem{1}=[1,6,7];   elem{2}=[1,7,2];   elem{3}=[2,7,8];   elem{4}=[2,8,3];
elem{5}=[3,8,9];   elem{6}=[3,9,4];   elem{7}=[4,9,10];  elem{8}=[4,10,5];
elem{9}=[6,11,12];  elem{10}=[6,12,7];  elem{11}=[7,12,13];  elem{12}=[7,13,8];
```

```
elem{13}=[8,13,14];   elem{14}=[8,14,9];   elem{15}=[9,14,15];   elem{16}=[9,15,10];
elem{17}=[11,16,17,12];   elem{18}=[12,17,18,13];
elem{19}=[16,19,20,17];   elem{20}=[17,20,21,18];
```

In the second step, we obtain the sparse matrix in the IJD format from the element nodes vectors. This is known as the element calculation in a finite element analysis.

```
iA = [];   jA = [];   dA = [];   n = 1;
ne = length(elem);
for j=1:ne
    e = elem{j};
    nn = length(e);
    iA = [iA, zeros(1,nn*nn)];
    jA = [jA, zeros(1,nn*nn)];
    dA = [dA, zeros(1,nn*nn)];
    for k=1:nn
        for l=1:nn
            iA(n) = e(k);   jA(n) = e(l);
            dA(n) = 10*e(k) + e(l);      %dA not important to the problem
            n = n + 1;
        end
    end
end
```

In the third step, we convert the sparse matrix from the IJD format to CSR format and the MATLAB internal sparse format. This is known as the matrix assembly in a finite element analysis.

```
A = sparse(iA,jA,dA);                    %to use spy(A)
%for assembly and to use the two algorithms
[dB,rB,jB,m,n] = ijd2csr_(dA,iA,jA,size(A,1),size(A,2));
```

Lastly we apply maxCut_ and minColor_ to reorder the sparse matrix. This step serves as a pre-processing step of the equation solution to speed up the equation solution in a finite element analysis.

```
>> p1=maxCut_(rB,jB)    %p1 a permutation vector
p1 =
     5     1    15    19    21     3    11    13     4    10     2     6     7
     9    14    16    17    20    18     8    12
>> p2=minColor_(rB,jB)  %p2 a permutation vector
p2 =
     1     3     5    11    13    15    19    21     2     4     6    14    16
    18     7     9    17     8    10    12    20
```

The effect of the reordering is shown in Fig. 1.3 by the MATLAB function spy.

```
subplot(1,3,1),spy(A),  title('A:before_reordering.');
subplot(1,3,2),spy(A(p1,p1)),  title('A:after_maxCut_.');
subplot(1,3,3),spy(A(p2,p2)),  title('A:after_minColor_.');
```

1.6 UTILITY CODES

In this section, we will present a few utility codes that are used in the algorithms to be presented in the subsequent chapters. They are simple and self-explanatory.

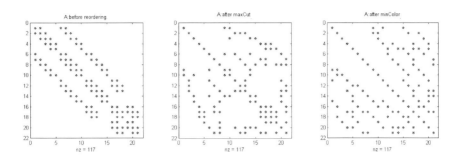

FIGURE 1.3

Sparsity pattern of Fig. 1.2 before and after reordering.

Algorithm 1.12

Swap two data of any types

```
function [a,b] = swap_(a,b)
c = a;   a = b;   b = c;
```

Algorithm 1.13

Find k, so v(k)=vk. k possible in (j1,j2).

```
%find k, so v(k)=vk.
function k = find_(v,vk,j1,j2)

if (exist('j1','var') == 0) j1 = 1; end
if (exist('j2','var') == 0) j2 = length(v); end

for i=j1:j2
    if (v(i) == vk) k = i; return; end
end
for i=1:j1-1
    if (v(i) == vk) k = i; return; end
end
for i=j2+1:length(v)
    if (v(i) == vk) k = i; return; end
end
k = 0;
```

Algorithm 1.14

Find k, so v(k)=maximum of v(j:end).

```
function k = argmax_(v,j,op)

if (exist('j','var') == 0) j = 1; end
if (exist('op','var') == 0) op = 0; end

k = j; n = length(v);
if (op == 0)        %abs
```

```
    ak = abs(v(k));
    for i=k+1:n
        ai = abs(v(i));
        if (ak < ai) ak = ai; k = i; end
    end
else                %noop
    ak = v(k);
    for i=k+1:n
        ai = v(i);
        if (ak < ai) ak = ai; k = i; end
    end
end
```

Algorithm 1.15

Find k,l, so A(k,l)=maximum of A(i1:i2,j1:j2).

```
function [k,l] = argsmax_(A,i1,j1,i2,j2,op)

if (exist('i1','var') == 0) i1 = 1; end
if (exist('j1','var') == 0) j1 = 1; end
if (exist('i2','var') == 0) i2 = size(A,1); end
if (exist('j2','var') == 0) j2 = size(A,2); end
if (exist('op','var') == 0) op = 0; end

k = i1;  l = j1;
if (op == 0)        %abs
    akl = abs(A(k,l));
    for i=i1:i2
        if (j2 == 0) j2 = i; end
        for j=j1:j2
            aij = abs(A(i,j));
            if (akl < aij) akl = aij;  k = i;  l = j; end
        end
    end
else                %noop
    akl = A(k,l);
    for i=i1:i2
        if (j2 == 0) j2 = i; end
        for j=j1:j2
            aij = A(i,j);
            if (akl < aij) akl = aij;  k = i;  l = j; end
        end
    end
end
```

In matrix computations, switching rows and columns are used in many algorithms to achieve better numerical stability. Row or column switching is presented as permutations of $1,2,3,\ldots$. Permutation forms a linear group. In matrix form, it is the orthogonal matrix obtained from switching the rows and columns of an identity matrix. The conversion between a permutation matrix and a permutation vector can clarify the relations between the two data forms of permutations.

Algorithm 1.16

Convert a permutation matrix to a permutation vector.

```
function p = pm2pv_(P)
```

```
m = size(P,1);    p = zeros(1,m);
for i=1:m
    for j = 1:m
        if(P(i,j) == 1)
            p(i) = j;   break;
        end
    end
end
```

Algorithm 1.17

Convert a permutation vector to a permutation matrix.

```
function P = pv2pm_(p)

m = length(p); P = zeros(m);
for i=1:m
    P(i,p(i)) = 1;
end
```

A permutation matrix is orthogonal, so its inverse is its transpose. If the permutation is represented as a permutation vector, its transpose is obtained in the following code.

Algorithm 1.18

Inverse permutation.

```
%vip = inverse permutation of piv.
function vip = inv_perm_(piv)

n = length(piv);    vip = piv;
for j=1:n
    vip(piv(j)) = j;
end
```

The sign of a permutation is positive if the permutation can be obtained from $1, 2, 3, \ldots$ in even number of steps, negative if in odd number of steps. The count of a permutation is found by the following code.

Algorithm 1.19

Count of a permutation.

```
%count number of permutations of a permutation array, piv
function count = perm_count_(piv)

s = length(piv);    p = 1:s;    count - 0,
for j=1:s
    if(p(j) ~= piv(j))
        k = find_(p,piv(j),j);
        pj = p(j);    p(j) = p(k);    p(k) = pj;
        count = count + 1;
    end
end
```

For a matrix $\mathbf{A} \in \mathbb{R}^{m \times n}$, row permutations are of the form $\mathbf{P}_1 \mathbf{A}$, and column permutations are of the form $\mathbf{AP}_2'$. Here, $\mathbf{P}_1$ is a permutation matrix of size m, and $\mathbf{P}_2$ is a permutation matrix of size n. Of course, the actual permutations are performed by the swapping of the rows or columns of the matrix or vector.

Algorithm 1.20

Row or column permutation. V=P*U or V=U*P'.

```
%rc='row': permute rows of u, P*U, ='col': permute column of U, U*P'.
function v = permute_(p,u,rc)

[m,n] = size(u);   s = length(p);   v = u;
if (exist('rc','var') == 0) rc = 'row'; end
if (m == 1) rc = 'col'; end
if (n == 1) rc = 'row'; end

if (strcmp(rc,'row'))                %V=U*P', side='right'
    for j=1:min(m,s)
        if (j ~= p(j)) v(j,:) = u(p(j),:); end
    end
else  %if (strcmp(rc,'col'))         %V=P*U , side='left'
    for j=1:min(n,s)
        if (j ~= p(j)) v(:,j) = u(:,p(j)); end
    end
end
```

To keep the symmetry of a symmetric matrix **A**, the permutations must be of the form **PAP'**, i.e. the same permutations are applied to the rows and columns of **A**. One special feature of the symmetric permutations is that any diagonal component of **A** cannot be permuted to become an off-diagonal component. The symmetric permutation with the data access restricted to the lower triangular part of **A** is done with the following code snippet:

```
if (i ~= j)     %swap row (i,j) and column (i,j)
    [A(i,1:i-1),A(j,1:i-1)] = swap_(A(i,1:i-1),A(j,1:i-1));
    [A(j+1:n,i),A(j+1:n,j)] = swap_(A(j+1:n,i),A(j+1:n,j));
    [A(i+1:j-1,i),A(j,i+1:j-1)] = swap_(A(i+1:j-1,i),A(j,i+1:j-1));
    [A(i,i),A(j,j)] = swap_(A(i,i),A(j,j));
    [p(i),p(j)] = swap_(p(i),p(j));
end
```

The efficiency of exploiting zero patterns of zero structured matrices is demonstrated by MATLAB functions calculating the matrix–vector product, where the unnecessary calculations with all the zeros are removed.

Algorithm 1.21

Calculate v=L*u or v=u*L, L Lower Triangle.

```
%side='right': v=L*u; ='left': u*L
function v = mtimesLowerTriangle_(L,u,side)

if (~exist('side','var') || isempty(side)) side = 'right'; end
[m,n] = size(L);   side = upper(side);

if (strcmp(side,'RIGHT'))    %v=L*u
    if (n ~= size(u,1)) error ('mtimesLowerTriangle_:␣size␣error'); end
    v = zeros(m,size(u,2));
    for i=1:m
        v(i,:) = L(i,1:min(i,n))*u(1:min(i,n),:);
```

```
        end
else %if(strcmp(side,'LEFT'))%v=u*L
    if (m ~= size(u,2)) error ('mtimesLowerTriangle_:_size_error'); end
    v = zeros(size(u,1),n);
    for j=1:n
        v(:,j) = u(:,j:m)*L(j:m,j);
    end
end
```

Algorithm 1.22

Calculate v=U*u or v=u*U, U Upper Triangle.

```
%side='right': v=U*u; ='left': u*U
function v = mtimesUpperTriangle_(U,u,side)

if (~exist('side','var') || isempty(side)) side = 'right'; end
[m,n] = size(U);    side = upper(side);

if (strcmp(side,'RIGHT'))      %v=U*u
    if (n ~= size(u,1)) error ('mtimesUpperTriangle_:_size_error'); end
    v = zeros(m,size(u,2));
    for i=1:m
        v(i,:) = U(i,i:n)*u(i:n,:);
    end
else %if(strcmp(side,'LEFT'))%v=u*U
    if (m ~= size(u,2)) error ('mtimesUpperTriangle_:_size_error'); end
    v = zeros(size(u,1),n);
    for j=1:n
        v(:,j) = u(:,1:min(j,m))*U(1:min(j,m),j);
    end
end
end
```

Algorithm 1.23

Calculate v=B*u or v=u*B, B in band matrix format.

```
%side='right': v=B*u; ='left': u*B
function v = mtimesBand_(B,lbw,ubw,m,n,u,side)

if (exist('m','var')==0 || isempty(m)) m = size(B,1); end
if (m > size(B,1)+lbw) m = size(B,1)+lbw; end
if (exist('n','var')==0 || isempty(n)) n = m; end
if (n > size(B,1)+ubw) n = size(B,1)+ubw; end
if (~exist('side','var') || isempty(side)) side = 'right'; end
side = upper(side);

if (strcmp(side,'RIGHT'))      %v=R*u
    if (n ~= size(u,1)) error ('mtimesBand_:_size_error'); end
    v = zeros(m,size(u,2));  lbw1 = lbw + 1;
    for i=1:m
        js = max(1,i-lbw):min(i+ubw,n);
        v(i,:) = B(i,js-(i-lbw1))*u(js,:);
    end
else %if(strcmp(side,'LEFT'))%v=u*B
    if (m ~= size(u,2)) error ('mtimesBand_:_size_error'); end
    v = zeros(size(u,1),n);    lbw1 = lbw + 1;
    for j=1:n
```

```
        for  i=max(1,j-ubw):min(j+lbw,m)
            v(:,j) = v(:,j) + u(:,i)*B(i,j-i+lbw1);
        end
    end
end
```

Algorithm 1.24

Calculate v=S*u or v=u*S, S in CSR format.

```
%side='right': v=B*u; ='left': u*B
function v = mtimesCSR_(dA,rA,jA,u,side)

m = length(rA)-1;   n = max(jA);
if (~exist('side','var') || isempty(side)) side = 'right'; end
side = upper(side);

if (strcmp(side,'RIGHT'))              %u=A*v
    if (n ~= size(u,1)) error ('mtimesCSR_:⌴size⌴error'); end
    v = zeros(m,size(u,2));
    for i=1:m
        v(i,:) = dA(rA(i):rA(i+1)-1) * u(jA(rA(i):rA(i+1)-1),:);
    end
else %if (strcmp(side,'LEFT'))     %u=v*A
    if (m ~= size(u,2)) error ('mtimesCSR_:⌴size⌴error'); end
    v = zeros(size(u,1),n);
    for i=1:m
        for k=rA(i):rA(i+1)-1
            j = jA(k);
            v(:,j) = v(:,j) + u(:,i)*dA(k);
        end
    end
end
```

Sometimes we need to transpose a band matrix or sparse matrix. The following is the MATLAB function to transpose a band matrix.

Algorithm 1.25

Transpose a band matrix.

```
function [Bt,lbwt,ubwt,mt,nt] = transposeBand_(B,lbw,ubw,m,n)

if (exist('m','var') == 0) m = size(B,1); end
if (exist('n','var') == 0) n = m; end

lbwt = ubw; ubwt = lbw; mt = n; nt = m; tbw1 = lbw+ubw+1;   mn = min(m,n);
Bt = zeros(min(n,mn+ubw),tbw1);

j = lbw + 1;   jt = lbwt + 1;
Bt(1:mn,jt) = B(1:mn,j);              %diagonal

if (m < n) k1 = min(n-m,ubw); else k1 = 0; end
for k=1:k1
    j = lbw + k + 1;   jt = lbwt - k + 1;
    Bt(k+1:m+k,jt) = B(:,j);          %sup-diagonals of B
end
for k=k1+1:ubw
```

```
      j = lbw + k + 1;   jt = lbwt - k + 1;
      Bt(k+1:n,jt) = B(1:n-k,j);      %sup-diagonals of B
end

if (m > n) k2 = min(m-n,lbw); else k2 = 0; end
for k=1:k2
      j = lbw - k + 1;   jt = lbwt + k + 1;
      Bt(1:n,jt) = B(k+1:n+k,j);      %sub-diagonals of B
end
for k=k2+1:lbw
      j = lbw - k + 1;   jt = lbwt + k + 1;
      Bt(1:m-k,jt) = B(k+1:m,j);      %sub-diagonals of B
end
```

To transpose a sparse matrix A in CSR format is easy, if we convert it to IJD format first, because in IJD format swapping (iA,jA) produces its transpose.

```
function [rB,cB,Brc,mb,nb] = transposeCSR_(rA,cA,Arc,ma,na)

[iA,jA,Aij,ma,na] = csr2ijd_(rA,cA,Arc,ma,na);
[rB,cB,Brc,mb,nb] = ijd2csr_(jA,iA,Aij,na,ma);
```

In some algorithms, it requires to find a vector perpendicular to a given set of vectors (or, columns of a matrix). This problem forms the basis of the Gram–Schimdt algorithm of QR. But in those algorithms, only the basic form of orthogonalization of an arbitrary vector to matrix columns is needed. Further the given matrix is not necessarily orthogonal among its columns. The following listed orthogonal_.m can serve that purpose.

Algorithm 1.26

Find a vector q perpendicular to all columns of a given matrix Q.

```
%Find a vector q, q'*Q=0. If no input q, q=randn(m,1).
%If w/o input P, Q'*Q=I. If w/ input P, P'*Q=I.
function q = orthogonal_(Q,q,P,unit)

[m,n] = size(Q);   eta = 0.5*sqrt(2.0);         %eta for reorthogonalization
if (m <= n) q = zeros(m,1); return; end         %no non0 q!
withq = exist('q','var') && ~isempty(q);
withP = exist('P','var') && ~isempty(P);
if (withq == 0) q = randn(m,1); q = q/norm(q); end
if (size(q,1)~=m || (withP~=0 && (size(P,1)~=m || size(P,2)~=n)))
      error('orthogonal_:_matrix_size_error.');
end
if (exist('unit','var') == 0) unit = 1; end
if (withP == 1) tol = max(abs(P(:,n)'*Q(:,n)-1.0),2.0*eps);
else            tol = max(abs(Q(:,n)'*Q(:,n)-1.0),2.0*eps); end

while(1)
      normq0 = realmax;  normq = norm(q);  qmax = norm(q,inf);
      while (normq < eta*normq0)
            normq0 = normq;
            if (withP) q = q - P*(Q'*q);
            else       q = q - Q*(Q'*q); end
            normq = norm(q);
      end
      if (withq==0 && normq<tol*max(1,qmax)) q = randn(m,1);   %try again
```

```
    else                                    break;  end
end
if (normq > tol)
    if (unit==1) q = q/normq; end
else
    q = zeros(m,1);
end
```

In multiplying algorithms, such as Lanczos and Arnoldi algorithms, it requires to calculate the product of a matrix and a vector. More generally it requires to calculate a vector under a linear transformation. The linear transformation can be in a factored form of a series of linear transformations, each of which is depicted by a matrix and an operator (a MATLAB function). The following `Ay_.m` shows the idea of the implementation that combines the common matrix–vector product and the more general linear transformation. In `Ay_.m`, the MATLAB functions starting with `mtimes` are functions for the matrix–vector product, **My** or **yM**. The MATLAB functions starting with `mdivide` are functions for the equation solution, $\mathbf{M^{-1}y}$ or $\mathbf{yM^{-1}}$. See Chapter 4 for the details of the MATLAB functions starting with names `mdivide`.

Algorithm 1.27

Find new y under a linear transformation A, A in factored form.

```
% Ay_(A,y,'left')=Ay_(A',y','right')'. r: A#x=a. l: y#A=b=>A'#y'=b' (no A').
% A = {{'op1',M1},{M2},....,{'opn',Mn}}. op2='mtimes'!
% M = F, {B,lbw,rbw,m,n}, {dA,rA,jA}, etc.
% op= 'mtimes','mtimesBand_','mtimesCSR_','mdivideByGauss_',etc, default='mtimes'.
function y = Ay_(A,y,side)

if (~iscell(A)) A = {'mtimes',A}; end   %F->{#,F}
if (ischar(A{1}) && strcmp(A{1},'full')) A = {'mtimes',A{2}}; end
if (ischar(A{1}) && strcmp(A{1},'band')) A = {'mtimesBand_',A{2}}; end
if (ischar(A{1}) && strcmp(A{1},'csr')) A = {'mtimesCSR_',A{2}}; end
if (~iscell(A{1})) A = {A}; end       %{#,F}->{{#,F}}; {#,{}}->{{#,{}}}
if (~exist('side','var') || isempty(side)) side = 'right'; end
if (strcmp(side,'right')) terms = length(A):-1:1; else terms = 1:length(A); end

for j=terms
    if (isempty(A{j}) || (iscell(A{j}) && strcmp(A{j}{1},'size'))) continue; end
    op = A{j}{1};  Mj = A{j}{2};
    if(strcmp(op,'mtimes') || strcmp(op,'mtimesFull_') || strcmp(op,
                                                    'mtimesOrthogonal_'))
        if (strcmp(side,'right')) y = Mj*y;
        else                      y = y*Mj; end
    elseif(strcmp(op,'mdivide') || strcmp(op,'mdivideFull_') || strcmp(op,
                                                    'mdivideByGauss_'))
        if (strcmp(side,'right')) y = mdivideByGauss_(Mj,y);
        else                      y = mdivideByGauss_(Mj',y')'; end
    elseif (strcmp(op,'mdivideByHouseholder_'))
        if (strcmp(side,'right')) y = mdivideByHouseholder_(Mj,y);
        else                      y = mdivideByHouseholder_(Mj',y')'; end
    elseif(strcmp(op,'mdivideOrthogonal_'))
        if (strcmp(side,'right')) y = Mj'*y;
        else                      y = y*Mj'; end
    elseif(strcmp(op,'mtimesDiagonal_'))
        y = y.*Mj;       %'left','right' same
    elseif(strcmp(op,'mdivideDiagonal_'))
```

```
            y = y./Mj;        %'left','right' same
        elseif (strcmp(op,'mtimesPermute_') || strcmp(op,'permute_'))
            if (strcmp(side,'right')) y = permute_(Mj,y,'row');
            else                      y = permute_(inv_perm_(Mj),y,'col'); end
        elseif (strcmp(op,'mdividePermute_'))
            if (strcmp(side,'right')) y = permute_(inv_perm_(Mj),y,'row');
            else                      y = permute_(Mj,y,'col'); end
        elseif(strcmp(op,'mtimesBand_'))
            if (length(Mj) >= 4) m = Mj{4}; else m = size(Mj{1},1); end
            if (length(Mj) >= 5) n = Mj{5}; else n = m; end
            y = mtimesBand_(Mj{1},Mj{2},Mj{3},m,n,y,side);
        elseif (strcmp(op,'mdivideBand_') || strcmp(op,'mdivideBandByGauss_'))
            if (length(Mj) >= 4) m = Mj{4}; else m = size(Mj{1},1); end
            if (length(Mj) >= 5) n = Mj{5}; else n = m; end
            if (strcmp(side,'right'))
                y = mdivideBandByGauss_(Mj{1},Mj{2},Mj{3},m,n,y);
            else
                Mjt = transposeBand_(Mj{1},Mj{2},Mj{3},m,n);
                y = mdivideBandByGauss_(Mjt,Mj{3},Mj{2},n,m,y')';
            end
        elseif (strcmp(op,'mdivideBandByGivens_'))
            if (length(Mj) >= 4) m = Mj{4}; else m = size(Mj{1},1); end
            if (length(Mj) >= 5) n = Mj{5}; else n = m; end
            if (strcmp(side,'right'))
                y = mdivideBandByGivens_(Mj{1},Mj{2},Mj{3},m,n,y);
            else
                Mjt = transposeBand_(Mj{1},Mj{2},Mj{3},m,n);
                y = mdivideBandByGivens_(Mjt,Mj{3},Mj{2},n,m,y')';
            end
        elseif(strcmp(op,'mtimesCSR_'))
            y = mtimesCSR_(Mj{1},Mj{2},Mj{3},y,side);
        elseif(strcmp(op,'mdivideCSR_'))
%           y = ???;          %not supported!!
        elseif (strcmp(op,'mtimesLowerTriangle_'))
            y = mtimesLowerTriangle_(Mj,y,side);
        elseif (strcmp(op,'mdivideLowerTriangle_'))
            if (strcmp(side,'right')) y = mdivideLowerTriangle_(Mj,y);
            else                      y = mdivideUpperTriangle_(Mj',y')'; end
        elseif (strcmp(op,'mtimesBandLowerTriangle_'))
            if (length(Mj) >= 3) m = Mj{3}; else m = size(Mj{1},1); end
            if (length(Mj) >= 4) n = Mj{4}; else n = m; end
            y = mtimesBand_(Mj{1},Mj{2},0,m,n,y,side);
        elseif (strcmp(op,'mdivideBandLowerTriangle_'))
            if (length(Mj) >= 3) m = Mj{3}; else m = size(Mj{1},1); end
            if (length(Mj) >= 4) n = Mj{4}; else n = m; end
            if (strcmp(side,'right'))
                y = mdivideBandLowerTriangle_(Mj{1},Mj{2},m,n,y);
            else
                Mjt = transposeBand_(Mj{1},Mj{2},0,m,n);
                y = mdivideBandUpperTriangle_(Mjt,Mj{2},n,m,y')';
            end
        elseif (strcmp(op,'mtimesUpperTriangle_'))
            y = mtimesUpperTriangle_(Mj,y,side);
        elseif (strcmp(op,'mdivideUpperTriangle_'))
            if (strcmp(side,'right')) y = mdivideUpperTriangle_(Mj,y);
            else                      y = mdivideLowerTriangle_(Mj',y')'; end;
        elseif (strcmp(op,'mtimesBandUpperTriangle_'))
```

```
        if (length(Mj) >= 3) m = Mj{3}; else m = size(Mj{1},1); end
        if (length(Mj) >= 4) n = Mj{4}; else n = m; end
        y = mtimesBand_(Mj{1},Mj{2},0,m,n,y,side);
    elseif (strcmp(op,'mdivideBandUpperTriangle_'))
        if (length(Mj) >= 3) m = Mj{3}; else m = size(Mj{1},1); end
        if (length(Mj) >= 4) n = Mj{4}; else n = m; end
        if (strcmp(side,'right'))
            y = mdivideBandUpperTriangle_(Mj{1},Mj{2},m,n,y);
        else
            Mjt = transposeBand_(Mj{1},0,Mj{2},m,n);
            y = mdivideBandLowerTriangle_(Mjt,Mj{2},n,m,y')';
        end
    elseif (strcmp(op,'Ay_'))
        y = Ay_(Mj,y,side);
    else
        warning('Ay_:_unknown_op.');
    end
end
```

The following simple examples demonstrate the functionality and application of Ay_.m. First we create a matrix in different formats and then a linear transformation in different formats.

```
>> A = [1    2    0    0    0;          %A in full matrix
        3    4    5    0    0;
        0    6    7    8    0;
        0    0    5    4    3;
        0    0    0    1    2];
>> [bA,lbw,ubw,m,n]=full2band_(A,1,1);    %A in band format
>> [sA,rA,jA]=full2csr_(A);               %A in csr format
>> [L,U,p]=LU_(A);                        %A=P'*L*U in factored form
>> x=(1:5)';                              %x=[1;2;3;4;5]

>> A1 = A;      %={'mtimes',A}            %A* in full format
>> A2 = {'mtimesBand_',{bA,lbw,ubw,m,n}};   %A* in band format
>> A3 = {'mtimesCSR_',{sA,rA,jA}};        %A* in csr format
>> A4 = {{'size',[5,5]},...               %A* in factored format
         {'mdividePermute_',p},...
         {'mtimesLowerTriangle_',L},...
         {'mtimesUpperTriangle_',U}};

>> B1 = {'mdivide',A};                    %A\ in full format
>> B2 = {'mdivideBand_',{bA,lbw,ubw,m,n}};  %A\ in band format
>>%B3 = {'mdivideCSR_',{sA,rA,jA}};       %A\ in csr format (not supported)
>> B4 = {{'size',[5,5]},...               %A\ in factored format
         {'mdivideUpperTriangle_',U},...
         {'mdivideLowerTriangle_',L},...
         {'mtimesPermute_',p}};
```

Then, we apply the matrix (or linear transformation) to Ay_.m. The output of zeros shows the equivalence of the application of Ay_.m and the original matrix **A**.

```
>> (Ay_(A1,x)-A*x)'                       =    0    0    0    0    0
=    0    0    0    0    0                >> Ay_(A2,x','left')-x'*A
>> Ay_(A1,x','left')-x'*A                 =    0    0    0    0    0
=    0    0    0    0    0                >> (Ay_(A3,x)-A*x)'
>> (Ay_(A2,x)-A*x)'                       =    0    0    0    0    0
```

```
>> Ay_(A3,x','left')-x'*A                        =      0      0      0      0      0
=      0      0      0      0      0            >> Ay_(A4,x','left')-x'*A
>> (Ay_(A4,x)-A*x)'                               =      0      0      0      0      0



>> (Ay_(B1,x)-A\x)'                               =    1.0e-015 *
=      0      0      0      0      0                         0      0    0.4441  -0.8882
>> Ay_(B1,x','left')-x'*inv(A)                           0
=    1.0e-014 *                                   >> Ay_(B2,x','left')-x'*inv(A)
 -0.1776    0.0711    0.0111   -0.0999            =    1.0e-014 *
-0.0666                                             -0.0666   0.0384   -0.0020   -0.0444
>> (Ay_(B2,x)-A\x)'                               -0.1332



>> (Ay_(B4,x)-A\x)'                               =    1.0e-014 *
=      0      0      0      0      0                -0.0888   0.0444        0   -0.0555
>> Ay_(B4,x','left')-x'*inv(A)                     -0.1332
```

If a linear transformation is not represented as an ordinary full matrix, we need a function to inquire its size. The following size_.m is an extension of the built-in MATLAB function size for a full matrix.

Algorithm 1.28

Get the size of a linear transformation.

```
function [m,n] = size_(A)

if (~iscell(A))
    [m,n] = size(A);                              %A=F
elseif (length(A)>1 && ischar(A{1}) && (strcmp(A{1},'full') ||...
        strcmp(A{1},'mtimes') || strcmp(A{1},'mdivide') ||...
        strcmp(A{1},'mtimesFull_') || strcmp(A{1},'mdivideFull_') ||...
        strcmp(A{1},'mdivideByGauss_') || strcmp(A{1},'mdivideByHouseholder_') ||...
        strcmp(A{1},'mdivideOrthogonal_')))
    [m,n] = size(A{2});                           %A={'full',F}
elseif (length(A)>1 && ischar(A{1}) && (strcmp(A{1},'band') ||...
        strcmp(A{1},'mtimesBand_') || strcmp(A{1},'mdivideBand_')))
    m = A{2}{4};   n = A{2}{5};                   %A={'band',{B,lbw,ubw,m,n}}
elseif (length(A)>1 && ischar(A{1}) && (strcmp(A{1},'csr') ||...
        strcmp(A{1},'mtimesCSR_') || strcmp(A{1},'mdivideCSR_')))
    m = length(A{2}{2}) - 1;   n = max(A{2}{3});  %A={'csr',{dA,rA,jA}}
elseif (length(A)>1 && iscell(A{1}) && strcmp(A{1}{1},'size'))
    m = A{1}{2}(1);   n = A{1}{2}(2);             %A={{'size',[m,n]},{...}}
else
    error('size_:  Input matrix error.');
end
```

Similarly for a linear transformation which is not represented as ordinary full matrix, we need a function to return its transpose. The following transpose_.m is an extension of the built-in MATLAB function transpose or its equivalent operator ' for a full matrix.

Algorithm 1.29

Get the size of a linear transformation.

```
function At = transpose_(A)

if (~iscell(A) || isempty(A))
    At = A';                        %A=F
elseif (length(A)>1 && ischar(A{1}) && (strcmp(A{1},'full') ||...
        strcmp(A{1},'mtimes') || strcmp(A{1},'mdivide') ||...
        strcmp(A{1},'mtimesFull_') || strcmp(A{1},'mdivideFull_') ||...
        strcmp(A{1},'mdivideByGauss_') || strcmp(A{1},'mdivideByHouseholder_') ||...
        strcmp(A{1},'mdivideOrthogonal_')))
    At = {A{1}, transpose_(A{2})};    %A={'full',F}
elseif (length(A)>1 && ischar(A{1}) && (strcmp(A{1},'band') ||...
        strcmp(A{1},'mtimesBand_') || strcmp(A{1},'mdivideBand_')))
    [Bt,lbwt,ubwt,mt,nt] = transposeBand_(A{2}{1},A{2}{2},A{2}{3},A{2}{4},A{2}{5});
    At = {A{1},{Bt,lbwt,ubwt,mt,nt}};
elseif (length(A)>1 && ischar(A{1}) && (strcmp(A{1},'csr') ||...
        strcmp(A{1},'mtimesCSR_') || strcmp(A{1},'mdivideCSR_')))
    [Brc,rB,cB,mb,nb] = transposeCSR_(A{2}{1},A{2}{2},A{2}{3},A{2}{4},A{2}{5});
    At = {A{1},{Brc,rB,cB,mb,nb}};
elseif (length(A)>1 && iscell(A{1}) && strcmp(A{1}{1},'size'))
    At = {'size',[A{1}{2}(2),A{1}{2}(1)]};
    for j=2:length(A)
        At = {At,transpose_(A{j})};
    end
else
    error('transpose_:_Input_matrix_error.');
end
```

Direct algorithms of decompositions of matrices by non-orthogonal transformations

2

INTRODUCTION

In this chapter and the next chapter, we will present various direct algorithms to decompose a matrix **A** into the form **UBV**. Matrix decompositions are usually the first step for other matrix algorithms, such as linear equation solutions, eigenvalues solutions, and singular value solutions. They also form an independent category of the matrix algorithms. As discussed in Section 1.4, the task of computing **A** = **UBV** can be classified into three forms, transforming, decomposing, and multiplying on one hand. It can also be classified according to the form of **U**, **V**, and **B** on the other hand. Both classifications are shaped strongly by the property and structure that **A** possesses. The complete coverage of computing **A** = **UBV** by direct algorithms is divided between two chapters. This chapter deals with the non-orthogonal **U** and **V**. The next chapter focuses on the exclusive use of orthogonal matrices for **U** and **V**.

Section 2.1 introduces the general elimination problem encountered in the direct algorithms of matrix decomposition. Then it presents the basic Gauss elimination matrix which all the algorithms of this chapter are built upon.

Section 2.2 presents LU algorithms: $\mathbf{PAQ}' = \mathbf{LU}$, where **A** is a general rectangular matrix, **L** is a lower triangular matrix, **U** is an upper triangular matrix, **P** and **Q** are permutation matrices.

Section 2.3 presents LDU algorithms: $\mathbf{PAQ}' = \mathbf{LDU}$, where **A** is a general rectangular matrix, **L** is a lower triangular matrix, **D** is a diagonal matrix, **U** is an upper triangular matrix, **P** and **Q** are permutation matrices.

Section 2.4 presents several decomposition algorithms of a symmetric matrix. The first is the specialization of LDU decomposition to the symmetric matrix, LDLt decomposition: $\mathbf{PAP}' = \mathbf{LDL}'$, where **L** is a lower triangular matrix, **D** is a diagonal matrix, **P** is a permutation matrix. The second and third are the numerically more stable algorithms, LTLt and LBLt decompositions: $\mathbf{PAP}' = \mathbf{LTL}'$ and $\mathbf{PAP}' = \mathbf{LBL}'$, where **T** is symmetric tri-diagonal, **B** is a diagonal of 1×1 and 2×2 blocks. The fourth decomposition is the specialization of LDLt to a symmetric positive definite matrix, LLt decomposition (commonly known as Cholesky decomposition): $\mathbf{A} = \mathbf{LL}'$. The fifth decomposition is the adaptation of the LLt decomposition to a symmetric positive indefinite matrix, xLLt decomposition (commonly known as modified Cholesky decomposition): $\mathbf{A} + \mathbf{E} = \mathbf{LL}'$, where **E** is a diagonal $\mathbf{E} \geq \mathbf{0}$.

Section 2.5 presents two similarity decomposition algorithms. The first is the LHLi decomposition: $\mathbf{PAP}' = \mathbf{LHL}^{-1}$, where **A** is a square matrix, **L** is lower triangular matrix, **H** is a Hessenberg matrix, **P** is permutation matrix. The second is the GTGi decomposition: $\mathbf{PAP}' = \mathbf{GTG}^{-1}$, where **A** is a square matrix, **G** is a square matrix, **T** is a tri-diagonal matrix, **P** is permutation matrix.

Section 2.6 presents GTJGt algorithm: $[\mathbf{A},\mathbf{B}] = \mathbf{G}[\mathbf{T},\mathbf{J}]\mathbf{G}'$, where $\mathbf{A}$ and $\mathbf{B}$ two are symmetric matrices, $\mathbf{G}$ is a square matrix, $\mathbf{T}$ is a symmetric tri-diagonal matrix, $\mathbf{J}$ is a diagonal matrix of only -1s, 0s, and $+1$s.

All the algorithms will be presented in more than one form, that is, transforming, decomposing, or multiplying discussed in Section 1.4. All the algorithms provide early exit and restart capability, so that the reader can run each algorithm step by step and check the output of computations. All the algorithms have four output formats: brief, compact, short, and long. The restart capability and output format will be explained in full detail in LU algorithm. They remain essentially same for all the other algorithms.

2.1 GAUSS ELIMINATION MATRIX

One central theme of all matrix computations is to introduce zeros to a given matrix. The following three problems are found in many matrix computation algorithms.

1. Given a column vector $\mathbf{u}$ of length m, we want to find a matrix $\mathbf{U}$ which satisfies the condition, Eq. (2.1),

$$
\mathbf{U}\begin{bmatrix} u_1 \\ \vdots \\ u_k \\ u_{k+1} \\ \vdots \\ u_m \end{bmatrix} = \begin{bmatrix} u_1 \\ \vdots \\ u_k \\ 0 \\ \vdots \\ 0 \end{bmatrix}. \tag{2.1}
$$

2. Given a row vector $\mathbf{v}$ of length n, we want to find a matrix $\mathbf{V}$ which satisfies the condition, Eq. (2.2),

$$
\left(v_1,\ldots,v_k,v_{k+1},\ldots,v_n\right)\mathbf{V} = \left(v_1,\ldots,v_k,0,\ldots,0\right). \tag{2.2}
$$

3. Given a column vector $\mathbf{u}$ and a row vector $\mathbf{v}$ from a column and row of a matrix, we want to find two matrices $\mathbf{U}$ and $\mathbf{V}$ which satisfy the condition, Eq. (2.3),

$$
\mathbf{U}\begin{bmatrix} & u_1 & \\ & \vdots & \\ v_1,\ldots, & w_j & ,\ldots,v_l,v_{l+1},\ldots,v_n \\ & \vdots & \\ & u_k & \\ & u_{k+1} & \\ & \vdots & \\ & u_m & \end{bmatrix} \quad \mathbf{V} = \begin{bmatrix} & u_1 & \\ & \vdots & \\ v_1,\ldots, & w_j & ,\ldots,v_l,0,\ldots,0 \\ & \vdots & \\ & u_k & \\ & 0 & \\ & \vdots & \\ & 0 & \end{bmatrix}. \tag{2.3}
$$

Problem 2 can be recast as problem 1, because $(\mathbf{vV})' = \mathbf{V}'\mathbf{v}'$, where $\mathbf{v}'$ is a column vector. For all three problems, $\mathbf{U}$ and $\mathbf{V}$ always exist and are non-unique. To find unique $\mathbf{U}$ and $\mathbf{V}$, we can put extra requirements on $\mathbf{U}$ and $\mathbf{V}$. For example, we may require them to have a simple form such as $\mathbf{I} + \mathbf{wI}(k,:)$ (Gauss elimination) or $\mathbf{I} - \alpha \mathbf{hh}'$ (Householder reflection), or $G(k,l,\theta)$ (Givens rotation). In problem 3, we may require $\mathbf{V} = \mathbf{U}^{-1}$ or $\mathbf{V} = \mathbf{U}'$.

Many matrix algorithms can be thought of clever and repeated applications of zeroing algorithms outlined above. The challenges are to keep the zeros introduced in earlier steps, and use only well conditioned $\mathbf{U}$ and $\mathbf{V}$.

LU decomposition and all the other decomposition algorithms of this chapter are built upon the Gauss elimination. We denote $\mathbf{G}$ for the zeroing matrix in Gauss elimination. $\mathbf{G}$ has the following form:

$$\mathbf{G} = \mathbf{I} + \mathbf{g}\mathbf{I}(k,:) = \left[\mathbf{I}(:,1),\dots,\mathbf{I}(:,k-1),\mathbf{g}+\mathbf{I}(:,k),\mathbf{I}(:,k+1),\dots,\mathbf{I}(:,n)\right], \tag{2.4a}$$

$$\mathbf{w} = \mathbf{G}\mathbf{v} = \mathbf{v} + v(k)\mathbf{g}. \tag{2.4b}$$

In order for $\mathbf{G}$ to eliminate $\mathbf{v}$ as in Eq. (2.4), $\mathbf{g}$ has to adopt the following values:

$$\mathbf{g}' = \left[0,\dots,0,0,-\frac{v(k+1)}{v(k)},\dots,-\frac{v(n)}{v(k)}\right]. \tag{2.5}$$

Because $g(k) = 0$, it can be verified that $(\mathbf{I}+\mathbf{g}\mathbf{I}(k,:))\,(\mathbf{I}-\mathbf{g}\mathbf{I}(k,:)) = \mathbf{I}$. Therefore,

$$\mathbf{G}^{-1} = \mathbf{I} - \mathbf{g}\mathbf{I}(k,:) = \left[\mathbf{I}(:,1),\dots,\mathbf{I}(:,k-1),-\mathbf{g}+\mathbf{I}(:,k),\mathbf{I}(:,k+1),\dots,\mathbf{I}(:,n)\right]. \tag{2.6}$$

$v(k)$ in Eq. (2.5) is called the pivot. Eqs. (2.4), (2.5), and (2.6) fail when $v(k) = 0$. When $|v(k)|$ is small compared to other components of $\mathbf{v}$, $\mathbf{g}$ will have components whose absolute values are larger than 1 – a condition that should be avoided in the matrix computations. We can show how cond($\mathbf{G}$) is determined by $\mathbf{g}$. For this purpose, we calculate the eigenvalues of $\mathbf{G}'\mathbf{G}$,

$$\begin{aligned}
\mathbf{G}'\mathbf{G}\mathbf{x} - \lambda\mathbf{x} &= (\mathbf{I} + \mathbf{g}\mathbf{I}(k,:) + \mathbf{I}(:,k)\mathbf{g}' + \mathbf{g}'\mathbf{g}\mathbf{I}(:,k)\mathbf{I}(k,:))\,\mathbf{x} - \lambda\mathbf{x} \\
&= (1-\lambda)\mathbf{x} + x_k\mathbf{g} + (\mathbf{g}'\mathbf{x} + x_k\mathbf{g}'\mathbf{g})\,\mathbf{I}(:,k) \\
&= \begin{bmatrix} (1-\lambda)\begin{bmatrix} x_1 \\ \vdots \\ x_{k-1} \end{bmatrix} \\ (1-\lambda)x_k + (\mathbf{g}'\mathbf{g})x_k + \mathbf{g}'\mathbf{x} \\ (1-\lambda)\begin{bmatrix} x_{k+1} \\ \vdots \\ x_n \end{bmatrix} + x_k\begin{bmatrix} g_{k+1} \\ \vdots \\ g_n \end{bmatrix} \end{bmatrix} = \begin{bmatrix} \mathbf{0} \\ 0 \\ \mathbf{0} \end{bmatrix}.
\end{aligned} \tag{2.7}$$

There are $n-2$ eigen pairs $\lambda = 1$ and $\mathbf{x}$ satisfying $x_k = 0$ and $\mathbf{g}'\mathbf{x} = 0$. The remaining two eigen pairs can be chosen to satisfy $\lambda \neq 1$ and $x_k \neq 0$. From Eq. (2.7), we can obtain the two eigenvalues as follows:

$$\lambda_1 = \frac{1}{2}\left[(\mathbf{g}'\mathbf{g}+2) - \sqrt{(\mathbf{g}'\mathbf{g}+2)^2 - 2^2}\right] \leq 1, \tag{2.8a}$$

$$\lambda_n = \frac{1}{2}\left[(\mathbf{g}'\mathbf{g}+2) + \sqrt{(\mathbf{g}'\mathbf{g}+2)^2 - 2^2}\right] \geq 1. \tag{2.8b}$$

By the definition of the 2-norm condition number of a matrix, we can calculate the 2-norm condition number of $\mathbf{G}$ as follows:

$$\kappa_2(\mathbf{G}) = \frac{\sigma_n(\mathbf{G})}{\sigma_1(\mathbf{G})} = \sqrt{\frac{\lambda_n(\mathbf{G})}{\lambda_1(\mathbf{G})}} = \frac{1}{2}\left[(\mathbf{g}'\mathbf{g}+2) + \sqrt{(\mathbf{g}'\mathbf{g}+2)^2 - 2^2}\right] = \lambda_n. \tag{2.9}$$

To reduce $\kappa_2\,(\mathbf{G})$, we can permute $\mathbf{v}$: $|v_k| = \max_{k \le j \le n}|v_j|$. Then $|g_j| \le 1, k+1 \le j \le n$. With such a permutation, we can guarantee the 2-norm condition number of the Gauss elimination matrix occurring in all the cases is bounded by

$$1 \le \kappa_2\,(\mathbf{G}) \le \frac{1}{2}\left[(n-k+2) + \sqrt{(n-k+2)^2 - 2^2}\right], \quad 1 \le k \le n-1. \tag{2.10}$$

Here is the detail of the MATLAB function for the Gauss elimination. It should be noted that the zeroing of a matrix using Gauss elimination is usually performed in line.

Algorithm 2.1

Calculate Gauss elimination matrix.
```
function g = gauss_(v,k,gj,format)

if (~exist('k','var') || isempty(k)) k = 1; end
if (~exist('gj','var') || isempty(gj)) gj = 1; end
if (~exist('format','var') || isempty(format)) format = 'short'; end
n = length(v);

if (strcmp(format,'short'))   %Gauss vector
    g = zeros(n,1);
    g(k+1:n) = -v(k+1:n)/v(k);
    if (gj==2 && k>1) g(1:k-1) = -v(1:k-1)/v(k); end
else                          %Gauss matrix
    g = eye(n);
    g(k+1:n,k) = -v(k+1:n)/v(k);
    if (gj==2 && k>1) g(1:k-1,k) = -v(1:k-1)/v(k); end
end
```

The usage of the MATLAB function gauss_ can be illustrated with a few examples.

The following two examples show the effect of permutation to the conditioning of the Gauss elimination matrix.

```
>> v1=[1;20;300];                          >> v2=[300;20;1];
>> G=gauss_(v1,1,1,'long')                 >> G=gauss_(v2,1,1,'long')
G =                                        G =
     1      0      0                          1.0000        0        0
   -20      1      0                         -0.0667   1.0000        0
  -300      0      1                         -0.0033        0   1.0000

>> G*v1                                    >> G*v2
=    1                                     =  300
     0                                        0
     0                                        0
>> cond(G)  %pivot=1, G bad conditioned    >> cond(G)  %pivot=300, G well conditioned
= 9.0402e+004                              =   1.0690
```

The effect of the second input argument (k) can be understood from the comparison of the previous two examples and the following two examples. k sets the position of the elimination. The third input argument z controls whether the elimination is only below row k (default by z=1) or both below and above row k (by z=2). z=1 corresponds to the Gauss elimination. z=2 corresponds to Gauss–Jordan elimination.

```
>> G=gauss_(v1,2,1,'long')              >> G=gauss_(v1,2,2,'long')
G =                                     G =
     1      0      0                          1.0000    -0.0500         0
     0      1      0                               0     1.0000         0
     0    -15      1                               0   -15.0000    1.0000

>> G*v1                                 >> G*v1
=      1                                =       0
      20                                       20
       0                                        0
```

The fourth input argument (`format`) determines whether the return value g is the Gauss vector (default by `format='short'`) or it is the Gauss matrix (by `format='long'`).

```
>> G=gauss_(v2,1,1,'long')              >> g=gauss_(v2,1,1,'short')
G =                                     g =
   1.0000        0        0                        0
  -0.0667   1.0000        0                  -0.0667
  -0.0033        0   1.0000                  -0.0033
```

2.2 LU DECOMPOSITION

Given a matrix, $\mathbf{A} \in \mathbb{R}^{m \times n}$, we want to find a lower triangular matrix $\mathbf{L}$ with 1s on the diagonal, an upper triangular matrix $\mathbf{U}$ and permutation matrices $\mathbf{P}$ and $\mathbf{Q}$ so that $\mathbf{PAQ}' = \mathbf{LU}$. $\mathbf{PA}$ is a row permutation of $\mathbf{A}$. $\mathbf{AQ}'$ is a column permutation of $\mathbf{A}$. Either $\mathbf{P}$, or $\mathbf{Q}$, or both can be the identity matrix. $\mathbf{PAQ}' = \mathbf{LU}$ is called LU decomposition.

2.2.1 LU DECOMPOSITION BY GAUSS ELIMINATION

To illustrate the procedure, let us look at a simple example,

$$\mathbf{A} = \begin{bmatrix} A_{11} & A_{12} & A_{13} & A_{14} & A_{15} \\ A_{21} & A_{22} & A_{23} & A_{24} & A_{25} \\ A_{31} & A_{32} & A_{33} & A_{34} & A_{35} \\ A_{41} & A_{42} & A_{43} & A_{44} & A_{45} \\ A_{51} & A_{52} & A_{53} & A_{54} & A_{55} \end{bmatrix}. \tag{2.11}$$

In the first step, depending on the input argument of `pivot`, we choose A_{11} so that $|A_{11}|$ is the maximum of $|A(:,1)|$ or the maximum of $|A(1:5,1:5)|$. We record the row switching or possibly column switching in the two permutation vectors, `p,q`. In the second step, we apply the Gauss elimination $\mathbf{G}_1 = \mathbf{I} - [0; \mathbf{g}]\mathbf{I}(1,:)$ to the permuted $\mathbf{P}_1\mathbf{AQ}_1'$,

$$\mathbf{g} = \frac{1}{A_{11}}\mathbf{A}(2:5,1),$$

$$\mathbf{G}_1\mathbf{P}_1\mathbf{AQ}_1' = \begin{bmatrix} A_{11} & A_{12} & A_{13} & A_{14} & A_{15} \\ \mathbf{0} & \mathbf{A}(2:5,2) - A_{12}\mathbf{g} & \mathbf{A}(2:5,3) - A_{13}\mathbf{g} & \mathbf{A}(2:5,4) - A_{14}\mathbf{g} & \mathbf{A}(2:5,5) - A_{15}\mathbf{g} \end{bmatrix}.$$

We can save the Gauss vector $\mathbf{g}$ in the zeroed $\mathbf{A}(2:5,1)$. The values of $\mathbf{G}_1\mathbf{P}_1\mathbf{AQ}_1'$ in the locations $(2:5,2:5)$ will overwrite $\mathbf{A}(2:5,2:5)$. The transformed $\mathbf{A}$ is of the following form, for clarity, the Gauss vector $\mathbf{g}$ is not shown,

$$\mathbf{G}_1\mathbf{P}_1\mathbf{AQ}_1' = \begin{bmatrix} A_{11} & A_{12} & A_{13} & A_{14} & A_{15} \\ 0 & A_{22} & A_{23} & A_{24} & A_{25} \\ 0 & A_{32} & A_{33} & A_{34} & A_{35} \\ 0 & A_{42} & A_{43} & A_{44} & A_{45} \\ 0 & A_{52} & A_{53} & A_{54} & A_{55} \end{bmatrix}. \tag{2.12}$$

Now we move to the second column of the transformed $\mathbf{A}$. The same two steps are applied to $\mathbf{A}(2:5,2:5)$. First, decide the pivot A_{22}, then apply the Gauss elimination,

$$\mathbf{g} = \frac{1}{A_{22}}\mathbf{A}(3:5,2),$$

$$\mathbf{G}_2\mathbf{P}_2\mathbf{G}_1\mathbf{P}_1\mathbf{AQ}_1'\mathbf{Q}_2' = \begin{bmatrix} A_{11} & A_{12} & A_{13} & A_{14} & A_{15} \\ 0 & A_{22} & A_{23} & A_{24} & A_{25} \\ 0 & 0 & \mathbf{A}(3:5,2) - A_{23}\mathbf{g} & \mathbf{A}(3:5,4) - A_{24}\mathbf{g} & \mathbf{A}(3:5,5) - A_{25}\mathbf{g} \end{bmatrix}.$$

The Gauss vector for the second column is saved to $\mathbf{A}(3:5,2)$. The values of $\mathbf{G}_2\mathbf{P}_2\mathbf{G}_1\mathbf{P}_1\mathbf{AQ}_1'\mathbf{Q}_2'$ in the locations $(3:5,3:5)$ will overwrite $\mathbf{A}(3:5,3:5)$. If the LU decomposition stops prematurely here, $\mathbf{L}$ and $\mathbf{U}$ can be read from $\mathbf{A}$ as illustrated below,

$$\mathbf{L} = \begin{bmatrix} 1 & 0 & 0 & 0 & 0 \\ A_{21} & 1 & 0 & 0 & 0 \\ A_{31} & A_{32} & 1 & 0 & 0 \\ A_{41} & A_{42} & 0 & 1 & 0 \\ A_{51} & A_{52} & 0 & 0 & 1 \end{bmatrix}, \quad \mathbf{U} = \begin{bmatrix} A_{11} & A_{12} & A_{13} & A_{14} & A_{15} \\ 0 & A_{22} & A_{23} & A_{24} & A_{25} \\ 0 & 0 & A_{33} & A_{34} & A_{35} \\ 0 & 0 & A_{43} & A_{44} & A_{45} \\ 0 & 0 & A_{53} & A_{54} & A_{55} \end{bmatrix}.$$

We can continue to apply the two steps to $\mathbf{A}(3:5,3:5)$ and then $\mathbf{A}(4:5,4:5)$ of the transformed $\mathbf{A}$. After $\mathbf{A}(4:5,4:5)$ is finished, the lower triangular part of $\mathbf{A}$ holds the $\mathbf{L}$ factor, while the upper triangular part of $\mathbf{A}$ holds the $\mathbf{U}$ factor.

In the algorithm LUbyGauss_ presented below, it provides four levels of pivoting. Among them, pivot=0,1,3 are not practically very useful. They are provided for the purpose to understand the effect of pivoting to the Gauss elimination.

- pivot=0: No switching of rows and columns is done in each step of the elimination. If a close to zero pivot occurs at some step, LU decomposition fails.
- pivot=1: Switching of rows is performed only when a close to zero pivot is found to allow the LU decomposition to continue. The first non-zero component among $\mathbf{A}(i:n,k)$ is permuted to row i.
- pivot=2: In each step, switching rows i and k, where k is determined by $|A(k,i)| = \max(|A(j,i)|), j = i,\ldots,m$. If $|A(k,i)|$ is close to zero, all the components in $\mathbf{A}(i:m,i)$ are close to zeros. The step is skipped. This kind of pivoting is called the partial pivoting and it is usually enough to make the LU decomposition stable.
- pivot=3: In each step, find k according to $|A(k,i)| = \max(|A(j,i)|), j = i,\ldots,m$. However, if $|A(k,i)|$ is close to zero, the step is not skipped. Instead it finds k from the maximum absolute component from the next column according to $|A(k,i+1)| = \max(|A(j,i+1)|), j = i,\ldots,m$. If $|A(k,i+1)|$ is still close to zero, it goes to $i+2$ column. Switch rows i and k and columns i and $i+1$ or $i+2$.

- `pivot=4`: In each step, switch rows i and k and columns i and l, where k and l are determined according to $|A(k,l)| = \max(|A(j_1, j_2)|), j_1 = i, \ldots, m$ and $j_2 = i, \ldots, n$. This kind of pivoting is called the complete pivoting. It is able to find the linearly independent rows and columns from $\mathbf{A}$. If the purpose is to find the rank of $\mathbf{A}$, the complete pivoting is needed.

For a general matrix $\mathbf{A} \in \mathbb{R}^{m \times n}$, the process to obtain the LU decomposition by Gauss elimination is shown below,

$$\mathbf{G}_i \left(\mathbf{P}_i \left(\cdots \mathbf{G}_2 \left(\mathbf{P}_2 \left(\mathbf{G}_1 \left(\mathbf{P}_1 \mathbf{A} \mathbf{Q}_1' \right) \right) \mathbf{Q}_2' \right) \cdots \right) \mathbf{Q}_i' \right) = \mathbf{U}_i, \quad i = 1, \ldots, \min(m, n). \tag{2.13}$$

The effect of the permutation of each Gauss elimination step from 1 to $\min(m, n)$ on $\mathbf{G}_k$ and $\mathbf{A}$ can be understood if we rewrite Eq. (2.13) as follows:

$$\mathbf{G}_i \left(\mathbf{P}_i \mathbf{G}_{i-1} \mathbf{P}_i \right) \left(\mathbf{P}_i \mathbf{P}_{i-1} \mathbf{G}_{i-2} \mathbf{P}_{i-1} \mathbf{P}_i \right) \cdots \left(\mathbf{P}_i \cdots \mathbf{P}_2 \mathbf{G}_1 \mathbf{P}_2 \cdots \mathbf{P}_i \right) \left(\mathbf{P}_i \cdots \mathbf{P}_1 \mathbf{A} \mathbf{Q}_1 \cdots \mathbf{Q}_i \right) = \mathbf{U}_i. \tag{2.14}$$

Because each row permutation $\mathbf{P}_i$ involves only rows i and $k, k \geq i$ and possibly each column permutation $\mathbf{Q}_i$ involves only i and l, $l \geq i$, $\mathbf{P}_i$ and $\mathbf{Q}_i$ are both symmetric and orthogonal. Row and column permutations of $\mathbf{P}_i \mathbf{P}_{i-1} \mathbf{G}_{i-2} \mathbf{P}_{i-1} \mathbf{P}_i$ only switch the components (i, k) of the Gauss vector in $\mathbf{G}_{i-1}$ and do no change the column positions. Eq. (2.14) tells us that the elimination can be done in place. In each step, we obtain a column of $\mathbf{L}$ and a row of $\mathbf{U}$. The columns of $\mathbf{L}$ can overwrite the zeroed part of $\mathbf{A}$. $\mathbf{U}$ occupies the remaining part of $\mathbf{A}$ that are not zeroed. The row permutation of i and k does not influence $\mathbf{U}$. It is done between the rows i and k of all previously obtained columns of $\mathbf{L}$ (Gauss vectors, lower left part of $\mathbf{A}$ from i) and between the rows i and k of the remaining part of $\mathbf{A}$ to be eliminated (lower right part of $\mathbf{A}$ from i). The column permutation of i and l does not influence $\mathbf{L}$. It is done between the columns i and l of all the previously obtained rows of $\mathbf{U}$ (upper right part of $\mathbf{A}$ from i) and between the columns i and l of the remaining part of $\mathbf{A}$ to be eliminated (lower right part of $\mathbf{A}$ from i). Because $\mathbf{L}$ and $\mathbf{U}$ overwrite $\mathbf{A}$, the permutation of both rows and columns is performed across entire rows and columns of the changed $\mathbf{A}$. It is not necessary to distinguish each area of $\mathbf{A}$ that the data actually belong to. At the end of Gauss elimination step $i = \min(m, n)$, the lower part below the diagonal of $\mathbf{A}$ contains all the columns of $\mathbf{L}$. The diagonal of $\mathbf{L}$ is 1s and is not saved. The diagonal and above the diagonal of $\mathbf{A}$ contains $\mathbf{U}$.

The implementation of LU decomposition is listed below. It can be seen that a large part of the code is the check of the input arguments and the handling of different pivoting. The core of LU decomposition is very small. The code will be further illustrated by examples at the end of the section.

Algorithm 2.2

P*A*Q'=L*U by Gauss, P,Q permutations, L lower, U upper triangle.

```
%function [A,p,q] = LUbyGauss_(A,pivot,tol,f1st,last,p,q)
%p*A*q'=L*U by Gauss, p,q permutations, L lower, U upper triangle.
%tol=tolerance to check 0. L,U overwrites A.
function [A,p,q] = LUbyGauss_(A,pivot,tol,f1st,last,p,q)

[m,n] = size(A);
if (~exist('pivot','var') || isempty(pivot)) pivot = 2; end
if (~exist('tol','var') || isempty(tol)) tol = sqrt(eps); end
if (~exist('f1st','var') || isempty(f1st)) f1st = 1; end
if (f1st < 1) f1st = 1; end
if (~exist('last','var') || isempty(last)) last = min(m,n); end
if (last > min(m,n)) last = min(m,n); end
```

```
if (~exist('p','var') || isempty(p)) p = 1:m; end
if (~exist('q','var') || isempty(q)) q = 1:n; end
tol = tol*max(1.0,norm(diag(A))/min(m,n));

for i=f1st:last
    k = i;   l = i;
    if (pivot == 0)              %no pivot
        if (abs(A(k,l))<tol && (norm(A(k+1:m,l))>tol || norm(A(k,l+1:n))>tol))
            error ('Zero␣pivot.␣Use␣1<=pivot<=4.');
        end
    elseif (pivot == 1)       %minimal pivot
        while (abs(A(k,l))<tol && k<m)
            A(k,l) = 0;   k = k + 1;     %next A(k,l)~=0 as pivot
        end
    elseif (pivot == 2)       %partial pivot
        k = argmax_(A(:,i),i);
    elseif (pivot == 3)       %partial pivot+
        k = argmax_(A(:,l),i);
        while (abs(A(k,l))<tol && l<n)
            l = l + 1;   k = argmax_(A(:,l),i);
        end
    else %if (pivot == 4)    %complete pivot
        [k,l] = argsmax_(A,i,i);
    end
    if (i ~= k)     %swap row i and row k
        [A(i,:), A(k,:)] = swap_(A(i,:), A(k,:));
        [p(i), p(k)] = swap_(p(i), p(k));
    end
    if (i ~= l)     %swap column i and column l
        [A(:,i), A(:,l)] = swap_(A(:,i), A(:,l));
        [q(i), q(l)] = swap_(q(i), q(l));
    end

    if (abs(A(i,i)) < tol)
        A(i:m,i) = 0.0;        %skip the step
    else
        g = A(i+1:m,i)/A(i,i);  A(i+1:m,i) = g;  %l: Gauss vector in zeroed A
        for j=i+1:n             %apply Gauss elimination to A(i+1:m,i+1:n)
            A(i+1:m,j) = A(i+1:m,j) - A(i,j)*g;  %u: overwrite A
        end
    end
end
```

2.2.2 LU DECOMPOSITION BY CROUT PROCEDURE

By Gauss eliminations, we see that $\mathbf{PA} = \mathbf{LU}$ always exist. We can obtain $\mathbf{P}$, $\mathbf{L}$, and $\mathbf{U}$ in a slightly different way. Let us look at a simple example,

$$
\begin{bmatrix} A_{11} & A_{12} & A_{13} & A_{14} & A_{15} \\ A_{21} & A_{22} & A_{23} & A_{24} & A_{25} \\ A_{31} & A_{32} & A_{33} & A_{34} & A_{35} \\ A_{41} & A_{42} & A_{43} & A_{44} & A_{45} \\ A_{51} & A_{52} & A_{53} & A_{54} & A_{55} \end{bmatrix} = \begin{bmatrix} L_{11} & 0 & 0 & 0 & 0 \\ L_{21} & L_{22} & 0 & 0 & 0 \\ L_{31} & L_{32} & L_{33} & 0 & 0 \\ L_{41} & L_{42} & L_{43} & L_{44} & 0 \\ L_{51} & L_{52} & L_{53} & L_{54} & L_{55} \end{bmatrix} \begin{bmatrix} U_{11} & U_{12} & U_{13} & U_{14} & U_{15} \\ 0 & U_{22} & U_{23} & U_{24} & U_{25} \\ 0 & 0 & U_{33} & U_{34} & U_{35} \\ 0 & 0 & 0 & U_{44} & U_{45} \\ 0 & 0 & 0 & 0 & U_{55} \end{bmatrix}. \quad (2.15)
$$

Equating the first column,

$$\begin{bmatrix} A_{11} \\ A_{21} \\ A_{31} \\ A_{41} \\ A_{51} \end{bmatrix} = \begin{bmatrix} U_{11}L_{11} \\ U_{11}L_{21} \\ U_{11}L_{31} \\ U_{11}L_{41} \\ U_{11}L_{51} \end{bmatrix},$$

we apply a row permutation $\mathbf{P}_1$ to $\mathbf{A}$ so that $|A_{11}| = \max(|A_{11}|, |A_{21}|, |A_{31}|, |A_{41}|, |A_{51}|)$. Then, we have

$$U_{11}L_{11} = A_{11},$$

$$U_{11} \begin{bmatrix} L_{21} \\ L_{31} \\ L_{41} \\ L_{51} \end{bmatrix} = \begin{bmatrix} A_{21} \\ A_{31} \\ A_{41} \\ A_{51} \end{bmatrix}.$$

In $A_{11} = U_{11}L_{11}$, U_{11} and L_{11} can be chosen arbitrarily. For simplicity, we can choose $L_{11} = 1$, then $U_{11} = A_{11}$ and $\mathbf{L}(2:5,1) = \frac{1}{U_{11}}\mathbf{A}(2:5,1)$. After this step, we obtained $\mathbf{L}(:,1)$ and $\mathbf{U}(:,1)$. Because $L_{11} = 1$ and $\mathbf{U}(2:5,1) = 0$, they do not need to be saved. U_{11} can overwrite A_{11} and $\mathbf{L}(2:5,1)$ can overwrite $\mathbf{A}(2:5,1)$.

Similarly equating the second column, we obtain $U_{12}, U_{22}, L_{22} = 1$ and $\mathbf{L}(3:5,2)$. At the end of the second step, $\mathbf{A}$ will look like the following:

$$\begin{bmatrix} U_{11} & U_{12} & A_{13} & A_{14} & A_{15} \\ L_{21} & U_{22} & A_{23} & A_{24} & A_{25} \\ L_{31} & L_{32} & A_{33} & A_{34} & A_{35} \\ L_{41} & L_{42} & A_{43} & A_{44} & A_{45} \\ L_{51} & L_{52} & A_{53} & A_{54} & A_{55} \end{bmatrix}.$$

The first two columns of $\mathbf{A}$ are overwritten by components of $\mathbf{L}$ and $\mathbf{U}$. The last three columns of $\mathbf{A}$ are still those of the original $\mathbf{A}$.

Equating the third column of Eq. (2.15),

$$\begin{bmatrix} 1 & 0 \\ L_{21} & 1 \end{bmatrix} \begin{bmatrix} U_{13} \\ U_{23} \end{bmatrix} = \begin{bmatrix} A_{13} \\ A_{23} \end{bmatrix},$$

$$U_{33} \begin{bmatrix} L_{33} \\ L_{43} \\ L_{53} \end{bmatrix} = \begin{bmatrix} A_{33} \\ A_{43} \\ A_{53} \end{bmatrix} - U_{13} \begin{bmatrix} L_{31} \\ L_{41} \\ L_{51} \end{bmatrix} - U_{23} \begin{bmatrix} L_{32} \\ L_{42} \\ L_{52} \end{bmatrix}.$$

The first equation is a lower triangular matrix, which can be easily solved by a forward substitution to obtain U_{13} and U_{23}. Then, we calculate the right hand side of the second equation and save the result back to $\mathbf{A}(3:5,3)$. Now we apply another row permutation $\mathbf{P}_3$ to $\mathbf{A}(3:5,3)$ so that $|A(3,3)|$ is the maximum. Remember to apply $\mathbf{P}_3$ to $\mathbf{L}(3:5,1:2)$ and $\mathbf{A}(3:5,4:5)$ as well. Because $\mathbf{L}(3:5,1:2)$ occupies $\mathbf{A}(3:5,1:2)$, $\mathbf{P}_3$ applies to entire $\mathbf{A}(3:5,:)$. Then $U_{33}L_{33} = A_{33}$. Again we choose $L_{33} = 1$, then $U_{33} = A_{33}$ and $\mathbf{L}(4:5,3) = \frac{1}{U_{33}}\mathbf{A}(4:5,3)$. For the same reason, $\mathbf{U}(1:3,3)$ and $\mathbf{L}(4:5,3)$ are saved to $\mathbf{A}(1:5,3)$.

For column j of $\mathbf{A}$, we go four steps. First, we solve a lower triangular equation to obtain
$\mathbf{U}(1:j-1,j)$. Then calculate $\mathbf{A}(j:m,j) = \mathbf{A}(j:m,j) - \mathbf{L}(j:m,1:j-1)\mathbf{U}(1:j-1,j)$. Third, perform
a permutation so that $|A(j,j)| = \max(|A(j:m,j)|)$. At last $U_{jj} = A_{jj}$ and $\mathbf{L}(j+1:m,j) = \frac{1}{U_{jj}}\mathbf{A}(j+1:$
$m,j)$. Continue these steps to the last column of $\mathbf{A}$, then we obtain $\mathbf{PA} = \mathbf{LU}$, where $\mathbf{P} = \mathbf{P}_5 \cdots \mathbf{P}_1$ and
$\mathbf{L}$ is below the diagonal of $\mathbf{A}$ and $\mathbf{U}$ is on and above the diagonal of $\mathbf{A}$. In this algorithm, at the step j,
$\mathbf{A}(1:j,j)$ tends to $\mathbf{U}(1:j,j)$ and $\mathbf{A}(j+1:m,j)$ tends to $\mathbf{L}(j+1:m,j)$. All the columns $\mathbf{A}(:,j+1:n)$
do not change. This makes it necessary to apply the above steps to the remaining columns of $\mathbf{A}$ if the
algorithm stops prematurely ($k = last + 1 \cdots n$) or a rectangular matrix of $m < n$ ($k = m + 1 \cdots n$) in
order to keep the identity $\mathbf{PA} = \mathbf{LU}$.

The column pivoting cannot be efficiently applied, but the row pivoting is enough to make the process
stable. The following is the list of the MATLAB code LUbyCrout_.

Algorithm 2.3

P*A=L*U by Crout, P row permutations. L lower, U upper triangle.

```
%function [A,p] = LUbyCrout_(A,pivot,tol,f1st,last,p)
%p*A=L*U by Crout, p row permutations. L lower, U upper triangle.
%tol=tolerance to check 0. L,U overwrites A.
function [A,p] = LUbyCrout_(A,pivot,tol,f1st,last,p)

[m,n] = size(A);
if (~exist('pivot','var') || isempty(pivot)) pivot = 2; end
if (~exist('tol','var') || isempty(tol)) tol = sqrt(eps); end
if (~exist('f1st','var') || isempty(f1st)) f1st = 1; end
if (f1st < 1) f1st = 1; end
if (~exist('last','var') || isempty(last)) last = min(m,n); end
if (last > min(m,n)) last = min(m,n); end
if (~exist('p','var') || isempty(p)) p = 1:m; end
tol = tol*max(1.0, norm(diag(A))/min(m,n));

for j=f1st:last
    k = j;
    for i=f1st:j-1    %U(f1st:j-1,j)=inv(L(f1st:j-1,f1st:j-1))*A(f1st:j-1,j)
        for l=f1st:i-1 %forward substitution
            A(i,j) = A(i,j) - A(i,l)*A(l,j);
        end
    end
    %U(j:m,j)=A(j:m,j)-L(j:m,f1st:j-1)*U(f1st:j-1,j)
    A(j:m,j) = A(j:m,j) - A(j:m,f1st:j-1)*A(f1st:j-1,j);
    if (pivot == 0)            %no pivot
        if (abs(A(j,j))<tol && norm(A(j+1:m,j))>tol)
            error ('Zero pivot. Use 1<=pivot<=2.');
        end
    elseif (pivot == 1)       %minimal pivot
        while (abs(A(k,j))<tol && k<m)
            A(k,j) = 0; k = k + 1;      %next A(k,l)~=0 as pivot
        end
    else  %if (pivot==2)      %partial pivot (column pivot not efficient)
        k = argmax_(A(:,j),j);
    end
    if (j ~= k)    %switch A(j,:) and A(k,:)
        [A(j,:),A(k,:)] = swap_(A(j,:),A(k,:));
        [p(j),p(k)] = swap_(p(j),p(k));
    end
```

```
        if (abs(A(j,j)) < tol) A(j+1:m,j) = 0.0;              %skip the step
        else                    A(j+1:m,j) = A(j+1:m,j)/A(j,j); end  %U
end

if (last < n)
    for j=last+1:n
        for i=f1st:last    %U = inv(L)*A
            for k=f1st:i-1 %forward substitution
                A(i,j) = A(i,j) - A(i,k)*A(k,j);
            end
        end
    end
    %U = A(j:m,j)-L(j:m,1:j-1)*U
A(last+1:m,last+1:n) = A(last+1:m,last+1:n) -...
                       A(last+1:m,f1st:last)*A(f1st:last,last+1:n);
end
```

2.2.3 DRIVER OF LU DECOMPOSITION

Both LUbyGauss_ and LUbyCrout_ output **L** and **U** in a compact form – **L** below the diagonal of **A** and **U** on and above the diagonal of **A**. LU_ outputs **L** and **U** separately as matrices for better readability. Its other major functions are to dispatch the call to LUbyGauss_ or LUbyCrout_ according to algo and set the size of **L** and **U** correctly according to format.

Algorithm 2.4

P*A*Q'=L*U. L lower,U upper triangle, P row, P column permutation.

```
%function [L,U,p,q] = LU_(A,algo,pivot,tol,format,f1st,last,p,q)
%LU: P*A*Q'=L*U.L lower,U upper triangle, P row, Q column permutation.
%algo='Gauss' or 'Crout'
%pivot=0, no pivot; =1 min row pivot to allow LU to finish;
%       =2 row pivot |lij|<=1; pivot=3, =2+column pivot;
%       =4, complete pivoting
%tol=tolerance to check 0s.
%format='long':  L(m,m),U(m,n), P,Q permutation matrices.
%       ='short': rows of U w/ zeros are removed. p,q in vector form.
%f1st,last,p,q: restart parameters.
function [L,U,p,q] = LU_(A,algo,pivot,tol,format,f1st,last,p,q)

[m,n] = size(A);
if (~exist('algo','var') || isempty(algo)) algo = 'Gauss'; end
algo = upper(algo);
if (~exist('pivot','var') || isempty(pivot)) pivot = 2; end
if (~exist('tol','var') || isempty(tol)) tol = sqrt(eps); end
if (~exist('format','var') || isempty(format)) format = 'short';  end
if (~exist('f1st','var') || isempty(f1st)) f1st = 1;  end
if (f1st < 1) f1st = 1; end
if (~exist('last','var') || isempty(last)) last = min(m,n); end
if (last > min(m,n)) last = min(m,n); end
if (~exist('p','var') || isempty(p)) p = 1:m; end
if (~exist('q','var')  || isempty(q)) q = 1:n; end
tol = tol*max(1.0, norm(diag(A))/min(m,n));
```

```
if (strcmp(algo,'GAUSS'))
    [A,p,q] = LUbyGauss_(A,pivot,tol,f1st,last,p,q);
else
    [A,p] = LUbyCrout_(A,pivot,tol,f1st,last,p);
end

L = tril(A);   U = triu(A);
for j=1:last L(j,j) = 1; end
if (last < min(m,n))
    for j=last+1:min(m,n) L(j,j) = 1; L(j+1:m,j) = 0; end
    U(last+1:m,last+1:n) = A(last+1:m,last+1:n);
end

[k,l] = size(U);   kmax = 0;   lmax = 0;
if (strcmp(format,'long'))
    kmax = k; lmax = l;
    p = pv2pm_(p);   q = pv2pm_(q);
end
if (strcmp(format,'short'))
    for i=k:-1:1
        for j=l:-1:min(i,last+1)
            if (abs(U(i,j)) > tol)
                kmax = max(kmax,i);   lmax = max(lmax,j);   break;
            end
        end
        if (lmax == l) break; end
    end
    if (size(U,1) > kmax) U = U(1:kmax,:); end
end

l2 = size(L,2);
if (l2 > kmax) L = L(:,1:kmax); end
if (l2 < kmax) L = [L, [zeros(l2,kmax-l2);eye(kmax-l2)]]; end
```

The LU decomposition is demonstrated with a few examples. The return values of LUbyGauss_ and LUbyCrout_ are in compact form where **L** and **U** overwrite **A** as described above.

```
>> A=randn(4);
>> [LU,p]=LUbyGauss_(A,2,100*eps)        >> [LU,p]=LUbyCrout_(A,2,100*eps)
LU =                                     LU =
    1.5929   -0.6817   -0.4293   0.3710      1.5929   -0.6817   -0.4293   0.3710
   -0.9921   -1.9106   -0.7938   2.4802     -0.9921   -1.9106   -0.7938   2.4802
   -0.0494   -0.1335   -0.5922  -1.0078     -0.0494   -0.1335   -0.5922  -1.0078
    0.6393    0.3081   -0.9708  -1.2515      0.6393    0.3081   -0.9708  -1.2515
p =                                      p =
    1     3     4     2                       1     3     4     2
```

The following two examples demonstrate the LU decomposition of a rank-deficient matrix. LU_ output **L** and **U** in two separate full matrices. The output format can be controlled by the input argument format='long' and format='short'. Note that the last two rows of **U** are zeros and removed if format='short'. And accordingly the last two columns of **L** are also removed.

```
>> A(1:2,:)=randn(2)*A(3:4,:);
>> [L,U,P,Q]=LU_(A,'gauss',4,100*eps,'long')
L =
      1.0000            0            0            0
     -0.2474       1.0000            0            0
      0.3851       0.6113       1.0000            0
      0.2784      -0.0314            0       1.0000
U =
      5.4852      -2.8570      -2.6307      -0.1559
           0      -0.7856      -0.3621      -0.5036
           0            0            0      -0.0000
           0            0            0            0
P =
      0       1       0       0
      0       0       0       1
      0       0       1       0
      1       0       0       0
```

```
Q =
      0       0       0       1
      1       0       0       0
      0       1       0       0
      0       0       1       0

>> [L,U,P]=LU_(A,'crout',2,100*eps,
                              'short')
L =
      1.0000            0
      0.0275       1.0000
      0.5532       0.6113
      0.2697      -0.0314
U =
     -2.8570      -2.6307      -0.1559       5.4852
           0       0.3612      -0.4607      -1.5083
P =
      2       4       3       1
```

The following two examples demonstrate the LU decomposition of rectangular matrices.

```
>> A=randn(4,3);
>> [L,U,p,q]=LU_(A,'gauss',4,100*eps,
                              'short')
L =
      1.0000            0            0
     -0.7499       1.0000            0
     -0.1606       0.1314       1.0000
     -0.1166       0.2288       0.0012
U =
      1.8861      -1.7378      -0.5696
           0      -2.8511      -0.8173
           0            0      -0.8283
p =
      1       3       4       2
q =
      1       3       2
```

```
>> A=randn(3,4);
>> [L,U,p,q]=LU_(A,'gauss',4,100*eps,'short')
L =
      1.0000            0            0
      0.3831       1.0000            0
      0.2193       0.1255       1.0000
U =
      2.3696      -0.1861      -0.7593       1.0526
           0       1.3664      -0.3668       0.0073
           0            0      -0.3826       0.1970
p =
      2       1       3
q =
      1       3       4       2
```

LU decomposition can be restarted. The following example demonstrates the correct way to restart LUbyGauss_ and LU_. The only requirement is that the input argument f1st of the subsequent restart must be equal to the value of the input argument last of the previous call to LUbyGauss_ plus one. The same rule of restart applies to LUbyCrout_ and combined use of LUbyCrout_ and LU_. Because LUbyGauss_ and LUbyCrout_ are mathematically equivalent, their mixed use in the restart for the same matrix will still produce the correct results.

```
>> A=randn(5);
>> [B,p]=LUbyGauss_(A,2,100*eps,1,2)
B =
      0.7435      -1.7273       0.9900      -1.9037      -0.2199
     -0.7356      -1.4326       1.4443      -3.1821      -0.5539
      0.0340      -0.6421       0.7089      -1.0885       1.4093
      0.3517      -0.4688      -0.4859      -1.2782      -0.9015
     -0.8139       0.6771      -0.1356       0.5613      -0.9109
```

```
p =
      5     1     3     4     2
>> [B,p]=LUbyGauss_(B,2,100*eps,3,3,p);              %3=2+1: restart from step 2
>> [L,U,p]=LU_(B,'crout',2,100*eps,'short',4,5,p)    %4=3+1: restart from step 3
L =
      1.0000         0         0         0         0
     -0.7356    1.0000         0         0         0
      0.0340   -0.6421    1.0000         0         0
      0.3517   -0.4688   -0.6854    1.0000         0
      0.8139    0.6771   -0.1913   -0.1744    1.0000
U =
      0.7435   -1.7273    0.9900   -1.9037   -0.2199
           0   -1.4326    1.4443   -3.1821   -0.5539
           0         0    0.7089   -1.0885    1.4093
           0         0         0   -2.0243    0.0644
           0         0         0         0   -0.6301
p =
      5     1     3     4     2
```

From the following example, we can see the form of **L** and **U** in the intermediate steps of the LU decomposition. The relation **PAQ′** = **LU** is satisfied in any LU decomposition step.

```
>> A=randn(5);
>> [L,U,p]=LU_(A,'gauss',2,100*eps,'short',1,2)
L =
      1.0000         0         0         0         0
      0.9039    1.0000         0         0         0
     -0.0418    0.3002    1.0000         0         0
     -0.4321    0.0862         0    1.0000         0
     -0.9135    0.5422         0         0    1.0000
U =
     -0.8139    0.6771   -0.1913    0.3530   -0.6414
           0   -2.0447    1.6172   -3.5012    0.0258
           0         0    0.2154   -0.0226    1.3747
           0         0   -0.9074   -1.5701   -0.2150
           0         0   -0.0617    0.3173   -0.8198
p =
      5     2     3     4     1
>> [L,U,p]=LU_(A,'gauss',2,100*eps,'short',1,3)
L =
      1.0000         0         0         0         0
      0.9039    1.0000         0         0         0
     -0.4321    0.0862    1.0000         0         0
     -0.0418    0.3002   -0.2374    1.0000         0
     -0.9135    0.5422    0.0680         0    1.0000
U =
     -0.8139    0.6771   -0.1913    0.3530   -0.6414
           0   -2.0447    1.6172   -3.5012    0.0258
           0         0   -0.9074   -1.5701   -0.2150
           0         0         0   -0.3953    1.3237
           0         0         0    0.4241   -0.8052
p =
      5     2     4     3     1
```

The efficiency of LU_ is compared against MATLAB built-in lu. The elapsed time is obtained to perform a LU decomposition of a 1000 × 1000 full matrix on an INSPIRON 1545 laptop. Because the MATLAB built-in lu is built on the optimized machine code of LAPACK and BLAS, its higher efficiency is expected, while the purpose of LU_ is to present the LU algorithm in a concise manner. Other output of zeros verifies the correctness of LU decompositions of LU_ and lu.

```
>> A=randn(1000);
>> tic                                    >> tic
>> [L,U,P]=LU_(A,'gauss',2,100*eps,'short');  >> [L,U,P]=lu(A);
>> toc                                    >> toc
Elapsed time is 6.573176 seconds.        Elapsed time is 0.215799 seconds.
>> norm(diag(L)-ones(1000,1))            >> norm(diag(L)-ones(1000,1))
=    0                                    =    0
>> norm(triu(L,1))                        >> norm(triu(L,1))
=    0                                    =    0
>> norm(tril(U,-1))                       >> norm(tril(U,-1))
=    0                                    =    0
>> norm(L*U-P*A)                          >> norm(L*U-P*A)
= 5.3326e-013                             = 4.3258e-013
```

2.2.4 LU DECOMPOSITION OF AN UPPER HESSENBERG MATRIX

An upper Hessenberg has all zeros below the sub-diagonal. Thus, to transform it to an upper triangle, only $n - 1$ components on the sub-diagonal need to be zeroed. Because the length of the Gauss elimination vector for each column is only one, the elimination can also be more efficient. A slight modification of LUbyGauss_.m gives us the specialized LU decomposition of upper Hessenberg matrix, LUhessenberg_.m. The pivoting is removed from LUhessenberg_.m, because the permutations destroys the Hessenberg structure. In LUhessenberg_.m, a slight generalization of an upper Hessenberg matrix is made—the number of nonzero sub-diagonals can be more than one.

The elimination process clearly shows that the number of nonzero sub-diagonals in the L factor equals the number of nonzero sub-diagonals in the Hessenberg matrix. If the decomposed matrix is an ordinary Hessenberg, the L factor has only one nonzero sub-diagonal. The input argument format controls the output format. The output format is demonstrated with the examples below.

Algorithm 2.5

H=L*U. L lower triangle, U upper triangle.
```
function [L,U] = LUhessenberg_(H,lbw,tol,format,f1st,last)

[m,n] = size(H);
tol = tol*max(1.0,norm(diag(H),inf));

for i=f1st:last
    k = min(i+lbw,m);
    if (abs(H(i,i)) < tol)
        if (norm(H(i+1:k,i),inf) > tol)
            error('LUhessenberg_:␣zero␣pivot.␣Use␣LU_␣w/␣pivot>0');
        end
    else
        H(i+1:k,i) = H(i+1:k,i)/H(i,i);
        for j=i+1:n
            H(i+1:k,j) = H(i+1:k,j) - H(i,j)*H(i+1:k,i);
        end
    end
end
end
```

```
if (strcmp(format,'long'))
    L = tril(H);   U = triu(H);
    if (m < n) L = L(:,1:m); end
    if (m > n) U = U(1:n,:); end
    for j=1:last L(j,j) = 1; end
elseif (strcmp(format,'short'))
    L = full2band_(H,lbw,0);   U = triu(H);
    if (m > n) U = U(1:n,:); end
    L(1:min(m,n),lbw+1) = 1;
end
```

The following example demonstrates the basic use of LUhessenberg_.m. The default input argument settings make its use very simple. format='short' by default. When format='short', L is in the band format.

```
>> A=randn(5);
>> H=triu(A);   H = H + diag(diag(A,-1),-1);     %one way to create a Hessenberg
>> [L,U]=LUhessenberg_(H)
L =
         0     1.0000
   35.1519     1.0000
    0.0085     1.0000
   -0.1681     1.0000
   -2.9043     1.0000
U =
   -0.0147     0.4573    -0.6201    -0.9841    -1.1435
         0   -15.0079    19.8720    35.9571    42.2421
         0          0    -1.5944     0.5613    -0.3513
         0          0          0    -0.3346     0.6877
         0          0          0          0     2.5369
```

The input matrix to LUhessenberg_.m is not necessary square and can have more than one nonzero sub-diagonals. In the next example, the input matrix **H** has eight rows and five columns and has two nonzero sub-diagonals.

```
>> H=[11,12,13,14,15;
      21,22,23,24,25;
      31,32,3.3,3.4,3.5;
       0,42,43,44,45;
       0, 0,53,54,5.5;
       0, 0, 0,55,65;
       0, 0, 0, 0,75;
       0, 0, 0, 0, 0];

>> [L,U]=LUhessenberg_(H,2,[],'long')   %lbw=2 must be explicitly set.
L =
    1.0000          0          0          0          0
    1.9091     1.0000          0          0          0
    2.8182     2.0000     1.0000          0          0
         0   -46.2000     1.3805     1.0000          0
         0          0    -1.7845     0.0152     1.0000
         0          0          0    -1.3834     0.9091
         0          0          0          0    -1.5152
         0          0          0          0          0
U =
   11.0000    12.0000    13.0000    14.0000    15.0000
```

```
0    -0.9091    -1.8182    -2.7273    -3.6364
0          0   -29.7000   -30.6000   -31.5000
0          0          0   -39.7576   -79.5152
0          0          0          0   -49.5000
```

Because `LUhessenberg_.m` has no pivoting, it can fail for rank-deficient input matrix. Should we change the Hessenberg matrix in the above example as follows, `LUhessenberg_.m` fails. However, the potential to fail is usually of no concern, because Hessenberg matrices arising in real applications are usually non-singular.

```
>> H(3,:)=[31,32,33,34,35];   %H(1:3,:) linearly dependent!

>> [L,U]=LUhessenberg_(H,2,[],'long')
??? Error using ==> LUhessenberg_ at 22
LUhessenberg_: zero pivot. Use LU_ w/ pivot>0
```

2.2.5 LU DECOMPOSITION OF A BAND MATRIX

A band matrix $\mathbf{B} \in \mathbb{R}^{m \times n}$ has b_l nonzero sub-diagonals and b_u nonzero sup-diagonals. For a band matrix, the efficiency of LU decomposition can be improved if taking the band structure into account. First, only $n \times b_l$ nonzeros below the diagonal need to be zeroed. Second, when applying one Gauss elimination, only $b_l \times b_u$ components need to be calculated. The elimination process clearly shows that the number of nonzero sub-diagonals in the L factor equals the number of nonzero sub-diagonals in $\mathbf{B}$, and the number of nonzero sup-diagonals in the U factor equals the number of nonzero sup-diagonals in $\mathbf{B}$.

A slight modification of `LUbyGauss_.m` gives us the specialized LU decomposition of a band matrix, `LUband_.m`. The pivoting is removed from `LUband_.m`, because the permutations destroys the band structure. The input matrix to `LUband_.m` must be in the band format. The format of the output matrices **L** and **U** is controlled by the input argument `format`. When `format='long'`, both **L** and **U** are in full matrix format. When `format='short'`, both **L** and **U** are in band matrix format.

Algorithm 2.6

B=L*U. L lower triangle, U upper triangle.

```
function [L,U] = LUband_(B,lbw,ubw,m,n,tol,format,f1st,last)
tol = tol*max(1.0,norm(B(:,lbw+1),inf));

for j=f1st:last
    if (abs(B(j,lbw+1)) < tol)
        bnorm = 0;
        for k=j+1:min(j+lbw,m) bnorm = max(bnorm,abs(B(k,j-k+lbw+1))); end
        if (bnorm > tol) error('LUband_:zero pivot.Use LU_ w/ pivot>0'); end
    else
        for i=j+1:min(j+lbw,m)
            B(i,j-i+lbw+1) = B(i,j-i+lbw+1)/B(j,lbw+1);
        end
        for k=j+1:min(j+lbw,m)
            for l=j+1:min(j+ubw,n)
                B(k,l-k+lbw+1) = B(k,l-k+lbw+1) - B(j,l-j+lbw+1)*B(k,j-k+lbw+1);
            end
        end
    end
end
end
```

```
if (strcmp(format,'long') || last<min(m,n))
    L = band2full_(B,lbw,0,m,n);
    if (m < n) L = L(:,1:m); end
    for j=1:last L(j,j) = 1; end
    U = band2full_(B(:,lbw+1:lbw+1+ubw),0,ubw,m,n);
    if (m > n) U = U(1:n,:); end
elseif (strcmp(format,'short'))
    L = B(:,1:lbw+1);   L(:,lbw+1) = 1;    U = B(:,lbw+1:lbw+1+ubw);
    for j=m:-1:1
        if (norm(U(j,:),inf) > tol) break; end
    end
    if (j < n)
        L(j+1:m,lbw+1) = 0;    U = U(1:j,:);
    end
end
```

One simple example demonstrates the basic use of LUband_.m. Note the zero patterns of **L** and **U** in the output.

```
>> A=randn(6);
>> B=diag(diag(A)); B=B+diag(diag(A,1),1);
>> B=B+diag(diag(A,-1),-1); B=B+diag(diag(A,-2),-2);   %one way to create a band matrix
>> B=full2band_(B,2,1);                                 %convert to band format!

>> [L,U]=LUband_(B,2,1,6,6,[],'long')      %Specify the layout of B correctly!
L =
    1.0000         0         0         0         0         0
    0.1245    1.0000         0         0         0         0
    1.3484   -2.8405    1.0000         0         0         0
         0   -4.0828    1.6760    1.0000         0         0
         0         0   -0.9234   -2.5577    1.0000         0
         0         0         0    0.9622   -0.2716    1.0000
U =
   -1.0036   -0.1269         0         0         0         0
         0    0.3196   -0.3186         0         0         0
         0         0   -1.4087    1.2967         0         0
         0         0         0   -1.0397    1.0934         0
         0         0         0         0    2.9322    0.2435
         0         0         0         0         0    0.4732
```

2.3 LDU DECOMPOSITION

Given a matrix, $\mathbf{A} \in \mathbb{R}^{m \times n}$, we want to find a lower triangular matrix $\mathbf{L}$ with 1s on the diagonal, a diagonal matrix $\mathbf{D}$, an upper triangular matrix $\mathbf{U}$ with 1s on the diagonal, and permutation matrices $\mathbf{P}$ and $\mathbf{Q}$ so that $\mathbf{PAQ}' = \mathbf{LDU}$. Depending on the chosen pivoting, either $\mathbf{P}$, or $\mathbf{Q}$ or both can be the identity matrix. $\mathbf{PAQ}' = \mathbf{LDU}$ is called a LDU decomposition. The LDU decomposition can be easily obtained from the LU decomposition by applying a simple transformation. Assuming $\mathbf{PAQ}' = \mathbf{LU}_1$ and $\mathbf{PAQ}' = \mathbf{LD}_2\mathbf{U}_2$, where $\mathbf{D}_2, \mathbf{U}_2$ can be obtained from $\mathbf{U}_1$ as follows:

$$D_2(j,j) = U_1(j,j), U_2(j,j) = 1; \quad U_2(j,j+1:n) = \frac{1}{D_2(j,j)}U_1(j,j+1:n). \tag{2.16}$$

Eq. (2.16) fails when $U_1(j, j) = 0$. This can happen in the following two cases:

1. $\mathbf{U}_1(j, j + 1 : n) = 0$. We can set $D_2(j, j) = 0$ and $U_2(j, j) = 1$.
2. $\mathbf{U}_1(j, j + 1 : n) \neq \mathbf{0}$. This case can be avoided with a column pivoting.

The LDU decomposition as presented in Eq. (2.16) is not very useful in practice nor very interesting as an algorithm. However, a LDU algorithm to calculate $\mathbf{L}, \mathbf{D}, \mathbf{U}$ directly will lead us to some new insights into the matrix decomposition algorithms. More importantly, it will build the stage for LDLt decomposition and other decomposition algorithms for symmetric matrices. In this section, we will extend the presentation of LU decomposition of the last section to LDU decomposition.

2.3.1 LDU DECOMPOSITION BY GAUSS ELIMINATION

We will use the same 5×5 matrix of Eq. (2.11) to illustrate the LDU decomposition.

The first step and second step are same as in LU. At the end of the second step, the transformed $\mathbf{A}$ of LU is of the form as shown in Eq. (2.12), which is reproduced below,

$$\mathbf{G}_1\mathbf{P}_1\mathbf{AQ}_1' = \begin{bmatrix} A_{11} & A_{12} & A_{13} & A_{14} & A_{15} \\ 0 & A_{22} & A_{23} & A_{24} & A_{25} \\ 0 & A_{32} & A_{33} & A_{34} & A_{35} \\ 0 & A_{42} & A_{43} & A_{44} & A_{45} \\ 0 & A_{52} & A_{53} & A_{54} & A_{55} \end{bmatrix}.$$

Differently from LU decomposition, we have a third step here. In this step, we choose another Gauss transformation $\mathbf{S}_1 = \mathbf{I} - [0; \mathbf{s}]\mathbf{I}(1, :)$ to eliminate $\mathbf{A}(1, 2 : 5)$,

$$\mathbf{s} = \frac{1}{A_{11}}\mathbf{A}(1, 2 : 5), \tag{2.17a}$$

$$\mathbf{G}_1\mathbf{P}_1\mathbf{AQ}_1'\mathbf{S}_1' = \begin{bmatrix} A_{11} & 0 & 0 & 0 & 0 \\ \mathbf{0} & \mathbf{A}(2:5,2) & \mathbf{A}(2:5,3) & \mathbf{A}(2:5,4) & \mathbf{A}(2:5,5) \end{bmatrix}. \tag{2.17b}$$

Because $\mathbf{A}(2 : 5, 1) = \mathbf{0}$, when $\mathbf{S}_1'$ is applied to $\mathbf{G}_1\mathbf{P}_1\mathbf{AQ}_1'$, it does not change $\mathbf{A}(2 : 5, 2 : 5)$. Again the Gauss vector $\mathbf{s}$ can overwrite the zeroed $\mathbf{A}(1, 2 : 5)$. Therefore, the third step amounts merely the overwriting of $\mathbf{A}(1, 2 : 5)$ by $\frac{1}{A_{11}}\mathbf{A}(1, 2 : 5)$.

If the complete pivoting was used in the first step and A_{11} is not zero, then absolute values of the components of $\mathbf{s}$ are less than 1. If the complete pivoting was used in the first step and A_{11} is zero, $\mathbf{A}$ is a zero matrix, we can set $\mathbf{L} = \mathbf{I}$, $\mathbf{D} = \mathbf{0}$, and $\mathbf{U} - \mathbf{I}$. This is the failure case 1 of Eq. (2.16). If the partial pivoting was used in the first step and A_{11} is zero, the second step of the usual LU decomposition can be skipped. But in case $\mathbf{A}(1, 2 : 5) \neq \mathbf{0}$, the LDU decomposition fails. This is the failure case 2 of Eq. (2.16). The remedy is to use the complete pivoting in the first step and return to the failure case 1.

The same three steps are repeated to $\mathbf{A}(2 : 5, 2 : 5)$, $\mathbf{A}(3 : 5, 3 : 5)$, $\mathbf{A}(4 : 5, 4 : 5)$, and $\mathbf{A}(5 : 5, 5 : 5)$. After $\mathbf{A}(5 : 5, 5 : 5)$ is finished, $\mathbf{L}$ is a lower triangular with 1s on the diagonal, $\mathbf{U}$ is an upper triangular with 1s on the diagonal, $\mathbf{D}$ is a diagonal with possibly some 0s on the diagonal. If the LDU decomposition stops prematurely after the second column and row are eliminated, $\mathbf{L}$, $\mathbf{D}$, and $\mathbf{U}$ are read from $\mathbf{A}$ as illustrated below. Remember the overwriting operation; A_{ij} shown below are not the original components of **A**,

$$L = \begin{bmatrix} 1 & 0 & 0 & 0 & 0 \\ A_{21} & 1 & 0 & 0 & 0 \\ A_{31} & A_{32} & 1 & 0 & 0 \\ A_{41} & A_{42} & 0 & 1 & 0 \\ A_{51} & A_{52} & 0 & 0 & 1 \end{bmatrix}, \quad D = \begin{bmatrix} A_{11} & 0 & 0 & 0 & 0 \\ 0 & A_{22} & 0 & 0 & 0 \\ 0 & 0 & A_{33} & A_{34} & A_{35} \\ 0 & 0 & A_{43} & A_{44} & A_{45} \\ 0 & 0 & A_{53} & A_{54} & A_{55} \end{bmatrix}, \quad U = \begin{bmatrix} A_{11} & A_{12} & A_{13} & A_{14} & A_{15} \\ 0 & A_{22} & A_{23} & A_{24} & A_{25} \\ 0 & 0 & 1 & 0 & 0 \\ 0 & 0 & 0 & 1 & 0 \\ 0 & 0 & 0 & 0 & 1 \end{bmatrix}.$$

The implementation of the LDU decomposition by Gauss elimination is very similar to that of LU decomposition by Gauss elimination. The only difference is to obtain **U** by Eq. (2.17a). The important point is that it must be done after the application of the column elimination by G_i to $A(i+1 : m, i+1 : n)$ not before it. In other words, step 3 must follow step 2.[1]

Algorithm 2.7

P*A*Q'=L*D*U by Gauss, P,Q permutations, L lower, U upper triangle, D diagonal.

```
function [A,p,q] = LDUbyGauss_(A,pivot,tol,f1st,last,p,q)

[m,n] = size(A);
tol = tol*max(1.0,norm(diag(A))/min(m,n));

for i=f1st:last
    k = i;   l = i;
    if (pivot == 0)            %no pivot
        if (abs(A(k,l))<tol && (norm(A(k+1:m,l))>tol || norm(A(k,l+1:n))>tol))
            error ('LDUbyGauss_:_Zero_pivot._Use_0<pivot<4.');
        end
    elseif (pivot == 1)        %minimal pivot
        while (abs(A(k,l))<tol && k<m)
            A(k,l) = 0;   k = k + 1;    %next A(k,l)~=0 as pivot
        end
    elseif (pivot == 2)        %partial pivot
        k = argmax_(A(:,l),i);
    elseif (pivot == 3)        %partial pivot+
        k = argmax_(A(:,l),i);
        while (abs(A(k,l))<tol && l<n)
            l = l + 1;   k = argmax_(A(:,l),i);
        end
    else %if(pivot==4)         %complete pivot
        [k,l] = argsmax_(A,i,i);
    end
    if (i ~= k)
        [A(i,:), A(k,:)] = swap_(A(i,:), A(k,:));
        [p(i),p(k)] = swap_(p(i),p(k));
    end
    if (i ~= l)
        [A(:,i), A(:,l)] = swap_(A(:,i), A(:,l));
        [q(i),q(l)] = swap_(q(i),q(l));
    end

    if (abs(A(i,i)) < tol)
        if (norm(A(i,i+1:n)) > tol)
```

```
            error ('LDUbyGauss_:_Zero_pivot._Increase_pivot.');
        end
        A(i:m,i) = 0.0;              %skip the step
    else
        g = A(i+1:m,i)/A(i,i);   A(i+1:m,i) = g;   %L: Gauss vector in zeroed A
        for j=i+1:n                  %apply Gauss elimination to A(i+1:m,i+1:n)
            A(i+1:m,j) = A(i+1:m,j) - A(i,j)*g;
        end
        A(i,i+1:n) = A(i,i+1:n)/A(i,i);              %U: overwrite A
    end
end
```

2.3.2 LDU DECOMPOSITION BY CROUT PROCEDURE

Similarly to the LU decomposition shown in Eq. (2.15), LDU decomposition can be written as follows:

$$
\begin{bmatrix} A_{11} & A_{12} & A_{13} & A_{14} & A_{15} \\ A_{21} & A_{22} & A_{23} & A_{24} & A_{25} \\ A_{31} & A_{32} & A_{33} & A_{34} & A_{35} \\ A_{41} & A_{42} & A_{43} & A_{44} & A_{45} \\ A_{51} & A_{52} & A_{53} & A_{54} & A_{55} \end{bmatrix} = \begin{bmatrix} 1 & & & & \\ L_{21} & 1 & & & \\ L_{31} & L_{32} & 1 & & \\ L_{41} & L_{42} & L_{43} & 1 & \\ L_{51} & L_{52} & L_{53} & L_{54} & 1 \end{bmatrix} \begin{bmatrix} D_1 & & \\ & \ddots & \\ & & D_5 \end{bmatrix} \begin{bmatrix} 1 & U_{12} & U_{13} & U_{14} & U_{15} \\ & 1 & U_{23} & U_{24} & U_{25} \\ & & 1 & U_{34} & U_{35} \\ & & & 1 & U_{45} \\ & & & & 1 \end{bmatrix}.
$$

Equating the first column,

$$
\begin{bmatrix} A_{11} \\ A_{21} \\ A_{31} \\ A_{41} \\ A_{51} \end{bmatrix} = \begin{bmatrix} D_1 \\ D_1 L_{21} \\ D_1 L_{31} \\ D_1 L_{41} \\ D_1 L_{51} \end{bmatrix},
$$

we apply a row permutation $\mathbf{P}_1$ to $\mathbf{A}$ so that $|A_{11}| = \max(|A_{11}|, |A_{21}|, |A_{31}|, |A_{41}|, |A_{51}|)$. Then, we have

$$
D_1 = A_{11},
$$

$$
\begin{bmatrix} L_{21} \\ L_{31} \\ L_{41} \\ L_{51} \end{bmatrix} = \frac{1}{D_1} \begin{bmatrix} A_{21} \\ A_{31} \\ A_{41} \\ A_{51} \end{bmatrix} = \frac{1}{A_{11}} \begin{bmatrix} A_{21} \\ A_{31} \\ A_{41} \\ A_{51} \end{bmatrix}.
$$

Similarly by equating the second column, we obtain $(D_1 U_{12})$, D_2, $\mathbf{L}(3:5,2)$, and U_{12}. At the end of the second step, $\mathbf{A}$ will look like the following:

$$
\begin{bmatrix} D_1 & U_{12} & A_{13} & A_{14} & A_{15} \\ L_{21} & D_2 & A_{23} & A_{24} & A_{25} \\ L_{31} & L_{32} & A_{33} & A_{34} & A_{35} \\ L_{41} & L_{42} & A_{43} & A_{44} & A_{45} \\ L_{51} & L_{52} & A_{53} & A_{54} & A_{55} \end{bmatrix}.
$$

The first two columns of $\mathbf{A}$ are overwritten by components of $\mathbf{L}$, $\mathbf{D}$, and $\mathbf{U}$. The last three columns of $\mathbf{A}$ are still those of the original $\mathbf{A}$.

Equating the third column,

$$\begin{bmatrix} 1 & 0 \\ L_{21} & 1 \end{bmatrix} \begin{bmatrix} (D_1 U_{13}) \\ (D_2 U_{23}) \end{bmatrix} = \begin{bmatrix} A_{13} \\ A_{23} \end{bmatrix},$$

$$D_3 \begin{bmatrix} 1 \\ L_{43} \\ L_{53} \end{bmatrix} = \begin{bmatrix} A_{33} \\ A_{43} \\ A_{53} \end{bmatrix} - (D_1 U_{13}) \begin{bmatrix} L_{31} \\ L_{41} \\ L_{51} \end{bmatrix} - (D_2 U_{23}) \begin{bmatrix} L_{32} \\ L_{42} \\ L_{52} \end{bmatrix}.$$

The first equation is a lower triangular matrix, which can be easily solved by a forward substitution to obtain $(D_1 U_{13})$ and $(D_2 U_{23})$. At this moment, we just write the product $(D_1 U_{13})$ to A_{13} and $(D_2 U_{23})$ to A_{23} and do not want to calculate U_{13} and U_{23}. Then we calculate the right hand side of the second equation and save the result back to $\mathbf{A}(3:5,3)$. Now we apply another row permutation $\mathbf{P}_3$ to $\mathbf{A}(3:5,3)$ so that $|A(3,3)|$ is the maximum. Remember to apply $\mathbf{P}_3$ to $\mathbf{L}(3:5,1:2)$ and $\mathbf{A}(3:5,4:5)$ as well. Because $\mathbf{L}(3:5,1:2)$ occupies $\mathbf{A}(3:5,1:2)$, $\mathbf{P}_3$ applies to the entire $\mathbf{A}(3:5,:)$. Then $D_3 = A_{33}$ and $\mathbf{L}(4:5,3) = \frac{1}{D_3}\mathbf{A}(4:5,3)$. Finally, we calculate $U_{13} = \frac{A_{13}}{D_1}$ and $U_{23} = \frac{A_{23}}{D_2}$. Remember that A_{13} is $(D_1 U_{13})$ and A_{23} is $(D_2 U_{23})$ calculated in the first step.

For column j of $\mathbf{A}$, we go five steps. At first we solve a lower triangular equation to obtain $\mathbf{D}(1:j-1,1:j-1)\mathbf{U}(1:j-1,j)$ and write the results back to $\mathbf{A}(1:j-1,j)$. Then calculate $\mathbf{A}(j:m,j) = \mathbf{A}(j:m,j) - \mathbf{L}(j:m,1:j-1)\mathbf{A}(1:j-1,j)$. Third perform a permutation so that $|A(j,j)| = \max(|A(j:m,j)|)$. In step 4, $D_j = A_{jj}$ and $\mathbf{L}(j+1:m,j) = \frac{1}{D_j}\mathbf{A}(j+1:m,j)$. Finally, $U_{1j} = \frac{A_{1j}}{D_1}, \ldots, U_{j-1,j} = \frac{A_{j-1,j}}{D_{j-1}}$. Continue these steps to the last column of $\mathbf{A}$, then we obtain $\mathbf{PA} = \mathbf{LDU}$, where $\mathbf{P} = \mathbf{P}_5 \cdots \mathbf{P}_1$ and $\mathbf{L}$ is below the diagonal of $\mathbf{A}$, $\mathbf{D}$ is on the diagonal of $\mathbf{A}$, and $\mathbf{U}$ is above the diagonal of $\mathbf{A}$. In the fourth step, if $D_j = 0$, in LU decomposition, this step can be skipped. But D_j is used to calculate in $U_{j,j+1} = \frac{A_{j,j+1}}{D_j}$ of column $j+1$ of $\mathbf{A}$, if $A_{j,j+1} \neq 0$, LDU decomposition fails. This is the failure case 2 for Eq. (2.16). Because the column pivoting cannot be implemented efficiently in the Crout algorithm, the failure poses a limitation of the LDU decomposition by Crout algorithm.

In this algorithm, at the step j, $\mathbf{A}(1:j-1,j)$ tends to $\mathbf{U}(1:j-1,j)$, A_{jj} becomes D_j, and $\mathbf{A}(j+1:m,j)$ tends to $\mathbf{L}(j+1:m,j)$. All the columns $\mathbf{A}(:,j+1:n)$ do not change. This makes it necessary to apply the above steps to the remaining columns of $\mathbf{A}$ if the algorithm stops prematurely $(k = last+1 \cdots n)$ or a rectangular matrix of $m < n$ $(k = m+1 \cdots n)$ in order to keep the identity $\mathbf{PA} = \mathbf{LDU}$.

The algorithm of LDU decomposition by Crout is very similar to the algorithm of LU decomposition by Crout. The MATLAB function LDUbyCrout_.m is listed below.

Algorithm 2.8

P*A=L*D*U by Crout, P permutations, L lower, U upper triangle, D diagonal.

```
function [A,p] = LDUbyCrout_(A,pivot,tol,f1st,last,p)

[m,n] = size(A);
tol = tol*max(1.0, norm(diag(A))/min(m,n));

for j=f1st:last
    k = j;
    for i=f1st:j-1        %1st:  D*U
        for l=f1st:i-1 A(i,j) = A(i,j) - A(i,l)*A(l,j); end
    end
    A(j:m,j) = A(j:m,j) - A(j:m,f1st:j-1)*A(f1st:j-1,j);    %2nd:  D*L
```

```
        for i=f1st:j-1      %3rd: U
            if (abs(A(i,i)) < tol)
                if (abs(A(i,j)) > tol) error('LDUbCrout__fails._Use_LDUbyGauss_.'); end
            else
                A(i,j) = A(i,j)/A(i,i);
            end
        end
        if (pivot == 0)
            if (abs(A(j,j))<tol && norm(A(j+1:m,j))>tol)
                error('LDUbyCrout_:_Zero_pivot._Use_1<=pivot<=2.');
            end
        elseif (pivot == 1)      %minimal pivot
            while (abs(A(k,j))<tol && k<m)
                A(k,j) = 0;   k = k + 1;      %next A(k,1)~=0 as pivot
            end
        else  %if (pivot==2)      %partial pivot (column pivot not efficient)
            k = argmax_(A(:,j),j);
        end
        if (j ~= k)    %switch A(j,:) and A(k,:)
            [A(j,:),A(k,:)] = swap_(A(j,:),A(k,:));
            [p(j),p(k)] = swap_(p(j),p(k));
        end

        if (abs(A(j,j)) < tol) A(j:m,j) = 0.0;                      %skip step
        else                   A(j+1:m,j) = A(j+1:m,j)/A(j,j); end %L: overwrite A
end

if (last < n)
    for i=f1st:last       %1st: L
        for j=last+1:n
            for k=f1st:i-1 A(i,j) = A(i,j) - A(i,k)*A(k,j); end
        end
    end
    A(last+1:m,last+1:n)=A(last+1:m,last+1:n)-...
                         A(last+1:m,f1st:last)*A(f1st:last,last+1:n);
    for i=f1st:last       %3rd: U
        if (abs(A(i,i)) > tol) A(i,last+1:n) = A(i,last+1:n)/A(i,i); end
    end
end
```

2.3.3 DRIVER OF LDU DECOMPOSITION

Both LDUbyGauss_ and LDUbyCrout_ output **L**, **D**, and **U** in a compact form – **L** below the diagonal of **A**, **D** on the diagonal, and **U** above the diagonal of **A**. LDU_ outputs **L**, **D**, and **U** separately as matrices for better readability. Its other major functions are to dispatch the call according to algo and to set the size of output arguments correctly according to format.

Algorithm 2.9

P*A*Q'=L*D*U. P,Q permutations, L lower, U upper triangle, D diagonal.

```
function [L,D,U,p,q] = LDU_(A,algo,pivot,tol,format,f1st,last,p,q)

[m,n] = size(A);
algo = upper(algo);   tol = tol*max(1.0, norm(diag(A))/min(m,n));

if (strcmp(algo,'GAUSS'))
```

```
    [A,p,q] = LDUbyGauss_(A,pivot,tol,f1st,last,p,q);
else
    [A,p] = LDUbyCrout_(A,pivot,tol,f1st,last,p);
end

L = tril(A);   D = diag(A);   U = triu(A);
for j=1:min(m,n) L(j,j) = 1.0;   U(j,j) = 1.0; end
if (last < min(m,n))
    for j=last+1:min(m,n) L(j+1:m,j) = 0.0;   U(j,j+1:n) = 0.0; end
    D = diag(D);   D(last+1:m,last+1:n) = A(last+1:m,last+1:n);
end

[k,l] = size(D);   kmax = 0;   lmax = 0;
if (strcmp(format,'long'))
    kmax = k;   lmax = l;
    if (k==1 || l==1) D = diag(D); end
    p = pv2pm_(p);   q = pv2pm_(q);
end
if (strcmp(format,'short'))
    for i=k:-1:1
        for j=l:-1:1
            if (abs(D(i,j)) > tol)
                kmax = max(kmax,i);   lmax = max(lmax,j);   break;
            end
        end
        if (lmax == l) break; end
    end
    if (kmax<k || lmax<l) D = D(1:kmax,1:lmax); end
    if (k>1 && l>1 && (kmax<=last || lmax<=last)) D = diag(D); end
end
if (k==1 || l==1) kmax = max(kmax,lmax);   lmax = kmax; end

l2 = size(L,2);   u1 = size(U,1);
if (l2 > kmax) L = L(:,1:kmax); end
if (l2 < kmax) L = [L, [zeros(l2,kmax-l2);eye(kmax-l2)]]; end
if (u1 > lmax) U = U(1:lmax,:); end
if (u1 < lmax) U = [U; [zeros(lmax-u1,u1),eye(lmax-u1)]]; end
```

The use of LDUbyGauss_, LDUbyCrout_, and LDU_ is similar to their LU counterpart. We show only two examples to demonstrate the importance of pivoting to the LDU decomposition.

In the following example, the U factor has large components if no column pivoting is used. The large components in the U factor are avoided if column pivoting is used.

```
>> A=randn(4,3);   A(:,3)=100*A(:,3);              0    1.0000 -371.4309
>> [L,d,U,p,q]=LDU_(A,'gauss',2,100*eps)           0         0    1.0000
L =
    1.0000         0         0            p =
   -0.5062    1.0000         0               3    2    4    1
   -0.4587    0.7997    1.0000            q =
    0.3062    0.0420   -0.3751               1    2    3
d =
   -2.6228
   -0.7058                                >> [L,d,U,p,q]=LDU_(A,'gauss',4,100*eps)
 -146.9218                                L =
U =                                            1.0000         0         0
    1.0000   -0.2032  -64.7004                 0.9627    1.0000         0
                                              -0.0857   -0.3376    1.0000
```

```
     0.6699     0.4339    -0.3751                        0     1.0000    -0.3774
d =                                                      0          0     1.0000
  176.2637                                  p =
   -3.9009                                      2     3     4     1
   -0.3956                                  q =
U =                                             3     1     2
    1.0000     0.0075    -0.0055
```

In the following example, column 2 of A is linearly dependent to column 1. LDU decomposition fails if no column pivoting is used. It is successful if column pivoting is used.

```
>> A(:,2)=rand*A(:,1);
>> [L,d,U,p,q]=LDU_(A,'gauss',2,100*eps)
??? Error using ==> LDUbyGauss_ at 49
LDUbyGauss_: Zero pivot. Increase pivot.

Error in ==> LDU_ at 27
    [A,p,q] = LDUbyGauss_(A,pivot,tol,f1st,last,p,q);

>> [L,d,U,p,q]=LDU_(A,'gauss',4,100*eps)
L =
    1.0000          0
    0.9627     1.0000
    0.6699     0.4339
   -0.0857    -0.3376
d =
  176.2637
   -3.9009
U =
    1.0000     0.0075     0.0040
         0     1.0000     0.5285
p =
    2     3     1     4
q =
    3     1     2
```

2.4 CONGRUENT DECOMPOSITION ALGORITHMS FOR SYMMETRIC MATRICES

In the last section, it is shown that $\mathbf{PAQ'} = \mathbf{LDU}$ exists and is stable if the complete pivoting is used. However, if the partial pivoting is used, the LDU decomposition has the potential to fail and the components in the $\mathbf{U}$ factor have the potential to grow without bounds. In this section, we will apply the LDU decomposition to symmetric matrices. The above conclusions are still valid to the LDU decomposition of symmetric matrices. Further the application of LDU decomposition to a symmetric matrix $\mathbf{A}$ raises two more issues.

1. To keep the symmetry, it is necessary to use only the congruent transformations. If the LDU decomposition exists and is stable, it must be of the form $\mathbf{PAP'} = \mathbf{LDL'}$. The decomposition of a symmetric matrix in this form is called LDLt decomposition.
2. For the symmetric matrices that LDLt decomposition does not exist or is not stable, lower the expectation of $\mathbf{LDL'}$ to the next closest simple forms. For example, $\mathbf{LTL'}$ or $\mathbf{LBL'}$, a symmetric

tri-diagonal **T** or a block diagonal **B** of 1×1 and symmetric 2×2 blocks is a good substitute for a diagonal **D**. We call **PAP′** = **LTL′** a LTLt decomposition and **PAP′** = **LBL′** a LBLt decomposition.

These two issues are addressed in this section. For LDLt and LTLt, we will present two mathematically equivalent algorithms. One is based on the Gauss or Parlett (transforming). The other is based on Crout or Aasen (decomposing). Two more special algorithms are presented to obtain $\mathbf{A} = \mathbf{LDL'} = \mathbf{L}\sqrt{\mathbf{D}}\left(\mathbf{L}\sqrt{\mathbf{D}}\right)' = \mathbf{LL'}$, if $\mathbf{D} \geq \mathbf{0}$ and $\mathbf{A} + \mathbf{E} = \mathbf{LDL'} = \mathbf{L}\sqrt{\mathbf{D}}\left(\mathbf{L}\sqrt{\mathbf{D}}\right)' = \mathbf{LL'}$, choosing a minimal diagonal $\mathbf{E} \geq \mathbf{0}$ so that $\mathbf{D} \geq \mathbf{0}$. We will call the later two decompositions LLt (commonly known as Cholesky decomposition) and xLLt (commonly known as modified Cholesky decomposition), respectively.

2.4.1 REDUCTION OF SYMMETRIC MATRIX TO DIAGONAL (LDLt)

For two classes of symmetric matrices, a diagonal dominant matrix where $|A_{ii}| \geq \sum_{j=1, j \neq i}^{n} |A_{ij}|$ and a positive definite matrix where $\mathbf{x'Ax} > 0, \forall \mathbf{x} \in \mathbb{R}^n \neq \mathbf{0}$, $\mathbf{A} = \mathbf{LDL'}$ exists and is stable. For a positive semi-definite matrix where $\mathbf{x'Ax} \geq 0, \forall \mathbf{x} \in \mathbb{R}^n \neq \mathbf{0}$, $\mathbf{PAP'} = \mathbf{LDL'}$ exists and is stable, see [29]. The above condition for the existence of LDLt decomposition is sufficient but not necessary. For a particular matrix **A**, **PAP′** = **LDL′** may or may not exist. At the step j eliminating $\mathbf{A}(j+1:n, j)$ and $\mathbf{A}(j, j+1:n)$, if $A_{jj} = 0$ but $\mathbf{A}(j+1:n, j) = \mathbf{A}(j, j+1:n)' \neq \mathbf{0}$, the LDLt decomposition does not exist. Note that A_{jj} and $\mathbf{A}(j+1:n, j) = \mathbf{A}(j, j+1:n)'$ are **A**'s components after applying $j-1$ steps of Gauss eliminations. The existence condition for the LDLt decomposition is difficult to state in terms of the original components of **A**. For a particular matrix **A**, even if **PAP′** = **LDL′**, there is no guarantee that $L_{ij} \leq 1$.

The algorithms for the LDLt decomposition presented in this subsection are specializations of LDUbyGauss_ and LDUbyCrout_ of the last subsection. If a zero pivot is found in the LDLt calculation, the algorithms stop with an error. If the algorithms are applied to a diagonal dominant matrix or a positive definite matrix, no permutations are performed.

Gauss Algorithm LDLtByGauss_ has three differences to LDUbyGauss_. (a) Only symmetric pivoting is performed. Pivot is found from the diagonal of **A**. (b) **U** = **L′**. The calculation of **U** is omitted by considering symmetry. (c) **D** is on the diagonal of **A**. **L** is below the diagonal of **A**. No change is made above the diagonal of **A**.[2]

Algorithm 2.10

```
P*A*P'=L*D*L' by Gauss, P, permutations, L lower triangle, D diagonal.
function [A,p] = LDLtByGauss_(A,pivot,tol,f1st,last,p)

[m,n] = size(A);
tol = tol*max(1.0,norm(diag(A))/m);

for i=f1st:last
    k = i;
    if (pivot > 0) k = argmax_(diag(A),i); end
    if (i ~= k)    %swap row (i,k) and column (i,k)
        [A(i,1:i-1),A(k,1:i-1)] = swap_(A(i,1:i-1),A(k,1:i-1));
        [A(k+1:n,i),A(k+1:n,k)] = swap_(A(k+1:n,i),A(k+1:n,k));
```

[2]For brevity, the heading code comments and input argument checks are not shown in the code presentation.

```
        [A(i+1:k-1,i),A(k,i+1:k-1)] = swap_(A(i+1:k-1,i),A(k,i+1:k-1));
        [A(i,i),A(k,k)] = swap_(A(i,i),A(k,k));
        [p(i),p(k)] = swap_(p(i),p(k));
    end
    if (abs(A(i,i)) > tol)
        g = A(i+1:m,i)/A(i,i);    %Gauss elimination vector
        for j=i+1:n
            A(j:m,j) = A(j:m,j) - A(j,i)*g(j-i:m-i);
        end
        A(i+1:m,i) = g;               %L
    elseif (norm(A(i+1:m,i)) > tol)
        error('LDLtByGauss_:_Zero_pivot._Use_pivot=1_or_ltl_,_lbl_.');
    end
end
```

Crout Algorithm LDLtByCrout_ has three differences to LDUbyCrout_. (a) No pivoting is performed. (b) $U = L'$. The calculation of U is omitted by considering symmetry. (c) D is on the diagonal of A. L is below the diagonal of A. No change is made above the diagonal of A.

Algorithm 2.11

A=L*D*L' by Crout, L lower triangle, D diagonal.

```
function A = LDLtByCrout_(A,tol,f1st,last)

[m,n] = size(A);   v = zeros(m,1);
tol = tol*max(1.0,norm(diag(A))/m);

for j=f1st:last
    for i=f1st:j-1
        v(i) = A(i,i)*A(j,i);
    end
    A(j:m,j) = A(j:m,j) - A(j:m,f1st:j-1)*v(f1st:j-1);
    if (abs(A(j,j)) > tol)
        A(j+1:m,j) = A(j+1:m,j)/A(j,j);
    elseif (norm(A(j+1:m,j)) > tol)
        error('LDLtByCrout_:_Zero_pivot._Use_LDLtByGauss_w/_pivot=1_or_LTLt_,_LBLt_.');
    end
end

if (last < n)
    for j=last+1:n
        for i=f1st:last
            v(i) = A(i,i)*A(j,i);
        end
        A(j:m,j) = A(j:m,j) - A(j:m,f1st:j-1)*v(f1st:j-1);
    end
end
```

LDLt Driver Both LDLtByGauss_ and LDLtByCrout_ output L and D in the compact format – L is below the diagonal of A and D is on the diagonal of A. The driver LDLt_ outputs D and L in two separate matrices according to the input argument format='short' or format='long'.

Algorithm 2.12

P*A*P'=L*D*L', L lower triangle, D diagonal.

```
function [L,D,p] = LDLt_(A,algo,pivot,tol,format,f1st,last,p)

[m,n] = size(A);

if (strcmp(algo,'GAUSS'))
    [A,p] = LDLtByGauss_(A,pivot,tol,f1st,last,p);
else
    A = LDLtByCrout_(A,tol,f1st,last);
end

L = tril(A);  D = diag(A);
for j=1:min(m,n) L(j,j) = 1.0; end
if (last < min(m,n))
    for j=last+1:min(m,n) L(j+1:m,j) = 0.0; end
    D = diag(D);
    for j=last+1:n-1
        D(j+1:n,j) = A(j+1:n,j);  D(j,j+1:n) = D(j+1:n,j)';
    end
end

if (strcmp(format,'long'))
    if (last == n) D = diag(D); end
    p = pv2pm_(p);
else  %if (strcmp(format,'short'))
    if (last == n)
        for i=m:-1:1
            if (abs(D(i)) > tol) kmax = i; break; end
        end
        if (kmax < m) D = D(1:kmax); end
    else
        for i=m:-1:1
            if (i <= last) j1 = i; j2 = i;
            else           j1 = last+1; j2 = n; end
            if (norm(D(i,j1:j2),inf) > tol) kmax = i; break; end
        end
        if (kmax < m) D = D(1:kmax,1:kmax); end
        if (kmax <= last) D = diag(D); end
    end
    if (size(L,2) > kmax) L = L(:,1:kmax); end
end
```

The use of LDLtByGauss_, LDLtByCrout_, and LDLt_ is similar to their counterparts of LDUbyGauss_, LDUbyCrout_, and LDU_. In the following, we will show four examples to emphasize the properties of the LDLt decomposition discussed above.

The first example is the LDLt decomposition of a diagonal dominant matrix.

```
>> A=randn(4);   A=A+A';
>> d=diag(abs(A)*(ones(4)-eye(4))).*sign(diag(A));
>> A=A+diag(d)      %one way to create a diagonal dominant matrix
A =
    -7.3809    2.0056    1.7543   -1.5263
     2.0056    6.2263   -0.2709    1.4011
```

```
    1.7543    -0.2709    -8.0191     1.3828
   -1.5263     1.4011     1.3828    -7.3800
>> [L,d]=LDLt_(A,'gauss',0,100*eps,'short')
L =                  %pivoting not needed, Lij < 1
    1.0000          0          0          0
   -0.2717     1.0000          0          0
   -0.2377     0.0304     1.0000          0
    0.2068     0.1457    -0.1301     1.0000
d =
   -7.3809     6.7713    -7.6084    -7.0792

>> [L,d]=LDLt_(A,'crout',0,100*eps,'short')
L =                  %'crout' same result to 'gauss'
    1.0000          0          0          0
   -0.2717     1.0000          0          0
   -0.2377     0.0304     1.0000          0
    0.2068     0.1457    -0.1301     1.0000
d =
   -7.3809     6.7713    -7.6084    -7.0792
```

Example 2 is the LDLt decomposition of a positive definite matrix.

```
>> A=randn(4);    A=A*diag([1;2;3;4])*A';
%positive definite matrix
>> [L,d,p]=LDLt_(A,'gauss',0,100*eps,           >> [L,d,p]=LDLt_(A,'gauss',1,100*eps,
                             'short')                                     'short')
L =       %without pivoting OK but Lij > 1       L =       %With pivoting, Lij <= 1
    1.0000          0          0          0          1.0000          0          0          0
   -0.2529     1.0000          0          0          0.1024     1.0000          0          0
   -0.4756     0.9817     1.0000          0          0.3697    -0.2454     1.0000          0
    2.1754    -0.3884     0.5773     1.0000         -0.0552     0.2611     0.3131     1.0000
d =       %d > 0                                 d =       %d > 0
    1.3000     4.0628     7.0011     2.0926         11.2107    11.0735     1.9466     0.3202
p =                                              p =
    1          2          3          4            3          4          2          1
```

Example 3 shows the case that a symmetric matrix may have no LDLt decomposition.

```
>> A=randn(5);    A=A+A';
>> [L,D,p]=LDLt_(A,'gauss',1,100*eps,'short',1,2)
L =
    1.0000          0          0          0          0
    0.1812     1.0000          0          0          0
    0.1968    -0.1309     1.0000          0          0
    0.5303    -0.1803          0     1.0000          0
   -0.4943    -0.5291          0          0     1.0000
D =
   -3.7255          0          0          0          0
         0    -2.1304          0          0          0
         0          0    -1.2865    -0.2870    -0.0369
         0          0    -0.2870     0.8246     0.1013
         0          0    -0.0369     0.1013     1.6902
p =
    2          1          3          4          5
>> D(3,3)=0; D(4,4) = 0; D(5,5) = 0;  %one way creating a matrix --
>> A=L*D*L';                           %that may have no LDLt decomposition
```

```
>> [L,D,p]=LDLt_(A,'gauss',1,100*eps,'short')
??? Error using ==> LDLtByGauss_ at 31
LDLtByGauss_: Zero pivot. Use pivot=1 or LTLt_, LBLt_.

Error in ==> LDLt_ at 30
    [A,p] = LDLtByGauss_(A,pivot,tol,f1st,last,p);
```

Example 4 shows the restart and partial LDLt decomposition.

```
>> A=rand(5);   A=A+A';
>> B=LDLtByCrout_(A,100*eps,1,2);
>> [L,D,p]=LDLt_(B,'gauss',1,100*eps,'short',3,3)
L =
    1.0000         0         0         0         0
   10.1911    1.0000         0         0         0
   14.5825    1.5303    1.0000         0         0
   11.0934    1.0915    0.2552    1.0000         0
    1.9808    0.1740    0.5256         0    1.0000
D =
    0.1079         0         0         0         0
         0  -10.2676         0         0         0
         0         0    2.1559         0         0
         0         0         0    0.3105   -0.1067
         0         0         0   -0.1067    0.9437
p =
    1     2     3     4     5
>> norm(L*D*L'-pv2pm_(p)*A*pv2pm_(p)')
= 3.6525e-015
```

2.4.2 CHOLESKY DECOMPOSITION (LLt)

A symmetric positive matrix has a weighty diagonal. Although the weight of the diagonal is not as profound as a diagonal dominant matrix, it is weighty enough to have a stable LDLt decomposition without the need of pivoting. Because of the positive definiteness, it has the property that $D > 0$. Therefore, A can be written as $A = LDL' = L\sqrt{D}\left(L\sqrt{D}\right)' = LL'$. This decomposition is best known as the Cholesky decomposition. Because of the importance of the symmetric positive definite matrices in many branches of science and engineering, there was vast amount of research in the Cholesky decomposition, see [29] for the theoretical analysis and many references cited there.

The equation $A = LDL' = L\sqrt{D}\left(L\sqrt{D}\right)' = LL', D > 0$ suggests a simple way for the LLt decomposition. First, calculate LDLt decomposition $A = LDL'$. Then calculate the square root $\sqrt{D} \Rightarrow D$. Third, form L by $LD \Rightarrow L$. However, the more efficient Cholesky algorithm to calculate L directly from A avoids the calculation of $LD \Rightarrow L$. The derivation of the Cholesky decomposition is very similar to that of LDUbyCrout_, see 2.3.2. Using a 5×5 symmetric matrix A, the LLt decomposition can be written as follows:

$$
\begin{bmatrix}
A_{11} & A_{21} & A_{31} & A_{41} & A_{51} \\
A_{21} & A_{22} & A_{32} & A_{42} & A_{52} \\
A_{31} & A_{32} & A_{33} & A_{43} & A_{53} \\
A_{41} & A_{42} & A_{43} & A_{44} & A_{54} \\
A_{51} & A_{52} & A_{53} & A_{54} & A_{55}
\end{bmatrix}
=
\begin{bmatrix}
L_{11} & 0 \\
L_{21} & L_{22} \\
L_{31} & L_{32} & L_{33} \\
L_{41} & L_{42} & L_{43} & L_{44} \\
L_{51} & L_{52} & L_{53} & L_{54} & L_{55}
\end{bmatrix}
\begin{bmatrix}
L_{11} & L_{21} & L_{31} & L_{41} & L_{51} \\
 & L_{22} & L_{32} & L_{42} & L_{52} \\
 & & L_{33} & L_{43} & L_{53} \\
 & & & L_{44} & L_{54} \\
 & & & & L_{55}
\end{bmatrix}.
\tag{2.18}
$$

Equating the first column of Eq. (2.18),

$$
L_{11}\begin{bmatrix} L_{11} \\ L_{21} \\ L_{31} \\ L_{41} \\ L_{51} \end{bmatrix} = \begin{bmatrix} A_{11} \\ A_{21} \\ A_{31} \\ A_{41} \\ A_{51} \end{bmatrix}.
$$

A is positive definite, $A_{11} > 0, L_{11} = \sqrt{A_{11}}$. Then $\mathbf{L}(2:5,1) = \frac{1}{L_{11}}\mathbf{A}(2:5,1)$.

Similarly equating the second column of Eq. (2.18), we obtain L_{22} and $\mathbf{L}(3:5,2)$. At the end of the second step, **A** will look like the following:

$$
\begin{bmatrix}
L_{11} & A_{12} & A_{13} & A_{14} & A_{15} \\
L_{21} & L_{22} & A_{23} & A_{24} & A_{25} \\
L_{31} & L_{32} & A_{33} & A_{34} & A_{35} \\
L_{41} & L_{42} & A_{43} & A_{44} & A_{45} \\
L_{51} & L_{52} & A_{53} & A_{54} & A_{55}
\end{bmatrix}.
$$

The first column of **A** is overwritten by $\mathbf{L}(:,1)$. A_{12} is not accessed. $\mathbf{A}(2:5,2)$ is overwritten by $\mathbf{L}(2:5,2)$. The last three columns of **A** are still those of the original **A**. If the LLt decomposition stops prematurely after finishing the calculation of the second column, the output matrix has the following form:

$$
\begin{bmatrix}
L_{11} & 0 & 0 & 0 & 0 \\
L_{21} & L_{22} & 0 & 0 & 0 \\
L_{31} & L_{32} & L_{33} & L_{34} & L_{35} \\
L_{41} & L_{42} & L_{43} & L_{44} & L_{45} \\
L_{51} & L_{52} & L_{53} & L_{54} & L_{55}
\end{bmatrix},
$$

where $\mathbf{L}(3:5,3:5) = \mathbf{A}(3:5,3:5) - \mathbf{L}(3:5,1:2)\mathbf{L}(3:5,1:2)'$. This output matrix has to be interpreted in the following sense:

$$
\begin{bmatrix}
A_{11} & A_{21} & A_{31} & A_{41} & A_{51} \\
A_{21} & A_{22} & A_{32} & A_{42} & A_{52} \\
A_{31} & A_{32} & A_{33} & A_{43} & A_{53} \\
A_{41} & A_{42} & A_{43} & A_{44} & A_{54} \\
A_{51} & A_{52} & A_{53} & A_{54} & A_{55}
\end{bmatrix} =
\begin{bmatrix}
L_{11} & 0 & 0 & 0 & 0 \\
L_{21} & L_{22} & 0 & 0 & 0 \\
L_{31} & L_{32} & L_{33} & L_{34} & L_{35} \\
L_{41} & L_{42} & L_{43} & L_{44} & L_{45} \\
L_{51} & L_{52} & L_{53} & L_{54} & L_{55}
\end{bmatrix}
\begin{bmatrix}
L_{11} & L_{21} & L_{31} & L_{41} & L_{51} \\
 & L_{22} & L_{32} & L_{42} & L_{52} \\
 & & 1 & 0 & 0 \\
 & & & 1 & 0 \\
 & & & & 1
\end{bmatrix}.
$$

Upon restart from the third column, only the lower triangular part of $\mathbf{A}(3:5,3:5)$ is accessed.

To continue the elimination, equating the third column of Eq. (2.18),

$$
\begin{bmatrix} L_{11} & 0 \\ L_{21} & L_{22} \end{bmatrix}\begin{bmatrix} L_{13} \\ L_{23} \end{bmatrix} = \begin{bmatrix} A_{13} \\ A_{23} \end{bmatrix},
$$

$$
L_{33}\begin{bmatrix} L_{33} \\ L_{43} \\ L_{53} \end{bmatrix} = \begin{bmatrix} A_{33} \\ A_{43} \\ A_{53} \end{bmatrix} - \begin{bmatrix} L_{31} & L_{32} \\ L_{41} & L_{42} \\ L_{51} & L_{52} \end{bmatrix}\begin{bmatrix} L_{31} \\ L_{32} \end{bmatrix}.
$$

The first equation is an identity because of the symmetry of **A**. We calculate the right hand side of the second equation and save the result back to $\mathbf{A}(3:5,3)$. By the positive definiteness of **A**, $A_{33} > 0$, then $L_{33} = \sqrt{A_{33}} \Rightarrow A_{33}$, $\mathbf{L}(4:5,3) = \frac{1}{L_{33}}\mathbf{A}(4:5,3) \Rightarrow \mathbf{A}(4:5,3)$.

For column j of $\mathbf{A}$, we go three steps. First, we calculate $\mathbf{A}(j : m, j) \Rightarrow \mathbf{A}(j : m, j) - \mathbf{L}(j, 1 : j-1)\mathbf{L}(j, 1 : j-1)'$. Second, we calculate the square root $A_{jj} \Rightarrow L_{jj} = \sqrt{A_{jj}}$. Third, $\mathbf{A}(j+1 : m, j) \Rightarrow \mathbf{L}(j+1 : m, j) = \frac{1}{A_{jj}}\mathbf{A}(j+1 : m, j).$[3] By the assumption of the positive definiteness, no pivoting is applied. If at any step $A_{jj} \leq 0$, the LLt decomposition stops with an error – $\mathbf{A}$ is not positive definite. The LLt decomposition can be used to test if a symmetric matrix is positive definite.

The following is MATLAB implementation of the Cholesky decomposition, which has merely a loop with two lines of operation codes. LLtByCholesky_ also handles the output. MATLAB built-in function chol does the same calculation.

Algorithm 2.13

A=L*L' by Cholesky, L lower triangle. L overwrites lower triangular part of A.

```
function A = LLtByCholesky_(A,flst,last)

[m,n] = size(A);

for j=flst:last
    A(j:n,j) = A(j:n,j) - A(j:m,flst:j-1)*A(j,flst:j-1)';
    if (A(j,j) <= 0)
        error('LLtByCholesky_:~(A>0).Use xLLt_,LDLt_,LTLt_,or LBLt_.');
    end
    A(j:n,j) = A(j:n,j)/sqrt(A(j,j));
end

if (last == n)      %complete LL'
    A = tril(A);    %L
else                %partial  LL'
    for j=flst:last A(j,j+1:n) = 0; end
    for j=last+1:n
        for i=flst:last
            A(j:m,j) = A(j:m,j) - A(j:m,i)*A(j,i);
        end
        A(j,j:n) = A(j:m,j)';
    end
end
```

The following simple example shows the use of LLtByCholesky_.

```
>> A=randn(4);   A=A*diag([1;2;3;4])*A';  %A positive definite
>> L=LLtByCholesky_(A)
L =
    5.3690         0         0         0
   -0.2073    1.7852         0         0
    4.0229   -2.0797    1.0038         0
    0.8177   -1.2564   -3.0428    1.3060

>> A=A*diag([1;-2;0;4])*A'; %A positive indefinite
>> L=LLtByCholesky_(A)
??? Error using ==> LLtByCholesky_ at 15
LLtByCholesky_:~(A>0).Use xLLt_,LDLt_,LTLt_,or LBLt_.
```

---

[3]Here some equations demonstrate the overwriting of the data, not necessarily the mathematical equivalence.

2.4.3 REDUCTION OF SYMMETRIC MATRIX TO TRI-DIAGONAL (LTLt)

When $\mathbf{A} = \mathbf{A}'$ but $\mathbf{PAP}' = \mathbf{LDL}'$ does not exist or is inaccurate to calculate, we can calculate $\mathbf{PAP}' = \mathbf{LTL}'$ instead, where $\mathbf{T}$ is symmetric tri-diagonal. Similarly to LU, LDU, and LDLt decomposition discussed previously, we have two mathematically equivalent algorithms. One is LTLtByParlett_, see [45]. It is a modification of the Gauss elimination LDLtByGauss_, which is of transforming nature. The other is LTLtByAasen_, see [1]. It is similar to LDLtByCrout_, which is of decomposing nature.

Algorithm of Parlett and Reid The algorithm can be illustrated with a 5×5 symmetric matrix $\mathbf{A}$. To start, we find a permutation $\mathbf{P}_1$ and apply $\mathbf{P}_1\mathbf{AP}'_1 \Rightarrow \mathbf{A}$ so that $|A_{21}| = \|\mathbf{A}(2:5,1)\|_\infty$. Then find a Gauss elimination matrix $\mathbf{G}_1$ and apply $\mathbf{G}_1\mathbf{AG}'_1 \Rightarrow \mathbf{A}$ so that $\mathbf{A}(3:5,1) = \mathbf{0}$ and $\mathbf{A}(1,3:5) = \mathbf{0}$. Now $\mathbf{A}$ has the following form:

$$\mathbf{A} = \begin{bmatrix} A_{11} & A_{21} & 0 & 0 & 0 \\ A_{21} & A_{22} & A_{32} & A_{42} & A_{52} \\ 0 & A_{32} & A_{33} & A_{43} & A_{53} \\ 0 & A_{42} & A_{43} & A_{44} & A_{54} \\ 0 & A_{52} & A_{53} & A_{54} & A_{55} \end{bmatrix}.$$

Next we apply the two steps of permutation and elimination to the second column and row. After the permutation $\mathbf{P}_2\mathbf{AP}'_2 \Rightarrow \mathbf{A}$, $|A_{32}| = \|\mathbf{A}(3:5,2)\|_\infty$. A Gauss elimination matrix $\mathbf{G}_2$ is chosen as follows:

$$\mathbf{G}_2 = \begin{bmatrix} 1 & 0 & 0 & 0 & 0 \\ 0 & 1 & 0 & 0 & 0 \\ 0 & 0 & 1 & 0 & 0 \\ 0 & 0 & -\frac{A_{42}}{A_{32}} & 1 & 0 \\ 0 & 0 & -\frac{A_{52}}{A_{32}} & 0 & 1 \end{bmatrix} = \mathbf{I} + \begin{bmatrix} \mathbf{0}^{2\times1} \\ \mathbf{g}_2 \end{bmatrix} \mathbf{I}(3,:), \quad \mathbf{g}_2 = \begin{bmatrix} 0 \\ -\frac{1}{A_{32}}\mathbf{A}(4:5,2) \end{bmatrix}.$$

The transformation of $\mathbf{G}_2\mathbf{AG}'_2$ leaves $\mathbf{A}(1:3,1:3)$ unaltered, sets $\mathbf{A}(4:5,2)$ and $\mathbf{A}(2,4:5)$ to 0s, while $\mathbf{A}(3:5,3:5)$ is overwritten by $\mathbf{A}(3:5,3:5) + \mathbf{g}_2\mathbf{A}(3,3:5) + \mathbf{A}(3:5,3)\mathbf{g}'_2 + A(3,3)\mathbf{g}_2\mathbf{g}'_2$. The partial LTLt decomposition at this moment takes the following form:

$$\begin{bmatrix} A_{11} & A_{21} & A_{31} & A_{41} & A_{51} \\ A_{21} & A_{22} & A_{32} & A_{42} & A_{52} \\ A_{31} & A_{32} & A_{33} & A_{43} & A_{53} \\ A_{41} & A_{42} & A_{43} & A_{44} & A_{54} \\ A_{51} & A_{52} & A_{53} & A_{54} & A_{55} \end{bmatrix} = \begin{bmatrix} 1 & 0 & 0 & 0 & 0 \\ 0 & 1 & 0 & 0 & 0 \\ 0 & L_{32} & 1 & 0 & 0 \\ 0 & L_{42} & L_{43} & 1 & 0 \\ 0 & L_{52} & L_{53} & 0 & 1 \end{bmatrix} \begin{bmatrix} T_{11} & T_{21} & 0 & 0 & 0 \\ T_{21} & T_{22} & T_{32} & 0 & 0 \\ 0 & T_{32} & T_{33} & T_{43} & T_{53} \\ 0 & 0 & T_{43} & T_{44} & T_{54} \\ 0 & 0 & T_{53} & T_{54} & T_{55} \end{bmatrix} \begin{bmatrix} 1 & 0 & 0 & 0 & 0 \\ 0 & 1 & L_{32} & L_{42} & L_{52} \\ 0 & 0 & 1 & L_{43} & L_{53} \\ 0 & 0 & 0 & 1 & 0 \\ 0 & 0 & 0 & 0 & 1 \end{bmatrix}.$$

Note that all the nonzeros components of $\mathbf{L}$ and $\mathbf{T}$ overwrite the original $\mathbf{A}$.

To continue the elimination, apply the permutation and elimination one more time to the third column and row, we obtain a symmetric triangular matrix $\mathbf{T}$. $\mathbf{P}$ and $\mathbf{L}$ are obtained as $\mathbf{P} = \mathbf{P}_3\mathbf{P}_2\mathbf{P}_1$ and $\mathbf{L} = \mathbf{G}_3\mathbf{P}_3\mathbf{G}_2\mathbf{P}_2\mathbf{G}_1$. In the implementation of LTLtByParlett_, the upper triangular above the diagonal of $\mathbf{A}$ is not touched and components of $\mathbf{L}$ take the positions of the zeroed $\mathbf{A}$ components. For the above 5×5 matrix $\mathbf{A}$, when LTLtByParlett_ finishes the calculation, $\mathbf{A}$ has the following data values:

$$\begin{bmatrix} T_{11} & A_{12} & A_{13} & A_{14} & A_{15} \\ T_{21} & T_{22} & A_{23} & A_{24} & A_{25} \\ L_{32} & T_{32} & T_{33} & A_{34} & A_{35} \\ L_{42} & L_{43} & T_{43} & T_{44} & A_{54} \\ L_{52} & L_{53} & L_{64} & T_{54} & T_{55} \end{bmatrix}.$$

Algorithm 2.14

P*A*P'=L*T*L' by Parlett and Reid, p permutations. L,T overwrites tril(A).

```
function [A,p] = LTLtByParlett_(A,tol,flst,last,p)

[m,n] = size(A);
tol = tol*max(1.0, norm(diag(A))/m);   v = zeros(m,1);

for j=flst:last
    k = argmax_(A(:,j),j+1);
    if (j+1 ~= k)
        [A(j+1,1:j),A(k,1:j)] = swap_(A(j+1,1:j),A(k,1:j));
        [A(j+2:k-1,j+1),A(k,j+2:k-1)] = swap_(A(j+2:k-1,j+1),A(k,j+2:k-1));
        [A(k+1:n,j+1),A(k+1:n,k)] = swap_(A(k+1:n,j+1),A(k+1:n,k));
        [A(j+1,j+1),A(k,k)] = swap_(A(j+1,j+1),A(k,k));
        [p(j+1),p(k)] = swap_(p(j+1),p(k));
    end
    if (abs(A(j+1,j)) < tol) A(j+1:m,j) = 0;   continue; end    %skip
% [1 0 0';   [A11 A12 a1';   [1 0 0';   [A11 A12 0';
% 0 1 0'; *  A21 A22 a2'; *  0 1 g'; =   A21 A22 b2';
% 0 g I]      a1  a2  A3]    0 0 I]       0   b2  B3];
% g=-a1/A21;  b2=a2+A22*g,  B3=A3+a2*g'+g*a2'+A22*g*g'=A3+g*a2'+b2*g'
    A(j+2:m,j) = A(j+2:m,j)/A(j+1,j);                           %g
    v(j+2:m) = A(j+2:m,j+1) - A(j+1,j+1)*A(j+2:m,j);            %b2
    for i=j+2:n
        A(i:m,i) = A(i:m,i) - A(i:m,j)*A(i,j+1) - v(i:m)*A(i,j);   %A3
    end
    A(j+2:m,j+1) = v(j+2:m);
end
```

Algorithm of Aasen For a symmetric matrix $\mathbf{A}$, $\mathbf{PAP'} = \mathbf{LTL'}$ always exists and is stable to calculate. Similarly to the Crout algorithms, each column of $\mathbf{L}$ and $\mathbf{T}$ can be obtained by equating each column of the two expressions of $\mathbf{PAP'}$ and $\mathbf{LTL'}$. Again we will illustrate the procedure with a 5×5 symmetric matrix $\mathbf{A}$. First we introduce an intermediate matrix $\mathbf{H} = \mathbf{TL'}$. $\mathbf{H}$ is an upper Hessenberg, because $\mathbf{T}$ is tri-diagonal and $\mathbf{L'}$ is upper triangular. Therefore, we have two sets of matrix equations,

$$
\mathbf{A} = \mathbf{LH}: \quad
\begin{bmatrix}
A_{11} & A_{21} & A_{31} & A_{41} & A_{51} \\
A_{21} & A_{22} & A_{32} & A_{42} & A_{52} \\
A_{31} & A_{32} & A_{33} & A_{43} & A_{53} \\
A_{41} & A_{42} & A_{43} & A_{44} & A_{54} \\
A_{51} & A_{52} & A_{53} & A_{54} & A_{55}
\end{bmatrix}
=
\begin{bmatrix}
1 & 0 & 0 & 0 & 0 \\
0 & 1 & 0 & 0 & 0 \\
0 & L_{32} & 1 & 0 & 0 \\
0 & L_{42} & L_{43} & 1 & 0 \\
0 & L_{42} & L_{53} & L_{54} & 1
\end{bmatrix},
\begin{bmatrix}
H_{11} & H_{12} & H_{13} & H_{14} & H_{15} \\
H_{21} & H_{22} & H_{23} & H_{24} & H_{25} \\
0 & H_{32} & H_{33} & H_{34} & H_{35} \\
0 & 0 & H_{43} & H_{44} & H_{45} \\
0 & 0 & 0 & H_{54} & H_{55}
\end{bmatrix}
$$

$$
\mathbf{H} = \mathbf{TL'}: \quad
\begin{bmatrix}
H_{11} & H_{12} & H_{13} & H_{14} & H_{15} \\
H_{21} & H_{22} & H_{23} & H_{24} & H_{25} \\
0 & H_{32} & H_{33} & H_{34} & H_{35} \\
0 & 0 & H_{43} & H_{44} & H_{45} \\
0 & 0 & 0 & H_{54} & H_{55}
\end{bmatrix}
=
\begin{bmatrix}
T_{11} & T_{21} & 0 & 0 & 0 \\
T_{21} & T_{22} & T_{32} & 0 & 0 \\
0 & T_{32} & T_{33} & T_{43} & 0 \\
0 & 0 & T_{43} & T_{44} & T_{54} \\
0 & 0 & 0 & T_{54} & T_{55}
\end{bmatrix}
\begin{bmatrix}
1 & 0 & 0 & 0 & 0 \\
0 & 1 & L_{32} & L_{42} & L_{52} \\
0 & 0 & 1 & L_{43} & L_{53} \\
0 & 0 & 0 & 1 & L_{54} \\
0 & 0 & 0 & 0 & 1
\end{bmatrix}.
$$

By $\mathbf{A}(:,1) = \mathbf{LH}(:,1)$, that is,

$$
\begin{bmatrix}
A_{11} \\
A_{21} \\
A_{31} \\
A_{41} \\
A_{51}
\end{bmatrix}
= \mathbf{LH}(:,1) =
\begin{bmatrix}
1 & 0 \\
0 & 1 \\
0 & L_{32} \\
0 & L_{42} \\
0 & L_{52}
\end{bmatrix}
\begin{bmatrix}
H_{11} \\
H_{21}
\end{bmatrix}
=
\begin{bmatrix}
H_{11} \\
H_{21} \\
L_{32}H_{21} \\
A_{42}H_{21} \\
A_{52}H_{21}
\end{bmatrix},
$$

we obtain the following:

$$H_{11} = A_{11},$$

$$\mathbf{P}_1\mathbf{A} \Rightarrow \mathbf{A} \text{ so that } |A_{21}| = \|\mathbf{A}(2:5,1)\|_\infty, \quad H_{21} = A_{21},$$

$$\begin{bmatrix} L_{32} \\ L_{42} \\ L_{52} \end{bmatrix} = \frac{1}{A_{21}} \begin{bmatrix} A_{31} \\ A_{41} \\ A_{51} \end{bmatrix}.$$

By $\mathbf{H}(:,1) = \mathbf{TL}(1,:)'$, that is,

$$\begin{bmatrix} H_{11} \\ H_{21} \\ \mathbf{0} \end{bmatrix} = \mathbf{TL}(1,:)' = \begin{bmatrix} T_{11} \\ T_{21} \\ \mathbf{0} \end{bmatrix},$$

we obtain $T_{11} = H_{11}$ and $T_{21} = H_{21}$. So now $\mathbf{L}(:,1:2)$ and $\mathbf{T}(:,1)$ are known after considering the relations $\mathbf{A}(:,1) = \mathbf{LH}(:,1)$ and $\mathbf{H}(:,1) = \mathbf{TL}(1,:)'$.

In a similar way, we obtain $\mathbf{L}(4:5,3)$, T_{22} and T_{32} by equations $\mathbf{A}(:,2) = \mathbf{LH}(:,2)$ and $\mathbf{H}(:,2) = \mathbf{TL}(2,:)'$.

Next we show how to calculate L_{54} and $\mathbf{T}(3:4,3)$ by equations $\mathbf{A}(:,3) = \mathbf{LH}(:,3)$ and $\mathbf{H}(:,3) = \mathbf{TL}(3,:)'$,

$$\begin{bmatrix} A_{13} \\ A_{23} \\ A_{33} \\ A_{43} \\ A_{53} \end{bmatrix} = \mathbf{LH}(:,3) = \begin{bmatrix} 1 & 0 & 0 & 0 \\ 0 & 1 & 0 & 0 \\ 0 & L_{32} & 1 & 0 \\ 0 & L_{42} & L_{43} & 1 \\ 0 & L_{42} & L_{53} & L_{54} \end{bmatrix} \begin{bmatrix} H_{13} \\ H_{23} \\ H_{33} \\ H_{43} \end{bmatrix}; \quad \begin{bmatrix} H_{13} \\ H_{23} \\ H_{33} \\ H_{43} \end{bmatrix} = \begin{bmatrix} T_{21} & 0 \\ T_{22} & T_{32} \\ T_{32} & T_{33} \\ 0 & T_{43} \end{bmatrix} \begin{bmatrix} L_{32} \\ 1 \end{bmatrix}.$$

From the above two equations for $\mathbf{A}(:,3)$ and $\mathbf{H}(:,3)$, we see that there are two ways to determine H_{13} and H_{23},

$$\begin{bmatrix} H_{13} \\ H_{23} \end{bmatrix} = \begin{bmatrix} 1 & 0 \\ 0 & 1 \end{bmatrix}^{-1} \begin{bmatrix} A_{13} \\ A_{23} \end{bmatrix}, \quad \begin{bmatrix} H_{13} \\ H_{23} \end{bmatrix} = \begin{bmatrix} T_{21} & 0 \\ T_{22} & T_{32} \end{bmatrix} \begin{bmatrix} L_{32} \\ 1 \end{bmatrix}.$$

We choose the second way, because the first way needs to access the data above $\mathbf{A}$'s diagonal. After H_{13} and H_{23} are determined, then $H_{33} = A_{33} - H_{23}L_{32}$. From the equations of the last two components of $\mathbf{A}(:,3)$, we have

$$\begin{bmatrix} H_{43} \\ H_{43}L_{54} \end{bmatrix} = \begin{bmatrix} A_{43} \\ A_{53} \end{bmatrix} - \begin{bmatrix} L_{42} & L_{43} \\ L_{52} & L_{53} \end{bmatrix} \begin{bmatrix} H_{23} \\ H_{33} \end{bmatrix} \Rightarrow \begin{bmatrix} A_{43} \\ A_{53} \end{bmatrix}.$$

We choose $\mathbf{P}_3$, $\mathbf{P}_3\mathbf{A} \Rightarrow \mathbf{A}$ so that $|A_{43}| = \|\mathbf{A}(4:5,3)\|_\infty$. So now we can calculate

$$H_{43} = A_{43}; \quad L_{54} = \frac{1}{H_{43}} A_{53}.$$

From the equations of the last two components of $\mathbf{H}(:,3)$, we have

$$\begin{bmatrix} T_{33} \\ T_{43} \end{bmatrix} = \begin{bmatrix} H_{33} \\ H_{43} \end{bmatrix} - L_{32} \begin{bmatrix} T_{32} \\ 0 \end{bmatrix}.$$

Until this step, all the components of $\mathbf{L}$ are determined. In $\mathbf{T}$ only T_{44}, T_{54}, and T_{55} are unknown. By considering $\mathbf{A}(:,4) = \mathbf{L}\mathbf{H}(:,4)$ and $\mathbf{H}(:,4) = \mathbf{T}\mathbf{L}(4,:)'$, we can determine T_{44} and T_{54}. In the last step, we determine T_{55} by considering $\mathbf{A}(:,5) = \mathbf{L}\mathbf{H}(:,5)$ and $\mathbf{H}(:,5) = \mathbf{T}\mathbf{L}(5,:)'$,

$$\begin{bmatrix} A_{15} \\ A_{25} \\ A_{35} \\ A_{45} \\ A_{55} \end{bmatrix} = \begin{bmatrix} 1 & 0 & 0 & 0 & 0 \\ 0 & 1 & 0 & 0 & 0 \\ 0 & L_{32} & 1 & 0 & 0 \\ 0 & L_{42} & L_{43} & 1 & 0 \\ 0 & L_{42} & L_{53} & L_{54} & 1 \end{bmatrix} \begin{bmatrix} H_{15} \\ H_{25} \\ H_{35} \\ H_{45} \\ H_{55} \end{bmatrix}, \quad \begin{bmatrix} H_{15} \\ H_{25} \\ H_{35} \\ H_{45} \\ H_{55} \end{bmatrix} = \begin{bmatrix} T_{21} & 0 & 0 & 0 \\ T_{22} & T_{32} & 0 & 0 \\ T_{32} & T_{33} & T_{43} & 0 \\ 0 & T_{43} & T_{44} & T_{54} \\ 0 & 0 & T_{54} & T_{55} \end{bmatrix} \begin{bmatrix} L_{52} \\ L_{53} \\ L_{54} \\ 1 \end{bmatrix}.$$

Similarly to the case of $\mathbf{A}(:,3)$, there are two ways to determine $\mathbf{H}(1:4,5)$. The first way is to use $\mathbf{H}(1:4,5) = \mathbf{L}(1:4,1:4)^{-1}\mathbf{A}(1:4,5)$, which needs to solve an equation of unit lower triangular matrix and needs to access the data above $\mathbf{A}$'s diagonal. The second way is to use $\mathbf{H}(1:4,5) = \mathbf{L}(2:5,1:4)\mathbf{L}(5,2:5)'$. We use the second way for $\mathbf{H}(1:4,5)$. Then from $A(5,5) = \mathbf{L}(5,1:5)\mathbf{H}(1:5,5)$, we obtain H_{55} as follows:

$$H_{55} = A_{55} - \mathbf{L}(5,2:4)\mathbf{H}(2:4,5).$$

From $H_{55} = \mathbf{T}(:,5)\mathbf{L}(5,:)' = T_{54}L_{54} + T_{55}$, we obtain T_{55},

$$T_{55} = H_{55} - T_{54}L_{54}.$$

For the general case of $n \times n$ symmetric matrix, the Aasen algorithm can be briefly summarized. Suppose $\mathbf{L}(:,1:j)$ and $\mathbf{T}(:,1:j-1)$ have been determined. $\mathbf{L}(:,j+1)$ and $\mathbf{T}(:,j)$ are determined by considering $\mathbf{A}(:,j) = \mathbf{L}\mathbf{H}(:,j)$ and $\mathbf{H}(:,j) = \mathbf{T}\mathbf{L}(j,:)'$. (a) Calculate $\mathbf{H}(1:j-1,j) = \mathbf{T}(1:j-1,:)\mathbf{L}(j,:)'$. (b) Calculate $H(j,j)$ through $A(j,j) = \mathbf{L}(j,:)\mathbf{H}(:,j)$. (c) Calculate $\mathbf{H}(j+1:m,j)$ and $\mathbf{L}(:,j)$ through $\mathbf{A}(j+1:m,j) = \mathbf{L}(j+1:m,:)\mathbf{H}(:,j)$. (d) Calculate $\mathbf{T}(:,j)$ through $\mathbf{H}(j+1:m,j) = \mathbf{T}(j+1:m,:)\mathbf{L}(j,:)'$. The proper layout of $\mathbf{L}$, $\mathbf{T}$, and $\mathbf{H}$ has to be taken into account for each column number j. For the partial LTLt decomposition, that is, the Aasen algorithm stops the calculation prematurely for $j < n$, the last $n - j$ columns of $\mathbf{A}$ are those of the original $\mathbf{A}$. To keep the identity, $\mathbf{PAP}' = \mathbf{LTL}'$, the deferred transformations to the last $n - j$ columns need to be done before exiting. These deferred transformations are same to those of the algorithm of Parlett and Reid.

The following is the MATLAB implementation of the algorithm of Aasen for $\mathbf{PAP}' = \mathbf{LTL}'$.

Algorithm 2.15

```
P*A*P'=L*T*L' by Aasen, p permutations, L, T overwrite tril(A).
function [A,p] = LTLtByAasen_(A,tol,flst,last,p)

[m,n] = size(A);
tol = tol*max(1.0, norm(diag(A))/m);
h = zeros(m,1);    g = zeros(m,1);    v = zeros(m,1);

for j=flst:last
    v(j+1:m) = A(j+1:m,j);   h(j) = A(j,j);
    if (j > 2)
        g(2:j-1) = A(j,1:j-2);   g(j) = 1;    %g=L(j,:)'
        for i=2:j-1                           %h(2:j)=T*L(j,2:j)'
            h(i) = A(i,i-1)*g(i-1) + A(i,i)*g(i) + A(i+1,i)*g(i+1);
            h(j) = h(j) - g(i)*h(i);
        end
        A(j,j) = h(j) - A(j,j-1)*A(j,j-2);
```

```
        end
        if (j < n)
            v(j+1:m) = v(j+1:m) - A(j+1:m,1:j-1)*h(2:j);
            k = argmax_(v, j+1);
            if (j+1 ~= k)
                [A(j+1,1:j),A(k,1:j)] = swap_(A(j+1,1:j),A(k,1:j));
                [A(j+2:k-1,j+1),A(k,j+2:k-1)] = swap_(A(j+2:k-1,j+1),A(k,j+2:k-1));
                [A(k+1:n,j+1),A(k+1:n,k)] = swap_(A(k+1:n,j+1),A(k+1:n,k));
                [A(j+1,j+1),A(k,k)] = swap_(A(j+1,j+1),A(k,k));
                [v(j+1),v(k)] = swap_(v(j+1),v(k));
                [p(j+1),p(k)] = swap_(p(j+1),p(k));
            end
            A(j+1,j) = v(j+1);
        end
        if (j < n-1)
            if (abs(v(j+1)) > tol) A(j+2:m,j) = v(j+2:m)/v(j+1);
            else                   A(j+2:m,j) = 0.0; end
        end
    end

    if (last < n)
        for j=f1st:last
            l1 = last + 1;  j1 = j + 1;  j2 = j + 2;
            if (j < last-1)
                g(l1:m) =-A(l1:m,j);   v(l1:m) = A(j2,j1)*A(l1:m,j1);   %b2
                h(l1:m) = v(l1:m) - A(j1,j1)*g(l1:m);                   %a2
            elseif (j == last-1)
                g(l1:m) =-A(l1:m,j); v(l1) = A(j2,j1); v(l1+1:m) = A(j2,j1)*A(l1+1:m,j1);
                h(l1:m) = v(l1:m) - A(j1,j1)*g(l1:m);                   %a2
            else %if(j==last)
                l1 = l1 + 1;
                g(l1:m) =-A(l1:m,j);   h(l1:m) = A(l1:m,j1);            %a2
                v(l1:m) = h(l1:m) + A(j1,j1)*g(l1:m);                   %b2
                A(l1:m,j1) = v(l1:m);
            end
            for i=l1:m
                A(i:m,i) = A(i:m,i) + g(i:m)*h(i) + v(i:m)*g(i);
            end
        end
    end
end
```

LTLt Driver LTLt_ dispatches the call to LTLtByParlett_ and LTLtByAasen_. Its another function handles the output according to the input argument format='short' or format='long'. When format='short', any columns and rows of zeros in **T** are removed from the output and **T** is output as band format.

Algorithm 2.16

P*A*P'=L*T*L', L lower triangle, D diagonal.

```
function [L,T,p] = LTLt_(A,algo,tol,format,f1st,last,p)

[m,n] = size(A);

if (strcmp(algo,'PARLETT'))
    [A,p] = LTLtByParlett_(A,tol,f1st,last,p);
else
    [A,p] = LTLtByAasen_(A,tol,f1st,last,p);
```

```
end

T = diag(diag(A));   L = eye(m);
for i=2:last
    T(i,i-1) = A(i,i-1);   T(i-1,i) = T(i,i-1);   L(i+1:m,i) = A(i+1:m,i-1);
end
if (last>1)
    T(last,last-1) = A(last,last-1);   T(last-1,last) = T(last,last-1);
end
if (last+1<m)
    L(last+2:m,last+1) = A(last+2:m,last);
end
if (last < m)
    T(last+1,last) = A(last+1,last);   T(last,last+1) = T(last+1,last);
    for i=last+1:m
        T(i:m,i) = A(i:m,i);   T(i,i:m) = T(i:m,i)';
    end
end

if (strcmp(format,'long')) p = pv2pm_(p); end
if (strcmp(format,'short'))
    tol = tol*max(1.0,norm(diag(T))/m);
    for j=m:-1:1
        if (last==m || j<=last)
            j1 = j-1;   j2 = j + 1;
            if (j2 > n) j2 = n;  end
        else
            j1 = last+1;  j2 = n;
        end
        if (norm(T(j,j1:j2),inf) > tol) k = j; break; end
    end
    if (k < m) L = L(:,1:k);   T = T(1:k,1:k); end
    if (last == m) T = full2band_(T,1,1); end
end
```

The following two examples demonstrate the use of the LTLt algorithms.

Example 1 shows that LTLt decomposition can be safely calculated where LDLt decomposition failed.

```
>> A=randn(5);   A=A+A';
>> [L,D,p]=LDLt_(A,'gauss',1,100*eps,'short',1,2);
>> D(3,3)=0;   D(4,4) = 0;   D(5,5) = 0;
>> A=L*D*L';        %One way creating a matrix having no LDLt decomposition
>> [L,D,p]=LDLt_(A,'gauss',1,100*eps,'short')
??? Error using ==> LDLtByGauss_ at 36
LDLtByGauss_: Zero pivot. Use pivot=1 or LTLt_, LBLt_.

Error in ==> LDLt_ at 29
    [A,p] = LDLtByGauss_(A,pivot,tol,f1st,last,p);

>> [L,T,p]=LTLt_(A,'aasen',100*eps,'short')
L =
    1.0000         0         0         0         0
         0    1.0000         0         0         0
         0   -0.3705    1.0000         0         0
         0   -0.6163   -0.5399    1.0000         0
         0   -0.3153   -0.2365    0.2068    1.0000
```

```
T =
             0      -3.6674      1.8650
        1.8650      -1.6840      1.2962
        1.2962      -2.2839     -1.4560
       -1.4560      -1.7484      0.3713
        0.3713      -0.2197           0
p =
        1      3      2      5      4
```

Example 2 shows the restart and partial LTLt decomposition, using the same matrix A in Example 1.

```
>> [B,p]=LTLtByParlett_(A,100*eps,1,1);
>> [L,T,P]=LTLt_(B,'parlett',100*eps,'long',2,2,p)
L =
        1.0000           0           0           0           0
             0      1.0000           0           0           0
             0     -0.3705      1.0000           0           0
             0     -0.3153     -0.2365      1.0000           0
             0     -0.6163     -0.5399           0      1.0000
T =
       -3.6674      1.8650           0           0           0
        1.8650     -1.6840      1.2962           0           0
             0      1.2962     -2.2839     -0.3011     -1.4560
             0           0     -0.3011     -0.1409      0.0097
             0           0     -1.4560      0.0097     -1.7484
P =
        1      0      0      0      0
        0      0      1      0      0
        0      1      0      0      0
        0      0      0      1      0
        0      0      0      0      1

>> norm(L*T*L'-P*A*P')
= 3.3566e-016
```

2.4.4 REDUCTION OF SYMMETRIC MATRIX TO BLOCK DIAGONAL (LBLt)

When $\mathbf{PAP}' = \mathbf{LDL}'$ does not exist or is inaccurate to calculate, another alternative to $\mathbf{PAP}' = \mathbf{LTL}'$ is to calculate $\mathbf{PAP}' = \mathbf{LBL}'$, where $\mathbf{B}$ is a block diagonal of 1×1 and symmetric 2×2 blocks. 1×1 and 2×2 blocks and their positions in $\mathbf{B}$'s diagonal are dynamically determined using the pivoting strategy of Bunch and Parlett, see [12] or Bunch and Kaufman, see [11]. The elimination algorithm is that of Gauss. The following discussion follows Golub and Loan [29].

If $\mathbf{A}$ is nonzero, it is always possible to find a permutation matrix $\mathbf{P}_1$ so that

$$\mathbf{P}_1\mathbf{AP}'_1 \Rightarrow \mathbf{A} = \begin{bmatrix} \mathbf{A}_{11} & \mathbf{A}'_{21} \\ \mathbf{A}_{21} & \mathbf{A}_{22} \end{bmatrix} = \begin{bmatrix} \mathbf{I}_s & \mathbf{0} \\ \mathbf{A}_{21}\mathbf{A}_{11}^{-1} & \mathbf{I}_{n-s} \end{bmatrix} \begin{bmatrix} \mathbf{A}_{11} & \mathbf{0} \\ \mathbf{0} & \mathbf{A}_{22} - \mathbf{A}_{21}\mathbf{A}_{11}^{-1}\mathbf{A}'_{21} \end{bmatrix} \begin{bmatrix} \mathbf{I}_s & \mathbf{A}_{11}^{-1}\mathbf{A}'_{21} \\ \mathbf{0} & \mathbf{I}_{n-s} \end{bmatrix}, \qquad (2.19)$$

where s is the size of the pivot $\mathbf{A}_{11}$, which can be 1 or 2. The pivot is chosen to make sure the components of $\mathbf{A}_{22} - \mathbf{A}_{21}\mathbf{A}_{11}^{-1}\mathbf{A}'_{21} \Rightarrow \mathbf{A}_{22}$ are properly bounded. For this purpose, we define $\alpha \in (0, 1)$ and $\mu_0 = \max_{i,j} |A_{ij}|$ and $\mu_1 = \max_i |A_{ii}|$.

Algorithm 2.1 Bunch–Parlett Pivot

1: **if** $\mu_1 \geq \alpha \mu_0$ **then**
2:    $s = 1$ and choose $\mathbf{P}_1$ so $A_{11} = \mu_1$.
3: **else**
4:    $s = 2$ and choose $\mathbf{P}_1$ so $A_{21} = \mu_0$.
5: **end if**

According to this pivoting strategy, after the elimination Eq. (2.19), the component of $\mathbf{A}_{22}$ has the following bound:

$$|\mathbf{A}_{22}| \leq \left(1 + \alpha^{-1}\right)\mu_0 \qquad \text{if } s = 1,$$
$$|\mathbf{A}_{22}| \leq \tfrac{3-\alpha}{1-\alpha}\mu_0 \qquad \text{if } s = 2.$$

By equating the growth factor of two consecutive $s = 1$ steps and one $s = 2$ step, i.e. $1 + \alpha^{-1} = (3 - \alpha)/(1 - \alpha)$, Bunch and Parlett concluded that $\alpha = (1 + \sqrt{17})/(8)$ is optimal to minimize the component growth in $\mathbf{A}_{22}$. The Bunch–Parlett pivoting is as stable as LU decomposition with complete pivoting. However, to find μ_0 in each elimination step requires a two dimensional search, which slows down considerably the performance. Bunch and Kaufman, [11], introduced a partial pivoting which avoids the two dimensional search. The Bunch–Parlett pivoting and Bunch–Kaufman pivoting are accessed in the MATLAB implementation LBLtByBunch_ by pivot=1 and pivot=2, respectively. In LBLtByBunch_, if pivot=0, it is equivalent to LDLtByGauss_.

Algorithm 2.17

```
P*A*P'=L*B*L', L,B overwrites tril(A). ib(j): 1x1 block; ib(j)=ib(j+1)=2 2x2 block.
function [A,ib,p] = LBLtByBunch_(A,pivot,tol,f1st,last,ib,p)

[m,n] = size(A);
tol = tol*max(1.0,norm(diag(A))/m);   tol2 = tol*tol;

g1 = zeros(m,1);   g2 = zeros(m,2);
alpha = (1.0+sqrt(17.0))/8.0;

j = f1st;
while (j <= last)
    if (pivot == 0)      %pivot from diagonal (ldl)
        k = argmax_(diag(A),j);
    elseif (pivot == 1) %Bunch-Kaufman pivot
        k = argmax_(A(:,j), j);
        lambda = abs(A(k,j));
        if (lambda < tol)
            j = j + 1;   continue;      %skip
        else
            if (abs(A(j,j)) >= alpha*lambda)  %diagonal large enough
                k = j;
            else
                k1 = argmax_(A(k,1:k-1),j);   k2 = argmax_(A(:,k),k);
                if (abs(A(k,k1)) > abs(A(k2,k))) l = k1;
                else                            k = k2;  l = k1; end
                sigma = abs(A(k,l));
                if(abs(A(j,j))*sigma >= alpha*lambda^2) k = j;
```

```
                        elseif(abs(A(k,k)) >= alpha*sigma)        k = k;
                        else                                      ib(j:j+1) = 2; end
                    end
                end
            else %if(pivot==2)  %Bunch_Parlett pivot
                k = argmax_(diag(A),j);  [k1,k2] = argsmax_(A,j,j,m,0);
                if (abs(A(k,k)) < alpha*abs(A(k1,k2))) k = k1;  l = k2;  ib(j:j+1) = 2; end
            end

            if (ib(j) == 1)     %1x1 pivot
                if (j < k)      %swap row (j,k) and column (j,k)
                    [A(j,1:j-1),A(k,1:j-1)] = swap_(A(j,1:j-1),A(k,1:j-1));
                    [A(j+1:k-1,j),A(k,j+1:k-1)] = swap_(A(j+1:k-1,j),A(k,j+1:k-1));
                    [A(k+1:n,j),A(k+1:n,k)] = swap_(A(k+1:n,j),A(k+1:n,k));
                    [A(j,j),A(k,k)] = swap_(A(j,j),A(k,k));
                    [p(j),p(k)] = swap_(p(j),p(k));
                end
                if (abs(A(j,j)) > tol)
                    g1(j+1:m) = A(j+1:m,j)/A(j,j);   %Gauss elimination vector
                    for i=j+1:n
                        A(i:m,i) = A(i:m,i) - A(i,j)*g1(i:m);
                    end
                    A(j+1:m,j) = g1(j+1:m);                %l
                end
                j = j + 1;
            else                %2x2 pivot
                if (j < l)
                    [A(j,1:j-1),A(l,1:j-1)] = swap_(A(j,1:j-1),A(l,1:j-1));
                    [A(j+1:l-1,j),A(l,j+1:l-1)] = swap_(A(j+1:l-1,j),A(l,j+1:l-1));
                    [A(l+1:n,j),A(l+1:n,l)] = swap_(A(l+1:n,j),A(l+1:n,l));
                    [A(j,j),A(l,l)] = swap_(A(j,j),A(l,l));
                    [p(j),p(l)] = swap_(p(j),p(l));
                end
                if (j+1 < k)
                    [A(j+1,1:j),A(k,1:j)] = swap_(A(j+1,1:j),A(k,1:j));
                    [A(j+2:k-1,j+1),A(k,j+2:k-1)] = swap_(A(j+2:k-1,j+1),A(k,j+2:k-1));
                    [A(k+1:n,j+1),A(k+1:n,k)] = swap_(A(k+1:n,j+1),A(k+1:n,k));
                    [A(j+1,j+1),A(k,k)] = swap_(A(j+1,j+1),A(k,k));
                    [p(j+1),p(k)] = swap_(p(j+1),p(k));
                end
                E = A(j:j+1,j:j+1);  E(1,2) = E(2,1);
                d = E(1,1)*E(2,2) - E(1,2)*E(2,1);                %=det(E)
                if (abs(d) > tol2)
                    E = [E(2,2),-E(1,2); -E(2,1), E(1,1)]/d;  %=inv(E)
                    g2(j+2:m,:) = A(j+2:m,j:j+1)*E;
                    for i=j+2:m
                        A(i:m,i) = A(i:m,i) - A(i,j)*g2(i:m,1) - A(i,j+1)*g2(i:m,2);
                    end
                    A(j+2:m,j:j+1) = g2(j+2:m,:);    %l
                end
                j = j + 2;
            end
        end
    end
```

The driver LBLt_ calls LBLtByBunch_ and then handles the output according to format='short' or format='long'.

Algorithm 2.18

P*A*P'=L*B*L', L lower triangle, B block diagonal.

```
function [L,B,p] = LBLt_(A,pivot,tol,format,f1st,last,ib,p)

[m,n] = size(A);

[A,ib,p] = LBLtByBunch_(A,pivot,tol,f1st,last,ib,p);
if (last<n && ib(last+1)==2) last = last + 1; end

L = eye(m);   B = [zeros(m,1),diag(A),zeros(m,1)];   j = 1;
while (j <= last)
    if (ib(j) == 1)
        L(j+1:m,j) = A(j+1:m,j);   j = j+1;
    else
        L(j+2:m,j:j+1) = A(j+2:m,j:j+1);   B(j+1,1) = A(j+1,j);
B(j,3) = B(j+1,1); j = j+2;
    end
end

if (strcmp(format,'long') || last<m)
    B = band2full_(B,1,1,m,n);   p = pv2pm_(p);
    for j=last+1:n
        B(j:m,j) = A(j:m,j);   B(j,j:n) = B(j:m,j)';
    end
elseif(strcmp(format,'short'))
    tol = tol*max(1.0,norm(B(:,2),inf));
    for j=last:-1:1
        if (max(abs(B(j,1)),abs(B(j,2))) > tol) break; end
    end
    if (j < last) L = L(:,1:j);   B = B(1:j,:); end
end
```

The following two examples demonstrate the use of the LBLt algorithms.

Example 1 shows that LBLt decomposition can be safely calculated where LDLt decomposition failed.

```
>> A=randn(5);   A=A+A';
>> [L,D,p]=LDLt_(A,'gauss',1,100*eps,'short',1,2);
>> D(3,3)=0;   D(4,4) = 0;   D(5,5) = 0;
>> A=L*D*L';      %One way creating a matrix that may have no LDLt decomposition
>> [L,D,p]=LDLt_(A,'gauss',1,100*eps,'short')
??? Error using ==> LDLtByGauss_ at 36
LDLtByGauss_: Zero pivot. Use pivot=1 or LTLt_, LBLt_.

Error in ==> LDLt_ at 29
    [A,p] = LDLtByGauss_(A,pivot,tol,f1st,last,p);

>> [L,B,p]=LBLt_(A,1,100*eps,'long')    %No permutation in this example.
L =                                      %P output suppressed for brevity.
     1.0000         0         0         0         0
     1.4691    1.0000         0         0         0
     0.0400   -0.1882    1.0000         0         0
    -0.9856   -0.4753         0    1.0000         0
    -0.5054   -0.4064    0.8376   -0.4994    1.0000
```

```
B =
     2.6375          0          0          0          0
          0    -6.3494          0          0          0
          0          0          0     1.3521          0
          0          0     1.3521          0          0
          0          0          0          0     1.1311
>> norm(L*B*L'-A)
= 4.4409e-016
```

Example 2 shows the restart and partial LBLt decomposition, using the same matrix A in Example 1.

```
>> [A1,ib,p]=LBLtByBunch_(A,1,100*eps,1,1);
>> [L,B]=LBLt_(A1,1,100*eps,'long',2,2)    %No permutation in this example.
L =                                        %P output suppressed for brevity.
     1.0000          0          0          0          0
     1.4691     1.0000          0          0          0
     0.0400    -0.1882     1.0000          0          0
    -0.5054    -0.4064          0     1.0000          0
    -0.9856    -0.4753          0          0     1.0000
B =
     2.6375          0          0          0          0
          0    -6.3494          0          0          0
          0          0          0    -0.6752     1.3521
          0          0    -0.6752          0     1.1326
          0          0     1.3521     1.1326          0
>> norm(L*B*L'-A)
=        0
```

2.4.5 MODIFIED CHOLESKY DECOMPOSITION (xLLt)

When $\mathbf{A}$ is symmetric but positive indefinite, $\mathbf{PAP}' = \mathbf{LL}'$ does not exist. But choosing a minimal diagonal $\mathbf{E} \geq \mathbf{0}$, $\mathbf{A} + \mathbf{E}$ can become positive definite. Then $\mathbf{P}(\mathbf{A} + \mathbf{E})\mathbf{P}' = \mathbf{LL}'$ is valid. The objective is to choose $\mathbf{E} \geq \mathbf{0}$ as small as possible to make $\mathbf{A} + \mathbf{E}$ positive definite. The algorithms for such a problem are commonly known as the modified Cholesky decomposition. Here, we name it xLLt decomposition to be compatible with other algorithms. The applications of such algorithms can be found in quadratic optimization problems, where a decent direction is found from a Newton step using a modified Hessian matrix. If the Hessian matrix is not positive definite, the direction from the Newton step can be non-decent. Using the algorithm of the modified Cholesky decomposition of the positive indefinite Hessian matrix, a decent direction of the function can be found.

If $\mathbf{E}$ is not restricted to be diagonal, the least possible $\mathbf{E}$ can be found by an eigenvalue analysis of $\mathbf{A}$, $\mathbf{AV} = \mathbf{V\Lambda}$. Because $\mathbf{A} = \mathbf{A}'$, all the eigenvalues are real. The eigenvalues are ordered as $\lambda_1 \leq \lambda_2 \cdots \leq \lambda_k < \lambda_{k+1} \cdots \leq \lambda_n$, where we assume $\lambda_1 < 0, \lambda_2 < 0, \ldots, \lambda_k < 0$. Then $\mathbf{E} = \mathbf{V}(:, 1 : k)\operatorname{diag}(|\lambda_1| + \delta, |\lambda_2| + \delta, \ldots, |\lambda_k| + \delta)\mathbf{V}(:, 1 : k)'$ is the least possible in terms of magnitude of components to render $\mathbf{A} + \mathbf{E}$ positive definite, where $\delta > 0$ is a tolerance for zeros. If $\mathbf{E}$ is restricted to be diagonal, $\mathbf{E} = (|\lambda_1| + \delta)\mathbf{I}$ can make $\mathbf{A} + \mathbf{E}$ positive definite. It is larger than the previous $\mathbf{E}$ in the sense that it is not necessarily large in the eigen directions other than $\mathbf{V}(:, 1)$. However, in any modified Cholesky decomposition algorithms, we have an extra requirement—the calculation of $\mathbf{E}$ should be a small multiple of n^2 operations in the overall Cholesky decomposition of $\frac{n^3}{3}$ operations. An eigenvalue analysis to find the λ_1 is usually 4 times slower than a Cholesky decomposition, which effectively excludes the eigenvalue analysis in an efficient implementation of any modified Cholesky decompositions.

The algorithm presented in this subsection is based on an improvement by Schnabel and Eskow [57] over the algorithm of Gill and Murray [47], and further revised by Schnabel and Eskow [58]. Again we take a 5×5 symmetric matrix $\mathbf{A}$ for a short exposition. To start, we assume $\mathbf{A}$ is positive definite. We find a permutation matrix $\mathbf{P}_1$ and perform $\mathbf{P}_1 \mathbf{A} \mathbf{P}_1' \Rightarrow \mathbf{A}$ so that $A_{11} = \max_{1 \le i \le 5}(A_{ii})$. If $A_{11} > 0$, we tentatively take a Cholesky decomposition step. According to LDLt decomposition, at the end of first Cholesky step, $\mathbf{A}(2:5, 2:5)$ will take the values of $\mathbf{A}(2:5, 2:5) - [\mathbf{A}(2:5, 1)\mathbf{A}(2:5, 1)']/A_{11}$. But this step is tentative, we do not calculate the whole $\mathbf{A}(2:5, 2:5)$ but only the diagonal part of $\mathbf{A}(2:5, 2:5)$. If all of the them are positive, $E_1 = 0$ and we will calculate the whole $\mathbf{A}(2:5, 2:5)$ and finish the first xLLt decomposition step. Otherwise, although $A_{11} > 0$, $\mathbf{A}$ is still positive indefinite. On the other hand if $A_{11} <= 0$, we immediately know $\mathbf{A}$ is positive indefinite. In case $\mathbf{A}$ is positive indefinite, we determine a large enough $E_1 > 0$ and add it to A_{11}. We can then safely take a Cholesky decomposition step with the pivot $A_{11} + E_1$, so that $\mathbf{A}(2:5, 2:5) - [\mathbf{A}(2:5, 1)\mathbf{A}(2:5, 1)']/(A_{11} + E_1) \Rightarrow \mathbf{A}(2:5, 2:5)$. Now we repeat the above steps to $\mathbf{A}(j:5, j:5), j = 2, 3, 4$. At any stage j, if $\mathbf{A}$ is found to be positive indefinite, the tentative Cholesky decomposition step with the pivot A_{jj} ($E_j = 0$) is skipped and goes directly to determine $E_j > 0$ and finish the Cholesky decomposition step with the pivot $A_{jj} + E_j$ ($E_j > 0$). If $\mathbf{A}$ is numerically positive definite, the result given by the xLLt algorithm is same as that given by the LLt algorithm. If $\mathbf{A}$ is found to be positive indefinite at the stage j, the question is to determine the right amount of E_j. For this purpose, we can use the Gerschgorin circle theorem [29] to estimate the smallest eigenvalues of $\mathbf{A}(j:5, j:5)$. It is proven in [57] that choosing $E_j = \max\left(0, \|\mathbf{A}(j+1:5, j)\|_\infty - A_{jj}\right)$ causes the Gerschgorin circles contract for $j = 1 \ldots, 4$. Therefore, this choice of E_j is enough to make sure $\mathbf{A} + \mathbf{E}$ is positive semi-definite. E_j is chosen a little bit larger for other considerations: to make sure $\mathbf{A} + \mathbf{E}$ is positive definite and its conditioning is not too bad. These details are controlled by the input argument tol to the MATLAB code xLLt_. The default value suggested by Schnabel and Eskow for tol is $\epsilon^{\frac{1}{3}}$.

In the MATLAB code xLLt_ listed below, algo='GAUSS0' is the ordinary LLt decomposition by Gauss elimination, which performs no permutations and fails if the input matrix is not positive definite. algo='GAUSS1' is also the ordinary LLt decomposition, which performs diagonal pivoting and is valid if the input matrix is positive semi-definite but fails if the input matrix is positive indefinite. algo='SCHNABEL1' is the algorithm by Schnabel and Eskow discussed in the last paragraph. In this algorithm, initially it tentatively tries $E_j = 0$ but switches to $E_j > 0$ immediately if it confirms the input matrix is positive indefinite. The phase corresponding to $E_j > 0$ corresponds to algo='SCHNABEL2'. Internally the algorithm does the switch from algo='SCHNABEL1' to algo='SCHNABEL2' if it confirms the input matrix is positive indefinite. algo='SCHNABEL2' can also be set from the very start in the input. If algo='SCHNABEL2' is set in the input, the code will not try the tentative Cholesky decomposition with $E_j = 0$ at the beginning. Therefore, the code for algo='SCHNABEL2' set in the input is similar to the algorithm by Gill and Murray [47], except that the determination of E_j is by Schnabel and Eskow. In xLLt_ listed below, there is a difference in the part of the code corresponding to algo='SCHNABEL2' to the algorithm by Schnabel and Eskow. In [57], the lower bounds of Gerschgorin circles are calculated and then updated for all the steps corresponding to algo='SCHNABEL2' and the symmetric row and column switching is made according to the maximum of lower Gerschgorin bounds. In xLLt_, these parts of the codes are commented out. The symmetric row and column switching is based on the maximum of the diagonals, which is same to algo='GAUSS1'. It is found that the two kinds of pivoting have little differences in terms of the bounds of $\mathbf{E}$ and conditioning of $\mathbf{L}$. If the pivoting based on the maximum diagonals is adopted, the calculation of the Gerschgorin lower bounds can be avoided.

Algorithm 2.19

P*(A+E)*P'=L*L', L lower triangle, E diagonal, P permutation.

```
%function [A,p,e] = xLLt_(A,algo,tol,format)
%P*(A+diag(e))*P'=L*L',A=A'. L=tril, e>=0,diagonal. L write tril(A).
%algo='gauss0': No permutation, e=0. A>0. If ~(A>0), exits. Normal Cholesky.
%algo='gauss1': L(i,i)=max(A(j,j)),j=1...n, e=0. A>=0. If ~(A>=0), exits.
%algo='schnabel1': Try algo=lll first, if find A<=0, switch to 'schnabel2'.
%algo='schnabel2': If A<=0, adding e>=0.
function [A,p,e] = xLLt_(A,algo,tol,format)

[m,n] = size(A);
if (m ~= n) error('xLLt_(A):_A_must_be_symmetric.'); end
if (~exist('algo','var') || isempty(algo)) algo = 'schnabel1'; end
if (~exist('tol','var') || isempty(tol)) tol = eps^(1.0/3.0); end
if (~exist('format','var') || isempty(format)) format = 'short'; end
algo = upper(algo);   tolbar = tol*tol;   mu = 100*tol;   p = 1:m;   e = zeros(1,m);

if (strcmp(algo,'SCHNABEL1') || strcmp(algo,'SCHNABEL2'))
    k = argmax_(diag(A),1);          %|A(k,k)| max
    gamma = abs(A(k,k));
    tolgamma = tol*gamma;   tolbargamma = tolbar*gamma;   mugamma = mu*gamma;
    k = argmax_(diag(A),1,1);        %A(k,k) max
    if (A(k,k) <= 0.0)  algo = 'SCHNABEL2'; end
%   g = zeros(m,1);        %Gerschgorin lower bound
end
if (strcmp(algo,'SCHNABEL2'))
%    for i=1:m            %Gerschgorin lower bound
%        g(i) = A(i,i);
%        for j=1:i-1 g(i) = g(i) - abs(A(i,j)); end
%        for j=i+1:m g(i) = g(i) - abs(A(j,i)); end
%    end
end


for j=1:m
    if (strcmp(algo,'GAUSS0'))         %L*L' = A, if A>0.
        if (A(j,j) < tol) error('xLLt_:_!(A>0)._Use_other_algos'); end
    elseif (strcmp(algo,'GAUSS1'))    %L*L' = P*A*P', if A>=0
        k = argmax_(diag(A),j);
        if (A(k,k) < tol)
            if (norm(A(j:n,j)) < tol) continue;
            else                      error('xLLt_:_!(A>=0)._Use_other_algos'); end
        elseif(j ~= k)
            [A(j,1:j-1),A(k,1:j-1)] = swap_(A(j,1:j-1),A(k,1:j-1));
            [A(k+1:n,j),A(k+1:n,k)] = swap_(A(k+1:n,j),A(k+1:n,k));
            [A(j+1:k-1,j),A(k,j+1:k-1)] = swap_(A(j+1:k-1,j),A(k,j+1:k-1));
            [A(j,j),A(k,k)] = swap_(A(j,j),A(k,k));
            [p(j),p(k)] = swap_(p(j),p(k));
        end
    elseif (strcmp(algo, 'SCHNABEL1'))  %L*L'=P*(A+E)*P', A >= 0??
        k = argmax_(diag(A),j,1);  %A(k,k) max
        if (j ~= k)
            [A(j,1:j-1),A(k,1:j-1)] = swap_(A(j,1:j-1),A(k,1:j-1));
            [A(k+1:n,j),A(k+1:n,k)] = swap_(A(k+1:n,j),A(k+1:n,k));
            [A(j+1:k-1,j),A(k,j+1:k-1)] = swap_(A(j+1:k-1,j),A(k,j+1:k-1));
            [A(j,j),A(k,k)] = swap_(A(j,j),A(k,k));
            [p(j),p(k)] = swap_(p(j),p(k));
```

```
          end
          Aii = A(j,j);
          if (Aii > tolgamma)    %Aii=min(|A(i,i)|),i=j+1...n of next Cholesky step
              for i=j+1:n  Aii = min(Aii, A(i,i)-A(i,j)*A(i,j)/A(j,j));   end
          end
          if (A(j,j)<tolbargamma || Aii<-mugamma) %KEY: phase 2. Aii<0 in R1
              algo = 'SCHNABEL2';
%             for i=j:n          %Calculate Gerschgorin lower bound
%                 g(i) = A(i,i);
%                 for k=j:i-1 g(i) = g(i) - abs(A(i,k)); end
%                 for k=i+1:n g(i) = g(i) - abs(A(k,i)); end
%             end
          end
      end
      if (strcmp(algo,'SCHNABEL2')) %L*L'=P*(A+E)*P', ~(A>0 || A=0)!!
          ej = e(p(j));
          if (j > 1) ej = e(p(j-1)); end
          if (j < n-1)
%             k = argmax_(g,j,1);          %Schnabel: g(k)=max(g(i)),i=j...n
              k = argmax_(diag(A),j,1); %trh: A(k,k)=max(diag(A(j:n)))
              if (j ~= k)
                  [A(j,1:j-1),A(k,1:j-1)] = swap_(A(j,1:j-1),A(k,1:j-1));
                  [A(k+1:n,j),A(k+1:n,k)] = swap_(A(k+1:n,j),A(k+1:n,k));
                  [A(j+1:k-1,j),A(k,j+1:k-1)] = swap_(A(j+1:k-1,j),A(k,j+1:k-1));
                  [A(j,j),A(k,k)] = swap_(A(j,j),A(k,k));
                  [p(j),p(k)] = swap_(p(j),p(k));
%                 [g(j),g(k)] = swap_(g(j),g(k));
              end
              normaj = 0.0;
              for i=j+1:n  normaj = normaj + abs(A(i,j));   end
              e(p(j)) = max(0.0, max(ej,max(normaj,tolgamma)-A(j,j)));
              A(j,j) = A(j,j) + e(p(j));
%             r = 1.0 - normaj/A(j,j);    %update Gerschgorin lower bound
%             for i=j+1:n
%                 g(i) = g(i) + abs(A(i,j))*r;
%             end
          elseif(j == n-1)  %last 2x2 block
              a11 = A(j,j);    a21 = A(j+1,j);    a22 = A(j+1,j+1);
              t1 = a11 + a22;  t2 = a11 - a22;  t3 = sqrt(t2*t2 + 4.0*A(j+1,j)*A(j+1,j));
              lambda1 = 0.5*min(t1-t3, t1+t3);   lambda2 = 0.5*max(t1-t3, t1+t3);
              ej = max(0.0, max(ej, -lambda1+...
                  max(tol*(lambda2 -lambda1)/(1.0-tol),tolbargamma)));
              eta = 1.0 + 0.25*(a11-a22)*(a11-a22)/a21/a21;

              eta1 = min(0.5,0.9*eta);
              a = eta1 - 1.0;
              b = 2.0*eta1*a11 - a11 - a22;
              c = eta1*a11*a11 - a11*a22 + a21*a21;
              d = sqrt(b*b-4.0*a*c);
              if (b > 0.0) q = -0.5*(b+d);
              else         q = -0.5*(b-d); end
              delta1 = max(q/a,c/q);

              eta2 = min(2.00,0.9*eta);
              a = eta2 - 1.0;
              b = 2.0*eta2*a11 - a11 - a22;
              c = eta2*a11*a11 - a11*a22 + a21*a21;
```

```
          d = sqrt(b*b-4.0*a*c);
          if (b > 0.0) q = -0.5*(b+d);
          else         q = -0.5*(b-d); end
          delta2 = max(q/a,c/q);

          ej = max(ej,min(delta1,delta2));  e(p(j)) = ej;   e(p(j+1)) = ej;
          A(j,j) = sqrt(A(j,j)+e(p(j)));
          A(j+1,j) = A(j+1,j)/A(j,j);
          A(j+1,j+1) = A(j+1,j+1) - A(j+1,j)*A(j+1,j);
          A(j+1,j+1) = sqrt(A(j+1,j+1)+e(p(j+1)));
          break;
        else %if(j==n) last block
          e(p(j)) = -A(j,j) + max(-tol*A(j,j)/(1.0-tol),tolbargamma);
          A(j,j) = sqrt(A(j,j)+e(p(j)));
          break;
        end
    end   %algo='schnabel2'
    A(j,j) = sqrt(A(j,j));
    A(j+1:m,j) = A(j+1:m,j)/A(j,j);
    for i=j+1:n
        A(i:m,i) = A(i:m,i) - A(i,j)*A(i:m,j);
    end
end

A = tril(A);
if (strcmp(format,'long'))
    p = pv2pm_(p);
    if (~isempty(e)) e = diag(e); end
else  %if (strcmp(format,'short'))
    for i=n:-1:1
        if (norm(A(i:m,i)) > tol) break; end
    end
    if (i < n) A = A(:,1:i); end
end
```

The first example is taken from [57]. The result from xLLt_ is listed below.

```
>> A = [0.3571, -0.1030,  0.0274, -0.0459;
        -0.1030,  0.2525,  0.0736, -0.3845;
         0.0274,  0.0736,  0.2340, -0.2878;
        -0.0459, -0.3845, -0.2878,  0.5549];

>> [L,p,e]=xLLt_(A,'schnabel1',eps^0.333,'short')
L =
    0.8475        0         0         0
   -0.0542    0.7194        0         0
   -0.3396    0.0125    0.5309        0
   -0.4537   -0.1773   -0.1474    0.3959
p =
    4    1    3    2
e =
    0.1633    0.1633    0.1633    0.1633
```

If the original pivoting of Schnabel and Eskow is used, the same result to [57] is obtained.

```
>> [L,p,e]=xLLt_(A,'schnabel1',eps^0.333,'short')
L =
    0.5976        0         0         0
```

```
   -0.0768      0.8258            0            0
    0.0459     -0.3442       0.4964            0
   -0.1724     -0.4816      -0.1698       0.3083
p =
     1      4      3      2
e =
              0       0.1330       0.1330       0.1330
```

The second example is taken from [58]. The result from xLLt_ is listed below. It is same to the result obtained if the pivoting based on the maximum of the Gerschgorin lower bounds is used.

```
>> A=[1890.3,  -1705.6,  -315.8,   3000.3;
      -1705.6,   1538.3,   284.9,  -2706.6;
       -315.8,    284.9,    52.5,   -501.2;
       3000.3,  -2706.6,  -501.2,   4760.8];

>> [L,p,e]=xLLt_(A,'schnabel1',eps^0.333,'short')
L =
    68.9986            0            0            0
    -7.2639       0.3194            0            0
   -39.2269      -0.1289       0.5596            0
    43.4835       0.1905       0.2659       0.3957
p =
     4      3      2      1
e =
    0.7803       0.7803       0.3666            0

>> cond(L)
= 448.6459
>> norm(L*L'-pv2pm_(p)*(A+diag(e))*pv2pm_(p)')
= 9.0949e-013
```

2.5 SIMILARITY DECOMPOSITION ALGORITHMS

In this section, we will discuss the algorithms to transform a general square matrix $\mathbf{A}$ to an upper Hessenberg matrix $\mathbf{H}$ or a tri-diagonal matrix $\mathbf{T}$ by using similarity transformations. More numerically stable orthogonal alternatives are discussed in Section 3.6. The non-orthogonal similarity transformations have the advantage of numerical efficiency. There are two main applications of transforming a square matrix to an upper Hessenberg or a tri-diagonal. One is the iterative equation solution and other is the eigenvalue solution. Both topics will be covered in the subsequent chapters.

2.5.1 REDUCTION OF SQUARE MATRIX TO HESSENBERG BY GAUSS ELIMINATION

Given a square matrix, $\mathbf{A} \in \mathbb{R}^{n \times n}$, we want to find a lower triangular matrix $\mathbf{L}$ with 1s on the diagonal, an upper Hessenberg matrix $\mathbf{H}$, and permutation matrices $\mathbf{P}$ so that $\mathbf{PAP}' = \mathbf{LHL}^{-1}$. Following the adopted algorithms naming conventions, $\mathbf{PAP}' = \mathbf{LHL}^{-1}$ is named as LHLi decomposition.

The algorithm is based on the Gauss elimination, and therefore it is similar to LDU and LTLt algorithms discussed in Sections 2.2 and 2.4.3. The differences to LDU and LTLt algorithms are outlined below. We take a 5×5 matrix $\mathbf{A}$ as the example. Similarly to LTLt, in the first step, we find a permutation

$\mathbf{P}_1$ and apply $\mathbf{P}_1 \mathbf{A} \mathbf{P}_1' \Rightarrow \mathbf{A}$ so that $|A_{21}| = \|\mathbf{A}(2:5,1)\|_\infty$. Then we find a Gauss elimination matrix $\mathbf{L}_1 = \mathbf{I} + \mathbf{l}_1 \mathbf{I}(2,:)$ and apply $\mathbf{L}_1 \mathbf{A} \Rightarrow \mathbf{A}$ so that $\mathbf{A}(3:5,1) = \mathbf{0}$. To keep the similarity, we also need to apply $\mathbf{A} \mathbf{L}_1^{-1} \Rightarrow \mathbf{A}$. Because $\mathbf{L}_1^{-1} = \mathbf{I} - \mathbf{l}_1 \mathbf{I}(2,:)$, $\mathbf{A} \mathbf{L}_1^{-1}$ only changes the second column of $\mathbf{A}$, which is overwritten by $\mathbf{A}(:,2) - \mathbf{A}(:,3:5)\mathbf{l}_1$. The transformation to the original $\mathbf{A}$ by $\mathbf{L}_1 \mathbf{P}_1 \mathbf{A} \mathbf{P}_1' \mathbf{L}_1^{-1} \Rightarrow \mathbf{A}$ takes the following form:

$$\mathbf{A} = \begin{bmatrix} A_{11} & A_{12} & A_{13} & A_{14} & A_{15} \\ A_{21} & A_{22} & A_{32} & A_{42} & A_{52} \\ 0 & A_{32} & A_{33} & A_{43} & A_{53} \\ 0 & A_{42} & A_{43} & A_{44} & A_{54} \\ 0 & A_{52} & A_{53} & A_{54} & A_{55} \end{bmatrix}.$$

The Gauss vector $\mathbf{l}_1$ can be saved to $\mathbf{A}(3:5,1)$. The calculation of $\mathbf{A}\mathbf{L}_1^{-1}$ tells us why an upper Hessenberg matrix is the simplest form which can be obtained by such an algorithm. Should we aim to zero $\mathbf{A}(2:5,1)$ with a Gauss elimination matrix $\mathbf{S}_1 = \mathbf{I} + \mathbf{s}_1 \mathbf{I}(1,:)$, $\mathbf{A}\mathbf{S}_1^{-1}$ immediately sets the zeroed $\mathbf{A}(2:5,1)$ to nonzeros.

To continue the algorithm, the same three steps, permutation, pre-multiplication by a Gauss elimination matrix, and post-multiplication by the inverse of the Gauss elimination matrix, are applied to the columns 2 and 3 of $\mathbf{A}$. For column 2, the aim is to zero $\mathbf{A}(4:5,2)$. For column 3, only $A(5,3)$ needs to be zeroed. Then, $\mathbf{A}$ is transformed to an upper Hessenberg matrix. The product of $\mathbf{P}_3\mathbf{P}_2\mathbf{P}_1$ is $\mathbf{P}$. The product of $\mathbf{L}_1\mathbf{L}_2\mathbf{L}_3$ is $\mathbf{L}$, a lower triangular matrix with 1s on the diagonal. Because of the special structure of each Gauss elimination matrix, $\mathbf{L}$ can be simply read from the saved Gauss vectors in the zeroed part of $\mathbf{A}$. The inverse of $\mathbf{L}$ is the product of $\mathbf{L}_3^{-1}\mathbf{L}_2^{-1}\mathbf{L}_1^{-1}$. For the efficiency, the product is accumulated in the order shown by the parentheses $(((\mathbf{L}_3^{-1})\mathbf{L}_2^{-1})\mathbf{L}_1^{-1})$.

For a general $n \times n$ square matrix $\mathbf{A}$, the transformations discussed above are applied to the columns 1 to $n-2$ of $\mathbf{A}$. The algorithm can stop at any column $l \le n-2$ and restart from $l+1$. If the algorithm stops at column $l < n-2$, the final $n-l$ columns of the output $\mathbf{H}$ are not in the upper Hessenberg form. However, at any step of the algorithm $j \le l, l \le n-2$, the following identities hold

$$\mathbf{P}\mathbf{A}\mathbf{P}' = \mathbf{L}\mathbf{H}\mathbf{L}^{-1}, \tag{2.20a}$$

$$\mathbf{P}\mathbf{A}\mathbf{P}'\mathbf{L}(:,1:j) = \mathbf{L}(:,1:j)\mathbf{H}(1:j,1:j) + H(j+1,j)\mathbf{L}(:,j+1)\mathbf{I}(j,:), \quad j = 1 \cdots l. \tag{2.20b}$$

The algorithm is numerically stable in the same sense of the LU decomposition with partial pivoting.

The MATLAB code LHLiByGauss_.m implementing the algorithm is listed below, in which over half of the code is handling the output according to format.

Algorithm 2.20

```
P*A*P'=L*H*inv(L), H upper Hessenberg, L lower triangle, P permutation.
function [H,L,Li,p] = LHLiByGauss_(A,tol,format,f1st,last,p)

[m,n] = size(A);
tol = tol*max(1.0,norm(diag(A),inf));

H = A;   L = [];   Li = [];
for j=f1st:last
    k = argmax_(H(:,j),j+1);
    if (j+1 ~= k)       %switch rows and columns (j+1,k)
        [H(j+1,:),H(k,:)] = swap_(H(j+1,:),H(k,:));
```

```
            [H(:,j+1),H(:,k)] = swap_(H(:,j+1),H(:,k));
            [p(j+1),p(k)] = swap_(p(j+1),p(k));
        end
        if (abs(H(j+1,j)) > tol)
            g = H(j+2:m,j)/H(j+1,j);  %Gauss vector
            for k=j+1:n                        %A=L*A
                H(j+2:m,k) = H(j+2:m,k) - H(j+1,k)*g;
            end
            H(j+2:m,j) = g;                    %save g
            H(:,j+1) = H(:,j+1) + H(:,j+2:n)*g;  %A=A*inv(L)
        end
end

if (strcmp(format,'long') || strcmp(format,'short'))
    L = eye(m);  Li = eye(m);
    for j=last:-1:1      %backward accumulation of L and Li
        L(j+2:m,j+1) = H(j+2:m,j);
        for k=j+2:n Li(k,j+1) = -Li(k,j+2:k)*H(j+2:k,j); end
    end
end

if (strcmp(format,'long') || strcmp(format,'short') || strcmp(format,'brief'))
    for j=last:-1:1 H(j+2:m,j) = 0.0; end
end

if (strcmp(format,'long'))
    p = pv2pm_(p);
elseif (strcmp(format,'short'))  %remove 0s from H
    l = n;
    for j=n:-1:1
        if (j > last) l1 = last; l2 = n;
        else          l1 = j-1;  l2 = j+1; end
        if (l1 < 1) l1 = 1; end
        if (l2 > n) l2 = n; end
        if (norm(H(j,l1:l2)) < tol) l = l - 1;
        else                        break; end
    end
    if (l < n) H = H(1:l,:);  L = L(:,1:l); end
end
```

The usage of LHLiByGauss_.m is demonstrated with a few examples.

```
>> A=randn(5);
>> [H,L,Li,p]=LHLiByGauss_(A,100*eps,'short')
H =
   -1.0133   -1.6955   -1.4712    0.2573   -1.0776
   -1.5902    1.4908    1.9370    0.3269    0.7090
         0   -1.4702    0.0063   -0.0147   -1.0606
         0         0    3.3205   -0.8199    1.0717
         0         0         0   -0.3336    1.5540
L =          %1st column and 1st row of L is I(:,1) and I(1,:)
    1.0000         0         0         0         0
         0    1.0000         0         0         0
         0    0.4411    1.0000         0         0
         0   -0.2779   -0.8060    1.0000         0
         0    0.2184    0.6395   -0.0264    1.0000
```

```
Li =              %1st column and 1st row of Li is I(:,1) and I(1,:)
    1.0000        0        0        0        0
         0   1.0000        0        0        0
         0  -0.4411   1.0000        0        0
         0  -0.0776   0.8060   1.0000        0
         0   0.0617  -0.6182   0.0264   1.0000
p =
    1    4    5    3    2
```

The identities Eq. (2.20) are verified to the machine precision.

```
>> P=pv2pm_(p);
>> norm(P*A*P'-L*H*Li)
= 4.4025e-016
>> norm(P*A*P'*L(:,1:2)-L(:,1:2)*H(1:2,1:2)-H(3,2)*L(:,3)*[0,1])
= 3.8459e-016
>> norm(P*A*P'*L(:,1:4)-L(:,1:4)*H(1:4,1:4)-H(5,4)*L(:,5)*[0,0,0,1])
= 4.4002e-016
```

The partial LHLi decomposition and restart are demonstrated below. Note the differences in the input arguments.

```
>> [H,L,Li,p]=LHLiByGauss_(A,100*eps,'compact',1,1)  %format='compact' !
H =
   -1.0133   -1.6955    0.2289   -1.0776   -0.5975
   -1.5902    1.4908    0.3456    0.7090    1.7621
   -0.2779    1.1849   -0.7572    1.9265    1.4730
    0.2184   -0.9402   -0.2990    0.8474   -0.8666
    0.4411   -1.4702   -0.0427   -1.0606    0.6502
L =
    []
Li =
    []
p =
    1    4    3    2    5
>> [H,L,Li,p]=LHLiByGauss_(H,100*eps,'short',2,2,p)  %H and p of previous as input !
H =
   -1.0133   -1.6955   -1.4712   -1.0776    0.2289
   -1.5902    1.4908    1.9370    0.7090    0.3456
         0   -1.4702    0.0063   -1.0606   -0.0427
         0         0   -0.0877    1.5257   -0.2717
         0         0    3.3205    1.0717   -0.7916
L =
    1.0000        0        0        0        0
         0   1.0000        0        0        0
         0   0.4411   1.0000        0        0
         0   0.2184   0.6395   1.0000        0
         0  -0.2779  -0.8060        0   1.0000
Li =
    1.0000        0        0        0        0
         0   1.0000        0        0        0
         0  -0.4411   1.0000        0        0
         0   0.0637  -0.6395   1.0000        0
         0  -0.0776   0.8060        0   1.0000
p =
    1    4    5    2    3
```

2.5.2 REDUCTION OF SQUARE MATRIX TO TRI-DIAGONAL BY GAUSS ELIMINATION

In LHLi decomposition discussed in the last subsection, after $\mathbf{A}(3:5,1)$ is zeroed with $\mathbf{L}_1 \mathbf{AL}_1^{-1} \Rightarrow \mathbf{A}$, we move to column 2 to zero $\mathbf{A}(4:5,2)$. With such a scheme, an upper Hessenberg is the simplest form that can be obtained. However, for the first column of $\mathbf{A}$, after $\mathbf{L}_1 \mathbf{AL}_1^{-1} \Rightarrow \mathbf{A}$ is performed, we can find another Gauss elimination matrix $\mathbf{U}_1$ to eliminate $\mathbf{A}(1,3:5)$. To keep the similarity, the actual calculation is $\mathbf{U}_1^{-1} \mathbf{AU}_1 \Rightarrow \mathbf{A}$. As illustrated in LHLi decomposition, $\mathbf{AL}_1^{-1}$ preserves the zeros of $\mathbf{A}(3:5,1)$ set by $\mathbf{L}_1 \mathbf{A}$. Similarly $\mathbf{U}_1^{-1} \mathbf{A}$ preserves the zeros of $\mathbf{A}(1,3:5)$ set by $\mathbf{AU}_1$. For the following discussion about the limitation of the algorithm, we write the transformation discussed so far in the following:

$$\mathbf{L}_1 = \begin{bmatrix} 1 & 0 & 0 & 0 & 0 \\ 0 & 1 & 0 & 0 & 0 \\ 0 & -\frac{A_{31}}{A_{21}} & 1 & 0 & 0 \\ 0 & -\frac{A_{41}}{A_{21}} & 0 & 1 & 0 \\ 0 & -\frac{A_{51}}{A_{21}} & 0 & 0 & 1 \end{bmatrix}, \quad \mathbf{L}_1 \mathbf{AL}_1^{-1} = \mathbf{H} = \begin{bmatrix} A_{11} & H_{12} & H_{13} & H_{14} & H_{15} \\ A_{21} & H_{22} & H_{23} & H_{24} & H_{25} \\ 0 & H_{32} & H_{33} & H_{34} & H_{35} \\ 0 & H_{42} & H_{43} & H_{44} & H_{45} \\ 0 & H_{52} & H_{53} & H_{54} & H_{55} \end{bmatrix}, \tag{2.21a}$$

$$\mathbf{U}_1 = \begin{bmatrix} 1 & 0 & 0 & 0 & 0 \\ 0 & 1 & -\frac{H_{13}}{H_{12}} & -\frac{H_{14}}{H_{12}} & -\frac{H_{15}}{H_{12}} \\ 0 & 0 & 1 & 0 & 0 \\ 0 & 0 & 0 & 1 & 0 \\ 0 & 0 & 0 & 0 & 1 \end{bmatrix}, \quad \mathbf{U}_1^{-1} \mathbf{HU}_1 = \mathbf{T} = \begin{bmatrix} A_{11} & H_{12} & 0 & 0 & 0 \\ A_{21} & T_{22} & T_{32} & T_{42} & T_{52} \\ 0 & T_{32} & T_{33} & T_{43} & T_{53} \\ 0 & T_{42} & T_{43} & T_{44} & T_{54} \\ 0 & T_{52} & T_{53} & T_{54} & T_{55} \end{bmatrix}. \tag{2.21b}$$

The algorithm has a potential numerical breakdown. To explain the potential numerical breakdown, let us see how $\mathbf{T}$ is calculated,

$$\begin{bmatrix} A_{21} \\ 0 \\ 0 \\ 0 \end{bmatrix} = \mathbf{L}_1(2:5,2:5) \begin{bmatrix} A_{21} \\ A_{31} \\ A_{41} \\ A_{51} \end{bmatrix}, \tag{2.22a}$$

$$\begin{bmatrix} H_{12} & H_{13} & H_{14} & H_{15} \end{bmatrix} = \begin{bmatrix} A_{12} & A_{13} & A_{14} & A_{15} \end{bmatrix} \mathbf{L}_1^{-1}(2:5,2:5), \tag{2.22b}$$

$$\begin{bmatrix} H_{12} & 0 & 0 & 0 \end{bmatrix} = \begin{bmatrix} H_{12} & H_{13} & H_{14} & H_{15} \end{bmatrix} \mathbf{U}_1(2:5,2:5), \tag{2.22c}$$

$$\begin{bmatrix} A_{21} \\ 0 \\ 0 \\ 0 \end{bmatrix} = \mathbf{U}_1(2:5,2:5)^{-1} \begin{bmatrix} A_{21} \\ 0 \\ 0 \\ 0 \end{bmatrix}. \tag{2.22d}$$

From Eq. (2.22), we can see that $A_{21} H_{12} = \mathbf{A}(1,2:5)\mathbf{A}(2:5,1)$, i.e. the algorithm preserves the inner product of the first column and first row of $\mathbf{A}$. If $\mathbf{A}(1,2:5)\mathbf{A}(2:5,1) \neq 0$, we have $A_{21} \neq 0$ and $H_{12} \neq 0$. The two Gauss elimination matrices $\mathbf{L}_1$ and $\mathbf{U}_1$ can be calculated with A_{21} and H_{12} as pivots, respectively. If $\mathbf{A}(1,2:5)\mathbf{A}(2:5,1) = 0$, we have the following three situations.

1. $\mathbf{A}(1,2:5)\mathbf{A}(2:5,1) = 0$ and $\mathbf{A}(2:5,1) = \mathbf{0}$, then $\mathbf{L}_1 = \mathbf{I}$, the first column is skipped. $\mathbf{A}$ is deflated at A_{21}. $\mathbf{L}(:,1)$ is a right eigenvector of $\mathbf{A}$.

2. $\mathbf{A}(1,2:5)\mathbf{A}(2:5,1) = 0$ and $\mathbf{A}(1,2:5) = \mathbf{0}$, then $\mathbf{U}_1 = \mathbf{I}$, the first row is skipped. $\mathbf{A}$ is deflated at A_{12}. $\mathbf{U}(1,:)'$ is a left eigenvector of $\mathbf{A}$.

3. $\mathbf{A}(1,2:5)\mathbf{A}(2:5,1) = 0$, $\mathbf{A}(1,2:5) \neq \mathbf{0}$ and $\mathbf{A}(2:5,1) \neq \mathbf{0}$, we have either $A_{21} = 0$ or $H_{12} = 0$, i.e. we have zero pivot in $\mathbf{L}_1$ or zero pivot in $\mathbf{U}_1$. The algorithm breaks down.

When case 3 happens, a possible way to avoid it is to apply an arbitrary similarity transformation to $\mathbf{A}$, such as $\mathbf{NAN}^{-1}$. Then apply the algorithm to $\mathbf{NAN}^{-1}$, hoping the breakdown will not happen again.

Even if a numerical breakdown never happens due to the inevitable rounding errors, very large numbers are likely to appear in the product of $\mathbf{U}_1^{-1}\mathbf{L}_1$. There are several heuristic pivoting strategies to improve the numerical stability of the algorithm, see [26]. In the MATLAB implementation GTGiByGeist_.m presented in this subsection, a pivoting proposed in [26] is implemented. For the first column of $\mathbf{A}$, the pivoting is to choose $\mathbf{A}_{21}$ to minimize the maximum element in $\mathbf{U}_1^{-1}\mathbf{L}_1$.

To transform an $n \times n$ matrix $\mathbf{A}$ to a tri-diagonal, repeat the above process of pivoting and two similarity transformations for $n-2$ steps. At the step j, we choose $A(j+1,j)$ to minimize the maximum element in $\mathbf{U}_j^{-1}\mathbf{L}_j$, then apply $\mathbf{U}_j^{-1}\mathbf{L}_j\mathbf{P}_j\mathbf{A}\mathbf{P}_j'\mathbf{L}_j^{-1}\mathbf{U}_j$ to zero $\mathbf{A}(j+2:n,j)$ and $\mathbf{A}(j,j+2:n)$. After the step $n-2$ finishes, the transformed $\mathbf{A}$ becomes a tri-diagonal $\mathbf{T}$. We accumulate a permutation matrix $\mathbf{P} = \mathbf{P}_{n-2}\cdots\mathbf{P}_2\mathbf{P}_1$ matrix and a full matrix $\mathbf{G}$ according to the following equation:

$$\mathbf{G} = \left(\mathbf{P}_{n-2}\cdots\mathbf{P}_2\mathbf{L}_1^{-1}\mathbf{U}_1\mathbf{P}_2\cdots\mathbf{P}_{n-2}\right)$$
$$\left(\mathbf{P}_{n-2}\cdots\mathbf{P}_3\mathbf{L}_2^{-1}\mathbf{U}_2\mathbf{P}_3\cdots\mathbf{P}_{n-2}\right)\cdots$$
$$\mathbf{P}_{n-2}\mathbf{L}_{n-3}^{-1}\mathbf{U}_{n-3}\mathbf{P}_{n-2}\mathbf{L}_{n-2}^{-1}\mathbf{U}_{n-2}.$$

Then, we have the relation $\mathbf{PAP}' = \mathbf{GTG}^{-1}$. Following the adopted algorithm naming convention, the algorithm is named GTGi decomposition. If the algorithm stops at $l \leq n-2$, the block $\mathbf{T}(l+1:n,l+1:n)$ is still a full matrix. But the relation $\mathbf{PAP}' = \mathbf{GTG}^{-1}$ still holds. Further we have the following identities for $j = 1\cdots l, l \leq n-2$:

$$\mathbf{PAP}'\mathbf{G}(:,1:j) = \mathbf{G}(:,1:j)\mathbf{T}(1:j,1:j) + T(j+1,j)\mathbf{G}(:,j+1)\mathbf{I}(j,:), \tag{2.23a}$$
$$\mathbf{G}^{-1}(1:j,:)\mathbf{PAP}' = \mathbf{T}(1:j,1:j)\mathbf{G}^{-1}(1:j,:) + T(j,j+1)\mathbf{I}(:,j)\mathbf{G}^{-1}(j+1,:). \tag{2.23b}$$

In the following, we first list the MATLAB code arg2max_.m for the pivoting used in GTGiByGeist_.m.

Algorithm 2.21

Pivoting algorithm for GTGi decomposition.

```
%Choose a pivot (k) for inv(u)*l*A*inv(l)*u to minimize the maximum of l*u.
%l,u are Gauss matrices to eliminate v1(flst:m) and v2(flst:n).
function [k,vk1,vk2] = arg2max_(v1,v2,flst,tol)

if (exist('flst','var') == 0) flst = 1; end
[m1,n1] = size(v1); n1 = max(m1,n1);  n = n1;
[m2,n2] = size(v2); n2 = max(m1,n2);
if (n1 ~= n2) k =-1; vk1 = realmax; vk2 = realmax; return; end       %input error

k1 = argmax_(v1,flst);  vk1 = abs(v1(k1));   %vk1=max of abs(v1)
k2 = argmax_(v2,flst);  vk2 = abs(v2(k2));   %vk2=max of abs(v2)
```

```
if (vk1<tol && vk2<tol) k = k1; vk1 = 0.0;  vk2 = 0.0; return; end
if (vk1<vk2 && vk1<tol) k = k2; vk1 = 0.0; return; end
if (vk2<vk1 && vk2<tol) k = k1; vk2 = 0.0; return; end
v1v2 = v1(f1st:n)'*v2(f1st:n);
if (v1v2 == 0.0) k = n+1;  vk1 = realmax; vk2 = realmax; return; end %breakdown

vj1 = 0.0;  vj2 = 0.0;  vk = realmax;
for j=f1st:n
    v1j = abs(v1(j));  v2j = abs(v2(j));
    if (j~=k1 && vj1<v1j) vj1 = v1j; end      %vj1=2nd max of abs(v1)
    if (j~=k2 && vj2<v2j) vj2 = v2j; end      %vj2=2nd max of abs(v2)
end

for j=f1st:n
    if (j ~= k1) v1j = abs(vk1/v1(j));           %mc
    else         v1j = abs(vj1/v1(j)); end       %mc
    if (j ~= k2) v2j = abs(v1(j)*vk2/v1v2);      %mr
    else         v2j = abs(v1(j)*vj2/v1v2); end  %mr
    vj = abs(v1(j)*v2(j)/v1v2);                   %gamma
    vj = max(vj, max(v1j,v2j));
    if (vj < vk) vk = vj;  k = j; end            %vk=max of abs(l*u)
end
vk1 = vk;  vk2 = vk;
```

Now the MATLAB implementation of GTGi decomposition, `GTGiByGeist_`.m.

Algorithm 2.22

P*A*P'=G*T*inv(G), T tri-diagonal, G full matrix, P permutation.

```
function [T,G,Gi,p] = GTGiByGeist_(A,tol,format,f1st,last,p)

[m,n] = size(A);
tol = tol*max(1.0,norm(diag(A),inf));  %small number

T = A;  G = [];  Gi = [];
for j=f1st:last
    [k,vk1,vk2] = arg2max_(T(:,j),T(j,:)',j+1,tol);  %pivot to min(max(|lu|))
%   k=j+1;  vk1 = max(abs(T(k:n,j)));  vk2 = max(abs(T(j,k:n))); %no pivot
    if (k == n+1)            %improvement: auto recover
        error('GTGiByGeist_ failed. Do N*A*inv(N) and call GTGiByGauss_ again.');
    end
    if (k>0 && j+1~=k)            %switch rows and columns (j+1,k)
        [T(j+1,:), T(k,:)] = swap_(T(j+1,:), T(k,:));
        [T(:,j+1), T(:,k)] = swap_(T(:,j+1), T(:,k));
        [p(j+1), p(k)] = swap_(p(j+1), p(k));
    end
    if (vk1 > tol)
        g = T(j+2:m,j)/T(j+1,j);  %Gauss vector
        for k=j+1:n
            T(j+2:m,k) = T(j+2:m,k) - T(j+1,k)*g;        %T=l*T
        end
        T(j+2:m,j) = g;              %save g in zeroed T
        T(j:m,j+1) = T(j:m,j+1) + T(j:m,j+2:n)*g;        %T=T*inv(l)
    end
    if (vk2 > tol)
        g = T(j,j+2:m)/T(j,j+1);  %Gauss vector
        for k=j+1:n
```

```
                T(k,j+2:m) = T(k,j+2:m) - T(k,j+1)*g;          %T=T*u
          end
          T(j,j+2:m) = g;                 %save g in zeroed T
          T(j+1,j+1:m) = T(j+1,j+1:m) + g*T(j+2:m,j+1:n);  %T=inv(r)*T
     end
end

if (strcmp(format,'long') || strcmp(format,'short'))
     G = eye(m);  Gi = eye(m);
     for j=last:-1:1       %backward accumulation of G and Gi
          for k=j+1:n
               G(j+1,k) = G(j+1,k) - T(j,j+2:n)*G(j+2:m,k);
               Gi(k,j+2:m) = Gi(k,j+2:m) + T(j,j+2:n)*Gi(k,j+1);
               G(j+2:m,k) = G(j+2:m,k) + G(j+1,k)*T(j+2:m,j);
               Gi(k,j+1) = Gi(k,j+1) - T(j+2:m,j)'*Gi(k,j+2:m)';
          end
     end
end

if (strcmp(format,'long') || strcmp(format,'short') || strcmp(format,'brief'))
     for j=last:-1:1
          T(j+2:m,j) = 0.0;   T(j,j+2:n) = 0.0;
     end
end

if (strcmp(format,'long'))
     p = pv2pm_(p);
elseif (strcmp(format,'short'))  %remove 0s from T
     l = n;
     for j=n:-1:1
          if (j > last) l1 = last; l2 = n;
          else          l1 = j-1;  l2 = j+1; end
          if (l1 < 1) l1 = 1; end
          if (l2 > n) l2 = n; end
          if (norm(T(j,l1:l2)) < tol) l = l - 1;
          else                        break; end
     end
     if (l < n) T = T(1:l,1:l);  G = G(:,1:l);  Gi = Gi(1:l,:); end
     if (last == m-2) T = full2band_(T,1,1); end
end
```

The usage of GTGiByGeist_.m is very similar to LHLiByGauss_.m. One example demonstrates the partial decomposition and restart.

```
>> A=randn(5);
>> [T,G,Gi,p]=GTGiByGeist_(A,100*eps,'compact',1,2);   %format='compact' !
>> [T,G,Gi,p]=GTGiByGeist_(T,100*eps,'short',3,5,p)    %T,p of previous as input !
T =       % T in band format
          0    -1.6636    -0.8136
    -0.7036     2.4243    -5.4188
     1.9423    -3.7743    -0.3051
    -0.8549    -1.1061     0.5085
     1.7011    -1.3400          0
G =       %Note G(:,1)=I(:,1), G(1,:)=I(1,:)
     1.0000          0          0          0          0
          0     1.0000    -1.5285    -0.1795    -0.4439
          0     0.7693    -0.1758     0.0450    -0.4080
```

```
         0    -0.3992     0.3484     1.0237    -0.3237
         0     1.8954    -3.1881     0.3908    -0.2284
Gi =       %Note Gi(:,1)=I(:,1),  Gi(1,:)=I(1,:)
    1.0000        0          0          0          0
         0    -1.3184     1.5445    -0.4874     0.4937
         0    -0.7412     0.9497    -0.1609    -0.0283
         0    -0.9810     0.3062     0.5935     0.5183
         0    -2.2743     0.0855    -0.7842     1.0000
p =        %p in permutation vector
      1      2      4      3      5
```

2.5.3 REDUCTION OF SQUARE MATRIX TO TRI-DIAGONAL BY LANCZOS PROCEDURE

From the last subsection, we see that a GTGi decomposition of $\mathbf{A}$ can be written as $\mathbf{A} = \mathbf{P}'\mathbf{GTG}^{-1}\mathbf{P}$. Let $\mathbf{P}'\mathbf{G} \Rightarrow \mathbf{G}$. Then $\mathbf{A} = \mathbf{GTG}^{-1}$. Equivalently $\mathbf{AG} = \mathbf{GT}$ and $\mathbf{G}^{-1}\mathbf{A} = \mathbf{TG}^{-1}$. The Lanczos algorithm based on these two identities is another way to reduce a square matrix to tri-diagonal form. According to the classification of matrix algorithms of Section 1.4, the Lanczos algorithm is of multiplying nature.

Introducing some notations for $\mathbf{G}$, $\mathbf{G}^{-1}$, and $\mathbf{T}$, we write the two identities as follows, where $m = n-1$ and $l = n - 2$:

$$\mathbf{A}\left[\mathbf{g}_1,\mathbf{g}_2,\ldots,\mathbf{g}_n\right] = \left[\mathbf{g}_1,\mathbf{g}_2,\ldots,\mathbf{g}_n\right]\begin{bmatrix} T_{11} & T_{12} & 0 & 0 & \cdots & 0 \\ T_{21} & T_{22} & T_{23} & 0 & \cdots & 0 \\ 0 & T_{32} & T_{33} & T_{34} & \cdots & 0 \\ \vdots & \vdots & \vdots & \vdots & & \vdots \\ 0 & 0 & \cdots & T_{ml} & T_{mm} & T_{mn} \\ 0 & 0 & \cdots & 0 & T_{nm} & T_{nn} \end{bmatrix}, \qquad (2.24a)$$

$$\begin{bmatrix} \mathbf{q}'_1 \\ \mathbf{q}'_2 \\ \vdots \\ \mathbf{q}'_n \end{bmatrix}\mathbf{A} = \begin{bmatrix} T_{11} & T_{12} & 0 & 0 & \cdots & 0 \\ T_{21} & T_{22} & T_{23} & 0 & \cdots & 0 \\ 0 & T_{32} & T_{33} & T_{34} & \cdots & 0 \\ \vdots & \vdots & \vdots & \vdots & \vdots & \vdots \\ 0 & 0 & \cdots & T_{ml} & T_{mm} & T_{mn} \\ 0 & 0 & \cdots & 0 & T_{nm} & T_{nn} \end{bmatrix}\begin{bmatrix} \mathbf{q}'_1 \\ \mathbf{q}'_2 \\ \vdots \\ \mathbf{q}'_n \end{bmatrix}. \qquad (2.24b)$$

$$\mathbf{q}'_i\mathbf{g}_j = I_{ij}, \quad i,j = 1\ldots,n \qquad (2.24c)$$

Compare the first column of Eq. (2.24a) and the first row of Eq. (2.24b),

$$\mathbf{A}\mathbf{g}_1 = T_{11}\mathbf{g}_1 + T_{21}\mathbf{g}_2, \qquad (2.25a)$$

$$\mathbf{q}'_1\mathbf{A} = T_{11}\mathbf{q}'_1 + T_{12}\mathbf{q}'_2. \qquad (2.25b)$$

Suppose we choose two arbitrary vectors $\mathbf{g}_1$ and $\mathbf{q}_1$ satisfying $\mathbf{q}'_1\mathbf{g}_1 = 1$. Then, we use $\mathbf{q}_1$ to pre-multiply Eq. (2.25a) or use $\mathbf{g}_1$ to post-multiply Eq. (2.25b), we obtain T_{11} as follows:

$$T_{11} = \mathbf{q}'_1\mathbf{A}\mathbf{g}_1. \qquad (2.26)$$

After T_{11} is determined, we write Eq. (2.25a) and Eq. (2.25b) as follows:

$$T_{21}\mathbf{g}_2 = \mathbf{c} = \mathbf{A}\mathbf{g}_1 - T_{11}\mathbf{g}_1, \qquad T_{12}\mathbf{q}'_2 = \mathbf{r}' = \mathbf{q}'_1\mathbf{A} - T_{11}\mathbf{q}'_1. \qquad (2.27)$$

Because we require $\mathbf{q}'_2\mathbf{g}_2 = 1$, from Eq. (2.27), we have $T_{21}T_{12} = \mathbf{r}'\mathbf{c}$. The condition of $T_{21}T_{12} = \mathbf{r}'\mathbf{c} = 0$ needs a lot of attention. It can happen in three situations.

1. $\mathbf{r}'\mathbf{c} = 0$ and $\mathbf{c} = \mathbf{0}$. $T_{21} = 0$ and choose any $\mathbf{g}_2$ which satisfies $\mathbf{q}'_1\mathbf{g}_2 = 0$ and $\mathbf{q}'_2\mathbf{g}_2 = 1$.

2. $\mathbf{r}'\mathbf{c} = 0$ and $\mathbf{r} = \mathbf{0}$. $T_{12} = 0$ and choose any $\mathbf{q}_2$ which satisfies $\mathbf{q}'_2\mathbf{g}_1 = 0$ and $\mathbf{q}'_2\mathbf{g}_2 = 1$.

3. $\mathbf{r}'\mathbf{c} = 0$, $\mathbf{r} \neq \mathbf{0}$ and $\mathbf{c} \neq \mathbf{0}$. The three equations of Eqs.(2.27) cannot hold at the same time. The algorithm breaks down.

This problem is exactly same to the numerical break down discussed in the last subsection. Possible ways to avoid it include choosing a different $\mathbf{g}_1$ and $\mathbf{q}_1$ to start, applying an arbitrary similarity transformation to $\mathbf{A}$ to start, and the block tri-diagonal Lanczos algorithm discussed in page 505 of [29]. In the following, we consider the case $\mathbf{r}'\mathbf{c} \neq 0$. To determine T_{21} and T_{12}, we need to supply an arbitrary condition between T_{21} and T_{12}. The possible choices are

$$T_{21} = A_{21}, \qquad T_{21} = 1, \qquad T_{21} = \|\mathbf{c}\|, \qquad T_{21} = \sqrt{|\mathbf{r}'\mathbf{c}|}, \cdots \tag{2.28a}$$

$$T_{12} = \frac{\mathbf{r}'\mathbf{c}}{T_{21}}. \tag{2.28b}$$

After T_{21} and T_{12} are determined, $\mathbf{g}_2$ and $\mathbf{q}'_2$ are simply calculated by Eq. (2.27). Following the same procedure, upon supplying supplementary conditions like Eq. (2.28), for $j = 2 \cdots n - 1, k = j + 1$, we determine $T_{jj}, T_{kj}, T_{jk}, \mathbf{g}_k, \mathbf{q}'_k$ from the following relations:

$$T_{jj} = \mathbf{q}'_j\mathbf{A}\mathbf{g}_j, \tag{2.29a}$$

$$T_{kj}\mathbf{g}_k = \mathbf{c} = \mathbf{A}\mathbf{g}_j - T_{ij}\mathbf{g}_i - T_{jj}\mathbf{g}_j, \tag{2.29b}$$

$$T_{jk}\mathbf{q}'_k = \mathbf{r}' = \mathbf{q}'_j\mathbf{A} - T_{ji}\mathbf{q}'_i - T_{jj}\mathbf{q}'_j. \tag{2.29c}$$

Finally from the last column of Eq. (2.24a) or the last row of Eq. (2.24b), we obtain $T_{nn} = \mathbf{q}'_n\mathbf{A}\mathbf{g}_n$. The GTGi decomposition by the Lanczos algorithm satisfies Eq. (2.23). We can see that the property is the result of the construction by Eqs. (2.27) and (2.29).

From the discussions made so far, we see that $\mathbf{A} = \mathbf{GTG}^{-1}$ exists but $\mathbf{G}$ and $\mathbf{T}$ are not unique. The non-uniqueness of $\mathbf{G}$ and $\mathbf{T}$ is due to the arbitrary choice of $\mathbf{g}_1$ and $\mathbf{q}_1$ and the arbitrary choice of the supplementary relation between T_{jk} and T_{kj}, see Eq. (2.28). Especially Eq. (2.28) shows that the claim made in [26] that the form of $\mathbf{GTG}^{-1}$ is unique once the first column and row of $\mathbf{G}$ are fixed is wrong. The question of making better choices to improve the numerical stability of the Lanczos algorithm and avoid the numerical break down remains unanswered.

Differently from other matrix decomposition algorithms presented so far, the input matrix $\mathbf{A}$ is not altered by the algorithm. $\mathbf{A}$ is used repeatedly by the algorithm to calculate $\mathbf{Ag}$ and $\mathbf{q}'\mathbf{A}$. Special algorithms to calculate $\mathbf{Ag}$ and $\mathbf{q}'\mathbf{A}$, for example, the matrix–vector product algorithms for band matrix and sparse matrix, can be considered in the algorithm. Furthermore, $\mathbf{A}$ is not necessary to be explicitly given. Any linear transformation, for example, a factored form of matrices and inverse matrices can be used instead of an ordinary full matrix. To be consistent with the input of an ordinary full matrix, in GTGiByLanczos_.m, the special matrix–vector product algorithm for the band or sparse matrix and the general linear transformation is compacted to a cell argument and passed to the first input argument A. The use of GTGiByLanczos_.m is demonstrated with examples.

Algorithm 2.23

A=G*T*inv(G), T tri-diagonal, G full matrix.

```
function [T,G,Gi] = GTGiByLanczos_(A,tol,flst,last,T,G,Gi)

[m,n] = size_(A);
if (m ~= n) error('GTGiByLanczos_:_Input_matrix_must_be_square.'); end
if (k+1 >= n) l = n - k; end
if (flst == 1)
    pg = Gi(1,:)*G(:,1);
    if (abs(pg) < tol)
        normq = norm(G(:,1));
        if (normq > eps) G(:,1) = G(:,1)/normq;  pg = pg/normq; end
        while(abs(pg) < tol) Gi(1,:) = randn(1,m); pg = Gi(1,:)*G(:,1); end
    end
    if (pg < 0) pg = -pg;  Gi(1,:) =-Gi(1,:); end
    pg = sqrt(pg);  G(:,1) = G(:,1)/pg;  Gi(1,:) = Gi(1,:)/pg;
    T = zeros(l+1,3);  G = [G(:,1),zeros(m,l)];  Gi = [Gi(1,:);zeros(l,n)];
    alpha0 = 0.0;  beta0 = 0.0;  g0 = zeros(m,1);  p0 = zeros(1,n);
else
    T = [T;zeros(l,3)];  G = [G,zeros(m,l)];  Gi = [Gi;zeros(l,n)];
    alpha0 = T(flst-1,3); beta0 = T(flst,1);  g0 = G(:,flst-1); p0 = Gi(flst-1,:);
end

for j=flst:last
    g = G(:,j);  p = Gi(j,:);
    Ag = Ay_(A,g,'right');  pA = Ay_(A,p,'left');      %Ag=A*g,  pA=p*A
    T(j,2) = p*Ag;
    g1 = Ag - alpha0*g0 - T(j,2)*g;  p1 = pA - beta0*p0  - T(j,2)*p;  pg = p1*g1;
    if (j == n)
        break;
    elseif(abs(pg) > tol)
        T(j+1,1) = sqrt(abs(pg));    T(j,3) = pg/T(j+1,1);  %T(j+1,j)*T(j,3)=1!!
        g1 = g1/T(j+1,1);  p1 = p1/T(j,3);
    elseif(norm(g1)>tol && norm(p1)<tol)
        T(j+1,1) = 1.0;
        p1 = orthogonal_(G(:,1:j),[],Gi(1:j,:)')';    p1 = p1/(p1*g1);
    elseif(norm(g1)<tol && norm(p1)>tol)
        T(j,3) = 1.0;
        g1 = orthogonal_(Gi(1:j,:)',[],G(:,1:j));     g1 = g1/(p1*g1);
    elseif(norm(g1)<tol && norm(p1)<tol)
        g1 = orthogonal_(Gi(1:j,:)',[],G(:,1:j));
        p1 = orthogonal_(G(:,1:j),[],Gi(1:j,:)')';    p1 = p1/(p1*g1);
    else %if(norm(g1)>tol & norm(p1)>tol & pg<tol) %Improvement here!
        error('GTGiByLanczos__failed._Choose_a_different_g_and_p_to_start.');
    end
    G(:,j+1) = g1;  Gi(j+1,:) = p1;
    g0 = g;  p0 = p;   alpha0 = T(j,3);  beta0  = T(j+1,1);
end
```

If the initial g_1 and q_1 are not input, GTGiByLanczos_.m generates random vectors for g_1 and q_1. This leads to different results from multiple runs of GTGiByLanczos_.m, which clearly shows the non-uniqueness of GTGi decompositions. The following is the output from two runs of GTGiByLanczos_.m for a same matrix.

```
>> A=randn(4);
>> [T,G,Gi]=GTGiByLanczos_(A,100*eps)        >> [T,G,Gi]=GTGiByLanczos_(A,100*eps)
T =                                          T =
        0     -3.2635    -4.5581                     0      6.4170    -3.0044
   4.5581      6.1947    -0.7888                 3.0044      5.6112    -7.5466
   0.7888      0.8608    -0.1262                 7.5466     -8.1420     0.0755
   0.1262      0.4422          0                 0.0755      0.3479          0
G =                                          G =
   0.5081      0.4651     0.2637     1.2603      -1.4728     1.9788    -1.3913     0.4103
  -0.6081     -1.0050     0.4523     0.0756       2.6578    -4.2709     3.1625     0.2151
  -0.6826     -0.7860     0.9935    -0.5558      -2.0384     2.1745    -1.4035    -0.0402
  -0.8875     -0.6841     0.0432     0.2685      -0.1787    -0.4924     0.7258     0.0235
Gi =                                         Gi =
  -0.0388      1.7821    -0.7221    -1.8146       0.3540    -1.3094    -2.5766     1.4016
   0.3123     -2.2584     0.9003     1.0338       0.6816    -2.5563    -4.2038     4.3155
   0.5448     -0.4457     1.0739    -0.2087       0.4829    -2.0756    -3.4630     4.6508
   0.5799      0.2083    -0.2658     0.3937       2.0582     0.5898    -0.7171    -0.0113
```

In the following, we create a simple sparse matrix **A** and use it to demonstrate the use of `mtimesCSR_.m` to calculate the matrix–vector product in `GTGiByLanczos_.m`. To use `mtimesCSR_.m`, we convert **A** to CSR format.

```
>> A = [11,  0,  0,  14;
        21,  0, 23,   0;
         0,  0,  0,  34;
        41, 42,  0,   0];
>> [dA,rA,jA,m,n] = full2csr_(A);
```

We create a cell array **S** to store the non-homogenous data of the sparse matrix **A**. **S** is used as the first input argument to `GTGiByLanczos_`. The name of the function `mtimesCSR_.m` is passed to `GTGiByLanczos_` by the last input argument `Ax`. To compare the output results of `GTGiByLanczos_` in two ways of matrix–vector calculation, we use the same $g_1 = [1; 0; 0; 0]$ and $q_1 = g_1$ in both runs.

```
>> S = {'mtimesCSR_',{dA,rA,jA}};
>> g1=[1;0;0;0]; q1=g1';
```

The following is the output from the run of `GTGiByLanczos_` using two ways of matrix–vector product.

```
>> [T1,G1,Gi1]=GTGiByLanczos_(A,100*eps,1,4,[],g1,q1)        %A*g, q'*A
T1 =
        0     11.0000    23.9583
  23.9583     21.5122   -21.5122
  21.5122    -92.4841   -81.0171
  81.0171     70.9719          0
G1 =
   1.0000          0          0     0.0000
        0     0.8765    -0.8765     0.0000
        0          0     2.7047     3.0875
        0     1.7113     0.0000     0.0000
Gi1 =
   1.0000          0          0          0
        0          0          0     0.5843
        0    -1.1409          0     0.5843
        0     0.9994     0.3239    -0.5119
```

```
>> [T2,G2,Gi2]=GTGiByLanczos_(S,100*eps,1,4,[],g1,q1)    %mtimesCSR_
T2 =
         0    11.0000    23.9583
   23.9583    21.5122   -21.5122
   21.5122   -92.4841   -81.0171
   81.0171    70.9719          0
G2 =
    1.0000          0          0     0.0000
         0     0.8765    -0.8765     0.0000
         0          0     2.7047     3.0875
         0     1.7113     0.0000     0.0000
Gi2 =
    1.0000          0          0          0
         0          0          0     0.5843
         0    -1.1409          0     0.5843
         0     0.9994     0.3239    -0.5119
```

In `GTGiByLanczos_.m`, we choose $T_{j+1,j} = \sqrt{|\mathbf{r}'\mathbf{c}|}$. This leads to $T_{j+1,j} = \pm T_{j,j+1}$ in the output $\mathbf{T}$ as shown in all the above examples. Choosing other relations will lead to different output of $\mathbf{T}$. The output $\mathbf{G}$ and $\mathbf{G}^{-1}$ of `GTGiByGeist_.m` will always have $\mathbf{I}(:,1)$ and $\mathbf{I}(1,:)$ in their first column and first row, respectively. We can run `GTGiByGeist_.m` with the sparse matrix $\mathbf{A}$ and compare its output to the output of `GTGiByLanczos_.m`. We can see $\mathbf{PG}_3$ is different from $\mathbf{G}_1$ and $\mathbf{G}_2$ from `GTGiByLanczos_.m`, since `GTGiByGeist_.m` does not enforce any relations between $T_{j+1,j}$ and $T_{j,j+1}$.

```
>> [T3,G3,Gi3,P]=GTGiByGeist_(A,100*eps,'long')
T3 =
   11.0000    14.0000          0          0
   41.0000    21.5122   -13.6110          0
         0    34.0000   -92.4841  -219.0006
         0          0    29.9715    70.9719
G3 =
    1.0000          0          0          0
         0     1.0000          0          0
         0          0     1.0000     3.0857
         0     0.5122    -0.3241     0.0000
Gi3 =
    1.0000          0          0          0
         0     1.0000          0          0
         0     1.5805     0.0000    -3.0857
         0    -0.5122     0.3241     1.0000
P =
    1          0          0          0
    0          0          0          1
    0          0          1          0
    0          1          0          0
```

2.6 REDUCTION OF A SYMMETRIC MATRIX TO TRI-DIAGONAL AND ANOTHER SYMMETRIC MATRIX TO DIAGONAL OF ±1s AND 0s

In this section, we study the problem of $[\mathbf{A}, \mathbf{B}] = \mathbf{G}[\mathbf{T}, \mathbf{J}]\mathbf{G}'$, where $\mathbf{A}$ and $\mathbf{B}$ are two symmetric matrices of the same size, $\mathbf{G}$ is a non-singular matrix, $\mathbf{T}$ is symmetric tri-diagonal, and $\mathbf{J}$ is diagonal of only +1s, −1s, and 0s. We name $[\mathbf{A}, \mathbf{B}] = \mathbf{G}[\mathbf{T}, \mathbf{J}]\mathbf{G}'$ the GTJGt decomposition. It is used in the first step reduction of a GJR iteration algorithm for the generalized eigenvalues of the symmetric indefinite pair $[\mathbf{A}, \mathbf{B}]$. See Section 6.11 for the GJR iteration algorithm. The GTJGt decomposition is studied in [13] for symmetric semi-positive $\mathbf{B}$ and in [71] for symmetric non-singular indefinite $\mathbf{B}$. If $\mathbf{B}$ is symmetric semi-definite, $\mathbf{J}$ includes only +1s and 0s. If $\mathbf{B}$ is symmetric indefinite and non-singular, $\mathbf{J}$ includes only +1s and -1s. The algorithm presented in this section is an extension to both [13] and [71]: $\mathbf{B}$ is symmetric and its eigenvalues can be positive, zero, and negative.

2.6.1 HYPER ROTATION AND HYPER REFLECTION

The algorithm of simultaneous reductions of the pair $[\mathbf{A}, \mathbf{B}]$ to $[\mathbf{T}, \mathbf{J}]$ is based on two zeroing matrices. The first is the hyperbolic rotation, an extension of the Givens rotation. The second is the hyperbolic reflection, an extension of the Householder reflection. See Section 3.1 for the Givens rotation and Householder reflection.

Hyperbolic Rotation First, we study the following elimination problem:

Problem I: Given $\mathbf{v} = \begin{bmatrix} v_1 \\ v_2 \end{bmatrix}$ and $\mathbf{D} = \begin{bmatrix} D_1 & 0 \\ 0 & D_2 \end{bmatrix}$, find a non-singular and best conditioned matrix

$$\mathbf{M} = \begin{bmatrix} M_{11} & M_{12} \\ M_{21} & M_{22} \end{bmatrix} \text{ so that } \mathbf{M}'\mathbf{v} = \begin{bmatrix} w \\ 0 \end{bmatrix} \text{ and } \mathbf{M}'\mathbf{D}\mathbf{M} = \begin{bmatrix} d_1 & 0 \\ 0 & d_2 \end{bmatrix}.$$

The conditions of zeroing and non-singularity are explicitly stated as follows:

$$\begin{aligned} M_{12}v_1 + M_{22}v_2 &= 0, \\ M_{11}M_{12}D_1 + M_{21}M_{22}D_2 &= 0, \\ M_{11}M_{22} - M_{12}M_{21} &= m \neq 0. \end{aligned} \tag{2.30}$$

For the following derivation, we introduce an auxiliary vector $\mathbf{u} = \begin{bmatrix} u_1 \\ u_2 \end{bmatrix} = \begin{bmatrix} D_2 & 0 \\ 0 & D_1 \end{bmatrix} \begin{bmatrix} v_1 \\ v_2 \end{bmatrix}$. The angle between $\mathbf{u}$ and $\mathbf{v}$ is denoted as θ: $\cos(\theta) = \mathbf{u}'\mathbf{v}/(\|\mathbf{u}\|\|\mathbf{v}\|)$.[4] Using the auxiliary vector $\mathbf{u}$, all the $\mathbf{M}$s satisfying Eq. (2.30) have the following form, where $M_{11} \neq 0$ and $m \neq 0$ are arbitrary,

$$\mathbf{M} = \begin{bmatrix} M_{11} & -\frac{m}{M_{11}} \frac{u_1 v_2}{\mathbf{u}'\mathbf{v}} \\ M_{11} \frac{u_2}{u_1} & \frac{m}{M_{11}} \frac{u_1 v_1}{\mathbf{u}'\mathbf{v}} \end{bmatrix}. \tag{2.31}$$

From all the possible $\mathbf{M}$s of the form Eq. (2.31), we want to find the $\mathbf{M}$ with the smallest condition number. The 2-norm condition number of a 2×2 matrix $\mathbf{M}$ can be calculated explicitly from its definition $\kappa(\mathbf{M}) = [\lambda_2(\mathbf{M}'\mathbf{M})]/[\lambda_1(\mathbf{M}'\mathbf{M})]$, where λ_2 and λ_1 are the larger and smaller eigenvalues of $\mathbf{M}'\mathbf{M}$,

$$\kappa(\mathbf{M}) = \frac{M_{11}^2 + M_{12}^2 + M_{21}^2 + M_{22}^2 + \sqrt{\left(M_{11}^2 + M_{12}^2 + M_{21}^2 + M_{22}^2\right)^2 - 4m^2}}{2m}. \tag{2.32}$$

Substituting Eq. (2.31) into Eq. (2.32), we obtain the 2-norm condition number of the zeroing matrix. The zeroing matrix has the minimum 2-norm condition when M_{11} assumes the following value:

$$M_{11} = u_1 \sqrt{\left| \frac{m}{\mathbf{u}'\mathbf{v}} \right| \frac{\|\mathbf{v}\|}{\|\mathbf{u}\|}} = \frac{u_1}{\|\mathbf{u}\|} \sqrt{\left| \frac{m}{\cos(\theta)} \right|}. \tag{2.33}$$

---

[4] All the vector norms in this subsection are 2-norm.

The corresponding minimum 2-norm condition number of the zeroing matrix is obtained as follows:

$$\kappa_{\min}(\mathbf{M}) = \frac{\|\mathbf{u} \times \mathbf{v}\| + \|\mathbf{u}\|\|\mathbf{v}\|}{|\mathbf{u}'\mathbf{v}|} = \frac{1 + |\sin(\theta)|}{|\cos(\theta)|}, \tag{2.34}$$

where $\mathbf{u} \times \mathbf{v}$ denotes the vector product. Eq. (2.34) shows that $\kappa_{\min}(\mathbf{M})$ does not depend on the determinant m. If we take $m = \mathbf{u}'\mathbf{v}/(\|\mathbf{u}\|\|\mathbf{v}\|) = \cos(\theta)$, the best conditioned zeroing matrix has the following form:

$$\mathbf{M} = \begin{bmatrix} c_u & -s_v \\ s_u & c_v \end{bmatrix}, \qquad c_u = \frac{u_1}{\|\mathbf{u}\|}, \qquad s_u = \frac{u_2}{\|\mathbf{u}\|}, \qquad c_v = \frac{v_1}{\|\mathbf{v}\|}, \qquad s_v = \frac{v_2}{\|\mathbf{v}\|}. \tag{2.35}$$

The form of Eq. (2.35) is similar to the Givens rotation matrix. Eq. (2.35) is also the zeroing matrix obtained in [13] for $D_1, D_2 \geq 0$. As can be seen from the above derivation, Eq. (2.35) can also be used for $D_1, D_2 \leq 0$.

Using the zeroing matrix $\mathbf{M}$ of Eq. (2.35), $\mathbf{M}'\mathbf{v}$ and $\mathbf{M}'\mathbf{DM}$ are calculated as follows:

$$\mathbf{M}'\mathbf{v} = \begin{bmatrix} \frac{\mathbf{u}'\mathbf{v}}{\|\mathbf{u}\|} \\ 0 \end{bmatrix} = \begin{bmatrix} \|\mathbf{v}\| \cos(\theta) \\ 0 \end{bmatrix}, \tag{2.36}$$

$$\mathbf{M}'\mathbf{DM} = \begin{bmatrix} D_1 D_2 \frac{\mathbf{u}'\mathbf{v}}{\mathbf{u}'\mathbf{u}} & 0 \\ 0 & \frac{\mathbf{u}'\mathbf{v}}{\mathbf{v}'\mathbf{v}} \end{bmatrix} = \begin{bmatrix} D_1 D_2 \frac{\|\mathbf{v}\|}{\|\mathbf{u}\|} \cos(\theta) & 0 \\ 0 & \frac{\|\mathbf{u}\|}{\|\mathbf{v}\|} \cos(\theta) \end{bmatrix}. \tag{2.37}$$

The following cases are special or exceptional to the general case of Eq. (2.35).

1. If $\mathbf{D} = \begin{bmatrix} D_1 & 0 \\ 0 & D_1 \end{bmatrix}$, $\mathbf{u} = \begin{bmatrix} D_1 & 0 \\ 0 & D_1 \end{bmatrix} \begin{bmatrix} v_1 \\ v_2 \end{bmatrix} = \begin{bmatrix} D_1 v_1 \\ D_1 v_2 \end{bmatrix}$, $\mathbf{M}$ is a Givens rotation matrix, see Section 3.1,

$$\mathbf{M} = \begin{bmatrix} \text{sign}(D_1)c_v & -s_v \\ \text{sign}(D_1)s_v & c_v \end{bmatrix}, \qquad \kappa(\mathbf{M}) = 1,$$

$$\mathbf{M}'\mathbf{v} = \begin{bmatrix} \text{sign}(D_1)\|\mathbf{v}\| \\ 0 \end{bmatrix}, \qquad \mathbf{M}'\mathbf{DM} = \mathbf{D}.$$

2. If $\mathbf{D} = \begin{bmatrix} D_1 & 0 \\ 0 & -D_1 \end{bmatrix}$, $\mathbf{u} = \begin{bmatrix} -D_1 & 0 \\ 0 & D_1 \end{bmatrix} \begin{bmatrix} v_1 \\ v_2 \end{bmatrix} = \begin{bmatrix} -D_1 v_1 \\ D_1 v_2 \end{bmatrix}$, $\mathbf{M}$ leads to the hyperbolic rotation matrix studied in [10, 71],

$$\mathbf{M} = \begin{bmatrix} -\text{sign}(D_1)c_v & -s_v \\ \text{sign}(D_1)s_v & c_v \end{bmatrix}, \qquad \kappa(\mathbf{M}) = \frac{|v_1| + |v_2|}{\|v_1| - |v_2\|},$$

$$\mathbf{M}'\mathbf{v} = \begin{bmatrix} \text{sign}(D_1)\frac{v_2^2 - v_1^2}{\|\mathbf{v}\|} \\ 0 \end{bmatrix}, \qquad \mathbf{M}'\mathbf{DM} = \left(c_v^2 - s_v^2\right)\mathbf{D}.$$

3. If $\mathbf{D} = \begin{bmatrix} D_1 & 0 \\ 0 & 0 \end{bmatrix}$, $\mathbf{u} = \begin{bmatrix} 0 & 0 \\ 0 & D_1 \end{bmatrix} \begin{bmatrix} v_1 \\ v_2 \end{bmatrix} = \begin{bmatrix} 0 \\ D_1 v_2 \end{bmatrix}$, $\mathbf{M}$ is simplified to the following form:

$$\mathbf{M} = \begin{bmatrix} 0 & -s_v \\ \text{sign}(D_1 v_2) & c_v \end{bmatrix}, \qquad \kappa(\mathbf{M}) = \frac{\|\mathbf{v}\| + |v_1|}{|v_2|},$$

$$\mathbf{M}'\mathbf{v} = \begin{bmatrix} \text{sign}(D_1)|v_2| \\ 0 \end{bmatrix}, \qquad \mathbf{M}'\mathbf{DM} = \begin{bmatrix} 0 & 0 \\ 0 & s_v^2 D_1 \end{bmatrix}.$$

4. If $\mathbf{D} = \begin{bmatrix} 0 & 0 \\ 0 & D_2 \end{bmatrix}$, $\mathbf{u} = \begin{bmatrix} D_2 & 0 \\ 0 & 0 \end{bmatrix}\begin{bmatrix} v_1 \\ v_2 \end{bmatrix} = \begin{bmatrix} D_2 v_1 \\ 0 \end{bmatrix}$, $\mathbf{M}$ is simplified to the following form:

$$\mathbf{M} = \begin{bmatrix} \text{sign}(D_2 v_1) & -s_v \\ 0 & c_v \end{bmatrix}, \qquad \kappa(\mathbf{M}) = \frac{\|\mathbf{v}\| + |v_2|}{|v_1|},$$

$$\mathbf{M'v} = \begin{bmatrix} \text{sign}(D_2)|v_1| \\ 0 \end{bmatrix}, \qquad \mathbf{M'DM} = \begin{bmatrix} 0 & 0 \\ 0 & c_v^2 D_2 \end{bmatrix}.$$

5. If $\mathbf{v} = \begin{bmatrix} 0 \\ v_2 \end{bmatrix}$, $\mathbf{u} = \begin{bmatrix} D_1 & 0 \\ 0 & D_2 \end{bmatrix}\mathbf{v} = \begin{bmatrix} 0 \\ D_1 v_2 \end{bmatrix}$, $\mathbf{M}$ is a permutation matrix,

$$\mathbf{M} = \begin{bmatrix} 0 & -\frac{v_2}{\|\mathbf{v}\|} \\ \frac{D_1 v_2}{|D_1 v_2|} & 0 \end{bmatrix} = \begin{bmatrix} 0 & \pm 1 \\ \pm 1 & 0 \end{bmatrix}, \qquad \kappa(\mathbf{M}) = 1,$$

$$\mathbf{M'v} = \begin{bmatrix} \pm v_2 \\ 0 \end{bmatrix}, \qquad \mathbf{M'DM} = \begin{bmatrix} D_2 & 0 \\ 0 & D_1 \end{bmatrix}.$$

6. If $\mathbf{u'v} = D_2 v_1^2 + D_1 v_2^2 = 0, v_1 v_2 \neq 0, D_1 D_2 < 0$, there is no solution to the basic elimination problem. If the nonzero $\mathbf{u}$ is increasingly perpendicular to the nonzero $\mathbf{v}$, the conditioning of $\mathbf{M}$ becomes worse and worse,

$$\mathbf{J} = \begin{bmatrix} J_1 & 0 \\ 0 & J_2 \end{bmatrix},$$ where $J_1, J_2 \in \{-1, 0, +1\}$, is called a sign matrix. If $\mathbf{D} = \mathbf{J}$, we have an extra requirement to the elimination problem.

Problem II: Given $\mathbf{v} = \begin{bmatrix} v_1 \\ v_2 \end{bmatrix}$ and $\mathbf{J} = \begin{bmatrix} J_1 & 0 \\ 0 & J_2 \end{bmatrix}$, find a non-singular and best conditioned matrix

$$\mathbf{G} = \begin{bmatrix} G_{11} & G_{12} \\ G_{21} & G_{22} \end{bmatrix}$$ so that $\mathbf{G'v} = \begin{bmatrix} w \\ 0 \end{bmatrix}$ and $\mathbf{G'JG} = \begin{bmatrix} j_1 & 0 \\ 0 & j_2 \end{bmatrix}$, where $j_1, j_2 \in \{-1, 0, +1\}$.

The elimination problem I is transformed to the elimination problem II by $\mathbf{L'v} \Rightarrow \mathbf{v}$ and $\mathbf{L'DL} = \mathbf{J}$, where $\mathbf{L} = \begin{bmatrix} L_1 & 0 \\ 0 & L_2 \end{bmatrix}$, $L_j = \begin{cases} \frac{1}{\sqrt{|D_j|}} & D_j \neq 0 \\ 1 & D_j = 0 \end{cases}$, $j = 1, 2$. The solution to problem II is obtained from the special cases 1,2,3, and 4 outlined above. First, using the zeroing matrix $\mathbf{M}$ of problem I, we have $\mathbf{M'v} = \begin{bmatrix} w \\ 0 \end{bmatrix}$ and $\mathbf{M'DM} = \begin{bmatrix} d_1 & 0 \\ 0 & d_2 \end{bmatrix}$. Then we define $\mathbf{N} = \begin{bmatrix} N_1 & 0 \\ 0 & N_2 \end{bmatrix}$, $N_j = \begin{cases} \frac{1}{\sqrt{|d_j|}} & d_j \neq 0 \\ 1 & d_j = 0 \end{cases}$, $j = 1, 2$.

$\mathbf{G} = \mathbf{MN}$ is the matrix sought.

The four cases listed below include all possible cases of $\mathbf{J}$ of 2×2.

1. If $\mathbf{J} = \pm \begin{bmatrix} 1 & 0 \\ 0 & 1 \end{bmatrix}$ or $\mathbf{J} = \pm \begin{bmatrix} 0 & 0 \\ 0 & 0 \end{bmatrix}$, $\mathbf{G}$ is the orthogonal Givens rotation matrix,

$$\mathbf{G} = \begin{bmatrix} c & -s \\ s & c \end{bmatrix}, \qquad c = \frac{v_1}{\|\mathbf{v}\|}, s = \frac{v_2}{\|\mathbf{v}\|}, \qquad \kappa(\mathbf{G}) = 1,$$

$$\mathbf{G'v} = \begin{bmatrix} \|\mathbf{v}\| \\ 0 \end{bmatrix}, \qquad \mathbf{G'JG} = \mathbf{J}.$$

2. If $\mathbf{J} = \pm \begin{bmatrix} 1 & 0 \\ 0 & -1 \end{bmatrix}$, $\mathbf{G}$ is the hyperbolic rotation matrix studied in [10, 71],

$$\mathbf{G} = \begin{bmatrix} J_1 c & -s \\ J_1 s & c \end{bmatrix}, \qquad c = \frac{v_1}{\sqrt{|v_1^2 - v_2^2|}}, s = \frac{v_2}{\sqrt{|v_1^2 - v_2^2|}}, \qquad \kappa(\mathbf{G}) = \frac{|v_1| + |v_2|}{||v_1| - |v_2||},$$

$$\mathbf{G}'\mathbf{v} = \begin{bmatrix} -J_1 \operatorname{sign}(v_1^2 - v_2^2) \sqrt{|v_1^2 - v_2^2|} \\ 0 \end{bmatrix}, \qquad \mathbf{G}'\mathbf{JG} = \begin{cases} \mathbf{J} & |v_1| > |v_2| \\ -\mathbf{J} & |v_1| < |v_2|. \end{cases}$$

If $|v_1| = |v_2|$, the elimination problem has no solution.

3. If $\mathbf{J} = \begin{bmatrix} \pm 1 & 0 \\ 0 & 0 \end{bmatrix}$, $\mathbf{G}$ takes the following form:

$$\mathbf{G} = \begin{bmatrix} 0 & -1 \\ J_1 & \frac{v_1}{v_2} \end{bmatrix}, \qquad \kappa(\mathbf{G}) = \frac{1}{2} \left[2 + \frac{v_1^2}{v_2^2} + \sqrt{\left(2 + \frac{v_1^2}{v_2^2}\right)^2 - 4} \right]$$

$$\mathbf{G}'\mathbf{v} = \begin{bmatrix} J_1 v_2 \\ 0 \end{bmatrix}, \qquad \mathbf{G}'\mathbf{JG} = \begin{bmatrix} 0 & 0 \\ 0 & J_1 \end{bmatrix}.$$

4. If $\mathbf{J} = \begin{bmatrix} 0 & 0 \\ 0 & \pm 1 \end{bmatrix}$, $\mathbf{G}$ takes the following form:

$$\mathbf{G} = \begin{bmatrix} J_2 & -\frac{v_2}{v_1} \\ 0 & 1 \end{bmatrix}, \qquad \kappa(\mathbf{G}) = \frac{1}{2} \left[2 + \frac{v_2^2}{v_1^2} + \sqrt{\left(2 + \frac{v_2^2}{v_1^2}\right)^2 - 4} \right],$$

$$\mathbf{G}'\mathbf{v} = \begin{bmatrix} J_2 v_1 \\ 0 \end{bmatrix}, \qquad \mathbf{G}'\mathbf{JG} = \mathbf{J}.$$

The following is the MATLAB implementation of the orthogonal Givens or hyperbolic Givens rotation for the different cases discussed so far.

Algorithm 2.24

```
G'*(v1;v2)=(x;0); G'*D1*G=D2
function [G,hyper] = xgivens_(v1,v2,d1,d2)

if (abs(v2)<eps*max(1.0,max(abs(v1),abs(d1)+abs(d2))))
    G = [1 0; 0 1];   hyper = 0;
elseif (exist('d1','var')==0 || exist('d2','var')==0 || d1==d2)
    [c,s] = givens_(v1,v2);   G = [c s; -s c];   hyper = 0;
elseif (d1 == -d2)          %hyper
    if (abs(v1) > abs(v2))  t = v2/v1;  c = 1.0/sqrt(1-t*t);  s = t*c;  hyper = 1;
    else                    t = v1/v2;  s = 1.0/sqrt(1-t*t);  c = t*s;  hyper = 2; end
    G = [c -s; -s c];
elseif (d1 == 0)
    G = [-sign(d2), -v2/abs(v1); 0.0, sign(v1)];  hyper = 3;
elseif (d2 == 0)
```

```
    G = [0.0, -sign(v2); sign(d1), v1/abs(v2)];  hyper = 4;
else                    %MDR
    u1 = d2*v1; u2 = d1*v2;  normu = sqrt(u1*u1+u2*u2);  normv = sqrt(v1*v1+v2*v2);
    G = [u1/normu -v2/normv; u2/normu v1/normv]; hyper = 5;
end
```

Given a vector $\mathbf{v}$ and a sign matrix $\mathbf{J}$ of a same size greater than 2, we want to find a non-singular $\mathbf{G}$ such that $\mathbf{G}'\mathbf{v}$ is zero except v_1 and $\mathbf{G}'\mathbf{J}\mathbf{G}$ remains a sign matrix. This problem can be solved by repeated transformations of $\mathbf{G}'_{n-1}\cdots\mathbf{G}'_1\mathbf{v}$ and $\mathbf{G}'_{n-1}\cdots\mathbf{G}'_1\mathbf{J}\mathbf{G}_1\cdots\mathbf{G}_{n-1}$, where each $\mathbf{G}_j, j = 1,\ldots,n-1$ is the best conditioned matrix determined for the elimination problem II or I. Obviously, the choice of the zeroing pair, i.e. the input arguments (v_1,v_2,d_1,d_2) to the MATLAB function xgivens_.m, influences the conditioning of each $\mathbf{G}_j$. However, there is no principle for the optimal zeroing pair. The following two ways to determine the zeroing pair for the elimination problem $[\mathbf{v},\mathbf{J}]$ suggested in [71] are reasonable:

1. $v(j)$ is zeroed in the order $j = n,n-1,\ldots,2$. $v(j)$ and $J(j)$ are the input arguments v_2 and d_2 to xgivens_.m. The other two input arguments v_1 and d_1 are the zeroing pair $v(i)$ and $J(i)$ to $v(j)$ and $J(j)$. $v(i)$ and $J(i)$ are determined so that $\begin{bmatrix} v(i) \\ v(j) \end{bmatrix}$ and $\begin{bmatrix} J(i) & 0 \\ 0 & J(j) \end{bmatrix}$ given the minimum $\kappa(\mathbf{G})$ among all the possible pairs $v(k), J(k), k = j-1,\ldots,2$. If $J(i) = J(j)$, $v(i)$ and $J(i)$ will be chosen, because an orthogonal Givens rotation can be used for the pair $(v(i),j(i),v(j),J(j))$.

2. Group the components of $\mathbf{v}$ and $\mathbf{J}$ into at most three sets. Within each set, the values of $\mathbf{J}$ are equal; therefore, the components of $\mathbf{v}$ in the set can be zeroed to only one component by orthogonal Givens rotations. Then, the remaining one pair or two pairs are zeroed with the algorithm of the hyperbolic Given rotations.

The orthogonal/hyperbolic Givens rotations and the above two choices for the zeroing pairs are implemented as algo='givens' and pivot=1 or pivot=2 in the MATLAB function GTJGt_.m.

Hyperbolic Reflection When the dimension of $\mathbf{v}$ and $\mathbf{J}$ is greater than 2 and $\mathbf{J} \neq \mathbf{0}$, instead of repeated applications of the orthogonal or hyperbolic Givens rotations, we can apply one hyperbolic reflection $\mathbf{H}$ so that $\mathbf{H}'\mathbf{v} = \beta\mathbf{I}(:,j)$ and $\mathbf{H}'\mathbf{J}\mathbf{H} = \mathbf{J}$, where the index j is to be determined later. Analogously to the Householder reflection, see 3.1, a hyperbolic reflection matrix $\mathbf{H}$ takes the following form:

$$\mathbf{H} = \mathbf{J} - \frac{2}{\mathbf{h}'\mathbf{J}\mathbf{h}}\mathbf{h}\mathbf{h}' = \mathbf{J} - \alpha\mathbf{h}\mathbf{h}'. \tag{2.38}$$

Given $\mathbf{H}$ in the above form, we can easily verify that $\mathbf{H}'\mathbf{J}\mathbf{H} = \mathbf{J}$ for any $\mathbf{h}$ noting that $\mathbf{J}\mathbf{J} = \mathbf{I}$. Because we want $\mathbf{H}'\mathbf{v} = \beta\mathbf{I}(:,j)$, we will assume $\mathbf{h} = \mathbf{J}\mathbf{v} + \gamma\mathbf{I}(:,j)$. Now we can calculate $\mathbf{H}'\mathbf{v}$ from the assumed $\mathbf{h}$,

$$\mathbf{H}'\mathbf{v} = \left(1 - \frac{2\mathbf{h}'\mathbf{v}}{\mathbf{h}'\mathbf{J}\mathbf{h}}\right)\mathbf{J}\mathbf{v} - \frac{2\mathbf{h}'\mathbf{v}}{\mathbf{h}'\mathbf{J}\mathbf{h}}\gamma\mathbf{I}(:,j) = \beta\mathbf{I}(:,j).$$

Therefore, we can write the condition of zeroing explicitly as follows, considering that $\mathbf{J}\mathbf{J} = \mathbf{I}$, $\mathbf{J}\mathbf{I}(:,j) = J_j\mathbf{I}(:,j)$, and $\mathbf{v}'\mathbf{I}(:,j) = v_j$,

$$2\mathbf{h}'\mathbf{v} = \mathbf{h}'\mathbf{J}\mathbf{h}, \text{ i.e. } 2\mathbf{v}'\mathbf{J}\mathbf{v} + 2\gamma v_j = \mathbf{v}'\mathbf{J}\mathbf{v} + 2\gamma v_j + \gamma^2 J_j.$$

The condition is satisfied if $\gamma = \pm\sqrt{|\mathbf{v}'\mathbf{J}\mathbf{v}|}$ and the index j is chosen according to $J_j = \text{sign}(\mathbf{v}'\mathbf{J}\mathbf{v})$. To avoid the possibility of numerical cancellation in the calculation of $\mathbf{h} = \mathbf{J}\mathbf{v} + \gamma\mathbf{I}(:,j)$, the sign of γ is chosen to be the sign of $J_j v_j$. The determined **H** zeros all the components of **v** except the jth component, which becomes $-\gamma$. The 2-norm condition number of the determined **H** is as follows, according to [10],

$$\kappa(\mathbf{H}) = \left(\frac{\mathbf{h'h}}{|\mathbf{h'Jh}|} + \sqrt{\left(\frac{\mathbf{h'h}}{\mathbf{h'Jh}}\right)^2 - 1} \right)^2.$$

$\kappa(\mathbf{H})$ is minimized if $|\mathbf{h'Jh}|$ is maximized. From $\mathbf{h} = \mathbf{Jv} + \text{sign}(J_j v_j) \sqrt{|\mathbf{v'Jv}|}\mathbf{I}(:,j)$, the best conditioned zeroing **H** is obtained when $J_j = \text{sign}(\mathbf{v'Jv})$ and $|v_j|$ is maximized. This way of determining j and **H** forms the algorithm for algo='householder' and pivot=1 in the MATLAB function GTJGt_.m. The algorithm has two noticeable pitfalls. The first is that **J** cannot include zeros, because we assume $\mathbf{J}^2 = \mathbf{I}$ when obtaining **h**. The second is that, even if **J** is non-singular but if $\mathbf{v'Jv} = 0$, the hyperbolic reflection does not exist. In GTJGt_.m, pivot=2 for algo='householder' is similar to pivot=2 for algo='givens'. We group **v** and **J** into at most three sets according to the values of the components of **J**. In each set, the components of **v** are zeroed to one component with the orthogonal Householder reflection, because the values of **J** are equal. The two remaining one pair or two pairs are zeroed according to the hyperbolic Givens rotations.

The following is the MATLAB implementation of the hyperbolic Householder reflection.

Algorithm 2.25

Calculate hyper reflection matrix H = J-alpha*h*h'

```
%H'*v = [0;...0;beta;0;...0] (H'*v)(j)=beta and H'*J*H=J.
%format='short': h=vector; ='long':h=matrix.
function [h,alpha,beta,j,hyper] = xhouseholder_(v,J,format)

if (~exist('format','var')) format = 'short'; end

n = size(v,1);   h = v;   hyper = 0;
if (exist('J','var') && length(J)==n)
    j = J(1);
    for i=1:n
        if (J(i) < 0) h(i) = -h(i); end          %h=J*v
        if (J(i) ~= j) j = J(i); hyper = 1; end
    end
end

if (hyper == 0)
    h = v;   alpha = 0.0; j = 1;
    normh = norm(h);
    if (v(1) > 0) beta = -normh; else beta = normh; end
    h(1) = h(1) - beta;
    if (normh > 0)
        alpha = h(1)*h(1)/(normh*(normh + abs(v(1))));   h = h/h(1);
    end
    if (strcmp(format,'long')) h = eye(n) - alpha*h*h'; end
else
    vJv = v'*h;   vv = v'*v;
    if (abs(vJv) < eps*vv) error('xhouseholder_:_No_hyper_reflection_exists.'); end

    absvJv = sqrt(abs(vJv));   vmax = 0.0;
    if (vJv > 0) sigma = 1; else sigma = -1; end
    for i=1:n
```

```
        if (J(i)==sigma && vmax<abs(v(i))) j = i;   vmax = abs(v(i)); end
    end

    if (v(j) < 0) sigma = -sigma; end        %sigma=sigma*sign(v(j))
    if (sigma > 0) beta =-absvJv;  h(j) = h(j) + absvJv;
    else           beta = absvJv;  h(j) = h(j) - absvJv; end

    % alpha = h(j)*h(j)/(absvJv*(absvJv+abs(v(j))));  h = h/h(j); %normalize h(j)=1
    alpha = 1.0/(absvJv*(absvJv+abs(v(j))));
    if (J(j) < 0) alpha = -alpha; end
    if (strcmp(format,'long')) h = diag(J) - alpha*h*h'; end
end
```

2.6.2 GTJGt DECOMPOSITION BY HYPERBOLIC ROTATION OR HYPERBOLIC REFLECTION

With the developed algorithms of hyperbolic rotation and hyperbolic reflection, now we start to illustrate the process of the simultaneous reduction of a symmetric pair $[\mathbf{A}, \mathbf{B}]$ into $[\mathbf{T}, \mathbf{J}]$, where $\mathbf{T}$ is symmetric tri-diagonal and $\mathbf{J}$ is a diagonal of only $+1$s, -1s, and 0s. We assume $\mathbf{A}$ and $\mathbf{B}$ to be two 5×5 symmetric matrices for the illustrative purpose.

In the first step, we transform $\mathbf{B}$ to diagonal. This can be done with either LDLt decomposition of Section 2.4.1 or numerically more stable LBLt decomposition of Section 2.4.4.[5] In both ways, the end transformation is presented as $\mathbf{G}_0'\mathbf{B}\mathbf{G}_0 = \mathbf{D}$. The same transformation is applied to $\mathbf{A}$: $\mathbf{G}_0'\mathbf{A}\mathbf{G}_0 \Rightarrow \mathbf{A}$,

$$\mathbf{G}_0'\mathbf{B}\mathbf{G}_0 = \begin{bmatrix} D_1 & 0 & 0 & 0 & 0 \\ 0 & D_2 & 0 & 0 & 0 \\ 0 & 0 & D_3 & 0 & 0 \\ 0 & 0 & 0 & D_4 & 0 \\ 0 & 0 & 0 & 0 & D_5 \end{bmatrix}, \quad \mathbf{G}_0'\mathbf{A}\mathbf{G}_0 \Rightarrow \begin{bmatrix} A_{11} & A_{21} & A_{31} & A_{41} & A_{51} \\ A_{21} & A_{22} & A_{32} & A_{42} & A_{52} \\ A_{31} & A_{32} & A_{33} & A_{43} & A_{53} \\ A_{41} & A_{42} & A_{43} & A_{44} & A_{54} \\ A_{51} & A_{52} & A_{53} & A_{54} & A_{55} \end{bmatrix}.$$

In the second step, we transform $\mathbf{D}$ to a sign matrix: $\mathbf{J} = \mathbf{G}_1'\mathbf{D}\mathbf{G}_1$, where $\mathbf{G}_1 = \text{diag}\left(\frac{1}{\sqrt{|D_1|}}, \ldots, \frac{1}{\sqrt{|D_5|}}\right)$. If a diagonal component of $\mathbf{D}$ is zero, the corresponding diagonal component of $\mathbf{G}_1$ should be replaced by 1,

$$\mathbf{G}_1'\mathbf{D}\mathbf{G}_1 = \begin{bmatrix} J_1 & 0 & 0 & 0 & 0 \\ 0 & J_2 & 0 & 0 & 0 \\ 0 & 0 & J_3 & 0 & 0 \\ 0 & 0 & 0 & J_4 & 0 \\ 0 & 0 & 0 & 0 & J_5 \end{bmatrix}, \quad \mathbf{G}_1'\mathbf{A}\mathbf{G}_1 \Rightarrow \begin{bmatrix} A_{11} & A_{21} & A_{31} & A_{41} & A_{51} \\ A_{21} & A_{22} & A_{32} & A_{42} & A_{52} \\ A_{31} & A_{32} & A_{33} & A_{43} & A_{53} \\ A_{41} & A_{42} & A_{43} & A_{44} & A_{54} \\ A_{51} & A_{52} & A_{53} & A_{54} & A_{55} \end{bmatrix}.$$

If $\mathbf{B}$ is positive definite, $\mathbf{J}$ is a 5×5 identity matrix. If $\mathbf{B}$ is indefinite, $J_1, \ldots, J_5$ are either $+1$ or -1. If $\mathbf{B}$ is singular, some of the diagonal components of $\mathbf{J}$ are 0s. The location of $-1, 0, +1$ in $\mathbf{J}$ is not known *a priori*.

In the third step, we apply the zeroing algorithms developed in the last subsection to $\mathbf{A}(2:5, 1)$ and $\mathbf{J}(2:5)$: $\mathbf{G}_2'\mathbf{A}\mathbf{G}_2 \Rightarrow \mathbf{A}$ and $\mathbf{G}_2'\mathbf{J}\mathbf{G}_2 \Rightarrow \mathbf{J}$, so that $\mathbf{A}(3:5, 1) = \mathbf{0}$, $\mathbf{A}(1, 3:5) = \mathbf{0}$ and $\mathbf{J}$ remains a sign matrix.

[5]If using LBLt decomposition, a simple eigenvalue analysis is needed for each 2×2 symmetric block diagonals.

In the fourth step, we perform $G_3'AG_3 \Rightarrow A$ and $G_3'JG_3 \Rightarrow J$. G_3 is obtained from the zeroing algorithm applied to $(A(3:5,2), J(3:5))$. Because $G_3(1:2,1:2) = I$, the zeroed $A(3:5,1)$ and $A(1,3:5)$ from the third step are not altered. Finally, we zero $A(5,3)$ and $A(3,5)$ by applying the zeroing algorithm to $(A(4:5,3), J(4:5))$. Now A becomes a tri-diagonal and B becomes a sign matrix. The whole transformations are accumulated in $G = G_1G_2G_3....$

The complete algorithm to transform $[A,B]$ to $[T,J]$ is implemented in the MATLAB function GTJGt_.m.

Algorithm 2.26

GTJGt: (A,B)=G*(T,J)*G', A,B symmetric, T tri-diagonal, J sign, G non-singular.

```
function [A,B,G] = GTJGt_(A,B,algo,pivot,tol,format,f1st,last,G)

[m,n] = size(A);   [k,l] = size(B);
if (~exist('algo','var') || isempty(algo)) algo = 'givens'; end
    [G,B,p]=LBLt_(B,1,tol,'short');                %L*B3*L'=P*B*P'
    [g1,g2] = size(G);
    if (g1 > g2)
        B = [B;zeros(g1-g2,3)];   %B = [B;zeros(g1-g2,1)]; %LDLt
        if (~strcmp(format,'brief')) G = [G,[zeros(g2,g1-g2);eye(g1-g2)]]; end
    end
A = permute_(p,A,'row');   A = permute_(p,A,'col');            %A=P*A*P'
A(1:g2,:) = mdivideLowerTriangle_(G(1:g2,1:g2),A(1:g2,:),1);   %A=inv(G)*A
if (g1 > g2)
    A(g2+1:g1,:) = A(g2+1:g1,:) - G(g2+1:g1,1:g2)*A(1:g2,:);   %A=inv(G)*A
end
for j=1:n                                          %lower half only:   A=A*inv(G)'
    for k=1:min(j-1,g2) A(j:n,j) = A(j:n,j) - G(j,k)*A(j:n,k); end
end
if (~strcmp(format,'brief'))
    for j=1:n
        for k=j+1:n G(j,k) =-G(k,j:k-1)*G(j,j:k-1)'; end
    end
    G = G - tril(G,-1);
    G = permute_(inv_perm_(p),G,'row');            %U=P'*inv(U)'
end
j = 1;
while (j < m)
    if (abs(B(j+1,1)) < tol*(abs(B(j,2))+abs(B(j+1,2)))) j = j + 1;
    else        %2x2 block
        [B12,X] = eig2x2_([B(j,2),B(j+1,1);B(j,3),B(j+1,2)]);
        B(j,2) = B12(1,1);   B(j+1,2) = B12(2,2);   B(j+1,1) = 0;   B(j,3) = 0;
        A(j,j+1) = A(j+1,j);
        A(j:j+1,1:j+1) = X'*A(j:j+1,1:j+1);   A(j:m,j:j+1) = A(j:m,j:j+1)*X;
        if (~strcmp(format,'brief')) G(:,j:j+1) = G(:,j:j+1)*X; end
        j = j + 2;
    end
end
J = B(:,2);   Jmax = norm(J,inf);
for j=1:m
    if (abs(J(j)) < tol*Jmax) J(j) = 0;
    else
        Jj = sqrt(abs(J(j)));
        if (J(j) > 0.0) J(j) = 1; else J(j) =-1; end
        A(j:m,j) = A(j:m,j)/Jj;   A(j,1:j) = A(j,1:j)/Jj;
```

```
                if (~strcmp(format,'brief')) G(:,j) = G(:,j)/Jj; end
            end
        end
        [J,p] = sort(J,'descend');   j1 = 0; j2 = 0; j3 = 0;
        for i=1:n
            if (J(i) >  0)      j1 = j1 + 1;
            elseif (J(i) ==0) j2 = j2 + 1;
            else              j3 = j3 + 1; end
        end
        if (j2 > 0)
            [J12,p12] = sort(J(1:j1+j2),'ascend');   p12 = [p12',j1+j2+1:n];
            p = permute_(p12,p);   J = permute_(p12,J);    %P'*J*P=[0...0;1...1;-1...-1]
        end
        A = A - triu(A,1);    A = A + tril(A,-1)';
        A = permute_(p,A,'row'); A = permute_(p,A,'col'); %P'*A*P=>A
        if (~strcmp(format,'brief')) G = permute_(p,G,'col');   %G*P=>G
        else                         G = []; end
    end

    if (strcmp(algo,'GIVENS')) Q = zeros(2);
    else                       h = zeros(m,1);   Ah = h;  h1 = h;  h2 = h; end

    for j=f1st:last
        z = 0; k02 = [0; 0]; k0 = 0;  algo = algo0;  algo00 = [];
        if (strcmp(algo,'GIVENS')) k2 = m+1; else k2 = j; end
        while (z < m-j-1)
            if (~isempty(algo00) && k0>0)  %zero pair (k1,k2)
                k1 = j+1;   k2 = k02(k0);   k0 = k0-1; algo = 'GIVENS';
            elseif (strcmp(algo,'GIVENS'))
                k2 = k2-1;   k1 = k2;
                for k=k2-1:-1:j+1
                    if (sign(J(k)) -- sign(J(k2))) k1 = k; break; end
                end
                if (k1 == k2)
                    if (pivot == 1)
                        Ak2j = A(k2,j);   kapamin = realmax;   v2v2 = Ak2j*Ak2j;
                        for k=j+1:k2-1
                            if (J(k) ==-J(k2))   %hyper=1 or 2
                                kapa = (abs(A(k,j))+abs(Ak2j))/abs(abs(A(k,j))-abs(Ak2j));
                            elseif (J(k) == 0)   %hyper=3
                                v1v1 = A(k,j)*A(k,j);   normv = v1v1 + v2v2;
                                kapa = 0.5*(1+normv/v1v1+sqrt((1+normv/v1v1)^2-4));
                            elseif (J(k2) == 0)   %hyper=4
                                v1v1 = A(k,j)*A(k,j);   normv = v1v1 + v2v2;
                                kapa = 0.5*(1+normv/v2v2+sqrt((1+normv/v2v2)^2-4));
                            else                 %hyper=5
                                v - [A(k,j); Ak2j];   u = [J(k2)*v(1); J(k)*v(2)];
                                kapa = (abs(u(1)*v(2)-u(2)*v(1))+norm(u)*norm(v))/
                                                                     abs(u'*v);
                            end
                            if (kapa < kapamin) kapamin = kapa; k1 = k; end
                        end
                    elseif (pivot==2 && k2 >j+1)
                        k0 = k0+1;   k02(k0) = k2;   continue;
                    elseif (pivot==2 && k2==j+1)
                        algo00 = 'GIVENS';   continue;
                    end
```

```
            end
    else  %if(strcmp(algo,'HOUSEHOLDER '))
        k1 = k2+1;   k2 = k1;
        if (pivot==1 && J(k1)~=0)
            k2 = m;    algo00 = 'GIVENS';
        elseif (pivot==2 || J(k1)==0)
            for k=k1+1:m
                if (J(k1) == J(k)) k2 = k2 + 1;
                else              k0 = k0+1;   k02(k0) = k; break; end
            end
            if (k2 == m) algo00 = 'GIVENS'; end
        end
    end                            %zero pair (k1,k2)

    if (strcmp(algo,'GIVENS'))
        [Q,hyper] = xgivens_(A(k1,j),A(k2,j),J(k1),J(k2));   z = z + 1;
        if (hyper == 2) J(k1) =-J(k1);  J(k2) =-J(k2);       %J=Q'*J*Q
        elseif (hyper == 4) J(k2) = J(k1);  J(k1) = 0;       %J=Q'*J*Q
        elseif (hyper == 5)                                  %D=Q'*D*Q
            v = [A(k1,j);A(k2,j)];  u = [J(k2)*v(1); J(k1)*v(2)];   uv = u'*v;
            J(k1) = J(k1)*J(k2)*uv/(u'*u);   J(k2) = uv/(v'*v);
        end
        A(k1,j) = Q(1,1)*A(k1,j) + Q(2,1)*A(k2,j);    A(k2,j) = 0;
        h1(j+1:k1) = A(k1,j+1:k1);   h1(k1+1:k2) = A(k1+1:k2,k1);
        h2(k1:k2)  = A(k2,k1:k2);    h2(k2+1:m)  = A(k2+1:m,k2);
        for k=j+1:k2      %A=Q'*A
            Ak1k = h1(k);
            A(k1,k) = Q(1,1)*Ak1k + Q(2,1)*A(k2,k);
            A(k2,k) = Q(1,2)*Ak1k + Q(2,2)*A(k2,k);
        end
        h2(k1) = A(k1,k2);   h2(k2) = A(k2,k2);
        for k=k1:m        %A=A*Q
            Akk1 = A(k,k1);
            A(k,k1) = Akk1*Q(1,1) + h2(k)*Q(2,1);
            A(k,k2) = Akk1*Q(1,2) + h2(k)*Q(2,2);
        end
        if (~strcmp(format,'brief'))   %G=G*Q
            Gk1 = G(:,k1);
            G(:,k1) = Gk1*Q(1,1) + G(:,k2)*Q(2,1);
            G(:,k2) = Gk1*Q(1,2) + G(:,k2)*Q(2,2);
        end
    else  %if (strcmp(algo,'HOUSEHOLDER '))
        [h(k1:k2),alpha,beta,l,hyper] = xhouseholder_(A(k1:k2,j),J(k1:k2));
                                                           z = z+k2-k1;
        if (hyper == 0)              %H=I-alpha*h*h'
            Ah(j+1:k1) = A(k1:k2,j+1:k1)'*h(k1:k2);
            for k=k1+1:k2
                Ah(k)  = A(k,k1:k)*h(k1:k) + A(k+1:k2,k)'*h(k+1:k2);
            end
            Ah(k2+1:m) = A(k2+1:m,k1:k2)*h(k1:k2);   hAh = h(k1:k2)'*Ah(k1:k2);
            h1(k1:k2) = alpha*h(k1:k2);   h2(k1:k2) = (alpha*hAh)*h1(k1:k2);
            A(k1,j) = beta;    A(k1+1:k2,j) = 0;   %H*A*H=>A
            A(k1:k2,j+1:k1-1) = A(k1:k2,j+1:k1-1)-h1(k1:k2)*Ah(j+1:k1-1)';
            for k=k1:k2
                A(k,k1:k) = A(k,k1:k)-Ah(k)*h1(k1:k)'-h1(k)*Ah(k1:k)'+h2(k)
                                                                *h(k1:k)';
            end
```

```
                    A(k2+1:m,k1:k2) = A(k2+1:m,k1:k2) - Ah(k2+1:m)*h1(k1:k2)';
                    if (~strcmp(format,'brief'))            %G*H=>G
                        h2 = G(:,k1:k2)*h(k1:k2);
                        G(:,k1:k2) = G(:,k1:k2) - h2*h1(k1:k2)';
                    end
                else   %if (hyper == 1)     %H=J-alpha*h*h'
                    Ah(j+1:k1-1) = (h(k1:k2)'*A(k1:k2,j+1:k1-1))';
                    for k=k1:k2
                        Ah(k) = A(k,k1:k-1)*h(k1:k-1) + A(k:k2,k)'*h(k:k2);
                    end
                    hAh = h(k1:k2)'*Ah(k1:k2);
                    h1(k1:k2) = alpha*h(k1:k2);   h2(k1:k2) = hAh*h1(k1:k2);
                    for k=k1:k2
                        if (J(k) < 0)
                            A(k,k1:k) =-A(k,k1:k);   A(k:k2,k) =-A(k:k2,k);
                            Ah(k) =-Ah(k);
                            A(k,j+1:k1-1) = -A(k,j+1:k1-1);
                        end
                    end
                    A(k1:k2,j) = 0;   A(k1+l-1,j) = beta;
                    A(k1:k2,j+1:k1-1) = A(k1:k2,j+1:k1-1) - h1(k1:k2)*Ah(j+1:k1-1)';
                    for k=k1:k2         %(J-alpha*h*h')*A*(J-alpha*h*h')=>A
                        A(k:k2,k) = A(k:k2,k)-Ah(k:k2)*h1(k)-h1(k:k2)*Ah(k)+h1(k:k2)
                                                                          *h2(k);
                    end
                    if (~strcmp(format,'brief'))       %G*H=>G
                        h2 = G(:,k1:k2)*h1(k1:k2);
                        for k=k1:k2     %G*J=>G
                            if (J(k) < 0) G(:,k) =-G(:,k); end
                        end
                        G(:,k1:k2) = G(:,k1:k2) - h2*h(k1:k2)';
                    end
                    if (l ~= 1)
                        i = k1; k = k1+l-1;
                        [A(i,1:i-1),A(k,1:i-1)] = swap_(A(i,1:i-1),A(k,1:i-1));
                        [A(k+1:n,i),A(k+1:n,k)] = swap_(A(k+1:n,i),A(k+1:n,k));
                        [A(i+1:k-1,i),A(k,i+1:k-1)] = swap_(A(i+1:k-1,i),A(k,i+1:k-1));
                        [A(i,i),A(k,k)] = swap_(A(i,i),A(k,k));
                        j1 = J(k1); J(k1) = J(k);   J(k) = j1;
                        if (~strcmp(format,'brief'))
                                      [G(:,i),G(:,k)] = swap_(G(:,i),G(:,k)); end
                    end
                end     %hyper
            end         %algo
        end     %while(z<m-j-1)
    end         %j=f1st...last

    if (last < n-2)    %partial GTJGt
        A = A - triu(A,1);   A = A + tril(A,-1)';   B = J';
    else
        if (strcmp(format,'long'))
            A = A - triu(A,1);   A = A + tril(A,-1)';   B = diag(J)';
        elseif (strcmp(format,'short') || strcmp(format,'brief'))
            for j=2:m A(j-1,j) = A(j,j-1); end
            A = full2band_(A,1,1);   B = J';
        end
    end
```

In the following, we give four examples demonstrating the use of GTJGt_.m. In the first example, **A** and **B** are both symmetric indefinite and non-singular. It shows the output of the same two matrices with different input arguments: algo='givens' and algo='householder'; pivot=1 and pivot=2; format='long' and format='short'.

```
>> A=randn(5);    A=0.5*(A+A');
>> B=randn(5);    B=0.5*(B+B');      %simple way to create a symmetric matrix

>> [T,J,G]=GTJGt_(A,B,'givens',1,100*eps,'long')
T =
      0.0616      1.6887           0           0           0
      1.6887     -6.8200      5.5792           0           0
           0      5.5792     -4.0186     -1.0736           0
           0           0     -1.0736     -0.0398     -0.2543
           0           0           0     -0.2543     -0.1102
J =
      1      0      0      0      0
      0      1      0      0      0
      0      0      1      0      0
      0      0      0     -1      0
      0      0      0      0     -1
G =
      1.0180           0           0           0           0
     -0.5956      0.2256      0.2103     -1.0892      0.2035
      0.2335      0.5834      0.7332      0.7036     -1.2138
     -0.8337      0.3462      1.0571     -0.3920      0.4892
     -0.4598     -0.5880     -0.2773     -1.0730     -0.8220

>> [T,J,G]=GTJGt_(A,B,'householder',2,100*eps,'short')
T =
           0      0.0616     -1.6887
     -1.6887     -6.8200      5.5792
      5.5792     -4.0186      1.0736
      1.0736     -0.0398      0.2543
      0.2543     -0.1102           0
J =
      1
      1
      1
     -1
     -1
G =
      1.0180           0           0           0           0
     -0.5956     -0.2256     -0.2103     -1.0892     -0.2035
      0.2335     -0.5834     -0.7332      0.7036      1.2138
     -0.8337     -0.3462     -1.0571     -0.3920     -0.4892
     -0.4598      0.5880      0.2773     -1.0730      0.8220
```

In the second example, **B** is symmetric indefinite and singular. **A** is the same matrix as in the first example. The output matrix **J** has +1s, −1s, and 0s.

```
>> d=[1;-2;3;0;0];    B=B'*diag(d)*B;    %simple way to create a symmetric matrix
                                         %with positive,zero and negative eigenvalues
>> [T,J,G]=GTJGt_(A,B,'givens',2,100*eps,'long')
T =
     -2.4128     -1.5310           0           0           0
     -1.5310      1.0426      0.6866           0           0
```

```
           0      0.6866     0.2648    -0.1203          0
           0          0     -0.1203    -1.1018    -1.0050
           0          0          0     -1.0050    -0.9475
J  =
      0     0     0     0     0
      0     0     0     0     0
      0     0     1     0     0
      0     0     0     1     0
      0     0     0     0    -1
G  =
           0     -0.4481    -1.1320    -3.0772     3.2005
           0     -1.0959     1.2401    -2.7981     2.4844
           0      0.0559    -0.5089     3.8513    -3.8087
      1.0000    -0.7057     2.6843    -1.2484     0.0551
           0      1.1859    -1.1115     0.4222     0.6866
```

In the third example, **A** is also symmetric indefinite and singular. **B** is the same matrix as in the second example. The output matrix **T** also has zeros on the diagonal.

```
>> d=[-10;20;0;30;0];    A=A'*diag(d)*A;

>> [T,J,G]=GTJGt_(A,B,'householder',1,100*eps,'long')
T  =
   104.8518   -15.7016          0          0          0
   -15.7016    -8.4105    16.9940          0          0
          0    16.9940    -6.6084    -7.9326          0
          0          0    -7.9326     3.1111    -0.0000
          0          0          0    -0.0000    -0.0000
J  =
      0     0     0     0     0
      0     0     0     0     0
      0     0    -1     0     0
      0     0     0     1     0
      0     0     0     0     1
G  =
           0      0.6611     0.8065    -0.0850     1.0729
           0      2.7562     1.9938     2.4834     1.0017
           0     -1.9138    -2.4171    -2.2625    -1.1439
      1.0000     1.4461     0.7300     2.7338     1.3492
           0     -0.1619     1.0109    -0.3596    -1.3546
```

The last example shows the correctness and efficiency of GTJGt decomposition of two relative large matrices. The two full symmetric matrices of a size 500×500 are created with the following piece of codes.

```
d1 = randn(500,1);    d1(100:150) = 0;
d2 = randn(500,1);    d2(300:320) =0;
[Q1,r] = QR_(randn(500));    [Q2,r] = QR_(randn(500));
A = Q1'*diag(d1)*Q1;   B = Q2'*diag(d2)*Q2;
```

The GTJGt decomposition of **A** and **B** is done with algo='householder',pivot=1 and algo='givens',pivot=2, respectively. The conditioning of the two transformation matrices G_1 and G_2 is close. The results of zeros show that **T** is a tri-diagonal and **J** is a diagonal. The results of close to zeros verify the correctness of the calculation and the difference to zeros measures the accuracy of the calculation. The calculation is done on an INSPIRON 1545 laptop.

```
>> tic                                    >> tic
>> [T1,J1,G1]=GTJGt_(A,B,'householder',...  >> [T2,J2,G2]=GTJGt_(A,B,'givens',2,...
                  1,100*eps,'long');                        100*eps,'long');
>> toc                                    >> toc
Elapsed time is 12.304127 seconds.        Elapsed time is 19.881355 seconds.

>> cond(G1)                               >> cond(G2)
= 4.7587e+006                             = 4.7587e+006
>> norm(G1*T1*G1'-A)                      >> norm(G2*T2*G2'-A)
= 1.7201e-008                             = 8.9605e-006
>> norm(G1*J1*G1'-B)                      >> norm(G2*J2*G2'-B)
= 7.9122e-011                             = 4.1992e-011
>> norm(tril(T1,-2))+norm(triu(T1,2))     >> norm(tril(T2,-2))+norm(triu(T2,2))
=    0                                    =    0
>> norm(tril(J1,-1))+norm(triu(J1,1))     >> norm(tril(J2,-1))+norm(triu(J2,1))
=    0                                    =    0
```

Direct algorithms of decompositions of matrices by orthogonal transformations

INTRODUCTION

The topic of this chapter is the direct algorithms to decompose a matrix $\mathbf{A}$ to the form $\mathbf{A} = \mathbf{UBV}$. It is the same topic of the last chapter. The difference is in the choice of $\mathbf{U}$ and $\mathbf{V}$. In the last chapter, $\mathbf{U}$ and $\mathbf{V}$ are non-orthogonal matrices. As discussed in the last chapter, the stability of the decomposition algorithm with non-orthogonal matrices has always an issue. To maintain the numerical stability, different pivoting strategies have been devised. Another way to maintain the numerical stability is to use exclusively orthogonal matrices. Orthogonal matrices keep the norm and dot product; thus, they will not magnify any numerical errors in calculations. But they require more computations and they may limit the form of $\mathbf{B}$ that can be reduced to. In this chapter, we use exclusively the orthogonal matrices in the decomposition. All the algorithms presented in this chapter have counterparts in the last chapter.

Section 3.1 presents two orthogonal zeroing matrices that are used in the chapter, Householder reflection matrix and Given rotation matrix.

Section 3.2 presents QR algorithms: $\mathbf{A} = \mathbf{QR}$ or $\mathbf{AP'} = \mathbf{QR}$, where $\mathbf{A}$ is a general rectangular matrix, $\mathbf{Q}$ is an orthogonal matrix, $\mathbf{R}$ is an upper triangular matrix, $\mathbf{P}$ is a permutation matrix.

Section 3.3 presents QLZ algorithms: $\mathbf{A} = \mathbf{QLZ}$, where $\mathbf{A}$ is a general rectangular matrix, $\mathbf{Q}$ is an orthogonal matrix, $\mathbf{L}$ is a lower triangular matrix, $\mathbf{Z}$ is another orthogonal matrix.

Section 3.4 presents QBZ algorithms: $\mathbf{A} = \mathbf{QBZ}$, where $\mathbf{A}$ is a general rectangular matrix, $\mathbf{Q}$ is an orthogonal matrix, $\mathbf{B}$ is a bi-diagonal matrix, $\mathbf{Z}$ is another orthogonal matrix.

Section 3.5 presents QHQt algorithms: $\mathbf{A} = \mathbf{QHQ'}$, where $\mathbf{A}$ is a general square matrix, $\mathbf{Q}$ is an orthogonal matrix, $\mathbf{H}$ is a Hessenberg matrix.

Section 3.6 presents QTQt algorithms: $\mathbf{A} = \mathbf{QTQ'}$, where $\mathbf{A}$ is a symmetric matrix, $\mathbf{Q}$ is an orthogonal matrix, $\mathbf{T}$ is a symmetric tri-diagonal matrix.

Section 3.7 presents QHRZ algorithms: $[\mathbf{A}, \mathbf{B}] = \mathbf{Q}[\mathbf{H}, \mathbf{R}]\mathbf{Z}$, where $\mathbf{A}$ and $\mathbf{B}$ are square matrices, $\mathbf{Q}$ is an orthogonal matrix, $\mathbf{H}$ is a Hessenberg matrix, $\mathbf{R}$ is an upper triangular matrix, $\mathbf{Z}$ is another orthogonal matrix.

All the algorithms will be presented in more than one form, that is, transforming or decomposing or multiplying discussed in Section 1.4. All the algorithms provide early exit and restart capability, so that the reader can run each algorithm step by step and check the output of computations. All the algorithms have four output formats, brief, compact, short, and long. The restart capability and output format will be explained in full detail in QR algorithm. They remain essentially the same for all the other algorithms.

Matrix Algorithms in MATLAB. DOI: 10.1016/B978-0-12-803804-8.00009-X

3.1 HOUSEHOLDER REFLECTION MATRIX AND GIVENS ROTATION MATRIX

Householder reflection matrix and Givens rotation matrix are orthogonal. All the algorithms to be presented in this chapter are built upon these two matrices.

A Householder reflection matrix $\mathbf{H}$ is of the following form:

$$\mathbf{H} = \mathbf{I} - \frac{2}{\mathbf{h}'\mathbf{h}}\mathbf{h}\mathbf{h}' = \mathbf{I} - \alpha\mathbf{h}\mathbf{h}'. \tag{3.1}$$

It can be easily verified that $\mathbf{H}$ has the following properties:

$$\mathbf{H} = \mathbf{H}', \quad \mathbf{H}'\mathbf{H} = \mathbf{H}\mathbf{H}' = \mathbf{I}, \quad \det(\mathbf{H}) = -1. \tag{3.2}$$

Given an arbitrary vector $\mathbf{v} \in \mathbb{R}^n$, we want to determine a Householder reflection matrix $\mathbf{H}$ so that $\mathbf{H}\mathbf{v} = \mathbf{v} - \frac{2\mathbf{h}'\mathbf{v}}{\mathbf{h}'\mathbf{h}}\mathbf{h} = \pm\|\mathbf{v}\|_2\mathbf{I}(:,1)$. From this requirement, we can assume $\mathbf{h} = \mathbf{v} + \gamma\mathbf{I}(:,1)$. Setting $\mathbf{h} = \mathbf{v} + \gamma\mathbf{I}(:,1)$ in $\mathbf{H}\mathbf{v}$ gives

$$\mathbf{H}\mathbf{v} = \frac{\gamma^2 - \mathbf{v}'\mathbf{v}}{\mathbf{v}'\mathbf{v} + 2\gamma v_1 + \gamma^2}\mathbf{v} - \gamma\frac{2\mathbf{v}'\mathbf{v} + 2\gamma v_1}{\mathbf{v}'\mathbf{v} + 2\gamma v_1 + \gamma^2}\mathbf{I}(:,1).$$

Setting $\gamma = \pm\|\mathbf{v}\|_2$, then $\mathbf{H}\mathbf{v} = \mp\|\mathbf{v}\|_2\mathbf{I}(:,1)$. To avoid the potential numerical cancelation in the calculation of $\mathbf{h} = \mathbf{v} + \gamma\mathbf{I}(:,1)$, we choose $\gamma = \text{sign}(v_1)\|\mathbf{v}\|_2$ and $\mathbf{H}\mathbf{v} = -\text{sign}(v_1)\|\mathbf{v}\|_2\mathbf{I}(:,1) = \beta\mathbf{I}(:,1)$. In the following listed MATLAB code householder_.m, $\mathbf{h}$ is normalized so that $h_1 = 1$. $\mathbf{h}(2:n)$ can be saved to the zeroed $\mathbf{v}(2:n)$. $h_1 = 1$ does not need to be saved.

Algorithm 3.1

Householder reflection matrix.

```
%Calculate Householder reflection matrix H=eye-alpha*h*h'
%H*v = [v(1);...;v(k-1);beta;0;...0] for z=1; or
%H*v = [0      ;...;0     ;beta;0;...0] for z=2
%format='short': h=Householder vector; ='long':h=Householder matrix.
function [h,alpha,beta] = householder_(v,k,z,format)

if (~exist('k','var')) k = 1; end
if (~exist('z','var')) z = 1; end
if (~exist('format','var')) format = 'short'; end

if (z==1 && k>1) v(1:k-1) = 0.0; end
alpha = 0.0;  normv = norm(v);
if (v(k) > 0) beta = -normv; else beta = normv; end
h = zeros(length(v),1);  h(1:end) = v(1:end);  h(k) = h(k) - beta;
if (normv > 0)
    alpha = h(k)*h(k)/(normv*(normv + abs(v(k))));  h = h/h(k);
end
if (strcmp(format,'long')) h = eye(length(v)) - alpha*h*h'; end
```

The following examples demonstrate the use of householder_.m. It should be noted that the Householder matrix $\mathbf{H}$ is rarely explicitly formed and only the Householder vector $\mathbf{h}$ is created and used.

```
>> v=[1;2;3];

>> H1=householder_(v,1,1,'long')
H1 =
   -0.2673   -0.5345   -0.8018
   -0.5345    0.7745   -0.3382
   -0.8018   -0.3382    0.4927
>> H1*v
=   -3.7417
     0.0000
          0

>> H2=householder_(v,2,1,'long')
H2 =
    1.0000         0         0
         0   -0.5547   -0.8321
         0   -0.8321    0.5547
>> H2*v
=    1.0000
    -3.6056
          0

>> H3=householder_(v,2,2,'long')
H3 =
```

```
    0.9535   -0.2673   -0.1396
   -0.2673   -0.5345   -0.8018
   -0.1396   -0.8018    0.5811
>> H3*v
=    0.0000
    -3.7417
     0.0000

>> h1=householder_(v,1,1,'short')
h1 =
    1.0000
    0.4218
    0.6327
>> h2=householder_(v,2,1,'short')
h2 =
         0
    1.0000
    0.5352
>> h3=householder_(v,2,2,'short')
h3 =
    0.1742
    1.0000
    0.5225
```

Householder reflection matrices can also be used to zero a selective component of a column or row vector. Now let us look at another example.

```
>> v=1:8
v =
     1     2     3     4     5     6     7     8
>> h=householder_([v(3);v(6)])
h =
    1.0000
    0.6180
>> h=[0;0;h(1);0;0;h(2);0;0];
>> H=eye(8)-(2.0/(h'*h))*h*h'
H =
    1.0000        0        0        0        0        0        0        0
         0   1.0000        0        0        0        0        0        0
         0        0  -0.4472        0        0  -0.8944        0        0
         0        0        0   1.0000        0        0        0        0
         0        0        0        0   1.0000        0        0        0
         0        0  -0.8944        0        0   0.4472        0        0
         0        0        0        0        0        0   1.0000        0
         0        0        0        0        0        0        0   1.0000
>> v*H
=    1.0000    2.0000   -6.7082    4.0000    5.0000    0.0000    7.0000    8.0000
```

The example demonstrates the way to zero v_6 and use v_3 as a pseudo-pivot. The calculation can be simplified by simple means. A more special algorithm for the task to zero a selective component of a vector is the Givens rotation.

Given a vector $\mathbf{v} = \begin{bmatrix} a \\ b \end{bmatrix}$, we want to determine a Givens rotation matrix $\mathbf{G} = \begin{bmatrix} c & -s \\ s & c \end{bmatrix}$ so that $\mathbf{u} = \mathbf{G'v} = \begin{bmatrix} \pm\sqrt{a^2 + b^2} \\ 0 \end{bmatrix}$, where $c = \cos(\theta)$ and $s = \sin(\theta)$ for some θ. The obvious choice of c

and s to set $u_2 = 0$ is the following:

$$c = \frac{a}{\sqrt{a^2 + b^2}} = \frac{1}{\sqrt{1 + \left(\frac{b}{a}\right)^2}}; \qquad s = -\frac{b}{\sqrt{a^2 + b^2}} = -\frac{1}{\sqrt{1 + \left(\frac{a}{b}\right)^2}}. \tag{3.3}$$

The following is the MATLAB code implementing the above equation.

Algorithm 3.2

Givens rotation matrix.

```
% [c -s; [a;    [x;
%  s  c]*  b] =  0]
function [c,s] = givens_(a,b)

if (b == 0)
    c = 1;  s = 0;
elseif (abs(b) > abs(a))
    tau = -a/b;
    s = 1.0/sqrt(1.0+tau*tau);  c = s*tau;
else
    tau = -b/a;
    c = 1.0/sqrt(1.0+tau*tau);  s = c*tau;
end
```

In practice, $\mathbf{G}'\mathbf{v}$ usually overwrites $\mathbf{v}$ and we want to save the information of the Givens rotation matrix $\mathbf{G}$ in the zeroed v_2. But $\mathbf{G}$ has two data c and s satisfying $c^2 + s^2 = 1$. c and s are saved and retrieved following a storage scheme devised by Stewart [67].

if $c = 0$ then
    $\rho = 1$.
else if $|c| < |s|$ then
    $\rho = \text{sign}(c)\frac{s}{2}$.
else
    $\rho = \text{sign}(s)\frac{2}{c}$.
end if

if $\rho = 1$ then
    $c = 1, s = 0$.
else if $|\rho| < 1$ then
    $s = 2\rho, c = \sqrt{1 - s^2}$.
else
    $c = \frac{2}{\rho}, s = \sqrt{1 - c^2}$.
end if

3.2 QR DECOMPOSITION

Given a matrix, $\mathbf{A} \in \mathbb{R}^{m \times n}$, we want to find an orthonormal matrix $\mathbf{Q}$ and a lower triangular matrix $\mathbf{R}$ so that $\mathbf{A} = \mathbf{QR}$. $\mathbf{A} = \mathbf{QR}$ is called a QR decomposition of $\mathbf{A}$. In the QR decomposition, $\mathbf{A}(j : m, j)$ is eliminated by Householder reflection matrices or Givens rotation matrices, where $j = 1 \cdots n - 1$ or $j = n - 1 \cdots 1$. To be specific, we choose $j = 1 \cdots n - 1$ in the algorithms presented in this section. Because Householder reflection matrices and Givens rotation matrices are orthogonal, the permutations of rows or columns are not needed for the QR decompositions. When the columns of $\mathbf{A}$ are not independent, the columns of $\mathbf{R}$ are not independent. A column permutation can be applied to $\mathbf{A}$ so that its dependent columns are moved to the right. In this way $\mathbf{AP}' = \mathbf{QR}$, all the independent columns of $\mathbf{R}$ are to its left.

3.2.1 QR DECOMPOSITION BY HOUSEHOLDER REFLECTIONS

The procedure of QR decomposition is illustrated with a 5×5 matrix,

$$\mathbf{A} = \begin{bmatrix} A_{11} & A_{12} & A_{13} & A_{14} & A_{15} \\ A_{21} & A_{22} & A_{23} & A_{24} & A_{25} \\ A_{31} & A_{32} & A_{33} & A_{34} & A_{35} \\ A_{41} & A_{42} & A_{43} & A_{44} & A_{45} \\ A_{51} & A_{52} & A_{53} & A_{54} & A_{55} \end{bmatrix}.$$

In the first step, we choose a Householder matrix $\mathbf{H}_1 = \mathbf{I} - \alpha_1 \mathbf{h}_1 \mathbf{h}_1'$ to zero $\mathbf{A}(2:5,1)$,

$$\mathbf{H}_1 \mathbf{A} = \mathbf{A} - (\alpha_1 \mathbf{h}_1)(\mathbf{h}_1' \mathbf{A}) = \begin{bmatrix} \beta_1 & A_{12} & A_{13} & A_{14} & A_{15} \\ 0 & A_{22} & A_{23} & A_{24} & A_{25} \\ 0 & A_{32} & A_{33} & A_{34} & A_{35} \\ 0 & A_{42} & A_{43} & A_{44} & A_{45} \\ 0 & A_{52} & A_{53} & A_{54} & A_{55} \end{bmatrix},$$

where α_1 and β_1 are the output arguments of householder_.m. The parentheses in $\mathbf{H}_1 \mathbf{A}$ show the grouping of the calculation of $\mathbf{H}_1 \mathbf{A}$. $\mathbf{H}_1 \mathbf{A}(:,2:4)$ overwrites $\mathbf{A}(:,2:4)$. $\mathbf{h}_1(2:5)$ is saved to $\mathbf{A}(2:5,1)$. The next step is to choose another Householder matrix $\mathbf{H}_2 = \mathbf{I} - \alpha_2 \mathbf{h}_2 \mathbf{h}_2'$ to zero $\mathbf{A}(3:5,2)$. The following equation shows the actual calculation. $\mathbf{A}$'s first row and column (now $\mathbf{A}(2:5,1) = \mathbf{0}$) is not altered by $\mathbf{H}_2 \mathbf{A}$. $\mathbf{h}_2(2:4)$ is saved to the zeroed $\mathbf{A}(3:5,2)$,

$$\mathbf{H}_2 \mathbf{A}(2:5,2:5) = \mathbf{A}(2:5,2:5) - (\alpha_2 \mathbf{h}_2)(\mathbf{h}_2' \mathbf{A}(2:5,2:5)) = \begin{bmatrix} \beta_2 & A_{23} & A_{24} & A_{25} \\ 0 & A_{33} & A_{34} & A_{35} \\ 0 & A_{43} & A_{44} & A_{45} \\ 0 & A_{53} & A_{54} & A_{55} \end{bmatrix}.$$

Continue the same steps to zero $\mathbf{A}(3:5,3)$ and $\mathbf{A}(4:5,4)$ with Householder matrices $\mathbf{H}_3$ and $\mathbf{H}_4$, respectively. Then, $\mathbf{H}_4 \mathbf{H}_3 \mathbf{H}_2 \mathbf{H}_1 \mathbf{A}$ becomes an upper triangular matrix denoted by $\mathbf{R}$. The product of $\mathbf{H}_4 \mathbf{H}_3 \mathbf{H}_2 \mathbf{H}_1$ is the orthogonal matrix denoted by $\mathbf{Q}$. For most calculations, $\mathbf{Q}$ can be kept as the factored form of $\mathbf{H}_4 \mathbf{H}_3 \mathbf{H}_2 \mathbf{H}_1$. If needed, $\mathbf{Q}$ can be explicitly formed. The calculation of $\mathbf{Q}$ is more efficient if calculated in the order $(((\mathbf{H}_4 \mathbf{H}_3) \mathbf{H}_2) \mathbf{H}_1)$.

Now let us assume $\mathbf{A}(:,3) = b_1 \mathbf{A}(:,1) + b_2 \mathbf{A}(:,2)$ for arbitrary b_1 and b_2 in the original $\mathbf{A}$ and we revisit the unexplored third step,

$$\mathbf{H}_2 \mathbf{H}_1 \mathbf{A}(:,3) = \begin{bmatrix} b_1 \beta_1 \\ 0 \\ 0 \\ 0 \\ 0 \end{bmatrix} + \begin{bmatrix} b_2 A_{12} \\ b_2 \beta_2 \\ 0 \\ 0 \\ 0 \end{bmatrix}.$$

As we see from the above calculation, if $\mathbf{A}(:,3)$ is linearly dependent to $\mathbf{A}(:,1)$ and/or $\mathbf{A}(:,2)$, $\mathbf{A}(3:5,3) = \mathbf{0}$ after $\mathbf{H}_2 \mathbf{H}_1$ is applied to $\mathbf{A}$. In this case, the third step can be skipped and the third column of $\mathbf{H}_2 \mathbf{H}_1 \mathbf{A}$ remains linearly dependent to its first and second columns. Sometimes it is useful to move the linearly dependent columns of $\mathbf{A}$ to the most right, for example, to reveal the column rank or to find the orthogonal bases of the range space of $\mathbf{A}$. If we want to do that and we find that $\mathbf{A}(3:5,3) = \mathbf{0}$, we can permute $\mathbf{A}(:,3)$ and $\mathbf{A}(:,5)$ or $\mathbf{A}(:,4)$. Then we apply a Householder matrix to zero $\mathbf{A}(3:5,3)$ from the permuted $\mathbf{A}(:,3)$. In the following MATLAB code QRbyHouseholder_.m, the decision to make the column permutations is controlled by pivot=1. However, if $\mathbf{A}$ has the full column rank, pivot=1 will make no difference to the QR decomposition. If $\mathbf{A}$ has column rank deficiency and the input argument pivot=1, the QR decomposition takes the form $\mathbf{AP'} = \mathbf{QR}$, where $\mathbf{P}$ is a permutation matrix.

Algorithm 3.3

```
A*P'=Q*R, Q orthogonal matrix, R upper triangular, P permutation.
function [A,p] = QRbyHouseholder_(A,pivot,tol,f1st,last,p)

[m,n] = size(A);
tol = tol*max(1.0,norm(diag(A),inf));

for j=f1st:last
    [h,alpha,beta] = householder_(A(j:m,j));
    if (pivot>0 && abs(beta)<tol)
        for k=n:-1:j+1
            if (p(k) ~= k) continue; end
            if (norm(A(j:m,k),inf) < tol) continue; end
            [h,alpha,beta] = householder_(A(j:m,k));
            [p(j),p(k)] = swap_(p(j),p(k));
            [A(:,j),A(:,k)] = swap_(A(:,j),A(:,k));
            break;
        end
    end
    A(j,j) = beta;   v = alpha*h;   %Apply H'*A
    for k=j+1:n
        ak = A(j:m,k);   A(j:m,k) = ak - (h'*ak)*v;
    end
    A(j+1:m,j) = h(2:m-j+1);       %Keep Householder vector
end
```

3.2.2 QR DECOMPOSITION BY GIVENS ROTATIONS

Givens rotations of Eq. (3.3) can also be used to compute the QR decomposition. The procedure is illustrated with a 4×3 matrix,

$$
\begin{bmatrix} A_{11} & A_{12} & A_{13} \\ A_{21} & A_{22} & A_{23} \\ A_{31} & A_{32} & A_{33} \\ A_{41} & A_{42} & A_{43} \end{bmatrix}
\xrightarrow{11,21}
\begin{bmatrix} A_{11} & A_{12} & A_{13} \\ 0 & A_{22} & A_{23} \\ A_{31} & A_{32} & A_{33} \\ A_{41} & A_{42} & A_{43} \end{bmatrix}
\xrightarrow{11,31}
\begin{bmatrix} A_{11} & A_{12} & A_{13} \\ 0 & A_{22} & A_{23} \\ 0 & A_{32} & A_{33} \\ A_{41} & A_{42} & A_{43} \end{bmatrix}
\xrightarrow{11,41}
\begin{bmatrix} A_{11} & A_{12} & A_{13} \\ 0 & A_{22} & A_{23} \\ 0 & A_{32} & A_{33} \\ 0 & A_{42} & A_{43} \end{bmatrix}
$$

$$
\xrightarrow{32,42}
\begin{bmatrix} A_{11} & A_{12} & A_{13} \\ 0 & A_{22} & A_{23} \\ 0 & A_{32} & A_{33} \\ 0 & 0 & A_{43} \end{bmatrix}
\xrightarrow{22,32}
\begin{bmatrix} A_{11} & A_{12} & A_{13} \\ 0 & A_{22} & A_{23} \\ 0 & 0 & A_{33} \\ 0 & 0 & A_{43} \end{bmatrix}
\xrightarrow{33,43}
\begin{bmatrix} A_{11} & A_{12} & A_{13} \\ 0 & A_{22} & A_{23} \\ 0 & 0 & A_{33} \\ 0 & 0 & 0 \end{bmatrix}.
$$

In the procedure shown above, we first take $a = A_{11}, b = A_{21}$ and construct a Givens rotation $\mathbf{G}_1$ according to Eq. (3.3) to zero A_{21}. $\mathbf{G}_1'\mathbf{A}$ only changes $\mathbf{A}(1:2,:)$. $\mathbf{A}(1:2,:)$ is overwritten by the change. The encoded $\begin{bmatrix} c,s \end{bmatrix}$ is saved to the zeroed A_{21}. Then, we zero A_{31} and A_{41} by using the rotation pair $(11,31)$ and $(11,41)$, respectively. Other orders of rotations can also be used. In the second column, we first zero A_{42} with the rotation pair $(32, 42)$, then zero A_{32} with the rotation pair $(22, 32)$. The column permutation of **A** in case of dependent columns is handled in the similar way to QRbyHouseholder_.m. Now we present the MATLAB implementation of QR decomposition by Givens rotations.

Algorithm 3.4

A*P'=Q*R, Q orthogonal matrix, R upper triangular, P permutation.

```
function [A,p] = QRbyGivens_(A,pivot,tol,f1st,last,p)

[m,n] = size(A);
tol = tol*max(1.0,norm(diag(A),inf));

for j=f1st:last
    normaj = norm(A(j:m,j),inf);
    if (pivot>0 && normaj<tol)        %column permutation
        for k=n:-1:j+1
            if (p(k) ~= k) continue; end
            normak = norm(A(j:m,k),inf);
            if (normak <= tol) continue; end
            [p(j),p(k)] = swap_(p(j),p(k));
            [A(:,j),A(:,k)] = swap_(A(:,j),A(:,k));
            normaj = normak;  break;
        end
    end
    if (normaj < tol) continue; end
    for k=j+1:m
        [c,s] = givens_(A(j,j),A(k,j));
        A(j,j) = c*A(j,j) - s*A(k,j);  %apply Givens transformation
        for l=j+1:n
            Ajl = A(j,l);  Akl = A(k,l);
            A(j,l) = c*Ajl - s*Akl;  A(k,l) = s*Ajl + c*Akl;
        end
        if (abs(c) < tol)         rho = 1;
        elseif(abs(s) < abs(c)) rho = sign(c)*s/2;
        else                    rho = sign(s)*2/c; end
        A(k,j) = rho;    %save encoded [c,s] at zeroed A(k,j)
    end
end
```

3.2.3 QR DECOMPOSITION BY GRAM–SCHMIDT ORTHOGONALIZATIONS

From the above two subsections, we see that QR decomposition of $\mathbf{A} = \mathbf{QR}$ always exists, where $\mathbf{A} \in \mathbb{R}^{m \times n}$, $\mathbf{Q}$ is orthogonal, and $\mathbf{R}$ is upper triangular. We can write $\mathbf{A} = \mathbf{QR}$ as a form of block column matrices,

$$\begin{bmatrix} \mathbf{A}(:,1) & \mathbf{A}(:,2) & \cdots & \mathbf{A}(:,n) \end{bmatrix} = \begin{bmatrix} \mathbf{Q}(:,1) & \mathbf{Q}(:,2) & \cdots & \mathbf{A}(:,m) \end{bmatrix} \begin{bmatrix} R_{11} & R_{12} & R_{13} & \cdots & R_{1n} \\ 0 & R_{22} & R_{23} & \cdots & R_{2n} \\ 0 & 0 & R_{33} & \cdots & R_{3n} \\ \vdots & \vdots & \vdots & \vdots & \vdots \\ 0 & 0 & 0 & \cdots & R_{mn} \end{bmatrix}. \quad (3.4)$$

By comparing the first column of the left and right hand sides, we obtain that

$$\mathbf{A}(:,1) = R_{11}\mathbf{Q}(:,1).$$

Since $\|\mathbf{Q}(:,1)\|_2 = 1$, the above equation determines that

$$R_{11} = \|\mathbf{A}(:,1)\|_2, \quad \mathbf{Q}(:,1) = \frac{1}{R_{11}}\mathbf{A}(:,1).$$

If $R_{11} = 0$, the above equation fails. We have two options to handle this case. The first option is to take $\mathbf{Q}(:,1)$ to be an arbitrary unit vector. The second one is to swap the column one and any other nonzero column of $\mathbf{A}$. Then calculate R_{11} and $\mathbf{Q}(:,1)$ from the first column of the permuted $\mathbf{A}$ according to the above equation. We need to record the permutation in $\mathbf{P}$.

Now we compare the second column of the left and right sides of Eq. (3.4),

$$\mathbf{A}(:,2) = R_{12}\mathbf{Q}(:,1) + R_{22}\mathbf{Q}(:,2).$$

Because we require $\mathbf{Q}(:,1)'\mathbf{Q}(:,2) = 0$ and $\mathbf{Q}(:,2)'\mathbf{Q}(:,2) = 1$, the above equation shows that

$$R_{12} = \mathbf{Q}(:,1)'\mathbf{A}(:,2), \quad R_{22} = \|\mathbf{A}(:,2) - R_{12}\mathbf{Q}(:,1)\|, \quad \mathbf{Q}_2 = \frac{1}{R_{22}}\left(\mathbf{A}(:,2) - R_{12}\mathbf{Q}(:,1)\right).$$

If $R_{22} = 0$, we again face the two options alluded in the above paragraph. But the option one must be slightly modified: the arbitrary unit vector $\mathbf{Q}(:,2)$ must be orthogonal to $\mathbf{Q}(:,1)$. See the discussion about `orthogonal_.m` in Section 1.6.

The third column of the left and right sides of Eq. (3.4) is $\mathbf{A}(:,3) = R_{13}\mathbf{Q}(:,1)+R_{23}\mathbf{Q}(:,2)+R_{33}\mathbf{Q}(:,3)$. Noting the orthonormality among $\mathbf{Q}(:,1:3)$, we calculate R_{13}, R_{33}, R_{33}, and $\mathbf{Q}(:,3)$ as follows:

$$R_{13} = \mathbf{Q}(:,1)'\mathbf{A}(:,3), \quad R_{23} = \mathbf{Q}(:,2)'\mathbf{A}(:,3),$$

$$R_{33} = \|\mathbf{A}(:,3) - R_{13}\mathbf{Q}(:,1) - R_{23}\mathbf{Q}(:,2)\|, \quad \mathbf{Q}_3 = \frac{1}{R_{33}}\left(\mathbf{A}(:,3) - R_{13}\mathbf{Q}(:,1) - R_{23}\mathbf{Q}(:,2)\right).$$

If $R_{33} = 0$, we follow the two options to treat the exception. We continue the same procedure to the last column of $\mathbf{A}$. Then, we obtain an $m \times m$ orthogonal matrix $\mathbf{Q}$ and an $m \times n$ upper triangular matrix $\mathbf{R}$, which satisfy $\mathbf{A} = \mathbf{QR}$ or $\mathbf{AP}' = \mathbf{QR}$, depending on the chosen option. The procedure we just described is the classical Gram–Schmidt orthogonalization.

The classical Gram–Schmidt orthogonalization is numerically unstable—the gradual loss of orthogonality among the columns of $\mathbf{Q}$. Let us take a look at $R_{23} = \mathbf{Q}(:,2)'\mathbf{A}(:,3)$. This expression is obtained by assuming $\mathbf{Q}(:,1)'\mathbf{Q}(:,2) = 0$. If we discard the assumption of $\mathbf{Q}(:,1)'\mathbf{Q}(:,2) = 0$, R_{23} should be calculated as $R_{23} = \mathbf{Q}(:,2)'(\mathbf{A}(:,3) - R_{13}\mathbf{Q}(:,1))$. In the calculation of $\mathbf{R}(1:j-1,j)$, we do not assume the orthogonality among $\mathbf{Q}(:,1:j-1)$ for $j = 3\cdots m$. The procedure is what is called the modified Gram–Schmidt orthogonalization. The modified Gram–Schmidt is implemented in the following `QRbyGramSchimdt_.m` with some rearrangement of the calculation. For $j = 1\cdots n$, when $\mathbf{Q}(:,j)$ is calculated, it overwrites $\mathbf{A}(:,j)$. The components of the columns of $\mathbf{A}$ from $j+1$ to the last column in the direction of $\mathbf{Q}(:,j)$, that is, $\mathbf{R}(j,j+1:n)$, are immediately calculated. Then, the components of $\mathbf{Q}(:,j)$ are removed from $\mathbf{A}(:,j+1:n)$. In `QRbyGramSchimdt_.m`, the two options of handling the exception of $R_{jj} = 0$ are controlled by the input argument `pivot`.

Algorithm 3.5

A*P'=Q*R, Q orthogonal matrix, R upper triangular, P permutation.

```
function [A,R,p] = QRbyGramSchimdt_(A,pivot,tol,f1st,last,R,p)

[m,n] = size(A);
tol = tol*max(1.0,norm(diag(A),inf));
R = [R;zeros(last-f1st+1,n)];

for j=f1st:last
    aj = A(:,j);  normaj = norm(aj);
    if (pivot>0 && normaj<tol)
        for k=n:-1:j+1
            if (p(k) ~= k) continue; end
            ak = A(:,k);  normak = norm(ak);
            if (normak <= tol) continue; end
            [p(j),p(k)] = swap_(p(j),p(k));
            [A(:,j),A(:,k)] = swap_(A(:,j),A(:,k));
            [R(1:j,j),R(1:j,k)] = swap_(R(1:j,j),R(1:j,k));
            aj = ak;  normaj = normak;
            break;
        end
    end
    R(j,j) = normaj;
    if (normaj > tol) qj = aj/normaj; else qj = orthogonal_(A(:,1:j-1)); end
    A(:,j) = qj;
    for k=j+1:n
        ak = A(:,k);  Rjk = qj'*ak;  R(j,k) = Rjk;
        A(:,k) = ak - Rjk*qj;
    end
end

if(m < n) A = A(:,1:m); end
```

3.2.4 DRIVER OF QR DECOMPOSITION

Both QRbyHouseholder_ and QRbyGivens_ output **Q** and **R** in a compact form—**Q** as Householder vectors or encoded Givens rotations below the diagonal of **A** and **R** on and above the diagonal of **A**. QR_ outputs **Q** and **R** separately as matrices for better readability. Its other major functions are to dispatch the call to QRbyHouseholder_, QRbyGivens_, or QRbyGramSchimdt_ according to algo and set the size of **Q** and **R** correctly according to format. All the three algorithms of QR have partial decomposition and restart capability. The functions of the three algorithms will be demonstrated by a few simple examples in the following.

Algorithm 3.6

A*P'=Q*R. Q orthogonal, R upper triangle, P permutation.

```
function [Q,R,p] = QR_(A,algo,pivot,tol,format,f1st,last,p)

if (iscell(A)) R = A{2}; A = A{1}; [m,n]=size(A); else R=[]; [m,n]=size(A); end
if (strcmp(format,'long') || strcmp(format,'short')) Q = eye(m); end

if(strcmp(algo,'HOUSEHOLDER'))
    [R,p] = QRbyHouseholder_(A,pivot,tol,f1st,last,p);
```

```
    if (strcmp(format,'long') || strcmp(format,'short'))
        for j=last:-1:1       %backward accumulation of Q
            qj = R(j+1:m,j);   R(j+1:m,j) = 0.0;
            h = [1; qj];   alpha = 2.0/(h'*h);   v = 2.0/(h'*h)*h;
            for k=j:m
                qk = Q(j:m,k);   beta = alpha*(h'*qk);   Q(j:m,k) = qk - beta*h;
            end
        end
    end
    if (strcmp(format,'brief')) Q = []; R = triu(R); end
    if (strcmp(format,'compact')) Q = []; end
elseif (strcmp(algo,'GIVENS'))
    [R,p] = QRbyGivens_(A,pivot,tol,f1st,last,p);
    if (strcmp(format,'long') || strcmp(format,'short'))
        for j=1:last          %accumulation of Q
            for k=j+1:m
                rho = R(k,j);    R(k,j) = 0.0;
                if (rho == 1)           c = 0;   s = 1;
                elseif(abs(rho) < 1) s = 2.0*rho;   c = sqrt(1.0-s*s);
                else                    c = 2.0/rho;   s = sqrt(1.0-c*c); end
                for l=1:m
                    Qlj = Q(l,j);    Qlk = Q(l,k);
                    Q(l,j) = c*Qlj - s*Qlk;   Q(l,k) = s*Qlj + c*Qlk;
                end
            end
        end
    end
    if (strcmp(format,'brief')) Q = []; R = triu(R); end
    if (strcmp(format,'compact')) Q = []; end
elseif (strcmp(algo,'GRAM-SCHIMDT'))
    [Q,R,p] = QRbyGramSchimdt_(A,pivot,tol,f1st,last,R,p);
    if (m>n && strcmp(format,'long'))
        R = [R;zeros(m-n,n)];
        for j=n+1:m Q = [Q,orthogonal_(Q)]; end
    end
else
    error ('QR_:_wrong_2nd_input_argument:_algo.');
end

if (strcmp(format,'long')) p = pv2pm_(p); end
if (strcmp(format,'short'))     %Remove Q(:,i),R(i,:) if R(i,:)=0
    if (m > n) Q = Q(:,1:n);   R = R(1:n,:); end
    [j1,j2] = size(R);   k = min(j1,j2);
    tol = tol*max(1.0,norm(diag(R),inf));
    for j=k:-1:1
        if (abs(R(j,j))>tol || norm(R(j,j+1:j2))>tol) break;
        else                                          k = j - 1; end
    end
    if (k < min(j1,j2)) Q = Q(:,1:k);   R = R(1:k,:); end
end
```

The output argument of `QRbyHouseholder_` and `QRbyGivens_` is in compact form where **Q** and **R** overwrite **A** as described in this section. In the following example, the output argument **p** (permutation vector) is omitted, because the input matrix **A** has full column rank.

```
>> A=randn(4);
>> QR1=QRbyHouseholder_(A)                      >> QR2=QRbyGivens_(A)
QR1 =                                           QR2 =
    1.3953     0.4221     0.2298    -1.7521         -1.3953    -0.4221    -0.2298     1.7521
    0.1099    -1.2325    -0.5081     0.5811         -0.1397    -1.2325    -0.5081     0.5811
   -0.2957    -0.4224     0.5113     0.8273          0.3005     7.2264    -0.5113    -0.8273
    0.3810     0.8550     0.1488     0.8174         -0.3061    -3.0945     5.7940    -0.8174
```

The following two examples show the effect of pivot=0 and pivot=1 to the QR decomposition of a column rank deficient matrix. If a matrix is column rank deficient, its **Q** and **R** factor can be non-unique, since arbitrary unit vector is chosen to complement the columns of **Q**. On the other hand, if a matrix has full column rank, the columns of **Q** are determined up to a sign difference. This can be observed from the output of two **Q**s. Compare their first column and also the two $R(1,1)$s.

```
>> A(:,2)=A(:,1)*randn; tol=100*eps;
>> [Q,R,P]=QR_(A,'householder',0,tol,'long')>> [Q,R,P]=QR_(A,'givens',1,tol,'long')
Q =                                           Q =
   -0.6069     0.1765    -0.6494    -0.4230        0.6069    -0.3629     0.6886    -0.1606
   -0.1765    -0.9806    -0.0713    -0.0465        0.1765     0.7044     0.0559    -0.6852
    0.4752    -0.0522    -0.7529     0.4523       -0.4752     0.3960     0.7073     0.3423
   -0.6122     0.0673     0.0799     0.7838        0.6122     0.4640    -0.1497     0.6225
R =                                           R =
    1.3953    -1.2608     0.2298    -1.7521       -1.3953     1.7521    -0.2298     1.2608
         0     0.0000     0.0590     0.9677            0    -1.3001    -0.0983     0.0000
         0          0     0.7184     0.0983            0          0    -0.7140     0.0000
         0          0          0    -0.8627            0          0          0     0.0000
P =                                           P =
    1     0     0     0                            1     0     0     0
    0     1     0     0                            0     0     0     1
    0     0     1     0                            0     0     1     0
    0     0     0     1                            0     1     0     0
```

The following two examples show the effect of format='long' and format='short' to the QR decomposition of rectangular matrices and rank deficient matrices.

```
>> A1=randn(4,3);  tol=100*eps;                   0.0678     0.6132     0.7870
>> [Q,R]=QR_(A1,'householder',0,tol,'long')      -0.2271     0.1669    -0.1206
Q =                                           R =
   -0.7376    -0.4996     0.4532     0.0310       -1.6697     2.1533    -0.5240
    0.6322    -0.5887     0.4010    -0.3049            0    -1.2894     0.3105
   -0.0678    -0.6132    -0.7870     0.0083            0          0     1.7360
    0.2271    -0.1669     0.1206     0.9518
R =
    1.6697    -2.1533     0.5240                 >> A2=randn(3,4);
         0     1.2894    -0.3105                 >> A2(2,:)=A2(1,:)*randn; tol=100*eps;
         0          0    -1.7360                 >> [Q,R]=QR_(A2,'givens',0,tol,'long')
         0          0          0                 Q =
                                                     0.2042    -0.8011    -0.5626
>> [Q,R]=QR_(A1,'givens',0,tol,'short')              0.1389    -0.5451     0.8268
Q =                                                 -0.9690    -0.2470          0
    0.7376     0.4996    -0.4532                 R =
   -0.6322     0.5887    -0.4010                     -0.0577    -0.3259    -1.8882     0.6265
```

```
         0     1.2988    -0.1365     0.8119         -0.1389    -0.5451
         0        0      -0.0000    -0.0000          0.9690    -0.2470
                                      R =
>> [Q,R]=QR_(A2,'gram-schimdt',0,tol,'short')      0.0577     0.3259     1.8882    -0.6265
Q =                                                    0      1.2988    -0.1365     0.8119
   -0.2042    -0.8011
```

The restart capability of QR decomposition is similar to that of LU decomposition, see Section 2.2. In the example, `[R,p]=QRbyHouseholder_(A,0,tol,1,2)` can also be `[R,p]=QR_(A, 'householder',0,tol,'compact',1,2)`. If `format='compact'`, `QR_` makes no change to the output by `QRbyHouseholder_`, `QRbyGivens_`, or `QRbyGramSchimdt_`.

```
>> A=randn(5); tol=100*eps;
>> [R,p]=QRbyHouseholder_(A,0,tol,1,2)                %R intermediate output
R =
    1.1822     0.6912    -0.4318     0.9005    -0.4880
   -0.1096     1.4766    -1.3017    -2.1972     1.2976
    0.0733    -0.1365     0.2640    -1.2169     1.2141
   -0.6719     0.6831     0.4926     1.1829    -0.8101
    0.1549    -0.4927    -0.3814     1.1565    -0.1348
p =
      1      2      3      4      5

>> [Q,R,p]=QR_(R,'householder',0,tol,'short',3,5,p)   %restart from column 3=2+1
Q =                                                   %R as input matrix
   -0.3398    -0.8687    -0.0010    -0.2622    -0.2475
    0.1469    -0.0622     0.8355     0.3674    -0.3761
   -0.0982     0.0943    -0.5042     0.4812    -0.7040
    0.9001    -0.2070    -0.1567    -0.2683    -0.2245
   -0.2076     0.4357     0.1519    -0.7019    -0.5013
R =
    1.1822     0.6912    -0.4318     0.9005    -0.4880
        0     1.4766    -1.3017    -2.1972     1.2976
        0         0     -0.6766     0.2654     0.0401
        0         0         0      -2.0364     1.2779
        0         0         0          0      -0.7169
p =
      1      2      3      4      5
```

If no restart from the third column is needed, the output of the partial QR decomposition can be checked by `QR_`. The output **R** is not completely upper triangular, but satisfying the relation $\mathbf{A} = \mathbf{QR}$.

```
>> [Q,R]=QR_(A,'givens',0,tol,'long',1,2)
Q =
    0.3398    -0.8687     0.0409    -0.0685     0.3516
   -0.1469    -0.0622     0.6190     0.7662     0.0657
    0.0982     0.0943     0.7844    -0.6011    -0.0702
   -0.9001    -0.2070         0     -0.2165     0.3163
    0.2076     0.4357         0          0      0.8759
R =                                                   %R not upper triangular
   -1.1822    -0.6912     0.4318    -0.9005     0.4880
        0     1.4766    -1.3017    -2.1972     1.2976
        0         0     -0.0823    -1.1777     1.3342
        0         0     -0.6612     0.1202    -0.0172
        0         0     -0.1174     1.6780    -0.6068
```

Because of the nature of modified Gram–Schmidt algorithm, the partial QR decomposition and its restart are arranged differently from that of Householder algorithm and Givens algorithm. The use of restart of QRbyGramSchimdt_ is explained with the following example.

```
>> [Q,R]=QR_(A,'gram-schimdt',0,tol,'compact',1,2)   %format='compact'
                                                      %for restart later
Q =                                                   %Q(:,3:5) intermediate result
   -0.3398   -0.8687    0.0007    0.5336   -0.1576
    0.1469   -0.0622   -0.5653   -0.5265    0.7727
   -0.0982    0.0943    0.3412   -1.1138    1.0995
    0.9001   -0.2070    0.1060    0.5047   -0.1882
   -0.2076    0.4357   -0.1028    1.4697   -0.5314
R =                                                   %R partial result
    1.1822    0.6912   -0.4318    0.9005   -0.4880
         0    1.4766   -1.3017   -2.1972    1.2976


>> C={Q;R}                                            %Use cell array to hold Q,R
C =
    [5x5 double]
    [2x5 double]
>> [Q,R]=QR_(C,'gram-schimdt',0,tol,'short',3,5)      %Pass [Q,R] as a cell array
Q =                                                   %This Q is final
   -0.3398   -0.8687    0.0010    0.2622    0.2475
    0.1469   -0.0622   -0.8355   -0.3674    0.3761
   -0.0982    0.0943    0.5042   -0.4812    0.7040
    0.9001   -0.2070    0.1567    0.2683    0.2245
   -0.2076    0.4357   -0.1519    0.7019    0.5013
R =                                                   %This R is final
    1.1822    0.6912   -0.4318    0.9005   -0.4880
         0    1.4766   -1.3017   -2.1972    1.2976
         0         0    0.6766   -0.2654   -0.0401
         0         0         0    2.0364   -1.2779
         0         0         0         0    0.7169
```

The efficiency of QR_ is compared against MATLAB built-in qr. The elapsed time is obtained to perform a QR decomposition of a 1000×1000 full matrix on an INSPIRON 1545 laptop. Because the MATLAB built-in qr is built on the optimized machine code of LAPACK and BLAS, its higher efficiency is expected, while the purpose of QR_ is to present the QR algorithm in a concise manner. Other output of zeros verifies the correctness of QR decompositions of QR_ and qr.

```
>> A=randn(1000);                      >> tic
>> tic                                 >> [Q,R]=qr(A);
>> [Q,R]=QR_(A);                        >> toc
>> toc                                 Elapsed time is 0.787308 seconds.
Elapsed time is 16.771341 seconds.     >> norm(Q'*Q-eye(1000))
>> norm(Q'*Q-eye(1000))                = 3.3645e-015
= 5.1318e-015                          >> norm(tril(R,-1))
>> norm(tril(R,-1))                    =    0
=    0                                 >> norm(Q*R-A)
>> norm(Q*R-A)                         = 9.6351e-014
= 1.2050e-013
```

3.2.5 QR DECOMPOSITION OF AN UPPER HESSENBERG MATRIX

An upper Hessenberg has all zeros below the sub-diagonal. Thus, to transform it to an upper triangle, only $n-1$ components on the sub-diagonal need to be zeroed. More efficient QR decomposition can be obtained if the zero pattern is exploited. We use Givens rotation to demonstrate the idea. In the following equation, $\xrightarrow{(22,32);(33,43)}$ means generating and applying Givens rotations from $a = H_{22}, b = H_{32}$ first and then $a = H_{33}, b = H_{43}$, respectively, by Eq. (3.3). From the Gram–Schmidt process, it can be shown that $\mathbf{Q}$ factor of an upper Hessenberg matrix is also upper Hessenberg,

$$\begin{bmatrix} H_{11} & H_{12} & H_{13} & H_{14} \\ H_{21} & H_{22} & H_{23} & H_{24} \\ 0 & H_{32} & H_{33} & H_{34} \\ 0 & 0 & H_{43} & H_{44} \end{bmatrix} \xrightarrow{(11,21)} \begin{bmatrix} H_{11} & H_{12} & H_{13} & H_{14} \\ 0 & H_{22} & H_{23} & H_{24} \\ 0 & H_{32} & H_{33} & H_{34} \\ 0 & 0 & H_{43} & H_{44} \end{bmatrix} \xrightarrow{(33,43);(22,32)} \begin{bmatrix} H_{11} & H_{12} & H_{13} & H_{14} \\ 0 & H_{22} & H_{23} & H_{24} \\ 0 & 0 & H_{33} & H_{34} \\ 0 & 0 & 0 & H_{44} \end{bmatrix}.$$

A slight modification of QRbyGivens_.m gives us the specialized QR decomposition of upper Hessenberg matrix, QRhessenberg_.m. The column permutations are removed from QRhessenberg_.m, because the permutations destroy the Hessenberg structure. In QRhessenberg_.m, a slight generalization of an upper Hessenberg matrix is made—the number of nonzero sub-diagonals can be more than one. Over half of the code of QRhessenberg_.m handles the output according to the input argument format.

Algorithm 3.7

```
H=Q*R. Q orthogonal, R upper triangle.
function [Q,R] = QRhessenberg_(H,lbw,tol,format,f1st,last)

[m,n] = size(H);   R = H;
tol = tol*max(1.0,norm(diag(H),inf));

for j=f1st:last
    for k=j+1:min(j+lbw,m)
        [c,s] = givens_(R(j,j),R(k,j));
        R(j,j) = c*R(j,j) - s*R(k,j);   %apply Givens transformation
        for l=j+1:n
            Rjl = R(j,l);    Rkl = R(k,l);
            R(j,l) = c*Rjl - s*Rkl;
            R(k,l) = s*Rjl + c*Rkl;
        end
        if (abs(c) < tol)        rho = 1;
        elseif(abs(s) < abs(c)) rho = sign(c)*s/2;
        else                    rho = sign(s)*2/c; end
        R(k,j) = rho;     %save encoded [c,s] at zeroed R(k,j)
    end
end

if (strcmp(format,'long') || strcmp(format,'short'))
    for j=1:last          %accumulation of Q
        for k=j+1:min(j+lbw,m)
            rho = R(k,j);   R(k,j) = 0.0;
            if (rho == 1)           c = 0;   s = 1;
            elseif(abs(rho) < 1) s = 2.0*rho;  c = sqrt(1.0-s*s);
            else                 c = 2.0/rho;  s = sqrt(1.0-c*c); end
            for l=1:m
                Qlj = Q(l,j);    Qlk = Q(l,k);
```

```
                    Q(1,j) = c*Q1j - s*Q1k;   Q(1,k) = s*Q1j + c*Q1k;
                end
            end
        end
end
if (strcmp(format,'short'))    %Remove Q(:,i),R(i,;) if R(i,:)=0
    if (m > n) Q = Q(:,1:n);   R = R(1:n,:); end
    [j1,j2] = size(R); k = min(j1,j2);
    for j=k:-1:1
        if (abs(R(j,j))>tol || norm(R(j,j+1:j2))>tol) break;
        else                                        k = j - 1; end
    end
    if (k < min(j1,j2)) Q = Q(:,1:k);   R = R(1:k,:); end
end
if (strcmp(format,'brief')) Q = []; R = triu(R); end
if (strcmp(format,'compact')) Q = []; end
```

The following example demonstrates the basic use of QRhessenberg_.m. The default input argument settings make its use very simple. Note the Hessenberg form of **Q** in the output.

```
>> A=randn(5);
>> H=triu(A);  H = H + diag(diag(A,-1),-1);    %one way to create a Hessenberg
>> [Q,R]=QRhessenberg_(H)
Q =                                    %Q also Hessenberg!
    0.2690    0.8410    0.0586   -0.1833   -0.4281
   -0.9631    0.2349    0.0164   -0.0512   -0.1196
         0    0.4873   -0.1090    0.3409    0.7965
         0         0   -0.9922   -0.0491   -0.1147
         0         0         0   -0.9193    0.3935
R =
    1.3969    0.4286    2.0322    0.0676    0.5421
         0   -1.5746   -1.7780   -0.0863    0.4402
         0         0   -0.2594    0.4672    0.9499
         0         0         0    0.7670    0.1879
         0         0         0         0    0.0679
```

The following example demonstrates the restart use of QRhessenberg_.m.

```
>> [Q,R]=QRhessenberg_(H,1,100*eps,'compact',1,2)   %format='compact' for restart.
Q =
    []
R =
    1.3969    0.4286    2.0322    0.0676    0.5421
    7.4355   -1.5746   -1.7780   -0.0863    0.4402
         0   -0.2437    0.0324    0.2411    0.0168
         0         0    0.2573   -0.5012   -0.9595
         0         0         0   -0.7051   -0.1460
>> [Q,R]=QRhessenberg_(R,1,100*eps,'long',3,5)      %Use immediate R, f1st=3, last=5
Q =                                    %same Q as previous example
    0.2690    0.8410    0.0586   -0.1833   -0.4281
   -0.9631    0.2349    0.0164   -0.0512   -0.1196
         0    0.4873   -0.1090    0.3409    0.7965
         0         0   -0.9922   -0.0491   -0.1147
         0         0         0   -0.9193    0.3935
R =                                    %same R as previous example
    1.3969    0.4286    2.0322    0.0676    0.5421
```

0	-1.5746	-1.7780	-0.0863	0.4402
0	0	-0.2594	0.4672	0.9499
0	0	0	0.7670	0.1879
0	0	0	0	0.0679

3.2.6 QR DECOMPOSITION OF A BAND MATRIX

A band matrix $\mathbf{B} \in \mathbb{R}^{m \times n}$ has b_l nonzero sub-diagonals and b_u nonzero sup-diagonals. For a band matrix, the efficiency of QR decomposition can be improved if taking the band structure into account. First, only $n \times b_l$ nonzeros below the diagonal need to be zeroed. Second, when applying one Givens rotation, only $2 \times b_u$ are altered. With the Gram–Schmidt process, it can be shown that the $\mathbf{Q}$ factor of $\mathbf{B}$ has zeros below the b_lth sub-diagonal. By direct calculation of $\mathbf{Q}'\mathbf{B}$, it can be shown that the $\mathbf{R}$ factor has zeros above the $b_l + b_u$th sup-diagonal.

The MATLAB code of QRband_.m is modified from QRbyGivens_.m. The column permutations are removed from QRband_.m, because the permutations destroy the band structure. In QRband_.m, the input band matrix $\mathbf{B}$ must be in the band format. Over half of the code of QRband_.m handles the output according to the input argument format.

Algorithm 3.8

B=Q*R. Q orthogonal, R upper triangle.

```
function [Q,R] = QRband_(B,lbw,ubw,m,n,tol,format,f1st,last)

if (~exist('m','var') || isempty(m)) m = size(B,1); end
Q = [];   R = [B,zeros(m,lbw)];    %R band w/ upper band width=ubw+lbw
if (strcmp(format,'long') || strcmp(format,'short')) Q = eye(m); end
lbw1 = lbw + 1;   tol = tol*max(1.0,norm(B(:,lbw1),inf));

for j=f1st:last
    for k=j+1:min(j+lbw,m)
        [c,s] = givens_(R(j,lbw1),R(k,j-k+lbw1));
        R(j,lbw1) = c*R(j,lbw1) - s*R(k,j-k+lbw1); %apply Givens transformation
        for l=j+1:min(k+ubw,n)
            Rjl = R(j,l-j+lbw1);   Rkl = R(k,l-k+lbw1);
            R(j,l-j+lbw1) = c*Rjl - s*Rkl;   R(k,l-k+lbw1) = s*Rjl + c*Rkl;
        end
        %save encoded Givens rotation [c,s] at zeroed R(k,j)
        if (abs(c) < tol)        rho = 1;
        elseif(abs(s) < abs(c)) rho = sign(c)*s/2;
        else                    rho = sign(s)*2/c; end
        R(k,j-k+lbw1) = rho;
    end
end

if (strcmp(format,'long') || strcmp(format,'short'))
    for j=1:last          %accumulation of Q
        for k=j+1:min(j+lbw,m)
            rho = R(k,j-k+lbw1); R(k,j-k+lbw1) = 0.0;
            if (rho == 1)         c = 0;   s = 1;
            elseif(abs(rho) < 1) s = 2.0*rho;   c = sqrt(1.0-s*s);
            else                 c = 2.0/rho;   s = sqrt(1.0-c*c); end
            for l=1:m
                Qlj = Q(l,j);   Qlk = Q(l,k);
```

```
                 Q(1,j) = c*Q1j - s*Q1k;   Q(1,k) = s*Q1j + c*Q1k;
          end
       end
    end
    R = R(:,lbw1:lbw1+ubw+lbw);
end
if (strcmp(format,'long')) R = band2full_(R,0,lbw+ubw,m,n); end
if (strcmp(format,'short'))
    if (m > n) Q = Q(:,1:n);   R = R(1:n,:); end
end
if (strcmp(format,'brief')) R = R(:,lbw1:lbw1+ubw+lbw); end
```

One simple example demonstrates the use of QRband_.m. Note the zero patterns of **Q** and **R** in the output.

```
>> A=randn(6);
>> B=diag(diag(A)); B=B+diag(diag(A,1),1);
>> B=B+diag(diag(A,-1),-1); B=B+diag(diag(A,-2),-2);  %one way to create a band matrix
>> B=full2band_(B,2,1);                               %convert to band format!

>> [Q,R]=QRband_(B,2,1,6,6,[],'long')       %Specify the layout of B correctly!
Q =                           %Q has zeros below 2nd sub-diagonal.
   -0.1427   -0.6245    0.1530    0.4041   -0.4909    0.4026
   -0.6275   -0.1163   -0.5567    0.0677    0.4450    0.2834
   -0.7655    0.2118    0.4278   -0.1308   -0.2732   -0.3073
         0   -0.7428    0.0805   -0.3876    0.2651   -0.4704
         0         0    0.6908    0.0912    0.6056    0.3843
         0         0         0   -0.8102   -0.2222    0.5424
R =                           %R has zeros above 3rd sup-diagonal. (3=2+1)
   -1.5885   -1.0053   -1.2599    1.0660         0         0
         0    0.7678    0.5700    0.6711    0.6599         0
         0         0    1.1510   -1.1184   -0.7530    0.4135
         0         0         0    1.8372    0.3124   -0.0647
         0         0         0         0   -0.8171    0.3298
         0         0         0         0         0    0.3098

>> norm(Q*R-band2full_(B,2,1,6,6))
= 5.8210e-016                          %Q*R-B=0.
```

3.3 COMPLETE ORTHOGONAL DECOMPOSITION (QLZ)

In the previous section, we showed $\mathbf{A} = \mathbf{QR}$, where $\mathbf{Q}$ is orthogonal and $\mathbf{R}$ is upper triangular. If we apply QR decomposition to $\mathbf{R}'$, we have $\mathbf{R}' = \mathbf{Z}'\mathbf{L}'$, where $\mathbf{Z}'$ is orthogonal and $\mathbf{L}'$ is upper triangular. Then, $\mathbf{A} = \mathbf{QR} = \mathbf{Q}(\mathbf{Z}'\mathbf{L}')' = \mathbf{QLZ}$. $\mathbf{A} = \mathbf{QLZ}$ is referred as the complete orthogonal decomposition in [29]. Following the naming convention of the book, we name it QLZ decomposition. It can be considered the counterpart of LDU decomposition discussed in Section 2.3 in the realm of orthogonal transformations. If applied to a full rank matrix, QLZ decomposition does not have much usefulness. But if applied to a rank deficient matrix, QLZ reveals the rank of the matrix, see the demonstrating examples of QLZ_.m in the following.

The MATLAB implementation of QLZ_.m closely follows the above discussion. The partial decomposition and restart are not implemented, because of their limited usefulness.

Algorithm 3.9

A=Q*L*Z. Q'*Q=I, Z'*Z=I, L lower triangle.
```
function [Q,L,Z] = QLZ_(A,algo,tol,format)

[m,n] = size(A);
if (~exist('algo','var') || isempty(algo)) algo = 'householder'; end
if (~exist('tol','var') || isempty(tol)) tol = sqrt(eps); end
if (~exist('format','var') || isempty(format)) format = 'short'; end
tol1 = tol*max(1.0,norm(diag(A),inf));

[Q,L,p] = QR_(A,algo,1,tol,format);

l = size(L,1);
for i=size(L,1):-1:1
    if (norm(L(i,:)) > tol1) l = i; break; end
end

[Z,L] = QR_(L(1:l,:)',algo,0,tol,format);   %chop off zeros from L

if (strcmp(format,'long')) p = pm2pv_(p); end
if (strcmp(format,'long') || strcmp(format,'short'))
    p = inv_perm_(p);  Z = permute_(p,Z);  L = L';  Z = Z';
end
if (strcmp(format,'long') && l<m) L = [L; zeros(m-l,n)]; end
```

The following example shows the QLZ decomposition of a full rank matrix. We can see the QLZ decomposition of the matrix does not reveal more information about it than its QR decomposition.

```
>> A=randn(4,3);   tol = 100*eps;
>> [Q,R]=QR_(A,'householder',0,tol,'long')   >> [Q,L,Z]=QLZ_(A,'householder',tol,'long')
Q =                                          Q =
   -0.6038    0.2515    0.2532    0.7128        -0.6038    0.2515    0.2532    0.7128
    0.5614   -0.1494   -0.4402    0.6846         0.5614   -0.1494   -0.4402    0.6846
   -0.1210    0.7518   -0.6321   -0.1432        -0.1210    0.7518   -0.6321   -0.1432
    0.5528    0.5909    0.5852    0.0519         0.5528    0.5909    0.5852    0.0519
R =                                          L =      %QLZ is almost identical to QR
   -2.2094   -0.3222   -1.2324                    2.5503         0         0
         0   -1.9157   -0.3729                    0.4222    1.9055         0
         0         0   -1.6447                    0.7947    0.1457   -1.4325
         0         0         0                         0         0         0
                                             Z =
                                                -0.8663    0.1920   -0.4611
                                                -0.1263   -0.9774   -0.1695
                                                -0.4832   -0.0886    0.8710
```

Now we do a QLZ decomposition of a rank deficient matrix. We can see its QLZ decomposition renders a simpler **L** factor than its **R** counterpart in QR decomposition.

```
>> A(3:4,:)=randn(2)*A(1:2,:);                   0.4753   -0.6925    0.0321    0.5418
>> [Q,R]=QR_(A,'householder',0,tol,'long')      -0.3117   -0.2869    0.8939   -0.1462
Q =                                          R =
   -0.6025   -0.6181   -0.4469   -0.2349        -2.2140    0.2723   -0.0023
    0.5602   -0.2369   -0.0105   -0.7937              0    0.1992   -0.3762
```

```
        0          0       0.0000               0.4753    -0.6925     0.0321     0.5418
        0          0         0                 -0.3117    -0.2869     0.8939    -0.1462
                                            L =
                                                2.2307         0          0
                                                0.0247    -0.4250         0
                                                     0         0          0
                                                     0         0          0
                                            Z =
>> [Q,L,Z]=QLZ_(A,'householder',tol,'long')   -0.9925    -0.0577     0.1076
Q =                                             0.1221    -0.4617     0.8786
   -0.6025    -0.6181    -0.4469    -0.2349     -0.0010     0.8852     0.4653
    0.5602    -0.2369    -0.0105    -0.7937
```

Now we see the QLZ decomposition of $\mathbf{A}'$. In the previous example, $\mathbf{A}$ is row rank deficient. In the following example, $\mathbf{A}'$ is column rank deficient. Note the effect of format='short' to the output.

```
>> [Q,R]=QR_(A','householder',0,tol,         >> [Q,L,Z]=QLZ_(A','householder',tol,
                              'short')                                      'short')
Q =                                           Q =
   -0.9636    -0.2449                            -0.9636    -0.2449
    0.2074    -0.4302                             0.2074    -0.4302
   -0.1689     0.8689                            -0.1689     0.8689
R =                                           L =
   -1.3845     1.2022     0.9684    -0.7128       2.1927         0
        0      0.3348     0.4868    -0.0135       0.4030    -0.4323
                                              Z =
                                                 -0.6314    -0.5885
                                                  0.5483    -0.2634
                                                  0.4416    -0.7144
                                                 -0.3251    -0.2717
```

3.4 REDUCTION OF MATRIX TO BI-DIAGONAL

Given a matrix $\mathbf{A} \in \mathbb{R}^{m \times n}$, an even simpler orthogonal decomposition than QR or QLZ, called QBZ, is possible: $\mathbf{A} = \mathbf{QBZ}$, where $\mathbf{Q}$ and $\mathbf{Z}$ are orthogonal matrices, $\mathbf{B}$ is a bi-diagonal matrix. We name this decomposition QBZ, also known bi-diagonalization of $\mathbf{A}$ in [29]. A bi-diagonal $\mathbf{B}$ is the simplest form that $\mathbf{A}$ can be transformed to by two-sided orthogonal transformations using a direct algorithm. It is usually used as the first step of an iterative algorithm to orthogonally transform $\mathbf{A}$ into a diagonal form, that is, a SVD of $\mathbf{A}$. In this section, we will present three algorithms to perform QBZ decomposition. The first one is based on the Householder reflections. The second is based on the Givens rotations. These two algorithms are transforming algorithms in terms of the algorithm classifications made in Section 1.4. The third algorithm is based on the Golub–Kahan–Lanczos bi-diagonalization procedure [5], which is multiplying according to the classifications made in Section 1.4.

3.4.1 QBZ DECOMPOSITION BY HOUSEHOLDER REFLECTIONS

In the QR decomposition of $\mathbf{A}$, we zero columns by columns using Householder Reflections, see Section 3.2.1. In the QBZ decomposition, after each column elimination, we have an extra step to zero the row. The trick is to keep the zeros obtained in all the previous steps. The idea can be illustrated with a simple example of $\mathbf{A}$ of 5×6. Suppose we applied a Householder reflection matrix $\mathbf{Q}_1$ to $\mathbf{A}$ to zero $\mathbf{A}(2:5,1)$. This is just the first step of QR discussed in 3.2.1,

$$\mathbf{Q}_1\mathbf{A} \Rightarrow \mathbf{A} = \begin{bmatrix} A_{11} & A_{12} & A_{13} & A_{14} & A_{15} & A_{16} \\ 0 & A_{22} & A_{23} & A_{24} & A_{25} & A_{26} \\ 0 & A_{32} & A_{33} & A_{34} & A_{35} & A_{36} \\ 0 & A_{42} & A_{43} & A_{44} & A_{45} & A_{46} \\ 0 & A_{52} & A_{53} & A_{54} & A_{55} & A_{56} \end{bmatrix}.$$

Next we find a Householder matrix $\mathbf{Z}_1$ to zero $\mathbf{A}(1,3:6)$,

$$\mathbf{A}\mathbf{Z}_1 \Rightarrow \mathbf{A} = \begin{bmatrix} A_{11} & A_{12} & 0 & 0 & 0 & 0 \\ 0 & A_{22} & A_{23} & A_{24} & A_{25} & A_{26} \\ 0 & A_{32} & A_{33} & A_{34} & A_{35} & A_{36} \\ 0 & A_{42} & A_{43} & A_{44} & A_{45} & A_{46} \\ 0 & A_{52} & A_{53} & A_{54} & A_{55} & A_{56} \end{bmatrix}.$$

To be more specific, we give a numerical example to demonstrate the exact operation of this step.

```
>> A=[11,12,13,14,15,16;
      0,22,23,24,25,26;
      0,32,33,34,35,36;
      0,42,43,44,45,46;
      0,52,53,54,55,56];

>> Z1=householder_(A(1,:),2,1,'long')  %to zero A(1,3:6)
Z1 =                 %Note Z1(:,1)=I(:,1), Z1(1,:)=I(1,:)
    1.0000         0         0         0         0         0
         0   -0.3814   -0.4132   -0.4449   -0.4767   -0.5085
         0   -0.4132    0.8764   -0.1331   -0.1426   -0.1521
         0   -0.4449   -0.1331    0.8567   -0.1536   -0.1638
         0   -0.4767   -0.1426   -0.1536    0.8355   -0.1755
         0   -0.5085   -0.1521   -0.1638   -0.1755    0.8128
>> A*Z1
ans =                %A(1,3:6) is zeroed, A(2:5,1) not altered.
   11.0000  -31.4643   -0.0000   -0.0000   -0.0000   -0.0000
         0  -53.7117    0.3549   -0.3870   -1.1290   -1.8709
         0  -75.9592    0.7098   -0.7741   -2.2579   -3.7418
         0  -98.2066    1.0647   -1.1611   -3.3869   -5.6127
         0 -120.4541    1.4196   -1.5481   -4.5158   -7.4835
```

It is important not to alter $\mathbf{A}(:,1)$ by $\mathbf{A}\mathbf{Z}_1$. This is achieved by having $\mathbf{I}(:,1)$ and $\mathbf{I}(:,1)$ as the first column and first row of $\mathbf{Z}_1$. To have such a $\mathbf{Z}_1$, the best we can do is to zero only $\mathbf{A}(1,3:6)$. Should we aim to zero $\mathbf{A}(1,2:6)$, $\mathbf{A}(:,1)$ will be changed by the transformation as the following example shows.

```
>> Y1=householder_(A(1,:),1,1,'long')  %to zero A(1,2:6)
Y1 =                 %Note 1st column and row of Y1
   -0.3300   -0.3600   -0.3900   -0.4200   -0.4500   -0.4800
   -0.3600    0.9025   -0.1056   -0.1137   -0.1218   -0.1299
   -0.3900   -0.1056    0.8856   -0.1232   -0.1320   -0.1408
   -0.4200   -0.1137   -0.1232    0.8674   -0.1421   -0.1516
   -0.4500   -0.1218   -0.1320   -0.1421    0.8477   -0.1624
   -0.4800   -0.1299   -0.1408   -0.1516   -0.1624    0.8268
>> A*Y1
ans =                %A(1,2:6) is zeroed, but A(:,1) altered.
```

```
 -33.3317    -0.0000    -0.0000    -0.0000    -0.0000    -0.0000
 -50.7025     8.2755     8.1318     7.9881     7.8444     7.7007
 -71.7036    12.5908    11.9733    11.3559    10.7385    10.1210
 -92.7046    16.9061    15.8149    14.7238    13.6326    12.5414
-113.7057    21.2214    19.6565    18.0916    16.5267    14.9618
```

We continue to apply the two steps of Householder transformations sequentially to $\mathbf{A}$: $\mathbf{Q}_2\mathbf{A} \Rightarrow \mathbf{A}$ to zero $\mathbf{A}(3:5,2)$, $\mathbf{A}\mathbf{Z}_2 \Rightarrow \mathbf{A}$ to zero $\mathbf{A}(2,4:6)$; $\mathbf{Q}_3\mathbf{A} \Rightarrow \mathbf{A}$ to zero $\mathbf{A}(4:5,3)$, $\mathbf{A}\mathbf{Z}_3 \Rightarrow \mathbf{A}$ to zero $\mathbf{A}(3,5:6)$; $\mathbf{Q}_4\mathbf{A} \Rightarrow \mathbf{A}$ to zero $\mathbf{A}(5,4)$. Then $\mathbf{A}$ becomes a bi-diagonal matrix $\mathbf{B}$. $\mathbf{Q}_4\mathbf{Q}_3\mathbf{Q}_2\mathbf{Q}_1$ becomes $\mathbf{Q}$ and $\mathbf{Z}_1\mathbf{Z}_2\mathbf{Z}_3$ becomes $\mathbf{Z}$. If the original matrix $\mathbf{A}$ is saved, it can be verified that $\mathbf{A} = \mathbf{QBZ}$. In the MATLAB implementation QBZbyHouseholder_.m, the special form of the Householder reflection matrix is taken into account when calculating the product of a Householder $\mathbf{H}$ to $\mathbf{A}$, $\mathbf{Q}$ or $\mathbf{Z}$, $\mathbf{HA}$ or $\mathbf{AH}$, etc. This consideration is discussed in Section 3.2.1.

Algorithm 3.10

A=Q*B*Z, Q,Z orthogonal matrix, B bi-diagonal.

```
function [Q,B,Z] = QBZbyHouseholder_(A,tol,format,f1st,last,Q,Z)

[m,n] = size(A);   B = A;
tol = tol*max(1.0,norm(diag(A),inf));

for j = f1st:last
    if (m-j>0 && norm(B(j+1:m,j),inf)>tol)
        [h,alpha,beta] = householder_(B(j:m,j),1,1);          %Q
        B(j,j) = beta;  v = alpha*h;      %apply A=Q'*A;
        for k=j+1:n
            bk = B(j:m,k);   B(j:m,k) = bk - (h'*bk)*v;
        end
        B(j+1:m,j) = h(2:m-j+1);              %save Householder vector
    end
    if (n-j>1 && norm(B(j,j+2:n),inf)>tol)
        [h,alpha,beta] = householder_(B(j,j+1:n),1,1);        %Z
        B(j,j+1) = beta;  v = alpha*h'; %apply A=A*Z'
        for k=j+1:m
            bk = B(k,j+1:n);   B(k,j+1:n) = bk - (bk*h)*v;
        end
        B(j,j+2:n) = h(2:n-j)';                %save Householder vector
    end
end

if (strcmp(format,'long') || strcmp(format,'short'))
    if (~exist('Q','var') || isempty(Q)) Q = eye(m); end
    if (~exist('Z','var') || isempty(Z)) Z = eye(n); end
    if (f1st == 1) js = last:-1:f1st; else js = f1st:last; end
    for j=js
        if (m-j > 0)
            q = B(j+1:m,j);   qq = q'*q;   B(j+1:m,j) = 0.0;
            if (qq > tol)
                h = [1; q];   hh = qq + 1.0;   alpha = 2.0/hh;
                if (f1st == 1)        %backward accumulation: Q=Qj*Q
                    v = alpha*h;
                    for k=j:m qk = Q(j:m,k);   Q(j:m,k) = qk - (h'*qk)*v; end
                else                 %forward accumulation: Q=Q*Qj
                    v = alpha*h';
```

```
                         for k=1:m qk = Q(k,j:m);   Q(k,j:m) = qk - (qk*h)*v; end
                   end
             end
       end
       if (n-j > 1)
             z = B(j,j+2:n)';   zz = z'*z;   B(j,j+2:n) = 0.0;
             if (zz > tol)
                   h = [1; z];   hh = zz + 1.0;   alpha = 2.0/hh;
                   if (flst == 1)      %forward   accumulation: Z=Z*Zj
                         v = alpha*h';
                         for k=j+1:n zk = Z(k,j+1:n); Z(k,j+1:n) = zk - (zk*h)*v; end
                   else                %backward accumulation: Z=Zj*Z
                         v = alpha*h;
                         for k=2:n zk = Z(j+1:n,k); Z(j+1:n,k) = zk - (h'*zk)*v; end
                   end
             end
       end
   end
end
if (strcmp(format,'short') && last==min(m,n))
   k = min(min(m,n),last); l = k + 1; Bkl = 0.0;
   if (m > k) B = B(1:k,:); end
   if (n > l) B = B(:,1:k+1); Bkl = B(k,k+1); end
   if (abs(Bkl) < tol)
         l = l - 1;
         if (abs(B(k,k)) < tol)
               k = k - 1;
               for j=k:-1:1
                     if (abs(B(j,j+1)) > tol) break; else l = l - 1; end
                     if (abs(B(j,j)) > tol) break; else k = k - 1; end
               end
         end
   end
   if (size(B,1) > k) B = B(1:k,:); end
   if (size(B,2) > l) B = B(:,1:l); end
   if (size(Q,2) > k) Q = Q(:,1:k); end
   if (size(Z,1) > l) Z = Z(1:l,:); end
   B = full2band_(B,0,1);
end
if (strcmp(format,'brief'))
   Q = []; b0 = diag(B);   b1 = diag(B,1); Z = [];
   if(length(b0) == length(b1)) B = [b0, b1];
   else                         B = [b0, [b1;0.0]]; end
end
if (strcmp(format,'compact')) Q = []; Z = []; end
```

The use of QBZbyHouseholder_.m is close to QRbyHouseholder_.m. We give a simple example in the following.

```
>> A=rand(5,6);
>> [Q,B,Z]=QBZbyHouseholder_(A,100*eps,'long')
Q =
   -0.5093    0.0479    0.8306   -0.1753   -0.1331
   -0.2456   -0.7711   -0.0686   -0.2297    0.5363
   -0.2780   -0.4895   -0.2198    0.2149   -0.7672
   -0.4972    0.3365   -0.4721   -0.6406   -0.0787
   -0.5965    0.2242   -0.1849    0.6781    0.3160
```

```
B =
   -1.6618      2.5367           0           0           0           0
         0      1.2163      1.0544           0           0           0
         0           0      0.4253     -0.4431           0           0
         0           0           0      0.3374     -0.2150           0
         0           0           0           0      0.2019     -0.1730
Z =
    1.0000           0           0           0           0           0
         0     -0.6148      0.1002      0.6329      0.3057     -0.3436
         0     -0.5157     -0.1470     -0.6141     -0.2845     -0.5043
         0     -0.4218      0.7103     -0.2185     -0.0476      0.5172
         0     -0.2976     -0.4201      0.3275     -0.6778      0.4102
         0     -0.2993     -0.5360     -0.2595      0.6033      0.4379
```

3.4.2 QBZ DECOMPOSITION BY GIVENS ROTATIONS

Just as in QR decomposition, a Householder reflection to zero multiple components of a matrix can be replaced by a series of Givens rotations, while each Givens rotation is to zero only one component of the matrix. In QBZ decomposition, we can also use Givens rotations. The essence of the algorithm is same as what we discussed in the last subsection and the QR decomposition by Givens rotation discussed in Section 3.2.2.

The following is the MATLAB implementation QBZbyGivens_.m, in which over half of the code is to handle the output according to the input argument format. Note that the part of the code handling the output is same to QBZbyHouseholder_.m.

Algorithm 3.11

A=Q*B*Z, Q,Z orthogonal matrix, B bi-diagonal.

```
function [Q,B,Z] = QBZbyGivens_(A,tol,format,f1st,last,Q,Z)

[m,n] = size(A); B = A;
tol = tol*max(1.0,norm(diag(A),inf));

for j = f1st:last
    if (m-j>0 && norm(B(j+1:m,j),inf)>tol)
        for k=j+1:m
            [c,s] = givens_(B(j,j),B(k,j));
            B(j,j) = c*B(j,j) - s*B(k,j);          %B=Q'*B
            for l=j+1:n
                Bjl = B(j,l);  Bkl = B(k,l);
                B(j,l) = c*Bjl - s*Bkl;  B(k,l) = s*Bjl + c*Bkl;
            end
            if (abs(c) < tol)           rho = 1;
            elseif(abs(s) < abs(c)) rho = sign(c)*s/2;
            else                        rho = sign(s)*2/c; end
            B(k,j) = rho;     %save encoded Givens [c,s] at zeroed B(k,j)
        end
    end
    if (n-j>1 && norm(B(j,j+2:n),inf) > tol)
        for k=j+2:n
            [c,s] = givens_(B(j,j+1),B(j,k));
            B(j,j+1) = c*B(j,j+1) - s*B(j,k);       %B=B*Z'
            for l=j+1:m
                Blj = B(l,j+1);  Blk = B(l,k);
```

```
                    B(l,j+1) = c*Blj - s*Blk;   B(l,k)   = s*Blj + c*Blk;
               end
               if (abs(c) < tol)          rho = 1;
               elseif(abs(s) < abs(c)) rho = sign(c)*s/2;
               else                      rho = sign(s)*2/c; end
               B(j,k) = rho;      %save encoded Givens [c,s] at zeroed B(j,k)
          end
     end
end

if (strcmp(format,'long') || strcmp(format,'short'))
     if (~exist('Q','var') || isempty(Q)) Q = eye(m); end
     if (~exist('Z','var') || isempty(Z)) Z = eye(n); end
     for j = flst:last
          if (m-j > 0)
               for k=j+1:m
                    rho = B(k,j);   B(k,j) = 0.0;
                    if (rho == 1)             c = 0;   s = 1;      %decode [c,s]
                    elseif(abs(rho) < 1) s = 2.0*rho;   c = sqrt(1.0-s*s);
                    else                      c = 2.0/rho;   s = sqrt(1.0-c*c); end
                    for l=1:m
                         Qlj = Q(l,j);   Qlk = Q(l,k);
                         Q(l,j) = c*Qlj - s*Qlk;   Q(l,k) = s*Qlj + c*Qlk;
                    end
               end
          end
          if (n-j > 1)
               for k=j+2:n
                    rho = B(j,k);   B(j,k) = 0.0;
                    if (rho == 1)             c = 0;   s = 1;      %decode [c,s]
                    elseif(abs(rho) < 1) s = 2.0*rho;   c = sqrt(1.0-s*s);
                    else                      c = 2.0/rho;   s = sqrt(1.0-c*c); end
                    for l=1:n
                         Zjl = Z(j+1,l);   Zkl = Z(k,l);
                         Z(j+1,l) = c*Zjl - s*Zkl;   Z(k,l) = s*Zjl + c*Zkl;
                    end
               end
          end
     end
end
if (strcmp(format,'short') && last==min(m,n))
     k = min(min(m,n),last); l = k + 1; Bkl = 0.0;
     if (m > k) B = B(1:k,:); end
     if (n > l) B = B(:,1:k+1); Bkl = B(k,k+1); end
     if (abs(Bkl) < tol)
          l = l - 1;
          if (abs(B(k,k)) < tol)
               k = k - 1;
               for j=k:-1:1
                    if (abs(B(j,j+1)) > tol) break; else l = l - 1; end
                    if (abs(B(j,j)) > tol) break; else k = k - 1; end
               end
          end
     end
     if (size(B,1) > k) B = B(1:k,:); end
     if (size(B,2) > l) B = B(:,1:l); end
     if (size(Q,2) > k) Q = Q(:,1:k); end
```

```
      if (size(Z,2) > 1) Z = Z(1:1,:); end
      B = full2band_(B,0,1);
end
if (strcmp(format,'brief'))
      Q = []; b0 = diag(B);  b1 = diag(B,1); Z = [];
      if(length(b0) == length(b1)) B = [b0, b1];
      else                         B = [b0, [b1;0.0]]; end
end
if (strcmp(format,'compact')) Q = []; Z = []; end
```

Now we give a simple example for QBZbyGivens_. The example demonstrates the partial QBZ decomposition of a non-square matrix. At any step of the QBZ decomposition, the identity $\mathbf{A} = \mathbf{QBZ}$ always holds. Before the QBZ decomposition completes, $\mathbf{B}$ is not completely bi-diagonal.

```
>> A=rand(6,5);
>> [Q,B,Z]=QBZbyGivens_(A,100*eps,'short',1,2)   %partial QBZ decomposition
Q =                       %Note special form of Q
   -0.4918   -0.0705    0.7460   -0.3717   -0.2198   -0.1006
   -0.5468   -0.0289   -0.6641   -0.4456   -0.2364   -0.0684
   -0.0767   -0.6804   -0.0491    0.3792   -0.1416   -0.6041
   -0.5514    0.3037         0    0.7207   -0.1850    0.2237
   -0.3817   -0.0681         0         0    0.9174   -0.0899
   -0.0589   -0.6591         0         0         0    0.7498
B =                       %B incomplete bi-diagonal
   -1.6565   -2.4564         0         0         0
         0   -2.0142   -0.5555         0         0
         0         0    0.1850    0.1469    0.3415
         0         0   -0.0155   -0.8493   -0.1144
         0         0   -0.1436    0.4458   -0.0541
         0         0    0.4237   -0.1662   -0.2383
Z =                       %
    1.0000         0         0         0         0
         0    0.4717    0.1694   -0.7944   -0.3430
         0    0.4440    0.5777    0.0939    0.6785
         0    0.5550    0.1339    0.6001   -0.5603
         0    0.5218   -0.7872         0    0.3288
```

To complete the partial QBZ decomposition, use the restart function of QBZbyGivens_. Note the output of $\mathbf{B}$ is in band format for the input argument format='short'. The use of partial QBZ decomposition, restart, and the input argument format for QBZbyGivens_ and QBZbyHouseholder_ is same.

```
>> [Q,B,Z]=QBZbyGivens_(B,100*eps,'short',3,5,Q,Z)     %f1st=2+1
Q =
   -0.4918   -0.0705   -0.2740   -0.4924   -0.6546
   -0.5468   -0.0289    0.2292   -0.0925    0.4704
   -0.0767   -0.6804    0.5173    0.3670   -0.3574
   -0.5514    0.3037   -0.2275    0.7076   -0.0825
   -0.3817   -0.0681    0.3505   -0.3347    0.3068
   -0.0589   -0.6591   -0.6558    0.0386    0.3486
B =
   -1.6565   -2.4564
   -2.0142   -0.5555
   -0.4843    0.2028
   -0.9764    0.0806
   -0.3971         0
Z =
    1.0000         0         0         0         0
```

0	0.4717	0.1694	-0.8595	-0.1003
0	0.4440	0.5777	0.2849	0.6229
0	0.5550	0.1339	0.4138	-0.7091
0	0.5218	-0.7872	0.0945	0.3149

3.4.3 QBZ DECOMPOSITION BY GOLUB–KAHAN–LANCZOS PROCEDURE

From the last two subsections, we see that the QBZ decomposition $\mathbf{A} = \mathbf{QBZ}$ for an arbitrary matrix $\mathbf{A}$ always exists, where $\mathbf{Q}$ and $\mathbf{Z}$ are orthogonal and $\mathbf{B}$ is bi-diagonal. We can write $\mathbf{A} = \mathbf{QBZ}$ in two equivalent forms: $\mathbf{AZ}' = \mathbf{QB}$ and $\mathbf{Q}'\mathbf{A} = \mathbf{BZ}$.

We take a 4×4 matrix $\mathbf{A}$ as an example. The two equivalent forms are written in terms of the columns and rows of $\mathbf{Z}$ and $\mathbf{Q}$, respectively,

$$\mathbf{A}\left[\mathbf{Z}(1,:)', \mathbf{Z}(2,:)', \mathbf{Z}(3,:)', \mathbf{Z}(4,:)'\right] = \left[\mathbf{Q}(:,1), \mathbf{Q}(:,2), \mathbf{Q}(:,3), \mathbf{Q}(:,4)\right] \begin{bmatrix} B_{11} & B_{12} & 0 & 0 \\ 0 & B_{22} & B_{23} & 0 \\ 0 & 0 & B_{33} & B_{34} \\ 0 & 0 & 0 & B_{44} \end{bmatrix}, \tag{3.5a}$$

$$\begin{bmatrix} \mathbf{Q}(:,1)' \\ \mathbf{Q}(:,2)' \\ \mathbf{Q}(:,3)' \\ \mathbf{Q}(:,4)' \end{bmatrix} \mathbf{A} = \begin{bmatrix} B_{11} & B_{12} & 0 & 0 \\ 0 & B_{22} & B_{23} & 0 \\ 0 & 0 & B_{33} & B_{34} \\ 0 & 0 & 0 & B_{44} \end{bmatrix} \begin{bmatrix} \mathbf{Z}(1,:) \\ \mathbf{Z}(2,:) \\ \mathbf{Z}(3,:) \\ \mathbf{Z}(4,:) \end{bmatrix}. \tag{3.5b}$$

Let us compare the first column of the left and right sides of Eq. (3.5a). Note that $\mathbf{Q}(:,1)'\mathbf{Q}(:,1) = 1$,

$$\mathbf{AZ}(1,:)' = B_{11}\mathbf{Q}(:,1), \tag{3.6}$$

$$B_{11} = \|\mathbf{AZ}(1,:)'\|_2, \quad \mathbf{Q}(:,1) = \frac{1}{B_{11}}\mathbf{AZ}(1,:)'. \tag{3.7}$$

Next let us compare the first row of the left and right sides of Eq. (3.5b). Note that $\mathbf{Z}(2,:)\mathbf{Z}(2,:)' = 1$,

$$\mathbf{Q}(:,1)'\mathbf{A} = B_{11}\mathbf{Z}(1,:) + B_{12}\mathbf{Z}(2,:),$$

$$B_{12} = \|\mathbf{Q}(:,1)'\mathbf{A} - B_{11}\mathbf{Z}(1,:)\|_2, \quad \mathbf{Z}(2,:) = \frac{1}{B_{12}}\left(\mathbf{Q}(:,1)'\mathbf{A} - B_{11}\mathbf{Z}(1,:)\right).$$

As shown below, we can verify that $\mathbf{Z}(2,:)\mathbf{Z}(1,:)' = 0$ if we choose $\mathbf{Z}(1,:)\mathbf{Z}(1,:)' = 1$,

$$\mathbf{Z}(2,:)\mathbf{Z}(1,:)' = \frac{1}{B_{12}}\mathbf{Q}(:,1)'\mathbf{AZ}(1,:)' - \frac{B_{11}}{B_{12}}\mathbf{Z}(1,:)\mathbf{Z}(1,:)' = \frac{B_{11}}{B_{12}}\left(\mathbf{Q}(:,1)'\mathbf{Q}(:,1) - \mathbf{Z}(1,:)\mathbf{Z}(1,:)'\right) = 0.$$

Now we compare the second column of the left and right sides of Eq. (3.5a). Note that $\mathbf{Q}(:,2)'\mathbf{Q}(:,2) = 1$,

$$\mathbf{AZ}(2,:)' = B_{12}\mathbf{Q}(:,1) + B_{22}\mathbf{Q}(:,2),$$

$$B_{22} = \|\mathbf{AZ}(2,:)' - B_{12}\mathbf{Q}(:,1)\|_2, \quad \mathbf{Q}(:,2) = \frac{1}{B_{22}}\left(\mathbf{AZ}(2,:)' - B_{12}\mathbf{Q}(:,1)\right).$$

Again we can verify that $\mathbf{Q}(:,1)'\mathbf{Q}(:,2) = 0$ as shown below,

$$\mathbf{Q}(:,1)'\mathbf{Q}(:,2) = \frac{1}{B_{22}}\left(B_{11}\mathbf{Z}(1,:) + B_{12}\mathbf{Z}(2,:)\right)\mathbf{Z}(2,:)' - \frac{B_{11}}{B_{22}}\mathbf{Q}(:,1)'\mathbf{Q}(:,1) = 0.$$

Similarly from the second row of Eq. (3.5b), we obtain B_{23} and $Z(3,:)$. Then from the third column of Eq. (3.5a), we obtain B_{33} and $Q(:,3)$. From the third row of Eq. (3.5b), we obtain B_{34} and $Z(4,:)$. Finally from the fourth column of Eq. (3.5a), we obtain B_{44} and $Q(:,4)$.

If we are given a unit row vector $Z(1,:)$ to start with, following the above procedure, we can obtain Q,Z and B. By construction, $Q'Q = I$, $ZZ' = I$, B is bi-diagonal, and $A = QBZ$. What we just described is the Golub–Kahan–Lanczos bi-diagonalization procedure in Section 6.3 of [5]. Two improvements must be made in order for the procedure to work correctly in practice. The first improvement is regarding the gradual loss of orthogonality among the columns of Q and among the rows of Z. In the above discussion, we can see that $Q'Q = I$ and $ZZ' = I$ are satisfied if $Z(1,:)Z(1,:)' = 1$ is satisfied. This observation is only true if the computation is exact. In reality, $Z(2,:)Z(1,:)' = 0$ and $Q(:,1)'Q(:,2) = 0$ are approximate. The small errors in these two identities tend to become bigger errors in all the identities which should satisfy in the subsequent steps of the algorithm: $Q'Q = I$, $ZZ' = I$, and $A = QBZ$. If the small errors in the orthogonality are left untreated, the algorithm will fail to produce the QBZ decomposition accurately. In the following MATLAB implementation QBZbyLanczos_.m, a simple full re-orthogonalization of $Q(:,j)$ to all the existing columns $Q(:,1 : j - 1)$ is adopted. A similar re-orthogonalization of $Z(j + 1,:)$ to $Z(1 : j,:)$ is performed. A full re-orthogonalization is not the most efficient. A selective re-orthogonalization similar to that in [46] may be possible, but it needs some research. The second is the exception regarding $B(j,j) = 0$ or $B(j,j+1) = 0$. If $B(j,j) = 0$, $Q(:,j)$ cannot be determined as described, we can take an arbitrary $Q(:,j)$ which satisfies $Q(:,1 : j - 1)'Q(:,j) = 0$. If $B(j,j + 1) = 0$, we take $Z(j + 1,:)$ to be arbitrary satisfying $Z(j + 1,:)Z(1 : j,:)' = 0$.

In this algorithm, differently from QBZ by Householder or Givens, A is not altered. A is only used in the matrix product calculations of Az' and $q'A$. As with all the algorithms of multiplying type, the algorithm is better suited to large and sparse or band matrices, where zero patterns can be taken into account in the calculation of Az and $q'A$. In the following QBZbyLanczos_.m, the matrix–vector product algorithms for band matrix and sparse matrix can be input through the last input argument Ax. Ax is a cell array, which can take the function name of the special matrix–vector product and any input arguments for that function. An example is provided below to demonstrate the usage of Ax. The use of QBZbyLanczos_.m is similar to GTGiByLanczos_.m presented in Section 2.5.3.

Algorithm 3.12

```
A=Q*B*Z', Q,Z orthogonal matrix, B bi-diagonal.
function [Q,B,Z] = QBZbyLanczos_(A,tol,f1st,last,Q,B,Z)

[m,n] = size_(A);
if (f1st == 1) z = Z(f1st,:);   q = zeros(m,1);    beta = 0.0;
else            z = Z(f1st,:);   q = Q(:,f1st-1);   beta = B(f1st-1,2); end

for j=f1st:last
    Az = Ay_(A,z','right');   q = Az - beta*q;   alpha = norm(q,inf);
    if (alpha > tol)
        q = q - Q(:,1:j-1)*(Q(:,1:j-1)'*q);   alpha = norm(q);
    end
    if (alpha > tol) q = q/alpha;
    else             q = orthogonal_(Q(:,1:j-1)); alpha = 0.0; end
    Q(:,j) = q;   B(j,1) = alpha;
    if (j < n)
        qA = Ay_(A,q','left');   z = qA - alpha*z;   beta = norm(z,inf);
        if (beta > tol)
            z = z - (z*Z(1:j,:)')*Z(1:j,:);   beta = norm(z);
```

```
            end
            if (beta > tol) z = z/beta;
            else            z = orthogonal_(Z(1:j,:)')')'; beta = 0; end
            B(j,2) = beta; Z(j+1,:) = z;
        end
    end

    if (B(end,2) == 0) B = band2full_(B,0,1,size(B,1),size(B,1));
    else               B = band2full_(B,0,1,size(B,1),size(B,1)+1); end
    if (m>n && last==min(m,n))
        for j=n+1:m Q = [Q,orthogonal_(Q)]; end
        B = [B;zeros(m-n,n)];
    end
    if (m<n && last==min(m,n))
        for j=m+2:n Z = [Z;orthogonal_(Z)']; end
        B = [B,zeros(m,n-m-1)];
    end
```

First, we present a simple example of full matrix to demonstrate the partial QBZ decomposition. Compare the output of the following example to the output of `[Q,B,Z]=QBZbyGivens_(A,100*eps,'short',1,2)` of the last subsection. Contrary to `QBZbyHouseholder_` and `QBZbyGivens_`, the shape of partial QBZ decomposition by `QBZbyLanczos_` is different. For the partial QBZ decomposition by `QBZbyLanczos_`, $\mathbf{A} \neq \mathbf{QBZ}$. But the following identities hold by construction,

$$
\begin{aligned}
\mathbf{AZ}(1:l,:)' &= \mathbf{QB}(:,1:l), \\
\mathbf{Q'A} &= \mathbf{B}(:,1:l)\mathbf{Z}(1:l,:) + B(l,l+1)\mathbf{I}(:,l)\mathbf{Z}(l+1,:),
\end{aligned}
\tag{3.8}
$$

where l is the value of the input argument `last` to `QBZbyLanczos_`. $l = 2$ in the example below.

```
>> A=rand(5,6);
>> [Q,B,Z]=QBZbyLanczos_(A,100*eps,1,2)
Q =
     0.3753     0.1454
     0.1130     0.2362
     0.7931    -0.4806
     0.3962     0.2687
     0.2457     0.7873
B =
     0.9838     1.7543          0
          0     1.6362     0.4570
Z =
     1.0000          0          0
          0     0.4989     0.4545
          0     0.4278     0.0578
          0     0.3315     0.3048
          0     0.5861    -0.7774
          0     0.3385     0.3048
```

A partial QBZ decomposition can be restarted. When QBZ decomposition is complete, the identity $\mathbf{A} = \mathbf{ABZ}$ recovers.

```
>> [Q,B,Z]=QBZbyLanczos_(A,100*eps,3,5,Q,B,Z)
Q =
     0.3753     0.1454    -0.5429     0.3227     0.6626
     0.1130     0.2362    -0.3523    -0.8979     0.0328
```

```
          0.7931      -0.4806      -0.0459      -0.0221      -0.3707
          0.3962       0.2687       0.7567      -0.1611       0.4151
          0.2457       0.7873      -0.0804       0.2513      -0.5002
B  =
          0.9838       1.7543            0            0            0            0
               0       1.6362       0.4570            0            0            0
               0            0       0.5359       0.4351            0            0
               0            0            0       0.2504       0.5001            0
               0            0            0            0       0.1153       0.1848
Z  =
          1.0000            0            0            0            0            0
               0       0.4989       0.4545       0.3059       0.1053       0.6632
               0       0.4278       0.0578      -0.3996       0.7523      -0.2966
               0       0.3315       0.3048       0.5464      -0.1898      -0.6802
               0       0.5861      -0.7774       0.1041      -0.1892       0.0738
               0       0.3385       0.3048      -0.6613      -0.5925      -0.0643
```

Next we present an example of QBZ decomposition of a band matrix. We show how to use the matrix product function mtimesBand_ in QBZbyLanczos_.

```
>> A = [5.5000       1.0000            0            0            0            0;
          1.0000       4.5000       1.0000            0            0            0;
               0       1.0000       3.5000       1.0000            0            0;
               0            0       1.0000       2.5000       1.0000            0;
               0            0            0       1.0000       1.5000       1.0000];

>> B = cell(5,1);    [B{1},B{2},B{3},B{4},B{5}]=full2band_(A,1,1);

>> [Q1,B1,Z1]=QBZbyLanczos_({'mtimesBand_',B},100*eps)
Q1  =
          0.9839      -0.1708       0.0495      -0.0177       0.0079
          0.1789       0.9394      -0.2723       0.0976      -0.0433
               0       0.2965       0.8600      -0.3739       0.1809
               0       0.0220       0.4233       0.7350      -0.5292
               0            0       0.0680       0.5568       0.8278
B1  =
          5.5902       1.7978            0            0            0            0
               0       4.5302       1.5954            0            0            0
               0            0       3.5431       1.3281            0            0
               0            0            0       2.5271       0.8371            0
               0            0            0            0       1.0942       0.3136
Z1  =
          1.0000            0            0            0            0            0
               0       0.9950      -0.0971       0.0209      -0.0062       0.0025
               0       0.0995       0.9705      -0.2091       0.0625      -0.0247
               0            0       0.2203       0.9080      -0.3275       0.1406
               0            0       0.0138       0.3588       0.7925      -0.4929
               0            0            0       0.0512       0.5106       0.8583

>> norm(Q1*B1*Z1-A)
= 9.9669e-016
```

In the example below, we convert the matrix **A** of the previous example to a sparse matrix of CSR format. Then use the matrix product function mtimeCSR_ in QBZbyLanczos_. Exactly the same results as the previous example which uses mtimeBand_ are obtained. It can be verified that $A = QBZ$.

```
>> S=cell(3,1);    [S{1},S{2},S{3}]=full2csr_(A);

>> [Q2,B2,Z2]=QBZbyLanczos_({'mtimesCSR_',S},100*eps)
Q2 =
    0.9839   -0.1708    0.0495   -0.0177    0.0079
    0.1789    0.9394   -0.2723    0.0976   -0.0433
         0    0.2965    0.8600   -0.3739    0.1809
         0    0.0220    0.4233    0.7350   -0.5292
         0         0    0.0680    0.5568    0.8278
B2 =
    5.5902    1.7978         0         0         0         0
         0    4.5302    1.5954         0         0         0
         0         0    3.5431    1.3281         0         0
         0         0         0    2.5271    0.8371         0
         0         0         0         0    1.0942    0.3136
Z2 =
    1.0000         0         0         0         0         0
         0    0.9950   -0.0971    0.0209   -0.0062    0.0025
         0    0.0995    0.9705   -0.2091    0.0625   -0.0247
         0         0    0.2203    0.9080   -0.3275    0.1406
         0         0    0.0138    0.3588    0.7925   -0.4929
         0         0         0    0.0512    0.5106    0.8583

>> norm(Q2*B2*Z2-A)
= 9.9669e-016
```

With QBZbyLanczos_.m, the first input argument A is not necessarily an explicit matrix. In the following examples, we apply QBZbyLanczos_.m to $A(:, 1 : 5)$ and $A(:, 1 : 5)^{-1}$. But $A(:, 1 : 5)$ is input as $\mathbf{LL}'$ and $A(:, 1 : 5)^{-1}$ is input as $\mathbf{L}'^{-1}\mathbf{L}^{-1}$, where $\mathbf{L}$ is the Cholesky factor of $A(:, 1 : 5)$.

```
>> L=LLtByCholesky_(A(:,1:5))
L =
    2.3452         0         0         0         0
    0.4264    2.0780         0         0         0
         0    0.4812    1.8079         0         0
         0         0    0.5531    1.4812         0
         0         0         0    0.6751    1.0219
>> Lb1=full2band_(L,1,0);    Lb2=full2band_(L',0,1);

>> A5 = {{'size',[5,5]},{'mtimesBand_',{Lb1,1,0,5,5}},{'mtimesBand_',{Lb2,0,1,5,5}}};
>> [Q3,B3,Z3]=QBZbyLanczos_(A5,100*eps);    %A5=A(:,1:5)=L*L'
>> norm(Q3*B3*Z3-A(:,1:5))
= 9.2066e-016

>> B5 = {{'size',[5,5]},{'mdivideBand_',{Lb2,0,1,5,5}},{'mdivideBand_',{Lb1,1,0,5,5}}};
>> [Q4,B4,Z4]=QBZbyLanczos_(B5,100*eps);    %B5=inv(A(:,1:5))=inv(L')*inv(L)
>> norm(Q4*B4*Z4-inv(A(:,1:5)))
= 3.4561e-016
```

3.5 REDUCTION OF SQUARE MATRIX TO HESSENBERG BY SIMILARITY TRANSFORMATIONS

In the last section, we showed that in a fixed number of steps a general matrix $\mathbf{A}$ can be transformed to a bi-diagonal $\mathbf{B}$ with two suitably chosen orthogonal transformations $\mathbf{Q}$ and $\mathbf{Z}$, that is, $\mathbf{A} = \mathbf{QBZ}$.

In this section, we will put a restriction on how we can choose $\mathbf{Z}$. The restriction is that $\mathbf{Z} = \mathbf{Q}'$. If we require $\mathbf{Z} = \mathbf{Q}'$, $\mathbf{A}$ is necessarily square. Under $\mathbf{Z} = \mathbf{Q}'$, the simplest form a square matrix $\mathbf{A}$ can be transformed into in a fixed number of steps is a Hessenberg matrix. Therefore, the topic of the section is that, given a square matrix $\mathbf{A} \in \mathbb{R}^{n \times n}$, we find an orthogonal matrix $\mathbf{Q}$, so that $\mathbf{H} = \mathbf{Q}'\mathbf{A}\mathbf{Q}$, where $\mathbf{H}$ is an upper Hessenberg. For brevity, we will name $\mathbf{A} = \mathbf{Q}\mathbf{H}\mathbf{Q}'$ the QHQt transformation. Similarly to QBZ decomposition, QHQt have three equivalent representations, by Householder, by Givens, and by Arnoldi. The corresponding non-orthogonal counterpart to $\mathbf{A} = \mathbf{Q}\mathbf{H}\mathbf{Q}'$ is the reduction of a square matrix to Hessenberg by Gauss elimination discussed in Section 2.5.

3.5.1 QHQt DECOMPOSITION BY HOUSEHOLDER REFLECTIONS

The exposition of the algorithm follows Sections 2.5, 3.2.1 and 3.4.1. We take a 5×5 matrix $\mathbf{A}$ as the example. In the first step, we find a Householder matrix $\mathbf{Q}_1 = \mathbf{I} - \alpha \mathbf{h}\mathbf{h}'$ and apply $\mathbf{G}_1 \mathbf{A} = \mathbf{A} - (\alpha \mathbf{h})(\mathbf{h}'\mathbf{A}) \Rightarrow \mathbf{A}$, so that $\mathbf{A}(3:5,1) = 0$,

$$
\begin{bmatrix} 1 & 0 & 0 & 0 & 0 \\ 0 & \alpha h_2 h_2 & \alpha h_2 h_3 & \alpha h_2 h_4 & \alpha h_2 h_5 \\ 0 & \alpha h_3 h_2 & \alpha h_3 h_3 & \alpha h_3 h_4 & \alpha h_3 h_5 \\ 0 & \alpha h_4 h_2 & \alpha h_4 h_3 & \alpha h_4 h_4 & \alpha h_4 h_5 \\ 0 & \alpha h_5 h_2 & \alpha h_5 h_3 & \alpha h_5 h_4 & \alpha h_5 h_5 \end{bmatrix}
\begin{bmatrix} A_{11} & A_{12} & A_{13} & A_{14} & A_{15} \\ A_{21} & A_{22} & A_{32} & A_{42} & A_{52} \\ A_{31} & A_{32} & A_{33} & A_{43} & A_{53} \\ A_{41} & A_{42} & A_{43} & A_{44} & A_{54} \\ A_{51} & A_{52} & A_{53} & A_{54} & A_{55} \end{bmatrix}
\Rightarrow
\begin{bmatrix} A_{11} & A_{12} & A_{13} & A_{14} & A_{15} \\ A_{21} & A_{22} & A_{32} & A_{42} & A_{52} \\ 0 & A_{32} & A_{33} & A_{43} & A_{53} \\ 0 & A_{42} & A_{43} & A_{44} & A_{54} \\ 0 & A_{52} & A_{53} & A_{54} & A_{55} \end{bmatrix}.
$$

To keep the similarity, it is necessary to apply $\mathbf{A}\mathbf{Q}_1' = \mathbf{A} - (\mathbf{A}\mathbf{h})(\alpha \mathbf{h}') \Rightarrow \mathbf{A}$. Because $\mathbf{Q}_1(:,1) = \mathbf{I}(:,1)$, the first column of $\mathbf{A}$ is not altered. This means that the zeros in $\mathbf{A}(3:5,1)$ set in $\mathbf{Q}_1 \mathbf{A}$ operation will not be altered in $(\mathbf{Q}_1 \mathbf{A})\mathbf{Q}_1'$ operation. In this way, the Householder vector $h(3:5)$ can be saved to the zeroed $A(3:5,1)$. Should we aim to zero $\mathbf{A}(2:5,1)$ by a Householder matrix $\mathbf{Z}_1$, $\mathbf{A}\mathbf{Z}_1'$ immediately sets the zeroed $\mathbf{A}(2:5,1)$ to nonzeros.

To continue the algorithm, the same two steps, pre-multiplication by a Householder matrix and post-multiplication by the same Householder matrix, are applied to columns 2 and 3 of $\mathbf{A}$. For column 2, the aim is to zero $\mathbf{A}(4:5,2)$. For column 3, only $A(5,3)$ needs to be zeroed. Then $\mathbf{A}$ is transformed to an upper Hessenberg matrix. The product of $\mathbf{Q}_1\mathbf{Q}_2\mathbf{Q}_3$ is $\mathbf{Q}$.

For a general $n \times n$ square matrix $\mathbf{A}$, the transformations discussed above are applied to columns 1 to $n-2$ of $\mathbf{A}$. The algorithm can stop at any column $l \leq n-2$ and restart from $l+1$. If the algorithm stops at column $l < n-2$, the final $n-l$ columns of the output $\mathbf{H}$ are not in the upper Hessenberg form. However at any step of the algorithm $j \leq l, l \leq n-2$, $\mathbf{A} = \mathbf{Q}\mathbf{H}\mathbf{Q}'$ holds.

The MATLAB code `QHQtByHouseholder_.m` implementing the algorithm is listed below, in which over half of the code is handling the output according to `format`.

Algorithm 3.13

```
A=Q*H*Q', H upper Hessenberg, Q orthogonal.
function [Q,H] = QHQtByHouseholder_(A,tol,format,f1st,last,Q)

[m,n] = size(A);   H = A;
tol = tol*max(1.0,norm(diag(A),inf));

for j=f1st:last
    [h,alpha,beta] = householder_(H(j+1:m,j));
    if (abs(beta) < tol) continue; end
    H(j+1,j) = beta;   H(j+2:m,j) = h(2:m-j);   v = alpha*h;
```

```
        for k=j+1:n              %H=(I-alpha*h*h')*H
            hk = H(j+1:m,k);  H(j+1:m,k) = hk - (h'*hk)*v;
        end
        for k=1:n                %H=H*(I-alpha*h*h')
            hk = H(k,j+1:n);  H(k,j+1:n) = hk - (hk*h)*v';
        end
    end

    if (strcmp(format,'long') || strcmp(format,'short'))
        if (~exist('Q','var') || isempty(Q)) back = 1; js = last:-1:1; Q = eye(m);
        else                                 back = 0; js = f1st:last; end
        for j=js
            q = H(j+2:m,j);  qq = q'*q;  H(j+2:m,j) = 0;
            if (qq < tol) continue; end
            h = [1; q];  alpha = 2.0/(qq+1.0);
            if (back == 1)           %backward accumulation of Q
                v = alpha*h;
                for k=j+1:m qk = Q(j+1:m,k); Q(j+1:m,k) = qk - (h'*qk)*v; end
            else                     %forward accumulation of Q
                v = alpha*h';
                for k=2:m qk = Q(k,j+1:m);  Q(k,j+1:m) = qk - (qk*h)*v; end
            end
        end
    end
    if (strcmp(format,'brief') || strcmp(format,'compact')) Q = []; end
    if (strcmp(format,'brief'))  %discard Q
        for j=last:-1:f1st H(j+2:m,j) = 0; end
    end
```

In the following, we show two ways to do restart with QHQtByHouseholder_. In the first way, we use format='long' to perform a partial **QHQt** decomposition at the beginning. Then finish the **QHQt** by a restart from the partial QHQt decomposition.

```
>> A=randn(5);
>> [Q,H]=QHQtByHouseholder_(A,100*eps,'long',1,2)      %partial QHQt, format='long'
Q =
    1.0000        0        0        0        0
         0  -0.3143  -0.5345  -0.6590   0.4258
         0  -0.0370  -0.7890   0.6086  -0.0759
         0  -0.8348   0.2876   0.3597   0.3016
         0   0.4505   0.0953   0.2569   0.8497
H =                                                   %H(3:5,3:5) full
    0.0412  -1.2115   1.4041   0.9118  -0.0250
    2.4063  -0.2214  -0.1711  -0.3178   0.8675
         0   2.6046   0.8102  -1.1511  -1.1665
         0        0   0.5677  -2.1278  -0.6176
         0        0   1.0097   0.2302  -0.7714

>> [Q,H]=QHQtByHouseholder_(H,100*eps,'long',3,5,Q)   %restart: input H AND Q.
Q =
    1.0000        0        0        0        0
         0  -0.3143  -0.5345  -0.0482   0.7831
         0  -0.0370  -0.7890  -0.2321  -0.5677
         0  -0.8348   0.2876  -0.4391  -0.1657
         0   0.4505   0.0953  -0.8666   0.1925
H =
    0.0412  -1.2115   1.4041  -0.4251  -0.8070
```

```
2.4063   -0.2214   -0.1711   -0.6004    0.7022
     0    2.6046    0.8102    1.5810    0.4317
     0         0   -1.1584   -1.2627   -0.2562
     0         0         0   -1.1040   -1.6365
```

The following is the second way, in which we use format='compact' at the beginning. Then finish the QHQt by a restart.

```
>> [Q,H]=QHQtByHouseholder_(A,100*eps,'compact',1,2)   %format='compact'
Q =
     []
H =
    0.0412   -1.2115    1.4041    0.9118   -0.0250
    2.4063   -0.2214   -0.1711   -0.3178    0.8675
    0.0282    2.6046    0.8102   -1.1511   -1.1665
    0.6352   -0.3535    0.5677   -2.1278   -0.6176
   -0.3427    0.0496    1.0097    0.2302   -0.7714

>> [Q,H]=QHQtByHouseholder_(H,100*eps,'long',3,5)      %restart: input H, but NOT Q.
Q =
    1.0000         0         0         0         0
         0   -0.3143   -0.5345   -0.0482    0.7831
         0   -0.0370   -0.7890   -0.2321   -0.5677
         0   -0.8348    0.2876   -0.4391   -0.1657
         0    0.4505    0.0953   -0.8666    0.1925
H =
    0.0412   -1.2115    1.4041   -0.4251   -0.8070
    2.4063   -0.2214   -0.1711   -0.6004    0.7022
         0    2.6046    0.8102    1.5810    0.4317
         0         0   -1.1584   -1.2627   -0.2562
         0         0         0   -1.1040   -1.6365
```

3.5.2 QHQt DECOMPOSITION BY GIVENS ROTATIONS

Just as in QR decomposition, a Householder reflection to zero multiple components of a matrix can be replaced by a series of Givens rotations, while each Givens rotation is to zero only one component of the matrix. In QHQt decomposition, we can also use Givens rotations. The essence of the algorithm is same as what we discussed in the last subsection and the QR decomposition by Givens rotation discussed in Section 3.2.2.

The following is the MATLAB implementation QHQtByGivens_.m, in which over half of the code is to handle the output according to the input argument format. Note that the part of the code handling the output is same to QHQtByHouseholder_.m.

Algorithm 3.14

A=Q*H*Q', , H upper Hessenberg, Q orthogonal.

```
function [Q,H] = QHQtByGivens_(A,tol,format,f1st,last,Q)

[m,n] = size(A);   H = A;
tol = tol*max(1.0,norm(diag(A),inf));

for j=f1st:last
    if (norm(H(j+1:m,j),inf) < tol) continue; end
    for k=j+2:m
```

```
            [c,s] = givens_(H(j+1,j),H(k,j));
            H(j+1,j) = c*H(j+1,j) - s*H(k,j);
            for l=j+1:n      %A=G*A
                Hjl = H(j+1,l);   Hkl = H(k,l);
                H(j+1,l) = c*Hjl - s*Hkl;   H(k,l) = s*Hjl + c*Hkl;
            end
            for l=1:m       %A=A*G
                Hlj = H(l,j+1);   Hlk = H(l,k);
                H(l,j+1) = c*Hlj - s*Hlk;   H(l,k) = s*Hlj + c*Hlk;
            end
            if (abs(c) < tol)          rho = 1;
            elseif(abs(s) < abs(c))  rho = sign(c)*s/2;
            else                       rho = sign(s)*2/c;  end
            H(k,j) = rho;      %save encoded Givens [c,s] at zeroed H(k,j)
        end
    end
end

if (strcmp(format,'long') || strcmp(format,'short'))
    if (~exist('Q','var') || isempty(Q)) js = 1:last;  Q = eye(m);
    else                                 js = f1st:last;   end
    for j=js      %accumulation of Q
        for k=j+2:m
            rho = H(k,j);   H(k,j) = 0;
            if (rho == 1)            c = 0;   s = 1;
            elseif(abs(rho) < 1) s = 2.0*rho;  c = sqrt(1.0-s*s);
            else                 c = 2.0/rho;  s = sqrt(1.0-c*c); end
            for l=1:m
                Qlj = Q(l,j+1);   Qlk = Q(l,k);
                Q(l,j+1) = c*Qlj - s*Qlk;   Q(l,k) = s*Qlj + c*Qlk;
            end
        end
    end
end
if (strcmp(format,'brief') || strcmp(format,'compact')) Q = []; end
if (strcmp(format,'brief'))  %discard Q
    for j=last:-1:f1st H(j+2:m,j) = 0; end
end
```

Now we give a simple example for QHQtByGivens_. The partial and restart of QHQtByGivens_ remain the same to those of QHQtByHouseholder_.

```
>> A=randn(5);
>> [Q,H]=QHQtByGivens_(A)
Q =
    1.0000         0         0         0         0
         0    0.9494    0.0483    0.2459   -0.1892
         0    0.0917    0.6599    0.0861    0.7407
         0   -0.1067   -0.4919    0.7855    0.3601
         0    0.2808   -0.5659   -0.5613    0.5347
H =
    1.0821   -0.4331    0.5646    0.5743    1.2942
    2.4991    1.9461    0.8711   -0.3855   -0.0939
         0    2.1228    0.0981   -0.1137    0.9981
         0         0   -1.3435   -0.3196   -0.5745
         0         0         0   -1.5044   -0.1967
```

3.5.3 QHQt DECOMPOSITION BY ARNOLDI PROCEDURE

The last two subsections showed that for a square matrix $\mathbf{A} \in \mathbb{R}^{n \times n}$, the QHQt decomposition $\mathbf{A} = \mathbf{QHQ'}$ exists, where $\mathbf{Q}$ is orthogonal and $\mathbf{H}$ is upper Hessenberg. We write $\mathbf{A} = \mathbf{QHQ'}$ in an equivalent form $\mathbf{AQ} = \mathbf{QH}$.

We illustrate the Arnoldi procedure with a 4×4 matrix $\mathbf{A}$. The equivalent form is written in terms of the columns of $\mathbf{Q}$,

$$\mathbf{A}\left[\mathbf{Q}(:,1), \mathbf{Q}(:,2), \mathbf{Q}(:,3), \mathbf{Q}(:,4)\right] = \left[\mathbf{Q}(:,1), \mathbf{Q}(:,2), \mathbf{Q}(:,3), \mathbf{Q}(:,4)\right] \begin{bmatrix} H_{11} & H_{12} & H_{13} & H_{14} \\ H_{21} & H_{22} & H_{23} & H_{24} \\ 0 & H_{32} & H_{33} & H_{34} \\ 0 & 0 & H_{43} & H_{44} \end{bmatrix}. \tag{3.9}$$

Assume $\mathbf{Q}(:,1)$ is an arbitrary unit vector of $\mathbb{R}^n$. We compare the first column of left and right sides of Eq. (3.9). Note that $\mathbf{Q}(:,1)'\mathbf{Q}(:,1) = 1$, $\mathbf{Q}(:,1)'\mathbf{Q}(:,2) = 0$, and $\mathbf{Q}(:,2)'\mathbf{Q}(:,2) = 1$,

$$\mathbf{AQ}(:,1) = H_{11}\mathbf{Q}(:,1) + H_{21}\mathbf{Q}(:,2),$$

$$H_{11} = \mathbf{Q}(:,1)'\mathbf{AQ}(:,1), \qquad H_{21} = \|\mathbf{AQ}(:,1) - H_{11}\mathbf{Q}(:,1)\|_2,$$

$$\mathbf{Q}(:,2) = \frac{1}{H_{21}}\left(\mathbf{AQ}(:,1) - H_{11}\mathbf{Q}(:,1)\right).$$

The equality of the second column of the left and right sides of Eq. (3.9) gives, noting the orthogonality of the columns of $\mathbf{Q}$,

$$\mathbf{AQ}(:,2) = \left[\mathbf{Q}(:,1), \mathbf{Q}(:,2)\right] \begin{bmatrix} H_{12} \\ H_{22} \end{bmatrix} + H_{32}\mathbf{Q}(:,3), \tag{3.10}$$

$$\begin{bmatrix} H_{12} \\ H_{22} \end{bmatrix} = \begin{bmatrix} \mathbf{Q}(:,1)' \\ \mathbf{Q}(:,2)' \end{bmatrix}(\mathbf{AQ}(:,2)), \qquad H_{32} = \|\mathbf{AQ}(:,2) - H_{12}\mathbf{Q}(:,1) - H_{22}\mathbf{Q}(:,2)\|_2, \tag{3.11}$$

$$\mathbf{Q}(:,3) = \frac{1}{H_{32}}\left(\mathbf{AQ}(:,2) - H_{12}\mathbf{Q}(:,1) - H_{22}\mathbf{Q}(:,2)\right). \tag{3.12}$$

Similarly, the equality of the third column of the left and right sides of Eq. (3.9) determines $\mathbf{H}(1:4,3)$ and $\mathbf{Q}(:,4)$. Finally, we compare the fourth column of the left and right sides of Eq. (3.9),

$$\mathbf{AQ}(:,4) = \left[\mathbf{Q}(:,1), \mathbf{Q}(:,2), \mathbf{Q}(:,3), \mathbf{Q}(:,4)\right] \begin{bmatrix} H_{14} \\ H_{24} \\ H_{34} \\ H_{44} \end{bmatrix}, \qquad \begin{bmatrix} H_{14} \\ H_{24} \\ H_{34} \\ H_{44} \end{bmatrix} = \begin{bmatrix} \mathbf{Q}(:,1)' \\ \mathbf{Q}(:,2)' \\ \mathbf{Q}(:,3)' \\ \mathbf{Q}(:,4)' \end{bmatrix}(\mathbf{AQ}(:,4)).$$

For a square matrix $\mathbf{A} \in \mathbb{R}^{n \times n}$, the following identities hold due to the construction of $\mathbf{Q}$ and $\mathbf{H}$ in the Arnoldi procedure. They are important relations for the applications of the Arnoldi procedure in the iterative equation solutions and eigenvalue solutions of non-symmetric matrices,

$$\mathbf{AQ}(:,1:j) = \mathbf{Q}(:,1:j)\mathbf{H}(1:j,1:j) + H(j+1,j)\mathbf{Q}(:,j+1)\mathbf{I}(j,:); \quad j = 1,2,\ldots,n, \tag{3.13}$$

$$\mathbf{Q}(:,1:j)'\mathbf{Q}(:,1:j) = \mathbf{I}; \quad j = 1,2,\ldots,n, \tag{3.14}$$

$$\mathbf{Q}(:,1:j)'\mathbf{Q}(:,j+1) = \mathbf{0}; \quad j = 1,2,\ldots,n-1. \tag{3.15}$$

If the Arnoldi procedure continues to $j = n$, two extra identities hold

$$\mathbf{AQ} = \mathbf{QH}, \qquad \mathbf{A} = \mathbf{QHQ}'. \tag{3.16}$$

Two improvements must be made in order for the Arnoldi procedure to work correctly in practice. The first improvement is regarding the gradual loss of orthogonality among the columns of $\mathbf{Q}$. In the above discussion, we can see that $\mathbf{Q}'\mathbf{Q} = \mathbf{I}$ is satisfied if $\mathbf{Q}(:,1)'\mathbf{Q}(:,1) = 1$ is satisfied. This observation is only true if the computation is exact. In reality, $\mathbf{Q}(:,1)'\mathbf{Q}(:,2) = 0$ is approximate. The small errors in the orthogonalities among $\mathbf{Q}(:,1:j)$ tend to become bigger errors in all the identities which should satisfy in the subsequent steps of the algorithm: $\mathbf{Q}'\mathbf{Q} = \mathbf{I}$ and $\mathbf{A} = \mathbf{QHQ}'$. If the small errors in the orthogonality are left untreated, the algorithm will fail to produce the QHQt decomposition accurately. In the following MATLAB implementation QHQtByArnoldi_.m, a re-orthogonalization based on a criterion proposed in [18] is implemented. Take the calculation of $\mathbf{Q}(:,3)$ in Eq. (3.12) as an example, the criterion is stated as if $H_{32} \leq \frac{1}{\sqrt{2}}\|\mathbf{AQ}(:,2) - H_{12}\mathbf{Q}(:,1) - H_{22}\mathbf{Q}(:,2)\|_2$, a re-orthogonalization of $\mathbf{Q}(:,3)$ to $\mathbf{Q}(:,1:2)$ will be performed. The second improvement is the exception handling regarding the possibility that $H(j+1,j) = 0$ for a j, $1 \leq j \leq 3$. If $H(j+1,j) = 0$, $\mathbf{Q}(:,j+1)$ cannot be determined as described. We can take an arbitrary unit vector $\mathbf{Q}(:,j+1)$ which satisfies $\mathbf{Q}(:,1:j)'\mathbf{Q}(:,j+1) = \mathbf{0}$. Note that if $H(j+1,j) = 0$, the equality of the jth column of the left and right sides of Eq. (3.9) still holds for an arbitrary unit vector $\mathbf{Q}(:,j+1)$.

For any matrix $\mathbf{A} \in \mathbb{R}^{n \times n}$, we can see from the above discussion that QHQt decomposition $\mathbf{A} = \mathbf{QHQ}'$ is not unique. The non-uniqueness hinges upon the arbitrary choice of $\mathbf{Q}(:,1)$. If $\mathbf{Q}(:,1)$ is fixed, $\mathbf{Q}$ and $\mathbf{H}$ become "essentially unique" if all $H(j+1,j) \neq 0, j = 1,2,\ldots,n-1$. What "essentially unique" means is that $H(j+1,j)$ can also take a negative value and so $\mathbf{Q}(:,j+1)$ can be $\pm\mathbf{Q}(:,j+1)$, for $j = 1,2,\ldots,n-1$. This is termed the implicit Q theorem. We need to exploit the implicit Q theorem in the QR iterations algorithm for eigenvalue analysis, see Section 6.4. If any $H(j+1,j) = 0$, the jth column $\mathbf{Q}(:,j)$ becomes non-unique, as well as $\mathbf{Q}(:,j+1:n)$ and $\mathbf{H}(j+1:n,j+1:n)$.

The MATLAB implementation of QHQt decomposition by the Arnoldi algorithm is listed below. Differently from other QHQt decomposition algorithms presented in this section, the input matrix $\mathbf{A}$ is not altered by the algorithm. $\mathbf{A}$ is used repeatedly by the algorithm to calculate $\mathbf{Aq}$. Special algorithms to calculate $\mathbf{Aq}$, for example, the matrix–vector product algorithms for band matrix and sparse matrix, can be input through the first input argument A, which can be be a cell array consisting of the function name of the special matrix–vector product and any input arguments for that function. See the demonstrating examples of QBZbyLanczos_.m in Section 3.4.3 and GTGiByLanczos_.m in Section 2.5.3 for the use of the cell form of the input matrix.

Algorithm 3.15

```
A=Q*H*Q', Q orthogonal matrix, H upper Hessenberg.
function [Q,H] = QHQtByArnoldi_(A,f1st,last,Q,H)

[m,n] = size_(A);   eta = 0.5*sqrt(2.0);     %eta for reorthogonalization
[qr0,qc0] = size(Q);   [hr0,hc0] = size(H);   lf1 = last-f1st+1;   lf = lf1;
if (m ~= qr0) error('QHQtByArnoldi_: Matrix size error.'); end
if (hr0 > 0) lf = lf1 - 1; end
qc = min(n,qc0+lf1);  hr = min(m,hr0+lf);   hc = min(n,hc0+lf1);
Q = [Q,zeros(m,qc-qc0)];   H = [H,zeros(hr0,hc-hc0);zeros(hr-hr0,hc)];

for j=f1st:last
    Aq = Ay_(A,Q(:,j),'right');
```

```
%      for l=1:2   %MGS: l=1:1 or l=1:2: w/o or w/ reorthogonalization
%          for k=1:j
%              qk = Q(:,k); Hkj = qk'*Aq; H(k,j) = H(k,j) + Hkj; Aq = Aq - Hkj*qk;
%          end
%      end
      normAq0 = norm(Aq);
      h = Q(:,1:j)'*Aq;   Aq = Aq - Q(:,1:j)*h;      %CGS
      normAq = norm(Aq);
      if (normAq < eta*normAq0)      %reorthogonalization
          s = Q(:,1:j)'*Aq;   Aq = Aq - Q(:,1:j)*s;   h = h + s;
          normAq0 = normAq;   normAq = norm(Aq);
      end
      H(1:j,j) = h;
      if (j == n)                    break;
      elseif(normAq>eta*normAq0) H(j+1,j) = normAq;   Q(:,j+1) = Aq/normAq;
      else                           H(j+1,j) = 0.0; Q(:,j+1) = orthogonal_(Q(:,1:j)); end
end
```

The use of QHQtByArnoldi_.m is similar to QBZbyLanczos_.m. Refer to Section 3.4.3 for more demonstrating examples. We give one example demonstrating the properties of Arnoldi procedure.

```
>> A=randn(5);     q=[1;0;0;0;0];
>> [Q1,H1]=QHQtByArnoldi_(A,1,5,q)
Q1 =     %Q1(:,1)=I(:,1).
   1.0000        0         0         0         0
        0   -0.1499    0.4528   -0.6526    0.5887
        0    0.5667   -0.5822   -0.5807   -0.0516
        0   -0.5838   -0.0324   -0.4790   -0.6547
        0   -0.5617   -0.6745    0.0862    0.4713
H1 =     %H1 is same as QHQtByHouseholder, sign may be different.
   0.5988    0.3598    0.1321    1.0386    0.4917
   0.5740   -0.8581   -0.1693   -0.5365   -0.8884
        0    2.3124   -0.0186   -0.1450    0.0728
        0         0    0.9682    1.3605    0.5000
        0         0         0    2.4020   -0.1481

>> q=randn(5,1);               %arbitrary q/norm(q) as Q(:,1)
>> [Q2,H2]=QHQtByArnoldi_(A,1,5,q)
Q2 =     %Q2 is different from Q1.
  -0.3577   -0.4038   -0.2943   -0.1585   -0.7728
   0.5848    0.2380   -0.6554    0.3527   -0.2178
   0.5473    0.1103    0.6297   -0.1348   -0.5231
  -0.2892    0.8344   -0.1248   -0.4197   -0.1685
   0.3834   -0.2680   -0.2679   -0.8100    0.2308
H2 =     %H2 is also different.
  -0.7172    0.2959    0.0303   -1.0945    0.5369
   1.6305    1.5205    0.6424   -0.0699   -1.2367
        0    1.8310   -1.1051   -1.1364   -0.5787
        0         0    1.1066    0.5306   -0.8314
        0         0         0    0.5471    0.7057

>> norm(Q1*H1*Q1'-Q2*H2*Q2')            %A=Q1*H1*Q1' and A=Q2*H2*Q2'
= 1.0994e-015
>> norm((Q1'*Q2)'*(Q1'*Q2)-eye(5))      %Q1 and Q2 differed by an orthogonal.
= 5.1543e-016
```

For `QHQtByArnoldi_.m`, the first input argument A is not necessarily an explicit matrix. In the following examples, we take $\mathbf{A} = \mathbf{A}_1\mathbf{A}_2$ and $\mathbf{A}^{-1} = \mathbf{A}_2^{-1}\mathbf{A}_1^{-1}$, respectively.

```
A1=randn(5);    A2=randn(5);
>> A={{'size',[5,5]},{'mtimes',A1},{'mtimes',A2}};    %A=A1*A2
>> B={{'size',[5,5]},{'mdivide',A2},{'mdivide',A1}};   %B=inv(A1*A2)

>> [Q1,H1]=QHQtByArnoldi_(A,[],[],q);
>> norm(Q1*H1*Q1'-A1*A2)
= 1.8336e-015

>> [Q2,H2]=QHQtByArnoldi_(B,[],[],q);
>> norm(Q2*H2*Q2'-inv(A1*A2))
= 3.1133e-015
```

3.6 REDUCTION OF SYMMETRIC MATRIX TO TRI-DIAGONAL BY CONGRUENT TRANSFORMATIONS

We specialize the QHQt decomposition algorithms presented in the last section to symmetric matrices. If $\mathbf{A} = \mathbf{QHQ}'$ and $\mathbf{A} = \mathbf{A}'$, then $\mathbf{H} = \mathbf{H}'$. If an upper Hessenberg is symmetric, it must be symmetric tri-diagonal. So we write $\mathbf{A} = \mathbf{QHQ}'$ as $\mathbf{A} = \mathbf{QTQ}'$ and name $\mathbf{A} = \mathbf{QTQ}'$ as QTQt decomposition. More importantly, $\mathbf{A}$ is symmetric and $\mathbf{T}$ is symmetric tri-diagonal, more efficient computations than QHQt decompositions are expected. The presentation of QTQt decomposition follows that of QHQt decomposition of the last section. Because the QTQt is the specialization of the QHQt, most of the discussion of the details is omitted. See the last section for all the details. The corresponding non-orthogonal counterpart to $\mathbf{A} = \mathbf{QTQ}'$ is the reduction of a general square matrix to tri-diagonal (GTGi) by Gauss elimination and Lanczos procedure discussed in Sections 2.5.2 and 2.5.3. Unlike the GTGi decomposition, QTQt decomposition is extremely stable.

3.6.1 QTQt DECOMPOSITION BY HOUSEHOLDER REFLECTIONS

For a symmetric matrix $\mathbf{A} \in \mathbb{R}^{n \times n}$, we choose a Householder matrix $\mathbf{Q}_1$ and apply $\mathbf{Q}_1\mathbf{A}$ so that $\mathbf{A}(2:n,1) = \mathbf{0}$. Because of the special structure of $\mathbf{Q}_1$: $\mathbf{Q}_1(:,1) = \mathbf{I}(:,1)$ and $\mathbf{Q}_1(1,:) = \mathbf{I}(1,:)$, $\mathbf{A}(1,:)$ is not altered by $\mathbf{Q}_1\mathbf{A}$. Therefore, the subsequent $(\mathbf{Q}_1\mathbf{A})\mathbf{Q}_1'$ will also set $\mathbf{A}(1,2:n)$ to zeros and keep $\mathbf{A}(:,1)$ unaltered. Repeat the process of alternatively eliminating $\mathbf{A}(j+1:n,j)$ and $\mathbf{A}(j,j+1:n)$ for $j = 1,2,\ldots,n-2$. $\mathbf{A}$ is then transformed to a symmetric tri-diagonal $\mathbf{T}$. The product of $\mathbf{Q}_1\mathbf{Q}_2\cdots\mathbf{Q}_{n-2}$ is $\mathbf{Q}$.

The MATLAB code `QTQtByHouseholder_.m` implementing the algorithm is listed below, in which over half of the code is handling the output according to `format`.

Algorithm 3.16

A=Q*T*Q', A=A', T symmetric tri-diagonal, Q orthogonal.

```
function [Q,A] = QTQtByHouseholder_(A,tol,format,flst,last,Q)

[m,n] = size(A);
tol = tol*max(1.0,norm(diag(A),inf));   Ah = zeros(m,1);    %temporary array

for j=flst:last
```

```
    [h,alpha,beta] = householder_(A(j+1:m,j));
    if (abs(beta) < tol) continue; end
    A(j+1,j) = beta;   A(j+2:m,j) = h(2:m-j);     %save Householder vector
    for k=j+1:n
        Ah(k) = A(k,j+1:k-1)*h(1:k-j-1) + A(k:n,k)'*h(k-j:n-j);
    end
    gamma  = (alpha*alpha)*(h(1:n-j)'*Ah(j+1:n)));
    for k=j+1:n                     %A=(I-beta*h*h')*A*(I-beta*h*h')
        A(k:n,k) = A(k:n,k) - alpha*(Ah(k:n)*h(k-j)+h(k-j:n-j)*Ah(k)) +...
                   gamma*h(k-j:n-j)*h(k-j);
    end
end
end

if (strcmp(format,'long') || strcmp(format,'short'))
    if (~exist('Q','var') || isempty(Q)) back = 1; js = last:-1:1; Q = eye(m);
    else                                 back = 0; js = f1st:last; end
    for j=js
        q = A(j+2:m,j);   qq = q'*q;   A(j+2:m,j) = 0;   A(j,j+2:n) = 0;
        if (qq < tol) continue; end
        h = [1; q];   alpha = 2.0/(qq+1.0);
        if (back == 1)        %backward accumulation of Q
            v = alpha*h;
            for k=j+1:m qk = Q(j+1:m,k); Q(j+1:m,k) = qk - (h'*qk)*v; end
        else                  %forward accumulation of Q
            v = alpha*h';
            for k=2:m qk = Q(k,j+1:m); Q(k,j+1:m) = qk - (qk*h)*v; end
        end
    end
    for j=1:n-1 A(j,j+1:n) = A(j+1:m,j); end
end
if (strcmp(format,'brief') || strcmp(format,'compact')) Q = []; end
if (strcmp(format,'brief')) %discard Q
    for j=last:-1:f1st A(j+2:m,j) = 0; A(j,j+2:m) = 0; end
    for j=1:n-1 A(j,j+1:n) = A(j+1:m,j); end
end
```

The use of QTQtByHouseholder_ is exactly same as QHQtByHouseholder_. One example serves to demonstrate the display of the actual form of the QTQt decomposition. See a demonstrating example for the partial QTQt decomposition in the next subsection.

```
>> A=randn(5);   A = 0.5*(A+A');          %one way to create a symmetric matrix
>> [Q,T]=QTQtByHouseholder_(A,100*eps,'long')
Q =
    1.0000         0         0         0         0
         0   -0.8806   -0.1559   -0.0949   -0.4374
         0    0.1011   -0.4256   -0.8882    0.1408
         0   -0.2210    0.8597   -0.4014    0.2256
         0   -0.4068   -0.2354    0.2027    0.8591
T =
   -0.1721    1.0417         0         0         0
    1.0417   -0.3745    0.9011         0         0
         0    0.9011   -0.2366    0.8331         0
         0         0    0.8331   -1.3917    0.7387
         0         0         0    0.7387   -0.3925

>> norm(Q*T*Q'-A)
= 2.0734e-015
```

3.6.2 **QTQt DECOMPOSITION BY GIVENS ROTATIONS**

In QTQt decomposition by Givens Rotations, we use the Givens rotation to zero one component at a time. For a full symmetric matrix, it does not have advantage or disadvantage to the QTQt decomposition by Householder reflections. For some structured matrices, such as band or sparse, the selective component zeroing function of Givens rotations has some advantage. But Householder reflections can also be used to zero selectively, see Section 3.1.

The following is the MATLAB implementation QTQtByGivens_.m, in which over half of the code is to handle the output according to the input argument format. Note that the part of the code handling the output is same to QTQtByHouseholder_.m.

Algorithm 3.17

A=Q*T*Q', A=A', T symmetric tri-diagonal, Q orthogonal.

```
function [Q,A] = QTQtByGivens_(A,tol,format,f1st,last,Q)

[m,n] = size(A);
tol = tol*max(1.0,norm(diag(A),inf));

for j=f1st:last
    if (norm(A(j+1:m,j),inf) < tol) continue; end
    for k=j+2:m
        [c,s] = givens_(A(j+1,j),A(k,j));
        A(j+1,j) = c*A(j+1,j) - s*A(k,j);    %A=G*A
        Aj1j1 = c*c*A(j+1,j+1) + s*s*A(k,k) - 2.0*s*c*A(k,j+1);
        Akk   = s*s*A(j+1,j+1) + c*c*A(k,k) + 2.0*s*c*A(k,j+1);
        Akj1  = (c*c-s*s)*A(k,j+1) + s*c*(A(j+1,j+1) - A(k,k));
        A(j+1,j+1) = Aj1j1;   A(k,k) = Akk;   A(k,j+1) = Akj1;
        for l=j+2:k-1
            Alj1 = A(l,j+1);   Alk  = A(k,l);
            A(l,j+1) = c*Alj1 - s*Alk;   A(k,l) = s*Alj1 + c*Alk;
        end
        for l=k+1:m
            Alj1 = A(l,j+1);   Alk  = A(l,k);
            A(l,j+1) = c*Alj1 - s*Alk;   A(l,k) = s*Alj1 + c*Alk;
        end
        if (abs(c) < tol)        rho = 1;
        elseif(abs(s) < abs(c)) rho = sign(c)*s/2;
        else                     rho = sign(s)*2/c; end
        A(k,j) = rho;    %save encoded Givens rotation [c,s] at zeroed A(k,j)
    end
end

if (strcmp(format,'long') || strcmp(format,'short'))
    if (~exist('Q','var') || isempty(Q)) js = 1:last;  Q = eye(m);
    else                                 js = f1st:last;  end
    for j=js    %accumulation of Q
        for k=j+2:m
            rho = A(k,j);  A(k,j) = 0;
            if (rho == 1)          c = 0;  s = 1;
            elseif(abs(rho) < 1) s = 2.0*rho;  c = sqrt(1.0-s*s);
            else                  c = 2.0/rho;  s = sqrt(1.0-c*c); end
            for l=1:m
                Qlj = Q(l,j+1);  Qlk = Q(l,k);
                Q(l,j+1) = c*Qlj - s*Qlk;   Q(l,k) = s*Qlj + c*Qlk;
```

```
              end
          end
      end
      for j=1:n-1 A(j,j+1:n) = A(j+1:m,j); end
end
if (strcmp(format,'brief') || strcmp(format,'compact')) Q = []; end
if (strcmp(format,'brief')) %discard Q
    for j=last:-1:f1st A(j+2:m,j) = 0; A(j,j+2:m) = 0; end
end
```

The use of QTQtByGivens_ is same as QTQtHouseholder_ and QHQtByGivens_. See Sections 3.6.1 and 3.5.2 for more demonstrating examples. An example is shown below for the partial QTQt decomposition. The same matrix **A** for the demonstrating example of QTQtByHouseholder_ is used below.

```
>> [Q,T]=QTQtByGivens_(A,100*eps,'long',1,2)      %partial QTQt
Q =
    1.0000         0         0         0         0
         0    0.8806    0.1559   -0.0081   -0.4475
         0   -0.1011    0.4256    0.8968   -0.0669
         0    0.2210   -0.8597    0.4425    0.1274
         0    0.4068    0.2354         0    0.8826
T =              %T incomplete tri-diagonal
   -0.1721   -1.0417         0         0         0
   -1.0417   -0.3745    0.9011         0         0
         0    0.9011   -0.2366    0.8108   -0.1913
         0         0    0.8108   -1.6692   -0.4375
         0         0   -0.1913   -0.4375   -0.1150

>> [Q,T]=QTQtByGivens_(T,100*eps,'long',3,5,Q)    %restart: T, Q as input.
Q =
    1.0000         0         0         0         0
         0    0.8806    0.1559    0.0949   -0.4374
         0   -0.1011    0.4256    0.8882    0.1408
         0    0.2210   -0.8597    0.4014    0.2256
         0    0.4068    0.2354   -0.2027    0.8591
T =
   -0.1721   -1.0417         0         0         0
   -1.0417   -0.3745    0.9011         0         0
         0    0.9011   -0.2366    0.8331         0
         0         0    0.8331   -1.3917   -0.7387
         0         0         0   -0.7387   -0.3925
```

3.6.3 QTQt DECOMPOSITION BY LANCZOS PROCEDURE

The derivation of the Lanczos procedure can be simplified from that of the Arnoldi procedure presented in Section 3.5.3. Write $\mathbf{A} = \mathbf{QTQ'}$ as $\mathbf{AQ} = \mathbf{QT}$. We illustrate the Lanczos procedure with a 4×4 matrix **A**. The equivalent form is written in terms of the columns of **Q**,

$$\mathbf{A}\left[\mathbf{Q}(:,1),\mathbf{Q}(:,2),\mathbf{Q}(:,3),\mathbf{Q}(:,4)\right] = \left[\mathbf{Q}(:,1),\mathbf{Q}(:,2),\mathbf{Q}(:,3),\mathbf{Q}(:,4)\right]\begin{bmatrix} T_{11} & T_{21} & 0 & 0 \\ T_{21} & T_{22} & T_{32} & 0 \\ 0 & T_{32} & T_{33} & T_{43} \\ 0 & 0 & T_{43} & T_{44} \end{bmatrix}. \quad (3.17)$$

We start the Lanczos with a given arbitrary unit vector $\mathbf{Q}(:,1)$. The equality of the first column of the left and right sides of Eq. (3.17) determines T_{11}, T_{21}, and $\mathbf{Q}(:,2)$. This step is exactly same as the first step of Arnoldi procedure,

$$\mathbf{AQ}(:,1) = T_{11}\mathbf{Q}(:,1) + T_{21}\mathbf{Q}(:,2),$$
$$T_{11} = \mathbf{Q}(:,1)'\mathbf{AQ}(:,1), \qquad T_{21} = \|\mathbf{AQ}(:,1) - T_{11}\mathbf{Q}(:,1)\|_2,$$
$$\mathbf{Q}(:,2) = \frac{1}{T_{21}}(\mathbf{AQ}(:,1) - T_{11}\mathbf{Q}(:,1)).$$

The subsequent steps have slight differences to the corresponding ones of Arnoldi procedure due to the consideration of the symmetry and tri-diagonal of **T**. For a 4 × 4 matrix, only three more Lanczos steps are needed to complete the QTQt decomposition. These steps are briefly reviewed in the following:

$$\mathbf{AQ}(:,2) = T_{21}\mathbf{Q}(:,1) + T_{22}\mathbf{Q}(:,2) + T_{32}\mathbf{Q}(:,3),$$
$$T_{22} = \mathbf{Q}(:,2)'\mathbf{AQ}(:,2), \qquad T_{32} = \|\mathbf{AQ}(:,2) - T_{21}\mathbf{Q}(:,1) - T_{22}\mathbf{Q}(:,2)\|_2,$$
$$\mathbf{Q}(:,3) = \frac{1}{T_{32}}(\mathbf{AQ}(:,2) - T_{21}\mathbf{Q}(:,1) - T_{22}\mathbf{Q}(:,2)).$$

The third step is similar to the second step. The last Lanczos step is obtained by the equality of the fourth column of the left and right of Eq. (3.17),

$$\mathbf{AQ}(:,4) = T_{43}\mathbf{Q}(:,3) + T_{44}\mathbf{Q}(:,4),$$
$$T_{44} = \mathbf{Q}(:,4)'\mathbf{AQ}(:,4).$$

Similarly to the Arnoldi procedure, two improvements are needed to make Lanczos procedure work correctly in practice. The first improvement is the gradual loss of orthogonality among the columns of **Q** due to the round off errors of the numerical calculation. The remedy to this well-known problem is well-studied. See [29, 46, 61, 62] and many references cited therein. The full re-orthogonalization is the most accurate and can be implemented easily, but it is the least efficient. Many selective re-orthogonalization schemes were proposed for the purpose of the eigenvalue solutions. In the MATLAB implementation QTQtByLanczos_.m presented below, a re-orthogonalization based on a criterion proposed in [18] is implemented. Take the calculation of $\mathbf{Q}(:,3)$ in Eq. (3.17) as an example, the criterion is stated as if $T_{32} \leq \frac{1}{\sqrt{2}}\|\mathbf{AQ}(:,2) - T_{21}\mathbf{Q}(:,1) - T_{22}\mathbf{Q}(:,2)\|_2$, a re-orthogonalization of $\mathbf{Q}(:,3)$ to $\mathbf{Q}(:,1:2)$ will be performed. The second improvement is the exception handling regarding the possibility that $T(j+1,j) = 0$ for a j, $1 \leq j \leq 3$. If $T(j+1,j) = 0$, $\mathbf{Q}(:,j+1)$ cannot be determined as described. We can take an arbitrary unit vector $\mathbf{Q}(:,j+1)$ which satisfies $\mathbf{Q}(:,1:j)'\mathbf{Q}(:,j+1) = \mathbf{0}$. Note that if $T(j+1,j) = 0$, the equality of the jth column of the left and right sides of Eq. (3.17) still holds for an arbitrary unit vector $\mathbf{Q}(:,j+1)$.

The identities similar to Eqs. (3.13) and (3.16) hold for the Lanczos procedure. They are important relations for the applications of the Lanczos procedure in the iterative equation solutions and eigenvalue solutions of symmetric matrices. They are reproduced here for references,

$$\mathbf{AQ}(:,1:j) = \mathbf{Q}(:,1:j)\mathbf{T}(1:j,1:j) + T(j+1,j)\mathbf{Q}(:,j+1)\mathbf{I}(j,:); \quad j = 1,2,\ldots,n, \tag{3.18}$$
$$\mathbf{Q}(:,1:j)'\mathbf{Q}(:,1:j) = \mathbf{I}; \quad j = 1,2,\ldots,n, \tag{3.19}$$
$$\mathbf{Q}(:,1:j)'\mathbf{Q}(:,j+1) = \mathbf{0}; \quad j = 1,2,\ldots,n-1. \tag{3.20}$$

If the Lanczos procedure continues to $j = n$, two extra identities hold

$$\mathbf{AQ} = \mathbf{QT}, \quad \mathbf{A} = \mathbf{QTQ}'. \tag{3.21}$$

For any symmetric matrix $\mathbf{A} \in \mathbb{R}^{n \times n}$, we can see from the above discussion that QTQt decomposition $\mathbf{A} = \mathbf{QTQ}'$ is not unique. The non-uniqueness hinges upon the arbitrary choice of $\mathbf{Q}(:, 1)$. If $\mathbf{Q}(:, 1)$ is fixed, $\mathbf{Q}$ and $\mathbf{T}$ become unique if all $T(j + 1, j) \neq 0, j = 1, 2, \ldots, n - 1$. If any $T(j + 1, j) = 0$, the jth column $\mathbf{Q}(:, j)$ becomes non-unique, as well as $\mathbf{Q}(:, j + 1 : n)$ and $\mathbf{T}(j + 1 : n, j + 1 : n)$.

The MATLAB implementation of QTQt decomposition by the Lanczos algorithm is listed below. Differently from other QTQt decomposition algorithms presented in this section, the input matrix $\mathbf{A}$ is not altered by the algorithm. $\mathbf{A}$ is used repeatedly by the algorithm to calculate $\mathbf{Aq}$. Special algorithms to calculate $\mathbf{Aq}$, for example, the matrix–vector product algorithms for symmetric band matrix and symmetric sparse matrix, can be specified through the first input argument A, which can be a cell array consisting of a function name of the special matrix–vector product and any input arguments for that function. See the demonstrating examples of QBZbyLanczos_.m in Section 3.4.3 and GTGiByLanczos_.m in Section 2.5.3 for the use of the cell form of the input matrix.

Algorithm 3.18

A=Q*T*Q', A=A', T symmetric tri-diagonal, Q orthogonal.

```
function [Q,T3] = QTQtByLanczos_(A,f1st,last,Q,T3)

[m,n] = size_(A);  eta = 0.5*sqrt(2.0)*0.0;    %eta for reorthogonalization
[qr0,qc0] = size(Q);  [tr0,tc0] = size(T3);  lf1 = last-f1st+1;  lf = lf1;
if (m~=qr0 || (tc0~=0 && tc0~=3)) error('QHQtByLanczos_:_Matrix_size_error.'); end
if (tr0 > 0) lf = lf1 - 1; end
qc = min(n,qc0+lf1); tr = min(m,tr0+lf);  tc = 3;
Q = [Q,zeros(m,qc-qc0)];  T3 = [T3; zeros(tr-tr0,tc)];

if (f1st == 1)
    beta0 = 0.0;  q0 = zeros(m,1);  q1 = Q(:,1);
else
    beta0 = T3(f1st,1);  q0 = Q(:,f1st-1);  q1 = Q(:,f1st);
    q1 = q1 - Q(:,1:f1st-1)*(Q(:,1:f1st-1)'*q1);  q1 = q1/norm(q1);  Q(:,f1st) = q1;
end

for j=f1st:last
    Aq1 = Ay_(A,q1,'right');      %Aq1=A*q1 or A#q1
    normAq1 = norm(Aq1);
    Aq2 = Aq1 - beta0*q0; beta1 = q1'*Aq2; Aq2 = Aq2 - beta1*q1;
    normAq2 = norm(Aq2);
    if (normAq2 < eta*normAq1)
        s = Q(:,1:j)'*Aq2;  Aq2 = Aq2 - Q(:,1:j)*s;
        if (j > 1) beta0 = beta0 + s(j-1); end
        beta1 = beta1 + s(j);
        normAq1 = normAq2;  normAq2 = norm(Aq2);
    end
    T3(j,2) = beta1;  beta2 = normAq2;
    if(j > 1) T3(j,1) = beta0;  T3(j-1,3) = beta0; end
    if (j == n)
        break;
    elseif (normAq2 > eta*normAq1)
        T3(j+1,1) = beta2; Q(:,j+1) = Aq2/beta2;
    else
        T3(j+1,1) = 0.0;   Q(:,j+1) = orthogonal_(Q(:,1:j));
    end
    beta0 = beta2; q0 = q1; q1 = Q(:,j+1); T3(j,3) = T3(j+1,1);
end
```

The use of `QTQtByLanczos_.m` is same as `QBZbyLanczos_.m` and `GTGiByLanczos_.m`. See Sections 3.4.3 and 2.5.3 for more demonstrating examples. In the following, we show an example of a partial QTQt decomposition of a sparse matrix by using the special sparse matrix–vector product function `mtimesCSR_.m`.

```
>> A=sprandsym(1000,0.1);    %a sparse symmetric matrix of about 0.1*1000*1000 nonzeros
>> [iA,jA,Aij] = find(A);    %convert A from MATLAB internal sparse format to IJD format
>> C=cell(3,1);    [C{1},C{2},C{3},m,n] = ijd2csr_(Aij,iA,jA,size(A,1),size(A,2));
>> q=zeros(m,1); q(1)=1;

>> [Q,T]=QTQtByLanczos_({'mtimesCSR_',C},1,10,q);       %A
>> T
T =
         0          0     8.7348
    8.7348     0.0323     9.6671
    9.6671    -0.3074    10.1443
   10.1443    -0.3723    10.1395
   10.1395     0.1492     9.8675
    9.8675     0.8241    10.1560
   10.1560     0.2732    10.4141
   10.4141     0.4796    10.5390
   10.5390    -0.0880    10.1662
   10.1662    -0.3800    10.4281
   10.4281          0          0
>> T=band2full_(T,1,1,11,10);
>> norm(A*Q(:,1:10)-Q(:,1:10)*T(1:10,1:10)-T(11,10)*Q(:,11)*[zeros(1,9),1])
= 7.5985e-015              %correct partial QTQt decomposition for A
>> norm(Q'*Q-eye(11))
= 4.9856e-016              %correct partial QTQt decomposition for A
```

In the second example, we apply `QTQtByLanczos_.m` to A^2, where A is the same sparse matrix in the previous example.

```
>> [Q,T]=QTQtByLanczos_({{'size',[m,n]},{'mtimesCSR_',C},{'mtimesCSR_',C}},1,10,q);
%A*A
>> T
T =
         0    76.2965    84.4407
   84.4407   196.4367   103.1037
  103.1037   200.8386   100.3278
  100.3278   211.4993   110.1619
  110.1619   216.8339   107.3818
  107.3818   217.1341   105.2238
  105.2238   199.3236    98.8700
   98.8700   201.1810   100.2582
  100.2582   206.0014   104.7298
  104.7298   208.2606   107.1723
  107.1723          0          0
>> T=band2full_(T,1,1,11,10);
>> norm(A*(A*Q(:,1:10))-Q(:,1:10)*T(1:10,1:10)-T(11,10)*Q(:,11)*[zeros(1,9),1])
= 1.0629e-013              %correct partial QTQt decomposition for A^2
>> norm(Q'*Q-eye(11))
= 4.3546e-015              %correct partial QTQt decomposition for A^2
```

3.7 REDUCTION OF A MATRIX TO UPPER HESSENBERG AND ANOTHER MATRIX TO UPPER TRIANGULAR

In this section, we simultaneously reduce two square matrices $\mathbf{A}$ and $\mathbf{B}$ to simpler forms by orthogonal transformations. Because of the restriction of the simultaneous reductions of two matrices, the simplest forms we can expect are a Hessenberg $\mathbf{H}$ for $\mathbf{A}$ and a triangular $\mathbf{R}$ for $\mathbf{B}$. The decomposition is expressed as $[\mathbf{A}, \mathbf{B}] = \mathbf{Q}[\mathbf{H}, \mathbf{R}]\mathbf{Z}$, where $\mathbf{Q}$ and $\mathbf{Z}$ are two orthogonal matrices. For brevity, we will name $[\mathbf{A}, \mathbf{B}] = \mathbf{Q}[\mathbf{H}, \mathbf{R}]\mathbf{Z}$ the QHRZ decomposition. It is used as the first-step reduction in the QZ algorithm of generalized eigenvalues of $\mathbf{A}\mathbf{x} = \lambda\mathbf{B}\mathbf{x}$. See Section 6.10 for the QZ algorithm.

3.7.1 QHRZ DECOMPOSITION BY ORTHOGONAL TRANSFORMATIONS

Applying QR decomposition of Section 3.2 to $\mathbf{B}$, we can find an orthogonal matrix $\mathbf{Q}_0$ so that $\mathbf{Q}_0'\mathbf{B}$ is an upper triangle. By the requirement, we also need to apply $\mathbf{Q}_0'\mathbf{A}$. $\mathbf{Q}_0'\mathbf{A}$ overwrites $\mathbf{A}$. $\mathbf{Q}_0'\mathbf{B}$ overwrites $\mathbf{B}$. Taking $\mathbf{A}$ and $\mathbf{B}$ to be 5×5 matrices, we illustrate the step by step reductions as follows:

$$\mathbf{Q}_0'\mathbf{A} \Rightarrow \mathbf{A} = \begin{bmatrix} A_{11} & A_{12} & A_{13} & A_{14} & A_{15} \\ A_{21} & A_{22} & A_{23} & A_{24} & A_{25} \\ A_{31} & A_{32} & A_{33} & A_{34} & A_{35} \\ A_{41} & A_{42} & A_{43} & A_{44} & A_{45} \\ A_{51} & A_{52} & A_{53} & A_{54} & A_{55} \end{bmatrix}, \qquad \mathbf{Q}_0'\mathbf{B} \Rightarrow \mathbf{B} = \begin{bmatrix} B_{11} & B_{12} & B_{13} & B_{14} & B_{15} \\ 0 & B_{22} & B_{23} & B_{24} & B_{25} \\ 0 & 0 & B_{33} & B_{34} & B_{35} \\ 0 & 0 & 0 & B_{44} & B_{45} \\ 0 & 0 & 0 & 0 & B_{55} \end{bmatrix}.$$

Now $\mathbf{B}$ is in upper triangular form. Next we need to reduce $\mathbf{A}$ to the upper Hessenberg form while keeping $\mathbf{B}$'s upper triangular form. First we find a Givens rotation $\mathbf{Q}_{45}$ and apply $\mathbf{Q}_{45}'\mathbf{A}$ to zero A_{51}. $\mathbf{Q}_{45}'\mathbf{A}$ changes only $\mathbf{A}(4:5,:)$. By the requirement, we need also to apply $\mathbf{Q}_{45}'\mathbf{B}$,

$$\mathbf{Q}_{45}'\mathbf{A} \Rightarrow \mathbf{A} = \begin{bmatrix} A_{11} & A_{12} & A_{13} & A_{14} & A_{15} \\ A_{21} & A_{22} & A_{23} & A_{24} & A_{25} \\ A_{31} & A_{32} & A_{33} & A_{34} & A_{35} \\ A_{41} & A_{42} & A_{43} & A_{44} & A_{45} \\ 0 & A_{52} & A_{53} & A_{54} & A_{55} \end{bmatrix}, \qquad \mathbf{Q}_{45}'\mathbf{B} \Rightarrow \mathbf{B} = \begin{bmatrix} B_{11} & B_{12} & B_{13} & B_{14} & B_{15} \\ 0 & B_{22} & B_{23} & B_{24} & B_{25} \\ 0 & 0 & B_{33} & B_{34} & B_{35} \\ 0 & 0 & 0 & B_{44} & B_{45} \\ 0 & 0 & 0 & B_{54} & B_{55} \end{bmatrix}.$$

$\mathbf{Q}_{45}'\mathbf{B}$ changes only $\mathbf{B}(4:5, 4:5)$, as a result B_{54} becomes non-zero. We find another Givens rotation $\mathbf{Z}_{45}$ and apply $\mathbf{B}\mathbf{Z}_{45}'$ to zero B_{54}. $\mathbf{B}(:, 4:5)$ changes due to $\mathbf{B}\mathbf{Z}_{45}'$. By the requirement, we also need to apply $\mathbf{A}\mathbf{Z}_{45}'$. The initially non-zero $\mathbf{A}(:, 4:5)$ is overwritten by $\mathbf{A}\mathbf{Z}_{45}'$,

$$\mathbf{A}\mathbf{Z}_{45}' \Rightarrow \mathbf{A} = \begin{bmatrix} A_{11} & A_{12} & A_{13} & A_{14} & A_{15} \\ A_{21} & A_{22} & A_{23} & A_{24} & A_{25} \\ A_{31} & A_{32} & A_{33} & A_{34} & A_{35} \\ A_{41} & A_{42} & A_{43} & A_{44} & A_{45} \\ 0 & A_{52} & A_{53} & A_{54} & A_{55} \end{bmatrix}, \qquad \mathbf{B}\mathbf{Z}_{45}' \Rightarrow \mathbf{B} = \begin{bmatrix} B_{11} & B_{12} & B_{13} & B_{14} & B_{15} \\ 0 & B_{22} & B_{23} & B_{24} & B_{25} \\ 0 & 0 & B_{33} & B_{34} & B_{35} \\ 0 & 0 & 0 & B_{44} & B_{45} \\ 0 & 0 & 0 & 0 & B_{55} \end{bmatrix}.$$

A_{41} is zeroed in the same way, first by pre-multiplying $\mathbf{Q}_{43}'$ for zeroing then by post-multiplying $\mathbf{Z}_{34}'$ for re-zeroing. Then the similar two steps are applied to zero A_{31}: the two Givens rotations used are $\mathbf{Q}_{23}$

and $\mathbf{Z}_{23}$,

$$\mathbf{Q}'_{23}\mathbf{A} \Rightarrow \mathbf{A} = \begin{bmatrix} A_{11} & A_{12} & A_{13} & A_{14} & A_{15} \\ A_{21} & A_{22} & A_{23} & A_{24} & A_{25} \\ 0 & A_{32} & A_{33} & A_{34} & A_{35} \\ 0 & A_{42} & A_{43} & A_{44} & A_{45} \\ 0 & A_{52} & A_{53} & A_{54} & A_{55} \end{bmatrix}, \quad \mathbf{Q}'_{23}\mathbf{B} \Rightarrow \mathbf{B} = \begin{bmatrix} B_{11} & B_{12} & B_{13} & B_{14} & B_{15} \\ 0 & B_{22} & B_{23} & B_{24} & B_{25} \\ 0 & B_{32} & B_{33} & B_{34} & B_{35} \\ 0 & 0 & B_{43} & B_{44} & B_{45} \\ 0 & 0 & 0 & 0 & B_{55} \end{bmatrix},$$

$$\mathbf{A}\mathbf{Z}'_{23} \Rightarrow \mathbf{A} = \begin{bmatrix} A_{11} & A_{12} & A_{13} & A_{14} & A_{15} \\ A_{21} & A_{22} & A_{23} & A_{24} & A_{25} \\ 0 & A_{32} & A_{33} & A_{34} & A_{35} \\ 0 & A_{42} & A_{43} & A_{44} & A_{45} \\ 0 & A_{52} & A_{53} & A_{54} & A_{55} \end{bmatrix}, \quad \mathbf{B}\mathbf{Z}'_{23} \Rightarrow \mathbf{B} = \begin{bmatrix} B_{11} & B_{12} & B_{13} & B_{14} & B_{15} \\ 0 & B_{22} & B_{23} & B_{24} & B_{25} \\ 0 & 0 & B_{33} & B_{34} & B_{35} \\ 0 & 0 & 0 & B_{44} & B_{45} \\ 0 & 0 & 0 & 0 & B_{55} \end{bmatrix}.$$

Now the first column of $\mathbf{A}$ is in the upper Hessenberg form and $\mathbf{B}$ keeps the upper triangular form. The reduction is completed by zeroing A_{52}, A_{42}, and A_{53}. To zero each component of $\mathbf{A}$, a pre-multiplying by a Givens rotation is applied to $\mathbf{A}$. Then a post-multiplying by another Givens rotation is applied to $\mathbf{B}$ to restore $\mathbf{B}$'s upper tri-angularity. By the requirement, the same Givens rotation is applied to both $\mathbf{A}$ and $\mathbf{B}$. The Givens rotation can be replaced by a 2×2 Householder reflection. The following MATLAB implementation of QHRZ decomposition qhrz_.m further clarifies the algorithm.

Algorithm 3.19

[A,B]=Q*[H,R]*Z, Q,Z orthogonal matrices, H upper Hessenberg, R upper Triangle.

```
%Q'*A*Z => H upper Hessenberg, Q'*B*Z => R upper triangle.
%format='long','short': H,R,Q,Z full matrices. ='brief': Q,Z not calculated.
function [A,B,Q,Z] = QHRZ_(A,B,format,f1st,last,Q,Z)

[m,n] = size(A);  [k,l] = size(B);
if (m~=n || m~=k || n~=l) error('QHRZ_:_Input_matrix_must_be_square.'); end
if (~exist('format','var')) format = 'short'; end
if (~exist('f1st','var')) f1st = 1; end
if (f1st < 1) f1st = 1; end
if (~exist('last','var')) last = n - 2; end
if (last > n-2) last = n - 2; end
if (strcmp(format,'brief'))
    Q = []; Z = [];
else
    if(~exist('Q','var') || isempty(Q)) Q = eye(m); end
    if(~exist('Z','var') || isempty(Z)) Z = eye(n); end
end

if (f1st == 1)    %Q'*B->R, upper triangle, H = Q'*A
    B = QRbyHouseholder_(B,0,100*eps);
    if (~strcmp(format,'brief'))
        for j=m:-1:1    %backward accumulation of Q
            h = [1; B(j+1:m,j)];  alpha = 2.0/(h'*h);  B(j+1:m,j) = 0;
            for k=j:m
                qk = Q(j:m,k);  beta = alpha*(h'*qk);  Q(j:m,k) = qk - beta*h;
            end
        end
        A = Q'*A;
    else
```

```
        for j=1:n
            h = [1; B(j+1:m,j)];   alpha = 2.0/(h'*h);   B(j+1:m,j) = 0;
            for k=1:n
                ak = A(j:m,k);   beta = alpha*(h'*ak);   A(j:m,k) = ak - beta*h;
            end
        end
    end
end

for j=flst:last    %Q'*H*Z'->H Hessenberg, Q'*R*Z'->R triangle
    for i=n:-1:j+2
        [c,s] = givens_(A(i-1,j), A(i,j));    G = [c s; -s c];
        A(i-1:i,j:n) = G'*A(i-1:i,j:n);   B(i-1:i,j:n) = G'*B(i-1:i,j:n);
        if (~strcmp(format,'brief')) Q(:,i-1:i) = Q(:,i-1:i)*G; end
        [c,s] = givens_(-B(i,i), B(i,i-1));   G = [c s; -s c];
        B(1:i,i-1:i) = B(1:i,i-1:i)*G;    A(1:n,i-1:i) = A(1:n,i-1:i)*G;
        if (~strcmp(format,'brief')) Z(i-1:i,:) = G'*Z(i-1:i,:); end
    end
end
```

The following simple example shows the basic use of QHRZ_.

```
>> A=randn(5);   B=randn(5);
>> [H,R,Q,Z]=QHRZ_(A,B)
H =
    0.2622     0.9870    -0.0843     0.3120    -0.8195
   -1.5203    -1.2081    -0.1410    -0.8798     0.0793
   -0.0000    -2.6280    -0.4191     1.5493     1.9065
         0          0    -0.5669     0.6355     0.7307
         0          0          0     0.4798     0.5905
R =
   -1.6711    -0.2341    -0.2073    -0.6012    -0.4971
         0    -0.4410    -0.4919    -2.5302     1.8192
         0     0.0000     1.4147    -1.8873     0.7390
         0     0.0000          0     1.6906    -0.3750
         0          0          0     0.0000     0.9345
Q =
   -0.0809     0.6577    -0.0815    -0.1794     0.7225
    0.0832     0.2785    -0.6775    -0.5069    -0.4466
    0.6962     0.0058     0.4858    -0.5285    -0.0038
   -0.7084    -0.0458     0.4024    -0.5629    -0.1320
    0.0092    -0.6983    -0.3694    -0.3387     0.5110
Z =
    1.0000          0          0          0          0
         0     0.3887     0.0293     0.6130    -0.6872
         0     0.2893     0.4351     0.5376     0.6618
         0     0.4084    -0.8569     0.1118     0.2941
         0     0.7736     0.2749    -0.5681    -0.0574
```

Use format='brief' to suppress the computation of **Q** and **Z**. **Q** and **Z** are not needed in case that only eigenvalues are calculated but not the eigenvectors. As alluded in the beginning of the section, the QHRZ decomposition is often used as the first step reduction for the QZ algorithm of the generalized eigenvalue analysis.

```
>> [H,R]=QHRZ_(A,B,'brief')
H =
    0.2622     0.9870    -0.0843     0.3120    -0.8195
```

$$
R = \begin{array}{rrrrr}
-1.5203 & -1.2081 & -0.1410 & -0.8798 & 0.0793 \\
0 & -2.6280 & -0.4191 & 1.5493 & 1.9065 \\
0 & 0.0000 & -0.5669 & 0.6355 & 0.7307 \\
0 & 0.0000 & 0.0000 & 0.4798 & 0.5905 \\
-1.6711 & -0.2341 & -0.2073 & -0.6012 & -0.4971 \\
0 & -0.4410 & -0.4919 & -2.5302 & 1.8192 \\
0 & 0.0000 & 1.4147 & -1.8873 & 0.7390 \\
0 & 0.0000 & 0 & 1.6906 & -0.3750 \\
0 & 0 & 0 & 0 & 0.9345
\end{array}
$$

The following example shows the partial QHRZ decomposition. Note the incomplete Hessenberg form for **H** and complete triangular form for **R**.

```
>> [H,R,Q,Z]=QHRZ_(A,B,'long',1,2);
>> H
H =
    0.2622    0.9870   -0.0843   -0.5791   -0.6585
   -1.5203   -1.2081   -0.1410   -0.3406    0.8150
   -0.0000   -2.6280   -0.4191    2.4093   -0.4801
         0         0   -0.2746    1.1095   -0.2370
         0         0    0.4959   -0.4634    0.1213
>> R
R =
   -1.6711   -0.2341   -0.2073   -0.7203    0.2996
         0   -0.4410   -0.4919    0.4276    3.0868
         0    0.0000    1.4147   -0.2275    2.0140
         0    0.0000         0    0.9447   -0.4274
         0         0         0         0    1.6725
```

To finish the QHRZ decomposition from the previous partial decomposition, use the restart as shown below. Note the positions of **H**, **R**, **Q**, and **Z** in the input argument list. The same output is obtained as the examples in the above, since the same matrices **A** and **B** are used in all the examples. For brevity, the calculation and output of **Q** and **Z** are suppressed.

```
>> [H,R]=QHRZ_(H,R,'brief',3,5,Q,Z)
H =
    0.2622    0.9870   -0.0843    0.3120   -0.8195
   -1.5203   -1.2081   -0.1410   -0.8798    0.0793
   -0.0000   -2.6280   -0.4191    1.5493    1.9065
         0         0   -0.5669    0.6355    0.7307
         0         0         0    0.4798    0.5905
R =
   -1.6711   -0.2341   -0.2073   -0.6012   -0.4971
         0   -0.4410   -0.4919   -2.5302    1.8192
         0    0.0000    1.4147   -1.8873    0.7390
         0    0.0000         0    1.6906   -0.3750
         0         0         0    0.0000    0.9345
```

3.7.2 QHRZ DECOMPOSITION BY ARNOLDI PROCEDURE

The Arnoldi algorithm for $\mathbf{A} = \mathbf{Q}\mathbf{H}\mathbf{Q}'$ discussed in Section 3.5.3 can be adapted for $[\mathbf{A},\mathbf{B}] = \mathbf{Q}[\mathbf{H},\mathbf{R}]\mathbf{Z}$. From the above subsection, we can see that $[\mathbf{A},\mathbf{B}] = \mathbf{Q}[\mathbf{H},\mathbf{R}]\mathbf{Z}$ always exists. As an illustrative example, for $\mathbf{A},\mathbf{B} \in \mathbb{R}^{4\times4}$, we write the QHRZ decomposition in the following form. We assume **B** is invertible for the following discussion:

$$\mathbf{A}\left[\mathbf{Z}(1,:)',\mathbf{Z}(2,:)',\mathbf{Z}(3,:)',\mathbf{Z}(4,:)'\right] = \left[\mathbf{Q}(:,1),\mathbf{Q}(:,2),\mathbf{Q}(:,3),\mathbf{Q}(:,4)\right]\begin{bmatrix} H_{11} & H_{12} & H_{13} & H_{14} \\ H_{21} & H_{22} & H_{23} & H_{24} \\ 0 & H_{32} & H_{33} & H_{34} \\ 0 & 0 & H_{43} & H_{44} \end{bmatrix}, \quad (3.22a)$$

$$\mathbf{B}\left[\mathbf{Z}(1,:)',\mathbf{Z}(2,:)',\mathbf{Z}(3,:)',\mathbf{Z}(4,:)'\right] = \left[\mathbf{Q}(:,1),\mathbf{Q}(:,2),\mathbf{Q}(:,3),\mathbf{Q}(:,4)\right]\begin{bmatrix} R_{11} & R_{12} & R_{13} & R_{14} \\ 0 & R_{22} & R_{23} & R_{24} \\ 0 & 0 & R_{33} & R_{34} \\ 0 & 0 & 0 & R_{44} \end{bmatrix}. \quad (3.22b)$$

We start from a given and arbitrary unit vector $\mathbf{Q}(:,1)$. The first column of Eq. (3.22b) shows that

$$\mathbf{B}\mathbf{Z}(1,:)' = R_{11}\mathbf{Q}(:,1),$$
$$\mathbf{Z}(1,:)' = R_{11}\mathbf{B}^{-1}\mathbf{Q}(:,1) = R_{11}\mathbf{v}_1.$$

We require $\mathbf{Z}(1,:)\mathbf{Z}(1,:)' = (\mathbf{v}_1'\mathbf{v}_1)R_{11}^2 = V_{11}R_{11}^2 = 1$, so $R_{11}^2 = V_{11}^{-1}$ and $\mathbf{Z}(1,:)' = R_{11}\mathbf{v}_1$. Substituting $\mathbf{Z}(1,:)$ into the first column of Eq. (3.22a), we obtain

$$\mathbf{A}\mathbf{Z}(1,:)' = \mathbf{u}_1 = H_{11}\mathbf{Q}(:,1) + H_{21}\mathbf{Q}(:,2).$$

Considering $\mathbf{Q}(:,1:2)'\mathbf{Q}(:,1:2) = \mathbf{I}$, we can calculate H_{11}, H_{21}, and $\mathbf{Q}(:,2)$ from the above equation,

$$H_{11} = \mathbf{Q}(:,1)'\mathbf{u}_1, \qquad H_{21} = \|\mathbf{u}_1 - H_{11}\mathbf{Q}(:,1)\|_2, \qquad \mathbf{Q}(:,2) = \frac{1}{H_{21}}\left(\mathbf{u}_1 - H_{11}\mathbf{Q}(:,1)\right).$$

Now introducing the known $\mathbf{Q}(:,1:2)$ into the second column of Eq. (3.22b), we have

$$\mathbf{B}\mathbf{Z}(2,:)' = R_{12}\mathbf{Q}(:,1) + R_{22}\mathbf{Q}(:,2),$$
$$\mathbf{Z}(2,:)' = R_{12}\mathbf{B}^{-1}\mathbf{Q}(:,1) + R_{22}\mathbf{B}^{-1}\mathbf{Q}(:,2) = R_{12}\mathbf{v}_1 + R_{22}\mathbf{v}_2.$$

The condition $\mathbf{Z}(1:2,:)\mathbf{Z}(1:2,:)' = \mathbf{I}$ gives the right equations to determine R_{12}, R_{22},

$$\mathbf{Z}(1,:)\mathbf{Z}(2,:)' = W_{11}R_{12} + W_{12}R_{22} = 0,$$
$$\mathbf{Z}(2,:)\mathbf{Z}(2,:)' = V_{11}R_{12}^2 + V_{12}R_{12}R_{22} + V_{22}R_{22}^2 = 1.$$

Then substituting $\mathbf{Z}(2,:)$ into the second column of Eq. (3.22a), we obtain

$$\mathbf{A}\mathbf{Z}(2,:)' = \mathbf{u}_2 = H_{12}\mathbf{Q}(:,1) + H_{22}\mathbf{Q}(:,2) + H_{32}\mathbf{Q}(:,3).$$

We calculate H_{12}, H_{22}, H_{32} by considering $\mathbf{Q}(:,1;3)'\mathbf{Q}(:,1;3) = \mathbf{I}$. After H_{12}, H_{22}, H_{32} are calculated, we calculate $\mathbf{Q}(:,3)$ from the above equation.

Now we introduce the known $\mathbf{Q}(:,1:3)$ into the third column of Eq. (3.22b),

$$\mathbf{B}\mathbf{Z}(3,:)' = R_{13}\mathbf{Q}(:,1) + R_{23}\mathbf{Q}(:,2) + R_{33}\mathbf{Q}(:,3),$$
$$\mathbf{Z}(3,:)' = R_{13}\mathbf{B}^{-1}\mathbf{Q}(:,1) + R_{23}\mathbf{B}^{-1}\mathbf{Q}(:,2) + R_{33}\mathbf{B}^{-1}\mathbf{Q}(:,3) = R_{13}\mathbf{v}_1 + R_{23}\mathbf{v}_2 + R_{33}\mathbf{v}_3.$$

$\mathbf{R}(1:3,3)$ is determined by the condition $\mathbf{Z}(1:3,:)\mathbf{Z}(1:3,:)' = \mathbf{I}$,

$$\mathbf{Z}(1,:)\mathbf{Z}(3,:)' = W_{11}R_{13} + W_{12}R_{23} + W_{13}R_{33} = 0,$$
$$\mathbf{Z}(2,:)\mathbf{Z}(3,:)' = W_{21}R_{13} + W_{22}R_{23} + W_{23}R_{33} = 0,$$
$$\mathbf{Z}(3,:)\mathbf{Z}(3,:)' = V_{11}R_{13}^2 + V_{12}R_{13}R_{23} + V_{22}R_{23}^2 + V_{13}R_{13}R_{33} + V_{23}R_{23}R_{33} + V_{33}R_{33}^2 = 1.$$

After $\mathbf{R}(1:3,3)$ is calculated from the above equation, we calculate $\mathbf{Z}(3,:)' = R_{13}\mathbf{v}_1 + R_{23}\mathbf{v}_2 + R_{33}\mathbf{v}_3$. Then we introduce the known $\mathbf{Z}(3,:)'$ into the third column of Eq. (3.22a) to determine $\mathbf{H}(1:4,3)$ and then $\mathbf{Q}(:,4)$.

Finally, we introduce the known $\mathbf{Q}(:,1:4)$ into the fourth column of Eq. (3.22b) to determine $\mathbf{R}(1:4,4)$ and then $\mathbf{Z}(4,:)'$. We then substitute the known $\mathbf{Z}(4,:)'$ into the fourth column of Eq. (3.22a) to determine $\mathbf{H}(1:4,4)$. Now all $\mathbf{Q}$, $\mathbf{H}$, $\mathbf{R}$, and $\mathbf{Z}$ are completely determined.

From the above discussion, we can see that the QHRZ decomposition is not unique: $\mathbf{Q}(:,1)$ is an arbitrary unit vector and further the sign of $H(j+1,j)$ and $R(j,j), j = 1,2,3$ can be arbitrarily chosen. The algorithm requires the inverse of a matrix $\mathbf{V}$ whose components are defined as $V_{ij} = \mathbf{Q}(:,i)'(\mathbf{BB}')^{-1}\mathbf{Q}(:,j), i,j = 1,2,3,4$. If $\mathbf{B}$ is invertible, $\mathbf{V}$ is also invertible. The situation that $\mathbf{B}$ is not invertible is not considered in the above discussion. In practice, QHRZ is used for the eigenvalue solutions of the pair $[\mathbf{A}, \mathbf{B}]$. For the practical purpose, the non-invertible or the ill-conditioned $\mathbf{B}$ can be replaced by a well-conditioned $\mathbf{A} - \sigma\mathbf{B}$ for a suitably chosen scalar σ. The implication of a non-invertible $\mathbf{B}$ has some theoretical importance. Even for a well-conditioned $\mathbf{B}$, the advantage of the above algorithm is not obvious. Therefore, the algorithm is not pursued further in this subsection.

Direct algorithms of solution of linear equations

INTRODUCTION

Given a matrix $\mathbf{A} \in \mathbb{R}^{m \times n}$ and a vector $\mathbf{b} \in \mathbb{R}^m$, the problem of the solution of the linear equations is to find a vector $\mathbf{x} \in \mathbb{R}^n$ such that $\mathbf{Ax} = \mathbf{b}$. The solving of linear equations is the inverse problem of the matrix multiplication: given the matrix $\mathbf{A}$ and the vector $\mathbf{x}$ and calculate $\mathbf{b} = \mathbf{Ax}$. The matrix multiplication is straight forward. The solving of linear equations is a lot more complicated. However as complicated it can be, it is the extension of the elementary scalar equation: $ax = b$. If $a \neq 0$, the unique solution is $x = a^{-1}b$. If $a = 0$ and $b = 0$, any number is a solution. Among all $x \in \mathbb{R}$, $x = 0$ is the minimum norm solution. If $a = 0$ and $b \neq 0$, $ax = b$ has no solution. For any $x \in \mathbb{R}$, the residual of the equation is the constant $|b|$. Among all $x \in \mathbb{R}$, $x = 0$ has the minimum norm. $\mathbf{Ax} = \mathbf{b}$ also has similar properties.

If $\operatorname{rank}(\mathbf{A}) = \operatorname{rank}([\mathbf{A}, \mathbf{b}])$, $\mathbf{Ax} = \mathbf{b}$ has a solution. If $\operatorname{rank}(\mathbf{A}) = \operatorname{rank}([\mathbf{A}, \mathbf{b}]) = n$, the solution is unique. If $\mathbf{A}$ is square and non-singular, $\mathbf{Ax} = \mathbf{b}$ has the unique solution $\mathbf{x} = \mathbf{A}^{-1}\mathbf{b}$. If $\operatorname{rank}(\mathbf{A}) = \operatorname{rank}([\mathbf{A}, \mathbf{b}]) < n$, $\dim(\operatorname{null}(\mathbf{A})) > 0$ and solutions are not unique. Among all $\mathbf{x}$ satisfying $\mathbf{Ax} = \mathbf{b}$, we want to find $\mathbf{x}_{01}$ such that $\|\mathbf{x}_{01}\|_2$ is minimum. $\mathbf{x}_{01}$ is called the minimum norm solution.

If $\operatorname{rank}(\mathbf{A}) = \operatorname{rank}([\mathbf{A}, \mathbf{b}]) - 1$, $\mathbf{Ax} = \mathbf{b}$ has no solution. Among all $\mathbf{x} \in \mathbb{R}^n$, we want to find $\mathbf{x}_{01}$ such that $\|\mathbf{b} - \mathbf{Ax}_{01}\|_2$ is minimum. $\mathbf{x}_{01}$ is called a minimum residual solution. If $\operatorname{rank}(\mathbf{A}) = \operatorname{rank}([\mathbf{A}, \mathbf{b}]) - 1 = n$, the minimum residual solution is unique. If $\operatorname{rank}(\mathbf{A}) = \operatorname{rank}([\mathbf{A}, \mathbf{b}]) - 1 < n$, $\dim(\operatorname{null}(\mathbf{A})) > 0$ and minimum residual solutions are not unique. Among all the minimum residual solutions, we want to find $\mathbf{x}_{01}$ such that $\|\mathbf{x}_{01}\|_2$ is minimum. $\mathbf{x}_{01}$ is called the minimum residual/norm solution.

In this chapter, we present several theoretical tools useful for the discussion of the solution of $\mathbf{Ax} = \mathbf{b}$ and several *direct* algorithms to find the solution of $\mathbf{Ax} = \mathbf{b}$. In each *direct* algorithm, we will consider all the possibilities as alluded above regarding the existence of a solution.

Section 4.1 presents the concept of the pseudo-inverse of a general matrix. We will need the pseudo-inverse to discuss the minimum norm or the minimum residual solution of $\mathbf{Ax} = \mathbf{b}$.

Section 4.2 discusses the addition of linear constraints $\mathbf{Bx} = \mathbf{b}$ to linear equations $\mathbf{Ax} = \mathbf{a}$. The contents of this section are of great importance to the understanding and solution of constrained multi-body mechanics and behavior of incompressible materials.

Section 4.3 presents solution algorithms to five special structured $\mathbf{A}$: zero, diagonal, orthogonal, lower triangular, and upper triangular.

Section 4.4 presents the elementary Gauss elimination algorithm and Gauss-Jordan elimination algorithm to $\mathbf{Ax} = \mathbf{b}$. Both full format $\mathbf{A}$ and band format $\mathbf{A}$ are covered.

Section 4.5 presents the Householder elimination algorithm to $\mathbf{Ax} = \mathbf{b}$ for the full format $\mathbf{A}$ and the Givens elimination algorithm to $\mathbf{Ax} = \mathbf{b}$ for the band format $\mathbf{A}$.

Matrix Algorithms in MATLAB. DOI: 10.1016/B978-0-12-803804-8.00010-6

Section 4.6 presents solution algorithms based on the decompositions of **A**. Most decomposition algorithms presented in Chapter 2 and Chapter 3 can be used for the purpose of the solution of $\mathbf{Ax} = \mathbf{b}$.

Section 4.7 presents several solution algorithms of special linear systems arising from the interpolation problem: notably Vandermonde matrix for the polynomial interpolation and fast Fourier transform for the trigonometric interpolation.

4.1 BRIEF INTRODUCTION OF PSEUDO-INVERSE

If **A** is square and non-singular, the unique solution of $\mathbf{Ax} = \mathbf{a}$ can be written as $\mathbf{x} = \mathbf{A}^{-1}\mathbf{a}$. If **A** is square but singular or rectangular, its inverse does not exist. If $\mathbf{Ax} = \mathbf{a}$ has a solution, its solution can be presented in a form $\mathbf{x} = \mathbf{Ba}$. If the solution is not unique, different solutions have different **B**s in their presentations of the form $\mathbf{x} = \mathbf{Ba}$. Specially the minimum norm solution corresponds to a particular **B**. Similarly if $\mathbf{Ax} = \mathbf{a}$ has no solution, the minimum residual solution can also be presented in a form $\mathbf{x} = \mathbf{Ba}$. If the minimum residual solution is not unique, different minimum residual solutions have different **B**s in their presentations of the form $\mathbf{x} = \mathbf{Ba}$. Specially the minimum residual/norm solution corresponds to a particular **B**. If $\mathbf{A} \in \mathbb{R}^{m \times n}$, then in all the cases $\mathbf{B} \in \mathbb{R}^{n \times m}$ and depends in some way on **A**. **B** is called the generalized inverse of **A**. **B**s in the presentations of different kinds of solution of $\mathbf{Ax} = \mathbf{a}$ are shown to satisfy some or all of the following four Moore-Penrose conditions, see [9, 34]:

$$\begin{aligned}\mathbf{ABA} &= \mathbf{A},\\ \mathbf{BAB} &= \mathbf{B},\\ (\mathbf{AB})' &= \mathbf{AB},\\ (\mathbf{BA})' &= \mathbf{BA}.\end{aligned} \tag{4.1}$$

For any $\mathbf{A} \in \mathbb{R}^{m \times n}$, the **B** satisfying all the four conditions *exists* and is *unique*. This special **B** is called the Moore-Penrose inverse or pseudo-inverse and is denoted as $\mathbf{A}^+$. When **A** is square and non-singular, $\mathbf{A}^+ = \mathbf{A}^{-1}$. The minimum norm solution or the minimum residual solution for $\mathbf{Ax} = \mathbf{b}$ can both be presented as $\mathbf{A}^+\mathbf{b}$. If $\mathbf{A}^+\mathbf{b}$ is the minimum norm solution, $\mathbf{AA}^+\mathbf{b} = \mathbf{b}$. If $\mathbf{A}^+\mathbf{b}$ is the minimum residual solution, $\mathbf{AA}^+\mathbf{b} \neq \mathbf{b}$. $\mathbf{AA}^+\mathbf{b} = \mathbf{b}$ is therefore the sufficient and necessary condition of the existence of solution of $\mathbf{Ax} = \mathbf{b}$.

From the definition of the pseudo-inverse, Eq. (4.1), we obtain directly the following identities:

$$\left(\mathbf{AA}^+\right)\left(\mathbf{AA}^+\right) = \mathbf{AA}^+, \tag{4.2a}$$
$$\left(\mathbf{A}^+\mathbf{A}\right)\left(\mathbf{A}^+\mathbf{A}\right) = \mathbf{A}^+\mathbf{A}, \tag{4.2b}$$
$$\left(\mathbf{AA}^+\right)^+ = \left(\mathbf{AA}^+\right), \tag{4.2c}$$
$$\left(\mathbf{A}^+\mathbf{A}\right)^+ = \left(\mathbf{A}^+\mathbf{A}\right). \tag{4.2d}$$

The pseudo-inverse of **A** provides a useful presentation to its null space. Because by the definition, we have the following identities:

$$\mathbf{A}\left(\mathbf{I}_n - \mathbf{A}^+\mathbf{A}\right) = \mathbf{0}_{mn}, \tag{4.3a}$$
$$\left(\mathbf{I}_m - \mathbf{AA}^+\right)\mathbf{A} = \mathbf{0}_{mn}. \tag{4.3b}$$

For the column null space of **A**, we have three useful representations, $\mathbf{I}_n - \mathbf{A}^+\mathbf{A}$, **N**, and **Z**: $\mathbf{A}(\mathbf{I}_n - \mathbf{A}^+\mathbf{A}) = \mathbf{0}_{mn}$, $\mathbf{AN}_{nr} = \mathbf{0}_{mr}$, and $\mathbf{AZ}_{nr} = \mathbf{0}_{mr}$. $\mathbf{N}_{nr}$ is an arbitrary independent set of bases of the null space of

A and $\mathbf{Z}_{nr}$ is an arbitrary set of orthogonal bases of the null space of **A**. If $\mathbf{z} \in \text{null}(\mathbf{A})$, that is, $\mathbf{Az} = \mathbf{0}$, we can write **z** in three forms: $\mathbf{z} = (\mathbf{I}_n - \mathbf{A}^+\mathbf{A})\mathbf{u}, \mathbf{u} \in \mathbb{R}^n$; $\mathbf{z} = \mathbf{N}_{mr}\mathbf{v}, \mathbf{v} \in \mathbb{R}^r$; and $\mathbf{z} = \mathbf{Z}_{mr}\mathbf{w}, \mathbf{w} \in \mathbb{R}^r$. Similar conclusions are valid for the row null space of **A**: $\mathbf{I}_m - \mathbf{A}\mathbf{A}^+$.

Now we discuss how to calculate $\mathbf{A}^+$.

First, the simplest case, the pseudo-inverse of a scalar α is simply

$$\alpha^+ = \begin{cases} \frac{1}{\alpha} & \alpha \neq 0 \\ 0 & \alpha = 0 \end{cases}. \tag{4.4}$$

Second, the pseudo-inverse of a diagonal matrix $\mathbf{D}_{mn}$ is a diagonal matrix of size $n \times m$, whose diagonal components are simply

$$D_{jj}^+ = \begin{cases} \frac{1}{D_{jj}} & D_{jj} \neq 0 \\ 0 & D_{jj} = 0 \end{cases}; j = 1, 2, \ldots, \min(m,n). \tag{4.5}$$

Third, the pseudo-inverse of an orthogonal matrix **U** is simply $\mathbf{U}^+ = \mathbf{U}'$, if $\mathbf{U}'\mathbf{U} = \mathbf{I}$ or $\mathbf{UU}' = \mathbf{I}$.

Suppose that **A** is decomposed as $\mathbf{A} = \mathbf{UV}$, where $\mathbf{U} \in \mathbb{R}^{m \times r}$, $\mathbf{V} \in \mathbb{R}^{r \times n}$, and $r = \text{rank}(\mathbf{A})$. This kind of decomposition is called a rank decomposition of **A**. The rank decomposition of **A** is not unique. For example, the LU decomposition by LU_.m and the QR decomposition by QR_.m in the short output format are both examples of the rank decomposition, see Sections 2.2 and 3.2. If $\mathbf{A} = \mathbf{UV}$ is a rank decomposition, we have the following important formula for $\mathbf{A}^+$,

$$\mathbf{A}^+ = \mathbf{V}'(\mathbf{VV}')^{-1}(\mathbf{U}'\mathbf{U})^{-1}\mathbf{U}'. \tag{4.6}$$

Because **U** and **V** are full rank, the inverse of both $(\mathbf{U}'\mathbf{U})$ and $(\mathbf{VV}')$ exists. By a direct verification, it can be shown that Eq. (4.6) satisfies all the four Moore-Penrose conditions of Eq. (4.1). Therefore, it is the pseudo-inverse of **A**.

In Eq. (4.6), **U** is full column rank, $\mathbf{U}^+ = (\mathbf{U}'\mathbf{U})^{-1}\mathbf{U}'$. Similarly **V** is full row rank, $\mathbf{V}^+ = \mathbf{V}'(\mathbf{VV}')^{-1}$. Both can be verified by a direct verification of Eq. (4.1) or by noticing $\mathbf{U} = \mathbf{UI}, \mathbf{V} = \mathbf{IV}$ and then applying Eq. (4.6). It is obvious that $\mathbf{U}^+\mathbf{U} = \mathbf{I}_m$ and $\mathbf{VV}^+ = \mathbf{I}_n$. $\mathbf{U}^+$ is also called the left inverse and $\mathbf{V}^+$ is also called the right inverse. For a square non-singular matrix, the left inverse and right inverse are equal to $\mathbf{A}^{-1}$. From Eq. (4.6), considering $\mathbf{U}^+ = (\mathbf{U}'\mathbf{U})^{-1}\mathbf{U}'$ and $\mathbf{V}^+ = \mathbf{V}'(\mathbf{VV}')^{-1}$, we obtain another important relation for $\mathbf{A}^+$,

If $\mathbf{A} = \mathbf{UV}$ is a rank decomposition, then $\mathbf{A}^+ = \mathbf{V}^+\mathbf{U}^+$. (4.7)

It must be emphasized that the relation $(\mathbf{UV})^+ = \mathbf{V}^+\mathbf{U}^+$ in general cases does not hold. In the following, we give a simple counterexample.

```
>> A=[7,8,9; 1,2,3; 4,5,6];

>> [L,U]=LU_(A,'gauss',2,100*eps,'long')
L =
   1.000000000000000                   0                   0
   0.142857142857143   1.000000000000000                   0
   0.571428571428571   0.500000000000000   1.000000000000000
U =
   7.000000000000000   8.000000000000000   9.000000000000000
                   0   0.857142857142857   1.714285714285714
                   0                   0                   0
```

Using the Matlab function `pinv` for the pseudo-inverse, we can calculate $U^+L^+ - A^+$ and $U(1:2,:)^+L(:,1:2)^+ - A^+$ as follows.

```
>> pinv(U)*pinv(L)-pinv(A)
= -0.083333333333334   -0.083333333333333    0.166666666666667
   0.000000000000000   -0.000000000000001   -0.000000000000000
   0.083333333333333    0.083333333333334   -0.166666666666667

>> pinv(U(1:2,:))*pinv(L(:,1:2))-pinv(A)
= 1.0e-014 *
  -0.005551115123126   -0.033306690738755    0.005551115123126
   0.047184478546569   -0.111022302462516   -0.029490299091606
  -0.033306690738755    0.088817841970013    0.016653345369377
```

From the output of U, we can see that rank(A) = 2. Therefore, $A = LU$ is not a rank decomposition; $A^+ \neq U^+L^+ = U^+L^{-1}$. The short output format of `LU_.m` removes the third row of U and the corresponding third column of L. $A = L(:,1:2)U(1:2,:)$ is indeed a rank decomposition of A. The calculation verifies that the relation $A^+ = U(1:2,:)^+L(1:2,:)^+$ indeed holds.

In $A = UV$, if $U'U = I$ (the column of U is orthogonal), then $A^+ = V^+U^+ = V^+U'$. This can also be easily verified by a direct verification of each identity of Eq. (4.1). Using the QR decomposition for A in the above counterexample, we can calculate the following.

```
>> [Q,R]=QR_(A,'givens',0,100*eps,'long')
Q =
   0.861640436855329   -0.301511344577763   -0.408248290463863
   0.123091490979333    0.904534033733291   -0.408248290463862
   0.492365963917331    0.301511344577763    0.816496580927726
R =
   8.124038404635961    9.601136296387953   11.078234188139945
                   0    0.904534033733291    1.809068067466582
                   0                    0                    0

>> pinv(R)*Q'-pinv(A)
= 1.0e-015 *
  -0.388578058618805   -0.111022302462516    0.499600361081320
   0.235922392732846   -0.645317133063372   -0.128369537222284
   0.055511151231258    0.555111512312578   -0.277555756156289

>> pinv(R(1:2,:))*Q(:,1:2)'-pinv(A)
= 1.0e-015 *
  -0.499600361081320    0.111022302462516    0.582867087928207
   0.326128013483640   -0.874300631892311   -0.197758476261356
   0.055511151231258    0.555111512312578   -0.277555756156289
```

The output of R also tells that rank(A) = 2; therefore, $A = QR$ is not a rank decomposition. But because Q is orthogonal, the relation $A^+ = R^+Q^+ = R^+Q'$ also holds. $A = Q(1:2,:)R(1:2,:)$ is another rank decomposition of A. The relation $A^+ = R(1:2,:)^+Q(:,1:2)^+ = R(1:2,:)^+Q(:,1:2)'$ holds.

Note that in $A = UV$, even if $UU' = I$ but $U'U \neq I$, $A^+ \neq V^+U^+$. Similarly, in $A = UV$, if $VV' = I$, $A^= V^+U^+ = V'U$. In $A = UV$, even if $V'V = I$ but not $VV' = I$, $A^+ \neq V^+U^+$.

The SVD of A is that $A = USV'$, where $U'U = I$, $V'V = I$, and S is diagonal. From the above discussions, $A^+ = VS^+U'$.

We summarize all the important relations about A^+ discussed so far and four new relations in Eq. (4.8). In Eq. (4.8), I denotes an identity matrix of a proper size and O denotes a zero matrix of a proper size. The relations expressed in Eq. (4.8) will be employed in the calculation of the minimum norm solution or the minimum residual solution of $\mathbf{Ax} = \mathbf{b}$. *It should be noted that the expression of* $\mathbf{x} = \mathbf{A}^{-1}\mathbf{b}$ *or* $\mathbf{x} = \mathbf{A}^{+}\mathbf{b}$ *does not mean the product of the inverse or the pseudo-inverse of* $\mathbf{A}$ *by* $\mathbf{b}$, *rather than any solution algorithm for the solution of* $\mathbf{Ax} = \mathbf{b}$. *Usually finding* $\mathbf{A}^{-1}$ *or* $\mathbf{A}^{+}$ *then calculating the matrix product is the least efficient to solve* $\mathbf{Ax} = \mathbf{b}$.

$$\text{If } \mathbf{A} \text{ is square and non-singular, } \mathbf{A}^{+} = \mathbf{A}^{-1}. \tag{4.8a}$$

$$\text{If } \mathbf{A} = \mathbf{UV} \text{ is a rank decomposition, then } \mathbf{A}^{+} = \mathbf{V}'(\mathbf{VV}')^{-1}(\mathbf{U}'\mathbf{U})^{-1}\mathbf{U}'. \tag{4.8b}$$

$$\text{If } \mathbf{U} \text{ has full column rank, then } \mathbf{U}^{+} = (\mathbf{U}'\mathbf{U})^{-1}\mathbf{U}'. \tag{4.8c}$$

$$\text{Especially if } \mathbf{U}'\mathbf{U} = \mathbf{I}, \text{ then } \mathbf{U}^{+} = \mathbf{U}'. \tag{4.8d}$$

$$\text{If } \mathbf{V} \text{ has full row rank, then } \mathbf{V}^{+} = \mathbf{V}'(\mathbf{VV}')^{-1}. \tag{4.8e}$$

$$\text{Especially if } \mathbf{VV}' = \mathbf{I}, \text{ then } \mathbf{V}^{+} = \mathbf{V}'. \tag{4.8f}$$

$$(\mathbf{UV})^{+} = \mathbf{V}^{+}\mathbf{U}^{+} \text{ holds when } \mathbf{UV} \text{ is a rank decomposition or } \mathbf{U}'\mathbf{U} = \mathbf{I}, \text{ or } \mathbf{VV}' = \mathbf{I}. \tag{4.8g}$$

$$\mathbf{O} \text{ is a zero matrix, } \mathbf{O}^{+} = \mathbf{O}'. \tag{4.8h}$$

$$[\mathbf{A} \ \mathbf{O}]^{+} = \begin{bmatrix} \mathbf{A}^{+} \\ \mathbf{O}' \end{bmatrix}. \tag{4.8i}$$

$$\begin{bmatrix} \mathbf{A} \\ \mathbf{O} \end{bmatrix}^{+} = [\mathbf{A}^{+} \ \mathbf{O}']. \tag{4.8j}$$

$$\begin{bmatrix} \mathbf{A} & \mathbf{O}_{12} \\ \mathbf{O}_{21} & \mathbf{O}_{22} \end{bmatrix}^{+} = \begin{bmatrix} \mathbf{A}^{+} & \mathbf{O}'_{21} \\ \mathbf{O}'_{12} & \mathbf{O}'_{22} \end{bmatrix}. \tag{4.8k}$$

4.2 LINEAR CONSTRAINTS TO LINEAR EQUATIONS

In this section, we study the following problem: we have a given set of linear equations $\mathbf{Ax} = \mathbf{a}$ and want the unknowns $\mathbf{x}$ to satisfy another set of linear equations $\mathbf{Bx} = \mathbf{b}$. $\mathbf{Bx} = \mathbf{b}$ is considered to be the linear constraints to the linear equations $\mathbf{Ax} = \mathbf{a}$. Obviously if $\mathbf{Bx} = \mathbf{b}$ does not have a solution, the posed problem does not have a solution. As a start point, we assume $\mathbf{Bx} = \mathbf{b}$ has a solution. If $\mathbf{x}$ verifies $\mathbf{Bx} = \mathbf{b}$, the same $\mathbf{x}$ is not likely to verify $\mathbf{Ax} = \mathbf{a}$. Therefore, the complete problem is posed as

$$\begin{aligned} &\text{Find } \mathbf{x} \in \mathbb{R}^{n} \text{ and } \mathbf{y} \in \mathbb{R}^{m} \\ &\text{to satisfy } \mathbf{Ax} + \mathbf{y} = \mathbf{a} \text{ and } \mathbf{Bx} = \mathbf{b}. \end{aligned} \tag{4.9}$$

    The constraint problem, Eq. (4.9), happens frequently in classical mechanics and is studied under many special conditions, [4, 39, 72–74]. That it is presented in many different forms poses a big challenge to people reading the literature. In this section, we will give a uniform presentation of the solution algorithms of Eq. (4.9), striping off all the complexities of mechanics. Eq. (4.9) has no other restrictions, except that we assume $\mathbf{Bx} = \mathbf{b}$ has a solution. This assumption is made for the sake of the well-posedness of the constraint problem. In the end of the section, we will study briefly the case when $\mathbf{Bx} = \mathbf{b}$ has no solution.

    In this section, we assume $\mathbf{B} \in \mathbb{R}^{c \times n}$ and $r = \text{rank}(\mathbf{B}) \leq \min(c, n)$.

4.2.1 WHEN A IS A RECTANGULAR MATRIX

First, we consider the general case when $\mathbf{A}$ is rectangular. We write the solution of $\mathbf{Bx} = \mathbf{b}$ as $\mathbf{x} = \mathbf{x}_1 + \mathbf{Oo}$, where $\mathbf{Bx}_1 = \mathbf{b}$, $\mathbf{BO} = \mathbf{0}$, and $\mathbf{o} \in \mathbb{R}^{n-r}$. $\mathbf{x}_1$ and $\mathbf{O}$ can be obtained using the algorithms presented in Sections 4.4–4.6. Introducing $\mathbf{x} = \mathbf{x}_1 + \mathbf{Oo}$ to $\mathbf{Ax} + \mathbf{y} = \mathbf{a}$, we have

$$(\mathbf{AO})\mathbf{o} + \mathbf{y} = \mathbf{a} - \mathbf{Ax}_1. \tag{4.10}$$

In general, solutions to Eq. (4.10) are not unique. Any solutions of Eq. (4.10) can be written as follows:

$$\mathbf{y} = \left(\mathbf{I} - (\mathbf{AO})(\mathbf{AO})^+\right)(\mathbf{a} - \mathbf{Ax}_1) + (\mathbf{AO})\mathbf{o}_0,$$
$$\mathbf{o} = (\mathbf{AO})^+(\mathbf{a} - \mathbf{Ax}_1) - \mathbf{o}_0. \tag{4.11}$$

Then, the general solutions to Eq. (4.9) are obtained as follows:

$$\mathbf{x} = \mathbf{x}_1 + \mathbf{O}(\mathbf{AO})^+(\mathbf{a} - \mathbf{Ax}_1) - \mathbf{Oo}_0,$$
$$\mathbf{y} = \left(\mathbf{I} - (\mathbf{AO})(\mathbf{AO})^+\right)(\mathbf{a} - \mathbf{Ax}_1) + (\mathbf{AO})\mathbf{o}_0, \tag{4.12}$$

where $\mathbf{o}_0 \in \mathbb{R}^{n-r}$. Obviously different $\mathbf{o}_0$ corresponds to different solution.

We can also write the solution of $\mathbf{Bx} = \mathbf{b}$ in the form of $\mathbf{x} = \mathbf{B}^+\mathbf{b} + (\mathbf{I} - \mathbf{B}^+\mathbf{B})\mathbf{o}$, where $\mathbf{o} \in \mathbb{R}^n$. Introducing this form of $\mathbf{x}$ into $\mathbf{Ax} + \mathbf{y} = \mathbf{a}$, we obtain an equation similar to Eq. (4.10),

$$(\mathbf{A}(\mathbf{I} - \mathbf{B}^+\mathbf{B}))\mathbf{o} + \mathbf{y} = \mathbf{a} - \mathbf{AB}^+\mathbf{b}. \tag{4.13}$$

Similar to Eq. (4.12), from Eq. (4.13) we obtain another form of the general solution to Eq. (4.9),

$$\mathbf{x} = \mathbf{B}^+\mathbf{b} + (\mathbf{I} - \mathbf{B}^+\mathbf{B})(\mathbf{A}(\mathbf{I} - \mathbf{B}^+\mathbf{B}))^+(\mathbf{a} - \mathbf{AB}^+\mathbf{b}) - (\mathbf{I} - \mathbf{B}^+\mathbf{B})\mathbf{o}_0,$$
$$\mathbf{y} = \left(\mathbf{I} - \mathbf{A}(\mathbf{I} - \mathbf{B}^+\mathbf{B})(\mathbf{A}(\mathbf{I} - \mathbf{B}^+\mathbf{B}))^+\right)(\mathbf{a} - \mathbf{AB}^+\mathbf{b}) + \mathbf{A}(\mathbf{I} - \mathbf{B}^+\mathbf{B})\mathbf{o}_0, \tag{4.14}$$

where $\mathbf{o}_0 \in \mathbb{R}^n$. Obviously different $\mathbf{o}_0$ corresponds to different solution.

Eqs. (4.12) and (4.14) are valid in all the possible cases. They apply equally well when $\mathbf{A}$ or $\mathbf{B}$ is rectangular or square, full rank, or deficient rank. The only requirement is $\mathbf{Bx} = \mathbf{b}$ has a solution, i.e. $\mathbf{Bx} = \mathbf{b}$ is consistent. Two trivial cases are worth mentioning: (a) $\mathbf{O} = \mathbf{0}$. (b) $\mathbf{I} - \mathbf{AO}(\mathbf{AO})^+ = \mathbf{0}$.

In Eqs. (4.12) and (4.14), $\mathbf{o}_0$ cannot be determined by the problem posed in Eq. (4.9). It needs other conditions to determine $\mathbf{o}_0$. In many scientific applications, $\mathbf{A}$ is usually square and there is extra condition that $\mathbf{y}$ must satisfy. In those applications, the extra condition can determine $\mathbf{o}_0$ uniquely. In the following, we will study Eq. (4.9) that arises in those applications in more detail.

4.2.2 WHEN A IS A SQUARE MATRIX

When $\mathbf{A}$ is square, we can pre-multiply Eq. (4.10) by $\mathbf{O}'$ or Eq. (4.13) by $\mathbf{I} - \mathbf{B}^+\mathbf{B}$, that is,[1]

$$(\mathbf{O}'\mathbf{AO})\mathbf{o} + \mathbf{O}'\mathbf{y} = \mathbf{O}'(\mathbf{a} - \mathbf{Ax}_1),$$
$$(\mathbf{I} - \mathbf{B}^+\mathbf{B})\mathbf{A}(\mathbf{I} - \mathbf{B}^+\mathbf{B})\mathbf{o} + (\mathbf{I} - \mathbf{B}^+\mathbf{B})\mathbf{y} = (\mathbf{I} - \mathbf{B}^+\mathbf{B})(\mathbf{a} - \mathbf{AB}^+\mathbf{b}). \tag{4.15}$$

Idealized Constraints In many scientific applications, it is reasonable to assume that $\mathbf{O}'\mathbf{y} = \mathbf{0}$. In a constraint motion of a mechanical system, this condition is known as the idealized constraint. The

---

[1] If $\mathbf{A}$ is not square, pre-multiply Eq. (4.10) by $\mathbf{O}'$ or Eq. (4.13) $\mathbf{I} - \mathbf{B}^+\mathbf{B}$ cannot be done, because the matrix size does not match.

motion equation of an unconstrained mechanical system is $\mathbf{Ax} = \mathbf{a}$. Constraints $\mathbf{Bx} = \mathbf{b}$ are applied to the unconstrained mechanical system. The effect of the constraints $\mathbf{Bx} = \mathbf{b}$ to the mechanical system is presented as the constraint forces $\mathbf{y}$. The motion equation of the constraint mechanical system becomes $\mathbf{Ax}+\mathbf{y} = \mathbf{a}$. The idealized constraint is commonly found in mechanical engineering, where the constraint forces $\mathbf{y}$ do no work in any virtual displacements allowed by the constraints. The condition of the idealized constraint is just $\mathbf{O'y} = \mathbf{0}$.

For the idealized constraint, we can use the condition $\mathbf{O'y} = \mathbf{0}$ to determine $\mathbf{o}_0$ in Eq. (4.12),

$$\mathbf{o}_0 = -(\mathbf{O'AO})\left(\mathbf{I} - (\mathbf{AO})(\mathbf{AO})^+\right)(\mathbf{a} - \mathbf{Ax}_1) + \left(\mathbf{I} - (\mathbf{O'AO})^+(\mathbf{O'AO})\right)\mathbf{o}_{00}. \tag{4.16}$$

If $\mathbf{O'AO}$ is non-singular, the second term of Eq. (4.16) is zero and $\mathbf{o}_0$ has the unique solution. Then $\mathbf{y}$ has the unique solution by the second equation of Eq. (4.12).

If we use $\mathbf{I} - \mathbf{B}^+\mathbf{B}$ for null($\mathbf{B}$), the condition of the idealized constraint is $(\mathbf{I} - \mathbf{B}^+\mathbf{B})\mathbf{y} = \mathbf{0}$. $\mathbf{o}_0$ in Eq. (4.14) can also be determined, which is in similar form to Eq. (4.16).

Method of Elimination For the idealized constraint, $\mathbf{y}$ is eliminated by considering $\mathbf{O'y} = \mathbf{0}$,

$$(\mathbf{O'AO})\mathbf{o} = \mathbf{O'}(\mathbf{a} - \mathbf{Ax}_1). \tag{4.17}$$

The solution of Eq. (4.17) is simply that

$$\mathbf{o} = (\mathbf{O'AO})^+\mathbf{O'}(\mathbf{a} - \mathbf{Ax}_1) + \left(\mathbf{I} - (\mathbf{O'AO})^+(\mathbf{O'AO})\right)\mathbf{o}_0, \tag{4.18}$$

where $\mathbf{o}_0 \in \mathbb{R}^{n-r}$. If $\mathbf{O'AO}$ is non-singular, the solution of Eq. (4.18) is unique. The solution $\mathbf{x}$ of Eq. (4.9) can, therefore, be uniquely determined if $\mathbf{O'AO}$ is non-singular. After $\mathbf{x}$ is uniquely determined, the solution $\mathbf{y}$ is also unique and can be calculated simply as $\mathbf{y} = \mathbf{a} - \mathbf{Ax}$.

In Eqs. (4.17) and (4.18), we can replace $\mathbf{O}_{n\times(n-r)}$ by $(\mathbf{I} - \mathbf{B}^+\mathbf{B})_{nn}$ and obtain two similar equations. Corresponding to Eq. (4.17), now we have

$$(\mathbf{I} - \mathbf{B}^+\mathbf{B})\mathbf{A}(\mathbf{I} - \mathbf{B}^+\mathbf{B})\mathbf{o} = (\mathbf{I} - \mathbf{B}^+\mathbf{B})(\mathbf{a} - \mathbf{AB}^+\mathbf{b}), \tag{4.19}$$

where $\mathbf{o}_0 \in \mathbb{R}^n$. Note that $(\mathbf{I} - \mathbf{B}^+\mathbf{B})\mathbf{o} = (\mathbf{I} - \mathbf{B}^+\mathbf{B})(\mathbf{x} - \mathbf{B}^+\mathbf{b}) = (\mathbf{I} - \mathbf{B}^+\mathbf{B})\mathbf{x}$ according to the definition of pseudo-inverse. Therefore, Eq. (4.19) can be written as

$$(\mathbf{I} - \mathbf{B}^+\mathbf{B})\mathbf{A}(\mathbf{I} - \mathbf{B}^+\mathbf{B})\mathbf{x} = (\mathbf{I} - \mathbf{B}^+\mathbf{B})(\mathbf{a} - \mathbf{AB}^+\mathbf{b}). \tag{4.20}$$

We write the constraint equation $\mathbf{Bx} = \mathbf{b}$ as

$$\mathbf{B}^+\mathbf{Bx} = \mathbf{B}^+\mathbf{b}. \tag{4.21}$$

The matrices of Eqs. (4.20) and (4.21) have same size. Adding them together, we obtain

$$\left((\mathbf{I} - \mathbf{B}^+\mathbf{B})\mathbf{A}(\mathbf{I} - \mathbf{B}^+\mathbf{B}) + \mathbf{B}^+\mathbf{B}\right)\mathbf{x} = (\mathbf{I} - \mathbf{B}^+\mathbf{B})(\mathbf{a} - \mathbf{AB}^+\mathbf{b}) + \mathbf{B}^+\mathbf{b}. \tag{4.22}$$

$\mathbf{x}$ is unique if $(\mathbf{I} - \mathbf{B}^+\mathbf{B})\mathbf{A}(\mathbf{I} - \mathbf{B}^+\mathbf{B}) + \mathbf{B}^+\mathbf{B}$ is non-singular. After $\mathbf{x}$ is uniquely determined, the solution $\mathbf{y}$ is also unique and can be calculated simply as $\mathbf{y} = \mathbf{a} - \mathbf{Ax}$.

As noted above, if $\mathbf{O'AO}$ or $(\mathbf{I} - \mathbf{B}^+\mathbf{B})\mathbf{A}(\mathbf{I} - \mathbf{B}^+\mathbf{B}) + \mathbf{B}^+\mathbf{B}$ is non-singular, $\mathbf{x}$ is unique. We give a short proof to that when $\mathbf{A}$ is symmetric positive semi-definite, the non-singularity condition of these two matrices is equivalent to the condition that $\begin{bmatrix} \mathbf{A} \\ \mathbf{B} \end{bmatrix}$ has full column rank.

For $x_0 \neq 0$, if $\begin{bmatrix} A \\ B \end{bmatrix} x_0 = \begin{bmatrix} Ax_0 \\ Bx_0 \end{bmatrix} = \begin{bmatrix} 0 \\ 0 \end{bmatrix}$, then $x_0 \in \text{null}(B)$, that is $x_0 = Oo_0$. $O'AOo_0 = O'Ax_0 = 0$; and $(I - B^+B)A(I - B^+B)x_0 + B^+Bx_0 = 0$. On the other hand, for $o_0 \neq 0$, if $O'AOo_0 = 0$, that is, $o_0'O'AOo_0 = 0$. Assume A is symmetric and positive semi-definite, we can write $A = A'^{\frac{1}{2}}A^{\frac{1}{2}}$. $o_0'O'A'^{\frac{1}{2}}A^{\frac{1}{2}}Oo_0 = 0$ means $A^{\frac{1}{2}}Oo_0 = 0$. Take $x_0 = Oo_0$. Then $Ax_0 = 0$. $Bx_0 = BOo_0 = 0$. From $(I - B^+B)A(I - B^+B)x_0 + B^+Bx_0 = 0$, we immediately obtain the two terms are both 0s, because the two terms are perpendicular. By $B^+Bx_0 = 0$, $BB^+Bx_0 = Bx_0 = 0$. By $(I - B^+B)A(I - B^+B)x_0 = 0$, assuming A positive semi-definite, we can obtain $A(I - B^+B)x_0 = 0 = Ax_0$. This proves the statement made in the last paragraph.

We note that if A is not symmetric positive semi-definite, the full rank of $\begin{bmatrix} A \\ B \end{bmatrix}$ is not equivalent to the non-singularity of $O'AO$. We give a counterexample. Suppose $B_{\frac{n}{2} \times n}$ is full rank. $O = \text{null}(B)$ has size of $n \times \frac{n}{2}$, so does its orthogonal complement Q. We take $A = QO'$. Then $\begin{bmatrix} A \\ B \end{bmatrix}$ is full rank. But $O'AO = O'QO'O = 0$.

Now we give a simple example to illustrate the operations by O and $I - B^+B$ in Eqs. (4.17) and (4.22).

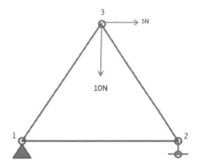

FIGURE 4.1

A truss structure.

The example is shown in Fig. 4.1. The truss structure is in equilibrium under the forces at node 3 and the supports at nodes 1 and 2. We want to find the displacements of the three nodes. The horizontal displacements of nodes 1, 2, 3 are denoted as x_1, x_3, x_5, respectively. The vertical displacements of nodes 1, 2, 3 are denoted as x_2, x_4, x_6, respectively. The known forces $a = [0,0,0,0,5,-10]'$ and unknown reaction forces y at each node follow the same order of numbering. The constraints (or boundary conditions) are $x_1 = 0, x_2 = 0, x_4 = 0$. The unknown displacements are x_3, x_5, x_6. The reaction forces are zeros where the displacements are unknown and are unknown where displacements are known. Under the constraints, for a particular choice of the material and dimension of the truss, the stiffness and the equilibrium equation of the truss structure is as follows. For a reference of forming the equilibrium equation of a structure, see [39, 44], but the detail is not relevant to the topic.

$$A = \begin{bmatrix} 0.3193 & 0.1201 & -0.2500 & 0 & -0.0693 & -0.1201; \\ 0.1201 & 0.2080 & 0 & 0 & -0.1201 & -0.2080; \end{bmatrix}$$

$$
\begin{bmatrix}
-0.2500 & 0 & 0.3193 & -0.1201 & -0.0693 & 0.1201; \\
0 & 0 & -0.1201 & 0.2080 & 0.1201 & -0.2080; \\
-0.0693 & -0.1201 & -0.0693 & 0.1201 & 0.1387 & 0; \\
-0.1201 & -0.2080 & 0.1201 & -0.2080 & 0 & 0.4160];
\end{bmatrix}
$$

$$
\begin{bmatrix}
A_{11} & A_{12} & A_{13} & A_{14} & A_{15} & A_{16} \\
A_{21} & A_{22} & A_{23} & A_{24} & A_{25} & A_{26} \\
A_{31} & A_{32} & A_{33} & A_{34} & A_{35} & A_{36} \\
A_{41} & A_{42} & A_{43} & A_{44} & A_{45} & A_{46} \\
A_{51} & A_{52} & A_{53} & A_{54} & A_{55} & A_{56} \\
A_{61} & A_{62} & A_{63} & A_{64} & A_{65} & A_{66}
\end{bmatrix}
\begin{bmatrix} 0 \\ 0 \\ x_3 \\ 0 \\ x_5 \\ x_6 \end{bmatrix}
+
\begin{bmatrix} y_1 \\ y_2 \\ 0 \\ y_4 \\ 0 \\ 0 \end{bmatrix}
=
\begin{bmatrix} 0 \\ 0 \\ 0 \\ 0 \\ 5 \\ -10 \end{bmatrix}.
$$

A is symmetric positive semi-definite. The form of the equilibrium equation is not the standard linear equation **Ax** = **b** to be presented in subsequent sections. An obvious way to transfer it to the standard form is to move the unknowns y_1, y_2, y_4 to the right hand side,

$$
\begin{bmatrix}
1 & 0 & A_{13} & 0 & A_{15} & A_{16} \\
0 & 1 & A_{23} & 0 & A_{25} & A_{26} \\
0 & 0 & A_{33} & 0 & A_{35} & A_{36} \\
0 & 0 & A_{43} & 1 & A_{45} & A_{46} \\
0 & 0 & A_{53} & 0 & A_{55} & A_{56} \\
0 & 0 & A_{63} & 0 & A_{65} & A_{66}
\end{bmatrix}
\begin{bmatrix} y_1 \\ y_2 \\ x_3 \\ y_4 \\ x_5 \\ x_6 \end{bmatrix}
=
\begin{bmatrix} 0 \\ 0 \\ 0 \\ 0 \\ 5 \\ -10 \end{bmatrix}.
$$

The disadvantage of this method is that it destroys the symmetric structure of **A**. The better ways are to follow Eqs. (4.17) and (4.22). The constraints of Fig. 4.1 are presented as the standard form of **Bx** = **b**,

$$
\begin{bmatrix}
1 & 0 & 0 & 0 & 0 & 0 \\
0 & 1 & 0 & 0 & 0 & 0 \\
0 & 0 & 0 & 1 & 0 & 0
\end{bmatrix}
\begin{bmatrix} x_1 \\ x_2 \\ x_3 \\ x_4 \\ x_5 \\ x_6 \end{bmatrix}
=
\begin{bmatrix} 0 \\ 0 \\ 0 \end{bmatrix}.
$$

The null space of **B** has two representations,

$$
\mathbf{O} =
\begin{bmatrix}
0 & 0 & 0 \\
0 & 0 & 0 \\
1 & 0 & 0 \\
0 & 0 & 0 \\
0 & 1 & 0 \\
0 & 0 & 1
\end{bmatrix},
\quad
\mathbf{I} - \mathbf{B}^+\mathbf{B} =
\begin{bmatrix}
0 & 0 & 0 & 0 & 0 & 0 \\
0 & 0 & 0 & 0 & 0 & 0 \\
0 & 0 & 1 & 0 & 0 & 0 \\
0 & 0 & 0 & 0 & 0 & 0 \\
0 & 0 & 0 & 0 & 1 & 0 \\
0 & 0 & 0 & 0 & 0 & 1
\end{bmatrix}.
$$

It should be noted that the choice of the bases of the null space of **B** can be arbitrary. For example, the following choices of **O** are equally valid, because $\mathbf{BO}_1 = \mathbf{0}$ and $\mathbf{BO}_2 = \mathbf{0}$. **O** in the above has the advantage of keeping the same base direction of **x**.

```
O1 = [    0           0           0;            O2 = [    0           0           0;
          0           0           0;                      0           0           0;
     -0.2270      0.1925     -0.9547;                -0.1077      0.6011      0.7919;
          0           0           0;                      0           0           0;
      0.2426     -0.9382     -0.2469;                -0.9373     -0.3270      0.1207;
     -0.9432     -0.2877      0.1662];               0.3315     -0.7292      0.5986];
```

It can be verified that $\mathbf{O}'\mathbf{y} = \mathbf{0}_3$, $(\mathbf{I} - \mathbf{B}^+\mathbf{B})\mathbf{y} = \mathbf{0}_6$, $\mathbf{O}_1'\mathbf{y} = \mathbf{0}_3$, and $\mathbf{O}_2'\mathbf{y} = \mathbf{0}_3$. This shows that the constraints of Fig. 4.1 are ideal. Following Eqs. (4.17) and (4.22), we can transform the equilibrium equation of the truss structure to the following:

$$\begin{bmatrix} A_{33} & A_{35} & A_{36} \\ A_{53} & A_{55} & A_{56} \\ A_{63} & A_{65} & A_{66} \end{bmatrix} \begin{bmatrix} x_3 \\ x_5 \\ x_6 \end{bmatrix} = \begin{bmatrix} 0 \\ 5 \\ -10 \end{bmatrix} \quad \text{or} \quad \begin{bmatrix} 1 & 0 & 0 & 0 & 0 & 0 \\ 0 & 1 & 0 & 0 & 0 & 0 \\ 0 & 0 & A_{33} & 0 & A_{35} & A_{36} \\ 0 & 0 & 0 & 1 & 0 & 0 \\ 0 & 0 & A_{35} & 0 & A_{55} & A_{56} \\ 0 & 0 & A_{63} & 0 & A_{65} & A_{66} \end{bmatrix} \begin{bmatrix} x_1 \\ x_2 \\ x_3 \\ x_4 \\ x_5 \\ x_6 \end{bmatrix} = \begin{bmatrix} 0 \\ 0 \\ 0 \\ 0 \\ 5 \\ -10 \end{bmatrix}.$$

In the first form, $\mathbf{O}$ is used as in Eq. (4.17). $\mathbf{O}'\mathbf{A}\mathbf{O}$ is just to remove the rows 1, 2, and 4 and columns 1, 2, and 4, from $\mathbf{A}$, where 1, 2, and 4 are the directions where x_1, x_2, x_4 are known. The unknowns are only x_3, x_5, and x_6. Should we use $\mathbf{O}_1$ or $\mathbf{O}_2$, not only we need to calculate $\mathbf{O}_1'\mathbf{A}\mathbf{O}_1$ and $\mathbf{O}_1'\mathbf{a}$, we also need to transform the solved unknowns back to x_3, x_5, x_6 by $\mathbf{O}_1$. In this form of using $\mathbf{O}$, we only need to solve smaller linear equations of 3×3 but we need to copy the coefficient matrix. In the second form, $\mathbf{I} - \mathbf{B}^+\mathbf{B}$ is used as in Eq. (4.22). $(\mathbf{I} - \mathbf{B}^+\mathbf{B})\mathbf{A}(\mathbf{I} - \mathbf{B}^+\mathbf{B}) + \mathbf{B}^+\mathbf{B}$ is just to set the off-diagonals of rows 1, 2, and 4 and columns 1, 2, and 4 to zeros while set the corresponding diagonals to ones, in $\mathbf{A}$. $(\mathbf{I} - \mathbf{B}^+\mathbf{B})\mathbf{a}$ does not change $\mathbf{a}$. The solved unknowns are still $\mathbf{x}$. In the second form, we solve linear equations of the same size and do not need to copy the coefficient matrix. The second form is commonly used to introduce the boundary conditions to equilibrium equations by finite element method, [39, 48].

When $\mathbf{A}$ is symmetric positive definite, we can use the condition $\mathbf{O}'\mathbf{y} = \mathbf{0}$ to show that $\mathbf{y}'\mathbf{A}^{-1}\mathbf{y}$ is the minimum of all $\hat{\mathbf{y}}'\mathbf{A}^{-1}\hat{\mathbf{y}} = (\mathbf{a} - \mathbf{A}\hat{\mathbf{x}})'\mathbf{A}^{-1}(\mathbf{a} - \mathbf{A}\hat{\mathbf{x}})$, where $\hat{\mathbf{x}}$ is any solution satisfying $\mathbf{B}\hat{\mathbf{x}} = \mathbf{b}$. This is known as Gauss principle of least constraint, [72] and . To prove it, note that $\hat{\mathbf{x}} - \mathbf{x} \in \text{span}(\mathbf{O})$ so $(\hat{\mathbf{x}} - \mathbf{x})'\mathbf{y} = \mathbf{0}$. We calculate the difference,

$$\begin{aligned} &\hat{\mathbf{y}}'\mathbf{A}^{-1}\hat{\mathbf{y}} - \mathbf{y}'\mathbf{A}^{-1}\mathbf{y} \\ &= (\mathbf{a} - \mathbf{A}\hat{\mathbf{x}})'\mathbf{A}^{-1}(\mathbf{a} - \mathbf{A}\hat{\mathbf{x}}) - (\mathbf{a} - \mathbf{A}\mathbf{x})'\mathbf{A}^{-1}(\mathbf{a} - \mathbf{A}\mathbf{x}) \\ &= \hat{\mathbf{x}}'\mathbf{A}\hat{\mathbf{x}} - \mathbf{x}'\mathbf{A}\mathbf{x} - 2(\hat{\mathbf{x}} - \mathbf{x})'\mathbf{a} = (\hat{\mathbf{x}} - \mathbf{x})'\mathbf{A}(\hat{\mathbf{x}} - \mathbf{x}) - 2(\hat{\mathbf{x}} - \mathbf{x})'(\mathbf{a} - \mathbf{A}\mathbf{x}) \\ &= (\hat{\mathbf{x}} - \mathbf{x})'\mathbf{A}(\hat{\mathbf{x}} - \mathbf{x}) - 2(\hat{\mathbf{x}} - \mathbf{x})'\mathbf{y} = (\hat{\mathbf{x}} - \mathbf{x})'\mathbf{A}(\hat{\mathbf{x}} - \mathbf{x}) \geq 0. \end{aligned} \quad (4.23)$$

The minimum condition of $(\mathbf{a} - \mathbf{A}\hat{\mathbf{x}})'\mathbf{A}^{-1}(\mathbf{a} - \mathbf{A}\hat{\mathbf{x}})$ under $\mathbf{B}\hat{\mathbf{x}} = \mathbf{b}$ is just Eq. (4.24) to be discussed in the next paragraph.

Method of Lagrange Multiplier If $\mathbf{O}'\mathbf{y} = \mathbf{0}$, we can write $\mathbf{y}$ as $\mathbf{y} = \mathbf{B}'\lambda$. In this form of $\mathbf{y}$, $\mathbf{O}'\mathbf{y} = \mathbf{O}'\mathbf{B}'\lambda = \mathbf{0}$ is satisfied because $\mathbf{B}\mathbf{O} = \mathbf{0}$ by construction. λ is commonly known as the Lagrange multipliers of the constraints $\mathbf{B}\mathbf{x} = \mathbf{b}$. Taking $\mathbf{y} = \mathbf{B}'\lambda$, the problem of Eq. (4.9) is transformed to find $\mathbf{x}$ and λ such that

$$\begin{bmatrix} \mathbf{A} & \mathbf{B}' \\ \mathbf{B} & \mathbf{0} \end{bmatrix} \begin{bmatrix} \mathbf{x} \\ \lambda \end{bmatrix} = \begin{bmatrix} \mathbf{a} \\ \mathbf{b} \end{bmatrix}. \quad (4.24)$$

To analyze the existence and uniqueness of the solution to Eq. (4.24), we follow the same procedure illustrated when studying Eq. (4.9). We write the solution of $\mathbf{Bx} = \mathbf{b}$ as $\mathbf{x} = \mathbf{Qq} + \mathbf{Oo}$, where $\mathbf{BO} = \mathbf{0}$ and $\mathbf{O'Q} = \mathbf{0}$. $\mathbf{O}$ is still the null space of $\mathbf{B}$, $\mathbf{Q}$ is the orthogonal complement of $\mathbf{O}$. In the presentation of $\mathbf{x} = \mathbf{Qq} + \mathbf{Oo}$, the vector $\mathbf{x} \in \mathbb{R}^n$ is decomposed to two orthogonal complementary bases of $\mathbb{R}^n$, $\mathbf{Q}$ and $\mathbf{O}$. $\mathbf{Q}$ or $\mathbf{O}$ can be orthogonal or non-orthogonal. Usually orthogonal bases are preferred due to their superior numerical properties. However, they need more computation to obtain. Introducing $\mathbf{x} = \mathbf{Qq} + \mathbf{Oo}$ into Eq. (4.24), we obtain

$$\begin{aligned} \mathbf{B}(\mathbf{Qq} + \mathbf{Oo}) &= \mathbf{b}, \\ \mathbf{A}(\mathbf{Qq} + \mathbf{Oo}) + \mathbf{B'}\lambda &= \mathbf{a}. \end{aligned} \tag{4.25}$$

Pre-multiply the second equation of Eq. (4.25) by $\begin{bmatrix} \mathbf{O'} \\ \mathbf{Q'} \end{bmatrix}$ and consider $\mathbf{BO} = \mathbf{0}$, we write Eq. (4.25) as

$$\begin{bmatrix} \mathbf{BQ} & \mathbf{0} & \mathbf{0} \\ \mathbf{O'AQ} & \mathbf{O'AO} & \mathbf{0} \\ \mathbf{Q'AQ} & \mathbf{Q'AO} & \mathbf{Q'B'} \end{bmatrix} \begin{bmatrix} \mathbf{q} \\ \mathbf{o} \\ \lambda \end{bmatrix} = \begin{bmatrix} \mathbf{b} \\ \mathbf{O'a} \\ \mathbf{Q'a} \end{bmatrix}. \tag{4.26}$$

Note that Eq. (4.26) is in block lower triangular form. The first equation of Eq. (4.26) is $\mathbf{BQq} = \mathbf{b}$. $\mathbf{q}$ always has a unique solution, because $\mathbf{Qq}$ is perpendicular to the null space of $\mathbf{B}$ by construction. The uniqueness of $\mathbf{o}$ is determined by the non-singularity of $\mathbf{O'AO}$. If $\mathbf{A}$ is non-singular, $\mathbf{O'AO}$ is also non-singular. Therefore, no matter what the constraints $\mathbf{Bx} = \mathbf{b}$ are, if $\mathbf{A}$ is non-singular, unique $\mathbf{x}$ can always be obtained. If $\mathbf{A}$ is singular, the uniqueness of $\mathbf{o}$ (or $\mathbf{x}$) has to be met by the non-singularity of $\mathbf{O'AO}$. The singularity of $\mathbf{A}$ has to be removed by the proper constraints of $\mathbf{B}$. In other words, if $\mathbf{A}$ is singular, in order to have a unique solution of $\mathbf{x}$ to Eq. (4.24), $\mathbf{A}$'s restriction in $\mathbf{B}$'s null space ($\mathbf{O'AO}$) must be non-singular. The non-singularity of $\mathbf{O'AO}$ is commonly known as the second LBB condition in the context of the finite element computation of incompressible materials, [4]. If $\mathbf{q}$ and $\mathbf{o}$ have unique solution, the uniqueness of λ is solely determined by $\mathbf{Q'B'}$. Let us assume $\mathbf{B} \in \mathbb{R}^{c \times n}$ and $\mathbf{Q} \in \mathbb{R}^{n \times r}$, that is, there are c linear constraints and r linearly independent constraints. $r \le c$ and $\mathbf{Q'B'} \in \mathbb{R}^{r \times c}$. If $r = c$, i.e. all the constraints of $\mathbf{Bx} = \mathbf{b}$ are linearly independent, $\mathbf{Q'B'}$ is square and non-singular, the solution of λ is unique. The non-singularity of $\mathbf{Q'B'}$ is commonly known as the first LBB condition in the context of the finite element computation of incompressible materials, [4]. If $r < c$, $\mathbf{Q'B'}$ is a wide matrix which has $c - r$ dimension of null space. We can add any vectors λ_0 belonging to the null space of $\mathbf{B'}$ to λ, $\mathbf{y} = \mathbf{B'}(\lambda + \lambda_0) = \mathbf{B'}\lambda$ is still the same. This conclusion is consistent with that following Eq. (4.18).

Should we use Eq. (4.24) to solve the equilibrium equation of Fig. 4.1, we need to solve linear equations of 9×9. The Lagrangian multipliers in this simple example are just the reaction forces y_1, y_2, and y_4.

Non-idealized Constraints In some applications, we have to consider $\mathbf{O'y} \ne \mathbf{0}$. If $\mathbf{O'y} \ne \mathbf{0}$, in the context of the constrained motion of a mechanical system, the constraints are termed as non-idealized constraints, [72], [74] and [73]. In the non-idealized constraints, further information of the non-idealized constraints is to specify $\mathbf{O'y} = \mathbf{O'\bar{y}}$ (or equivalently $(\mathbf{I} - \mathbf{B^+B})\mathbf{y} = (\mathbf{I} - \mathbf{B^+B})\bar{\mathbf{y}}$). The non-idealized constraints are completely determined by $\mathbf{B}, \mathbf{b}$, and $\bar{\mathbf{y}}$. In the idealized constraints, we take $\bar{\mathbf{y}} = \mathbf{0}$. It is noted generally $\mathbf{y} \ne \bar{\mathbf{y}}$, because $\mathbf{O'}$ has null space (or to say $\mathbf{I} - \mathbf{B^+B}$ is not full rank).

One way to treat the non-idealized constraints is to decompose the constraint forces to two parts: $\mathbf{y} = \mathbf{Q}\lambda + \mathbf{O}\gamma$. $\mathbf{O'y} = \mathbf{O'O}\gamma = \mathbf{O'\bar{y}}$. $\mathbf{x}$ is still written as $\mathbf{x} = \mathbf{Qq} + \mathbf{Oo}$. Following the same procedure to obtain Eqs. (4.26), $\mathbf{Bx} = \mathbf{b}$ and $\mathbf{Ax} + \mathbf{y} = \mathbf{a}$ is transformed to

$$\begin{bmatrix} \mathbf{BQ} & \mathbf{0} & \mathbf{0} & \mathbf{0} \\ \mathbf{O'AQ} & \mathbf{O'AO} & \mathbf{0} & \mathbf{O'O} \\ \mathbf{Q'AQ} & \mathbf{Q'AQ} & \mathbf{Q'Q} & \mathbf{0} \end{bmatrix} \begin{bmatrix} \mathbf{q} \\ \mathbf{o} \\ \lambda \\ \gamma \end{bmatrix} = \begin{bmatrix} \mathbf{b} \\ \mathbf{O'a} \\ \mathbf{Q'a} \end{bmatrix}. \tag{4.27}$$

Eq. (4.27) is supplemented by the condition $\mathbf{O'O}\lambda = \mathbf{O'\bar{y}}$. One way to specify $\bar{\mathbf{y}}$ is to assume $\gamma = \mathbf{C}\lambda$, where $\mathbf{C}$ is a another matrix to identify the constraints in addition to $\mathbf{Bx} = \mathbf{b}$. Introducing $\gamma = \mathbf{C}\lambda$ into Eq. (4.27), we obtain

$$\begin{bmatrix} \mathbf{BQ} & \mathbf{0} & \mathbf{0} \\ \mathbf{O'AQ} & \mathbf{O'AO} & \mathbf{O'OC} \\ \mathbf{Q'AQ} & \mathbf{Q'AQ} & \mathbf{Q'Q} \end{bmatrix} \begin{bmatrix} \mathbf{q} \\ \mathbf{o} \\ \lambda \end{bmatrix} = \begin{bmatrix} \mathbf{b} \\ \mathbf{O'a} \\ \mathbf{Q'a} \end{bmatrix}. \tag{4.28}$$

Because $\mathbf{Qq}$ is perpendicular to null($\mathbf{B}$), $\mathbf{q}$ always has a unique solution. Further if $\mathbf{O'AO}$ is non-singular, the unique solution of $\mathbf{y}$ is determined by the non-singularity of $\mathbf{Q'Q} - \mathbf{Q'AO}(\mathbf{O'AO})^{-1}\mathbf{O'OC}$.

When $\mathbf{A}$ is symmetric positive definite and the constraints are non-idealized, Gauss principle of least constraint has the following extension, [74]. $(\mathbf{y} - \bar{\mathbf{y}})'\mathbf{A}^{-1}(\mathbf{y} - \bar{\mathbf{y}})$ is the minimum of all $(\hat{\mathbf{y}} - \bar{\mathbf{y}})'\mathbf{A}^{-1}(\hat{\mathbf{y}} - \bar{\mathbf{y}}) = (\mathbf{a} - \mathbf{A}\hat{\mathbf{x}})'\mathbf{A}^{-1}(\mathbf{a} - \mathbf{A}\hat{\mathbf{x}})$, where $\hat{\mathbf{x}}$ is any solution satisfying $\mathbf{B}\hat{\mathbf{x}} = \mathbf{b}$. To prove it, note that $\hat{\mathbf{x}} - \mathbf{x} \in \text{span}(\mathbf{O})$ so $(\hat{\mathbf{x}} - \mathbf{x})'(\mathbf{y} - \bar{\mathbf{y}}) = \mathbf{0}$. We calculate the difference,

$$\begin{aligned} & (\hat{\mathbf{y}} - \bar{\mathbf{y}})'\mathbf{A}^{-1}(\hat{\mathbf{y}} - \bar{\mathbf{y}}) - (\mathbf{y} - \bar{\mathbf{y}})'\mathbf{A}^{-1}(\mathbf{y} - \bar{\mathbf{y}}) \\ & = (\mathbf{a} - \mathbf{A}\hat{\mathbf{x}} - \bar{\mathbf{y}})'\mathbf{A}^{-1}(\mathbf{a} - \mathbf{A}\hat{\mathbf{x}} - \bar{\mathbf{y}}) - (\mathbf{a} - \mathbf{Ax} - \bar{\mathbf{y}})'\mathbf{A}^{-1}(\mathbf{a} - \mathbf{Ax} - \bar{\mathbf{y}}) \\ & = \hat{\mathbf{x}}'\mathbf{A}\hat{\mathbf{x}} - \mathbf{x}'\mathbf{Ax} - 2(\hat{\mathbf{x}} - \mathbf{x})'(\mathbf{a} - \bar{\mathbf{y}}) = (\hat{\mathbf{x}} - \mathbf{x})'\mathbf{A}(\hat{\mathbf{x}} - \mathbf{x}) - 2(\hat{\mathbf{x}} - \mathbf{x})'(\mathbf{a} - \mathbf{Ax} - \bar{\mathbf{y}}) \\ & = (\hat{\mathbf{x}} - \mathbf{x})'\mathbf{A}(\hat{\mathbf{x}} - \mathbf{x}) - 2(\hat{\mathbf{x}} - \mathbf{x})'(\mathbf{y} - \bar{\mathbf{y}}) = (\hat{\mathbf{x}} - \mathbf{x})'\mathbf{A}(\hat{\mathbf{x}} - \mathbf{x}) \geq 0. \end{aligned} \tag{4.29}$$

4.2.3 WHEN Bx = b HAS NO SOLUTION

When $\mathbf{Bx} = \mathbf{b}$ has no solution, we may have two different tasks. One is to find the inconsistent equations from $\mathbf{Bx} = \mathbf{b}$ and remove them from the set. The other is to solve a different problem from Eq. (4.9) when $\mathbf{Bx} = \mathbf{b}$ has no solution.

Remove redundancy and inconsistency from Bx = b   There are various reasons $\mathbf{Bx} = \mathbf{b}$ include redundant equations, redundant unknowns, and inconsistent equations. For example, when $\mathbf{Bx} = \mathbf{b}$ is generated from a set of parameters, the rank of $[\mathbf{B}, \mathbf{b}]$ changes due to the change of the parameters. All the equation solution algorithms presented in Sections 4.4–4.6 can be used to find the redundancy and inconsistency from $\mathbf{Bx} = \mathbf{b}$. The MATLAB codes presented in Sections 4.4–4.6 need minor modifications to output the information of the redundancy and inconsistency in $\mathbf{Bx} = \mathbf{b}$.

When two equations include redundancy or inconsistency, treating which equation as redundant or inconsistent can be arbitrary. In some applications, it may have bias toward treating one of the equation as redundant or inconsistent. We use a simple example to illustrate how this problem can be solved. In the following, $\mathbf{Bx} = \mathbf{b}$ are obviously two inconsistent linear constraints.

```
>> B = [2    4    6    8;
        1    2    3    4];
>> b = [10;
        100];
```

Either a LU decomposition or QR decomposition of $[\mathbf{B},\mathbf{b}]$ will reveal the second equation is inconsistent to the first equation. The second equation is likely to be discarded.

```
>> [L,U,p,q]=LU_([B,b])
L =                                      >> [Q,R,p]=QR_([B,b])
     1.0000          0                   Q =
     0.5000     1.0000                        -0.8944      0.4472
U =                                           -0.4472     -0.8944
     2      4      6      8     10        R =
     0      0      0      0     95        -2.2361   -4.4721   -6.7082   -8.9443  -53.6656
p =                                            0    -0.0000   -0.0000   -0.0000   84.9706
     1      2                             p =
q =                                            1      2      3      4      5
     1      2      3      4      5
```

However, if we want to keep the second equation, we can scale the second equation upward. Then LU decomposition of $[\mathbf{B},\mathbf{b}]$ will favor it. The trick is to foul the pivoting in LU.

```
>> B(2,:) = 10*B(2,:);
>> b(2) = 10*b(2);

>> [L,U,p,q]=LU_([B,b])
L =
     1.0000          0
     0.2000     1.0000
U =
          10          20          30          40        1000
           0           0           0           0        -190
p =
     2      1
q =
     1      2      3      4      5
```

Accept Bx = b has no solution   When $\mathbf{Bx} = \mathbf{b}$ has no solution, the problem stated in Eq. (4.9) is not well posed. The following problem is proposed instead.

> Given positive definite $\mathbf{Y},\mathbf{Z}$: find $\mathbf{y} \in \mathbb{R}^m$ and $\mathbf{z} \in \mathbb{R}^c$ to minimize $\mathbf{y}'\mathbf{Yy} + \mathbf{z}'\mathbf{Zz}$
>
> subject to $\mathbf{Ax} + \mathbf{y} = \mathbf{a}$ and $\mathbf{Bx} + \mathbf{z} = \mathbf{b}$ $\qquad(4.30)$

The minimization condition is simply

$$(\mathbf{A}'\mathbf{YA} + \mathbf{B}'\mathbf{ZB})\,\mathbf{x} = \mathbf{A}'\mathbf{Ya} + \mathbf{B}'\mathbf{Zb},$$
$$\mathbf{y} = \mathbf{a} - \mathbf{Ax}, \qquad(4.31)$$
$$\mathbf{z} = \mathbf{b} - \mathbf{Bx}.$$

4.3 SOLUTION OF FIVE ELEMENTARY LINEAR EQUATIONS

Linear equations of a zero matrix, or a diagonal matrix, orthogonal matrix, lower triangular matrix, upper triangular matrix are easy. The solution algorithms of these elementary linear equations form the foundation of solving hard linear equations.

4.3.1 LINEAR EQUATIONS OF A ZERO MATRIX: $\mathbf{Ox} = \mathbf{b}$

$$\mathbf{Ox} = \begin{bmatrix} 0 & 0 & \cdots & 0 \\ 0 & 0 & \cdots & 0 \\ \vdots & \vdots & \cdots & \vdots \\ 0 & 0 & \cdots & 0 \end{bmatrix} \begin{bmatrix} x_1 \\ x_2 \\ \vdots \\ x_n \end{bmatrix} = \begin{bmatrix} b_1 \\ b_2 \\ \vdots \\ b_m \end{bmatrix} = \mathbf{b}. \tag{4.32}$$

Eq. (4.32) is trivia. However, it is an essential building block to the solution of linear equations.

The null space of $\mathbf{O}$ is $\mathbb{R}^n$. A set of the orthogonal basis for the null space can be taken as $\mathbf{I}$.

If $\mathbf{b} \neq \mathbf{0}$, there is no solution. For any $\mathbf{x} \in \mathbb{R}^n$, the residual of Eq. (4.32) is $\mathbf{y} = \mathbf{b} - \mathbf{Ox} = \mathbf{b}$. In all $\mathbf{x} \in \mathbb{R}^n$, $\mathbf{x}_{01} = \mathbf{0}$ has the minimum norm ($\|\mathbf{x}_{01}\|_2 = 0$).

If $\mathbf{b} = \mathbf{0}$, any $\mathbf{x} \in \mathbb{R}^n$ are solutions. In all $\mathbf{x} \in \mathbb{R}^n$, $\mathbf{x}_{01} = \mathbf{0}$ has the minimum norm ($\|\mathbf{x}_{01}\|_2 = 0$).

The usefulness of $\mathbf{Ox} = \mathbf{b}$ appears in the solution of general linear equations. It can appear in one of the following three forms:

$$\begin{bmatrix} \mathbf{A} & \mathbf{O} \end{bmatrix} \begin{bmatrix} \mathbf{x} \\ \mathbf{x}_0 \end{bmatrix} = \mathbf{b}, \tag{4.33a}$$

$$\begin{bmatrix} \mathbf{A} \\ \mathbf{O} \end{bmatrix} \mathbf{x} = \begin{bmatrix} \mathbf{b} \\ \mathbf{b}_0 \end{bmatrix} \tag{4.33b}$$

$$\begin{bmatrix} \mathbf{A} & \mathbf{O}_{12} \\ \mathbf{O}_{21} & \mathbf{O}_{22} \end{bmatrix} \begin{bmatrix} \mathbf{x} \\ \mathbf{x}_0 \end{bmatrix} = \begin{bmatrix} \mathbf{b} \\ \mathbf{b}_0 \end{bmatrix}. \tag{4.33c}$$

In Eqs. (4.33a) and (4.33c), the unknown $\mathbf{x}_0$ is redundant. It can be removed from Eqs. (4.33a) and (4.33c). If we assume $\mathbf{x}_0 = \mathbf{0}$, actually we try to calculate the minimum norm solutions of Eqs. (4.33a) and (4.33c). In Eqs. (4.33b) and (4.33c), if $\mathbf{b}_0 = \mathbf{0}$, the second equation of Eqs. (4.33b) and (4.33c) is redundant. It can be removed from Eqs. (4.33b) and (4.33c). Assuming $\mathbf{x}_0 = \mathbf{0}$ gives the minimum norm solution to Eqs. (4.33b) and (4.33c). If $\mathbf{b}_0 \neq \mathbf{0}$, Eqs. (4.33b) and (4.33c) are not consistent. They have no solutions. $\mathbf{Ax} = \mathbf{b}$ gives the minimum residual solution for Eq. (4.33b) and $\begin{bmatrix} \mathbf{A} & \mathbf{O}_{12} \end{bmatrix} \mathbf{x} = \mathbf{b}$ gives the minimum residual solution for Eq. (4.33c). Assuming $\mathbf{x}_0 = \mathbf{0}$ gives the minimum residual/norm solution to Eqs. (4.33b) and (4.33c).

Using Eqs. (4.8i)–(4.8k), the above conclusions are succinctly expressed in

$$\text{Minimum norm solution of Eq. (4.33a): } \begin{bmatrix} \mathbf{x} \\ \mathbf{x}_0 \end{bmatrix} = \begin{bmatrix} \mathbf{A} & \mathbf{O} \end{bmatrix}^+ \mathbf{b} = \begin{bmatrix} \mathbf{A}^+ \mathbf{b} \\ \mathbf{0} \end{bmatrix}, \tag{4.34a}$$

$$\text{Minimum residual solution of Eq. (4.33b): } \mathbf{x} = \begin{bmatrix} \mathbf{A} \\ \mathbf{O} \end{bmatrix}^+ \begin{bmatrix} \mathbf{b} \\ \mathbf{b}_0 \end{bmatrix} = \mathbf{A}^+ \mathbf{b}, \tag{4.34b}$$

$$\text{Minimum residual/norm solution of Eq. (4.33c): } \begin{bmatrix} \mathbf{x} \\ \mathbf{x}_0 \end{bmatrix} = \begin{bmatrix} \mathbf{A} & \mathbf{O}_{12} \\ \mathbf{O}_{21} & \mathbf{O}_{22} \end{bmatrix}^+ \begin{bmatrix} \mathbf{b} \\ \mathbf{b}_0 \end{bmatrix} = \begin{bmatrix} \mathbf{A}^+ \mathbf{b} \\ \mathbf{0} \end{bmatrix}. \tag{4.34c}$$

4.3.2 LINEAR EQUATIONS OF A DIAGONAL MATRIX: $\mathbf{Dx} = \mathbf{b}$

$$\mathbf{Dx} = \begin{bmatrix} D_1 & & & \\ & D_2 & & \\ & & \ddots & \\ & & & D_n \end{bmatrix} \begin{bmatrix} x_1 \\ x_2 \\ \vdots \\ x_n \end{bmatrix} = \begin{bmatrix} b_1 \\ b_2 \\ \vdots \\ b_n \end{bmatrix} = \mathbf{b}; \quad D_j \neq 0, j = 1, 2, \ldots, n. \tag{4.35}$$

Eq. (4.35) is the simplest linear equations. Each unknown is decoupled with other unknowns. The unique solution is calculated by the simplest algorithm, a loop of division.

```
for j=1:n
    x(j) = b(j)/D(j);
end
```

If the diagonal matrix $\mathbf{D}$ is stored in the format of a vector, the solution of $\mathbf{x}$ can be simply calculated by the element-by-element operator of MATLAB, x=b./D.

In Eq. (4.35), if $\mathbf{D}_j$ is a matrix, $\mathbf{D}$ is block diagonal. $\mathbf{x}_j$ is solved independently: $\mathbf{D}_j\mathbf{x}_j = \mathbf{b}_j, j = 1, 2, \ldots, n$.

4.3.3 LINEAR EQUATIONS OF AN ORTHOGONAL MATRIX: Qx = b

$$\mathbf{Qx} = \begin{bmatrix} Q_{11} & Q_{12} & \cdots & Q_{1n} \\ Q_{21} & Q_{22} & \cdots & Q_{2n} \\ \vdots & \vdots & \cdots & \vdots \\ Q_{m1} & Q_{m2} & \cdots & Q_{mn} \end{bmatrix} \begin{bmatrix} x_1 \\ x_2 \\ \vdots \\ x_n \end{bmatrix} = \begin{bmatrix} b_1 \\ b_2 \\ \vdots \\ b_m \end{bmatrix} = \mathbf{b}. \tag{4.36}$$

$m < n$: Rows of $\mathbf{Q}$ are orthogonal, $\mathbf{QQ}' = \mathbf{I}_m$. Solutions always exist and are not unique. Any solution can be written as $\mathbf{x} = \mathbf{x}_1 + \mathbf{Zz}$. $\mathbf{x}_1$ is an arbitrary particular solution, $\mathbf{Qx}_1 = \mathbf{b}$. $\mathbf{Z}$ is a set of basis of the null space of $\mathbf{Q}$. Here we take $\mathbf{Z}$ to be an orthogonal complement of the rows of $\mathbf{Q}$. We can use the MATLAB function orthogonal_.m (see Section 1.6) to construct $\mathbf{Z}$.

```
Z = orthogonal(Q');
for j=2:n-m
    z = orthogonal_(Q');
    Z = [Z, orthogonal_(Z,z)];
end
```

Among all the particular solutions, we want to find one particular solution $\mathbf{x}_{01} = \mathbf{x}_1 + \mathbf{Zz}_{01}$ with the minimum norm. $\mathbf{z}_{01}$ is determined to minimize $\mathbf{x}'_{01}\mathbf{x}_{01}$,

$$\mathbf{x}'_{01}\mathbf{x}_{01} = \mathbf{z}'_{01}\mathbf{Z}'\mathbf{Zz}_{01} + 2\mathbf{z}'_{01}\mathbf{Z}'\mathbf{x}_1 + \mathbf{x}'_1\mathbf{x}_1,$$

$$\frac{\partial (\mathbf{x}'_{01}\mathbf{x}_{01})}{\partial \mathbf{z}_{01}} = 2\mathbf{Z}'\mathbf{Zz}_{01} + 2\mathbf{Z}'\mathbf{x}_1 = 2\mathbf{z}_{01} + 2\mathbf{Z}'\mathbf{x}_1 = \mathbf{0}, \tag{4.37}$$

$$\mathbf{z}_{01} = -\mathbf{Z}'\mathbf{x}_1.$$

Therefore, the unique particular solution with the minimum norm is given by

$$\mathbf{x}_{01} = (\mathbf{I} - \mathbf{ZZ}')\mathbf{x}_1 = \mathbf{Q}'\mathbf{Qx}_1 = \mathbf{Q}'\mathbf{b} = \mathbf{Q}^+\mathbf{b}. \tag{4.38}$$

$m = n$: $\mathbf{Q}'\mathbf{Q} = \mathbf{QQ}' = \mathbf{I}$. $\mathbf{Z}$ is null. The unique solution is $\mathbf{Q}^{-1}\mathbf{b} = \mathbf{Q}'\mathbf{b}$.

$m > n$: Columns of $\mathbf{Q}$ are orthogonal, $\mathbf{Q}'\mathbf{Q} = \mathbf{I}_n$. In general, no solution exists. In such a case, we want to find an $\mathbf{x}_{01}$ such that $\|\mathbf{y}\|_2 = \|\mathbf{b} - \mathbf{Qx}_{01}\|_2$ is minimum,

$$\mathbf{y}'\mathbf{y} = \mathbf{x}'_{01}\mathbf{Q}'\mathbf{Qx}_{01} - 2\mathbf{x}'_{01}\mathbf{Q}'\mathbf{b} + \mathbf{b}'\mathbf{b},$$

$$\frac{\partial (\mathbf{y}'\mathbf{y})}{\partial \mathbf{x}_{01}} = -2\mathbf{Q}' (\mathbf{b} - \mathbf{Qx}_{01}) = 2\mathbf{x}_{01} - 2\mathbf{Z}'\mathbf{b} = \mathbf{0}, \tag{4.39}$$

$$\mathbf{x}_{01} = \mathbf{Q}'\mathbf{b} = \mathbf{Q}^+\mathbf{b}.$$

The minimum residual is then $\mathbf{b} - \mathbf{Q}\mathbf{Q}'\mathbf{b} = (\mathbf{I} - \mathbf{Q}\mathbf{Q}')\mathbf{b} = \mathbf{Z}\mathbf{Z}'\mathbf{b}$, where $\mathbf{Z}$ is an orthogonal complement of the columns of $\mathbf{Q}$. $\mathbf{Z}$ can be constructed using orthogonal_.m of Section 1.6.

```
Z = orthogonal_(Q);
for j=2:m-n
    z = orthogonal_(Q);
    Z = [Z,orthogonal_(Z,z)];
end
```

If $\mathbf{b} \in \text{range}(\mathbf{Q})$ (that is $\mathbf{b} = \mathbf{Q}\mathbf{c}$ for some $\mathbf{c}$), the minimum residual is $\mathbf{b} - \mathbf{Q}\mathbf{Q}'\mathbf{b} = \mathbf{Q}\mathbf{c} - \mathbf{Q}\mathbf{Q}'\mathbf{Q}\mathbf{c} = 0$. In this particular case, $\mathbf{Q}'\mathbf{b}$ is the unique solution.

In all the three cases, $\mathbf{x}_{01}$ and possibly $\mathbf{Z}$ for $m < n$ or $m > n$ are calculated by mdivideOrthogonal_.m.

Algorithm 4.1

Linear equations of orthogonal matrix: Qx=b

```
%m=n:  |b-Q*x01|=0,  Z=null
%m<n:  |b-Q*x01|=0,  |x01| minimum ,  Q*Z=0
%m>n:  |b-Q*x01| minimum ,  b-Q*x01=Z*Z'*b
function [x01,Z] = mdivideOrthogonal_(Q,b)

[m,n] = size(Q);
if (m ~= size(b,1)) error('mdivideOrthogonal_:_matrix_size_error'); end

x01 = Q'*b;   Z = [];
if (m < n)
    for j=1:n-m Z = [Z,orthogonal_([Q',Z])]; end
end
if (m > n)
    for j=1:m-n Z = [Z,orthogonal_([Q,Z])]; end
end
```

Based on the discussions of Sections 4.1 and 4.3.1–4.3.3, we have another useful way to calculate the pseudo-inverse. Suppose $\mathbf{A} = \mathbf{U}\mathbf{S}\mathbf{V}'$ is the singular value decomposition of $\mathbf{A}$. Then $\mathbf{A}^+ = (\mathbf{U}\mathbf{S}\mathbf{V}')^+ = \mathbf{V}'^+\mathbf{S}^+\mathbf{U}^+ = \mathbf{V}\mathbf{S}^+\mathbf{U}'$, where $\mathbf{S}^+$ follows Eq. (4.8k).

4.3.4 LINEAR EQUATIONS OF A LOWER TRIANGULAR MATRIX: Lx = b

$$\mathbf{Lx} = \begin{bmatrix} L_{11} & & & & \\ L_{21} & L_{22} & & & \\ \vdots & \vdots & \ddots & & \\ L_{n1} & L_{n2} & \cdots & L_{nn} & \\ \vdots & \vdots & \cdots & \vdots & \\ L_{m1} & L_{m2} & \cdots & L_{mn} & \end{bmatrix} \begin{bmatrix} x_1 \\ x_2 \\ \vdots \\ x_n \end{bmatrix} = \begin{bmatrix} b_1 \\ b_2 \\ \vdots \\ b_n \\ \vdots \\ b_m \end{bmatrix} = \mathbf{b}; \quad L_{jj} \neq 0, j = 1,2,\ldots,n. \tag{4.40}$$

If $m = n$, Eq. (4.40) has an unique solution. In mdivideLowerTriangle_.m, the unique solution $\mathbf{x}_{01} = \mathbf{L}^{-1}\mathbf{b}$ is calculated by the forward substitution, see [29]. If $L_{jj} = 1, j = 1,2,\ldots,n$, the division by L_{jj} in the forward substitution is omitted.

If $m > n$, in general Eq. (4.40) does not have a solution. In such a case, we want to find an $\mathbf{x}_{01}$ such that $\|\mathbf{y}\|_2 = \|\mathbf{b} - \mathbf{L}\mathbf{x}_{01}\|_2$ is minimum,

$$\mathbf{y}'\mathbf{y} = \mathbf{x}'_{01}\mathbf{L}'\mathbf{L}\mathbf{x}_{01} - 2\mathbf{x}'_{01}\mathbf{L}'\mathbf{b} + \mathbf{b}'\mathbf{b},$$

$$\frac{\partial\,(\mathbf{y}'\mathbf{y})}{\partial\mathbf{x}_{01}} = -2\mathbf{L}'(\mathbf{b} - \mathbf{L}\mathbf{x}_{01}) = 2\mathbf{L}'\mathbf{L}\mathbf{x}_{01} - 2\mathbf{L}'\mathbf{b} = 0, \tag{4.41}$$

$$\mathbf{x}_{01} = (\mathbf{L}'\mathbf{L})^{-1}\,\mathbf{L}'\mathbf{b} = \mathbf{L}^{+}\mathbf{b}.$$

If $\mathbf{b} \in \text{range}(\mathbf{L})$, that is, $\mathbf{b} = \mathbf{L}\mathbf{c}$ for some $\mathbf{c} \in \mathbb{R}^n$, then $\mathbf{x}_{01}$ calculated in Eq. (4.41) is also the unique solution $\mathbf{x}_{01} = \mathbf{c}$ satisfying $\mathbf{L}\mathbf{x}_{01} = \mathbf{b}$. In this particular case, $\mathbf{L}(1:n,:)^{-1}\mathbf{b}(1:n) = \mathbf{L}^{+}\mathbf{b}$. If $\mathbf{b} \notin \text{range}(\mathbf{L})$, the two calculations $\mathbf{L}(1:n,:)^{-1}\mathbf{b}(1:n)$ and $\mathbf{L}^{+}\mathbf{b}$ are different. The latter gives the minimum residual. In mdivideLowerTriangle_.m, two ways are presented to calculate $\mathbf{L}^{+}\mathbf{b}$ (for $m > n$).

The first way is based on the QR decomposition of $\mathbf{L}$,

$$\mathbf{L} = \mathbf{QR}: \quad \mathbf{x}_{01} = (\mathbf{L}'\mathbf{L})^{-1}\,\mathbf{L}'\mathbf{b} = (\mathbf{R}'\mathbf{Q}'\mathbf{QR})^{-1}\,\mathbf{R}'\mathbf{Q}'\mathbf{b} = \mathbf{R}^{-1}\mathbf{Q}'\mathbf{b}.$$

The second way is based on the Cholesky decomposition of $\mathbf{L}'\mathbf{L}$. In mdivideLowerTriangle_.m, the second way is commented,

$$\mathbf{L}'\mathbf{L} = \mathbf{CC}': \quad \mathbf{x}_{01} = (\mathbf{L}'\mathbf{L})^{-1}\,\mathbf{L}'\mathbf{b} = (\mathbf{CC}')^{-1}\,\mathbf{L}'\mathbf{b} = \mathbf{C}'^{-1}\left(\mathbf{C}^{-1}\,(\mathbf{L}'\mathbf{b})\right).$$

Algorithm 4.2

Linear equations of a lower triangular matrix: Lx=b

```
function x01 = mdivideLowerTriangle_(L,b,unitDiagonal)

[m,n] = size(L);
if (m ~= size(b,1)) error('mdivideLowerTriangle_:_matrix_size_error.'); end
if (exist('unitDiagonal','var') == 0) unitDiagonal = 0; end
x01 = zeros(n,size(b,2));

if (m == n)        %forward substitution: inv(L)*b
    x01(1,:) = b(1,:);
    if (unitDiagonal == 0) x01(1,:) = x01(1,:)/L(1,1); end
    for i=2:n
        x01(i,:) = b(i,:) - L(i,1:i-1)*x01(1:i-1,:);
        if (unitDiagonal == 0) x01(i,:) = x01(i,:)/L(i,i); end
    end
else %if(m > n) %normal equation:        inv(L'*L)*L'*b
    [Q,R] = QR_(L,'householder',0,100*eps,'short');    %Way 1: L=QR
    x01 = mdivideUpperTriangle_(R,Q'*b);
%        C = zeros(n);   x01 = zeros(n,1);                %Way 2: L'L=CC'
%        for i=1:n
%            x01(i) = L(i:m,i)'*b(i:m);    %x01 = L'*b
%            for j=i:n                     %C = L'*L
%                C(i,j) = L(j:m,i)'*L(j:m,j);   C(j,i) = C(i,j);
%            end
%        end
%        C = LLtByCholesky_(C);            %C*C'=L'*L
%        x01 = mdivideLowerTriangle_(C, x01);    x01 = mdivideUpperTriangle_(C',x01);
end
```

`mdivideLowerTriangle_.m` admits a specialization for a band lower triangular matrix.

Algorithm 4.3

Linear equations of a banded lower triangular matrix: Lx=b

```
function x01 = mdivideBandLowerTriangle_(L,lbw,m,n,b,unitDiagonal)

lbw1 = lbw + 1;
x01 = zeros(n,size(b,2));

if (m == n)        %forward substitution: inv(L)*b
    x01(1,:) = b(1,:);
    if (unitDiagonal == 0) x01(1,:) = x01(1,:)/L(1,lbw1); end
    for i=2:n
        js = max(1,i-lbw):min(i-1,n);
        x01(i,:) = b(i,:) - L(i,js-(i-lbw1))*x01(js,:);
        if (unitDiagonal == 0) x01(i,:) = x01(i,:)/L(i,lbw1); end
    end
else %if(m > n) %normal equation: QR=L, inv(L'*L)*L'*b=inv(R)*Q'*b
    [Q,R] = QRband_(L,lbw,0,m,n,100*eps,'short');
    x01 = mdivideBandUpperTriangle_(R,lbw,n,n,Q'*b,0);
end
```

4.3.5 LINEAR EQUATIONS OF AN UPPER TRIANGULAR MATRIX: Ux = b

$$\mathbf{Ux} = \begin{bmatrix} U_{11} & U_{12} & \cdots & U_{1m} & \cdots & U_{1n} \\ & U_{22} & \cdots & U_{2m} & \cdots & U_{2n} \\ & & \ddots & \vdots & \vdots & \vdots \\ & & & U_{mm} & \cdots & U_{mn} \end{bmatrix} \begin{bmatrix} \mathbf{x}_1 \\ \mathbf{x}_2 \\ \vdots \\ \mathbf{x}_m \\ \vdots \\ \mathbf{x}_n \end{bmatrix} = \begin{bmatrix} \mathbf{b}_1 \\ \mathbf{b}_2 \\ \vdots \\ \mathbf{b}_m \end{bmatrix} = \mathbf{b}; \quad U_{jj} \neq 0, j = 1, 2, \ldots, m. \tag{4.42}$$

If $m = n$, Eq. (4.42) has an unique solution. In `mdivideUpperTriangle_.m`, the unique solution $\mathbf{x}_{01} = \mathbf{U}^{-1}\mathbf{b}$ is calculated by the backward substitution, see [29]. If $U_{jj} = 1, j = 1, 2, \ldots, n$, the division by U_{jj} in the backward substitution is omitted.

If $m < n$, solutions of Eq. (4.42) are not unique. In such a case, we want to find an $\mathbf{x}_{01}$ such that $\|\mathbf{x}_{01}\|_2$ is minimum among all the solutions satisfying $\mathbf{Ux} = \mathbf{b}$,

$$\text{minimize } \mathbf{x}'\mathbf{x}$$
$$\text{subject to } \mathbf{Ux} = \mathbf{b}. \tag{4.43}$$

The solution of Eq. (4.43) is obtained by introducing Lagrangian multipliers,

$$L(\mathbf{x}, \lambda) = \mathbf{x}'\mathbf{x} + (\mathbf{b} - \mathbf{Ux})'\lambda,$$

$$\frac{\partial L}{\partial \mathbf{x}} = 2\mathbf{x} + \mathbf{U}'\lambda = \mathbf{0}, \quad \frac{\partial L}{\partial \lambda} = \mathbf{b} - \mathbf{Ux} = \mathbf{0}, \tag{4.44}$$

$$\mathbf{x}_{01} = \mathbf{U}'\left(\mathbf{UU}'\right)^{-1}\mathbf{b} = \mathbf{U}^{+}\mathbf{b}.$$

At least two ways are possible to calculate $\mathbf{U}^+\mathbf{b}$ (for $m < n$). The first way is based on the QR decomposition of $\mathbf{U}'$,

$$\mathbf{U}' = \mathbf{QR}: \quad \mathbf{x}_{01} = \mathbf{U}'(\mathbf{UU}')^{-1}\mathbf{b} = \mathbf{QR}(\mathbf{R}'\mathbf{Q}'\mathbf{QR})^{-1}\mathbf{b} = \mathbf{QR}'^{-1}\mathbf{b}.$$

The second way is based on the Cholesky decomposition of $\mathbf{UU}'$,

$$\mathbf{UU}' = \mathbf{CC}': \quad \mathbf{x}_{01} = \mathbf{U}'(\mathbf{UU}')^{-1}\mathbf{b} = \mathbf{U}'(\mathbf{CC}')^{-1} = \mathbf{U}'\mathbf{C}'^{-1}\left(\mathbf{C}^{-1}\mathbf{b}\right).$$

In the following, we derive a third way to solve $\mathbf{Ux} = \mathbf{b}$. Any particular solution $\mathbf{x}_1$ of Eq. (4.42) satisfies $\mathbf{Ux}_1 = \mathbf{b}$. The general solutions of Eq. (4.42) can be written as the sum of an arbitrary particular solution $\mathbf{x}_1$ and a homogeneous solution $\mathbf{x}_0$,

$$\mathbf{x} = \mathbf{x}_1 + \mathbf{x}_0 = \mathbf{x}_1 + \mathbf{Nz} = \mathbf{U}^-\mathbf{b}. \tag{4.45}$$

In Eq. (4.45), $\mathbf{N}$ is an arbitrary set of basis of the null space of $\mathbf{U}$; $\mathbf{U}^-$ is a generalized inverse satisfying only the first condition of the Moore-Penrose condition Eq. (4.1), see [34].

One special particular solution $\mathbf{x}_1$ is chosen as follows. We take $\mathbf{x}_1(m+1:n) = 0$. Then $\mathbf{x}_1(1:m) = \mathbf{U}(:, 1:m)^{-1}\mathbf{b}$. $\mathbf{U}(:, 1:m)^{-1}\mathbf{b}$ is calculated by the backward substitution.

$\mathbf{N}$ is also specially chosen. We take $\mathbf{N}(m+1:n,:) = \mathbf{I}$. Then $\mathbf{N}(1:m,:) = -\mathbf{U}(:, 1:m)^{-1}\mathbf{U}(:, m+1:n)$. $\mathbf{U}(:, 1:m)^{-1}\mathbf{U}(:, m+1:n)$ are also calculated by the backward substitution.

An orthogonal set of basis $\mathbf{Z}$ can be chosen for null($\mathbf{U}$). Once an arbitrary set of basis $\mathbf{N}$ is determined, $\mathbf{Z}$ can be constructed directly from $\mathbf{N}$ using the MATLAB function orthogonal_.m.

```
Z = N(:,1)/norm(N(:,1));
for j=2:size(N,2)
    Z = [Z,orthogonal_(Z,N(:,j))];
end
```

We write the minimum norm solution $\mathbf{x}_{01}$ in the form of Eq. (4.45): $\mathbf{x}_{01} = \mathbf{x}_1 + \mathbf{Nz}_{01}$. $\mathbf{z}_{01}$ is determined by the minimum condition of $\mathbf{x}'_{01}\mathbf{x}_{01}$,

$$\begin{aligned} \mathbf{x}'_{01}\mathbf{x}_{01} &= \mathbf{z}'_{01}\mathbf{N}'\mathbf{Nz}_{01} + 2\mathbf{z}'_{01}\mathbf{N}'\mathbf{x}_1 + \mathbf{x}'_1\mathbf{x}_1, \\ \frac{\partial\left(\mathbf{x}'_{01}\mathbf{x}_{01}\right)}{\partial\mathbf{z}_{01}} &= 2\mathbf{N}'\mathbf{Nz}_{01} + 2\mathbf{N}'\mathbf{x}_1 = \mathbf{0}, \\ \mathbf{z}_{01} &= -(\mathbf{N}'\mathbf{N})^{-1}\mathbf{N}'\mathbf{x}_1, \\ \mathbf{x}_{01} &= \left(\mathbf{I} - \mathbf{N}(\mathbf{N}'\mathbf{N})^{-1}\mathbf{N}'\right)\mathbf{x}_1. \end{aligned} \tag{4.46}$$

If an orthogonal set of basis $\mathbf{Z}$ is used for null($\mathbf{U}$), $\mathbf{x}_{01}$ can be more easily calculated as

$$\mathbf{x}_{01} = \left(\mathbf{I} - \mathbf{Z}(\mathbf{Z}'\mathbf{Z})^{-1}\mathbf{Z}'\right)\mathbf{x}_1 = (\mathbf{I} - \mathbf{ZZ}')\mathbf{x}_1. \tag{4.47}$$

$\mathbf{x}_{01}$ calculated in Eq. (4.44) is a particular solution. Substituting it as $\mathbf{x}_1$ into the last equation of Eq. (4.46) and noticing that $\mathbf{UN} = \mathbf{0}$, we show that $\mathbf{x}_{01}$ calculated in Eqs. (4.44) and (4.46) are identical. In mdivideUpperTriangle_.m, $\mathbf{x}_{01} = \mathbf{U}^+\mathbf{b}$ is calculated according to Eq. (4.47). The choice is made because $\mathbf{Z}$ is also calculated in mdivideUpperTriangle_.m.

Algorithm 4.4

Linear equations of an upper triangular matrix: Ux=b

```
function [x01,Z] = mdivideUpperTriangle_(U,b,unitDiagonal)

[m,n] = size(U);
if (m ~= size(b,1)) error('mdivideUpperTriangle_:_matrix_size_error.'); end
if (exist('unitDiagonal','var') == 0) unitDiagonal = 0; end
x01 = zeros(n,size(b,2));   Z = [];

x01(m,:) = b(m,:);         %Backward substitution: x01=inv(U(:,1:m))*b
if (unitDiagonal == 0) x01(m,:) = x01(m,:)/U(m,m); end
for i=m-1:-1:1
    x01(i,:) = b(i,:) - U(i,i+1:m)*x01(i+1:m,:);
    if (unitDiagonal == 0) x01(i,:) = x01(i,:)/U(i,i); end
end

if (m < n)
    Z = [zeros(m,n-m); eye(n-m)];          %U*Z=0
    for j=1:n-m            %Backward substitution: Z=inv(U(:,1:m))*U(:,m+1:n)
        Z(m,j) =-U(m,m+j);
        if (unitDiagonal == 0) Z(m,j) = Z(m,j)/U(m,m); end
        for i=m-1:-1:1
            Z(i,j) =-U(i,m+j) - U(i,i+1:m)*Z(i+1:m,j);
            if (unitDiagonal == 0) Z(i,j) = Z(i,j)/U(i,i); end
        end
    end
    Z(:,1) = Z(:,1)/norm(Z(:,1));       %orthogalize Z, Z'*Z=I
    for j=2:n-m
        Z(:,j) = orthogonal_(Z(:,1:j-1),Z(:,j));
    end
    x01 = x01 - Z*(Z'*x01);             %min norm: x01=(I-Z*Z')*x01
%       [Q,R] = QR_(U','householder',0,100*eps,'short');   %Way 1: U'=QR
%       x01 = Q*mdivideLowerTriangle_(R',b);
end
```

mdivideUpperTriangle_.m admits a specialization for a band upper triangular matrix.

Algorithm 4.5

Linear equations of a banded upper triangular matrix: Ux=b

```
function [x01,Z] = mdivideBandUpperTriangle_(U,ubw,m,n,b,unitDiagonal)

% ubw = size(U,2) - 1;
x01 = zeros(n,size(b,2));   Z = [];

x01(m,:) = b(m,:);
if (unitDiagonal == 0) x01(m,:) = x01(m,:)/U(m,1); end
for i=m-1:-1:1
    js = i+1:min(m,min(i+ubw,n));
    x01(i,:) = b(i,:) - U(i,js-(i-1))*x01(js,:);
    if (unitDiagonal == 0) x01(i,:) = x01(i,:)/U(i,1); end
end

if (m < n)
    Z = [zeros(m,n-m); eye(n-m)];          %U*Z=0
```

```
  for j=1:n-m      %backward substitution: Z=inv(U(:,1:m))*U(:,m+1:n)
      Z(m,j) =-U(m,j+1);
      if (unitDiagonal == 0) Z(m,j) = Z(m,j)/U(m,1); end
      for i=m-1:-1:1
          js = i+1:min(m,min(i+ubw,n));
          if (m+j <= min(i+ubw,n)) Z(i,j) =-U(i,m+j-i+1); end
          Z(i,j) = Z(i,j) - U(i,js-(i-1))*Z(js,j);
          if (unitDiagonal == 0) Z(i,j) = Z(i,j)/U(i,1); end
      end
  end
  Z(:,1) = Z(:,1)/norm(Z(:,1));      %orthogalize Z, Z'*Z=I
  for j=2:n-m
      Z(:,j) = orthogonal_(Z(:,1:j-1),Z(:,j));
  end
  x01 = x01 - Z*(Z'*x01);            %min norm: x01=(I-Z*Z')*x01
%     U = transposeBand_(U,0,ubw,m,n);
%     [Q,R] = QRband_(U,ubw,0,n,m,'householder',0,100*eps,'short');   %1: U'=QR
%     x01 = Q*mdivideBandLowerTriangle_(R',ubw,m,m,b,0);
end
```

4.4 GAUSS AND GAUSS-JORDAN ELIMINATION ALGORITHMS

The solution of $\mathbf{Ax} = \mathbf{b}$ is equivalently transformed as shown below,

$$
\begin{aligned}
\mathbf{Ax} &= \mathbf{b}, \\
\left(\mathbf{UAV}^{-1}\right)(\mathbf{Vx}) &= \mathbf{Ub} = \mathbf{c}, \\
\mathbf{By} &= \mathbf{c}, \\
\mathbf{Vx} &= \mathbf{y}.
\end{aligned}
\tag{4.48}
$$

$\mathbf{U}$ is the non-singular linear transformations applied to the rows of $[\mathbf{A},\mathbf{b}]$, i.e. the sets of the linear equations $\mathbf{Ax} = \mathbf{b}$. $\mathbf{V}$ is the non-singular linear transformations applied to the columns of $\mathbf{A}$, i.e. the sets of unknowns $\mathbf{x}$. Choosing well-conditioned $\mathbf{U}$ and $\mathbf{V}$, we want to transform the original equations $\mathbf{Ax} = \mathbf{b}$ to one set or two sets of significantly simpler equations $\mathbf{By} = \mathbf{c}$ and $\mathbf{Vx} = \mathbf{y}$ that are discussed in Section 4.3.

In the Gauss elimination algorithm, $\mathbf{U}$ is chosen as the product of $r = \text{rank}(\mathbf{A})$ Gauss elimination matrices, $\mathbf{U} = \mathbf{G}_r \cdots \mathbf{G}_2\mathbf{G}_1$, see Section 2.1. To reduce the numerical errors, we may switch the rows of $[\mathbf{A},\mathbf{b}]$, i.e. reorder the equations, and/or switch the columns of $\mathbf{A}$, i.e. relabel the unknowns. At the step j, $\mathbf{G}_j$ is chosen to zero $\mathbf{A}(j+1:m,j)$. After r steps, $\mathbf{A}$ is reduced to an upper triangular matrix. To illustrate each step more clearly, let us look at a simple example,

$$
\begin{aligned}
x_1 + 2x_2 + 3x_3 + 4x_4 &= 40, \\
2x_1 + 4x_2 + 6x_3 + 8x_4 &= 30, \\
3x_1 + 6x_2 + x_3 + 2x_4 &= 20, \\
4x_1 + 8x_2 + 3x_3 + 4x_4 &= 10.
\end{aligned}
$$

The coefficients of the equations and the right hand side of the equations are arranged in the augmented matrix $[\mathbf{A},\mathbf{b}]$,

$$\begin{bmatrix} 1 & 2 & 3 & 4 & 40 \\ 2 & 4 & 6 & 8 & 30 \\ 3 & 6 & 1 & 2 & 20 \\ 4 & 8 & 3 & 4 & 10 \end{bmatrix}.$$

The Gauss elimination is applied to $[\mathbf{A},\mathbf{b}]$. At first, we choose a permutation $\mathbf{P}_1$ to switch the first and fourth equation to put A_{41} at A_{11}. Then we select the Gauss elimination matrix $\mathbf{G}_1$ to zero $A(2:4,1)$. The multiplication of $\mathbf{G}_1\mathbf{P}_1[\mathbf{A},\mathbf{b}]$ produces

```
   4.0000        8.0000       3.0000       4.0000      10.0000
        0             0       4.5000       6.0000      25.0000
        0             0      -1.2500      -1.0000      12.5000
        0             0       2.2500       3.0000      37.5000
```

Because $\mathbf{A}(:,1)$ and $\mathbf{A}(:,2)$ are linearly dependent, $\mathbf{G}_1$ that zeros $A(2:4,1)$ also zeros $A(2:4,2)$. To continue the Gauss elimination, we need to switch $\mathbf{A}(:,2)$ and $\mathbf{A}(:,3)$. The switch is denoted as $\mathbf{Q}_2$. After the switch, $A_{22}=4.5000$, which is the largest of $A(2:4,2)$. We do not need to switch the equations. We select $\mathbf{G}_2$ to zero $A(3:4,2)$. The multiplication of $\mathbf{G}_2[\mathbf{AQ}_2,\mathbf{b}]$ produces the following:

```
G2 = gauss_(A(:,2),2,1,'long')          G2*[A,b]
1.0000        0            0        0    4.0000   3.0000   8.0000   4.0000   10.0000
     0   1.0000            0        0         0   4.5000        0   6.0000   25.0000
     0   0.2778       1.0000        0         0        0        0   0.6667   19.4444
     0  -0.5000            0   1.0000         0        0        0        0   25.0000
```

Since $A_{33}=0$, we switch $\mathbf{A}(:,3)$ and $\mathbf{A}(:,4)$. The switch is denoted as $\mathbf{Q}_3$. The column switch is expressed as $[\mathbf{AQ}_3,\mathbf{b}]$.

```
[A*Q3,b]
   4.0000        3.0000       4.0000       8.0000      10.0000
        0        4.5000       6.0000            0      25.0000
        0             0       0.6667            0      19.4444
        0             0            0            0      25.0000
```

Now $\mathbf{A}$ is an upper triangular matrix, the solution of $\mathbf{Uy} = \mathbf{c}$ can be obtained by mdivideUpperTriangle_.m of the last section. After $\mathbf{y}$ is obtained, performing the inverse of the permutations $(\mathbf{Q}_2\mathbf{Q}_3)'\mathbf{y}$, we obtain the solution of the original equation: $x_1 = y_1, x_2 = y_3, x_3 = y_4, x_4 = y_2$.

From the above discussion, we can see that the Gauss elimination algorithm is the LU decomposition applied to the augmented matrix $[\mathbf{A},\mathbf{b}]$: all the row transformations applied to $\mathbf{A}$ are applied to $\mathbf{b}$ simultaneously, but any column transformations applied to $\mathbf{A}$ are not applied to $\mathbf{b}$. The product of all the Gauss elimination matrices is the $\mathbf{L}$ factor in the LU decomposition of $\mathbf{A}$. The Gauss elimination algorithm reduces $\mathbf{A}$ to the $\mathbf{U}$ factor of the LU decomposition of $\mathbf{A}$. For the sake of the solution of $\mathbf{Ax} = \mathbf{b}$, all the row permutations and the elimination matrices are not needed to be saved. Unlike the LU decomposition, we do not need to require each Gauss elimination matrix to be lower triangular. At the step j, $\mathbf{G}_j$ can be chosen to zero both $A(j+1:m,j)$ and $A(1:j-1,j)$. This choice of $\mathbf{G}_j$ is often refereed as Gauss-Jordan elimination algorithm, [2]. After r steps, $\mathbf{A}$ is reduced to a diagonal matrix. To illustrate the Gauss-Jordan elimination algorithm further, let us look at the above simple example again.

The Gauss-Jordan elimination performed to the first column of $\mathbf{A}$ is exactly same as that of the Gauss elimination. Starting from the second column, the Gauss-Jordan elimination differs from the Gauss elimination in the choice of the elimination matrix. For the above example, after switching columns 2 and 3, the Gauss-Jordan elimination matrix $\mathbf{J}_2$ is chosen as follows.

```
J2=gauss_(A(:,2),2,2,'long')
    1.0000   -0.6667         0         0
         0    1.0000         0         0
         0    0.2778    1.0000         0
         0   -0.5000         0    1.0000
```

$\mathbf{J}_2 [\mathbf{A},\mathbf{b}]$, that is, the Jordan elimination, consists of a forward elimination, i.e. the Gauss elimination, and a backward elimination (missing in the Gauss elimination). The forward elimination eliminates x_2 from the third and fourth equations and the backward elimination eliminates x_2 from the first equation.

```
J2*[A,b]
    4.0000         0    8.0000         0   -6.6667
         0    4.5000         0    6.0000   25.0000
         0         0         0    0.6667   19.4444
         0         0         0         0   25.0000
```

Since $A_{33} = 0$, we need to switch columns 3 and 4. After the column switching, $\mathbf{A}$ is in the upper triangular form. The Gauss elimination stops here and starts the backward substitution. But the Jordan elimination continues to eliminate x_3 from the first and second equations. A Jordan elimination $\mathbf{J}_3$ is chosen and $\mathbf{J}_3 [\mathbf{A},\mathbf{b}]$ eliminates x_3 from the first and second equations.

```
J3 = gauss_(A(:,3),3,2,'long')          J3*[A,b]
1.0000        0         0        0       4.0000        0        0   8.0000    -6.6667
     0   1.0000   -9.0000        0            0   4.5000   0.0000        0  -150.0000
     0        0    1.0000        0            0        0   0.6667        0    19.4444
     0        0         0   1.0000            0        0        0        0    25.0000
```

Then $\mathbf{A}$ is reduced to a diagonal form. The solution of $\mathbf{Ax} = \mathbf{b}$ can be easily calculated.

Suppose $\mathbf{A} \in \mathbb{R}^{m \times n}$, $\mathbf{x} \in \mathbb{R}^n$, $\mathbf{b} \in \mathbb{R}^m$, the end result of the Gauss elimination applied to $\mathbf{Ax} = \mathbf{b}$ can be written in Eq. (4.49), where $\mathbf{G}_j^{-1}$ is the Gauss elimination matrix chosen to zero $A(j+1:m,j), j = 1,2,\ldots,r$,

$$
\mathbf{G}_r^{-1} \cdots \mathbf{G}_2^{-1} \mathbf{G}_1^{-1} [\mathbf{PAQ'},\mathbf{P}_1\mathbf{b}] =
\begin{bmatrix}
U_{11} & U_{12} & \cdots & U_{1r} & U_{1,r+1} & \cdots & U_{1n} & c_1 \\
 & U_{22} & \cdots & U_{2r} & U_{2,r+1} & \cdots & U_{2n} & c_2 \\
 & & \ddots & \vdots & \vdots & \vdots & \vdots & \vdots \\
 & & & U_{rr} & U_{r,r+1} & \cdots & U_{rn} & c_r \\
 & & & & & & & c_{r+1} \\
 & & & & & & & \vdots \\
 & & & & & & & c_m
\end{bmatrix}.
\tag{4.49}
$$

Eq. (4.49) is composed of two sets of linear equations $\mathbf{U}(\mathbf{Qx}) = \mathbf{c}(1:r)$ and $\mathbf{O}(\mathbf{Qx}) = \mathbf{c}(r+1:m)$ that are discussed in the last section.

Similarly, the end result of the Gauss-Jordan elimination applied to $\mathbf{Ax} = \mathbf{b}$ can be written in Eq. (4.50), where $\mathbf{J}_j^{-1}$ is the Gauss elimination matrix chosen to zero $\mathbf{A}(j+1:m,j)$ and $\mathbf{A}(1:j-1,j)$, $j = 1, 2, \ldots, r$,

$$
\mathbf{J}_r^{-1} \cdots \mathbf{J}_2^{-1} \mathbf{J}_1^{-1} [\mathbf{PAQ}', \mathbf{P}_1 \mathbf{b}] =
\begin{bmatrix}
U_{11} & 0 & \cdots & 0 & U_{1,r+1} & \cdots & U_{1n} & c_1 \\
 & U_{22} & \cdots & 0 & U_{2,r+1} & \cdots & U_{2n} & c_2 \\
 & & \ddots & \vdots & \vdots & \vdots & \vdots & \vdots \\
 & & & U_{rr} & U_{r,r+1} & \cdots & U_{rn} & c_r \\
 & & & & & & & c_{r+1} \\
 & & & & & & & \vdots \\
 & & & & & & & c_m
\end{bmatrix}. \tag{4.50}
$$

Eq. (4.50) is composed of two sets of linear equations $\mathbf{U}(\mathbf{Qx}) = \mathbf{c}(1:r)$ and $\mathbf{O}(\mathbf{Qx}) = \mathbf{c}(r+1:m)$ that are discussed in Section 4.3.

From the structure of $\mathbf{U}$ and $\mathbf{c}$ of Eq. (4.49) or Eq. (4.50), the solution of $\mathbf{Ax} = \mathbf{b}$ should be considered according to the following five cases.

1. If $r = m = n$, $\mathbf{Ax} = \mathbf{b}$ has a unique solution for any $\mathbf{b}$. The unique solution $\mathbf{x}_{02}$ is calculated by $\mathbf{U}(\mathbf{Qx}_{02}) = \mathbf{c}$.

2. If $r = m < n$, $\mathbf{Ax} = \mathbf{b}$ has non-unique solutions for any $\mathbf{b}$. The minimum norm solution $\mathbf{x}_{02}$ is calculated by $\mathbf{U}(\mathbf{Qx}_{02}) = \mathbf{c}$.

3. If $r < m$ and $\mathbf{c}(r+1:m) = \mathbf{0}$, the minimum norm solution $\mathbf{x}_{02}$ is calculated by $\mathbf{U}(\mathbf{Qx}_{02}) = \mathbf{c}(1:r)$.

4. If $r < m$ and $\mathbf{c}(r+1:m) \neq \mathbf{0}$, Eq. (4.49) or Eq. (4.50), i.e. $\mathbf{Ax} = \mathbf{b}$ has no solution. $\mathbf{U}(\mathbf{Qx}_{02}) = \mathbf{c}(1:r)$ gives the minimum residual solution $\mathbf{Qx}_{02}$ for Eq. (4.49) or Eq. (4.50). However, $\mathbf{x}_{02}$ *is not the minimum residual solution of* $\mathbf{Ax} = \mathbf{b}$. This important point poses as a limitation of the Gauss elimination algorithm and the Gauss-Jordan elimination algorithm to find the minimum residual solution of $\mathbf{Ax} = \mathbf{b}$. For brevity, we call $\mathbf{x}_{02}$ the pseudo-minimum residual solution of $\mathbf{Ax} = \mathbf{b}$.[2]

5. If $r < n$, $\dim(\text{null}(\mathbf{A})) = n - r > 1$. $\text{null}(\mathbf{A})$ is calculated by $\mathbf{U}(\mathbf{QZ}) = \mathbf{0}$.

Gauss elimination algorithm and Gauss-Jordan elimination algorithm are implemented in `mdivideByGauss_.m`. The third input argument, `gj=1` or `gj=2`, controls which algorithm is used. The default algorithm is `gj=1` for the Gauss elimination algorithm.

Algorithm 4.6

Find (x,Z) to A*x = b and A*Z=0. Gauss elimination.

```
%gj=1: Gauss elimination; gj=2: Gauss-Jordan elimination.
function [x02,Z] = mdivideByGauss_(A,b,gj,tol)
```

---

[2]Because $\mathbf{P}'(\mathbf{LU})\mathbf{Qx} = \mathbf{b}$, the minimum residual solution of $\mathbf{Ax} = \mathbf{b}$ is $\mathbf{x}_{01} = \mathbf{A}^+\mathbf{b} = (\mathbf{P}'(\mathbf{LU})\mathbf{Q})^+ \mathbf{b} = \mathbf{Q}'(\mathbf{LU})^+ \mathbf{Pb}$. $\mathbf{x}_{02}$ calculated by the Gauss elimination is actually $\mathbf{Q}'\mathbf{U}^+\mathbf{L}^{-1}\mathbf{Pb}$. In the Gauss elimination and Gauss-Jordan elimination, $\mathbf{L}$ is a non-singular matrix of size $m \times m$. If rank($\mathbf{A}$) $= r < m$, $(\mathbf{LU})^+ \neq \mathbf{U}^+\mathbf{L}^{-1}$ as explained in Section 4.1. That explains why $\mathbf{x}_{02} \neq \mathbf{x}_{01}$.

```
[m,n] = size(A);
if (m ~= size(b,1)) error('mdivideByGauss_:_size_differ.'); end
if (exist('gj','var') ==0) gj = 1; end
if (exist('tol','var') == 0) tol = sqrt(eps); end
epslon = tol*max(1.0,norm(diag(A),inf));  piv = 1:m;  pjv = 1:n;

for i=1:min(m,n)
    k = argmax_(A(:,i),i);  l = i;
    while (abs(A(k,l))<epslon && l<n)
        l = l + 1;  k = argmax_(A(:,l),i);
    end
    if (i ~= k)     %switch A(i,:) and A(k,:); b(i,:) and b(k,:)
        [A(i,:), A(k,:)] = swap_(A(i,:), A(k,:));
        [b(i,:), b(k,:)] = swap_(b(i,:), b(k,:));
        [piv(i), piv(k)] = swap_(piv(i), piv(k));
    end
    if (i ~= l)     %switch A(:,i) and A(:,l)
        [A(:,i), A(:,l)] = swap_(A(:,i), A(:,l));
        [pjv(i), pjv(l)] = swap_(pjv(i), pjv(l));
    end
    if (abs(A(i,i)) > epslon)
        if (gj==2 && i>1) A(1:i-1,i) = A(1:i-1,i)/A(i,i); end
        if (i<m) A(i+1:m,i) = A(i+1:m,i)/A(i,i); end
        for j=i+1:n                          %elimination
            if (gj==2 && i>1) A(1:i-1,j) = A(1:i-1,j) - A(i,j)*A(1:i-1,i); end
            if (i<m) A(i+1:m,j) = A(i+1:m,j) - A(i,j)*A(i+1:m,i); end
        end
        for j=1:size(b,2)                    %elimination
            if (gj==2 && i>1) b(1:i-1,j) = b(1:i-1,j) - b(i,j)*A(1:i-1,i); end
            if(i<m) b(i+1:m,j) = b(i+1:m,j) - b(i,j)*A(i+1:m,i); end
        end
        r = i;
    end
end

if (gj == 2)
    for i=1:r
        if (r < n) A(i,r+1:n) = A(i,r+1:n)/A(i,i); end
        b(i,:) = b(i,:)/A(i,i);  A(i,i) = 1.0;
    end
end

for j=1:size(b,2)
    if (r<m && norm(b(r+1:m,j))>tol*max(1.0,norm(b(:,j),inf)))
        warning('mdivideByGauss_:_A*x=b(:,%d)_inconsistent.',j);
    end
end

if (gj == 1)
    [x02,Z] = mdivideUpperTriangle_(A(1:r,:),b(1:r,:));
else
    x02 = b(1:r,:);  Z = [];
    if (r < n)
        Z = [-A(1:r,r+1:n);eye(n-r)];     %A*Z=0
        Z(:,1) = Z(:,1)/norm(Z(:,1));      %orthogonalize Z
        for j=2:n-r
            Z(:,j) = orthogonal_(Z(:,1:j-1),Z(:,j));
```

```
            end
            x02 = [x02; zeros(n-r,size(x02,2))];    x02 = x02 - Z*(Z'*x02);
        end
    end

pjv = inv_perm_(pjv);
x02 = permute_(pjv,x02);
if (~isempty(Z)) Z = permute_(pjv,Z); end
```

Now we give several simple examples demonstrating the properties of solutions under different cases. The first example demonstrates the unique solution under a non-singular square matrix.

```
>> A=randn(5); b=randn(5,2);    %A non-singular square, b suitable size
>> [x02,Z]=mdivideByGauss_(A,b)
x02 =
    -1.1802    -0.4959
    -0.3440    -0.1908
    -0.6314    -0.6812
    -1.3974    -0.7872
     0.2782    -0.2257
Z =
     []                    %r=n, Z empty, x02 unique solution

>> norm(b-A*x02)
= 1.2406e-015           %x02 is indeed the solution.
```

The second example demonstrates the solutions of consistent equations and no solutions of non-consistent equations of a singular square matrix.

```
>> A(:,4:5)=A(:,1:2)*randn(2);   %Make A singular
>> b(:,1)=A*randn(5,1);          %b's column 1 in A's range
>> [x02,Z]=mdivideByGauss_(A,b,2)    %Use Gauss-Jordan elimination
Warning: mdivideByGauss_: A*x=b(:,2) inconsistent.   %because b's column 2 arbitrary
> In mdivideByGauss_ at 38
x02 =
    -1.3439     0.1868
     0.7572     0.4890
     0.4409     0.7102
     0.0654    -0.3062
    -0.0840    -0.0922
Z =                       %because A's columns 4,5 dependent on A's columns 1,2
     0.0354     0.2814    %so dim(null(A)) = 2
     0.1720     0.4159
    -0.0000     0.0000
          0     0.8608
     0.9845    -0.0828

>> norm(b(:,1)-A*x02(:,1))
= 1.0370e-015           %Ax=b(:,1) has non-unique solutions. x02 has minimum norm.
>> norm(b(:,2)-A*x02(:,2))
=    1.9182             %Ax=b(:,2) has no solution. x02 pseudo minimum residual.
>> norm(A*Z)
= 1.8491e-016           %Z in null(A)
>> norm(Z'*Z-eye(2))
= 2.2291e-016           %Z: orthogonal unit basis for null(A)
```

Linear equations of a wide matrix (less equations than unknowns) always have null spaces. The third example demonstrates the non-unique solutions of a wide rectangular matrix with a full rank.

```
>> A=randn(5,8); b=randn(5,2);      %arbitrary b
>> [x02,Z]=mdivideByGauss_(A,b)        %Use Gauss elimination
x02 =                              %x02 minimum norm
      0.7680    -0.8481
     -0.0384     0.4077
     -0.1757     0.4486
     -0.3197     0.6765
      0.4626    -0.0801
      0.4640    -0.6828
     -0.3076    -0.2568
      0.3894     0.0104
Z =                                %solutions non-unique
     -0.5981     0.1150    -0.2106
      0.2809    -0.2822    -0.0530
     -0.5425    -0.2661     0.1114
     -0.1645     0.2446    -0.4050
      0.3446     0.6105    -0.1459
      0.3509    -0.4744    -0.1907
           0     0.4228     0.3231
           0          0     0.7838

>> norm(b-A*x02)                   %x02 is minimum norm solution.
= 1.0243e-015
```

If a wide matrix is rank deficient, its range is reduced. Example 4 demonstrates the non-unique solutions of consistent equations and no solutions of non-consistent equations of a wide rank deficient matrix.

```
>> A(4:5,:)=randn(2)*A(1:2,:);
>> b(:,1)=A*randn(8,1);
>> [x02,Z]=mdivideByGauss_(A,b,2)
Warning: mdivideByGauss_: A*x=b(:,2) inconsistent.
> In mdivideByGauss_ at 38
x02 =
      0.8547    -0.3922
      0.9890     0.1161
     -0.2787     0.7701
     -0.2603     0.1950
      0.0178     0.5359
      0.0946    -0.0057
      0.4833    -0.2242
      0.0288     0.0846
Z =
     -0.7166    -0.0186    -0.1367    -0.2127     0.0877
      0.4837     0.1728    -0.0281    -0.1960    -0.2655
     -0.4601    -0.1155     0.0554     0.1507    -0.4491
           0     0.6375    -0.3249     0.1415    -0.0956
           0          0          0          0     0.8374
           0          0     0.8873     0.0224    -0.0269
           0          0          0     0.9326     0.0567
      0.2023    -0.7417    -0.2910     0.0579    -0.0763

>> norm(b(:,1)-A*x02(:,1))         %x02(:,1) is minimum norm solution.
= 1.9004e-015
```

```
>> norm(b(:,2)-A*x02(:,2))          %x02(:,2) is pseudo minimum residual solution.
=    1.8570
```

Linear equations of high matrices (more equations than unknowns) usually have no solutions. Example 5 demonstrates the unique solution of consistent equations and no solution of non-consistent equations of a high matrix with a full rank.

```
>> A=randn(8,5);  b=[A*randn(5,1),randn(8,1)];
>> [x02,Z]=mdivideByGauss_(A,b)
Warning: mdivideByGauss_: A*x=b(:,2) inconsistent.
> In mdivideByGauss_ at 38
x02 =
     -0.1669        0.1304
     -0.8162        0.4474
      2.0941       -0.2647
      0.0802        0.7510
     -0.9373        0.6808
Z =
       []

>> norm(b(:,1)-A*x02(:,1))          %x02(:,1) is unique solution.
= 6.4974e-016
>> norm(b(:,2)-A*x02(:,2))          %x02(:,2) is pseudo minimum residual solution.
=    1.7625
```

If a high matrix is rank deficient, it starts to have null space. Example 6 demonstrates the non-unique solutions of consistent equations and no solution of non-consistent equations of a high rank deficient matrix.

```
>> A(5:8,:)=randn(4)*A(1:4,:);  b=[A*randn(5,1),randn(8,1)];
>> [x02,Z]=mdivideByGauss_(A,b,2)
Warning: mdivideByGauss_: A*x=b(:,2) inconsistent.
> In mdivideByGauss_ at 38
x02 =
     -1.6187       -0.6626
     -1.0700       -1.3418
     -0.7592       -0.5606
      2.1778       -0.8307
      0.5919        0.0598
Z =
      0.4478
     -0.1972
      0.0245
      0.0075
      0.8718

>> norm(b(:,1)-A*x02(:,1))          %x02(:,1) is minimum norm solution.
= 2.0592e-015
>> norm(b(:,2)-A*x02(:,2))          %x02(:,2) is pseudo minimum residual solution.
=    1.7642
```

mdivideByGauss_.m admits a specialization for a band matrix. In mdivideBandByGauss_.m, no row or column permutation is done, because permutations destroy the band structure of the input matrix **B**. The Gauss-Jordan elimination is not implemented, because its backward elimination also destroys the band structure of **B**.

Algorithm 4.7

Find (x,Z) to B*x = b and B*Z=0. B band matrix, Gauss elimination.

```
function [x02,Z] = mdivideBandByGauss_(B,lbw,ubw,m,n,b,tol)

lbw1 = lbw + 1;    normB = max(1.0,norm(B(:,lbw1),inf));

for j=1:min(m,n)
    if (abs(B(j,lbw1)) < tol*normB)
        bnorm = 0;
        for i=j+1:min(m,j+lbw) bnorm = max(bnorm,abs(B(i,j-i+lbw1))); end
        if (bnorm > tol*normB)
            error('mdivideBandByGauss_:_zero_pivot._Use_mdivideByGauss_');
        end
    else
        for i=j+1:min(m,j+lbw) B(i,j-i+lbw1) = B(i,j-i+lbw1)/B(j,lbw1); end
        for k=j+1:min(m,j+lbw)              %elimination
            for l=j+1:min(j+ubw,n)
                B(k,l-k+lbw1) = B(k,l-k+lbw1) - B(j,l-j+lbw1)*B(k,j-k+lbw1);
            end
        end
        for l=1:size(b,2)
            for k=j+1:min(m,j+lbw)          %elimination
                b(k,l) = b(k,l) - b(j,l)*B(k,j-k+lbw1);
            end
        end
        r = j;
    end
end

for j=1:size(b,2)
    if (r<m && norm(b(r+1:m,j))>tol*max(1.0,norm(b(:,j),inf)))
        warning('mdivideByGauss_:_B*x=b(:,%d)_inconsistent.',j);
    end
end

[x02,Z] = mdivideBandUpperTriangle_(B(1:r,lbw1:lbw1+ubw),ubw,r,n,b(1:r,:));
```

Finally, we compare the efficiency of mdivideByGauss_.m against the MATLAB built-in functions A\b and inv(A)*b. The elapsed time is obtained to perform the solution of **Ax = b** of a 1000 × 1000 on an INSPIRON 1545 laptop.

We create a 1000 × 1000 band matrix with a lower bandwidth 2 and an upper bandwidth 3.

```
A=diag(randn(1000,1));
A=A+diag(randn(999,1),1); A=A+diag(randn(999,1),-1);
A=A+diag(randn(998,1),2); A=A+diag(randn(998,1),-2);
A=A+diag(randn(997,1),3);    %A in full format
b=randn(1000,1);             %right hand side
```

First, we solve the equation **Ax = b** with **A** in the full format.

```
>> tic                                =  6.5704e-011
>> x1 = mdivideByGauss_(A,b,1);
>> toc                                >> tic
Elapsed time is 9.237545 seconds.     >> x2 = mdivideByGauss_(A,b,2);
>> norm(b-A*x1)                        >> toc
```

```
Elapsed time is 14.680799 seconds.         =  5.6061e-011
>> norm(b-A*x2)
=  5.1923e-009                               >> tic
                                             >> x4 = inv(A)*b;
>> tic                                       >> toc
>> x3 = A\b;                                 Elapsed time is 0.665595 seconds.
>> toc                                       >> norm(b-A*x4)
Elapsed time is 0.333143 seconds.            =  4.0577e-009
>> norm(b-A*x3)
```

Next we solve the same equation with **A** in the band format.

```
B=full2band_(A,2,3);          %B in band format

>> tic
>> x5=mdivideBandByGauss_(B,2,3,1000,1000,b);
>> toc
Elapsed time is 0.015855 seconds.
>> norm(b-A*x5)
=  3.4673e-010
```

4.5 HOUSEHOLDER AND GIVENS ELIMINATION ALGORITHMS

For solving $\mathbf{Ax} = \mathbf{b}$, the Householder elimination is very similar to the Gauss elimination. In this section, only the differences are outlined. For the elimination procedure and the different cases of solutions, refer to the last section.

Because we use the orthogonal Householder matrix to zero columns of **A**, we do not need row permutations. But if $\mathbf{A}(j : m, j)$ is zero and $\mathbf{A}(j : m, k), j < k <= n$ is nonzero, we need to switch the columns j and k. The goal of the elimination is to reduce **A** to an upper triangular form. The Householder elimination algorithm is the QR Householder decomposition algorithm applied to the augmented matrix $[\mathbf{A}, \mathbf{b}]$. To show the process step by step, we use the same equation that was used in the last section. For the convenience, $[\mathbf{A}, \mathbf{b}]$ is reproduced below,

$$\begin{bmatrix} 1 & 2 & 3 & 4 & 40 \\ 2 & 4 & 6 & 8 & 30 \\ 3 & 6 & 1 & 2 & 20 \\ 4 & 8 & 3 & 4 & 10 \end{bmatrix}.$$

To zero $\mathbf{A}(2 : 4, 1)$, a Householder matrix $\mathbf{H}_1$ is chosen. $\mathbf{H}_1 [\mathbf{A}, \mathbf{b}]$ is shown below.

```
>> H1=householder_(A(:,1),1,1,'long')    >> H1*[A,b]
-0.1826   -0.3651   -0.5477   -0.7303    -5.4772  -10.9545   -5.4772   -7.6681  -36.5148
-0.3651    0.8873   -0.1691   -0.2255     0.0000    0.0000    3.3825    4.3972    6.3742
-0.5477   -0.1691    0.7463   -0.3382     0.0000    0.0000   -2.9263   -3.4042  -15.4387
-0.7303   -0.2255   -0.3382    0.5490     0.0000    0.0000   -2.2351   -3.2056  -37.2516
```

Because $\mathbf{A}(:, 1)$ and $\mathbf{A}(:, 2)$ are linearly dependent, $\mathbf{H}_1$ that zeros $\mathbf{A}(2 : 4, 1)$ also zeros $\mathbf{A}(2 : 4, 2)$. To continue the Householder elimination, we need to switch $\mathbf{A}(:, 2)$ and $\mathbf{A}(:, 3)$. The switch is denoted as $\mathbf{Q}_2$. After the switch, we choose another Householder matrix to zero $\mathbf{A}(3 : 4, 2)$.

```
>> H2=householder_(A(:,2),2,1,'long')      >> H2*[A,b]
1.0000      0         0         0           -5.4772  -5.4772 -10.9545  -7.6681 -36.5148
     0  -0.6765    0.5853    0.4470          0.0000  -5.0000   0.0000  -6.4000 -30.0000
     0   0.5853    0.7957   -0.1561          0.0000  -0.0000   0.0000   0.3651  -2.7404
     0   0.4470   -0.1561    0.8808          0.0000  -0.0000   0.0000  -0.3267 -27.5528
```

Because $\mathbf{H}_2(:,1) = \mathbf{I}_1$ and $\mathbf{H}_2(1,:) = \mathbf{I}'_1$, $\mathbf{A}(2:4,1)$ remains $\mathbf{0}$. Should we aim to zero A_{21} also as in the Gauss-Jordan elimination by a different Householder matrix $\mathbf{H}_b$, $\mathbf{H}_b\mathbf{A}$ sets $\mathbf{A}(2:4,1)$ to nonzero.

```
>> Hb=householder_(A(:,2),2,2,'long')      >> Hb*[A,b]
 0.6254    0.7385   -0.2001   -0.1529       -3.4254  -0.0000  -6.8509  -0.3767  -9.3443
 0.7385   -0.4561    0.3946    0.3014       -4.0452  -7.4162  -8.0904  -9.9782 -47.1940
-0.2001    0.3946    0.8931   -0.0817        1.0962  -0.0000   2.1924   0.4914  -0.9223
-0.1529    0.3014   -0.0817    0.9376        0.8373  -0.0000   1.6745  -0.2302 -26.1641
```

After performing $\mathbf{H}_2[\mathbf{A},\mathbf{b}]$ as shown above, $A_{43} = 0$ but $A_{44} \neq 0$, to continue the Householder elimination, we need to switch $\mathbf{A}(:,3)$ and $\mathbf{A}(:,4)$. The switch is denoted as $\mathbf{Q}_3$. After switching columns 3 and 4, a Householder matrix $\mathbf{H}_3$ is chosen to zero A_{43}.

```
>> H3=householder_(A(:,3),3,1,'long')      >> H3*[A,b]
1.0000      0         0         0           -5.4772  -5.4772  -7.6681 -10.9545 -36.5148
     0  1.0000       0         0            0.0000  -5.0000  -6.4000   0.0000 -30.0000
     0       0   -0.7452    0.6668         -0.0000   0.0000  -0.4899  -0.0000 -16.3299
     0       0    0.6668    0.7452          0.0000  -0.0000   0.0000   0.0000 -22.3607
```

Now $\mathbf{A}$ is an upper triangular matrix, the solution of $\mathbf{U}\mathbf{y} = \mathbf{c}$ can be obtained by mdivideUpperTriangle_.m of Section 4.3.5. After $\mathbf{y}$ is obtained, performing the inverse of the permutations $(\mathbf{Q}_2\mathbf{Q}_3)'\mathbf{y}$, we obtain the solution of the original equation: $x_1 = y_1, x_2 = y_3, x_3 = y_4, x_4 = y_2$.

The end result of the Householder elimination applied to $[\mathbf{A},\mathbf{b}]$ has the same form as Eq. (4.49), which for the convenience is reproduced below,

$$\mathbf{H}_r^{-1} \cdots \mathbf{H}_2^{-1}\mathbf{H}_1^{-1}[\mathbf{AQ'},\mathbf{b}] = \begin{bmatrix} U_{11} & U_{12} & \cdots & U_{1r} & U_{1,r+1} & \cdots & U_{1n} & c_1 \\ & U_{22} & \cdots & U_{2r} & U_{2,r+1} & \cdots & U_{2n} & c_2 \\ & & \ddots & \vdots & \vdots & \vdots & \vdots & \vdots \\ & & & U_{rr} & U_{r,r+1} & \cdots & U_{rn} & c_r \\ & & & & & & & c_{r+1} \\ & & & & & & & \vdots \\ & & & & & & & c_m \end{bmatrix}. \tag{4.51}$$

There are five cases for the solutions, see Section 4.4. Case 4 has an important difference.

4. If $r < m$ and $\mathbf{c}(r+1:m) \neq \mathbf{0}$, Eq. (4.51), i.e. $\mathbf{Ax} = \mathbf{b}$ has no solution. $\mathbf{U}(\mathbf{Qx}_{01}) = \mathbf{c}(1:r)$ gives the minimum residual solution $\mathbf{Qx}_{01}$ for Eq. (4.51). $\mathbf{x}_{01}$ *is also the minimum residual solution of* $\mathbf{Ax} = \mathbf{b}$. This important point poses as an advantage of the Householder elimination algorithm to find the minimum residual solution of $\mathbf{Ax} = \mathbf{b}$.[3]

---

[3] Because $(\mathbf{HU})\mathbf{Qx} = \mathbf{b}$, the minimum residual solution of $\mathbf{Ax} = \mathbf{b}$ is $\mathbf{x}_{01} = \mathbf{A}^+\mathbf{b} = ((\mathbf{HU})\mathbf{Q})^+\mathbf{b} = \mathbf{Q}'(\mathbf{HU})^+\mathbf{b}$. $\mathbf{x}_{01}$ calculated by the Householder elimination is actually $\mathbf{Q}'\mathbf{U}^+\mathbf{H}'\mathbf{b}$. The Householder matrix $\mathbf{H}$ is orthogonal. $(\mathbf{HU})^+ = \mathbf{U}^+\mathbf{H}'$ as explained in Section 4.1.

The Householder elimination algorithm is implemented in mdivideByHouseholder_.m.

Algorithm 4.8

Find (x,Z) to A*x = b and A*Z=0. Householder elimination.

```
function [x01,Z] = mdivideByHouseholder_(A,b,tol)

[m,n] = size(A);
normA = max(1.0, norm(diag(A),inf));   pjv = 1:n;

for j=1:min(m,n)
    [h,alpha,beta] = householder_(A(j:m,j));
    if (abs(beta) < tol*normA)
        for k=n:-1:j+1
            if (pjv(k) ~= k) continue; end
            if (norm(A(j:m,k),inf) < tol*normA) continue; end
            [h,alpha,beta] = householder_(A(j:m,k));
            [pjv(j),pjv(k)] = swap_(pjv(j),pjv(k));
            [A(:,j),A(:,k)] = swap_(A(:,j),A(:,k));
            break;
        end
    end
    if (abs(beta) < tol*normA) continue; end
    r = j;   A(j,j) = beta;   v = alpha*h;   %Apply H'*A
    for k=j+1:n
        ak = A(j:m,k);   A(j:m,k) = ak - (h'*ak)*v;
    end
    for k=1:size(b,2)
        bk = b(j:m,k);   b(j:m,k) = bk - (h'*bk)*v;
    end
end
```

mdivideByHouseholder_.m admits a specialization for a band matrix. For a band matrix, the Householder elimination can also be used. But in mdivideBandByGivens_.m, the Givens elimination is adopted. In mdivideBandByGivens_.m, no column permutation is done, because permutations destroy the band structure of the input matrix **B**.

Algorithm 4.9

Find (x,Z) to B*x = b and B*Z=0. B band matrix. Givens elimination.

```
function [x01,Z] = eqsBandByGivens_(B,lbw,ubw,m,n,b,tol)
if (exist('tol','var') == 0) tol = sqrt(eps); end
B = [B,zeros(m,lbw)];   %B band w/ upper band width=ubw+lbw

for j=1:min(m,n)
    for k=j+1:min(j+lbw,m)
        [c,s] = givens_(B(j,lbw1),B(k,j-k+lbw1));
        B(j,lbw1) = c*B(j,lbw1) - s*B(k,j-k+lbw1); %apply Givens elimination
        for l=j+1:min(k+ubw,n)
            Bjl = B(j,l-j+lbw1);   Bkl = B(k,l-k+lbw1);
            B(j,l-j+lbw1) = c*Bjl - s*Bkl;   B(k,l-k+lbw1) = s*Bjl + c*Bkl;
        end
        bj = b(j,:);   bk = b(k,:);
        b(j,:) = c*bj - s*bk;   b(k,:) = s*bj + c*bk;
    end
    if (abs(B(j,lbw1)) > tol*normB) r = r + 1; end
```

```
end

for j=1:size(b,2)
    if (r<m && norm(b(r+1:m,j))>tol*max(1.0,norm(b(:,j),inf)))
        warning('eqsBandByGivens_:␣B*x=b(:,%d)␣inconsistent.',j);
    end
end

[x01,Z] = eqsBandUpperTriangle_(B(1:r,lbw1:lbw1+ubw+lbw),ubw+lbw,r,n,b(1:r,:));
```

Now we use mdivideByHouseholder_.m and mdivideBandByGivens_.m to solve the same equation of the 1000×1000 band matrix that was used in Section 4.4.

```
>> tic                                    >> tic
>> x6=mdivideByHouseholder_(A,b);         >> x7=mdivideBandByGivens_(B,2,3,1000,
>> toc                                                            1000,b);
Elapsed time is 7.926679 seconds.         >> toc
>> norm(b-A*x6)                           Elapsed time is 0.040995 seconds.
=   3.7698e-009                           >> norm(b-A*x7)
                                          =   2.4559e-009
```

4.6 SOLUTION ALGORITHMS BASED ON MATRIX DECOMPOSITIONS

In Chapters 2 and 3, we presented various algorithms of matrix decomposition: $\mathbf{A} = \mathbf{UBV}$. In the decomposition, $\mathbf{U}$ and $\mathbf{V}$ are full rank; their numerical conditioning is usually as good as it can get under each decomposition algorithm. Any rank deficiency and bad numerical conditioning in $\mathbf{A}$ are condensed in $\mathbf{B}$ only. Introducing the decomposition to the linear equations $\mathbf{Ax} = \mathbf{b}$, the solution of $\mathbf{Ax} = \mathbf{b}$ can be obtained in stages,

$$(\mathbf{UBV})\,\mathbf{x} = \mathbf{b}, \tag{4.52a}$$

$$(\mathbf{BV})\,\mathbf{x} = \mathbf{U}^+\mathbf{b} = \mathbf{c}, \tag{4.52b}$$

$$(\mathbf{V})\,\mathbf{x} = \mathbf{B}^+\mathbf{c} = \mathbf{d}, \tag{4.52c}$$

$$\mathbf{x} = \mathbf{V}^+\mathbf{d}. \tag{4.52d}$$

In theory, any decomposition can be used. But in practice, only those decompositions are useful: $\mathbf{A} = \mathbf{UBV}$ can be efficiently calculated and the solutions of the three linear equations $\mathbf{U}^+\mathbf{b}, \mathbf{B}^c$, and $\mathbf{V}^d$ are significantly easier than $\mathbf{Ax} = \mathbf{b}$. Practically, these three linear equations are one of the five elementary linear equations discussed in Section 4.3. If $\mathbf{A}$ has a null space, the null space can be obtained by Eq. (4.52). If $\mathbf{Ax} = \mathbf{b}$ has a solution, the unique or the minimum norm solution obtained in Eq. (4.52) is also the corresponding solution of $\mathbf{Ax} = \mathbf{b}$. If $\mathbf{Ax} = \mathbf{b}$ does not have a solution, the minimum residual solution obtained in Eq. (4.52) may or may not be the minimum residual solution of $\mathbf{Ax} = \mathbf{b}$. See the discussion of case 4 in Sections 4.4 and 4.5. The conclusion is that if all the factors are full rank or the decomposition is orthogonal, the minimum residual solution of $\mathbf{Ax} = \mathbf{b}$ can be obtained by Eq. (4.52).

For $\mathbf{A} \in \mathbb{R}^{m \times n}$, the long format of $\mathbf{A}$'s decomposition is $\mathbf{A}_{mn} = \mathbf{U}_{mm}\mathbf{B}_{mn}\mathbf{V}_{nn}$, where the subscript denotes the size of each matrix. The short format of $\mathbf{A}$'s decomposition has three possible forms:

$A_{mn} = U_{mm}B_{mr}V_{rn}$, or $A_{mn} = U_{mr}B_{rn}V_{nn}$, or $A_{mn} = U_{mr}B_{rr}V_{rn}$, where $r = $ rank (A). The exact form of the short format is determined by the decomposition algorithm and the rank condition of A ($r < \min(m,n), m < n, m = n$ or $m > n$). In the short format of the decomposition, all the factors are in full rank.

For the uniformity of the presentation and the convenience in coding, only the short format of the decomposition is considered in the following and in the MATLAB implementation mdivideByDecomposing_.m. The following decomposition algorithms are implemented in mdivideByDecomposing_.m. As presented in Sections 2.2 and 3.2, LU and QR decompositions admit specializations of Hessenberg and band matrices, respectively. These specializations are allowed in mdivideByDecomposing_.m.

1. LU decomposition, see Section 2.2. For a general matrix A: $A = P_1'LUP_2$,

$$\left(P_1'LUP_2\right)x = b, \tag{4.53a}$$
$$x = P_2'\left(U^+\left(L^+\left(P_1 b\right)\right)\right); \qquad \text{null}(A) = P_2'\left(I_n - U^+U\right). \tag{4.53b}$$

2. LDU decomposition, see Section 2.3. For a general matrix A: $A = P_1'LDUP_2$,

$$\left(P_1'LDUP_2\right)x = b, \tag{4.54a}$$
$$x = P_2'\left(U^+\left(D^{-1}\left(L^+\left(P_1 b\right)\right)\right)\right); \qquad \text{null}(A) = P_2'\left(I_n - U^+U\right). \tag{4.54b}$$

3. LDLt decomposition, see Section 2.4. For a symmetric matrix A: $A = P'LDL'P$,

$$\left(P'LDL'P\right)x = b, \tag{4.55a}$$
$$x = P'\left(L'^+\left(D^{-1}\left(L^+\left(Pb\right)\right)\right)\right); \qquad \text{null}(A) = P'\left(I - L'^+L'\right). \tag{4.55b}$$

4. LLt decomposition, see Section 2.4. For a symmetric positive matrix A: $A = LL'$,

$$\left(LL'\right)x = b, \tag{4.56a}$$
$$x = L'^{-1}\left(L^{-1}b\right). \tag{4.56b}$$

5. LBLt[4] decomposition, see Section 2.4. For a symmetric matrix A: $A = P'LBL'P$,

$$\left(P'LBL'P\right)x = b, \tag{4.58a}$$
$$x = P'\left(L'^+\left(B^{-1}\left(L^+\left(Pb\right)\right)\right)\right); \qquad \text{null}(A) = P'\left(I - L'^+L'\right). \tag{4.58b}$$

---

[4] LTLt decomposition, see Section 2.4. For a symmetric matrix A: $A = P'LTL'P$.

$$\left(P'LTL'P\right)x = b \tag{4.57a}$$
$$x = P'\left(L'^+\left(T^+\left(L^+\left(Pb\right)\right)\right)\right); \qquad \text{null}(A) = \begin{bmatrix} P'\left(I - L'^+L'\right) \\ P'\left(L'^+\left(I - T^+T\right)\right) \end{bmatrix}. \tag{4.57b}$$

Unfortunately, even the short format of the LTLt decomposition for a rank deficient symmetric matrix A is not a rank decomposition. This happens when the tri-diagonal matrix T has a one-dimensional null space. When $A = P'LTL'P$ is not a rank decomposition and $b \notin$ range (A), x calculated in Eq. (4.57) is not the minimum residual solution of $Ax = b$. For this reason. The code corresponding to the LTLt decomposition is commented out in mdivideByDecomposing_.m.

6. QR decomposition, see Section 3.2. For a general matrix $\mathbf{A}$: $\mathbf{A} = \mathbf{QRP}$,

$$(\mathbf{QRP})\,\mathbf{x} = \mathbf{b}, \tag{4.59a}$$

$$\mathbf{x} = \mathbf{P}'\left(\mathbf{R}^{+}\left(\mathbf{Q}'\mathbf{b}\right)\right); \qquad \text{null}(\mathbf{A}) = \mathbf{P}'\left(\mathbf{I}_{n} - \mathbf{R}^{+}\mathbf{R}\right). \tag{4.59b}$$

7. QLZ decomposition, see Section 3.3. For a general matrix $\mathbf{A}$: $\mathbf{A} = \mathbf{QLZ}$,

$$(\mathbf{QLZ})\,\mathbf{x} = \mathbf{b}, \tag{4.60a}$$

$$\mathbf{x} = \mathbf{Z}'\left(\mathbf{L}^{-1}\left(\mathbf{Q}'\mathbf{b}\right)\right); \qquad \text{null}(\mathbf{A}) = \mathbf{I}_{n} - \mathbf{Z}'\mathbf{Z}. \tag{4.60b}$$

8. QBZ decomposition, see Section 3.4. For a general matrix $\mathbf{A}$: $\mathbf{A} = \mathbf{QBZ}$,

$$(\mathbf{QBZ})\,\mathbf{x} = \mathbf{b}, \tag{4.61a}$$

$$\mathbf{x} = \mathbf{Z}'\left(\mathbf{B}^{-1}\left(\mathbf{Q}'\mathbf{b}\right)\right); \qquad \text{null}(\mathbf{A}) = \mathbf{I}_{n} - \mathbf{Z}'\mathbf{Z}. \tag{4.61b}$$

In the above Eqs. (4.53)–(4.61), the pseudo-inverse symbol $+$ on a matrix means the matrix can be a high matrix or a wide matrix. The inverse symbol -1 on a matrix means the matrix is a square matrix.

Algorithm 4.10

Find (x,Z) to A*x = b and A*Z=0. Decomposition algorithms.

```
%decomposer: cell array, decomposer{1}(A,...)
%tol=tolerance to check 0s.
function [x01,Z] = mdivideByDecomposing_(A,b,decomposer,tol)

[m,n] = size(A);
if (m ~= size(b,1)) error('mdivideByDecomposing_:_size_differ.'); end
if (~exist('decomposer','var') || isempty(decomposer))
    decomposer = {'LU_', 'gauss', 3};
end
decomposer{1} = upper(decomposer{1});
if (exist('tol','var') == 0) tol = sqrt(eps); end

if (strcmp(decomposer{1},'LU_'))
%    [L,U,p,q] = LU_(A,algo,pivot,tol,format,f1st,last,p,q)
    [L,U,p,q] = LU_(A,decomposer{2},decomposer{3},tol);
    x01 = permute_(p,b);
    x01 = mdivideLowerTriangle_(L,x01,1);
    [x01,Z] = mdivideUpperTriangle_(U,x01,0);
    q = inv_perm_(q);
    x01 = permute_(q,x01);
    if (~isempty(Z)) Z = permute_(q,Z); end
elseif(strcmp(decomposer{1},'LUHESSENBERG_'))
%    [L,U] = LUhessenberg_(H,lbw,tol,format,f1st,last)
    [L,U] = LUhessenberg_(A,decomposer{2},tol);
    x01 = mdivideBandLowerTriangle_(L,decomposer{2},m,n,b,1);
    [x01,Z] = mdivideUpperTriangle_(U,x01,0);
elseif(strcmp(decomposer{1},'LUBAND_'))
%    [L,U] = LUband_(B,lbw,ubw,m,n,tol,format,f1st,last)
    [L,U] = LUband_(A,decomposer{2},decomposer{3},decomposer{4},decomposer{5},tol);
    x01 = mdivideBandLowerTriangle_(L,decomposer{2},decomposer{4},decomposer{4},b,1);
```

```
          [x01,Z] = mdivideBandUpperTriangle_(U,decomposer{3},decomposer{4},decomposer{5},...
                                                x01,0);
elseif(strcmp(decomposer{1},'LDU_'))
%     [L,D,U,p,q] = LDU_(A,algo,pivot,tol,format,f1st,last,p,q)
      [L,D,U,p,q] = LDU_(A,decomposer{2},decomposer{3},tol);
      x01 = permute_(p,b);
      x01 = mdivideLowerTriangle_(L,x01,1);
      x01 = x01./D;
      [x01,Z] = mdivideUpperTriangle_(U,x01,0);
      q = inv_perm_(q);
      x01 = permute_(q,x01);
      if (~isempty(Z)) Z = permute_(q,Z); end
elseif (strcmp(decomposer{1},'LDLT_'))
%     [L,D,p] = LDLt_(A,algo,pivot,tol,format,f1st,last,p)
      [L,D,p] = LDLt_(A,decomposer{2},decomposer{3},tol);
      x01 = permute_(p,b);
      x01 = mdivideLowerTriangle_(L,x01,1);
      x01 = x01./D;
      [x01,Z] = mdivideUpperTriangle_(L',x01,1);
      p = inv_perm_(p);
      x01 = permute_(p,x01);
      if (~isempty(Z)) Z = permute_(p,Z); end
elseif (strcmp(decomposer{1},'LLT_'))
%     L = LLt_(A,f1st,last)
      L = LLt_(A);
      x01 = mdivideLowerTriangle_(L,b,0);
      x01 = mdivideUpperTriangle_(L',x01,0);   Z = [];
% elseif (strcmp(decomposer{1},'LTLT_'))
% %     [L,T,p] = LTLt_(A,algo,tol,format,f1st,last,p)
%       [L,T,p] = LTLt_(A,decomposer{2},tol);
%       x01 = permute_(p,b);
%       x01 = mdivideLowerTriangle_(L,x01,1);
%       [x01,z] = mdivideBandByGauss_(T,1,1,size(T,1),size(T,1),x01,tol);
% %     [x01,z] = mdivideBandByGivens_(T,1,1,size(T,1),size(T,1),x01,tol);
%       [x01,Z] = mdivideUpperTriangle_(L',x01,1);
%       if (~isempty(z)) Z = [Z,mdivideUpperTriangle_(L',z,1)]; end
%       p = inv_perm_(p);
%       x01 = permute_(p,x01);
%       if (~isempty(Z)) Z = permute_(p,Z); end
elseif (strcmp(decomposer{1},'LBLT_'))
%     [L,B,p] = LBLt_(A,pivot,tol,format,f1st,last,ib,p)
      [L,B,p] = LBLt_(A,decomposer{2},tol);
      x01 = permute_(p,b);
      x01 = mdivideLowerTriangle_(L,x01,1);
      k = size(x01,1);   i = 1;
      while(i <= k)
          if (B(i,3) == 0)
              x01(i,:) = x01(i,:)/B(i,2);   i = i+1;
          else
              B11 = B(i,2);   B22 = B(i+1,2);   B12 = B(i,3);   B21 = B12;
              detB = B11*B22-B12*B21;
              x01(i+1,:) = (B11*x01(i+1,:) - B12*x01(i,:))/detB;
              x01(i,:) = (x01(i,:) - B12*x01(i+1,:))/B11;
              i = i + 2;
          end
      end
      [x01,Z] = mdivideUpperTriangle_(L',x01,1);
```

```
      p = inv_perm_(p);
      x01 = permute_(p,x01);
      if (~isempty(Z)) Z = permute_(p,Z); end
elseif (strcmp(decomposer{1},'QR_'))
%     [Q,R,p] = QR_(A,algo,perm,tol,format,f1st,last,p)
      [Q,R,p] = QR_(A,decomposer{2},decomposer{3},tol);
      x01 = Q'*b;
      [x01,Z] = mdivideUpperTriangle_(R,x01,0);
      p = inv_perm_(p);
      x01 = permute_(p,x01);
      if (~isempty(Z)) Z = permute_(p,Z); end
elseif (strcmp(decomposer{1},'QRHESSENBERG_'))
%     [Q,R] = QRhessenberg_(H,lbw,tol,format,f1st,last)
      [Q,R] = QRhessenberg_(A,decomposer{2},tol);
      x01 = Q'*b;
      [x01,Z] = mdivideUpperTriangle_(R,x01,0);
elseif(strcmp(decomposer{1},'QRBAND_'))
%     [Q,R] = QRband_(B,lbw,ubw,m,n,tol,format,f1st,last)
      [Q,R] = QRband_(A,decomposer{2},decomposer{3},decomposer{4},decomposer{5},tol);
      [x01,Z] = mdivideBandUpperTriangle_(R,decomposer{2}+decomposer{3},decomposer{5},...
                                    decomposer{5},Q'*b,0);
elseif(strcmp(decomposer{1},'QLZ_'))
%     [Q,L,Z] = QLZ_(A,algo,tol,format)
      [Q,L,Z] = QLZ_(A,decomposer{2},tol);
      x01 = Q'*b;
      x01 = mdivideLowerTriangle_(L,x01,0);
      [x01,Z] = mdivideOrthogonal_(Z,x01);
elseif(strcmp(decomposer{1},'QBZ_'))
      decomposer{2} = upper(decomposer{2});
      if (strcmp(decomposer{2},'HOUSEHOLDER'))
%         [Q,B,Z] = QBZbyHouseholder_(A,tol,format,f1st,last,Q,Z)
          [Q,B,Z] = QBZbyHouseholder_(A,tol);
      elseif (strcmp(decomposer{2},'GIVENS'))
%         [Q,B,Z] = QBZbyGivens_(A,tol,format,f1st,last,Q,Z)
          [Q,B,Z] = QBZbyGivens_(A,tol);
%       elseif (strcmp(decomposer{2},'LANCZOS'))
% %         [Q,B,Z] = QBZbyLanczos_(A,tol,f1st,last,Q,B,Z,Ax)
%           [Q,B,Z] = QBZbyLanczos_(A,tol);
      else
          ('mdivideByDecomposing:_unknown_QBZ_algo.');
      end
      [x01,z] = mdivideBandUpperTriangle_(B,1,size(Q,2),size(Z,1),Q'*b,0);
      if (~isempty(z)) z = Z'*z; end
      [x01,Z] = mdivideOrthogonal_(Z,x01);
      if (~isempty(z)) Z = [z,Z]; end
else
      error('mdivideByDecomposing:_unknown_decomposer.');
end
```

The third input argument to mdivideByDecomposing_.m is a cell array decomposer, containing the name of the decomposition function and the input arguments to the decomposition function. Refer to each section discussing the decomposition for the details of the input arguments. As shown in mdivideByDecomposing_.m, its default input is decomposer={'LU_', 'gauss', 3}. To explain how to specify decomposer, let us look at QR decomposition in more detail. The part of code corresponding to QR is shown as follows.

```
elseif (strcmp(decomposer{1},'QR_'))            %decomposer{1}='QR_'
%    [Q,R,p] = QR_(A,algo,perm,tol,format,f1st,last,p)    %List of input arguments of QR_
     [Q,R,p] = QR_(A,decomposer{2},decomposer{3},tol);    %decomposer{2}=algo, {3}=perm
     x01 = Q'*b;
     [x01,Z] = mdivideUpperTriangle_(R,x01,0);
     p = inv_perm_(p);
     x01 = permute_(x01,p);
     if (~isempty(Z)) Z = permute_(Z,p); end
```

To use QR decomposition for $\mathbf{Ax} = \mathbf{b}$, the input commands are the following.

```
>> A=randn(8,10);  b=randn(8,1);          %Arbitrary A and b for demonstration
>> decomposer = {'qr_','householder',1};  %Use {} to create cell array
>> tol = 100*eps;                         %tolerance to check 0s
>> [x01,Z]=mdivideByDecomposing_(A,b,decomposer,tol)    %Ax=b ==> (Q*R*P)*x=b
```

Set decomposer{1}='qr_' to access QR_.m. From the input commands and the listed code for the
QR decomposition, we can see that input values of algo and perm for QR_.m are set by decomposer{2}=
'householder' and decomposer{3}=1. The input value of tol for QR_.m is set by the fourth input argument
of mdivideByDecomposing_. The other input arguments for QR_.m: format,f1st,last,p need not to be set
explicitly. They take the default values set in QR_.m. See Section 3.2. The alphabetic values for decomposer
are not case sensitive. The settings of decomposer for other decomposition algorithms are similar. The
list of input arguments for each decomposition function is shown and commented. The matching of the
input arguments and decomposer can be easily understood.

Now we give three simple examples to demonstrate the use of mdivideByDecomposing_. The first
example shows how to set the values of decomposer correctly.

```
>> A=randn(5); b=randn(5,2);          %A non-singular square, b suitable size
>> x1=mdivideByGauss_(A,b);               %use defaults
>> x2=mdivideByHouseholder_(A,b);         %use defaults

>> x3=mdivideByDecomposing_(A,b);         %It's easy to use default decomposer values

>> decomposer={'qr','householder_',1}; %wrong function name, wrong QR algo
>> x4=mdivideByDecomposing_(A,b,decomposer,100*eps);
??? Error using ==> mdivideByDecomposing_ at 134
mdivideByDecomposing: unknown decomposer.

>> decomposer{1}='qr_';                %correct function name
>> x4=mdivideByDecomposing_(A,b,decomposer,100*eps);
??? Error using ==> QR_ at 62
QR_: wrong 2nd input argument: algo.

Error in ==> mdivideByDecomposing_ at 92
    [Q,R,p] = QR_(A,decomposer{2},decomposer{3},tol);

>> decomposer{2}='householder';        %correct QR_ algo
>> x4=mdivideByDecomposing_(A,b,decomposer,100*eps);
                                       %It's harder to set decomposer values.
                                       %After two tries, we got it right.
>> [norm(b-A*x1),norm(b-A*x2),norm(b-A*x3),norm(b-A*x4)]
= 1.0e-014 *                           %All 4 solutions are right!
    0.4146    0.9256    0.4146    0.8158
```

The second example demonstrates the solutions of consistent equations and no solutions of non-consistent equations of a singular square matrix. Compare with second example of Section 4.4.

```
>> A(:,4:5)=A(:,1:2)*randn(2);    %Make A singular
>> b(:,1)=A*randn(5,1);           %b's column 1 in A's range

>> x = pinv(A)*b                  %MATLAB built-in function for singular A
    -0.6540   -0.0182             %x(:,1) minimum norm solution
     0.6930    0.0481             %x(:,2) minimum residual solution
    -2.2499    0.8582
    -0.5573   -0.0673
    -0.6660   -0.0467


>> [x1,Z1]=mdivideByGauss_(A,b)
Warning: mdivideByGauss_: A*x=b(:,2) inconsistent.
> In mdivideByGauss_ at 50                    >> [x3,Z3]=mdivideByDecomposing_(A,b)
x1 =                                          x3 =
    -0.6540    0.0916  %(:,1) min norm            -0.6540   -0.0182  %(:,1) min norm
     0.6930   -0.0304  %(:,2) not min residual     0.6930    0.0481  %(:,2) min residual
    -2.2499    0.7689                             -2.2499    0.8582
    -0.5573   -0.0419                             -0.5573   -0.0673
    -0.6660    0.0280                             -0.6660   -0.0467
Z1 =                                          Z3 =
     0.0137    0.5366                              0.0137    0.5366
     0.6996    0.4706                              0.6996    0.4706
          0         0                                   0         0
          0    0.5184                                   0    0.5184
     0.7144   -0.4710                              0.7144   -0.4710
```

The third example compares the efficiency of different decomposition algorithms against the MATLAB built-in function A\b. The elapsed time is obtained to perform the solution of $\mathbf{Ax} = \mathbf{b}$ of a 1000×1000 on an INSPIRON 1545 laptop.

```
>> A=randn(1000); d=rand(1000,1); A = A*diag(d)*A';    %A positive definite
>> b=randn(1000,1);

>> tic
>> x1=A\b;
>> toc
Elapsed time is 0.204821 seconds.
>> norm(b-A*x1)
=   2.1251e-008

%Consider symmetry & positive definite
>> tic
>> x2=mdivideByDecomposing_(A,b,{'LLt_'});
>> toc
Elapsed time is 2.156594 seconds.
>> norm(b-A*x2)
=   2.0606e-008

%Consider symmetry & ignore positive definite
>> tic
>> x3=mdivideByDecomposing_(A,b,{'LDLt_','gauss',1});
>> toc
Elapsed time is 6.142507 seconds.
```

```
>> norm(b-A*x3)
=   2.5269e-008


%Ignore symmetry & positive definite
>> decomposer = {'LU_','gauss',2};
>> tic
>> x4=mdivideByDecomposing_(A,b,decomposer);
>> toc
Elapsed time is 6.453157 seconds.
>> norm(b-A*x4)
=   2.4509e-008


%Ignore symmetry & positive definite
>> decomposer = {'QR_','householder',0};
>> tic
>> x5=mdivideByDecomposing_(A,b,decomposer);
>> toc
Elapsed time is 16.796331 seconds.
>> norm(b-A*x5)
=   2.7775e-008


%Ignore symmetry & positive definite
>> decomposer = {'LDU_','gauss',2};
>> tic
>> x6=mdivideByDecomposing_(A,b,decomposer);
>> toc
Elapsed time is 6.757830 seconds.
>> norm(b-A*x6)
=   2.4283e-008


%Ignore symmetry & positive definite
>> decomposer = {'QBZ_','householder'};
tol = 100*eps;
>> tic
>> x7=mdivideByDecomposing_(A,b,decomposer,tol);
>> toc
Elapsed time is 48.728098 seconds.
>> norm(b-A*x7)
=   3.8295e-008
```

4.7 LINEAR SYSTEMS ARISING FROM INTERPOLATION

For the convenience of notations, all indices in this section start from 0.

4.7.1 INTRODUCING FUNCTION INTERPOLATION

In a domain $[x_0, x_n]$, for an univariate known or unknown function $y(x)$, the usual one-dimensional interpolation problem is stated as follows:

1. Choose $n + 1$ known functions $f_0(x), f_1(x), f_2(x), \ldots, f_n(x)$ as function bases for the $n + 1$-dimensional univariate function space $\mathbb{F}(x)$. The common choices for $\mathbb{F}(x)$ are nth order polynomial $P_n(x)$ and nth order trigonometric function $T_n(x)$. The common choices for $[f_0(x), f_1(x), f_2(x), \ldots, f_n(x)]$ can be one of the following:

a. $\left[\frac{(x-x_1)(x-x_2)\cdots(x-x_n)}{(x_0-x_1)(x_0-x_1)\cdots(x_0-x_n)}, \frac{(x-x_0)(x-x_1)\cdots(x-x_n)}{(x_1-x_0)(x_1-x_2)\cdots(x_1-x_n)}, \ldots, \frac{(x-x_0)(x-x_1)\cdots(x-x_{n-1})}{(x_n-x_0)(x_n-x_1)\cdots(x_n-x_{n-1})}\right]$ for $P_n(x)$.

b. $\left[1, (x-x_0), (x-x_0)(x-x_1), \ldots, (x-x_0)(x-x_1)\cdots(x-x_{n-1})\right]$ for $P_n(x)$.

c. $\left[1, x, x^2, \ldots, x^n\right]$ for $P_n(x)$.

d. $\left[1, (x-x_0), \frac{1}{2!}(x-x_0)^2, \ldots, \frac{1}{n!}(x-x_0)^n\right]$ for $P_n(x)$.

e. $\left[1, e^{ik\theta}, e^{i2k\theta}, \ldots, e^{i(n-1)k\theta}\right]$ for $T_n(x)$, where $i = \sqrt{-1}$, $e = 2.718281828459046\cdots$, $\theta = 2\pi/n$ and $k = (x-x_0)/\Delta$.

f. $\left[\sin(k\theta), \sin(2k\theta), \ldots, \sin((n-1)k\theta)\right]$ for $T_n(x)$, $\theta = \pi/n$ and $k = (x-x_0)/\Delta$.

g. $\left[\frac{1}{2}, \cos(k\theta), \cos(2k\theta), \ldots, \cos((n-1)k\theta), \frac{1}{2}\cos(nk\theta)\right]$ for $T_n(x)$, $\theta = \frac{\pi}{n}$ and $k = (x-x_0)/\Delta$.

h. etc.

2. We approximate $y(x)$ in the following form:

$$y(x) \approx f(x) = c_0 f_0(x) + c_1 f_1(x) + c_2 f_2(x) + \cdots + c_n f_n(x), \tag{4.62}$$

where $c_0, c_1, \ldots, c_n$ are $n+1$ unknown coefficients independent of the univariate x.

3. To determine the $n+1$ unknown coefficients $c_0, c_1, \ldots, c_n$, we introduce $n+1$ independent arbitrarily chosen conditions. The common chosen conditions can be one of the following:

a. $y_k = y(x_k) = f(x_k), k = 0, 1, 2, \ldots, n$.

b. $y_k = y(x_k) = f(x_k), y'_k = y'(x_k) = f'(x_k), k = 0, 1, \ldots, n/2$.

c. $y_0 = f(x_0), y'_0 = f'(x_0), y''_0 = f''(x_0), \ldots, y_0^{(n)} = f^{(n)}(x_0)$.

d. etc.

   The approximation of $y(x)$ by the interpolation $f(x)$ is solely determined by the choice of the function space $\mathbb{F}(x)$. The choice of $\mathbb{F}(x)$ should be determined based on the full or limited understanding of $y(x)$. If $y(x)$ happens to be inside $\mathbb{F}(x)$, then $y(x) = f(x)$. The choice of the function bases and the specification of $n+1$ independent conditions are a matter of convenience: easy calculation of $n+1$ coefficients $c_0, c_1, \ldots, c_n$ from the specified conditions of $y(x)$ and easy calculation of $f(x)$ from the determined $c_0, c_1, \ldots, c_n$, according to Eq. (4.62). Once the function bases $\left[f_0(x), f_1(x), \ldots, f_n(x)\right]$ are decided, the interpolation can be conveniently expressed as matrix computations. The matrix arising from the interpolation has a special structure. The special structure is exploited for the calculations of the interpolation,

$$\mathbf{y} = \begin{bmatrix} y_0 \\ y_1 \\ \vdots \\ y_n \end{bmatrix} = \begin{bmatrix} f_0(x_0) & f_1(x_0) & \cdots & f_n(x_0) \\ f_0(x_1) & f_1(x_1) & \cdots & f_n(x_1) \\ \vdots & \vdots & \cdots & \vdots \\ f_0(x_n) & f_1(x_n) & \cdots & f_n(x_n) \end{bmatrix} \begin{bmatrix} c_0 \\ c_1 \\ \vdots \\ c_n \end{bmatrix} = \mathbf{Fc}, \tag{4.63a}$$

$$y(x) \approx f(x) = \left[f_0(x), f_1(x), \ldots, f_n(x)\right] \mathbf{c}. \tag{4.63b}$$

The matrix computations arising from the general function bases $[f_0(x), f_1(x), f_2(x), \ldots, f_n(x)]$ and the conditions 3a are summarized below.[5]

-1. Inverse (Lagrange, Newton, Vandermonde, Fourier, Sine, Cosine) Transform: $\mathbf{c} = \mathbf{F}^{-1}\mathbf{y}$.

0. Function Interpolation: $y(x) \approx f(x) = f_k(x)c_k$.

1. (Lagrange, Newton, Vandermonde, Fourier, Sine, Cosine) Transform: $\mathbf{y} = \mathbf{Fc}$.

4.7.2 POLYNOMIAL INTERPOLATION

Lagrange Interpolation It is specified as the interpolation of function bases 1a and conditions 3a, of Section 4.7.1, that is,

$$\text{Find } f(x) = \sum_{l=0}^{n} c_l \frac{(x - x_0) \cdots (x - x_{l-1})(x - x_{l+1}) \cdots (x - x_n)}{(x_l - x_0) \cdots (x_l - x_{l-1})(x_l - x_{l+1}) \cdots (x_l - x_n)} \tag{4.64}$$

to satisfy $f(x_k) = y_k, k = 0, 1, 2, \ldots, n$.

Following Eq. (4.63a), from Eq. (4.64), we obtain $\mathbf{y} = \mathbf{Ic} = \mathbf{c}$.

Newton Interpolation It is specified as the interpolation of function bases 1b and conditions 3a of Section 4.7.1, that is,

$$\text{Find } f(x) = c_0 + c_1(x - x_0) + c_2(x - x_0)(x - x_1) + \cdots + c_n(x - x_0)(x - x_1) \cdots (x - x_{n-1})$$
$$\text{to satisfy } f(x_k) = y_k, k = 0, 1, 2, \ldots, n. \tag{4.65}$$

From the chosen function bases and the conditions, we obtain the following equations:

$$\mathbf{y} = \begin{bmatrix} y_0 \\ y_1 \\ y_2 \\ \vdots \\ y_n \end{bmatrix} = \begin{bmatrix} 1 & 0 & 0 & 0 & \cdots & 0 \\ 1 & N_{11} & 0 & 0 & \cdots & 0 \\ 1 & N_{21} & N_{22} & 0 & \cdots & 0 \\ \vdots & \vdots & \vdots & \vdots & \vdots & \vdots \\ 1 & N_{n1} & N_{n2} & N_{n3} & \cdots & N_{nn} \end{bmatrix} \begin{bmatrix} c_0 \\ c_1 \\ c_2 \\ \vdots \\ c_n \end{bmatrix} = \mathbf{Nc}, \tag{4.66a}$$

$$N_{kl} = (x_k - x_0)(x_k - x_1) \cdots (x_k - x_{l-1}), \quad k \geq l. \tag{4.66b}$$

---

[5] 'Transform' and 'Inverse Transform' may be defined in the opposite sense, for example, in [51]. The exponential in the Fourier function bases may also have a difference in sign. These differences are not important in theory and in practice.
In Eq. (4.63a), if $\mathbf{F}$ is orthogonal, we say c_l is the component of $\mathbf{y}$ on $\mathbf{F}(:, l)$ and y_k is the component of $\mathbf{c}$ on $\mathbf{F}(k, :)'$.

$\mathbf{c} = \mathbf{N}^{-1}\mathbf{y}$ can be calculated by the forward substitution,

$$c_0 = y_0,$$

$$c_1 = \frac{y_1 - y_0}{x_1 - x_0} = y_{01},$$

$$c_2 = \frac{1}{x_2 - x_1}\left(\frac{y_2 - y_0}{x_2 - x_0} - y_{01}\right) = y_{012},$$

$$c_3 = \frac{1}{x_3 - x_2}\left(\frac{1}{x_3 - x_1}\left(\frac{y_3 - y_0}{x_3 - x_0} - y_{01}\right) - y_{012}\right) = y_{0123}, \tag{4.67}$$

$$\vdots$$

$$c_n = \frac{1}{x_n - x_{n-1}}\left(\cdots\left(\frac{1}{x_n - x_1}\left(\frac{y_n - y_0}{x_n - x_0} - y_{01}\right) - y_{012}\right) - \cdots - y_{012\cdots(n-1)}\right) = y_{012\cdots n}.$$

The right hand side, $y_{012\cdots k}$, is called the kth order divided difference of $f(x)$ at $x_0, x_1, \ldots, x_k$. It is the coefficient of x^k of the unique kth order polynomial passing through $(x_l, y_l), l = 0, 1, 2, \ldots, k$. The unique kth order polynomial can also be represented by the Lagrange interpolation, that is,

$$\sum_{l=0}^{k} y_l \frac{(x - x_0)(x - x_1)\cdots(x - x_{l-1})(x - x_{l+1})\cdots(x - x_k)}{(x_l - x_0)(x_l - x_1)\cdots(x_l - x_{l-1})(x_l - x_{l+1})\cdots(x_l - x_k)}.$$

Comparing the coefficient of x^k, we obtain another expression for c_k,

$$c_k = y_{012\cdots k} = \sum_{l=0}^{k} \frac{y_l}{(x_l - x_0)(x_l - x_1)\cdots(x_l - x_{l-1})(x_l - x_{l+1})\cdots(x_l - x_k)} \tag{4.68}$$

Either Eq. (4.67) or Eq. (4.68) can be used to calculate c_k. But the recursive relationship derived below is what is implemented in the MATLAB function `polynomialInterpolation_.m`.

The same nth order polynomial passing through $(x_k, y_k), k = 0, 1, 2, \ldots, n$ can also be written as

$$f(x) = b_0 + b_1(x - x_n) + b_2(x - x_n)(x - x_{n-1}) + \cdots + b_n(x - x_n)(x - x_{n-1})\cdots(x - x_1). \tag{4.69}$$

Comparing the coefficient of x^n of Eqs. (4.65) and (4.69), we see that $b_n = c_n$. Subtracting Eq. (4.65) from Eq. (4.69), we obtain

$$(x - x_1)(x - x_2)\cdots(x - x_{n-2})(c_n(x - x_0) - b_n(x - x_n)) + (c_{n-1} - b_{n-1})x^{n-1} + P_{n-2}(x) \equiv 0.$$

The coefficient of x^{n-1} is 0, therefore $c_n = \frac{b_{n-1} - c_{n-1}}{x_n - x_0}$. Using the notation of the divided difference,

$$c_n = y_{012\cdots n} = \frac{y_{n\cdots 21} - y_{01\cdots(n-1)}}{x_n - x_0} = \frac{y_{12\cdots n} - y_{01\cdots(n-1)}}{x_n - x_0}. \tag{4.70}$$

The last equality holds because $y_{n\cdots 21}$ is symmetrical with respect to any two indices as seen in Eq. (4.68).

To summarize, $\mathbf{c} = \mathbf{N}^{-1}\mathbf{y}$ is calculated recursively as shown in the following divided difference table:

$$
\begin{array}{llll}
x_0 \ y_0 \\
\quad\quad y_{01} \\
x_1 \ y_1 \quad\quad y_{012} \\
\quad\quad y_{12} \quad\quad y_{0123} \\
x_2 \ y_2 \quad\quad y_{123} \quad\quad y_{01234} \\
\quad\quad y_{23} \quad\quad y_{1234} \\
x_3 \ y_3 \quad\quad y_{234} \\
\quad\quad y_{34} \\
x_4 \ y_4 \\
\quad \vdots \quad \vdots
\end{array}
$$

Vandermonde Interpolation It is specified as the interpolation of function bases 1c and conditions 3a of Section 4.7.1, that is,

$$
\begin{aligned}
&\text{Find } f(x) = c_0 + c_1 x + c_2 x^2 + \cdots + c_n x^n \\
&\text{to satisfy } f(x_k) = y_k, k = 0,1,2,\ldots,n.
\end{aligned}
\tag{4.71}
$$

Following Eq. (4.63a), the conditions $f(x_k) = y_k, k = 0,1,2,\ldots,n$ are expressed as follows:

$$
\mathbf{y} = \begin{bmatrix} y_0 \\ y_1 \\ y_2 \\ \vdots \\ y_n \end{bmatrix} = \begin{bmatrix} 1 & x_0 & x_0^2 & \cdots & x_0^n \\ 1 & x_1 & x_1^2 & \cdots & x_1^n \\ 1 & x_2 & x_2^2 & \cdots & x_2^n \\ \vdots & \vdots & \vdots & \cdots & \vdots \\ 1 & x_n & x_n^2 & \cdots & x_n^n \end{bmatrix} \begin{bmatrix} c_0 \\ c_1 \\ c_2 \\ \vdots \\ c_n \end{bmatrix} = \mathbf{Vc}.
\tag{4.72}
$$

The solution of $\mathbf{c} = \mathbf{V}^{-1}\mathbf{y}$ is very economically obtained by comparing the coefficients of the like powers of x in the interpolation polynomial expressed in Vandermonde's form and Newton's form,

$$
\begin{aligned}
&c_0 + c_1 x + c_2 x^2 + \cdots + c_n x^n = \\
&b_0 + b_1(x - x_0) + b_2(x - x_0)(x - x_1) + \cdots + b_n(x - x_0)(x - x_1)\cdots(x - x_{n-1}) = \\
&b_0 + (x - x_0)(b_1 + (x - x_1)(b_2 + (x - x_2)(b_3 + \cdots(x - x_{n-2})(b_{n-1} + (x - x_{n-1})b_n)))).
\end{aligned}
\tag{4.73}
$$

By equating the coefficients of x^n of both sides, we obtain $c_n = b_n$. Then equating the coefficients of x^k, we obtain the recursive relation $c_k = b_k - c_{k+1}x_{k+1}, k = n - 1,\ldots,2,1,0$.

Listing of MATLAB Function for Polynomial Interpolation The two kinds of polynomial interpolations (Newton, Vandermonde) discussed in this subsection are collectively implemented in one MATLAB function polynomialInterpolation_.m. In polynomialInterpolation_.m, the two interpolations are accessed by the input argument algo='newton' or algo='vandermonde'. The three kinds of calculations (inverse transform, interpolation, transform) are accessed by the input argument iw=-1,0,+1. Depending on the input values of algo and iw, the input and output arguments of interpolation_.m take different meanings. They will be explained with the example below.

Algorithm 4.11

Matrix computations arising from polynomial function interpolation

```
%algo='newton','vandermonde'.
%iw=-1: inv(P)*y->y; =0: f_l(chi)y_l->y; =+1: P*y->y
function y = polynomialInterpolation_(x,y,algo,iw,chi)

n = length(x);
if (n ~= length(y)) error('polynomialInterpolation_:␣size␣error'); end
if (~exist('algo','var') || isempty(algo)) algo = 'newton'; end
algo = lower(algo);
if (~exist('iw','var') || isempty(iw)) iw = 0; end
if (iw==0 && (~exist('chi','var') || isempty(chi))) chi = 0.0; end

if(strcmp(algo,'newton') && iw==-1)                    %c = inv(N)*y
    for k=1:n-1
        for l=n:-1:k+1 y(l) = (y(l)-y(l-1))/(x(l)-x(l-k)); end
    end
elseif(strcmp(algo,'newton') && iw==0)
    c = y;   y = c(1);   fl = 1.0;
    for l=2:n   fl = fl*(chi-x(l-1));   f = f + fl*c(l);   end
elseif(strcmp(algo,'newton') && iw==+1)
    c = y;   y(1:n) = y(1);
    for k=2:n
        fl = 1.0;
        for l=2:k   fl = fl*(x(k)-x(l-1));   y(k) = y(k) + fl*c(l);   end
    end
elseif(strcmp(algo,'vandermonde') && iw==-1)
    y = interpolation_(x,y,'newton',iw);
    for k=n-1:-1:1
        for l=k:n-1 y(l) = y(l) - y(l+1)*x(k); end
    end
elseif(strcmp(algo,'vandermonde') && iw==0)
    c = y;   fl = 1.0;   y = c(1);
    for l=2:n   fl = fl*chi;   y = y + fl*c(l);   end
elseif(strcmp(algo,'vandermonde') && iw==+1)
    c = y;   y(1:n) = c(1);
    for k=1:n
        fl = 1.0;
        for l=2:n   fl = fl*x(k);   y(k) = y(k) + fl*c(l);   end
    end
else
    error('polynomailInterpolation_:␣wrong␣input␣argument.');
end
```

We use the following three polynomials to demonstrate the use of `polynomialInterpolation_.m`.

$$p_2(x) = 0 - (x + 2) + \frac{1}{2}(x + 2)(x + 1) = -1 + \frac{1}{2}x + \frac{1}{2}x^2$$

$$p_3(x) = p_2(x) - \frac{1}{4}(x + 2)(x + 1)(x - 1) = -\frac{1}{2} + \frac{3}{4}x - \frac{1}{4}x^3 \qquad (4.74)$$

$$p_4(x) = p_3(x) + \frac{1}{8}(x + 2)(x + 1)(x - 1)(x - 2) = -\frac{1}{2} + \frac{3}{4}x - \frac{1}{4}x^3$$

The three polynomials are plotted with the following MATLAB script. In Fig. 4.2, the curve $p_{04}(x)$ is the cubic polynomial interpolation constructed from $p_4(x)$, see the discussion below.

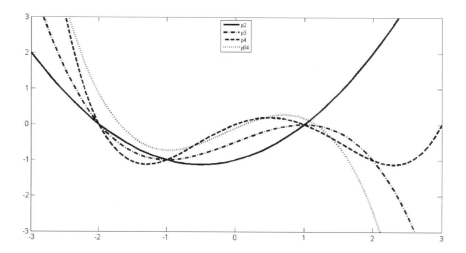

FIGURE 4.2

Polynomials: $p_2(x), p_3(x), p_4(x), y_4(x)$.

```
x = zeros(61,1); p2 = zeros(61,1); p3 = zeros(61,1); p4 = zeros(61,1);

x(1) = -3;
for k=1:61
    xk = x(k);
    p2(k) = -(xk+2) + 0.5*(xk+2)*(xk+1);
    p3(k) = p2(k) -0.25*(xk+2)*(xk+1)*(xk-1);
    p4(k) = p3(k) +0.125*(xk+2)*(xk+1)*(xk-1)*(xk-2);
    x(k+1) = x(k) + 0.1;
end
x = x(1:61);

hold off;
plot(x,p2,'red');
hold on;
plot(x,p3,'green');
hold on;
plot(x,p4,'blue');
axis([-3,3,-3,3]);
legend('p2','p3','p4','Location','North');
```

We use four points from each curve to construct an interpolation for the approximation of each curve.

```
>> x2=[x(11);x(21);x(41);x(51)]'
   -2.0000   -1.0000    1.0000    2.0000
>> y2=[p2(11);p2(21);p2(41);p2(51)]'
   -0.0000   -1.0000    0.0000    2.0000
>> c2=polynomialInterpolation_(x2,y2,'newton',-1)
   -0.0000   -1.0000    0.5000   -0.0000        %Newton form of p2(x), c2(4)=0!
```

```
>> b2=polynomialInterpolation_(x2,y2,'vandermonde',-1)
   -1.0000     0.5000     0.5000    -0.0000        %Vandermonde form of p2(x), b2(4)=0!

>> x3=[x(11);x(21);x(41);x(51)]'
   -2.0000    -1.0000     1.0000     2.0000
>> y3=[p3(11);p3(21);p3(41);p3(51)]'
   -0.0000    -1.0000     0.0000    -1.0000
>> c3=polynomialInterpolation_(x3,y3,'newton',-1)
   -0.0000    -1.0000     0.5000    -0.2500        %Newton form of p3(x)
>> b3=polynomialInterpolation_(x3,y3,'vandermonde',-1)
   -0.5000     0.7500          0    -0.2500        %Vandermonde form of p3(x)

>> x4=[x(11);x(21);x(41);x(51)]'
   -2.0000    -1.0000     1.0000     2.0000
>> y4=[p4(11);p4(21);p4(41);p4(51)]'
   -0.0000    -1.0000    -0.0000    -1.0000
>> c4=polynomialInterpolation_(x4,y4,'newton',-1)
   -0.0000    -1.0000     0.5000    -0.2500      %Newton form: interpolated p4(x)
>> b4=polynomialInterpolation_(x4,y4,'vandermonde',-1)
   -0.5000     0.7500     0.0000    -0.2500      %Vandermonde form: interpolated p4(x)
```

The outputs of $p_2(x)$ and $p_3(x)$ match the coefficients of $p_2(x)$ and $p_3(x)$ given in Eq. (4.74). This shows that four points are enough to present either a quadratic or cubic polynomial. The output of $p_4(x)$ does not match the coefficients of $p_4(x)$ given in Eq. (4.74). Actually the output is same as the output for $p_3(x)$. This is not surprising, because x3,y3 and x4,y4 are just the four intersections of $p_3(x)$ and $p_4(x)$ shown in Fig. 4.2. To present a quartic polynomial, at least five points are required.

Now we use different four points from each curve to construct the interpolation function for each curve. The interpolation function constructed from any four points from $p_2(x)$ is exactly same as $p_2(x)$. For $p_2(x)$, the Newton form constructed from any four different points will have different coefficients. Because the Vandermonde form is unique $p_2(x)$, the Vandermonde coefficients from any four different points will be exactly same. The same conclusion is true for $p_3(x)$. The conclusion is not true for $p_4(x)$. For $p_4(x)$, different cubic polynomials are obtained from four different points.

```
>> x2=[x(3);x(50);x(10);x(20)]'
   -2.8000     1.9000    -2.1000    -1.1000
>> y2=[p2(3);p2(50);p2(10);p2(20)]'
    1.5200     1.7550     0.1550    -0.9450
>> c2=polynomialInterpolation_(x2,y2,'newton',-1)
    1.5200     0.0500     0.5000          0        %Same p2(x), different Newton form
>> b2=polynomialInterpolation_(x2,y2,'vandermonde',-1)
   -1.0000     0.5000     0.5000          0        %Same Vandermonde form

>> x3=[x(61);x(40);x(20);x(1)]'
    3.0000     0.9000    -1.1000    -3.0000
>> y3=[p3(61);p3(40);p3(20);p3(1)]'
   -5.0000    -0.0072    -0.9923     4.0000
>> c3=polynomialInterpolation_(x3,y3,'newton',-1)
   -5.0000    -2.3775    -0.7000    -0.2500        %Same p3(x), different Newton form
>> b3=polynomialInterpolation_(x3,y3,'vandermonde',-1)
   -0.5000     0.7500    -0.0000    -0.2500        %Same Vandermonde form

>> x4=[x(5);x(25);x(35);x(45)]'
   -2.6000    -0.6000     0.4000     1.4000
>> y4=[p4(5);p4(25);p4(35);p4(45)]'
```

```
     3.9312    -0.6048     0.1872    -0.3808
>> c4=polynomialInterpolation_(x4,y4,'newton',-1)
     3.9312    -2.2680     1.0200    -0.4250        %Different interpolated p4(x)
>> b4=polynomialInterpolation_(x4,y4,'vandermonde',-1)
    -0.1092     0.8770    -0.1700    -0.4250        %Different interpolated p4(x)
```

To show the cubic polynomial constructed from x4,y4, we plot it by the following script. From Fig. 4.2, it is neither $p_3(x)$ nor $p_4(x)$.

```
p04 = zeros(61,1);
for k=1:61
    xk = x(k);
    p04(k) = polynomialInterpolation_(x4,b4,'vandermonde',0,xk);      %iw=0
end
plot(x,p04,'black');
```

Contrarily, to use iw=+1 in polynomialInterpolation_ with c4 or b4 will produce the original y4.

```
>> y04=polynomialInterpolation_(x4,c4,'newton',1)               %iw=+1
     3.9312    -0.6048     0.1872    -0.3808        %Same as y4
>> y004=polynomialInterpolation_(x4,b4,'vandermonde',1)         %iw=+1
     3.9312    -0.6048     0.1872    -0.3808        %Same as y4
```

4.7.3 TRIGONOMETRIC INTERPOLATION

For the practical purpose, we consider only the case that n is an integer power of 2, such as $n = 2,4,8,16$. The reason for this restriction will be clear later.

Complex Valued Fourier Interpolation (Complex Valued FFT) It is specified as the interpolation of function bases 1e and conditions 3a of Section 4.7.1, that is,

$$\text{Find } f(x) = c_0 + c_1 e^{ik\theta} + c_2 e^{ik2\theta} + \cdots + c_{n-1}e^{ik(n-1)\theta}, \quad \text{where } i = \sqrt{-1}, \theta = \frac{2\pi}{n} \text{ and}$$
$$k = \frac{x - x0}{\Delta}, \text{ to satisfy } f(x_0 + k\Delta)) = y_k, k = 0,1,2,\ldots,n-1. \tag{4.75}$$

Following Eq. (4.63a), the conditions $f(x_0 + k\Delta) = y_k, k = 0,1,2,\ldots,n-1$ are expressed as follows. $n-1$ is denoted as m below,

$$\mathbf{y} = \begin{bmatrix} y_0 \\ y_1 \\ y_2 \\ \vdots \\ y_m \end{bmatrix} = \begin{bmatrix} 1 & 1 & 1 & 1 & \cdots & 1 \\ 1 & \omega & \omega^2 & \omega^3 & \cdots & \omega^m \\ 1 & \omega^2 & \omega^4 & \omega^6 & \cdots & \omega^{2m} \\ \vdots & \vdots & \vdots & \vdots & \cdots & \vdots \\ 1 & \omega^m & \omega^{m2} & \omega^{m3} & \cdots & \omega^{mm} \end{bmatrix} \begin{bmatrix} c_0 \\ c_1 \\ c_2 \\ \vdots \\ c_m \end{bmatrix} = \mathbf{Fc}, \tag{4.76a}$$

$$\omega = e^{i\frac{2\pi}{n}}; \quad F_{kl} = e^{\frac{i2\pi}{n}k \times l} = \omega^{kl} = \omega^{kl \bmod n}, \tag{4.76b}$$

$$\mathbf{F}(k,:) = e^{\frac{i2\pi}{n}k[0,1,2,\ldots,m]}; \quad \mathbf{F}(:,l) = e^{\frac{i2\pi}{n}[0,1,2,\ldots,m]'l}, \tag{4.76c}$$

$$y_n = y_0; \quad c_n = c_0. \tag{4.76d}$$

The efficiency of calculating $\mathbf{c} = \mathbf{F}^{-1}\mathbf{y}$ and $\mathbf{y} = \mathbf{Fc}$ can be vastly improved by taking advantage of the simple relation Eq. (4.76b). In fact, the improvement is a reduction of computation from $O(n^3)$ to $O(n\log_2 n)$ for $\mathbf{c} = \mathbf{F}^{-1}\mathbf{y}$, and from $O(n^2)$ to $O(n\log_2 n)$ for $\mathbf{y} = \mathbf{Fc}$.

First, we show that $\mathbf{F}^{-1} = \frac{1}{n}\mathbf{F}' = \frac{1}{n}\overline{\mathbf{F}}$.[6] This is because[7]

$$\mathbf{F}(k,:)\overline{\mathbf{F}}(:,l) = e^{i0(k-l)\theta} + e^{i1(k-l)\theta} + e^{i2(k-l)\theta} + \cdots + e^{i(n-1)(k-l)\theta}$$

$$= 1 + 2\left(\cos\left((k-l)\theta\right) + \cos\left(2(k-l)\theta\right) + \cdots + \cos\left(\frac{n-2}{2}(k-l)\theta\right)\right) + \cos\left(\frac{n}{2}(k-l)\theta\right)$$

$$= \begin{cases} n & k = l \\ 0 & k \neq l. \end{cases}$$

Therefore, $\mathbf{c} = \mathbf{F}^{-1}\mathbf{y} = \frac{1}{n}\overline{\mathbf{F}}\mathbf{y}$, which has the same amount of calculation as $\mathbf{y} = \mathbf{F}\mathbf{c}$.

Second, we show that $\mathbf{y} = \mathbf{F}\mathbf{c}$ can be calculated recursively. We write Eq. (4.76a) as follows:

$$y_k = \sum_{l=0}^{n-1} c_l e^{i\frac{2\pi}{n}kl} = \sum_{l=0}^{n/2-1} c_{2l} e^{i\frac{2\pi}{n}k(2l)} + \sum_{l=0}^{n/2-1} c_{2l+1} e^{i\frac{2\pi}{n}k(2l+1)}$$

$$= \sum_{l=0}^{n/2-1} c_{2l} e^{i\frac{2\pi}{n/2}kl} + e^{i\frac{2\pi}{n}k} \sum_{l=0}^{n/2-1} c_{2l+1} e^{i\frac{2\pi}{n/2}kl}; \quad k = 0,1,2,\ldots,n/2-1, \qquad (4.77)$$

$$y_{n/2+k} = \sum_{l=0}^{n/2-1} c_{2l} e^{i\frac{2\pi}{n/2}kl} - e^{i\frac{2\pi}{n}k} \sum_{l=0}^{n/2-1} c_{2l+1} e^{i\frac{2\pi}{n/2}kl}; \quad k = 0,1,2,\ldots,n/2-1.$$

In Eq. (4.77), the first term is the Fourier transform from the even numbered points, while the second term is the Fourier transform from the odd numbered points. We write Eq. (4.77) in the following matrix form, where the subscript of a matrix, such as n in $\mathbf{F}_n$, denotes the size of the matrix

$$\mathbf{y} = \mathbf{F}_n\mathbf{c} = \begin{bmatrix} \mathbf{I}_{n/2} & \mathbf{\Omega}_{n/2} \\ \mathbf{I}_{n/2} & -\mathbf{\Omega}_{n/2} \end{bmatrix} \begin{bmatrix} \mathbf{F}_{n/2}\mathbf{c}(0:2:n-1) \\ \mathbf{F}_{n/2}\mathbf{c}(1:2:n-1) \end{bmatrix}, \qquad (4.78a)$$

$$\mathbf{\Omega}_{n/2} = \begin{bmatrix} 1 & & & & \\ & \omega_n^1 & & & \\ & & \omega_n^2 & & \\ & & & \ddots & \\ & & & & \omega_n^{n/2-1} \end{bmatrix}; \qquad \omega_n = e^{i\frac{2\pi}{n}}. \qquad (4.78b)$$

Similarly, we can apply Eq. (4.78) to $\mathbf{F}_{n/2}\mathbf{c}(0:2:n-1)$ and $\mathbf{F}_{n/2}\mathbf{c}(1:2:n-1)$ with n replaced by $n/2$. We continue to apply Eq. (4.78) to $\mathbf{c}$ of the halved length until we reach $\mathbf{F}_2[c_a; c_b]$. Here, $0 \leq a,b \leq n$, the indices obtained by repeated even-odd partitions of $(0,1,2,\ldots,n-1)$. But $\mathbf{F}_2[c_a; c_b]$ is just

$$\mathbf{F}_2\begin{bmatrix} c_a \\ c_b \end{bmatrix} = \begin{bmatrix} 1 & 1 \\ 1 & -1 \end{bmatrix}\begin{bmatrix} c_a \\ c_b \end{bmatrix} = \begin{bmatrix} c_a + c_b \\ c_a - c_b \end{bmatrix}.$$

---

[6]$\overline{\mathbf{F}}$ means taking the complex conjugate of each component of $\mathbf{F}$. $\overline{\mathbf{F}}'$ is usually denoted as $\mathbf{F}^H$.

[7]The equality can be verified by using the Lagrange trigonometric identity, see [37].

$$\sum_{k=0}^{n} \cos(k\theta) = -\frac{1}{2} + \frac{\sin\left(n + \frac{1}{2}\right)\theta}{2\sin\left(\frac{1}{2}\theta\right)}.$$

To illustrate the recursive process more clearly, we take $n = 8$ as an example. For the reason to be clear shortly, we will use the binary to denote the index of $\mathbf{c}$. Note that the symbol $\otimes$ in Eq. (4.79) is the outer product introduced in Section 1.1.1,

$$
\mathbf{F}_8 \begin{bmatrix} c_{000} \\ c_{001} \\ c_{010} \\ c_{011} \\ c_{100} \\ c_{101} \\ c_{110} \\ c_{111} \end{bmatrix} = \left(\mathbf{I}_1 \otimes \begin{bmatrix} \mathbf{I}_4 & \Omega_4 \\ \mathbf{I}_4 & -\Omega_4 \end{bmatrix} \right) \begin{bmatrix} \mathbf{F}_4 \begin{bmatrix} c_{000} \\ c_{010} \\ c_{100} \\ c_{110} \end{bmatrix} \\ \mathbf{F}_4 \begin{bmatrix} c_{001} \\ c_{011} \\ c_{101} \\ c_{111} \end{bmatrix} \end{bmatrix}
$$

$$
= \left(\mathbf{I}_1 \otimes \begin{bmatrix} \mathbf{I}_4 & \Omega_4 \\ \mathbf{I}_4 & -\Omega_4 \end{bmatrix} \right) \left(\mathbf{I}_2 \otimes \begin{bmatrix} \mathbf{I}_2 & \Omega_2 \\ \mathbf{I}_2 & -\Omega_2 \end{bmatrix} \right) \begin{bmatrix} \mathbf{F}_2 \begin{bmatrix} c_{000} \\ c_{100} \end{bmatrix} \\ \mathbf{F}_2 \begin{bmatrix} c_{010} \\ c_{110} \end{bmatrix} \\ \mathbf{F}_2 \begin{bmatrix} c_{010} \\ c_{101} \end{bmatrix} \\ \mathbf{F}_2 \begin{bmatrix} c_{011} \\ c_{111} \end{bmatrix} \end{bmatrix} \tag{4.79}
$$

$$
= \left(\mathbf{I}_1 \otimes \begin{bmatrix} \mathbf{I}_4 & \Omega_4 \\ \mathbf{I}_4 & -\Omega_4 \end{bmatrix} \right) \left(\mathbf{I}_2 \otimes \begin{bmatrix} \mathbf{I}_2 & \Omega_2 \\ \mathbf{I}_2 & -\Omega_2 \end{bmatrix} \right) \left(\mathbf{I}_4 \otimes \begin{bmatrix} 1 & 1 \\ 1 & -1 \end{bmatrix} \right) \begin{bmatrix} c_{000} \\ c_{100} \\ c_{010} \\ c_{110} \\ c_{001} \\ c_{101} \\ c_{011} \\ c_{111} \end{bmatrix}.
$$

From Eq. (4.79), to calculate $\mathbf{y} = \mathbf{F}_8\mathbf{c}$, first we permute $\mathbf{c}$ from $(0,1,2,3,4,5,6,7)$ to $(0,4,2,6,1,5,3,7)$. In binary, the permutation is $000 \to 000$, $001 \to 100$, $010 \to 010$, $011 \to 110$, $100 \to 001$, $101 \to 101$, $110 \to 011$, $111 \to 111$. The permutation is based on the bit reversal, that is, $b_2 b_1 b_0 \to b_0 b_1 b_2$. Each digit b equals 0 or 1. This is correct because each test of even and odd is to test each b equals 0 or 1 from the lowest bit to the highest bit. After permuting $\mathbf{c}$ by bit reversal, $\mathbf{F}_8$ is decomposed into $\log_2 8 = 3$ sparse factors. Each sparse factor has only two nonzeros per row. The product of each sparse factor with $\mathbf{c}$ takes $O(8)$ operations. Therefore, the total operations for $\mathbf{y} = \mathbf{F}_8\mathbf{c}$ are $O(8 \log_2 8)$. For $\mathbf{y} = \mathbf{F}_n\mathbf{c}$, the conclusion is obtained with 8 replaced by n.

Real Valued Fourier Interpolation (Real Valued FFT) In the following, we consider the calculation of $\mathbf{y} = \mathbf{Fc}$ when $\mathbf{c}$ or $\mathbf{y}$ is real.

When $\mathbf{c}$ is real, from Eq. (4.76), $y_{n-k} = \overline{y}_k, k = 0,1,2,n/2$. This property warrants further efficiency in calculating $\mathbf{y} = \mathbf{Fc}$. We still follow Eq. (4.78) to calculate $\mathbf{y}$. But now we stop the further partition of $\mathbf{c}$. Instead $\mathbf{u} = \mathbf{F}_{n/2}\mathbf{c}(0 : 2 : n - 1)$ and $\mathbf{v} = \mathbf{F}_{n/2}\mathbf{c}(1 : 2 : n - 1)$ are obtained by calculating $\mathbf{z} = \mathbf{F}_{n/2}(\mathbf{c}(0 : 2 : n - 1) + i\mathbf{c}(1 : 2 : n - 1))$, which is an ordinary complex valued FFT just discussed,

$$\mathbf{z} = \mathbf{F}_{n/2}(\mathbf{c}(0 : 2 : n - 1) + i\mathbf{c}(1 : 2 : n - 1)) = \mathbf{u} + i\mathbf{v}, \tag{4.80a}$$

$$z_k = u_k + iv_k; \quad \overline{z}_{n/2-k} = \overline{u}_{n/2-k} + \overline{iv}_{n/2-k} = u_k - iv_k; \quad k = 0,1,2,\ldots,n/4, \tag{4.80b}$$

$$u_k = \frac{1}{2}\left(z_k + \overline{z}_{n/2-k}\right); \quad v_k = \frac{1}{2i}\left(z_k - \overline{z}_{n/2-k}\right); \quad k = 0,1,2,\ldots,n/4, \tag{4.80c}$$

$$u_{n/2-k} = \overline{u}_k; \quad v_{n/2-k} = \overline{v}_k; \quad k = 0,1,2,\ldots,n/4, \tag{4.80d}$$

$$\mathbf{y} = \begin{bmatrix} \mathbf{I}_{n/2} & \Omega_{n/2} \\ \mathbf{I}_{n/2} & -\Omega_{n/2} \end{bmatrix} \begin{bmatrix} \mathbf{u} \\ \mathbf{v} \end{bmatrix}. \tag{4.80e}$$

If $\mathbf{c}$ is real, $\mathbf{y} = \mathbf{F}^{-1}\mathbf{c}$ also satisfies $y_{n-k} = \overline{y}_k, k = 0,1,2,n/2$. $\mathbf{y}$ is calculated as $\mathbf{F}^{-1}\mathbf{c} = \frac{1}{n}\overline{\mathbf{F}\mathbf{c}} = \frac{1}{n}\overline{\mathbf{F}\overline{\mathbf{c}}}$, where $\mathbf{F}\mathbf{c}$ is calculated following Eq. (4.80).

Contrarily, given a complex array $\mathbf{c}$ which satisfies $c_{n-k} = \overline{c}_k, k = 0,1,2,\ldots,n/2$, $\mathbf{y} = \mathbf{F}_n^{-1}\mathbf{c}$ is real. To calculate the real $\mathbf{y}$, we reverse the calculation of Eq. (4.80),

$$\begin{bmatrix} \mathbf{u} \\ \mathbf{v} \end{bmatrix} = \begin{bmatrix} \mathbf{F}_{n/2}\mathbf{y}(0 : 2 : n - 1) \\ \mathbf{F}_{n/2}\mathbf{y}(1 : 2 : n - 1) \end{bmatrix} = \frac{1}{2}\begin{bmatrix} \mathbf{I}_{n/2} & \mathbf{I}_{n/2} \\ \Omega_{n/2} & -\Omega_{n/2} \end{bmatrix}\begin{bmatrix} \mathbf{c}(0 : n/2 - 1) \\ \overline{\mathbf{c}}(n - (n/2 : -1 : 0)) \end{bmatrix}, \tag{4.81a}$$

$$\mathbf{y}(0 : 2 : n - 1) + i\mathbf{y}(1 : 2 : n - 1) = \mathbf{F}_{n/2}^{-1}(\mathbf{u} + i\mathbf{v}). \tag{4.81b}$$

If $\mathbf{c}$ satisfies $c_{n-k} = \overline{c}_k, k = 0,1,2,\ldots,n/2$, $\mathbf{y} = \mathbf{F}\mathbf{c}$ is also real. We use Eq. (4.81) to calculate $\mathbf{F}\mathbf{c}$: $\mathbf{F}\mathbf{c} = \left(\mathbf{F}^{-1}\right)^{-1}\mathbf{c} = \frac{1}{n}\overline{\mathbf{F}^{-1}} = \frac{1}{n}\overline{\mathbf{F}^{-1}\overline{\mathbf{c}}}$.

Sine Interpolation (FsinT) It is specified as the interpolation of function bases of 1g and conditions 3a of Section 4.7.1, that is,

Find $f(x) = c_1 \sin(\check{k}\theta) + c_2 \sin(\check{k}2\theta) + \cdots + c_{n-1}\sin(\check{k}(n-1)\theta)$, where $\theta = \dfrac{\pi}{n}$ and $\check{k} = \dfrac{x - x_0}{\Delta}$

to satisfy $f(x_0 + k\Delta) = y_k, k = 1,2,\ldots,n - 1$.

$$\tag{4.82}$$

Following Eq. (4.63a), the conditions $f(x_0 + k\Delta) = y_k, k = 1,2,\ldots,n - 1$ are expressed as follows. $n - 1$ is denoted as m below,

$$\mathbf{y} = \begin{bmatrix} y_1 \\ y_2 \\ \vdots \\ y_m \end{bmatrix} = \begin{bmatrix} \sin(\theta) & \sin(2\theta) & \sin(3\theta) & \cdots & \sin(m\theta) \\ \sin(2\theta) & \sin(4\theta) & \sin(6\theta) & \cdots & \sin(2m\theta) \\ \vdots & \vdots & \vdots & \cdots & \vdots \\ \sin(m\theta) & \sin(m2\theta) & \sin(m3\theta) & \vdots & \sin(m^2\theta) \end{bmatrix}\begin{bmatrix} c_1 \\ c_2 \\ \vdots \\ c_m \end{bmatrix} = \mathbf{S}\mathbf{c}. \tag{4.83}$$

Using trigonometric product-to-sum and Lagrange identity we can show that $\mathbf{S}(k,:)\mathbf{S}(:,l) = \frac{n}{2}$ if $k = l$ otherwise 0. This means $\mathbf{S}^{-1} = \frac{2}{n}\mathbf{S}$. Therefore, $\mathbf{c} = \mathbf{S}^{-1}\mathbf{y} = \frac{2}{n}\mathbf{S}\mathbf{y}$.

Now we show how to use Eq. (4.80) for real valued FFT to calculate $\mathbf{y} = \mathbf{S}\mathbf{c}$. First we introduce an auxiliary array,

$$b_0 = 0,$$

$$b_l = \sin\left(\frac{l\pi}{n}\right)(c_l + c_{n-l}) + \frac{1}{2}(c_l - c_{n-l}), \quad l = 1,2,\ldots,n - 1.$$

Then we calculate the real valued FFT of $b_0, b_1, b_2, \ldots, b_{n-1}$: $z_k = \sum_{l=0}^{n-1} d_l e^{i\frac{2\pi}{n}kl} = u_k + iv_k$. Notice that the first term of d_l is symmetric about $l = \frac{n}{2}$ and the second term of d_l is anti-symmetric about $l = n/2$. Considering the symmetric and anti-symmetric valued FFT, u_k and v_k can be represented as follows:

$$
\begin{aligned}
u_k &= \sum_{l=1}^{n-1} \sin\left(\frac{l\pi}{n}\right)(c_l + c_{n-l})\cos\left(\frac{2\pi}{n}kl\right) \\
&= \sum_{l=1}^{n-1} c_l \left(\sin\left((2k+1)l\frac{\pi}{n}\right) - \sin\left((2k-1)l\frac{\pi}{n}\right)\right) = y_{2k+1} - y_{2k-1}, \\
v_k &= \sum_{l=1}^{n-1} \frac{1}{2}(c_l - c_{n-l})\sin\left(\frac{2\pi}{n}kl\right) \\
&= \sum_{l=1}^{n-1} c_l \sin\left(\frac{2\pi}{n}kl\right) = y_{2k}.
\end{aligned}
\tag{4.84}
$$

Therefore, the components of $\mathbf{y} = \mathbf{S}\mathbf{c}$ can be determined as follows:

$$
y_{2k} = v_k, \quad y_{2k+1} = y_{2k-1} + u_k \quad k = 0, 1, 2, \ldots, \frac{n}{2} - 1.
\tag{4.85}
$$

For $k = 0$, $y_1 = y_{-1} + u_0$. According to the definition of Eq. (4.83), $y_1 = -y_{-1}$, therefore,

$$
y_1 = \frac{1}{2}u_0.
\tag{4.86}
$$

Cosine Interpolation (FcosT) It is specified as the interpolation of function bases 1g and conditions 3a of Section 4.7.1, that is,

Find $f(x) = \frac{1}{2}c_0 + \cos(\hat{k}\theta)c_1 + \cos(\hat{k}2\theta)c_2 + \cdots + \cos(\hat{k}(n-1)\theta)c_{n-1} + \frac{1}{2}\cos(\hat{k}n\theta)c_n$;

to satisfy $f(x_0 + k\Delta) = y_k, k = 0, 1, 2, \ldots, n$; where $\theta = \frac{\pi}{n}$ and $\hat{k} = \frac{x - x_0}{\Delta}$.
$$\tag{4.87}$$

Following Eq. (4.63a), the conditions $f(x_0 + k\Delta) = y_k, k = 0, 1, 2, \ldots, n$ are expressed as follows:

$$
\mathbf{y} = \begin{bmatrix} y_0 \\ y_1 \\ y_2 \\ \vdots \\ y_n \end{bmatrix} = \begin{bmatrix} 1/2 & 1 & 1 & \cdots & 1 & 1/2 \\ 1/2 & \cos\theta & \cos 2\theta & \cdots & \cos(n-1)\theta & -1/2 \\ 1/2 & \cos 2\theta & \cos 4\theta & \cdots & \cos 2(n-1)\theta & 1/2 \\ \vdots & \vdots & \vdots & \cdots & \vdots & \vdots \\ 1/2 & \cos(n-1)\theta & \cos(n-1)2\theta & \cdots & \cos(n-1)^2\theta & -1/2 \\ 1/2 & \cos n\theta & \cos n2\theta & \cdots & \cos n(n-1)\theta & 1/2 \end{bmatrix} \begin{bmatrix} c_0 \\ c_1 \\ c_2 \\ \vdots \\ c_n \end{bmatrix} = \mathbf{C}\mathbf{c}.
\tag{4.88}
$$

Using trigonometric product-to-sum and Lagrange identity we can show that $\mathbf{C}(k,:)\mathbf{C}(:,l) = \frac{n}{2}$ if $k = l$ otherwise 0. This means $\mathbf{C}^{-1} = \frac{2}{n}\mathbf{C}$. Therefore, $\mathbf{c} = \mathbf{C}^{-1}\mathbf{y} = \frac{2}{n}\mathbf{C}\mathbf{y}$.

Now we show how to use Eq. (4.80) for real valued FFT to calculate $\mathbf{y} = \mathbf{C}\mathbf{c}$. First we introduce an auxiliary array,

$$
b_l = \frac{1}{2}(c_l + c_{n-l}) - \sin\left(l\frac{\pi}{n}\right)(c_l - c_{n-l}); \quad l = 0, 1, 2, \ldots, n-1.
$$

Then we calculate the real valued FFT of $b_0, b_1, b_2, \ldots, b_{n-1}$: $z_k = \sum_{l=0}^{n-1} d_l e^{i\frac{2\pi}{n}kl} = u_k + iv_k$. Follow the same procedure of obtaining Eq. (4.85), now we obtain

$$y_{2k} = u_k; \quad y_{2k+1} = y_{2k-1} + v_k \quad k = 0, 1, 2, \ldots, \frac{n}{2} - 1. \tag{4.89}$$

For $k = 0$, $y_1 = y_{-1} + v_0 = y_{-1}$. Instead we have to use the definition Eq. (4.88) to calculate y_1 directly,

$$y_1 = \frac{1}{2}(c_0 - c_n) + \sum_{l=0}^{n-1} c_l \cos\left(l\frac{\pi}{n}\right). \tag{4.90}$$

The sum is accumulated during the generation of $b_0, b_1, \ldots, b_{n-1}$.

Listing of MATLAB Function for Trigonometric Interpolation The three kinds of interpolations (Fourier, sine, and cosine) discussed in this subsection are collectively implemented in one MATLAB function `trigonometricInterpolation_.m`. In `trigonometricInterpolation_.m`, the three interpolations are accessed by the input argument algo='fourier',algo='sine', or algo='cosine'. The three kinds of calculations (inverse transform, interpolation, and transform) are accessed by the input argument iw=-1,0,+1, respectively. Depending on the input values of algo and iw, the input and output arguments of interpolation_.m take different meanings. They will be explained with the examples below.

In `trigonometricInterpolation_.m`, the calculation of the trigonometric functions follows the suggestion of Section 5.5 of [51] for the efficiency and accuracy,

$$\alpha = 2\sin^2\frac{\theta}{2}, \quad \beta = \sin\theta,$$
$$\cos(l+1)\theta = \cos(l\theta + \theta) = \cos l\theta - (\alpha\cos l\theta + \beta\sin l\theta),$$
$$\sin(l+1)\theta = \sin(l\theta + \theta) = \sin l\theta - (\alpha\sin l\theta - \beta\cos l\theta).$$

Algorithm 4.12

Matrix computations arising from trigonometric function interpolation

```
%algo='fourier','sine','cosine'
%iw=-1: inv(F)*y->y.  = 0: f_1(kbar)y_1->y.  =+1: F*y->y.
function y = trigonometricInterpolation_(y,algo,iw,kbar)

if (iscell(y)) y2 =y(2:end);  y = y{1};  else y2 = []; end
if (~exist('algo','var')) algo = 'fourier'; end
algo = lower(algo);
if (~exist('iw','var')) iw = 0; end
if (iw==0 && ~exist('kbar','var')) kbar = 0.0; end
if (strcmp(algo,'sine'))       n0 = size(y,1)+1;
elseif (strcmp(algo,'cosine')) n0 = size(y,1)-1;
else                           n0 = size(y,1); end
n = 2^ceil(log2(n0));
if (n > n0) y = [y; zeros(n-n0,size(y,2))]; end
twopi = 2.0*pi;      %function base: e^(+1i*2.0*pi/n)
%twopi =-2.0*pi;     %function base: e^(-1i*2.0*pi/n)

if(strcmp(algo,'fourier') && (iw==-1 || iw==+1))
    if (~isreal(y))       %complex valued FFT
        bits = log2(n);  p = zeros(n,1);
        for i=1:n
```

```
            for j=1:bits
                bj = bitget(i-1,j);
                if (bj == 1) p(i) = bitset(p(i), bits+1-j, 1); end
            end
        end
        y = permute_(p+1,y);    %bit reversal y
        twopi = iw*twopi;  n1 = 1;   n2 = 2;
        while (n2 <= n)
            theta = twopi/n2;    w = 1.0;
            alpha = sin(0.5*theta); alpha = 2.0*alpha*alpha;  beta = sin(theta);
            for l1=1:n1
                for l2=l1:n2:n
                    k1 = l2;  k2 = k1 + n1;   wyk2 = w*y(k2);
                    y(k2) = y(k1) - wyk2;  y(k1) = y(k1) + wyk2;      %recursive
                end
                c = real(w);  s = imag(w);  c0 = c;
                c = c - (alpha*c+beta*s); s = s - (alpha*s-beta*c0);   w = c+s*1i;
            end
            n1 = n2;  n2 = n2*2;
        end
        if (iw ==-1) y = y/n; end
    else %if(isreal(y)) %real valued FFT
        if(isempty(y2)) real2 = 1; else real2 = strcmp(y2{1},'real'); end
        if (real2 == 1)
            z = complex(y(1:2:n),y(2:2:n));
            z = trigonometricInterpolation_(z,'fourier',1);
            y(1) = real(z(1)) + imag(z(1));  y(2) = real(z(1)) - imag(z(1));
        else
            if (iw == 1) y(4:2:n) =-y(4:2:n);  y = y*n; end
            z = [0.5*(y(1)+y(2))+0.5*(y(1)-y(2))*1i; zeros(n/2-1,1)];
        end
        theta = twopi/n;
        alpha = sin(0.5*theta);  alpha = 2.0*alpha*alpha;  beta = sin(theta);
        W = (1.0-alpha) + beta*1i;      %cos(1*theta)+i*sin(1*theta)
        for k=2:n/2
            if (real2==1) iW = 1i*W; else iW = conj(1i*W); end
            a = 0.5*(1.0-iW);  b = 0.5*(1.0 + iW);
            if (real2 == 1)
                zk = a*z(k) + b*conj(z(n/2-k+2));
                y(2*k-1) = real(zk);  y(2*k) = imag(zk);
            else
                yk1 = y(2*k-1) + y(2*k)*1i;  yk2 = y(n-2*k+3) - y(n-2*k+4)*1i;
                z(k) = a*yk1 + b*yk2;
            end
            c = real(W);    s = imag(W);  c0 = c;
            c = c - (alpha*c + beta*s);  s = s - (alpha*s - beta*c0);
            W = c + s*1i;                 %cos(k*theta)+i*sin(k*theta)
        end
        if (real2 == 1)
            if (iw ==-1) y(4:2:n) =-y(4:2:n);  y = y/n; end
            y = {y; 'complex'};
        else
            z = trigonometricInterpolation_(z,'fourier',-1);
            y(1:2:n) = real(z);  y(2:2:n) = imag(z);
            y = {y; 'real'};
        end
    end
end
```

```
elseif(strcmp(algo,'fourier') && iw==0)
    if(isempty(y2)) real2 = 0; else real2 = strcmp(y2{1},'real'); end
    x = y;   theta = kbar*twopi/2.0;   c = cos(theta);   s = sin(theta);
    if (real2 == 0) y = x(1) + (c+s*1i)*x(n/2+1);
    else            y = x(1) + (c+s*1i)*x(2);   end
    W0 = (c*c-s*s) + (2.0*s*c)*1i;      %e^(1i*kbar*twopi)
    theta = kbar*twopi/n;
    alpha = sin(0.5*theta); alpha = 2.0*alpha*alpha; beta = sin(theta);
    W = (1.0-alpha) + beta*1i;          %cos(1*theta)+i*sin(1*theta)
    for l=2:n/2
        if (real2 == 0) x1 = x(l);      x2 = x(n-l+2);
        else            x1 = x(2*l-1) + x(2*l)*1i;   x2 = conj(x1);   end
        y = y + W*x1 + W0*conj(W)*x2;
        c = real(W);    s = imag(W);   c0 = c;
        c = c - (alpha*c + beta*s);    s = s - (alpha*s - beta*c0);
        W = c + s*1i;               %cos(l*theta)+i*sin(l*theta)
    end
elseif(strcmp(algo,'sine') && (iw==-1 || iw==+1))
    theta = twopi/2.0/n;
    alpha = sin(0.5*theta); alpha = 2.0*alpha*alpha; beta = sin(theta);
    c = 1.0 - alpha;   s = beta;   z = zeros(n,1);
    for k=2:n
        z(k) = s*(y(k-1)+y(n-k+1)) + 0.5*(y(k-1)-y(n-k+1));
        c0 = c;   c = c - (alpha*c + beta*s); s = s - (alpha*s - beta*c0);
    end
    z = trigonometricInterpolation_(z,'fourier',1);   z = z{1};
    y(1) = 0.5*real(z(1));
    for k=2:n/2
        y(2*k-2) = z(2*k);   y(2*k-1) = y(2*k-3) + z(2*k-1);
    end
    if (iw ==-1) y = y/(n/2); end
elseif(strcmp(algo,'sine') && iw==0)
    theta = kbar*twopi/2.0/n;
    x = y;   alpha = sin(0.5*theta); alpha = 2.0*alpha*alpha; beta = sin(theta);
    c = 1.0 - alpha;   s = beta;   y = 0.0;
    for k=1:n-1
        y = y + s*x(k);
        c0 = c;   c = c - (alpha*c + beta*s); s = s - (alpha*s - beta*c0);
    end
elseif(strcmp(algo,'cosine') && (iw==-1 || iw==+1))
    theta = twopi/2.0/n;
    alpha = sin(0.5*theta); alpha = 2.0*alpha*alpha; beta = sin(theta);
    c = 1.0 - alpha; s = beta;   z = zeros(n,1);
    z(1) = 0.5*(y(1) + y(n+1));   y2 = 0.5*(y(1) - y(n+1));
    for k=2:n
        z(k) = 0.5*(y(k)+y(n-k+2)) - s*(y(k)-y(n-k+2));   y2 = y2 + c*y(k);
        c0 = c;   c = c - (alpha*c + beta*s); s = s - (alpha*s - beta*c0);
    end
    z = trigonometricInterpolation_(z,'fourier',1);   z = z{1};
    y(1) = z(1);   y(2) = y2;   y(n+1) = z(2);
    for k=2:n/2
        y(2*k-1) = z(2*k-1);   y(2*k) = y(2*k-2) + z(2*k);
    end
    if (iw ==-1) y = y/(n/2); end
elseif(strcmp(algo,'cosine') && iw==0)
    theta = kbar*twopi/2.0/n;
    x = y;   alpha = sin(0.5*theta); alpha = 2.0*alpha*alpha; beta = sin(theta);
```

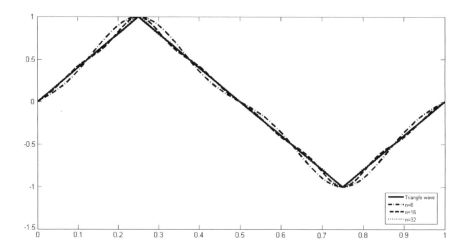

FIGURE 4.3

Sine interpolation of triangle wave.

```
    c = 1.0 - alpha;   s = beta;   y = 0.5*(x(1)+cos(n*theta)*x(n+1));
    for k=2:n
        y = y + c*x(k);
        c0 = c;   c = c - (alpha*c + beta*s);   s = s - (alpha*s - beta*c0);
    end
else
    error('trigonometricInterpolation_:␣wrong␣input␣argument.');
end
```

We give two simple examples for the trigonometric interpolations. The first example is shown in Fig. 4.3, which is produced by the following MATLAB script.

```
n = 8;           %number of sine functions
y1 = zeros(n,1);
d = 1/(n/4);
             %generate points on triangle wave
for k=2:n/4+1 y1(k) = y1(k-1)+d; end
for k=n/4+2:3*n/4+1 y1(k) = y1(k-1)-d; end
for k=3*n/4+2:n y1(k) = y1(k-1)+d; end
             %calculate coefficients of sine functions
c1=trigonometricInterpolation_(y1(2:n),'sine',-1);

m = 10*n;   x2 = zeros(m,1);   y2 = zeros(m,1);
d = 1/m;    xk = 0.0;

for k=1:m
    x2(k) = xk;
    y2(k) = trigonometricInterpolation_(c1,'sine',0,xk*n);
    xk = xk + d;
end

hold on;
plot(x2,y2,'red');      %interpolation by sine functions
```

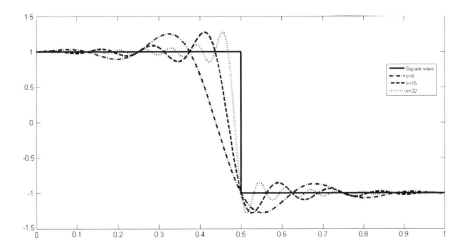

FIGURE 4.4

Cosine interpolation of square wave.

The second example is the cosine function interpolation of a square wave, shown in Fig. 4.4. The curve is produced with the following MATLAB script.

```
n = 8;          %number of cosine functions
y1 = zeros(n+1,1);
                %points on square wave
y1(1:n/2) = 1;
y1(n/2+1:n+1) = -1;
                %calculate coefficients of cosine functions
c1=trigonometricInterpolation_(y1,'cosine',-1);

m = 10*n;   x2 = zeros(m,1);   y2 = zeros(m,1);
d = 1/m;    xk = 0.0;

for k=1:m
    x2(k) = xk;
    y2(k) = trigonometricInterpolation_(c1,'cosine',0,xk*n);
    xk = xk + d;
end

hold on;
plot(x2,y2,'red');
```

Iterative algorithms of solution of linear equations

5

INTRODUCTION

We studied the solution of the general linear equations $\mathbf{A}_{mn}\mathbf{x}_n = \mathbf{b}_m$ in Chapter 4: the existence and uniqueness of solutions and many direct algorithms. In this chapter, we direct our attention to a less general problem: the solution of $\mathbf{A}_{nn}\mathbf{x}_n = \mathbf{b}_n$, where $\mathbf{A}$ is *square and non-singular*.[1] However, the algorithms are *iterative*. Just as the applicability of a direct algorithm depends on the property that $\mathbf{A}$ possesses, the applicability (convergence, convergence rate, etc.) of an iterative algorithm is solely determined by $\mathbf{A}$'s property. We will emphasize the applicability issue of iterative algorithms with numerical examples and counterexamples.

In Section 5.1, we give an overview of iterative algorithms. The simple Newton-Raphson iteration algorithm is used as an example to illustrate the basic components of an iterative algorithm.

Section 5.2 presents the details of the classical stationary methods: Richardson iteration, Jacobi iteration, Gauss-Seidel iteration, their corresponding acceleration techniques, and convergence properties.

Section 5.3 presents an overview of the non-stationary methods: the projection method, approximation subspace and projection subspace, and the construction of bases of the subspaces.

Section 5.4 presents the details of non-stationary methods applied to a symmetric (positive definite and indefinite) matrix: conjugate gradient method, the minimum residual method, the minimum error method and their connection to the Lanczos tri-diagonal matrix decomposition, and so forth.

Section 5.5 presents the details of non-stationary algorithms applied to a non-symmetric matrix: the Arnoldi projection method, the minimum residual method, the Lanczos projection method, the quasi-minimum residual method, and the variants of conjugate gradient method adapted to the non-symmetric matrix.

Section 5.6 presents four special iterative algorithms for normal equations: $\mathbf{A}'\mathbf{A}\mathbf{x} = \mathbf{A}'\mathbf{b}$ and $\mathbf{A}\mathbf{A}'\mathbf{y} = \mathbf{b}$.

Section 5.7 briefly addresses four remaining important topics related to the iterative algorithms of linear equation solution: pre-conditioning techniques, parallel computation, algebraic multigrid method, and domain decomposition method. Their brief exposure in this section is more conceptual. The reader is encouraged to consult [56] and the many references cited therein for the full discussion of these topics.

The discussions in Sections 5.2–5.6 are all supplemented by MATLAB codes and numerical examples. In all the MATLAB codes presented in this chapter, the user can optionally supply a MATLAB function to calculate the matrix-vector product and/or another MATLAB function to be used

---

[1] The comparative "less general" is by no means less important. In fact, almost all linear equation solution problems encountered in any scientific and engineering disciplines belong to this category. In another word, in those application fields, the problem is formulated to be in this form.

Matrix Algorithms in MATLAB. DOI: 10.1016/B978-0-12-803804-8.00011-8

as a pre-conditioner. Examples are provided to demonstrate the use of the optional MATLAB function input for the matrix-vector product and pre-conditioning, the two most intensive computations in the iterative algorithms of solving linear equations.

The test matrices used in most of the numerical examples are small full matrices generated by the MATLAB program. They are for the purpose of demonstrating the property of the algorithm and the usage of the MATLAB function. Note that iterative algorithms are usually used to solve sparse and large scale linear equations. Only a few relatively large sparse matrices are tested to demonstrate the efficiency of the code implementation.

5.1 OVERVIEW OF ITERATIVE ALGORITHMS

An iterative algorithm is usually the only way to solve nonlinear equations. But there are no universal iterative algorithms applicable to all kinds of nonlinear equations. For general nonlinear equations, Newton-Raphson algorithm is the simplest to implement. It works well (converges) if an initial guess of the solution is close to the real solution. It fails badly (diverges) if no such an initial guess is available. We will use Newton-Raphson algorithm to illustrate the essential features of an iterative algorithm.

Algorithm 5.1

Newton-Raphson iteration algorithm

```
%Newton Raphson: y=f(x)=f(x0) + df/dx0*dx = 0, x = x0 + dx
function x = newtonRaphson_(F,x,tolx,toly,last)

if (~iscell(F)) error('newtonRaphson_:_input_argument_error'); end
[y,Dy]   = feval(F{1},F{2:end},x);
dx = -(Dy\y);
x = x + dx;
d0norm = max(1.0,norm(dx,inf));    y0norm = max(1.0,norm(y,inf)); l = 1;

while((norm(dx,inf)>tolx*d0norm || norm(y,inf)>toly*y0norm) && l<last)
    [y,Dy]   = feval(F{1},F{2:end},x);
    dx = -(Dy\y);
    x = x + dx;
    l = l + 1;
end
```

The input arguments to `newtonRaphson_` are `F,x,tolx,toly,last`. F is a cell array defining the nonlinear equations $f = 0$: `F{1}` the name of a MATLAB function calculating f and its derivatives, `F{2:end}` are parameters defining the nonlinear equations. `x` is the initial guess of the solution. `tolx,toly` are tolerances for the convergence of x and f. `last` is the maximum iteration number, which is useful only to provide an exit to an otherwise endless iteration. The output x is the calculated solution. Newton-Raphson iteration algorithm consists of four major constituents: a tolerance check, the calculation of the nonlinear functions (also derivatives), the calculation of the increment (`dx`) of the solution variable, and the update of the solution variable (`x`). The convergence of Newton-Raphson algorithm is reflected by the fact that the iteration ends with `l<last`. The convergence rate reaches quadratic in a close neighborhood of a root. Whether Newton-Raphson algorithm converges depends on the nonlinear equations and the initial guess of the solution.

As an example, finding the root of a polynomial by Newton-Raphson algorithm can be realized by the following listed MATLAB function, `polynomial_.m`.

Algorithm 5.2

Horner algorithm calculating polynomial and its derivative

```
%a = [a0,a1,a2,...,an] polynomial coefficients.
%Horner: f = a0+a1*x+a2*x^2+...+an*x^n, Df = a1+2*a2*x+...+n*an*x^(n-1)
function [f,Df] = polynomial_(a,x)

n = length(a);
f = a(n);   Df = 0.0;
for j=n-1:-1:1
    Df = Df*x + f;   f = f*x + a(j);
end
```

The usage of `newtonRaphson_.m` and `polynomial_.m` is demonstrated by the following simple example. Note that a formula is available to find the root of the polynomial with an order less or equal to 4.

```
>> a=[-2;1;1];              %quadratic: -2+x+x^2=(x-1)(x+2)=0
>> F={'polynomial_',a};     %F{1}='polynomial_', function name
                            %F{2}=a, defining a quadratic function
>> x=0.5;                    %initial guess
>> x=newtonRaphson_(F,x,1.0e-8,1.0e-8,10)
x =
    1.0000                   %root x=1
>> x=-1;                     %initial guess
>> x=newtonRaphson_(F,x,1.0e-8,1.0e-8,10)
x =
    -2                       %root x=-2
```

Linear equations can be solved by direct algorithms as discussed in Chapter 4. For large scale of sparse linear equations, due to the efficiency requirement and computer memory limitation, iterative algorithms are often used. There are two major types of iterative algorithms for solving linear equations: stationary methods and non-stationary methods. Both can be interpreted in terms of projection schemes. The code structure of iterative algorithms of linear equations shares many similarities to the four major constituents of Newton-Raphson. Convergence and convergence rate are decided by the property of the matrix and the algorithm.

5.2 STATIONARY ITERATIONS: JACOBI, GAUSS-SEIDEL, AND MORE

Jacobi and Gauss-Seidel iteration algorithms, see [56] and [7], belong to a category called stationary iterative algorithms, which are based on the matrix splitting,

$$\mathbf{Ax} = (\mathbf{B} - \mathbf{C})\mathbf{x} = \mathbf{a}, \tag{5.1a}$$

$$\mathbf{Bx} - \mathbf{Cx} + \mathbf{a}. \tag{5.1b}$$

Iteratively, Eq. (5.1b) is relaxed to hold approximately as follows:

$$\mathbf{Bx}_{i+1} \approx \mathbf{Cx}_i + \mathbf{a}, \tag{5.2}$$

where $i + 1$ and i are iteration numbers. If in the splitting, we assume $\mathbf{B}$ is non-singular, then an approximation $\mathbf{x}_{i+1}$ of $\mathbf{x}$ presumably more accurate than $\mathbf{x}_i$ can be calculated as follows:

$$\mathbf{x}_{i+1} = \mathbf{B}^{-1}\mathbf{Cx}_i + \mathbf{B}^{-1}\mathbf{a} = \mathbf{Gx}_i + \mathbf{g}. \tag{5.3}$$

Eq. (5.3) can also be written as an increment form as follows:

$$\mathbf{x}_{i+1} = \mathbf{B}^{-1}(\mathbf{B} - \mathbf{A})\mathbf{x}_i + \mathbf{B}^{-1}\mathbf{a} = \mathbf{x}_i + \mathbf{B}^{-1}(\mathbf{a} - \mathbf{A}\mathbf{x}_i) = \mathbf{x}_i + \mathbf{B}^{-1}\mathbf{r}_i, \tag{5.4}$$

where $\mathbf{r}_i = \mathbf{a} - \mathbf{A}\mathbf{x}_i$ is the residual of $\mathbf{A}\mathbf{x} = \mathbf{a}$ at $\mathbf{x}_i$. When $\mathbf{r}_i \Rightarrow \mathbf{0}$, Eq. (5.4) converges.

Further we have two homogeneous equations by subtracting Eq. (5.3) from the equation satisfied by the real solution $\mathbf{x} = \mathbf{G}\mathbf{x} + \mathbf{g}$ and the equation satisfied by the iterations i and $i - 1$ $\mathbf{x}_i = \mathbf{G}\mathbf{x}_{i-1} + \mathbf{g}$,

$$\mathbf{x}_{i+1} - \mathbf{x} = \mathbf{G}(\mathbf{x}_i - \mathbf{x}), \tag{5.5a}$$

$$\mathbf{x}_{i+1} - \mathbf{x}_i = \mathbf{G}(\mathbf{x}_i - \mathbf{x}_{i-1}). \tag{5.5b}$$

Repeatedly applying Eq. (5.5), we obtain a serious of equations leading to the initial guess of the solution $\mathbf{x}_0$,

$$\mathbf{x}_{i+1} - \mathbf{x} = \mathbf{G}(\mathbf{x}_i - \mathbf{x}) = \mathbf{G}^2(\mathbf{x}_{i-1} - \mathbf{x}) = \cdots = \mathbf{G}^{i+1}(\mathbf{x}_0 - \mathbf{x}) \tag{5.6a}$$

$$\mathbf{x}_{i+1} - \mathbf{x}_i = \mathbf{G}(\mathbf{x}_i - \mathbf{x}_{i-1}) = \mathbf{G}^2(\mathbf{x}_{i-1} - \mathbf{x}_{i-2}) = \cdots = \mathbf{G}^i(\mathbf{x}_1 - \mathbf{x}_0) = \mathbf{G}^i(\mathbf{g} - (\mathbf{I} - \mathbf{G})\mathbf{x}_0). \tag{5.6b}$$

Now we can see that the convergence of the iteration Eq. (5.3) for any initial guess $\mathbf{x}_0$ is determined by $\mathbf{G}^i \Rightarrow \mathbf{0}$ or equivalently $|\lambda_{\max}(\mathbf{G})| < 1$. $|\lambda_{\max}(\mathbf{G})|$ means the eigenvalue of $\mathbf{G}$ with the maximum magnitude. A theorem proved in [56] states that for a regular splitting[2] $\mathbf{A} = \mathbf{B} - \mathbf{C}$, $|\lambda_{\max}(\mathbf{G})| = |\lambda_{\max}(\mathbf{B}^{-1}\mathbf{C})| < 1$ if and only if $\mathbf{A}$ is non-singular and $\mathbf{A}^{-1}$ is non-negative.[3] For a non-regular splitting, the convergence of the iteration Eq. (5.3) is not known except in some special cases enumerated when we discuss Jacobi and Gauss-Seidel iterations in the following.

Another useful form of Eq. (5.3) is the pre-conditioned form

$$\mathbf{x}_{i+1} = \left(\mathbf{I} - \mathbf{B}^{-1}\mathbf{A}\right)\mathbf{x}_i + \mathbf{B}^{-1}\mathbf{a} \quad \text{or} \quad \mathbf{B}^{-1}\mathbf{A}\mathbf{x}_i = \mathbf{B}^{-1}\mathbf{a}. \tag{5.7}$$

$\mathbf{B}$ in this case is called the pre-conditioner of $\mathbf{A}$; its role is to make $\mathbf{B}^{-1}\mathbf{A}$ better conditioned than $\mathbf{A}$. From this view, the iteration Eq. (5.3) or Eq. (5.4) can be considered as the fixed point iteration on the pre-conditioned linear system.

We partition $\mathbf{A}$ along the diagonal and lower/upper triangle,

$$\mathbf{A} = \mathbf{D} + \mathbf{L} + \mathbf{U}$$

$$= \begin{bmatrix} A_{11} & & & \\ & A_{22} & & \\ & & \ddots & \\ & & & A_{nn} \end{bmatrix} + \begin{bmatrix} 0 & & & \\ A_{21} & 0 & & \\ \vdots & \vdots & \ddots & \\ A_{n1} & A_{n2} & \cdots & 0 \end{bmatrix} + \begin{bmatrix} 0 & A_{12} & \cdots & A_{1n} \\ & 0 & \cdots & A_{2n} \\ & & \ddots & \vdots \\ & & & 0 \end{bmatrix}. \tag{5.8}$$

In terms of the splitting Eq. (5.1b), Richardson iteration is defined as Eq. (5.9a), Jacobi iteration is defined as Eq. (5.9b), and Gauss-Seidel iteration is defined as Eq. (5.9c). Whether these two splittings are regular is the property of $\mathbf{A}$,

$$\text{Richardson } \mathbf{B} = \mathbf{I}; \quad \mathbf{C} = \mathbf{I} - \mathbf{A}, \tag{5.9a}$$

$$\text{Jacobi } \mathbf{B} = \mathbf{D}; \quad \mathbf{C} = -\mathbf{L} - \mathbf{U}, \tag{5.9b}$$

---

[2] $\mathbf{A} = \mathbf{B} - \mathbf{C}$ is a regular splitting, if $\mathbf{B}$ is non-singular and $\mathbf{B}^{-1}$ and $\mathbf{C}$ are non-negative.

[3] Let $\mathbf{A}, \mathbf{B} \in \mathbb{R}^{m \times n}$. $\mathbf{A} \le \mathbf{B}$ means $A_{ij} \le B_{ij}$ for $1 \le i \le m, 1 \le j \le n$. Let $\mathbf{O}$ is a $m \times n$ zero matrix. $\mathbf{A}$ is non-negative if $\mathbf{A} \ge \mathbf{O}$, positive if $\mathbf{A} > \mathbf{O}$.

$$\text{Gauss-Seidel } \mathbf{B} = \mathbf{D} + \mathbf{L}; \quad \mathbf{C} = -\mathbf{U}. \tag{5.9c}$$

Then, the iteration Eq. (5.3) can be written, respectively, as follows for Jacobi and Gauss-Seidel iterations:

$$\text{Richardson } \mathbf{x}_{i+1} = (\mathbf{I} - \mathbf{A})\mathbf{x}_i + \mathbf{a} = \mathbf{G}_{rk}\mathbf{x}_i + \mathbf{g}_{rk} = \mathbf{x}_i + \mathbf{y}_i, \tag{5.10a}$$

$$\text{Jacobi } \mathbf{x}_{i+1} = -\mathbf{D}^{-1}(\mathbf{L} + \mathbf{U})\mathbf{x}_i + \mathbf{D}^{-1}\mathbf{a} = \mathbf{G}_{ja}\mathbf{x}_i + \mathbf{g}_{ja} = \mathbf{x}_i + \mathbf{D}^{-1}\mathbf{y}_i, \tag{5.10b}$$

$$\text{Gauss-Seidel } \mathbf{x}_{i+1} = -(\mathbf{D} + \mathbf{L})^{-1}\mathbf{U}\mathbf{x}_i + (\mathbf{D} + \mathbf{L})^{-1}\mathbf{a} = \mathbf{G}_{gs}\mathbf{x}_i + \mathbf{g}_{gs} = \mathbf{x}_i + (\mathbf{D} + \mathbf{L})^{-1}\mathbf{y}_i. \tag{5.10c}$$

Whether $|\lambda_{\max}(\mathbf{G}_{rk})| < 1$, $|\lambda_{\max}(\mathbf{G}_{ja})| < 1$, and $|\lambda_{\max}(\mathbf{G}_{gs})| < 1$ are the properties of $\mathbf{A}$. Eq. (5.10b) is linear equations with a diagonal matrix. Eq. (5.10c) is linear equations with a tri-diagonal matrix. $\mathbf{x}_{i+1}(j)$ denotes the component j of $\mathbf{x}_{i+1}$, which is calculated, respectively, as follows:

$$\text{Jacobi } \mathbf{x}_{i+1}(j) = \frac{1}{A_{jj}}\left(\mathbf{a}(j) - \sum_{k=1}^{j-1}A_{jk}\mathbf{x}_i(k) - \sum_{k=j+1}^{n}A_{jk}\mathbf{x}_i(k)\right), \quad j = 1,\ldots,n, \tag{5.11a}$$

$$\text{Gauss-Seidel } \mathbf{x}_{i+1}(j) = \frac{1}{A_{jj}}\left(\mathbf{a}(j) - \sum_{k=1}^{j-1}A_{jk}\mathbf{x}_{i+1}(k) - \sum_{k=j+1}^{n}A_{jk}\mathbf{x}_i(k)\right), \quad j = 1,\ldots,n. \tag{5.11b}$$

From Eqs. (5.11), we see that the only difference between Jacobi and Gauss-Seidel iterations is the calculation of the second term within the bracket. For Jacobi iteration, we need to have two arrays for $\mathbf{x}$; one for $\mathbf{x}_i$ and the other for $\mathbf{x}_{i+1}$. For Gauss-Seidel iteration, one array is enough; the components of $\mathbf{x}$ are updated in place.

After $\mathbf{x}_{i+1}(j)$ is calculated by Eq. (5.10a), Eq. (5.11a), or Eq. (5.11b), we can calculate the following weighted sum:

$$\omega_j\mathbf{x}_{i+1}(j) + (1 - \omega_j)\mathbf{x}_i(j) \tag{5.12}$$

and use this weighted sum for $\mathbf{x}_{i+1}(j)$ in the subsequent calculations. This leads to the weighted form for Richardson, Jacobi, and Gauss-Seidel iterations [weighted Gauss-Seidel iteration is commonly known as successive over relaxation (SOR) method]. Their matrix forms are written as follows:

$$\text{Weighted Richardson } \mathbf{x}_{i+1} = \mathbf{x}_i + \Omega\mathbf{y}_i, \tag{5.13a}$$

$$\text{Weighted Jacobi } \mathbf{x}_{i+1} = \mathbf{D}^{-1}(-\Omega(\mathbf{L} + \mathbf{U}) + (\mathbf{I} - \Omega)\mathbf{D})\mathbf{x}_i + \mathbf{D}^{-1}\Omega\mathbf{a}, \tag{5.13b}$$

$$\text{Weighted Gauss-Seidel } \mathbf{x}_{i+1} = (\mathbf{D} + \Omega\mathbf{L})^{-1}(-\Omega\mathbf{U} + (\mathbf{I} - \Omega)\mathbf{D})\mathbf{x}_i + (\mathbf{D} + \Omega\mathbf{L})^{-1}\Omega\mathbf{a}, \tag{5.13c}$$

where Ω is a diagonal matrix consisting of $\omega_j, j = 1,\ldots,n$. In most applications, $\omega_j = \omega, j = 1,\ldots,n$.

Gauss-Seidel iteration defined in Eq. (5.10c) (or equivalently as Eq. (5.11b) or Eq. (5.13c)) is the forward Gauss-Seidel iteration. The backward Gauss-Seidel iteration can be similarly defined as follows:

$$\mathbf{B} = \mathbf{D} + \mathbf{U}; \quad \mathbf{C} = -\mathbf{L}, \tag{5.14a}$$

$$\mathbf{x}_{i+1} = -(\mathbf{D} + \mathbf{U})^{-1}\mathbf{L}\mathbf{x}_i + (\mathbf{D} + \mathbf{U})^{-1}\mathbf{a} = \mathbf{G}_{gs}\mathbf{x}_i + \mathbf{g}_{gs} = \mathbf{x}_i + (\mathbf{D} + \mathbf{U})^{-1}\mathbf{r}_i, \tag{5.14b}$$

$$\mathbf{x}_{i+1}(j) = \frac{1}{A_{jj}}\left(\mathbf{a}(j) - \sum_{k=n}^{j+1}A_{jk}\mathbf{x}_{i+1}(k) - \sum_{k=j-1}^{1}A_{jk}\mathbf{x}_i(k)\right), \quad j = n,\ldots,1. \tag{5.14c}$$

The symmetric successive over relaxation (SSOR) step is composed of one weighted forward Gauss-Seidel step followed by a weighted backward Gauss-Seidel step:

$$\text{Weighted Forward } \mathbf{x}_{i+1/2} = (\mathbf{D} + \Omega\mathbf{L})^{-1}(-\Omega\mathbf{U} + (\mathbf{I} - \Omega)\mathbf{D})\mathbf{x}_i + (\mathbf{D} + \Omega\mathbf{L})^{-1}\Omega\mathbf{a}, \qquad (5.15\text{a})$$

$$\text{Weighted Backward } \mathbf{x}_{i+1} = (\mathbf{D} + \Omega\mathbf{U})^{-1}(-\Omega\mathbf{L} + (\mathbf{I} - \Omega)\mathbf{D})\mathbf{x}_{i+1/2} + (\mathbf{D} + \Omega\mathbf{U})^{-1}\Omega\mathbf{a}. \qquad (5.15\text{b})$$

In terms of the concept of the pre-conditioner introduced in Eq. (5.7), we can deduce the corresponding pre-conditioner for each of the following iteration schemes:

$$\text{Richardson or Weighted Richardson } \mathbf{B} = \mathbf{I},$$
$$\text{Jacobi or Weighted Jacobi } \mathbf{B} = \mathbf{D},$$
$$\text{Forward Gauss-Sedel } \mathbf{B} = \mathbf{D} + \mathbf{L},$$
$$\text{Weighted Forward Gauss-Sedel (SOR) } \mathbf{B} = \mathbf{D} + \Omega\mathbf{L}, \qquad (5.16)$$
$$\text{Backward Gauss-Sedel } \mathbf{B} = \mathbf{D} + \mathbf{U},$$
$$\text{Weighted Backward Gauss-Sedel } \mathbf{B} = \mathbf{D} + \Omega\mathbf{U},$$
$$\text{SSOR } \mathbf{B} = (\mathbf{D} + \Omega\mathbf{L})\mathbf{D}^{-1}(\mathbf{D} + \Omega\mathbf{U}).$$

About the convergence of Richardson, Jacobi, and SOR, it is proved in [56] that Richardson iteration is convergent for any initial $\mathbf{x}_0$ is $\mathbf{A}$ is positive definite and $0 < \omega < 2/\lambda_{\max}(\mathbf{A})$, where $\lambda_{\max}(\mathbf{A})$ is the maximum eigenvalue of $\mathbf{A}$. For the fastest convergence, the optimal $\omega = [\lambda_{\max}(\mathbf{A}) - \lambda_{\min}(\mathbf{A})]/[\lambda_{\max}(\mathbf{A}) + \lambda_{\min}(\mathbf{A})]$. If the eigenvalues of $\mathbf{A}$ are condensed closely, i.e. $\mathbf{A}$ is well-conditioned, Richardson iteration converges quickly. In [56], it also proves that Jacobi iteration is convergent for any initial $\mathbf{x}_0$ if $\mathbf{A}$ is diagonally dominant and SOR iteration is convergent for any initial $\mathbf{x}_0$ and $0 < \omega < 2$ if $\mathbf{A}$ is symmetric positive definite. However, the necessary conditions for the convergence of Richardson, Jacobi, and Gauss-Seidel iterations are not known. It is observed that Jacobi iteration is convergent even if $\mathbf{A}$ is not diagonally dominant for certain choices of $\mathbf{x}_0$. A similar conclusion is also true for Richardson and Gauss-Seidel iterations.

With the theoretical information of these iterative algorithms presented, now we present their MATLAB implementations, eqsStationary_.m, including Richardson, Jacobi, Gauss-Seidel, and their variants (weighted, forward/backward, etc.) accessed by the input arguments (algo and omega). The argument algo can take two types of values, character strings or cell arrays. See the comments in eqsStationary_.m. If algo takes cell arrays, for example, algo={'mdivideByGauss_',B}, B works as a pre-conditioner and uses mdivideByGauss_.m to solve linear equations like $\mathbf{By} = \mathbf{b}$. See examples below.

Algorithm 5.3

Stationary iterations for Ax=a

```
%Find x to A*x=a: |x1-xk|<tol*|x1-x0|, |a-A*x|<tol*|a-A*x0|, input x=x0.
% algo = 'richardson', 'jacobi', 'gauss-seidel' (default)
%       = 'forward-gauss-seidel'='gauss-seidel','backward-gauss-seidel', 'ssor'
%       = cell array: algo{1}= user function for inv(B)*; algo{2}=B
%last=max number of iterations, default=infinity.
%omega= weight, x = x + omega*d, d calculated according to algo
%Convergence: depends on A and algo specification. (A,B full).
function x = eqsStationary_(A,a,x,algo,tol,last,omega)

m = size(a,1);  n = m;
if (exist('x','var')==0 || isempty(x)) x = zeros(n,size(a,2)); end    %randn(n,1);
if (n~=size(x,1) || size(a,2)~=size(x,2)) error('eqsStationary_:_size_error.'); end
```

```
if (exist('algo','var')==0 || isempty(algo)) algo = 'gauss-seidel'; end
if (ischar(algo))
    if(strcmp(algo,'gauss-seidel')) gs = 1; end
    if(strcmp(algo,'forward-gauss-seidel')) algo = 'gauss-seidel'; gs = 1; end
    if(strcmp(algo,'backward-gauss-seidel')) algo = 'gauss-seidel'; gs =-1; end
    if(strcmp(algo,'ssor')) algo = 'gauss-seidel'; gs = 2; end
end
if (exist('tol','var')==0 || isempty(tol)) tol = sqrt(eps); end
if (exist('last','var')==0 || isempty(last)) last = intmax; end
if (exist('omega','var')==0 || isempty(omega)) omega = 1; end

if (ischar(algo) && strcmp(algo,'richardson'))        %richardson
    y = a - A*x;   dx = y;
    epslonx = tol*max(1.0,norm(dx,inf));   epslony = tol*max(1.0,norm(y,inf)); l = 0;
    while((norm(dx,inf)>epslonx || norm(y,inf)>epslony) && l<last)
        if (omega==1) x = x + dx; else x = x + omega*dx; end
        y = a - A*x;   dx = y;   l = l + 1;
    end
elseif (ischar(algo) && strcmp(algo,'jacobi'))         %jacobi
    y = a - A*x;   dx = zeros(n,size(a,2));
    for j=1:n dx(j,:) = y(j,:)/A(j,j); end
    if (omega==1) x = x + dx; else x = x + omega*dx; end
    epslonx = tol*max(1.0,norm(dx,inf));   epslony = tol*max(1.0,norm(y,inf)); l = 1;
    while((norm(dx,inf)>epslonx || norm(y,inf)>epslony) && l<last)
        y = a - A*x;
        for j=1:n dx(j,:) = y(j,:)/A(j,j); end
        if (omega==1) x = x + dx; else x = x + omega*dx; end
        l = l + 1;
    end
elseif (ischar(algo) && strcmp(algo,'gauss-seidel'))  %gauss-seidel
    y = a - A*x;
    epslon = tol*max(1.0,norm(y,inf));   dmax = 2.0*epslon;   l = 0;
    while (dmax>epslon && l<last)
        dmax = 0.0;   l = l + 1;
        for k=1:abs(gs)
            if (gs==-1 || k==2) loop = n:-1:1; else loop = 1:n; end
            for j=loop
                y(j,:) = a(j,:) - A(j,1:j-1)*x(1:j-1,:) - A(j,j:n)*x(j:n,:);
                d = y(j,:)/A(j,j);   dmax = max(dmax,norm(d,inf));
                if (omega == 1) x(j,:) = x(j,:) + d;
                else              x(j,:) = x(j,:) + omega*d; end
            end
        end
    end
elseif (iscell(algo))                                %x=x+omega*inv(B)*(a-A*x)
    y = a - A*x;   dx = feval(algo{1},algo{2},y);
    if (omega==1) x = x + dx; else x = x + omega*dx; end
    epslonx = tol*max(1.0,norm(dx,inf));   epslony = tol*max(1.0,norm(y,inf)); l = 1;
    while((norm(dx,inf)>epslonx || norm(y,inf)>epslony) && l<last)
        y = a - A*x;   dx = feval(algo{1},algo{2},y);
        if (omega==1) x = x + dx; else x = x + omega*dx; end
        l = l + 1;
    end
else
    error('eqsStationary_:_input_error.');
end
l
```

Now we give a few examples demonstrating how to use `eqsStationary_.m`.
The following are **A** and **a** for the first example.

```
>> A = [ 3.2379   -0.7837   -1.4722    0.3539   -0.7404   -0.4116    0.7138   -0.7395;
         -0.7837    3.4437    0.0182   -0.2024    0.1539   -1.0706    0.0119   -0.3450;
         -1.4722    0.0182    2.4814   -0.3643    0.5938    0.4763    0.2375    0.2707;
          0.3539   -0.2024   -0.3643    4.4725    0.0922   -0.6030    0.5484   -0.8374;
         -0.7404    0.1539    0.5938    0.0922    3.6565   -0.9065   -0.5724   -0.5546;
         -0.4116   -1.0706    0.4763   -0.6030   -0.9065    3.8057   -0.5302   -0.6180;
          0.7138    0.0119    0.2375    0.5484   -0.5724   -0.5302    2.9271    0.1662;
         -0.7395   -0.3450    0.2707   -0.8374   -0.5546   -0.6180    0.1662    2.1458];
>> a = [0.5529, -0.2037, -2.0543, 0.1326, 1.5929, 1.0184, -1.5804, -0.0787]';
```

A is positive definite, as can be seen by its eigenvalues. But it is not diagonally dominant.

```
>> eig(A)'
ans =          %> 0: positive definite.
    0.5646    1.0670    5.8259    5.3746    2.4953    4.2038    3.4852    3.1541

>> (2*diag(A)-abs(A)*ones(8,1))'
ans =          %< 0: not diagonally dominant.
   -1.9772    0.8580   -0.9516    1.4709    0.0427   -0.8105    0.1467   -1.3856
```

The shortest input takes full advantage of the default input values, it uses Gauss-Seidel iterations.

```
>> x1=eqsStationary_(A,a)'   %Other inputs are defaults!
l = 39               %number of Gauss-Seidel iterations
x1 =
          0.3757    0.3884   -1.0642    0.2464    0.9922    0.9385   -0.2820    0.9342

>> (a-A*x1')'               %=0, is the solution.
  1.0e-007 *
    0.5992    0.2922   -0.2065    0.3494    0.2910    0.1376   -0.0441   -0.0000
```

To use Jacobi iterations, input `algo='jacobi'`.

```
>> x2=eqsStationary_(A,a,[],'jacobi')'
l = 88               %slower convergence than Gauss-Seidel
x2 =
          0.3757    0.3884   -1.0642    0.2464    0.9922    0.9385   -0.2820    0.9342
```

Fig. 5.1 shows the change of the base-10 logarithm of the residuals of the above two iterations.

Next we compare the effect of different `omega` values in Gauss-Seidel iterations. Their effects in Jacobi iterations are similar.

```
>> x3=eqsStationary_(A,a,[],'gauss-seidel',[],[],0.9)';
l = 54               %omega=0.9<1, under relaxation: convergence rate reduces.

>> x4=eqsStationary_(A,a,[],'gauss-seidel',[],[],1.0)';
l = 42               %omega=1.0

>> x5=eqsStationary_(A,a,[],'gauss-seidel',[],[],1.1)';
l = 33               %omega=1.1>1, over relaxation: convergence rate increases.

>> x6=eqsStationary_(A,a,[],'gauss-seidel',[],[],1.3)';
l = 18               %a better omega then previous

>> x7=eqsStationary_(A,a,[],'gauss-seidel',[],[],1.4)';
l = 22               %a worse omega than previous
```

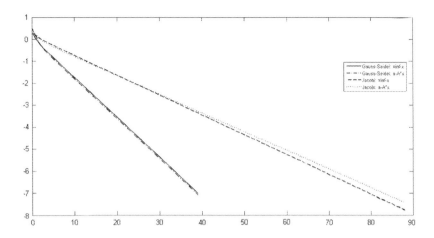

FIGURE 5.1

Errors and residuals of Jacobi and Gauss-Seidel iterations.

```
>> x8=eqsStationary_(A,a,[],'gauss-seidel',[],[],1.9)';
l = 173            %omega=1.9 too big

>> x9=eqsStationary_(A,a,[],'gauss-seidel',[],1000,2.0)';
l = 1000           %omega=2, not converging
>> (a-A*x2')'      %This is not the solution.
   1.5755    -6.3274    -4.1589    -3.8872     2.1337     1.3981    -3.8619    -0.3372

>> x10=eqsStationary_(A,a,[],'gauss-seidel',[],1000,2.1)'
l = 1000                %omega>2, diaverge
x2 =
1.0e+046 *
   0.4416     1.3927     3.0243     0.6721    -0.7341    -1.8134    -3.1116    -1.5204
```

Fig. 5.2 shows the change of the base-10 logarithm of the residuals of the iterations 3-7.

For the tested matrix, the initial guess of the solution only changes the iterations slightly. Higher accuracy of the solution can be achieved by tighter error tolerances with more iterations.

```
>> x0=randn(8,1);
>> x11=eqsStationary_(A,a,x0,'gauss-seidel')';     %tolx=toly=sqrt(eps)=1.4901e-008
l = 37             %omega=1, different initial x0
>> (a-A*x11')'     %=0
  1.0e 007 *
  -0.4476    -0.2183     0.1542    -0.2610    -0.2174    -0.1028     0.0329    -0.0000

>> x12=eqsStationary_(A,a,x0,'gauss-seidel',eps)';
l = 81             %smaller tolerance, more iterations.
>> (a-A*x12')'     %more accurate than the previous
  1.0e-015 *
        0    -0.0833     0.4441     0.3053          0          0          0    -0.0971
```

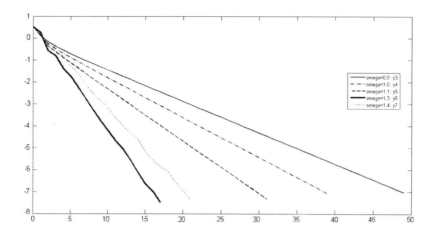

FIGURE 5.2

Residuals of Gauss-Seidel iterations under different ω.

Now we show how to use the pre-conditioner form of the stationary iterations. If the pre-conditioner takes `diag(A)`, it is equivalent to Jacobi iterations. If the pre-conditioner takes `tril(A)`, it is equivalent to Gauss-Seidel iterations. If the pre-conditioner is close to **A**, convergence is faster. In the extreme case, if the pre-conditioner is equal to **A**, it converges in one iteration if there are no numerical errors.

```
>> algo = {'mdivideByGauss_',tril(A)};        %algo{2}=tril(A): same as Gauss-Seidel!
>> x13=eqsStationary_(A,a,x0,algo,eps)'
l = 81              %same convergence rate
x3 =
    0.3757     0.3885    -1.0642     0.2464     0.9922     0.9385    -0.2820     0.9343
>> (a-A*x13')'      %same accuracy
    1.0e-015 *
    -0.1110    -0.1943     0.8882    -0.2498          0          0          0    -0.0971

>> algo{1}='mdivideLowerTriangle_';           %more efficient by tril(A)\a!
>> x14=eqsStationary_(A,a,x0,algo,eps)'
l = 81              %again same convergence rate
x14 =               %same solution
    0.3757     0.3885    -1.0642     0.2464     0.9922     0.9385    -0.2820     0.9343

>> B=randn(8);      %used as a perturbation to A
>> algo={'mdivideByGauss_',A+0.1*B};
>> x15=eqsStationary_(A,a,x0,algo,eps)';
l = 33              %Convergence improves, 81==>33

>> algo{2}=A+0.001*B;    %even closer to A
>> x16=eqsStationary_(A,a,x0,algo,eps)';
l = 7               %Convergence greatly improves, 81==>7

>> algo{2}=A;       %just A
>> x17=eqsStationary_(A,a,x0,algo,eps)';
l = 3               %It should converges in 1 iteration. But numerical errors...
```

The second example shows the convergence property of the stationary iterations if the matrix is not positive and diagonally dominant.

```
>> A=A+B;

>> eig(A)                    %not  symmetric,  positive  indefinite
  -1.1300
   6.5515
   5.0541 + 1.8940i
   5.0541 - 1.8940i
   3.9504
   1.4897
   2.5519 + 1.0051i
   2.5519 - 1.0051i
>> (2*diag(A)-abs(A)*ones(8,1))'   %not  diagonally  dominant
  -3.6918    -4.3399   -2.5853   -2.1994   -1.3601    2.0833    -2.0918    -6.1374


>> x18=eqsStationary_(A,a,x0,'jacobi')'
l = 2158
x18 =                    %Jacobi diverges.
   NaN   NaN   NaN   NaN   NaN   NaN   NaN   NaN

>> x19=eqsStationary_(A,a,x0,'gauss-seidel')'
l = 1264
x19 =                    %Gauss-Seidel diverges.
   NaN   NaN   NaN   NaN   NaN   NaN   NaN   NaN

>> algo={'mdivideByGauss_',A+0.1*C};
>> x20=eqsStationary_(A,a,x0,algo)'
l = 10
x20 =                    %Pre-conditioner helps  converging.
   0.1911     0.1410    -0.2762    0.2296     0.6284    0.2648    -0.3379    -0.3272
>> (a-A*x20')'       %It is the solution
  1.0e-008 *
   0.0819    -0.3885    -0.0323   -0.2757   -0.1450    0.2575     0.1871    -0.1753
```

As a transition to the subsequent sections, we point out that the stationary iterations can be interpreted as the special cases of the method of projection. The method of projection provides a framework unifying many different iteration algorithms.

For the $i + 1$th iteration, we assume the increment is in the direction $\mathbf{I}(:,j), j = 1,\dots,n$. The new iteration and residual are calculated as follows:

$$\mathbf{x}_{i+1} = \mathbf{x}_{0i} + \mathbf{I}(:,j)d_j,$$
$$\mathbf{y}_{i+1} = \mathbf{b} - \mathbf{A}\left(\mathbf{x}_{0i} + \mathbf{I}(:,j)d_j\right) = \mathbf{y}_{0i} + \mathbf{A}(:,j)d_j.$$

To determine d_j, we assume $\mathbf{I}(:,j)'\mathbf{y}_{i+1} = 0$. This gives

$$d_j = -\frac{\mathbf{I}(:,j)'\mathbf{y}_{0i}}{\mathbf{I}(:,j)'\mathbf{A}(:,j)} = -\frac{\mathbf{y}_{0i}(j)}{A_{jj}},$$
$$\mathbf{x}_{i+1}(j) = \mathbf{x}_{0i}(j) - d_j \quad \text{or} \quad \text{if } \omega \neq 1: \mathbf{x}_{i+1}(j) = \mathbf{x}_{0i}(j) - \omega d_j.$$

The above process is the Galerkin projection, see [56] and [39], which consists of the following four key steps:

1. Assume a form of an approximate solution:
$$\mathbf{x}_{i+1} = \mathbf{x}_{0i} + \mathbf{I}(:,j)d_j, j = 1,\ldots,n.$$

2. Obtain a formula for the residual corresponding to the approximate solution:
$$\mathbf{y}_{i+1} = \mathbf{a} - \mathbf{A}\left(\mathbf{x}_{0i} + \mathbf{I}(:,j)d_j\right) = (\mathbf{a} - \mathbf{A}\mathbf{x}_0) - \mathbf{A}(:,j)d_j = \mathbf{y}_0 - \mathbf{A}(:,j)d_j.$$

3. Assume the projected residual of $\mathbf{y}_{i+1}$ in $\mathbf{I}(:,j)$ is zero:
$$\mathbf{I}(:,j)'\left(\mathbf{y}_0 - \mathbf{A}(:,j)d_j\right) = 0, \Rightarrow d_j = \frac{y_0(j)}{A_{jj}}.$$

4. Update the approximate solution:
$$\mathbf{x}_{i+1}(j) = \mathbf{x}_{0i}(j) + \omega d_j.$$

The four steps are iteratively applied to drive the residual $\mathbf{y}$ to zero. Further we can see that, for $j = 1,\ldots,n$ and when $j = n + 1$ then $j = 1,\ldots,n$ starting over

$$\mathbf{x}_{0i}(1:j-1) = \begin{cases} \mathbf{x}_i(1:j-1) & \text{Jacobi iterations} \\ \mathbf{x}_{i+1}(1:j-1) & \text{Gauss-Seidel iterations} \end{cases}; \quad \mathbf{x}_{0i}(j:n) = \mathbf{x}_i(j:n).$$

From the next section, we will choose more general subspaces $\mathbf{V}$ and $\mathbf{W}'$ instead of $\mathbf{I}(:,j)$ and $\mathbf{I}(:,j)'$. Further $\mathbf{V} = \mathbf{W}$ or $\mathbf{V} \neq \mathbf{W}$ and $\mathbf{V}$ and $\mathbf{W}$ are dynamically updated with more information obtained in the iteration process to improve the convergence rate. These iteration algorithms belong to the non-stationary iterations. We will first treat their applications in symmetric matrix in Section 5.4, then unsymmetric matrix in Section 5.5.

5.3 GENERAL METHODOLOGY OF NON-STATIONARY ITERATIONS

The central theme of the next three sections is the scale reduction of presumably large scale linear equations $\mathbf{A}_{nn}\mathbf{x}_n = \mathbf{a}_n$, n is large and $\mathbf{A}$ is sparse or full. The general methodology is the method of projection, which consists the following four key steps, see also the end of the previous section.

1. Assume a form of an approximate solution:
$$\mathbf{x}_m = \mathbf{x}_0 + \mathbf{V}(1:n,1:m)\mathbf{v}(1:m), m \ll n, \mathbf{x}_0 \text{ and } \mathbf{V} \text{ are assumed and } \mathbf{v} \text{ is unknown.}$$

2. Obtain a formula for the residual corresponding to the approximate solution:
$$\mathbf{y}_m = \mathbf{a} - \mathbf{A}\left(\mathbf{x}_0 + \mathbf{V}\mathbf{v}\right) = (\mathbf{a} - \mathbf{A}\mathbf{x}_0)g - \mathbf{A}\mathbf{V}\mathbf{v} = \mathbf{y}_0 - \mathbf{A}\mathbf{V}\mathbf{v}.$$

3. Assume the projected residual of $\mathbf{y}_m$ onto $\mathbf{W}$ is zero (Galerkin condition):
$$\mathbf{W}'\left(\mathbf{y}_0 - \mathbf{A}\mathbf{V}\mathbf{v}\right) = \mathbf{0}, \mathbf{W} \in \mathbb{R}^{n\times m} \Rightarrow (\mathbf{W}'\mathbf{A}\mathbf{V})\mathbf{v} = \mathbf{W}'\mathbf{y}_0.$$

4. Update the approximate solution and new residual:
$$\mathbf{x}_m = \mathbf{x}_0 + \mathbf{V}\mathbf{v}; \mathbf{y}_m = \mathbf{y}_0 - \mathbf{A}\mathbf{V}\mathbf{v}.$$

The four steps are iteratively applied to drive the residual $\mathbf{y}$ to zero. At step 1 of the new iteration, $\mathbf{x}_m$ of step 4 of the old iteration replaces $\mathbf{x}_0$. In the new iteration, span($\mathbf{V}$) and span($\mathbf{W}$) can take different subspaces. For the convenience of calculation, any convenient bases $\mathbf{V}$ and $\mathbf{W}$ can be chosen. The chosen subspaces determine the convergence rate. The chosen bases determine the efficiency of the iteration.

At step 3, $\mathbf{v}$ is solved from the scale reduced linear equations $(\mathbf{W}'\mathbf{A}\mathbf{V})\,\mathbf{v} = \mathbf{W}'\mathbf{y}_0$, $\mathbf{W}'\mathbf{A}\mathbf{V} \in \mathbb{R}^{m \times m}$. To determine $\mathbf{v}$ uniquely, $\mathbf{W}'\mathbf{A}\mathbf{V}$ must be non-singular, which sets the criteria for the choice of the subspaces that $\mathbf{V}$ and $\mathbf{W}$ present. $\mathbf{V}$ and $\mathbf{W}$ are the chosen bases of the chosen subspaces $\mathbb{R}^m$ in $\mathbb{R}^n$. In practice, the following six forms of span($\mathbf{V}$) and span($\mathbf{W}$) are commonly used. See [56].

1. span($\mathbf{W}$) = span($\mathbf{V}$). If $\mathbf{A}$ is positive definite, step 3 is equivalent to minimizing the A-norm of the error: $(\mathbf{x}_\infty - \mathbf{x}_m)'\,\mathbf{A}\,(\mathbf{x}_\infty - \mathbf{x}_m)$ for all $\mathbf{x}_m$ defined in step 1, where $\mathbf{x}_\infty$ satisfies $\mathbf{A}\mathbf{x}_\infty = \mathbf{a}$. If $\mathbf{A}$ is not positive definite, it does not correspond to any extrema, rather it is merely a stationary condition.

2. span($\mathbf{W}$) = $\mathbf{A}$ span($\mathbf{V}$). Step 3 is equivalent to minimizing the 2-norm of the residual: $(\mathbf{a} - \mathbf{A}\mathbf{x}_m)'\,(\mathbf{a} - \mathbf{A}\mathbf{x}_m)$ for all $\mathbf{x}_m$ defined in step 1.

3. span($\mathbf{V}$) = $\mathbf{A}'$ span($\mathbf{W}$). Step 3 is equivalent to minimizing the 2-norm of the error: $(\mathbf{x}_\infty - \mathbf{x}_m)'\,(\mathbf{x}_\infty - \mathbf{x}_m)$ for all $\mathbf{x}_m$ defined in step 1, where $\mathbf{x}_\infty$ satisfies $\mathbf{A}\mathbf{x}_\infty = \mathbf{a}$.

4. span($\mathbf{V}$) = ?. $\mathbf{W}$ is unspecified. For the convenience of solution, $\mathbf{W}$ is chosen to render $(\mathbf{W}'\mathbf{A}\mathbf{V})\,\mathbf{v} = \mathbf{W}'\mathbf{y}_0$ a simple form. The explicit form of $\mathbf{W}$ is not needed.

5. span($\mathbf{V}$) = ?. $\mathbf{V}$ is unspecified. For the convenience of solution, $\mathbf{V}$ is chosen to render $(\mathbf{W}'\mathbf{A}\mathbf{V})\,\mathbf{v} = \mathbf{W}'\mathbf{y}_0$ a simple form. The explicit form of $\mathbf{V}$ is not needed.

6. span($\mathbf{V}$) = ? and span($\mathbf{W}$) = ?. Both $\mathbf{V}$ and $\mathbf{W}$ are determined backwardly to make the projection condition equivalent to an established algorithm, although the explicit form of $\mathbf{V}$ and $\mathbf{W}$ is not needed.

In most algorithms, we need to construct one or two Krylov subspaces of $\mathrm{span}\{\mathbf{r}, \mathbf{A}\mathbf{r}, \mathbf{A}^2\mathbf{r}, \dots, \mathbf{A}^{m-1}\mathbf{r}\}$ and/or $\mathrm{span}\{\mathbf{q}, \mathbf{A}'\mathbf{q}, \mathbf{A}'^2\mathbf{q}, \dots, \mathbf{A}'^{m-1}\mathbf{q}\}$. We denote these subspace as $\mathbb{K}(\mathbf{A}, \mathbf{r}, m)$ and $\mathbb{K}(\mathbf{A}', \mathbf{q}, m)$, respectively. From how it is constructed, we can see that $\mathbb{K}(\mathbf{A}, \mathbf{r}, m) = P_k(\mathbf{A})\mathbf{r}$, where P_k is a polynomial of order $k, k \leq m$. The order k depends on the distinctions of $\mathbf{A}$'s eigenvalues corresponding to the eigenvectors that are not orthogonal to $\mathbf{r}$. Similarly $\mathbb{K}(\mathbf{A}', \mathbf{q}, m) = P_l(\mathbf{A}')\mathbf{q}$, where P_l is another polynomial of order $l, l \leq m$. The order l depends on the distinctions of $\mathbf{A}'$'s eigenvalues corresponding to the eigenvectors that are not orthogonal to $\mathbf{q}$. The eigenvalues of $\mathbf{A}$ and $\mathbf{A}'$ are same, but for a non-symmetric $\mathbf{A}$, their eigenvectors are different.

We need to choose bases to present $\mathbb{K}(\mathbf{A}, \mathbf{r}, m)$ and/or $\mathbb{K}(\mathbf{A}', \mathbf{q}, m)$. There are three common choices: (a) orthogonal bases, (b) incomplete orthogonal bases, (c) bi-orthogonal bases.

If $\mathbf{A}$ is symmetric, the complexities of choosing span($\mathbf{V}$), span($\mathbf{W}$), and their bases are greatly reduced. It is possible to choose only the full orthogonal bases $\mathbf{V}$ for the Krylov subspace $\mathbb{K}(\mathbf{A}, \mathbf{r}, m)$. $\mathbf{V}$ can be constructed by calling the MATLAB function QTQtByLanczos_.m, see Section 3.6.3. To be consistent with the notations used in this chapter, we changed the output arguments [Q,T3] of GTGiByLanczos_.m to [V,T]. V is an orthogonal matrix of size $n \times (m + 1)$. T is a symmetric tri-diagonal matrix of size $(m + 1) \times m$. $\mathbf{V}$ and $\mathbf{T}$ satisfy Eqs. (3.18) and (3.21). For the reference, we re-write them in the following:

$$\mathbf{A}\mathbf{V}(:, 1:m) = \mathbf{V}(:, 1:m)\mathbf{T}(1:m, 1:m) + T(m+1, m)\mathbf{V}(:, m+1)\mathbf{I}(m, :) = \mathbf{V}\mathbf{T}, \qquad (5.17a)$$

$$\mathbf{V}(:, 1:m)'\mathbf{V}(:, 1:m) = \mathbf{I}, \qquad (5.17b)$$

$$\mathbf{V}(:, 1:m)'\mathbf{V}(:, m+1) = \mathbf{0}. \qquad (5.17c)$$

If the Lanczos procedure continues to $m = n$, two extra identities hold

$$\mathbf{AV} = \mathbf{VT}; \quad \mathbf{A} = \mathbf{VTV}'. \tag{5.18}$$

For the non-symmetric matrix $\mathbf{A}$, the orthogonal bases of $\mathbb{K}(\mathbf{A}, \mathbf{r}, m)$ are constructed by calling the MATLAB function QHQtByArnoldi_.m, see Section 3.5. To be consistent with the notations used in this chapter, we changed the output arguments [Q,H] of QHQtByArnoldi_.m to [V,H]. V is an orthogonal matrix of size $n \times (m + 1)$. H is an upper Hessenberg matrix of size $(m + 1) \times m$. $\mathbf{V}$ and $\mathbf{H}$ satisfy Eqs. (3.13) and (3.16). For the reference, we rewrite Eqs. (3.13) and (3.16) in the following:

$$\mathbf{AV}(:, 1 : m) = \mathbf{V}(:, 1 : m)\mathbf{H}(1 : m, 1 : m) + H(m + 1, m)\mathbf{V}(:, m + 1)\mathbf{I}(m, :) = \mathbf{VH}, \tag{5.19a}$$
$$\mathbf{V}(:, 1 : m)'\mathbf{V}(:, 1 : m) = \mathbf{I}, \tag{5.19b}$$
$$\mathbf{V}(:, 1 : m)'\mathbf{V}(:, m + 1) = \mathbf{0}. \tag{5.19c}$$

If the Arnoldi procedure continues to $m = n$, two extra identities hold

$$\mathbf{AV} = \mathbf{VH}; \quad \mathbf{A} = \mathbf{VHV}'. \tag{5.20}$$

Similar statements can be made regarding the orthogonal bases of $\mathbb{K}(\mathbf{A}', \mathbf{q}, m)$.

When constructing the incomplete orthogonal bases of $\mathbb{K}(\mathbf{A}, \mathbf{r}, m)$, the orthogonality is *not* enforced among all the columns of $\mathbf{V}$, but only among at most $l, l < m$ neighboring columns. In this case, $\mathbf{V}$ is incompletely orthogonal and $\mathbf{H}$ is a band matrix with lower bandwidth 1 and upper bandwidth $l, l < m$. Eq. (5.19a) is still valid, because $\mathbf{V}$ and $\mathbf{H}$ are constructed based on it. However, Eqs. (5.19b) and (5.19c) are not valid anymore. The purpose of the incomplete orthogonalization is to reduce the computation, because the computation of orthogonalization increases linearly to the number of orthogonal columns. Similar statements can be made regarding the incomplete orthogonal bases of $\mathbb{K}(\mathbf{A}', \mathbf{q}, m)$.

When constructing the bi-orthogonal bases, we construct two bases, $\mathbf{V}$ for $\mathbb{K}(\mathbf{A}, \mathbf{r}, m)$, $\mathbf{W}$ for $\mathbb{K}(\mathbf{A}', \mathbf{q}, m)$. Both $\mathbf{V}$ and $\mathbf{W}$ are not orthogonal, but $\mathbf{W}'\mathbf{V} = \mathbf{I}$. If $\mathbf{V}$ and $\mathbf{W}$ are square, the relation implies $\mathbf{W}' = \mathbf{V}^{-1}$. Such bi-orthogonal bases can be calculated by calling the MATLAB function GTGiByLanczos_.m, see Section 2.5.3. To be consistent with the notations used in this chapter, we changed the output arguments [T,G,Gi] of GTGiByLanczos_.m to [T,V,W]. T is a tri-diagonal matrix of size $(m+1) \times m$. V is a matrix of size $n \times (m + 1)$. W is a matrix of size $(m + 1) \times n$. $\mathbf{T}$, $\mathbf{V}$, and $\mathbf{W}$ satisfy Eqs. (2.23). For the reference, we write Eqs. (2.23) in the following:

$$\mathbf{AV}(:, 1 : m) = \mathbf{V}(:, 1 : m)\mathbf{T}(1 : m, 1 : m) + T(m + 1, m)\mathbf{V}(:, m + 1)\mathbf{I}(m, :) = \mathbf{VT}, \tag{5.21a}$$
$$\mathbf{A}'\mathbf{W}(1 : m, :)' = \mathbf{W}(1 : m, :)'\mathbf{T}(1 : m, 1 : m)' + T(m, m + 1)\mathbf{W}(m + 1, :)'\mathbf{I}(m, :) = \mathbf{W}'\mathbf{T}'. \tag{5.21b}$$

If $m = n$, two extra identities hold

$$\mathbf{AV} = \mathbf{VT}; \quad \mathbf{A} = \mathbf{VTW}'. \tag{5.22}$$

Considering the properties of $\mathbf{A}$, we choose different $\mathbf{V}$, $\mathbf{W}$, different ways to generate them, different ways to solve the scale reduced linear equations generated at step 3, and different ways to update the approximate solutions at step 4. All of these different choices produce the different algorithms presented in the next three sections.

5.4 NON-STATIONARY ITERATIONS APPLIED TO SYMMETRIC MATRIX

5.4.1 CG: CONJUGATE GRADIENT V IS FULL ORTHOGONAL BASES OF $\mathbb{K}(A, y_0, m)$ AND $W = V$

Using the relations of Eqs. (5.17), the Galerkin projection condition can be simplified as follows:

$$\mathbf{W}(:,1:m)'\mathbf{y}_m = \mathbf{V}(:,1:m)'\,(\mathbf{y}_0 - \mathbf{A}\mathbf{V}(:,1:m)\mathbf{v})$$
$$= \|\mathbf{y}_0\|_2\mathbf{I}(:,1) - \mathbf{T}(1:m,1:m)\mathbf{v} = \mathbf{0}. \tag{5.23}$$

Then $\mathbf{v} = \|\mathbf{y}_0\|_2\mathbf{T}(1:m,1:m)^{-1}\mathbf{I}(:,1)$, where $\mathbf{T}_m$ is a symmetric tri-diagonal matrix. In the following, we denote $\beta = \|\mathbf{y}_0\|_2$.

There are many ways to solve $\mathbf{v} = \beta\mathbf{T}_m^{-1}\mathbf{I}(:,1)$, for example, eqsBandByGauss_.m, eqsBandByGivens_.m or mdivideByDecomposing_ with the input decomposer='LUband_' or decomposer='QRband_', see Section 4.4–4.6.

After $\mathbf{v}$ is calculated, we can calculate the new approximate solution $\mathbf{x}_m = \mathbf{x}_0 + \mathbf{V}(:,1:m)\mathbf{v}$ and then calculate the new residual $\mathbf{y}_m$,

$$\mathbf{y}_m = \mathbf{a} - \mathbf{A}\mathbf{x}_m = \mathbf{y}_0 - \mathbf{A}\mathbf{V}(:,1:m)\mathbf{v}$$
$$= \mathbf{y}_0 - \mathbf{V}(:,1:m)\mathbf{T}(1:m,1:m)\mathbf{v} - T(m+1,m)\mathbf{V}(:,m+1)\mathbf{I}(m,:)\mathbf{v} \tag{5.24}$$
$$= -T(m+1,m)v(m)\mathbf{V}(:,m+1),$$

where in the second equality the first two terms are canceled because of Eq. (5.23). The new residual $\mathbf{y}_m$ is in the direction of $\mathbf{V}(:,m+1)$. To check the convergence by $\|\mathbf{y}_m\|_2$, we do not need to form $\mathbf{y}_m$ according to Eq. (5.24). Instead the simple relation $\|\mathbf{y}_m\|_2 = T(m+1,m)|v(m)|$ can be used.

If $m = n$, $T(n+1,n) = 0$. It takes only one iteration to converge. If QTQtByLanczos_.m breaks down when generating $\mathbf{V}$ at an immediate step $l, l \leq m$, then $T(l+1,l) = 0$. The current iteration will converge. If $\mathbf{A}$ is positive definite, the iteration can converge for any $m \geq 1$. If $\mathbf{A}$ is not positive definite, the convergence property is not known. To improve the convergence, we can apply the iterations to the preconditioned form of $\mathbf{A}\mathbf{x} = \mathbf{a}$. See the discussion of numerical examples below.

Although the process outlined above works well, a more elegant process, the so-called conjugate gradient method, is discussed below.

Because $\mathbf{T}(1:m,1:m)$ is a symmetric tri-diagonal matrix, its LU decomposition without pivoting has a fixed format. We take $m = 5$ as an example. $\mathbf{T}_5 = \mathbf{L}_5\mathbf{U}_5$ is shown below,

$$\begin{bmatrix} T_{11} & T_{12} & & & \\ T_{12} & T_{22} & T_{23} & & \\ & T_{23} & T_{33} & T_{34} & \\ & & T_{34} & T_{44} & T_{45} \\ & & & T_{45} & T_{55} \end{bmatrix} = \begin{bmatrix} 1 & & & & \\ L_{21} & 1 & & & \\ & L_{32} & 1 & & \\ & & L_{43} & 1 & \\ & & & L_{54} & 1 \end{bmatrix}\begin{bmatrix} U_{11} & T_{12} & & & \\ & U_{22} & T_{23} & & \\ & & U_{33} & T_{34} & \\ & & & U_{44} & T_{45} \\ & & & & U_{55} \end{bmatrix}.$$

We write the new approximate solution $\mathbf{x}_m$ in terms of $\mathbf{T}_m = \mathbf{L}_m\mathbf{U}_m$ as follows:

$$\mathbf{x}_m = \mathbf{x}_0 + \mathbf{V}_{nm}\mathbf{v} = \mathbf{x}_0 + \mathbf{V}_{nm}\,(\mathbf{L}_m\mathbf{U}_m)^{-1}\,\beta\mathbf{I}(:,1)$$
$$= \mathbf{x}_0 + \left(\mathbf{V}_{nm}\mathbf{U}_m^{-1}\right)\left(\mathbf{L}_m^{-1}\beta\mathbf{I}(:,1)\right) = \mathbf{x}_0 + \mathbf{P}\mathbf{s}, \tag{5.25}$$

where $\mathbf{P} = \mathbf{V}_{nm}\mathbf{U}_m^{-1}$ and $\mathbf{s} = \mathbf{L}_m^{-1}\beta\mathbf{I}(:,1)$. For $\mathbf{P} = \mathbf{V}_{nm}\mathbf{U}^{-1}$, equating the last column of both sides of $\mathbf{PU} = \mathbf{V}(:,1:m)$, we obtain

$$\mathbf{P}(:,m) = \frac{1}{U(m,m)} \left(\mathbf{V}(:,m) - T(m-1,m)\mathbf{P}(:,m-1) \right). \tag{5.26}$$

For $\mathbf{s} = \mathbf{L}^{-1}\beta\mathbf{I}(:,1)$, equating the last row of both sides of $\mathbf{Ls} = \beta\mathbf{I}(:,1)$, we obtain

$$s(m) = -L(m,m-1)s(m-1). \tag{5.27}$$

By construction, we can see that the following identities hold:

$$\mathbf{P}'\mathbf{AP} = \mathbf{U}'^{-1}\mathbf{V}'_{nm}\mathbf{AV}_{nm}\mathbf{U}^{-1} = \mathbf{U}'^{-1}\mathbf{T}_m\mathbf{U}^{-1} = \mathbf{U}'^{-1}\mathbf{LUU}^{-1} = \mathbf{U}'^{-1}\mathbf{L}. \tag{5.28}$$

$\mathbf{P}'\mathbf{AP}$ is symmetric and $\mathbf{U}'^{-1}\mathbf{L}$ is a lower triangular and also symmetric. This means both must be diagonal, in other words, $\mathbf{P}(:,k)'\mathbf{AP}(:,l) = \mathbf{0}, k,l = 1,\ldots,m, k \neq l$. The columns of $\mathbf{P}$ are *A-orthogonal* or *conjugate*.

Instead of constructing the whole $\mathbf{V}_{nm}$ and $\mathbf{T}_m$ and then constructing the whole $\mathbf{P}(:,1:m)$, we can also calculate $\mathbf{V}(:,k)$, $T(k,k), T(k+1,k) = T(k,k+1)$ and $\mathbf{P}(:,k)$ for $k = 1,\ldots,m$ and calculate the approximate solutions $\mathbf{x}_k$ for $k = 1,\ldots,m$. From Eq. (5.25), we can see that

$$\begin{aligned}\mathbf{x}_k &= \mathbf{x}_0 + \mathbf{P}(:,1:k)\mathbf{s}(1:k) = \mathbf{x}_0 + \mathbf{P}(:,1:k-1)\mathbf{s}(1:k-1) + \mathbf{P}(:,k)s(k) \\ &= \mathbf{x}_{k-1} + \mathbf{P}(:,k)s(k); \quad k = 1,\ldots,m.\end{aligned} \tag{5.29}$$

Then the residuals $\mathbf{y}_k = \mathbf{a} - \mathbf{Ax}_k$ are calculated as follows:

$$\mathbf{y}_k = \mathbf{y}_{k-1} - \mathbf{AP}(:,k)s(k) = -T(k+1,k)v(k)\mathbf{V}(:,k+1); \quad k = 1,\ldots,m, \tag{5.30}$$

where the last equality is from Eq. (5.24). By construction, we see that $\mathbf{y}'_k\mathbf{y}_l = 0, k,l = 0,1,\ldots,m, k \neq l$. In other words, the residuals in different steps are orthogonal.

Following Eqs. (5.26), (5.29), and (5.30) and considering the orthogonality among $\mathbf{y}_k$s and A-orthogonal among $\mathbf{P}(:,k)$s, in fact, we do not need to keep all the columns of $\mathbf{V}$ and $\mathbf{P}$. Introducing a vector $\mathbf{p}_k$ which has a scale difference to $\mathbf{P}(:,k)$, we can write Eqs. (5.26), (5.29), and (5.30) more succinctly as follows:

$$\mathbf{x}_{k+1} = \mathbf{x}_k + \alpha_k\mathbf{p}_k; \quad \mathbf{y}_{k+1} = \mathbf{y}_k - \alpha_k\mathbf{Ap}_k; \quad \mathbf{p}_{k+1} = \mathbf{y}_{k+1} + \beta_k\mathbf{p}_k. \tag{5.31}$$

The scalars α_k, β_k are determined by the conditions $\mathbf{y}'_{k+1}\mathbf{y}_k = 0$ and $\mathbf{p}'_{k+1}\mathbf{Ap}_k = 0$,

$$\alpha_k = \frac{\mathbf{y}'_k\mathbf{y}_k}{\mathbf{p}'_k\mathbf{Ap}_k}; \quad \beta_k = \frac{\mathbf{y}'_{k+1}\mathbf{y}_{k+1}}{\mathbf{y}'_k\mathbf{y}_k}. \tag{5.32}$$

At the start, $\mathbf{p}_0 = \mathbf{y}_0$. This defines the CG iteration which requires only one matrix-vector product ($\mathbf{Ap}$), two vector inner-products ($\mathbf{y}'\mathbf{y}$ and $\mathbf{p}'\mathbf{Ap}$), and four vectors ($\mathbf{x}, \mathbf{y}, \mathbf{p}, \mathbf{Ap}$).

The following is the MATLAB implementation of Eqs. (5.31) and (5.33).

Algorithm 5.4

Conjugate Gradient iterations for Symmetric Ax=a

```
% A=A', input x=x0, output x: L*(A)*R*(R^{-1}*x)=L*a, default L=I, R=I.
function x = eqsCG_(A,a,x,tol,last,L,R)

[m,n] = size_(A);
y = Ay_(A,y,'right');
if (exist('L','var') && ~isempty(L)) y = Ay_(L,a-y,'right'); else y = a-y; end
p = y;  yy = y'*y;  epslon = tol*max(1.0,sqrt(yy));  l = 0;

while(sqrt(yy)>epslon && l<last)
    if (exist('R','var') && ~isempty(R)) Ap = Ay_(R,p,'right'); else Ap = p; end
    Ap = Ay_(A,Ap,'right');
    if (exist('L','var') && ~isempty(L)) Ap = Ay_(L,Ap,'right'); end
    alpha = yy/(p'*Ap);
    x = x + alpha*p;  y = y - alpha*Ap;
    yy0 = yy;  yy = y'*y;  beta = yy/yy0;
    p = y + beta*p;  l = l + 1;
end
if (exist('R','var') && ~isempty(R)) x = Ay_(R,x,'right'); end
```

5.4.2 CR: CONJUGATE RESIDUAL V IS FULL ORTHOGONAL BASES OF $\mathbb{K}(\mathbf{A}, \mathbf{y_0}, m)$ AND $\mathbf{W} = \mathbf{AV}$

Using the relations of Eqs. (5.17), the Galerkin projection condition now takes the following form:

$$
\begin{aligned}
\mathbf{W}(:,1:m)'\mathbf{y}_m &= (\mathbf{AV}(:,1:m))'\,(\mathbf{a} - \mathbf{A}\,(\mathbf{x}_0 + \mathbf{V}(:,1:m)\mathbf{v})) \\
&= (\mathbf{VT})'\,(\mathbf{y}_0 - (\mathbf{VT})\,\mathbf{v}) \\
&= \beta\mathbf{T}(1:m+1,1:m)'\mathbf{I}(:,1) - \mathbf{T}(1:m+1,1:m)'\mathbf{T}(1:m+1,1:m)\mathbf{v} = 0.
\end{aligned}
\tag{5.33}
$$

If $\mathbf{T}(1:m+1,1:m)'\mathbf{T}(1:m+1,1:m)$ is formed explicitly, then $\mathbf{v} = (\mathbf{T}'\mathbf{T})^{-1}\beta\mathbf{T}'\mathbf{I}(:,1)$ can be solved by many algorithms of Chapter 4.

A better way is not to form $\mathbf{T}'\mathbf{T}$. As can be seen from Eq. (5.33), $\mathbf{v}$ is the solution of the over-determined linear equations $\mathbf{T}(1:m+1,1:m)\mathbf{v} = \beta\mathbf{I}(:,1)$. The over-determined linear equations can be solved by QR,

$$
\mathbf{v} = \beta\mathbf{T}_{(m+1)m}^{+}\mathbf{I}(:,1) = \beta\left(\mathbf{Q}_{m+1}\mathbf{R}_{(m+1)m}\right)^{+}\mathbf{I}(:,1) = \beta\mathbf{R}^{+}\mathbf{Q}'\mathbf{I}(:,1) = \beta\mathbf{R}^{+}\mathbf{Q}(1,:)'.
\tag{5.34}
$$

In the above steps, $\mathbf{QR} = \mathbf{T}_{(m+1)m}$ is a QR decomposition of $\mathbf{T}_{(m+1)m}$ performed by calling QRband_, see Section 3.2.6. $\mathbf{R}^{+}\mathbf{Q}(1,:)'$ is the least square solution performed by calling eqsUpperTriangle_, see Section 4.3.5. LU decomposition of $\mathbf{T}(1:m+1,1;m)$ is not suitable for the minimum residual solution. See the discussion of pseudo-inverse in Section 4.1.

After $\mathbf{v}$ is calculated, we can calculate the new approximate solution $\mathbf{x}_m = \mathbf{x}_0 + \mathbf{V}(:,1:m)\mathbf{v}$ and then calculate the new residual $\mathbf{y}_m$,

$$
\begin{aligned}
\mathbf{y}_m &= \mathbf{y}_0 - \mathbf{AV}(:,1:m)\mathbf{v} = \mathbf{V}(:,1:m+1)\left(\beta\mathbf{I}(:,1) - \mathbf{T}_{(m+1)m}\mathbf{v}\right) \\
&= \beta\mathbf{Q}(1,m+1)\mathbf{V}(:,1:m+1)\mathbf{QI}(:,m+1).
\end{aligned}
\tag{5.35}
$$

However, for the purpose of the check of convergence of iterations, $\mathbf{y}_m$ is not needed. If $\|\mathbf{y}_m\|_2$ is needed to check the convergence of iterations, we can see that it is equal to $\beta\mathbf{Q}(1,m+1)$, which is readily available when solving the minimum residual equations of Eq. (5.34).

Similarly to CG method discussed in the last subsection, we can combine the solution of $\mathbf{v}$ and the update of $\mathbf{x}_m$ to obtain a more elegant method: conjugate residual (CR) method.

$$
\begin{aligned}
\mathbf{x}_m &= \mathbf{x}_0 + \mathbf{V}(:, 1:m)\mathbf{v} = \mathbf{x}_0 + \left(\mathbf{V}(:, 1:m)\mathbf{R}^+\right)\left(\beta \mathbf{Q}(1,:)'\right) = \mathbf{x}_0 + \mathbf{Ps} \\
&= (\mathbf{x}_0 + \mathbf{P}(:, 1:m-1)\mathbf{s}(1:m-1)) + \mathbf{P}(:,m)\mathbf{s}(m) = \mathbf{x}_{m-1} + \mathbf{P}(:,m)\mathbf{s}(m),
\end{aligned}
\tag{5.36}
$$

where $\mathbf{P} = \mathbf{V}(:, 1:m)\mathbf{R}^+$ and $\mathbf{s} = \beta \mathbf{Q}(1,:)'$. It can be verified that $(\mathbf{AP})'(\mathbf{AP}) = \mathbf{I}$ and $\mathbf{y}_k' \mathbf{Ay}_l = 0, k, l = 1, \ldots, m, k \neq l$.

To illustrate the procedure more clearly, we study a simple example of $m = 4$. The partial Lanczos reduction starting with $\mathbf{V}(:, 1) = \frac{\mathbf{y}_0}{\beta}$ has the following form:

$$
\mathbf{A}\left[\mathbf{V}(:, 1), \mathbf{V}(:, 2), \mathbf{V}(:, 3), \mathbf{V}(:, 4)\right] = \left[\mathbf{V}(:, 1), \mathbf{V}(:, 2), \mathbf{V}(:, 3), \mathbf{V}(:, 4), \mathbf{V}(:, 5)\right]
\begin{bmatrix}
T_{11} & T_{21} & & & \\
T_{21} & T_{22} & T_{32} & & \\
& T_{32} & T_{33} & T_{43} & \\
& & T_{43} & T_{44} & \\
& & & T_{54} &
\end{bmatrix}.
$$

The first approximation is $\mathbf{x}_1 = \mathbf{x}_0 + \mathbf{V}(:, 1)\mathbf{v}_1$. $\mathbf{v}_1$ is determined by minimizing $\|\mathbf{y}_1\|_2$,

$$
\mathbf{y}_1 = \mathbf{y}_0 - \mathbf{AV}(:, 1)\mathbf{v}_1 = \mathbf{V}(:, 1:2)\left(\begin{bmatrix}\beta \\ 0\end{bmatrix} - \begin{bmatrix}T_{11} \\ T_{21}\end{bmatrix}\mathbf{v}_1\right) = \mathbf{V}(:, 1:2)\mathbf{Q}_1\left(\beta \begin{bmatrix}c_1 \\ s_1\end{bmatrix} - \begin{bmatrix}R_{11} \\ 0\end{bmatrix}\mathbf{v}_1\right). \tag{a}
$$

In Eq. (a), $\mathbf{Q}_1$ is the Givens rotation eliminating T_{21} and is equal to $\begin{bmatrix} c_1 & s_1 \\ -s_1 & c_1 \end{bmatrix}$. From Eq. (a), we can obtain the following results:

$$
\text{1st solution } \mathbf{x}_1 = \mathbf{x}_0 + \left(\mathbf{V}(:, 1)\frac{1}{R_{11}}\right)(c_1\beta) = \mathbf{x}_0 + \mathbf{P}(:, 1)\mathbf{s}(1),
$$

$$
\text{1st residual } \mathbf{y}_1 = \mathbf{V}(:, 1:2)\mathbf{Q}_1 s_1 \beta \begin{bmatrix} 0 \\ 1 \end{bmatrix}.
$$

The second approximation is $\mathbf{x}_2 = \mathbf{x}_0 + \mathbf{V}(:, 1:2)\mathbf{v}_2$. $\mathbf{v}_2$ is determined by minimizing $\|\mathbf{y}_2\|_2$,

$$
\begin{aligned}
\mathbf{y}_2 = \mathbf{y}_0 - \mathbf{AV}(:, 1:2)\mathbf{v}_2 &= \mathbf{V}(:, 1:3)\left(\begin{bmatrix}\beta \\ 0 \\ 0\end{bmatrix} - \begin{bmatrix}T_{11} & T_{21} \\ T_{21} & T_{22} \\ & T_{32}\end{bmatrix}\mathbf{v}_2\right) \\
&= \mathbf{V}(:, 1:3)\mathbf{Q}_1\mathbf{Q}_2\left(\beta \begin{bmatrix}c_1 \\ s_1 c_2 \\ s_1 s_2\end{bmatrix} - \begin{bmatrix}R_{11} & R_{12} \\ & R_{22} \\ & 0\end{bmatrix}\mathbf{v}_2\right).
\end{aligned}
\tag{b}
$$

In Eq. (b), $\mathbf{Q}_2$ is the Givens rotation eliminating T_{32} and is equal to $\begin{bmatrix} c_2 & s_2 \\ -s_2 & c_2 \end{bmatrix}$. From Eq. (b), we can obtain the following results:

$$
\text{2nd solution } \mathbf{x}_2 = \mathbf{x}_0 + \left(\mathbf{V}(:, 1:2)\begin{bmatrix}R_{11} & R_{12} \\ & R_{22}\end{bmatrix}^{-1}\right)\left(\beta \begin{bmatrix}c_1 \\ s_1 c_2\end{bmatrix}\right) = \mathbf{x}_0 + \mathbf{P}(:, 1:2)\mathbf{s}(1:2),
$$

$$
\text{2nd residual } \mathbf{y}_2 = \mathbf{V}(:, 1:2)\mathbf{Q}_1\mathbf{Q}_2 s_1 s_2 \beta \begin{bmatrix} 0 \\ 0 \\ 1 \end{bmatrix}.
$$

We can continue the above procedure two more steps to reach $\mathbf{V}(:, 1:5)$ and $\mathbf{T}(1:5, 1:4)$. Then we either increase $\mathbf{V}$ and $\mathbf{T}$ or generate a new $\mathbf{V}(:, 1:5)$ with the newly calculated $\mathbf{x}_4$ as $\mathbf{x}_0$ and $\mathbf{y}_4$ as $\mathbf{y}_0$.

We can verify the following identities:

$$\mathbf{y}_0'\mathbf{A}\mathbf{y}_1 = s_1\beta^2 (\mathbf{A}\mathbf{V}(:, 1))' \, \mathbf{V}(:, 1:2)\mathbf{Q}_1 \begin{bmatrix} 0 \\ 1 \end{bmatrix} = s_1\beta^2 (\mathbf{Q}_1\mathbf{R}(1:2, 1))' \, \mathbf{Q}_1 \begin{bmatrix} 0 \\ 1 \end{bmatrix}$$

$$= s_1\beta^2 [R_{11} 0] \begin{bmatrix} 0 \\ 1 \end{bmatrix} = 0,$$

$$\mathbf{y}_0'\mathbf{A}\mathbf{y}_2 = s_1^2 s_2\beta^2 (\mathbf{A}\mathbf{V}(:, 1))' \, \mathbf{V}(:, 1:3)\mathbf{Q}_1\mathbf{Q}_2 \begin{bmatrix} 0 \\ 0 \\ 1 \end{bmatrix}$$

$$= s_1^2 s_2\beta^2 \mathbf{R}(1:2, 1)' \mathbf{Q}_1' \mathbf{V}(:, 1:2)' \mathbf{V}(:, 1:3)\mathbf{Q}_1\mathbf{Q}_2 \begin{bmatrix} 0 \\ 0 \\ 1 \end{bmatrix} = s_1^2 s_2\beta^2 [R_{11} 0] \begin{bmatrix} 0 \\ -s_2 \end{bmatrix} = 0,$$

$$\mathbf{y}_1'\mathbf{A}\mathbf{y}_2 = s_1^2 s_2\beta^2 [0\ 1] \mathbf{Q}_1' \mathbf{V}(:, 1:2)' \mathbf{A}\mathbf{V}(:, 1:2)\mathbf{Q}_1\mathbf{Q}_2 \begin{bmatrix} 0 \\ 0 \\ 1 \end{bmatrix}$$

$$= s_1^2 s_2\beta^2 [0\ 1] \mathbf{Q}_1' \mathbf{V}(:, 1:2)' \mathbf{Q}(:, 1:3)\mathbf{Q}_1\mathbf{Q}_2 \begin{bmatrix} R_{11} & R_{12} \\ 0 & R_{22} \\ 0 & 0 \end{bmatrix} \begin{bmatrix} 0 \\ 0 \\ 1 \end{bmatrix} = 0,$$

$$(\mathbf{A}\mathbf{P})'\,(\mathbf{A}\mathbf{P}) = \left(\mathbf{A}\mathbf{V}(:, 1:2)\mathbf{R}(1:2, 1:2)^{-1}\right)' \left(\mathbf{A}\mathbf{V}(:, 1:2)\mathbf{R}(1:2, 1:2)^{-1}\right)$$

$$= \mathbf{R}(1:2, 1:2)'^{-1}\mathbf{R}(1:3, 1:2)'\mathbf{R}(1:3, 1:2)\mathbf{R}(1:2, 1:2)^{-1} = \mathbf{I}.$$

From the above discussion, we can build the CR method. The scalars α_k, β_k in Eq. (5.31) are now determined by the conditions $\mathbf{y}_k'\mathbf{A}\mathbf{y}_l = 0, k \neq l$ and $(\mathbf{A}\mathbf{P})'\,(\mathbf{A}\mathbf{P}) = \mathbf{I}$,

$$\alpha_k = \frac{\mathbf{y}_k'\mathbf{A}\mathbf{y}_k}{(\mathbf{A}\mathbf{p}_k)'\,(\mathbf{A}\mathbf{p}_k)}; \quad \beta_k = \frac{\mathbf{y}_{k+1}'\mathbf{A}\mathbf{y}_{k+1}}{\mathbf{y}_k'\mathbf{A}\mathbf{y}_k}. \tag{5.37}$$

At the start, $\mathbf{p}_0 = \mathbf{y}_0$. This defines the CR iteration which requires only one matrix-vector product ($\mathbf{A}\mathbf{y}$), two vector inner-products ($\mathbf{y}'\mathbf{A}\mathbf{y}$ and $(\mathbf{A}\mathbf{p})'(\mathbf{A}\mathbf{p})$), and five vectors ($\mathbf{x}, \mathbf{y}, \mathbf{p}, \mathbf{A}\mathbf{y}, \mathbf{A}\mathbf{p}$). The vector $\mathbf{A}\mathbf{p}$ is calculated as $\mathbf{A}\mathbf{p}_{k+1} = \mathbf{A}\mathbf{y}_{k+1} + t\mathbf{A}\mathbf{y}_k$.

CR shows similar convergence to CG method, but it requires one more vector storage and $2n$ more operations for $\mathbf{A}\mathbf{p}$. That is why CG method is often preferred.

The following is the MATLAB implementation of Eqs. (5.31) and (5.37).

Algorithm 5.5

Conjugate residual iterations for symmetric Ax=a

```
% A=A', input x=x0, output x: L*(A)*R*(R^{-1}*x)=L*a, default L=I, R=I.
function x = eqsCR_(A,a,x,tol,last,L,R)

[m,n] = size_(A);

if (exist('R','var') && ~isempty(R)) y = Ay_(R,x,'right'); else y = x; end
y = Ay_(A,y,'right');
```

```
if (exist('L','var') && ~isempty(L)) y = Ay_(L,a-y,'right'); else y = a-y; end
if (exist('R','var') && ~isempty(R)) Ay = Ay_(R,y,'right'); else Ay = y; end
Ay = Ay_(A,Ay,'right');
if (exist('L','var') && ~isempty(L)) Ay = Ay_(L,Ay,'right'); end

p = y;   Ap = Ay;  yAy = y'*Ay;  epslon = tol*max(1.0,norm(y,inf));   l = 0;
while (norm(y,inf)>epslon && l<last)
    alpha = yAy/(Ap'*Ap);
    x = x + alpha*p;  y = y - alpha*Ap;
    if (exist('R','var') && ~isempty(R)) Ay = Ay_(R,y,'right'); else Ay = y; end
    Ay = Ay_(A,Ay,'right');
    if (exist('L','var') && ~isempty(L)) Ay = Ay_(L,Ay,'right'); end
    yAy0 = yAy;   yAy = y'*Ay;
    beta = yAy/yAy0;
    p = y + beta*p;   Ap = Ay + beta*Ap;
    l = l + 1;
end
if (exist('R','var') && ~isempty(R)) x = Ay_(R,x,'right'); end
```

5.4.3 'C'E: 'CONJUGATE' ERROR $\mathbf{W}$ IS FULL ORTHOGONAL BASES OF $\mathbb{K}(\mathbf{A}, \mathbf{y}_0, m)$ AND $\mathbf{V} = \mathbf{AW}$

Using the relations of Eqs. (5.17), the Galerkin projection condition now takes the following form, see [22, 79]:

$$
\begin{aligned}
\mathbf{W}(:,1:m)'\mathbf{y}_m &= \mathbf{W}(:,1:m)'\mathbf{AA}^{-1}(\mathbf{a} - \mathbf{Ax}_m) = \mathbf{V}(:,1:m)'(\mathbf{x}_\infty - \mathbf{x}_m) \\
&= \mathbf{W}(:,1:m)'\mathbf{y}_0 - (\mathbf{AW}(:,1:m))'(\mathbf{AW}(:,1:m))\mathbf{v} \\
&= \beta\mathbf{I}(:,1) - \mathbf{T}(1:m+1,1:m)'\mathbf{T}(1:m+1,1:m)\mathbf{v} = \mathbf{0}.
\end{aligned}
\tag{5.38}
$$

The first line of equalities shows that $\mathbf{x}_m$ is the minimum error solution for all $\mathbf{x}_m$ with the presumed form. The last line of equalities is the formula to determine $\mathbf{v}$. If $\mathbf{T}(1:m+1,1:m)'\mathbf{T}(1:m+1,1:m)$ is formed explicitly, then $\mathbf{v} = (\mathbf{T}'\mathbf{T})^{-1}\beta\mathbf{I}(:,1)$ can be solved by many algorithms of Chapter 4.

A better way is not to form $\mathbf{T}'\mathbf{T}$. If we introduce $\mathbf{u}$ that satisfies $\mathbf{u} = \mathbf{T}(1:m+1,1:m)\mathbf{v}$, then $\mathbf{u}$ is the solution of the under-determined linear equations $\mathbf{T}(1:m+1,1:m)'\mathbf{u} = \beta\mathbf{I}(:,1)$. Therefore,

$$
\mathbf{u} = \beta\mathbf{T}(1:m+1,1:m)'^{+}\mathbf{I}(:,1) = \beta\left(\mathbf{Q}_{m+1}\mathbf{R}_{(m+1)m}\right)'^{+}\mathbf{I}(:,1) = \beta\mathbf{QR}'^{+}\mathbf{I}(:,1).
\tag{5.39}
$$

In the above steps, $\mathbf{Q}_{m+1}\mathbf{R}_{(m+1)m} = \mathbf{T}(1:m+1,1:m)$ is the QR decomposition of $\mathbf{T}(1:m+1,1:m)$ performed by calling QRband_, see Section 3.2.6. $\mathbf{R}'^{+}_{(m+1)m}\mathbf{I}(:,1)$ is the minimum norm solution performed by calling eqsLowerTriangle_, see Section 4.3.4.

After $\mathbf{v}$ is calculated, we can calculate the new approximate solution $\mathbf{x}_m$ and then calculate the new residual $\mathbf{y}_m$ as follows:

$$
\begin{aligned}
\mathbf{x}_m &= \mathbf{x}_0 + \mathbf{AW}(:,1:m)\mathbf{v} = \mathbf{x}_0 + \mathbf{WTv} = \mathbf{x}_0 + \mathbf{W}(:,1:m+1)\mathbf{u}, \\
\mathbf{y}_m &= \mathbf{y}_0 - \mathbf{AW}(:,1:m+1)\mathbf{u}.
\end{aligned}
\tag{5.40}
$$

Unlike CG and CR, the calculation of $\mathbf{y}_m$ cannot be simplified. The convergence check can be based on the change of $\mathbf{x}_m$ between two successive iterations. In this setting, the calculation of $\mathbf{y}_m$ can be omitted.

Similarly to CG method discussed in Section 5.4.1 and CR method discussed in the last subsection, we can combine the solution of $\mathbf{v}$ and the update of $\mathbf{x}_m$ to obtain an incremental form to update $\mathbf{x}_m$ and $\mathbf{y}_m$,

$$\begin{aligned}
\mathbf{x}_m &= \mathbf{x}_0 + \mathbf{W}(:,1:m+1)\mathbf{u} \\
&= \mathbf{x}_0 + (\mathbf{W}(:,1:m+1)\mathbf{Q}(1:m+1,1:m))\left(\mathbf{R}(1:m+1,1:m)'^{+}\beta\mathbf{I}(:,1)\right) \\
&= \mathbf{x}_0 + \mathbf{Ps} = (\mathbf{x}_0 + \mathbf{P}(:,1:m-1)\mathbf{s}(1:m-1)) + \mathbf{P}(:,m)s(m) = \mathbf{x}_{m-1} + \mathbf{P}(:,m)s(m), \\
\mathbf{y}_m &= \mathbf{y}_{m-1} - \mathbf{AP}(:,m)s(m),
\end{aligned}$$

(5.41)

where $\mathbf{P} = \mathbf{W}(:,1:m+1)\mathbf{Q}(1:m+1,1:m)$ and $\mathbf{s} = \mathbf{R}(1:m,:)'^{-1}\beta\mathbf{I}(:,1)$. Unfortunately, a two-term recursive corresponding to Eq. (5.31) is not known.

In the following, eqsCE_.m gives two mathematically equivalent implementations of the 'C'E algorithm. One is based on Eq. (5.40) by setting the internal parameter inc=0. The other is based on Eq. (5.41) by setting inc=1.

Algorithm 5.6

Conjugate error iterations for symmetric Ax=a

```
% A=A', input x=x0, output x: L*(A)*R*(R^{-1}*x)=L*a, default L=I, R=I.
function x = eqsCE_(A,a,x,tol,last,L,R)

[m,n] = size_(A);  inc = 0;  tsal = min(floor(m/2),100);    %inc, tsal: internal args!
if (~iscell(A)) A = {'mtimes',A}; end

if (~isempty(R)) y = Ay_(R,x,'right'); else y = x; end
y = Ay_(A,y,'right');
if (~isempty(L)) y = Ay_(L,a-y,'right'); else y = a-y; end
beta = norm(y);   epslon = tol*max(1.0,beta);   l = 0;

if (inc == 0)      %block update of x,y
    w = [norm(y);zeros(tsal,1)];
    while(beta>epslon && l<last)
        [W,T3] = QTQtByLanczos_({{'size',[m,n]},L,A,R},1,tsal,y,[]);
        [Q,QR] = QRband_(T3,1,1,tsal+1,tsal,[],'compact');           %Q*R=T
        QR = transposeBand_(QR,1,2,tsal+1,tsal+1);
        w(1:tsal) = eqsBandLowerTriangle_(QR,2,tsal,tsal,w(1:tsal)); %w=inv(R')*w
        for k=tsal:-1:1                                             %w=Q*w
            rho = QR(k,4);        w1 = w(k);    w2 = w(k+1);
            if (rho == 1)         c = 0; s = 1;
            elseif(abs(rho) < 1)  s = 2.0*rho; c = sqrt(1.0-s*s);
            else                  c = 2.0/rho; s = sqrt(1.0-c*c); end
            w(k) = c*w1 + s*w2;   w(k+1) =-s*w1 + c*w2;
        end
        x = x + W*w;
        if (~isempty(R)) y = Ay_(R,x,'right'); else y = x; end
        y = Ay_(A,y,'right');
        if (~isempty(L)) y = Ay_(L,a-y,'right'); else y = a-y; end
        beta = norm(y);  w(1) = beta;  w(2:tsal+1) = 0;  l = l + 1;
    end
else %if(inc=1)    %incremental update of x,y
    while(beta>epslon && l<last) %Same iterations as inc=0, less memory.
        H = zeros(4,2);        %H(:,1)=H(:,k) or R of H=Q*R, H(:,2)=rho of Q
        w0 = zeros(n,1);  w1 = y/beta;  p = w1;  y0 = 0.0; y1 = 0.0; y2 = beta;
        for k = 1:tsal
            if (~isempty(R)) Aw1 = Ay_(R,w1,'right'); else Aw1 = w1; end
            Aw1 = Ay_(A,Aw1,'right');
            if (~isempty(L)) Aw1 = Ay_(L,Aw1,'right'); end
            H(3,1) = w1'*Aw1;
```

```
            w2 = Aw1 - H(2,1)*w0 - H(3,1)*w1;
            H(4,1) = norm(w2);
            if (H(4,1) > tol) w2 = w2/H(4,1); end
            for j=1:2    %Apply 2 previous [c,s] to H(:,k), ie, H(:,1)
                rho = H(j+1,2);    h1 = H(j,1);    h2 = H(j+1,1);
                if (rho == 1)          c = 0; s = 1;
                elseif(abs(rho) < 1) s = 2.0*rho; c = sqrt(1.0-s*s);
                else                   c = 2.0/rho; s = sqrt(1.0-c*c); end
                H(j,1)   = c*h1 - s*h2;   H(j+1,1) = s*h1 + c*h2;
            end
            [c,s] = givens_(H(3,1),H(4,1));
            H(3,1) = c*H(3,1) - s*H(4,1);
            if (abs(c) < tol)       H(4,2) = 1;
            elseif(abs(s) < abs(c)) H(4,2) = sign(c)*s/2;
            else                    H(4,2) = sign(s)*2/c; end
            y2 = (y2 - y0*H(1,1) - y1*H(2,1))/H(3,1);
            x = x + (c*p - s*w2)*y2;
            p = s*p + c*w2;   w0 = w1;   w1 = w2;
            H(1,1) = 0.0;   H(2,1) = H(4,1);   H(2,2) = H(3,2);   H(3,2) = H(4,2);
            y0 = y1;   y1 = y2;   y2 = 0.0;
        end
        if (exist('R','var') && ~isempty(R)) y = Ay_(R,x,'right'); else y = x; end
        y = Ay_(A,y,'right');
        if (exist('L','var') && ~isempty(L)) y = Ay_(L,a-y,'right'); else y = a-y; end
        beta = norm(y);   l = l + 1;
    end
end
if (~isempty(R)) x = Ay_(R,x,'right'); end
```

5.4.4 NUMERICAL EXAMPLES FOR CG,CR, AND CE

The numerical properties of the three algorithms and the use of eqsCG_.m, eqsCR_.m, and eqsCE_.m are demonstrated with the following simple examples.

The following are $\mathbf{A}$ and $\mathbf{a}$ for the first example. This is the same matrix and vector used in Section 5.2. $\mathbf{A}$ is symmetric and positive definite.

```
>> A = [ 3.2379  -0.7837  -1.4722   0.3539  -0.7404  -0.4116   0.7138  -0.7395;
        -0.7837   3.4437   0.0182  -0.2024   0.1539  -1.0706   0.0119  -0.3450;
        -1.4722   0.0182   2.4814  -0.3643   0.5938   0.4763   0.2375   0.2707;
         0.3539  -0.2024  -0.3643   4.4725   0.0922  -0.6030   0.5484  -0.8374;
        -0.7404   0.1539   0.5938   0.0922   3.6565  -0.9065  -0.5724  -0.5546;
        -0.4116  -1.0706   0.4763  -0.6030  -0.9065   3.8057  -0.5302  -0.6180;
         0.7138   0.0119   0.2375   0.5484  -0.5724  -0.5302   2.9271   0.1662;
        -0.7395  -0.3450   0.2707  -0.8374  -0.5546  -0.6180   0.1662   2.1458];
>> a = [0.5529, -0.2037, -2.0543, 0.1326, 1.5929, 1.0184, -1.5804, -0.0787]';
```

We use the following two initial guesses for the solution of $\mathbf{Ax} = \mathbf{a}$.

```
>> x01=zeros(8,1);    x02=(1:8)';
```

CG and CR show similar convergence pattern. Convergence pattern of CE is different from CG or CR. The change of $\|\mathbf{x}_\infty - \mathbf{x}_k\|_2$ and $\|\mathbf{y}_k\|_2$ is shown in Figs. 5.3–5.5.

The second example is a full 200×200 symmetric indefinite matrix. It is created in the way shown below. The largest magnitude of the eigenvalue is 100, while the smallest is 0.01. The condition number is 10,000.

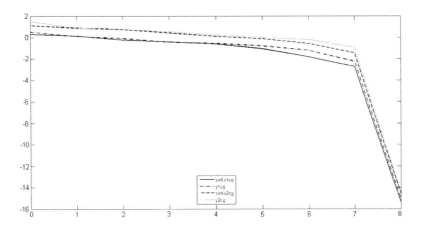

FIGURE 5.3

Errors and residuals of CG iterations.

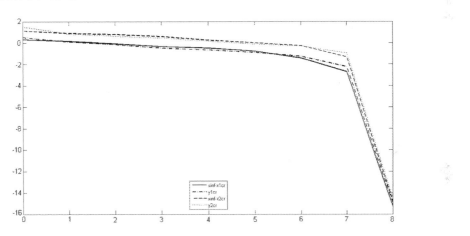

FIGURE 5.4

Errors and residuals of CR iterations.

```
>> d=[-100:1:-1,1:100];  d(100)=-0.01;  d(101) = 0.01;  [Q,R]=QR_(randn(200));
>> A=Q*diag(d)*Q';  a=randn(200,1);  x0=ones(200,1);
```

For the positive indefinite matrix, CG and CR iterations can converge for an arbitrarily initial solution. Theoretically, they can converge at most 200 (the size of the matrix) iterations. But due to the numerical errors, they usually require more iterations than 200.

```
>> x1=eqsCG_(A,a,x0,100*eps,1000);        >> norm(a-A*x1)
   534           %number of iterations      2.1833e-011
```

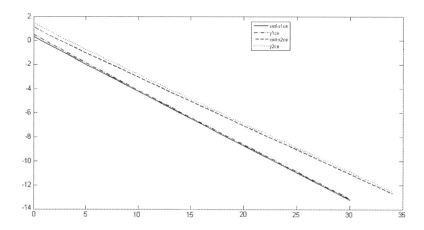

FIGURE 5.5

Errors and residuals of CE iterations.

```
>> x2=eqsCR_(A,a,x0,100*eps,1000);          >> norm(a-A*x2)
   539                 %number of iterations    3.1099e-011
```

CE iterations cannot converge for the same matrix.

```
>> x3=eqsCE_(A,a,x0,[],10000);              >> norm(a-A*x3)
      10000          %number of iterations       2.0519
```

In the third example, we create a band matrix **B** from the full matrix **A** of the second example.

```
>> A=A-tril(A,-11)-triu(A,11);
>> [B,lbw,ubw,m,n]=full2band_(A,10,10);          %A in band format
```

The way to use CG, CR, and CE for the band matrix is shown below. {'mtimesBand_',{B,lbw,ubw,m,n}} creates a linear transformation which contains the data of the band matrix, see Section 1.3. 'mtimesBand_' uses mtimesBand_.m to calculate the matrix-vector product, see Section 1.6.

```
>> x1=eqsCG_({'mtimesBand_',{B,lbw,ubw,m,n}},a,x0,[],1000);   >> norm(a-A*x1)
   324                                                           2.1996e-006
```

```
>> x2=eqsCR_({'mtimesBand_',{B,lbw,ubw,m,n}},a,x0,[],1000);   >> norm(a-A*x2)
   316                                                           2.9422e-006
```

CE iterations also converge in this example of the band matrix, however at a lot more iterations.

```
>> x3=eqsCE_({'mtimesBand_',{B,lbw,ubw,m,n}},a,x0,[],10000);   >> norm(a A*x3)
   841                                                              3.6114e-006
```

In the last example, we transfer the band matrix **B** into the sparse format. {dA,rA,dA} creates a cell array which contains the data for the sparse matrix, see Section 1.3. 'mtimesCSR_' uses mtimesCSR_.m to calculate the matrix-vector product, see Section 1.6. When CG, CR, and CE are applied to the same band matrix in the sparse format, they have exactly the same iterations and output as the third example.

```
>> [dA,rA,jA]=full2csr_(A);          %dA,rA,jA: CSR data of A.
>> x1=eqsCG_({'mtimesCSR_',{dA,rA,jA}},a,x0,[],10000);   %same as x1 for band format
>> x2=eqsCR_({'mtimesCSR_',{dA,rA,jA}},a,x0,[],10000);   %same as x2 for band format
>> x3=eqsCE_({'mtimesCSR_',{dA,rA,jA}},a,x0,[],10000);   %same as x3 for band format
```

CG, CR, and CE iterations can be improved by a proper choice of pre-conditioners. We show how to use the pre-conditioners in CG, CR, and CE. The pre-conditioners are applied to **Ax** = **a** as follows:

$$\left(\mathbf{L}^{-1}\mathbf{A}\mathbf{L}'^{-1}\right)\left(\mathbf{L}'\mathbf{x}\right) = \mathbf{L}^{-1}\mathbf{a}.$$

L is chosen to make $\mathbf{L}^{-1}\mathbf{A}\mathbf{L}'^{-1}$ better conditioned. **L** is the left pre-conditioner and **L'** is the right pre-conditioner. To keep the symmetry of **A**, the left and right pre-conditioners are transpose matrices. If **A** is not symmetric, the left and right pre-conditioners can be independently chosen. The left or right pre-conditioner can even be an identity matrix.

In eqsCG_.m, the last two input arguments are L and R which takes the input for the pre-conditioners. The input format for eqsCR_.m and eqsCE_.m is exactly same as eqsCG_.m. In the following examples, L={'mdivideByGauss_',U1} and R={'mdivideByGauss_',U1'}; contains the information of the pre-conditioners. The left pre-conditioner matrix is U1, the right is U1'. For both the left and right pre-conditioners, it uses 'mdivideByGauss_' to calculate $\mathbf{U}_1^{-1}\mathbf{b}$ or $\mathbf{U}_1'^{-1}\mathbf{b}$. The format of L and R is same as A.

Note that the way we choose to construct and apply the pre-conditioners in the following examples is not practical in real applications. For the practical ways to create and apply pre-conditioners, see [56].

```
>> [V,D]=eig(A);              %[D,V] eigenvalues and eigenvectors of A
>> U1=V*sqrt(abs(D));         %U1^{-1}*A*U1^{-T} = diag([-1,1])
>> D(1:10)=randn(10,1);
>> U2=V*sqrt(abs(D));         %U2^{-1}*A*U2^{-T} = diag([x,-1,1])
>> V(:,1)=randn(200,1);
>> U3=V*sqrt(abs(D));         %(U3^{-1}'*A*U3^{-T})(1,:), (:,1) arbitrary
                             %(U3^{-1}'*A*U3^{-T})(2:200,2:200)=diag([x,-1,1])
```

The use of the three pre-conditioners U1, U2, and U3 is demonstrated below. Their abilities of reducing the number of iterations are the direct outcome of their abilities of making $\mathbf{U}^{-1}\mathbf{A}\mathbf{U}'^{-1}$ better conditioned. But is observed that the condition number of $\mathbf{U}^{-1}\mathbf{A}\mathbf{U}'^{-1}$ is not a good indicator for the reduction of the number of iterations. The observation is the following.

```
>> A1 = inv(U1)*A*inv(U1)';
>> A2 = inv(U2)*A*inv(U2)';
>> A3 = inv(U3)*A*inv(U3)';

>> cond(A)
   118.6231          %not bad conditioning

>> cond(A1)
```

```
   1.0000           %perfect conditioned!

>> cond(A2)
  145.5928          %worse conditioned than A
>> cond(A2(1:10,1:10))
   8.0557           %bad conditioning only in A2(1:10,1:10)
>> cond(A2(11:200,11:200))
   1.0000           %majority of A2 perfect conditioned!

>> cond(A3)
  3.4911e+004       %worst conditioned
>> cond(A3(1:10,1:10))
  249.5805          %every part of A3 is bad conditioned
>> cond(A3(11:100,11:100))
  7.4372e+003       %every part of A3 is bad conditioned
>> cond(A3(101:200,101:200))
  2.8253e+004       %every part of A3 is bad conditioned

>> L={'mdivideByGauss_',U1}; R={'mdivideByGauss_',U1'};
>> x1=eqsCG_({'mtimesCSR_',{dA,rA,jA}},a,x0,[],100,L,R);
      4        %cond(A1)=1
>> norm(a-A*x1)
=   3.5688e-012

>> L={'mdivideByGauss_',U2}; R={'mdivideByGauss_',U2'};
>> x2=eqsCG_({'mtimesCSR_',{dA,rA,jA}},a,x0,[],100,L,R);
     13        %cond(A2(11:200,11:200))=1
>> norm(a-A*x2)
=   1.8968e-006

>> L={'mdivideByGauss_',U3}; R={'mdivideByGauss_',U3'};
>> x3=eqsCG_({'mtimesCSR_',{dA,rA,jA}},a,x0,[],100,L,R);
     19        %but cond(A3)=3.4911e+004. ???
>> norm(a-A*x3)
=   4.7575e-005
```

The change of errors and residuals of the original linear equations with the use of the three pre-conditioned linear systems are shown in Fig. 5.6.

5.5 NON-STATIONARY ITERATIONS APPLIED TO UNSYMMETRIC MATRIX

We extend the non-stationary iterations from symmetric matrix to unsymmetric matrix. In the extension, the more complex relations, Eqs. (5.19) or Eqs. (5.21), replace the simpler relations, Eqs. (5.17). But the four-steps general methodology discussed in Section 5.3 remains the same.

5.5.1 FOM: FULL ORTHOGONALIZATION METHOD V IS FULL ORTHOGONAL BASES OF $\mathbb{K}(A, y_0, m)$ AND $W = V$

Using the relations of Eqs. (5.19), the Galerkin projection condition can be simplified as follows:

$$
\begin{aligned}
W(:,1:m)'y_m &= V(:,1:m)'(y_0 - AV(:,1:m)v) \\
&= \|y_0\|_2 I(:,1) - H(1:m,1:m)v = 0.
\end{aligned}
\tag{5.42}
$$

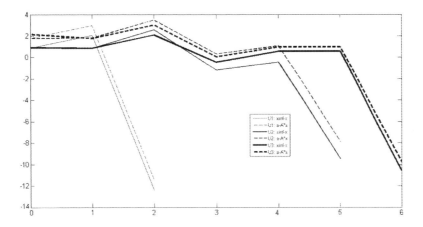

FIGURE 5.6

Errors and residuals of CG iterations with different pre-conditioners.

Then $\mathbf{v} = \|\mathbf{y}_0\|_2 \mathbf{H}_m^{-1} \mathbf{I}(:, 1)$, where $\mathbf{H}_m$ is an upper Hessenberg matrix. In the following, we denote $\beta = \|\mathbf{y}_0\|_2$. $\mathbf{v}$ is solved from Eq. (5.42) by following the steps below,

$$\mathbf{v} = \beta \mathbf{H}(1 : m, 1 : m)^{-1} \mathbf{I}(:, 1) = \beta (\mathbf{QR})^{-1} \mathbf{I}(:, 1) = \beta \mathbf{R}^{-1} \mathbf{Q}(1, :)'. \tag{5.43}$$

In the above steps, $\mathbf{QR} = \mathbf{H}(1 : m, 1 : m)$ is the QR decomposition of $\mathbf{H}(1 : m, 1; m)$ performed by calling QRhessenberg_, see Section 3.2.5. $\mathbf{R}^{-1}\mathbf{Q}(1, :)'$ is an equation solution performed by calling eqsUpperTriangle_, see Section 4.3.5. Another option is to solve Eq. (5.42) by performing the LU decomposition of $\mathbf{H}(1 : m, 1; m)$ (calling LUhessenberg_, see Section 2.2.4) and then solving upper triangular equations (calling eqsUpperTriangle_, see Section 4.3.5).

After $\mathbf{v}$ is calculated, we can calculate the new approximate solution $\mathbf{x}_m = \mathbf{x}_0 + \mathbf{V}(:, 1 : m)\mathbf{v}$ and then calculate the new residual $\mathbf{y}_m$,

$$\begin{aligned} \mathbf{y}_m &= \mathbf{a} - \mathbf{A}\mathbf{x}_m = \mathbf{y}_0 - \mathbf{A}\mathbf{V}(:, 1 : m)\mathbf{v} \\ &= \mathbf{y}_0 - \mathbf{V}(:, 1 : m)\mathbf{H}(1 : m, 1 : m)\mathbf{v} - H(m + 1, m)\mathbf{V}(:, m + 1)\mathbf{I}(m, :)\mathbf{v} \\ &= -H(m + 1, m)v(m)\mathbf{V}(:, m + 1), \end{aligned} \tag{5.44}$$

where in the second equality the first two terms are canceled because of Eq. (5.42). The residual $\mathbf{y}_m$ is in the direction of $\mathbf{V}(:, m + 1)$ and its magnitude is $H(m + 1, m)|v(m)|$. To check the convergence by $\|\mathbf{y}_m\|_2$, we do not need to form $\mathbf{y}_m$ according to Eq. (5.44). Instead the simple relation $\|\mathbf{y}_m\|_2 = H(m + 1, m)|v(m)|$ can be used.

If $m = n$, $H(n + 1, n) = 0$. It takes only one iteration to converge. If QHQtbyArnoldi_.m breaks down when generating $\mathbf{V}$ at an immediate step $l, l \leq m$, then $H(l + 1, l) = 0$. The current iteration will converge. If $\mathbf{A}$ is positive definite, the iteration can converge for any $m \geq 1$. In other cases, the convergence property is not known. To improve the convergence, we can apply the iterations to the pre-conditioned form of $\mathbf{Ax} = \mathbf{a}$. See the discussion of numerical examples below.

Similarly to Eqs. (5.29) and (5.30), we can combine the update of $\mathbf{x}_m$ and the solution of $\mathbf{v}$ to obtain an incremental form for $\mathbf{x}_m$. But the U factor or the R factor of LU or QR of $\mathbf{H}(1:m,1:m)$ is a full upper triangle, no advantage can be gained from the incremental form.

Algorithm 5.7

Full orthogonalization method for unsymmetric Ax=a

```
% A/=A', input x=x0, output x: L*(A)*R*(R^{-1}*x)=L*a, default L=I, R=I.
function x = eqsFOM_(A,a,x,tol,last,L,R)

[m,n] = size_(A);   tsal = m-1;    %= floor(m/2); %tsal: internal arg!
if (~iscell(A)) A = {'mtimes',A}; end

if (~isempty(R)) y = Ay_(R,x,'right'); else y = x; end
y = Ay_(A,y,'right');
if (~isempty(L)) y = Ay_(L,a-y,'right'); else y = a-y; end
beta = norm(y);   epslon = tol*max(1.0,beta);   v = [beta;zeros(tsal-1,1)];   l = 0;

while(beta>epslon && l<last)
    [V,H] = QHQtByArnoldi_({{'size',[m,n]},L,A,R},1,tsal,y,[]);
    [Q,QR] = QRhessenberg_(H(1:tsal,1:tsal),1,[],'compact');
    for k=1:tsal-1           %v=beta*Q'*[1;0]
        rho = QR(k+1,k);
        if (rho == 1)         c = 0; s = 1;
        elseif(abs(rho) < 1) s = 2.0*rho; c = sqrt(1.0-s*s);
        else                 c = 2.0/rho; s = sqrt(1.0-c*c); end
        v(k+1) = s*v(k);      v(k) = c*v(k);
    end
    v = mdivideUpperTriangle_(QR,v);   %v=beta*R^{-1}*Q(1,:)'
    x = x + V(:,1:tsal)*v;
    if (~isempty(R)) y = Ay_(R,x,'right');    else y = x; end
    y = Ay_(A,y,'right');
    if (~isempty(L)) y = Ay_(L,a-y,'right'); else y = a-y; end
    beta = abs(H(tsal+1,tsal)*v(tsal));   v(1) = beta;   v(2:tsal) = 0;   l = l + 1;
end
if (~isempty(R)) x = Ay_(R,x,'right'); end
```

5.5.2 GMRES: GENERALIZED MINIMUM RESIDUAL V IS FULL ORTHOGONAL BASES OF $\mathbb{K}(A, y_0, m)$ AND $W = AV$

Utilizing Eqs. (5.19), the projection condition now takes the following form:

$$\begin{aligned}\mathbf{W}(:,1:m)'\mathbf{y}_m &= (\mathbf{AV}(:,1:m))'\,(\mathbf{y}_0 - \mathbf{AV}(:,1:m)\mathbf{v})\\ &= (\mathbf{VH})'\,(\beta\mathbf{VI}(:,1) - \mathbf{VHv}) = \beta\mathbf{H}'\mathbf{I}(:,1) - \mathbf{H}'\mathbf{Hv} = 0.\end{aligned} \quad (5.45)$$

The first line of equalities shows that $\mathbf{x}_m$ is the solution that minimizes $\|\mathbf{y}_m\|_2$ for all $\mathbf{x}_m$ with the presumed form. The last line of equality is the formula to determine $\mathbf{v}$: $\mathbf{v}$ is the solution of the over-determined linear equations $\mathbf{Hv} = \beta\mathbf{I}(:,1)$,

$$\mathbf{v} = \beta\mathbf{H}(1:m+1,1:m)^+\mathbf{I}(:,1) = \beta\left(\mathbf{Q}_{m+1}\mathbf{R}_{(m+1)m}\right)^+\mathbf{I}(:,1) = \beta\mathbf{R}^+\mathbf{Q}'\mathbf{I}(:,1) = \beta\mathbf{R}^+\mathbf{Q}(1,:)'. \quad (5.46)$$

In the above steps, $\mathbf{Q}_{m+1}\mathbf{R}_{(m+1)m} = \mathbf{H}(1:m+1,1:m)$ is the QR decomposition of $\mathbf{H}(1:m+1,1;m)$ performed by calling QRhessenberg_, see Section 3.2.5. $\mathbf{R}^+\mathbf{Q}(1,:)'$ is the least square solution performed by calling eqsUpperTriangle_, see Section 4.3.5. LU decomposition of $\mathbf{H}(1:m+1,1;m)$ is not suitable for the minimum residual solution. See the discussion of pseudo-inverse in Section 4.1.

After $\mathbf{v}$ is calculated, we can calculate the new approximate solution $\mathbf{x}_m = \mathbf{x}_0 + \mathbf{V}(:,1:m)\mathbf{v}$ and then calculate the new residual $\mathbf{y}_m$.

$$\begin{aligned}\mathbf{y}_m &= \mathbf{y}_0 - \mathbf{AV}(:,1:m)\mathbf{v} = \mathbf{V}(:,1:m+1)'\,(\beta\mathbf{I}(:,1) - \mathbf{H}(1:m+1,1:m)\mathbf{v})\\ &= \beta Q(1,m+1)\mathbf{V}(:,1:m+1)\mathbf{QI}(:,m+1).\end{aligned} \tag{5.47}$$

However, for the purpose of iterations, $\mathbf{y}_m$ is not needed. If $\|\mathbf{y}_m\|_2$ is needed to check the convergence of iterations, we can see that $\|\mathbf{y}_m\|_2 = \beta Q(1,m+1)$, which is readily available when solving the minimum residual equations of Eq. (5.46).

The convergence property of GMRES is similar to FOM discussed in the last subsection. There is no advantage in adopting the incremental form similar to Eq. (5.36).

The following is the MATLAB implementation of GMRES. Note the small difference to eqsFOM_.m.

Algorithm 5.8

Generalized residual method for unsymmetric Ax=a

```
% A/=A', input x=x0, output x: L*(A)*R*(R^{-1}*x)=L*a, default L=I, R=I.
function x = eqsGMRES_(A,a,x,tol,last,L,R)

[m,n] = size_(A);   tsal = m-1;   %= floor(m/2); %tsal: internal arg!
if (~iscell(A)) A = {'mtimes',A}; end

if (~isempty(R)) y = Ay_(R,x,'right'); else y = x; end
y = Ay_(A,y,'right');
if (~isempty(L)) y = Ay_(L,a-y,'right'); else y = a-y; end
beta = norm(y);   epslon=tol*max(1.0,beta);   v = [beta;zeros(tsal,1)];   ql=1.0; l=0;

while(beta>epslon && l<last)
    [V,H] = QHQtByArnoldi_({{'size',[m,n]},L,A,R},1,tsal,y,[]);
    [Q,QR] = QRhessenberg_(H,1,[],'compact');
    for k=1:min(tsal,n-1)
        rho = QR(k+1,k);
        if (rho == 1)           c = 0; s = 1;
        elseif(abs(rho) < 1) s = 2.0*rho; c = sqrt(1.0-s*s);
        else                    c = 2.0/rho; s = sqrt(1.0-c*c); end
        v(k+1) = s*v(k);        v(k)   = c*v(k);   ql = ql*s;
    end
    v(1:tsal) = mdivideUpperTriangle_(QR(1:tsal,1:tsal),v(1:tsal));
    x = x + V(:,1:tsal)*v(1:tsal);
    if (~isempty(R)) y = Ay_(R,x,'right'); else y = x; end
    y = Ay_(A,y,'right');
    if (~isempty(L)) y = Ay_(L,a-y,'right'); else y = a-y; end
    beta = abs(beta*ql);   v(1) = beta;   v(2:tsal+1) = 0.0;   ql = 1.0;   l = l + 1;
end
if (~isempty(R)) x = Ay_(R,x,'right'); end
```

5.5.3 GMERR: GENERALIZED MINIMUM ERROR W IS FULL ORTHOGONAL BASES OF $\mathbb{K}(A', y_0, m)$ AND $V = A'W$

The projection condition now takes the following form, see [22] and [79]:

$$
\begin{aligned}
\mathbf{W}(:,1:m)'\mathbf{y}_m &= \mathbf{W}(:,1:m)'\mathbf{AA}^{-1}(\mathbf{a} - \mathbf{Ax}_m) = \mathbf{V}(:,1:m)'(\mathbf{x}_\infty - \mathbf{x}_m) \\
&= \mathbf{W}(:,1:m)'\mathbf{y}_0 - (\mathbf{A}'\mathbf{W}(:,1:m))'(\mathbf{A}'\mathbf{W}(:,1:m))\mathbf{v} \\
&= \mathbf{W}(:,1:m)'\mathbf{y}_0 - (\mathbf{WH})'(\mathbf{WH})\mathbf{v} = \beta\mathbf{I}(:,1) - \mathbf{H}'\mathbf{Hv} = \mathbf{0}.
\end{aligned}
\tag{5.48}
$$

The first line of equalities shows that $\mathbf{x}_m$ is the minimum error solution for all $\mathbf{x}_m$ with the presumed form. The last line of equality is the formula to determine $\mathbf{v}$. If $\mathbf{H}(1:m+1,1:m)'\mathbf{H}(1:m+1,1:m)$ is formed explicitly, then $\mathbf{v} = \beta\,(\mathbf{H}'\mathbf{H})^{-1}\mathbf{I}(:,1)$ can be solved by many algorithms of Chapter 4.

A better way is not to form $\mathbf{H}'\mathbf{H}$. If we introduce $\mathbf{u}$ that satisfies $\mathbf{u} = \mathbf{Hv}$, then $\mathbf{u}$ is the solution of the under-determined linear equations $\mathbf{H}(1:m+1,1:m)'\mathbf{u} = \beta\mathbf{I}(:,1)$, which we solve by a QR decomposition of $\mathbf{H}$,

$$
\mathbf{u} = \beta\mathbf{H}(1:m+1,1:m)'^{+}\mathbf{I}(:,1) = \beta\left(\mathbf{Q}_{m+1}\mathbf{R}_{(m+1)m}\right)'^{+}\mathbf{I}(:,1) = \beta\mathbf{QR}'^{+}\mathbf{I}(:,1).
\tag{5.49}
$$

After $\mathbf{u}$ is determined, the new approximation is $\mathbf{x}_m = \mathbf{x}_0 + \mathbf{W}(:,1:m+1)\mathbf{u}$ and the new residual is $\mathbf{y}_m = \mathbf{y}_0 - \mathbf{AW}(:,1:m+1)\mathbf{u}$. Unlike FOM and GMRES, the calculation of $\mathbf{y}_m$ cannot be simplified. The convergence check can be based on the change of $\mathbf{x}_m$ between the successive iterations. In this setting, the calculation of $\mathbf{y}_m$ can be omitted.

The convergence property of GMERR is similar to GMRES discussed in the last subsection, see [79]. There is no advantage in adopting the incremental form similar to Eq. (5.41).

Algorithm 5.9

Generalized error method for unsymmetric Ax=a

```
% A/=A', input x=x0, output x: L*(A)*R*(R^{-1}*x)=L*a, default L=I, R=I.
function x = eqsGMERR_(A,a,x,tol,last,L,R)

[m,n] = size_(A);  tsal = m-1; %floor(m/2);        %tsal: internal arg!
if (~iscell(A)) A = {'mtimes',A}; end

At = transpose_(A);  Lt = transpose_(L);  Rt = transpose_(R);

if (~isempty(R)) y = Ay_(R,x,'right'); else y = x; end
y = Ay_(A,y,'right');
if (~isempty(L)) y = Ay_(L,a-y,'right'); else y = a-y; end
beta = norm(y);  epslon=tol*max(1.0,beta);  w = [beta;zeros(tsal,1)];  l = 0;

while(beta>epslon && l<last)
    [W,H] = QHQtByArnoldi_({{'size',[n,m]},Lt,At,Rt},1,tsal,y,[]);
    [Q,QR] = QRhessenberg_(H,1,[],'compact');
    w(1:tsal) = mdivideLowerTriangle_(QR(1:tsal,:)',w(1:tsal));        %y=W'*r
    for k=min(tsal,n-1):-1:1
        rho = QR(k+1,k);      w1 = w(k);    w2 = w(k+1);
        if (rho == 1)         c = 0; s = 1;
        elseif(abs(rho) < 1)  s = 2.0*rho; c = sqrt(1.0-s*s);
        else                  c = 2.0/rho; s = sqrt(1.0-c*c); end
        w(k) = c*w1 + s*w2;   w(k+1) =-s*w1 + c*w2;
    end
```

```
    x = x + W*w;
    if (~isempty(R)) y = Ay_(R,x,'right'); else y = x; end
    y = Ay_(A,y,'right');
    if (~isempty(L)) y = Ay_(L,a-y,'right'); else y = a-y; end
    beta = norm(y); w(1) = beta;  w(2:tsal+1) = 0;  l = l + 1;
end
if (~isempty(R)) x = Ay_(R,x,'right'); end
```

5.5.4 DIOM: DIRECT INCOMPLETE ORTHOGONALIZATION METHOD V IS INCOMPLETE ORTHOGONAL BASES OF $\mathbb{K}(A, y_0, m)$ AND W = ?

We consider how to construct $(\mathbf{W}'\mathbf{A}\mathbf{V})\,\mathbf{v} = \mathbf{W}'\mathbf{y}_0$ and how to solve it. If we simply choose $\mathbf{W} = \mathbf{V}$, although Eq. (5.19a) is still valid, but because $\mathbf{V}(:,1:m)'\mathbf{V}(:,1:m) \neq \mathbf{I}$ and $\mathbf{V}(:,1:m)'\mathbf{V}(:,m+1) \neq \mathbf{0}$, then $\mathbf{V}(:,1:m)'\mathbf{A}\mathbf{V}(:,1:m) \neq \mathbf{H}(1:m,1:m)$ and $\mathbf{W}'\mathbf{y}_0 \neq \beta\mathbf{I}(:,1)$. Because the orthogonality is not enforced among all the columns of $\mathbf{V}$, $\mathbf{H}$ now is a band matrix with lower bandwidth of 1 and upper bandwidth of $l, l \leq m$.

We decide to determine $\mathbf{v}$ by the simple equation $\mathbf{H}(1:m,1:m)\mathbf{v} = \beta\mathbf{I}(:,1)$ and determine what $\mathbf{W}$ can give rise to this equation. From Eq. (5.19a), we see that the conditions $\mathbf{W}$ must satisfy the following:

$$\mathbf{W}'\mathbf{V}(:,1:m) = \mathbf{I}_m, \tag{5.50a}$$
$$\mathbf{W}'\mathbf{V}(:,m+1) = \mathbf{0}. \tag{5.50b}$$

Although it does not need to construct $\mathbf{W}$ explicitly, it is easy to verify that the following $\mathbf{W}$ satisfies Eqs. (5.50),

$$\text{Define } \mathbf{U} = (\mathbf{V}(:,1:m)')^{+} \text{ and } \mathbf{N} = \text{null}\,(\mathbf{V}(:,1:m)')\,,$$
$$\mathbf{u} = \mathbf{U}'\mathbf{V}(:,m+1) \text{ and } \mathbf{n} = \mathbf{N}'\mathbf{V}(:,m+1),$$
$$\mathbf{Z} = -\frac{\mathbf{n}\mathbf{u}'}{\mathbf{n}'\mathbf{n}}, \tag{5.51}$$
$$\text{Final Result } \mathbf{W} = \mathbf{U} + \mathbf{N}\mathbf{Z} \neq \mathbf{V}.$$

Because the pseudo-inverse of $\mathbf{V}(:,1:m)'$ is unique and the null space of $\mathbf{V}(:,1:m)'$ is also unique, the subspace span($\mathbf{W}$) defined by Eq. (5.51) is unique. However, its bases $\mathbf{W}$ defined by Eq. (5.51) are not, as the presentation of $\mathbf{N}$ is not unique.

Now we explore how to solve $\mathbf{H}(1:m,1:m)\mathbf{v} = \beta\mathbf{I}(:,1)$. Solving this equation is easy, many algorithms presented in Chapter 4 can be used, but eqsByDecomposing_(A,b,decomposer,tol) with the input decomposer='LUband_' or decomposer='QRband_' are more suitable. After $\mathbf{v}$ is calculated, the new iteration $\mathbf{x}_m = \mathbf{x}_0 + \mathbf{V}\mathbf{v}$ according to step 4 of Section 5.3 and the new residual $\mathbf{y}_m$ is still Eq. (5.44).

Similarly to the CG method that takes advantage of the tri-diagonal structure of $\mathbf{T}$, we can take advantage of the band structure of $\mathbf{H}$ to obtain an incremental form to update $\mathbf{x}_m$ and $\mathbf{y}_m$.

Because $\mathbf{H}(1:m,1:m)$ is a band matrix, its LU decomposition without pivoting has a fixed format, see Section 2.2. We take $m-5, l=3$ as an example. $\mathbf{H}(1:5,1:5) = \mathbf{L}_5\mathbf{U}_5$ is shown below,

$$
\begin{bmatrix} H_{11} & H_{12} & H_{13} \\ H_{21} & H_{22} & H_{23} & H_{24} \\ & H_{32} & H_{33} & H_{34} & H_{35} \\ & & H_{43} & H_{44} & H_{45} \\ & & & H_{54} & H_{55} \end{bmatrix} = \begin{bmatrix} 1 \\ L_{21} & 1 \\ & L_{32} & 1 \\ & & L_{43} & 1 \\ & & & L_{54} & 1 \end{bmatrix} \begin{bmatrix} U_{11} & U_{12} & U_{13} \\ & U_{22} & U_{23} & U_{24} \\ & & U_{33} & U_{34} & U_{35} \\ & & & U_{44} & U_{45} \\ & & & & U_{55} \end{bmatrix}.
$$

Based on the LU decomposition, $\mathbf{x}_5$ is calculated as follows:

$$
\begin{aligned}
\mathbf{x}_5 &= \mathbf{x}_0 + \mathbf{V}(:,1:5)(\mathbf{L}_5\mathbf{U}_5)^{-1}\beta\mathbf{I}(:,1) \\
&= \mathbf{x}_0 + \left(\mathbf{V}(:,1:5)\mathbf{U}_5^{-1}\right)\left(\mathbf{L}_5^{-1}\beta\mathbf{I}(:,1)\right) \\
&= \mathbf{x}_0 + \mathbf{Ps},
\end{aligned}
$$

where $\mathbf{P} = \mathbf{V}(:,1:5)\mathbf{U}_5^{-1}$ and $\mathbf{s} = \mathbf{L}_5^{-1}\beta\mathbf{I}(:,1)$.

We write $\mathbf{P} = \mathbf{V}(:,1:5)\mathbf{U}_5^{-1}$ as $\mathbf{PU}_5 = \mathbf{V}(:,1:5)$ and equate the fifth column of both sides, obtaining

$$
\mathbf{P}(:,5) = \frac{1}{U_{55}}\left(\mathbf{V}(:,5) - U_{35}\mathbf{P}(:,3) - U_{45}\mathbf{P}(:,4)\right).
$$

We write $\mathbf{s} = \mathbf{L}_5^{-1}\beta\mathbf{I}(:,1)$ as $\mathbf{L}_5\mathbf{s} = \beta\mathbf{I}(:,1)$ and equate the fifth row of both sides, obtaining

$$
s(5) = -L_{54}s(4).
$$

We write $\mathbf{x}_5 = \mathbf{x}_0 + \mathbf{Ps}$ as follows:

$$
\mathbf{x}_5 = (\mathbf{x}_0 + \mathbf{P}(:,1:4)s(1:4)) + \mathbf{P}(:,5)s(5) = \mathbf{x}_4 + \mathbf{P}(:,5)s(5).
$$

For the general case, replace 5 by m in the above three equations. They provide an incremental update formula for $\mathbf{x}_m$, which only needs to access the most recent column of $\mathbf{V}$. For the construction of new column of $\mathbf{V}$ and $\mathbf{H}$, only at most l recent columns of $\mathbf{V}$ are needed.

No general convergence property for DIOM is known. In practice, DIOM shows similar convergence behaviors to FOM. When FOM converges, DIOM can also converge. When FOM diverges, DIOM also diverges.

Algorithm 5.10

Direct incomplete orthogonalization method for unsymmetric Ax=a

```
% A/=A', input x=x0, output x: L*(A)*R*(R^{-1}*x)=L*a, default L=I, R=I.
function x = eqsDIOM_(A,a,x,tol,last,L,R)

[m,n] = size_(A);  tsal = m-1;  kth=floor(tsal/2);    %tsal,kth: internal args!
if (~iscell(A)) A = {'mtimes',A}; end

V = zeros(n,min(kth+1,n));   H = zeros(tsal+1,2);  P = zeros(n,min(kth+1,n));
eta = 0.5*sqrt(2.0);         %eta for reorthogonalization

if (~isempty(R)) y = Ay_(R,x,'right'); else y = x; end
y = Ay_(A,y,'right');
if (~isempty(L)) y = Ay_(L,a-y,'right'); else y = a-y; end
beta = norm(y);  epslon = tol*max(1.0,beta);  V(:,1) = y/beta; v = [beta;0.0]; l = 0;
```

```
while(beta>epslon && l<last)
    for k = 1:tsal
        kV = mod(k,kth+1);
        if (kV == 0) kV = kth+1;  end
        if (~isempty(R)) Avk = Ay_(R,V(:,kV),'right'); else Avk = V(:,kV); end
        Avk = Ay_(A,Avk,'right');
        if (~isempty(L)) Avk = Ay_(L,Avk,'right'); end
        normAvk0 = norm(Avk);
        for j=max(1,k-kth+1):k
            jV = mod(j,kth+1);
            if (jV == 0) jV = kth+1; end
            vj = V(:,jV);
            H(j,1) = vj'*Avk;
            Avk = Avk - H(j,1)*vj;
        end
        normAvk = norm(Avk);
        if (normAvk < eta*normAvk0)    %reorthogonalization
            for j=max(1,k-kth+1):k
                jV = mod(j,kth+1);
                if (jV == 0) jV = kth+1; end
                vj = V(:,jV);
                Hj1 = vj'*Avk;    H(j,1) = H(j,1) + Hj1;
                Avk = Avk - Hj1*vj;
            end
            normAvk = norm(Avk);
        end
        H(k+1,1) = normAvk;
        kV1 = mod(k+1,kth+1);
        if (kV1 == 0) kV1 = kth+1; end
        if (normAvk > tol) V(:,kV1) = Avk/normAvk;
        else               V(:,kV1) = 0.0;   end
        if (k-kth >= 1) H(k-kth,1) = 0; end %unwanted data from k-1
        for j=max(1,k-kth):k-1   %Apply old [c,s] to H(:,1), ie H(:,k)
            rho = H(j+1,2);      h1 = H(j,1);   h2 = H(j+1,1);
            if (rho == 1)        c = 0; s = 1;
            elseif(abs(rho) < 1) s = 2.0*rho; c = sqrt(1.0-s*s);
            else                 c = 2.0/rho; s = sqrt(1.0-c*c); end
            H(j,1) = c*h1 - s*h2;   H(j+1,1) = s*h1 + c*h2;
        end
        if (k < tsal)    %if (1 || k<tsal) => DQGMRES_
            [c,s] = givens_(H(k,1),H(k+1,1));      %zero H(k+1,k), ie H(k+1,1)
            H(k,1) = c*H(k,1) - s*H(k+1,1);
            if (abs(c) < tol)        H(k+1,2) = 1;
            elseif(abs(s) < abs(c)) H(k+1,2) = sign(c)*s/2;
            else                     H(k+1,2) = sign(s)*2/c; end
            v(2) = s*v(1);   v(1) = c*v(1);
        end
        P(:,kV) = V(:,kV);
        for j=max(1,k-kth+1):k-1
            jP = mod(j,kth+1);
            if (jP == 0) jP = kth+1; end
            P(:,kV) = P(:,kV) - H(j,1)*P(:,jP);
        end
        P(:,kV) = P(:,kV)/H(k,1);
        x = x + v(1)*P(:,kV);
        v(1) = v(2);    %l = l + 1; %beta = abs(v(2)); %beta ~=|b-A*x|
        if (abs(v(2)) < epslon) break; end  %lucky breakdown
```

```
      end
      if (~isempty(R)) y = Ay_(R,x,'right'); else y = x; end
      y = Ay_(A,y,'right');
      if (~isempty(L)) y = Ay_(L,a-y,'right'); else y = a-y; end
      beta = norm(y);  V(:,1) = y/beta;  v(1) = beta;  v(2) = 0.0;  l = l + 1;
   end
   if (~isempty(R)) x = Ay_(R,x,'right'); end
```

5.5.5 DQGMRES: DIRECT QUASI-GENERALIZED MINIMUM RESIDUAL V IS INCOMPLETE ORTHOGONAL BASES OF $\mathbb{K}(\mathbf{A}, \mathbf{y_0}, m)$ AND $\mathbf{W} = ?$

In an analogy to the relation between DIOM and FOM, we can obtain DQGMRES from GMRES by allowing $\mathbf{V}$ to be incomplete orthogonal bases of $\mathbb{K}(\mathbf{A}, \mathbf{y}_0, m)$. Had we chosen $\mathbf{W} = \mathbf{AV}$ as in GMRES, the projection condition is in the same form as Eq. (5.45), but the last equality cannot be obtained, because $\mathbf{V}(:, 1 : m)'\mathbf{V}(:, 1 : m) \neq \mathbf{I}$. Instead the projection condition takes the following form:

$$\mathbf{W}(:, 1 : m)'\mathbf{y}_m = \mathbf{H}'\mathbf{V}'(\mathbf{y}_0 - \mathbf{VHv}) = \mathbf{0}. \tag{5.52}$$

We decide to solve $\mathbf{v}$ by the simple equation $\mathbf{H}'\mathbf{Hv} = \beta\mathbf{H}'\mathbf{I}(:, 1)$ and determine what $\mathbf{W}$ can give rise to this equation. It is easy to see that choosing $\mathbf{W} = \mathbf{V}(:, 1 : m + 1)'^+\mathbf{H}(1 : m + 1, 1 : m) \neq \mathbf{AV}(:, 1 : m)$ satisfies the requirement. By $\mathbf{W} = \mathbf{V}'^+\mathbf{H}$, $\mathbf{W}$ is also unique. For the purpose of iterations, $\mathbf{W}$ does not need to be formed explicitly.

Now we explore how to solve the over-determined linear equations $\mathbf{Hv} = \beta\mathbf{I}(:, 1)$. In DIOM, the linear equations $\mathbf{H}(1 : m, 1 : m)\mathbf{v} = \beta\mathbf{I}(:, 1)$ are solved by a LU decomposition of $\mathbf{H}(1 : m, 1 : m)$. Its advantage is that only the most recent column of $\mathbf{V}$ is needed to update $\mathbf{x}_m$. To solve $\mathbf{v} = \beta\mathbf{H}^+\mathbf{I}(:, 1)$, a LU decomposition of $\mathbf{H}$ is not suitable. See the discussion of the pseudo-inverse in Section 4.1. Instead we use a QR decomposition of $\mathbf{H}$,

$$\begin{aligned}\mathbf{x}_m &= \mathbf{x}_0 + \mathbf{V}(:, 1 : m)\beta\left(\mathbf{Q}_{m+1}\mathbf{R}_{(m+1)m}\right)^+\mathbf{I}(:, 1) \\ &= \mathbf{x}_0 + \left(\mathbf{V}(:, 1 : m)\mathbf{R}^+\right)(\beta\mathbf{Q}(1, :)') = \mathbf{x}_0 + \mathbf{Ps} \\ &= (\mathbf{x}_0 + \mathbf{P}(:, 1 : m - 1)\mathbf{s}(1 : m - 1)) + \mathbf{P}(:, m)\mathbf{s}(m) = \mathbf{x}_{m-1} + \mathbf{P}(:, m)\mathbf{s}(m),\end{aligned} \tag{5.53}$$

where $\mathbf{P} = \mathbf{V}(:, 1 : m)\mathbf{R}^+_{(m+1)m}$ and $\mathbf{s} = \beta\mathbf{Q}(1, :)'$.

Similarly to IDOM, the third line of Eq. (5.53) is adopted to calculate $\mathbf{x}_m$, where an advantage is taken of the band structure of $\mathbf{H}$ to derive an incremental form of $\mathbf{x}_m$. $\mathbf{H}(1 : m + 1, 1 : m)$ has a lower bandwidth of 1 and an upper bandwidth of $l, l \leq m$. Its QR decomposition has a fixed format, see Section 3.2.6. We take $m = 4, l = 2$ as an example. $\mathbf{H}_{54} = \mathbf{Q}_{55}\mathbf{R}_{54}$ is shown below,

$$\begin{bmatrix} H_{11} & H_{12} & & & \\ H_{21} & H_{22} & H_{23} & & \\ & H_{32} & H_{33} & H_{34} & \\ & & H_{43} & H_{44} & \\ & & & H_{54} \end{bmatrix} = \begin{bmatrix} Q_{11} & Q_{12} & Q_{13} & Q_{14} & Q_{15} \\ Q_{21} & Q_{22} & Q_{23} & Q_{24} & Q_{25} \\ & Q_{23} & Q_{33} & Q_{34} & Q_{35} \\ & & Q_{43} & Q_{44} & Q_{45} \\ & & & Q_{54} & Q_{55} \end{bmatrix} \begin{bmatrix} R_{11} & R_{12} & R_{13} & \\ & R_{22} & R_{23} & R_{24} \\ & & R_{33} & R_{34} \\ & & & R_{44} \\ & & & 0 \end{bmatrix}.$$

Because of the band structure, we use Givens rotations to calculate the QR decomposition, see Section 3.2.5. To derive the incremental form of $\mathbf{x}_m$, the Givens rotations are applied differently from

Section 3.2.5. The reason is that each column of $\mathbf{H}$ is calculated one at a time. For example, when the Givens rotation $\mathbf{G}_1$ is applied to eliminate $H(2,1)$, $\mathbf{H}(:,2:4)$ is not available. The detailed process is illustrated below with the simple example of $\mathbf{H}_{54}$.

After $\mathbf{V}(:,1)$ and $\mathbf{H}(1:2,1)$ are calculated, we perform the following calculations:

$$\text{Find Givens rotation } \mathbf{G}_1 = \begin{bmatrix} c_1 & -s_1 \\ s_1 & c_1 \end{bmatrix} \text{ to eliminate } H_{21},$$

$$\mathbf{G}_1\mathbf{H}(1:2,1) = \mathbf{G}_1 \begin{bmatrix} H_{11} \\ H_{21} \end{bmatrix} \Rightarrow \begin{bmatrix} R_{11} \\ 0 \end{bmatrix}; \quad \mathbf{G}_1 \begin{bmatrix} 1 \\ 0 \end{bmatrix} = \begin{bmatrix} c_1 \\ s_1 \end{bmatrix}.$$

Now we go to calculate $\mathbf{V}(:,2)$ and $\mathbf{H}(1:3,2)$. Then, we continue to apply Givens rotations to $\mathbf{H}(1:3,2)$,

$$\text{First apply } \mathbf{G}_1\mathbf{H}(1:2,2) = \mathbf{G}_1 \begin{bmatrix} H_{12} \\ H_{22} \end{bmatrix} \Rightarrow \begin{bmatrix} R_{12} \\ H_{22} \end{bmatrix},$$

$$\text{Find Givens rotation } \mathbf{G}_2 = \begin{bmatrix} c_2 & -s_2 \\ s_2 & c_2 \end{bmatrix} \text{ to eliminate } H_{32},$$

$$\mathbf{G}_2\mathbf{H}(2:3,2) = \mathbf{G}_2 \begin{bmatrix} H_{22} \\ H_{32} \end{bmatrix} = \begin{bmatrix} R_{22} \\ 0 \end{bmatrix}; \quad \mathbf{G}_2 \begin{bmatrix} s_1 \\ 0 \end{bmatrix} = \begin{bmatrix} s_1 c_2 \\ s_1 s_2 \end{bmatrix}.$$

For $\mathbf{H}(1:4,3)$, we need to apply $\mathbf{G}_1$ and $\mathbf{G}_2$ then find $\mathbf{G}_3$ to eliminate H_{43},

$$\text{First apply } \mathbf{G}_1\mathbf{H}(1:2,3) = \mathbf{G}_1 \begin{bmatrix} 0 \\ H_{23} \end{bmatrix} \Rightarrow \begin{bmatrix} R_{13} \\ H_{23} \end{bmatrix},$$

$$\text{Second apply } \mathbf{G}_2\mathbf{H}(2:3,3) = \mathbf{G}_2 \begin{bmatrix} H_{23} \\ H_{33} \end{bmatrix} \Rightarrow \begin{bmatrix} R_{23} \\ H_{33} \end{bmatrix},$$

$$\text{Find Givens rotation } \mathbf{G}_3 = \begin{bmatrix} c_3 & -s_3 \\ s_3 & c_3 \end{bmatrix} \text{ to eliminate } H_{43}$$

$$\mathbf{G}_3\mathbf{H}(3:4,3) = \mathbf{G}_3 \begin{bmatrix} H_{33} \\ H_{43} \end{bmatrix} = \begin{bmatrix} R_{33} \\ 0 \end{bmatrix}; \quad \mathbf{G}_3 \begin{bmatrix} s_1 s_2 \\ 0 \end{bmatrix} = \begin{bmatrix} s_1 s_2 c_3 \\ s_1 s_2 s_3 \end{bmatrix}.$$

For $\mathbf{H}(3:5,4)$, we do not need to apply $\mathbf{G}_1$, because $\mathbf{H}(1:2,4) = \mathbf{0}$. We need to apply $\mathbf{G}_2$ and $\mathbf{G}_3$ then find $\mathbf{G}_4$ to eliminate H_{54}. In the following, only the calculations related to $\mathbf{G}_4$ are shown,

$$\mathbf{G}_4\mathbf{H}(4:5,4) = \mathbf{G}_4 \begin{bmatrix} H_{44} \\ H_{54} \end{bmatrix} = \begin{bmatrix} R_{44} \\ 0 \end{bmatrix}; \quad \mathbf{G}_4 \begin{bmatrix} s_1 s_2 s_3 \\ 0 \end{bmatrix} = \begin{bmatrix} s_1 s_2 s_3 c_4 \\ s_1 s_2 s_3 s_4 \end{bmatrix}.$$

After four steps of Givens rotations, the over-determined linear equations $\mathbf{H}_{54}\mathbf{v} = \beta\mathbf{I}(:,1)$ are transformed to the following form:

$$\begin{bmatrix} R_{11} & R_{12} & R_{13} & \\ & R_{22} & R_{23} & R_{24} \\ & & R_{33} & R_{34} \\ & & & R_{44} \\ & & & 0 \end{bmatrix} \begin{bmatrix} v_1 \\ v_2 \\ v_3 \\ v_4 \end{bmatrix} = \beta \begin{bmatrix} c_1 \\ s_1 c_2 \\ s_1 s_2 c_3 \\ s_1 s_2 s_3 c_4 \\ s_1 s_2 s_3 s_4 \end{bmatrix}.$$

The least residual of the above equation is simply $\beta s_1 s_2 s_3 s_4 \mathbf{I}(:,5)$. Therefore, the residual of the original equation is as follows:

$$\mathbf{y}_4 = \mathbf{a} - \mathbf{A}\,(\mathbf{x}_0 + \mathbf{V}(:,1:4)\mathbf{v}) = \mathbf{y}_0 - \mathbf{V}(:,1:5)\mathbf{H}_{54}\mathbf{v}$$
$$= \mathbf{V}(:,1:5)\mathbf{Q}_{55}\left(\beta \mathbf{Q}_{55}'\mathbf{I}(:,1) - \mathbf{R}_{54}\mathbf{v}\right) = \beta s_1 s_2 s_3 s_4 \mathbf{V}(:,1:5)\mathbf{Q}_{55}\mathbf{I}(:,5).$$

Because $\mathbf{V}(:,1:5)'\mathbf{V}(:,1:5) \neq \mathbf{I}$, $\|\mathbf{y}_4\|_2 \neq \beta s_1 s_2 s_3 s_4$. If $\mathbf{V}(:,1:5)$ is close to orthogonal, $\beta s_1 s_2 s_3 s_4$ is a good estimate of $\|\mathbf{y}_4\|_2$ and can be used to check the convergence of the residual.

Finally, we are able to show how to calculate $\mathbf{P}$ in Eq. (5.53). For the cited simple example, we write $\mathbf{P} = \mathbf{V}(:,1:4)\mathbf{R}(1:4,1:4)^{-1}$ as $\mathbf{V}(:,1:4) = \mathbf{PR}(1:4,1:4)$ and equate the last column of both sides. We obtain

$$\mathbf{P}(:,4) = \frac{1}{R_{44}}\left(\mathbf{V}(:,4) - R_{24}\mathbf{P}(:,2) - R_{34}\mathbf{P}(:,3)\right).$$

$s(4)$ is just $\beta s_1 s_2 s_3 s_4$ and can be calculated as $s_4 s(3)$.

For the general case, replace 4 by m and 2 by l. In this way, we do not need to keep $\mathbf{V}(:,1:m)$ and only need to keep l recent columns of $\mathbf{P}$.

The MATLAB implementation of DQGMRES, `eqsDQGMRES_.m`, only has a small difference to `eqsDIOM_.m`. Removal of Lines 57 and 64, i.e. `'if␣(k␣<␣tsal)'` and its matching `'end'`, from `eqsDIOM_.m`, we have `eqsDQGMRES_.m`. There is a mathematically equivalent implementation based on the block update of $\mathbf{x}$ and $\mathbf{y}$, which is similar to `eqsQMR_.m`. See Section 5.5.8.

5.5.6 DQGMERR: DIRECT QUASI-GENERALIZED MINIMUM ERROR $\mathbf{W}$ IS INCOMPLETE ORTHOGONAL BASES OF $\mathbb{K}(\mathbf{A}', \mathbf{y}_0, m)$ AND $\mathbf{V} = ?$

Although it is not found in the literature, DQGMERR can be obtained from GMERR in the same way as we obtain DQGMRES from GMRES by allowing $\mathbf{W}$ to be incomplete bases of $\mathbb{K}(\mathbf{A}', \mathbf{y}_0, m)$.

Had we chosen $\mathbf{V} = \mathbf{A}'\mathbf{W}$ as in GMERR, the projection condition is in a similar form to Eq. (5.48). Because now $\mathbf{W}(:,1:m)'\mathbf{W}(:,1:m) \neq \mathbf{I}$, the last equality of Eq. (5.48) cannot be obtained.

We keep $\mathbf{V}$ unknown and write the projection condition as follows:

$$\mathbf{W}(:,1:m)'\mathbf{y}_m = \mathbf{W}(:,1:m)'\mathbf{A}\mathbf{A}^{-1}\,(\mathbf{a} - \mathbf{A}\mathbf{x}_1) = (\mathbf{A}'\mathbf{W})'\,(\mathbf{x}_\infty - \mathbf{x}_1)$$
$$= \mathbf{W}(:,1:m)'\mathbf{y}_0 - (\mathbf{A}'\mathbf{W}(:,1:m))'\,\mathbf{V}\mathbf{v} \qquad (5.54)$$
$$= \mathbf{W}(:,1:m)'\mathbf{y}_0 - \mathbf{H}(1:m+1,1:m)'\mathbf{W}(:,1:m+1)'\mathbf{V}\mathbf{v} = \mathbf{0}.$$

We choose $\mathbf{V} = \mathbf{W}(:,1:m+1)'^{+}\mathbf{H}(1:m+1,1:m)$. By this choice of $\mathbf{V}$, the above projection condition is simplified to

$$\mathbf{W}(:,1:m)'\mathbf{y}_m = \mathbf{W}(:,1:m)'\mathbf{y}_0 - \mathbf{H}(1:m+1,1:m)'\mathbf{H}(1:m+1,1:m)\mathbf{v} = \mathbf{0}. \qquad (5.55)$$

Note that $\mathbf{W}(:,1:m)'\mathbf{y}_0 \neq \beta \mathbf{I}(:,1)$. $\mathbf{H}(1:m+1,1:m)$ is a band matrix with a lower bandwidth of 1 and an upper band width of $l, l \leq m$. The remaining calculation is similar to DQGMRES, see Section 5.5.5.

The MATLAB implementation of DQGMERR, `eqsDQGMERR_.m`, is close to `eqsDQGMRES_.m`. But the difference is not negligible. The following lists `eqsDQGMERR_.m`.

Algorithm 5.11

Direct quasi-generalized minimum error method for unsymmetric Ax=a

```
% A/=A', input x=x0, output x: L*(A)*R*(R^{-1}*x)=L*a, default L=I, R=I.
function x = eqsDQGMERR_(A,a,x,tol,last,L,R)

[m,n] = size_(A);  tsal = m-1;  kth=floor(tsal/2);  %tsal,kth: internal args!
if (~iscell(A)) A = {'mtimes',A}; end

At = transpose_(A);  Lt = transpose_(L);  Rt = transpose_(R);

W = zeros(n,min(kth+1,n));  H = zeros(tsal+1,2);  w = zeros(tsal+1,1);
eta = 0.5*sqrt(2.0);          %eta for reorthogonalization

if (~isempty(R)) y = Ay_(R,x,'right'); else y = x; end
y = Ay_(A,y,'right');
if (~isempty(L)) y = Ay_(L,a-y,'right'); else y = a-y; end
beta = norm(y);  epslon = tol*max(1.0,beta);
W(:,1) = y/beta;  p = W(:,1);  w(1) = beta;  l = 0;

while(beta>epslon && l<last)
    for k = 1:tsal
        kW = mod(k,kth+1);
        if (kW == 0) kW = kth+1; end
        if (~isempty(Lt)) Atwk = Ay_(Lt,W(:,kW),'right'); else Atwk = W(:,kW); end
        Atwk = Ay_(At,Atwk,'right');
        if (~isempty(Rt)) Atwk = Ay_(Rt,Atwk,'right'); end
        normAtwk0 = norm(Atwk);
        for j=max(1,k-kth+1):k
            jW = mod(j,kth+1);
            if (jW == 0) jW = kth+1; end
            wj = W(:,jW);
            H(j,1) = wj'*Atwk;
            Atwk = Atwk - H(j,1)*wj;
        end
        normAtwk = norm(Atwk);
        if (normAtwk < eta*normAtwk0)  %reorthogonalization
            for j=max(1,k-kth+1):k
                jW = mod(j,kth+1);
                if (jW == 0) jW = kth+1; end
                wj = W(:,jW);
                Hj1 = wj'*Atwk;   H(j,1) = H(j,1) + Hj1;
                Atwk = Atwk - Hj1*wj;
            end
            normAtwk = norm(Atwk);
        end
        H(k+1,1) = normAtwk;
        kW1 = mod(k+1,kth+1);
        if (kW1 == 0) kW1 = kth+1; end
        if (normAtwk > tol) W(:,kW1) = Atwk/normAtwk;
        else                W(:,kW1) = 0.0;    end
        if (k-kth >= 1) H(k-kth,1) = 0; end %unwanted data from k-1
        for j=max(1,k-kth):k-1 %Apply old [c,s] to H(:,k), ie H(:,1)
            rho = H(j+1,2);   h1 = H(j,1);   h2 = H(j+1,1);
            if (rho == 1)         c = 0; s = 1;
            elseif(abs(rho) < 1) s = 2.0*rho; c = sqrt(1.0-s*s);
            else                 c = 2.0/rho; s = sqrt(1.0-c*c); end
```

```
        H(j,1) = c*h1 - s*h2;   H(j+1,1) = s*h1 + c*h2;
    end
    [c,s] = givens_(H(k,1),H(k+1,1));     %to zero H(k+1,k), ie H(k+1,1)
    H(k,1) = c*H(k,1) - s*H(k+1,1);
    if (abs(c) < tol)         H(k+1,2) = 1;
    elseif(abs(s) < abs(c)) H(k+1,2) = sign(c)*s/2;
    else                      H(k+1,2) = sign(s)*2/c; end
    w(k) = (w(k) - H(max(1,k-kth):k-1,1)'*w(max(1,k-kth):k-1))/H(k,1);
    x = x + (c*p - s*W(:,kW1))*w(k);
    p = s*p + c*W(:,kW1);
    if (normAtwk < tol) break; end        %lucky breakdown
  end
  if (~isempty(R)) y = Ay_(R,x,'right'); else y = x; end
  y = Ay_(A,y,'right');
  if (~isempty(L)) y = Ay_(L,a-y,'right'); else y = a-y; end
  beta = norm(y);
  W(:,1) = y/beta;  p = W(:,1);  w(1) = beta;  w(2:end) = 0.0;  l = l + 1;
end
if (~isempty(R)) x = Ay_(R,x,'right'); end
```

5.5.7 BCG: BI-CONJUGATE GRADIENT V AND W ARE BI-ORTHOGONAL BASES OF $\mathbb{K}(A, y_0, m)$ AND $\mathbb{K}(A', y_0, m)$

BCG is similar to DIOM in content: $\mathbf{V}$ and $\mathbf{W}$ are not orthogonal. It is similar to CG in form: two-term recursions. See Sections 5.5.4 and 5.4.1.

Using the relations of Eqs. (5.21), the Galerkin projection condition can be simplified as follows:

$$\mathbf{W}(:,1:m)'\mathbf{y}_m = \mathbf{W}(:,1:m)'(\mathbf{y}_0 - \mathbf{A}\mathbf{V}(:,1:m)\mathbf{v})$$
$$= \beta \mathbf{I}(:,1) - \mathbf{T}(1:m,1:m)\mathbf{v} = \mathbf{0}. \tag{5.56}$$

Then, $\mathbf{v} = \beta \mathbf{T}_m^{-1}\mathbf{I}(:,1)$, where $\mathbf{T}_m$ is a tri-diagonal matrix.

$\mathbf{v}$ can be solved by calling eqsByDecomposing_(A,b,decomposer,tol) with decomposer='LUband_' or 'QRband_'. After $\mathbf{v}$ is calculated, we can calculate the new approximate solution $\mathbf{x}_m$ and new residual $\mathbf{y}_m$,

$$\mathbf{x}_m = \mathbf{x}_0 + \mathbf{V}(:,1:m)\mathbf{v} = \mathbf{x}_0 + \mathbf{V}(:,1:m)(\mathbf{L}_m\mathbf{U}_m)^{-1}\mathbf{v}$$
$$= \mathbf{x}_0 + \left(\mathbf{V}(:,1:m)\mathbf{U}_m^{-1}\right)\left(\mathbf{L}_m^{-1}\beta\mathbf{I}(:,1)\right) = \mathbf{x}_0 + \mathbf{Ps}$$
$$= ((\mathbf{x}_0 + \mathbf{P}(:,1:m-1)\mathbf{s}(1:m-1)) + \mathbf{P}(:,m)\mathbf{s}(m) = \mathbf{x}_{m-1} + \mathbf{P}(:,m)\mathbf{s}(m), \tag{5.57}$$
$$\mathbf{y}_m = \mathbf{a} - \mathbf{A}\mathbf{x}_m = \mathbf{y}_0 - \mathbf{A}\mathbf{V}(:,1:m)\mathbf{v} = -T(m+1,m)v(m)\mathbf{V}(:,m+1)$$
$$= \mathbf{y}_0 - \mathbf{APs} = \mathbf{y}_{m-1} - \mathbf{AP}(:,m)\mathbf{s}(m).$$

The new residual $\mathbf{y}_m$ is in the direction of $\mathbf{V}(:,m+1)$. To check the convergence by $\|\mathbf{y}_m\|_2$, we do not need to form $\mathbf{y}_m$ according to Eq. (5.24). Instead the simple relation $\|\mathbf{y}_m\|_2 = T(m+1,m)|v(m)|\|\mathbf{V}(:,m+1)\|_2$ can be used.

All the above discussions are parallel to those of CG to emphasize their similarities, see Section 5.4.1. We again follow the presentation of CG to derive the two-term recursion for the present case that $\mathbf{V}$ and $\mathbf{W}$ are bi-orthogonal.

We want to have a two-term recursive formula same as Eq. (5.31). But now because $\mathbf{y}_k'\mathbf{y}_l \neq 0, k \neq l$, and $\mathbf{P}'\mathbf{AP} \neq \mathbf{I}$, the scalars α_k, β_k in Eq. (5.31) cannot be determined as in Eq. (5.33). In order to obtain a formula to determine α_k, β_k similarly to Eq. (5.33), we introduce another iteration based on $\mathbf{A}'\chi = \alpha$,

$$
\begin{aligned}
\mathbf{V}(:,1:m)'\boldsymbol{\eta}_m &= \mathbf{V}(:,1:m)'(\alpha - \mathbf{A}'\chi_m) \\
&= \mathbf{V}(:,1:m)'(\alpha - \mathbf{A}'(\chi_0 + \mathbf{W}(:,1:m)\mathbf{w})) \\
&= \mathbf{V}(:,1:m)'(\boldsymbol{\eta}_0 - \mathbf{A}'\mathbf{W}(:,1:m)\mathbf{w}) = \gamma\mathbf{I}(:,1) - \mathbf{T}(1:m,1:m)'\mathbf{w} = \mathbf{0}.
\end{aligned}
\tag{5.58}
$$

After $\mathbf{w} = \mathbf{T}(1:m,1:m)'^{-1}\gamma\mathbf{I}(:,1) = (\mathbf{U}'_m\mathbf{L}'_m)^{-1}\gamma\mathbf{I}(:,1)$ is calculated, the new approximation and residual are updated as follows:

$$
\begin{aligned}
\chi_m &= \chi_0 + \mathbf{W}(:,1:m)\mathbf{w} = \chi_0 + \left(\mathbf{W}(:,1:m)\mathbf{L}'^{-1}_m\right)\left(\mathbf{U}'^{-1}_m\gamma\mathbf{I}(:,1)\right) \\
&= \chi_0 + \mathbf{\Pi}\sigma = (\chi_0 + \mathbf{\Pi}(:,1:m-1)\sigma(1:m-1)) + \mathbf{\Pi}(:,m)\sigma(m) = \chi_{m-1} + \mathbf{\Pi}(:,m)\sigma(m), \\
\boldsymbol{\eta}_m &= \alpha - \mathbf{A}'\chi_m = \boldsymbol{\eta}_0 - \mathbf{A}'\mathbf{W}(:,1:m)\mathbf{w} = -T(m,m+1)\mathbf{W}(:,m+1)\mathbf{I}(m,:) \\
&= \boldsymbol{\eta}_0 - \mathbf{A}'\mathbf{\Pi}\sigma = \boldsymbol{\eta}_{m-1} - \mathbf{A}'\mathbf{\Pi}(:,m)\sigma(m),
\end{aligned}
\tag{5.59}
$$

where $\mathbf{\Pi} = \mathbf{W}(:,1:m)\mathbf{L}'^{-1}_m$ and $\sigma = \mathbf{U}'^{-1}_m\gamma\mathbf{I}(:,1)$.

We can verify that $\boldsymbol{\eta}'_k\mathbf{y}_l = 0, k, l = 1, \ldots, m, k \neq l$ and $\mathbf{\Pi}'\mathbf{AP} = \mathbf{I}$.

Using these two properties and following CG, we do not need to keep all the columns of $\mathbf{V}, \mathbf{W}$ and $\mathbf{P}, \mathbf{\Pi}$. Introducing a vector $\mathbf{p}_k$ which has a scale difference to $\mathbf{P}(:,k)$ and $\boldsymbol{\pi}_l$ which has a scale difference to $\mathbf{\Pi}(:,l)$, we can write the two iterations for $\mathbf{Ax} = \mathbf{a}$ and $\mathbf{A}'\chi = \alpha$ more succinctly as follows:

$$
\begin{aligned}
\mathbf{x}_{k+1} &= \mathbf{x}_k + \alpha_k\mathbf{p}_k; & \mathbf{y}_{k+1} &= \mathbf{y}_k - \alpha_k\mathbf{Ap}_k; & \mathbf{p}_{k+1} &= \mathbf{y}_{k+1} + \beta_k\mathbf{p}_k, \\
\chi_{k+1} &= \chi_k + \alpha_k\boldsymbol{\pi}_k; & \boldsymbol{\eta}_{k+1} &= \boldsymbol{\eta}_k - \alpha_k\mathbf{A}'\boldsymbol{\pi}_k; & \boldsymbol{\pi}_{k+1} &= \mathbf{y}_{k+1} + \beta_k\mathbf{p}_k.
\end{aligned}
\tag{5.60}
$$

The scalars α_k, β_k are determined by the conditions $\boldsymbol{\eta}'_k\mathbf{y}_l = 0, k, l = 1, \ldots, m, k \neq l$ and $\mathbf{\Pi}'\mathbf{AP} = \mathbf{I}$,

$$
\alpha_k = \frac{\boldsymbol{\eta}'_k\mathbf{y}_k}{\boldsymbol{\pi}'_k\mathbf{Ap}_k}; \quad \beta_k = \frac{\boldsymbol{\eta}'_{k+1}\mathbf{y}_{k+1}}{\boldsymbol{\eta}'_k\mathbf{y}_k}.
\tag{5.61}
$$

At the start, $\mathbf{p}_0 = \mathbf{y}_0$ and $\boldsymbol{\pi}_0 = \boldsymbol{\eta}_0$. It requires that $\boldsymbol{\eta}'_0\mathbf{y}_0 \neq 0$. This defines the BCG iteration which requires two matrix-vector products ($\mathbf{Ap}, \mathbf{A}'\boldsymbol{\pi}$), two vector inner-products ($\boldsymbol{\eta}'\mathbf{y}$ and $\boldsymbol{\pi}'\mathbf{Ap}$) and seven vectors ($\mathbf{x}, \mathbf{y}, \boldsymbol{\eta}, \mathbf{p}, \mathbf{Ap}, \boldsymbol{\pi}, \mathbf{A}'\boldsymbol{\pi}$). If $\mathbf{A}'\chi = \alpha$ is solved at the same time, choosing $\boldsymbol{\eta}_0 = \alpha - \mathbf{A}'\chi_0$, one more vector ($\chi$) is needed.

It can be seen that BCG actually solves two linear equations ($\mathbf{Ax} = \mathbf{a}$ and $\mathbf{A}'\chi = \alpha$) at the same time. If only $\mathbf{Ax} = \mathbf{a}$ needs to be solved, half of the calculation is wasted. In Sections 5.5.10–5.5.11, we will discuss the iterations which do not require the calculations related to $\mathbf{A}'$. But in the next two subsections, we will discuss the topics corresponding to minimum residual and minimum error in the case of bi-orthogonality.

Algorithm 5.12

Bi-Conjugate gradient method for unsymmetric Ax=a

```
% A/=A', input x=x0, output x: L*(A)*R*(R^{-1}*x)=L*a, default L=I, R=I.
function x = eqsBCG_(A,a,x,tol,last,L,R)

[m,n] = size_(A);
if (~iscell(A)) A = {'mtimes',A}; end
```

```
At = transpose_(A);  Lt = transpose_(L);  Rt = transpose_(R);

if (~isempty(R)) y = Ay_(R,x,'right'); else y = x; end
y = Ay_(A,y,'right');
if (~isempty(L)) y = Ay_(L,a-y,'right'); else y = a-y; end
p = y;  normy = norm(y);  epslon = tol*max(1.0,normy);  l = 0;

if (~isempty(Lt)) z = Ay_(Lt,x,'right'); else z = x; end
z = Ay_(At,z,'right');
if (~isempty(Rt)) z = Ay_(Rt,z,'right'); end
yz = y'*z;  q = z;
while(yz < tol) z = normy*rand(n,size(a,2)); yz = y'*z; q = z; end

while(normy>epslon && l<last)
    if (~isempty(R)) Ap = Ay_(R,p,'right'); else Ap = p; end
    Ap = Ay_(A,Ap,'right');
    if (~isempty(L)) Ap = Ay_(L,Ap,'right'); end
    alpha = yz/(q'*Ap);
    x = x + alpha*p;  y = y - alpha*Ap;
    if (~isempty(Lt)) Aq = Ay_(Lt,q,'right'); else Aq = q; end
    Aq = Ay_(At,Aq,'right');
    if (~isempty(Rt)) Aq = Ay_(Rt,Aq,'right'); end
    z = z - alpha*Aq;
    yz0 = yz;  yz = y'*z;
    beta = yz/yz0;
    p = y + beta*p;  q = z + beta*q;
    normy = norm(y);  l = l + 1;
end
if (~isempty(R)) x = Ay_(R,x,'right'); end
```

5.5.8 QMR: QUASI-MINIMAL RESIDUAL V IS BI-ORTHOGONAL BASES OF $\mathbb{K}(A, y_0, m)$ TO $\mathbb{K}(A', y_0, m)$ AND W = ?

QMR is similar to DQGMRES, where $\mathbf{V}$ is chosen to be non-orthogonal bases of $\mathbb{K}(\mathbf{A}, \mathbf{y}_0, m)$. The difference is that in DQGMRES $\mathbf{V}$ is partially orthogonal bases of $\mathbb{K}(\mathbf{A}, \mathbf{y}_0, m)$ and in QMR $\mathbf{V}$ is bi-orthogonal bases of $\mathbb{K}(\mathbf{A}, \mathbf{y}_0, m)$ to $\mathbb{K}(\mathbf{A}', \mathbf{y}_0, m)$.

We keep $\mathbf{W}$ in unknown form. The projection condition takes the usual form

$$
\begin{aligned}
\mathbf{W}(:, 1:m)'\mathbf{y}_m &= \mathbf{W}(:, 1:m)' (\mathbf{y}_0 - \mathbf{AV}(:, 1:m)\mathbf{v}) \\
&= \mathbf{W}(:, 1:m)'\mathbf{V}(:, 1:m+1)(\beta\mathbf{I}(:, 1) - \mathbf{T}(1:m+1, 1:m)\mathbf{v}) = \mathbf{0}.
\end{aligned}
\tag{5.62}
$$

In order to obtain the same simple form of "minimum" residual linear equations $\mathbf{T}(1:m+1, 1:m)\mathbf{v} = \beta\mathbf{I}(:, 1)$ as that of GMRES, we should choose $\mathbf{W} = \mathbf{V}(:, 1:m+1)'^{+}\mathbf{T}(1:m+1, 1:m) \neq \mathbf{AV}(:, 1:m)$. But we do not need to form $\mathbf{W}$ explicitly.

We use QR to solve $\mathbf{T}(1:m+1, 1:m)\mathbf{v} = \beta\mathbf{I}(:, 1)$, where $\mathbf{T}(1:m+1, 1:m)$ is tri-diagonal. $\mathbf{v}$ is indeed the minimum residual solution to this over-determined linear equations. Because $\mathbf{V}(:, 1:m+1)$ is not orthogonal, the norm of $\mathbf{y}_0 - \mathbf{AV}(:, 1:m)\mathbf{v}$ is not the minimum. This is where "quasi-minimum" comes from. See Sections 5.5.2 and 5.5.5 for more details.

The following lists the MATLAB implementation of QMR, eqsQMR_.m. There is a mathematically equivalent implementation based on the incremental update of $\mathbf{x}$ and $\mathbf{y}$, which is similar to eqsDQGMRES_.m. See Section 5.5.5.

Algorithm 5.13

Quasi-minimum residual method for unsymmetric Ax=a

```
% A/=A', input x=x0, output x: L*(A)*R*(R^{-1}*x)=L*a, default L=I, R=I.
function x = eqsQMR_(A,a,x,tol,last,L,R)

[m,n] = size_(A);    tsal = m;      %= floor(m/2); %tsal: internal input arg!
if (~iscell(A)) A = {'mtimes',A}; end

At = transpose_(A);  Lt = transpose_(L);  Rt = transpose_(R);
H = zeros(5,2);     %H(:,1)=H or R of H=Q*R, H(:,2)=rho of Q

if (~isempty(R)) y = Ay_(R,x,'right'); else y = x; end
y = Ay_(A,y,'right');
if (~isempty(L)) y = Ay_(L,a-y,'right'); else y = a-y; end
beta = norm(y);  epslon = tol*max(1.0,beta);  l = 0;

while(beta>epslon && l<last)
    v0 = zeros(n,1);  v1 = y/beta;  w0 = zeros(n,1);  w1 = v1;
    p0 = zeros(n,1);  p1 = p0;      r = [w1'*y; 0.0];
    for k = 1:tsal
        if (~isempty(R)) Av1 = Ay_(R,v1,'right'); else Av1 = v1; end
        Av1 = Ay_(A,Av1,'right');
        if (~isempty(L)) Av1 = Ay_(L,Av1,'right'); end
        if (~isempty(Lt)) Aw1 = Ay_(Lt,w1,'right'); else Aw1 = w1; end
        Aw1 = Ay_(At,Aw1,'right');
        if (~isempty(Rt)) Aw1 = Ay_(Rt,Aw1,'right'); end
        H(3,1) = w1'*Av1;
        v2 = Av1 - H(2,1)*v0 - H(3,1)*v1;
        w2 = Aw1 - H(5,1)*w0 - H(3,1)*w1;
        vw = v2'*w2;
        if (abs(vw) < tol) break; end
        H(4,1) = sqrt(abs(vw));  H(5,1) = vw/H(4,1);
        v2 = v2/H(4,1);  w2 = w2/H(5,1);
        for j=1:2  %Apply old [c,s] to H(:,k)=H(:,1)
            rho = H(j+1,2);    h1 = H(j,1);   h2 = H(j+1,1);
            if (rho == 1)       c = 0; s = 1;
            elseif(abs(rho) < 1) s = 2.0*rho; c = sqrt(1.0-s*s);
            else                c = 2.0/rho; s = sqrt(1.0-c*c); end
            H(j,1) = c*h1 - s*h2;    H(j+1,1) = s*h1 + c*h2;
        end
        [c,s] = givens_(H(3,1),H(4,1));    %to zero H(k+1,k), ie H(k+1,1)
        H(3,1) = c*H(3,1) - s*H(4,1);
        if (abs(c) < tol)       H(4,2) = 1;
        elseif(abs(s) < abs(c)) H(4,2) = sign(c)*s/2;
        else                    H(4,2) = sign(s)*2/c; end
        r(2) = s*r(1);  r(1) = c*r(1);
        p2 = (v1 - H(1,1)*p0 - H(2,1)*p1)/H(3,1);
        x = x + r(1)*p2;
        r(1) = r(2);  beta = abs(r(2));    %=|a-A*x| <-: convergence difficulty!
        H(1,1) = 0.0;  H(2,1) = H(5,1);   H(2,2) = H(3,2);  H(3,2) = H(4,2);
        v0 = v1;  v1 = v2;  w0 = w1;  w1 = w2;  p0 = p1;  p1 = p2;  l = l + 1;
    end
    if (~isempty(R)) y = Ay_(R,x,'right'); else y = x; end
    y = Ay_(A,y,'right');
    if (~isempty(L)) y = Ay_(L,a-y,'right'); else y = a-y; end
    beta = norm(y);                        %=|a-A*x|  ->: convergence difficulty!
```

```
end
if (~isempty(R)) x = Ay_(R,x,'right'); end
```

5.5.9 QME: QUASI-MINIMAL ERROR W IS BI-ORTHOGONAL BASES OF $\mathbb{K}(\mathbf{A}, \mathbf{y}_0, m)$ TO $\mathbb{K}(\mathbf{A}', \mathbf{y}_0, m)$ AND $\mathbf{V} = ?$

QME is similar to DQGMERR, where $\mathbf{W}$ is chosen to be non-orthogonal bases of $\mathbb{K}(\mathbf{A}, \mathbf{y}_0, m)$. The difference is that in DQGMERR $\mathbf{W}$ is partially orthogonal bases of $\mathbb{K}(\mathbf{A}', \mathbf{y}_0, m)$ and in QME $\mathbf{W}$ is bi-orthogonal bases of $\mathbb{K}(\mathbf{A}', \mathbf{y}_0, m)$ to $\mathbb{K}(\mathbf{A}, \mathbf{y}_0, m)$.

We keep $\mathbf{V}$ in unknown form. The projection condition takes the usual form

$$
\begin{aligned}
\mathbf{W}(:, 1:m)' \mathbf{y}_m &= \mathbf{W}(:, 1:m)' \mathbf{y}_0 - (\mathbf{A}'\mathbf{W}(:, 1:m))' \mathbf{V}(:, 1:m)\mathbf{v} \\
&= \mathbf{W}(:, 1:m)' \mathbf{y}_0 - \mathbf{T}(1:m+1, 1:m)\mathbf{W}(:, 1:m+1)'\mathbf{V}(:, 1:m)\mathbf{v} = \mathbf{0}.
\end{aligned}
\tag{5.63}
$$

In order to obtain the same simple form of "minimum" error linear equations $\mathbf{T}(1:m+1, 1:m)'\mathbf{T}(1:m+1, 1:m)'\mathbf{v} = \beta\mathbf{I}(:, 1)$ as that of GMERR, we should choose $\mathbf{V} = \mathbf{W}(:, 1:m+1)'^+\mathbf{T}(1:m+1, 1:m) \neq \mathbf{A}'\mathbf{W}(:, 1:m)$. But we do not need to form $\mathbf{V}$ explicitly.

We use QR to solve $\mathbf{T}(1:m, 1:m+1)\mathbf{u} = \beta\mathbf{I}(:, 1)$, where $\mathbf{T}(1:m, 1:m+1)$ is tri-diagonal. $\mathbf{u}$ is indeed the minimum error solution to this under-determined linear equations. Then $\mathbf{v} = \mathbf{T}(1:m+1, 1:m)'\mathbf{u}$ and $\mathbf{x}_m = \mathbf{x}_0 + \mathbf{W}(:, 1:m+1)^+\mathbf{u}$. Because $\mathbf{W}(:, 1:m+1)$ is not orthogonal, the norm of $\mathbf{x}_\infty - \mathbf{x}_m$ is not the minimum. This is where "quasi-minimum" comes from. See Sections 5.5.3 and 5.5.6 for more details. The calculation of $\mathbf{x}_m$ requires $\mathbf{W}(:, 1:m+1)^+$, which makes this implementation of QME impractical. There is a mathematically equivalent implementation based on the incremental update of $\mathbf{x}$ and $\mathbf{y}$, which is similar to eqsDQGMERR_.m. See Section 5.5.6. The following lists the MATLAB implementation of QME, eqsQME_.m.

Algorithm 5.14

Quasi-minimum error method for unsymmetric Ax=a

```
% A/=A', input x=x0, output x: L*(A)*R*(R^{-1}*x)=L*a, default L=I, R=I.
function x = eqsQME_(A,a,x,tol,last,L,R)

[m,n] = size_(A);    tsal = m-1;  %floor(m/2);        %tsal: internal input arg!
if (~iscell(A)) A = {'mtimes',A}; end

if (~isempty(R)) y = Ay_(R,x,'right'); else y = x; end
y = Ay_(A,y,'right');
if (~isempty(L)) y = Ay_(L,a-y,'right'); else y = a-y; end
beta = norm(y);   epslon = tol*max(1.0,beta);   w = [beta;zeros(tsal,1)];   l = 0;

while(beta>epslon && l<last)
    [T3,V,W] = GTGiByLanczos_({{'size',[n,m]},L,A,R},tol,1,tsal,[],y,y');
    [Q,QR] = QRband_(T3(1:tsal,:),1,1,tsal,tsal+1,[],'compact');
    for k=1:tsal-1
        rho = QR(k+1,1);      w1 = w(k);    w2 = w(k+1);
        if (rho == 1)         c = 0; s = 1;
        elseif(abs(rho) < 1)  s = 2.0*rho; c = sqrt(1.0-s*s);
        else                  c = 2.0/rho; s = sqrt(1.0-c*c); end
        w(k) = c*w1 - s*w2;   w(k+1) = s*w1 + c*w2;
    end
    w = mdivideBandUpperTriangle_(QR(:,2:end),2,tsal,tsal+1,w(1:tsal));
```

```
      x = x + pinv(W)*w;
      if (~isempty(R)) y = Ay_(R,x,'right'); else y = x; end
      y = Ay_(A,y,'right');
      if (~isempty(L)) y = Ay_(L,a-y,'right'); else y = a-y; end
      beta = norm(y);   y = y/beta;   w(1) = beta;   w(2:tsal+1) = 0;   l = l + 1;
end
if (~isempty(R)) x = Ay_(R,x,'right'); end
```

5.5.10 TFBCG: TRANSPOSED FREE BI-CONJUGATE GRADIENT $V = ?$ AND $W = ?$ TO MAKE IT EQUIVALENT TO BICGSTAB

In BCG, two matrix-vector products ($\mathbf{Ap}$, $\mathbf{A}'\boldsymbol{\pi}$) are needed, see Eqs. (5.60) and (5.61). In this section, we discuss an algorithm corresponding to BCG but without $\mathbf{A}'\boldsymbol{\pi}$. The purpose of eliminating $\mathbf{A}'\boldsymbol{\pi}$ is to improve the efficiency and overcome the unavailability of $\mathbf{A}'$ in some applications, where $\mathbf{A}$ is not given explicitly, for example, $\mathbf{A}$ is given only through the matrix-vector product $\mathbf{Ap}$. Even if $\mathbf{A}'$ is available, to consider the matrix-vector product of $\mathbf{A}'\mathbf{v}$ doubles the coding work in eqsGMERR_.m, DQGMERR_.m, eqsBCG_.m, eqsQMR_.m, eqsQME_.m, and GTGiByLanczos_.m. In these functions, if a function for the matrix-vector product of $\mathbf{Ap}$ is needed, another function for $\mathbf{A}'\boldsymbol{\pi}$ is also needed. If a pre-conditioner for $\mathbf{Ax} = \mathbf{a}$ is needed, the transposed pre-conditioner for $\mathbf{A}'\chi = \alpha$ is also needed. It is not easy to construct the transposed pre-conditioner from a given pre-conditioner within the scope of these functions.

From $\mathbf{y}_k, \mathbf{p}_k, \boldsymbol{\eta}_k$, and $\boldsymbol{\pi}_k$ defined in Eqs. (5.60), we see that they can be equivalently represented as two k-th order polynomials Y_k and P_k and further that the coefficients of $\mathbf{A}^k$ (or $\mathbf{A}'^k$) of Y_k and P_k are same,

$$
\begin{aligned}
\mathbf{y}_k &= Y_k(\mathbf{A})\mathbf{y}_0 = \left(a_k\mathbf{A}^k + a_{k-1}\mathbf{A}^{k-1} + \cdots\right)\mathbf{y}_0; \quad \boldsymbol{\eta}_k = Y_k(\mathbf{A}')\boldsymbol{\eta}_0, \\
\mathbf{p}_k &= P_k(\mathbf{A})\mathbf{y}_0 = \left(a_k\mathbf{A}^k + b_{k-1}\mathbf{A}^{k-1} + \cdots\right)\mathbf{y}_0; \quad \boldsymbol{\pi}_k = P_k(\mathbf{A}')\boldsymbol{\eta}_0.
\end{aligned}
\tag{5.64}
$$

Then the scalars α_k, β_k defined in Eqs. (5.61) can be calculated in terms of the two polynomials $Y_k(\mathbf{A})$ and $P_k(\mathbf{A})$. In the following, we omit the argument $\mathbf{A}$ and change Y_k and P_k to $\mathbf{Y}_k$ and $\mathbf{P}_k$ to emphasize their matrix nature,

$$
\alpha_k = \frac{(Y_k(\mathbf{A}')\boldsymbol{\eta}_0)' Y_k(\mathbf{A})\mathbf{y}_0}{(P_k(\mathbf{A}'))' \mathbf{A}P_k(\mathbf{A})\mathbf{y}_0} = \frac{\boldsymbol{\eta}_0'\mathbf{Y}_k^2\mathbf{y}_0}{\boldsymbol{\eta}_0'\mathbf{A}\mathbf{P}_k^2\mathbf{y}_0}, \qquad \beta_k = \frac{(Y_{k+1}(\mathbf{A}')\boldsymbol{\eta}_0)' Y_{k+1}(\mathbf{A})\mathbf{y}_0}{(Y_k(\mathbf{A}')\boldsymbol{\eta}_0)' Y_k(\mathbf{A})\mathbf{y}_0} = \frac{\boldsymbol{\eta}_0'\mathbf{Y}_{k+1}^2\mathbf{y}_0}{\boldsymbol{\eta}_0'\mathbf{Y}_k^2\mathbf{y}_0}. \tag{5.65}
$$

If we can find the iteration formula for the new iterates $\mathbf{y}_k = \mathbf{Y}_k^2\mathbf{y}_0$ and $\mathbf{p}_k = \mathbf{P}_k^2\mathbf{y}_0$, then the new algorithm which is equivalent to BCG simply replaces $Y_k'(\mathbf{A}')Y_k(\mathbf{A})$ by $Y_k^2(\mathbf{A})$, and $P_k'(\mathbf{A}')\mathbf{A}P_k(\mathbf{A})$ by $\mathbf{A}P_k^2(\mathbf{A})$. The new algorithm is known as CGS (conjugate gradient squared) in the literature, see [56, 63]. *In the following we use the same symbols $\mathbf{y}_k$ and $\mathbf{p}_k$, but their meanings are different from BCGs.* Based on their new definitions and Eqs. (5.60), the new iterates $\mathbf{y}_k$ and $\mathbf{p}_k$ are defined as follows:

$$
\begin{aligned}
\mathbf{y}_{k+1} &= \mathbf{Y}_k^2\mathbf{y}_0 - 2\alpha_k\mathbf{A}\mathbf{Y}_k\mathbf{P}_k\mathbf{y}_0 + \alpha_k^2\mathbf{A}^2\mathbf{P}_k^2\mathbf{y}_0 = \mathbf{y}_k - 2\alpha_k\mathbf{A}\mathbf{Y}_k\mathbf{P}_k\mathbf{y}_0 + \alpha_k^2\mathbf{A}^2\mathbf{p}_k, \\
\mathbf{p}_{k+1} &= \mathbf{Y}_{k+1}^2\mathbf{y}_0 + 2\beta_k\mathbf{Y}_{k+1}\mathbf{P}_k\mathbf{y}_0 + \beta_k^2\mathbf{P}_k^2\mathbf{y}_0 = \mathbf{y}_{k+1} + 2\beta_k\mathbf{Y}_{k+1}\mathbf{P}_k\mathbf{y}_0 + \beta_k^2\mathbf{p}_k.
\end{aligned}
\tag{5.66}
$$

For the two cross terms in Eqs. (5.66), we introduce two new iterates $\mathbf{q}_k = \mathbf{Y}_k\mathbf{P}_k\mathbf{y}_0$ and $\mathbf{r}_k = \mathbf{Y}_{k+1}\mathbf{P}_k\mathbf{y}_0$. Then, we have the following two recursive updates:

$$
\begin{aligned}
\mathbf{q}_k &= \mathbf{Y}_k\mathbf{P}_k\mathbf{y}_0 = \mathbf{Y}_k\left(\mathbf{Y}_k + \beta_{k-1}\mathbf{P}_{k-1}\right)\mathbf{y}_0 = \mathbf{y}_k + \beta_{k-1}\mathbf{Y}_k\mathbf{P}_{k-1}\mathbf{y}_0 = \mathbf{y}_k + \beta_{k-1}\mathbf{r}_{k-1}, \\
\mathbf{r}_k &= \mathbf{Y}_{k+1}\mathbf{P}_k\mathbf{y}_0 = \left(\mathbf{Y}_k - \alpha_k\mathbf{A}\mathbf{P}_k\right)\mathbf{P}_k\mathbf{y}_0 = \mathbf{y}_k + \beta_{k-1}\mathbf{r}_{k-1} - \alpha_k\mathbf{A}\mathbf{p}_k = \mathbf{q}_k - \alpha_k\mathbf{A}\mathbf{p}_k.
\end{aligned}
\tag{5.67}
$$

At the start, we have $\mathbf{y}_0 = \mathbf{a} - \mathbf{A}\mathbf{x}_0$, $\mathbf{p}_0 = \mathbf{q}_0 = \mathbf{y}_0$, and an arbitrary η_0 but $\eta_0'\mathbf{y}_0 \neq 0$. Then we can list the complete CGS iterations as follows:

$$\alpha_k = \frac{\eta_0'\mathbf{y}_k}{\eta_0'\mathbf{A}\mathbf{p}_k}, \tag{5.68a}$$

$$\mathbf{r}_k = \mathbf{q}_k - \alpha_k\mathbf{A}\mathbf{p}_k, \tag{5.68b}$$

$$\mathbf{x}_{k+1} = \mathbf{x}_k + \alpha_k\,(\mathbf{q}_k + \mathbf{r}_k), \tag{5.68c}$$

$$\mathbf{y}_{k+1} = \mathbf{y}_k - \alpha_k\mathbf{A}\,(\mathbf{q}_k + \mathbf{r}_k), \tag{5.68d}$$

$$\beta_k = \frac{\eta_0'\mathbf{y}_{k+1}}{\eta_0'\mathbf{y}_k}, \tag{5.68e}$$

$$\mathbf{q}_{k+1} = \mathbf{y}_{k+1} + \beta_k\mathbf{r}_k, \tag{5.68f}$$

$$\mathbf{p}_{k+1} = \mathbf{q}_{k+1} + \beta_k\,(\beta_k\mathbf{p}_k + \mathbf{r}_k). \tag{5.68g}$$

CGS works well in many cases and is about twice as efficient as BCG. But the squared polynomials in $\mathbf{y}_k = \mathbf{Y}_k^2\mathbf{y}_0$ and $\mathbf{p}_k = \mathbf{P}_k^2\mathbf{y}_0$ cause more rounding errors than BCG. To rectify the problem of rounding errors, an improvement called BICGSTAB (Bi-Conjugate Gradient STABilized) was established, see [56, 76]. Following our naming convention, it is named as TFBCG in this book.

In TFBCG, $\mathbf{y}_k = \mathbf{Y}_k^2\mathbf{y}_0$ and $\mathbf{p}_k = \mathbf{P}_k^2\mathbf{y}_0$ are modified to $\mathbf{y}_k = \mathbf{S}_k\mathbf{Y}_k\mathbf{y}_0$ and $\mathbf{p}_k = \mathbf{S}_k\mathbf{P}_k\mathbf{y}_0$. *In the following we use the same symbols $\mathbf{y}_k$ and $\mathbf{p}_k$, but their meanings are different from BCGs and CGSs.* $S_k\,(\mathbf{A})$ is another k-th order polynomial of $\mathbf{A}$, stabilizing the growth of errors in $\mathbf{y}_k$ and $\mathbf{p}_k$. A particular choice of S_k is the following:

$$S_{k+1}\,(\mathbf{A}) = (\mathbf{I} - \omega_k\mathbf{A})\,S_k\,(\mathbf{A}), \tag{5.69}$$

where ω_k is another scalar to be determined to minimize $\|\mathbf{y}_{k+1}\|_2$. Based on their new definitions and Eqs. (5.60) and (5.69), the iterates $\mathbf{y}_k$ and $\mathbf{p}_k$ for TFBCG are defined as follows:

$$\mathbf{y}_{k+1} = (\mathbf{I} - \omega_k\mathbf{A})\,S_k\,(\mathbf{Y}_k - \alpha_k\mathbf{A}\mathbf{P}_k)\,\mathbf{y}_0 = (\mathbf{I} - \omega_k\mathbf{A})\,(\mathbf{y}_k - \alpha_k\mathbf{A}\mathbf{p}_k) = (\mathbf{I} - \omega_k\mathbf{A})\,\mathbf{s}_k, \tag{5.70a}$$

$$\mathbf{p}_{k+1} = S_{k+1}\,(\mathbf{Y}_{k+1} + \beta_k\mathbf{P}_k)\,\mathbf{y}_0 = \mathbf{y}_{k+1} + \beta_k\,(\mathbf{I} - \omega_k\mathbf{A})\,\mathbf{p}_k. \tag{5.70b}$$

From the first of Eqs. (5.70), the optimal value of ω_k is given by

$$\omega_k = \frac{\mathbf{s}_k'\mathbf{A}\mathbf{s}_k}{\mathbf{s}_k'\mathbf{A}'\mathbf{A}\mathbf{s}_k}. \tag{5.71}$$

For the recursive update of α_k and β_k, we cannot use the new $\mathbf{y}_k$ and $\mathbf{p}_k$ in either Eqs. (5.61) or Eqs. (5.65). However, we can show they are related to the new $\mathbf{y}_k$ and $\mathbf{p}_k$. At first, we note that polynomials of $Y_k\,(\mathbf{A})$ and $P_k\,(\mathbf{A})$ are as shown in Eqs. (5.64), where the coefficients of $\mathbf{A}^k$ in both polynomials are a_k. Second, we write $S_k\,(\mathbf{A})$ as $S_k\,(\mathbf{A}) = c_k\mathbf{A}^k + c_{k-1}\mathbf{A}^{k-1} + \cdots$. Third, by the definition of Y_{k+1} according to Eq. (5.60) and S_{k+1} according to Eq. (5.69), we have $a_{k+1} = -\alpha_k a_k$ and $c_{k+1} = -\omega_k c_k$. Finally, we know that $\mathbf{A}'^k Y_l\,(\mathbf{A}) = 0, k, l = 1, \ldots, m, k < l$ by the construction of GTGiByLanczos_.m, i.e. bi-orthogonality. Based on these four observations, we can obtain the following relations:

$$\eta_0' Y_k' (\mathbf{A}') Y_k (\mathbf{A}) \mathbf{y}_0 = \eta_0' \frac{a_k}{c_k} \left(c_k \mathbf{A}'^k + \frac{c_k}{a_k} a_{k-1} \mathbf{A}'_{k-1} + \cdots \right)' Y_k (\mathbf{A}) \mathbf{y}_0$$

$$= \frac{a_k}{c_k} \eta_0' S_k (\mathbf{A}) Y_k (\mathbf{A}) \mathbf{y}_0 = \frac{a_k}{c_k} \eta_0' \mathbf{y}_k,$$

$$\eta_0' P_k' (\mathbf{A}') \mathbf{A} P_k (\mathbf{A}) \mathbf{y}_0 = \eta_0' \frac{a_k}{c_k} \left(c_k \mathbf{A}'^k + \frac{c_k}{a_k} b_{k-1} \mathbf{A}'^{k-1} + \cdots \right)' \mathbf{A} P_k (\mathbf{A}) \mathbf{y}_0$$

$$= \frac{a_k}{c_k} \eta_0' \mathbf{A} S_k (\mathbf{A}) P_k (\mathbf{A}) \mathbf{y}_0 = \frac{a_k}{c_k} \eta_0' \mathbf{A} \mathbf{p}_k.$$

From the above relations, α_k, β_k as defined in Eqs. (5.61) are obtained as follows:

$$\alpha_k = \frac{\eta_0' Y_k' (\mathbf{A}') Y_k (\mathbf{A}) \mathbf{y}_0}{\eta_0' P_k' (\mathbf{A}') \mathbf{A} P_k (\mathbf{A}) \mathbf{y}_0} = \frac{\eta_0' \mathbf{y}_k}{\eta_0' \mathbf{A} \mathbf{p}_k},$$

$$\beta_k = \frac{\eta_0' Y_{k+1}' (\mathbf{A}') Y_{k+1} (\mathbf{A}) \mathbf{y}_0}{\eta_0' Y_k' (\mathbf{A}') Y_k (\mathbf{A}) \mathbf{y}_0} = \frac{\alpha_k}{\omega_k} \frac{\eta_0' \mathbf{y}_{k+1}}{\eta_0' \mathbf{y}_k}.$$

At the start, we have $\mathbf{y}_0 = \mathbf{a} - \mathbf{A}\mathbf{x}_0$, $\mathbf{p}_0 = \mathbf{y}_0$, and an arbitrary η_0 but $\eta_0' \mathbf{y} \neq 0$. The complete iterations of TFBCG are listed below,

$$\alpha_k = \frac{\eta_0' \mathbf{y}_k}{\eta_0' \mathbf{A} \mathbf{p}_k}, \tag{5.72a}$$

$$\mathbf{s}_k = \mathbf{y}_k - \alpha_k \mathbf{A} \mathbf{p}_k, \tag{5.72b}$$

$$\omega_k = \frac{\mathbf{s}_k' \mathbf{A} \mathbf{s}_k}{\mathbf{s}_k' \mathbf{A}' \mathbf{A} \mathbf{s}_k}, \tag{5.72c}$$

$$\mathbf{x}_{k+1} = \mathbf{x}_k + \alpha_k \mathbf{p}_k + \omega_k \mathbf{s}_k, \tag{5.72d}$$

$$\mathbf{y}_{k+1} = \mathbf{s}_k - \omega_k \mathbf{A} \mathbf{s}_k, \tag{5.72e}$$

$$\beta_k = \frac{\alpha_k}{\omega_k} \frac{\eta_0' \mathbf{y}_{k+1}}{\eta_0' \mathbf{y}_k}, \tag{5.72f}$$

$$\mathbf{p}_{k+1} = \mathbf{y}_{k+1} + \beta_k (\mathbf{p}_k - \omega_k \mathbf{A} \mathbf{p}_k). \tag{5.72g}$$

Now we write Eqs. (5.72) in the form of the projection condition to extend TFBCG to another algorithm, TFQMR discussed in the next subsection.

First, we introduce the following notations:

$$\mathbf{V} = [\mathbf{p}_0, \mathbf{s}_0, \mathbf{p}_1, \mathbf{s}_1, \ldots], \tag{5.73a}$$

$$\mathbf{v} = [\alpha_0, \omega_0, \alpha_1, \omega_1, \ldots]', \tag{5.73b}$$

$$\mathbf{U} = \left[\frac{\mathbf{y}_0}{\|\mathbf{y}_0\|_2}, \frac{\mathbf{q}_0}{\|\mathbf{q}_0\|_2}, \frac{\mathbf{y}_1}{\|\mathbf{y}_1\|_2}, \frac{\mathbf{q}_1}{\|\mathbf{q}_1\|_2}, \ldots \right]. \tag{5.73c}$$

Then $\mathbf{x}_m$ and $\mathbf{y}_m$ can be written as follows:

$$\mathbf{x}_m = \mathbf{x}_0 + \mathbf{V} \mathbf{v}, \tag{5.74a}$$

$$\mathbf{y}_m = \mathbf{y}_0 - \mathbf{A} \mathbf{V} \mathbf{v}. \tag{5.74b}$$

Third, from the second and fifth equations of Eqs. (5.72), we obtain

$$\mathbf{AV}(:,1:m) = \left[\frac{1}{\alpha_0}(\mathbf{y}_0 - \mathbf{q}_0), \frac{1}{\omega_0}(\mathbf{q}_0 - \mathbf{y}_1), \frac{1}{\alpha_1}(\mathbf{y}_1 - \mathbf{q}_1), \frac{1}{\omega_1}(\mathbf{q}_1 - \mathbf{y}_2), \ldots\right]$$

$$= \mathbf{U}\,\mathrm{diag}\,(\|\mathbf{y}_0\|_2, \|\mathbf{q}_0\|_2, \ldots) \begin{bmatrix} 1 & & & \\ -1 & 1 & & \\ & -1 & 1 & \\ & & -1 & 1 \\ & & & -1 \\ & & & & \ddots \end{bmatrix} \mathrm{diag}\left(\frac{1}{\alpha_0}, \frac{1}{\omega_0}, \ldots\right) \qquad (5.75)$$

$$= \mathbf{U}(:,1:m)\mathbf{H}(1:m,1:m) + H(m+1,m)\mathbf{U}(:,m+1)\mathbf{I}(m,:)$$
$$= \mathbf{U}(:,1:m+1)\mathbf{H}(1:m+1,1:m).$$

Finally, using Eq. (5.75) in Eq. (5.74b), we have

$$\mathbf{y}_m = \mathbf{y}_0 - (\mathbf{U}(:,1:m)\mathbf{H}(1:m,1:m) + H(m+1,m)\mathbf{U}(:,m+1)\mathbf{I}(m,:))\,\mathbf{v}(1:m)$$
$$= \mathbf{U}(:,1:m+1)\,(\|\mathbf{y}_0\|_2\mathbf{I}(1:m+1,1) - \mathbf{H}(1:m+1,1:m)\mathbf{v}(1:m)). \qquad (5.76)$$

We can see that TFBCG iterations of Eqs. (5.72) correspond to the following projection conditions:

$$\mathbf{W}(:,1:m)'\,(\mathbf{y}_0 - (\mathbf{U}(:,1:m)\mathbf{H}(1:m,:) + H(m+1,m)\mathbf{U}(:,m+1)\mathbf{I}(m,:))\,\mathbf{v}) = \mathbf{0}, \qquad (5.77a)$$

$$\mathbf{W}(:,1:m)'\begin{bmatrix} \mathbf{y}_0 \\ \mathbf{U}(:,1:m) \\ \mathbf{U}(:,m+1) \end{bmatrix} = \begin{bmatrix} \|\mathbf{y}_0\|_2\mathbf{I}(:,1) \\ \mathbf{I} \\ \mathbf{0} \end{bmatrix}. \qquad (5.77b)$$

The following lists eqsTFBCG_.m. Compare with eqsBCG_.m to see the differences and commonalities. $\mathbf{z}$ can be chosen arbitrarily. If we choose $\mathbf{z} = \mathbf{I}(:,1)$, then we can save two vector dot products in $\mathbf{z}'\mathbf{Ap}$ and $\mathbf{z}'\mathbf{y}$. But this particular choice of $\mathbf{z}$ may introduce potential calculation failure due to $\mathbf{z}'\mathbf{Ap} = 0$ or $\mathbf{z}'\mathbf{y} = 0$.

Algorithm 5.15

Transpose free bi-conjugate gradient method for unsymmetric Ax=a

```
% A/=A', input x=x0, output x: L*(A)*R*(R^{-1}*x)=L*a, default L=I, R=I.
function x = eqsTFBCG_(A,a,x,tol,last,L,R)

[m,n] = size_(A);
if (~iscell(A)) A = {'mtimes',A}; end

if (exist('R','var') && ~isempty(R)) y = Ay_(R,x,'right'); else y = x; end
y = Ay_(A,y,'right');
if (exist('L','var') && ~isempty(L)) y = Ay_(L,a-y,'right'); else y = a-y; end
z = randn(n,1);     %= [1.0;zeros(n-1,1)];
p = y;   normy = norm(y);   epslon = tol*max(1.0,normy);   yz = y'*z;   l = 0;

while(normy>epslon && l<last)
    if (exist('R','var') && ~isempty(R)) Ap = Ay_(R,p,'right'); else Ap = p; end
    Ap = Ay_(A,Ap,'right');
    if (exist('L','var') && ~isempty(L)) Ap = Ay_(L,Ap,'right'); end
    alpha = yz/(z'*Ap);      %alpha = yz/Ap(1);
```

```
        q = y - alpha*Ap;
        if (exist('R','var') && ~isempty(R)) Aq = Ay_(R,q,'right'); else Aq = q; end
        Aq = Ay_(A,Aq,'right');
        if (exist('L','var') && ~isempty(L)) Aq = Ay_(L,Aq,'right'); end
        qAq = q'*Aq;    AqAq = Aq'*Aq;
        omega = qAq/AqAq;
        x = x + alpha*p + omega*q;
        y = q - omega*Aq;
        yz0 = yz;    yz = y'*z;    %yz = y(1);
        beta = alpha/omega*yz/yz0;
        p = y + beta*(p - omega*Ap);
        normy = norm(y);    l = l + 1;
end
if (exist('R','var') && ~isempty(R)) x = Ay_(R,x,'right'); end
```

5.5.11 TFQMR: TRANSPOSE FREE QUASI-MINIMAL RESIDUAL V = ? AND W = ? TO MAKE IT EQUIVALENT TO TFQMR

It is noted that TFQMR presented in [25] corresponds to CGS, while TFQMR presented below corresponds to BICGSTAB.

TFQMR corresponds to the following projection conditions, see Eq. (5.76):

$$\mathbf{W}(:,1:m+1)'\mathbf{U}(:,1:m+1)\left(\|\mathbf{y}_0\|_2\mathbf{I}(:,1)-\mathbf{H}(1:m+1,1:m)\mathbf{v}\right)=\mathbf{0}, \tag{5.78a}$$

$$\mathbf{W}(:,1:m+1)'\mathbf{U}(:,1:m+1)=\mathbf{H}(1:m+1,1:m)'. \tag{5.78b}$$

$\mathbf{H}(1:m+1,1:m)\mathbf{v}=\|\mathbf{y}_0\|_2\mathbf{I}(:,1)$ defines an over-determined problem, where $\mathbf{H}(1:m+1,1:m)$ is a bi-diagonal matrix defined in Eq. (5.75). The solution procedure is similar to DQGMRES, see Section 5.5.5. Because the columns of $\mathbf{U}(:,1:m+1)$ are not orthogonal, the minimization of the over-determined problem does not correspond to the minimization of $\|\mathbf{y}_m\|_2$. This is where "quasi-minimum residual" comes from.

Algorithm 5.16

Transpose free quasi-minimal method for unsymmetric Ax=a

```
% A/=A', input x=x0, output x: L*(A)*R*(R^{-1}*x)=L*a, default L=I, R=I.
function x = eqsTFQMR_(A,a,x,tol,last,L,R)

[m,n] = size_(A);
if (~iscell(A)) A = {'mtimes',A}; end

if (exist('R','var') && ~isempty(R)) y = Ay_(R,x,'right'); else y = x; end
y = Ay_(A,y,'right');
if (exist('L','var') && ~isempty(L)) y = Ay_(L,a-y,'right'); else y = a-y; end
normy = norm(y);    normy0 = normy;    epslon = tol*max(1.0,normy);    l = 0;
V = [y,zeros(n,1)];    P = zeros(n,2);    v = [normy;0.0];    u = [0;0;0];
c = 1.0;    s = 0.0;    z = randn(n,1);    %=[1;zeros(n-1,1)];

while(normy>epslon && l<last)
    for k = 1:2
        if (norm(V(:,k),inf) < tol) break; end
        Av = V(:,k);
        if (exist('R','var') && ~isempty(R)) Av = Ay_(R,Av,'right'); end
        Av = Ay_(A,Av,'right');
```

```
      if (exist('L','var') && ~isempty(L)) Av = Ay_(L,Av,'right'); end
      if (k == 1)
          Av1 = Av;  yz = y'*z;  u(1) = yz/(Av'*z);
          y = y - u(1)*Av;    V(:,2) = y;
      else
          u(2) = (y'*Av)/(Av'*Av);
          y = y - u(2)*Av;
          yz0 = yz;   yz = y'*z;   u(3) = yz/yz0*u(1)/u(2);
          V(:,1) = y + u(3)*(V(:,1)-u(2)*Av1);
      end
      normy = norm(y);   h = [0.0; normy0; -normy];   normy0 = normy;
      h(2:3) = h(2:3)/u(k);
      h(1) = -s*h(2);    h(2) = c*h(2);     %Apply old Givens rotation
      [c,s] = givens_(h(2),h(3));
      h(2) = c*h(2) - s*h(3);                %Apply new Givens rotation
      v(2) = s*v(1);   v(1) = c*v(1);
      if (k == 1) P(:,1) = (V(:,1)-h(1)*P(:,2))/h(2);
      else          P(:,2) = (V(:,2)-h(1)*P(:,1))/h(2); end
      x = x + P(:,k)*v(1);    v(1) = v(2);
   end
   l = l + 1;
end
if (exist('R','var') && ~isempty(R)) x = Ay_(R,x,'right'); end
```

5.5.12 NUMERICAL EXAMPLES

The numerical properties and usage of the 11 algorithms discussed in this section are demonstrated with the following simple examples.

The following are $\mathbf{A}$ and $\mathbf{a}$ for the first example.

```
>> A = [-0.8099    1.0562   -1.2276    1.0377    0.9291    1.5352   -0.0352    0.9390;
         -0.6967    1.2791   -1.5684    0.3636    0.0208    1.2677   -0.0175   -1.1496;
         -1.6603   -0.7969   -2.4280   -1.5947   -0.5394    1.9951   -0.0995    2.6229;
          0.7216    0.8557   -1.1658   -0.0718    0.4037    0.2236    0.5688    2.3756;
          1.3094   -0.8298    0.1879   -1.5433    0.3578   -1.3153    0.5492    0.0564;
         -1.2559    0.9281    0.0961   -1.1173   -1.6693    0.1815    0.1328   -0.5879;
          0.3058   -0.6929    1.4178    0.8162   -0.0798   -1.2785   -1.2299   -0.9830;
         -0.1890    0.1884    0.4202    0.5067    0.7377   -1.5095    1.6455   -1.3790];
>> a  = ones(8,1);   x0 = zeros(8,1);
```

The base-10 logarithms of the norms of errors $\mathbf{x}_\infty - \mathbf{x}_k$ and residuals $\mathbf{a} - \mathbf{A}\mathbf{x}_k$ are displayed in Figs. 5.7 and 5.8. For the given matrix, DIOM and DQGMERR do not converge within 50 iterations. For DIOM, DQGMRES, and DQGMERR, there are two internal input parameters tsal and kth. The former controls the number of iterations to restart the algorithm and the latter sets the number of orthogonal columns of the bases of the Krylov subspace. The values of two parameters have a significant impact on the convergence of the three algorithms. For FOM, GMRES, and GMERR, there is one internal input parameter tsal which sets the size of the Hessenberg matrix $\mathbf{H}$ in these algorithms. The value of tsal has a significant impact on the convergence of the three algorithms. To keep the uniformity of the input arguments for all the algorithms, the crucial input arguments tsal and kth are hard coded. The reader is advised to pay attention to this important point.

Among the 11 algorithms, TFBCG and TFQMR are found to have the best convergence properties.

In the second example, we apply TFBCG and TFQMR to $\mathbf{A}\mathbf{x} = \mathbf{a}$, where $\mathbf{A}$ is a 1000×1000 band matrix with a lower bandwidth of 3 and an upper bandwidth of 2. The input script is shown below. When

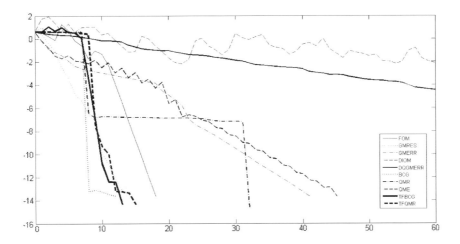

FIGURE 5.7

Errors of the 11 algorithms.

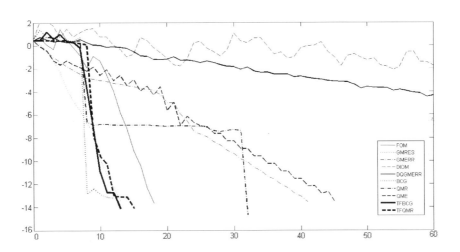

FIGURE 5.8

Residuals of the 11 algorithms.

calling TFBCG and TFQMR, **A** is in CSR format and mtimesCSR_.m is used to calculate the matrix-vector product **Av**. The errors and residuals are shown in Fig. 5.9.

```
>> d0 = 3*ones(1000,1);    d1 = ones(999,1);    d2 = ones(998,1);    d3 = ones(997,1);
>> A = diag(d0) + diag(d1,1) + diag(-d1,-1) + diag(-d2,2) + diag(d2,-2) + diag(d3,-3);
```

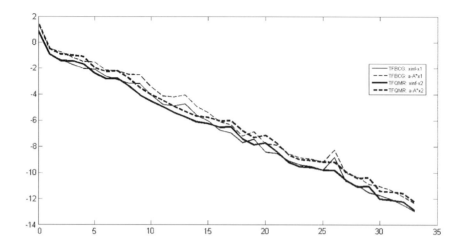

FIGURE 5.9

Errors and residuals of TFBCG and TFQMR.

```
>> [dA,rA,jA,m,n] = full2csr_(A);              %save A in CSR format
>> a = ones(1000,1);
>> x0= zeros(1000,1);                          %initial solution
>> x1 = eqsTFBCG_({'mtimesCSR_',{dA,rA,jA}},a,x0,100*eps,100);    %CSR by TFBCG
    33    %33 iterations to converge with tol=100*eps=2.2204e-014
>> x2 = eqsTFQMR_({'mtimesCSR_',{dA,rA,jA}},a,x0,100*eps,100);    %CSR by TFQMR
    33    %33 iterations to converge with tol=100*eps=2.2204e-014
```

The number of iterations is reduced if proper pre-conditioners are applied. For the purpose of the demonstration, we create and apply a pre-conditioner as the following script shows.

```
>> B = full2band_(A,3,2);
>> [L,R]=LUband_(B,3,2,1000,1000);
>> L = {'mdivideBandLowerTriangle_',{L,3,1000,1000}};    %left  conditioner
>> R = {'mdivideBandUpperTriangle_',{R,2,1000,1000}};    %right conditioner
>> x1 = eqsTFBCG_({'mtimesCSR_',{dA,rA,jA}},a,x0,100*eps,100,L,R);   %CSR by TFBCG
     1    %1 iteration to converge, because L*R=A is exact numerically
>> x2 = eqsTFQMR_({'mtimesCSR_',{dA,rA,jA}},a,x0,100*eps,100,L,R);   %CSR by TFQMR
     1    %1 iteration to converge, because L*R=A is exact numerically
```

5.6 SPECIAL ALGORITHMS FOR NORMAL EQUATIONS

As Sections 5.4 and 5.5 show, the algorithms for linear equations of a symmetric matrix (especially symmetric positive definite matrix) have better numerical properties and also easier to implement than an unsymmetric matrix. In some cases, it may be advantageous to transform linear equations of an unsymmetric matrix to equivalent linear equations of a symmetric matrix and then apply the algorithms for the symmetric matrix to the symmetrized linear equations.

5.6.1 SYMMETRIZING TRANSFORMATIONS

Given $\mathbf{Ax} = \mathbf{a}$ where $\mathbf{A} \in \mathbb{R}^{m \times n}, m < n, m = n$ or $m > n$ and $\mathbf{A} \neq \mathbf{A}'$. *We assume* $\mathbf{A}$ *has full rank.* There exist following symmetrizing transformations:

$$\text{If } m \geq n: \mathbf{A}'\mathbf{Ax} = \mathbf{A}'\mathbf{a}, \tag{5.79a}$$

$$\text{If } m \geq n: \begin{bmatrix} \mathbf{I} & \mathbf{A} \\ \mathbf{A}' & \mathbf{O} \end{bmatrix} \begin{bmatrix} \mathbf{a} - \mathbf{Ax} \\ \mathbf{x} \end{bmatrix} = \begin{bmatrix} \mathbf{a} \\ \mathbf{0} \end{bmatrix}, \tag{5.79b}$$

$$\text{If } m = n: \begin{bmatrix} \mathbf{O} & \mathbf{A} \\ \mathbf{A}' & \mathbf{O} \end{bmatrix} \begin{bmatrix} \mathbf{Ax} \\ \mathbf{x} \end{bmatrix} = \begin{bmatrix} \mathbf{a} \\ \mathbf{A}'\mathbf{a} \end{bmatrix}, \tag{5.79c}$$

$$\text{If } m \leq n: \mathbf{AA}'\mathbf{z} = \mathbf{a}; \ \mathbf{x} = \mathbf{A}'\mathbf{z}, \tag{5.80a}$$

$$\text{If } m \leq n: \begin{bmatrix} \mathbf{I} & \mathbf{A}' \\ \mathbf{A} & \mathbf{O} \end{bmatrix} \begin{bmatrix} \mathbf{x} \\ -\mathbf{z} \end{bmatrix} = \begin{bmatrix} \mathbf{0} \\ \mathbf{a} \end{bmatrix}. \tag{5.80b}$$

Under the assumptions, all the square matrices on the left hand side of equations are symmetric and non-singular. Further $\mathbf{A}'\mathbf{A}$ and $\mathbf{AA}'$ are symmetric positive definite. When solving Eqs. (5.79) or Eqs. (5.80) by algorithms for a symmetric matrix, in all cases, we do not need to form explicitly the symmetric matrices on the left hand side. But there is still price to pay for the symmetrization. The price is the larger condition number of the symmetric matrices and/or the increase of the size of the equations.

Using the SVD of $\mathbf{A} = \mathbf{USV}'$, we can obtain the condition number of each matrix of Eqs. (5.79) and Eqs. (5.80).

For Eqs. (5.79a) and (5.80a), we can easily obtain $\mathbf{A}'\mathbf{A} = \mathbf{VS}'\mathbf{SV}'$ and $\mathbf{AA}' = \mathbf{USS}'\mathbf{U}'$. This shows that

$$\text{cond}(\mathbf{A}'\mathbf{A}) = \text{cond}(\mathbf{AA}') = \text{cond}(\mathbf{A})^2. \tag{5.81}$$

If $\text{cond}(\mathbf{A})$ is 10^8, then $\text{cond}(\mathbf{A}'\mathbf{A})$ or $\text{cond}(\mathbf{AA}')$ is 10^{16} and any iterative solution algorithms for Eq. (5.79a) or Eq. (5.80a) will fail.

For Eq. (5.79c), we have

$$\begin{bmatrix} \mathbf{O} & \mathbf{A} \\ \mathbf{A}' & \mathbf{O} \end{bmatrix} = \begin{bmatrix} \mathbf{U} & \mathbf{O} \\ \mathbf{O} & \mathbf{V} \end{bmatrix} \begin{bmatrix} \mathbf{O} & \mathbf{S} \\ \mathbf{S} & \mathbf{O} \end{bmatrix} \begin{bmatrix} \mathbf{U}' & \mathbf{O} \\ \mathbf{O} & \mathbf{V}' \end{bmatrix} = \begin{bmatrix} \mathbf{U} & \mathbf{O} \\ \mathbf{O} & \mathbf{V} \end{bmatrix} \mathbf{P} \begin{bmatrix} \mathbf{S} & \mathbf{O} \\ \mathbf{O} & \mathbf{S} \end{bmatrix} \mathbf{P}' \begin{bmatrix} \mathbf{U}' & \mathbf{O} \\ \mathbf{O} & \mathbf{V}' \end{bmatrix}, \tag{5.82}$$

where $\mathbf{P}$ is a permutation matrix. Eq. (5.82) shows that the matrix for Eq. (5.79c) has the same condition number as $\mathbf{A}$.

For Eq. (5.79b), we also have

$$\begin{bmatrix} \mathbf{I} & \mathbf{A} \\ \mathbf{A}' & \mathbf{O} \end{bmatrix} = \begin{bmatrix} \mathbf{U} & \mathbf{O} \\ \mathbf{O} & \mathbf{V} \end{bmatrix} \begin{bmatrix} \mathbf{I} & \mathbf{S} \\ \mathbf{S}' & \mathbf{O} \end{bmatrix} \begin{bmatrix} \mathbf{U}' & \mathbf{O} \\ \mathbf{O} & \mathbf{V}' \end{bmatrix}. \tag{5.83}$$

Now we calculate the singular values of $\mathbf{B} = \begin{bmatrix} \mathbf{I} & \mathbf{S} \\ \mathbf{S}' & \mathbf{O} \end{bmatrix}$. It is enough to consider only the nonzeros in the diagonal $\mathbf{S}$. Because $\mathbf{B}^2 = \mathbf{B}'\mathbf{B} = \mathbf{BB}' = \begin{bmatrix} \mathbf{I} + \mathbf{S}^2 & \mathbf{S} \\ \mathbf{S} & \mathbf{S}^2 \end{bmatrix}$, the eigenvalue λ of $\mathbf{B}^2$ can be calculated as follows:

$$\det \begin{bmatrix} \mathbf{I} + \mathbf{S}^2 - \lambda\mathbf{I} & \mathbf{S} \\ \mathbf{S} & \mathbf{S}^2 - \lambda\mathbf{I} \end{bmatrix} = \det \left(\left(\mathbf{I} + \mathbf{S}^2 - \lambda\mathbf{I} \right) \left(\mathbf{S}^2 - \lambda\mathbf{I} \right) - \mathbf{S}^2 \right) = \det \left(\lambda^2\mathbf{I} - \lambda \left(\mathbf{I} + 2\mathbf{S}^2 \right) + \mathbf{S}^4 \right) = 0,$$

where the second equality is obtained by Theorem 3 in [60]. From the above equation, one singular value of $\mathbf{A}$ corresponds to two eigenvalues of $\mathbf{B}$,

$$\lambda_{1,2} = \frac{1 + 2s^2 \pm \sqrt{1 + 4s^2}}{2}; \quad \lambda_1 \geq s, \ \lambda_2 \leq s.$$

Therefore, $\mathrm{cond}(\mathbf{B}) \geq \mathrm{cond}(\mathbf{A})$, i.e. $\mathrm{cond} \begin{bmatrix} \mathbf{I} & \mathbf{A} \\ \mathbf{A}' & \mathbf{O} \end{bmatrix} \geq \mathrm{cond}(\mathbf{A})$. Similarly, $\mathrm{cond} \begin{bmatrix} \mathbf{I} & \mathbf{A}' \\ \mathbf{A} & \mathbf{O} \end{bmatrix} \geq \mathrm{cond}(\mathbf{A})$.

In this section, we will design special algorithms for Eq. (5.79a), Eq. (5.80a), Eq. (5.79b) and Eq. (5.80b). Eq. (5.79c) is not treated, because it is numerically equivalent to Eq. (5.79a). Eq. (5.79a) and Eq. (5.80a) are commonly known as normal equations. They are the minimizing conditions of the least residuals $\|\mathbf{a} - \mathbf{A}\mathbf{x}\|_2$ and errors $\|\mathbf{x}_\infty - \mathbf{A}'\mathbf{z}\|_2$, respectively. Eq. (5.79b) and Eq. (5.80b) are special cases of linear equations with linear constraints discussed in Section 4.2.

5.6.2 STATIONARY ITERATIONS FOR NORMAL EQUATIONS

In Section 5.2, we see that all the stationary iteration algorithms are projection methods employing $\mathbf{I}(:,i)$. We apply the projection method employing $\mathbf{I}(:,i)$ to Eq. (5.79a) and Eq. (5.80a),
For Eq. (5.79a),

$$\mathbf{x}_{i+1} = \mathbf{x}_{0i} + d_i\mathbf{I}(:,i), \tag{5.84a}$$

$$\mathbf{y}_{i+1} = \mathbf{a} - \mathbf{A}\left(\mathbf{x}_{0i} + d_i\mathbf{I}(:,i) \right) = \mathbf{y}_{0i} - d_i\mathbf{A}\mathbf{I}(:,i), \tag{5.84b}$$

$$\mathbf{I}(:,i)'\mathbf{A}'\mathbf{y}_{i+1} = \mathbf{A}(:,i)'\left(\mathbf{y}_{0i} - d_i\mathbf{A}(:,i) \right) = 0, \tag{5.84c}$$

$$d_i = \frac{\mathbf{A}(:,i)'\mathbf{y}_{0i}}{\mathbf{A}(:,i)'\mathbf{A}(:,i)}. \tag{5.84d}$$

If each column of $\mathbf{A}$ is normalized, i.e. $\mathbf{A}(:,i)'\mathbf{A}(:,i) = 1$, then $d_i = \mathbf{A}(:,i)'\mathbf{y}_{0i}$.
For Eq. (5.80a),

$$\mathbf{z}_{i+1} = \mathbf{z}_{0i} + d_i\mathbf{I}(:,i), \tag{5.85a}$$

$$\mathbf{y}_{i+1} = \mathbf{a} - \mathbf{A}\mathbf{A}'\left(\mathbf{z}_{0i} + d_i\mathbf{I}(:,i) \right) = \mathbf{y}_{0i} - d_i\mathbf{A}\mathbf{A}'\mathbf{I}(:,i), \tag{5.85b}$$

$$\mathbf{I}(:,i)'\mathbf{y}_{i+1} = \mathbf{I}(:,i)'\left(\mathbf{y}_{0i} - d_i\mathbf{A}\mathbf{A}'\mathbf{I}(:,i) \right) = 0, \tag{5.85c}$$

$$d_i = \frac{\mathbf{I}(:,i)'\mathbf{y}_{0i}}{\mathbf{A}(i,:)\mathbf{A}(i,:)'}. \tag{5.85d}$$

If each row of $\mathbf{A}$ is normalized, i.e. $\mathbf{A}(i,:)\mathbf{A}(i,:)' = 1$, then $d_i = \mathbf{I}(:,i)'\mathbf{y}_{0i}$. If we base the iterations on the variable $\mathbf{x}$, Eq. (5.85a) is then replaced by the following equation:

$$\mathbf{x}_{i+1} = \mathbf{x}_{0i} + d_i\mathbf{A}'\mathbf{I}(:,i) = \mathbf{x}_{0i} + d_i\mathbf{A}(i,:)'. \tag{5.85a}$$

See Section 5.2 for the difference in $\mathbf{x}_{0i}$ between Jacobi and Gauss-Seidel iterations, and the application of an acceleration parameter ω. If $\mathbf{A}$ is full rank, $\mathbf{A}'\mathbf{A}$ or $\mathbf{A}\mathbf{A}'$ is symmetric positive definite. Gauss-Seidel iterations for $\mathbf{A}'\mathbf{A}$ or $\mathbf{A}\mathbf{A}'$ converge for arbitrary $\mathbf{x}_0$ and $0 < \omega < 2$. The convergence property of Richardson and Jacobi iterations for normal equations is not easy to apply, because it requires an eigenvalue analysis of $\mathbf{A}'\mathbf{A}$ or $\mathbf{A}\mathbf{A}'$.

The following listed `eqsStationaryNormal_.m` implements the stationary iteration algorithms for the normal equations. The input arguments and structure of `eqsStationaryNormal_.m` are similar to `eqsStationary_.m`. The input argument `eq = 1` solves Eq. (5.79a) and `eq = 2` solves Eq. (5.80a). The pre-conditioner for normal equations is not implemented in `eqsStationaryNormal_.m`. It is noted that `eqsStationaryNormal_.m` can be applied to a rectangular long or wide full rank matrix. When the solution converges, the output of `eqsStationaryNormal_.m` for a rectangular full rank matrix is $\mathbf{A}^{+}\mathbf{a}$.

Algorithm 5.17

Stationary iterations for A'*A*x=A'*a or A*A'*z=a,x=A'*z

```
% eq = 1: A'*A*x=A'*a;  = 2: A*A'*z=a, x = A'*z
% algo = 'richardson', 'jacobi', 'gauss-seidel' (default)
%      = 'forward-gauss-seidel'='gauss-seidel','backward-gauss-seidel', 'ssor'
function x = eqsStationaryNormal_(A,eq,a,x,algo,tol,last,omega)

[m,n] = size(A);

if (strcmp(algo,'richardson'))          %richardson
    y = a - A*x;   dx = A'*y;
    epslon = tol*max(1.0,norm(dx,inf));  l = 0;
    while(norm(dx,inf)>epslon && l<last)
        if (omega == 1) x = x + dx; else x = x + omega*dx; end
        y = a - A*x;    dx = A'*y;  l = l + 1;
    end
elseif (strcmp(algo,'jacobi'))          %jacobi
    if (eq == 1) s = zeros(n,1); else s = zeros(m,1); end
    if (eq == 1)
        for j=1:n s(j)=norm(A(:,j));  A(:,j)=A(:,j)/s(j);  x(j,:)=s(j)*x(j,:); end
    else
        for i=1:m s(i)=norm(A(i,:));  A(i,:)=A(i,:)/s(i);  a(i,:)=a(i,:)/s(i); end
    end
    y = a - A*x;    dx = A'*y;
    epslon = tol*max(1.0,norm(dx,inf));  l = 0;
    while(norm(dx,inf)>epslon && l < last)
        if (omega == 1) x = x + dx;  else x = x + omega*dx; end
        y = a - A*x;    dx = A'*y;  l = l + 1;
    end
    if (eq==1)
        for j=1:n x(j,:) = x(j,:)/s(j); end
    end
else %if (strcmp(algo,'gauss-seidel')) %gauss-seidel
    if (eq == 1) mn = n; else mn = m; end
    s = zeros(mn,1);    y = a - A*x;
    if (eq == 1)
        for j=1:n s(j)=norm(A(:,j));  A(:,j)=A(:,j)/s(j);  x(j,:)=s(j)*x(j,:); end
    else
        for i=1:m s(i)=norm(A(i,:));  A(i,:)=A(i,:)/s(i);  a(i,:)=a(i,:)/s(i); end
    end
    epslon = tol*max(1.0,norm(y,inf));  dmax = 2.0*epslon;  l = 0;
    while (dmax>epslon && l<last)
        dmax = 0.0;  l = l + 1;
        for k=1:abs(gs)
            if (gs==-1 || k==2) loop = mn:-1:1; else loop = 1:mn; end
```

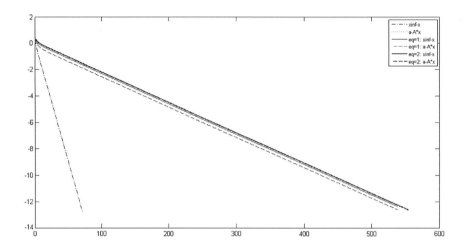

FIGURE 5.10

Errors and residuals of Gauss-Seidel iterations for normal equations.

```
        for j=loop
            if (eq == 1) d = y'*A(:,j); else d = a(j)-A(j,:)*x; end
            dmax = max(dmax,abs(d));   d = omega*d;
            if (eq == 1) x(j) = x(j) + d;  y = y - d*A(:,j);
            else           x = x + d*A(j,:)';   end
        end
    end
  end
  if (eq==1)
      for j=1:n x(j,:) = x(j,:)/s(j); end
  end
end
```

In the following, we give three numerical examples solved by eqsStationaryNormal_.m.

In the first example, the matrix **A** and right hand side **a** are listed in Section 5.2. The Gauss-Seidel for normal equations takes more iterations, because cond(**A**) = 10.3181, but cond(**A′A**) = cond(**AA′**) = 106.4632.

```
>> x=eqsStationary_(A,a,zeros(8,1),'gauss-seidel',100*eps,1000);
l =    71
>> x1=eqsStationaryNormal_(A,1,a,zeros(8,1),'gauss-seidel',100*eps,1000);
l =    538
>> x2=eqsStationaryNormal_(A,2,a,zeros(8,1),'gauss-seidel',100*eps,1000);
l =    554
```

The errors and residuals of **Ax** = **a** in the iterations by Gauss-Seidel and Gauss-Seidel for normal equations are displayed in Fig. 5.10.

In the second example, the matrix **A** and right hand side **a** are listed in Section 5.5.12. The Gauss-Seidel iterations cannot converge for this example. But the Gauss-Seidel iterations for normal equations converge, because **A′A** and **AA′** are symmetric definite and omega=1 in the solutions.

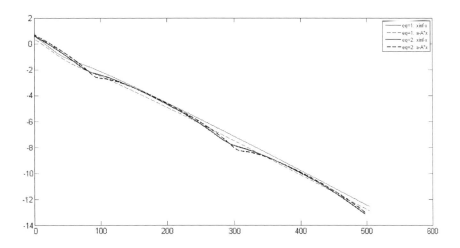

FIGURE 5.11

Errors and residuals of Gauss-Seidel iterations for normal equations.

```
>> x1=eqsStationaryNormal_(A,1,a,x0,'gauss-seidel',100*eps,4000);
l = 504
>> x2=eqsStationaryNormal_(A,2,a,x0,'gauss-seidel',100*eps,4000);
l = 497
```

The errors and residuals of $\mathbf{Ax} = \mathbf{a}$ in the iterations are displayed in Fig. 5.11.

The third example is the Gauss-Seidel iterations applied to normal equations of rectangular matrices.

```
>> A1 = [-0.2200   -0.4495    0.4288    0.0695   -0.1064;
         -1.4144   -1.5479    1.2951   -1.8337    0.3388;
         -0.3028   -0.0958   -0.1861    1.8274    1.0335;
         -0.5696    0.9077    0.1307    0.6541   -1.4048;
         -0.1215    2.3696   -0.6576   -1.5448   -1.0306;
         -0.3902    0.5198   -0.7593   -0.3751   -0.6434;
         -0.8443    0.4105   -0.5952    0.2077    0.1708;
         -1.7378    1.0526    0.8124   -0.7656    1.3448];
>> a1 = ones(8,1);   x01 = zeros(5,1);

>> A2 = [1.9363   -0.8001    0.2171    0.5213   -1.0923    0.6464    0.7925   -1.3528;
         0.7413    0.4932    0.6307   -0.6160   -0.3257   -1.1294    0.6034    0.4570;
         0.8120    1.2376   -0.5485    1.3458   -2.0122    0.1970   -0.0584    0.3912;
        -0.1428    1.2960    0.2296    0.9749    1.5677    1.6969   -1.1087    2.0730;
        -0.0999   -0.2782    0.3553   -2.3779    0.2333    0.7260    2.1442   -0.3233];
>> a2 = ones(5,1);   x02 = zeros(8,1);

>> x1=eqsStationaryNormal_(A1,1,a1,x01,'gauss-seidel',100*eps,1000);
l = 56
>> x2=eqsStationaryNormal_(A2,2,a2,x02,'gauss-seidel',100*eps,1000);
l = 48
```

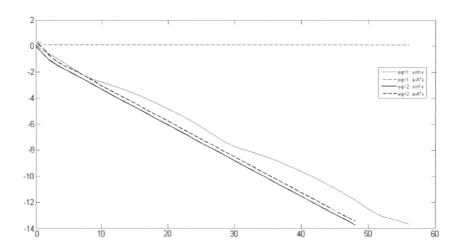

FIGURE 5.12

Errors and residuals of Gauss-Seidel iterations for normal equations.

The errors and residuals of $\mathbf{Ax} = \mathbf{a}$ in the iterations are displayed in Fig. 5.12. $\mathbf{y}_1 = \mathbf{a}_1 - \mathbf{A}_1\mathbf{x}_1$ does not converge to zero, because the linear equations are over-determined.

5.6.3 CONJUGATE GRADIENT FOR NORMAL EQUATIONS

If $\mathbf{A}$ is symmetric positive definite, CG converges from an arbitrary $\mathbf{x}_0$. At any intermediate iteration k, the intermediate solution $\mathbf{x}_k$ minimizes $(\mathbf{x}_\infty - \mathbf{x}_k)'\, \mathbf{A}\, (\mathbf{x}_\infty - \mathbf{x}_k)$ for all $\mathbf{x} \in \mathbf{x}_0 + \mathbb{K}\,(\mathbf{A}, \mathbf{y}_0, k)$.

When CG is applied to Eq. (5.79a) or Eq. (5.80a), because $\mathbf{A}'\mathbf{A}$ in Eq. (5.79a) and $\mathbf{AA}'$ in Eq. (5.80a) are symmetric positive definite, the CG algorithms inherit the property of CG for a positive definite matrix.

For Eq. (5.79a), the CG iteration formula equations (5.31) and (5.33) are specialized as follows:

$$\mathbf{x}_{k+1} = \mathbf{x}_k + \alpha_k\mathbf{p}_k; \qquad \mathbf{z}_{k+1} = \mathbf{A}'\mathbf{y}_{k+1} = \mathbf{A}'\,(\mathbf{y}_k - \alpha_k\mathbf{Ap}_k)\,; \qquad \mathbf{p}_{k+1} = \mathbf{z}_{k+1} + \beta_k\mathbf{p}_k\,. \qquad (5.86)$$

The scalars α_k and β_k are determined by the conditions $\mathbf{z}'_{k+1}\mathbf{z}_k = 0$ and $\mathbf{p}'_{k+1}\mathbf{A}'\mathbf{Ap}_k = 0$,

$$\alpha_k = \frac{\mathbf{z}'_k\mathbf{z}_k}{\mathbf{p}'_k\mathbf{A}'\mathbf{Ap}_k}\,; \qquad \beta_k = \frac{\mathbf{z}'_{k+1}\mathbf{z}_{k+1}}{\mathbf{z}'_k\mathbf{z}_k}\,. \qquad (5.87)$$

$\mathbf{x}_k$ minimizes $(\mathbf{x}_\infty - \mathbf{x}_k)'\, \mathbf{A}'\mathbf{A}\, (\mathbf{x}_\infty - \mathbf{x}_k) = (\mathbf{a} - \mathbf{Ax}_k)'\,(\mathbf{a} - \mathbf{Ax}_k) = \mathbf{y}'_k\mathbf{y}_k$ for all $\mathbf{x} \in \mathbf{x}_0 + \mathbb{K}\,(\mathbf{A}'\mathbf{A}, \mathbf{A}'\mathbf{y}_0, k)$. Comparing with CR and GMRES, the minimizing function, i.e. the norm of the residual, is same, but the subspace in which to seek the argument of the minimum is different. For CR and GMRES, the subspace is $\mathbf{x}_0 + \mathbb{K}\,(\mathbf{A}, \mathbf{y}_0, k)$. Due to the similarity to CR and GMRES, the specialized CG for Eq. (5.79a) is commonly known as CGNR.[4]

---

[4]Conjugate Gradient Normal Residual.

For Eq. (5.80a), the CG iteration formula equations (5.31) and (5.33) are specialized as follows:

$$\mathbf{x}_{k+1} = \mathbf{A}'\mathbf{w}_{k+1} = \mathbf{A}'(\mathbf{w}_k + \alpha_k\mathbf{p}_k) = \mathbf{x}_k + \alpha_k\mathbf{q}_k, \tag{5.88a}$$

$$\mathbf{y}_{k+1} = \mathbf{y}_k - \alpha_k\mathbf{A}\mathbf{A}'\mathbf{p}_k = \mathbf{y}_k - \alpha_k\mathbf{A}\mathbf{q}_k, \tag{5.88b}$$

$$\mathbf{q}_{k+1} = \mathbf{A}'\mathbf{p}_{k+1} = \mathbf{A}'(\mathbf{y}_{k+1} + \beta_k\mathbf{p}_k) = \mathbf{A}'\mathbf{y}_{k+1} + \beta_k\mathbf{q}_k. \tag{5.88c}$$

The scalars α_k and β_k are determined by the conditions $\mathbf{y}'_{k+1}\mathbf{y}_k = 0$ and $\mathbf{p}'_{k+1}\mathbf{A}\mathbf{A}'\mathbf{p}_k = 0$,

$$\alpha_k = \frac{\mathbf{y}'_k\mathbf{y}_k}{\mathbf{p}'_k\mathbf{A}\mathbf{A}'\mathbf{p}_k} = \frac{\mathbf{y}'_k\mathbf{y}_k}{\mathbf{q}'_k\mathbf{q}_k}; \qquad \beta_k = \frac{\mathbf{y}'_{k+1}\mathbf{y}_{k+1}}{\mathbf{y}'_k\mathbf{y}_k}. \tag{5.89}$$

$\mathbf{z}_k$ minimizes $(\mathbf{z}_\infty - \mathbf{z}_k)'\,\mathbf{A}\mathbf{A}'\,(\mathbf{z}_\infty - \mathbf{z}_k)$ for all $\mathbf{z} \in \mathbf{z}_0 + \mathbb{K}(\mathbf{A}\mathbf{A}',\mathbf{y}_0,k)$. In terms of $\mathbf{x}_k$, $\mathbf{x}_k$ minimizes $(\mathbf{x}_\infty - \mathbf{x}_k)'(\mathbf{x}_\infty - \mathbf{x}_k)$ for all $\mathbf{x} \in \mathbf{x}_0 + \mathbf{A}'\mathbb{K}(\mathbf{A}\mathbf{A}',\mathbf{y}_0,k) = \mathbf{x}_0 + \mathbb{K}(\mathbf{A}'\mathbf{A},\mathbf{A}'\mathbf{y}_0,k)$. Comparing with CGNR, the minimizing function, i.e. the norm of the error, is different, but the subspace for the argument of the minimum is same. Comparing with CE and GMERR, the minimizing function is same, but the subspace for the argument of the minimum is different. Due to the similarity to CE and GMERR, the specialized CG for Eq. (5.80a) is commonly known as CGNE.[5]

The MATLAB function eqsCGNormal_.m implements both CGNR and CGNE. The input argument eq = 1 sets CGNR and eq = 2 sets CGNE. Access to a special matrix-vector product function and to a pre-conditioner is not implemented in eqsCGNormal_.m.

Algorithm 5.18

Conjugate gradient iterations for A'*A*x=A'*a or A*A'*z=a,x=A'*z

```
%Find  x  to  A*x=a:  |x1-xk|<tol*|x1-x0|,  |a-A*x|<tol*|a-A*x0|,  input x=x0.
% eq = 1: A'*A*x=A'a;   = 2: A*A'*z=a,  x = A'*z
function x = eqsCGNormal_(A,eq,a,x,tol,last)
y = a - A*x;

if (eq == 1)        %A'*A*x = A'*a
    z = A'*y;  p = z;
    zz = z'*z;  epslon = tol*max(1.0,sqrt(zz));  l = 0;
    while(sqrt(zz)>epslon && l<last)
        Ap = A*p;
        alpha = zz/(Ap'*Ap);
        x = x + alpha*p;  y = y - alpha*Ap;  z = A'*y;
        zz0 = zz;  zz = z'*z;  beta = zz/zz0;
        p = z + beta*p;  l = l + 1;
    end
else %if(eq == 2)  %A*A'*z = a,  x=A'*z
    q = A'*y;
    yy = y'*y;  epslon = tol*max(1.0,sqrt(yy));  l = 0;
    while(sqrt(yy)>epslon && l<last)
        Aq = A*q;
        alpha = yy/(q'*q);
        x = x + alpha*q;  y = y - alpha*Aq;
        yy0 = yy;  yy = y'*y;  beta = yy/yy0;
        q = A'*y + beta*q;  l = l + 1;
    end
end
l
```

---

[5]Conjugate Gradient Normal Error.

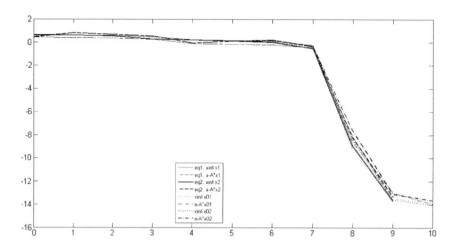

FIGURE 5.13

Errors and residuals of CG iterations for normal equations.

The first example for eqsCGNormal_.m is same as the second example of eqsStationaryNormal_.m of the last subsection. See Section 5.5.12 for the matrix **A** and right hand side **a**. The solutions are verified by the following script.

```
>> x1=eqsCGNormal_(A,1,a,x0,100*eps,1000);
l = 9
>> x2=eqsCGNormal_(A,2,a,A'*x0,100*eps,1000);
l = 9
>> x01=eqsCG_(A'*A,A'*a,x0,100*eps,1000);
l = 10
>> x02=eqsCG_(A*A',a,x0,100*eps,1000);
l = 10

>> norm(a-A*x1)
ans = 1.4518e-015        %x1 is the solution
>> norm(x1-x2)
ans = 8.9896e-016        %x1 = x2
>> norm(x1-x01)
ans = 7.9704e-016        %x1 = x01
>> norm(x2-A'*x02)
ans = 1.2824e-015        %x2 = A'*x02
```

The errors and residuals of $\mathbf{Ax} = \mathbf{a}$ in the iterations are displayed in Fig. 5.13.

The second example of eqsCGNormal_.m solves the third example of eqsStationaryNormal_.m. The errors and residuals of the two equations $\mathbf{A}_1\mathbf{x}_1 = \mathbf{a}_1$ and $\mathbf{A}_2\mathbf{x}_2 = \mathbf{a}_2$ in the iterations are displayed in Fig. 5.14. See the list of $\mathbf{A}_1$, $\mathbf{A}_2$, $\mathbf{a}_1$, and $\mathbf{a}_2$ in the last subsection. $\mathbf{y}_1 = \mathbf{a}_1 - \mathbf{A}_1\mathbf{x}_1$ does not converge to zero, because the linear equations are over-determined.

Comparing Figs. 5.13 and 5.14 with Figs. 5.11 and 5.12, we clearly see the difference of convergence in Gauss-Seidel and CG. For the Gauss-Seidel iterations, the errors and residuals gradually reduce in long iterations, due to the consecutive zeroing of each component of residuals. While for the CG

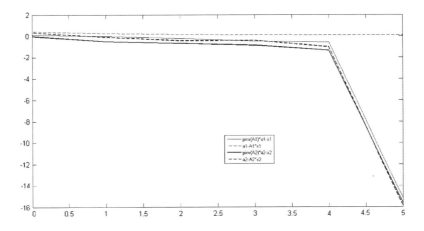

FIGURE 5.14

Errors and residuals of CG iterations for normal equations.

iterations, the minimum of the residuals or errors is searched in a gradually increasing Krylov subspace. When the dimension of the Krylov subspace reaches n (the number of columns of $\mathbf{A}$), the solution of the linear equations is found and then both residuals and errors drop suddenly.

5.6.4 REMARKS ON ITERATION ALGORITHMS FOR CONSTRAINED LINEAR EQUATIONS

In the last subsection, we study the iterative solution of the following form of linear equations that are studied in Section 4.2,

$$\begin{bmatrix} \mathbf{A} & \mathbf{B}' \\ \mathbf{B} & \mathbf{O} \end{bmatrix} \begin{bmatrix} \mathbf{x} \\ \mathbf{y} \end{bmatrix} = \begin{bmatrix} \mathbf{a} \\ \mathbf{b} \end{bmatrix}. \tag{5.90}$$

Because Eq. (5.90) is more general than Eqs. (5.79b) and (5.80b), the discussion of Eq. (5.90) applies to Eqs. (5.79b) and (5.80b) as well.

The Jacobi and Gauss-Seidel algorithms discussed in Section 5.2 cannot be applied to Eq. (5.90), because the diagonal or the lower/upper triangular part of the matrix is singular. No matter what properties $\mathbf{A}$ and $\mathbf{B}$ possess, the matrix of Eq. (5.90) is positive indefinite. The Richardson algorithm if applied to the whole Eq. (5.90), the iterations will not converge. Nothing in non-stationary iteration algorithms can prevent their applications to Eq. (5.90), but the convergence of the non-stationary iteration algorithms for Eq. (5.90) is not known in general. Typically, $\mathbf{A}$ and $\mathbf{B}$ are stored separately. When a non-stationary iteration algorithm is applied to Eq. (5.90), a special function of the matrix-vector product can be conveniently built. The iteration should be easily specialized taking account of the block structure of Eq. (5.90).

In the following, we assume $\mathbf{A}$ is square and non-singular, and Eq. (5.90) can be solved in the form of block matrices,

$$\mathbf{x} = \mathbf{A}^{-1}\left(\mathbf{a} - \mathbf{B}'\mathbf{y}\right), \tag{5.91a}$$

$$\mathbf{BA}^{-1}\mathbf{B}'\mathbf{y} = \mathbf{BA}^{-1}\mathbf{a} - \mathbf{b}. \tag{5.91b}$$

If $\mathbf{B}$ has full rank, $\mathbf{BA}^{-1}\mathbf{B}'$ is non-singular, which guarantees the unique solution of $\mathbf{y}$. Further to the non-singular assumption for $\mathbf{A}$, we assume $\mathbf{B}$ has full rank. Under the assumption, we can introduce the unique $\mathbf{y}$ from Eq. (5.91b) into Eq. (5.91a). The obtained equation for $\mathbf{x}$ is as follows:

$$\mathbf{x} = \mathbf{A}^{-1}\left(\mathbf{a} - \mathbf{B}'\left(\mathbf{BA}^{-1}\mathbf{B}'\right)^{-1}\left(\mathbf{BA}^{-1}\mathbf{a} - \mathbf{b}\right)\right). \tag{5.92}$$

Eqs. (5.91b) and (5.92) are too complicated to solve numerically. Eq. (5.91b) is the key to the difficulty of solving Eq. (5.90). It is not economical or even impossible to form $\mathbf{BA}^{-1}\mathbf{B}'$ explicitly. If a non-stationary algorithm is applied to Eq. (5.91b), to calculate a matrix-vector product of $\mathbf{BA}^{-1}\mathbf{B}'\mathbf{y}$, we need to calculate $\mathbf{B}'\mathbf{y}$ and then solve linear equations $\mathbf{A}^{-1}\left(\mathbf{B}'\mathbf{y}\right)$ and then calculate $\mathbf{B}\left(\mathbf{A}^{-1}\left(\mathbf{B}'\mathbf{y}\right)\right)$. The amount of calculation can be prohibitive. The Uzawa iteration algorithm [75] introduces the following simplification to solve Eq. (5.90): to relax the strong coupling between $\mathbf{x}$ and $\mathbf{y}$ and use the simple Richardson iteration for Eq. (5.91b),

$$\mathbf{x}_{k+1} = \mathbf{A}^{-1}\left(\mathbf{a} - \mathbf{B}'\mathbf{y}_k\right), \tag{5.93a}$$

$$\mathbf{y}_{k+1} = \mathbf{y}_k + \omega\left(\mathbf{BA}^{-1}\mathbf{a} - \mathbf{b} - \mathbf{BA}^{-1}\mathbf{By}_k\right) = \mathbf{y}_k + \omega\left(\mathbf{Bx}_{k+1} - \mathbf{b}\right). \tag{5.93b}$$

If $\mathbf{y}_k$ is known, Eq. (5.93a) can be easily solved by any suitable algorithm (direct or iterative, considering the property of $\mathbf{A}$). Eq. (5.93b) is simply the Richardson iteration applied to Eq. (5.91b). Its convergence hinges on the positive definiteness of $\mathbf{BA}^{-1}\mathbf{B}'$ and $0 < \omega < 2/\lambda_{\max}\left(\mathbf{BA}^{-1}\mathbf{B}'\right)$. If $\mathbf{A}$ is positive definite and $\mathbf{B}$ has full rank, $\mathbf{BA}^{-1}\mathbf{B}'$ is positive definite. But to guarantee the convergence, ω must satisfy the inequality, requiring an eigenvalue analysis of $\mathbf{BA}^{-1}\mathbf{B}'$. Except in special situations, to conduct an eigenvalue analysis of $\mathbf{BA}^{-1}\mathbf{B}'$ is also prohibitive.

5.7 OTHER IMPORTANT TOPICS

Iterative algorithms are mainly used to solve large scale sparse linear equations encountered in the discretization of partial differential equations (PDEs). To make iterative algorithms practical for these problems, we need one more important ingredient: pre-conditioner. In previous sections, several demonstrative examples are provided to show how to create a pre-conditioner and apply it in an iterative algorithm. The method shown is not practical for real problems.

To quote from [56]: "To find a good preconditioner to solve a given sparse linear system is often viewed as a combination of art and science. Theoretical results are rare and some methods work surprisingly well, often beyond expectations. A preconditioner can be defined as any subsidiary approximate solver that is combined with an outer iteration technique, typically one of the Krylov subspace iterations...."

[56] gives a good account of preconditioning techniques. Other than preconditioning, [56] also discusses three other important topics related to iterative algorithms but are not covered in this book:

parallel computation, algebraic multigrid method, and domain decomposition method. A full coverage of these four important topics is beyond the scope of this book. However, in order to present a more complete picture of the iterative algorithms, we want to give a brief review of these four important topic in this section. Their brief exposure in this section is more conceptual. The reader should consult [56] and many references cited therein for more information on these topics.

5.7.1 PRECONDITIONING TECHNIQUES

A preconditioning technique is any equivalent transformations applied to $\mathbf{Ax} = \mathbf{a}$, such that the equivalently transformed linear equations $\mathbf{U}^{-1}\mathbf{AV}^{-1}(\mathbf{Vx}) = \mathbf{U}^{-1}\mathbf{a}$ take less time to solve by an iterative algorithm. Here, either $\mathbf{U}$ or $\mathbf{V}$ can be an identity matrix. If $\mathbf{U}$ or $(\mathbf{V})$ is an identity matrix, the preconditioning is right sided (or left sided), otherwise both sided. $\mathbf{U}^{-1}$ does a row transformation of $\mathbf{A}$ and $\mathbf{a}$, that is, the linear equations. $\mathbf{V}^{-1}$ does a column transformation of $\mathbf{A}$, that is, the unknowns $\mathbf{x}$. If $\mathbf{V}$ is not an identity matrix, after the solution of the equivalent linear equations $\mathbf{U}^{-1}\mathbf{AV}^{-1}\mathbf{w} = \mathbf{U}^{-1}\mathbf{a}$ is obtained, the solution to the original equation $\mathbf{Ax} = \mathbf{a}$ is obtained by $\mathbf{x} = \mathbf{V}^{-1}\mathbf{w}$.

If an iterative algorithm requires the matrix-product calculation in the form of $\mathbf{Av}$, when it is applied to $\mathbf{U}^{-1}\mathbf{AV}^{-1}\mathbf{w} = \mathbf{U}^{-1}\mathbf{a}$, it works in the following order:

$$\mathbf{w} \Leftarrow \mathbf{V}^{-1}\mathbf{w}, \tag{5.94a}$$

$$\mathbf{w} \Leftarrow \mathbf{Aw}, \tag{5.94b}$$

$$\mathbf{w} \Leftarrow \mathbf{U}^{-1}\mathbf{w}. \tag{5.94c}$$

Here, $\mathbf{V}^{-1}\mathbf{w}$ and $\mathbf{U}^{-1}\mathbf{w}$ are two linear equations, which can be solved by any direct or iterative algorithms discussed in Chapter 4 and this chapter. $\mathbf{Aw}$ is a matrix-vector product. When either $\mathbf{U}$ or $\mathbf{V}$ is an identity matrix, the corresponding step of the solution of the linear equations is not taken.

If $\mathbf{A}$ is symmetric, it is necessary to keep $\mathbf{U}^{-1}\mathbf{AV}^{-1}$ a symmetric matrix in order to apply the algorithms for the symmetric matrix, such as CG, CR, or CE discussed in Section 5.4. This makes it necessary that $\mathbf{U}$ and $\mathbf{V}$ are of the form $\mathbf{V} = \mathbf{U}'$. In this case, the equivalent linear equations are $\mathbf{U}^{-1}\mathbf{AU}'^{-1}\mathbf{w} = \mathbf{U}^{-1}\mathbf{a}$. The requirement clearly limits the choices of $\mathbf{U}$ and increases the calculation. When solving $\mathbf{Ax} = \mathbf{a}$ by CG or CR, an inner product of the form $\mathbf{u}'\mathbf{Av}$ involving $\mathbf{A}$ is calculated. The symmetry of $\mathbf{A}$ is manifested by the property that $\mathbf{u}'(\mathbf{Av}) = (\mathbf{Au})'\mathbf{v}$. If the inner product satisfies the symmetry property, all the formulas of CG and CR are valid. This allows us to require the symmetry in the inner product instead. Consider two preconditioning techniques for the symmetric $\mathbf{A}$,

$$\mathbf{U}^{-1}\mathbf{Ax} = \mathbf{U}^{-1}\mathbf{a}, \quad \mathbf{U} = \mathbf{U}', \tag{5.95a}$$

$$\mathbf{AV}^{-1}\mathbf{w} = \mathbf{a}, \quad \mathbf{V} = \mathbf{V}'. \tag{5.95b}$$

For Eq. (5.95a), in the inner product calculation, if we choose the following $\mathbf{U}$-based inner product:

$$\left(\mathbf{u}'\mathbf{U}^{-1}\mathbf{Av}\right)_{\mathbf{U}} = \mathbf{u}'\mathbf{UU}^{-1}\mathbf{Av} = \mathbf{u}'\mathbf{Av} = (\mathbf{Au})'\mathbf{v} = \left(\mathbf{UU}^{-1}\mathbf{Au}\right)'\mathbf{v} = \left(\left(\mathbf{U}^{-1}\mathbf{Au}\right)'\mathbf{v}\right)_{\mathbf{U}}, \tag{5.96}$$

the inner product satisfies the symmetry.

For Eq. (5.95b), in the inner product calculation, if we choose the following $\mathbf{V}^{-1}$-based inner product,

$$\left(\mathbf{u}'\mathbf{AV}^{-1}\mathbf{v}\right)_{\mathbf{V}^{-1}} = \left(\mathbf{V}^{-1}\mathbf{u}\right)'\mathbf{AV}^{-1}\mathbf{v} = \left(\mathbf{AV}^{-1}\mathbf{u}\right)'\mathbf{V}^{-1}\mathbf{v} = \left(\left(\mathbf{AV}^{-1}\mathbf{u}\right)'\mathbf{v}\right)_{\mathbf{V}^{-1}}, \tag{5.97}$$

the inner product also satisfies the symmetry.

Therefore, for symmetric $\mathbf{A}$, we can also choose a different inner product in CG or CR, and use the preconditioning in the form of Eq. (5.95a) or (5.95b).

How can we guarantee the solution of $\mathbf{U}^{-1}\mathbf{A}\mathbf{V}^{-1}(\mathbf{V}\mathbf{x}) = \mathbf{U}^{-1}\mathbf{a}$ takes less time by an iteration algorithm? Clearly when the iterative algorithm is applied to the equivalent linear system, the number of iterations must be less than that of the original linear system. Because in each iteration, more calculations are needed (extra one or two solutions of auxiliary linear equations), the reduction of the iteration must outweigh the increase in the calculation of an iteration. This sets the first requirement that either $\mathbf{U}^{-1}\mathbf{w}$ or $\mathbf{V}^{-1}\mathbf{w}$ must be easy to solve. The second requirement is to reduce the iteration number as much as possible.

Clearly both requirements hinge on the choice of $\mathbf{U}$ and $\mathbf{V}$. Unfortunately, there are no general rules to choose $\mathbf{U}$ and $\mathbf{V}$. Because when an iterative algorithm is applied to $\mathbf{I}\mathbf{x} = \mathbf{a}$, it requires only one iteration to converge to the solution. It is natural to choose $\mathbf{U}\mathbf{V}$ as close to $\mathbf{A}$ as possible. Under such a vague condition, the following choices are possible.

1. $\mathbf{U} = \mathbf{A}$ or $\mathbf{V} = \mathbf{A}$, $\mathbf{U}^{-1}\mathbf{w}$ or $\mathbf{V}^{-1}\mathbf{w}$ is solved by any stationary iteration algorithms under a rough tolerance. If $\mathbf{A}$ is symmetric, use SSOR with $\mathbf{U}$-based inner product of Eq. (5.96) or $\mathbf{V}^{-1}$-based inner product of Eq. (5.97) to keep the symmetry.

2. Any approximate decompositions of $\mathbf{A}$ such that $\mathbf{E} = \mathbf{U}\mathbf{V} - \mathbf{A}$ is as small as possible. $\mathbf{A}$ is usually sparse and large, an accurate decomposition $\mathbf{U}\mathbf{V} = \mathbf{A}$ will lead to full $\mathbf{U}$ and $\mathbf{V}$. Then the solution of $\mathbf{U}^{-1}\mathbf{w}$ and $\mathbf{V}^{-1}\mathbf{w}$ also takes more time. This is not acceptable. The common choice is to drop "insignificant" numbers from $\mathbf{U}$ and $\mathbf{V}$ to make $\mathbf{U}$ and $\mathbf{V}$ as sparse as possible. There are many ways to decide what numbers in $\mathbf{U}$ and $\mathbf{V}$ are "insignificant." Usually any numbers of $\mathbf{U}$ and $\mathbf{V}$ in the same locations of nonzeros of $\mathbf{A}$ are considered to be significant. The significance of other numbers of $\mathbf{U}$ and $\mathbf{V}$ in other locations is determined by the level of fill, or the magnitude of the number, or the combination of both. The concept of the level of fill comes naturally when we examine the nonzero patterns of the product of $\mathbf{U}\mathbf{V}$. For example, when we do a LU decomposition of a sparse $\mathbf{A}$, we drop any nonzeros from $\mathbf{L}$ and $\mathbf{U}$ from (i, j) where $\mathbf{A}(i, j) = 0$. We get an incomplete LU decomposition of level 0 (ILU(0)) of $\mathbf{A}$. The product $\mathbf{L}_0\mathbf{U}_0 = \mathbf{A}_0 \neq \mathbf{A}$ and $\mathbf{A}_0$ has more nonzeros than $\mathbf{A}$. If we keep all the nonzeros in $\mathbf{L}$ and $\mathbf{U}$ where $\mathbf{A}_0$ are not zeros, we get ILU(1) of $\mathbf{A}$: $\mathbf{L}_1\mathbf{U}_1 = \mathbf{A}_1 \neq \mathbf{A}$ and $\mathbf{A}_1$ has more nonzeros than $\mathbf{A}$ and $\mathbf{A}_0$. Similarly ILU(2) of $\mathbf{A}$: $\mathbf{L}_2\mathbf{U}_2 = \mathbf{A}_2 \neq \mathbf{A}$, where $\mathbf{L}_2$ and $\mathbf{U}_2$ has the same zero pattern as $\mathbf{A}_1$. Presumably, $\mathbf{L}_2\mathbf{U}_2$ is closer to $\mathbf{A}$ than $\mathbf{L}_1\mathbf{U}_1$, and $\mathbf{L}_1\mathbf{U}_1$ is closer to $\mathbf{A}$ than $\mathbf{L}_0\mathbf{U}_0$. Usually the zero pattern of ILU(l), $l \geq 0$ can be determined by the sparsity of $\mathbf{A}$ using the standard techniques from graph theories.

3. Choose $\mathbf{U}$ or $\mathbf{V}$ such that $\|\mathbf{I} - \mathbf{U}\mathbf{A}\|_2$, or $\|\mathbf{I} - \mathbf{A}\mathbf{V}\|_2$ or $\|\mathbf{I} - \mathbf{U}\mathbf{A}\mathbf{V}\|_2$ as small as possible. Because only a crude $\mathbf{U}$ or $\mathbf{V}$ is needed, these minimization problems are solved very approximately to save the computation time.

4. Any special structures in $\mathbf{A}$ should be exploited in the above choices to save the computation time.

It is exactly because the usefulness of the preconditioning $\mathbf{U}^{-1}\mathbf{A}\mathbf{V}^{-1}\mathbf{w} = \mathbf{U}^{-1}\mathbf{a}$ depends on the property and sparsity of $\mathbf{A}$, there is no universal rule to determine what is a good preconditioning. The necessity of preconditioning and the information of a good preconditioning must be obtained from the application problem where $\mathbf{A}\mathbf{x} = \mathbf{a}$ comes from. This question in turn is answered by how we model the application problem by $\mathbf{A}\mathbf{x} = \mathbf{a}$. Some modeling of the problem gives a linear system $\mathbf{A}\mathbf{x} = \mathbf{a}$ that is easy to solve. Another modeling of the same problem gives another linear system $\mathbf{A}\mathbf{x} = \mathbf{a}$ that is difficult to solve. Usually all the preconditioning techniques studied in the context of matrix computations are based only on $\mathbf{A}$ without regard to the better numerical modeling of the application problem.

5.7.2 PARALLEL COMPUTATIONS

Because of the need to solve very large scale of sparse linear equation systems, parallel computations are becoming increasingly important. Parallel computations intrinsically depend on the hardware configurations, shared memory, or distributed memory, etc. Fortunately, the emergence of message passing interface (MPI) and a number of libraries handling data communications between different processors, computers, or clusters of computers hide the complexity of hardware configurations from the implementation of parallel computations. See [24].

The efficiency of parallel computations depends on four factors: the distribution of computations among different processors, the processing speed of each processor, the amount of data that must be transmitted between different processors, and the speed of data communication between different processors.

In an algorithm, parallelism can be extracted in different levels and areas of the algorithm. Sometimes, the usual algorithm suitable for sequential computations must be reordered in order to reveal more parallelism. Usually the parallelism in an algorithm can be revealed by the standard topological sorting algorithm in graph theories.

The parallelism in some elementary matrix computations, such as the inner product and matrix-vector product, can be easily extracted. For example, if we want to distribute the inner product calculation of two large vectors in two processors, it can be easily achieved as follows:

$$w = \mathbf{u}'\mathbf{v} = \mathbf{u}(1:i)'\mathbf{v}(1:i) + \mathbf{u}(i+1:n)'\mathbf{u}(i+1:n), \tag{5.98}$$

where $\mathbf{u}(1:i)'\mathbf{v}(1:i)$ is calculated in one processor and $\mathbf{u}(i+1:n)'\mathbf{u}(i+1:n)$ is calculated in another processor at the same time. The addition calculation can be done in either processor. The partition of the task, measured in this case by i, is determined by the ratio of the processing speed of the two processors. If the processing speed of two process is same, $i = n/2$ so that the two calculations finish at the same time. Each processor only needs to store half of the data of $\mathbf{u}$ and $\mathbf{v}$.

As another example, the matrix-vector product calculation can be arranged between the two processors in the following two ways:

$$\mathbf{w} = \mathbf{A}\mathbf{v} = \begin{bmatrix} \mathbf{A}(1:i,:)\mathbf{v} \\ \mathbf{A}(i+1:m,:)\mathbf{v} \end{bmatrix} = \mathbf{A}(:,1:j)\mathbf{v}(1:j) + \mathbf{A}(:,j+1:n)\mathbf{v}(j+1:n). \tag{5.99}$$

The parallel computations of many of these elementary matrix computations are supported by the computer hardware.

In $\mathbf{A}\mathbf{x} = \mathbf{a}$, if $\mathbf{A}$ is sparse, several groups of $\mathbf{x}$ may be decoupled from each other. These groups of $\mathbf{x}$ can then be solved in parallel. To reveal the independence of the unknowns, the standard coloring algorithm in the graph theories can be used. See algorithms `maximalIndependent_.m` and `maximalIndependents_.m` presented in Section 1.5.

The Jacobi iteration can be easily made to run in parallel, in fact, it is similar to the matrix-vector product discussed above. But after each Jacobi iteration, the most recent iteration $\mathbf{x}_k(i_1:i_2)$ in each processor is broadcast to all the other processors. The Gauss-Seidel iteration requires more data communication: in the interval of each iteration it needs to send the data $\mathbf{x}(1:i)$ to other processors which are used to solve $\mathbf{x}(k), k > j$. At the end of each iteration, each processor should also send its most recently calculated components of $\mathbf{x}$ to all the other processors. In the non-stationary iteration algorithms, the major calculation is the calculation of the matrix-vector product and the inner vector product. Some parallelism can be extracted according to Eqs. (5.99) and (5.98). Other parallelism can be extracted by the study of each algorithm.

5.7.3 ALGEBRAIC MULTIGRID METHOD

In Section 5.2, we showed that the error of a stationary algorithm (Jacobi, Gauss-Seidel iterations, etc.) changes in the iteration according to the following equation:

$$\mathbf{x}_\infty - \mathbf{x}_i = \mathbf{G}^i \left(\mathbf{x}_\infty - \mathbf{x}_0 \right), \tag{5.100}$$

where $\mathbf{x}_\infty$ satisfies $\mathbf{A}\mathbf{x}_\infty = \mathbf{a}$, $\mathbf{x}_0$ is the initial guess of the solution, $\mathbf{x}_i$ is the approximate solution of the i-th iteration and $\mathbf{G}$ is the iteration matrix of the stationary algorithm. For the form of $\mathbf{G}$, see Eqs. (5.10) and (5.13). For Jacobi, $\mathbf{G} = \mathbf{I} - \mathbf{D}^{-1}\mathbf{A}$. For Gauss-Seidel, $\mathbf{G} = \mathbf{I} - (\mathbf{D} + \mathbf{L})^{-1}\mathbf{A}$. In general,

$$\mathbf{G} = \mathbf{I} - f(\mathbf{A}, \omega) \tag{5.101}$$

where f is some simple function determined by the stationary algorithm, ω is the weighting factor defined in Eq. (5.11). In order that the iteration converges, it is necessary that $\mathbf{G}^i \Rightarrow \mathbf{0}$ or equivalently $|\lambda_{\max}(\mathbf{G})| < 1$. If $|\lambda_{\max}(\mathbf{G})|$ is close to zero, the convergence is fast. $|\lambda_{\max}(\mathbf{G})|$ is close to one, the convergence is slow. Obviously the eigenvalues of $\mathbf{G}$ and $\mathbf{A}$ are related by

$$\lambda(\mathbf{G}) = 1 - f(\lambda(\mathbf{A}), \omega). \tag{5.102}$$

We can take a closer look at the convergence patterns if we decompose $\mathbf{x}_\infty - \mathbf{x}_0$ along the eigenvectors $\mathbf{V}$ of $\mathbf{G}$, where e_j is the component of $\mathbf{x}_\infty - \mathbf{x}_0$ along the j-th eigenvector $\mathbf{V}(:, j)$ of $\mathbf{G}$,

$$\mathbf{x}_\infty - \mathbf{x}_0 = \mathbf{V}e = \sum_{j=1}^{n} \mathbf{V}(:, j)e_j. \tag{5.103}$$

From Eqs. (5.100), (5.102), and (5.103), we can obtain

$$\mathbf{x}_\infty - \mathbf{x}_i = \sum_{j=1}^{n} \left(1 - f(\lambda_j(\mathbf{A}), \omega) \right)^i \mathbf{V}(:, j)e_j. \tag{5.104}$$

The speed of convergence of $\mathbf{x}_\infty - \mathbf{x}_i$ in the direction $\mathbf{V}(:, j)$ is determined by $1 - f(\lambda_j(\mathbf{A}), \omega)$. If $f(\lambda_j(\mathbf{A}), \omega)$ is close to one, the convergence along $\mathbf{V}(:, j)$ is fast. If $f(\lambda_j(\mathbf{A}), \omega)$ is close to zero, the convergence along $\mathbf{V}(:, j)$ is slow.

In many applications, the linear equations $\mathbf{A}\mathbf{x} = \mathbf{a}$ come from the discretization of a PDE in a physical domain. To illustrate the property of $f(\lambda_j(\mathbf{A}), \omega)$, we study the central difference discretization of a 1-dimensional Poisson equation in $[0, 1]$,

$$x''(s) = a(s) \quad \text{for } s \in (0, 1),$$
$$x(0) = x(1) = 0.$$

The interval $[0, 1]$ is discretized uniformly with $n + 2$ points $s_k = kh, k = 0, 1, 2, \ldots, n + 1$ with $(n + 1)h = 1$. The second order derivative $x''(s)$ is approximated with the central difference. After introducing the boundary conditions at $x_0 = x_{n+1} = 0$, the Poisson equation is approximately transformed into the following linear equations:

$$
\begin{bmatrix}
2 & -1 & & & \\
-1 & 2 & -1 & & \\
& \ddots & \ddots & \ddots & \\
& & -1 & 2 & -1 \\
& & & -1 & 2
\end{bmatrix}
\begin{bmatrix}
x_1 \\
x_2 \\
\vdots \\
x_{n-1} \\
x_n
\end{bmatrix}
=
\begin{bmatrix}
a(s_1) \\
a(s_2) \\
\vdots \\
a(s_{n-1}) \\
a(s_n)
\end{bmatrix}.
\tag{5.105}
$$

The eigenvalues and eigenvectors of the matrix $\mathbf{A}$ in the above linear equations can be shown to be the following:

$$
\theta_k = \frac{k\pi}{n+1} = k\pi s_k,
$$

$$
\lambda_k(\mathbf{A}) = 4\sin^2\left(\frac{\theta_k}{2}\right), \quad k = 1, 2, \ldots, n,
$$

$$
\mathbf{V}(:, k) =
\begin{bmatrix}
\sin(\theta_k) \\
\sin(2\theta_k) \\
\vdots \\
\sin(n\theta_k)
\end{bmatrix}.
\tag{5.106}
$$

For the model problem of Eq. (5.105), we can obtain the eigenvalues of $\mathbf{G}$ as follows:

$$
\lambda_k(\mathbf{G}) = 1 - f\left(4\sin^2\left(\frac{\theta_k}{2}\right), \omega\right).
$$

For both Richardson and Jacobi iterations, with a proper choice of ω, it can be shown that $0 < \lambda_k(\mathbf{G}) < 1/2$ for $k > n/2$ and $1/2 \leq \lambda_k(\mathbf{G}) < 1$ for $k < n/2$. Therefore, the components of the error of the iteration are reducing more quickly along the higher frequency modes of $\mathbf{G}$. The convergence pattern of the Gauss-Seidel iterations is different—the components of the error are reducing more quickly along the middle spectrum of the eigenvectors of $\mathbf{G}$. If we measure the error reductions in the directions of the eigenvectors of $\mathbf{A}$, it can be shown that for Richardson, Jacobi, and Gauss-Seidel iterations, the error all reduces more quickly in high frequency modes. The convergence pattern of the stationary iterations is irrespective of n. Therefore, if we switch between the fine and coarse discretizations, some components of the error that are hard to reduce in the lower spectrum in a fine discretization can be reduced more quickly by transforming the error to high spectrum in a coarse discretization. This is the essence of the multigrid method—switch the stationary iterative solution of given PDEs among multiple grids (or discretizations). There are different ways of switching among the multiple grids, such as V-cycles, W-cycles, or a combination of both. When switching between two grids, we need to transfer the approximate solution, for example, the values of $x_j = x(s_j)$ of the Poisson equation, from one grid to another grid. This can be done easily for the cited example. If we double n, i.e. switch from a coarse grid to a fine grid, x_j at an old coarse grid point assume the original value and x_j at a new fine grid can be interpolated from the neighboring old coarse grids. The general idea of the multigrid method can be extended to 2-dimensional and 3-dimensional Poisson equations and other PDEs.

If we are given only linear equations $\mathbf{A}x = \mathbf{a}$ without any knowledge of the PDEs and the grids, the multigrid method discussed above cannot be used. However, the notion of fine and coarse grids can be based on the maximal independent set ordering, i.e. `maximalIndependent_.m` presented in Section 1.5. The complement set of the independent set thus obtained is called the coarse set. Then, the components of the approximate solution at the fine set must be defined in terms of the components of the approximate solution at the coarse set. The interpolation from the coarse set to the fine set is based on the notion of the eigenvector of the lower frequency of $\mathbf{A}$. If an eigenvalue λ of $\mathbf{A}$ is small, the corresponding eigenvector $\mathbf{v}$ has the property that $\mathbf{Av} \approx \mathbf{0}$. As illustrated in the example of 1-dimensional Poisson equation, $\mathbf{G}^i \mathbf{v}$ approaches zero slowly. Therefore, we want to approximate $\mathbf{v}$ in the coarse set. For j in the fine set, from the property $\mathbf{Av} \approx \mathbf{0}$, we can write

$$A_{jj}v_j \approx -\sum_{k \neq j} A_{kj}v_k = -\sum_{k \in C_j} A_{kj}v_k - \sum_{k \in F_j^s} A_{kj}v_k - \sum_{k \in F_j^w} A_{kj}v_k; \quad j \in F,$$

where we use C_j for the coarse set which has connection to j, F_j^s for the fine set which has strong connection to j, and F_j^w for the fine set which has weak connection to j. The strong or weak connection is determined the value of A_{kj}. Further we assume the following relations:

$$v_k = v_j, \quad k \in C_j^w,$$

$$\left(\sum_{l \in C_j} A_{kl}\right) v_k = \sum_{l \in C_j} A_{kl}v_l, \quad k \in C_j^s.$$

Combining the above two equations, we obtain the interpolation from the coarse set to the fine set,

$$v_j = \sum_{k \in C_j} w_{jk}v_k, \quad \text{with } w_{jk} = \frac{A_{jk} + \sum_{l \in F_j^s} \frac{A_{jl}A_{lk}}{\sum_{l \in C_j} A_{jl}}}{A_{jj} + \sum_{l \in F_j^s} A_{jl}}.$$

Once we have the definition for the fine set and coarse set and an interpolation from the coarse set to the fine set, we can extend the multigrid method to the stationary iterative solution of $\mathbf{Ax} = \mathbf{a}$. The extension is based purely on the information from $\mathbf{A}$. The method obtained is termed algebraic multigrid method.

5.7.4 DOMAIN DECOMPOSITION METHOD

$\mathbf{Ax} = \mathbf{a}$ is often obtained from the numerical solution of PDEs defined on a physical domain. $\mathbf{A}$ is obtained from the discretization of the PDEs. $\mathbf{a}$ is obtained from the known function in the PDEs and the boundary conditions. $\mathbf{x}$ is the unknown function values defined at points in the domain. It is natural to divide the physical domain into several sub-domains. We will study two strategies of Domain Decomposition Method.

Coupling Neighboring Sub-domains along Neighboring Nodes   As an example, we consider an L-shaped domain shown in Fig. 5.15. The L-shaped domain Ω partitioned into three sub-domains. A similar example is shown in Fig. 1.2 in Section 1.5, where we used a different node numbering for the same meshes. Another difference is that we consider two unknowns for each node in the example here instead of one unknown in the example in Section 1.5. It is natural to number $\mathbf{x}$ consecutively for all the nodes of the same sub-domain. Usually the discretization of the PDEs determines that $\mathbf{A}$ is a sparse matrix. $A_{ij} = 0$ if i, j do not belong to the same sub-domain or not the same element within the same sub-domain. Corresponding to the nodes interfacing two neighboring sub-domains, the nonzero

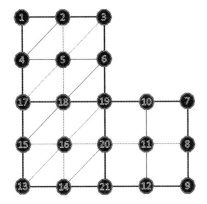

FIGURE 5.15

Finite element mesh of three sub-domains
coupled on nodes.

A_{ij} couples the two sub-domains. The five nodes 17, 18, 19, 20, and 21 are on the interfaces between
the two sub-domains.

The sparsity pattern of **A** for the meshes shown in Fig. 5.15 is obtained by the following steps.

In the first step, we use the following script to create the mesh shown in Fig. 5.15.

```
elem=cell(1,20);    %We use cell array, because of different length of members of elem
elem{1}=[1,4,2];    elem{2}=[4,5,2];    elem{3}=[2,5,3];    elem{4}=[5,6,3];
elem{5}=[4,17,5];   elem{6}=[17,18,5];  elem{7}=[5,18,6];   elem{8}=[18,19,6];
elem{9}=[7,10,11,8];    elem{10}=[8,11,12,9];
elem{11}=[10,19,20,11]; elem{12}=[11,20,21,12];
elem{13}=[13,16,15];    elem{14}=[13,14,16];    elem{15}=[14,20,16];
elem{16}=[14,21,20];
elem{17}=[15,18,17];    elem{18}=[15,16,18];    elem{19}=[16,19,18];
elem{20}=[16,20,19];
```

In the second step, we obtain the sparse matrix **A** in the IJD format from the element nodes vectors.

```
iA = [];  jA = [];  dA = [];  n = 1;
ne = length(elem);
for j=1:ne
    e = elem{j};
    nn = length(e);
    iA = [iA, zeros(1,2*2*nn*nn)];    %2 unknowns for each node
    jA = [jA, zeros(1,2*2*nn*nn)];
    dA = [dA, zeros(1,2*2*nn*nn)];
    for k=1:nn
        for l=1:nn
            iA(n) = 2*e(k)-1;  jA(n) = 2*e(l)-1;  dA(n) = randn;  n = n + 1;
            iA(n) = 2*e(k)-1;  jA(n) = 2*e(l);    dA(n) = randn;  n = n + 1;
            iA(n) = 2*e(k);    jA(n) = 2*e(l)-1;  dA(n) = randn;  n = n + 1;
            iA(n) = 2*e(k);    jA(n) = 2*e(l);    dA(n) = randn;  n = n + 1;
        end
    end
end
```

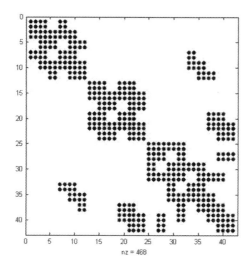

FIGURE 5.16

Sparsity pattern of Fig. 5.15.

In the third step, we convert the sparse matrix from the IJD format to the MATLAB internal sparse format and then use the MATLAB function spy to display the sparsity pattern as shown in Fig. 5.16.

`A = sparse(iA,jA,dA);    spy(A);`

In general, we divide a domain into s sub-domains. If we number $\mathbf{x}$ consecutively for all the internal nodes first for each sub-domain from $j = 1, 2, \ldots, s$, then number $\mathbf{x}$ for all the interface nodes, we will have the following block and sparse structure:

$$\begin{bmatrix} \mathbf{A}_1 & & & & \mathbf{B}_{1s} \\ & \mathbf{A}_2 & & & \mathbf{B}_{2s} \\ & & \ddots & & \vdots \\ & & & \mathbf{A}_s & \mathbf{B}_{ss} \\ \mathbf{C}_{s1} & \mathbf{C}_{s2} & \cdots & \mathbf{C}_{ss} & \mathbf{D} \end{bmatrix} \begin{bmatrix} \mathbf{x}_1 \\ \mathbf{x}_2 \\ \vdots \\ \mathbf{x}_s \\ \mathbf{x}_{s+1} \end{bmatrix} = \begin{bmatrix} \mathbf{a}_1 \\ \mathbf{a}_2 \\ \vdots \\ \mathbf{a}_s \\ \mathbf{a}_{s+1} \end{bmatrix}. \tag{5.107}$$

Each $\mathbf{A}_j, j = 1, 2, \ldots, s$ is a sparse matrix for the internal nodes of each sub-domain. Each $\mathbf{B}_{js}$ and each $\mathbf{C}_{sj}, j = 1, 2, \ldots, s$ are the sparse coupling terms of neighboring sub-domains. $\mathbf{D}$ is also sparse relating the unknowns of the nodes on the interfaces. If the numbering of $\mathbf{x}$ is based on other schemes, the sparse pattern will be different. Specially, the sparse patterns obtained by applying maximalIndependent_.m or maximalIndependents_.m are of great interest, since they offer greater parallelism for the linear equations solution. See Section 1.5.

There are three possible ways to solve Eq. (5.107). The first way is just to solve it as it is written, $\mathbf{x} = \mathbf{A}^{-1}\mathbf{a}$. The second way is to eliminate $\mathbf{x}_j, j = 1, 2, \ldots, s$ and obtain reduced linear equations $\mathbf{S}\mathbf{x}_{s+1} = \mathbf{s}$. In both ways, we should take the sparse and block structure of $\mathbf{A}$ into account to speed up the calculation. Both ways can be either direct or iterative. The third way is to apply the block Jacobi iterations. For each block $\mathbf{A}_j\mathbf{x}_j = \mathbf{a}_j - \mathbf{B}_{js}\mathbf{x}_{s+1}, j = 1, 2, \ldots, s$, $\mathbf{x}_{s+1}$ assumes the values of

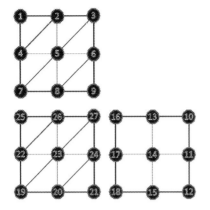

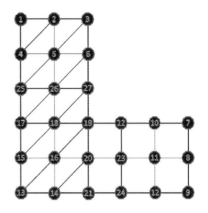

FIGURE 5.17

Finite element mesh of three sub-domains coupled on nodes.

FIGURE 5.18

Finite element mesh of three sub-domains coupled on elements.

the previous iteration. These s sets of linear equations can be solved in parallel. For $\mathbf{x}_{s+1}$, we have $\mathbf{D}\mathbf{x}_{s+1} = \mathbf{a}_{s+1} - \mathbf{C}_{s1}\mathbf{x}_1 - \mathbf{C}_{s2}\mathbf{x}_2 - \cdots - \mathbf{C}_{ss}\mathbf{x}_s$.

For the coupling problem of Fig. 5.15, we can have an alternative that is based on the constraint equations. For each interface node in Fig. 5.15, we create two nodes in the same position belonging to different sub-domains. We illustrate the method in Fig. 5.17. The constrains are $\mathbf{x}_7 = \mathbf{x}_{25}, \mathbf{x}_8 = \mathbf{x}_{26}, \mathbf{x}_9 = \mathbf{x}_{27}, \mathbf{x}_{16} = \mathbf{x}_{27}, \mathbf{x}_{17} = \mathbf{x}_{24}$, and $\mathbf{x}_{18} = \mathbf{x}_{21}$. The advantage of the method of Fig. 5.17 is that linear equations of each sub-domain can be generated in parallel. Further if the two sub-domains of the triangular meshes are identical, their linear equations are also identical.

The linear equations of Fig. 5.17 have a structure of the form as shown in Eq. (5.108). See Sections 4.2.2 and 5.6.4 for the solution of

$$
\begin{bmatrix}
\mathbf{A}_1 & & & \mathbf{I} & \\
& \mathbf{A}_2 & & & \mathbf{I} \\
& & \mathbf{A}_3 & -\mathbf{I} & -\mathbf{I} \\
\mathbf{I} & & -\mathbf{I} & 0 & 0 \\
& \mathbf{I} & -\mathbf{I} & 0 & 0
\end{bmatrix}
\begin{bmatrix}
\mathbf{x}_1 \\ \mathbf{x}_2 \\ \mathbf{x}_3 \\ \lambda_{13} \\ \lambda_{23}
\end{bmatrix}
=
\begin{bmatrix}
\mathbf{a}_1 \\ \mathbf{a}_2 \\ \mathbf{a}_3 \\ \mathbf{b}_{13} \\ \mathbf{b}_{23}
\end{bmatrix}.
\tag{5.108}
$$

Coupling Neighboring Sub-domains along Neighboring Elements   In Fig. 5.15, the neighboring sub-domains are coupled along the element edges. Another possibility is to couple the neighboring sub-domain along a band of elements as Fig. 5.18 shows. The six elements (17,26,25), (17,18,26), (18,27,26), (18,19,27), (19,20,23,22), and (20,21,24,23) are on the interface between the two sub-domains. The sparsity pattern of $\mathbf{A}$ of Fig. 5.18 is displayed in Fig. 5.19.

In general, we divide a domain into s sub-domains. If we number $\mathbf{x}$ consecutively for all the nodes of the internal elements first for each sub-domain from $j = 1, 2, \ldots, s$, then number $\mathbf{x}$ for all the

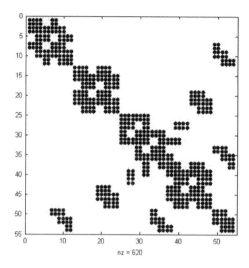

FIGURE 5.19

Sparsity pattern of Fig. 5.18.

unnumbered nodes of the interface elements, we will have the following block and sparse structure:

$$
\begin{bmatrix}
\mathbf{A}_{11} & \mathbf{A}_{12} & \cdots & \mathbf{A}_{1s} \\
\mathbf{A}_{21} & \mathbf{A}_{22} & \cdots & \mathbf{A}_{2s} \\
\vdots & \vdots & \cdots & \vdots \\
\mathbf{A}_{s1} & \mathbf{A}_{s2} & \cdots & \mathbf{A}_{ss}
\end{bmatrix}
\begin{bmatrix}
\mathbf{x}_1 \\
\mathbf{x}_2 \\
\vdots \\
\mathbf{x}_s
\end{bmatrix}
=
\begin{bmatrix}
\mathbf{a}_1 \\
\mathbf{a}_2 \\
\vdots \\
\mathbf{a}_s
\end{bmatrix}. \tag{5.109}
$$

Each diagonal block $\mathbf{A}_{jj}, j = 1,2,\ldots,s$ has a structure in the form of $\mathbf{A}_{jj} = \begin{bmatrix} \mathbf{A}_j & \mathbf{B}_j \\ \mathbf{C}_j & \mathbf{D}_j \end{bmatrix}$, where $\mathbf{A}_j$ is a sparse matrix for the internal nodes of each sub-domain. Each $\mathbf{B}_j$ and each $\mathbf{C}_j$ are the sparse coupling terms between internal element nodes and the interface element nodes belonging to the j-th sub-domain. $\mathbf{D}_j$ is also sparse relating the unknowns between the interface element nodes belonging to the j-th sub-domain. Notice the similarity of $\mathbf{A}_{jj}$ to $\mathbf{A}$ in Eq. (5.107). Each $\mathbf{A}_{ij}, i, j = 1,2,\ldots,s, i \neq j$ is a sparse matrix coupling the interface nodes belonging to the i-th and j-th sub-domains. If the i-th and j-th sub-domains are not neighboring, $\mathbf{A}_{ij}$ is zero. If the numbering of $\mathbf{x}$ is based on other schemes, the sparse pattern will be different. Specially, the sparse patterns obtained by applying `maximalIndependent_.m` or `maximalIndependents_.m` are of great interest, since they offer greater parallelism for the linear equations solution. See Section 1.5.

Similarly to Eq. (5.107), we have three possible ways to solve Eq. (5.109). The first way is just to solve it as it is written, $\mathbf{x} = \mathbf{A}^{-1}\mathbf{a}$. The second way is to eliminate the unknowns of the internal nodes for each sub-domain and obtain the reduced linear equations $\mathbf{Sw} = \mathbf{s}$ for all the nodes of the interface elements. In both ways, we should take the sparse and block structure of $\mathbf{A}$ into account to speed up the calculation. Both ways can be either direct or iterative. The third way is to apply the block Jacobi or Gauss-Seidel iterations. For each block $\mathbf{A}_{jj}\mathbf{x}_j = \mathbf{a}_j - \mathbf{A}_{jk}\mathbf{x}_k, k = 1,2,\ldots,s, k \neq j, j = 1,2,\ldots,s.$

$\mathbf{x}_j$ includes the unknowns of the internal nodes and interface element nodes. In block Gauss-Seidel iterations, the new approximate unknowns in $\mathbf{x}_j$ for the interface element nodes are used for the block iterations of the remaining sub-domains. In block Jacobi iterations, these unknowns keep the approximate values of the previous iteration. Therefore, in the block Jacobi iteration, all the sub-domains can be iterated in parallel.

Direct algorithms of solution of eigenvalue problem

INTRODUCTION

In the last two chapters, we studied the algorithms for linear equations $\mathbf{Ax} = \mathbf{b}$. In this and next chapter, we study the algorithms for an eigenvalue problem. The eigenvalue problem is to find λ and $\mathbf{x}$ from the equation $\mathbf{Ax} = \lambda\mathbf{x}$ or $\mathbf{Ax} = \lambda\mathbf{Bx}$, where $\mathbf{A}$ and $\mathbf{B}$ are two square matrices. About the mathematical theories and properties of an eigenvalue problem, see Section 1.4 for a brief exposition or [29] for a more detailed discussion.

For $\mathbf{A} \in \mathbb{R}^{n \times n}$, the eigenvalue λ is the root of the nth order polynomial $\det(\mathbf{A} - \lambda\mathbf{I}) = 0$. Similarly for $\mathbf{A}, \mathbf{B} \in \mathbb{R}^{n \times n}$, the generalized eigenvalue λ is the root of the nth order polynomial $\det(\mathbf{A} - \lambda\mathbf{B}) = 0$. If $n = 1$, the calculation of the eigenvalue is truly trivial. If $n = 2, 3, 4$, direct algorithms are possible. These direct algorithms actually can be used as building blocks for iterative algorithms for $n > 4$. In Section 6.1, we list two MATLAB functions to calculate the eigenvalues for the case $n = 2$. If $n > 4$, no direct algorithms are possible. However, the algorithms presented in this chapter are like direct algorithms in real applications: the experience shows that they (nearly) never fail to converge in a fixed number of iterations. In the next chapter, we study the other iterative algorithms that do not have these preferred characteristics.

In Section 6.2, we present four useful auxiliary algorithms for the symmetric eigenvalue problem. For a symmetric matrix $\mathbf{A} \in \mathbb{R}^{n \times n}$, its eigenvalues are real and thus can be ordered ascendingly, $\lambda_1 \leq \lambda_2 \leq \cdots \leq \lambda_{n-1} \leq \lambda_n$. The first algorithm, which is implemented in neig_.m, calculates an integer pair $[k, l], k \leq l$ from a given interval $[\alpha, \beta], \alpha \leq \beta$, such that $\alpha \leq \lambda_k$ and $\lambda_l \leq \beta$. The second algorithm, which is implemented in veig_.m, is the inverse function of neig_.m. The two algorithms are useful when only approximate bound for an eigenvalue is needed. There are two similar algorithms, vxeig_.m and nxeig_.m, for the symmetric positive definite generalized eigenvalue problem.

The key algorithm of the chapter is QR iteration algorithm, which is presented in Section 6.4. QR iteration is an extension of the power iteration and subspace iteration method. The power iteration and subspace iteration methods do not belong to the 'direct' eigenvalue algorithms that are the topic of this chapter. We defer their full presentation in the next chapter. However, we start the presentation of QR algorithm with a brief introduction of the two algorithms in Section 6.3. Two algorithms, eigUnsymByQR_.m and eigSymByQR_.m, are presented in Section 6.4. The second one is a specialized QR algorithm for symmetric matrices.

Section 6.5 presents the inverse iteration algorithm to calculate the eigenvectors from the given eigenvalues. Section 6.6 presents an orthogonal similarity transformation to order the eigenvalues in real Schur form of an unsymmetric matrix. The algorithm is useful to obtain the invariant subspace corresponding to the given eigenvalues of an unsymmetric matrix.

Matrix Algorithms in MATLAB. DOI: 10.1016/B978-0-12-803804-8.00012-X

Section 6.7 presents two special algorithms for symmetric tri-diagonal matrix: eigenvalues by bisection and divide-and-conquer (or more figuratively tearing and stitching). Section 6.8 presents the classical Jacobi iteration for a symmetric matrix. Jacobi iteration algorithm is inherently parallel and has superior accuracy for symmetric positive definite matrix. The algorithms presented in Sections 6.7 and 6.8 are useful as an alternative to the QR iteration algorithm.

The last three sections present algorithms for $\mathbf{Ax} = \lambda \mathbf{Bx}$. Section 6.9 treats symmetric $\mathbf{A}$ and $\mathbf{B}$, and further $\mathbf{B}$ is positive definite. Section 6.10 treats unsymmetric $\mathbf{A}$ and $\mathbf{B}$. Section 6.11 treats symmetric $\mathbf{A}$ and $\mathbf{B}$, and $\mathbf{B}$ can be positive indefinite.

6.1 ALGORITHMS OF SOLUTION OF 2×2 EIGENVALUE PROBLEMS

The eigenvalues of 2×2 matrices are elementary. Yet they are one of the building blocks of the eigenvalues of the general $n \times n$ matrices. In this section, we present two MATLAB functions, eig2x2_.m for $\mathbf{Ax} = \lambda \mathbf{x}$ and xeig2x2_.m for $\mathbf{Ax} = \lambda \mathbf{Bx}$, where $\mathbf{A}, \mathbf{B} \in \mathbb{R}^{2 \times 2}$.

For $\mathbf{A} \in \mathbb{R}^{2 \times 2}$, the eigenvalues of $\mathbf{Ax} = \lambda \mathbf{x}$ are determined as follows:

$$\det\left(\begin{bmatrix} A_{11} - \lambda & A_{12} \\ A_{21} & A_{22} - \lambda \end{bmatrix}\right) = 0, \quad \text{i.e. } \lambda^2 - \text{tr}(\mathbf{A})\lambda + \det(\mathbf{A}) = 0. \tag{6.1}$$

The eigenvalues are real if $d = \text{tr}^2(\mathbf{A}) - 4\det(\mathbf{A}) = (A_{11} - A_{22})^2 + 4A_{12}A_{21} \geq 0$. This is the case when $A_{12}A_{21} \geq 0$ (off-diagonals have same sign) or when $A_{11}A_{22} - A_{12}A_{21} = 0$ ($\mathbf{A}$ is singular). The real eigenvalues are calculated in eig2x2_.m. According to algo='schur' or algo='eig', the orthogonal Schur vectors or eigenvectors are calculated in eig2x2_.m as X. If the input matrix A is symmetric, the Schur vectors are also the eigenvectors. If $(A_{11} - A_{22})^2 + 4A_{12}A_{21} < 0$, the two eigenvalues are conjugate complex. Because we want to keep all the calculations in real arithmetic, no eigenvalues and eigenvectors are calculated. The results of different cases are distinguished by the output argument res=0,1,2,3. See the comments in eig2x2_.m for more details.

Algorithm 6.1

$\mathbf{AX} = \mathbf{X}\lambda$ of a 2×2 matrix by direct calculation.

```
%A is a 2x2 matrix. algo='eig' for X=eigenvectors, ='schur' for X=Schur vectors.
%res=0: X is eigenvectors and also Schur vectors (i.e. orthogonal, A=A').
%    =1: X is Schur vectors but not eigenvectors (i.e. orthogonal, A/=A').
%    =2: X is eigenvectors but not orthogonal (i.e. not Schur vectors, A/=A').
%    =3: A has no real eigenvalues, Lambda,X not calculated.
function [Lambda,X,res] = eig2x2_(A,algo)

if (A(1,2) == A(2,1))                    %X'*A*X = [Lambda(1),0;0,Lambda(2)]
    if (A(1,2) == 0)
        c = 1.0;   s = 0.0;
    else
        tau = 0.5*(A(2,2)-A(1,1))/A(1,2);
        if (tau >= 0)  t = 1.0/(tau+sqrt(1+tau*tau));
        else           t = 1.0/(tau-sqrt(1+tau*tau)); end
        c = 1.0/sqrt(1.0+t*t);   s = t*c;
    end
    X = [c,s; -s,c]; Lambda = [X(:,1)'*A*X(:,1),0; 0,X(:,2)'*A*X(:,2)];   res = 0;
```

```
else
    d = (A(1,1)-A(2,2))*(A(1,1)-A(2,2)) + 4.0*A(1,2)*A(2,1);
    if (d < 0) Lambda = []; X = []; res = 3; return; end
    if (exist('algo','var')==0 || isempty(algo)) algo = 'eig'; end
    if (strcmp(algo,'eig'))                  %A*X = X*Lambda
        e = A(1,1) + A(2,2);  d = sqrt(d);  Lambda = [0.5*(d+e); 0.5*(-d+e)];
        [tmax,jmax] = max(abs([A(1,1)-Lambda(1),A(1,2),A(2,2)-Lambda(1)]));
        if (jmax == 1)    x1 = [-A(1,2)/(A(1,1)-Lambda(1));1.0];
        elseif (jmax == 2) x1 = [1.0;-(A(1,1)-Lambda(1))/A(1,2)];
        else              x1 = [1.0;-A(2,1)/(A(2,2)-Lambda(1))]; end
        [tmax,jmax] = max(abs([A(1,1)-Lambda(1),A(1,2),A(2,2)-Lambda(2)]));
        if (jmax == 1)    x2 = [-A(1,2)/(A(1,1)-Lambda(2));1.0];
        elseif (jmax == 2) x2 = [1.0;-(A(1,1)-Lambda(1))/A(1,2)];
        else              x2 = [1.0;-A(2,1)/(A(2,2)-Lambda(2))]; end
        X = [x1/norm(x1),x2/norm(x2)];  res = 1;
    else %if (strcmp(algo,'schur'))   %X'*A*X = [Lambda(1),x; 0,Lambda(2)]
        if (abs(A(2,1)) < eps*(abs(A(1,1))+abs(A(2,2))))
            c = 1.0;   s = 0.0;
        elseif (abs(A(1,2)) < eps*(abs(A(1,1))+abs(A(2,2))))
            t = A(2,1)/(A(1,1)-A(2,2));  c = 1.0/sqrt(1.0+t*t);  s =-t*c;
        else  %eta*t^2 + 2*tau*t-1=0
            eta = A(1,2)/A(2,1);    tau = 0.5*(A(2,2)-A(1,1))/A(2,1);
            if (tau >= 0.0) t = 1.0/(tau+sqrt(eta+tau*tau));
            else            t = 1.0/(tau-sqrt(eta+tau*tau)); end
            c = 1.0/sqrt(1.0+t*t);  s = t*c;
        end
        X = [c,s; -s,c];  Lambda = X'*A*X;  Lambda(2,1)=0.0;  res=2;
    end
end
```

For $\mathbf{A}, \mathbf{B} \in \mathbb{R}^{2 \times 2}$, the eigenvalues of $\mathbf{A}\mathbf{x} = \lambda \mathbf{B}\mathbf{x}$ are determined as follows:

$$
\det\left(\begin{bmatrix} A_{11} - \lambda B_{11} & A_{12} - \lambda B_{12} \\ A_{21} - \lambda B_{21} & A_{22} - \lambda B_{22} \end{bmatrix}\right) = 0, \quad \text{i.e. } \det(\mathbf{B})\lambda^2 - \det(\mathbf{A},\mathbf{B})\lambda + \det(\mathbf{A}) = 0,
$$

$$
\text{where } \det(\mathbf{A},\mathbf{B}) = \det\left(\begin{bmatrix} A_{11} & A_{12} \\ B_{21} & B_{22} \end{bmatrix}\right) + \det\left(\begin{bmatrix} B_{11} & B_{12} \\ A_{21} & A_{22} \end{bmatrix}\right).
$$

(6.2)

The eigenvalues are real if $d = \det^2(\mathbf{A},\mathbf{B}) - 4\det(\mathbf{A})\det(\mathbf{B}) \geq 0$. If the eigenvalues are real, it is possible to find two well-conditioned matrices $\mathbf{U}, \mathbf{V} \in \mathbb{R}^{2 \times 2}$ such that $\mathbf{U}'\mathbf{A}\mathbf{V}$ and $\mathbf{U}'\mathbf{B}\mathbf{V}$ are both diagonal. If $\mathbf{A}$ and $\mathbf{B}$ are symmetric, we further require $\mathbf{V} = \mathbf{U} = \mathbf{G}$ to keep the symmetry of $\mathbf{G}'\mathbf{A}\mathbf{G}$ and $\mathbf{G}'\mathbf{B}\mathbf{G}$. In the following, we focus the discussion to the simpler case that both $\mathbf{A}$ and $\mathbf{B}$ are symmetric. The conditions of the diagonalization of $\mathbf{G}'\mathbf{A}\mathbf{G}$ and $\mathbf{G}'\mathbf{B}\mathbf{G}$ and non-singularity of $\mathbf{G}$ are expressed as follows:

$$
A_{11}G_{11}G_{12} + A_{21}(G_{11}G_{22} + G_{12}G_{21}) + A_{22}G_{21}G_{22} = 0,
$$
$$
B_{11}G_{11}G_{12} + B_{21}(G_{11}G_{22} + G_{12}G_{21}) + B_{22}G_{21}G_{22} = 0,
$$
$$
G_{11}G_{22} - G_{12}G_{21} = g \neq 0.
$$

(6.3)

When $d = (A_{11}B_{22} - A_{22}B_{11})^2 + 4(A_{21}B_{11} - A_{11}B_{21})(A_{21}B_{22} - A_{22}B_{21}) \geq 0$, there are two solutions to Eq. (6.3),

$$\mathbf{G} = \begin{bmatrix} G_{11} & \pm \frac{k_1 g}{Q_{11}} \\ k_2 G_{11} & \frac{k_3 g}{Q_{11}} \end{bmatrix}.$$

$$k_1 = \frac{A_{22}B_{21} - A_{21}B_{22}}{\sqrt{d}}, \qquad k_2 = \frac{A_{11}B_{22} - A_{22}B_{11} \pm \sqrt{d}}{2(A_{22}B_{21} - A_{21}B_{22})}, \qquad k_3 = 1 \mp k_1 k_2.$$

(6.4)

In Eq. (6.4), G_{11} and d can be arbitrary. When $G_{11} = \sqrt[4]{(k_1^2 + k_3^2)/(1 + k_2^2)}$, $\mathbf{G}$ has the minimum condition number.

In xeig2x2_.m, this best conditioned $\mathbf{G}$ with $g = 1$ is calculated, where different cases are handled for the efficiency and accuracy.

Algorithm 6.2

A=A',B=B', 2x2 matrix. Find best G: G'*A*G and G'*B*G are both diagonal and det(G)=1.

```
% res=-1:no solution, G=[],M=[].
% res=0: A=A',B=B',B(1,1)=B(2,2), B(2,1)=0: G'*M=I, a12=b12=0.
% res=1: A=A',B=B',B(1,1)=-B(2,2),B(2,1)=0: G'*B*M=B; =2, G'*B*M=-B. a12=b12=0.
% res=3: A=A',B=B',M=G'. a12=b12=0.
% res=4: other case. G'*G=I, M'*M=I.
function [G,M,res] = xeig2x2_(A,B)

b = A(1,1)*B(2,2) + A(2,1)*B(1,2) - A(2,2)*B(1,1) - A(1,2)*B(2,1);
a = A(1,1)*B(1,2) - A(1,2)*B(1,1);   c = A(2,1)*B(2,2) - A(2,2)*B(2,1);
d = b*b-4*a*c;
if (d < 0) G = []; M = []; res = -1; return; end

if (A(1,2)==A(2,1) && B(1,2)==B(2,1))   %symmetric
    if (B(2,1)==0 && B(1,1)==B(2,2))         %ortho
        d = sqrt((A(1,1)-A(2,2))*(A(1,1)-A(2,2)) + 4.0*A(2,1)*A(2,1));
        c = sqrt(0.5*(1.0+(A(1,1)-A(2,2))/d));   s = -A(2,1)/d/c;
        G = [c s; -s c];   M = G';   res = 0;
    elseif (B(2,1)==0 && B(1,1)==-B(2,2))    %hyper
        a12 = A(1,1) + A(2,2);   d = sqrt(a12*a12-4.0*A(2,1)*A(2,1));
        if (a12 < -d)
            k3 = 0.5*(1.0 - a12/d);   c = sqrt(k3);   s = sqrt(k3-1);
            if (A(2,1) > 0) s = -s; end
        elseif (a12 > d)
            k3 = 0.5*(1.0 + a12/d);   c = sqrt(k3);   s = sqrt(k3-1);
            if (A(2,1) < 0) s = -s; end
        else
            c = 1; s = 0;
        end
        G = [c -s; -s c];   M = G';   res = 1;   %=2 not listed!
    else                                     %GBR
        a = A(1,1)*B(2,2)-A(2,2)*B(1,1);   b = A(2,2)*B(2,1)-A(2,1)*B(2,2);
        c = A(1,1)*B(2,1)-A(2,1)*B(1,1);   d = sqrt(a*a+4.0*b*c);
        k1 = b/d; k2 = 0.5*(a-d)/b; k3 = 1 + k1*k2;
        G11 = power((k1*k1+k3*k3)/(1+k2*k2),0.25);
        G = [G11 k1/G11; k2*G11 k3/G11];   M = G';   res = 3;
    end
else                                     %nonsymmetric
    if (abs(a) > 100*eps)
        if (b >= 0.0) tanc = -0.5*(b + sqrt(d))/a;
        else          tanc = -0.5*(b - sqrt(d))/a; end
```

```
        if (tanc*tanc > abs(c/a)) tanc = c/a/tanc; end
    else
        tanc = -c/b;
    end
    theta = atan(tanc);  c = cos(theta);  s = sin(theta);  G = [c s;-s c];
    tanc = (A(1,1)*tanc+A(2,1))/(A(1,2)*tanc+A(2,2));
    theta = atan(tanc);  c = cos(theta);  s = sin(theta);  M = [c s;-s c];
    res = 4;
end
```

6.2 BOUND ESTIMATION OF SYMMETRIC EIGENVALUE PROBLEMS

For $\mathbf{Ax} = \lambda\mathbf{x}, \mathbf{A} = \mathbf{A}'$ and $\mathbf{Ax} = \lambda\mathbf{Bx}, \mathbf{A} = \mathbf{A}', \mathbf{B} = \mathbf{B}'$ and $\mathbf{B}$ is positive semi-definite, the eigenvalues are real. We order the eigenvalues ascendingly $\lambda_1 \le \lambda_2 \cdots \le \lambda_k \cdots \le \lambda_l \cdots \lambda_{n-1} \le \lambda_n$.

In engineering applications or in some eigenvalue algorithms, we may need to get a quick estimate of the lower and upper bound of an eigenvalue or the number of eigenvalues in a given interval. For this purpose, we can apply Sylvester law of inertia [29]. For a symmetric matrix $\mathbf{A} \in \mathbb{R}^{n \times n}$, the matrix inertia is a triplet (m, z, p), where m is the number of negative eigenvalues of $\mathbf{A}$, z is the number of zero eigenvalues, p is the number of positive eigenvalues. The Sylvester law of inertia states that the matrix inertia does not change under any congruent transformations. Therefore, we can obtain the matrix inertia by LDLt decomposition discussed in Section 2.4.

If $\mathbf{A} - \alpha\mathbf{I} = \mathbf{LDL}'$, $m(\mathbf{A} - \alpha\mathbf{I}) = m(\mathbf{D})$. Therefore, the number of negative values in $\mathbf{D}$ is the number of eigenvalues of $\mathbf{A}$ that is less than α. Similarly if $\mathbf{A} - \beta\mathbf{I} = \mathbf{LDL}'$, $m(\mathbf{A} - \beta\mathbf{I}) = m(\mathbf{D})$. If $\alpha \le \beta$, $m(\mathbf{A} - \beta\mathbf{I}) - m(\mathbf{A} - \alpha\mathbf{I})$ is the number of eigenvalues of $\mathbf{A}$ in the interval $[\alpha, \beta]$. By a simple index transformation, from $m(\mathbf{A} - \alpha\mathbf{I})$ and $m(\mathbf{A} - \beta\mathbf{I})$, we can obtain a duplet $[k, l]$, such that $\alpha \le \lambda_k \le \lambda_l \le \beta$.

The calculation of $[k, l]$ from the given $[\alpha, \beta]$ is implemented in neig_.m.

Algorithm 6.3

$\mathbf{A} - \lambda\mathbf{I}, \mathbf{A} = \mathbf{A}'$: Calculate (k, l), so that $\alpha \le \lambda_k \le \lambda_l \le \beta$.

```
function [k,l] = neig_(A,alpha,beta)

[m,n]=size(A);
tol = 100*eps;

for j=1:n A(j,j) = A(j,j) - alpha; end
[L,d,p] = LDLt_(A,'gauss',1,tol,'short');
ld = length(d); k = 0;
for j=1:ld
    if (d(j) < 0) k = k + 1; end
end
k = min(k+1,n);

if (abs(alpha-beta)<eps*max(abs(alpha)+abs(beta),1))
    l = k + n - ld + 1;
else
    beta = beta - alpha;
    for j=1:n A(j,j) = A(j,j) - beta; end
    [L,d,p] = LDLt_(A,'gauss',1,tol,'short');
    ld = length(d);  l = n - ld;
    for j = 1:ld
```

```
        if (d(j) < 0) l = l + 1; end
    end
end
```

The following simple example shows the output of `neig_.m` from a symmetric matrix. The output results are shown with comments.

```
>> [Q,R]=QR_(randn(8));   d = 1:8;
>> A=Q*diag(d)*Q';        %A's eigenvalues are 1,2,3,4,5,6,7,8

>> [k,l]=neig_(A,2.0,5.0);
>> [k,l] =
    2     5                 %2.0<=2<5<5.0

>> [k,l]=neig_(A,2.5,5.5);
>> [k,l] =
    3     5                 %2.5<3<5<5.5

>> [k,l]=neig_(A,1.5,4.5);
>> [k,l] =
    2     4                 %1.5<2<4<4.5
```

The inverse function of `neig_.m` is `veig_.m`. Given a duplet $[k,l]$, we calculate an interval $[\alpha,\beta]$, so that $\alpha \le \lambda_k \le \lambda_l \le \beta$. This calculation is not as straightforward as `neig_.m`. At first we calculate a coarse estimation of $[\alpha,\beta]$ by applying Gershgorin theorem [29]. Then $[\alpha,\beta]$ is continuously refined by bisection.

Algorithm 6.4

$\mathbf{A} - \lambda\mathbf{I}, \mathbf{A} = \mathbf{A}'$: Calculate (α,β), so that $\alpha \le \lambda_k \le \lambda_l \le \beta$.

```
function [alpha,beta] = veig_(A,k,l)

[m,n]=size(A);
tol = 100*eps;

alpha = realmax; beta =-realmax;      %Apply Gershgorin theorem
for i=1:n
    ri = 0.0;
    for j=1:i-1 ri = ri + abs(A(i,j)); end
    for j=i+1:n ri = ri + abs(A(i,j)); end
    alpha = min(alpha, A(i,i)-ri);   beta = max(beta, A(i,i)+ri);
end

beta1 = beta;  gamma0 = 0.0; k1 = 0;   %Determine lower bound alpha
while(k1 ~= k-1)
    gamma = 0.5*(alpha+beta1);   k1 = 0;
    for j=1:n A(j,j) = A(j,j) - (gamma - gamma0); end
    gamma0 = gamma;
    [L,d,p] = LDLt_(A,'gauss',1,tol,'short');
    for j = 1:length(d)
        if (d(j) < 0) k1 = k1 + 1; end
    end
    if (k1 == k-1)  alpha = gamma;
    elseif (k1 < k) alpha = gamma;
    elseif (k1 > l) beta  = gamma;  beta1 = gamma;
    else            beta1 = gamma; end
end
```

```
alpha2 = alpha; k2 = 0;                    %Determine upper bound beta
while(k2 ~= 1)
   gamma = 0.5*(alpha2+beta);   k2 = 0;
   for j=1:n A(j,j) = A(j,j) - (gamma - gamma0); end
   gamma0 = gamma;
   [L,d,p] = LDLt_(A,'gauss',1,tol,'short');
   for j = 1:length(d)
      if (d(j) < 0) k2 = k2 + 1; end
   end
   if (k2 == 1)     beta = gamma;
   elseif (k2 < k) alpha = gamma; alpha2 = gamma;
   elseif (k2 > 1) beta = gamma;
   else            alpha2 = gamma; end
end
```

The same matrix applied in `neig_.m` is applied in `veig_.m`. The output results are shown with comments.

```
>> [alpha,beta]=veig_(A,2,5);
>> [alpha,beta] =
     1.3440     5.8857        %1.3440<2<5<5.8857
>> [alpha,beta]=veig_(A,3,5);
>> [alpha,beta] =
     2.8579     5.6965        %2.8579<3<5<5.6965
>> [alpha,beta]=veig_(A,2,4);
>> [alpha,beta] =
     1.3440     4.7503        %1.3440<2<4<4.7503
```

The above two algorithms `neig_.m` and `veig_.m` can be extended to the generalized eigenvalue problem $\mathbf{A} - \lambda\mathbf{B}$ if $\mathbf{A} = \mathbf{A}', \mathbf{B} = \mathbf{B}'$ and $\mathbf{B}$ is positive definite. When $\mathbf{B}$ is positive definite, $\mathbf{A} - \lambda\mathbf{B}$ can be transformed into the standard eigenvalue problem,

$$\mathbf{A} - \alpha\mathbf{B} = \mathbf{A} - \lambda\mathbf{C}\mathbf{C}' = \mathbf{C}\left(\mathbf{C}^{-1}\mathbf{A}\mathbf{C}'^{-1} - \alpha\mathbf{I}\right)\mathbf{C}' = \mathbf{L}\mathbf{D}\mathbf{L}'.$$

Therefore, $m(\mathbf{A} - \alpha\mathbf{B}) = m(\mathbf{D})$ measures the number of eigenvalues of $\mathbf{A} - \lambda\mathbf{B}$ that are less than α. If $\alpha \leq \beta$, $m(\mathbf{A} - \beta\mathbf{B}) - m(\mathbf{A} - \alpha\mathbf{B})$ is the number of eigenvalues of $\mathbf{A} - \lambda\mathbf{B}$ in the interval $[\alpha, \beta]$. If $\mathbf{A} - \lambda\mathbf{B}$ is not symmetric positive definite, the eigenvalues can be complex. Even if all the eigenvalues are real, the conclusions are not valid.

The MATLAB implementations `nxeig_.m` and `vxeig_.m` are listed as follows. In both functions, we do not check the symmetric positive definiteness. If $\mathbf{A} - \lambda\mathbf{B}$ is not symmetric positive definite, the output result is simply wrong.

Algorithm 6.5

$\mathbf{A} - \lambda\mathbf{B}, \mathbf{A} = \mathbf{A}', \mathbf{B} = \mathbf{B}', \mathbf{B} > 0$: Calculate (k,l), so that $\alpha \leq \lambda_k \leq \lambda_l \leq \beta$.

```
function [k,l] = nxeig_(A,B,alpha,beta)

[m,n]=size(A);   [k,l] = size(B);
tol = 100*eps;

[L,d,p] = LDLt_(A-alpha*B,'gauss',1,tol,'short');
ld = length(d); k = 0;
for j=1:ld
    if (d(j) < 0) k = k + 1; end
```

```
end
k = min(k+1,n);

if (abs(alpha-beta)<eps*max(abs(alpha)+abs(beta),1))
    l = k + n - ld + 1;
else
    [L,d,p] = LDLt_(A-beta*B,'gauss',1,tol,'short');
    ld = length(d);  l = n - ld;
    for j = 1:ld
        if (d(j) < 0) l = l + 1; end
    end
end
```

We present a simple example to demonstrate the use of nxeig_.m. **A** is the same matrix used in the above examples. **B** is created below. The output results are shown with comments.

```
>> [Q,R]=QR_(randn(8));    d = 8:-1:1;
>> B=Q*diag(d)*Q';          %B=B', B>0
>> sort(eig(A,B))'
    0.1693     0.4637     0.5389     0.7925     1.2146     1.6298     2.7722     5.4334

>> [k,l]=nxeig_(A,B,0.2,1.5);
>> [k,l] =
    2      5                  %0.2<0.4637<1.2146<1.5

>> [k,l]=nxeig_(A,B,0.5,1.5);
>> [k,l] =
    3      5                  %0.5<0.5389<1.2146<1.5

>> [k,l]=nxeig_(A,B,0.5,1.0);
>> [k,l] =
    3      4                  %0.5<0.5389<0.7925<1.0
```

Algorithm 6.6

$\mathbf{A} - \lambda\mathbf{B}, \mathbf{A} = \mathbf{A}', \mathbf{B} = \mathbf{B}', \mathbf{B} > \mathbf{0}$: Calculate (α, β), so that $\alpha \le \lambda_k \le \lambda_l \le \beta$.

```
function [alpha,beta] = vxeig_(A,B,k,l)

[m,n]=size(A);   [mB,nB] = size(B);
tol = 100*eps;   inf = 1.0/tol;

alpha = realmax;  beta =-realmax;       %Apply Gershgorin theorem
for i=1:n
    ri = 0.0;
    for j=1:i-1 ri = ri + abs(A(i,j)); end
    for j=i+1:n ri = ri + abs(A(i,j)); end
    alpha = min(alpha, A(i,i)-ri);  beta = max(beta, A(i,i)+ri);
end

[L,d,p] = LDLt_(B,'gauss',1,tol,'short');
nz = n - length(d); ninf = 0; pinf = 0;
while(nz > 0)                           %Make sure inf large enough
    [L,d,p] = LDLt_(A+inf*B,'gauss',1,tol,'short');
    for j=1:length(d)
        if (d(j) < 0) ninf = ninf + 1; end
    end
    [L,d,p] = LDLt_(A-inf*B,'gauss',1,tol,'short');
```

```
        for j=1:length(d)
            if (d(j) > 0) pinf = pinf + 1; end
        end
        if (ninf + pinf <= nz) break; end
        inf = 2.0*inf; ninf = 0; pinf = 0;
    end

    k1 = n; k2 = 0; delta = 0;              %Determine lower bound alpha
    if (k <= ninf)        alpha =-inf;
    elseif (k > n-pinf) alpha = inf;
    else
        while (k1 >= k)
            alpha = alpha - delta;  k1 = 0;
            [L,d,p] = LDLt_(A-alpha*B,'gauss',1,tol,'short');
            for j=1:length(d)
                if (d(j) < 0) k1 = k1 + 1; end
            end
            delta = beta - alpha;
        end
        delta = 0;
        while(k2 < k)
            beta = beta + delta;  k2 = 0;
            [L,d,p] = LDLt_(A-beta*B,'gauss',1,tol,'short');
            for j=1:length(d)
                if (d(j) < 0) k2 = k2 + 1; end
            end
            delta = beta - alpha;
        end
        beta1 = beta;
        while(k1 ~= k-1)
            gamma = 0.5*(alpha+beta1); k1 = 0;
            [L,d,p] = LDLt_(A-gamma*B,'gauss',1,tol,'short');
            for j = 1:length(d)
                if (d(j) < 0) k1 = k1 + 1; end
            end
            if (k1 == k-1)  alpha = gamma;
            elseif (k1 < k) alpha = gamma;
            elseif (k1 > l) beta = gamma; beta1 = gamma;
            else            beta1 = gamma; end
        end
    end

    if (l <= ninf)        beta =-inf;        %Determine upper bound beta
    elseif (l > n-pinf) beta = inf;
    else
        delta = beta - alpha;
        while(k2 < l)
            beta = beta + delta; k2 = 0;
            [L,d,p] = LDLt_(A-beta*B,'gauss',1,tol,'short');
            for j=1:length(d)
                if (d(j) < 0) k2 = k2 + 1; end
            end
            delta = beta - alpha;
        end
        alpha2 = alpha;
        while(k2 ~= l)
            gamma = 0.5*(alpha2+beta); k2 = 0;
```

```
    [L,d,p] = LDLt_(A-gamma*B,'gauss',1,tol,'short');
    for j = 1:length(d)
        if (d(j) < 0) k2 = k2 + 1; end
    end
    if (k2 == 1)    beta = gamma;
    elseif (k2 < k) alpha = gamma; alpha2 = gamma;
    elseif (k2 > 1) beta = gamma;
    else            alpha2 = gamma; end
  end
end
```

We use the same **A** and **B** in veig2_.m in the following example. The output results are shown with comments.

```
>> [alpha,beta]=vxeig_(A,B,2,5);
>> [alpha,beta] =
    0.2085     1.2493        %0.2085<0.4637<1.2146<1.2493
>> [alpha,beta]=vxeig_(A,B,3,5);
>> [alpha,beta] =
    0.4924     1.4622        %0.4924<0.5389<1.2146<1.4622
>> [alpha,beta]=vxeig_(A,B,2,4);
>> [alpha,beta] =
    0.2085     1.0601        %0.2085<0.4637<0.7925<1.0601
```

6.3 POWER ITERATIONS AND SUBSPACE ITERATIONS

Suppose $\mathbf{A} \in \mathbb{R}^{n \times n}$ is diagonalizable. We order **A**'s eigenvalues as $|\lambda_1| \leq |\lambda_2| \cdots \leq |\lambda_{n-1}| < |\lambda_n|$. We order **A**'s eigenvectors $\mathbf{V}(:, 1 : n)$ following the order of **A**'s eigenvalues.

Given an arbitrary vector $\mathbf{u} \in \mathbb{R}^n$. We decompose **u** in terms of $\mathbf{V}(:, 1 : n)$, i.e.

$$\mathbf{u} = \mathbf{V}(\mathbf{V}'\mathbf{u}) = \mathbf{V}\mathbf{w} = w_1\mathbf{V}(:,1) + w_2\mathbf{V}(:,2) + \cdots + w_{n-1}\mathbf{V}(:,n-1) + w_n\mathbf{V}(:,n).$$

Au can be presented as follows:

$$\mathbf{Au} = \mathbf{AVw} = \mathbf{V}\lambda\mathbf{w} = \lambda_1 w_1\mathbf{V}(:,1) + \lambda_2 w_2\mathbf{V}(:,2) + \cdots + \lambda_{n-1}w_{n-1}\mathbf{V}(:,n-1) + \lambda_n w_n\mathbf{V}(:,n)$$

$$= \lambda_n \left(\frac{\lambda_1}{\lambda_n}w_1\mathbf{V}(:,1) + \frac{\lambda_2}{\lambda_n}w_2\mathbf{V}(:,2) + \cdots + \frac{\lambda_{n-1}}{\lambda_n}w_{n-1}\mathbf{V}(:,n-1) + w_n\mathbf{V}(:n) \right).$$

Similarly $\mathbf{A}^k\mathbf{u}, k \to \infty$ can be presented as follows:

$$\mathbf{A}^k\mathbf{u} = \lambda_n^k \left(\left(\frac{\lambda_1}{\lambda_n}\right)^k w_1\mathbf{V}(:,1) + \left(\frac{\lambda_2}{\lambda_n}\right)^k w_2\mathbf{V}(:,2) + \cdots + \left(\frac{\lambda_{n-1}}{\lambda_n}\right)^k w_{n-1}\mathbf{V}(:,n-1) + w_n\mathbf{V}(:n) \right).$$

In order to avoid the overflow or underflow when calculating $\mathbf{A}^k\mathbf{u}$, we can normalize it for each k and save the result to **u**. This forms the algorithm of the power iteration. It is useful for calculating λ_n.

1. If $|\lambda_1| \leq |\lambda_2| \cdots \leq |\lambda_{n-1}| < |\lambda_n|$, $\mathbf{A}^k\mathbf{u} \Rightarrow \mathbf{u} \to \text{span}(\mathbf{V}(:,n))$ and $\frac{\mathbf{u}'\mathbf{Au}}{\mathbf{u}'\mathbf{u}} \to \lambda_n$.
2. If $|\lambda_{n-1}| < |\lambda_n|$ but the difference is small, the convergence is slow.
3. If $|\lambda_{n-1}| = |\lambda_n|$, we have three situations:

    a. If $\lambda_{n-1} = \lambda_n$, $\mathbf{A}^k\mathbf{u} \Rightarrow \mathbf{u} \to \text{span}(\mathbf{V}(:,n-1), \mathbf{V}(:,n))$ and $\frac{\mathbf{u}'\mathbf{Au}}{\mathbf{u}'\mathbf{u}} \to \lambda_n$.

    b. If $\lambda_{n-1} = -\lambda_n$, $\mathbf{A}^k\mathbf{u}$ will not converge to any subspace. But $\mathbf{A}^{2k}\mathbf{u}$ converges to the invariant subspace of $\mathbf{A}^2$.

    c. If λ_{n-1} and λ_n are conjugate complex, $\mathbf{A}^k\mathbf{u}$ will not converge to any subspace. This will never happen when $\mathbf{A}$ is symmetric. When $\mathbf{A}$ is unsymmetric, we can use a $\mathbf{u}$ with two columns.

To calculate λ_{n-1}, we can deflate $\mathbf{V}(:,n)$ from $\mathbf{A}^k\mathbf{u}$ for each k, i.e. $\mathbf{A}^k\mathbf{u} \Rightarrow \mathbf{u}, \mathbf{u} - \mathbf{V}(:,n)(\mathbf{V}(:,n)'\mathbf{u}) \Rightarrow \mathbf{u}$. An alternative is to use the shift and invert. We know $1/(\lambda_{n-1} - \sigma)$ is an eigenvalue of $(\mathbf{A} - \sigma\mathbf{I})^{-1}$. If σ is close to λ_{n-1}, $1/(\lambda_{n-1} - \sigma)$ is likely the extremal eigenvalue of $(\mathbf{A} - \sigma\mathbf{I})^{-1}$. Therefore, $(\mathbf{A} - \sigma\mathbf{I})^{-k}\mathbf{u} \rightarrow \mathrm{span}(\mathbf{V}(:,n-1))$. The deflation or the shift and invert is also applicable for other eigenvalues.

If $\mathbf{u}$ has two columns(for notational purpose, we denote it as $\mathbf{U}$), we can intuitively imagine $\mathbf{A}^k\mathbf{U}$ converges to $\mathrm{span}(\mathbf{V}(:,n-1:n))$ when $k \rightarrow \infty$. Under some mild conditions, this is really the case, see [29]. To avoid the overflow and underflow of $\mathbf{A}^k\mathbf{U}$, we use QR decomposition on $\mathbf{A}^k\mathbf{U}$. Note that if $\mathbf{A}^k\mathbf{U} = \mathbf{QR}$, $\mathbf{A}^k\mathbf{U}$ and $\mathbf{Q}$ span the same subspace. We also need to replace the Rayleigh quotient calculation of $\mathbf{u}'\mathbf{Au}$ by a small scale eigenvalue problem for $\mathbf{U}'\mathbf{AU}$. This forms the algorithm of the subspace iteration. The number of columns of $\mathbf{U}$ can also be any integer in the interval of $[1, n]$. The power iteration is a special case of the subspace iteration, where the dimension of the subspace is one. Both algorithms are implemented in one MATLAB function, eigSubspace_.m. When the number of columns of $\mathbf{U}$ is less than n, the subspace iterations belong to the class of iterative algorithms of approximating the invariant subspace of $\mathbf{A}$ with a gradually improving lower dimensional subspace, which is the topic of the next chapter. Therefore, we defer the list of eigSubspace_.m to the next chapter. The brief discussion of this section paves the way to the QR algorithm of the following section.

6.4 QR ITERATIONS

In the subspace iterations, if the rank of the starting $\mathbf{U}$ (denoted as $\mathbf{U}_0$ in this section) is n, and the eigenvalues of $\mathbf{A}$ satisfy $|\lambda_1| < |\lambda_2| < \cdots < |\lambda_{n-1}| < |\lambda_n|$, then $\mathrm{span}(\mathbf{A}^k\mathbf{U}_0)$, i.e. $\mathrm{span}(\mathbf{U}_k)$ converges to the span of the eigenvectors of $\mathbf{A}$. This means $\mathbf{A}_k = \mathbf{U}_k'\mathbf{AU}_k$ converges to an upper triangular form ($\mathbf{A}$'s Schur form), or a quasi-upper triangular form (Real Schur form), at a rate approximately $\frac{|\lambda_l|}{|\lambda_{l+1}|}, l = 1, 2, \ldots, n-1$. See Sections 1.1 and 1.4 for a brief account or [29] for more details. Following the subspace iterations, let us check $\mathbf{A}_{k-1}$ and $\mathbf{A}_k$,

$$\mathbf{A}_{k-1} = \mathbf{U}_{k-1}'(\mathbf{AU}_{k-1}) = \mathbf{U}_{k-1}'(\mathbf{U}_k\mathbf{R}_k) = (\mathbf{U}_{k-1}'\mathbf{U}_k)\mathbf{R}_k = \mathbf{Q}_k\mathbf{R}_k,$$
$$\mathbf{A}_k = \mathbf{U}_k'\mathbf{AU}_k = (\mathbf{U}_k'\mathbf{AU}_{k-1})(\mathbf{U}_{k-1}'\mathbf{U}_k) = \mathbf{R}_k\mathbf{Q}_k = \mathbf{Q}_k'\mathbf{A}_{k-1}\mathbf{Q}_k.$$

Therefore, $\mathbf{A}_k$ is determined by computing the QR decomposition of $\mathbf{A}_{k-1}$ and then multiplying the factors in reverse order. Equivalently, it can be determined by applying an orthogonal similarity transformation to $\mathbf{A}_{k-1}$. The orthogonal transformation is $\mathbf{Q}_k$, the Q factor of QR decomposition of $\mathbf{A}_{k-1}$,

$$\mathbf{A}_k = \mathbf{R}_k\mathbf{Q}_k = (\mathbf{Q}_k'\mathbf{A}_{k-1})\mathbf{Q}_k = \mathbf{Q}_k'\mathbf{A}_{k-1}\mathbf{Q}_k. \tag{6.5}$$

Eq. (6.5) forms the essence of QR iteration. Under the assumed conditions, $\mathbf{A}_k$ converges to the Schur form of $\mathbf{A}$. The drawbacks of Eq. (6.5) are the high cost of computation (each QR is $O(n^3)$ operation) and the assumed conditions. In the following, we discuss four practical improvements, which together form the most efficient algorithm of QR iterations to find eigenvalues of a full matrix.

In this section, we use the following simple 4×4 unsymmetric matrix $\mathbf{A}$ to illustrate each step of QR iterations. To illustrate the QR iterations for the symmetric matrix, we use $\mathbf{B} = \frac{1}{2}(\mathbf{A} + \mathbf{A}')$.

```
>> A=[1,2,3,4;5,6,7,8;2,1,4,3;8,7,5,6];      >> B=0.5*(A+A');
>> eig(A)'                                    >> eig(B)'
=   18.1697    -2.9685    0.4351    1.3637     =   -3.3637    -0.1120    1.4759    18.9999
```

6.4.1 REDUCE A TO HESSENBERG FORM

The high cost of $O(n^3)$ operation of a QR step $\mathbf{A}_k = \mathbf{Q}'_k \mathbf{A}_{k-1} \mathbf{Q}_k$ can be reduced to $O(n^2)$, if $\mathbf{A}_{k-1}$ is an upper Hessenberg matrix. If $\mathbf{A}_{k-1}$ is an upper Hessenberg matrix $\mathbf{H}_{k-1}$, the Q factor of its QR decomposition $\mathbf{Q}_k$ is also upper an Hessenberg matrix, and $\mathbf{Q}'_k \mathbf{A}_{k-1} \mathbf{Q}_k$ keeps the upper Hessenberg form $\mathbf{H}_k$.

The orthogonal similarity reduction of $\mathbf{A}$ to a Hessenberg matrix is a direct algorithm, QHQt for a general square matrix discussed in Section 3.5, or QTQt for a symmetric matrix discussed in Section 3.6. For QHQt, we have three MATLAB implementations QHQtByHouseholder_.m, QHQtByGivens_.m, and QHQtByArnoldi_.m. For QTQt, we also have three MATLAB codes QTQtByHouseholder_.m, QTQtByGivens_.m, and QHQtByLanczos_.m.

```
>> [U0,H0]=QHQtByHouseholder_(A)             >> [U00,T0]=QTQtByHouseholder_(B)
U0 =                                         U00 =
    1.0000         0         0         0         1.0000         0         0         0
         0   -0.5185   -0.8130   -0.2650              0   -0.4741   -0.7475   -0.4652
         0   -0.2074   -0.1811    0.9613              0   -0.3386   -0.3329    0.8801
         0   -0.8296    0.5534   -0.0747              0   -0.8127    0.5748   -0.0953
H0 =                                         T0 =
    1.0000   -4.9774    0.0442    2.0552         1.0000   -7.3824         0         0
   -9.6437   14.6022    3.5834   -5.1275        -7.3824   15.0367    4.2350         0
         0    4.4628   -0.4380   -2.9149              0    4.2350   -0.2065   -0.7468
         0         0    0.8181    1.8359              0         0   -0.7468    1.1698
```

6.4.2 A QR ITERATION STEP FOR A HESSENBERG MATRIX

A QR iteration step as shown in Eq. (6.5) consists of two sub-steps: first, an orthogonal reduction of $\mathbf{H}_{k-1}$ to an upper triangular form $\mathbf{Q}'_k \mathbf{H}_{k-1} \Rightarrow \mathbf{R}_k$; second, $\mathbf{R}_k \mathbf{Q}_k \Rightarrow \mathbf{H}_k$. The first sub-step is discussed in Section 3.2.5 for a Hessenberg matrix and in Section 3.2.6 for a band matrix. In the following, we use $\mathbf{H}$ and $\mathbf{T}$ obtained in this last subsection to illustrate the whole QR iteration step.

The following is the sub-step for k=1, $\mathbf{Q}'\mathbf{H}_0 \Rightarrow \mathbf{R}$.

```
>> [Q,R]=QRhessenberg_(H0)
Q =
    0.1031    0.6078   -0.0574    0.7853
   -0.9947    0.0630   -0.0059    0.0814
         0   -0.7916   -0.0445    0.6094
         0         0   -0.9973   -0.0729
R =
    9.6954  -15.0376   -3.5597    5.3121
         0   -5.6377    0.5994    3.2334
         0         0   -0.8203   -1.7886
         0         0         0   -0.7137
```

The second sub-step is simply $\mathbf{RQ}$. Because of the upper Hessenberg structure of of $\mathbf{Q}$, $\mathbf{RQ}$ is again an upper Hessenberg form.

```
>> H=R*Q
H =
    15.9574      7.7627     -5.6063      3.8329
     5.6076     -0.8298     -3.2180     -0.3294
          0      0.6494      1.8204     -0.3696
          0           0      0.7118      0.0520
```

If we repeat the above two sub-steps another time, $\mathbf{H}$ is transformed to the following.

```
H =      %H keeps upper Hessenberg, with sub-diagonal reduced.
    18.2943      2.2307     -4.0464      5.6952
    -1.1334     -2.8814     -2.5136     -0.4846
          0     -0.3263      1.2940     -1.2286
          0           0      0.1335      0.2932
```

If we repeat the QR iteration step for 10 times more, $\mathbf{H}$ is almost upper triangular. The diagonal components are the approximate eigenvalues of the original matrix $\mathbf{A}$.

```
H =      %H is almost upper triangular.
    18.1697      3.0408     -3.4726      6.1675
    -0.0000     -2.9684     -2.4193      0.0013
    -0.0000     -0.0002      1.3636     -1.3432
    -0.0000      0.0000      0.0000      0.4351
```

For the symmetric matrix $\mathbf{B}$, we can use QRband_.m for the tri-diagonal matrix $\mathbf{T}$. The applications of QR iterations to $\mathbf{T}$ are shown for three iterations.

```
T =          %1st iteration
    16.7477      6.7207      0.0000      0.0000
     6.7207     -1.0688     -0.4818     -0.0000
          0     -0.4818      1.3891      0.2623
          0           0      0.2623     -0.0680
T =          %2nd iteration
    18.9224     -1.3139      0.0000     -0.0000
    -1.3139     -3.2780      0.1995     -0.0000
          0      0.1995      1.4674     -0.0204
          0           0     -0.0204     -0.1117
T =          %12th iteration
    18.9999     -0.0000      0.0000     -0.0000
    -0.0000     -3.3637      0.0001      0.0000
          0      0.0001      1.4759     -0.0000
          0           0     -0.0000     -0.1120
```

6.4.3 DEFLATION

The sub-diagonal components of $\mathbf{H}$ converge to zero when $k \to \infty$. But each component converges to zero at a different rate. When the sub-diagonal component $H(o+1,o)$ is small enough, i.e. $|H(o+1,o)| < \tau\left(|H(o,o)| + |H(o+1,o+1)|\right)$, we set $H(o+1,o) = 0$, where $1 \leq o < n$,

$$\mathbf{H} = \begin{bmatrix} \mathbf{H}(1:o,1:o) & \mathbf{H}(1:o,o+1:n) \\ \mathbf{0} & \mathbf{H}(o+1:n,o+1:n) \end{bmatrix}.$$

Then, from now, on we can solve two smaller eigenvalue problems for $\mathbf{H}(1:o,1:o)$ and $\mathbf{H}(o+1:n,o+1:n)$. Both $\mathbf{H}$ are upper Hessenberg. If only eigenvalues are sought, $\mathbf{H}(1:o,o+1:n)$ can be dropped from any further calculations. Otherwise, the pre-orthogonal transformations applied to $H(1 : o, 1 : o)$ and post orthogonal transformations applied to $H(o + 1 : n, o + 1 : n)$ are applied to $H(1 : o, o + 1 : n)$.

For a symmetric matrix, when $|T(o + 1, o)| < \tau (|T(o,o)| + |T(o + 1, o + 1)|)$ for some $1 \leq o < n$, we set $T(o, o + 1) = T(o + 1, o) = 0$,

$$\mathbf{T} = \begin{bmatrix} T(1 : o, 1 : o) & \mathbf{0} \\ \mathbf{0} & T(o + 1 : n, o + 1 : n) \end{bmatrix}.$$

Then from now on we can solve two smaller eigenvalue problems for $\mathbf{T}(1 : o, 1 : o)$ and $\mathbf{T}(o + 1 : n, o + 1 : n)$. Both $\mathbf{T}$ are symmetric tri-diagonal.

6.4.4 SHIFT

In the subspace iterations presented in the last section, we see that if σ is close to an eigenvalue λ_l of $\mathbf{A}$, the subspace iterations for $(\mathbf{A} - \sigma \mathbf{I})^{-1}$ converge to λ_l quickly. In QR iteration, the shift is applied as follows:

$$\begin{aligned} \mathbf{H}_1 - \sigma \mathbf{I} &= \mathbf{QR}, \\ \mathbf{H}_2 &= \mathbf{RQ} + \sigma \mathbf{I} = \mathbf{Q}'\mathbf{H}_1\mathbf{Q}. \end{aligned} \tag{6.6}$$

If the sub-diagonal of $\mathbf{H}_1$ does not contain zeros and σ is one eigenvalue of $\mathbf{H}_1$, the above QR iteration with σ as the shift will converge to σ in one step, with $\mathbf{H}_2(n, n - 1) = 0$ and $\mathbf{H}_2(n, n) = \sigma$. First we note that the rank of $\mathbf{H}_1 - \sigma \mathbf{I}$ is $n - 1$. This means the first $n - 1$ diagonal components of $\mathbf{R}$ does not contain zeros and $\mathbf{R}(n, n) = 0$. The direct calculation of $\mathbf{RQ} + \sigma \mathbf{I}$ leads to the conclusion. The conclusion is illustrated with the following simple example. From eig(A), we see that 18.1697 is an approximate eigenvalue of $\mathbf{A}$. We apply 18.1697 as the shift in one QR iteration step for $\mathbf{H}_0$.

```
>> H=H0;   sigma=18.1697;
>> [Q,R]=QR_(H-sigma*eye(4),'householder',0,100*eps,'long');

>> H=R*Q+sigma*eye(4)
H =
   -1.9807    -1.1266     0.8599    -4.5312
   -2.2102    -1.0685     1.5807     1.7119
        0     -0.8594     1.8804    -5.9749
        0          0     -0.0024    18.1688        %H(4,3)~=0,  H(4,4)~=lambda_4
```

The above calculation based on Eq. (6.6) is called the QR iteration with the explicit shift. The QR iteration with explicit zero shift is discussed in Section 6.4.2. The actual operation does not need to follow Eq. (6.6). The actual operation is called the QR iteration with the implicit shift. Again we illustrate the implicit shift with an example. For the symmetric matrix, the Hessenberg matrix $\mathbf{H}$ in the following is replaced by the symmetric tri-diagonal matrix $\mathbf{T}$.

```
>> G0=eye(4);   G1=eye(4);   G2=eye(4);     H=H0;   sigma=18.1697;

>> [c,s]=givens_(H(1,1)-sigma,H(2,1));   G=[c,s;-s,c];   G0(1:2,1:2)=G;
>> H=G0'*H*G0
H =       %H(3,1) becomes nonzero.
   -1.9807     4.3367     1.7934    -0.7191
   -0.3296    17.5829     3.1027    -5.4770
```

```
    2.1855     3.8911    -0.4380    -2.9149
         0          0     0.8181     1.8359

>> [c,s]=givens_(H(2,1),H(3,1));   G=[c,s;-s,c];  G1(2:3,2:3)=G;
>> H=G1'*H*G1
H =      %H(3,1)->0, H(4,2) becomes nonzero.
   -1.9807    -1.1266     4.5556    -0.7191
   -2.2102    -1.0685    -1.0783     2.0656
         0    -0.2899    18.2134    -5.8505
         0    -0.8090     0.1220     1.8359

>> [c,s]=givens_(H(3,2),H(4,2));   G=[c,s;-s,c];  G2(3:4,3:4)=G;
>> H=G2'*H*G2
H =      %H(4,2)=0, H(4,3)~0 by almost exact shift.
   -1.9807    -1.1266    -0.8599     4.5312
   -2.2102    -1.0685    -1.5807    -1.7119
         0     0.8594     1.8804    -5.9749
         0    -0.0000    -0.0024    18.1688
```

In both the explicit and implicit shifts, we see that first column of both $\mathbf{Q}$s are determined by the call to givens_(H(1,1)-sigma,H(2,1)). The final $\mathbf{H}$ by the implicit shift is essentially equal to the final $\mathbf{H}$ by the explicit shift. More precisely the two $\mathbf{H}$s are related by $\mathbf{D}'\mathbf{H}\mathbf{D}$, where $\mathbf{D} = \text{diag}(\pm 1, \pm 1, \ldots, \pm 1)$. This is the implicit Q theorem, which is discussed in Section 3.5.

In reality, we do not know the exact shift. We use the eigenvalues of $\mathbf{H}(n-1:n, n-1:n)$ to estimate the shift. For an unsymmetric real matrix, its eigenvalues can be complex conjugate. Using a real σ as the shift in the QR iteration will not accelerate the convergence. If we want to keep the real arithmetic, we can use the double shifts,

$$
\begin{aligned}
\mathbf{H}_1 - \sigma_1 \mathbf{I} &= \mathbf{Q}_1 \mathbf{R}_1, \\
\mathbf{H}_{1.5} &= \mathbf{R}_1 \mathbf{Q}_1 + \sigma_1 \mathbf{I} = \mathbf{Q}_1' \mathbf{H}_1 \mathbf{Q}_1, \\
\mathbf{H}_{1.5} - \sigma_2 \mathbf{I} &= \mathbf{Q}_2 \mathbf{R}_2, \\
\mathbf{H}_2 &= \mathbf{R}_2 \mathbf{Q}_2 + \sigma_2 \mathbf{I} = \mathbf{Q}_2' \mathbf{H}_{1.5} \mathbf{Q}_2 = \mathbf{Q}_2' \mathbf{Q}_1' \mathbf{H}_1 \mathbf{Q}_1 \mathbf{Q}_2.
\end{aligned}
\tag{6.7}
$$

Using Eq. (6.7), we can show that

$$
\mathbf{Q}_{12} \mathbf{R}_{12} = \mathbf{Q}_1 \mathbf{Q}_2 \mathbf{R}_2 \mathbf{R}_1 = \mathbf{Q}_1 \left(\mathbf{H}_{1.5} - \sigma_2 \mathbf{I} \right) \mathbf{R}_1 = \mathbf{H}_1^2 - (\sigma_1 + \sigma_2) \mathbf{H}_1 + \sigma_1 \sigma_2 \mathbf{I}.
$$

If σ_1 and σ_2 are the complex conjugate eigenvalues of $\mathbf{H}(n-1:n, n-1:n)$, then

$$
\begin{aligned}
s &= \sigma_1 + \sigma_2 = H(n-1, n-1) + H(n, n), \\
t &= \sigma_1 \sigma_2 = H(n-1, n-1)H(n, n) - H(n-1, n)H(n, n-1)
\end{aligned}
$$

are real numbers. If we form the matrix $\mathbf{M} = \mathbf{H}_1^2 - (\sigma_1 + \sigma_2) \mathbf{H}_1 + \sigma_1 \sigma_2 \mathbf{I}$ and apply a QR decomposition $\mathbf{M} = \mathbf{Q}_{12} \mathbf{R}_{12}$, then $\mathbf{H}_2 = \mathbf{Q}_{12}' \mathbf{H}_1 \mathbf{Q}_{12}$ is the Hessenberg matrix obtained by the QR iteration with double shifts. This is the explicit double shift, which is illustrated as follows:

```
>> H=H0;   s=H(3,3)+H(4,4);   t=H(3,3)*H(4,4)-H(3,4)*H(4,3);
>> M=H*H-s*H+t*eye(4)
M =
    49.1828   -70.5027   -16.1916    28.3479
  -136.9813   258.3841    41.1256  -107.3832
```

```
  -43.0381    56.9740    15.9923   -22.8832
         0     3.6512          0          0
```

```
>> [Q12,R12]=QR_(M);
```

```
>> H=Q12'*H*Q12
H =
    18.2958     1.3591     5.4817     4.4442
    -1.9030    -3.1281    -0.6443     1.9439
     0.0000     0.1623     0.2863    -0.2547
    -0.0000     0.0000     1.2043     1.5460
```

It is expensive to form $\mathbf{M}$ explicitly. The better alternative is to use the implicit double shifts based on the implicit Q theorem. In $\mathbf{H}_2 = \mathbf{Q}'\mathbf{H}_1\mathbf{Q}$, if we keep $\mathbf{H}_1$ and $\mathbf{H}_2$ the Hessenberg forms and $\mathbf{Q}(:,1)$ equals to $\mathbf{Q}_{12}(:,1)$ within $\mathbf{Q}_{12}\mathbf{R}_{12} = \mathbf{M}$, then $\mathbf{Q}'\mathbf{H}_1\mathbf{Q}$ and $\mathbf{Q}'_{12}\mathbf{H}_1\mathbf{Q}_{12}$ are essentially equal.

First, we show that $\mathbf{M}(:,1) = (\mathbf{H}_1 - \sigma_1\mathbf{I})(\mathbf{H}_1 - \sigma_2\mathbf{I})\mathbf{I}(:,1)$ can be calculated in $O(1)$ operations as follows:

$$\mathbf{M}(:,1) = (\mathbf{H}_1 - \sigma_1\mathbf{I})\begin{bmatrix} H_{11} - \sigma_2 \\ H_{21} \\ 0 \\ \vdots \\ 0 \end{bmatrix} = \begin{bmatrix} H_{11}^2 + H_{12}H_{21} - (\sigma_1 + \sigma_2)H_{11} + \sigma_1\sigma_2 \\ H_{21}(H_{11} + H_{22} - \sigma_1 - \sigma_2) \\ H_{21}H_{32} \\ 0 \\ \vdots \\ 0 \end{bmatrix}. \qquad (6.8)$$

Second, we construct an orthogonal matrix $\mathbf{G}_0$ such that $\mathbf{G}_0'\mathbf{M}(:,1) = \|\mathbf{M}(:,1)\|_2\mathbf{I}(:,1)$. Then we calculate $\mathbf{G}_0'\mathbf{H}_1\mathbf{G}_0$. Third, we apply $n-2$ orthogonal similarity transformations to recover the destroyed Hessenberg form of $\mathbf{G}_0'\mathbf{H}_1\mathbf{G}_0$. In the following, we use a simple example to illustrate the implicit double shifts.

```
>> H=H0;   s=H(3,3)+H(4,4);   t=H(3,3)*H(4,4)-H(3,4)*H(4,3);
%s=sigma1+sigma2, t=sigma1*sigma2
>> m1=[H(1,1)*H(1,1)+H(1,2)*H(2,1)-s*H(1,1)+t;
      H(2,1)*(H(1,1)+H(2,2)-s);
      H(2,1)*H(3,2);
      0];
```

```
>> G0=householder_(m1,1,1,'long');
>> G0'*m1
ans =    %just verify
  -151.7732
          0
    -0.0000
          0
```

```
>> H=G0'*H*G0
H =     %H(3:4,1) becomes nonzero.
    18.2958    -2.5677    -2.7562    -6.1203
     1.5744    -2.7236     0.5648     0.4453
    -1.0435     2.1331    -0.4081    -1.1640
     0.2320    -0.1581     0.7684     1.8359
```

```
>> G1=householder_(H(:,1),2,1,'long');
>> H=G1'*H*G1
```

```
H =        %H(3,1)=>0
   18.2958     1.3591    -3.9345    -5.8584
   -1.9030    -3.1281     1.1869    -1.6688
    0.0000    -0.1551     0.1283    -0.6903
         0    -0.0477     0.7687     1.7040

>> G2=householder_(H(:,2),3,1,'long');
>> H=G2'*H*G2
H =        %H restores upper Hessenberg, with sub-diagonal reduced.
   18.2958     1.3591     5.4817    -4.4442
   -1.9030    -3.1281    -0.6443    -1.9439
   -0.0000     0.1623     0.2863     0.2547
   -0.0000     0.0000    -1.2043     1.5460
```

Note the commonality of this **H** and the **H** obtained by the explicit double shift.

6.4.5 MATLAB IMPLEMENTATIONS OF QR ITERATIONS ALGORITHMS

We put everything we discussed in this section together to two MATLAB functions, eigUnsymByQR_.m for unsymmetric matrices, and eigSymByQR_.m for symmetric matrices. In each function, the economy is made in the matrix product by the Givens or Householder matrix. Each function contains an input argument format, which controls the calculation of the Schur vectors (for unsymmetric matrix) and eigenvectors (for symmetric matrix). If format='long', the Schur vectors or eigenvectors are calculated. If format='brief', the Schur vectors or eigenvectors are not calculated.

Algorithm 6.7

$\mathbf{AV} = \mathbf{V}\lambda$, A = A' by QR iterations.

```
function [A,U] = eigUnsymByQR_(A,tol,format)

[m,n] = size(A);
[U,A] = QHQtByHouseholder_(A,tol,format);

k = 1;  l = m;  o = 0;
while k<l-1        %Apply QR step to A(k:l,k:l)
    k = 1;  o = 0;
    for i=l:-1:2        %find lower subdiagonal=0
        if (abs(A(i,i-1)) > tol*(abs(A(i-1,i-1))+abs(A(i,i))))
            if (o == 0) o = 1; else l = i + 1; break; end
        else
            if (o == 0) l = l - 1; else l = l - 2; end
            A(i,i-1) = 0;   o = 0;
        end
    end
    for i=l:-1:2        %find upper subdiagonal=0
        if (abs(A(i,i-1)) <= tol*(abs(A(i-1,i-1))+abs(A(i,i))))
            A(i,i-1) = 0;   k = i;  break;
        end
    end
    if (k >= l-1) continue; end
    A1 = A(l-1,l-1);   A2 = A(l,l-1);   A3 = A(l-1,l);   A4 = A(l,l);
    eta = A1 + A4;   tau = A1*A4 - A2*A3;        %double shifts
    h1 = A(k,k)*A(k,k) + A(k,k+1)*A(k+1,k) - eta*A(k,k) + tau;
    h2 = A(k+1,k)*(A(k,k)+A(k+1,k+1)-eta);
    h3 = A(k+1,k)*A(k+2,k+1);
```

```
      for i=k:l-1
          if (i < l-1) [h,beta] = householder_([h1;h2;h3]);   rc = i:i+2;
          else         [h,beta] = householder_([h1;h2]);      rc = i:i+1;  end
          betah = beta*h;
          for j=max(k,i-1):l    %H22=Z*H22
              Hj = A(rc,j);    A(rc,j) = Hj - (h'*Hj)*betah;
          end
          for j=k:l             %H22=H22*Z
              Hj = A(j,rc);    A(j,rc) = Hj - (Hj*h)*betah';
          end
          if (~strcmp(format,'brief'))
              for j=1:k-1       %H12=H12*Z
                  Hj = A(j,rc);    A(j,rc) = Hj - (Hj*h)*betah';
              end
              for j=l+1:n       %H23=Z*H23
                  Hj = A(rc,j);    A(rc,j) = Hj - (h'*Hj)*betah;
              end
              for j=1:m         %U=U*Z
                  Uj = U(j,rc);    U(j,rc) = Uj - (Uj*h)*betah';
              end
          end
          h1 = A(i+1,i);
          if (i < l-1) h2 = A(i+2,i); end
          if (i < l-2) h3 = A(i+3,i); end
      end
end

k = 1;  l = m;
while k < l    %Reduce 2x2 diagonal blocks to triangle if possible
    if (abs(A(l,l-1)) > tol*(abs(A(l-1,l-1))+abs(A(l,l))))
        [Lambda,G,res] = eig2x2_(A(l-1:l,l-1:l),'schur');
        if (res < 3)     %res=3: cannot reduce
            A(l-1:l,l-1:l) = Lambda;
            if (~strcmp(format,'brief'))
                A(l-1:l,l+1:n) = G'*A(l-1:l,l+1:n);
                A(1:l-2,l-1:l) = A(1:l-2,l-1:l)*G;
                U(:,l-1:l) = U(:,l-1:l)*G;
            end
        end
        l = l - 2;
    else %if(eta*eta-4.0*tau < 0.0)       %complex eigenvalues
        A(l,l-1) = 0;   l = l - 1;
    end
end

if (strcmp(format0,'long')) [A,U] = eigvec_(A0,A,[],tol); end %eigenvector
```

Algorithm 6.8

$\mathbf{AV} = \mathbf{V}\lambda, A=A'$ by QR iterations.

```
function [A,U] = eigSymByQR_(A,tol,format)

if (exist('tol','var') == 0) tol = sqrt(eps); end
if (~exist('format','var') || isempty(format)) format = 'long'; end
if (~iscell(A))
    [m,n] = size(A);
```

```
        [U,A] = QTQtByHouseholder_(A,tol,format);  A=full2band_(A,1,1);
else    %A in band: {B,1,1,m,n}
    m = A{4};  n = A{5};  A = A{1};
    if (strcmp(format,'long')) U = eye(m); end
end
if (m ~= n) error('eigSymByQR_:_matrix_size_error.'); end

k = 1; l = m;
while k<l     %Apply QR step to A(k:l,k:l)
    k = 1;
    for i=l:-1:2
        if (abs(A(i,1)) > tol*(abs(A(i-1,2))+abs(A(i,2)))) l = i; break; end
        l = l - 1;
    end
    for i=l:-1:2
        if (abs(A(i,1)) <= tol*(abs(A(i-1,2))+abs(A(i,2)))) k = i; break; end
    end
    if (k >= l) break; end
    T11 = A(l-1,2); T21 = A(l,1);  T22 = A(l,2);
    d = 0.5*(T11-T22);  e = sqrt(d*d+T21*T21);
    if (d >= 0.0) sigma = T22-T21*T21/(d+e); else sigma = T22-T21*T21/(d-e); end
    a1 = A(k,2)-sigma;  a2 = A(k+1,1);
    for i=k:l-1
        [c,s] = givens_(a1,a2);                %Z=[c s;-s c].
        cc = c*c; ss = s*s; cs2 = 2*c*s;   %A(i:i+1,i:i+1)=Z'*A(i:i+1,i:i+1)*Z
        if (i > k) A(i,1) = c*A(i,1) - s*a2; end
        T11 = A(i,2); T21 = A(i+1,1);  T22 = A(i+1,2);
        A(i,2)   = cc*T11 + ss*T22 - cs2*T21;
        A(i+1,2) = ss*T11 + cc*T22 + cs2*T21;
        A(i+1,1) = (cc-ss)*T21 + c*s*(T11-T22);
        a1 = A(i+1,1);
        if (i < l-1) a2 = -s*A(i+2,1); A(i+2,1) = c*A(i+2,1); end
        if (strcmp(format,'long'))     %U(:,i:i+1)=U(:,i:i+1)*Z
            for j=1:m
                Uji = U(j,i);   Uji1 = U(j,i+1);
                U(j,i) = c*Uji - s*Uji1;  U(j,i+1) = s*Uji + c*Uji1;
            end
        end
    end
end
A = A(:,2);
```

We use the unsymmetric matrix **A** in eigUnsymByQR_.m and the symmetric matrix **B** in eigUnsymByQR_.m. The output is shown below.

```
>> [S,U]=eigUnsymByQR_(A,100*eps,'short')
S =
    18.1697    3.0407    0.6509    7.0480
         0   -2.9685   -1.9892    1.3768
    0.0000         0    0.4351   -1.3432
         0         0         0    1.3637
U =
    0.2696    0.5797    0.7037    0.3097
    0.6699    0.3874   -0.3408   -0.5339
    0.2239    0.1750   -0.5694    0.7714
    0.6546   -0.6951    0.2537    0.1549
```

```
>> norm(U'*U-eye(4))
=   2.5183e-015              %right U
>> norm(U*S*U'-A)
=   2.1027e-014              %right S
>> [D,U]=eigSymByQR_(B,100*eps,'long')
D =
   18.9999
   -3.3637
   -0.1120
    1.4759
U =
    0.3718      0.6987      0.5807     -0.1909
    0.5755      0.2793     -0.7538     -0.1501
    0.3810     -0.0315      0.0962      0.9190
    0.6208     -0.6579      0.2920     -0.3105

>> norm(U'*U-eye(4))
=   8.0212e-016              %right U
>> norm(U*diag(D)*U'-B)
=   5.1650e-015              %right D
```

For `format='brief'`, the output is the following. Notice the difference of S to the S calculated for `format='long'`.

```
>> [S,U]=eigUnsymByQR_(A,100*eps,'brief')      >> [D,U]=eigSymByQR_(B,100*eps,'brief')
S =                                            D =
   18.1697      3.0407      1.1003     6.9920      18.9999
        0      -2.9685     -1.8971     1.5011      -3.3637
    0.0000           0      0.4351    -1.3432      -0.1120
        0           0           0     1.3637       1.4759
U =                                            U =
     []                                             []
```

6.5 CALCULATION OF EIGENVECTORS BY INVERSE ITERATIONS

In `eigUnsymByQR_.m` and `eigSymByQR_.m`, if the input argument `format='brief'`, the Schur vectors U in $U'AU = S$ are not calculated. Approximately, the total computation is proportional to $10n^3$. If `format='long'`, the Schur vectors are accumulated in QR iterations. Approximately, the total computation is proportional to $25n^3$. Thus, if only eigenvalues are needed, setting `format='brief'` is very economical. Even if less than 25% eigenvectors are sought, it is still more economical not to accumulate the Schur vectors in QR iterations. Instead the inverse iteration algorithm presented below should be followed.

Assume $A \in R^{n \times n}$ is diagonalizable. $V^{-1}AV = \lambda$, where V are the eigenvectors and λ are the eigenvalues. An arbitrary vector $v \in R^n$ can be decomposed in the directions of V, that is, $v = V(V'v) = Vu$.

Let $\mu \in R$ and $A - \mu I$ is non-singular. $w = (A - \mu I)^{-1} v$ is decomposed in the directions of V,

$$w = (A - \mu I)^{-1} v = \left(V\lambda V^{-1} - \mu I\right)^{-1} v = V(\lambda - \mu I)^{-1} u = \sum_{i=1}^{n} \frac{u_i}{\lambda_i - \mu} V(:,i).$$

Similarly $(A - \mu I)^{-k} v, k = 1,2,\ldots$ is decomposed in the directions of V,

$$w = (A - \mu I)^{-k} v = \sum_{l=1}^{n} \frac{u_l}{(\lambda_l - \mu)^k} V(:,l). \tag{6.9}$$

Clearly if μ is much closer to λ_j than to the other eigenvalues and $u_j \neq 0$, $(\mathbf{A} - \mu \mathbf{I})^{-k} \mathbf{v}$ is very close to $\mathbf{V}(:,j)$. Eq. (6.9) is the basis of inverse iteration algorithm to find the eigenvector from the corresponding eigenvalue of $\mathbf{A}$. The inverse iteration algorithm is just the power iteration applied to $(\mathbf{A} - \mu \mathbf{I})^{-1}$. To avoid the overflow, $\mathbf{w}$ is normalized for each k. If μ is the calculated eigenvalue by `eigUnsymByQR_.m` or `eigSymByQR_.m`, $k = 1$ is enough to converge $\|\mathbf{A}\mathbf{V}(:,j) - \mathbf{V}(:,j)\mu\|_2 < \tau\|\mathbf{A}\|_\infty$.

For the unsymmetric $\mathbf{A} \in \mathbb{R}^{n \times n}$, λ_j and $\mathbf{V}(:,j)$ can be complex. We write $\lambda_j = \xi + i\eta$ and $\mathbf{V}(:,j) = \mathbf{v}_1 + i\mathbf{v}_2$. The eigen pair satisfy the following equation:

$$\mathbf{A}\,(\mathbf{v}_1 + i\mathbf{v}_2) = (\mathbf{v}_1 + i\mathbf{v}_2)\,(\xi + i\eta)$$

or equivalently,

$$\begin{bmatrix} \mathbf{A} - \xi\mathbf{I} & \eta\mathbf{I} \\ -\eta\mathbf{I} & \mathbf{A} - \xi\mathbf{I} \end{bmatrix} \begin{bmatrix} \mathbf{v}_1 \\ \mathbf{v}_2 \end{bmatrix} = \begin{bmatrix} \mathbf{0} \\ \mathbf{0} \end{bmatrix}. \tag{6.10}$$

The inverse iteration is now applied to $\begin{bmatrix} \mathbf{A} - \xi\mathbf{I} & \eta\mathbf{I} \\ -\eta\mathbf{I} & \mathbf{A} - \xi\mathbf{I} \end{bmatrix}$.

`eigvec_.m` implements the inverse iteration algorithm. For the conciseness, only the Gauss elimination algorithm is adopted for the equation solution. The input argument `algo` is not used in `eigvec_.m` but can be used for its extension to consider many other equation solution algorithms. Especially more efficient algorithms should be used if the input matrix A to `eigvec_.m` is symmetric or upper Hessenberg.

Algorithm 6.9

Find eigenvector **V**, $\mathbf{AV} = \mathbf{VS}$, inverse iterations.

```
function [Lambda,V] = eigvec_(A,S,V,tol)

[m,n] = size(A);  [k0,l0] = size(S);  k = max(k0,l0);  l = min(k0,l0);
Lambda = zeros(k,1);  D = diag(A);  smax = max(1.0, max(abs(D)));  j = 1;

while (j <= k)
    if (l == 1)
        s = S(j);   t = 0;
    elseif (k>=2 && l==2)
        if (j==k || abs(S(j,2))<tol*abs(S(j,1)))
            s = S(j,1);   t = 0.0;
        else
            s = S(j,1)+S(j+1,2);   t = S(j,1)*S(j+1,2)-S(j,2)*S(j+1,1);
        end
    else %if(k == 1)
        if(j==k || abs(S(j+1,j))<tol*(abs(S(j,j))+abs(S(j+1,j+1))))  %real
            s = S(j,j);   t = 0;
        else
            s = S(j,j)+S(j+1,j+1);   t = S(j,j)*S(j+1,j+1)-S(j,j+1)*S(j+1,j);
        end
    end
    if (t == 0)      %real
        for i=1:m A(i,i) = D(i) - s; end
        smax = max(smax,abs(s));
        v = V(:,j);   normv = norm(v);   v = v/normv;
        v = mdivideByGauss_(A,v,1,tol*tol);            %Gauss
        normv = norm(v);   v = v/normv;   Av = A*v;   s = s+v'*Av;
        for i=1:m A(i,i) = D(i) - s; end
        Lambda(j,1) = s;   V(:,j) = v;   j = j + 1;
```

```
    else %if(t~=0) %complex eigenvalue
        sr = 0.5*s;   si = 0.5*sqrt(4.0*t-s*s);   smax = max(smax,sqrt(sr*sr+si*si));
        uv = [V(:,j); V(:,j+1)];   uvnorm = norm(uv);
        u = uv(1:n)/uvnorm;   v = uv(n+1:2*n)/uvnorm;
        for i=1:m A(i,i) = D(i) - sr; end
        uv = mdivideByGauss_([A,si*eye(n);-si*eye(n),A],[u;v],1,tol*tol);
        normuv = norm(uv);   u = uv(1:n)/normuv;   v = uv(n+1:2*n)/normuv;
        Auv = [A*u+si*v;-si*u+A*v];
        sr = sr + [u',v']*Auv;   si = si + [-v',u']*Auv;
        for i=1:m A(i,i) = D(i) - sr; end
        if (size(Lambda,2) == 1) Lambda = [Lambda,zeros(k,1)]; end
        Lambda(j:j+1,:) = [sr,si; -si,sr];   V(:,j) = u;   V(:,j+1) = v;   j = j + 2;
    end
end
```

The following shows the testing matrices for `eigvec_.m`.

```
>> A = [0.8147    0.9575    0.4218    0.6787    0.2769    0.4387    0.7094    0.9597;
        0.9058    0.9649    0.9157    0.7577    0.0462    0.3816    0.7547    0.3404;
        0.1270    0.1576    0.7922    0.7431    0.0971    0.7655    0.2760    0.5853;
        0.9134    0.9706    0.9595    0.3922    0.8235    0.7952    0.6797    0.2238;
        0.6324    0.9572    0.6557    0.6555    0.6948    0.1869    0.6551    0.7513;
        0.0975    0.4854    0.0357    0.1712    0.3171    0.4898    0.1626    0.2551;
        0.2785    0.8003    0.8491    0.7060    0.9502    0.4456    0.1190    0.5060;
        0.5469    0.1419    0.9340    0.0318    0.0344    0.6463    0.4984    0.6991];
>> B = 0.5*(A+A');
```

Only eigenvalues are calculated for **A** and **B**. Because `format='brief'`, no Schur vectors are calculated.

```
>> S=eigUnsymByQR_(A,100*eps,'brief')
S =       %Schur form: diagonal blocks show eigenvalues.
    4.3239    0.2843   -0.4169   -0.9137   -0.1842    0.4017    0.7651   -0.6979
         0   -0.8288   -0.0191    0.0157    0.1249    0.0206   -0.0232    0.0913
    0.0000         0   -0.3810   -0.1379   -0.0902    0.2839   -0.3360   -0.7244
    0.0000         0         0    0.2571    0.7113   -0.2575    0.0983   -0.1327
   -0.0000         0    0.0000   -0.2569    0.1442   -0.4415   -0.3623   -0.0317
    0.0000    0.0000   -0.0000         0         0    0.6249   -0.6125    0.1349
    0.0000   -0.0000    0.0000   -0.0000         0         0    0.4147    0.0253
    0.0000    0.0000   -0.0000   -0.0000         0    0.0000   -0.0923    0.4117
```

```
>> D=eigSymByQR_(B,100*eps,'brief')'
D =       %Diagonal form: eigenvalues
    4.4792   -0.8413    0.8552   -0.1415    0.5829    0.2072    0.4142   -0.5892
```

To calculate the selected eigenvectors, we apply `eigvec_.m` in the following way.

```
>> [s1,v1]=eigvec_(A,S(1,1))       %S(1,1) is real.
s1 =       %s1 is slightly more accurate than S(1,1).
    4.3239
v1 =       %eigenvector corresponding to s1.
    0.4178
    0.4096
    0.2398
    0.4538
    0.4277
    0.1511
    0.3702
    0.2268
```

```
>> norm(A*v1-v1*s1)
ans =          %verified.
  5.4390e-016

>> [S45,V45]=eigvec_(A,S(4:5,4:5))  %S(4:5,4:5) is conjugate complex.
S45 =          %(1,1)+/-(1i)(1,2) eigenvalues
    0.2007    0.4237
   -0.4237    0.2007
V45 =          %v4(:,1)+/-(1i)v4(:,2) eigenvectors/.
    0.3662    0.1259
   -0.3830    0.0271
   -0.3962   -0.2864
    0.2918   -0.2104
    0.2845    0.2853
    0.2898   -0.0452
    0.0399    0.0751
   -0.1841    0.2115
>> norm(A*V45-V45*S45)
ans =          %verified.
  2.7904e-016
```

The following shows the way to calculate eigenvectors corresponding to both real and complex eigenvalues. The second input argument to eigvec_.m has two columns. For the real eigenvalue, set zero to the corresponding second column.

```
>> [S145,V145]=eigvec_(A,[S(1,1),0;S(4:5,4:5)])
S145 =
    4.3239         0    %S145(1,2)=0 => S145(1,1) real eigenvalue
    0.2007    0.4237    %S145(2:3,:) complex conjugate eigenvalue
   -0.4237    0.2007
V145 =
    0.4178   -0.1132    0.3703
    0.4096   -0.0404   -0.3818
    0.2398    0.2725   -0.4059
    0.4538    0.2204    0.2844
    0.4277   -0.2753    0.2942
    0.1511    0.0552    0.2880
    0.3702   -0.0737    0.0425
    0.2268   -0.2178   -0.1767

>> norm(A*V145(:,1)-V145(:,1)*S145(1,1))
=   2.4425e-015
>> norm(A*V145(:,2:3)-V145(:,2:3)*S145(2:3,:))
=   7.0037e-016
```

The call of eigvec_(A,S) calculates all the eigenvectors of **A** from **S**.

```
>> [Sv,V]=eigvec_(A,S)
Sv =
    4.3239         0    %real
   -0.8288         0    %real
   -0.3810         0    %real
    0.2007    0.4237    %complex
   -0.4237    0.2007
    0.6249         0    %real
    0.4132    0.0483    %complex
   -0.0483    0.4132
```

```
V =
   -0.4178    0.3696    0.2445   -0.0960    0.3751   -0.2681   -0.2688   -0.4411
   -0.4096   -0.0955    0.2569   -0.0579   -0.3796    0.4780    0.4530    0.1807
   -0.2398    0.3609    0.2023    0.2536   -0.4179   -0.0399    0.1381    0.1905
   -0.4538   -0.6842   -0.1344    0.2332    0.2739    0.3134   -0.0271    0.1203
   -0.4277    0.1759    0.0636   -0.2615    0.3066   -0.1895   -0.4084   -0.0501
   -0.1511    0.1083   -0.0397    0.0684    0.2852    0.1978    0.1685    0.0154
   -0.3702    0.1620   -0.8936   -0.0717    0.0459    0.0767   -0.1159    0.2200
   -0.2268   -0.4324    0.1055   -0.2257   -0.1665   -0.7204   -0.2324   -0.3332

>> norm(A*V(:,1:3)-V(:,1:3)*diag(Sv(1:3,1)))
=   3.0507e-015
>> norm(A*V(:,4:5)-V(:,4:5)*Sv(4:5,:))
=   5.2260e-016
>> norm(A*V(:,6)-V(:,6)*Sv(6,1))
=   9.3353e-016
>> norm(A*V(:,7:8)-V(:,7:8)*Sv(7:8,:))
=   6.8325e-016
```

For the symmetric matrix, the second input argument of eigvec_.m is simply one column or row vector.

```
>> [d125,V125]=eigvec_(B,[D(1:2);D(5)])
d125 =
    4.4792
   -0.8413
    0.5829
V125 =
    0.3894   -0.3900   -0.6683
    0.4296    0.1130   -0.1277
    0.3577   -0.3707    0.3858
    0.3978    0.6363    0.2571
    0.3368   -0.1063    0.3628
    0.2382   -0.1578    0.0650
    0.3432   -0.2300    0.1648
    0.2993    0.4513   -0.3989
>> norm(B*V125-V125*diag(d125))
=   1.2027e-013

>> [d,V]=eigvec_(B,D);
>> norm(B*V-V*diag(d))
=   3.0125e-014
```

6.6 CALCULATION OF INVARIANT SUBSPACE BY EIGENVALUE REORDERING

In Section 6.4, we presented the QR iteration algorithms eigUnsymByQR_.m and eigSymByQR_.m to calculate the Schur form of a general square matrix or a symmetric matrix. For a real square matrix $\mathbf{A}$, there exists a real orthogonal matrix $\mathbf{U}$, such that $\mathbf{A} = \mathbf{U}\mathbf{S}\mathbf{U}'$, where $\mathbf{S}$ is a real upper quasi-triangular matrix, called $\mathbf{A}$'s real Schur form. If $\mathbf{A}$ is symmetric, $\mathbf{S}$ must be diagonal.

If we partition $\mathbf{U}$ and $\mathbf{S}$ conformally as

$$\mathbf{A}\begin{bmatrix} \mathbf{U}_1 & \mathbf{U}_2 \end{bmatrix} = \begin{bmatrix} \mathbf{U}_1 & \mathbf{U}_2 \end{bmatrix} \begin{bmatrix} \mathbf{S}_{11} & \mathbf{S}_{12} \\ \mathbf{0} & \mathbf{S}_{22} \end{bmatrix}$$

the first column of the left and right hand sides shows that

$$\mathbf{A}\mathbf{U}_1 = \mathbf{U}_1\mathbf{S}_{11}.$$

If we assume $\lambda(\mathbf{S}_{11}) \cup \lambda(\mathbf{S}_{22}) = \varnothing$, the above equation means that $\mathbf{U}_1$ is the orthogonal bases of the invariant subspace of $\mathbf{A}$ corresponding to the eigenvalues contained in $\mathbf{S}_{11}$.

If we need to calculate the orthogonal bases of $\mathbf{A}$ corresponding to the requested eigenvalues $\lambda_{en}(\mathbf{A})$, we need that $\lambda(\mathbf{S}_{11}) = \lambda_{en}(\mathbf{A})$ and the eigenvalues of $\mathbf{S}_{11}$ are ordered as specified in en. Unfortunately, QR iteration algorithm cannot order the eigenvalues in a specified way. Clearly we need to perform further orthogonal similarity transformations to $\mathbf{S}$ that preserve its upper quasi-triangular form with the requested eigenvalues ordering. An iterative algorithm to achieve this goal is discussed in [66]. A direct algorithm is also possible, see [21, 54]. The MATLAB code reorderSchur_.m presented below is based on an improved direct algorithm discussed in [6].

First, we see that $\mathbf{S}$ can be block diagonalized by the following non-orthogonal similarity transformation:

$$\begin{bmatrix} \mathbf{S}_{11} & \mathbf{S}_{12} \\ \mathbf{0} & \mathbf{S}_{22} \end{bmatrix} = \begin{bmatrix} \mathbf{I}_1 & -\mathbf{X} \\ \mathbf{0} & \mathbf{I}_2 \end{bmatrix} \begin{bmatrix} \mathbf{S}_{11} & \mathbf{0} \\ \mathbf{0} & \mathbf{S}_{22} \end{bmatrix} \begin{bmatrix} \mathbf{I}_1 & \mathbf{X} \\ \mathbf{0} & \mathbf{I}_2 \end{bmatrix}, \tag{6.11}$$

where $\mathbf{X}$ is the solution of the Sylvester equation

$$\mathbf{S}_{11}\mathbf{X} - \mathbf{X}\mathbf{S}_{22} = \mathbf{S}_{12}. \tag{6.12}$$

Under the condition that $\lambda(\mathbf{S}_{11}) \cup \lambda(\mathbf{S}_{22}) = \varnothing$, the solution $\mathbf{X}$ exists and is unique.

Second, we determine an orthogonal matrix $\mathbf{Q}$ such that

$$\mathbf{Q}' \begin{bmatrix} -\mathbf{X} \\ \mathbf{I}_2 \end{bmatrix} = \begin{bmatrix} \mathbf{R} \\ \mathbf{0} \end{bmatrix}. \tag{6.13}$$

Third, we apply the following similarity transformation by $\mathbf{Q}$:

$$\begin{aligned} \mathbf{Q}'\mathbf{S}\mathbf{Q} &= \mathbf{Q}' \begin{bmatrix} \mathbf{I}_1 & -\mathbf{X} \\ \mathbf{0} & \mathbf{I}_2 \end{bmatrix} \begin{bmatrix} \mathbf{S}_{11} & \mathbf{0} \\ \mathbf{0} & \mathbf{S}_{22} \end{bmatrix} \begin{bmatrix} \mathbf{I}_1 & \mathbf{X} \\ \mathbf{0} & \mathbf{I}_2 \end{bmatrix} \mathbf{Q} = \begin{bmatrix} \mathbf{Q}'_{11} & \mathbf{R} \\ \mathbf{Q}'_{12} & \mathbf{0} \end{bmatrix} \begin{bmatrix} \mathbf{S}_{11} & \mathbf{0} \\ \mathbf{0} & \mathbf{S}_{22} \end{bmatrix} \begin{bmatrix} \mathbf{0} & \mathbf{Q}'^{-1}_{12} \\ \mathbf{R}^{-1} & -\mathbf{R}^{-1}\mathbf{Q}'_{11}\mathbf{Q}'^{-1}_{12} \end{bmatrix} \\ &= \begin{bmatrix} \mathbf{R}\mathbf{S}_{22}\mathbf{R}^{-1} & -\mathbf{R}\mathbf{S}_{22}\mathbf{R}^{-1}\mathbf{Q}'_{11}\mathbf{Q}'^{-1}_{12} \\ \mathbf{0} & \mathbf{Q}'_{12}\mathbf{S}_{11}\mathbf{Q}'^{-1}_{12} \end{bmatrix}. \end{aligned} \tag{6.14}$$

Notice that in Eq. (6.14), the position of eigenvalues of $\mathbf{S}_{11}$ and $\mathbf{S}_{22}$ is swapped.

We can apply Eqs. (6.12)–(6.14) to any two consecutive diagonal blocks of $\mathbf{S}$. Each application will swap the eigenvalues of the two consecutive diagonal blocks. A diagonal block can be either 1×1 or 2×2. Therefore, the eigenvalues swapping have four cases: $1 \times 1 \leftrightarrow 1 \times 1$, $1 \times 1 \leftrightarrow 2 \times 2$, $2 \times 2 \leftrightarrow 1 \times 1$, and $2 \times 2 \leftrightarrow 2 \times 2$. Repeating Eqs. (6.12)–(6.14) to the chosen two consecutive diagonal blocks will put the eigenvalues in any specified order.

The only remaining issue is the solution of Eq. (6.12). It can be shown Eq. (6.12) is equivalent to the following linear equations:

$$(\mathbf{I}_2 \otimes \mathbf{S}_{11} - \mathbf{S}'_{22} \otimes \mathbf{I}_1)[\mathbf{X}(:,1); \mathbf{X}(:,2); \cdots] = [\mathbf{S}_{12}(:,1); \mathbf{S}_{12}(:,2); \cdots], \tag{6.15}$$

where $\otimes$ is the outer product symbol, see Section 1.1.

Algorithm 6.10

Reorder Schur Form **S** so that eigenvalues specified in en to upper left of **S**.

```
function [S,U] = reorderSchur_(S,U,en,tol)

[m,n] = size(S);
if (n == 1)    %S is diagonal
    [S,p] = sort(S);    p0 = 1:m;
    for j=1:length(en)
        if(p0(j) ~= en(j))
            k = find_(p0,en(j),j);
            p0j = p0(j);   p0(j) = p0(k);   p0(k) = p0j;
            sj = S(j);     S(j) = S(k);     S(k) = sj;
            pj = p(j);     p(j) = p(k);     p(k) = pj;
        end
    end
    if (~isempty(U)) U = permute_(p,U,'col'); end
else %if(m==n)%S is quasi upper triangle
    s = zeros(m,1);   pair = zeros(m,1);   j = 1;
    while j <= m    %Check block 1x1 or 2x2
        if j==m || abs(S(j+1,j)) < tol*(abs(S(j,j))+abs(S(j+1,j+1)))
            s(j) = S(j,j);   pair(j) = j;    j = j + 1;
        else
            s(j) = sqrt(S(j,j)*S(j+1,j+1)-S(j,j+1)*S(j+1,j));  s(j+1) = s(j);
            pair(j) = j+1;   pair(j+1) = j;   j = j + 2;
        end
    end
    [s,p] = sort(s);    invp = inv_perm_(p');   rn = [];
    for j=1:length(en)  %en(j)=eig order=>rn(j)=row order
        if (en(j) == 0) continue; end
        l = p(en(j));    pairl = pair(l);
        if (pairl == l)        rn = [rn,l];   k = j;
        elseif (pairl == l-1) rn = [rn,l-1];  k = find_(en,invp(pairl),j);
        elseif (pairl == l+1) rn = [rn,l];    k = find_(en,invp(pairl),j); end
        if (k > j) en(k) = 0; end %keep conjugate complex eig in one block
    end
    rnj = 1;
    for j=1:length(rn)
        l = rn(j);
        if (l == pair(l)) rn12 = 1; else rn12 = 2; end
        while (rnj < l) %permute rn(j) (1x1 or 2x2) to j
            k = l - 1;    %in each step, permute adajacent blocks (k,l)
            if (l==pair(l) && k==pair(k))            %1<->1
                A = S(k,k);   B = S(l,l);   C = S(k,l);
                [q,r] = QR_([C;B-A],'householder',0,tol,'long');
                pair(k:k+1) = [k; k+1];   enk = k + 1;   ll = l;
            elseif(l==pair(l) && k~=pair(k))         %1<->2
                k = k - 1;
                A = S(k:k+1,k:k+1); B = S(l,l); C = S(k:k+1,l);
                A(1,1) = A(1,1) - B;  A(2,2) = A(2,2) - B;
                X = eqs_(A,-C);  [q,r] = QR_([X;1.0],'householder',0,tol,'long');
                pair(k:k+2) = [k; k+2; k+1];   enk = k+1; ll = 1;
            elseif(l~=pair(l) && k==pair(k))         %2<->1
                A = S(k,k);   B = S(l:l+1,l:l+1);   C = S(k,l:l+1);
                B(1,1) = B(1,1) - A;  B(2,2) = B(2,2) - A;
                X = eqs_(B',C');  [q,r] = QR_([X';eye(2)],'householder',0,tol,'long');
                pair(k:k+2) = [k+1; k; k+2];   enk = k+2;   ll = l+1;
```

```
    else %if(l~=pair(l) && k~=pair(k))    %2<->2
        k = k - 1;
        A = S(k:k+1,k:k+1);   B = S(l:l+1,l:l+1);   C = S(k:k+1,l:l+1);
        F = [A(1,1)-B(1,1) A(1,2)        -B(2,1)          0.0;
                A(2,1)        A(2,2)-B(1,1)  0.0          -B(2,1);
                -B(1,2)        0.0        A(1,1)-B(2,2) A(1,2);
                0.0         -B(1,2)        A(2,1)        A(2,2)-B(2,2)];
        f = [C(1,1);C(2,1);C(1,2);C(2,2)];
        x = eqs_(F,-f);   X = [x(1) x(3); x(2) x(4)];
        [q,r] = QR_([X;eye(2)],'householder',0,tol,'long');
        pair(k:k+3) = [k+1; k; k+3; k+2];   enk = k+2; ll = l+1;
    end
    S(k:ll,:) = q'*S(k:ll,:);   S(:,k:ll) = S(:,k:ll)*q;
    if (~isempty(U)) U(:,k:ll) = U(:,k:ll)*q; end
    for i=j+1:length(rn)
        if (rn(i) == k) rn(i) = enk; break; end
    end
    rn(j) = k;  l = k;
    end    %while (j<l)
    rnj = rnj + rn12;
    end   %for j=1:length(rn)
end
```

The input argument en specifies the requested eigenvalues for which the invariant subspaces are sought. Each eigenvalue is identified as its order in the eigenvalue spectrum ordered from small to large. Conjugate complex eigenvalues are ordered according to their absolutes.

In the following, we use the unsymmetric 8×8 matrix $\mathbf{A}$ and symmetric 8×8 matrix $\mathbf{B}$ used in Section 6.5 to demonstrate the reordering of eigenvalues. The eigenvalues are ordered as follows. $\lambda_1(\mathbf{A}) = -0.8288$, $\lambda_8(\mathbf{A}) = 4.3239$. $\lambda_3(\mathbf{A}) = 0.4132 + 0.0483i$, and $\lambda_4(\mathbf{A}) = 0.4132 - 0.0483i$ are conjugate complex and ordered consecutively. Because $\mathbf{B}$ is symmetric, all its eigenvalues are real. $\lambda_1(\mathbf{B}) = -0.8413$, $\lambda_8(\mathbf{B}) = 4.4792$, $\lambda_3(\mathbf{B}) = -0.1415$, $\lambda_4(\mathbf{B}) = 0.2072$.

```
eig(A) =                              eig(B) =
  -0.8288                               -0.8413
  -0.3810                               -0.5892
   0.4132 + 0.0483i                     -0.1415
   0.4132 - 0.0483i                      0.2072
   0.2007 + 0.4237i                      0.4142
   0.2007 - 0.4237i                      0.5829
   0.6249                                0.8552
   4.3239                                4.4792
```

First, we can see that the Schur form of $\mathbf{A}$ is not ordered in $[1,8,3,4]$. That means $\mathbf{U}(:,1:4)$ is not the orthogonal bases of the invariant subspace corresponding to the eigenvalues of $\lambda_{[1,8,3,4]}(\mathbf{A})$.

```
>> [S,U]=eigUnsymByQR_(A,100*eps,'short')
S =
    4.3239     0.2843    -0.4169    0.9137     0.1842     0.4017    -0.7651     0.6979
         0    -0.8288    -0.0191   -0.0157    -0.1249     0.0206     0.0247    -0.0877
    0.0000          0    -0.3810   -0.1379    -0.0902    -0.2834    -0.3090    -0.7327
    0.0000          0          0    0.2571     0.7113     0.3499    -0.2819     0.0255
   -0.0000          0     0.0000   -0.2569     0.1442    -0.3730    -0.2748    -0.0824
    0.0000     0.0000    -0.0000         0          0     0.6249    -0.6151     0.1342
    0.0000    -0.0000     0.0000   -0.0000          0          0     0.4147     0.0253
    0.0000     0.0000    -0.0000   -0.0000          0     0.0000    -0.0923     0.4117
```

U =

0.4178	0.3932	-0.2671	-0.4055	0.0719	0.2021	0.4774	0.4014
0.4096	-0.0730	-0.2987	0.4475	-0.2431	-0.6563	0.0507	0.2122
0.2398	0.3747	-0.2093	0.6170	0.3825	0.3993	-0.1530	-0.2202
0.4538	-0.6602	0.0655	-0.1168	0.5436	0.0042	0.1364	-0.1616
0.4277	0.1998	-0.0944	-0.3708	-0.3192	-0.0852	-0.2541	-0.6760
0.1511	0.1168	0.0311	-0.2505	0.2853	-0.1279	-0.7811	0.4382
0.3702	0.1826	0.8721	0.1721	-0.1443	0.0253	0.0812	0.1063
0.2268	-0.4205	-0.1446	0.1053	-0.5383	0.5872	-0.2151	0.2427

If we need the orthogonal bases of the invariant subspace corresponding to the eigenvalues of $\lambda_{[1,8,3,4]}(\mathbf{A})$, we have to apply some orthogonal similarity transformations to $\mathbf{A}$ to move $\lambda_{[1,8,3,4]}(\mathbf{A})$ to $\mathbf{S}(1:4,1:4)$. The needed orthogonal similarity transformations are calculated by reorderSchur_.m by setting en=[1,8,3,4] in the call to reorderSchur_.m.

```
>> [S,U]=reorderSchur_(S,U,[1,8,3,4],100*eps)
```
S =

-0.8288	-0.2843	0.1058	-0.0939	-0.0564	0.0459	0.1099	-0.0743
-0.0000	4.3239	-0.5302	0.7797	0.0188	-0.7391	0.0644	0.9048
0.0000	0.0000	0.4182	0.0980	0.2430	-0.1571	0.3834	0.0630
-0.0000	0.0000	-0.0241	0.4081	0.6878	-0.2780	-0.1712	-0.0801
-0.0000	0.0000	0.0000	-0.0000	-0.3810	0.2703	0.1586	0.1347
-0.0000	-0.0000	0.0000	-0.0000	-0.0000	0.4673	0.4653	-0.7343
-0.0000	0.0000	0.0000	-0.0000	0.0000	-0.5388	-0.0660	-0.1093
0.0000	0.0000	-0.0000	0.0000	0.0000	0.0000	0.0000	0.6249

U =

0.3696	0.4389	0.4982	0.4323	0.1180	-0.0218	-0.3080	-0.3556
-0.0955	0.4050	-0.5467	0.4693	-0.0972	0.1860	0.4570	-0.2344
0.3609	0.2601	-0.3210	-0.0464	-0.3851	-0.6760	-0.1698	0.2506
-0.6842	0.4167	-0.1024	-0.1886	-0.0975	-0.0067	-0.5316	-0.1413
0.1759	0.4380	0.2823	-0.4542	-0.4701	0.4199	0.2627	0.1576
0.1083	0.1573	-0.1679	0.2688	0.2447	0.3948	-0.3246	0.7362
0.1620	0.3797	-0.1596	-0.4725	0.7269	-0.1389	0.1719	-0.0602
-0.4324	0.2032	0.4539	0.2312	0.0975	-0.3957	0.4254	0.4066

The updated $\mathbf{S}$ displays $\lambda_{[1,8,3,4]}(\mathbf{A})$ in $\mathbf{S}(1:4,1:4)$ and updated $\mathbf{U}(:,1:4)$ is the orthogonal bases of the invariant subspace corresponding to the eigenvalues of $\lambda_{[1,8,3,4]}(\mathbf{A})$.

Because the Schur form of a symmetric matrix is diagonal, its reorder is very simple. We only need to permute the columns of $\mathbf{S}$ and $\mathbf{U}$ according to en=[1,8,3,4].

6.7 SPECIAL ALGORITHMS FOR SYMMETRIC TRI-DIAGONAL MATRIX

A symmetric tri-diagonal matrix which is shown below

$$\mathbf{T} = \begin{bmatrix} T_{11} & T_{12} & & \cdots & & 0 \\ T_{12} & T_{22} & T_{23} & \cdots & & \vdots \\ & \ddots & \ddots & \ddots & & \\ \vdots & & \ddots & \ddots & T_{n-1,n} \\ 0 & \cdots & & T_{n-1,n} & T_{nn} \end{bmatrix} \tag{6.16}$$

can be obtained by QHQt decomposition of a full symmetric matrix. It can also occur naturally in many practical problems. Its eigenvalues can be efficiently found by QR iteration algorithm `eigSymByQR_.m`, see Section 6.4.

In this section, two special algorithms are presented. The first is an algorithm based on the bisection, in which the bisection is determined by the calculation of the determinant. This algorithm is more efficient when only a portion of the eigenvalues is sought. The second algorithm is the divide-and-conquer method that has high parallelism to obtain the whole eigenvalues.

6.7.1 EIGENVALUES BY BISECTION

As it was discussed in Section 1.1.4, the characteristic polynomial of a square matrix is $P_n(x) = \det(\mathbf{A} - x\mathbf{I})$. The eigenvalues of $\mathbf{A}$ are the roots of the nth order polynomial $P_n(x) = 0$. When $\mathbf{A}$ is symmetric tri-diagonal, the calculation of $P_n(x)$ for any x can be recursively calculated. Define $P_0(x) = 1, P_k(x) = \det(\mathbf{T}(1:k,1:k) - x\mathbf{I}), k = 1,\ldots,n$. A direct expansion of the determinant of Eq. (6.16) shows that

$$P_k(x) = (T_{kk} - x)P_{k-1}(x) - T_{k-1,k}^2 P_{k-2}(x). \tag{6.17}$$

According to Eq. (6.17), $P_n(s)$ or $P_n(t)$ can be calculated in $O(n)$ operations. $P_n(\lambda) = 0, \lambda \in [s,t]$, if $P_n(s)P_n(t) \leq 0$. The root λ is found iteratively by the bisection. Assume $\lambda = \frac{s+t}{2}$. The interval $[s,t]$ is continuously reducing size: if $P_n(\lambda)P_n(s) < 0, t = \lambda$; otherwise $s = \lambda$.

To start the bisection, $[s,t]$ is calculated as follows:

$$s = \min_{1 \leq i \leq n} T_{ii} - |T_{i,i+1}| - |T_{i+1,i}|, \quad t = \max_{1 \leq i \leq n} T_{ii} + |T_{i,i+1}| + |T_{i+1,i}|. \tag{6.18}$$

Gershgorin theorem, [29], states that $s \leq \lambda_i \leq t, i = 1,\ldots,n$. Therefore $[s,t]$ defined in Eq. (6.18) provides an initial valid interval for all the eigenvalues.

The efficiency of the bisection for an eigenvalue λ can be improved if more accurate estimation of $[s,t]$ can be obtained. The improved $[s,t]$ for λ can be obtained by using Sturm sequence theorem, also see [29]. In the bisection discussed so far, only the values $P_n(s)$ or $P_n(t)$ are used for halving the interval. However, $P_k(s)$ or $P_k(t), k = 0,1,\ldots,n-1$ also provides the information about the locations of other eigenvalues. Sturm sequence theorem states that $a(s)$ equals to the number of eigenvalues that are less than s, where $a(s)$ is the number of sign changes in the sequence

$$P_0(s), P_1(s), P_2(s),\ldots, P_{n-1}(s), P_n(s).$$

When counting the sign changes, if $P_k(s) = 0$, it is counted as having a different sign to $P_{k-1}(s)$.

Suppose the eigenvalues are ordered as $\lambda_1 \leq \lambda_2 \leq \cdots \lambda_{n-1} \leq \lambda_n$. If $s < \lambda_1, a(s) = 0$. If $\lambda_1 < s < \lambda_2, a(s) = 1, \ldots$. If $\lambda_{n-1} < s < \lambda_n, a(s) = n - 1$. If $\lambda_n < s, a(s) = n$. Therefore, $a(s)$ provides the information about locations of all the eigenvalues. This information is used to update $[s,t]$ for all the eigenvalues.

$a(s)$ defined based on $P_k(s)$ is prone to overflow and underflow. In [8], $a(s)$ is defined based on

$$Q_k(s) = \frac{P_k(s)}{P_{k-1}(s)}, \quad k = 1,\ldots,n.$$

$a(s)$ is now given by the number of negative $Q_k(s)$ for $k = 1,\ldots,n$.

More details of the algorithm are illustrated by the following MATLAB code `eigTridByDet_.m` and the numerical examples.

Algorithm 6.11

Calculate eigenvalues of a tri-diagonal matrix by bisection.

```
function S = eigTridByDet_(T,k,l,tol)

[m,n] = size(T);
smin = T(m,2)-abs(T(m,1));   smax = T(m,2)+abs(T(m,1));       %Gershgorin
for j=m-1:-1:2
    rmax = abs(T(j,1)) + abs(T(j,3));
    smin = min(smin,T(j,2)-rmax);   smax = max(smax,T(j,2)+rmax);
end
smin = min(smin, T(1,2)-abs(T(1,3)));   smax = max(smax, T(1,2)+abs(T(1,3)));
j = l-k+1;   Smin(1:j) = smin;   Smax(1:j) = smax;   S(1:j) = 0.5*(smin+smax);

for j=2:m T(j,1) = T(j,1)*T(j-1,3); end    %algorithm requires product >=0.

for j=l:-1:k              %Calculate S(1:l-k+1)=[Sk...Sl]
    sminj = Smin(j-k+1);    smaxj = Smax(j-k+1);   sj = 0.5*(sminj + smaxj);
    while (smaxj-sminj > 2.0*eps*(abs(sminj)+abs(smaxj)) + tol)
        a = 0;   q = 1;   %S(1:a(sj)) <= sj
        for i=1:m
            if (q ~= 0) q = T(i,2)-sj - T(i,1)/q;
            else        q = T(i,2)-sj - sqrt(T(i,1))/eps; end
            if (q < 0)  a = a + 1; end
        end
        if (a < k)
            for i=k:j
                if (Smin(i-k+1) < sj) Smin(i-k+1) = sj; end   %better s
            end
        elseif (k<=a && a<j)
            for i=k:a
                if (Smax(i-k+1) > sj) Smax(i-k+1) = sj; end %better t
            end
            for i=a+1:j
                if (Smin(i-k+1) < sj) Smin(i-k+1) = sj; end %better s
            end
        else    %a>=j
            for i=k:j
                if (Smax(i-k+1) > sj) Smax(i-k+1) = sj; end %better t
            end
        end
        sminj = Smin(j-k+1);    smaxj = Smax(j-k+1);   sj = 0.5*(sminj+smaxj);
    end
    S(j-k+1) = sj;  %jth smallest eigen value
end
```

The use of eigTridByDet_.m is illustrated with the following simple symmetric tri-diagonal matrix.

```
>> A=rand(8);   A=0.5*(A+A');   [Q,T]=QTQtByHouseholder_(A,100*eps,'long');
>> T=full2band_(T,1,1)
T =
         0      0.8909    -1.2442
   -1.2442      2.7509     1.5280
    1.5280      0.5532     0.6790
    0.6790      0.1054    -0.3283
   -0.3283     -0.2714     0.5428
    0.5428     -0.3707    -0.2003
```

```
      -0.2003    -0.1108     0.1118
       0.1118    -0.3855          0
>> eig(A)'
=    -0.9979    -0.7618    -0.4235    -0.1215     0.1068     0.3993     0.9963     3.9641
```

The input matrix T to eigTridByDet_.m must be in band format. The same eigenvalues are obtained as MATLAB built-in eigenvalue function eig.

```
>> S=eigTridByDet_(T)
S =
     -0.9979    -0.7618    -0.4235    -0.1215     0.1068     0.3993     0.9963     3.9641
```

If only the third to the sixth eigenvalues are sought, the input to eigTridByDet_.m is shown below.

```
>> S=eigTridByDet_(T,3,6)
S =
     -0.4235    -0.1215     0.1068     0.3993
```

The last input argument tol controls the convergence of the bisection.

6.7.2 A DIVIDE-AND-CONQUER ALGORITHM

The symmetric tri-diagonal matrix shown in Eq. (6.16) can be written as follows:

$$\mathbf{T} = \begin{bmatrix} \mathbf{T}_1 & \mathbf{0} \\ \mathbf{0} & \mathbf{T}_2 \end{bmatrix} + \rho\mathbf{u}\mathbf{u}'. \tag{6.19}$$

If we assume $u(m) = u(m + 1) = 1$ and the other components are zeros, that is,

$$\mathbf{u}' = [0, \ldots, 0, 1, 1, 0, \ldots, 0]$$

and further assume $\rho = T(m + 1, m)$, then $T_1(m, m) = T(m, m) - \rho$, $T_2(1, 1) = T(m + 1, m + 1) - \rho$ and other components of $\mathbf{T}_1$ and $\mathbf{T}_2$ are same as the corresponding components of $\mathbf{T}$.

In Eq. (6.19), $\mathbf{T}_1$ and $\mathbf{T}_2$ are two symmetric tri-diagonal matrices with the sizes $m \times m$ and $(n - m) \times (n - m)$, respectively. Suppose we have found the eigen solutions for $\mathbf{T}_1$ and $\mathbf{T}_2$, that is, we have found two orthogonal matrices $\mathbf{Q}_1$ and $\mathbf{Q}_2$ such that $\mathbf{Q}_1'\mathbf{T}_1\mathbf{Q}_1 = \mathbf{D}_1$ and $\mathbf{Q}_2'\mathbf{T}_2\mathbf{Q}_2 = \mathbf{D}_2$ are each diagonal. If we set

$$\mathbf{Q} = \begin{bmatrix} \mathbf{Q}_1 & \mathbf{0} \\ \mathbf{0} & \mathbf{Q}_2 \end{bmatrix} \quad \text{and} \quad \mathbf{D} = \begin{bmatrix} \mathbf{D}_1 & \mathbf{0} \\ \mathbf{0} & \mathbf{D}_2 \end{bmatrix},$$

then

$$\mathbf{Q}'\mathbf{T}\mathbf{Q} = \mathbf{Q}' \left(\begin{bmatrix} \mathbf{T}_1 & \mathbf{0} \\ \mathbf{0} & \mathbf{T}_2 \end{bmatrix} + \rho\mathbf{u}\mathbf{u}' \right) \mathbf{Q} = \mathbf{D} + \rho\mathbf{z}\mathbf{z}', \tag{6.20}$$

where $\mathbf{z} = \mathbf{Q}'\mathbf{u} = \begin{bmatrix} \mathbf{Q}_1(m, :)' \\ \mathbf{Q}_2(1, :)' \end{bmatrix}$.

If we can find the eigen solutions of $\mathbf{D} + \rho\mathbf{z}\mathbf{z}'$, then the eigen solutions of $\mathbf{T}$ can be obtained by Eq. (6.20). The eigen solutions of $\mathbf{T}_1$ and $\mathbf{T}_2$ can be found in parallel. Further their eigen solutions can be recursively computed according to Eqs. (6.19) and (6.20). The recursion stops when the size of $\mathbf{T}$ is equal to 1 or 2 when its eigen solutions are easily calculated. The recursion can stop earlier when the size of $\mathbf{T}$ is smaller than a given value, when its eigen solutions are found by any algorithms presented in previous sections. The algorithm based on Eqs. (6.19) and (6.20) is implemented in eigTridByR1U_.m, in which the algorithm for Eq. (6.20) is implemented in eigDiagByR1U_.m.

Algorithm 6.12

Eigenvalues of tri-diagonal symmetric matrix, by rank-1 update.

```
function [S,Q] = eigTridByR1U_(T,tol,format,minm)

[m,n] = size(T);

if (m == 1)
    S = T(1,2);   Q = 1.0;
elseif (m == 2)
    T11 = T(1,2);   T22 = T(2,2);   T12 = T(1,3);   %T21 = T(2,1);
    [c,s] = eig22_(T11,T22,T12);   cc = c*c;   ss = s*s;   cs = 2.0*c*s;
    S = [cc*T11+ss*T22-cs*T12; cc*T22+ss*T11+cs*T12];
    Q = [c,s;-s,c];
elseif (m<=minm || m+1<minm)
    [S,Q] = eigSymByQR_(T,tol,format);
%   S = eigTridByDET_(T,tol,format);   Q = [];
%   if (strcmp(format,'long'))
%       A = band2full_(T,1,1,m,m,1);   [S,Q] = eigvec_(A,S,Q,'gauss',tol);
%   end
elseif(abs(T(n+1,1)) < tol*(abs(T(n,2))+abs(T(n+1,2))))
    [S1,Q1] = eigTridByR1U_(T(1:n,:),tol,format,minm);
    [S2,Q2] = eigTridByR1U_(T(n+1:m,:),tol,format,minm);
    S = [S1;S2];   Q = [];   k = size(Q1,1);   l = size(Q2,2);
    if (strcmp(format,'long')) Q = [Q1,zeros(k,l);zeros(l,k),Q2];   end
else                          %recursive eigTridByR1U_
    if (T(n+1,1) > 0) theta = 1.0; else theta = -1.0; end
    rho = T(n+1,1)/theta;   %rho>0
    T(n,2) = T(n,2)-rho;     T(n+1,2) = T(n+1,2)-rho*theta*theta;
    [D1,Q1] = eigTridByR1U_(T(1:n,:),tol,format,minm);
    [D2,Q2] = eigTridByR1U_(T(n+1:m,:),tol,format,minm);
    T(n,2) = T(n,2)+rho;     T(n+1,2) = T(n+1,2)+rho*theta*theta;
    D = [D1;D2];   z = [Q1(n,:)';theta*Q2(1,:)'];
    [S,Q] = eigDiagByR1U_(D,z,rho,tol,format);
    if (strcmp(format,'long'))
        Q(1:n,:) = Q1*Q(1:n,:);   Q(n+1:m,:) = Q2*Q(n+1:m,:);
    end
end
```

Now we discuss an efficient algorithm for the eigen solution of $\mathbf{D} + \rho\mathbf{zz}'$, see [29].
Let λ be an eigenvalue of $\mathbf{D} + \rho\mathbf{zz}'$ and the corresponding eigenvector be $\mathbf{v}$. Then,

$$(\mathbf{D} - \lambda\mathbf{I})\mathbf{v} + \rho(\mathbf{z}'\mathbf{v})\mathbf{z} = \mathbf{0}. \tag{6.21}$$

If $\mathbf{D} - \lambda\mathbf{I}$ is not singular, then

$$\mathbf{v} = -\rho(\mathbf{z}'\mathbf{v})(\mathbf{D} - \lambda\mathbf{I})^{-1}\mathbf{z}. \tag{6.22}$$

Pre-multiply Eq. (6.21) by $\mathbf{z}'(\mathbf{D} - \lambda\mathbf{I})^{-1}$, we obtain

$$(\mathbf{z}'\mathbf{v})\left(1 + \rho\mathbf{z}'(\mathbf{D} - \lambda\mathbf{I})^{-1}\mathbf{z}\right) = 0.$$

If $\mathbf{z}'\mathbf{v} \neq 0$, then

$$f(\lambda) = 1 + \rho\mathbf{z}'(\mathbf{D} - \lambda\mathbf{I})^{-1}\mathbf{z} = 1 + \rho\left(\frac{z_1^2}{D_1 - \lambda} + \frac{z_2^2}{D_2 - \lambda} + \cdots + \frac{z_n^2}{D_n - \lambda}\right) = 0. \tag{6.23}$$

Eq. (6.23) is the nth order polynomial to determine λ. Once λ is determined, the eigenvector $\mathbf{v}$ with the unit length is obtained by Eq. (6.22),

$$\mathbf{v} = \frac{(\mathbf{D} - \lambda \mathbf{I})^{-1} \mathbf{z}}{\|(\mathbf{D} - \lambda \mathbf{I})^{-1} \mathbf{z}\|_2}.\tag{6.24}$$

The calculation of λ by Eq. (6.23) and $\mathbf{v}$ by Eq. (6.24) depends on the assumption that $\mathbf{D} - \lambda \mathbf{I}$ is not singular and $\mathbf{z}'\mathbf{v} \neq 0$. If all components of $\mathbf{z}$ are not zero and all components of $\mathbf{D}$ are distinct, the assumption is valid.[1]

If the components of $\mathbf{D}$ are not distinct or some components of $\mathbf{z}$ are zeros, we can choose an orthogonal matrix $\mathbf{U}$ to transform $\mathbf{D} + \rho \mathbf{z}\mathbf{z}'$ to the following standard form:

$$\mathbf{U}'(\mathbf{D} + \rho \mathbf{z}\mathbf{z}')\mathbf{U} = \begin{bmatrix} \bar{\mathbf{D}}(1:m) & \mathbf{0} \\ \mathbf{0} & \bar{\mathbf{D}}(m+1:n) \end{bmatrix} + \rho \begin{bmatrix} \bar{\mathbf{z}}(1:m) \\ \mathbf{0} \end{bmatrix} \begin{bmatrix} \bar{\mathbf{z}}(1:m)' & \mathbf{0}' \end{bmatrix}.\tag{6.25}$$

$\bar{\mathbf{D}}(1:m)$ are distinct and $\bar{\mathbf{z}}(1:m)$ are nonzero; therefore, the eigenvalues and eigenvectors of $\bar{\mathbf{D}}(1:m,1:m) + \rho \bar{\mathbf{z}}(1:m)\bar{\mathbf{z}}(1:m)'$ can be obtained by Eqs. (6.23) and (6.24). The eigenvalues of $\bar{\mathbf{D}}(m+1:n,m+1:n) + \rho \bar{\mathbf{z}}(m+1:n)\bar{\mathbf{z}}(m+1:n)'$ are simply $\bar{\mathbf{D}}(m+1:n)$ and the corresponding eigenvectors are $\mathbf{I}(:,m+1:n)$. In Eq. (6.25), $\mathbf{U}$ is determined by following Eqs. (6.26) and (6.27).

In $\mathbf{D}$, if $D_i = D_j, 1 \leq i < j \leq n$, we can choose an orthogonal matrix $\mathbf{G}$ (Givens rotation or Householder reflection) to zero z_j,

$$\mathbf{G}'\left(\begin{bmatrix} D_i & 0 \\ 0 & D_j \end{bmatrix} + \rho \begin{bmatrix} z_i \\ z_j \end{bmatrix} \begin{bmatrix} z_i & z_j \end{bmatrix} \right)\mathbf{G} = \begin{bmatrix} D_i & 0 \\ 0 & D_j \end{bmatrix} + \rho \begin{bmatrix} \pm\sqrt{z_i^2 + z_j^2} \\ 0 \end{bmatrix} \begin{bmatrix} \pm\sqrt{z_i^2 + z_j^2} & 0 \end{bmatrix}.\tag{6.26}$$

In $\mathbf{z}$, if $z_i = 0, z_j \neq 0, 1 \leq i < j \leq n$, we can choose a permutation matrix $\mathbf{P}$ to switch z_i and z_j,

$$\mathbf{P}'\left(\begin{bmatrix} D_i & 0 \\ 0 & D_j \end{bmatrix} + \rho \begin{bmatrix} 0 \\ z_j \end{bmatrix} \begin{bmatrix} 0 & z_j \end{bmatrix} \right)\mathbf{P} = \begin{bmatrix} D_j & 0 \\ 0 & D_i \end{bmatrix} + \rho \begin{bmatrix} z_j \\ 0 \end{bmatrix} \begin{bmatrix} z_j & 0 \end{bmatrix}.\tag{6.27}$$

For the convenience of the following discussion, we assume $\mathbf{D}$ and $\mathbf{z}$ are of the form in the parenthesis of Eq. (6.28) and $\mathbf{D}$ is sorted ascendingly and $\mathbf{D} - \lambda \mathbf{I}$ is not singular,

$$\mathbf{D} + \rho \mathbf{z}\mathbf{z}' = \rho(\mathbf{z}'\mathbf{z})\left(\frac{1}{\rho(\mathbf{z}'\mathbf{z})}\mathbf{D} + \frac{1}{(\mathbf{z}'\mathbf{z})}\mathbf{z}\mathbf{z}' \right).\tag{6.28}$$

As an example, D=[0;0.3226;0.9677;1.1290;2.2581;2.5806] and z=[0.5680;0.1136;0.3408;0.2840;0.5112; 0.4544]. The graph of $f(\lambda)$ of Eq. (6.23) is shown in Fig. 6.1. $f(\lambda)$ is monotone and has exactly n zeros between the poles. The ith root $\lambda_i \in (D_i, D_{i+1})$. If $f[(D_i + D_{i+1})/2] > 0$, $\lambda_i \in [D_i, (D_i + D_{i+1})/2]$; otherwise $\lambda_i \in [(D_i + D_{i+1})/2, D_{i+1}]$. For better numerical accuracy, when $\lambda_i \in [D_i, (D_i + D_{i+1})/2]$,

---

[1] If $\mathbf{D} - \lambda \mathbf{I}$ is singular, then $\lambda = D_i$ for some i and thus

$$\mathbf{I}(i,:)((\mathbf{D} - \lambda \mathbf{I})\mathbf{v} + \rho(\mathbf{z}'\mathbf{v})\mathbf{z}) = \rho(\mathbf{z}'\mathbf{v})z_i = 0.$$

By the assumption $\rho \neq 0$ and $z_i \neq 0$, then $\mathbf{z}'\mathbf{v} = 0$ and therefore $\mathbf{D}\mathbf{v} = \lambda \mathbf{v}$. However the components of $\mathbf{D}$ are distinct, $\mathbf{v}$ must be equal to $\mathbf{I}(:,i)$. But $\mathbf{z}'\mathbf{v} = z_i = 0$, a contradiction. Thus if $\mathbf{D}$ are distinct and $\mathbf{z}$ are nonzero, $\mathbf{D} - \lambda \mathbf{I}$ must be non-singular and $\mathbf{z}'\mathbf{v} \neq 0$.

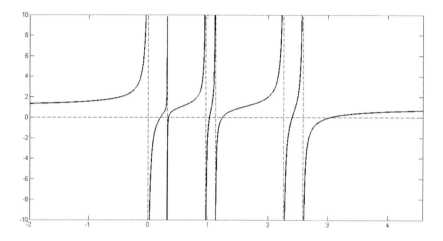

FIGURE 6.1

Graph of $1 + \frac{z_1^2}{D_1-\lambda} + \frac{z_2^2}{D_2-\lambda} + \frac{z_3^2}{D_3-\lambda} + \frac{z_4^2}{D_4-\lambda} + \frac{z_5^2}{D_5-\lambda} + \frac{z_6^2}{D_6-\lambda}$.

we shift the origin of the real axis to D_i. Thus Eq. (6.23) is as follows:

$$g(\mu) = 1 + \sum_{j=1}^{n} \frac{z_j^2}{(D_j - D_i) - (\lambda - D_i)} = 1 + \sum_{j=1}^{n} \frac{z_j^2}{d_j - \mu}$$

$$= 1 + \sum_{j=1}^{i} \frac{z_j^2}{d_j - \mu} + \sum_{j=i+1}^{n} \frac{z_j^2}{d_j - \mu} = 1 + g_1(\mu) + g_2(\mu). \qquad (6.29)$$

The root of $g(\mu) = 0$ can be found by Newton-Raphson iterations, see Section 5.1, where a linear function is used to approximate $g(\mu)$ in the neighborhood of the approximate root. However in Eq. (6.29), $g(\lambda)$ is the sum of rational functions. When finding the root in $(0, d_{i+1}/2)$, a better algorithm than Newton-Raphson is to approximate $g(\mu)$ by the sum of three rational functions as follows, see [41]:

$$h(\mu) = 1 + h_1(\mu) + h_2(\mu) = 1 + \left(a_1 + \frac{b_1}{0 - \mu}\right) + \left(a_2 + \frac{b_2}{d_{i+1} - \mu}\right). \qquad (6.30)$$

a_1 and b_1 are chosen such that $h_1(\mu) = g_1(\mu)$ and $h_1'(\mu) = g_1'(\mu)$. Similarly a_2 and b_2 are chosen such that $h_2(\mu) = g_2(\mu)$ and $h_2'(\mu) = g_2'(\mu)$. Eq. (6.30) is a quadratic function; one of its roots μ_i is in $(0, d_{i+1}/2)$. μ_i is an approximate root of $g(\mu) = 0$. μ_i is used again in Eq. (6.30) to find a better estimation of the root. When $|g(\mu_i)|$ is small enough, $\lambda_i = \mu_i + D_i$.

λ_i that $\lambda_i \in [(D_i + D_{i+1})/2, D_{i+1}]$ is obtained similarly.

For a more precise discussion, we denote the eigenvalue of $\mathbf{D} + \mathbf{z}\mathbf{z}'$ as λ and the calculated eigenvalue by the above procedure as $\bar{\lambda}$. If $\bar{\lambda}$ is very close to D_i (that is, $|z_i|$ is very small), the calculated v_i according to Eq. (6.24) is not accurate. As a result, $\mathbf{V}$ calculated using all the $\bar{\lambda}$ in Eq. (6.24) is not orthogonal. A remedy to this problem is addressed in [30]. $\bar{\lambda}$ is the approximate eigenvalue of $\mathbf{D} + \mathbf{z}\mathbf{z}'$

but the exact eigenvalue of $\mathbf{D} + \bar{\mathbf{z}}\bar{\mathbf{z}}'$. If we use $\bar{\lambda}$ and $\bar{\mathbf{z}}$ in Eq. (6.24), the calculated $\bar{\mathbf{v}}$ is the exact corresponding eigenvector of $\mathbf{D} + \bar{\mathbf{z}}\bar{\mathbf{z}}'$. $\bar{z}_i$ is calculated as follows:

$$\det\left(\mathbf{D} + \bar{\mathbf{z}}\bar{\mathbf{z}}' - D_i\mathbf{I}\right) = \left(1 + \sum_{j=1}^{n}\frac{\bar{z}_j^2}{D_j - D_i}\right)\prod_{j=1}^{n}(D_j - D_i) = \prod_{j=1}^{n}(\bar{\lambda}_j - D_i), \qquad (6.31a)$$

$$\bar{z}_i = \operatorname{sign}(z_i)\sqrt{\frac{\displaystyle\prod_{j=1}^{n}(\bar{\lambda}_j - D_i)}{\displaystyle\prod_{j=1, j\neq i}^{n}(D_j - D_i)}}. \qquad (6.31b)$$

eigDiagByR1U_.m listed below is based on the algorithm based on Eqs. (6.24), (6.29), (6.30) and (6.31b).

Algorithm 6.13

Calculate eigenvalues of a diagonal plus rank-1 matrix.

```
function [S,Q] = eigDiagByR1U_(D,z,rho,tol,format)

m = length(D);
normz = norm(z);   z = z/normz;   rho = rho*normz*normz;   Dmax = max(abs(D));
if (rho < tol*Dmax)      %rho=0: S=D,Q=I
    if (strcmp(format,'long')) Q = eye(m); else Q = []; end
    S = D;   return;
end
D = D/rho;   Dmax = Dmax/rho;   rho0 = rho;   rho = 1.0;      %standardize: rho=1
tolD = tol*max(1.0, Dmax);

[D,p1] = sort(D);     z = permute_(p1,z);    p1 = inv_perm_(p1);
Hp = [];     Hv = zeros(m,1);     j = 1;     k = 0;
while (j < m)
    for l=j+1:m
        if (D(l)-D(j) < tolD) k = k + 1; else break; end
    end
    if (k > 0) %D(j)=D(j+1)=...=D(j+k)
        [h,beta] = householder_(z(j:j+k));
        z(j) = z(j) - beta*(h'*z(j:j+k))*h(1);   z(j+1:j+k) = 0.0;
        Hp = [Hp;[j,k]];    Hv(j:j+k) = h;    Hv(j) = beta;
    end
    j = j + k + 1;    k = 0;
end

p2 = 1:m;    last = m;
for j=1:m        %P2: permute all z(j)=0 to bottom of z
    if (abs(z(j)) < tolD)
        while(abs(z(last))<tolD && last>0) last = last - 1; end
        if (last > j)
            z(j) = z(last);    z(last) = 0.0;
            p2j = p2(j);   p2(j) = p2(last);   p2(last) = p2j;   last = last-1;
        end
    end
end
```

```
D = permute_(p2,D);
[D(1:last),p3] = sort(D(1:last));    %reorder D
S = D;  D = D(1:last);   D = [D(1:last);D(last)+z'*z];   Q = [];
z(1:last) = permute_(p3,z(1:last));      zz = z.*z;
p3 = inv_perm_(p3);     p3 = [p3',last+1:m];

for j=1:last  %zero finder for lambda: rational approximation for f(lambda)
    s = 0.5*(D(j)+D(j+1));   f = 0.0;
    for k=1:last f = f + zz(k)/(D(k)-s); end
    f = 1.0 + f;
    if (f > 0.0) dj = D(j); else dj = D(j+1); end
    dD = D - dj;          %shift: D+z*z'==>(D-dj*I)+z*z'
    eta = 0.5*(s+dj) - dj;    f1 = 0.0;    f2 = 0.0;
    for k=1:j f1 = f1 + zz(k)/(dD(k)-eta); end
    for k=j+1:last f2 = f2 + zz(k)/(dD(k)-eta); end
    f = 1.0 + f1 + f2;
    while (abs(f) > tol*last*(1.0+abs(f1)+abs(f2)))
        df1 = 0.0;    df2 = 0.0;
        for k=1:j df1 = df1 + zz(k)/(dD(k)-eta)^2; end
        for k=j+1:last df2 = df2 + zz(k)/(dD(k)-eta)^2; end
        c1 = (dD(j)-eta)^2 * df1;
        c2 = (dD(j+1)-eta)^2 * df2;
        c3 = 1.0 + f1-c1/(dD(j)-eta) + f2-c2/(dD(j+1)-eta);
        a = c3;
        b = -c1 - c2 - c3*dD(j) - c3*dD(j+1);
        c = c1*dD(j+1) + c2*dD(j) + c3*dD(j)*dD(j+1);
        if (b > 0) eta = -0.5*(b+sqrt(b*b-4.0*a*c))/a;
        else       eta = -2.0*c/(b-sqrt(b*b-4.0*a*c)); end   %eta: Newton correction
        f1 = 0.0;    f2 = 0.0;
        for k=1:j f1 = f1 + zz(k)/(dD(k)-eta); end
        for k=j+1:last f2 = f2 + zz(k)/(dD(k)-eta); end
        f = 1.0 + f1 + f2;
    end
    S(j) = eta + dj;
end

if (strcmp(format,'long'))    %calculate Q
    Q = eye(m);
    for j=1:last
        d1 = 1.0;    d2 = 1.0;
        for k=1:j-1 d1 = d1*(S(k)-D(j))/(D(k)-D(j)); end
        for k=j+1:last d2 = d2*(S(k)-D(j))/(D(k)-D(j)); end
        z(j) = sign(z(j))*sqrt(d1*d2*(S(j)-D(j)));    %Gu & Einstat's formua
    end
    for j=1:last
        if (S(j)==D(j) || S(j)==D(j+1)) continue; end
        for k=1:last q(k) = z(k)/(D(k)-S(j)); end    %eigvector
        Q(1:last,j) = q/norm(q);
    end

    [S,p4] = sort(S);
    Q = permute_(p4,Q,'col');   Q = permute_(p3,Q,'row');   Q = permute_(p2,Q,'row');
    for l=1:size(Hp,1)               %Q=H*P3*P2*(Q*P4)
        j = Hp(l,1);   k = Hp(l,2);
        h = Hv(j:j+k); h(1) = 1.0;   beta = Hv(j);
        Q(j:j+k,:) = Q(j:j+k,:) - (beta*h)*(h'*Q(j:j+k,:));
```

```
    end
    Q - permute_(p1,Q,'row');        %Q=P1*Q
end
S = S*rho0;
```

Using the same symmetric tri-diagonal matrix **T** of the last subsection in `eigTridByDET_.m`, we obtain the following output.

```
>> [S,Q]=eigTridByR1U_(T);
>> S' =
   -0.9978   -0.7618   -0.4235   -0.1215    0.1068    0.3993    0.9963    3.9641
>> Q =
    0.1220   -0.2646   -0.0345   -0.1716    0.4044    0.4549   -0.6291    0.3438
    0.1852   -0.3514   -0.0364   -0.1396    0.2548    0.1797    0.0533   -0.8493
   -0.3549    0.5925    0.0476    0.1227   -0.1117    0.0938   -0.5735   -0.3944
    0.3941   -0.3566    0.0135    0.1922   -0.5000   -0.4257   -0.4942   -0.0699
    0.5903    0.2835    0.1201    0.3867   -0.2288    0.5752    0.1551    0.0055
   -0.5516   -0.4718   -0.0255    0.2231   -0.4618    0.4532    0.0633    0.0007
   -0.1275   -0.1530    0.3187    0.7703    0.4812   -0.1837   -0.0115   -0.0000
    0.0233    0.0454   -0.9372    0.3262    0.1093   -0.0262   -0.0009   -0.0000
```

The above eigen solutions of **T** are verified as follows.

```
>> B=band2full_(T,1,1,8,8,1);
>> norm(Q'*Q-eye(8))
=   5.3357e-016
>> norm(Q'*B*Q-diag(S))
=   3.5680e-008
```

6.8 JACOBI ITERATIONS FOR SYMMETRIC MATRIX

The eigenvalues and eigenvectors of a 2×2 symmetric matrix can be calculated *directly* using `eig2x2_.m`: `function [Lambda,G,res] = eig2x2_(A,algo)`, see Section 6.1,

$$\mathbf{G}' \begin{bmatrix} A_{11} & A_{12} \\ A_{12} & A_{22} \end{bmatrix} \mathbf{G} = \begin{bmatrix} \lambda_1 & 0 \\ 0 & \lambda_2 \end{bmatrix}. \tag{6.32}$$

For an $n \times n$ symmetric matrix **A**, we can apply Eq. (6.32) with `[Lambda,G,res]=eig22_([A(i,i),A(i,j);A(j,i),A(j,j)]);`, $1 \leq i < j \leq n$. The Jacobi rotation matrix is denoted as $\mathbf{J}(i,j,G)$: $\mathbf{J} = \mathbf{I}$, but $J_{ii} = G_{11} = c, J_{jj} = G_{22} = c, J_{ij} = G_{12} = s, J_{ji} = G_{21} = -s$. The orthogonal similarity transformation is illustrated in

$$\mathbf{J}'\mathbf{AJ} = \bar{\mathbf{A}} = \begin{bmatrix} A_{11} & \cdots & \bar{A}_{1i} & \cdots & \bar{A}_{1j} & \cdots & A_{1n} \\ \vdots & & \vdots & & \vdots & & \vdots \\ \bar{A}_{i1} & \cdots & \bar{A}_{ii} & \cdots & \bar{A}_{ij} & \cdots & \bar{A}_{in} \\ \vdots & & \vdots & & \vdots & & \vdots \\ \bar{A}_{j1} & \cdots & \bar{A}_{ji} & \cdots & \bar{A}_{jj} & \cdots & \bar{A}_{jn} \\ \vdots & & \vdots & & \vdots & & \vdots \\ A_{n1} & \cdots & \bar{A}_{ni} & \cdots & \bar{A}_{nj} & \cdots & A_{nn} \end{bmatrix}. \tag{6.33}$$

$\mathbf{J'AJ}$ only changes $\mathbf{A}$'s ith and jth rows and columns and $\bar{A}_{ij} = \bar{A}_{ji} = 0$.

Let us compare the Frobenius norm of the off diagonal of $\mathbf{A}$ and $\bar{\mathbf{A}}$. Note that the Frobenius norm does not change in the orthogonal similarity transformation,

$$\text{off}(\bar{\mathbf{A}}) = \|\bar{\mathbf{A}}\|_F^2 - \sum_{k=1}^{n} \bar{A}_{kk}^2 = \|\mathbf{A}\|_F^2 - \sum_{k=1}^{n} A_{kk}^2 + \left(A_{ii}^2 + A_{jj}^2 - \bar{A}_{ii}^2 - \bar{A}_{jj}^2\right) = \text{off}(\mathbf{A}) - 2A_{ij}^2.$$

This shows the continuous application of Eq. (6.33) with different (i, j) drives $\mathbf{A}$ closer to a diagonal form.

The choice of (i, j) is not unique. In `eigByJacobi_.m`, a parallel ordering is used. For example, $n = 4$, we group the 6 [=$(4 \times 3)/2$] rotations: $\{(1,2),(3,4)\}$; $\{(1,4),(2,3)\}$; $\{(1,3),(2,4)\}$. In each group, the two rotations can be applied simultaneously. Each rotation costs $O(n)$ operations. The $[n(n-1)]/2$ rotations make one Jacobi sweep. [53] shows heuristically the number of sweeps to reach convergence of off$(\mathbf{A})$ is proportional to $\log(n)$.

Algorithm 6.14

Calculate eigenvalues of a symmetric matrix by Jacobi iterations.

```
function [A,U] = eigByJacobi_(A,tol,format)

[m,n] = size(A);
offA = norm(A-diag(diag(A)),'fro')/sqrt(2.0);    %Frobenius norm of off-diagonals of A.
offA = offA*offA;      offA0 = tol*offA;
if (mod(m,2) == 0)   top = 1:2:n;   bot = 2:2:n;    n2 = n/2;
else               top = 1:2:n+1; bot = 2:2:n+1;  n2 = (n+1)/2; end

while(offA > offA0)
    for k = 1:n2
        p = min(top(k),bot(k));    q = max(top(k),bot(k));
        if (q == n+1) continue; end
        A(p+1:q-1,p) = A(p,p+1:q-1);    A(q,p+1:q-1) = A(p+1:q-1,q);
        App = A(p,p);    Aqq = A(q,q);    Apq = A(p,q);  offA = offA - Apq*Apq;
        [Lambda,G] = eig2x2_([App,Apq;Apq,Aqq]);   c = G(1,1);   s =-G(2,1);
        A(p,p) = Lambda(1,1);   A(q,q) = Lambda(2,2);   A(p,q)=0.0;   A(q,p) = 0.0;
        for i=1:p-1
            Aip = A(i,p);    Aiq = A(i,q);
            A(i,p) = c*Aip - s*Aiq;   A(i,q) = s*Aip + c*Aiq;
        end
        for i=p+1:q-1
            A(i,q) = s*A(i,p) + c*A(i,q);   A(p,i) = c*A(p,i) - s*A(q,i);
        end
        for i=q+1:n
            Api = A(p,i);    Aqi = A(q,i);
            A(p,i) = c*Api - s*Aqi;   A(q,i) = s*Api + c*Aqi;
        end
        if (strcmp(format,'long'))
            for i=1:n
                Uip = U(i,p);   Uiq = U(i,q);
                U(i,p) = c*Uip - s*Uiq;   U(i,q) = s*Uip + c*Uiq;
            end
        end
    end
    top0 = top;   bot0 = bot;
```

```
        for k = 1:n2
            if (k == 2) top(k) = bot0(1); end
            if (k >  2) top(k) = top0(k-1); end
            if (k == n2) bot(k) = top0(k); end
            if (k <  n2) bot(k) = bot0(k+1); end
        end
end
A = diag(A);
```

The following simple example verifies `eigByJacobi_.m`.

```
>> A = randn(8);   A = 0.5*(A+A');
>> [S,Q]=eigByJacobi_(A,100*eps,'long');
>> norm(Q'*A*Q-diag(S))
=   1.2002e-008
>> norm(Q'*Q-eye(8))
=   2.1134e-015
```

6.9 ALGORITHMS FOR SYMMETRICAL POSITIVE DEFINITE $\mathbf{A}\mathbf{x} = \lambda \mathbf{B}\mathbf{x}$

For two matrices $\mathbf{A},\mathbf{B} \in \mathbb{R}^{n \times n}$, an eigenvalue λ is defined as the root of the nth order polynomial $\det(\mathbf{A} - \lambda\mathbf{B}) = 0$. Given any two non-singular matrices $\mathbf{U}$ and $\mathbf{V}$, we have the following:

$$\det(\mathbf{A} - \lambda\mathbf{B}) = \det(\mathbf{U}'\mathbf{A}\mathbf{V} - \lambda\mathbf{U}'\mathbf{B}\mathbf{V}) = \det(\bar{\mathbf{A}} - \lambda\bar{\mathbf{B}}) = 0. \tag{6.34}$$

According to the properties of $\mathbf{A}$ and $\mathbf{B}$, we can choose appropriate and well-conditioned $\mathbf{U}$ and $\mathbf{V}$, so that $\det(\bar{\mathbf{A}} - \lambda\bar{\mathbf{B}}) = 0$ can be solved directly or by an established algorithm.

In this section, we consider the particular case that $\mathbf{B}$ is symmetric positive definite. When $\mathbf{B} = \mathbf{B}'$ and $\mathbf{B} > 0$, $\mathbf{B} = \mathbf{L}\mathbf{L}'$, see Section 2.4.2. We choose $\mathbf{U} = \mathbf{L}'^{-1}$ and $\mathbf{V} = \mathbf{L}^{-1}$,

$$\det(\mathbf{A} - \lambda\mathbf{B}) = \det(\mathbf{L}'^{-1}\mathbf{A}\mathbf{L}^{-1} - \lambda\mathbf{I}) = \det(\bar{\mathbf{A}} - \lambda\mathbf{I}) = 0. \tag{6.35}$$

By the transformation of Eq. (6.35), the generalized eigen problem $\mathbf{A}\mathbf{v} = \lambda\mathbf{B}\mathbf{v}$ is reduced to the standard eigen problem $\bar{\mathbf{A}}\mathbf{w} = \lambda\mathbf{w}$, so that the algorithms discussed in the previous sections of this chapter can be applied.

When $\mathbf{A} = \mathbf{A}'$, we also have $\bar{\mathbf{A}} = \bar{\mathbf{A}}'$. In this case, `eigSymByQR_.m` can be applied to $\bar{\mathbf{A}}\mathbf{w} = \lambda\mathbf{w}$. The following is the list of `xeigSym1ByQR_.m` which implements Eq. (6.35) for the case $\mathbf{A} = \mathbf{A}', \mathbf{B} = \mathbf{B}'$, and $\mathbf{B} > 0$.

Algorithm 6.15

Solution of generalized symmetric positive eigen problem $\mathbf{A}\mathbf{v} = \lambda\mathbf{B}\mathbf{v}$ by QR iteration.

```
function [A,U] = xeigSym1ByQR_(A,B,tol,format)

[m,n] = size(A);   [k,l] = size(B);
if (m~=n || m~=k || n~=l) error('xeigSym1ByQR_:_Matrix_size_error.'); end
if (exist('tol','var') == 0) tol = sqrt(eps); end
if (~exist('format','var') || isempty(format)) format = 'long'; end

L = LLtByCholesky_(B);            %B=L*L'
```

```
A = eqsLowerTriangle_(L,A,0);        %A=inv(B)*A

for j=1:n                            %A=A*inv(L)', lower half of A calculated.
    for k=1:j-1
        A(j:n,j) = A(j:n,j) - L(j,k)*A(j:n,k);
    end
    A(j:n,j) = A(j:n,j)/L(j,j);
end


[A,U] = eigSymByQR_(A,tol,format);
if (strcmp(format,'long')) U = eqsUpperTriangle_(L',U,0); end
```

The following simple example verifies xeigSym1ByQR_.m, in which tol=1.4901e-008 and tol=2.2204e-014 are used as the convergence tolerance of QR algorithms. The result shows that $\mathbf{AV} = \mathbf{BV\Lambda}$ is satisfied to higher accuracy if a tighter convergence tolerance is used.

```
>> A = randn(8);  A = 0.5*(A+A');                        %A=A'
>> [Q,R]=QR_(randn(8));   d = rand(8,1);   B = Q*diag(d)*Q';   %B=B' & B>0

>> [DA,VA] = eigSymByQR_(A);
>> DA'
=   -4.2337     2.7608     1.9123    -2.2509    -1.3635    -1.1412     1.0285    -0.0655
>> [DB,VB] = eigSymByQR_(B);
>> DB          %DB=d,  VB=+/-Q
=    0.1190     0.1626     0.2760     0.4984     0.7547     0.7094     0.6551     0.6797

>> [S,U]=xeigSym1ByQR_(A,B)
S =
   -23.5006    -8.2850     4.6734     3.4864     2.2931    -0.1860    -2.4187    -2.5399
U =
    -2.0532    -0.4493    -0.1908    -0.1215     0.2819     0.0743    -0.6606    -0.5406
     0.6285    -1.7270    -0.9254    -0.0827     0.0533    -0.6479     0.1499     0.3521
     1.3325    -0.2433    -0.1469    -0.8017     0.2073     0.4422    -0.2652    -0.3897
    -0.0555     1.0455     0.2244    -0.0613     0.4869     0.7074    -0.2452     1.0769
     0.4740     0.7060    -0.7739    -0.3835    -0.4137    -0.7713    -0.4783     0.2167
    -0.4784     0.6988    -0.6241     0.7515     0.3265     0.9080     0.8176    -0.2885
    -0.0330    -0.2361    -0.0400    -0.7784    -1.1156     0.2689    -0.1764     0.4032
     0.2572    -0.0931    -0.0580     1.0167    -0.1087     0.4817    -0.5875    -0.1232

>> norm(A*U-B*U*diag(S))
= 7.1181e-010       %less accurate for tol=sqrt(eps)=1.4901e-008.

>> [S,U]=xeigSym1ByQR_(A,B,100*eps);
>> norm(A*U-B*U*diag(S))
= 8.9978e-015       %more accurate for tol=100*eps=2.2204e-014.
```

Now we discuss another algorithm for the symmetric positive definite eigen problem. In Eq. (6.34), we choose $\mathbf{U}$ and $\mathbf{V}$ so that $\bar{\mathbf{A}}$ and $\bar{\mathbf{B}}$ are approaching diagonals. The algorithm is similar to eigJacobi_.m but is based on xeig2x2_.m instead, see Section 6.1,

$$\mathbf{G}'\begin{bmatrix} A_{11} & A_{12} \\ A_{12} & A_{22} \end{bmatrix}\mathbf{G} = \begin{bmatrix} \bar{A}_{11} & 0 \\ 0 & \bar{A}_{22} \end{bmatrix}, \qquad \mathbf{G}'\begin{bmatrix} B_{11} & B_{12} \\ B_{12} & B_{22} \end{bmatrix}\mathbf{G} = \begin{bmatrix} \bar{B}_{11} & 0 \\ 0 & \bar{B}_{22} \end{bmatrix}. \tag{6.36}$$

For two $n \times n$ symmetric matrices $\mathbf{A}$ and $\mathbf{B}$, we apply Eq. (6.36) with

```
[G,res]=xeig2x2_([A(i,i),A(i,j);A(j,i),A(j,j)],[B(i,i),B(i,j);B(j,i),B(j,j)]);, 1 ≤ i < j ≤ n.
```

The extended Jacobi rotation matrix is denoted as $\mathbf{J}(i,j,\mathbf{Q})$: $\mathbf{J} = \mathbf{I}$, but $J_{ii} = Q_{11}, J_{ij} = Q_{12}, J_{ji} = Q_{21}, J_{jj} = Q_{22}$. The congruent transformation $\mathbf{J'AJ}$ is similar to Eq. (6.33), so is $\mathbf{J'BJ}$. The choice of (i,j) is same as that in eqsByJacobi_.m, see Section 6.8. This extended Jacobi iteration algorithm is implemented in the following xeigByJacobi_.m.

Algorithm 6.16

Solution of generalized symmetric positive eigen problem $\mathbf{Av} = \lambda\mathbf{Bv}$ by Jacobi iteration.

```
function [A,B,U] = xeigByJacobi_(A,B,tol,format)

[m,n] = size(A);  [k,l] = size(B);    converged = 0;
if (mod(m,2) == 0) top = 1:2:n;    bot = 2:2:n;    n2 = n/2;
else               top = 1:2:n+1; bot = 2:2:n+1;  n2 = (n+1)/2; end

while(~converged)
    converged = 1;
    for k = 1:n2
        p = min(top(k),bot(k));    q = max(top(k),bot(k));
        if (q == n+1) continue; end
        A(p+1:q-1,p) = A(p,p+1:q-1);    A(q,p+1:q-1) = A(p+1:q-1,q);
        B(p+1:q-1,p) = B(p,p+1:q-1);    B(q,p+1:q-1) = B(p+1:q-1,q);
        App = A(p,p);    Aqq = A(q,q);    Apq = A(p,q);
        Bpp = B(p,p);    Bqq = B(q,q);    Bpq = B(p,q);
        if (sqrt(abs(Apq*Apq/App*Aqq))<tol && sqrt(abs(Bpq*Bpq/Bpp*Bqq))<tol)
            A(p,q) = 0; B(p,q) = 0; continue;
        end
        [G,M,res] = xeig2x2_([App,Apq;Apq,Aqq],[Bpp,Bpq;Bpq,Bqq]);
        if (res ==-1) error('xeigByJacobi_:_xeig2x2__has_no_solution.'); end
        G11 = G(1,1);    G12 = G(1,2);    G21 = G(2,1);    G22 = G(2,2);
        A(p,p) = (G11*App+G21*Apq)*G11 + (G11*Apq+G21*Aqq)*G21;
        A(q,q) = (G12*App+G22*Apq)*G12 + (G12*Apq+G22*Aqq)*G22;
        B(p,p) = (G11*Bpp+G21*Bpq)*G11 + (G11*Bpq+G21*Bqq)*G21;
        B(q,q) = (G12*Bpp+G22*Bpq)*G12 + (G12*Bpq+G22*Bqq)*G22;
        A(p,q) = 0.0;    A(q,p) = 0.0;    B(p,q) = 0.0;    B(q,p) = 0.0;    converged=0;
        for i=1:p-1
            Aip = A(i,p);    Aiq = A(i,q);
            A(i,p) = Aip*G11 + Aiq*G21;    A(i,q) = Aip*G12 + Aiq*G22;
            Bip = B(i,p);    Biq = B(i,q);
            B(i,p) = Bip*G11 + Biq*G21;    B(i,q) = Bip*G12 + Biq*G22;
        end
        for i=p+1:q-1
            A(i,q) = A(i,p)*G12 + A(i,q)*G22; A(p,i) = G11*A(p,i) + G21*A(q,i);
            B(i,q) = B(i,p)*G12 + B(i,q)*G22; B(p,i) = G11*B(p,i) + G21*B(q,i);
        end
        for i=q+1:n
            Api = A(p,i);    Aqi = A(q,i);
            A(p,i) = G11*Api + G21*Aqi;    A(q,i) = G12*Api + G22*Aqi;
            Bpi = B(p,i);    Bqi = B(q,i);
            B(p,i) = G11*Bpi + G21*Bqi;    B(q,i) = G12*Bpi + G22*Bqi;
        end
        if (strcmp(format,'long'))        %U=U*G
            for i=1:n
                Uip = U(i,p);    Uiq = U(i,q);
                U(i,p) = Uip*G11 + Uiq*G21;    U(i,q) = Uip*G12 + Uiq*G22;
            end
        end
```

```
      end
      top0 = top;    bot0 = bot;
      for k = 1:n2
          if (k == 2) top(k) = bot0(1); end
          if (k >  2) top(k) = top0(k-1); end
          if (k == n2) bot(k) = top0(k); end
          if (k <  n2) bot(k) = bot0(k+1); end
      end
      if (converged==0 || bot(1)~= 2) converged = 0; end
end
A = diag(A)';   B = diag(B)';
```

Because **G** in Eq. (6.36) is not orthogonal, we cannot prove the norm of off-diagonals of **A** or **B** is approaching zero monotonically. But the practical calculations show that xeigByJacobi_.m is always convergent when $A = A', B = B'$ and $B > 0$. xeigByJacobi_.m is even convergent occasionally when **B** is positive indefinite!

The same **A** and **B** that are used in xeigSym1ByQR_ are used again in xeigByJacobi_.m. The following are the outputs.

```
>> [S,T,U]=xeigByJacobi_(A,B)
S =
    0.1529    0.0470    0.0014   -0.0008   -0.0021   -0.0001   -0.0077   -0.3656
T =
    0.0327    0.0135    0.0006    0.0043    0.0009    0.0000    0.0009    0.0156
U =
    0.0345    0.0141   -0.0071    0.0049   -0.0194    0.0029    0.0137   -0.2561
    0.1674    0.0096   -0.0013   -0.0424    0.0044   -0.0019    0.0528    0.0784
    0.0266    0.0931   -0.0052    0.0289   -0.0078    0.0021    0.0074    0.1662
   -0.0406    0.0071   -0.0122    0.0463   -0.0073   -0.0058   -0.0319   -0.0069
    0.1400    0.0445    0.0103   -0.0505   -0.0141   -0.0012   -0.0216    0.0591
    0.1129   -0.0873   -0.0082    0.0594    0.0241    0.0015   -0.0213   -0.0597
    0.0072    0.0904    0.0279    0.0176   -0.0052   -0.0022    0.0072   -0.0041
    0.0105   -0.1181    0.0027    0.0315   -0.0173    0.0007    0.0028    0.0321

>> norm(A*U*diag(T)-B*U*diag(S))
= 1.7353e-006        %less accurate for tol=sqrt(eps)=1.4901e-008.
>> [S,T,U]=xeigByJacobi_(A,B,100*eps);
>> norm(A*U*diag(T)-B*U*diag(S))
= 1.0259e-010        %more accurate for tol=100*eps=2.2204e-014.
```

If we apply xeigByJacobi_.m to two randomly generated symmetric matrices, most likely we get a failure.

```
>> A=randn(8);   A = 0.5*(A+A');   B=randn(8);   B = 0.5*(B+B');
>> [S,T,U]=xeigByJacobi_(A,B,100*eps)
??? Error using ==> xeigByJacobi_ at 29
xeigByJacobi_: B is not positive definite.
```

But xeigByJacobi_.m works for the following two symmetric matrices, where **B** is symmetric indefinite. The necessary condition that the Jacobi iteration is convergent is not known.

```
A=[-1.3868    -1.1038    -3.4136     0.5804     0.7407     1.5451    -1.7457    -1.5058;
   -1.1038    -3.4357    -0.3355     0.8407     0.0263     1.0571     0.8146    -1.8848;
   -3.4136    -0.3355   -10.1789     5.0447     2.0872     3.7564    -2.3035    -3.5354;
    0.5804     0.8407     5.0447    -2.3595    -0.6091    -1.2710     1.2396     1.9854;
    0.7407     0.0263     2.0872    -0.6091    -1.4479     0.6730    -0.2697     3.0598;
    1.5451     1.0571     3.7564    -1.2710     0.6730    -3.4842     1.5921     1.8510;
```

```
           -1.7457    0.8146   -2.3035    1.2396   -0.2697    1.5921   -2.5701   -2.9890;
           -1.5058   -1.8848   -3.5354    1.9854    3.0598    1.8510   -2.9890    1.4021];

B=[-4.5453   -1.6110    0.6778   -0.1267    1.1489    0.6352    1.7148    0.0586;
   -1.6110   -4.3734   -0.3734    0.2053    0.4745    0.6256    1.3989    0.3791;
    0.6778   -0.3734    0.2853   -2.6448   -2.7523   -0.7915    3.7029    2.2115;
   -0.1267    0.2053   -2.6448   -2.4346    0.8836    0.7518   -2.0289   -2.4225;
    1.1489    0.4745   -2.7523    0.8836   -1.4905   -0.6042   -0.9320   -2.5673;
    0.6352    0.6256   -0.7915    0.7518   -0.6042   -3.1592   -1.2943   -0.3173;
    1.7148    1.3989    3.7029   -2.0289   -0.9320   -1.2943   -2.9376    1.7419;
    0.0586    0.3791    2.2115   -2.4225   -2.5673   -0.3173    1.7419   -4.5026];

>> [S,T,U]=xeigByJacobi_(A,B,100*eps)
S =
  -11.5488   -5.0487   -3.5361   -2.6417   -1.0471   -0.4783    1.3383    5.6568
T =
    7.4726   -1.3566   -3.4661   -4.6031   -4.0974   -3.3468   -4.4028   -6.3779
U =
    0.4946    0.3627    0.2186   -0.4155   -0.3275    0.6454   -0.5399    0.3522
   -0.1586   -0.0087   -0.8996    0.1041    0.0556    0.1874    0.2794   -0.3642
   -0.5201    0.0428    0.2926    0.3358   -0.1663    0.2415    0.4058   -0.2871
    0.3180   -0.0886    0.1343   -0.3291   -0.6631    0.0829    0.5794   -0.1631
    1.0098    0.8865    0.0598    0.1944    0.3112    0.4488    0.0990    0.5969
   -0.1101   -0.5567    0.0800   -0.1878    0.3469    0.6330    0.1833    0.0534
   -0.5607    0.3620   -0.1145   -0.6840    0.3644    0.0526    0.1725   -0.5151
   -0.3405   -0.2198   -0.2776   -0.2319    0.0320   -0.2398    0.1862    0.7044
>> norm(A*U*diag(T)-B*U*diag(S))
= 9.2708e-007
```

6.10 ALGORITHMS FOR UNSYMMETRICAL $\mathbf{Ax} = \lambda\mathbf{Bx}$

For two matrices $\mathbf{A},\mathbf{B} \in \mathbb{R}^{n \times n}$, an eigenvalue λ is defined as the root of the nth order polynomial $\det(\mathbf{A} - \lambda\mathbf{B}) = 0$. Given any two non-singular matrices $\mathbf{U}$ and $\mathbf{V}$, we have the following:

$$\det(\mathbf{A} - \lambda\mathbf{B}) = \det(\mathbf{U}'\mathbf{AV} - \lambda\mathbf{U}'\mathbf{BV}) = \det(\bar{\mathbf{A}} - \lambda\bar{\mathbf{B}}) = 0. \qquad (6.37)$$

According to the properties of $\mathbf{A}$ and $\mathbf{B}$, we can choose appropriate and well-conditioned $\mathbf{U}$ and $\mathbf{V}$, so that $\det(\bar{\mathbf{A}} - \lambda\bar{\mathbf{B}}) = 0$ can be solved directly or by an established algorithm.

In this section, we consider the general square matrices $\mathbf{A}$ and $\mathbf{B}$. In this case, the independent choice of $\mathbf{U}$ and $\mathbf{V}$ is acceptable. For the purpose of eigenvalue calculation, we can require that $\mathbf{U}'\mathbf{AV}$ and $\mathbf{U}'\mathbf{BV}$ are upper triangular. It is indeed possible to find two orthogonal matrices $\mathbf{U}$ and $\mathbf{V}$ such that $\mathbf{U}'\mathbf{AV}$ and $\mathbf{U}'\mathbf{BV}$ are both upper triangular. When $\mathbf{A}$ and $\mathbf{B}$ are real matrices and contain conjugal complex eigenvalues and we want to keep only the real arithmetic, a slight modification of this rule has to be made to allow $\mathbf{U}'\mathbf{AV}$ to be pseudo-upper triangular: its diagonal can be 1×1 or 2×2 blocks. See [29]. This is the QZ algorithm, which is discussed in more detail in the following.

6.10.1 HESSENBERG-TRIANGULAR REDUCTION

The MATLAB function qhrz_.m that is presented in Section 3.7 can be used to simultaneously reduce $\mathbf{A}$ to an upper Hessenberg form and $\mathbf{B}$ to an upper triangular form.

```
>> A=[1,2,3,4;5,6,7,8;2,1,4,3;8,7,5,6];    B=A';
```

```
>> [H,R,U,V]=QHRZ_(A,B)
H =                                          U =
   -8.9461   -7.3613   -3.0831  -13.3218        -0.1826    0.1695   -0.4550    0.8549
   -3.7372   -2.9272    1.0910   -4.6522        -0.3651   -0.4638   -0.7182   -0.3683
         0   -1.7273   -2.6554   -5.5155        -0.5477    0.7760   -0.0658   -0.3058
         0    0.0000   -0.4790    0.8645        -0.7303   -0.3925    0.5222    0.1998
R =                                          V =
   -5.4772   -7.8790    2.5735  -15.6460         1.0000         0         0         0
         0    1.4368    1.1975    0.0932              0    0.7209    0.5767   -0.3845
         0         0    0.9510   -6.4657              0   -0.5947    0.7995    0.0843
         0         0         0    4.2759              0    0.3560    0.1678    0.9193
```

6.10.2 DEFLATION

If $H(o+1,o)=0, 1 \le o < n$, we can split the eigenvalue problem $H - \lambda R$ into two smaller eigenvalue problems $H(1:o,1:o) - \lambda R(1:o,1:o)$ and $H(o+1:n,o+1:n) - \lambda R(o+1:n,o+1:n)$,

$$H - \lambda R = \begin{bmatrix} H(1:o,1:o) - \lambda R(1:o,1:o) & H(1:o,o+1:n) - \lambda R(1:o,o+1:n) \\ 0 & H(o+1:n,o+1:n) - \lambda R(o+1:n,o+1:n) \end{bmatrix}.$$

On the other hand, if $R(o,o)=0, 1 \le o < n$, we can find two orthogonal matrices Q and Z, $Q'HZ \Rightarrow H$ and $Q'RZ \Rightarrow R$, so that $H(n,n-1) = 0$ and $R(n,n) = 0$, and then deflate. We take the following simple example to illustrate the process.

```
H = [1    2    3    4;        R = [1    2    3    4;
     4    3    2    1;             0    0    4    3;    %R(2,2)=0
     0    2    3    4;             0    0    3    4;
     0    0    4    3]             0    0    0    4];
```

First we zero R(3,3) with Q23'*R, at same time we also calculate Q23'*H.
```
>> Q23=eye(4);   [c,s]=givens_(R(2,3),R(3,3));   Q23(2:3,2:3)=[c s;-s c];
```

```
>> H=Q23'*H                           >> R=Q23'*R
=   1.0000    2.0000    3.0000    4.0000    =   1.0000    2.0000    3.0000    4.0000
    3.2000    3.6000    3.4000    3.2000             0         0    5.0000    4.8000
   -2.4000   -0.2000    1.2000    2.6000             0         0         0    1.4000
         0         0    4.0000    3.0000             0         0         0    4.0000
```

Because H(3,1) becomes nonzero, in the second step, we use Z12 to recover H's Hessenberg form.
```
>> Z12=eye(4);   [c,s]=givens_(H(3,2),H(3,1));   Z12(1:2,1:2)=[c -s;s c];
```

```
>> H=H*Z12                            >> R=R*Z12
=   1.9100   -1.1626    3.0000    4.0000    =   1.9100   -1.1626    3.0000    4.0000
    3.3218   -3.4879    3.4000    3.2000             0         0    5.0000    4.8000
         0    2.4083    1.2000    2.6000             0         0         0    1.4000
         0         0    4.0000    3.0000             0         0         0    4.0000
```

We repeat the above two steps to zero R(4,4) by pre-multiplication of Q34', then to recover H's Hessenberg form by post-multiplication of Z23.

```
>> Q34=eye(4);  [c,s]=givens_(R(3,4),R(4,4));  Q34(3:4,3:4)=[c s;-s c];
```

```
>> H=Q34'*H                              >> R=Q34'*R
=    1.9100    -1.1626     3.0000    4.0000   =    1.9100    -1.1626    3.0000    4.0000
     3.3218    -3.4879     3.4000    3.2000        0          0         5.0000    4.8000
     0         -0.7956    -4.1719   -3.6905        0          0         0        -4.2379
     0          2.2731    -0.1888    1.4630        0          0         0         0
```

```
>> Z23=eye(4);  [c,s]=givens_(H(4,3),H(4,2));  Z23(2:3,2:3)=[c -s;s c];
```

```
>> H=H*Z23                               >> R=R*Z23
=    1.9100     2.8935     1.4069    4.0000   =    1.9100     2.8935    1.4069    4.0000
     3.3218     3.0997     3.7573    3.2000        0          4.9828    0.4138    4.8000
     0         -4.2234     0.4476   -3.6905        0          0         0        -4.2379
     0          0         -2.2809    1.4630        0          0         0         0
```

Finally we can zero H(4,3) by post-multiplication of Z34. Because of the structure of R, this operation does not change R(4,:).

```
>> Z34=eye(4);  [c,s]=givens_(H(4,4),H(4,3));  Z34(3:4,3:4)=[c -s;s c];
```

```
>> H=H*Z34                               >> R=R*Z34
=    1.9100     2.8935     4.1265    0.9753   =    1.9100     2.8935    4.1265    0.9753
     3.3218     3.0997     4.7221   -1.4351        0          4.9828    4.2637    2.2431
     0         -4.2234    -2.8648   -2.3692        0          0        -3.5672   -2.2880
     0          0          0         2.7098        0          0         0         0
```

Now $\mathbf{H} - \lambda\mathbf{R}$ is deflated at $o = n - 1$,

$$\mathbf{H} - \lambda\mathbf{R} = \begin{bmatrix} \mathbf{H}(1:n-1,1:n-1) - \lambda\mathbf{R}(1:n-1,1:n-1) & \mathbf{H}(1:n-1,n) - \lambda\mathbf{R}(1:n-1,n) \\ 0 & H_{nn} \end{bmatrix}.$$

6.10.3 SHIFT

We can assume without loss of generality that $\mathbf{H}$ has no zeros in its sub-diagonal and $\mathbf{R}$ has no zeros in its diagonal, because if they do, we can deflate to two or more smaller eigenvalue problems. Therefore, we can assume $\mathbf{R}$ is non-singular and the eigenvalue problem $\mathbf{Hx} - \lambda\mathbf{Rx}$ can be equivalently transformed into $(\mathbf{HR}^{-1})(\mathbf{Rx}) = \lambda(\mathbf{Rx})$. When we apply shift, we can assume the shift is implicitly applied to the Hessenberg matrix $\mathbf{M} = \mathbf{HR}^{-1}$. We do not need to form $\mathbf{M}$ explicitly. To apply the implicit Q theorem, see Sections 3.5 and 6.4.4, all we need is to determine the two eigenvalues σ_1 and σ_2 of $\mathbf{M}(n-1:n, n-1:n)$ and calculate $\mathbf{v} = (\mathbf{M} - \sigma_1\mathbf{I})(\mathbf{M} - \sigma_2\mathbf{I})\mathbf{I}(:,1)$. Then we find a Householder matrix $\mathbf{Q}_0$ so that $\mathbf{Q}_0\mathbf{v} = \pm\|\mathbf{v}\|_2\mathbf{I}(:,1)$. Next we apply $\mathbf{Q}_0\mathbf{H} \Rightarrow \mathbf{H}$ and $\mathbf{RQ}_0 \Rightarrow \mathbf{R}$. Finally, we apply the steps of QHRZ algorithm (see Section 3.7) to recover the upper Hessenberg form to $\mathbf{H}$ and upper triangular form to $\mathbf{R}$.

v can be calculated in $O(1)$ flops as follows:

$$\mathbf{v} = \begin{bmatrix} M_{11}^2 + M_{12}M_{21} - (\sigma_1 + \sigma_2) M_{11} + \sigma_1\sigma_2 \\ M_{21} (M_{11} + M_{22} - \sigma_1 - \sigma_2); \\ M_{21} M_{32} 0 \\ \vdots \\ 0 \end{bmatrix},$$

$$\sigma_1 + \sigma_2 = M_{n-1,n-1} + M_{nn},$$

$$\sigma_1\sigma_2 = M_{n-1,n-1}M_{nn} - M_{n-1,n}M_{n,n-1},$$

$$\mathbf{M}(n-1:n,n-1:n) = \mathbf{H}(n-1:n,n-2:n)\,(\mathbf{R}(n-2:n,n-2:n))^{-1},$$

$$\mathbf{M}(1:3,1:2) = \mathbf{H}(1:3,1:2)\,(\mathbf{R}(1:2,1:2))^{-1}.$$

6.10.4 MATLAB IMPLEMENTATION OF QZ ALGORITHM

We put everything we discussed in this section together to a MATLAB functions, xeigUnSymByQZ_.m. In the function, the economy is made in the matrix product by the Givens or Householder matrix. The function contains an input argument format, which controls the calculation of the two orthogonal matrices **U** and **V**. If format='long', **U** and **V** are calculated. If format='brief', **U** and **V** are not calculated.

Algorithm 6.17

Solution of generalized eigenvalue problem $\mathbf{Av} = \lambda\mathbf{Bv}$ by QZ iteration.

```
function [A,B,U,V] = xeigUnsymByQZ_(A,B,tol,format)

[m,n] = size(A);  [k,l]= size(B);
[A,B,U,V] = QHRZt_(A,B,'long');    %A==>Upper Hessenberg, B==>Upper Triangular.

k = 1;  l = m;
while k<l-1
    k = 1; o = 0;
    for i=l:-1:2   %Find deflation due to H(1,l-1)=0
        if (abs(A(i,i-1)) > tol*(abs(A(i-1,i-1))+abs(A(i,i))))
            if (o == 0) o = 1; else l = i + 1; break; end
        else
            if (o == 0) l = l - 1; else l = l - 2; end
            o = 0;
        end
    end
    for i=l:-1:2   %Find deflation due to H(k,k-1)=0
        if (abs(A(i,i-1)) <= tol*(abs(A(i-1,i-1))+abs(A(i,i))))
            k = i; break;
        end
    end
    o = k;          %Find deflation due to T(o,o)=0
    while (o < l)
        tnorm = 0.0;    o = l + 1;
        for j=k:l tnorm = tnorm + abs(B(j,j)); end
        for j=k:l
            if (abs(B(j,j)) < tol*tnorm) o = j; break; end
        end
```

```
          p = k;  q = 1;
          if (strcmp(format,'long')) p = 1; q = n; end
          if (o == k)
              [c,s] = givens_(B(k,k+1),B(k+1,k+1));   G = [c s;-s c];
              B(k:k+1,k+1:q) = G'*B(k:k+1,k+1:q);
              A(k:k+1,k:q) = G'*A(k:k+1,k:q);
              if (strcmp(format,'long')) U(:,k:k+1) = U(:,k:k+1)*G; end
              o = o + 1;
          end
          for j=o:1-1
              [c,s] = givens_(B(j,j+1),B(j+1,j+1));   G = [c s;-s c];
              B(j:j+1,j+1:q) = G'*B(j:j+1,j+1:q);
              A(j:j+1,j-1:q) = G'*A(j:j+1,j-1:q);
              if (strcmp(format,'long')) U(:,j:j+1) = U(:,j:j+1)*G; end
              [c,s] = givens_(-A(j+1,j),A(j+1,j-1));   G = [c s; -s c];
              A(p:j+1,j-1:j) = A(p:j+1,j-1:j)*G;
              B(p:j-1,j-1:j) = B(p:j-1,j-1:j)*G;
              if (strcmp(format,'long')) V(:,j-1:j) = V(:,j-1:j)*G; end
              o = o + 1;
          end
          if (o == 1)
              [c,s] = givens_(-A(1,1),A(1,1-1));   G = [c s; -s c];
              A(p:1,1-1:1) = A(p:1,1-1:1)*G;
              B(p:1-1,1-1:1) = B(p:1-1,1-1:1)*G;
              if (strcmp(format,'long')) V(:,1-1:1) = V(:,1-1:1)*G; end
              1 = 1 - 1;  o = k;
          end
      end
 end  %while(p<1)
 %Apply QZ to [A(k:1,k:1),B(k:1,k:1)]
 if (k >= 1-1) break; end
 B33 = 1.0/B(1,1);
 B23 = -B(1-1,1)*B33/B(1-1,1-1);
 B13 = -(B(1-2,1-1)*B23+B(1-2,1)*B33)/B(1-2,1-2);
 B22 = 1.0/B(1-1,1-1);
 B12 = -B(1-2,1-1)*B22/B(1-2,1-2);
 M11 = A(1-1,1-2)*B12 + A(1-1,1-1)*B22;
 M12 = A(1-1,1-2)*B13 + A(1-1,1-1)*B23 + A(1-1,1)*B33;
 M21 = A(1,1-1)*B22;      M22 = A(1,1-1)*B23 + A(1,1)*B33;
 s = M11 + M22;  t = M11*M22 - M12*M21;        %double shifts
 a0 = 1.0/B(k,k);
 a1 = A(k,k)*a0;      b1 = A(k+1,k)*a0;   %H*inv(T)*e1=[a1;b1;0;...0]
 b2 = b1/B(k+1,k+1); a2 = (a1 - B(k,k+1)*b2)/B(k,k);
 a3 = A(k,k)*a2 + A(k,k+1)*b2;
 b3 = A(k+1,k)*a2 + A(k+1,k+1)*b2;
 c3 = A(k+2,k+1)*b2;
 v = [a3-s*a1+t; b3-s*b1; c3];                 %
 for j=k:1-1
     [h,beta] = householder_(v,1,2);    bh = beta*h;
     p = max(1,j-1);  q = 1;   ij = j:j+length(v)-1;
     if (strcmp(format,'long')) q = m; end
     A(ij,p:q) = A(ij,p:q) - bh*(h'*A(ij,p:q));
     B(ij,p:q) = B(ij,p:q) - bh*(h'*B(ij,p:q));
     if (strcmp(format,'long')) U(:,ij) = U(:,ij)-(U(:,ij)*h)*bh'; end
     if (j < 1-1)
         v = [B(j+2,j);B(j+2,j+1);B(j+2,j+2)];
         [h,beta] = householder_(v,3,2);      bh = beta*h;
         p = k;   q = min(j+3,1);
```

```
            if (strcmp(format,'long')) p = 1;   q = min(j+3, m);   end
            A(p:q,j:j+2) = A(p:q,j:j+2) - (A(p:q,j:j+2)*h)*bh';
            B(p:q,j:j+2) = B(p:q,j:j+2) - (B(p:q,j:j+2)*h)*bh';
            if (strcmp(format,'long')) V(:,j:j+2)=V(:,j:j+2)-(V(:,j:j+2)*h)*bh'; end
        end
        v = [B(j+1,j);B(j+1,j+1)];
        [h,beta] = householder_(v,2,2);       bh = beta*h;
        p = k;   q = min(j+3,l);
        if (strcmp(format,'long'))  p = 1;   q = min(j+3, m);  end
        A(p:q,j:j+1) = A(p:q,j:j+1) - (A(p:q,j:j+1)*h)*bh';
        B(p:q,j:j+1) = B(p:q,j:j+1) - (B(p:q,j:j+1)*h)*bh';
        if (strcmp(format,'long')) V(:,j:j+1) = V(:,j:j+1)-(V(:,j:j+1)*h)*bh'; end
        if (j < l-2) v = [A(j+1,j);A(j+2,j);A(j+3,j)]; end
        if (j == l-2) v = [A(j+1,j);A(j+2,j)]; end
    end
end       %while(k<l-1)


k = 1;  l = m;
while k < l    %Reduce 2x2 diagonal blocks to triangle if possible
    if (abs(A(l,l-1)) > tol*(abs(A(l-1,l-1))+abs(A(l,l))))
        [G,M,res] = xeig2x2_(A(l-1:l,l-1:l),B(l-1:l,l-1:l));
        if (res ~= -1)
            if (strcmp(format,'long')) q = n; else q = l; end
            A(l-1:l,l-1:q) = G'*A(l-1:l,l-1:q);
            B(l-1:l,l-1:q) = G'*B(l-1:l,l-1:q);
            if (strcmp(format,'long')) U(:,l-1:l) = U(:,l-1:l)*G; end
            if (strcmp(format,'long')) p = 1; else p = l-1; end
            A(p:l,l-1:l) = A(p:l,l-1:l)*M;
            B(p:l,l-1:l) = B(p:l,l-1:l)*M;
            if (strcmp(format,'long')) V(:,l-1:l) = V(:,l-1:l)*M; end
        end
        l = l - 2;
    else
        A(l,l-1) = 0;   l = l - 1;
    end
end
```

Following examples use the two matrices: A=[1,2,3,4;5,6,7,8;2,1,4,3;8,7,5,6]; B=A';.
The verification of xeigUnsymByQZ_(A,B) applied to the two 4 × 4 matrices is listed below.

```
>> [S,T,U,V]=xeigUnsymByQZ_(A,B)          U =
S =                                            0.0626   -0.1305   -0.4121    0.8995
     5.5886   -7.0079    6.1416   14.9822      0.4472    0.1846   -0.7940   -0.3681
          0   -1.3156   -2.0178   -0.7656      0.2300   -0.9592   -0.0178   -0.1633
          0        0    -3.1847   -6.8609      0.8621    0.1696    0.4465    0.1692
    -0.0000   -0.0000        0     1.3666  V =
T =                                            0.8995   -0.4121    0.1305    0.0626
     1.3666   -6.8609    0.7656   14.9822     -0.3681   -0.7940   -0.1846    0.4472
          0    3.1847   -2.0178   -6.1416     -0.1633   -0.0178    0.9592    0.2300
          0        0     1.3156   -7.0079      0.1692    0.4465   -0.1696    0.8621
     0.0000   -0.0000    0.0000    5.5886

>> norm(U'*U-eye(4))                      >> norm(U'*A*V-S)
=   1.2877e-015                           =   2.2944e-009
>> norm(V'*V-eye(4))                      >> norm(U'*B*V-T)
=   2.1012e-015                           =   1.0254e-015
```

We make a change to $\mathbf{A}$ and $\mathbf{B}$: `A(1,:)=A(4,:); B(:,1)=B(:,4); ,` so that both $\mathbf{A}$ and $\mathbf{B}$ are singular. Now $\mathbf{A} - \lambda \mathbf{B}$ has two conjugate complex eigenvalues, one zero eigenvalue and one infinity eigenvalue, as the following output shows.

```
>> [S,T,U,V]=xeigUnsymByQZ_(A,B)          U =
S =                                           0.5182     0.0645    -0.8077    -0.2738
   -4.4737    17.7605     0.9871    13.4746    0.5686    -0.6261     0.1404     0.5147
    1.7664    -1.7703     0.4496    -1.4964    0.3735     0.7744     0.1345     0.4928
         0          0    -0.0000    -1.3246    0.5182     0.0645     0.5567    -0.6461
   -0.0000    -0.0000          0    -4.8540  V =
T =                                           0.3730     0.1426     0.4772     0.7828
   -7.9512    13.5130     2.3558    16.6309   -0.3816     0.1179    -0.7027     0.5888
    0.0000     2.9496    -2.0495     1.2125    0.3943     0.8649    -0.2372    -0.2008
    0.0000     0.0000    -3.1096     0.0231   -0.7482     0.4667     0.4713    -0.0158
         0          0          0     0.0000
```

It is interesting to apply `[S,T,U,V]=xeigUnsymByQZ_(A,eye(4))` and `[S,T,U,V]=xeigUnsymByQZ_(A,A)`. For brevity, their output is not listed.

6.11 ALGORITHMS FOR SYMMETRIC POSITIVE INDEFINITE $\mathbf{Ax} = \lambda \mathbf{Bx}$

For two matrices $\mathbf{A}, \mathbf{B} \in \mathbb{R}^{n \times n}$, an eigenvalue λ is defined as the root of the nth order polynomial $\det(\mathbf{A} - \lambda \mathbf{B}) = 0$. Given any two non-singular matrices $\mathbf{U}$ and $\mathbf{V}$, we have the following:

$$\det(\mathbf{A} - \lambda \mathbf{B}) = \det(\mathbf{U}'\mathbf{A}\mathbf{V} - \lambda \mathbf{U}'\mathbf{B}\mathbf{V}) = \det(\bar{\mathbf{A}} - \lambda \bar{\mathbf{B}}) = 0. \qquad (6.38)$$

According to the properties of $\mathbf{A}$ and $\mathbf{B}$, we can choose appropriate and well-conditioned $\mathbf{U}$ and $\mathbf{V}$, so that $\det(\bar{\mathbf{A}} - \lambda \bar{\mathbf{B}}) = 0$ can be solved directly or by an established algorithm.

In this section, we consider the particular case that $\mathbf{A}$ and $\mathbf{B}$ are symmetric but $\mathbf{B}$ is positive indefinite. To keep the symmetry, it is necessary that $\mathbf{V} = \mathbf{U}$. Because $\mathbf{B}$ is not positive definite, the roots of $\det(\bar{\mathbf{A}} - \lambda \bar{\mathbf{B}}) = 0$ can be conjugate complex. If we want to keep the real arithmetic, the simplest form of $\bar{\mathbf{A}}$ is a pseudo-diagonal of 1×1 and 2×2 blocks and $\bar{\mathbf{B}}$ is diagonal. The algorithm to achieve this simplest form is similar to the algorithms `eigSymByQR_.m` and `eigUnsymByQR_.m` discussed in Section 6.4. In the first step, we transform $\mathbf{A}$ and $\mathbf{B}$ to a symmetric tri-diagonal $\hat{\mathbf{A}}$ and a sign matrix $\hat{\mathbf{J}}$.[2] The first step is a direct procedure, that is `GTJGt_.m`, see Section 2.6. In the second step, the symmetric tri-diagonal matrix $\hat{\mathbf{A}}$ is congruently transformed into the pseudo-diagonal $\bar{\mathbf{A}}$ and the sign matrix $\hat{\mathbf{J}}$ is congruently transformed into another sign matrix $\bar{\mathbf{J}}$. Because the congruent transformation does not change the inertia of a matrix, the number of $+1$, 0, and -1 in $\hat{\mathbf{J}}$ and $\bar{\mathbf{J}}$ is same but the locations of $+1$, 0, and -1 in $\hat{\mathbf{J}}$ and $\bar{\mathbf{J}}$ can be different. Each 2×2 diagonal block of $\bar{\mathbf{A}}$ and the corresponding diagonal of $\pm(+1, -1)$ of $\bar{\mathbf{J}}$ form a pair of conjugate complex eigenvalues. Each 1×1 diagonal block of $\bar{\mathbf{A}}$ and the corresponding diagonal of $+1, 0, -1$ of $\bar{\mathbf{J}}$ form a real eigenvalue. The second step is an iterative procedure. To keep it analogous to QR iteration, we refer the algorithm of this section as GJR iteration.

---

[2] A sign matrix is a diagonal matrix. The diagonal components can be only $+1$, 0 or -1. See Section 2.6. If $\mathbf{B}$ is positive definite, $\hat{\mathbf{J}}$ is simply an identity matrix. The number of $+1$, 0 and -1 in $\hat{\mathbf{B}}$ are the inertia of $\mathbf{B}$.

6.11.1 A GJR ITERATION STEP FOR A TRI-DIAGONAL AND SIGN PAIR

To keep the discussion concise, we apply a GJR iteration step to a 4×4 tri-diagonal and sign matrix pair generated as follows.

```
>> A=randn(4);   A = 0.5*(A+A');   B=randn(4);   B = 0.5*(B+B');
>> G1=eye(4);   G2=eye(4);   G3=eye(4);
>> [T,J,G]=GTJGt_(A,B);
```

```
>> T=band2full_(T,1,1,4,4)                >> J=diag(J)
T =                                       J =
   -0.4394    0.5814         0        0        1    0    0    0
    0.5814    2.9106    3.9144         0        0   -1    0    0
         0    3.9144    4.5468   -0.0115        0    0    1    0
         0         0   -0.0115    0.4810        0    0    0    1
```

The GJR iteration is similar to QR iteration that is discussed in Section 6.4. The difference is that xgivens_.m is used in GJR iteration while givens_.m is used in QR iteration. At first, we find a non-singular matrix **G** such that $G'T \Rightarrow T$ is lower triangular and $G'JG$ is still a sign matrix.

```
>> [G1(1:2,1:2),hyper] = xgivens_(T(1,1),T(2,1),J(1,1),J(2,2));   G=G1;
```

```
>> T=G1'*T                                >> J=G1'*J*G1
T =       %T(2,1)==>0                      J =       %J is still a sign matrix.
   -0.3807   -5.1156   -5.9775        0      -1.0000        0        0        0
         0   -4.2468   -4.5175        0            0   1.0000        0        0
         0    3.9144    4.5468   -0.0115          0        0   1.0000        0
         0         0   -0.0115    0.4810          0        0        0   1.0000
```

```
>> [G2(2:3,2:3),hyper] = xgivens_(T(2,2),T(3,2),J(2,2),J(3,3));   G=G*G2;
```

```
>> T=G2'*T                                >> J=G2'*J*G2
T =       %T(3,2)==>0                      J =       %J is still a sign matrix.
   -0.3807   -5.1156   -5.9775        0      -1.0000        0        0        0
         0    5.7757    6.4033   -0.0078          0   1.0000        0        0
         0    0.0000   -0.2815    0.0085          0   0.0000   1.0000        0
         0         0   -0.0115    0.4810          0        0        0   1.0000
```

```
>> [G3(3:4,3:4),hyper] = xgivens_(T(3,3),T(4,3),J(3,3),J(4,4))
G3 =
    1.0000         0         0         0
         0    1.0000         0         0
         0         0    0.9992   -0.0408
         0         0    0.0408    0.9992
hyper =
     0           %hyper=0 means G3 is Givens rotation matrix.
```

```
>> G=G*G3
G =       %Note G's Hessenberg form.
   -1.1541    1.1228    1.0341   -0.0422
   -1.5270    0.8486    0.7815   -0.0319
         0    0.6777   -0.7347    0.0300
         0         0    0.0408    0.9992
```

```
>> T=G3'*T                                    >> J=G3'*J*G3
T =     %T(4,3)=>0. Now T is lower triangularJ =      %J is still a sign matrix.
   -0.3807    -5.1156    -5.9775         0      -1.0000         0         0         0
         0     5.7757     6.4033    -0.0078           0    1.0000         0         0
         0     0.0000    -0.2818     0.0281           0    0.0000    1.0000         0
         0    -0.0000    -0.0000     0.4803           0   -0.0000         0    1.0000
```

Second, $\mathbf{TG} \Rightarrow \mathbf{T}$. Now $\mathbf{T}$ recovers its initial symmetric tri-diagonal form.

```
>> T=T*G
T =
    8.2511    -8.8197    -0.0000     0.0000
   -8.8197     9.2409    -0.1910     0.0000
   -0.0000    -0.1910     0.2081     0.0196
    0.0000    -0.0000     0.0196     0.4799
```

If we apply the above two sub-steps for 200 times, we get the following output, where $\mathbf{T}$ becomes pseudo-diagonal and $\mathbf{J}$ remains a sign matrix.

```
>> T                                   >> J
T =    %T32=>5.9038e-016, T43=>-1.0352e-010 J =
    2.4011    -2.9876         0         0      -1    0    0    0
   -2.9876     3.1462     0.0000         0       0    1    0    0
         0     0.0000     0.4905    -0.0000       0    0    1    0
         0          0    -0.0000     0.4423       0    0    0    1
```

The two real eigenvalues are T(3,3)/J(3,3) and T(4,4)/J(4,4). The two complex eigenvalues are determined by $\det(\mathbf{T}(1:2,1:2) - \lambda\mathbf{J}(1:2,1:2)) = 0$. The eigenvalues of the original pair $(\mathbf{A},\mathbf{B})$ and the reduced pair $(\mathbf{T},\mathbf{J})$ can be compared as follows:

```
>> eig(A,B)                          >> eig(T,J)
ans =                                ans =
   0.3725 + 1.1103i                     0.3725 + 1.1103i
   0.3725 - 1.1103i                     0.3725 - 1.1103i
   0.4905                               0.4905
   0.4423                               0.4423
```

6.11.2 DEFLATION

When an off-diagonal component of $\mathbf{T}$ is small enough, we set it to zero. Then the eigen problem is deflated to two smaller eigen problems. See Section 6.4.3 for the discussion on deflation. A deflation algorithm to treat $\mathbf{J}$ with zeros, which is similar to that discussed in Section 6.10.2, is not known.

6.11.3 SHIFT

The validity of the shift strategy of GJR presented in this subsection cannot be proved mathematically. But it is quite effective in practical calculations. The gist of shift in same in GJR algorithm and in QR algorithm. See Section 6.4.4 for the discussion on shift in QR algorithm.

The following is the single shift GJR iteration:

$$\mathbf{G}_1'(\mathbf{T}_0 - \sigma\mathbf{J}_0) = \mathbf{R}_1, \quad \mathbf{J}_1 = \mathbf{G}_1'\mathbf{J}_0\mathbf{G}_1,$$
$$\mathbf{T}_1 = \mathbf{R}_1\mathbf{G}_1 + \sigma\mathbf{J}_1 = \mathbf{G}_1'(\mathbf{T}_0 - \sigma\mathbf{J}_0)\mathbf{G}_1 + \sigma\mathbf{J}_1 = \mathbf{G}_1'\mathbf{T}_0\mathbf{G}_1. \tag{6.39}$$

If the off-diagonal of $\mathbf{T}_0$ does not contain zeros and σ is one eigenvalue of the pair $(\mathbf{T}_0, \mathbf{J}_0)$, the above GJR step with σ as the shift will converge to σ in one step, with $\mathbf{T}_1(n, n-1) = \mathbf{T}_1(n-1, n) = 0$ and $\mathbf{T}_1(n, n) = \sigma$.

The double shift GJR iteration is expressed as follows:

$$
\begin{aligned}
&\mathbf{G}'_1 (\mathbf{T}_0 - \sigma_1 \mathbf{J}_0) = \mathbf{R}_1, \quad \mathbf{J}_1 = \mathbf{G}'_1 \mathbf{J}_0 \mathbf{G}_1, \\
&\mathbf{T}_1 = \mathbf{R}_1 \mathbf{G}_1 + \sigma \mathbf{J}_1 = \mathbf{G}'_1 (\mathbf{T}_0 - \sigma \mathbf{J}_0) \mathbf{G}_1 + \sigma \mathbf{J}_1 = \mathbf{G}'_1 \mathbf{T}_0 \mathbf{G}_1, \\
&\mathbf{G}'_2 (\mathbf{T}_1 - \sigma_2 \mathbf{J}_1) = \mathbf{R}_2, \quad \mathbf{J}_2 = \mathbf{G}'_2 \mathbf{J}_1 \mathbf{G}_2, \\
&\mathbf{T}_2 = \mathbf{R}_2 \mathbf{G}_2 + \sigma_2 \mathbf{J}_2 = \mathbf{G}'_2 (\mathbf{T}_1 - \sigma_2 \mathbf{J}_1) \mathbf{G}_2 + \sigma_2 \mathbf{J}_2 = \mathbf{G}'_2 \mathbf{T}_1 \mathbf{G}_2 = \mathbf{G}'_2 \mathbf{G}'_1 \mathbf{T}_0 \mathbf{G}_2 \mathbf{G}_1.
\end{aligned}
\tag{6.40}
$$

A double shift algorithm, which is similar to that discussed in Sections 6.4.4 and 6.10.2, is not known. And the validity of the implicit Q theorem is not known.

In xeigByxgivens_.m, the shift is determined by the eigenvalues of $\mathbf{T}(n-1:n, n-1:n) - \lambda \mathbf{J}(n-1:n, n-1:n)$. If the eigenvalues are real, the implicit single shift is used,

$$
\mathbf{v} = (\mathbf{T} - \sigma \mathbf{J}) \mathbf{I}(:, 1) =
\begin{bmatrix}
T_{11} - \sigma J_{11} \\
T_{21} \\
0 \\
\vdots \\
0
\end{bmatrix}.
$$

If the eigenvalues are conjugate complex, the implicit double shift is used. The complex eigenvalues can only occur when $J(n-1, n-1)J(n, n) = -1$,

$$
\mathbf{v} =
\begin{bmatrix}
T_{11}^2 + T_{22}^2 - J_{11} s T_{11} + t J_{11}^2 \\
(T_{11} + T_{22}) T_{21} - \frac{1}{2}(J_{11} + J_{22}) s T_{21} \\
T_{32} T_{21} \\
0 \\
\vdots \\
0
\end{bmatrix},
$$

$$
s = \frac{T(n-1, n-1)}{J(n-1, n-1)} + \frac{T(n, n)}{J(n, n)},
$$

$$
t = \frac{T(n-1, n-1)T(n, n) - T(n-1, n)T(n, n-1))}{J(n-1, n-1)J(n, n)}.
$$

In both cases, a non-singular matrix $\mathbf{G}_0$ is determined so that $\mathbf{G}'_0 \mathbf{v} = \mu \mathbf{I}(:, 1)$ and $\mathbf{G}'_0 \mathbf{J} \mathbf{G}_0 \Rightarrow \mathbf{J}$ keeps the sign matrix form. The calculated $\mathbf{G}'_0 \mathbf{T} \mathbf{G}_0 \Rightarrow \mathbf{T}$ loses the tri-diagonal form. The subsequent GJR steps are to recover the tri-diagonal form to $\mathbf{T}$ and keep $\mathbf{J}$ a sign matrix.

6.11.4 MATLAB IMPLEMENTATIONS OF GJR ITERATIONS ALGORITHMS

We put everything we discussed in this section together to a MATLAB function, xeigByxgivens_.m. In the function, the economy is made in the matrix product by the extended Givens matrix. The function contains an input argument format, which controls the calculation of the matrix $\mathbf{G}$. If format='long', $\mathbf{G}$ is calculated. If format='brief', $\mathbf{G}$ is not calculated.

Algorithm 6.18

Solution of generalized symmetric eigen problem $\mathbf{Av} = \lambda\mathbf{Bv}$ by GJR iteration.

```
function [T,J,G] = xeigByxgivens_(A,B,tol,format)

[m,n] = size(A); [k,l] = size(B);
[T,J,G] = GTJGt_(A,B,'givens',1,tol,'short');
tnorm = norm(T(:,2))/sqrt(m);

k = 1;  l = m;  o = 0;
while k<l-1    %Apply xGivens step to T(k:l,k:l)
    k = 1;  o = 0;
    for i=l:-1:2
        if (abs(T(i,1))>tol*max(abs(T(i-1,2))+abs(T(i,2)),tnorm))
            if (o == 0) o = 1; else l = i + 1; break; end
        else
            if (o == 0) l = l - 1; else l = l - 2; end
            T(i,1) = 0;  o = 0;
        end
    end
    for i=l:-1:2
        if (abs(T(i,1))< tol*min(abs(T(i-1,2))+abs(T(i,2)),tnorm))
            T(i,1) = 0;  k = i;  break;
        end
    end
    if (k >= l-1) break; end
    T11 = T(l-1,2); T21 = T(l,1); T22 = T(l,2);  T12 = T21;  d1=J(l-1);  d2=J(l);
    a = d1*d2;    b = -d2*T11 - d1*T22;   c = T11*T22 - T12*T21;
    delta = 0.5*(d2*T11-d1*T22);  d = delta*delta + d1*d2*T12*T21;
    Tk = T(k,2);   Tk1 = T(k+1,1);
    if (d1 == d2)
        d = 0.5*(T11-T22);  e = sqrt(d*d+T21*T21);
        if (d >= 0.0) miu = T22-T21*T21/(d+e); else miu = T22-T21*T21/(d-e); end
        h = [Tk-miu; Tk1; 0; 0];
    elseif (a==0 && b~=0) %d1*d2=0
        miu = -c/b;  h = [Tk-miu*J(k); Tk1; 0; 0];
    elseif (a~=0 && d>=0) %d1*d2~=0
        miu = T22/d2 + (delta - sign(delta)*sqrt(d))/(d1*d2);
        h = [Tk-miu*J(k); Tk1; 0; 0];
    else
        eta = T11/d1 + T22/d2;  tau = c/(d1*d2);  dk = J(k); dk1 = J(k+1);
        h = [Tk*Tk + Tk1*Tk1 - eta*dk*Tk + tau*dk*dk;
            (Tk+T(k+1,2))*Tk1 - 0.5*eta*(dk+dk1)*Tk1; T(k+2,1)*Tk1; 0];
    end

    for i=k:l-1
        if (h(3)==0 || i==l-1)     rc = [1,2];
        elseif(J(i) == J(i+1))     rc = [1,2;1,3];
        elseif (J(i) ~= J(i+2))    rc = [1,3;1,2];
        elseif (J(i+1) == J(i+2))  rc = [2,3;1,2];
        elseif (J(i)*J(i+1) ~= 0)  rc = [1,2;1,3];
        elseif (J(i)*J(i+2) ~= 0)  rc = [1,3;1,2];
        elseif (J(i+1)*J(i+2) ~= 0) rc = [2,3;1,2];
        else
            error('eig2Byxgivens_:impossible case.');
        end
        S = zeros(4,3);
```

```
S(1,1) = T(i,2);   S(2,2) = T(i+1,2);   S(2,1) = T(i+1,1);   S(1,2) = S(2,1);
if (i < l-1) S(3,2) = T(i+2,1);   S(2,3) = S(3,2);   end
if (size(rc,1) == 2)
    S(3,3) = T(i+2,2);   S(3,1) = h(4);   S(1,3) = S(3,1);
    if (i < l-2) S(4,3) = T(i+3,1); end
end
for j=1:size(rc,1)
    j1 = rc(j,1);   j2 = rc(j,2);   i1 = i+j1-1;   i2 = i+j2-1;
    [Q,hyper] = xgivens_(h(j1),h(j2),J(i1),J(i2));
    h(j1) = Q(1,1)*h(j1) + Q(2,1)*h(j2);   h(j2) = 0.0;
    if (hyper == 0)        %rotation
        s1 = S(j1,:);
        S(j1,:) = Q(1,1)*s1 + Q(2,1)*S(j2,:);
        S(j2,:) = Q(1,2)*s1 + Q(2,2)*S(j2,:);
        s2 = S(:,j2);
        S(:,j2) = S(:,j1)*Q(1,2) + s2*Q(2,2);
        S(:,j1) = S(:,j1)*Q(1,1) + s2*Q(2,1);
        if (strcmp(format,'long'))
            u1 = G(:,i1);
            G(:,i1) = u1*Q(1,1) + G(:,i2)*Q(2,1);
            G(:,i2) = u1*Q(1,2) + G(:,i2)*Q(2,2);
        end
    elseif (hyper == 1)    %hyper rotation 1
        c = Q(1,1);   s =-Q(1,2);
        S(j1,:) = c*S(j1,:) - s*S(j2,:);
        S(j2,:) =-s/c*S(j1,:) + S(j2,:)/c;
        S(:,j1) = S(:,j1)*c - S(:,j2)*s;
        S(:,j2) =-S(:,j1)*s/c + S(:,j2)/c;
        if (strcmp(format,'long'))
            G(:,i1) = G(:,i1)*c - G(:,i2)*s;
            G(:,i2) =-G(:,i1)*s/c + G(:,i2)/c;
        end
    elseif(hyper == 2)     %hyper rotation 2
        c = Q(1,1);   s =-Q(1,2);
        s1 = S(j1,:);
        S(j1,:) = c*s1 - s*S(j2,:);   S(j2,:) =-c/s*S(j1,:) - s1/s;
        s2 = S(:,j1);
        S(:,j1) = s2*c - S(:,j2)*s;   S(:,j2) =-S(:,j1)*c/s - s2/s;
        if (strcmp(format,'long'))
            u1 = G(:,i1);
            G(:,i1) = u1*c - G(:,i2)*s;   G(:,i2) =-G(:,i1)*c/s - u1/s;
        end
        J(i1) =-J(i1);   J(i2) =-J(i2);
    else                        %MDR
        d1 = J(i1)*Q(1,1)*Q(1,1) + J(i2)*Q(2,1)*Q(2,1);
        d2 = J(i1)*Q(1,2)*Q(1,2) + J(i2)*Q(2,2)*Q(2,2);
        J(i1) = sign(d1);   J(i2) = sign(d2);
        d1 = sqrt(abs(d1)); d2 = sqrt(abs(d2));
        if (d1 > 0) Q(:,1) = Q(:,1)/d1; end
        if (d2 > 0) Q(:,2) = Q(:,2)/d2; end
        s1 = S(j1,:);
        S(j1,:) = Q(1,1)*s1 + Q(2,1)*S(j2,:);
        S(j2,:) = Q(1,2)*s1 + Q(2,2)*S(j2,:);
        s2 = S(:,j2);
        S(:,j2) = S(:,j1)*Q(1,2) + s2*Q(2,2);
        S(:,j1) = S(:,j1)*Q(1,1) + s2*Q(2,1);
        if (strcmp(format,'long'))
```

```
                        u1 = G(:,i1);
                        G(:,i1) = u1*Q(1,1) + G(:,i2)*Q(2,1);
                        G(:,i2) = u1*Q(1,2) + G(:,i2)*Q(2,2);
                    end
                end
            end   %j=1:1:size(rc,1)
            if (i > k) T(i,1) = h(1); end
            T(i,2) = S(1,1);  T(i+1,2) = S(2,2);  T(i+1,1) = S(2,1);  h(1) = S(2,1);
            if (i < l-1) h(2) = S(3,1);  T(i+2,1) = S(3,2); end
            if (size(rc,1) == 2)
                T(i+2,2) = S(3,3);  h(3) = S(4,1);  h(4) = S(4,2);
                if (i < l-2) T(i+3,1) = S(4,3); end
            end
        end   %i=k:l-1
end

k = 1;  l = m;
while k < l   %Reduce 2x2 diagonal blocks to diagonal if possible
    if (abs(T(l,1)) > tol*(abs(T(l-1,2))+abs(T(l,2))))
        T11 = T(l-1,2); T21 = T(l,1); T22 = T(l,2); T12 = T21;  d1=J(l-1); d2=J(l);
        [Q,M,hyper] = xeig2x2_([T11,T12;T21,T22],[d1,0;0,d2]);
        if (hyper == -1) l = l-2; continue; end
        if (hyper == 2) J(l-1) =-J(l-1); J(l) =-J(l); end
        if (hyper == 3)
            d1 = J(l-1)*Q(1,1)*Q(1,1) + J(l)*Q(2,1)*Q(2,1);
            d2 = J(l-1)*Q(1,2)*Q(1,2) + J(l)*Q(2,2)*Q(2,2);
            J(l-1) = sign(d1);  J(l) = sign(d2);
            d1 = sqrt(abs(d1)); d2 = sqrt(abs(d2));
            if(d1 > 0) Q(:,1) = Q(:,1)/d1; end
            if(d2 > 0) Q(:,2) = Q(:,2)/d2; end
        end
        T(l-1,2) = (Q(1,1)*T11+Q(2,1)*T21)*Q(1,1)+(Q(1,1)*T12+Q(2,1)*T22)*Q(2,1);
        T(l,2)   = (Q(1,2)*T11+Q(2,2)*T21)*Q(1,2)+(Q(1,2)*T12+Q(2,2)*T22)*Q(2,2);
        T(l,1) = 0;
        if (strcmp(format,'long'))
            u1 = G(:,l-1);
            G(:,l-1) = u1*Q(1,1) + G(:,l)*Q(2,1); G(:,l) = u1*Q(1,2) + G(:,l)*Q(2,2);
        end
        l = l - 2;
    else
        T(l,1) = 0;    l = l - 1;
    end
end
T(1:m-1,3) = T(2:m,1);
```

In the following example, xeigByxgivens_.m is applied to a symmetric positive definite pair. For the symmetric positive definite pair, xeigSym1ByQR_.m produces the same output.

```
>> [Q,R]=QR_(randn(8));   da = randn(8,1);  A = Q*diag(da)*Q';   %A=A'
>> [Q,R]=QR_(randn(8));   db = rand(8,1);   B = Q*diag(db)*Q';   %B=B' & B>0

>> [T,J,U]=xeigByxgivens_(A,B,100*eps,'long');
>> T       %T(:,1)=0, all eigenvalus are real.
=         0     4.0420         0
          0    -7.3633         0
          0    -3.7786         0
          0     1.1581         0
```

```
          0    -1.1389              0
          0    -0.5656              0
          0    -0.3055              0
          0    -0.0535              0
>> J      %B=B' & B>0, then J=I.
=    1    1    1    1    1    1    1    1

>> [D,V]=xeigSym1ByQR_(A,B,100*eps);
>> D      %same as T(:,2).
=  -7.3633    4.0420   -3.7786    1.1581   -1.1389   -0.5656   -0.3055   -0.0535
```

Now we change **B** to a positive indefinite matrix. For a symmetric positive indefinite pair, its eigenvalues can be conjugate complex. The following shows the result output by xeigByxgivens_.m and its result verification.

```
>> db(1)=-db(1);  db(5)=-db(5);  db(8)=-db(8);   %3 negatives.
>> B = Q*diag(db)*Q';   %B=B', B has 3 negative eigenvalues.
>> [T,J,U]=xeigByxgivens_(A,B,100*eps,'long')
T =        %(A,B) has 2 pairs of conjugate complex eigenvalues.
          0    -7.0710              0
          0    -0.2008        -3.0434
    -3.0434    -3.8762              0
          0    -0.9090        -1.3896
    -1.3896    -1.2771              0
          0    -0.9937              0
          0    -0.3468              0
          0    -0.0861              0
J =        %J has 3 -1s.
    1    1    -1    1    -1    1    1    -1
U =
     0.3576   -0.4143   -0.4571   -0.5256   -0.0350    0.5652    0.7878   -0.2770
     1.0000   -1.1921   -0.1936    0.3411    0.6036   -1.2005    0.2573    0.2350
    -0.2816   -0.7057   -2.1386   -0.9728   -0.1265    0.3869   -0.2972    0.3403
     0.7298    0.6522    0.6360    0.3502    0.2952    0.0961   -0.0435   -0.1271
     0.6200   -0.8498    0.5876    0.7019    0.7380    0.4930   -0.4636   -0.7370
     0.2672   -0.1038   -0.3022   -1.0052   -1.1011   -0.6210   -0.2691   -0.3475
     0.3613   -1.3752   -0.9649    1.3246    1.2931   -0.1281    0.2776   -0.9305
     1.2262   -0.6978   -1.7758   -1.1648   -1.0429   -0.0303   -0.1103    0.3784

>> norm(U'*A*U-band2full_(T,1,1))
=    6.8138e-013       %=0, correct result.
>> norm(U'*B*U-diag(J))
=    7.1443e-014       %=0, correct result.
```

xeigByxgivens_.m can be used to a symmetric pair (**A**,**B**), where **A** and **B** can be singular. The following shows the application of xeigByxgivens_.m to such a pair and its result verification.

```
>> [Q,R]=QR_(randn(8)); da(1)=0; da(8)=0; A=Q*diag(da)*Q';   %A=A'
>> [Q,R]=QR_(randn(8)); db(1)=0; db(7)=0; B=Q*diag(da)*Q';   %B=B'

>> [T,J,U]=xeigByxgivens_(A,B,100*eps,'long')
T =        %That T(7,2)=T(8,2)=0 singifies da(1)=da(8)=0.
          0    -5.1173              0
          0     0.4005              0
          0   -16.7251              0
          0     0.0684        -0.2896
```

```
    -0.2896    -0.6222           0
          0    -0.0183           0
          0    -0.0000           0
          0     0.0000           0
J =        %That J has 2 zeors signifies db(1)=db(7)=0.
     0      0     -1     -1      1      1     -1     -1
U =
     1.7500    -0.0196    -3.2573     0.4689    -0.4544     1.3448     1.2164     0.6419
    -0.1599    -0.3947    -3.6736     0.3688     0.3322     1.2925     1.3846    -0.1584
     1.8575     0.2516    -1.0743     0.7798     2.0358     1.9555     2.3539    -1.9609
     1.2299    -0.0075    -2.6102     0.1211     1.4621    -1.0731    -0.8503    -1.7399
    -0.6687     0.3847     6.5085    -0.5885    -0.4573    -2.0624    -1.8549     0.1919
    -0.8644    -0.5028    -4.6271    -0.7905    -0.4695    -0.0636     0.1136    -0.5209
    -0.5028     0.8644     5.7583    -0.8235     0.4168    -3.1404    -2.9255     0.0016
    -0.3186    -0.4879    -0.3793    -1.3249    -1.4901    -0.1396     0.3413     1.2313

>> norm(U'*A*U-band2full_(T,1,1))
=   1.4699e-012      %=0, correct result.
>> norm(U'*B*U-diag(J))
=   5.0440e-013      %=0, correct result.


>> eig(band2full_(T,1,1),diag(J))        >> eig(A,B)     %same as (T,J)!
= -0.3453 + 0.0848i                      = 16.7251
  -0.3453 - 0.0848i                        -0.0000
     -Inf                                  -0.0183
      Inf                                  -0.3453 + 0.0848i
  16.7251                                  -0.3453 - 0.0848i
  -0.0183                                  -0.0000
   0.0000                                      Inf
  -0.0000                                      Inf
```

Of course we can apply xeigUnsymByQZ_.m to all the examples of this section. Because in xeigUnsymByQZ_.m only orthogonal transformations are used, the calculations are perfectly stable, but the symmetry of the pair is not taken into account.

Iterative algorithms of solution of eigenvalue problem

7

INTRODUCTION

For an eigenvalue problem $\mathbf{Ax} = \lambda\mathbf{x}$ or $\mathbf{Ax} = \lambda\mathbf{Bx}$, $\mathbf{A},\mathbf{B} \in \mathbb{R}^{n \times n}$, the iterative algorithm is to find λ and $\mathbf{x}$ through the solution of a smaller eigenvalue problem $(\mathbf{U}'\mathbf{AU})\,\mathbf{y} = \lambda\mathbf{y}$ or $(\mathbf{U}'\mathbf{AU})\,\mathbf{y} = \lambda\,(\mathbf{U}'\mathbf{BU})\,\mathbf{y}$, $\mathbf{U} \in \mathbb{R}^{n \times m}$. For many practical problems, n is usually large and $m \ll n$. The smaller eigenvalue problem is usually solved by some direct algorithm that is presented in Chapter 6.

In Section 7.1, we discuss the general methodology to reduce a large scale eigenvalue problem to a smaller scale eigenvalue problem: the projection method, approximation subspace and projection subspace and the construction of bases of the subspaces. The projection method discussed in Section 7.1 has a close similarity to that discussed in Section 5.3. To speed up the convergence, spectral transformation, restart and lock and purge of converged eigenvalues [40, 65], are needed. The spectral transformation is to algebraically transform an eigenvalue problem to another one that converges faster toward the sought-after eigenvalues. The most commonly used spectral transformation is the shift and inverse. The restart, lock and purge are all the techniques to update the approximation (and/or projection) subspace so that the projection method converges faster toward the sought-after eigenvalues.

Section 7.2 presents the basic power iteration and subspace iteration algorithms. The basic formulation of the two algorithms is discussed in Section 6.3, while Section 7.2 focuses on the code implementation and demonstrates the numerical properties of the two algorithms by examples. The power iteration and subspace iteration algorithms can be seen as a bridge between the direct and iterative algorithms of eigenvalue problems.

Section 7.3 presents the celebrated Lanczos algorithm for symmetric eigenvalue problems. Also see Sections 3.6.3 and 5.4 for the partial QTQt decomposition by Lanczos procedure and the Lanczos algorithm for symmetric linear equations. For symmetric eigenvalue problems, the Lanczos algorithm simplifies the calculation by choosing the orthogonal bases of the Krylov subspace $\mathbb{K}\,(\mathbf{A},\mathbf{v},m)$ as the approximation (also the projection) subspace. The resulted smaller scale eigenvalue problem is symmetric tri-diagonal, which can be solved by any of the algorithms, `eigSymByQR_.m`, `eigTridByR1U_.m` or `eigTridByDet_.m`, that are presented in Chapter 6.

Section 7.4 discusses the Arnoldi algorithm for unsymmetric eigenvalue problems. The Arnoldi algorithm is an extension of the Lanczos algorithm to the unsymmetric matrix. Also see Sections 3.5.3 and 5.5 for the partial QHQt decomposition by Arnoldi procedure and the Arnoldi algorithm for unsymmetric linear equations. The resulted smaller scale eigenvalue problem is upper Hessenberg, which can be solved by the algorithm `eigUnsymByQR_.m` that is presented in Chapter 6.

Only the common iterative eigenvalue solution algorithms are presented in this chapter. In the last section, Section 7.5, several important omitted topics, such as, generalized eigenvalue problem, nonlinear eigenvalue problem and Jacobi-Davidson iterations are briefly touched.

Matrix Algorithms in MATLAB. DOI: 10.1016/B978-0-12-803804-8.00013-1

The discussions in Sections 7.2–7.4 are all supplemented by MATLAB codes and numerical examples. The test matrices used in most of the numerical examples are small full matrices generated by the MATLAB program. They are for the purpose of demonstrating the property of the algorithm and the usage of the MATLAB function. Note that iterative algorithms are usually used to solve sparse and large scale eigenvalue problems. Only a few relatively large sparse matrices are tested to demonstrate the efficiency of the code implementation.

7.1 GENERAL METHODOLOGY OF ITERATIVE EIGENVALUE ALGORITHMS

7.1.1 BASIC IDEAS

The central theme of the next three sections is the scale reduction of presumably large scale eigenvalue problems $\mathbf{A}_{nn}\mathbf{x}_n = \lambda\mathbf{x}_n$, n is large and $\mathbf{A}$ is sparse or full. The mathematical foundation is fully discussed in [29, 55] and the large amount of references cited therein. In this section, we take a very different approach to explore the mathematical foundation of the iterative algorithms of eigenvalue problems. We use a few numerical examples to explain the essence of the iterative eigenvalue algorithms.

At first, we study the property of eigenvalues and eigenvectors of a symmetric matrix.

```
>> [Q,R]=QR_(randn(8));   d = [1;2;2;3;3;3;4;5];   A=Q*diag(d)*Q';
%A=A', eig(A) is d.
>> tol = 100*eps;

>> [lambda,V] = eigSymByQR_(A,tol);
>> lambda'    %eigenvalues of A
=  1.0000    2.0000    3.0000    5.0000    4.0000    2.0000    3.0000    3.0000
```

The eigenvalues and eigenvectors satisfy the following equations, see Section 1.1.4:

$$\mathbf{V}'\mathbf{A}\mathbf{V} = \lambda, \quad \mathbf{V}'\mathbf{V} = \mathbf{I}. \tag{7.1}$$

These equations can be easily verified for the calculated v and lambda from A.

```
>> norm(V'*A*V-diag(lambda))              >> norm(V'*V-eye(8))
= 4.5520e-015                             = 1.4221e-015
```

Eq. (7.1) can also be written for each column of $\mathbf{V}$, that is,

$$\mathbf{V}(:,j)'\mathbf{A}\mathbf{V}(:,j) = \lambda_j, \quad \mathbf{V}(:,j)'\mathbf{V}(:,j) = 1; \quad j = 1,\ldots,n. \tag{7.2}$$

And numerically, Eq. (7.2) is verified as follows:

```
>> V(:,4)'*A*V(:,4)-lambda(4)            >> V(:,4)'*V(:,4)-1.0
= 2.6645e-015                            = 4.4409e-016
>> V(:,4)'*A*V(:,5)                      >> V(:,4)'*V(:,5)
=-3.3307e-016                            = 4.5103e-017
```

Further, Eq. (7.1) can be written for any subset of columns of $\mathbf{V}$, for example,

$$\begin{bmatrix} \mathbf{V}(:,j)' \\ \mathbf{V}(:,k)' \end{bmatrix} \mathbf{A} \left[\mathbf{V}(:,j), \mathbf{V}(:,k)\right] = \begin{bmatrix} \lambda_j & 0 \\ 0 & \lambda_k \end{bmatrix}; \quad \begin{bmatrix} \mathbf{V}(:,j)' \\ \mathbf{V}(:,k)' \end{bmatrix} \left[\mathbf{V}(:,j), \mathbf{V}(:,k)\right] = \begin{bmatrix} 1 & 0 \\ 0 & 1 \end{bmatrix}. \tag{7.3}$$

And numerically, Eq. (7.3) is exemplified by the following calculations:

```
>> V45 = [V(:,4),V(:,5)];
>> A45=V45'*A*V45                    >> V45'*V45
=    5.0000   -0.0000          =    1.0000    0.0000
     0.0000    4.0000               0.0000    1.0000
```

In Section 6.5, we studied the problem to find the eigenvector from the given eigenvalue. The algorithm is the inverse iteration. From Eqs. (7.1) to (7.3), we can see that the calculation of eigenvalues is very simple if the corresponding eigenvectors are given. In reality, the eigenvectors are unknown. Eqs. (7.1)–(7.3) cannot be applied to find the eigenvalues as they are shown.

The subspace spanned by the eigenvectors of A is A's invariant subspace. This statement is made from the definition of eigenvectors, since span $(AV(:,j:k)) \subset$ span $(V(:,j:k))$. The eigenvectors are a set of bases (orthogonal, if the matrix is symmetric) of the invariant subspace. If the invariant subspace is spanned by a single eigenvector, it is 1-dimensional and its base is just the eigenvector. If the invariant subspace is spanned by multiple eigenvectors, the choice of bases is not unique. For example, the subspace spanned by V45 and the subspace spanned by V45*randn(2) are exactly same. Another set of orthogonal bases of this invariant subspace of A can be obtained by QR_(V45*randn(2)). In the following calculations, we create two arbitrary sets of orthogonal bases of the same invariant subspace, U45a and U45b. We see that U45a'*A*U45a and U45b'*A*U45b give the eigenvalues corresponding to the invariant subspace and both U45a*Q45a and U45b*Q45b are the eigenvectors. From this simple example, we see that if we know the invariant subspace span $(V(:,4:5))$, the eigenvalues and eigenvectors corresponding to the invariant subspace can be found by solving a 2×2 eigenvalue problem. For the given matrix A, the whole $\mathbb{R}^8$ is its invariant space. If we choose an arbitrary orthogonal bases U of $\mathbb{R}^8$, we know the eigenvalues of A and $U'AU$ are same. But $U'AU$ does not simplify the calculation of its eigenvalues. For the purpose of simplifying the calculation of the eigenvalues, the dimension of the invariant subspace should be small. For the purpose of finding the right eigenvalues, the invariant subspace should be chosen appropriately. If we want to find $\lambda = 4,5$, span $(V(:,4:5))$ is the perfect choice. Any higher dimensional space containing span $(V(:,4:5))$ is equally valid, for example, span $(V(:,1),V(:,4:5))$. But span $(V(:,1:3))$ is not a good choice—this choice corresponds to $\lambda = 1,2,3$. In reality, the invariant subspace corresponding to the wanted eigenvalues is still unknown. The calculations of eigenvalues as shown in the following simple examples cannot be applied.

```
>> U45a=QR_(V45*randn(2));
>> [s45a,Q45a]=eigSymByQR_(U45a'*A*U45a,tol)
s45a =           %eigenvalues
     5.0000
     4.0000
Q45a =
     0.9813    0.1925
    -0.1925    0.9813
>> U45a*Q45a   % eigenvectors ~ V45
=   -0.1533    0.2285
     0.5051   -0.2319
    -0.0076   -0.2087
    -0.1389    0.6552
    -0.0049   -0.3722
     0.3051    0.5161
     0.6068    0.0371
    -0.4905   -0.1221
>> U45b=QR_(V45*randn(2));
```

```
>> [s45b,Q45b]=eigSymByQR_(U45b'*A*U45b,tol)
s45b =          %still eigenvalues
    4.0000
    5.0000
Q45b =
    0.8217    -0.5699
    0.5699     0.8217
>> U45b*Q45b   %still eigenvectors ~ V45
=  -0.2285     0.1533
    0.2319    -0.5051
    0.2087     0.0076
   -0.6552     0.1389
    0.3722     0.0049
   -0.5161    -0.3051
   -0.0371    -0.6068
    0.1221     0.4905
```

In the above calculations, if span(U45a) and span(U45b) are not exactly the invariant subspace of A corresponding to $\lambda = 4, 5$, we can expect that the eigenvalues of U45a'*A*U45a and U45b'*A*U45b will not be $\lambda = 4, 5$. The more difference of span(U45) to span(V45), the more difference of the eigenvalues of U45'*A*U45 to $\lambda = 4, 5$. This is supported by the following calculations.

```
>> v1=randn(2);    v2a=randn(6,2);    v2b=0.01*v2a;
%span(U45a) large deviation to span(V45)
>> [U45a,R]=QR_(V45*v1+[V(:,1:3),V(:,6:8)]*v2a);

%span(U45b) small deviation to span(V45)
>> [U45b,R]=QR_(V45*v1+[V(:,1:3),V(:,6:8)]*v2b);

>> [s45a,Q45a]=eigSymByQR_(U45a'*A*U45a,tol)
s45a =    %large difference to lambda=4,5
    3.0869
    2.8132
Q45a =
    0.9720     0.2348
   -0.2348     0.9720
>> [s45b,Q45b]=eigSymByQR_(U45b'*A*U45b,tol)
s45b =    %small difference to lambda=4,5
    3.9995
    4.9992
Q45b =
    0.9994    -0.0341
    0.0341     0.9994
```

The observations about the eigenvalues we made to the symmetric matrix are also valid to an unsymmetric matrix. For an unsymmetric matrix, eigenvectors are not orthogonal but Schur vectors are. For brevity, we demonstrate the observations with a simple unsymmetric matrix.

```
>> A(2:8,1)=-A(2:8,1);    A(1:7,8)=-A(1:7,8);      %To make A unsymmetric
>> v1=randn(3);    v2a=randn(5,3);    v2b=v2a*0.01;  %To create orthogonal bases
```

First we check the observations by using eigenvalues and eigenvectors.

```
>> [Lambda,V] = eigUnsymByQR_(A,tol,'long');      %eigenvalues and eigenvectors
>> Lambda
=    3.5756     0.8386
    -0.8386     3.5756
```

```
      1.4288            0      %real      eigenvalue :3    = lambda(1)     ordered
      3.8753            0
      2.7723       0.3004      %complex eigenvalues:5,6 = lambda(3,4) ordered
     -0.3004       2.7723
      2.0001            0
      3.0000            0

>> [U356,R]=QR_([V(:,3),V(:,5:6)]*v1);        %span(U356)=span(V(:,3),V(:,5:6))
>> [L356,Q356]=eigUnsymByQR_(U356'*A*U356,tol,'long');
>> L356
=     1.4288            0      %real      eigenvalue
      2.7723       0.3004      %complex eigenvalues
     -0.3004       2.7723
>> V356=U356*Q356;           %eigenvectors , ~ [V(:,3),V(:,5:6)]
>> norm(A*V356-V356*[L356(1,:),0;[0;0],L356(2:3,:)])
=     1.2319e-014            %exact for span(U356)=span(V(:,3),V(:,5:6))

                             %span(U356a) far from span(V(:,3),V(:,5:6))
>> [U356a,R]=QR_([V(:,3),V(:,5:6)]*v1+[V(:,1:2),V(:,4),V(:,7:8)]*v2a);
>> [L356a,Q356a]=eigUnsymByQR_(U356a'*A*U356a,tol,'long');
>> L356a                %large difference to Lamba
=     3.7662
      1.8688
      2.6338
>> V356a=U356a*Q356a;
>> norm(A*V356a-V356a*diag(L356a))
=     0.8577                 %L356a , V356a far from eigenvalues(vectors)

                             %span(U356b) close to span(V(:,3),V(:,5:6))
>> [U356b,R]=QR_([V(:,3),V(:,5:6)]*v1+[V(:,1:2),V(:,4),V(:,7:8)]*v2b);
>> [L356b,Q356b]=eigUnsymByQR_(U356b'*A*U356b,tol,'long');
>> L356b                %small difference to Lambda
=     1.4310            0
      2.7735       0.3105
     -0.3105       2.7735
>> V356b=U356b*Q356b;
>> norm(A*V356b-V356b*[L356b(1,:),0;[0;0],L356b(2:3,:)])
=     0.0274                 %L356b , V356b close to eigenvalues(vectors)
```

Next we check the observations by using eigenvalues and Schur vectors. In order to obtain the same invariant subspace of span($V(:,3),V(:,5:6)$) in the previous calculations using eigenvectors, we need to reorder the Schur vectors W calculated by eigUnsymByQR_, so that span($W(:,1:3)$) = span($V(:,3),V(:,5:6)$). See Section 6.6 about the calculation of the invariant subspace by eigenvalue reordering.

```
>> [S,W] = eigUnsymByQR_(A,100*eps,'short');
                             %pseudo upper triangle and Schur vectors
>> [S,W]=reorderSchur_(S,W,[1,3,4],100*eps);
>> S       %Reorder S,W. W(:,1:3) => invariant subspace of A to lambda(1,3,4)
=     1.4288     0.3711    -0.0375     0.6799     0.7143     0.0290    -0.0024     0.0000
      0.0000     2.8585     0.3628     0.9125     0.0677    -0.3549     0.0059     0.0000
     -0.0000    -0.2693     2.6861    -0.6385    -0.3287    -0.3878     0.0062    -0.0000
      0.0000    -0.0000     0.0000     3.9706    -1.5496    -0.1060     0.0022    -0.0000
      0.0000     0.0000    -0.0000     0.5546     3.1806    -0.0769    -0.0072     0.0000
      0.0000     0.0000     0.0000    -0.0000    -0.0000     3.8753     0.0043    -0.0000
     -0.0000     0.0000    -0.0000     0.0000     0.0000     0.0000     2.0001     0.0000
           0          0          0          0          0          0          0     3.0000
```

```
>> [U356,R]=QR_(W(:,1:3)*v1);      %span(U356)=span(W(:,1:3))
>> [S356,Q356]=eigUnsymByQR_(U356'*A*U356,tol,'short');
>> S356
=    1.4288    -0.3470     0.1369    %real eigenvalue      (1,1)
          0     2.7841    -0.4133    %complex eigenvalues (2:3,2:3)
     0.0000     0.2187     2.7605
>> W356=U356*Q356;       %Schur vectors, ~ W(:,1:3)
>> norm(A*W356-W356*S356)
=    3.7679e-015           %exact for span(U356)=span(W(:,1:3))


                          %span(U356a) far from span(W(:,1:3))
>> [U356a,R]=QR_(W(:,1:3)*v1+W(:,4:8)*v2a);
>> [S356a,Q356a]=eigUnsymByQR_(U356a'*A*U356a,tol,'short');
>> S356a               %large difference to S(1:3,1:3)
=    1.5621    -0.1915    -0.5041
          0     3.8109     0.5972
          0          0     2.7266
>> W356a=U356a*Q356a;
>> norm(A*W356a-W356a*S356a)
=    1.4947               %S356a, W356a far from eigenvalues and Schur vectors


                          %span(U356b) close to span(W(:,1:3))
>> [U356b,R]=QR_(W(:,1:3)*v1+W(:,4:8)*v2b);
>> [S356b,Q356b]=eigUnsymByQR_(U356b'*A*U356b,tol,'short');
>> S356b               %small difference to S(1:3,1:3)
=    1.4257    -0.3570     0.0769
          0     2.8013    -0.4273
          0     0.2276     2.7245
>> W356b=U356b*Q356b;
>> norm(A*W356b-W356b*S356b)
=    0.0532               %S356b, W356b close to eigenvalues and Schur vectors
```

Using the orthogonal columns U356 calculated above from QR_(W(:,1:3)*v1), we can construct an orthogonal matrix **U** that satisfies **U**(:,1 : 3) =U356. Such a **U** is not unique. One simple way is to use orthogonal_.m to generate it.

```
>> U=U356;
>> for j=4:8 U=[U,orthogonal_(U,randn(8,1))]; end

>> norm(U(:,1:3)-U356)
=    0
>> norm(U'*U-eye(8))
=    4.8070e-016
```

Such a **U** possesses a useful property to deflate **U′AU**.

```
>> B=U'*A*U
B =  1.9841     0.0644     0.6914    -0.2966     0.1386    -0.3853     0.7054    -0.2179
     0.7073     2.7246    -0.0906    -0.5712    -0.3405     0.5694    -0.9212    -0.1515
     0.4287    -0.3279     2.2647    -0.1010     0.2250     0.0304     0.2309     0.2208
     0.0000    -0.0000    -0.0000     3.8154    -0.0109    -0.1406    -0.3894     0.5016
     0.0000    -0.0000     0.0000    -0.0030     3.3436     0.2534    -0.0945     0.6809
     0.0000     0.0000     0.0000    -0.6655    -0.3310     2.4723    -0.4206    -0.0175
     0.0000     0.0000     0.0000     0.2758     0.6316     0.0587     3.1231     1.2010
     0.0000    -0.0000     0.0000     0.1448     0.2791     0.7715    -0.1094     3.2722

>> norm(B(4:8,1:3))
=    3.4077e-015
```

From the above discussions, we see that the eigenvalues of a matrix can be accurately calculated by solving a smaller scale eigenvalue problem if we can find a subspace which accurately contains the invariant subspace corresponding to the sought-after eigenvalues.

Algebraically, the ideas discussed so far can be succinctly presented with the help of the orthogonal projection method, see also Section 5.3. Given a column orthogonal matrix $\mathbf{U} \in \mathbb{R}^{n \times m}$, if an eigenvector $\mathbf{v}$ of $\mathbf{A}$ can be represented as $\mathbf{v} = \mathbf{U}\mathbf{y}$, then $\mathbf{A}\mathbf{v} = \mathbf{A}\mathbf{U}\mathbf{y} = \lambda\mathbf{v} = \lambda\mathbf{U}\mathbf{y}$. Because $\mathbf{U}'\mathbf{U} = \mathbf{I}$, $(\mathbf{U}'\mathbf{A}\mathbf{U})\mathbf{y} = \lambda\mathbf{y}$. If $\mathbf{v}$ cannot be presented as $\mathbf{U}\mathbf{y}$, $\mathbf{A}\mathbf{U}\mathbf{y} - \lambda\mathbf{U}\mathbf{y} \neq \mathbf{0}$. To determine $(\lambda, \mathbf{y})$, we assume the projections of the nonzero residual on $\mathbf{U}$ are zeros, that is, $(\mathbf{U}'\mathbf{A}\mathbf{U})\mathbf{y} = \lambda\mathbf{y}$. The pair $(\lambda, \mathbf{y})$ is called the Ritz value and Ritz vector, which is the eigenvalue and eigenvector of the small scale eigenvalue problem $(\mathbf{U}'\mathbf{A}\mathbf{U})\mathbf{y} = \lambda\mathbf{y}$. The efficiency and accuracy of this method depends on the chosen $\mathbf{U}$. In the iterative algorithms, $\mathbf{U}$ is made to approach the desired invariant subspace of $\mathbf{A}$ by employing a series of numerical techniques, some of which are briefly discussed below.

7.1.2 TWO WAYS TO APPROXIMATE DOMINANT INVARIANT SUBSPACE

Given a matrix $\mathbf{Q} \in \mathbb{R}^{n \times m}$, from the discussion in Section 6.3, we know $\mathbf{A}^k\mathbf{Q}$ approximately represents the invariant subspace corresponding to the dominant eigenvalues of $\mathbf{A}$ for a large k. If $\mathbf{Q}$ has large components in the dominant invariant subspace, $\mathbf{A}^k\mathbf{Q}$ can approximately represent it for even a small k. If $\mathbf{Q}$ happens to represent an invariant subspace of $\mathbf{A}$, it can be used directly to simplify the calculation of eigenvalues as the above examples show. A set of orthogonal bases $\mathbf{V}$ for the subspace spanned by $\mathbf{A}^k\mathbf{Q}$ can be obtained by its QR decomposition. If $\mathbf{Q}$ has only one column, the QR decomposition of $\mathbf{A}^k\mathbf{Q}$ is just the normalization of $\mathbf{A}^k\mathbf{Q}$. The resulted $\mathbf{V}'\mathbf{A}\mathbf{V}$ is usually a full matrix. Using $\mathbf{A}^k\mathbf{Q}$ to approximate the dominant subspace is the algorithm of power iteration and subspace iteration presented in Sections 6.3 and 7.2.

Given a vector $\mathbf{q} \in \mathbb{R}^n$, the Krylov subspace $\mathbb{K}(\mathbf{A}, \mathbf{q}, m) = \mathrm{span}\left(\mathbf{q}, \mathbf{A}\mathbf{q}, \mathbf{A}^2\mathbf{q}, \ldots, \mathbf{A}^{m-1}\mathbf{q}\right)$ usually has a better representation of a dominant subspace of $\mathbf{A}$ than $\mathbf{A}^k\mathbf{Q}$, because the former forms a space by a complete $(m-1)$th order polynomial of $\mathbf{A}$, while the latter forms a space by a single term $\mathbf{A}^k$ only. The orthogonal bases $\mathbf{V}$ of $\mathbb{K}(\mathbf{A}, \mathbf{q}, m)$ are formed in a step by step construction, that is, QTQtByLanczos_.m for a symmetric matrix and QHQtByArnoldi_.m for an unsymmetric matrix. The resulted $\mathbf{V}'\mathbf{A}\mathbf{V}$ is symmetric tri-diagonal or upper Hessenberg. See Sections 3.6.3 and 3.5.3, respectively. Using $\mathbb{K}(\mathbf{A}, \mathbf{q}, m)$ to approximate the dominant subspace is the algorithm of Lanczos for a symmetric matrix of Section 7.3 and Arnoldi for an unsymmetric matrix of Section 7.4.

7.1.3 SHIFT AND INVERSE TO APPROXIMATE NON-DOMINANT INVARIANT SUBSPACE

The iterative algorithms outlined above are efficient to converge to the maximum modulus of eigenvalues, since the dominant invariant subspace is best approximated by $\mathbf{A}^k\mathbf{Q}$ or $\mathbb{K}(\mathbf{A}, \mathbf{q}, m)$. If we need to find other eigenvalues that are interior in the spectrum of a matrix, the iterative algorithms may need many iterations to converge to the desired eigenvalues. In these situations, we may instead try to apply the iterative algorithms to a transformed eigenvalue problem,

$$(\mathbf{A} - \sigma\mathbf{I})^{-1} \mathbf{w} = \theta\mathbf{w}. \tag{7.4}$$

382   **CHAPTER 7** Iterative algorithms of solution of eigenvalue problem

The eigenpair $(\theta, \mathbf{w})$ of this transformed eigenvalue problem and the eigenpair $(\lambda, \mathbf{v})$ of the original eigenvalue problem $\mathbf{Av} = \lambda \mathbf{v}$ are related by

$$\theta = \frac{1}{\lambda - \sigma}, \quad \mathbf{w} = \mathbf{v}. \tag{7.5}$$

If the desired eigenvalue λ is close to σ, θ is then the maximum modulus eigenvalue of $(\mathbf{A} - \sigma \mathbf{I})^{-1}$. Applying the iterative algorithms to Eq. (7.4) leads to a fast convergence.

In the subspace iterations, an invariant subspace is approximated by $(\mathbf{A} - \sigma \mathbf{I})^{-k} \mathbf{Q}$. In the Lanczos or Arnoldi iterations, an invariant subspace is approximated by $\mathbb{K}\left((\mathbf{A} - \sigma \mathbf{I})^{-1}, \mathbf{q}, m\right)$. In both cases, we need to solve linear equations $(\mathbf{A} - \sigma \mathbf{I})^{-1} \mathbf{b}$, see Chapters 4 and 5 for the algorithms. In Sections 7.2–7.4, numerical examples are provided to demonstrate the use of the method.

7.1.4 BETTER APPROXIMATING AN INVARIANT SUBSPACE

At the start of the iterations, an invariant subspace is approximated by either $\mathbf{C}^k \mathbf{Q}$ or $\mathbb{K}(\mathbf{C}, \mathbf{q}, m)$, where $\mathbf{C} = \mathbf{A}$ or $\mathbf{C} = (\mathbf{A} - \sigma \mathbf{I})^{-1}$. If any information about the interested invariant subspace is known, the initial $\mathbf{Q}$ or $\mathbf{q}$ should be constructed to include enough components of the subspace. If no information is available, $\mathbf{Q}$ or $\mathbf{q}$ can be randomly generated. In later iterations, the invariant subspace is still approximated by the same form $\mathbf{C}^k \mathbf{Q}$ or $\mathbb{K}(\mathbf{C}, \mathbf{q}, m)$. However, with more information available from the calculations of eigenvalues of $(\mathbf{U}'\mathbf{C}\mathbf{U}) \mathbf{v} = \lambda \mathbf{v}$, we can use better $\mathbf{Q}$ or $\mathbf{q}$ to start each iteration. Based on the information available, three techniques are applied individually or collectively:

1. Filtering of non-converged and undesired spectrum.
2. Purging of converged and undesired spectrum.
3. Locking of converged and desired spectrum.

These techniques will be discussed in more detail in Lanczos and Arnoldi algorithms of Sections 7.3 and 7.4.

7.2 POWER ITERATIONS AND SUBSPACE ITERATIONS FOR $\mathbf{Ax} = \lambda \mathbf{x}$

The formulation of the power iteration and subspace iteration is discussed in Section 6.3. As pointed out in Section 7.1, in $(\mathbf{U}'\mathbf{A}\mathbf{U}) \mathbf{y} = \lambda \mathbf{y}$, $\mathbf{U}$ is the orthogonal bases of the subspace spanned by $\mathbf{A}^k \mathbf{Q}$, where $\mathbf{Q}$ is the user input or randomly generated matrix. If the column of $\mathbf{Q}$ is only one, the algorithm is simply the power iteration, otherwise subspace iteration. This section focuses on the code implementation of eigBySubspace_.m and demonstrates the application of eigBySubspace_.m by a few numerical examples.

Algorithm 7.1

$\mathbf{AV} = \mathbf{V}\lambda$ by Subspace iteration.

```
function [lambda,V] = eigBySubspace_(A,algo,Q,tol,nv,lambda,V)

[m,n] = size_(A);  nlambda = 0;    normA = norm(Ay_(A,ones(m,1)));
eqsALGO = 'mtimes';  eigALGO = 'eigUnsymByQR_';
if (length(algo)>=1 && ~isempty(algo{1})) sigma   = algo{1}; end
if (length(algo)>=2 && ~isempty(algo{2})) eqsALGO = algo{2}; end
if (length(algo)>=3 && ~isempty(algo{3})) eigALGO = algo{3}; end
```

```
if (~isempty(nv) && strcmp(nv{1},'n'))
    l1 = nv{2}; l2 = nv{3};
    if (strcmp(eigALGO,'eigSymByQR_')) [v1,v2] = veig_(A,l1,l2);   %full A=A'!!
    else                              v1 =-realmax;  v2 = realmax; end
elseif (~isempty(nv) && strcmp(nv{1},'v'))
    v1 = nv{2};   v2 = nv{3};
    if (strcmp(eigALGO,'eigSymByQR_')) [l1,l2] = neig_(A,v1,v2);   %full A=A'!!
    else                              l1 = 1;  l2 = n; end
else
    l1 = n;   l2 = n;   v1 =-realmax;   v2 = realmax;
end
l12 = l2 - l1 + 1;
if(~exist('Q','var') || isempty(Q)) Q = randn(m,min([fix(n/2),2*l12,l12+8])); end
if (exist('sigma','var')) A = A_(A,sigma,eqsALGO); end

AQ = Ay_(A,Q);  nq0 = size(Q,2);  tol1 = 1000.0*tol;
while(nlambda<l12 && length(lambda)<n)
    nq0 = min(nq0,n-size(V,2));   nq = size(AQ,2);
    if (nq < nq0) AQ = [AQ, randn(m,nq0-nq)]; end
    if (size(V,2) > 0) AQ = AQ - V*(V'*AQ); end  %deflation: not good for A~=A'
    if (size(AQ,2)==1) r = norm(AQ); Q = AQ/r;
    else               [Q,r] = QR_(AQ,'householder',0,tol,'short'); end
    AQ = Ay_(A,Q);
    sita = Q'*AQ; j = 0;  k = 1;  l = size(sita,1);   [ml,nl] = size(lambda);
    if (size(AQ,2) > 1)
        if(strcmp(eigALGO,'eigSymByQR_')) [sita,S] = eigSymByQR_(sita,tol,'long');
        else                              [sita,S] = eigUnsymByQR_(sita,tol,'long');
                                                                              end
        Q = Q*S;  AQ = Ay_(A,Q);     %AQ for error check
    end
    while k <= l  %check convergence
        if (size(sita,2)==1 || k==l || sita(k,2)==0)  %real
            if (norm(AQ(:,k)-Q(:,k)*sita(k,1)) <= tol1*normA)
                if (exist('sigma','var')) sita(k) = sigma + 1.0/sita(k,1); end
                if (nl ~= 2) lambda = [lambda;sita(k,1)];
                else         lambda = [lambda;[sita(k,1),0]]; end
                V = [V,Q(:,k)];
                if (v1<=sita(k) && sita(k)<=v2) nlambda = nlambda + 1; end
            else
                j = j + 1;
                if (j < k) AQ(:,j) = AQ(:,k); end
            end
            k = k + 1;
        else                                        %complex
            if (norm(AQ(:,k:k+1)-Q(:,k:k+1)*sita(k:k+1,:)) < tol1*normA)
                if (exist('sigma','var'))
                    sita3 = sita(k,1)*sita(k,1)+sita(k,2)*sita(k,2);
                    sita(k,1) = sigma+sita(k,1)/sita3;  sita(k,2) =-sita(k,2)/sita3;
                    sita(k+1,1) =  sita(k,2);  sita(k+1,2) = sita(k,1);
                end
                if (nl == 1) lambda = [lambda,zeros(ml,1)]; end
                lambda = [lambda; sita(k:k+1,:)];  V = [V,Q(:,k:k+1)];
                nlambda = nlambda + 2;
            else
                j = j + 1;
                if (j < k) AQ(:,j:j+1) = AQ(:,k:k+1); end
                j = j + 1;
```

```
            end
            k = k + 2;
        end
    end
    if (j < size(AQ,2)) AQ = AQ(:,1:j); end
end
```

The optional second input argument algo is a cell array, defining the shift (sigma), the algorithm for solving $(\mathbf{A} - \sigma\mathbf{I})^{-1}$ and the algorithm for the reduced eigenvalue problem. As an example, algo={2.1,'LDLt_','eigSymByQR_'} If the third input argument Q is a vector, eigBySubspace_.m implements the power iteration algorithm. If Q is a matrix with more than one column, eigBySubspace_.m implements the subspace iteration algorithm. The optional fifth argument nv defines the range of the eigenvalues sought by eigBySubspace_.m. For example, nv={'n',2,5} directs eigBySubspace_.m to calculate the eigenvalues $\lambda_2 \le \lambda_3 \le \lambda_4 \le \lambda_5$. nv={'v',2.0,5.0} directs eigBySubspace_.m to calculate the eigenvalues $2.0 \le \lambda \le 5.0$. eigBySubspace_.m uses veig_.m or neig_.m to determine the range of the sought eigenvalues. Because veig_.m and neig_.m are applicable to symmetrical matrices and implemented for full symmetrical matrices only, the fifth input argument nv is not used for other types of matrices.

The use of eigBySubspace_.m is demonstrated by following examples. The first example is a symmetrical matrix.

```
>> [Q,R]=QR_(randn(8));   d = [1;2;2;3;3;3;4;5];   A=Q*diag(d)*Q';     %eig(A) is d.
>> q = randn(8,1);    tol = 100*eps;

>> [lambda,V]=eigBySubspace_(A,{},q,tol);
>> lambda
=    5.0000
>> V'
=   0.1387     0.4871     0.2780    -0.1950     0.4368    -0.1199    -0.5749     0.3040

>> norm(A*V-V*lambda)=1.2570e-010                    %correct eigenvalue and eigenvector
```

Because 5 is the eigenvalue of the maximum modulus, the power iteration converges to 5. If we start from a different **q**, we will most likely get the same (more precisely, numerically close) $\lambda = 5$ and the same **V**.

In order to obtain $\lambda = 4$ and its corresponding eigenvector, we have to pass $(\lambda = 5, \mathbf{V})$ as the input arguments to eqsSubSpace_.m. The eigenvector corresponding to $\lambda = 5$ is deflated in each iteration.

```
>> [lambda,V]=eigBySubspace_(A,{},q,tol,{},lambda,V);
>> lambda'
=    5.0000     4.0000
>> V'
=   0.1387     0.4871     0.2780    -0.1950     0.4368    -0.1199    -0.5749     0.3040
   -0.0389    -0.3744    -0.0192     0.4135    -0.3592     0.1428    -0.4909     0.5446
```

In the following example, we want to calculate $\lambda(3:5) = [3; 3; 3]$. We can set the input argument nv to {'n',2,6}. In the iterations, the extremal eigenvalues converge first. Then, the eigenvectors corresponding to the extremal eigenvalues are deflated in order to calculate the eigenvalues in the middle of the spectrum. In the output, the extremal eigenvalues and their eigenvectors are included.

```
>> [lambda,V]=eigBySubspace_(A,{},randn(8,1),tol,{'n',2,6});
>> lambda'
=    5.0000     4.0000     3.0000     3.0000     3.0000
>> V
```

```
=    -0.1387     0.0389    -0.3434     0.7924     0.1005
     -0.4871     0.3744    -0.2070    -0.1627     0.3248
     -0.2780     0.0192     0.0479    -0.3088     0.5333
      0.1950    -0.4135    -0.7287    -0.0665     0.1092
     -0.4368     0.3592    -0.1608     0.0313    -0.6331
      0.1199    -0.1428    -0.1489    -0.3878    -0.4180
      0.5749     0.4909     0.1733     0.1675     0.0984
     -0.3040    -0.5446     0.4773     0.2578    -0.0529
```

In order to calculate the eigenvalues in the middle of the spectrum in few iterations, we can use the input argument `algo` to set a shift and then use the inverse subspace iterations. For example, if we want to calculate $\lambda(2:4) = [2; 2; 3]$, we can set the shift to 2.1. Because 2.1 is close to $\lambda = 2$, $\lambda = 2$ converges first.

```
>> [lambda,V]=eigBySubspace_(A,{2.1,'LDLt_'},randn(8,1),tol,{'n',2,4});
>> lambda'
=    2.0000     2.0000     3.0000
>> V'
=    0.0425     0.1670    -0.5113    -0.3604    -0.4414    -0.0094    -0.5002    -0.3660
    -0.4263    -0.1451    -0.2212     0.2424     0.2173    -0.7833    -0.1385    -0.0982
     0.1476     0.3464     0.5211     0.1966    -0.6086    -0.3997     0.0779    -0.1086
```

We can apply `eqsSubSpace_.m` to an unsymmetric matrix. As another example, we create an unsymmetric matrix from $\mathbf{A}$ used in the above examples as follows.

```
>> A = A-2*tril(A,-1);          %A=-A'
>> [lambda,V]=eigBySubspace_(A,{[],[],'eigUnsymByQR_'},randn(8,2),tol);
>> lambda
=    2.9366     1.8483
    -1.8483     2.9366
>> V'     %V can change w/ randn(8,2), but span(V) does not.
=    0.0375    -0.4916    -0.1526     0.0911    -0.2300    -0.0363     0.2190     0.3916
     0.0523     0.3211    -0.3412     0.1672    -0.1387     0.1430     0.4184    -0.0704

>> norm(A*V-V*lambda)=1.7373e-010               %correct eigenvalue and eigenvector
```

The matrix can be banded or sparse. For an example, we create the following band matrix from `A` in the above example. The input `{'band',{B,2,1,8,8}}` presents the complete information of the banded matrix.

```
>> A=A-tril(A,-3)-triu(A,2);
>> B=full2band_(A,2,1)
B =
          0          0     2.7769     0.3326
          0    -0.3326     2.7682     0.9371
     0.1860    -0.9371     2.3847    -0.0222
     0.5454     0.0222     2.9486    -0.4827
     0.0258     0.4827     3.2478     0.0235
    -0.2614    -0.0235     2.4268    -0.0853
     0.4549     0.0853     3.4499    -1.0631
     0.1299     1.0631     2.9971          0

>> [lambda,V]=eigBySubspace_({'band',{B,2,1,8,8}},{[],[],'eigUnsymByQR_'},...
                 randn(8,2),tol);
>> lambda
=    3.2192     1.0388
    -1.0388     3.2192
```

```
>> V'    %V can change w/ randn(8,2), but span(V) does not.
=   -0.0000     0.0000     0.0000    -0.0004    -0.0008    -0.0384     0.0460     0.6968
    -0.0000    -0.0000     0.0000    -0.0005     0.0011    -0.0256     0.7063     0.1068

>> norm(A*V-V*lambda)=1.7824e-010             %correct eigenvalue and eigenvector
```

The following example shows the way to use the shift algorithm for an unsymmetric band matrix.

```
>> [lambda,V]=eigBySubspace_({'band',{B,2,1,8,8}},{2.8,'LU_','eigUnsymByQR_'},...
                      randn(8,2),tol);
>> lambda
=    2.7919
>> V'    %+/- V does not change w/ randn(8,2).
=   -0.9375    -0.0424    -0.3338     0.0610    -0.0435    -0.0429     0.0085    -0.0168

>> norm(A*V-V*lambda)=6.5284e-013             %correct eigenvalue and eigenvector
```

It should be noted that for the unsymmetric matrix the eigenvalue deflation is not implemented in eigBySubspace_.m. To implement the deflation, we have to use the Schur vectors instead of the eigenvectors.

7.3 LANCZOS ITERATIONS FOR $Ax = \lambda x$ OF A SYMMETRIC MATRIX
7.3.1 BASIC LANCZOS ALGORITHM

An orthogonal bases $\mathbf{U}$ of the Krylov subspace $\mathbb{K}(\mathbf{A},\mathbf{q},m) = \mathrm{span}\left(\mathbf{q},\mathbf{Aq},\mathbf{A}^2\mathbf{q},\dots,\mathbf{A}^{m-1}\mathbf{q}\right)$ can be constructed by QTQtByLanczos_.m. By the construction of $\mathbf{U}$, $\mathbf{U}$ and a symmetric tri-diagonal matrix $\mathbf{T}$ satisfy the following important relations, see Section 3.6.3:

$$\mathbf{AU}(:,1:m) = \mathbf{U}(:,1:m)\mathbf{T}(1:m,1:m) + T(m+1,m)\mathbf{U}(:,m+1)\mathbf{I}(m,:), \tag{7.6a}$$

$$\mathbf{U}(:,1:m)'\mathbf{U}(:,1:m) = \mathbf{I}, \tag{7.6b}$$

$$\mathbf{U}(:,1:m)'\mathbf{U}(:,m+1) = \mathbf{0}. \tag{7.6c}$$

Suppose an eigenpair of $\mathbf{A}$ is $(\lambda,\mathbf{v})$, where $\mathbf{v}$ can be approximately presented as $\mathbf{v} = \mathbf{U}(:,1:m)\mathbf{u}$. To determine the two unknowns $(\lambda,\mathbf{u})$, we introduce the following Galerkin conditions:

$$\mathbf{U}(:,1:m)'\mathbf{y} = \mathbf{U}(:,1:m)'\left(\mathbf{AU}(:,1:m)\mathbf{u} - \lambda\mathbf{U}(:,1:m)\mathbf{u}\right) = \mathbf{0}. \tag{7.7}$$

Considering Eq. (7.6), the above Galerkin conditions are simplified to

$$\mathbf{T}(1:m,1:m)\mathbf{u} = \lambda\mathbf{u}. \tag{7.8}$$

From Eq. (7.8), $(\lambda,\mathbf{u})$ can be found by any eigenvalue algorithms for a symmetric tri-diagonal matrix, such as eigSymByQR_.m, eigTridByDet_.m, or eigTridByR1U_.m, see Sections 6.4 and 6.7. Once $(\lambda,\mathbf{u})$ is determined, the residual $\mathbf{r}$ can be numerically calculated,

$$\begin{aligned}
\mathbf{r} = \mathbf{Av} - \lambda\mathbf{v} &= \mathbf{AU}(:,1:m)\mathbf{u} - \lambda\mathbf{U}(:,1:m)\mathbf{u} \\
&= \left(\mathbf{U}(:,1:m)\mathbf{T}(1:m,1:m) + T(m+1,m)\mathbf{U}(:,m+1)\mathbf{I}(m,:)\right)\mathbf{u} - \lambda\mathbf{U}(:,1:m)\mathbf{u} \\
&= \mathbf{U}(:,1:m)\left(\mathbf{T}(1:m,1:m)\mathbf{u} - \lambda\mathbf{u}\right) + T(m+1,m)u(m)\mathbf{U}(:,m+1) \\
&= T(m+1,m)u(m)\mathbf{U}(:,m+1).
\end{aligned} \tag{7.9}$$

From Eq. (7.9), the residual, i.e. the error measurement of $(\lambda, \mathbf{U}(:, 1 : m)\mathbf{u})$ as an eigenpair of $\mathbf{A}$, is in the direction of $\mathbf{U}(:, m + 1)$. Its magnitude $\|\mathbf{r}\|_2$ is simply $|T(m + 1, m)u(m)|$. $|T(m + 1, m)u(m)|$ provides an efficient check of the convergence of the eigenpair. Only when $|T(m + 1, m)u(m)|$ is small enough, we form the eigenvector $\mathbf{U}(:, 1 : m)\mathbf{u}$. A small $|T(m + 1, m)u(m)|$ indicates either $T(m + 1, m)$ or $u(m)$ is small. If $T(m + 1, m)$ is small, $\mathbb{K}(\mathbf{A}, \mathbf{q}, m)$ forms an accurate m-dimensional invariant subspace of $\mathbf{A}$. All the m eigenvalues of $\mathbf{U}(:, 1 : m)'\mathbf{A}\mathbf{U}(:, 1 : m)$ are also the eigenvalues of $\mathbf{A}$. If $T(m + 1, m)$ is not small but $u(m)$ is, $\mathbb{K}(\mathbf{A}, \mathbf{q}, m)$ contains a 1-dimensional invariant space of $\mathbf{A}$ and $\lambda = \mathbf{u}'\mathbf{A}\mathbf{u}$ is an eigenvalue. See the discussion in Section 7.1.1.

7.3.2 ORTHOGONALITY OF U

The brief discussion of the previous subsection is the classical Lanczos algorithm. Its correct implementation hinges on the two implied conditions Eqs. (7.6b) and (7.6c) which we used to obtain Eq. (7.8). These two conditions are the orthogonality among the columns of $\mathbf{U}$.

From Eq. (7.6), we can calculate the following:

$$\mathbf{U}(:, 1 : j)'\mathbf{U}(:, j + 1) = \frac{\mathbf{U}(:, 1 : j)' \left(\mathbf{A}\mathbf{U}(:, i) - T(j, j - 1)\mathbf{U}(:, j - 1) - T(j, j)\mathbf{U}(:, j)\right)}{T(j + 1, j)}. \qquad (7.10)$$

If $|T(j + 1, j)|$ is small, a significant loss of orthogonality between $\mathbf{U}(:, 1 : j)$ and $\mathbf{U}(:, j + 1)$ can occur, even when the orthogonality of $\mathbf{U}(:, 1 : j)$ is accurate. The small $|T(j + 1, j)|$ occurs when $\mathbf{U}(:, 1 : j)$ is close to an invariant subspace of $\mathbf{A}$, that is, when all the eigenvalues of $\mathbf{T}(1 : j, 1 : j)$ are close to the eigenvalues of $\mathbf{A}$.

From Eq. (7.9), we can calculate the following:

$$\mathbf{v}'\mathbf{U}(:, j + 1) = \frac{\mathbf{v}' (\mathbf{A}\mathbf{v} - \lambda\mathbf{v})}{T(j + 1, j)u(j)}. \qquad (7.11)$$

If $|T(j + 1, j)|$ is not small, but $\mathbf{v}$ is a converged Ritz vector, then $|u(j)|$ must be small. Eq. (7.11) tells us that a small $|u(j)|$ means $\mathbf{v}'\mathbf{U}(:, j + 1)$ can be significantly from zero. But $\mathbf{v} = \mathbf{U}(:, 1 : j)\mathbf{u}$, this means $\mathbf{U}(:, 1 : j)'\mathbf{U}(:, j + 1)$ can be significantly from zero.

In Eqs. (7.10) and (7.11), j can be any number between 1 and m, the limiting number of Lanczos steps.

If the loss of orthogonality is not treated, a duplicate copy of the converged eigenpair $(\lambda, \mathbf{u})$ will soon appear in the tri-diagonal $\mathbf{T}(1 : m, 1 : m)$. This is because the newly calculated columns of $\mathbf{U}$ have non-negligible components in the converged Ritz vectors. There are four different ways to remedy the loss of orthogonality.

Half Re-orthogonalization Fig. 7.1 illustrates the three vectors in a Lanczos step. If the angle θ is small, $\mathbf{A}\mathbf{U}(:, j)$ has a significant component in span $(\mathbf{U}(:, j - 1), \mathbf{U}(:, j))$; in other words $\mathbf{A}\mathbf{U}(:, j)$ is close to invariant. For better accuracy, in this case $\mathbf{U}(:, j + 1)$ is orthogonalized to $\mathbf{U}(:, 1 : j - 1)$. If the two vectors denoted as $\mathbf{A}\mathbf{U}(:, j)$ and $T_{j-1,j}\mathbf{U}(:, j - 1) + T_{j,j}\mathbf{U}(:, j)$ are randomly chosen, taking $\theta = 45°$ will have 50% chance of re-orthogonalization. $\theta = 45°$ corresponds to setting `eta=0.5*sqrt(2.0)` in `QTQtByLanczos_.m`. For a given symmetric matrix $\mathbf{A}$ and an initial vector $\mathbf{q}$, setting `eta=0.5*sqrt(2.0)` does not mean re-orthogonalization is performed in half of the Lanczos steps. Using `eta=0.5*sqrt(2.0)` as the criterion is studied in [18].

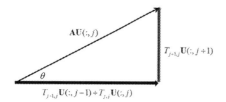

FIGURE 7.1

Three vectors in a Lanczos step.

Full Re-orthogonalization Re-orthogonalize the newly calculated column of **U** against all the previous columns of **U**. First calculate $U(:, j + 1)$ by the three-term recursive formula of Lanczos, Eq. (7.6). Then modify it according to $U(:, j + 1) = U(:, j + 1) - U(:, 1 : j)(U(:, 1 : j)'U(:, 1 : j + 1))$. With the growth of j, the increase of calculation is prohibitive. In QTQtByLancos_.m, setting eta=realmax corresponds to this scheme.

No Orthogonalization See [15]. In this scheme, only the orthogonalization between $U(:, j - 1)$ and $U(:, j), j = 2, \ldots, m + 1$ is explicitly performed according to the Lanczos three term recursion. In QTQtByLanczos_.m, setting eta=0 corresponds to the local orthogonalization. When $U(:, 1 : j)'U(:, 1 : j) \neq I(1 : j, 1 : j)$, duplicate eigenpairs appear in $U(:, 1 : j)'AU(:, 1 : j)$.

For the illustration, we look at the following simple example.

```
>> [Q,R]=QR_(randn(8));   d = [1;2;2;3;3;3;4;5];   A=Q*diag(d)*Q';
%A=A', eig(A) is d.

>> [lambda,V] = eigSymByQR_(A,100*eps);
>
> lambda'    %eigenvalues of A
=  5.0000    4.0000    3.0000    2.0000    1.0000    3.0000    2.0000    3.0000
```

We choose an initial vector q that belongs to the 2-dimensional invariant subspace corresponding to lambda=3,1,3. As expected, $T_{32} \approx 0$. Because of only local orthogonalizations, $U(:, 3 : 4)'U(:, 1 : 2) \neq 0$. As a result, Eq. (7.6) becomes invalid.

```
>> q=[V(:,3),V(:,5:6)]*randn(3,1);      %q belongs to span([V(:,3),V(:,5:6)])
>> [U,T3]=QTQtByLanczos_(A,1,4,q);      %set eta=0 in QTQtByLanczos_.m

>> T=band2full_(T3,1,1,5,5)          %Note T(3,2)=1.7644e-015=8*eps
T =  1.7766       0.9747          0            0            0
     0.9747       2.2234       0.0000          0            0
        0         0.0000       4.1254       1.0298          0
        0            0         1.0298       3.1650       1.0655
        0            0            0         1.0655          0
>> U(:,1:4)'*U(:,1:4)                    %not equal to I
=  1.0000       0.0000       0.0508      -0.2348
   0.0000       1.0000      -0.1256       0.2801
   0.0508      -0.1256       1.0000      -0.0000
  -0.2348       0.2801      -0.0000       1.0000
>> U(:,1:4)'*A*U(:,1:4)                  %not equal to T
=  1.7766       0.9747      -0.0322      -0.1440
```

```
    0.9747     2.2234    -0.2298     0.3940
   -0.0322     0.2298     4.1254     1.0298
   -0.1440     0.3940     1.0298     3.1650
```

If we calculate the eigenvalues of T(2:4,2:4) and T(3:4,3:4), we will find that they have common eigenvalues, lambda=4.7815,2.5089. They can only happen when T(3,2)=0. This can be verified by using the recursive formula of a tri-diagonal matrix, see Section 6.7.1. The common eigenvalues are introduced by $\mathbf{U}(:,3:4)$ and should be discarded.

```
>> eigSymByQR_(T(1:4,1:4),100*eps,'short')'
=    1.0000     3.0000     4.7815     2.5089
>> eigSymByQR_(T(2:4,2:4),100*eps,'short')'
=    2.2234     4.7815     2.5089
>> eigSymByQR_(T(3:4,3:4),100*eps,'short')'
=    4.7815     2.5089
```

Selective Re-orthogonalization   See [61]. We rewrite the first two Lanczos recursive formula as follows, including the floating point errors:

$$T_{21}\mathbf{U}(:,2) = \mathbf{AU}(:,1) - T_{11}\mathbf{U}(:,1) + \boldsymbol{\epsilon}_2,$$
$$T_{32}\mathbf{U}(:,3) = \mathbf{AU}(:,2) - T_{21}\mathbf{U}(:,1) - T_{22}\mathbf{U}(:,2) + \boldsymbol{\epsilon}_3.$$

Now we calculate $T_{32}\mathbf{U}(:,1)'\mathbf{U}(:,3) - T_{21}\mathbf{U}(:,2)'\mathbf{U}(:,2)$, considering $\mathbf{U}(:,1)'\mathbf{AU}(:,2) = \mathbf{U}(:,2)'\mathbf{AU}(:,1)$, $\mathbf{U}(:,1)'\mathbf{U}(:,1) = \mathbf{U}(:,2)'\mathbf{U}(:,2) = 1$, and $\mathbf{U}(:,1)'\mathbf{U}(:,2) = \mathbf{U}(:,2)'\mathbf{U}(:,1) = \epsilon$, because of the symmetry of $\mathbf{A}$ and the explicit normalization and orthogonalization,

$$T_{32}\mathbf{U}(:,1)'\mathbf{U}(:,3) = (T_{11} - T_{22})\,\epsilon + \mathbf{U}(:,1)'\boldsymbol{\epsilon}_3 - \mathbf{U}(:,2)'\boldsymbol{\epsilon}_2.$$

The last two terms are in the order of $\epsilon\|\mathbf{A}\|$. With an estimation for $\|\mathbf{A}\|$, $\mathbf{U}(:,1)'\mathbf{U}(:,3)$ can be estimated as follows:

$$|\mathbf{U}(:,1)'\mathbf{U}(:,3)| = \epsilon\frac{|T_{11} - T_{22}| + \|\mathbf{A}\|}{T_{32}}. \tag{7.12}$$

In the same way, $\mathbf{U}(:,j-1)'\mathbf{U}(:,j) = \epsilon, \mathbf{U}(:,j)'\mathbf{U}(:,j) = 1$ for $j = 1,\ldots,m$, while $|\mathbf{U}(:,i)'\mathbf{U}(:,j)|, i = 1,\ldots,j-1$ can be estimated by a recursive formula similar to Eq. (7.12).

When any $|\mathbf{U}(:,i)'\mathbf{U}(:,j)|, i = 1,\ldots,j-1$ reaches a threshold, an explicit re-orthogonalization of $\mathbf{U}(:,i)$ to $\mathbf{U}(:,j)$ is done. Then $|\mathbf{U}(:,i)'\mathbf{U}(:,j)|$ is set to ϵ and the Lanczos recursion continues. A threshold of $\sqrt{\epsilon}$ is enough to guarantee the calculated $\mathbf{T}$ is a fully accurate projection of $\mathbf{A}$ on the subspace span $\mathbf{U}$, [],

$$\mathbf{T}(1:j,1:j) = \mathbf{N}'\mathbf{AN} + \mathbf{E}, \qquad \|\mathbf{E}\| = O\left(\epsilon\|\mathbf{A}\|\right).$$

Here, $\mathbf{N}$ is an orthogonal basis of the subspace spanned by $\mathbf{U}(:,1:j)$. Although $\mathbf{N}$ is not known explicitly, we know the eigenvalues of $\mathbf{T}(1:j,1:j)$ fully approximate those of $\mathbf{A}$ to the restricted subspace spanned by $\mathbf{U}(:,1:j)$.

7.3.3 IMPLICIT RESTART FOR A BETTER APPROXIMATE INVARIANT SUBSPACE

With the orthogonality of $\mathbf{U}(:,1:m)$ satisfied to $\sqrt{\epsilon}$, whether $\mathbf{T}(1:m,1:m)$ can approximate the desired eigenvalues of $\mathbf{A}$ depends entirely on whether $\mathbf{U}(:,1:m)$ contains the desired invariant subspace of $\mathbf{A}$. If the initial vector $\mathbf{q}$ belongs to the desired invariant subspace of $\mathbf{A}$, $T(m+1,m) = 0$ for some

$m < n$ and we get an invariant subspace. Increase of m will increase the richness of span $(\mathbf{U}(:,1:m))$, thus the chance of its containing the desired invariant subspace. In the extreme case, taking $m = n$ gives the whole space of $\mathbb{R}^n$. But this is entirely unnecessary. The goal is to use $m \ll n$. The strategy is to restart the basic Lanczos algorithm with a better $\mathbf{q}$ based on the information available from the solution of the eigenvalues of $\mathbf{T}(1:m,1:m)$. The implicit restart is the better strategy that provides not only a better $\mathbf{q}$ but also saves the recursion steps in the Lanczos three term recursions.

We assume the new $\mathbf{q}$ for the restart, denoted as $\mathbf{q}_+$, is chosen from the span of the Lanczos vectors $\mathbf{Q}(:,1:m)$,

$$\mathbf{q}_+ = \mathbf{Q}(:,1:m)\mathbf{p} = p(\mathbf{A})\mathbf{q} = \mathbf{V}p(\mathbf{\Lambda})\mathbf{V}'\mathbf{q}, \tag{7.13}$$

for some array $\mathbf{p} \in \mathbb{R}^m$ or some polynomial p of degree $m-1$, where $\mathbf{\Lambda}$ and $\mathbf{V}$ are the eigenvalues and eigenvectors of $\mathbf{A}$. Suppose the polynomial is of the following form, where the subscript denotes the polynomial degree,

$$p_m(\lambda) = (\lambda - \theta_1)(\lambda - \theta_2)\cdots(\lambda - \theta_k)p_l(\lambda) = p_k(\lambda)p_l(\lambda), \quad m = k+l. \tag{7.14}$$

If $\theta_j, j = 1,\ldots,k$ is undesired eigenvalues, $p(\lambda)$ has small values around them and $\mathbf{q}_+$ has small components in the corresponding eigenvectors. Thus to choose a better $\mathbf{q}$ is to choose a polynomial p that emphasizes the components of the desired invariant subspace and de-emphasizes the components of the undesired invariant subspace.

Given a set of eigenvalues $\lambda_j, j = 1,\ldots,m$, deciding which is undesired should be made by the user of the program. A user can decide to write a function to pick a particular λ_j based on some specification. Such a function should look like the following.

```
function pick = user_pick_(spec,neig,lambda,lambdaj)

pick = 0;
if (lambdaj belongs to lambda that satisfies spec and neig)
   pick = 1;
end
```

The following examples of picking k eigenvalues from m eigenvalues may have practical importance to many users.

1. Largest Modulus ('LM') or Smallest Modulus ('SM').
2. Largest Real part ('LR') or Smallest Real part ('SR').
3. Largest absolute Real part ('LRM') or Smallest absolute Real part ('SRM').
4. Largest Imaginary part ('LI') or Smallest Imaginary part ('SI').
5. Largest absolute Imaginary part ('LIM') or Smallest absolute Imaginary part ('SIM').

The following lists the code for the picking based on these picking specification.

Algorithm 7.2

Pick vj from v based on spec = 'LM','SM',....,'SIM'

```
% order v according to spec. If (vj->[v(1),v(k)]) pick=1; else pick=0.
function pick = pick_(spec,k,v,vj)

[m,n] = size(v);  spec = upper(spec);
if (n == 2)   %complex conjugate [vr,vi;-vi,vr] ==> [vr,vi;vr,vi]
    if (vj(1,2) ~= 0) vj(2,1) = vj(1,1); vj(2,2) = vj(1,2); end
```

```
      j = 1;
      while (j < m)
         if (v(j,2) ~= 0) v(j+1,1) = v(j,1);   v(j+1,2) = v(j,2); j = j + 1; end
         j = j + 1;
      end
end

if (strcmp(spec,'LM') || strcmp(spec,'SM'))               %Larg(Small)est Modulus
   u = zeros(m,1);
   for j=1:m u(j) = norm(v(j,:)); end
elseif (strcmp(spec,'LR') || strcmp(spec,'SR'))           %Larg(Small)est Real
   u = v(:,1);
elseif (strcmp(spec,'LRM') || strcmp(spec,'SRM'))         %Larg(Small)est |Real|
   u = abs(v(:,1));
elseif (n==2 && (strcmp(spec,'LI') || strcmp(spec,'SI'))) %Larg(Small) Imag
   u = v(:,2);
elseif (n==2 && (strcmp(spec,'LIM') || strcmp(spec,'SIM')))%Larg(Small)est |Imag|
   u = abs(v(:,2));
else
   error('pick_:_invalid_3rd_argument.');
end

if (spec(1) == 'L') [u,p] = sort(u,'descend');
else                [u,p] = sort(u,'ascend'); end
v = permute_(p,v,'row'); j = 1;  pick = 0;
while (j<=k)
   if (n==1 && vj(1,1)==v(j,1) ||...
       n==2 && vj(1,1)==v(j,1) && vj(1,2)==v(j,2))
       pick = 1; break;
   end
   if (n==1 || v(j,2)==0) j = j + 1; else j = j + 2; end
end
```

The polynomial p shown in Eq. (7.13) is generated according to Eq. (7.14) as the product of $p_k(\mathbf{T})p_l(\mathbf{T})$.

$p_k(\mathbf{T}(1:m,1:m)) = (\mathbf{T} - \theta_1\mathbf{I})(\mathbf{T} - \theta_2\mathbf{I})\cdots(\mathbf{T} - \theta_k\mathbf{I})$ is generated by the implicit QR shift strategy, see [29, 78]. We can either apply the implicit single QR shift (see Section 6.4.4) k times or apply implicit QR k shifts once. In the later way, first we calculate a vector $\mathbf{z} = p_k(\mathbf{T}(1:m,1:m))\mathbf{I}(:,1)$. Note that $p_k(\mathbf{T})$ does not need to be formed explicitly. It is easy to verify that $\mathbf{z}(k+2:m) = \mathbf{0}$. Then we find an orthogonal matrix $\mathbf{Z}_0$ (by Householder or Givens, see Section 3.1) such that $\mathbf{Z}_0'\mathbf{z} = \pm\|\mathbf{z}\|_2\mathbf{I}(:,1)$. At the same time, we calculate $\mathbf{Z}_0'\mathbf{T}(1:m,1:m)\mathbf{Z}_0 \Rightarrow \mathbf{T}(1:m,1:m)$. It is easy to verify that $\mathbf{T}(1:k+1,1:k+1)$ becomes full. Third, we find another orthogonal matrix $\mathbf{Z}_1$ such that $\mathbf{Z}_1'\mathbf{T}(1:m,1:m)\mathbf{Z}_1$ returns to symmetric tri-diagonal (see Section 3.6). Write $\mathbf{Z} = \mathbf{Z}_0\mathbf{Z}_1$. By the construction of $\mathbf{Z}$, we can show that $\mathbf{Z}(:,1) = \mathbf{z}/\|\mathbf{z}\|$ and $\mathbf{Z}(i:m,j) = \mathbf{0}, i = k+j, j = 1:l-1$. To make it more explicit, we calculate a simple example in the following.

```
>> A = randn(8);   A = 0.5*(A+A');
>> [Q,T]=QTQtByHouseholder_(A,100*eps,'long');

>> T
=  -0.9250     2.0522          0          0          0          0          0          0
    2.0522     0.6988    -1.8009          0          0          0          0          0
         0    -1.8009    -0.1612     1.3722          0          0          0          0
         0          0     1.3722    -2.1639     1.0428          0          0          0
```

0	0	0	1.0428	-0.3129	-0.8419	0	0
0	0	0	0	-0.8419	0.2010	0.9838	0
0	0	0	0	0	0.9838	0.3932	0.4206
0	0	0	0	0	0	0.4206	0.0119

```
>> theta1 = randn;  theta2 = randn;  theta3 = randn;   e1=[1;zeros(7,1)];
>> z=(T-theta3*eye(8))*e1;   %Note p3(T) is not explicitly formed.
>> z=(T-theta2*eye(8))*z;
>> z=(T-theta1*eye(8))*z;
>> z'                          %Note z(3+2:8)=0
= -11.2178    15.2486    6.3436   -5.0715        0        0        0        0

>> Z0=householder_(z,1,1,'long');
>> (Z0'*z)'                    %Just verify
=  20.5990   -0.0000   -0.0000   -0.0000        0        0        0        0

>> T=Z0'*T*Z0                  %T(1:3+2,1:3+2) full
= -2.7216    1.1190   -0.7747    0.1991   -0.2567        0        0        0
   1.1190    2.0060   -1.0719   -0.3814    0.1230        0        0        0
  -0.7747   -1.0719    0.2192    1.1520    0.0512        0        0        0
   0.1991   -0.3814    1.1520   -2.0548    1.0018        0        0        0
  -0.2567    0.1230    0.0512    1.0018   -0.3129   -0.8419        0        0
        0         0         0         0   -0.8419    0.2010    0.9838        0
        0         0         0         0         0    0.9838    0.3932    0.4206
        0         0         0         0         0         0    0.4206    0.0119

>> [Z1,T]=QTQtByHouseholder_(T,100*eps,'long');
>> T                          %T in tri-diagonal
= -2.7216   -1.3992        0         0         0         0         0         0
  -1.3992    1.9009    1.9168        0         0         0         0         0
        0    1.9168   -2.1239    0.1204        0         0         0         0
        0         0    0.1204   -0.3262    0.7797        0         0         0
        0         0         0    0.7797   -0.0463   -0.6631        0         0
        0         0         0         0   -0.6631    0.7877   -0.7566        0
        0         0         0         0         0   -0.7566    0.2509   -0.1519
        0         0         0         0         0         0   -0.1519    0.0204

>> Z=Z0*Z1                    %Note Z(:,1)=z/norm(z) and zeros in Z.
= -0.5446   -0.3865   -0.4857   -0.0576   -0.0157    0.2973    0.4178   -0.2274
   0.7403   -0.6145   -0.0806   -0.0513   -0.1247    0.0992    0.1466   -0.1357
   0.3080    0.6307   -0.0223   -0.0354   -0.0107    0.3496    0.5427   -0.2978
  -0.2462   -0.2039    0.8040   -0.0711   -0.3536    0.0779    0.1956   -0.2775
        0    0.1835   -0.3228   -0.2502   -0.8066   -0.1566   -0.2775   -0.2179
        0         0   -0.0806    0.7012   -0.0742   -0.5834    0.2480   -0.3075
        0         0         0   -0.6584    0.2773   -0.6226    0.2713   -0.1683
        0         0         0         0   -0.3552   -0.1447    0.5090    0.7706
```

Now we post-multiply the calculated $\mathbf{Z}$ to Eq. (7.6a),

$$\mathbf{AQ}(:,1:m)\mathbf{Z} = \mathbf{Q}(:,1:m)\mathbf{Z}'\,(\mathbf{Z}'\mathbf{T}(1:m,1:m)\mathbf{Z}) + T(m+1,m)\mathbf{Q}(:,m+1)\mathbf{I}(m,:)\mathbf{Z}. \qquad (7.15)$$

Denote $\mathbf{Q}_+(:,1:m) = \mathbf{Q}(:,1:m)\mathbf{Z}$ and $\mathbf{T}_+(1:m,1:m) = \mathbf{Z}'\mathbf{T}(1:m,1:m)\mathbf{Z}$. We rewrite the above equation as follows:

$$\mathbf{AQ}_+(:,1:m) = \mathbf{Q}_+(:,1:m)\mathbf{T}_+(1:m,1:m) + T(m+1,m)\mathbf{Q}(:,m+1)\mathbf{Z}(m,:). \qquad (7.16)$$

Note Eq. (7.16) is not a new m-step Lanczos partial decomposition because of the last term. However, $\mathbf{Z}(m, 1 : l - 1) = \mathbf{0}$, $\mathbf{Q}_+(:,1 : l)'\mathbf{Q}_+(:,l + 1) = \mathbf{0}$ and $\mathbf{Q}_+(:,1 : l)'\mathbf{Z}(:,m + 1) = \mathbf{0}$, the first l column of Eq. (7.17) is really a new l-step Lanczos partial decomposition,

$$\mathbf{AQ}_+(:,1 : l) = \mathbf{Q}_+(:,1 : l)\mathbf{T}_+(1 : l, 1 : l) + (T_+(l + 1, l)\mathbf{Q}_+(:,l + 1)$$
$$+ \, T(m + 1, m)Z(m, j)\mathbf{Q}(:,m + 1))\,\mathbf{I}(l,:).$$

Denote the term in the bracket still as $T_+(l + 1, l)\mathbf{Q}_+(:,l + 1)$. We can rewrite the above equation as the standard l-step Lanczos partial decomposition,

$$\mathbf{AQ}_+(:,1 : l) = \mathbf{Q}_+(:,1 : l)\mathbf{T}_+(1 : l, 1 : l) + T_+(l + 1, l)\mathbf{Q}_+(:,l + 1)\mathbf{I}(l,:). \tag{7.17}$$

The l-step Lanczos partial decomposition as shown in Eq. (7.17) is restarted and continued for k more steps to reach an m-step Lanczos partial decomposition, which is of the same form as Eq. (7.6), with $\mathbf{Q}$ replaced by $\mathbf{Q}_+$ and $\mathbf{T}$ by $\mathbf{T}_+$. The k-step restart of Eq. (7.17) makes the polynomial $p_l(\lambda)$ of Eq. (7.13). The new starting vector of Eq. (7.17) is $\vartheta\mathbf{q}_+ = \vartheta\mathbf{Q}_+(:,1) = \vartheta\mathbf{Q}(:,1 : m)\mathbf{Z}(:,1) = \mathbf{Q}_+(:,1 : m)\mathbf{z}$, which can be shown to be of the following form:

$$\begin{aligned}
\vartheta\mathbf{q}_+ &= \mathbf{Q}(:,1 : m)p_k(\mathbf{T})\mathbf{I}(:,1) \\
&= \mathbf{Q}(:,1 : m)(\mathbf{T}(1 : m,:) - \theta_k\mathbf{I})(\mathbf{T}(1 : m,:) - \theta_{k-1}\mathbf{I})\cdots(\mathbf{T}(1 : m,:) - \theta_1\mathbf{I})\mathbf{I}(:,1) \\
&= [(\mathbf{A} - \theta_k\mathbf{I})\mathbf{Q}(:,1 : m) - T(m + 1,m)\mathbf{Q}(:,m + 1)\mathbf{I}(m,:)]\,p_{k-1}(\mathbf{T})\mathbf{I}(:,1) \\
&= (\mathbf{A} - \theta_k\mathbf{I})\mathbf{Q}(:,1 : m)p_{k-1}(\mathbf{T})\mathbf{I}(:,1) \\
&= (\mathbf{A} - \theta_k\mathbf{I})\cdots(\mathbf{A} - \theta_1\mathbf{I})\mathbf{Q}(:,1 : m)\mathbf{I}(:,1) = p_k(\mathbf{A})\mathbf{q}.
\end{aligned} \tag{7.18}$$

Since $\theta_j, j = 1\cdots k$ are undesired eigenvalues, the components of $\mathbf{q}_+$ tend to be small in the directions of eigenvectors corresponding to the undesired eigenvalues.

7.3.4 PURGING OF CONVERGED UNDESIRED EIGENVECTORS

Suppose $(\boldsymbol{\Theta},\mathbf{Y})$ are a subset of the eigenpairs of $\mathbf{T},\mathbf{Y} \in \mathbb{R}^{m\times l}, 1 \le l < m$. From $\mathbf{Y}$ we can construct a full orthogonal matrix $\mathbf{Z} = [\mathbf{Y}^\perp,\mathbf{Y}]$, where $\mathbf{Y}^\perp$ is the orthogonal complement to $\mathbf{Y}$. $\mathbf{Y}^\perp$ is not unique. One simple choice is to use orthogonal_(Y) and then permute $\mathbf{Y}$ toward the end of the columns, see Section 7.1.1 for the construction of such a $\mathbf{Z}$. Post-multiplying $\mathbf{Z}$ to Eq. (7.6) and denoting $\mathbf{Q}_+ = \mathbf{Q}(:,1 : m)\mathbf{Z}, \mathbf{T}_+ = \mathbf{Z}'\mathbf{T}(1 : m, 1 : m)\mathbf{Z}, k = m - l$, we write the resultant equation in the sub-matrix form,

$$\mathbf{A}\left[\mathbf{Q}_+(:,1 : k),\mathbf{Q}_+(:,k + 1 : m)\right]$$
$$= \left[\mathbf{Q}_+(:,1 : k),\mathbf{Q}_+(:,k + 1 : m)\right]\begin{bmatrix} \mathbf{T}_+(1 : k,1 : k) & \mathbf{T}_+(1 : k,k + 1 : m) \\ \mathbf{0} & \boldsymbol{\Theta} \end{bmatrix} \tag{7.19}$$
$$+ \, T(m + 1,m)\mathbf{Q}(:,m + 1)\mathbf{Z}(m,:).$$

If $\boldsymbol{\Theta}$ are undesired eigenvalues, we can simply drop the last l columns of Eq. (7.19). The first k columns of Eq. (7.19) are rewritten as follows:

$$\mathbf{AQ}_+(:,1 : k) = \mathbf{Q}_+(:,1 : k)\mathbf{T}_+(1 : k,1 : k) + T(m + 1,m)\mathbf{Q}(:,m + 1)\mathbf{Z}(m,1 : k). \tag{7.20}$$

Note that Eq. (7.20) is not a k-step Lanczos partial decomposition, because $\mathbf{T}_+(1:k,1:k)$ is full and $\mathbf{Z}(m,1:k)$ is not a multiple of $\mathbf{I}(k,:)$.

In order that Eq. (7.20) is a k-step Lanczos partial decomposition, we choose a special $\mathbf{Y}^\perp$ that is due to Sorensen [64, 65]. We first consider the case that $\mathbf{Y}$ has only one column. For the notation, we rename $\mathbf{Y}$ as $\mathbf{y}$. The special $\mathbf{y}^\perp$ is chosen as follows.

The first column,

$$\mathbf{Z}(:,1) = \begin{bmatrix} a_1 \mathbf{y}(1:1) \\ b_1 y_2 \\ 0\mathbf{y}(3:m) \end{bmatrix}; \qquad \mathbf{Z}(:,1)'\mathbf{y} = 0, \qquad \mathbf{Z}(:,1)'\mathbf{Z}(:,1) = 1;$$

$$a_1 = \pm\frac{\|\mathbf{y}(2:2)\|_2}{\|\mathbf{y}(1:1)\|_2\|\mathbf{y}(1:2)\|_2}, \qquad b_1 = \mp\frac{\|\mathbf{y}(1:1)\|_2}{\|\mathbf{y}(2:2)\|_2\|\mathbf{y}(1:2)\|_2};$$

If $y_1 = 0$, then $Z_{11} = 1$ and $\mathbf{Z}(2:m,1) = \mathbf{0}$.

The second column,

$$\mathbf{Z}(:,2) = \begin{bmatrix} a_2 \mathbf{y}(1:2) \\ b_2 y_3 \\ 0\mathbf{y}(4:m) \end{bmatrix}; \qquad \mathbf{Z}(:,2)'\mathbf{y} = 0, \qquad \mathbf{Z}(:,2)'\mathbf{Z}(:,2) = 1;$$

$$a_2 = \pm\frac{\|\mathbf{y}(3:3)\|_2}{\|\mathbf{y}(1:2)\|_2\|\mathbf{y}(1:3)\|_2}, \qquad b_2 = \mp\frac{\|\mathbf{y}(1:2)\|_2}{\|\mathbf{y}(3:3)\|_2\|\mathbf{y}(1:3)\|_2};$$

If $\mathbf{y}(1:2) = \mathbf{0}$, then $Z_{12} = 0, Z_{22} = 1$ and $\mathbf{Z}(3:m,2) = \mathbf{0}$.

The $(m-1)$th column,

$$\mathbf{Z}(:,m-1) = \begin{bmatrix} a_{m-1}\mathbf{y}(1:m-1) \\ b_{m-1} y_m \end{bmatrix}; \qquad \mathbf{Z}(:,m-1)'\mathbf{y} = 0, \qquad \mathbf{Z}(:,m-1)'\mathbf{Z}(:,m-1) = 1;$$

$$a_{m-1} = \pm\frac{\|\mathbf{y}(m:m)\|_2}{\|\mathbf{y}(1:m-1)\|_2\|\mathbf{y}(1:m)\|_2}, \qquad b_{m-1} = \mp\frac{\|\mathbf{y}(1:m-1)\|_2}{\|\mathbf{y}(m:m)\|_2\|\mathbf{y}(1:m)\|_2};$$

If $\mathbf{y}(1:m-1) = \mathbf{0}$, then $\mathbf{Z}(1:m-1,m-1) = 0, Z(m-1,m) = 1$.

It is easy to verify that $\mathbf{Z}(:,i)'\mathbf{Z}(:,j) = a_j\left(a_i\mathbf{y}(1:i)'\mathbf{y}(1:i) + b_i y_{i+1}^2\right) = 0, j = 2\cdots m-1,$ $\forall i < j$. Thus, $\mathbf{Z}$ is an orthogonal matrix. $\mathbf{Z}$ constructed in this way has the following properties:

$$\mathbf{Z} = \mathbf{R} + \mathbf{y}\mathbf{I}(m,:) \sim \begin{bmatrix} R_{11} & R_{12} & R_{13} & R_{14} & y_1 \\ R_{21} & R_{22} & R_{23} & R_{24} & y_2 \\ 0 & R_{32} & R_{33} & R_{34} & y_3 \\ 0 & 0 & R_{43} & R_{44} & y_4 \\ 0 & 0 & 0 & R_{54} & y_5 \end{bmatrix}, \tag{7.21}$$

$\mathbf{H}(j+1:m,j) = 0, j = 1\cdots m-2, \mathbf{R}(:,m) = \mathbf{0}, \mathbf{Z}(:,m) = \mathbf{y}, \mathbf{R}'\mathbf{y} = 0, \mathbf{Z}'\mathbf{y} = \mathbf{I}(:,m).$

If $y_1 \neq 0$, $\mathbf{Z}$ has the following further properties:

$$
\mathbf{Z} = \mathbf{G} + \mathbf{yg} \sim
\begin{bmatrix}
0 & 0 & 0 & 0 & 0 \\
G_{21} & 0 & 0 & 0 & 0 \\
G_{31} & G_{32} & 0 & 0 & 0 \\
G_{41} & G_{42} & G_{43} & 0 & 0 \\
G_{51} & G_{52} & G_{53} & G_{54} & 0
\end{bmatrix}
+
\begin{bmatrix}
y_1 \\
y_2 \\
y_3 \\
y_4 \\
y_5
\end{bmatrix}
[g_1, g_2, g_3, g_4, g_5];
$$

$$g_m = 1, \qquad \mathbf{g}(1:m-1) = \frac{1}{y_1}\mathbf{R}(1, 1:m-1);$$

$$G_{21} = R_{21} - \frac{y_2}{y_1}R_{11}, \qquad \mathbf{G}(3:m, 1) = -\frac{1}{y_1}\mathbf{y}(3:m);$$

$$R_{22} \equiv y_2 z_2, \qquad G_{32} = R_{32} - \frac{y_3}{y_1}R_{22}, \qquad \mathbf{G}(4:m, 2) = -\frac{1}{y_1}\mathbf{y}(4:m); \cdots$$

$$\mathbf{R}(2:m-1, m-1) \equiv \mathbf{y}(2:m-1)z_{m-1}, \qquad G_{m,m-1} = R_{m,m-1} - \frac{y_m}{y_1}R_{m-1,m-1}.$$

(7.22)

Now using this specially chosen $\mathbf{Z}$ in Eq. (7.19), $\mathbf{T}_+$ can be written as follows:

$$
\begin{aligned}
\mathbf{T}_+(1:m, 1:m) &= \mathbf{Z'T}(1:m, 1:m)\mathbf{Z} = \mathbf{Z'T}(\mathbf{R} + \mathbf{yI}(m,:)) = \mathbf{Z'TR} + \theta\mathbf{I}(:,m)\mathbf{I}(m,:) \\
&= (\mathbf{G'} + \mathbf{gy'})\mathbf{TR} + \theta\mathbf{I}(:,m)\mathbf{I}(m,:) = \mathbf{G'TR} + \theta\mathbf{I}(:,m)\mathbf{I}(m,:).
\end{aligned}
$$

(7.23)

From the structure of $\mathbf{R}, \mathbf{G}$, and $\mathbf{T}$, we know $\mathbf{G'TR}$ is upper Hessenberg and its mth column and row are both zeros. But $\mathbf{T}_+(1:m, 1:m)$ must be symmetric, therefore $\mathbf{T}_+(1:m, 1:m)$ is symmetric and tri-diagonal.

Further if θ is a converged eigenvalue of $\mathbf{A}$, the residual by Eq. (7.9) is zero. Assume $y_m = 0$, from Eq. (7.21), we can obtain immediately $\mathbf{Z}(m-1,:) = [\mathbf{I}(m-1,:), 0]$. In this case, Eq. (7.20) becomes a $(m-1)$-step Lanczos partial decomposition.

Note that $\mathbf{T}_+(1:m, 1:m)$ calculated in Eq. (7.23) is a symmetric tri-diagonal based on $\mathbf{G}$ and $\mathbf{g}$ calculated in Eq. (7.22). If $y_1 = 0$, $\mathbf{G}$ and $\mathbf{g}$ cannot be calculated. In real calculations, because of round-off errors, $y_1 = 0$ rarely happens. But if $|y_1|$ is small, $\mathbf{G}$ and $\mathbf{g}$ are in the order of $|y_1|^{-1}$. $\mathbf{gy'TR} \approx \theta\mathbf{gy'R}$ can be significantly from zeros, due to numerical errors in $\mathbf{Ty} = \theta\mathbf{y}$ and $\mathbf{R'y} = 0$. To avoid this from happening, the algorithm of Eq. (7.21) is slightly modified, see [65]. The modification essentially replaces a 2×2 identity sub-matrix in $\mathbf{R}$ by another 2×2 orthogonal matrix by maintaining two conditions $\mathbf{Z'y} = \mathbf{I}(:,m)$ and $\mathbf{y'TZ} = \theta\mathbf{I}(m,:)$. Remember that the orthogonal complement $\mathbf{y}^\perp$ to $\mathbf{y}$ is not unique.

If $\mathbf{Y}$ has more than one column, the procedure illustrated above can be applied sequentially. Suppose $\mathbf{Y}$ has two columns, the two-step procedure works as follows:

$$
\mathbf{y} = \mathbf{Y}(:, 2), \qquad \mathbf{Z}_2 = \mathbf{R} + \mathbf{yI}(m,:); \sim
\begin{bmatrix}
R_{11} & R_{12} & R_{13} & R_{14} & y_1 \\
R_{21} & R_{22} & R_{23} & R_{24} & y_2 \\
0 & R_{32} & R_{33} & R_{34} & y_3 \\
0 & 0 & R_{43} & R_{44} & y_4 \\
0 & 0 & 0 & R_{54} & y_5
\end{bmatrix};
$$

$$\mathbf{y} = \mathbf{Z}_2\mathbf{Y}(:,1), \qquad \mathbf{Z}_1 = \mathbf{U} + \mathbf{I}(:,m)\mathbf{I}(m-1) + \mathbf{yI}(m,:); \sim \begin{bmatrix} U_{11} & U_{12} & U_{13} & 0 & y_1 \\ U_{21} & U_{22} & U_{23} & 0 & y_2 \\ 0 & U_{32} & U_{33} & 0 & y_3 \\ 0 & 0 & U_{43} & 0 & y_4 \\ 0 & 0 & 0 & 1 & 0 \end{bmatrix};$$

$$\mathbf{Z} = \mathbf{Z}_2\mathbf{Z}_1 = \mathbf{RZ} + \mathbf{Y}(:,1)\mathbf{I}(m-1,:) + \mathbf{Y}(:,2)\mathbf{I}(m,:).$$

Given $\mathbf{Y}$ with $\mathbf{Y}'\mathbf{Y} = \mathbf{I}$, creating the orthogonal matrix $\mathbf{Z}$ based on Eqs. (7.21) and (7.22) is implemented in sorensen_.m. Its use in purging a converged undesired eigenvalue is based on Eqs. (7.19) and (7.20).

Algorithm 7.3

Given Y'*Y=I, find Q(:,1:k)=Y and Q'*Q=Q*Q'=I. If A*Y=Y*D, Y'*A*Q=(D;0).

```
function Q = sorensen_(Y,A)

[m,n] = size(Y);   Q = eye(m);   y = zeros(m,1);
if (~exist('A','var') || isempty(A))
    for j=n:-1:1
        y(1:n-j) = 0;
        for i=n-j+1:m y(i) = Q(1:i,i)'*Y(1:i,j); end
        Qj = [y,zeros(m,m-1)];
        sigma = y(1)*y(1);   tau0 = abs(y(1));
        for i=2:m
            sigma = sigma + y(i)*y(i);   tau = sqrt(sigma);
            if (tau0 == 0)
                Qj(i-1,i) = 1;
            else
                gamma = (y(i)/tau)/tau0;   rho = tau0/tau;
                Qj(1:i-1,i) =-y(1:i-1)*gamma;   Qj(i,i) = rho;
            end
            tau0 = tau;
        end
        Q = Q*Qj;
    end
else     %A={'band',T3}, A={'hess',H} or A={'full',F}
    format = A{1};   A = A{2};   tiny = 0.01*sqrt(eps);
    for j=n:-1:1
        Qj = zeros(m);
        for i=1:n-j
            y(i) = 0;   Qj(i,i+1) = 1;
        end
        for i=n-j+1:m
            y(i) = Q(1:i,i)'*Y(1:i,j);
            if (y(i) == 0) y(i) = eps/m; end
        end
        sigma = y(n-j+1)*y(n-j+1);   tau0 = abs(y(n-j+1));
        for i=n-j+2:m
            sigma = sigma + y(i)*y(i);   tau = sqrt(sigma);
            gamma = (y(i)/tau)/tau0;   rho = tau0/tau;
            Qj(1:i-1,i) =-y(1:i-1)*gamma;   Qj(i,i) = rho;
            if (i<m && tau<0.05)
                tau1 = sqrt(sigma+y(i+1)*y(i+1));
                if (strcmp(format,'band'))
```

```
              alpha = y(1:i)'*Ay_({'band',{A(1:i,:),1,1,i,i}},Qj(1:i,i));
              beta  = y(i+1)*A(i+1,1)*rho;
          elseif(strcmp(format,'hess'))
              alpha = y(1:i)'*Ay_({'hess',A(1:i,1:i)},Qj(1:i,i));
              beta  = y(i+1)*A(i+1,i)*rho;
          else %if(strcmp(format,'full'))
              alpha = y(1:i)'*(A(1:i,1:i)*Qj(1:i,i));
              beta = y(i+1)*A(i+1,i)*rho;
          end
          if(alpha*beta < 0) s = 1; else s =-1; end
          if (abs(alpha+beta) < eps*tau1)
              if (rho < tiny)
                  Qj(i,i) = Qj(i,i)*s*(abs(alpha)+eps*tau1)/abs(beta);
              elseif (abs(alpha) > abs(beta))
                  phi = s*(abs(beta)+eps*tau1)/abs(alpha);
                  sigma = sigma*phi*phi;   tau = tau*abs(phi);
                  y(1:i) = y(1:i)*phi;
              else
                  psi = s*(abs(alpha)+eps*tau1)/abs(beta);
                  y(i+1:m) = y(i+1:m)*psi;
              end
          end
      end
      tau0 = tau;
    end
    Qj(:,1) = y/norm(y);   Q = Q*Qj;
  end
end
```

7.3.5 LOCKING OF CONVERGED DESIRED EIGENVECTORS

If $(\mathbf{\Theta}, \mathbf{Y})$ are converged desired eigenpairs of $\mathbf{A}$, we create the orthogonal matrix $\mathbf{Z}$ by calling sorensen_(Y) and permute $\mathbf{Y}$ to the first k column of $\mathbf{Z}$. Post-multiplying this special $\mathbf{Z}$ in Eq. (7.6) and denoting $\mathbf{Q}_+ = \mathbf{Q}(:,1 : m)\mathbf{Z}, \mathbf{T}_+ = \mathbf{Z}'\mathbf{T}(1 : m,1 : m)\mathbf{Z}$, we write the resultant equation in the sub-matrix form

$$\mathbf{A}\left[\mathbf{Q}_+(:,1:k),\mathbf{Q}_+(:,k+1:m)\right]$$

$$= \left[\mathbf{Q}_+(:,1:k),\mathbf{Q}_+(:,k+1:m)\right]\begin{bmatrix} \mathbf{\Theta} & \mathbf{0} \\ \mathbf{0} & \mathbf{T}_+(k+1:m,k+1:m) \end{bmatrix} \tag{7.24}$$

$$+ T(m+1,m)\mathbf{Q}(:,m+1)\mathbf{Z}(m,:).$$

Note that $\mathbf{Y}(m,:) = 0$ (converged). By construction of $\mathbf{Z}$, $\mathbf{Z}(m,:) = \mathbf{I}(m,:)$ and $\mathbf{T}_+(k+1:m,k+1:m)$ is also symmetric tri-diagonal. Eq. (7.24) remains an m-step Lanczos partial decomposition. The first k columns $\mathbf{T}_+(1:k,1:k),\mathbf{Q}_+(:,1:k)$ are the eigenvalues and eigenvectors of $\mathbf{A}$. $\mathbf{T}_+(1:k,1:k) = \mathbf{\Theta}$ does not need to participate in the Lanczos recursion. If re-orthogonalization is needed, the new Lanczos vector will be orthogonalized against $\mathbf{Q}_+(:,1:k)$.

7.3.6 MATLAB IMPLEMENTATION OF LANCZOS ALGORITHM

The contents of Section 7.1 and this section are succinctly implemented in eigByLanczos_.m of few than 150 lines of MATLAB codes. Most of the input arguments to eigByLanczos_.m are same to those to eigBySubspace_.m, see Section 7.2 for the explanation of these same input arguments. The differences

are the second input argument q, the fifth input argument pick, and the extra sixth input argument
m. q can be only a column vector. A multiple column matrix Q, such as used in eigBySubspace_.m,
corresponds to the implementation of block Lanczos algorithm, see [5], which is not implemented in
eigByLanczos_.m. In eigByLanczos_.m, we use pick to replace nv in eigBySubspace_.m. An example of pick
is pick={'pick_', 'LM', 3}, which uses pick_.m to pick three largest modulus eigenvalues. A general
input of pick can be pick={'user_pick_', 'user_spec', neig}. The extra input argument m is the step of
Lanczos partial decomposition, that is, m in Eq. (7.6). All input arguments except the first one can take
default values. For the most common usage, to calculate the largest modulus eigenvalue of a full matrix
A to the precision of $\sqrt{\epsilon}\|A\|$, the call can be simply [lambda,V]=eigByLanczos_(A).

Algorithm 7.4

AV = **V**λ by Lanczos iteration.

```
%lambda,V: i=eigenvalue(vector)s from previous run; o=new ones append to input.
function [lambda,V] = eigByLanczos_(A,algo,q,tol,pick,m,lambda,V)
if (~iscell(algo)) error('eigByLanczos_:_algo_format_error.'); end
eqsALGO = 'mtimes';  eigALGO = 'eigSymByQR';
if (length(algo)>=1 && ~isempty(algo{1})) sigma  = algo{1}; end
if (length(algo)>=2 && ~isempty(algo{2})) eqsALGO = algo{2}; end
if (~exist('V','var')) V = []; end
if (neig <= neig1) warning('eigByLanczos_:_no_operation.'); return; end
if (m < n) m1 = m + 1; else m1 = n; end

if (exist('sigma','var'))
    A = A_(A,sigma,eqsALGO);   normA = max(1.0,1.0/abs(normA-sigma));
end
if (neig1 == 0)
    Q = q/norm(q);  T3 = [];
else
    normq0 = norm(q);  q = q - V*(V'*q);  normq = norm(q);  eta = 0.5*sqrt(2.0);
    if (normq < eta*normq0)    %reorthogonalization
        normq0 = normq;  q = q-V*(V'*q);  normq = norm(q);
    end
    if (normq > eta*normq0) q = q/normq;
    else                    q = orthogonal_(V); end
    Q = [V,q];  T3 = zeros(neig1+1,3);  T3(1:neig1,2) = lambda;
    if (exist('sigma','var')) T3(1:neig1,2) = 1.0./(T3(1:neig1,2) - sigma); end
    normA = max(normA,max(abs(T3(1:neig1,2))));
end
[Q,T3] = QTQtByLanczos_(A,neig1+1,m,Q,T3);
q = Q(:,m1);  t = [zeros(1,m-1),T3(m1,1)];  V0 = [];  %V0: undesired eigenvectors
if (m == n) beta = 0; else beta = abs(t(m)); end

while(neig1 < neig)
    [sita,Y] = eigSymByQR_({'band',{T3(neig1+1:m,:),1,1,m-neig1,m-neig1}},tol,'long');
    if (exist('sigma','var')) lmd = sigma + 1.0./sita;  else lmd = sita; end
    neig0 = neig1;  sita11 = [];  sita21 = [];  sita22 = [];  Y11 = [];  Y21 = [];
    for k=1:size(sita,1)    %check convergence of eigs
        normA = max(normA,abs(sita(k)));
        if (feval(pick{1},pick{2},neig-neig0,lmd,lmd(k)) == 1)
            if (beta*norm(Y(m-neig0,k)) < tol*normA)             %to be locked
                sita11 = [sita11;sita(k)];  Y11 = [Y11,Y(:,k)];  neig1 = neig1 + 1;
            end
        elseif (beta*norm(Y(m-neig0,k)) < tol*normA)
            sita21 = [sita21;sita(k)];  Y21 = [Y21,Y(:,k)];        %to be purged
```

```
        else
            sita22 = [sita22;sita(k)];                            %to be filtered
        end
    end
end
l2 = length(sita21);   l3 = length(sita22);

if (~isempty(sita11))    %lock converged wanted eigs(sita11)
    j1 = size(Y11,2); j2 = m-neig0;
    W = sorensen_(Y11,{'band',T3(neig0+1:m,:)});
    Q(:,neig0+1:m) = Q(:,neig0+1:m)*W;
    t(neig0+1:neig1) = t(m)*W(j2,1:j1);   t(m) = t(m)*W(j2,j2);
    Tw = mtimesBand_(T3(neig0+1:m,:),1,1,m-neig0,m-neig0,W(:,j1+1:j2));
    for j=j1+1:j2
        T3(neig0+j,2) = W(1:j,j)'*Tw(1:j,j-j1);
        if (j < j2)
            T3(neig0+j+1,1) = W(1:j+1,j+1)'*Tw(1:j+1,j-j1);
            T3(neig0+j,3) = T3(neig0+j+1,1);
        end
    end
    T3(neig0+1:neig1,2) = sita11;  %lock sita11
    T3(neig0+2:neig1+1,1) = 0.0; T3(neig0+1:neig1,3) = 0.0;
end
if (neig1 >= neig) break; end

if (~isempty(sita21))     %purge unwanted converged eigs(sita21)
    if (neig1 > neig0)     %(W'*T*W)*(W'*Y21)=sita21*(W'*Y21)
        Y21 = W'*Y21;    Y21 = Y21(neig1-neig0+1:m-neig0,:);
    end
    W = sorensen_(Y21,{'band',T3(neig1+1:m,:)});
    W = permute_([l2+1:m-neig1,1:l2],W,'col');
    Q(:,neig1+1:m) = Q(:,neig1+1:m)*W;    V0 = [V0,Q(:,m-neig1+1:m)];
    t(neig0+1:neig1) = 0.0;   t(m-l2:m) = t(m)*W(m-neig1,m-neig1-l2:m-neig1);
    Tw = mtimesBand_(T3(neig1+1:m,:),1,1,m-neig1,m-neig1,W(:,1:m-neig1-l2));
    for j=1:m-neig1-l2
        T3(neig1+j,2) = W(1:j+l2,j)'*Tw(1:j+l2,j);
        if (j < m-neig1-l2)
            T3(neig1+j+1,1) = W(1:j+l2+1,j+1)'*Tw(1:j+l2+1,j);
            T3(neig1+j,3) = T3(neig1+j+1,1);
        end
    end
    T3(m-l2+1:m,2) = sita21;  %purge sita21
    T3(m-l2+1:m,1) = 0.0;   T3(m-l2:m-1,3) = 0.0;
end

if (~isempty(sita22))     %shift nonconverged unwanted eigs (sita22)
    j1 = neig1+1;   j2 = m-l2;   W = eye(j2-j1+1);
    for k=1:size(sita22,1)
        a1 = T3(neig1+1,2)-sita22(k);   a2 = T3(neig1+2,1);
        for j=j1:j2-1
            [c,s] = givens_(a1,a2);   cc = c*c;   ss = s*s;   cs2 = 2.0*c*s;
            if (j > j1)
                T3(j,1) = c*T3(j,1) - s*a2;   T3(j-1,3) = T3(j,1);
            end
            T11 = T3(j,2); T21 = T3(j+1,1);   T22 = T3(j+1,2);
            T3(j,2)   = cc*T11 + ss*T22 - cs2*T21;
            T3(j+1,2) = ss*T11 + cc*T22 + cs2*T21;
            T3(j+1,1) = (cc-ss)*T21 + c*s*(T11-T22);   T3(j,3) = T3(j+1,1);
```

```
                     a1 = T3(j+1,1);
                     if (j < j2-1)
                         a2 = -s*T3(j+2,1);
                         T3(j+2,1) = c*T3(j+2,1);   T3(j+1,3) = T3(j+2,1);
                     end
                     W(:,j-j1+1:j-j1+2) = W(:,j-j1+1:j-j1+2)*[c,s;-s,c];
                 end
             end
             Q(:,j1:j2) = Q(:,j1:j2)*W;   t(j1:j2) = t(j2)*W(m-neig1-12,:);
         end

         if (l2 + l3 > 0)      %implicit restart
             l = m - l2 - l3;
             q = T3(l+1,1)*Q(:,l+1) + t(l)*Q(:,m1);
             T3(l+1,1) = norm(q);   T3(l,3) = T3(l+1,1);   Q(:,l+1) = q/T3(l+1,1);
             [Q,T3] = QTQtByLanczos_(A,l+1,m,Q(:,1:l+1),T3(1:l+1,:),V0);
         else                     %explicit restart
             [y,l] = min(abs(Y(m-neig0,neig1-neig0+1:m-neig0)));
             Q(:,neig1+1) = Q(:,neig0+1:m)*Y(:,neig1-neig0+1);
             [Q,T3] = QTQtByLanczos_(A,neig1+1,m,Q(:,1:neig1+1),T3(1:neig1,:),V0);
         end
         q = Q(:,m+1);   t = [zeros(1,m-1),T3(m+1,1)];   beta = abs(t(m));
     end

lambda = T3(1:neig1,2);   V = Q(:,1:neig1);
if (exist('sigma','var')) lambda = sigma + 1.0./lambda; end
```

To show the property of the Lanczos algorithm and the way to use `eigByLanczos_.m`, we apply `eigByLanczos_.m` to the following two examples.

The first example is a full matrix of 100×100. As shown below, its eigenvalues are scattered in $[-1000, +1000]$ with 94 of them condensed in $[-1, +1]$. As explained in Sections 6.3 and 7.1, the extremal eigenvalues converge very fast in the Lanczos algorithm. The eigenvalues in the middle of the spectrum converge slowly. If the input argument m, i.e. m in Eq. (7.6), is larger, the convergence is faster. To calculate the eigenvalues in the middle of the spectrum in few iterations, we can use the shift and inverse.

```
>> d=[-1000;  -100;  -10;  -1;  -0.1;  -0.01;  -0.001;  0.0;  -rand(42,1);
       1000;   100;   10;   1;   0.1;   0.01;   0.001;  0.0;   rand(42,1)];
>> [V,r]=QR_(randn(100));
>> A=V'*diag(d)*V;      q=randn(100,1);     tol=100*eps;      %(d,V) eigs of A.
```

The code snippets and calculated results are listed below. The convergence patterns for the first eight extremal eigenvalues, that is, $(\pm 1000, \pm 100, \pm 10, \pm 1)$, are shown in Fig. 7.2, where the abscissa is the accumulated number of times of solving Eq. (7.8) and the ordinate is the logarithm of the error calculated in Eq. (7.9). When $m = 8$, ± 1000 converge in two iterations and ± 100 converge in three iterations. When $m = 16$, all the first six largest modulus eigenvalues $\pm 1000, \pm 100$, and ± 10 converge in the first iteration. But ± 1 take 17 iterations to converge, because they are very close to other eigenvalues $0.9593, 0.9597, -0.9706, -0.9649$. After calculating the first 8 largest modulus eigenvalues, if we want to calculate these four eigenvalues, we can restart from the end of the calculation of the second call to `eigByLanczos_.m`. Of course, we can calculate all the first 12 largest modulus eigenvalues by only one call to `eigByLanczos_.m`. If we want to calculate only the first six largest eigenvalues, we can pass `pick={'pick_','LR',6}` to `eigByLanczos_.m`. If we want to calculate the six smallest modulus eigenvalues, we can pass `algo={0.0011,'LDLt_'}` and `pick={'pick_','SM',6}` to `eigByLanczos_.m`.

```
     %Calculate 1st 4 largest modulus eigenvalues through a subspace of dimension of 8.
>> [lambda4,V4]=eigByLanczos_(A,[],q,tol,{'pick_','LM',4},8);
>> lambda4'
=  1.0e+003 *
    1.0000    -1.0000     0.1000    -0.1000
>> norm(A*V4-V4*diag(lambda4))=6.6542e-013  %correct eigenvalues and eigenvectors
>> norm(V4'*V4-eye(4))=8.3257e-016            %correct eigenvalues and eigenvectors
     %Calculate 1st 8 largest modulus eigenvalues through a subspace of dimension of 16.
>> [lambda8,V8]=eigByLanczos_(A,[],q,tol,{'pick_','LM',8},16);
>> lambda8'
=  1.0e+003 *
    1.0000    -1.0000     0.1000    -0.1000    -0.0100     0.0100     0.0010    -0.0010
>> norm(A*V8-V8*diag(lambda8))=1.9891e-010  %correct eigenvalues and eigenvectors
>> norm(V8'*V8-eye(8))=1.9292e-011            %correct eigenvalues and eigenvectors
     %Restart from [lambda8,V8]. Dimension of subspace increased to 20.
>> [lambda12,V12]=eigByLanczos_(A,[],q,tol,{'pick_','LM',12},20,lambda8,V8);
>> lambda12(9:12)'
=  0.9593     0.9597    -0.9706    -0.9649
>> norm(A*V12-V12*diag(lambda12))=1.9980e-010    %correct eigenvalues and eigenvectors
>> norm(V12'*V12-eye(12))=2.0269e-011            %correct eigenvalues and eigenvectors
     %Obtain lambda12,V12 by only one call.
>> [lambda12,V12]=eigByLanczos_(A,[],q,tol,{'pick_','LM',12},20);
>> lambda12(1:8)'
=  1.0e+003 *
   -1.0000     1.0000    -0.1000     0.1000     0.0100    -0.0100     0.0010    -0.0010
>> lambda12(9:12)'
=  0.9593     0.9597    -0.9706    -0.9649
>> norm(A*V12-V12*diag(lambda12))=1.1366e-010    %correct eigenvalues and eigenvectors
>> norm(V12'*V12-eye(12))=7.9808e-013            %correct eigenvalues and eigenvectors
     %Calcculate 1st 6 largest eigenvalues.
>> [lambda6,V6]=eigByLanczos_(A,[],q,tol,{'pick_','LR',6},20);
>> lambda6(1:3)'
=  1.0e+003 *
    1.0000     0.1000     0.0100
>> lambda6(4:6)'
=  1.0000     0.9593     0.9597
>> norm(A*V6-V6*diag(lambda6))=2.4277e-011  %correct eigenvalues and eigenvectors
>> norm(V6'*V6-eye(6))=2.6669e-014            %correct eigenvalues and eigenvectors
     %Calcculate 6 smallest modulus eigenvalues using shift and inverse.
>> [lambda6,V6]=eigByLanczos_(A,{0.0011,'LDLt_'},q,tol,{'pick_','SM',6},20);
>> lambda6'
=  0.0010    -0.0010    -0.0000    -0.0000     0.0100    -0.0100
>> norm(A*V6-V6*diag(lambda6))=5.9362e-012  %correct eigenvalues and eigenvectors
>> norm(V6'*V6-eye(6))=8.8980e-014            %correct eigenvalues and eigenvectors
```

The second example is a 1000×1000 tri-diagonal matrix, whose diagonal is all 2 and the two off-diagonals are all -1, see Section 5.7.3 for a discussion of such a matrix. It is generated in the following code scripts.

```
>> B=[[0;-ones(999,1)],2*ones(1000,1),[-ones(999,1);0]];
>> F=band2full_(B,1,1,1000,1000);        %full format, for verification only.
```

Its eigenvalues and eigenvectors are as shown in Eq. (5.106). They can be obtained in eigSymByQR_.m.

```
>> tic
>> [lambda,V]=eigSymByQR_({'band',{B,1,1,1000,1000}},100*eps);
>> toc
Elapsed time is 50.986598 seconds.
```

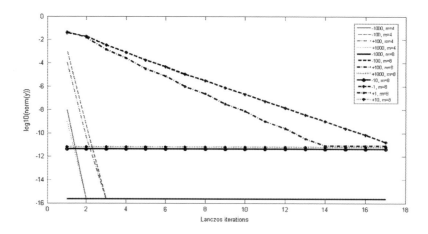

FIGURE 7.2

Errors of Lanczos iterations.

```
>> norm(F*V-V*diag(lambda))=1.9126e-013      %correct eigenvalues and eigenvectors
>> norm(V'*V-eye(1000))=1.8913e-014          %correct eigenvalues and eigenvectors
>> lambda=sort(lambda);
>> lambda(1:10)'       %smallest eigenvalues
=   1.0e-003 *
    0.0098    0.0394    0.0886    0.1576    0.2462    0.3546    0.4826    0.6304    0.7978
0.9849
>> lambda(496:505)'       %medium eigenvalues
=   1.9718    1.9780    1.9843    1.9906    1.9969    2.0031    2.0094    2.0157    2.0220
2.0282
>> lambda(991:1000)'       %largest eigenvalues
=   3.9990    3.9992    3.9994    3.9995    3.9996    3.9998    3.9998    3.9999    4.0000
4.0
```

The three groups of eigenvalues are calculated by `eigByLanczos_.m` with the band format of the matrix.

```
>> q=ones(1000,1);   tol=100*eps;   m = 50;   n = 1000;   pick={'pick_','LM',10};

>> [lambda1,V1]=eigByLanczos_({'band',{B,1,1,n,n}},{},q,tol,pick,m);
>> lambda1'   %largest eigenvalues
=   4.0000    3.9998    3.9996    3.9994    3.9990    3.9986    3.9981    3.9975    3.9968
3.9961
>> norm(F*V1-V1*diag(lambda1))=5.6896e-013   %correct eigenvalues and eigenvectors
>> norm(V1'*V1-eye(10))=1.3722e-013          %correct eigenvalues and eigenvectors
   %shift and inverse with shift=0. Solve B^{-1}*v = lambda*v.
>> [lambda2,V2]=eigByLanczos_({'band',{B,1,1,n,n}},{0.0,'mdivideBandByGivens_'},...
                          q,tol,{'pick_','SR',10},50);
>> lambda2'   %smallest eigenvalues.
=   1.0e-003 *
    0.0098    0.0886    0.0394    0.2462    0.1576    0.4826    0.3546    0.7978    0.6304
0.9849
   %shift and inverse with shift=2. Resolve (B-2I)^{-1}*v = lambda*v.
>> B(:,2)=B(:,2)-2;
```

```
>> [lambda3,V3]=eigByLanczos_({'mdivideBandByGivens_',{B,1,1,n,n}},{},q,tol,pick,60);
>> lambda3=2.0+1.0./lambda3;        %Recover eiegnvalues of B
>> lambda3'
=   2.0031    1.9969    1.9906    2.0094    2.0157    1.9843    1.9780    2.0282    2.0220
1.9718
>> norm(F*V3-V3*diag(lambda3))=1.1143e-015   %correct eigenvalues and eigenvectors
>> norm(V3'*V3-eye(10))=5.8913e-015          %correct eigenvalues and eigenvectors
```

The three groups of the eigenvalues can also be calculated with the CSR format of the matrix. In the shift and inverse algorithm, we have to use the iterative equation solution algorithm for the matrix-vector product.

```
>> B(:,2)=2;  %restore the original B
>> [S,r,c]=band2csr_(B,1,1,1000,1000);

>> [lambda1,V1]=eigByLanczos_({'csr',{S,r,c}},{},q,tol,pick,50);
>> lambda1'   %largest eigenvalues
=   4.0000    3.9998    3.9996    3.9994    3.9990    3.9986    3.9981    3.9975    3.9968
3.9961
>> norm(F*V1-V1*diag(lambda1))=5.6896e-013   %correct eigenvalues and eigenvectors
>> norm(V1'*V1-eye(10))=1.3722e-013          %correct eigenvalues and eigenvectors
   %shift and inverse with shift=0. Solve B^{-1}*v = lambda*v.
>> [lambda2,V2]=eigByLanczos_({'csr',{S,r,c}},{0.0,'eqsCG_'},q,tol,...
                            {'pick_','SR',10},50);
>> lambda2'   %smallest eigenvalues
=   0.0000    0.0001    0.0002    0.0005    0.0008    0.0012    0.0017    0.0022    0.0028
0.0036
>> norm(F*V2-V2*diag(lambda2))=5.4052e-011   %correct eigenvalues and eigenvectors
>> norm(V2'*V2-eye(10))=1.3508e-015          %correct eigenvalues and eigenvectors
   %shift and inverse with shift=2. Resolve (B-2I)^{-1}*v = lambda*v.
>> B(:,2)=B(:,2)-2;
>> [lambda3,V3]=eigByLanczos_({'eqsCG_',{'csr',{S,r,c}}},{},q,tol,pick,60);
>> lambda3=2.0+1.0./lambda3;        %Recover eiegnvalues of B
>> lambda3'   %medium eigenvalues
=   2.0031    1.9906    2.0157    1.9780    2.0282    1.9655    2.0408    1.9529    2.0533
1.9404
>> norm(F*V3-V3*diag(lambda3))=1.0214e-010   %correct eigenvalues and eigenvectors
>> norm(V3'*V3-eye(10))=1.1687e-015          %correct eigenvalues and eigenvectors
```

7.4 ARNOLDI ITERATIONS FOR $\mathbf{Ax} = \lambda\mathbf{x}$ OF AN UNSYMMETRIC MATRIX

For the eigenvalue problem of an unsymmetric matrix $\mathbf{A}$, $\mathbf{Ax} = \lambda\mathbf{x}$, the Arnoldi iterative algorithm is an extension of the Lanczos algorithm discussed in the previous section. The discussion of the Arnoldi algorithm in this section focuses only on the differences.

7.4.1 BASIC ARNOLDI ALGORITHM

The form of Eq. (7.6) remains the same, but with $\mathbf{T}$ replaced by $\mathbf{H}$, an upper Hessenberg matrix. In Eq. (7.25), $\mathbf{Q}$ and $\mathbf{H}$ are generated in QHQtByArnoldi_.m,

$$\mathbf{AQ}(:,1:m) = \mathbf{Q}(:,1:m)\mathbf{H}(1:m,1:m) + H(m+1,m)\mathbf{Q}(:,m+1)\mathbf{I}(m,:), \quad (7.25a)$$

$$\mathbf{Q}(:,1:m)'\mathbf{Q}(:,1:m) = \mathbf{I}, \quad (7.25b)$$

$$\mathbf{Q}(:, 1 : m)'\mathbf{Q}(:, m + 1) = \mathbf{0}. \tag{7.25c}$$

Suppose an eigenpair of $\mathbf{A}$ is $(\lambda, \mathbf{v})$, where $\mathbf{v}$ can be approximately presented as $\mathbf{v} = \mathbf{Q}(:, 1 : m)\mathbf{u}$. To determine the two unknowns $(\lambda, \mathbf{u})$, we introduce the following Galerkin conditions:

$$\mathbf{Q}(:, 1 : m)'\mathbf{y} = \mathbf{Q}(:, 1 : m)'\,(\mathbf{AQ}(:, 1 : m)\mathbf{u} - \lambda\mathbf{Q}(:, 1 : m)\mathbf{u}) = \mathbf{0}. \tag{7.26}$$

Considering Eq. (7.25), the above Galerkin conditions are simplified to

$$\mathbf{H}(1 : m, 1 : m)\mathbf{u} = \lambda\mathbf{u}. \tag{7.27}$$

From Eq. (7.27), $(\lambda, \mathbf{u})$ can be found by any eigenvalue algorithms for a Hessenberg matrix, such as `eigUnsymByQR_.m`. Once $(\lambda, \mathbf{u})$ is determined, the residual $\mathbf{y}$ can be numerically calculated,

$$
\begin{aligned}
\mathbf{y} = \mathbf{Av} - \lambda\mathbf{v} &= \mathbf{AQ}(:, 1 : m)\mathbf{u} - \lambda\mathbf{Q}(:, 1 : m)\mathbf{u} \\
&= (\mathbf{Q}(:, 1 : m)\mathbf{H}(1 : m, 1 : m) + H(m + 1, m)\mathbf{Q}(:, m + 1)\mathbf{I}(m, :))\,\mathbf{u} - \lambda\mathbf{Q}(:, 1 : m)\mathbf{u} \\
&= \mathbf{Q}(:, 1 : m)\,(\mathbf{H}(1 : m, 1 : m)\mathbf{u} - \lambda\mathbf{u}) + H(m + 1, m)u(m)\mathbf{U}(:, m + 1) \\
&= H(m + 1, m)u(m)\mathbf{Q}(:, m + 1).
\end{aligned} \tag{7.28}
$$

From Eq. (7.28), the residual, i.e. the error measurement of $(\lambda, \mathbf{Q}(:, 1 : m)\mathbf{u})$ as an eigenpair of $\mathbf{A}$, is in the direction of $\mathbf{Q}(:, m + 1)$. Its magnitude $\|\mathbf{y}\|_2$ is simply $|H(m + 1, m)u(m)|$. $|H(m + 1, m)u(m)|$ provides an efficient check of the convergence of the eigenpair. Only when $|H(m + 1, m)u(m)|$ is small enough, we form the eigenvector $\mathbf{Q}(:, 1 : m)\mathbf{u}$. A small $|H(m + 1, m)u(m)|$ indicates either $H(m + 1, m)$ or $u(m)$ is small. If $H(m + 1, m)$ is small, $\mathbb{K}(\mathbf{A}, \mathbf{q}, m)$ forms an accurate m-dimensional invariant subspace of $\mathbf{A}$. All the m eigenvalues of $\mathbf{Q}(:, 1 : m)'\mathbf{AQ}(:, 1 : m)$ are also the eigenvalues of $\mathbf{A}$. If $H(m + 1, m)$ is not small but $u(m)$ is, $\mathbb{K}(\mathbf{A}, \mathbf{q}, m)$ contains a 1-dimensional invariant space of $\mathbf{A}$ and $\lambda = \mathbf{u}'\mathbf{Au}$ is an eigenvalue. See the discussion in Section 7.1.1.

7.4.2 ORTHOGONALITY OF Q

Refer to Section 7.3.

7.4.3 IMPLICIT RESTART FOR A BETTER APPROXIMATE INVARIANT SUBSPACE

Refer to Section 7.3. In the implicit restart, both single shift and double shift should be considered. The double shifts are for the case of complex eigenvalues. See Section 6.4.4 for the implicit QR.

7.4.4 PURGING OF CONVERGED UNDESIRED EIGENVECTORS

Refer to Section 7.3 for the orthogonal matrix $\mathbf{Z}$ calculated by `sorensen_(y)`, where $\mathbf{y}'\mathbf{y} = 1$. Post-multiplying $\mathbf{Z}$ to Eq. (7.25a), we obtain

$$\mathbf{AQ}(:, 1 : m)\mathbf{Z} = \mathbf{Q}(:, 1 : m)\mathbf{ZZ}'\mathbf{H}(1 : m, 1 : m)\mathbf{Z} + H(m + 1, m)\mathbf{Q}(:, m + 1)\mathbf{I}(m, :)\mathbf{Z}. \tag{7.29}$$

If $\mathbf{Hy} = \mathbf{y}\theta$,

$$
\begin{aligned}
\mathbf{H}_+(1 : m, 1 : m) = \mathbf{Z}'\mathbf{H}(1 : m, 1 : m)\mathbf{Z} &= \mathbf{Z}'\mathbf{H}\,(\mathbf{R} + \mathbf{y}\mathbf{I}(m, :)) = \mathbf{Z}'\mathbf{HR} + \theta\mathbf{I}(:, m)\mathbf{I}(m, :) \\
&= (\mathbf{G}' + \mathbf{g}\mathbf{y}')\,\mathbf{HR} + \theta\mathbf{I}(:, m)\mathbf{I}(m, :) = \mathbf{G}'\mathbf{HR} + \mathbf{g}\mathbf{y}'\mathbf{HR} + \theta\mathbf{I}(:, m)\mathbf{I}(m, :).
\end{aligned} \tag{7.30}
$$

From the structure of $\mathbf{R}, \mathbf{G}$, and $\mathbf{H}$, we know $\mathbf{G'HR}$ is upper Hessenberg and its mth column and row are both zeros. But the first $(m-1)$ columns of $\mathbf{gy'HR}$ are full and only its mth column is zero. In this case, Eq. (7.29) is not an m-step Arnoldi partial decomposition.

If $\mathbf{y'H} = \theta\mathbf{y'}$, then

$$\begin{aligned}
\mathbf{H}_+(1:m, 1:m) &= \mathbf{Z'H}(1:m, 1:m)\mathbf{Z} = (\mathbf{G'} + \mathbf{gy'})\,\mathbf{HZ} = \mathbf{G'HZ} + \theta\mathbf{gI}(m,:)\\
&= \mathbf{G'H}\,(\mathbf{R} + \mathbf{yI}(m,:)) + \theta\mathbf{gI}(m,:) = \mathbf{G'HR} + (\mathbf{G'Hy} + \theta\mathbf{g})\,\mathbf{I}(m,:)\\
&= \begin{bmatrix} \mathbf{H}_+(1:m-1, 1:m-1) & \mathbf{H}_+(1:m-1, m)\\ \mathbf{0} & \theta \end{bmatrix}.
\end{aligned} \tag{7.31}$$

Note again that $\mathbf{G'HR}$ is upper Hessenberg and its mth column and row are both zeros, and the last column of $\mathbf{G'}$ is zero and $g_m = 1$. Obviously, in Eq. (7.29), $\mathbf{Z}(m,:) = [0,\ldots,0, Z_{m,m-1}, y_m]$. Therefore with $\mathbf{y'H} = \theta\mathbf{y'}$ and z=sorensen_(y), after removing the last column, the first $m-1$ columns of Eq. (7.29) remain $(m-1)$-step Arnoldi partial decomposition. It does not require $y_m = 0$ for the conclusion to hold. If $|y_m|$ is not small, the implicit restart with θ as shift can purge θ as well.

If $\mathbf{Y'H} = \mathbf{\Theta Y'}$, $\mathbf{\Theta}$ a $k \times k$ block diagonal with 1×1 (real eigenvalues) or 2×2 (complex conjugate eigenvalues) blocks, to apply sorensen_(Y) to calculate $\mathbf{Z}$ is not correct, since $\mathbf{Y}$ is not orthogonal. In this case, the following procedure is used:

$$\begin{aligned}
&\text{QR decomposition of } \mathbf{Y} : \mathbf{Y} = \mathbf{WR}\\
&\mathbf{R'W'H} = \mathbf{\Theta R'W'}\\
&\mathbf{R'} \text{ is non-singular: } \mathbf{W'H} = \left(\mathbf{R'^{-1}\Theta R'}\right)\mathbf{W'} = \mathbf{EW'}.
\end{aligned} \tag{7.32}$$

After we obtain the orthogonal $\mathbf{W}$, we can calculate $\mathbf{Z}$ =sorensen_(W). If we apply the $\mathbf{Z}$ to Eq. (7.25), the new $\mathbf{H}_+$ can be obtained,

$$\mathbf{H}_+(1:m, 1:m) = \begin{bmatrix} \mathbf{H}_+(1:l, 1:l) & \mathbf{H}_+(1:l, l+1:m)\\ \mathbf{0} & \mathbf{E} \end{bmatrix}. \tag{7.33}$$

Obviously $\mathbf{Z}(m,:) = [Z(m,l)\mathbf{I}(l,:), \mathbf{W}(k,:)]$. The first $l(=m-k)$ columns of Eq. (7.25) remain l-step partial Arnoldi decomposition.

7.4.5 LOCKING OF CONVERGED DESIRED EIGENVECTORS

If $(\theta, \mathbf{y})$ is a converged desired eigenpair, i.e. $\mathbf{Hy} = \mathbf{y}\theta$ and $|y_m|$ is small, we want to lock the relation $\mathbf{AQy} = \mathbf{Qy}\theta$. To do this, we calculate $\mathbf{Z}$ by sorensen_(y) with $\mathbf{Z}(:,1) = \mathbf{y}$. Because $|y_m|$ is small, $\mathbf{Z}(m,:) \approx \mathbf{I}(m,:)$. We apply the $\mathbf{Z}$ to Eq. (7.25). The new $\mathbf{H}_+$ in this case takes the following form:

$$\begin{aligned}
\mathbf{H}_+(1:m, 1:m) &= \mathbf{Z'H}(1:m, 1:m)\mathbf{Z} - \mathbf{Z'II}\,(\mathbf{R} + \mathbf{yI}(1,:)) = \mathbf{Z'HR} + \theta\mathbf{I}(:,1)\mathbf{I}(1,:)\\
&= (\mathbf{G'} + \mathbf{gy'})\,\mathbf{HR} + \theta\mathbf{I}(:,1)\mathbf{I}(1,:) = \mathbf{G'HR} + \mathbf{gy'HR} + \theta\mathbf{I}(:,1)\mathbf{I}(1,:)\\
&\sim \begin{bmatrix} 0 & 0 & 0 & 0 & 0\\ 0 & B_{22} & B_{23} & B_{24} & B_{25}\\ 0 & B_{32} & B_{33} & B_{34} & B_{35}\\ 0 & 0 & B_{43} & B_{44} & B_{45}\\ 0 & 0 & 0 & B_{54} & B_{55} \end{bmatrix} + \begin{bmatrix} y_1\\ y_2\\ y_3\\ y_4\\ 0 \end{bmatrix}[0, b_2, b_3, b_4, b_5] + \begin{bmatrix} \theta & 0 & 0 & 0 & 0\\ 0 & 0 & 0 & 0 & 0\\ 0 & 0 & 0 & 0 & 0\\ 0 & 0 & 0 & 0 & 0\\ 0 & 0 & 0 & 0 & 0 \end{bmatrix}.
\end{aligned} \tag{7.34}$$

The structure of the three terms $\mathbf{G}'\mathbf{HR}$, $\mathbf{gy}'\mathbf{HR}$, and $\theta\mathbf{I}(:,1)\mathbf{I}(1,:)$ is exemplified in Eq. (7.34). Because of the term $\mathbf{gy}'\mathbf{HR}$, $\mathbf{H}_+(1:m, 2:m)$ is full. Now we want to transform Eq. (7.25) under the $\mathbf{Z}$ to a partial Arnoldi decomposition. To do this, we need to transform $\mathbf{H}_+(2:m, 2:m)$ to upper Hessenberg, i.e. a QHQt decomposition of $\mathbf{H}_+(2:m, 2:m)$, see Section 3.5. At the same time, we need to keep $\mathbf{Z}(m,:) \approx \mathbf{I}(m,:)$ in Eq. (7.29) intact. This can be achieved with an orthogonal similarity transformation $\mathbf{W}'_j\mathbf{H}_+(1:m, 1:m)\mathbf{W}_j \Rightarrow \mathbf{H}_+(1:m, 1:m)$ to zero $\mathbf{H}_+(j, 2:j-2), j = m:-1:3$. Each $\mathbf{W}_j$ satisfies $\mathbf{W}_j(:,1) = \mathbf{W}_j(1,:)' = \mathbf{I}(:,1)$ and $\mathbf{W}_j(:,m) = \mathbf{W}_j(m,:)' = \mathbf{I}(:,m)$. This guarantees $\mathbf{H}_+(:,1)$ and $\mathbf{Z}(:,m)$ intact.

If $\mathbf{HY} = \mathbf{Y\Theta}$, $\|\mathbf{Y}(m,:)\|_2$ is small and $\mathbf{\Theta}$ are the desired eigenvalues, we want to lock the relation $\mathbf{AQ}(:,1:m)\mathbf{Y} = \mathbf{Q}(:,1:m)\mathbf{Y\Theta}$. Follow Eq. (7.32) to generate the orthogonal matrix $\mathbf{Z}$ and apply it to Eq. (7.25). The new $\mathbf{H}_+(1:m, 1:m)$ is deflated.

$$\text{QR decomposition of } \mathbf{Y}: \mathbf{Y} = \mathbf{WR},$$
$$\mathbf{HWR} = \mathbf{WR\Theta},$$
$$\mathbf{R} \text{ is non-singular: } \mathbf{HW} = \left(\mathbf{R}^{-1}\mathbf{WR}\right)\mathbf{W}'\mathbf{\Theta} = \mathbf{WE},$$
$$\mathbf{Z} = \text{sorensen\_}(\mathbf{W}), \ \mathbf{Z}(:,1:k) = \mathbf{W}, \ \mathbf{Z}(m,:) \approx \mathbf{I}(m,:),$$
$$\mathbf{H}_+(1:m, 1:m) = \begin{bmatrix} \mathbf{E} & \mathbf{H}_+(1:k, k+1:m) \\ \mathbf{0} & \mathbf{H}_+(k+1:m, k+1:m) \end{bmatrix}. \tag{7.35}$$

In Eq. (7.35), $\mathbf{H}_+(k+1:m, k+1:m)$ is full. We use an orthogonal similarity transformation $\mathbf{W}'_j\mathbf{H}_+(1:m, 1:m)\mathbf{W}_j \Rightarrow \mathbf{H}_+(1:m, 1:m)$ to zero $\mathbf{H}_+(j, 2:j-2), j = m:-1:k+2$. Each $\mathbf{W}_j$ satisfies $\mathbf{W}_j(:,1:k) = \mathbf{W}_j(1:k,:)' = \mathbf{I}(:,1:k)$ and $\mathbf{W}_j(:,m) = \mathbf{W}_j(m,:)' = \mathbf{I}(:,m)$. This guarantees $\mathbf{H}_+(:,1:k)$ and $\mathbf{Z}(:,m)$ intact.

7.4.6 MATLAB IMPLEMENTATION OF ARNOLDI ALGORITHM

The contents of Section 7.1 and this section are succinctly implemented in `eigByArnoldi_.m` of few than 180 lines of MATLAB codes. All of the input arguments to `eigByArnoldi_.m` are same to those to `eigByLanczos_.m`, see Section 7.3.6 for the explanation of these input arguments. Of course, the input and output arguments S,V in the context of an unsymmetric matrix refer to the partial Schur decomposition factors.

Algorithm 7.5

$\mathbf{AV} = \mathbf{V}\lambda$ by Arnoldi iteration.

```
function [S,V] = eigByArnoldi_(A,algo,v,tol,pick,m,S,V)

[n1,n] = size_(A);   normA = max(1.0,norm(Ay_(A,ones(n1,1))));   %est. norm(A)
eqsALGO = 'mtimes';   eigALGO = 'eigUnsymByQR';
if (length(algo)>=1 && ~isempty(algo{1})) sigma   = algo{1}; end
if (length(algo)>=2 && ~isempty(algo{2})) eqsALGO = algo{2}; end
if (length(algo)>=3 && ~isempty(algo{3})) eigALGO = algo{3}; end
if (~exist('m','var') || isempty(m) || m<neig || m>n)
    A = A_(A,sigma,eqsALGO);   normA = max(1.0,1.0/abs(normA-sigma));
end
if (neig1 == 0)
    V = v;   S = [];
else
    normv0 = norm(v);   v = v - V*(V'*v);   normv = norm(v);   eta = 0.5*sqrt(2.0);
```

```
    if (normv < eta*normv0)         %reorthogonalization
        normv0 =normv;   v = v - V*(V'*v);   normv = norm(v);
    end
    if (normv > eta*normv0) V = [V,v/normv];
    else                    V = [V,orthogonal_(V)]; end
    if(exist('sigma','var'))        %S=(S-sigma*I)^{-1}
        for j=1:neig1 S(j,j) = S(j,j) - sigma; end
        S = eqsUpperTriangle_(S,eye(neig1));
    end
    normA = max(normA,max(abs(diag(S))));
end
[V,S] = QHQtByArnoldi_(A,neig1+1,m,V,S);
v = V(:,m1);   s = [zeros(1,m-1),S(m1,m)];   V0 = [];   %V0: undesired Schur vectors
if (m == n) beta = 0; else beta = abs(s(m)); end

while(neig1 < neig)
    neig0 = neig1;   l2 = 0;   l3 = 0;
    [Sita,Y] = eigUnsymByQR_({'hess',S(neig1+1:m,neig1+1:m)},tol,'long');
    Lmd = Sita;   [k1,k2] = size(Lmd);   k = 1;
    if (exist('sigma','var'))       %Lmd of unshifted, as pick based on unshifted
        while (k <= k1)
            if (k2==1 || Lmd(k,2)==0)
                Lmd(k,1) = sigma + 1.0/Lmd(k,1);   k = k + 1;
            else
                Lmdk = sigma + 1.0/(Lmd(k,1)+1i*Lmd(k,2));
                Lmd(k:k+1,:) = [real(Lmdk),imag(Lmdk); -imag(Lmdk),real(Lmdk)];
                k = k + 2;
            end
        end
    end
    k = 1;  Sita11 = [];  Sita21 = [];  Sita22 = [];  Y11 = [];  Y21 = [];
    while (k <= k1)
        normA = max(normA,norm(Lmd(k,:)));
        if (k2==1 || Lmd(k,2)==0) l = k;  else l = k + 1; end
        if (isempty(pick) || feval(pick{1},pick{2},neig-neig0,Lmd,Lmd(k:l,:))==1)
            if(beta*norm(Y(m-neig0,k:l)) < tol*normA)      %to be locked
                Sita11 = [Sita11; Sita(k,:)];   Y11 = [Y11,Y(:,k:l)];
                if (l == k) neig1 = neig1 + 1; else neig1 = neig1 + 2; end
            end
        elseif (beta*norm(Y(m-neig0,k:l)) < tol*normA)     %to be purged
            Sita21 = [Sita21; Sita(k,:)];   Y21 = [Y21,Y(:,k:l)];
            if (k2==2 && Sita(k,2)~=0) Sita21 = [Sita21; [-Sita(k,2),Sita(k,1)]]; end
        else                                        %to be filtered
            Sita22 = [Sita22; Sita(k,:)];
        end
        if (l == k) k = k + 1; else k = k + 2; end
    end

    [k1,k2] = size(Sita11);
    if (k1 > 0)    %lock converged wanted eigs(Sita11)
        j1 = size(Y11,2); j2 = m-neig0;
        [W,r] = QR_(Y11,'householder',0,tol,'short');
        W = sorensen_(W,{'hess',S(neig0+1:m,neig0+1:m)});
        V(:,neig0+1:m) = V(:,neig0+1:m)*W;
        S(1:neig0,neig0+1:m) = S(1:neig0,neig0+1:m)*W;
        S(neig0+1:m,neig0+1:m) = W'*S(neig0+1:m,neig0+1:m)*W;
        S(neig1+1:m,neig0+1:neig1) = 0.0;                    %lock sita11
```

```
        s(neig0+1:neig1) = s(m)*W(j2,1:j1);   s(m) = s(m)*W(j2,j2);
        for k=m:-1:neig1+3           %S(neig1+1:m,neig1+1:m)=>Hessenberg
            sk = S(k,neig1+1:k-1);   sk = sk'/norm(sk);
            p = [2:k-neig1-1,1];     W = permute_(p,sorensen_(sk),'col');
            S(:,neig1+1:k-1) = S(:,neig1+1:k-1)*W;
            S(neig1+1:k-1,:) = W'*S(neig1+1:k-1,:);
            S(k,neig1+1:k-2) = 0.0;
            V(:,neig1+1:k-1) = V(:,neig1+1:k-1)*W;
        end
    end
    if (neig1 >= neig) break; end

    if (~isempty(Sita21))   %purge unwanted converged eigs(Sita21) change S' eigvec_
        if (size(Sita21,2)==2 && norm(Sita21(:,2))<tol*norm(Sita21(:,1)))
            Sita21 = Sita21(:,1);
        end
        [Sita21,Y21]=eigvec_(S(neig1+1:m,neig1+1:m)',Sita21,[],tol);
        l2 = size(Y21,2);   p = [l2+1:m-neig1,1:l2];
        [W,r] = QR_(Y21,'householder',0,tol,'short');
        W = sorensen_(W,{'full',S(neig1+1:m,neig1+1:m)'});
        W = permute_(p,W,'col');
        V(:,neig1+1:m) = V(:,neig1+1:m)*W;   V0 = [V0,V(:,m-neig1-l2+1:m-neig1)];
        S(1:neig1,neig1+1:m) = S(1:neig1,neig1+1:m)*W;
        S(neig1+1:m,neig1+1:m) = W'*S(neig1+1:m,neig1+1:m)*W;
        S(m-l2+1:m,neig1+1:m-l2) = 0.0;
        s(neig0+1:neig1) = 0.0;
        s(m-l2:m) = s(m)*W(m-neig1,m-neig1-l2:m-neig1);
    end

    [k1,k2] = size(Sita22);
    if (k1 > 0)    %shift nonconverged unwanted eigs (Sita22)
        W = eye(m-neig1-l2);   G = eye(2);   j1 = neig1+1;   j2 = m-l2;
        for k=1:k1
            sr = Sita22(k,1);   si = 0;
            if (k2 == 2) si = Sita22(k,2); end
            if (si == 0)       %single shift
                l3 = l3 + 1;   miu = sr;
                s1 = S(neig1+1,neig1+1)-miu;   s2 = S(neig1+2,neig1+1);
                for j=j1:j2-1
                    [G(1,1),G(1,2)] = givens_(s1,s2);
                    G(2,1) = -G(1,2);   G(2,2) = G(1,1);   rc = j:j+1;
                    if (j == j1) rc1 = j1:j2;   else rc1 = j-1:j2; end
                    if (j <j2-2) rc2 = j1:j+2;   else rc2 = j1:j2;   end
                    S(rc,rc1) = G'*S(rc,rc1);   S(rc2,rc) = S(rc2,rc)*G;
                    W(:,j-neig1:j-neig1+1) = W(:,j-neig1:j-neig1+1)*G;
                    s1 = S(j+1,j);
                    if (j < j2-1) s2 = S(j+2,j); end
                end
            else            %double shift
                l3 = l3 + 2;   eta = 2.0*sr;    tau = sr*sr + si*si;
                s1 = S(j1,j1)*S(j1,j1)+S(j1,j1+1)*S(j1+1,j1)-eta*S(j1,j1)+tau;
                s2 = S(j1+1,j1)*(S(j1,j1)+S(j1+1,j1+1)-eta);
                s3 = S(j1+1,j1)*S(j1+2,j1+1);
                for j=j1:j2-1
                    if (j < j2-1)
                        [sj,beta] = householder_([s1;s2;s3]);   rc = j:j+2;
                    else
```

```
                [sj,beta] = householder_([s1;s2]);      rc = j:j+1;
            end
            if (j == j1) rc1 = j1:j2;  else rc1 = j-1:j2; end
            if (j <j2-2) rc2 = j1:j+3; else rc2 = j1:j2;  end
            betasj = beta*sj;
            S(rc,rc1) = S(rc,rc1) - betasj*(sj'*S(rc,rc1));
            S(rc2,rc) = S(rc2,rc) - (S(rc2,rc)*sj)*betasj';
            W(:,rc-neig1) = W(:,rc-neig1) - (W(:,rc-neig1)*sj)*betasj';
            s1 = S(j+1,j);
            if (j < j2-1) s2 = S(j+2,j); end
            if (j < j2-2) s3 = S(j+3,j); end
          end
        end
      end
      S(1:neig1,j1:j2) = S(1:neig1,j1:j2)*W;  V(:,j1:j2) = V(:,j1:j2)*W;
      S(j1:j2,j2+1:m) = W'*S(j1:j2,j2+1:m);
      s(j1:j2) = s(j2)*W(m-neig1-12,:);
    end

    if (12 + 13 > 0)     %implicit restart
       1 = m - 12 - 13;
       if (s(1) < 0.0) s(1) =-s(1);  v=-v; end
       V(:,1+1) = v;  S(1+1,1) = s(1);
       [V,S] = QHQtByArnoldi_(A,1+1,m,V(:,1:1+1),S(1:1+1,1:1),V0);
    else                 %explicit restart
       [y,1] = min(abs(Y(m-neig0,neig1-neig0+1:m-neig0)));
       V(:,neig1+1) = V(:,neig0+1:m)*Y(:,neig1-neig0+1);
       [V,S] = QHQtByArnoldi_(A,neig1+1,m,V(:,1:neig1+1),S(1:neig1,:),V0);
    end
    v = V(:,m1);  s = [zeros(1,m-1),S(m1,m)];  beta = abs(s(m));
  end

  S = S(1:neig1,1:neig1);  V = V(:,1:neig1);
  if (exist('sigma','var'))
     S = eqsByGauss_(S,eye(neig1));
     for j=1:neig1 S(j,j) = S(j,j) + sigma; end
  end
```

To compare with `eigByLanczos_.m`, we apply `eigByArnoldi_.m` to two similar numerical examples that are presented in Section 7.3.6.

The first example is a full matrix of 100×100. As shown below, its eigenvalues are scattered in $[-1000, +1000]$ with 94 of them condensed in $[-1, +1]$. As explained in Sections 6.3 and 7.1, the extremal eigenvalues converge very fast in the Arnoldi algorithm. The eigenvalues in the middle of the spectrum converge slowly. If the input argument m, i.e. m in Eq. (7.6), is larger, the convergence is faster. To calculate the eigenvalues in the middle of the spectrum in few iterations, we can use the shift and inverse.

```
>> d=[-1000; -100; -10; -1; -0.1; -0.01; -0.001; 0.0; -rand(42,1);
       1000;  100;  10;  1;  0.1;  0.01;  0.001; 0.0;  rand(42,1)];
>> B=randn(100);
>> A=inv(B)*diag(d)*B;   q=randn(100,1);   tol=100*eps;   %(d,B) eigs of A.
```

The code snippets and calculated results are listed below. The convergence patterns for the first 8 extremal eigenvalues, that is, $(\pm 1000, \pm 100, \pm 10, \pm 1)$, are shown in Fig. 7.3, where the abscissa is the accumulated number of times of solving Eq. (7.27) and the ordinate is the logarithm of the error calculated in Eq. (7.28). When $m = 8$, ± 1000 and ± 100 converge in two iterations. When $m = 16$, all the first six largest modulus eigenvalues $\pm 1000, \pm 100$, and ± 10 converge in the first iteration. But ± 1 take 17 iterations to converge, because they are very close to other eigenvalues $0.9797, -0.9390, 0.9631, -0.9294$. After calculating the first eight largest modulus eigenvalues, if we want to calculate these four eigenvalues, we can restart from the end of the calculation of the second call to eigByArnoldi_.m. Of course, we can calculate all the first 12 largest modulus eigenvalues by only one call to eigByArnoldi_.m. If we want to calculate only the first six largest eigenvalues, we can pass pick={'pick_','LR',6} to eigByArnoldi_.m. If we want to calculate the six smallest modulus eigenvalues, we can pass algo={0.0011,'LU_'} and pick={'pick_','SM',6} to eigByArnoldi_.m.

```
   %Calculate 1st 4 largest modulus eigenvalues through a subspace of dimension of 8.
>> [S4,V4]=eigByArnoldi_(A,[],q,tol,{'pick_','LM',4},8);
>> S4
=  1.0e+003 *
     1.0000      0.1212    -1.6585      1.8912
    -0.0000     -1.0000    -0.4067      0.1178
    -0.0000     -0.0000     0.1000     -0.0998
    -0.0000      0.0000    -0.0000     -0.1000
>> norm(A*V4-V4*S4))=1.7522e-010          %correct eigenvalues and Schur vectors
>> norm(V4'*V4-eye(4))=7.9259e-016        %correct eigenvalues and Schur vectors
   %Calculate 1st 8 largest modulus eigenvalues through a subspace of dimension of 16.
>> [S8,V8]=eigByArnoldi_(A,[],q,tol,{'pick_','LM',8},16);
>> S8
=  1.0e+003 *
     1.0000     -0.1212    -1.6585    -1.8912     1.4017     1.6241    -2.1678     0.8366
    -0.0000     -1.0000     0.4067     0.1178     1.0916     0.7411     0.3583     0.1113
     0.0000      0.0000     0.1000     0.0998    -0.0956    -0.0047    -0.0818     0.1240
     0.0000     -0.0000     0.0000    -0.1000    -0.0472    -0.1237     0.2210    -0.1675
    -0.0000      0.0000    -0.0000    -0.0000     0.0100    -0.0136     0.0069     0.0011
    -0.0000     -0.0000     0.0000     0.0000     0.0000    -0.0100     0.0032    -0.0012
          0           0          0          0          0          0    -0.0010    -0.0040
          0           0          0          0          0          0          0     0.0010
>> norm(A*V8-V8*S8)=3.0638e-009           %correct eigenvalues and Schur vectors
>> norm(V8'*V8-eye(8))=6.2249e-015        %correct eigenvalues and Schur vectors
   %Restart from [S8,V8]. Dimension of subspace increased to 20.
>> [S12,V12]=eigByArnoldi_(A,[],q,tol,{'pick_','LM',12},20,S8,V8);
>> S12(9:12,9:12)
=    0.9797     -0.4166    -0.1262      0.8449
          0     -0.9390    -0.5869     -0.0037
          0           0     0.9631     -0.0013
          0           0          0     -0.9294
>> norm(S12(1:8,1:8)-S8)=0    %no change
>> norm(V12(:,1:8)-V8)=0      %no change
>> norm(A*V12-V12*S12)=3.0639e-009        %correct eigenvalues and Schur vectors
>> norm(V12'*V12-eye(12))=6.2332e-015     %correct eigenvalues and Schur vectors
   %Obtain S12,V12 by only one call.
>> [S12,V12]=eigByArnoldi_(A,[],q,tol,{'pick_','LM',12},20);
>> diag(S12(1:8,1:8))'
=  1.0e+003 *
     1.0000     -1.0000     0.1000    -0.1000     0.0100    -0.0100    -0.0010     0.0010
>> diag(S12(9:12,9:12))'
=    0.9797     -0.9390     0.9631    -0.9294
>> norm(A*V12-V12*S12)=1.2765e-010        %correct eigenvalues and Schur vectors
>> norm(V12'*V12-eye(12))=4.4833e-015     %correct eigenvalues and Schur vectors
   %Calcculate 6 smallest modulus eigenvalues using shift and inverse.
```

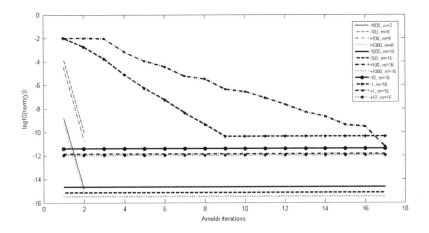

FIGURE 7.3

Errors of Arnoldi iterations.

```
>> [S6,V6]=eigByArnoldi_(A,{0.0011,'LU_'},q,tol,{'pick_','SM',6},20);
>> S6
=    0.0010   -0.0010   -0.0041   -0.0153    0.0018   -0.0826
     0.0000   -0.0010    0.0011   -0.0022   -0.0230    0.0148
    -0.0000   -0.0000   -0.0000   -0.0000    0.0020   -0.0062
     0.0000    0.0000    0.0000    0.0000   -0.0004   -0.0038
          0         0         0         0    0.0100   -0.0009
          0         0         0         0         0   -0.0100
>> norm(A*V6-V6*S6)=3.7535e-010          %correct eigenvalues and Schur vectors
>> norm(V6'*V6-eye(6))=1.5639e-015       %correct eigenvalues and Schur vectors
```

The second example is a 200×200 band matrix generated in the following code scripts.

```
>> B=[[0;-ones(199,1)],2*ones(200,1),[-ones(199,1);0]];
%symmetric tri-diagonal
>> B=[B, [-ones(99,1);ones(99,1);0;0],[ones(99,1);-ones(98,1);0;0;0]];
%sup-diagonals
>> F=band2full_(B,1,3,200,200);                                   %full format
```

The eigenvalues of **B** include both real and complex conjugates. First, the whole spectrum is calculated by eigUnsymByQR_.m with the full format of the matrix.

```
>> tic
>> [S,V]=eigUnsymByQR_({'hess',F},100*eps,'short');
>> toc
Elapsed time is 402.220080 seconds.
>> S(1:8,1:8)
=    4.8319    0.9799   -0.5060    0.1674   -0.0003   -0.0010   -0.0002   -0.0015
          0    4.8245   -0.8116    0.4087   -0.0007   -0.0039   -0.0014   -0.0047
          0         0    4.8120   -0.7627   -0.0029    0.0038    0.0035    0.0063
          0         0         0    4.7946   -0.0141   -0.0172   -0.0033   -0.0199
     0.0000         0    0.0000         0    3.8355    1.1615   -0.5758   -0.6645
     0.0000   -0.0000         0   -0.0000   -1.3345    3.6445   -0.8199    0.3019
```

```
     0.0000      0.0000      0.0000          0    -0.0000          0     3.7172    -1.3311
    -0.0000     -0.0000     -0.0000    -0.0000     0.0000    -0.0000     1.1466     3.7534
```

```
>> norm(tril(S,-2))=1.1211e-015
>> norm(F*V-V*S)=1.7894e-013              %correct  eigenvalues  and  Schur  vectors
>> norm(V'*V-eye(200))=2.7344e-014        %correct  eigenvalues  and  Schur  vectors
```

Second, the first eight largest modulus of eigenvalues and first eight smallest modulus of eigenvalues are calculated by `eigByArnoldi_.m` with the band format of the matrix.

```
>> q=ones(200,1);   tol=100*eps;   m = 20;   n = 200;
>> pick1={'pick_','LM',8};    pick2={'pick_','SM',8};
```

```
>> [S1,V1]=eigByArnoldi_({'band',{B,1,3,n,n}},{},q,tol,pick1,m);
>> S1
=    4.9659      1.1110      0.2021      0.2564      0.2615      0.0858     -0.0996     -0.1631
    -0.0019      4.9730      0.9836      0.0685     -0.0534      0.1720      0.1012      0.0220
          0           0      5.2506     -0.7732     -0.6082     -0.2867      0.0709      0.1497
          0           0      0.1503      4.6232      0.5970      0.4398      0.1762     -0.0294
          0           0           0           0      4.7337      0.8251      0.2248      0.0595
          0           0           0           0     -0.0795      5.0124      0.8397      0.4507
          0           0           0           0           0           0      4.7701      0.7835
          0           0           0           0           0           0     -0.1045      4.7908
>> norm(F*V1-V1*S1)=1.8912e-012           %correct  eigenvalues  and  Schur  vectors
>> norm(V1'*V1-eye(8))=9.4926e-015        %correct  eigenvalues  and  Schur  vectors
```

```
>> [S2,V2]=eigByArnoldi_({'band',{B,1,3,n,n}},{0.0,'mdivideBandByGivens_'},q,tol,
                                                                          pick2,m);
>> S2
=    0.0327     -0.3423      0.0915      0.2869     -0.0379     -0.1150      0.1894      0.1552
    -0.0000     -0.0276     -0.0295     -0.3928      0.0092      0.1102     -0.2097     -0.1770
          0           0     -0.0794      0.0108      0.1191     -0.0701     -0.0181      0.0293
          0           0           0      0.0851     -0.0334     -0.2500      0.4141      0.2752
          0           0           0           0     -0.0692      0.0768      0.0607     -0.0742
          0           0           0           0     -0.0130     -0.1017     -0.1779     -0.2327
          0           0           0           0           0           0      0.0864      0.3917
          0           0           0           0           0           0           0      0.0921
>> norm(F*V2-V2*S2)=4.8720e-007           %correct  eigenvalues  and  Schur  vectors
>> norm(V2'*V2-eye(8))=4.0750e-015        %correct  eigenvalues  and  Schur  vectors
```

7.5 OTHER IMPORTANT TOPICS

In this section, we briefly discuss several important topics of iterative eigenvalue algorithms that are not covered in Sections 7.1–7.4. For more in-depth presentations of these topics, the reader can consult the references cited.

7.5.1 ITERATIVE ALGORITHMS OF GENERALIZED EIGENVALUE PROBLEMS

Most of the iterative algorithms of the generalized eigenvalue problem $\mathbf{Av} = \lambda\mathbf{Bv}$ is to transform it to the standard eigenvalue problem $\mathbf{Cv} = \lambda\mathbf{v}$ and then apply the iterative algorithms of the Sections 7.1–7.4. In most algorithms, $\mathbf{C}$ is not explicitly formed. See [5, 55]. Possible transformations include the following:

$$\mathbf{Au} = \left(\sigma + \frac{1}{\theta}\right)\mathbf{Bu} \Rightarrow (\mathbf{A} - \sigma\mathbf{B})^{-1}\mathbf{Bu} = \theta\mathbf{u}.$$

$$\lambda = \sigma + \frac{1}{\theta}; \qquad \mathbf{v} = \mathbf{u}.$$

(7.36)

$$\mathbf{Av} = \left(\sigma + \frac{1}{\theta}\right)\mathbf{Bv} \Rightarrow \mathbf{B}(\mathbf{A} - \sigma\mathbf{B})^{-1}\mathbf{u} = \theta\mathbf{u}.$$

$$\lambda = \sigma + \frac{1}{\theta}; \qquad \mathbf{v} = (\mathbf{A} - \sigma\mathbf{B})^{-1}\mathbf{u}.$$

(7.37)

$$\mathbf{Au} = \frac{\theta}{1 + \sigma\theta}\mathbf{Bu} \Rightarrow (\mathbf{B} - \sigma\mathbf{A})^{-1}\mathbf{Au} = \theta\mathbf{u}.$$

$$\lambda = \frac{\theta}{1 + \sigma\theta}; \qquad \mathbf{v} = \mathbf{u}.$$

(7.38)

$$\mathbf{Av} = \frac{\theta}{1 + \sigma\theta}\mathbf{Bv} \Rightarrow \mathbf{A}(\mathbf{B} - \sigma\mathbf{A})^{-1}\mathbf{u} = \theta\mathbf{u}.$$

$$\lambda = \frac{\theta}{1 + \sigma\theta}; \qquad \mathbf{v} = (\mathbf{B} - \sigma\mathbf{A})^{-1}\mathbf{u}.$$

(7.39)

$$\mathbf{Au} = \left(\sigma + \frac{1}{\theta}\right)\mathbf{Bu}; \qquad \mathbf{A} - \sigma\mathbf{B} = \mathbf{GP} \Rightarrow \mathbf{G}^{-1}\mathbf{BP}^{-1}\mathbf{u} = \theta\mathbf{u}.$$

$$\lambda = \sigma + \frac{1}{\theta}; \qquad \mathbf{v} = \mathbf{P}^{-1}\mathbf{u}.$$

(7.40)

$$\mathbf{Av} = \frac{\theta}{1 + \sigma\theta}\mathbf{Bv}; \qquad \mathbf{B} - \sigma\mathbf{A} = \mathbf{GP} \Rightarrow \mathbf{G}^{-1}\mathbf{AP}^{-1}\mathbf{u} = \theta\mathbf{u}.$$

$$\lambda = \frac{\theta}{1 + \sigma\theta}; \qquad \mathbf{v} = \mathbf{P}^{-1}\mathbf{u}.$$

(7.41)

In Eqs. (7.36)–(7.41), $\mathbf{A} - \sigma\mathbf{B}$ or $\mathbf{B} - \sigma\mathbf{A}$ is assumed non-singular. In Eq. (7.36), $\mathbf{C} = (\mathbf{A} - \sigma\mathbf{B})^{-1}\mathbf{B}$; in Eq. (7.41), $\mathbf{C} = \mathbf{G}^{-1}\mathbf{AP}^{-1}$, etc. In iterative algorithms, we need to repeatedly calculate $\mathbf{Cx}$. It does not need to explicitly form $\mathbf{C}$. The calculation of $\mathbf{Cx}$ should proceed as follows.

For Eq. (7.36),
$$\mathbf{Bx} \Rightarrow \mathbf{x}, \qquad (\mathbf{A} - \sigma\mathbf{B})^{-1}\mathbf{x} \Rightarrow \mathbf{x}.$$

For Eq. (7.41),
$$\mathbf{P}^{-1}\mathbf{x} \Rightarrow \mathbf{x}, \qquad \mathbf{Ax} \Rightarrow \mathbf{x}, \qquad \mathbf{G}^{-1}\mathbf{x} \Rightarrow \mathbf{x}, \quad \text{etc.}$$

If the resulted matrix $\mathbf{C}$ is symmetric, we can apply eigByLanczos_.m to the transformed eigenvalue problem. Otherwise, we should apply eigByArnoldi_.m to the transformed eigenvalue problem.

When $\mathbf{A} - \sigma\mathbf{B}$ is symmetric positive definite for some σ, $\mathbf{A} - \sigma\mathbf{B}$ has the Cholesky decomposition $\mathbf{LL}'$. Using the Cholesky decomposition in Eq. (7.40), the corresponding $\mathbf{C}$ is symmetric. Even when $\mathbf{A} - \sigma\mathbf{B}$ is symmetric positive definite, but if we apply $(\mathbf{A} - \sigma\mathbf{B})^{-1}$ to Eq. (7.36) or Eq. (7.37), the corresponding $\mathbf{C}$ is unsymmetric. Similar conclusions apply to Eqs. (7.41), (7.38) and (7.39) when $\mathbf{B} - \sigma\mathbf{A}$ is symmetric positive definite.

If we apply QTQtByLanczos_.m to such a $\mathbf{C}$, the obtained $\mathbf{Q}$ and $\mathbf{T}$ will not satisfy the important Lanczos relation, Eq. (7.6). It is interesting to check the output of QTQtByLanczos_.m applied to an unsymmetric matrix. From the following output, we see that for an unsymmetric matrix the satisfaction of Eqs. (7.6a)–(7.6c) depends on the initial vector q to start the Lanczos recursion. But under any q, Eqs. (7.6a)–(7.6c) are not satisfied simultaneously.

```
>> A
A = 8.5437    -1.8708     2.2184     2.0870    -0.1988    -2.2129    -0.6556    -0.2742
    -1.8708     0.5457     0.2167    -1.4853    -1.5776    -0.4899     1.8494    -2.8551
     2.2184     0.2167     4.1098     0.8632    -1.2347     0.9203     2.3702    -0.5469
     2.0870    -1.4853     0.8632     7.8822     3.6870    -1.4296     0.2042    -1.9046
    -0.1988    -1.5776    -1.2347     3.6870     5.5400     0.2456     0.1570     0.0039
    -2.2129    -0.4899     0.9203    -1.4296     0.2456     4.1490     0.5754     2.8132
    -0.6556     1.8494     2.3702     0.2042     0.1570     0.5754     5.0560     0.3425
    -0.2742    -2.8551    -0.5469    -1.9046     0.0039     2.8132     0.3425     2.6021
>> B
B = 1.2929    -0.6445     0.6586     1.0816    -0.0604    -1.3116    -1.0102     0.1580
    -0.6445    -1.6313     0.1531    -0.2630    -0.2989    -0.1009     0.7592    -1.6410
     0.6586     0.1531    -0.2751     0.2949    -0.4791     0.2693     0.9787    -0.1831
     1.0816    -0.2630     0.2949     1.9565     1.7150    -0.6765     0.0745    -0.5273
    -0.0604    -0.2989    -0.4791     1.7150     0.6588    -0.2711    -0.0398     0.5648
    -1.3116    -0.1009     0.2693    -0.6765    -0.2711     0.1585     0.3846     1.7084
    -1.0102     0.7592     0.9787     0.0745    -0.0398     0.3846     1.0501     0.2904
     0.1580    -1.6410    -0.1831    -0.5273     0.5648     1.7084     0.2904    -0.4913
>> eigSymByQR_(A-2*B)'    %A-2*B is positive definite.
=    7.4133     6.1151     1.8344     4.4534     4.1993     2.4219     3.4479     3.1048
>> C=inv(A-2*B)*B;        %C is unsymmetric.
>> q1'
=    1.3458     0.9749    -2.3779    -1.0923    -0.3257    -2.0122     1.5677     0.2333
>> q2'
=    0.7413     0.8120    -0.1428    -0.0999    -0.8001     0.4932     1.2376     1.2960
>> q3'
=   -0.4033     0.0841    -0.4353    -0.5626     0.8781    -0.8146    -0.2584     0.4933

>> [Q,T3]=QTQtByLanczos_(C,1,4,q1);
>> T=band2full_(T3,1,1)
T =-0.1104     0.4835          0          0          0
    0.4835     0.2665     0.4123          0          0
         0     0.4123    -0.2202     0.3533          0
         0          0     0.3533     0.4499     1.2716
         0          0          0     1.2716          0
>> C*Q(:,1:4)-Q(:,1:4)*T(1:4,1:4)-T(5,4)*Q(:,5)*[0,0,0,1]
=         0     0.0222     0.0013          0
          0     0.1217     0.0009          0
          0     0.0600    -0.0023          0
          0     0.0718    -0.0010          0
          0    -0.0164    -0.0003     0.0000
          0     0.0345    -0.0019          0
          0    -0.1723     0.0015          0
          0     0.0029     0.0002          0
>> Q'*Q-eye(5)
=         0     0.0000    -0.4285    -0.0000     0.0883
     0.0000          0    -0.0000     0.0000    -0.2377
    -0.4285    -0.0000    -0.0000     0.0047     0.5529
    -0.0000     0.0000     0.0047          0     0.0000
     0.0883    -0.2377     0.5529     0.0000    -0.0000

>> [Q,T3]=QTQtByLanczos_(C,1,4,q2);
>> T=band2full_(T3,1,1)
T =-0.0253     0.9663          0          0          0
    0.9663     0.2140     0.6686          0          0
         0     0.6686    -0.0167     0.5104          0
         0          0     0.5104    -0.3633     0.5247
```

```
            0          0          0      0.5247        0
>> norm(C*Q(:,1:4)-Q(:,1:4)*T(1:4,1:4)-T(5,4)*Q(:,5)*[0,0,0,1])
=   6.0385e-017                        %1st Lanczos relation holds.
>> Q'*Q-eye(5)
=        0    -0.0000    -0.6395     0.3143     0.1360
   -0.0000    -0.0000    -0.0000    -0.6217     0.2362
   -0.6395    -0.0000    -0.0000    -0.0000    -0.6998
    0.3143    -0.6217    -0.0000    -0.0000    -0.0000
    0.1360     0.2362    -0.6998    -0.0000         0

>> [Q,T3]=QTQtByLanczos_(C,1,4,q3);
>> T=band2full_(T3,1,1)
T =-0.1296     0.3494          0          0          0
    0.3494    -0.3268     0.5028          0          0
         0     0.5028    -0.2386     0.3406          0
         0          0     0.3406     0.1006     0.2839
         0          0          0     0.2839          0
>> C*Q(:,1:4)-Q(:,1:4)*T(1:4,1:4)-T(5,4)*Q(:,5)*[0,0,0,1]
=   -0.0020     0.0003     0.0200     0.0024
    -0.0056     0.0013    -0.0807    -0.0666
    -0.0081    -0.0004     0.0597    -0.0640
    -0.0031     0.0001    -0.0456    -0.0011
    -0.0003    -0.0003    -0.0590    -0.0556
     0.0042     0.0014     0.0014     0.0951
    -0.0022    -0.0026    -0.0269    -0.0089
    -0.0051     0.0013     0.0296    -0.0856
>> norm(Q'*Q-eye(5))
=   2.9564e-016              %2nd Lanczos relation holds.
```

For the symmetric positive definite $\mathbf{A} - \sigma\mathbf{B}$, instead of the transformations Eqs. (7.36), (7.37) and (7.40), we can apply the following generalized Lanczos iteration:

$$\mathbf{B}\mathbf{U}(:,1:m) = (\mathbf{A} - \sigma\mathbf{B})\,\mathbf{U}(:,1:m)\mathbf{T}(1:m,1:m) + T(m+1,m)\,(\mathbf{A} - \sigma\mathbf{B})\,\mathbf{U}(:,m+1)\mathbf{I}(m,:), \quad (7.42a)$$

$$\mathbf{U}(:,1:m)'\,(\mathbf{A} - \sigma\mathbf{B})\,\mathbf{U}(:,1:m) = \mathbf{I}, \tag{7.42b}$$

$$\mathbf{U}(:,1:m)'\,(\mathbf{A} - \sigma\mathbf{B})\,\mathbf{U}(:,m+1) = \mathbf{0}. \tag{7.42c}$$

$\mathbf{T}(1:m,1:m)$ is symmetric. Similarly to the standard Lanczos algorithm discussed in Section 7.3, the eigenvalues and eigenvectors of $\mathbf{T}(1:m,1:m)$ can approximate the eigenvalues and eigenvectors of $(\mathbf{A} - \sigma\mathbf{B})^{-1}\mathbf{B}$. Suppose $\mathbf{T}(1:m,1:m)\mathbf{u} = \theta\mathbf{u}$ and $\mathbf{v} = \mathbf{U}(:,1:m)\mathbf{u}$, we calculate $\mathbf{r} = (\mathbf{A} - \sigma\mathbf{B})^{-1}\mathbf{B}\mathbf{v} - \theta\mathbf{v}$ in the following:

$$\begin{aligned}
\mathbf{r} &= (\mathbf{A} - \sigma\mathbf{B})^{-1}\,(\mathbf{B}\mathbf{U}(:,1:m)\mathbf{u} - \theta\,(\mathbf{A} - \sigma\mathbf{B})\,\mathbf{U}(:,1:m)\mathbf{u}) \\
&= T(m+1,m)u(m)\mathbf{U}(:,m+1).
\end{aligned} \tag{7.43}$$

If $\mathbf{T}(1:m,1:m)\mathbf{u} = \theta\mathbf{u}$ and taking $(\theta, \mathbf{U}(:,1:m)\mathbf{u})$ as the eigenpair of $(\mathbf{A} - \sigma\mathbf{B})^{-1}\mathbf{B}$, the error is in the direction of $\mathbf{U}(:,m+1)$. If $|T(m+1,m)u(m)|$ is small enough, $(\theta, \mathbf{U}(:,1:m)\mathbf{u})$ is an accurate approximation of the eigenpair of $(\mathbf{A} - \sigma\mathbf{B})^{-1}\mathbf{B}$.

If $\mathbf{A} - \sigma\mathbf{B}$ is symmetric indefinite for all σ, Eq. (7.42) can be formally applied. But it can fail for some starting $\mathbf{U}(:,1)$, because no $\mathbf{U}$ can be found to satisfy Eqs. (7.42b) and (7.42c) for such $\mathbf{U}(:,1)$.[1] A

---

[1] Suppose $\mathbf{U}(:,1)$ belongs to the subspace spanned by eigenvectors corresponding to both positive and negative eigenvalues.

theoretically sound algorithm is another generalized Lanczos iteration,

$$(\mathbf{A} - \sigma\mathbf{B})^{-1}\,\mathbf{B}\mathbf{U}(:,1:m) = \mathbf{U}(:,1:m)\mathbf{S}^{-1}\mathbf{T}(1:m,1:m) + \frac{T(m+1,m)}{s_{m+1}}\mathbf{U}(:,m+1)\mathbf{I}(m,:), \quad (7.44a)$$

$$\mathbf{U}(:,1:m)'\mathbf{B}\mathbf{U}(:,1:m) = \mathbf{S} = \text{diag}(s_1, s_2, \ldots, s_m), \quad (7.44b)$$

$$\mathbf{U}(:,1:m)'\mathbf{B}\mathbf{U}(:,m+1) = \mathbf{0}. \quad (7.44c)$$

Then $(\mathbf{A} - \sigma\mathbf{B})^{-1}\,\mathbf{B}\mathbf{v} = \theta\mathbf{v}$ is reduced to $\mathbf{T}(1:m,1:m)\mathbf{u} = \theta\mathbf{S}(1:m,1:m)\mathbf{u}$.

If $\mathbf{A} - \sigma\mathbf{B}$ is singular for all σ or if $\mathbf{A}$ and $\mathbf{B}$ are non-square, the eigenvalue problem is more complicated. For a brief account, see [5] and references cited therein.

7.5.2 NONLINEAR EIGENVALUE PROBLEMS

$(\mathbf{A} - \lambda\mathbf{I})\mathbf{x} = \mathbf{0}$ or $(\mathbf{A} - \lambda\mathbf{B})\mathbf{x} = \mathbf{0}$ is extended to

$$\left(\lambda^p\mathbf{A}_p + \lambda^{p-1}\mathbf{A}_{p-1} + \cdots + \lambda\mathbf{A}_1 + \mathbf{A}_0\right)\mathbf{v} = \mathbf{P}(\lambda)\mathbf{v} = \mathbf{0}. \quad (7.45)$$

In Eq. (7.45), $\mathbf{P}(\lambda)$ is an $n \times n$ matrix of pth order polynomial of λ. $(\lambda, \mathbf{v} \neq \mathbf{0})$ satisfying Eq. (7.45) is an eigenpair of $\mathbf{P}$, with λ satisfying $\det(\mathbf{P}(\lambda)) = 0$. Therefore $\mathbf{P}(\lambda)\mathbf{v} = \mathbf{0}$ has $n \times p$ eigenvalues and eigenvectors. In $\mathbb{C}^n$, the $n \times p$ eigenvectors are linearly dependent.

The general strategy to solve Eq. (7.45) is to transform it to the form $\mathbf{A}\mathbf{y} = \lambda\mathbf{B}\mathbf{y}$, commonly known as the linearization. There are two common ways to do it,

$$\mathbf{A} = \begin{bmatrix} \mathbf{0} & \mathbf{I} & \mathbf{0} & \cdots & \mathbf{0} \\ \mathbf{0} & \mathbf{0} & \mathbf{I} & \cdots & \mathbf{0} \\ \vdots & \vdots & \ddots & \ddots & \vdots \\ \vdots & \vdots & \ddots & \ddots & \mathbf{I} \\ -\mathbf{A}_0 & -\mathbf{A}_1 & -\mathbf{A}_2 & \cdots & -\mathbf{A}_{p-1} \end{bmatrix}, \quad \mathbf{B} = \begin{bmatrix} \mathbf{I} & & & \\ & \mathbf{I} & & \\ & & \ddots & \\ & & & \mathbf{I} \\ & & & & \mathbf{A}_p \end{bmatrix}, \quad (7.46)$$

$$\mathbf{A} = \begin{bmatrix} \mathbf{0} & \mathbf{0} & \cdots & \mathbf{0} & \mathbf{A}_0 \\ \mathbf{0} & \mathbf{0} & \cdots & \mathbf{A}_0 & \mathbf{A}_1 \\ \vdots & \vdots & & \vdots & \vdots \\ \mathbf{0} & \mathbf{A}_0 & \cdots & \mathbf{0} & \mathbf{A}_{p-2} \\ \mathbf{A}_0 & \mathbf{A}_1 & \cdots & \mathbf{A}_{p-2} & \mathbf{A}_{p-1} \end{bmatrix}, \quad \mathbf{B} = \begin{bmatrix} \mathbf{0} & \cdots & \mathbf{0} & \mathbf{A}_0 & \mathbf{0} \\ \mathbf{0} & \cdots & \mathbf{A}_0 & \mathbf{A}_1 & \mathbf{0} \\ \vdots & \mathbf{A}_0 & \cdots & \vdots & \vdots \\ \mathbf{A}_0 & \mathbf{A}_1 & \cdots & \mathbf{A}_{p-2} & \mathbf{0} \\ \mathbf{0} & \cdots & & \mathbf{0} & -\mathbf{A}_p \end{bmatrix}. \quad (7.47)$$

For both Eqs. (7.46) and (7.47), the eigenpair is $(\lambda, [\mathbf{v}; \lambda\mathbf{v}; \ldots; \lambda^{p-1}\mathbf{v}])$.

If $\mathbf{A}_p$ is symmetric positive definite, $\mathbf{B}$ in Eq. (7.46) is also symmetric positive definite, but $\mathbf{A}$ in Eq. (7.46) is unsymmetric. On the other hand, $\mathbf{A}$ and $\mathbf{B}$ in Eq. (7.47) are symmetric, but positive indefinite.

7.5.3 JACOBI–DAVIDSON'S METHOD

In Section 7.1, the reduced eigenvalue problem is expressed as the Galerkin condition $\mathbf{U}'(\mathbf{A}\mathbf{U}\mathbf{u} - \theta\mathbf{U}\mathbf{u}) = 0$. In the Lanczos and Arnoldi algorithms, $\mathbf{U}$ is taken as the orthogonal bases of the Krylov subspace $\mathbb{K}(\mathbf{A}, \mathbf{U}(:,1), m)$. The advantage of choosing such particular orthogonal bases is that $\mathbf{U}'\mathbf{AU}$ is in a simple form, symmetric tri-diagonal if $\mathbf{A}$ is symmetric or upper Hessenberg if $\mathbf{A}$ is unsymmetric. Other choices of $\mathbf{U}$ are equally valid. One such $\mathbf{U}$ is discussed by Davidson in [19].

Taking such orthogonal bases $\mathbf{U}$, the reduced eigenvalue problem $(\mathbf{U}'\mathbf{AU})\mathbf{u} = \theta\mathbf{u}$ can be solved by `eigSymByQR_.m` for the symmetric $\mathbf{A}$ or `eigUnsymByQR_.m` for the unsymmetric $\mathbf{A}$. The Ritz pair $(\theta, \mathbf{v} = \mathbf{Uu})$ is used as an approximation of an eigenpair of $\mathbf{A}$. From the Galerkin condition, $\mathbf{U}$ is orthogonal to the residual $\mathbf{r} = \mathbf{Av} - \theta\mathbf{v}$.

If the residual $\mathbf{r}$ is not small enough, we assume $\mathbf{A}(\mathbf{v} + \mathbf{d}) - \theta(\mathbf{v} + \mathbf{d}) = \mathbf{0}$ and $\mathbf{d} \perp \mathbf{u}$, that is,

$$(\mathbf{A} - \theta\mathbf{I})\mathbf{d} = -(\mathbf{A} - \theta\mathbf{I})\mathbf{v} = -\mathbf{r}. \tag{7.48}$$

Because $\mathbf{d} \perp \mathbf{v}$, we express $\mathbf{d}$ as $(\mathbf{I} - \mathbf{vv}')\mathbf{d}$. Further $\mathbf{v}'\mathbf{r} = 0$ due to $\mathbf{U}'\mathbf{r} = \mathbf{0}$. Therefore, we can write Eq. (7.48) as follows:

$$(\mathbf{I} - \mathbf{vv}')(\mathbf{A} - \theta\mathbf{I})(\mathbf{I} - \mathbf{vv}')\mathbf{d} = -\mathbf{r}. \tag{7.49}$$

Eqs. (7.48) and (7.49) were originated in Jacobi [36].

After $\mathbf{d}$ is solved from Eq. (7.49), $\mathbf{v}$ is updated to $\mathbf{v} + \mathbf{d}$ and θ is updated using the Rayleigh quotient. Eq. (7.49) is iterated until $\mathbf{r}$ is small enough.

The Jacobi-Davidson method can be extended to the generalized eigenvalue problem $\mathbf{Ax} = \lambda\mathbf{Bx}$. The Petrov-Galerkin condition for the reduced eigenvalue problem is $\mathbf{W}'(\mathbf{AUu} - \theta\mathbf{BUu}) = 0$. If $\mathbf{W}'\mathbf{BU}$ can chosen to be $\mathbf{I}$, i.e. $\mathbf{B}$-orthogonal, we solve a reduced standard eigenvalue problem; otherwise we solve a reduced generalized eigenvalue problem. The Ritz pair $(\theta, \mathbf{v} = \mathbf{Uu})$ is used as an approximation of an eigenpair of $(\mathbf{A}, \mathbf{B})$. From the Petrov-Galerkin condition, $\mathbf{W}$ is orthogonal to the residual $\mathbf{r} = \mathbf{Av} - \theta\mathbf{Bv}$.

If the residual $\mathbf{r}$ is not small enough, we assume $\mathbf{A}(\mathbf{v} + \mathbf{d}) - \theta\mathbf{B}(\mathbf{v} + \mathbf{d}) = \mathbf{0}$ and $\mathbf{d} \perp \mathbf{u}$, that is,

$$(\mathbf{A} - \theta\mathbf{B})\mathbf{d} = -(\mathbf{A} - \theta\mathbf{B})\mathbf{v} = -\mathbf{r}. \tag{7.50}$$

Because $\mathbf{d} \perp \mathbf{v}$, we express $\mathbf{d}$ as $(\mathbf{I} - \mathbf{vv}')\mathbf{d}$. Further we choose a $\mathbf{w}$ such that $\mathbf{w}'\mathbf{r} = 0$. Therefore, we can write Eq. (7.50) as follows.

$$(\mathbf{I} - \mathbf{ww}')(\mathbf{A} - \theta\mathbf{B})(\mathbf{I} - \mathbf{vv}')\mathbf{d} = -\mathbf{r}. \tag{7.51}$$

After $\mathbf{d}$ is solved from Eq. (7.51), $\mathbf{v}$ is updated to $\mathbf{v} + \mathbf{d}$ and θ is updated using the Rayleigh quotient. Eq. (7.51) is iterated until $\mathbf{r}$ is small enough.

There is no restriction of choosing $\mathbf{U}$, $\mathbf{W}$, and $\mathbf{w}$. If $(\mathbf{A}, \mathbf{B})$ is a symmetric positive definite pair, we can simply choose $\mathbf{W} = \mathbf{V}$, $\mathbf{V}'\mathbf{BV} = \mathbf{I}$, and $\mathbf{w} = \mathbf{v}$. If $(\mathbf{A}, \mathbf{B})$ is not a symmetric positive definite pair, we can adopt a particular choice of $\mathbf{W}$ and $\mathbf{w}$ that was studied in [17]. The choice was motivated by the partial generalized Schur decomposition of $(\mathbf{A}, \mathbf{B})$,

$$\mathbf{Z}(:, 1:m)'\mathbf{AQ}(:, 1:m) = \mathbf{S}, \qquad \mathbf{Z}(:, 1:m)'\mathbf{BQ}(:, 1:m) = \mathbf{T}, \tag{7.52}$$

where $\mathbf{Q}, \mathbf{Z}$ are column orthogonal; $\mathbf{S}, \mathbf{T}$ are upper triangle. This means $T(j,j)\mathbf{AQ}(:,j) - S(j,j)\mathbf{BQ}(:,j) \perp \mathbf{Z}(:,j), j = 1, \ldots, m$. This suggests we should adopt the Petrov-Galerkin condition, i.e. $\mathbf{W} \neq \mathbf{V}$. The reduced pair $(\mathbf{W}'\mathbf{AV}, \mathbf{W}'\mathbf{BV})$ also admits the generalized Schur decomposition,

$$\mathbf{Y}'(\mathbf{W}'\mathbf{AV})\mathbf{G} = \bar{\mathbf{S}}, \qquad \mathbf{Y}'(\mathbf{W}'\mathbf{BV})\mathbf{G} = \bar{\mathbf{T}}, \tag{7.53}$$

where $\mathbf{Y}, \mathbf{G}$ are orthogonal; $\bar{\mathbf{S}}, \bar{\mathbf{T}}$ are upper triangle. We wish to approximate $\mathbf{Z}$ by $\mathbf{WY}$, $\mathbf{Q}$ by $\mathbf{VG}$, $\mathbf{S}$ by $\bar{\mathbf{S}}$, and $\mathbf{T}$ by $\bar{\mathbf{T}}$. By Eq. (7.53), we see that $\text{span}(\mathbf{Y}) = \text{span}(\mathbf{W}'\mathbf{AVG}) = \text{span}(\mathbf{W}'\mathbf{BVG})$. This relation holds if

$$\text{span}(\mathbf{W}) = \text{span}(\alpha\mathbf{AV} + \beta\mathbf{BV}), \quad \forall \alpha, \beta \in \mathbb{R}. \tag{7.54}$$

Accordingly in Eq. (7.51), $\mathbf{w}$ can be chosen as

$$\mathbf{w} = \frac{\alpha \mathbf{Av} + \beta \mathbf{Bv}}{\|\alpha \mathbf{Av} + \beta \mathbf{Bv}\|_2}. \tag{7.55}$$

α, β can be chosen to speed up the convergence. If we want the approximate eigenvalues that are close to σ, we can choose α, β according to the following:

$$\alpha = \frac{1}{\sqrt{1 + \sigma^2}}, \qquad \beta = -\alpha \sigma. \tag{7.56}$$

Algorithms of solution of singular value decomposition

8

INTRODUCTION

In this chapter, we present the algorithms of SVD. For an arbitrary matrix $\mathbf{A} \in \mathbb{R}^{m \times n}$, we find two orthogonal matrices $\mathbf{U} \in \mathbb{R}^{m \times m}$ and $\mathbf{V} \in \mathbb{R}^{n \times n}$ and a diagonal matrix $\mathbf{S}$ with entries $S_{jj} = s_j, j = 1, 2, \ldots, \min(m, n)$ such that $\mathbf{A} = \mathbf{USV}$. The number of non zeros of s_j is the rank of $\mathbf{A}$. Because $r = \text{rank}(\mathbf{A}) \leq \min(m, n)$, in the short format of the decomposition, $\mathbf{U} \in \mathbb{R}^{m \times r}, \mathbf{V} \in \mathbb{R}^{r \times n}$, and $\mathbf{S}$ is a diagonal matrix with only nonzero entries $s_j, j = 1, 2, \ldots, r$. The short format of the decomposition can be written as $\mathbf{A} = \sum_{j=1}^{r} s_j \mathbf{U}(:, j) \mathbf{V}(j, :)$, where each s_j is called the singular value of $\mathbf{A}$, $\mathbf{U}(:, j)$ is called the left singular vector and $\mathbf{V}(j, :)$ is called the right singular vector. Each $(s_j, \mathbf{U}(:, j), \mathbf{V}(j, :))$ is called the singular triplet of $\mathbf{A}$.

The matrix $\mathbf{A} \in \mathbb{R}^{m \times n}$ defines a set of linear multivariate functions, whose domain is $\mathbb{R}^n$ and range is $\mathbb{R}^m$. Under the corresponding orthogonal bases $\mathbf{I}_n$ and $\mathbf{I}_m$, the linear multivariate functions are represented by $\mathbf{A}$. The set of functions is usually coupled, that is, $\mathbf{A}$ is not diagonal. The SVD of $\mathbf{A}$ is to find two sets of orthogonal bases for the domain and range, $\mathbf{V}'$ and $\mathbf{U}$, such that the set of linear functions is decoupled. That is, under the orthogonal bases $\mathbf{V}'$ and $\mathbf{U}$, the given set of linear multivariate functions can be represented by a diagonal matrix $\mathbf{S}$.

In Section 8.1, we discuss the connection between the SVD and eigenvalue decomposition of a symmetric matrix. The connection also provides the proof of the existence of the SVD as well as the method to build the numerical algorithms. The reader can find many commonalities among the algorithms discussed in this chapter and Chapters 6 and 7.

Section 8.2 presents the algorithms for the simplest $\mathbf{A}$, $\mathbf{A} \in \mathbb{R}^{m \times 1}$, $\mathbf{A} \in \mathbb{R}^{1 \times n}$, and $\mathbf{A} \in \mathbb{R}^{2 \times 2}$. These simple algorithms are also the building blocks of the algorithms of the subsequent subsections.

Built upon the simple SVD algorithm of Section 8.2, Section 8.3 presents the relatively simple Jacobi SVD algorithm, which has the useful property that tiny singular values can be calculated accurately.

Section 8.4 is the counter part of Section 6.4 in SVD. It presents the QR iteration algorithm for SVD.

Section 8.5 corresponds to Section 6.7 in SVD. It presents two special SVD algorithms for a bi-diagonal matrix.

Algorithms presented in Sections 8.4 and 8.5 are so-called *direct* SVD algorithms, because in practice they nearly always converge in a fixed number of iterations. The *direct* SVD algorithms are usually applied to small size full matrices. For large and sparse matrices, the *iterative* algorithm is better suited. Section 8.6 presents the Lanczos SVD algorithm. Refer to Section 7.3 for Lanczos algorithm in eigenvalue decomposition.

For the theoretical discussion and the QR iteration, refer [29]. Chapter 6 of [5] presents a survey of SVD algorithms. [20, 23] discuss the numerical subtlety of QR iteration. The divide and conquer algorithm in Section 8.5.1 is based on [31, 38]. The bisection algorithm in Section 8.5.2 and the Lanczos

Matrix Algorithms in MATLAB. DOI: 10.1016/B978-0-12-803804-8.00014-3

algorithm for SVD in the last section are the products made based on their counterparts in the symmetric eigenvalue decomposition that are discussed in Sections 6.7.2 and 7.3.

8.1 INTRODUCTION OF SVD AND ITS ALGORITHMS

Given an arbitrary matrix $\mathbf{A} \in \mathbb{R}^{m \times n}$, we assume its SVD exists: $\mathbf{A} = \mathbf{USV}$, $\mathbf{U}'\mathbf{U} = \mathbf{I}_m$, $\mathbf{VV}' = \mathbf{I}_n$, and $\mathbf{S}$ is diagonal. If the assumption is correct, then we can write a series of equivalent identities $\mathbf{A}' = \mathbf{V}'\mathbf{S}'\mathbf{U}'$ and $\mathbf{AV}' = \mathbf{US}$ and $\mathbf{A}'\mathbf{U} = \mathbf{V}'\mathbf{S}'$, etc.

From the assumed identities, we can further form the following identities:

$$m \leq n: \quad \mathbf{AA}' = \mathbf{U}\left(\mathbf{SS}'\right)\mathbf{U}', \tag{8.1}$$

$$m \geq n: \quad \mathbf{A}'\mathbf{A} = \mathbf{V}'\left(\mathbf{S}'\mathbf{S}\right)\mathbf{V}, \tag{8.2}$$

$$
m \leq n: \quad
\mathbf{W} = \begin{bmatrix} \frac{1}{\sqrt{2}}\mathbf{U} & \frac{1}{\sqrt{2}}\mathbf{U} & \mathbf{0}_{m\times(m-n)} \\ \frac{1}{\sqrt{2}}\mathbf{V}(1:m,:)' & -\frac{1}{\sqrt{2}}\mathbf{V}(1:m,:)' & \mathbf{V}(m+1:n,:)' \end{bmatrix},
$$
$$
\begin{bmatrix} \mathbf{0}_{m\times m} & \mathbf{A} \\ \mathbf{A}' & \mathbf{0}_{n\times n} \end{bmatrix} \mathbf{W} = \mathbf{W}\begin{bmatrix} \mathbf{S}_m & & \\ & -\mathbf{S}_m & \\ & & \mathbf{0}_{n-m} \end{bmatrix}, \tag{8.3}
$$

$$
m \geq n: \quad
\mathbf{W} = \begin{bmatrix} \frac{1}{\sqrt{2}}\mathbf{V}' & \frac{1}{\sqrt{2}}\mathbf{V}' & \mathbf{0}_{n\times(m-n)} \\ \frac{1}{\sqrt{2}}\mathbf{U}(:,1:n) & -\frac{1}{\sqrt{2}}\mathbf{U}(:,1:n) & \mathbf{U}(:,n+1:m) \end{bmatrix}
$$
$$
\begin{bmatrix} \mathbf{0}_{n\times n} & \mathbf{A}' \\ \mathbf{A} & \mathbf{0}_{m\times m} \end{bmatrix} \mathbf{W} = \mathbf{W}\begin{bmatrix} \mathbf{S}_n & & \\ & -\mathbf{S}_n & \\ & & \mathbf{0}_{m-n} \end{bmatrix}. \tag{8.4}
$$

Eqs. (8.1)–(8.4) are the eigenvalue decompositions of the symmetric matrices $\mathbf{AA}'$, $\mathbf{A}'\mathbf{A}$, etc.

$\mathbf{AA}'$ is symmetric positive semi definite. Its eigenvalue decomposition is $\mathbf{AA}' = \mathbf{U}\boldsymbol{\Lambda}\mathbf{U}'$. By Eq. (8.1), $\mathbf{U}$ is the left singular vectors, $s_j = \sqrt{\lambda_j} > 0$, $j = 1, 2, \ldots, r = \text{rank}(\mathbf{A}) \leq \min(m,n)$. Using $\mathbf{A}'\mathbf{U} = \mathbf{V}'\mathbf{S}'$, for s_j, the corresponding right singular vector can be calculated as $\mathbf{V}(j,:)' = \frac{1}{s_j}\mathbf{A}'\mathbf{U}(:,j)$. If $r < n$, $\mathbf{V}(r+1:n,:)'$ can be chosen as any orthogonal complementary vectors to $\mathbf{V}(1:r,:)'$.

$\mathbf{A}'\mathbf{A}$ is symmetric positive semi definite. Its eigenvalue decomposition is $\mathbf{A}'\mathbf{A} = \mathbf{V}'\boldsymbol{\Lambda}\mathbf{V}$. By Eq. (8.2), $\mathbf{V}$ is the right singular vectors, $s_j = \sqrt{\lambda_j} > 0$, $j = 1, 2, \ldots, r = \text{rank}(\mathbf{A}) \leq \min(m,n)$. Using $\mathbf{AV}' = \mathbf{US}$, for s_j, the corresponding left singular vector can be calculated as $\mathbf{U}(:,j) = \frac{1}{s_j}\mathbf{AV}(j,:)'$. If $r < m$, $\mathbf{U}(:,r+1:m)$ can be chosen as any orthogonal complementary vectors to $\mathbf{U}(:,1:r)$.

By Eq. (8.3) or Eq. (8.4), the nonzero singular values s_j are the positive eigenvalues, $\lambda_j > 0$, $j = 1, 2, \ldots, r$. The corresponding left and right singular vectors $\mathbf{U}(:,1:r)$ and $\mathbf{V}(1:r,:)'$ can be directly read from $\mathbf{W}$. $\mathbf{U}(:,r+1:m)$ can be taken as an arbitrary orthogonal complement to $\mathbf{U}(:,1:r)$. $\mathbf{V}(r+1:n,:)'$ can be taken as an arbitrary orthogonal complement to $\mathbf{V}(1:r,:)'$.

The discussions made above clearly show the existence of the SVD and the method to calculate it. If the amount of the computation of $\mathbf{AA}'$ and $\mathbf{A}'\mathbf{A}$ is close, for $m \leq n$, Eq. (8.1) is more efficient than Eq. (8.2), because the size of the eigenvalue decomposition is smaller. In Eqs. (8.1) and (8.2), the eigenvalues are the squares of the singular values. If $\mathbf{A}$ has some singular values that are much less than 1, the corresponding eigenvalues are even smaller than 1. To find these tiny eigenvalues accurately poses a challenge to many eigenvalue algorithms. The size of eigenvalue decomposition of Eqs. (8.3) and (8.4) is $m + n$, larger than both Eqs. (8.1) and (8.2). But they are better suited to find tiny singular values.

Eqs. (8.1)–(8.4) can be applied directly to find SVD as it was discussed above. But for the efficiency, we will take two steps.

In the first step, we calculate $\mathbf{A}$'s QBZ decomposition, $\mathbf{A} = \mathbf{QBZ}$, using QBZbyHouseholder_.m or QBZbyGivens_.m. In the QBZ decomposition, $\mathbf{Q}$ is column orthogonal, $\mathbf{Z}$ is row orthogonal, and $\mathbf{B}$ is bi-diagonal. See Section 3.4. In the second step, we calculate $\mathbf{B}$'s SVD, $\mathbf{B} = \mathbf{XSY}$, using one of the methods shown in Eqs. (8.1)–(8.4). Then $\mathbf{A} = \mathbf{Q}(\mathbf{XSY})\mathbf{Z} = (\mathbf{QX})\mathbf{S}(\mathbf{YZ}) = \mathbf{USV}$. If adopting Eq. (8.1) or Eq. (8.2), we do not need to form explicitly $\mathbf{BB}'$ or $\mathbf{B}'\mathbf{B}$. Instead all the calculations are applied to $\mathbf{B}$ directly. Sections 8.4 and 8.5 present three different such algorithms. If adopting Eq. (8.3) or Eq. (8.4), $\begin{bmatrix} 0 & \mathbf{B} \\ \mathbf{B}' & 0 \end{bmatrix}$ or $\begin{bmatrix} 0 & \mathbf{B}' \\ \mathbf{B} & 0 \end{bmatrix}$ is permuted to one of the following tri-diagonal forms:

$$\mathbf{P}\begin{bmatrix} 0 & \mathbf{B} \\ \mathbf{B}' & 0 \end{bmatrix}\mathbf{P}' = \begin{bmatrix} 0 & B_{11} & & & & \\ B_{11} & 0 & B_{12} & & & \\ & B_{12} & 0 & B_{22} & & \\ & & B_{22} & 0 & \ddots & \\ & & & \ddots & \ddots & B_{rs} \\ & & & & B_{rs} & 0 \end{bmatrix} ; \quad r = \text{rank}(\mathbf{A}),\ s = r \text{ or } s = r + 1. \quad (8.5)$$

Then, we can apply the eigenvalue decomposition algorithm for the symmetric tri-diagonal matrices presented in Sections 6.4 and 6.7. In Eq. (8.5), the permutation is

$$\mathbf{p} = \begin{bmatrix} r + 1, 1, r + 2, 2, \ldots, 2r - 2, r - 1, 2r, r \end{bmatrix} \quad \text{if } s = r,$$
$$\mathbf{p} = \begin{bmatrix} r + 1, 1, r + 2, 2, \ldots, 2r - 2, r - 1, 2r, r, 2r + 1 \end{bmatrix} \quad \text{if } s = r + 1. \quad (8.6)$$

In the first step, we can also apply the partial QBZ decomposition of $\mathbf{A}$ using QBZbyLanczos_.m. See Section 3.4. In such a case, $\mathbf{A} \ne \mathbf{QBZ}$, but the following equations are satisfied, where l is the input argument last to QBZbyLanczos_.m,

$$\mathbf{AZ}(1:l,:)' = \mathbf{Q}(:,1:l)\mathbf{B}(:,1:l),$$
$$\mathbf{A}'\mathbf{Q}(:,1:l) = \mathbf{Z}(1:l,:)'\mathbf{B}(:,1:l)' + B(l,l+1)\mathbf{Z}(l+1,:)'\mathbf{I}(l,:). \quad (8.7)$$

In the second step, we calculate the SVD of $\mathbf{B}(:,1:l)$, $\mathbf{B}(:,1:l) = \mathbf{XSY}$, using one of the methods shown in Eqs. (8.1)–(8.4). Introducing this expression of $\mathbf{B}(:,1:l)$ into Eq. (8.7), we can establish

$$\mathbf{A}(\mathbf{YZ}(1:l,:))' = (\mathbf{Q}(:,1:l)\mathbf{X})\mathbf{S},$$
$$\mathbf{A}'(\mathbf{Q}(:,1:l)\mathbf{X}) = (\mathbf{YZ}(1:l,:))'\mathbf{S}' + B(l,l+1)\mathbf{Z}(l+1,:)'\mathbf{X}(l,:). \quad (8.8)$$

Therefore, taking the triplet $(S(j,j), \mathbf{Q}(:,1:l)\mathbf{X}(:,j), \mathbf{Y}(j,:)\mathbf{Z}(1:l,:)), j = 1, \ldots, l$ as the approximate singular triplet of $\mathbf{A}$, the residual is simply $B(l,l+1)|X(l,j)|$. One implementation of such an algorithm is presented in Section 8.6.

8.2 SVD ALGORITHMS OF A MATRIX OF $1 \times n$ OR $m \times 1$ OR 2×2

As shown in Eqs. (8.1) and (8.2), $\mathbf{A}$'s SVD can be obtained as the eigenvalue decomposition of $\mathbf{AA}'$ or $\mathbf{A}'\mathbf{A}$. From the discussion of characteristic polynomials in Chapters 1 and 6, for $\mathbf{A} \in \mathbb{R}^{m \times n}$, $\mathbf{A}$'s SVD can be obtained analytically, if $1 \leq m \leq 4$ or $1 \leq n \leq 4$. The cases $m = 1$, $n = 1$, and $m = n = 2$ are elementary but enlightening.

If $m = n = 1$, that is, $\mathbf{A}$ is a scalar a, obviously $a = (\text{sign}(a) \pm 1)|a|(\mp 1)$. This means $(|a|, \text{sign}(a) \pm 1, \pm 1)$ is the singular triplet of the scalar a.

If $m = 1, n > 1$, that is, $\mathbf{A}$ is a row vector $\mathbf{a}$, obviously

$$\mathbf{a} = [a_1, a_2, \ldots, a_n] = (\pm 1)\left[\|\mathbf{a}\|_2, 0, \ldots, 0\right]\begin{bmatrix} \mathbf{a}_1 = \pm\frac{\mathbf{a}}{\|\mathbf{a}\|_2} \\ \mathbf{a}_1^{\perp} \end{bmatrix},$$

where $\mathbf{a}_1^{\perp}$ is an arbitrary orthogonal complement to the unit row vector $\mathbf{a}_1$. This means $(\|\mathbf{a}\|_2, \pm 1, \mathbf{a}_1)$ and $(0, 1, \mathbf{a}_1^{\perp}(j,:)), j = 1, 2, \ldots, n-1$ are the singular triplet of the row vector $\mathbf{a}$.

If $m > 1, n = 1$, that is, $\mathbf{A}$ is a column vector $\mathbf{a}$, obviously

$$\mathbf{a} = \begin{bmatrix} a_1 \\ a_2 \\ \vdots \\ a_m \end{bmatrix} = \begin{bmatrix} \mathbf{a}_1 = \pm\frac{\mathbf{a}}{\|\mathbf{a}\|_2}, & \mathbf{a}_1^{\perp} \end{bmatrix}\begin{bmatrix} \|\mathbf{a}\|_2 \\ 0 \\ \vdots \\ 0 \end{bmatrix}(\pm 1),$$

where $\mathbf{a}_1^{\perp}$ is an arbitrary orthogonal complement to the unit column vector $\mathbf{a}_1$. This means $(\|\mathbf{a}\|_2, \mathbf{a}_1, \pm 1)$ and $(0, \mathbf{a}_1^{\perp}(:,j), 1), j = 1, 2, \ldots, m-1$ are the singular triplet of the column vector $\mathbf{a}$.

If $m = n = 2$, that is, $\mathbf{A} = \begin{bmatrix} A_{11} & A_{12} \\ A_{21} & A_{22} \end{bmatrix}$. The characteristic polynomial of Eq. (8.1) or Eq. (8.2) is $\det(\lambda \mathbf{I}_{2\times 2} - \mathbf{AA'}) = 0$, i.e.

$$\lambda^2 - \left(A_{11}^2 + A_{12}^2 + A_{21}^2 + A_{22}^2\right)\lambda + (A_{11}A_{22} - A_{12}A_{21})^2 = 0. \tag{a}$$

The characteristic polynomial of Eq. (8.3) or Eq. (8.4) is $\det\left(\lambda \mathbf{I}_{4\times 4} - \begin{bmatrix} \mathbf{0} & \mathbf{A} \\ \mathbf{A'} & \mathbf{0} \end{bmatrix}\right) = 0$, i.e.

$$\lambda^4 - \left(A_{11}^2 + A_{12}^2 + A_{21}^2 + A_{22}^2\right)\lambda^2 + (A_{11}A_{22} - A_{12}A_{21})^2 = 0. \tag{b}$$

It can be verified that both roots of Eq. (a) are non-negative, the square roots of which are the two singular values, s_1, s_2. While the four roots of Eq. (b) are $s_1, s_2, -s_1, -s_2$. The left and singular vectors are obtained following the discussions of Eqs. (8.1)–(8.4).

For $m = n = 2$, the SVD of $\mathbf{A}$ is implemented in the following svd2x2_.m. The input argument algo=1,2,3,4 corresponds to Eqs. (8.1)–(8.4).

Algorithm 8.1

Singular value decomposition of a 2 × 2 matrix.

```
function [U,S,V] = svd2x2_(A,algo)

if (~exist('algo','var')) algo = 1; end
tol = 100*eps;

if(algo == 1)               %eig(A*A')
    [S,U] = eig2x2_(A*A');  [S,p]=sort(abs(diag(S)),'descend');
U=permute_(p,U,'col');
```

```
   if (S(2) < tol*S(1)) S(2) = 0; end
   S = sqrt(S);   V = eye(2);
   if (S(1) > tol) V(1,:) = (U(:,1)'/S(1))*A; end
   if (S(2) > tol*S(1))
       V(2,:) = (U(:,2)'/S(2))*A;
   else
       V2 = U(:,2)';   V2 = V2-V(1,:)*(V(1,:)*V2');   V(2,:) = V2/norm(V2);
   end
elseif (algo == 2)      %eig(A'*A)
   [S,V]=eig2x2_(A'*A);   [S,p]=sort(abs(diag(S)),'descend');
V=permute_(p,V','row');
   if (S(2) < tol*S(1)) S(2) = 0; end
   S = sqrt(S);   U = eye(2);
   if (S(1) > tol) U(:,1) = A*(V(1,:)'/S(1)); end
   if (S(2) > tol*S(1))
       U(:,2) = A*(V(2,:)'/S(2));
   else
       U2 = V(2,:)';   U2 = U2-U(:,1)*(U(:,1)'*U2);   U(:,2) = U2/norm(U2);
   end
elseif(algo == 3)        %eig([zeros(2),A;A' zeros(2)])
   normA2 = A(1,1)*A(1,1)+A(2,2)*A(2,2)+A(1,2)*A(1,2)+A(2,1)*A(2,1);
   detA = A(1,1)*A(2,2)-A(1,2)*A(2,1);
   sigma = sqrt(normA2*normA2-4.0*detA*detA);
   S = [sqrt(0.5*(normA2+sigma)); sqrt(0.5*(normA2-sigma))];   U = eye(2);   V = U;
   B = zeros(4);   B(1:2,3:4) = A;   B(3:4,1:2) = A';   z = zeros(4,1);
   B(1,1) = S(1);   B(2,2) = S(1);   B(3,3) = S(1);   B(4,4) = S(1);
   [x01,Z1] = eqsByHouseholder_(B,z,tol);
   B(1,1) = S(2);   B(2,2) = S(2);   B(3,3) = S(2);   B(4,4) = S(2);
   [x01,Z2] = eqsByHouseholder_(B,z,tol);
   if (size(Z1,2) == 1) U(:,1) = sqrt(2.0)*Z1(1:2);   V(1,:) = sqrt(2.0)*Z1(3:4)';
   else                 U(:,1) = Z1(1:2,2);   V(1,:) = Z1(3:4,1)';   end
   if (size(Z2,2) == 1) U(:,2) = sqrt(2.0)*Z2(1:2);   V(2,:) = sqrt(2.0)*Z2(3:4)';
   else                 U(:,2) = Z2(1:2,2);   V(2,:) = Z2(3:4,1)';   end
   if (norm(A*V(1,:)'-S(1)*U(:,1)) > tol*S(2)) V(1,:) =-V(1,:); end
   if (norm(A*V(2,:)'-S(2)*U(:,2)) > tol*S(2)) V(2,:) =-V(2,:); end
else %if(algo == 4)      %eig([zeros(2),A';A zeros(2)])
   normA2 = A(1,1)*A(1,1)+A(2,2)*A(2,2)+A(1,2)*A(1,2)+A(2,1)*A(2,1);
   detA = A(1,1)*A(2,2)-A(1,2)*A(2,1);
   sigma = sqrt(normA2*normA2-4.0*detA*detA);
   S = [sqrt(0.5*(normA2+sigma)); sqrt(0.5*(normA2-sigma))];   U = eye(2);   V = U;
   B = zeros(4);   B(1:2,3:4) = A';   B(3:4,1:2) = A;   z = zeros(4,1);
   B(1,1) = S(1);   B(2,2) = S(1);   B(3,3) = S(1);   B(4,4) = S(1);
   [x01,Z1] = eqsByHouseholder_(B,z,tol);
   B(1,1) = S(2);   B(2,2) = S(2);   B(3,3) = S(2);   B(4,4) = S(2);
   [x01,Z2] = eqsByHouseholder_(B,z,tol);
   if (size(Z1,2) == 1) V(1,:) = sqrt(2.0)*Z1(1:2)';   U(:,1) = sqrt(2.0)*Z1(3:4);
   else                 V(1,:) = Z1(1:2,2)';   U(:,1) = Z1(3:4,1);   end
   if (size(Z2,2) == 1) V(2,:) = sqrt(2.0)*Z2(1:2)';   U(:,2) = sqrt(2.0)*Z2(3:4);
   else                 V(2,:) = Z2(1:2,2)';   U(:,2) = Z2(3:4,1);   end
   if (norm(A*V(1,:)'-S(1)*U(:,1)) > tol*S(2)) V(1,:) =-V(1,:); end
   if (norm(A*V(2,:)'-S(2)*U(:,2)) > tol*S(2)) V(2,:) =-V(2,:); end
end
```

An algorithm with higher accuracy than svd2x2_.m is obtained by treating different cases differently. Two 2×2 rotation matrices $\mathbf{G}_1 = \begin{bmatrix} c_1 & s_1 \\ -s_1 & c_1 \end{bmatrix}$ and $\mathbf{G}_2 = \begin{bmatrix} c_2 & s_2 \\ -s_2 & c_2 \end{bmatrix}$ are determined to diagonalize $\mathbf{A}$,

$$\begin{bmatrix} c_1 & -s_1 \\ s_1 & c_1 \end{bmatrix} \begin{bmatrix} A_{11} & A_{12} \\ A_{21} & A_{22} \end{bmatrix} \begin{bmatrix} c_2 & -s_2 \\ s_2 & c_2 \end{bmatrix} = \begin{bmatrix} \sigma_1 & 0 \\ 0 & \sigma_2 \end{bmatrix}. \tag{8.9}$$

The conditions to determine c_1, s_1 and c_2, s_2 are as follows:

$$(s_1 A_{11} + c_1 A_{21}) c_2 + (s_1 A_{12} + c_1 A_{22}) s_2 = 0,$$
$$(c_1 A_{12} - s_1 A_{22}) c_2 - (c_1 A_{11} - s_1 A_{21}) s_2 = 0,$$
$$c_1^2 + s_1^2 = 1,$$
$$c_2^2 + s_2^2 = 1.$$

The following listed $givens2\_.m$ implements this higher accuracy algorithm.

Algorithm 8.2

Singular value decomposition of a 2×2 matrix.

```
% [c1 -s1; [a1 a2; [c2 s2; [x 0;       %Different cases handled
%  s1  c1]* a3 a4]*-s2 c2]= 0 y];       %differently for accuracy!
function [c1,s1,c2,s2] = givens2_(a1,a2,a3,a4)

a = max(max(abs(a1),abs(a3)),max(abs(a2),abs(a4)));   tol = 10*eps;
if (abs(a3) < tol*a) a3 = 0.0; end
if (abs(a2) < tol*a) a2 = 0.0; end
if (abs(a4) < tol*a) a4 = 0.0; end

if (a2==0 && a3==0)
    c1 = 1.0;   s1 = 0.0;   c2 = 1.0;   s2 = 0.0;
elseif (a1==0 && a4==0)
    c1 = 1.0;   s1 = 0.0;   c2 = 0.0;   s2 = 1.0;
elseif (a1==0 && a2==0)
    c1 = 1.0;   s1 = 0.0;   [c2,s2] = givens_(a4,a3);   s2 = -s2;
elseif (a3==0 && a4==0)
    c1 = 1.0;   s1 = 0.0;   [c2,s2] = givens_(a1,a2);
elseif (a1==0 && a3==0)
    [c1,s1] = givens_(a4,a2);   s1 = -s1;   c2 = 1.0;   s2 = 0.0;
elseif (a2==0 && a4==0)
    [c1,s1] = givens_(a1,a3);   c2 = 1.0;   s2 = 0.0;
elseif (a3 == 0)
    tau = 0.5*(a2*a2+a4*a4-a1*a1)/(a1*a2);   sigma = sqrt(1.0+tau*tau);
    if (tau >= 0.0) t2 = 1.0/(tau+sigma); else t2 = 1.0/(tau-sigma); end
    t1 = (a1*t2+a2)/a4;
    c1 = 1.0/sqrt(1.0+t1*t1);   s1 = t1*c1;   c2 = 1.0/sqrt(1.0+t2*t2);   s2 = t2*c2;
elseif (a2 == 0)
    tau = 0.5*(a3*a3+a4*a4-a1*a1)/(a1*a3);   sigma = sqrt(1.0+tau*tau);
    if (tau >= 0.0) t1 = 1.0/(tau+sigma); else t1 = 1.0/(tau-sigma); end
    t2 = (a1*t1+a3)/a4;
    c1 = 1.0/sqrt(1.0+t1*t1);   s1 = t1*c1;   c2 = 1.0/sqrt(1.0+t2*t2);   s2 = t2*c2;
elseif (a1*a3+a2*a4 == 0.0)
    t2 = (a3*a3-a2*a2)/(a1*a2+a3*a4);   t1 = (a1*t2+a2)/(a3*t2+a4);
    c1 = 1.0/sqrt(1.0+t1*t1);   s1 = t1*c1;   c2 = 1.0/sqrt(1.0+t2*t2);   s2 = t2*c2;
else
    c = a1*a3 + a2*a4;   a = (a1*a2+a3*a4)/c;   b = (a2*a2-a3*a3)/c;
d = a*a3;   e = a*a2;
    if ((abs(a3) > abs(a2))) tau = 0.5*(a*a4+b*a3-a1)/d;   sigma = (a2-b*a4)/d;
    else                     tau = 0.5*(b*a2+a4-a*a1)/e;   sigma = (a3+b*a1)/e; end
```

```
      if (tau >= 0.0) t2 = sigma/(tau + sqrt(sigma+tau*tau));
      else            t2 = sigma/(tau - sqrt(sigma+tau*tau)); end
      t1 = a*t2 + b;
      c1 = 1.0/sqrt(1.0+t1*t1);   s1 = t1*c1;   c2 = 1.0/sqrt(1.0+t2*t2);   s2 = t2*c2;
end
```

8.3 JACOBI ITERATION ALGORITHM FOR SVD

The Jacobi algorithm for SVD is similar to the Jacobi algorithm for the symmetric eigenvalue, see Section 6.8.

For a square matrix $\mathbf{A}$, we can apply Eq. (8.9) with `[c1,s1,c2,s2]=givens2_(A(i,i),A(i,j);` `A(j,i),A(j,j));`, $1 \leq i, j \leq n$. The two Givens rotations $\mathbf{J}_1, \mathbf{J}_2, \mathbf{J}_1 = \mathbf{I}, J_1(i,i) = J_1(j,j) = c_1, J_1(i,j) = -J_1(j,i) = s_1$ and $\mathbf{J}_2 = \mathbf{I}, J_2(i,i) = J_2(j,j) = c_2, J_2(i,j) = -J_2(j,i) = s_2$. The orthogonal transformation $\mathbf{J}_1'\mathbf{A}\mathbf{J}_2'$ is illustrated in

$$\mathbf{J}_1'\mathbf{A}\mathbf{J}_2' = \bar{\mathbf{A}} = \begin{bmatrix} A_{11} & \cdots & \bar{A}_{1k} & \cdots & \bar{A}_{1l} & \cdots & A_{1n} \\ \vdots & & \vdots & & \vdots & & \vdots \\ \bar{A}_{i1} & \cdots & \bar{A}_{ik} & \cdots & \bar{A}_{il} & \cdots & \bar{A}_{in} \\ \vdots & & \vdots & & \vdots & & \vdots \\ \bar{A}_{j1} & \cdots & \bar{A}_{jk} & \cdots & \bar{A}_{jl} & \cdots & \bar{A}_{jn} \\ \vdots & & \vdots & & \vdots & & \vdots \\ A_{m1} & \cdots & \bar{A}_{mk} & \cdots & \bar{A}_{ml} & \cdots & A_{mn} \end{bmatrix}. \tag{8.10}$$

$\mathbf{J}_1'\mathbf{A}\mathbf{J}_2'$ only changes $\mathbf{A}$'s ith and jth rows and columns, with $\bar{A}_{ij} = \bar{A}_{ji} = 0$. The Frobenius norm of the off diagonal of $\bar{\mathbf{A}}$ is reduced by $A_{ij}^2 + A_{ji}^2$, which means the continuous application of Eq. (8.10) with different (i, j) drives $\mathbf{A}$ closer to a diagonal form. The choice of (i, j) follows the same rule as Jacobi iteration for symmetric eigenvalue problems. The algorithm is converged when the Frobenius norm of the off diagonals does not change between the Jacobi sweeps. The product of all $\mathbf{J}_1$s is the left singular vectors. The product of all $\mathbf{J}_2$s is the right singular vector.

The aforementioned Jacobi algorithm cannot be applied to a non-square matrix. For such a matrix $\mathbf{A}$, first we apply QLZ decomposition, $\mathbf{A} = \mathbf{QLZ}$, see Section 3.4. $\mathbf{L}$ is a lower triangular matrix which reveals the rank of $\mathbf{A}$. Then we apply the aforementioned Jacobi algorithm to $\mathbf{L}(1 : r, 1 : r), r = \text{rank}(\mathbf{A})$. The product of $\mathbf{Q}$ and all the $\mathbf{J}_1$s is the left singular vector. The product of $\mathbf{Z}$ and all the $\mathbf{J}_2$s is the right singular vector.

Algorithm 8.3

Singular value decomposition by Jacobi iterations.
```
function [U,S,V] = svdByJacobi_(A,tol,format)

[m,n] = size(A);
if(m == n)
    if(strcmp(format,'brief')) U = []; V = [];   else U = eye(m); V = U; end
    S = A;   r = m;
else
    [U,S,V] = QLZ_(A,'householder',tol,format);
```

```
      for r=min(size(S,1),size(S,2)):-1:1
          if (norm(S(r,1:r),inf) > 0) break; end
      end
      S = S(1:r,1:r);
end
offS = norm(S-diag(diag(S)),'fro')^2;   offS0 = 0;

if (mod(r,2) == 0) top = 1:2:r;    bot = 2:2:r;      r2 = r/2;
else               top = 1:2:r+1;  bot = 2:2:r+1;    r2 = (r+1)/2; end

while(abs(offS-offS0) > 0)
    offS0 = offS;
    for k = 1:r2
        p = min(top(k),bot(k));    q = max(top(k),bot(k));
        if (q == r+1) continue; end
        offS = offS - S(p,q)*S(p,q) - S(q,p)*S(q,p);
        [c1,s1,c2,s2] = givens2_(S(p,p),S(p,q),S(q,p),S(q,q));   %more accuracy
        G1 = [c1,s1;-s1,c1];   G2 = [c2,-s2;s2,c2];
%       [G1,s,G2] = svd2x2_([S(p,p),S(p,q);S(q,p),S(q,q)],3);   %less accuracy
        Sp = S(p,:);   S(p,:) = G1(:,1)'*[Sp;S(q,:)];   S(q,:) = G1(:,2)'*[Sp;S(q,:)];
        Sp = S(:,p);   S(:,p) = [Sp,S(:,q)]*G2(1,:)';   S(:,q) = [Sp,S(:,q)]*G2(2,:)';
        if (~strcmp(format,'brief'))
            Up = U(:,p);   U(:,p) = [Up,U(:,q)]*G1(:,1);   U(:,q) = [Up,U(:,q)]*G1(:,2);
            Vp = V(p,:);   V(p,:) = G2(1,:)*[Vp;V(q,:)];   V(q,:) = G2(2,:)*[Vp;V(q,:)];
        end
    end
    top0 = top;  bot0 = bot;
    for k = 1:r2
        if (k == 2) top(k) = bot0(1); end
        if (k >  2) top(k) = top0(k-1); end
        if (k == r2) bot(k) = top0(k); end
        if (k <  r2) bot(k) = bot0(k+1); end
    end
end

for j=1:r
    if(S(j,j) < 0.0)
        S(j,j) =-S(j,j);
        if (j <= size(V,1)) V(j,:) =-V(j,:); end
    end
end
S = diag(S);  [S,p] = sort(S,'descend');   r = min(m,n);   l = size(S,1);
if (~strcmp(format,'brief')) U = permute_(p,U,'col');   V = permute_(p,V,'row'); end
if (strcmp(format,'long'))
    if (r > 1)  S = [S;zeros(r-1,1)]; end
    if (m >= n) S = [diag(S);zeros(m-n,n)]; end
    if (m <  n) S = [diag(S),zeros(m,n-m)]; end
elseif (strcmp(format,'short'))
    for l=size(S,1):-1:1
        if (S(l) > tol*S(1)) break; end
    end
    if (l < size(S,1)) S = S(1:l);   U = U(:,1:l);   V = V(1:l,:); end
end
```

Following three simple examples demonstrates the high accuracy and efficiency of svdByJacobi_.m.

```
>> A=randn(8,5);   A(:,4:5)=A(:,1:2)*randn(2);    %non-square and rank deficient matrix
```

```
>> [U,S,V]=svdByJacobi_(A,100*eps,'short');
>> S'                    %non-zero singular values
=   7.6631     2.5585     2.0668
>> norm(U*diag(S)*V-A)
=   6.4021e-015
>> norm(U'*U-eye(3))
=   5.1674e-016
>> norm(V*V'-eye(3))
=   9.1696e-016

>> A=randn(5,8);  A(4:5,:)=randn(2)*A(1:2,:);   %non-square and rank deficient matrix
>> [U,S,V]=svdByJacobi_(A,100*eps,'short');
>> S'                    %non-zero singular values
=   4.4760     3.4220     2.3546
>> norm(U*diag(S)*V-A)
=   3.8197e-015
>> norm(U'*U-eye(3))
=   9.3014e-016
>> norm(V*V'-eye(3))
=   2.5847e-016

>> A=randn(100);         %100x100 full matrix
>> tic
>> [U,S,V]=svdByJacobi_(A,100*eps,'short');
>> toc
Elapsed time is 3.901344 seconds.
>> norm(S-svd(A))
= 1.6285e-012            %S equals MATLAB built-in svd.
>> norm(U*diag(S)*V-A)
=   1.5771e-011          %A=U*S*V
>> norm(U'*U-eye(100))
= 2.7965e-014            %U'*U=I
>> norm(V*V'-eye(100))
=   2.7253e-014          %V*V'=I
```

8.4 QR ITERATION ALGORITHM FOR SVD

As shown in Section 8.1, the QR iteration algorithm for the symmetric eigenvalue decomposition can be directly applied to Eqs. (8.1)–(8.4) to find the SVD of $\mathbf{A}$. However, the direct application requires the explicit formation of $\mathbf{AA}'$ or $\begin{bmatrix} \mathbf{0} & \mathbf{A} \\ \mathbf{A}' & \mathbf{0} \end{bmatrix}$, etc., which has hinder effect in both efficiency and accuracy. QR iteration algorithm for SVD is an adaptation of QR iteration algorithm that was discussed in Section 6.4.

We use the following simple matrix and $\mathbf{A}'\mathbf{A}$ (Eq. (8.2)) as the example for the presentation of the QR iteration algorithm.

```
>> A = [-1.0284     0.1394    -0.8309    -1.2367     0.6205;
        -0.0259     0.9228     0.7847     0.3900     1.0982;
         0.8801    -0.6208     0.9698    -0.7157    -0.6531;
         0.4778     0.0726    -0.0965    -0.2824     1.8969;
         1.1449     1.3409     0.1917     0.0370    -1.1560;
         0.4397     0.4162    -0.0822     1.0517     0.0335;
        -0.1530    -1.4609     1.8527     0.5098    -1.6310;
        -0.3123     0.0867     0.2697    -0.9725     0.3115];
```

To calculate the eigenvalue of $\mathbf{A}'\mathbf{A}$ by the QR iteration algorithm, in the first step, we calculate its QTQt decomposition, $\mathbf{T} = \mathbf{Q}'\mathbf{A}'\mathbf{A}\mathbf{Q}$.

```
>> [Q,T]=QTQtByHouseholder_(A'*A,100*eps,'long')
Q = 1.0000        0         0         0         0
          0   -0.4548    0.8202   -0.0064   -0.3468
          0   -0.5364   -0.0816    0.6765    0.4980
          0   -0.4518   -0.0429   -0.7346    0.5043
          0    0.5490    0.5645    0.0511    0.6143

T = 3.6862   -2.7169        0         0         0
   -2.7169    7.8203    4.5013        0         0
         0    4.5013    9.8175   -2.0431        0
         0         0   -2.0431    3.7827    0.1976
         0         0         0    0.1976    4.0559
```

A tri-diagonal matrix can also be obtained by A's QBZ decomposition, $\mathbf{B} = \mathbf{Q}'\mathbf{A}\mathbf{Z}'$, because $\mathbf{B}'\mathbf{B} = \mathbf{Z}\mathbf{A}'\mathbf{Q}\mathbf{Q}'\mathbf{A}\mathbf{Z}' = \mathbf{Z}\mathbf{A}'\mathbf{A}\mathbf{Z}'$.

```
>> [Q,B,Z]=QBZbyGivens_(A);
>> B=band2full_(B,0,1)
=  -1.9200    1.4151        0         0         0
          0   -2.4120   -1.8662        0         0
          0         0   -2.5169   -0.8118        0
          0         0         0   -1.7674    0.1118
          0         0         0         0   -2.0108
>> Z           %Z(j,:) and Q(:,j) of A'*A can differ by +/-.
=   1.0000        0         0         0         0
          0   -0.4548   -0.5364   -0.4518    0.5490
          0    0.8202   -0.0816   -0.0429    0.5645
          0    0.0064   -0.6765    0.7346   -0.0511
          0   -0.3468    0.4980    0.5043    0.6143
>> B'*B        %B'*B and T can differ by +/-.
=   3.6862   -2.7169        0         0         0
   -2.7169    7.8203    4.5013        0         0
         0    4.5013    9.8175    2.0431        0
         0         0    2.0431    3.7827   -0.1976
         0         0         0   -0.1976    4.0559
```

The second step of the QR iteration algorithm consists of a series of the following QR steps, $j = 0, 1, 2, \ldots$:

$$\mathbf{T}_0 = \mathbf{T},$$
$$\mathbf{T}_j - \theta\mathbf{I} = \mathbf{Q}_j\mathbf{R}_j; \qquad \mathbf{T}_{j+1} = \mathbf{R}_j\mathbf{Q}_j + \theta\mathbf{I} = \mathbf{Q}_j'\mathbf{T}_j\mathbf{Q}_j,$$
$$\mathbf{T}_{j+1} \Rightarrow \mathrm{diag}(s_1^2, s_2^2, \ldots, s_n^2).$$

In each step, the shift θ is chosen as the eigenvalue of $\mathbf{T}(n-1:n, n-1:n)$ that is closer to $T(n,n)$. The actual QR and RQ calculations shown above are implicitly performed, see Section 6.4.

For brevity, the first QR step for $\mathbf{T}$ is *explicitly* performed and shown below.

```
>> theta = eig2x2_(T(4:5,4:5))
=    3.6790        0
          0    4.1596    %theta(2,2) is closer to T(5,5).
>> [Q,R]=QR_(T-theta(2,2)*eye(5));
>> Q                      %To be compared with G1*G2*G3*G4 below.
=   -0.1716    0.5830   -0.6354   -0.4677   -0.0900
```

```
   -0.9852    -0.1016     0.1107     0.0815     0.0157
         0    -0.8061    -0.4736    -0.3486    -0.0671
         0          0     0.5998    -0.7857    -0.1512
         0          0          0     0.1890    -0.9820
>> T=R*Q+theta(2,2)*eye(5)    %To be compared with B'*B below.
=    6.7797     5.5015          0     0.0000    -0.0000
     5.5015     8.7716     2.7458     0.0000          0
          0     2.7458     6.2174     0.6272          0
          0          0     0.6272     3.3049     0.0136     %T(4,5) reduced.
          0          0          0     0.0136     4.0890
```

The QR step can also be equivalently applied to $\mathbf{B}'\mathbf{B}$ implicitly. θ is chosen as the eigenvalue of $(n-1:n, n-1:n)$ block of $\mathbf{B}'\mathbf{B}$ that is closer to $B(n-1,n)^2 + B(n,n)^2$,

$$\begin{bmatrix} B(n-2,n-1)^2 + B(n-1,n-1)^2 & B(n-1,n-1)B(n-1,n) \\ B(n-1,n)B(n-1,n-1) & B(n-1,n)^2 + B(n,n)^2. \end{bmatrix}$$

The first column of $\mathbf{B}'\mathbf{B} - \theta\mathbf{I}$ is simply

$$\mathbf{b}_1 = \begin{bmatrix} B(1,1)^2 - \theta \\ B(1,2)B(1,1) \\ 0 \\ \vdots \\ 0 \end{bmatrix}.$$

A Givens rotation $\mathbf{Q}_1$ is found that is to zero $b_1(2,1)$, i.e. $\mathbf{Q}'_1\mathbf{b}_1 = \|\mathbf{b}_1\|_2\mathbf{I}(:,1)$. Then Givens rotations $\mathbf{G}_1, \mathbf{Q}_2, \mathbf{G}_2, \mathbf{Q}_3, \ldots, \mathbf{G}_{n-1}, \mathbf{Q}_{n-1}$ are found such that $\mathbf{G}'_{n-1}\cdots\mathbf{G}'_2\mathbf{G}'_1\left(\mathbf{BQ}'_1\right)\mathbf{Q}'_2\cdots\mathbf{Q}'_{n-1}$ remains the bi-diagonal form. Therefore, $\mathbf{Q}_{n-1}\cdots\mathbf{Q}_1\left(\mathbf{B}'\mathbf{B}\right)\mathbf{Q}'_1\cdots\mathbf{Q}'_{n-1}$ remains the tri-diagonal form.

The first QR step for $\mathbf{B}$ is *implicitly* performed and shown below.

```
>> T45=[B(3,4)*B(3,4)+B(4,4)*B(4,4),B(4,4)*B(4,5);
        B(4,5)*B(4,4),               B(4,5)*B(4,5)+B(5,5)*B(5,5)]
=    3.7827    -0.1976
    -0.1976     4.0559

>> theta=eig2x2_(T45)
=    3.6790          0
          0     4.1596     %theta(2,2) is closer to T45(2,2).
>> [c,s]=givens_(B(1,1)*B(1,1)-theta(2,2),B(1,2)*B(1,1));
>> G1=eye(5);   G1(1:2,1:2)=[c,s;-s,c];
>> B=B*G1          %B(2,1) nonzero.
=   -1.0646    -2.1343          0          0          0
     2.3762     0.4140    -1.8662          0          0
          0          0    -2.5169    -0.8118          0
          0          0          0    -1.7674     0.1118
          0          0          0          0    -2.0108
>> [c,s]=givens_(B(1,1),B(2,1)); Q1=eye(5);   Q1(1:2,1:2)=[c,s;-s,c];
>> B=Q1'*B          %B(1,3) nonzero.
=   -2.6038    -1.2504     1.7031          0          0
          0     1.7785    -0.7630          0          0
          0          0    -2.5169    -0.8118          0
          0          0          0    -1.7674     0.1118
          0          0          0          0    -2.0108
```

```
>> [c,s]=givens_(B(1,2),B(1,3));   G2=eye(5);   G2(2:3,2:3)=[c,s;-s,c];
>> B=B*G2            %B(3,2) nonzero.
=   -2.6038    -2.1129         0         0         0
          0    -0.4375    -1.8852         0         0
          0     2.0288    -1.4896    -0.8118         0
          0         0         0    -1.7674     0.1118
          0         0         0         0    -2.0108
>> [c,s]=givens_(B(2,2),B(3,2));   Q2=eye(5);   Q2(2:3,2:3)=[c,s;-s,c];
>> B=Q2'*B            %B(2,4) nonzero.
=   -2.6038    -2.1129         0         0         0
          0    -2.0754     1.0586     0.7935         0
          0         0    -2.1569    -0.1711         0
          0         0         0    -1.7674     0.1118
          0         0         0         0    -2.0108
>> [c,s]=givens_(B(2,3),B(2,4));   G3=eye(5);   G3(3:4,3:4)=[c,s;-s,c];
>> B=B*G3            %B(4,3) nonzero.
=   -2.6038    -2.1129         0         0         0
          0    -2.0754     1.3230     0.0000         0
          0         0    -1.8285     1.1567         0
          0         0    -1.0601    -1.4142     0.1118
          0         0         0         0    -2.0108
>> [c,s]=givens_(B(3,3),B(4,3));   Q3=eye(5);   Q3(3:4,3:4)=[c,s;-s,c];
>> B=Q3'*B            %B(3,5) nonzero.
=   -2.6038    -2.1129         0         0         0
          0    -2.0754     1.3230     0.0000         0
          0         0    -2.1135     0.2914     0.0561
          0         0         0    -1.8036     0.0967
          0         0         0         0    -2.0108
>> [c,s]=givens_(B(3,4),B(3,5));   G4=eye(5);   G4(4:5,4:5)=[c,s;-s,c];
>> B=B*G4            %B(5,4) nonzero.
=   -2.6038    -2.1129         0         0         0
          0    -2.0754     1.3230     0.0000    -0.0000
          0         0    -2.1135     0.2967         0
          0         0         0    -1.7528     0.4359
          0         0         0    -0.3801    -1.9746
>> [c,s]=givens_(B(4,4),B(5,4));   Q4=eye(5);   Q4(4:5,4:5)=[c,s;-s,c];
>> B=Q4'*B            %B recovers bi-diagonal form.
=   -2.6038    -2.1129         0         0         0
          0    -2.0754     1.3230     0.0000    -0.0000
          0         0    -2.1135     0.2967         0
          0         0         0    -1.7936     0.0076
          0         0         0    -0.0000    -2.0221
```

It is clear that the two computations applied to **T** and **B** are equivalent. Especially the first column of the product of $G_1 G_2 G_3 G_4$ equals to $Q(:, 1)$. The diagonal of $B'B$ and **T** is same and the off-diagonals can have different signs.

```
>> G1*G2*G3*G4              %Compare with Q above. Columns can differ by +/-.
=   -0.1716    0.5830    0.6354    -0.4677     0.0900
    -0.9852   -0.1016   -0.1107     0.0815    -0.0157
          0   -0.8061    0.4736    -0.3486     0.0671
          0         0    0.5998     0.7857    -0.1512
          0         0         0     0.1890     0.9820
>> B'*B                     %Compare with T above. Off-diagonal can differ by +/-.
=    6.7797    5.5015         0         0         0
     5.5015    8.7716   -2.7458    -0.0000     0.0000
          0   -2.7458    6.2174    -0.6272    -0.0000
```

```
0    -0.0000    -0.6272    3.3049    -0.0136    %(4,5) reduced.
0     0.0000    -0.0000   -0.0136     4.0890
```

If the QR steps are repeatedly applied to **T**, **T** converges to a diagonal with entries of the square of the singular values of **A**. If the QR steps are applied equivalently to **B**, **B** converges to a diagonal with entries of the positive or negative of the singular values of **A**. For the negative entries, we take their absolute and move the negative to their left or right singular vectors. When a super-diagonal of **B** approaches zero, the **B** is deflated to two halves. The whole algorithm is concisely implemented in the following svdByQR_.m.

Algorithm 8.4

Singular value decomposition by QR iterations.

```
function [U,S,V] = svdByQR_(A,tol,format)

[m,n] = size_(A);
if (exist('tol','var') == 0) tol = sqrt(eps); end
if (~exist('format','var') || isempty(format)) format = 'long'; end
if (~strcmp(format,'brief')) fmt = 'short'; else fmt = 'brief'; end
if (~iscell(A))
    [U,S,V] = QBZbyHouseholder_(A,tol,fmt);
elseif (ischar(A{1}) && ~strcmp(A{1},'band'))
    [U,S,V] = QBZbyHouseholder_(A{2},tol,fmt);
elseif (ischar(A{1}) && strcmp(A{1},'band'))
    lbw = A{2}{2};   ubw = A{2}{3};   A = A{2}{1};
    if (lbw~=0 && ubw~=1)
        [U,S,V] = QBZbyHouseholder_(band2full_(A,lbw,ubw,m,n),tol,fmt);
    elseif (~strcmp(format,'brief'))
        U = eye(m);   V = eye(n);   S = A;
    else
        U = [];   V = [];   S = A;
    end
else
    error('svdByQR_:␣unknown␣matrix␣format.');
end
if (S(end,2) ~= 0) S = [S;[0,0]]; U = [U,orthogonal_(U)]; end

k = 1; l = size(S,1);   smax = max(max(abs(S(:,1))),max(abs(S(:,2))));
while (k < l)
    for i=l-1:-1:k                %find S(i,i)=0
        if (abs(S(i,1)) < tol*smax) break; end
    end
    if (abs(S(i,1)) < tol*smax)   %S(i,i)=0, Z'*S => S(i,:)=0, then deflate
        b = S(i,2);   S(i,2) = 0.0;
        for j=i+1:l
            [c,s] = givens_(S(j,1),b); %Z=[c,-s;s c]
            S(j,1) =-s*b + c*S(j,1);   b = s*S(j,2);   S(j,2) = c*S(j,2);
            if (~isempty(U))
                for p=1:size(U,1)
                    Upi = U(p,i);   Upj = U(p,j);
                    U(p,i) = Upi*c + Upj*s;   U(p,j) =-Upi*s + Upj*c;
                end
            end
        end
    end
    end
    for i=l:-1:2     %find block S(k:l,k:l) to apply QR
```

```
            if (abs(S(i-1,2)) > tol*(abs(S(i-1,1))+abs(S(i,1))))
                l = i; break;
            else
                S(i-1,2) = 0.0;  l = l - 1;
            end
        end
        k0 = k;  k = 1;
        for i=l:-1:2
            if (abs(S(i-1,2)) <= tol*(abs(S(i-1,1))+abs(S(i,1)))) k = i; break; end
        end
        if (k >= l) break; end
        if (k < k0) continue; end
        T11 = S(l-1,1)*S(l-1,1);          %apply QR step to S(k:l,k:l)
        if (k < l-1) T11 = T11 + S(l-1,2)*S(l-1,2); end
        T22 = S(l,1)*S(l,1) + S(l-1,2)*S(l-1,2);   T21 = S(l-1,1)*S(l-1,2);
        d = 0.5*(T11 - T22);   T21T21 = T21*T21;   e = sqrt(d*d + T21T21);
        if (d >= 0) miu = T22 - T21T21/(d+e); else miu = T22 - T21T21/(d-e); end
        a1 = S(k,1)*S(k,1)-miu; a2 = S(k,1)*S(k,2);
        [c,s] = givens_(a1,a2); b1 = S(k,1);   b2 = S(k,2);
        S(k,1) = b1*c - b2*s;   S(k,2) = b1*s + b2*c;
        a1 = S(k,1);   a2 =-S(k+1,1)*s;   S(k+1,1) = S(k+1,1)*c;
        if (~isempty(V))
            vk = V(k,:);
            V(k,:) = c*vk - s*V(k+1,:);   V(k+1,:) = s*vk + c*V(k+1,:);
        end
        for i=k:l-2
            [c,s] = givens_(a1,a2); b1 = S(i,2);   b2 = S(i+1,1);
            S(i,1) = c*a1 - s*a2;   S(i,2) = c*b1 - s*b2;   S(i+1,1) = s*b1 + c*b2;
            a1 = S(i,2);   a2 =-s*S(i+1,2);   S(i+1,2) = c*S(i+1,2);
            if (~isempty(U))
                ui = U(:,i);
                U(:,i) = ui*c - U(:,i+1)*s;   U(:,i+1) = ui*s + U(:,i+1)*c;
            end
            [c,s] = givens_(a1,a2); b1 = S(i+1,1);   b2 = S(i+1,2);
            S(i,2) = a1*c - a2*s;   S(i+1,1) = b1*c - b2*s;   S(i+1,2) = b1*s + b2*c;
            a1 = S(i+1,1);   a2 =-S(i+2,1)*s;   S(i+2,1) = S(i+2,1)*c;
            if (~isempty(V))
                vi1 = V(i+1,:);
                V(i+1,:) = c*vi1 - s*V(i+2,:);   V(i+2,:) = s*vi1 + c*V(i+2,:);
            end
        end
        [c,s] = givens_(a1,a2); b1 = S(l,1);   b2 = S(l-1,2);
        S(l-1,1) = c*a1 - s*a2;   S(l,1) = s*b2 + c*b1;   S(l-1,2) = c*b2 - s*b1;
        if (~isempty(U))
            ul1 = U(:,l-1);
            U(:,l-1) = ul1*c - U(:,l)*s;   U(:,l) = ul1*s + U(:,l)*c;
        end
    end

    for j=1:size(S,1)
        if (S(j,1) < 0)  %singular values >= 0
            S(j,1) =-S(j,1);
            if (~isempty(V)) V(j,:) =-V(j,:); end
        end
    end
    S = S(:,1);  [S,p] = sort(S,'descend');   mn = min(m,n);  l = size(S,1);
    if (~strcmp(format,'brief')) U = permute_(p,U,'col');   V = permute_(p,V,'row'); end
```

```
if (mn < 1) S = S(1:mn,:);   U = U(:,1:mn);   V = V(1:mn,:);   l = mn; end
if (strcmp(format,'long'))
    if (mn > 1) S = [S;zeros(mn-1,1)]; end
    S = diag(S);
    if (m > n) S = [S;zeros(m-n,n)]; end
    if (m < n) S = [S,zeros(m,n-m)]; end
    for j=l+1:m U = [U,orthogonal_(U)]; end
    for j=l+1:n V = [V;orthogonal_(V')']; end
end
```

Following three examples of medium sized full matrices demonstrate the efficiency and high accuracy of svdByQR_.m.

```
>> A=randn(500,800);   A(400:500,:)=randn(101)*A(100:200,:);
>> tic
>> [U,S,V]=svdByQR_(A,100*eps,'long');      %format='long'
>> toc
Elapsed time is 16.296169 seconds.
>> norm(U*S*V-A)
=   3.3387e-011            %A=U*S*V
>> norm(U'*U-eye(500))
=   4.1228e-014            %U'*U=I
>> norm(V*V'-eye(800))
=   3.8930e-014            %V*V'=I
>> norm(S(400:500,400:500))
=   1.5839e-013      %A has 101 zero singular values.
>> S(400,400)
=   8.9039e-014
>> S(500,500)
=   0

>> A=randn(800,500);   A(:,400:500)=A(:,100:200)*randn(101);
>> tic
>> [U,S,V]=svdByQR_(A,100*eps,'short');      %format='short'
>> toc
Elapsed time is 14.051717 seconds.
>> norm(U*diag(S)*V-A)
=   2.5835e-011
>> norm(U'*U-eye(399))
=   7.1262e-014            %A has 101 zero singular values.
>> norm(V*V'-eye(399))
=   7.5927e-014            %U,V do not include singular vectors w/ s=0.

>> A=randn(1000);
>> tic
>> [U,S,V]=svdByQR_(A,100*eps,'brief');      %format='brief', U,V not calculated.
>> toc
Elapsed time is 28.138716 seconds.
>> norm(S-svd(A))
=   2.6295e-011            %S equals MATLAB built-in svd
```

8.5 SPECIAL SVD ALGORITHMS OF BI-DIAGONAL MATRIX

Two special eigenvalue algorithms for symmetric tri-diagonal matrices are presented in Section 6.7, bisection algorithm and divide-conquer algorithm. The SVD of a bi-diagonal matrix **B** can be turned into an eigenvalue of a tri-diagonal matrix $\mathbf{T}$ as shown in Eqs. (8.1)–(8.4). Therefore, the two algorithms of Section 6.7 can be directly applied to the SVD of a bi-diagonal matrix. However, for both the efficiency and accuracy, the tri-diagonal matrices, $\mathbf{B'B}$, etc, in Eqs. (8.1)–(8.4), are not explicitly formed. The two special SVD algorithms for the bi-diagonal matrix are the adaption of the two algorithms of Section 6.7.

8.5.1 SVD BY BISECTION

svdBidByDet_.m listed below is the application of eigTridByDet_.m to the tri-diagonal matrix $\mathbf{B'B}$. For a 5×5 bi-diagonal $\mathbf{B}$, $\mathbf{B'B}$ is as follows:

$$\mathbf{B'B} = \begin{bmatrix} B_{11}^2 & B_{11}B_{12} & & & \\ B_{12}B_{11} & B_{12}^2 + B_{22}^2 & B_{22}B_{23} & & \\ & B_{23}B_{22} & B_{23}^2 + B_{33}^2 & B_{33}B_{34} & \\ & & B_{34}B_{33} & B_{34}^2 + B_{44}^2 & B_{44}B_{45} \\ & & & B_{45}B_{55} & B_{45}^2 + B_{55}^2 \end{bmatrix}.$$

svdBidByDet_.m accesses the components of $\mathbf{B'B}$ as the above equation shows without forming the tri-diagonal $\mathbf{B'B}$ explicitly. Refer to Section 6.7.1 for a more detailed discussion of the bisection algorithm and eigTridByDet_.m.

Algorithm 8.5

Singular value decomposition by bisection.

```
function S = svdBidByDet_(B,tol,flst,last)

[m,n] = size(B);
if (B(m,2) ~= 0) B = [B;[0,0]]; m = m + 1; flst = flst + 1; last = last + 1; end

%Gershgorin estimation of eig(B'*B)
B2 = B.*B;   r1 = abs(B(1,1)*B(1,2)); smin = B2(1,1)-r1;   smax = B2(1,1)+r1;
for j=2:m-1
    r2 = abs(B(j,1)*B(j,2));   o = B2(j,1) + B2(j-1,2);
    smin = min(smin, o-r1-r2);   smax = max(smax,o+r1+r2);   r1 = r2;
end
r2 = abs(B(m,1)*B(m-1,2));   o = B2(m,1) + B2(m-1,2);
smin = min(smin, o-r2);   smax = max(smax, o+r2);

Smin(1:last-flst+1,1) = smin;   Smax(1:last-flst+1,1) = smax;
S(1:last-flst+1,1) = 0.5*(smin+smax);

for j=last:-1:flst  %calculate S(1:last-flst+1) = [Sk,...,Sl]
    sminj = Smin(j-flst+1);   smaxj = Smax(j-flst+1);   sj = 0.5*(sminj+smaxj);
    while (smaxj-sminj > 2.0*eps*(abs(sminj)+abs(smaxj)) + tol)
        a = 0;   t = sj;   q = B2(1,1) - t;
        if (q < 0) a = a + 1; end
        for i=2:m
            if(q ~= 0) t = t*B2(i-1,2)/q+sj; else t = t*B2(i-1,2)/eps+sj; end
            q = B2(i,1) - t;
            if (q < 0) a = a + 1; end
        end
        if (a < flst)
            for i=flst:j
                if (Smin(i-flst+1) < sj) Smin(i-flst+1) = sj; end
```

```
            end
        elseif (f1st<=a && a<j)
            for i=f1st:a
                if (Smax(i-f1st+1) > sj) Smax(i-f1st+1) = sj; end
            end
            for i=a+1:j
                if (Smin(i-f1st+1) < sj) Smin(i-f1st+1) = sj; end
            end
        else %a>=j
            for i=f1st:j
                if (Smax(i-f1st+1) > sj) Smax(i-f1st+1) = sj; end
            end
        end
        sminj = Smin(j-f1st+1);  smaxj = Smax(j-f1st+1);  sj = 0.5*(sminj+smaxj);
    end  %while(smaxj-sminj > 2.0*eps*(abs(sminj)+abs(smaxj)) + tol)
    S(j-f1st+1) = sj;
end
```

The input matrix to svdBidByDet_.m must be in a band format with lbw=0,ubw=1. The use of svdBidByDet_.m is illustrated with the following examples.

```
>> A=randn(1000);
>> [Q,B,Z]=[Q,B,Z]=QBZbyHouseholder_(A,100*eps,'brief');
%format='brief',Q,Z not calculated.
>> S=svdBidByDet_(B,100*eps);
>> tic
>> S=svdBidByDet_(B,100*eps);
>> toc
Elapsed time is 3.115636 seconds.
>> tic
>> s=svd(A);      %MATLAB built-in svd function.
>> toc
Elapsed time is 1.977421 seconds.
>> norm(s-S)
=  1.1328e-012    %S equals MATLAB built-in svd
```

If only the first eight singular values are needed, the input to svdBidByDet_.m is as follows. The singular values are ordered from small to large.

```
>> Sa=svdBidByDet_(B,100*eps,1,8)'        %f1st=1,last=8.
Sa = 0.3454    0.3212    0.2726    0.2023    0.1642    0.0979    0.0772    0.0377
>> s(991:1000)'    %MATLAB svd.
=    0.3454    0.3212    0.2726    0.2023    0.1642    0.0979    0.0772    0.0377
```

The last eight singular values are calculated similarly.

```
>> Sb=svdBidByDet_(B,100*eps,993,1000)'    %f1st=993,last=1000.
Sb = 62.7253    62.3645    62.1172    61.9164    61.5313    61.2801    61.1762    60.9062
>> s(1:10)'      %MATLAB svd.
=    62.7253    62.3645    62.1172    61.9164    61.5313    61.2801    61.1762    60.9062
```

8.5.2 A DIVIDE-AND-CONQUER ALGORITHM

For the details of the divide-and-conquer algorithm for the symmetric tri-diagonal matrix, see Section 6.7.2. We take a 6×6 bi-diagonal matrix to illustrate the divide-and-conquer algorithm for its SVD,

$$\mathbf{B} = \begin{bmatrix} \begin{array}{cc|c} B_{11} & B_{12} & \\ & B_{22} & B_{23} \\ & & 0 & 0 \\ \hline & & & B_{44} & B_{45} \\ & & & & B_{55} & B_{56} \\ & & & & & B_{66} \end{array} \end{bmatrix} + \begin{bmatrix} & & B_{33} & B_{34} & \\ & & & & \end{bmatrix}$$

$$= \begin{bmatrix} \mathbf{B}_1 & \\ \hline & \mathbf{B}_2 \end{bmatrix} + B_{33} \begin{bmatrix} \mathbf{I}_3 \\ \mathbf{0} \end{bmatrix} [\, \mathbf{I}_3' \,|\, \mathbf{0}' \,] + B_{34} \begin{bmatrix} \mathbf{I}_3 \\ \mathbf{0} \end{bmatrix} [\, \mathbf{0}' \,|\, \mathbf{I}_1' \,]$$

$$= \begin{bmatrix} \mathbf{U}_1 \mathbf{S}_1 \mathbf{V}_1 & \\ \hline & \mathbf{U}_2 \mathbf{S}_2 \mathbf{V}_2 \end{bmatrix} + B_{33} \begin{bmatrix} \mathbf{I}_3 \\ \mathbf{0} \end{bmatrix} [\, \mathbf{I}_3' \,|\, \mathbf{0}' \,] + B_{34} \begin{bmatrix} \mathbf{I}_3 \\ \mathbf{0} \end{bmatrix} [\, \mathbf{0}' \,|\, \mathbf{I}_1' \,]$$

$$= \begin{bmatrix} \mathbf{U}_1 & \\ & \mathbf{U}_2 \end{bmatrix} \left(\begin{bmatrix} \mathbf{S}_1 & \\ & \mathbf{S}_2 \end{bmatrix} + \begin{bmatrix} \mathbf{U}_1' & \\ & \mathbf{U}_2' \end{bmatrix} \begin{bmatrix} \mathbf{I}_3 \\ \mathbf{0} \end{bmatrix} [\, B_{33} \mathbf{I}_3' \,|\, B_{34} \mathbf{I}_1' \,] \begin{bmatrix} \mathbf{V}_1' & \\ & \mathbf{V}_2' \end{bmatrix} \right) \begin{bmatrix} \mathbf{V}_1 & \\ & \mathbf{V}_2 \end{bmatrix}$$

$$= \begin{bmatrix} \mathbf{U}_1 & \\ & \mathbf{U}_2 \end{bmatrix} \left(\begin{bmatrix} \mathbf{S}_1 & \\ & \mathbf{S}_2 \end{bmatrix} + \begin{bmatrix} \mathbf{I}_3 \\ \mathbf{0} \end{bmatrix} [\, B_{33} \mathbf{V}_1(:,3)' \,|\, B_{34} \mathbf{V}_2(:,1)' \,] \right) \begin{bmatrix} \mathbf{V}_1 & \\ & \mathbf{V}_2 \end{bmatrix}.$$

In the above equations $\mathbf{B}_1 = \mathbf{U}_1 \mathbf{S}_1 \mathbf{V}_1$ and $\mathbf{B}_2 = \mathbf{U}_2 \mathbf{S}_2 \mathbf{V}_2$ are SVDs. $\mathbf{S}_1$ and $\mathbf{S}_2$ are diagonal and are denoted as follows:

$$\mathbf{S}_1 = \begin{bmatrix} S_1(1) & & \\ & S_1(2) & \\ & & 0 \end{bmatrix}, \qquad \mathbf{S}_2 = \begin{bmatrix} S_2(1) & & \\ & S_2(2) & \\ & & S_2(3) \end{bmatrix}.$$

Because $S_1(3) = 0$, we have $\mathbf{U}_1' \mathbf{I}_3 = \mathbf{I}_3$. This important relation is used in the last line of the above equations. The term in the parenthesis of the last line is written as follows, where $\mathbf{z}(1:3)' = B_{33} \mathbf{V}_1(:,3)'$ and $\mathbf{z}(4:6)' = B_{34} \mathbf{V}_2(:,1)'$:

$$\mathbf{E} = \begin{bmatrix} S_1(1) & & & & & \\ & S_1(2) & & & & \\ z_1 & z_2 & z_3 & z_4 & z_5 & z_6 \\ & & & S_2(1) & & \\ & & & & S_2(2) & \\ & & & & & S_2(3) \end{bmatrix}.$$

If we can find the SVD of $\mathbf{E}$, $\mathbf{E} = \mathbf{U}_3 \mathbf{S} \mathbf{V}_3$, then the SVD of $\mathbf{B}$ is simply

$$\mathbf{B} = \begin{bmatrix} \mathbf{U}_1 & \\ & \mathbf{U}_2 \end{bmatrix} \mathbf{U}_3 \mathbf{S} \mathbf{V}_3 \begin{bmatrix} \mathbf{V}_1 & \\ & \mathbf{V}_2 \end{bmatrix} = \mathbf{U} \mathbf{S} \mathbf{V}.$$

The SVD of $\mathbf{E}$ can be found by the eigenvalue decomposition of $\mathbf{E}'\mathbf{E} = \mathbf{V}_3' \mathbf{S}^2 \mathbf{V}_3$. However, $\mathbf{E}'\mathbf{E}$ has the following form:

$$\mathbf{E}'\mathbf{E} = \begin{bmatrix} \mathbf{S}_1^2 & \\ & \mathbf{S}_2^2 \end{bmatrix} + \mathbf{z}\mathbf{z}' + \begin{bmatrix} \mathbf{S}_1 & \\ & \mathbf{S}_2 \end{bmatrix} \begin{bmatrix} \mathbf{I}_3 \\ \mathbf{0} \end{bmatrix} \mathbf{z}' + \mathbf{z} [\, \mathbf{I}_3' \ \mathbf{0}' \,] \begin{bmatrix} \mathbf{S}_1 & \\ & \mathbf{S}_2 \end{bmatrix} = \begin{bmatrix} \mathbf{S}_1^2 & \\ & \mathbf{S}_2^2 \end{bmatrix} + \mathbf{z}\mathbf{z}'.$$

In the above equation, the last two terms of the first equality vanish because $S_1(3) = 0$ and $\mathbf{S}_1 \mathbf{i}_3 = \mathbf{0}$. This form of $\mathbf{E}'\mathbf{E}$ is same as Eq. (6.20) and therefore its eigenvalue decomposition can be solved by `eigDiagByR1U_.m`, see Section 6.7.2 for the formulation and implementation. However, for the numerical accuracy, $\mathbf{E}'\mathbf{E}$ is not explicitly formed as it is shown. The SVD of $\mathbf{E}$ is calculated directly based on $\mathbf{E}$. The MATLAB implementation `svdDiagByR1U_.m` is an adaptation of `eigDiagByR1U_.m`.

Algorithm 8.6

Singular value decomposition of a diagonal plus a rank-1 matrix.

```
function [U,S,V] = svdDiagByR1U_(D,z,tol,format)

m = length(D);
S = sort(D,'ascend');
if (strcmp(format,'brief')) U = [];  V = [];
else                        U = eye(m);  V = U; end

zmax = max(abs(z));  dmax = max(max(D),zmax);
if (zmax < tol*dmax) return; end

%P1*(diag(D)+I(:,k)*z')*P1'=diag(D)+I(:,1)*z': D(1)=0,D ascending
[D,p1] = sort(D,'ascend');  z = permute_(p1,z);  p1 = inv_perm_(p1);

Hp = [];  Hv = zeros(m,1);  j = 2;      %zero z(j+1:k) if D(j:k) equals
while (j < m)
    for k=j+1:m
        if (D(k)-D(j) > tol*dmax) k = k - 1;  break; end
    end
    if (k-j>0 && D(k)-D(j)<tol*dmax)    %D(j:k-1)=D(j)
        [h,alpha,beta] = householder_(z(j:k));   %H*(D+I(:,1)*z')*H'=D+I(:,1)*z'
        z(j) = beta;  z(j+1:k) = 0.0;            %H*I(:,1)=I(:,1), z(j:k)'*H'=[zj,0]
        Hp = [Hp;[j,k]];  Hv(j:k) = h;  Hv(j) = alpha;   %save Householder data
    end
    j = k + 1;
end
Gp = [];  Gv = zeros(m,2);              %zero z(j) if D(j)=0
for j = 2:m
    if (D(j) < tol*dmax)
        [c,s] = givens_(z(1),z(j));              %G=[c,s;-s,c]
        z(1) = z(1)*c - z(j)*s;  z(j) = 0.0;     %[0,0;0,Dj]*G=0; [z1,zj]*G=[z1,0]
        Gp = [Gp;j];  Gv(j,1) = c;  Gv(j,2) = s;         %save Givens data
    end
end

p2 = 1:m;  l = m;    %P2: permute all z(j)=0 to the bottom
for j=2:m
    if (abs(z(j)) < tol*dmax)
        while(l>0 && abs(z(l))<tol*dmax) l = l - 1; end
        if (l > j)
            z(j) = z(l);  z(l) = 0.0;
            p2j = p2(j);  p2(j) = p2(l);  p2(l) = p2j;
            l = l - 1;
        end
    end
end
D = permute_(p2,D);       %apply same permututation to D

S(l+1:m) = D(l+1:m);      %z(l+1:m)=0, diag(D(1:l))+I(:,1)*z(1:l)' standard form.
[D,p3] = sort(D(1:l),'ascend');  z = permute_(p3,z(1:l));
p3 = [inv_perm_(p3)',l+1:m];
D2 = D.*D;  z2 = z.*z;  D2 = [D2; D2(l)+z'*z];

for j=1:l
    s = 0.5*(D2(j)+D2(j+1));
```

```
      f = 1.0;
      for k=1:l f = f + z2(k)/(D2(k)-s); end
      if (f > 0.0) dj = D2(j); else dj = D2(j+1); end
      dD = D2 - dj;      etamin = max(eps,max(tol*dj,tol*(D2(j+1)-D2(j))));
      eta = 0.5*(s+dj) - dj;
      f1 = 0.0;    f2 = 0.0;
      for k=1:j f1 = f1 + z2(k)/(dD(k)-eta); end
      for k=j+1:l f2 = f2 + z2(k)/(dD(k)-eta); end
      f = 1.0 + f1 + f2;
      while (abs(f) > tol*l*(1.0+abs(f1)+abs(f2)))
          df1 = 0.0;    df2 = 0.0;
          for k=1:j df1 = df1 + z2(k)/(dD(k)-eta)^2; end
          for k=j+1:l df2 = df2 + z2(k)/(dD(k)-eta)^2; end
          c1 = (dD(j)-eta)^2 * df1;
          c2 = (dD(j+1)-eta)^2 * df2;
          c3 = 1.0 + f1-c1/(dD(j)-eta) + f2-c2/(dD(j+1)-eta);
          a = c3;
          b =-c1 - c2 - c3*dD(j) - c3*dD(j+1);
          c = c1*dD(j+1) + c2*dD(j) + c3*dD(j)*dD(j+1);
          if (b > 0) eta = -0.5*(b+sqrt(b*b-4.0*a*c))/a;
          else       eta = -2.0*c/(b-sqrt(b*b-4.0*a*c));   end
          f1 = 0.0;    f2 = 0.0;
          for k=1:j f1 = f1 + z2(k)/(dD(k)-eta); end
          for k=j+1:l f2 = f2 + z2(k)/(dD(k)-eta); end
          f = 1.0 + f1 + f2;
      end
      if (abs(eta) < etamin) eta = sign(eta)*etamin; end      %interlacing
      S(j) = eta + dj;
end

if (~strcmp(format,'brief'))        %U,V by Ming Gu & Stanley Eisenstat method
    u = zeros(l,1);   v = zeros(l,1);
    for j=1:l
        d1 = 1.0;    d2 = 1.0;
        for k=1:j-1 d1 = d1*(S(k)-D2(j))/(D2(k)-D2(j)); end
        for k=j+1:l d2 = d2*(S(k)-D2(j))/(D2(k)-D2(j)); end
        z(j) = sign(z(j))*sqrt(d1*d2*(S(j)-D2(j)));
    end
    for j=1:l
        for k=1:l v(k) = z(k)/(D2(k)-S(j)); end
        u = D.*v;   u(1) =-1;
        U(1:l,j) = u/norm(u);   V(j,1:l) = v'/norm(v);
    end
    S(1:l) = sqrt(S(1:l));    [S,p4] = sort(S,'descend');

    %U = P1*H*P2*P3*U*P4';    V = P4*V*P3'*P2'*G'*H'*P1'
    U = permute_(p4,U,'col');   V = permute_(p4,V,'row');
    p3 = permute_(p2,p3);
    U = permute_(p3,U,'row');   V = permute_(p3,V,'col');
    for k=1:size(Gp)
        j = Gp(k);  c = Gv(j,1);  s = Gv(j,2);  V1 = V(:,1);
        V(:,1) = c*V1 + s*V(:,j);  V(:,j) = -s*V1 + c*V(:,j);
    end
    for l=1:size(Hp,1)
        j = Hp(l,1);  k = Hp(l,2);
        h = Hv(j:k); h(1) = 1.0;  alpha = Hv(j);  alphah = alpha*h;
        U(j:k,:) = U(j:k,:) - alphah*(h'*U(j:k,:));
```

```
        V(:,j:k) = V(:,j:k) - (V(:,j:k)*h)*alphah';
    end
    U = permute_(p1,U,'row');   V = permute_(p1,V,'col');
else       %if(strcmp(format,'brief'))
    S(1:l) = sqrt(S(1:l));     S = sort(S,'descend');
end
```

From the above discussion, we know the following way to split **B** does not work:

$$
\mathbf{B} =
\left[
\begin{array}{ccc|ccc}
B_{11} & B_{12} & & & & \\
 & B_{22} & B_{23} & & & \\
 & & B_{33} & & & \\
\hline
 & & & B_{44} & B_{45} & \\
 & & & & B_{55} & B_{56} \\
 & & & & & B_{66}
\end{array}
\right]
+
\left[
\begin{array}{c|c}
 & B_{34} \\
\hline
 & \\
\end{array}
\right]
$$

$$
=
\left[
\begin{array}{c|c}
\mathbf{B}_1 & \\
\hline
 & \mathbf{B}_2
\end{array}
\right]
+ B_{34}
\left[
\begin{array}{c}
\mathbf{I}_3 \\
\mathbf{0}
\end{array}
\right]
\left[\, \mathbf{0}' \,|\, \mathbf{I}_1' \,\right]
$$

$$
=
\left[
\begin{array}{c|c}
\mathbf{U}_1\mathbf{S}_1\mathbf{V}_1 & \\
\hline
 & \mathbf{U}_2\mathbf{S}_2\mathbf{V}_2
\end{array}
\right]
+ B_{34}
\left[
\begin{array}{c}
\mathbf{I}_3 \\
\mathbf{0}
\end{array}
\right]
\left[\, \mathbf{0}' \,|\, \mathbf{I}_1' \,\right]
$$

$$
=
\left[
\begin{array}{cc}
\mathbf{U}_1 & \\
 & \mathbf{U}_2
\end{array}
\right]
\left(
\left[
\begin{array}{cc}
\mathbf{S}_1 & \\
 & \mathbf{S}_2
\end{array}
\right]
+
\left[
\begin{array}{cc}
\mathbf{U}_1' & \\
 & \mathbf{U}_2'
\end{array}
\right]
\left[
\begin{array}{c}
\mathbf{I}_3 \\
\mathbf{0}
\end{array}
\right]
\left[\, \mathbf{0}' \,|\, B_{34}\mathbf{I}_1' \,\right]
\left[
\begin{array}{cc}
\mathbf{V}_1' & \\
 & \mathbf{V}_2'
\end{array}
\right]
\right)
\left[
\begin{array}{cc}
\mathbf{V}_1 & \\
 & \mathbf{V}_2
\end{array}
\right]
$$

$$
=
\left[
\begin{array}{cc}
\mathbf{U}_1 & \\
 & \mathbf{U}_2
\end{array}
\right]
\left(
\left[
\begin{array}{cc}
\mathbf{S}_1 & \\
 & \mathbf{S}_2
\end{array}
\right]
+
\left[
\begin{array}{c}
\mathbf{U}_1(3,:)' \\
\mathbf{0}
\end{array}
\right]
\left[\, \mathbf{0}' \;\; B_{34}\mathbf{V}_2(:,1)' \,\right]
\right)
\left[
\begin{array}{cc}
\mathbf{V}_1 & \\
 & \mathbf{V}_2
\end{array}
\right].
$$

If we still denote the term in the parenthesis as $\mathbf{E}$, $\mathbf{E}'\mathbf{E}$ is not in the form of Eq. (6.20), because now $S_1(3) \neq 0$ and $\mathbf{U}_1'\mathbf{i}_3 \neq \mathbf{i}_3$.

For an arbitrary size of a bi-diagonal matrix, it can be recursively split until the trivial 1×1, 1×2, or 2×2 matrix or some specified small size matrix. The SVD of the bi-diagonal matrix of the specified small size can be solved by any algorithms that are presented in previous sections. The SVD of the whole matrix is related to the SVDs of the split ones by those of **E**s. This type of algorithm is recursive. `svdBidByR1U_.m` is an adaptation of `eigTridByR1U_.m`.

Algorithm 8.7

Singular value decomposition of bi-diagonal matrix by divide-and-conquer.

```
function [U,S,V] = svdBidByR1U_(B,tol,format)

[m,n] = size(B);  l = 4;  %or any #<=m
if (mod(m,2)) k = (m+1)/2; else k = m/2; end        %B to 2 halves + 1

if (m==1 && B(1,2)==0)
    S = abs(B(1,1));   U - 1.0;  V - 1.0;
    if (B(1,1) < 0.0) V =-1.0; end
elseif (m == 1)
    s1 = norm(B);  v1 = B/s1;  v2= randn(1,2);  v2 = v2 - (v2*v1')*v1;
    S  = [s1, 0];  U = 1.0;  V = [v1;v2/norm(v2)];
elseif (m == 2)
    [U,S,V] = svd2x2_([B(1,1),B(1,2);0.0,B(2,1)]);
elseif (m<=l || m+1<l)
    [U,S,V] = svdByQR_({'band',{B,0,1,m,m}},tol,'long');   S = diag(S);
```

```
elseif(abs(B(k,2)) < tol*(abs(B(k,1))+abs(B(k+1,1))))
      [U1,S1,V1] = svdBidByR1U_(B(1:k,:),   tol,format);
      [U2,S2,V2] = svdBidByR1U_(B(k+1:m,:),tol,format);
      [S,p] = sort([S1;S2],'descend');
      if (~strcmp(format,'brief'))
            U = [U1,zeros(k,m-k);zeros(m-k,k),U2];  U = permute_(p,U,'col');
            V = [V1,zeros(k,m-k);zeros(m-k,k),V2];  V = permute_(p,V,'row');
      else
            U = [];  V = [V1(:,1), V2(:,end)];
      end
else       %recursive svdBidByR1U_
      alpha = B(k,1);  beta = B(k,2);  B(k,1:2) = 0;
      [U1,S1,V1] = svdBidByR1U_(B(1:k,:),tol,format);  S1(k) = 0;
      [U2,S2,V2] = svdBidByR1U_(B(k+1:m,:),tol,format);
      [U,S,V] = svdDiagByR1U_([S1;S2],[alpha*V1(:,end);beta*V2(:,1)],tol,'long');
      if (~strcmp(format,'brief'))
            U1(k,k) = 1;    %U1(k,k)=-1 not good for svdBidByR1U_
            U(1:k,:) = U1*U(1:k,:);   U(k+1:m,:) = U2*U(k+1:m,:);
            V(:,1:k) = V(:,1:k)*V1;   V(:,k+1:m) = V(:,k+1:m)*V2;
      else
            U = [];  V = [V(:,1:k)*V1(:,1),V(:,k+1:m)*V2(:,end)];
      end
end
```

The input matrix to svdBidByR1U_.m must be in a band format with lbw=0,ubw=1. The use of svdBidByR1U_.m is illustrated with the following examples.

```
>> A=randn(1000);
>> [Q,B,Z]=QBZbyHouseholder_(A,100*eps,'long');  %format='long', B in full format.
>> B=full2band_(B,0,1);                          %convert B to band format.
>> tic
>> [U,S,V]=svdBidByR1U_(B,100*eps,'long');
>> toc
Elapsed time is 3.361023 seconds.
>> norm(U*diag(S)*V-band2full_(B,0,1))
=   1.4931e-005
>> norm(U'*U-eye(1000))
=   7.4167e-015
>> norm(V*V'-eye(1000))
=   7.0666e-015
>> U=Q*U;
>> V=V*Z;
>> norm(U*diag(S)*V-A)
=   1.4931e-005
>> norm(U'*U-eye(1000))
=   7.7232e-015
>> norm(V*V'-eye(1000))
=   7.2658e-015

>> [Q,B,Z]=QBZbyHouseholder_(A,100*eps,'brief');  %B in band format, Q,Z not
                                                                 calculated.
>> tic
>> [U,S,V]=svdBidByR1U_(B,100*eps,'brief');       %U,V not calculated.
>> toc
Elapsed time is 2.125435 seconds.
>> tic
>> s=svd(A);                                      %MATLAB built in svd
```

```
>> toc
Elapsed time is 1.923082 seconds.
>> norm(S-s)
=  6.7893e-008            %S equals MATLAB built in svd.
```

8.6 LANCZOS ALGORITHM FOR SVD

In the Lanczos algorithm for the symmetric eigenvalues decomposition, eigByLanczos_.m, we perform a partial QTQt decomposition to a symmetric matrix **A** and obtain a symmetric tri-diagonal matrix **T**. The eigenvalues of **T** are used to approximate the eigenvalues of **A**. To improve the efficiency and accuracy, we have to consider the orthogonality, restart, and lock and purge. See Section 7.3.

The Lanczos algorithm for SVD is based on Eqs. (8.7) and (8.8). In svdByLanczos_.m, we perform a partial QBZ decomposition to an arbitrary matrix **A** and obtain a bi-diagonal matrix **B**. The singular values of **B** are used to approximate the singular values of **A**. To improve the efficiency and accuracy, all the considerations for eigByLanczos_.m should be equally applied in svdByLanczos_.m.

However, in svdByLanczos_.m listed below, the more complicated implicit restart and picking of singular values are not implemented. As a result, the code is remarkably concise, less than 60 lines, which has the benefits of presenting the Lanczos SVD algorithm more clearly. A more complete implementation of svdByLanczos_.m is considered for a future edition. Refer to the comments in svdByLanczos_.m and the subsequent examples for the meanings of the input arguments.

Algorithm 8.8

Singular value decomposition by Lanczos algorithm.

```
%A*V'-U*diag(S), U'*U=I, V*V'=I by Lanczos. z: initial arbitrary vector A*z'.
%ns: =length(S), S output. l: # of Lanczos steps.
%Input U,S,V previous run of svdByLanczos_; Output U,S,V appended to Input U,S,V.
function [U,S,V] = svdByLanczos_(A,z,tol,ns,l,U,S,V)

[m,n] = size_(A);   normA = max(1.0,norm(Ay_(A,ones(n,1))));    %est. norm(A)
if (~exist('z','var') || isempty(z)) z = ones(1,n); end         %=randn(1,n)
if (size(z,2) == 1) z = z'; end
if (~exist('tol','var') || isempty(tol)) tol = sqrt(eps); end
if (~exist('ns','var') || isempty(ns)) ns = min(m,n); end
if (~exist('l','var') || isempty(l)) l = min(m,n); end
if (l > min(m,n)) l = min(m,n); end
if (ns > l) ns = l; end
if (~exist('U','var') || isempty(U)) U = []; end
if (~exist('S','var') || isempty(S)) S = []; end
if (~exist('V','var') || isempty(V)) V = []; end
[ns0,ns1] = size(S);   [mu,nu] = size(U);   [mv,nv] = size(V);
if (ns0~=nu || ns0~=mv || (ns0>0 && (mu~=m || nv~=n)))
    error('svdByLanczos_:Input singular values and vectors size differ.');
end
if (ns1 == 1) S = [S,zeros(ns0,1)]; end
if (l < n) ll = l + 1; else ll = n; end

while(1)
    if (ns0 > 0) z = z - (z*V')*V; end
    normz = norm(z);
    if (normz > tol) z = z/norm(z);   break;
```

```
          else              z = randn(1,n);  end
    end
    [Q,S,Z] = QBZbyLanczos_(A,tol,'short',ns0+1,ns0+1,U,S,[V;z]);
    beta = S(ns0+1,2);  S(ns0+1,2) = 0;
    while(ns0 < ns)
        [X,sita,Y] = svdByQR_({'band',{S(ns0+1:ns0+1,:),0,1,1,1}},tol,'short');
%       [X,sita,Y] = svdBdByR1U_(S(ns0+1:ns0+1,:),tol,'long ');
        sc = realmax; ott = 0.0;  ls = 0;  lo = 0;  ns1 = ns0;
        for j=1:l
            normA = max(normA,abs(sita(j)));  ds = abs(beta*X(1,j));
            if (ds < tol*normA)
                U = [U,Q(:,ns0+1:ns0+1)*X(:,j)];   V = [V;Y(j,:)*Z(ns0+1:ns0+1,:)];
                ns1 = ns1 + 1;  S(ns1,1:2) = [sita(j),0];  continue;
            end
            if (ds < sc)  sc = ds;  ls = j; end          %min residual
            if (sita(j) > ott) ott = sita(j);  lo = j; end     %max singular value
        end
        if (ns1 >= ns) break; end
        z = Y(ls,:)*Z(ns0+1:ns0+1,:);                    %explicit restart
        ns0 = ns1;
        while(1)
            if (ns0 > 0) z = z - (z*V')*V; end
            normz = norm(z);
            if (normz > tol) z = z/normz;  break;
            else            z = randn(1,n); end
        end
        [Q,S,Z] = QBZbyLanczos_(A,tol,'short',ns0+1,ns0+1,U(:,1:ns0),S(1:ns0,:),
                                                        [V(1:ns0,:);z]);
        beta = S(ns0+1,2);   S(ns0+1,2) = 0;
    end
    S = S(1:ns1,1);
```

The use of svdByLanczos_.m is demonstrated in the following two examples.
The first example is a full non-square matrix.

```
>> B=randn(1000,101);   z = randn(101,1);
>> s = svd(B);
>> s(1:8)'         %f1st 8 largest singular values by MATLAB svd.
=  41.2682    41.1019    40.2503    39.8087    39.6425    39.4702    38.9679    38.7160
>> s(94:101)'      %last 8 smallest nonzero singular values by MATLAB svd.
=  23.6515    23.4801    23.2248    23.1368    22.9422    22.3238    22.2458    21.4877
>> [U,S,V]=svdByLanczos_(B,z,100*eps,8,20);
>> S'             %8 singular values obtained by z.
=  41.1019    21.4877    41.2682    22.2458    40.2503    22.3238    39.8087    38.9679
>> [U,S,V]=svdByLanczos_(B,randn(101,1),100*eps,8,20);
>> S'             %8 singular values obtained by randn(101,1).
=  41.1019    41.2682    40.2503    39.8087    21.4877    39.6425    22.2458    22.3238
>> [U,S,V]=svdByLanczos_(B',randn(1000,1),100*eps,8,20);
>> S'             %8 singular values obtained by B' and randn(1000,1).
=  41.1019    41.2682    40.2503    39.8087    39.6425    38.7160    39.4702    38.9679
>> [U,S,V]=svdByLanczos_(B',randn(1000,1),100*eps,16,40,U,S,V);   %restart
>> S(1:8)'         %f1st 8 has no change from the previous.
=  41.1019    41.2682    40.2503    39.8087    39.6425    38.7160    39.4702    38.9679
>> S(9:16)'         %8 more singular values calculated.
=  21.4877    22.2458    38.4422    38.3187    38.0206    37.7949    37.8942    37.4485
>> norm(U'*U-eye(16))
=  9.3328e-015    %U'*U=I
```

```
>> norm(V*V'-eye(16))
=   9.3328e-015      %V*V'=I
>> norm(B'*V'-U*diag(S))
=   2.8791e-012     %correct U,S,V
```

In the second example, we interpret the non-square matrix **B** in the first example as a band matrix with a lower bandwidth of 40 and a upper bandwidth of 60. We store the band matrix as a full matrix **A** and a sparse matrix **C**.

```
>> A=band2full_(B,40,60,1000,1000);     %full format
>> [dA,rA,jA]=full2csr_(A);
>> B = {'band',{B,40,60,1000,1000}};    %band format
>> C = {'csr',{dA,rA,jA}};              %csr format
>> z = randn(1000,1);                   %initial vector for Lanczos
```

The SVD of the same 1000×1000 matrix is calculated with the three formats, full, band, and sparse.

```
>> [U1,S1,V1]=svdByLanczos_(A,z,100*eps,8,20);              %full
>> [U1,S1,V1]=svdByLanczos_(A,z,100*eps,16,50,U1,S1,V1);   %restart
>> [U2,S2,V2]=svdByLanczos_(B,z,100*eps,8,20);              %band
>> [U2,S2,V2]=svdByLanczos_(B,z,100*eps,16,50,U2,S2,V2);   %restart
>> [U3,S3,V3]=svdByLanczos_(C,z,100*eps,8,20);              %csr
>> [U3,S3,V3]=svdByLanczos_(C,z,100*eps,16,50,U3,S3,V3);   %restart

>> norm(U1'*U1-eye(16))
=   4.6736e-015
>> norm(V1*V1'-eye(16))
=   7.8687e-015
>> norm(A*V1'-U1*diag(S1))
=   2.3208e-012
>> norm(U2'*U2-eye(16))
=   2.6977e-015
>> norm(V2*V2'-eye(16))
=   4.7151e-015
>> norm(A*V2'-U2*diag(S2))
=   2.4361e-012
>> norm(U3'*U3-eye(16))
=   2.6977e-015
>> norm(V3*V3'-eye(16))
=   4.7151e-015
>> norm(A*V3'-U3*diag(S3))
=   2.4361e-012
```

Bibliography

REFERENCES

1. Aasen JO. On the reduction of a symmetric matrix to tridiagonal form. BIT 1971;11:233–42.
2. Althoen Steven C, Mclaughlin Renate. Gauss-jordan reduction: A brief history. Amer Math Monthly 1987;94:130–42.
3. Anderson E, Bai Z, Bischof C, Demmel J, Dongarra J, Ducroz J, et al. LAPACK UsersǴuide, Release 2.0. 2nd ed. Philadelphia (Pennsylvania): SIAM; 1999.
4. Arnold Douglas N. Mixed finite element methods for elliptic problems. Comput Methods Appl Mech Engrg 1990;82:281–300.
5. Bai Zhaojun, Demmel James, Dongarra Jack, Ruhe Axel, van der Vorst Henk. Templates for the solution of algebraic eigenvalue problems: a practical guide. Philadelphia (Pennsylvania): SIAM; 2000.
6. Bai Zhaojun, Demmel James W. On swapping diagonal blocks in real schur form. Linear Algebra Appl 1993;186:73–95.
7. Barrett Richard, Barry Michael, Chan Tony F, Demmel James, Donato June, Dongarra Jack, et al. Templates for the solution of linear systems: building blocks for iterative methods. Philadelphia (Pennsylvania): SIAM; 1994.
8. Barth W, Martin RS, Wilkinson JH. Calculation of the eigenvalues of a symmetric tridiagonal matrix by the method of bisection. Numer Math 1967;9:386–93.
9. Ben-Israel Adi, Greville Thomas NE. Generalized inverses: theory and applications. New York: Springer; 2003.
10. Bojanczyk Adam W, Qiao Sanzhen, Steinhardt Allan O. Unifying unitary and hyperbolic transformations. Linear Algebra Appl 2000;316:183–97.
11. Bunch JR, Kaufman L, Parlett BN. Decomposition of a symmetric matrix. Numer Math 1976;27:95–109.
12. Bunch JR, Parlett BN. Direct methods for solving symmetric indefinite systems of linear equations. SIAM J Num Anal 1971;8:639–55.
13. Bunse-Gerstner A. An algorithm for the symmetric generalized eigenvalue problem. Linear Algebra Appl 1984;58(1):43–68.
14. Cooperstein Bruce. Advanced linear algebra. 6000 Broken Sound Park Way (Boca Raton, FL): CRC Press; 2010.
15. Cullum JK, Willoughby RA. Computing eigenvalues of very large symmetric matrices – an implementation of a lanczos algorithm with no reorthogonalization. J Comput Phys 1981;44:329–58.
16. Cuthill E, Mckee J. Reducing the bandwidth of sparse symmetric matrices. In: Proceedings of 24th Nat. Conf. ACM; 1969. pp. 157–72.
17. van der vorst HA, Fokkema DR, Sleijpen GLG. Jacobi-davidson style qr and qz algorithms for the partial reduction of matrix pencils. SIAM J Sci Comput 1998;20:94–125.
18. Daniel JW, Gragg WB, Kaufman L, Stewart GW. Reorthogonalization and stable algorithms for updating the Gram-Schmidt qr factorization. Math Comp 1976;30(136):772–95.
19. Davidson ER. The iterative calculation of a few of the lowest eigenvalues the corresponding eigenvectors of large real symmetric matrices. J Comput Phys 1975;17:87–94.
20. Demmel J, Kahan W. Accurate singular values bidiagonal matrices. SIAM J Sci Stat Comp 1990;11:873–912.
21. Dongarra J, Hammarling S, Wilkinson J. Numerical considerations in computing invariant subspaces. SIAM J Math Appl 1992;13:145–61.
22. Ehrig Rainald, Deuflhard Peter. Gmerr - an error minimizing variant of gmres, In: of GMRES, Preprint SC 97-63, Konrad-Zuse-Zentrum fur Informationstechnik. 1997.
23. Fernando KV, Parlett BN. Accurate singular values and differential qd algorithms. Numer Math 1994;67:191–229.
24. Message Passing Interface Forum. MPI: A Message-Passing Interface Standard, Version 3.0. High Performance Computing Center Stuttgart (HLRS); 2012.
25. Freund RW. A transpose-free quasi-minimum residual algorithm for non-hermitian linear system. SIAM J Sci Comput 1993;14:470–82.
26. Geist GA. Reduction of a general matrix to tridiagonal form. SIAM J Matrix Anal Appl 1991;12:362–73.
27. George A, Liu JW-H. Computer implementation of the finite element method, tech. rep. stan-cs-208. Technical report, Department of Computer Science, Standford University. 1971.

28. Gibbs NE, Poole Jr WG, Stockmeyer PK. An algorithm for reducing the bandwidth and profile of a sparse matrix. SIAM J Numer Anal 1976;13:236–50.

29. Golub Gene H, Van Loan Charles F. Matrix computations. Baltimore (Maryland): The Johns Hopkins University Press; 1996.

30. Gu M, Eisenstat SC. A divide-and-conquer algorithm for the symmetric tridiagonal eigenproblem. SIAM J Matrix Anal Appl 1995;16:172–91.

31. Gu Ming, Demmel James, Dhillon Inderjit. Efficient computation of the singular value decomposition with applications to least squares problems. Technical report, University of Tennessee. 1994.

32. Higham Nicholas J. Newton's method for the matrix square root. Math Comp 1986;46(174):537–49.

33. Higham NJ. Accuracy and stability of numerical algorithms. Philadelphia (Pennsylvania): SIAM; 1996.

34. Huang YZ, Zhong SM, Li ZL. Ju Zheng Li Lun (Matrix Theory, in Chinese). Beijing (China): Higher Education Press; 2003.

35. The Mathworks Inc. MATLAB users' guide. Natick (Massachusetts): The MathWorks Inc.; 1999.

36. Jacobi CGJ. Ueber ein leichtes verfahren, die in der theorie der sacularstorungen vorkommenden gleichungen numerisch aufzulosen. J Reine Angew Math 1846;30:51–94.

37. Jeffrey Alan, Dai Hui hui. Handbook of mathematical formulas and integrals. Academic Press; 2008.

38. Jessup ER, Sorensen DC. A parallel algorithm for computing the singular value decomposition of a matrix: A revision of argonne national laboratory tech. report anl/mcs-tm-102. Technical report, University of Colorado. 1992.

39. Hughes Thomas JR. The finite element method, linear static and dynamic element analysis. Dover Publications Inc.; 2000.

40. Lehoucq RB, Sorensen DC. Deflation techniques for an implicitly restarted arnoldi iteration. SIAM J Matrix Anal Appl 1996;14(4):789–821.

41. Li R-C. Solving secular equations stably and efficiently, technical report ut-cs-94-260. Technical report, University of Tennessee, Knoxville, TN. 1994.

42. Van Loan Charles F. Introduction to scientific computing, a matrix-vector approach using MATLAB. Upper Saddle River (New Jersey): Prentice Hall; 1997.

43. Marcus M. Matrices and MATLAB: a tutorial. Upper Saddle River (New Jersey): Prentice Hall; 1993.

44. Zienkiewicz OC, Taylor RL. The finite element method, volume 1 basic formulation and linear problems. 4th ed.: McGraw-Hill Book Company; 1994.

45. Parlett BN, Reid JK. On the solution of a system of linear equations whose matrix is symmetric but not definite. BIT 1970;10:386–97.

46. Parlett BN, Scott DS. The lanczos algorithm with selective orthogonalization. Math Comp 1979;33(145):217–38.

47. Gill PE, Murray W, Wright MH. Practical optimization. London: Academic Press; 1981.

48. Pfeiffer Friedrich, Glocker Christopher. Multibody dynamics with unilateral contacts. Wien (New York): Springer; 2000.

49. Poole David. Linear algebra, a modern introduction. 20 Channel Street (Boston, MA): Brooks/Cole; 2011.

50. Pratap R. Getting started with MATLAB. Fort Worth (Taxas): Saunders College Publications; 1995.

51. Press William H, Teukolsky Saul A, Vetterling William T, Flannery Brian P. Numerical recipes in c: the art of scientific computing. Cambridge (UK): Cambridge University Press; 1992.

52. Karp RM. Reducibility among combinatorial problems. In: Miller RE, Thatcher JW, editors. Complexity of computer computations. New York: Plenum Press; 1972. pp. 85–104.

53. Brent RP, Luk FT. The solution of singular value and symmetric eigenvalue problems on multiprocessor arrays. SIAM J Sci Stat Comp 1985;6:69–84.

54. Ruhe A. An algorithm for numerical determination of the structure of a geneal matrix. BIT 1970;10:196–216.

55. Saad Yousef. Numerical methods for large eigenvalue problems: theory and algorithms. New York: John Wiley and Sons; 1996.

56. Saad Yousef. Iterative methods for sparse linear systems. Philadelphia (Pennsylvania): SIAM; 2003.

57. Schnabel RB, Eskow E. A new modified cholesky factorization. SIAM J Sci Stat Comp 1990;11:1136–58.

58. Schnabel RB, Eskow E. A revised modified cholesky factorization algorithm. SIAM J Optim 1999;9:1135–48.

59. Shilov Georgi E. Linear algebra. New York (NY): Dover Publications; 1977.

60. Silvester John R. Determinants of block matrices. Math Gazette 2000;84:460–7.

61. Simon H. Analysis of the symmetric lanczos algorithm with reorthogonalization methods. Linear Algebra Appl 1984;61:101–32.
62. Simon H. The lanczos algorithm with partial reorthogonalization. Math Comp 1984;42:115–42.
63. Sonneveld P. Cgs: A fast lanczos-type solver for nonsymmetric linear systems. SIAM J Sci Stat Comp 1989;10:36–52.
64. Sorensen DC. Implicit application of polynomial filters in a k-step arnoldi method. SIAM J Matrix Anal Appl 1982;13:357–85.
65. Sorensen DC. Deflation for implicitly restarted arnoldi methods. Technical report. SIAM J Matrix Anal Appl, 1998.
66. Stewart GW. Algorithm 506 hqr3 and exchang: Fortran subroutine for calculating and ordering the eigenvalues of a real upper hessenberg matrix. ACM Trans Math Software 1976;2:275–80.
67. Stewart GW. The economical storage of plane rotations. Numer Math 1976;25:137–8.
68. Stewart GW. Matrix algorithms: volume I, basic decompositions. Philadelphia (Pennsylvania): SIAM; 1998.
69. Stewart GW. Matrix algorithms: volume II, eigensystems. Philadelphia (Pennsylvania): SIAM; 2001.
70. Stewart GW, Sun JG. Matrix perturbation theory. San Diego (CA): Academic Press; 1990.
71. Tisseur Francoise. Tridiagonal diagonal reduction of symmetric indefinite pairs. SIAM J Matrix Anal Appl 2004;26(1):215–32.
72. Udwadia Firdaus E. Fundamental principles of lagrangian dynamics: Mechanical systems with non-ideal, holonomic and nonholonomic constraints. J Math Anal Appl 2000;251:341–55.
73. Udwadia Firdaus E, Phomomsiri Phailaung. Explicit equations of motion for constrained mechanical systems with singular mass matrices and applications to multi-body dynamics. Proc R Soc A 2006;462:2097–117.
74. Udwadia Firdaus E, Kalaba RE. On the foundations of analytical mechanics. Internat J Nonlinear Mech 2002;37:1090–7.
75. Uzawa Hirofumi. Iterative methods for concave programming. In: Studies in linear and nonlinear programming. Stanford University Press; 1958.
76. van der vorst HA. Bi-cgstab: A fast and smoothly converging variant of bi-cg for the solution of non-symmetric linear systems. SIAM J Sci Stat Comp 1992;13:631–44.
77. Wang Q, Guo YC, Shi XW. An improved algorithm for matrix bandwidth and profile reduction in finite element method. Progr Electromagnetics Res Lett 2009;9:29–38.
78. Watkins DS, Elsner L. Chasing algorithms for the eigenvalue problem. SIAM J Matrix Anal Appl 1991;12(2):374–84.
79. Weiss R. Error-minimizing krylov subspace methods. SIAM J Sci Comp 1994;15:511–27.

Index

Note: Page numbers followed by "f" indicate figures, "t" indicate tables.

460

Printed in the United States
By Bookmasters